COAL CITY PUBLIC LIBRARY DISTRICT
3 5920 00009 4258
P9-CRM-325

5-1-91

Illustrated REVERSE DICTIONARY

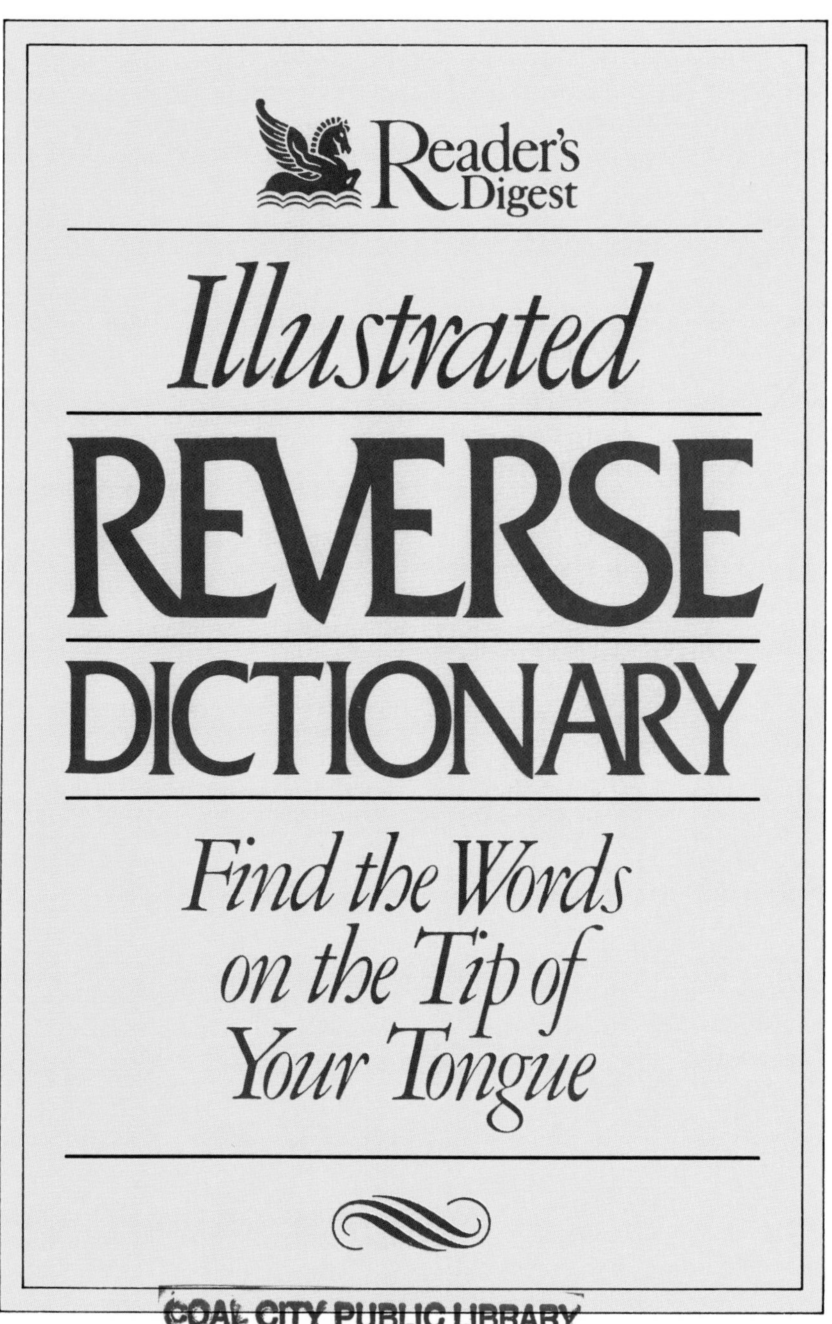

The Reader's Digest Association, Inc. Pleasantville, New York • Montreal

CONTRIBUTORS

Editor: John Ellison Kahn, MA, DPhil

Consultant Editor: Robert Ilson, MA, PhD
Associate Director of The Survey of English Usage
Honorary Research Fellow, University College, London
Editor, *International Journal of Lexicography*

The publishers thank the following for their valuable editorial and lexicographic contributions to this book:

Faye Carney, MA
Sylvia Chalker, MA
Emily Driver, BA
Nicholas Jones, MA

READER'S DIGEST GENERAL BOOKS

Editor in Chief: John A. Pope, Jr.
Managing Editor: Jane Polley
Executive Editor: Susan J. Wernert
Art Director: David Trooper
Group Editors: Will Bradbury, Norman B. Mack, Kaari Ward
Group Art Editors: Evelyn Bauer, Joel Musler
Chief of Research: Monica Borrowman
Copy Chief: Edward W. Atkinson
Picture Editor: Richard Pasqual
Rights and Permissions: Pat Colomban
Head Librarian: Jo Manning

ILLUSTRATED REVERSE DICTIONARY

Based on *Reader's Digest Reverse Dictionary,* published by The Reader's Digest Association Limited, London, with text compiled by WordCraft Editing and Writing Limited.

Americanized and expanded by Walter D. Glanze.

The acknowledgments that appear on page 608 are hereby made a part of this copyright page.

Library of Congress Cataloging in Publication Data

Illustrated reverse dictionary / [editor, John Ellison Kahn]. —
Americanized and expanded ed. / by Walter D. Glanze.
p. cm. — (Reader's Digest general books)
"Based on Reader's digest reverse dictionary, published by the Reader's Digest Association Limited, London"—T.p. verso.
ISBN 0-89577-352-X
1. English language—Synonyms and antonyms. I. Kahn, John Ellison. II. Glanze, Walter D. III. Reader's Digest Association. IV. Reader's digest. V. Reader's digest reverse dictionary.
PE1591.I4 1990
423'.1—dc20 90-39606

Printed in the United States of America

From the Idea to the Word

The Reverse Dictionary and How It Works

Everyone has experienced the frustration of mislaying a familiar word. You know what you want to say; you know that the precise word exists that would enable you to say it; and you know that you *know* this word ... but when you reach for it, it's not there. That's when the pantomime of exasperation begins: You snap your fingers, you frown, you rummage about in your mental attic, you say "It's on the tip of my tongue" or "What's that word—oh, *you* know." But the word, hovering just out of reach, continues to elude and tantalize you.

Psychologists studying this phenomenon compare it to being on the brink of a sneeze. Anticipation ... concentration ... and—frustration. What's needed, so to speak, is a pinch of snuff. The *Illustrated Reverse Dictionary* provides one. It's a linguistic snuffbox, helping to release that pent-up sneeze. The relief it affords should be considerable.

Several Angles of Attack

The *Illustrated Reverse Dictionary* is above all a word finder. Its purpose is to identify the precise word for an idea that may be in your mind but that you can't express. You have the idea; the book provides the word. It does this by directing you from a familiar word connected with the idea to the elusive word you are looking for—*from the word you know to the word you need.*

The familiar "cue word" leads to the tricky "target word" in any of three different ways:

—by means of a definition leading you directly to the target word,

—by referring you to a chart of terms on a particular subject, with the target word among them,

—by referring you to an illustration on which the target word is pinpointed.

Suppose you are trying to recall or discover the name for the sculpture of a woman that serves as a column supporting the roof of a building in ancient Greece. Various words come to mind as possible cues—**woman,** say, or **sculpture,** or **column.** Look up any of these cue words, and it will lead you to the target word CARYATID. **Woman** takes you there by way of a definition, **sculpture** by way of a chart of sculpture terms, and **column** by way of a definition and an illustration.

Note the distinctive feature of this approach in each case: Instead of starting with a headword and moving on to the definition, as in a conventional dictionary, the *Illustrated Reverse Dictionary* starts with the definition, so to speak, and leads from there to the word you are seeking—hence the title of the book.

Hitting the Target

Most target words can be approached from several directions. First, you can look up any of several *synonyms.* If you're trying to reach for the word TRAJECTORY, for instance, you'll find it if you look up **path** or **curve** ("curved flight path ...") or **flight** ("flight path ..."). Or you may approach the target word from its cluster of *associations* rather than its synonyms: A ball thrown through the air has a TRAJECTORY, so you might aim at this target word by looking up **ball** or **throw.** And because missiles, too, have trajectories, you could use the cue word **missile** to hit the target.

The linguistic side of the human mind works by lateral thinking as well as straight-line logical thinking, and many cue words have been selected to make provision for this. You can often approach a target word through its *collocations*—that is, through phrases in which it commonly occurs, phrases such as *connubial bliss, a sedentary job,* and *rancid butter.* You might accordingly look up the cue words **bliss, job,** and **butter** to find the respective target words CONNUBIAL, SEDENTARY, and RANCID.

A target word may even be cued by its *opposite* if that seems a promising approach. So the term RELEGATION could be found by looking up **promotion,** and LEVITY could be found by looking up **serious.**

Clearly it would be impracticable to provide every single possible approach to a target word, but the most promising and productive approaches will be there. If you don't find the cue word you want first time, just try again. "What's the word for that tiny Japanese tree—a sort of pot plant? ... oh, *you* know." You won't find the answer if you look up **tiny**—there are hundreds of tiny things, so **tiny** isn't really a useful cue word. But if you try again, and look up **miniature,** or **dwarf,** or simply **tree,** or **pot plant,** or the chart at the cue word **Japanese ...** you'll hit the target each time: BONSAI!

Enriching Your Vocabulary

The *Illustrated Reverse Dictionary* is more than just a word finder. It's a vocabulary builder too. It sets out to extend your command of words—to bring into the center of your working vocabulary those words that have up to now been only on its fringes. And it goes a step further—venturing beyond the fringes of the familiar, to give you access to the hinterland of the English language.

For the most part, the target words are moderately tricky, words at the level of TRAJECTORY, CONNUBIAL, and RELEGATION, or CORUSCATING, CRUSTACEAN, EUTHANASIA, ECLECTIC, PARSIMONIOUS, NONCHALANT, METAMORPHOSIS, EXUBERANT, PANACEA ...

But some target words seem to fall outside this middle range, and to be either very familiar or very obscure. This is often because the *meaning,* rather than the word, is under consideration. Take the terms STAR, CROWN, and PEEL—extremely simple terms surely, and yet not so simple when it comes to connecting them with special meanings that you might have in mind. The term STAR can mean the white spot on a horse's forehead (you'll find it at the cue word **horse**). The small, notched winding knob on an old-fashioned watch is a CROWN (at the cue word **watch**). And when a **baker** (at this cue word) uses a long flat shovel to take bread or pies out of the oven, the implement that he or she is wielding is a PEEL.

Words You Didn't Know

Conversely, the words RETIARIUS, AUTOTOMY, ENTASIS, and ROWEL may be utterly unfamiliar to you. But you probably are familiar with their meanings—with *the ideas underlying the words.* A RETIARIUS was the gladiator in ancient Rome who went into the arena armed with a net and trident rather than a sword (see chart at **Roman**). When a lizard sheds its tail to escape an attacker, the process is known as AUTOTOMY (see **lizard**). The slight bulge that makes a column on a Greek temple appear straight when viewed from below is called an ENTASIS (see **column**). And the small toothed wheel on the end of the spur on a cowboy's boot is a ROWEL (see **cowboy**).

Sometimes even the idea, not just the word, may be unfamiliar to you, as with MOXIBUSTION perhaps, referring to a kind of alternative therapy that involves setting fire to herbs placed on the patient's skin. (You'll find it in the chart at **therapy,** but also at the cue word **acupuncture** because the two procedures are related.)

There's a sprinkling of such complex terms spicing the text throughout—*words you didn't know you didn't know.*

Entertaining Words

Some of these unfamiliar terms are just highfalutin synonyms for perfectly familiar words: ANTHROPOPHAGI for **cannibals,** or LYCANTHROPE for **werewolf.** Some are the unfamiliar technical terms for all-too-familiar realities. The adventurous-sounding BORBORYGMUS is merely the less-than-heroic condition of tummy rumbling (see **stomach**). The grandiose SINGULTUS is just the humble **hiccup** (at this cue word). And the resonant STERNUTATION is simply—sneezing (at **sneeze**).

Such words would, of course, sound very pompous if used freely in conversation, and tend to be pretentious even in formal writing, but they're certainly worth *knowing.* And they're fun. This points to a third function of the *Illustrated Reverse Dictionary:* providing enjoyment. Supplementing the book's value as a word finder and a vocabulary builder is its entertainment value. Many of the obscurer terms in the text have been included for sheer fun—swashbuckling, cheeky, invigorating, their claims are irresistible. A tightrope walker can be called a FUNAMBULIST (see **tightrope**), and a striptease artist an ECDYSIAST (see **stripteaser**). (The word ECDYSIS is the technical term for the sloughing of skin, as by a snake or insect, so you'll find it at **skin.**) A DIASTEMA is a wide gap between the **teeth** (at this cue word), and a DEIPNOSOPHIST is an expert at dinner-table conversation—see **dinner table.** (Try dropping that casually into the conversation at the table!)

In addition, the crossword devotee will quickly discover that the *Illustrated Reverse Dictionary* is an ideal tool, a great source of solutions to those baffling clues across and down. And it was mainly with crossword puzzle enthusiasts in mind that the editors included a sizable number of stimulating (but perhaps not very familiar) British terms among the target words.

Never at a Loss for Words

Finally, the book affords you an opportunity for some linguistic creativity of your own. Hundreds of the target words are word elements rather than full-fledged words—combining forms, including prefixes and suffixes, mostly from Greek and Latin roots—terms such as the fairly familiar ULTRA-, at "**beyond** (combining form)," along with EXO-, HYPER-, META-, PARA-, SUPER-, SUPRA-, SUR-, and TRANS-; and PSEUDO-, at "**false** (combining form)"; and the less familiar -DENDRO-, referring to a tree (as in *rhododendron*), at "**tree** (combining form)," along with ARBOR- and SILV-; and -LATRY, meaning worship (as in *idolatry*), at "**worship** (combining form)." These are the materials on which you as wordsmith can get to work if the word you are groping for persists in eluding you. From the last two elements just mentioned, for instance, you could forge the term *dendrolatry*—that is, tree worship, as practiced by various pagan cultures in ancient times. Suppose you want to describe an insect or reptile that eats ants: Look up "**ant** (combining form)" to find MYRMECO-, and "**eat** (combining form)" to find -PHAGOUS (along with -VOROUS) —and there you have it, *myrmecophagous.* Or if you want to refer to a seven-sided disc: "**seven** (combining form)" gives you HEPTA-, and "**-sided** (combining form)" gives you -GON—yielding *heptagon.*

So you can use the *Illustrated Reverse Dictionary* inventively, as well as for reference. Use it for fun, as well as for illumination. Consider it a linguistic treasure chest, as well as a linguistic snuffbox. Rummage among its pages from time to time—you never know what you might find next!—and enjoy some of the coruscating jewels of the English vocabulary.

Happy browsing then—and successful sternutation.

—The Editors

PRONUNCIATION KEY

a	as in *trap* /trap/	**h**	as in *hat* /hat	**owr**	as in *sour* /sowr/
aa	as in *calm* /kaam/, *rod* /raad/	**i**	as in *grid* /grid/	**oy**	as in *boy* /boy/
air	as in *scarce* /skairs/	**ī**	as in *price* /prīs/	**p**	as in *crop* /kraap/
aar	as in *cart* /kaart	**īr**	as in *fire* /fīr/	**r**	as in *red* /red/
aw	as in *thought* /thawt/	**j**	as in *judge* /juj/	**s**	as in *sauce* /saws/
ay	as in *face* /fays/	**k**	as in *kick* /kik/	**sh**	as in *ship* /ship/
b	as in *stab* /stab/	**kh** (underlined)	as in *loch* /laakh/, *Bach* /baakh/	**t**	as in *state* /stayt/
ch	as in *church* /church/, *nature* /náychər	**l**	as in *fill* /fil/	**th**	as in *thick* /thik/
d	as in *dead* /ded/	**m**	as in *man* /man/	**th** (underlined)	as in *smooth* /smo͞oth/
e	as in *ten* /ten/	**n**	as in *fan* /fan/	**u**	as in *cut* /kut/
ee	as in *meat* /meet/	**ng**	as in *tank* /tangk/, *finger* /fíng-gər/	**ur**	as in *turn* /turn/
ew	as in *few* /few/	**ō**	as in *goat* /gōt/	**v**	as in *valve* /valv/
ə	as in *about* /ə-bówt/, *cannon* /kánnən/	**o͝o**	as in *would* /wo͝od	**w**	as in *wet* /wet/
f	as in *sofa* /sófə/	**o͞o**	as in *shoe* /sho͞o/	**y**	as in *yes* /yes/
g	as in *stag* /stag/	**ow**	as in *stout* /stowt/	**z**	as in *zoo* /zo͞o/
				zh (underlined)	as in *vision* /vizh'n/

Charts and Illustrations

Quick-Reference Features That Pinpoint the Word You Need

Page numbers in regular type refer to charts.
Page numbers in **bold** type refer to illustrations.

a or **an** in English grammar, or equivalent word in other languages, introducing without strictly identifying the noun following it INDEFINITE ARTICLE
- "a" or first letter of the Greek alphabet ALPHA

A-Z, or similar full range of a series GAMUT

abandon See also **depart, give up, energy, enthusiasm**
- give up an idea, habit, or friendship RENOUNCE, REPUDIATE
- give up a position RESIGN, ABDICATE
- give up something valued for something else FORGO
- give up to someone else RELINQUISH
- give up under compulsion SURRENDER
- leave by breaking the bonds of faithfulness DESERT, DEFECT, ABSCOND, APOSTATIZE
- leave by no longer seeking or staying with FORSAKE, REJECT

abandoned child or baby, of unknown parentage FOUNDLING

abandoning or voluntary relinquishment of a claim, right, or privilege WAIVER

abbey See illustration, page 12
- abbey or cathedral in some cities MINSTER
- head of a convent, abbey, or similar kind of religious community SUPERIOR

abbot, bishop, or clergyman of similar standing PRELATE

abbreviate, cut short TRUNCATE

abbreviation, such as *USA*, that unlike an acronym is pronounced letter by letter LETTERWORD, INITIALISM
- abbreviation, such as *AWOL* or *radar*, that is pronounced as a word ACRONYM
- abbreviation in the form of a symbol or letter, such as &, representing an entire word or phrase LOGOGRAM, LOGOGRAPH

abdomen, abdomen's upper area, below the ribs HYPOCHONDRIUM
- membrane lining the abdominal cavity and covering most of the organs PERITONEUM
- network of nerves in the abdomen, spreading to the intestines and liver SOLAR PLEXUS
- relating to the abdomen CELIAC

abdominal, relating to the front of the body VENTRAL
- abdominal pain COLIC

ability, power of mind or body born in us FACULTY, ENDOWMENT, GIFT
- easy power to carry out some specific task SKILL, DEXTERITY
- exceptional ability TALENT
- natural or acquired ability in a certain direction APTITUDE
- power that is equal to the demand COMPETENCE
- power to do quickly and well EFFICIENCY
- ability or character CALIBER
- ability or expertise, especially in judging shrewdly ACUMEN
- ability that has still not proved itself in actual successes POTENTIAL

able See also **skillful, clever, expert**
- able, capable, properly equipped or suitably qualified COMPETENT, PROFICIENT
- extremely able, deft, expert ADROIT, ADEPT

abnormal See also **odd**
- abnormal, as in sexual behavior DEVIANT, DEVIATE
- abnormal, departing from the norm or convention ECCENTRIC, BIZARRE, GROTESQUE, IDIOSYNCRATIC, OUTRÉ, ABERRANT, DIVERGENT, HETERODOX, HETEROCLITE, HERETICAL
- abnormal, differing from what is natural and usual or expected PRETERNATURAL
- abnormal, inconsistent, out of keeping, odd ANOMALOUS, INCONGRUOUS
- abnormal, through being corrupted PERVERTED
- abnormal sexual behavior or act PERVERSION

abnormal (combining form) DYS-, PARA-

abnormality such as a disease or disturbed mental state PATHOLOGY

abnormality (combining form) -OSIS, TERAT-, TERATO-

abolish See **destroy, get rid of**

abominable snowman YETI

aboriginal, original inhabitant NATIVE, INDIGENE, ABORIGINE, AUTOCHTHON

aboriginal terms See chart at **Australian terms**

abortion - bring on an abortion artificially, especially by the use of medical drugs INDUCE, TERMINATE

about, concerning, regarding, relating to APROPOS, APROPOS OF, RE, IN RE
- about or approximately, as written before an uncertain date CIRCA

about, around (combining form) PERI-, AMB-

about to happen IMMINENT, IMPENDING

about-turn, about-face, U-turn, reversal of attitude or policy VOLTE-FACE

above, term used to refer to a previous section or earlier part of a text SUPRA
- above, overlooking, or on top of SURMOUNTING
- superior in quality PARAMOUNT, PAR EXCELLENCE

above, beyond (combining form) EPI-, HYPER-, SUPER-, SUPRA-, SUR-, TRANS-, ULTRA-

abrasive mineral, aluminum oxide CORUNDUM

abrupt in manner CURT

abscess - abnormal opening or passage between a hollow organ and the skin FISTULA

absence or departure that is without permission or notification AWOL, FRENCH LEAVE
- absence of life ABIOSIS
- absence of rules or laws ANARCHY
- absence or opposite of something positive or real NEGATION

absent - while absent, although absent IN ABSENTIA

absentee, especially from school or work TRUANT

absentminded, inattentive, daydreaming, distracted DISTRAIT, ABSTRACTED, PREOCCUPIED
- absentminded through being excessively idealistic or romantic QUIXOTIC
- absentmindedness, daydreaming WOOLGATHERING

absolute, certain, without reservation, as a denial might be CATEGORICAL
- absolute, complete, utter outright RANK, UNADULTERATED, UNEQUIVOCAL
- absolute power, nondemocratic

rule, dictatorship or tyranny DESPOTISM, TOTALITARIANISM, AUTARCHY, AUTOCRACY
- absolute ruler who is enlightened and well-disposed toward his subjects BENEVOLENT DESPOT

absolution granted or confession heard by a priest SHRIFT
- obtain or give absolution at confession SHRIVE

absorb, cause to become a full member, part, or participant INTEGRATE, ASSIMILATE, INCORPORATE
- absorb by or as if by swallowing INGEST
- absorbing gas or liquid POROUS
- process, unlike absorption, by which a thin film of substance accumulates on the surface of a solid ADSORPTION

absorbed See **interested**

abstract, simplified, stylized, as a painting or design might be CONVENTIONALIZED
- abstract, subtle, or complex, often excessively so METAPHYSICAL
- abstract or imaginary rather than actual NOTIONAL
- abstract sculpture CONSTRUCTION
- nonabstract, realistic or representational, as a painting might be FIGURATIVE
- treat an idea or abstraction as a real or concrete thing REIFY

absurd See also **ridiculous**
- absurd or apparently self-contradictory statement that is not necessarily untrue PARADOX
- following through an idea or principle to an absurd extreme REDUCTIO AD ABSURDUM

absurdity, gross misrepresentation, farce, or caricature TRAVESTY, CHARADE

abundance See **plenty, excess**

abundant (combining form) -ULENT

academic
- academic conference or discussion COLLOQUIUM, SEMINAR
- academic retreat from everyday life, as a university is sometimes

Abbey Buildings

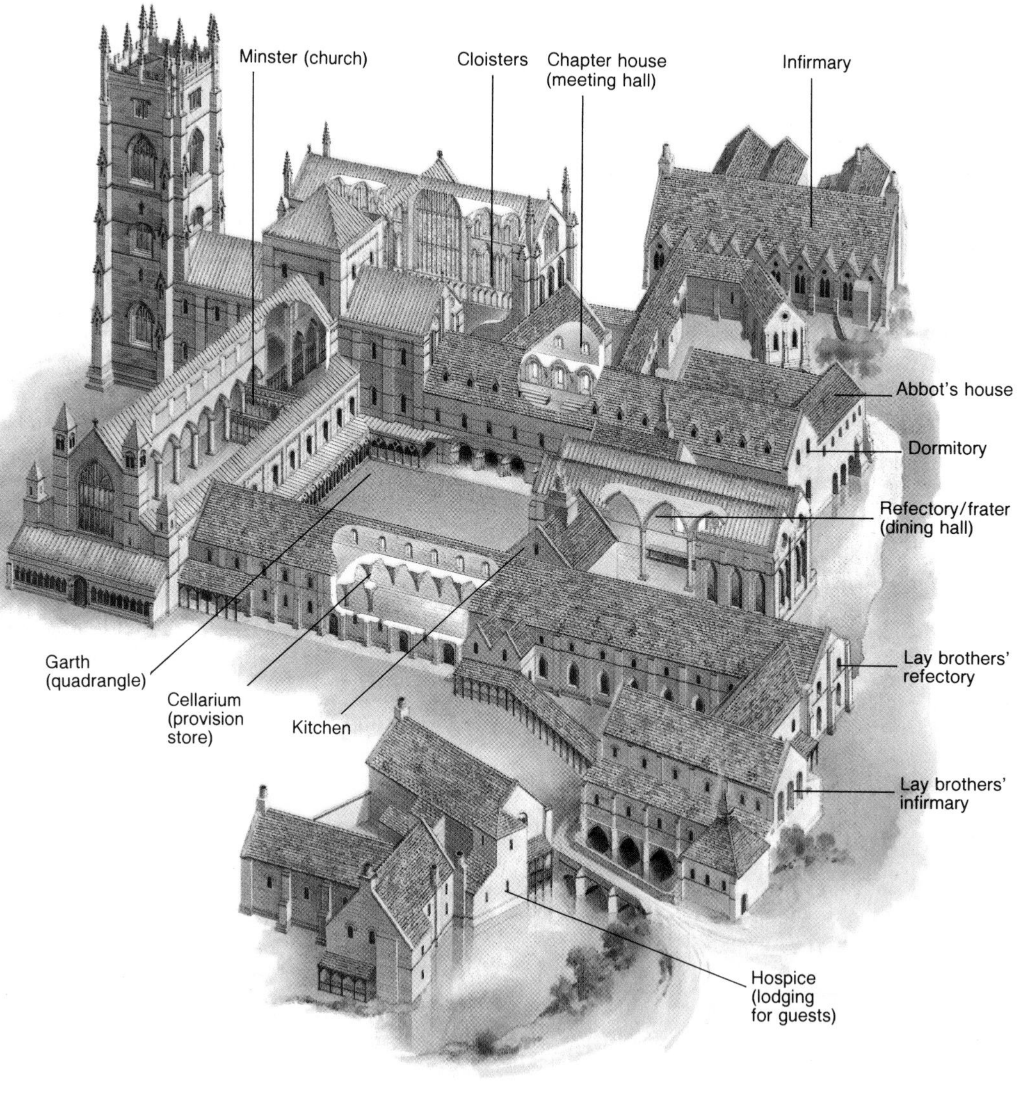

considered to be IVORY TOWER
- academic treatise or thesis, as for a higher degree DISSERTATION
- half an academic year SEMESTER
- relating to two or more academic subjects or fields of study INTERDISCIPLINARY
- strips of white cloth on academic robes GENEVA BANDS

accelerated (combining form) TACH-, TACHY-, TACHEO-

accent, vocabulary, and general form of a language used by a particular regional or social group DIALECT
- accent of a strong regional kind, especially Irish BROGUE
- accent mark consisting of a wavy line (ñ) TILDE
- accent mark consisting of two dots (ë) DIERESIS, UMLAUT
- accent mark that is roof-shaped (ê) CIRCUMFLEX ACCENT
- accent mark that is slanted from left to right (è) GRAVE ACCENT
- accent mark that is slanted from right to left (é) ACUTE ACCENT
- accented, carrying the principal stress in a word, as a syllable might be TONIC
- throaty and harsh, as some accents or languages are GUTTURAL
- word having an accent on the last syllable OXYTONE

accept, abide by, or reconcile oneself to, a ruling, decision, or the like COMPLY WITH, ACCEDE TO, ACQUIESCE IN

acceptable See also **mediocre**
- acceptable, effective, or sound, as an argument, title, or passport might be VALID
- acceptable to one's taste or ideas PALATABLE
- meet the required standards of acceptability PASS MUSTER
- model of behavior, standard of acceptability, or the like NORM

acceptance as true, belief CREDENCE
- acceptance of an agreement or treaty ACCESSION
- acceptance or approval, as of a decision or course of action SANCTION, ENDORSEMENT

accepted widely, generally believed, time-honored, as a theory or view might be RECEIVED

accepting, as of misfortune or unfair treatment, passive or submissive RESIGNED, ACQUIESCENT

accident, as caused by bad luck rather than negligence MISHAP
- accident or occurrence causing death FATALITY
- tendency to make lucky discoveries by accident SERENDIPITY

accidental, by chance, unexpected or unplanned ADVENTITIOUS, FORTUITOUS
- accidental, chance, occurring randomly CONTINGENT, ALEATORY, HAPHAZARD
- accidental, unintended, or impulsive UNPREMEDITATED
- accidental developments, or changes of fortune VICISSITUDES
- accidental yet unlawful killing MANSLAUGHTER

accidentally, unintentionally, without meaning to INADVERTENTLY, UNWITTINGLY

accommodation - assign accommodation to military officers or troops BILLET, QUARTER, CANTON

accompany or escort someone, especially a young unmarried woman, for protection and propriety CHAPERON
- accompany troops, ships, or land vehicles for protection CONVOY
- accompanying, associated with, occurring together CONCOMITANT

accomplished fact, something that cannot be undone FAIT ACCOMPLI

accomplishment showing great skill TOUR DE FORCE

account, score, or recorded reckoning, as of accidents TALLY
- account, typically detailing the goods or services provided INVOICE, STATEMENT
- alter a document, accounts, evidence, or the like in order to deceive FALSIFY
- clearly described in vivid or exciting detail, as an account of an accident might be GRAPHIC
- examine, adjust, or certify accounts or other records AUDIT
- settling of a bill or account RECKONING

accuracy or strict adherence to the truth VERACITY
- demanding and determined person, insisting on obedience, tidiness, accuracy, or the like STICKLER

accurate See also **precise**
- accurate or indisputably true statement, belief, principle, or the like VERITY

accusation See also **charge**
- accusation or a veiled criticism IMPUTATION
- accusations of a bitter, mutual kind RECRIMINATIONS
- acknowledgment of a telling point, argument, or accusation made against one TOUCHÉ
- false report or accusation, slander, slur ASPERSION, CALUMNY
- reject or deny a claim or accusation REPUDIATE
- stop and confront a person, as with an accusation ACCOST

accuse, confront, or criticize TAX
- accuse of a crime, especially treason IMPEACH
- accuse of or charge with an offense or crime, especially before a court of law INDICT, ARRAIGN
- accuse or inform against DENOUNCE

accustomed to, used to HABITUATED, INURED, ACCLIMATIZED, ATTUNED, WONT

aces - two aces, the lowest throw in playing dice AMBSACE

achieve or obtain, manage COMPASS, ENCOMPASS

achievement of a final stage or development, high point PINNACLE, ZENITH, MERIDIAN, SUMMIT
- achievement or exploit showing great skill or strength TOUR DE FORCE
- achievement or success of a brilliant kind ÉCLAT

acid See chart, page 14
- acid-alkali indicator PHENOLPHTHALEIN, LITMUS PAPER, PH TEST
- acid as used for etching on a printing plate MORDANT
- acidlike substance, the universal solvent that dissolves anything, believed by alchemists to be possible and discoverable ALKAHEST
- acid or other destructive chemical CORROSIVE
- able to react as both an acid and a base, as some chemicals are AMPHOTERIC, AMPHIPROTIC
- bottle for acids and other corrosive liquids CARBOY
- chemical compound that reacts with acids to form salts BASE
- soluble base that can neutralize an acid ALKALI

acidic or harsh, as in smell, manner, or effect ASTRINGENT

acknowledged, candidly admitted, self-confessed AVOWED

acorn - acorn's cuplike base, or other cup-shaped structure CUPULE
- acorns and beech nuts used as pig food MAST
- acorns and other pasturage for pigs, as in a forest PANNAGE

acquaintance, personal knowledge CONVERSANCE, CONVERSANCY, COGNIZANCE
- close relationship, often with mutual understanding INTIMACY

acrobat or entertainer who twists his limbs and body into abnormal positions CONTORTIONIST
- acrobat or gymnast specializing in turning somersaults or cartwheels TUMBLER
- acrobats' bar suspended from free-swinging ropes TRAPEZE

acronym See **abbreviation**

across, from side to side, crossways

TRANSVERSELY, ATHWART

across (combining form) DIA-, TRANS-, TRA-

act or adventure, especially a noble or heroic one EXPLOIT

- act or behave in a specified way, conduct oneself COMPORT ONESELF

acting See also **theater** and chart at **drama**

- acting, especially excessively dramatic acting HISTRIONICS
- acting, provisional, being a temporary substitute for INTERIM, SURROGATE
- acting or speaking beyond the range of one's ability or expertise ULTRACREPIDARIAN
- acting profession, the stage, the "boards," dramatics FOOTLIGHTS
- acting ruler during a monarch's illness, minority, or other disqualifying condition REGENT

acting (combining form) -FEX, -FAX, -OR, -TRIX, -ICIAN, -IST

- acting in place of PRO-

action aimed at resisting change or warding off likely defeat REARGUARD ACTION

- action taken to avoid likely trouble or problems EVASIVE ACTION
- automatic or involuntary action AUTOMATISM
- behavior or mental activity directed toward change or action, including desire or striving CONATION
- stimulation, impulse, or spur to action, drive or prompting MOTIVATION, INCENTIVE, INDUCEMENT

activate a mechanism by releasing a catch, trigger, or switch TRIP, ACTUATE

active See also **energetic, enthusiastic**

- active, easy, and skillful AGILE
- active, easy, and swift NIMBLE
- active, lively, and vigorous, typically in spite of being old SPRY, SPRIGHTLY
- active, tireless, and unfailingly energetic INDEFATIGABLE
- active, vigorous, and enthusiastic ANIMATED, VIVACIOUS
- active, watchful, and ready ALERT, VIGILANT
- active and faithful to the task in hand INDUSTRIOUS, DILIGENT
- active in an excessive or uncontrolled way HYPERACTIVE, MANIC, HECTIC, FRENETIC
- actively promoting and committed to a moral or political cause ENGAGÉ
- inactive but still arousable, potentially active LATENT, DORMANT
- no longer active, as a volcano might be EXTINCT
- receiving or being subjected to an

ACIDS

acetic acid	found in vinegar
amino acid	basis of proteins
ascorbic acid	vitamin C
bile acid	active in absorbing fat from intestine
carbolic acid	phenol; used in disinfectant soap
citric acid	found in lemons and other citrus fruits
conjugate acid	from addition of a proton to a base
deoxyribonucleic acid	DNA; basis of chromosomes, and hence of genetic transmission
essential fatty acid	vitamin F
fatty acid	associated with fat in the body
folic acid	vitamin B_c or vitamin M
formic acid	naturally occurring in ants
free fatty acid	found in the blood
hydrochloric acid	spirits of salt; found in dilute form in the digestive juices; wide industrial application
lactic acid	found in sour milk
linoleic acid	needed in the diet but not produced by the body
malic acid	found in unripe apples and other fruit
metenoic acid	vitamin U; provides relief for ulcers
mineral acid	strong substance, such as hydrochloric acid or sulfuric acid
monobasic acid	only one molecule of base is needed to neutralize one molecule of the substance
nitric acid	aqua fortis; corrosive acid used in making explosives and rocket fuels
nitrohydrochloric acid	aqua regia; used for dissolving platinum and gold, and for testing metals
pangamic acid	vitamin B_{15}
para-aminobenzoic acid	PABA; vitamin B_x prevents sunburn
polyunsaturated fatty acid	helps in lowering blood cholesterol, but increases the need for vitamin E
prussic acid/ hydrocyanic acid	cyanide compound, a favorite poison of mystery writers
ribonucleic acid	RNA; found in all living cells; essential for protein production
salicylic acid	basis of aspirin
sulfuric acid	highly dangerous and corrosive acid, with wide industrial application
tannic acid	tannin; found in tea; used in tanning and clarifying wine and beer
tartaric acid	used in baking powder
uric acid	cause, when unregulated, of gout

action rather than being active or taking the initiative PASSIVE
activity, amusement, or hobby, interesting pursuit DIVERSION, DISTRACTION, AVOCATION
- activity, such as spacewalking, outside the spacecraft while away from earth EXTRAVEHICULAR ACTIVITY
actor in an old-fashioned masque or mime MUMMER
- actor, especially in dramas THESPIAN
- actor or comedian who overacts HAM
- actor or other performer having considerable experience, veteran artiste TROUPER
- actor who conveys ideas by the use of expression and gesture rather than words MIME
- actor who has a nonspeaking role in a play or movie, such as an extra or walk-on SUPERNUMERARY
- actor who knows a role and can replace the regular actor in an emergency UNDERSTUDY
- actor's cue to speak or enter CATCHWORD
- actor's first public appearance DEBUT
- actor's lengthy speech when alone on stage MONOLOGUE, SOLILOQUY
- reappearance of an actor, cast, choir, or the like, to acknowledge applause CURTAIN CALL
- relating to an actor always cast in the same type of role TYPECAST
actress playing a young woman, especially a flirtatious lady's maid in a comedy or comic opera SOUBRETTE
- actress playing the role of a naive young woman INGENUE
actual See also **real**
actually, really, in fact DE FACTO
acupuncture STYLOSTIXIS
- gentle cauterizing of the skin by burning a small piece of a woolly or downy substance as a means of therapy, sometimes used as a supplement to acupuncture MOXIBUSTION, BYSSOCAUSIS
acute or piercing, as a pain might be LANCINATING
A.D. or Christian era as referred to by non-Christians COMMON ERA, C.E.
adapt See also **change**
- adapt, become integrated or absorbed ASSIMILATE
- adapt, familiarize, adjust to new circumstances ORIENTATE
- adapt or arrange a musical item for different instruments, voices, or the like TRANSCRIBE
adaptable, adjusting to changed conditions PLIABLE, VERSATILE
- adaptable or variable, as working hours might be FLEXIBLE
add, attach, or tack on AFFIX, ANNEX
- add or attach at the end APPEND, SUFFIX, SUBJOIN
- add to, complete, make perfect COMPLEMENT
- add to or aggravate an error or difficulty COMPOUND
- number or quantity that is added to another ADDEND
- number or quantity to which another is added AUGEND
added, supplementary, incidental rather than essential or belonging ADSCITITIOUS, ADVENTITIOUS, EXTRANEOUS, EXTRINSIC
- added clause, amendment, or qualification to a legal document, verdict, parliamentary bill, or the like RIDER, CODICIL
- added material at the end of a book, message, or the like AFTERTHOUGHT, POSTSCRIPT, APPENDIX, ANNEX, SUPPLEMENT, ADDENDUM
- added or growing by a series of steps or additions INCREMENTAL, CUMULATIVE
- added or related feature that is not essential but only incidental ADJUNCT
- added unnecessary words PLEONASM
- added repetitious words TAUTOLOGY
addiction to alcohol or drugs DEPENDENCE
adding device, as used in Asia, operated by moving beads on rods ABACUS
addition bit by bit and a gradual increase, build-up ACCRETION
- addition of a syllable at the end of a word SUFFIX
- addition of a syllable in front of a word PREFIX
- addition of a syllable inside a word INFIX
- addition or amendment to a will CODICIL
- addition or increase INCREMENT
- addition or newly acquired possession, as in a library or other collection ACCESSION
- addition or the total reached by it SUMMATION
additional, extra SUPPLEMENTARY, SUPERVENIENT
- additional, supplementary, or accompanying item, as to an automobile FITMENT, ACCESSORY, FITTINGS
- additional charge or cost SURCHARGE
- additional or supplementary part, typically added to something more important APPENDAGE, APPURTENANCE, PENDANT
- additional proposition following from the proof of another proposition COROLLARY
- additional section at the end of a novel, piece of music, or the like CODA
- additional sum of money, such as a bonus or an increase in price PREMIUM
additional (combining form) EPI-, EP-, EPH-
address See also **speech**
- address a book or other work specifically to a person or group as a mark of respect or affection DEDICATE
- address to an imaginary or absent person or a personified thing when digressing in a formal speech APOSTROPHE
- phrase used in the address on a letter that is to be kept at a particular post office for collection by the addressee GENERAL DELIVERY, POSTE RESTANTE
adequate See also **mediocre**
- adequate but modest income or standard of living SUFFICIENCY, COMPETENCE
adjective or adverb in grammar MODIFIER, QUALIFIER
- adjective and noun, such as *stormy weather*, replaced by two nouns plus "and," such as *storm and weather* HENDIADYS
- adjective or descriptive term, often a scornful or disparaging one EPITHET
- degrees of comparison of adjectives and adverbs POSITIVE, COMPARATIVE, SUPERLATIVE
- referring or relating to an adjective typically directly in front of the noun, as in *the lonely child*, rather than separated from it by a verb ATTRIBUTIVE
- referring or relating to an adjective that is separated from the noun by a linking verb, as in *the child is lonely* PREDICATIVE
- word, such as *the*, *six*, or *your*, that limits a noun and is placed before any descriptive adjectives DETERMINER
adjust See also **change, correct, improve**
- adjust, adapt, or tailor, as to improve or harmonize MODIFY, REGULATE
- adjust, alter, or tinker with, as to improve the relationship between corresponding parts of a machine ALIGN
- adjust, familiarize, adapt to new circumstances ORIENTATE
- adjust and correct, set right RECTIFY, REMEDY, REDRESS

- adjust organ pipes or a wind instrument to perfect the tone and pitch VOICE
- adjust to a new environment, harmonize ASSIMILATE, ACCULTURATE

admiration See also **praise**
- admiration, great regard, high esteem APPROBATION, VENERATION
- deserving admiration, admirable COMMENDABLE, LAUDABLE, ESTIMABLE
- excessive admiration, doting devotion, hero worship IDOLATRY

admire greatly, hold in very high esteem REVERE, IDOLIZE

admired or beloved person or thing, focus of attention CYNOSURE

admirers - group of ardent admirers CLAQUE

admission of guilt, acknowledgment of wrongdoing or sin PECCAVI, MEA CULPA
- admission qualifications, exams, or ceremony for a university or college MATRICULATION
- admission ritual or ceremony INITIATION

admit, confess, acknowledge AVOW, CONCEDE
- admit defeat in an election CONCEDE
- admitting of or permitting something, such as an interpretation SUSCEPTIBLE

adolescence in its early stages, in which adult reproductive characteristics develop PUBERTY

adorn See **decorate, ornament**

adult insect IMAGO

adultery or other sexual unfaithfulness INFIDELITY, CRIMINAL CONVERSATION
- adulterous, referring or relating to a spouse's sexual relationship outside marriage EXTRAMARITAL
- man whose wife has committed adultery CUCKOLD
- man who tolerates his wife's adultery WITTOL
- person cited in a divorce case as having committed adultery with the partner being sued CORESPONDENT
- tacit encouragement of a wrongful act, such as the adultery of one's spouse CONNIVANCE

advance arrival or announcer, forerunner PREDECESSOR, PRECURSOR, HARBINGER, HERALD, BELLWETHER
- advance explorer, reconnoiterer, scout OUTRIDER
- advance or intrusion into the territory or time of another INROAD, ENCROACHMENT, INCURSION, TRESPASS, INFRINGEMENT
- advance payment, as in a poker game or financial venture ANTE
- advance to a higher level or a more important role GRADUATE
- advancing by degrees or stages, as from one tone or color to the next GRADATION
- person giving advance notice of doom or disaster CASSANDRA
- sudden and dramatic advance or change QUANTUM LEAP, QUANTUM JUMP

advanced or clever beyond his years as a sophisticated child seems to be PRECOCIOUS

advantage, benefit, blessing BOON
- advantage of a temporary or uncertain kind TOEHOLD
- anything that can be turned to one's profit or advantage GRIST
- be of help or advantage AVAIL
- exploited person, person who is taken advantage of, dupe STOOGE, PATSY, MARK, CAT'S-PAW
- have a specified effect, as to one's credit or advantage REDOUND
- person who exploits or takes advantage of another's generosity PARASITE, LEECH, SPOONER
- person who takes advantage of an opportunity, often unscrupulously OPPORTUNIST
- take advantage of an opportunity, turn something to advantage UTILIZE, CAPITALIZE ON
- take advantage of, especially selfishly and unjustly EXPLOIT

advantageous, favorable, healthy BENEFICIAL, BENIGN, BENIGNANT, EXPEDIENT

adventure, deed, or feat, especially a noble or heroic one EXPLOIT
- adventure story CONTE
- mischievous adventure, spree, prank ESCAPADE, CAPER

adventurer, rogue PICARO, PICAROON

adventurous, flamboyant, daredevil, swaggering SWASHBUCKLING

adventurous spirit See **energy**

adverb See **adjective**

advertise a product by using one's name to recommend it ENDORSE

advertisement, notice, or leaflet distributed widely, handout HANDBILL, CIRCULAR, FLIER
- measurement of advertising space AGATE LINE
- person who writes the text of advertisements COPYWRITER
- simple catchphrase, motto, or the like used repeatedly, as in advertisements SLOGAN
- simple, catchy tune or rhyme as used in advertisements JINGLE

advertising and its philosophy MADISON AVENUE
- advertising and publicity language that is exaggerated, misleading, or bewildering HYPE
- advertising display board BILLBOARD
- advertising or publicity campaign, or advertising in general PROMOTION
- advertising or publicity that is brash and sensational BALLYHOO, RAZZLE-DAZZLE, RAZZMATAZZ, HYPE
- advertising or selling of an aggressive kind HARD SELL
- advertising technique in film and television using flashed images, too quick to be consciously registered, supposedly to influence the viewer SUBLIMINAL ADVERTISING

advice, guidance COUNSEL
- advice or warning MONITION
- observer, as at a card game, offering uninvited comments or advice KIBITZER
- remedial, improving, beneficial, as advice might be SALUTARY
- seeking of or meeting for advice, as from a doctor or lawyer CONSULTATION

advisable, prudent JUDICIOUS, EXPEDIENT

advise, give clear directions INSTRUCT
- advise strongly EXHORT
- gently criticize errors and faults to prevent them in the future ADMONISH
- give considered opinion on a serious matter COUNSEL

adviser, assistant, right-hand person AIDE
- adviser or wise teacher MENTOR
- adviser to an editor or publisher on the suitability for publication of an academic article REFEREE
- advisers, unofficial yet influential, to a government or business leader KITCHEN CABINET

advocate See **lawyer**

aerial, as for a radio or television ANTENNA
- aerial in the form of a straight metal rod, supported in the middle DIPOLE
- aerial maneuvers in aerobatics SNAP ROLL, BARREL ROLL, WINGOVER, CHANDELLE
- directional aerial with several parallel elements, as used in radio astronomy and television reception YAGI

aerosol - liquid or gas for dispersing substances, as in an aerosol DISPERSANT, PROPELLANT

affair, sexual relationship LIAISON
- referring or relating to a spouse's sexual relationship outside marriage EXTRAMARITAL, ADULTEROUS

affect See also **influence**
- have a favorable or unfavorable result or effect REDOUND
- affect, influence, serve as evidence MILITATE

affected See also **pompous, high-**

falutin, artificial
- affected, fussily dainty, overrefined, as in movement or behavior MINCING, NIMINY-PIMINY, EFFETE
- affected, overelegant, as manner or speech PRECIOUS, GENTEEL, PRETENTIOUS, LA-DI-DA
- affected, overrefined, overelaborate, as with ideas or styles RECHERCHÉ
- affected readily or moved easily SUSCEPTIBLE
- affectedly pretty or fashionable CHICHI

affected, suffering (combining form) -OTIC

affecting or touching POIGNANT, PATHETIC

affection See also **liking**
- antagonize, alienate, lose the affection of ESTRANGE

afflicted, as by a disease or disaster STRICKEN

afraid See **scared, cowardly**

afraid (combining form) -PHOBE, -PHOBIA, -PHOBIC

Africa - bard or oral historian in a West African community GRIOT
- boss or employer in East Africa, or a respectful term of address BWANA
- charm, amulet, or fetish in Africa, or its supposed supernatural powers JUJU
- brightly colored cloth strip used as a garment in Africa KANGA, KENTE, KIKOI
- independence or freedom in Africa, or a rallying cry invoking it UHURU
- plantation or garden plot in East Africa SHAMBA
- region of northwest Africa between the Sahara and the Mediterranean MAGHREB
- shirt of a bright pullover style worn in Africa DASHIKI

African - having tightly curled hair on the head, as black Africans have ULOTRICHOUS
- dark pigment in the skin, as among Africans MELANIN

African lily AGAPANTHUS

after, later in time, following POSTERIOR, SUBSEQUENT, EX POST FACTO

after (combining form) EPI-, POST-

afterbirth PLACENTA, SECUNDINES

aftereffects, complications, or condition following a disease SEQUELA

afterlife - region or state after death between heaven and hell, in which venial sinners can atone PURGATORY
- region or state in the afterlife for the souls of unbaptized babies and of just pre-Christians LIMBO

afternoon show, as of a theatrical performance MATINEE

AGES OF HUMANS	PERSON AGED
quinquagenarian	50+
sexagenarian	60+
septuagenarian	70+
octogenarian	80+
nonagenarian	90+
centenarian	100+

- afternoon sleep or rest, especially in hot southern countries SIESTA
- relating to the afternoon POSTMERIDIAN

again, audience's enthusiastic demand for a further performance, as by a musician ENCORE
- again and again, to a sickening extent AD NAUSEAM
- musical direction to perform again a passage DA CAPO

again (combining form) ANA-, RE-, PALIM-

against one's interests, unfavorable ADVERSE
- strive against MILITATE
- vote or argument against CON

against (combining form) ANTI-, CONTRA-, COUNTER-, OB-

against the law ILLICIT, ILLEGAL, ILLEGITIMATE

age See chart
- age, long life LONGEVITY
- age according to years lived, in contrast to mental age, as used to assess IQ CHRONOLOGICAL AGE
- aging, growing old SENESCENCE
- discrimination against the aged or elderly AGEISM
- dominant outlook and spirit of a particular age ZEITGEIST
- historical period, era EPOCH
- period of being legally under age MINORITY, NONAGE
- person of the same age as another CONTEMPORARY, COEVAL
- retired or discharged because of old age or illness SUPERANNUATED
- study of aging and the aged GERONTOLOGY, GERIATRICS

aged artificially, as some furniture or leather is DISTRESSED

agent, as of a university, in business matters SYNDIC
- agent, representative, or deputy performing duties for someone else MINISTER, PROXY, ASSIGNEE, VICAR
- agent inciting illegal activity AGENT PROVOCATEUR
- agent in former times, as for collecting tithes or conducting a case in court PROCTOR
- agent legally entitled to control or administer the property or funds of someone else TRUSTEE
- agent or go-between in a sexual relationship PIMP, PANDER, PANDERER, PROCURER, MAQUEREAU
- agent or means mediating between people or things, go-between INTERMEDIARY, OMBUDSMAN
- agent or messenger sent on a mission, typically by a government or head of state EMISSARY, AMBASSADOR
- agent or middleman in business dealings BROKER, FACTOR
- agent or representative, as at a conference DELEGATE
- agent secretly representing another FRONT, DUMMY
- agent who runs a landowner's estate STEWARD, BAILIFF
- agent's fee or percentage charged for successfully completed services COMMISSION
- appoint as one's agent, substitute, or representative DEPUTE
- deputy administrative officer or agent assisting a king, magistrate, or the like VICEGERENT
- powerful agent giving secret or unofficial advice ÉMINENCE GRISE

aggravate, worsen, or intensify something, such as a pain or difficulty EXACERBATE

aggressive See also **hostile**
- aggressive, energetic, pushy, or go-getting COMBATIVE, ASSERTIVE
- aggressive and antisocial person, typically suffering from an unstable personality and lack of conscience PSYCHOPATH, SOCIOPATH
- aggressively or ruthlessly seeking to increase one's own influence, wealth, or the like SELF-AGGRANDIZING

agitation of the mind or the feelings TUMULT

agony See also **pain**
- occasion or place of great agony GETHSEMANE

agree, approve, or assent to a belief, opinion, or the like SUBSCRIBE
- agree, correspond, match, be alike or parallel TALLY, ACCORD, COINCIDE, COMPORT, CHIME, HARMONIZE, QUADRATE, SQUARE, EQUATE
- agree, in a haughty way, to do something DEIGN, CONDESCEND
- agree, share an opinion or conclusion CONCUR
- agree to a request, comply with a demand, or the like ACCEDE, ACQUIESCE, YIELD
- express an agreement regarding action ASSENT
- express willingness or compli-

ance CONSENT
agreeable See also **friendly, kind**
- agreeable, open to suggestion or ideas AMENABLE, RECEPTIVE

agreed to by everybody UNANIMOUS
agreeing, harmonious IN UNISON, IN CONCERT, CONGRUENT
- agreeing or assenting, as by answering yes AFFIRMATIVE
- agreeing with, conforming to PURSUANT TO

agreement, as between rival nations PACT, TREATY, ACCORD
- agreement, especially one by which creditors settle for partial payment of a debt COMPOSITION
- agreement, settlement, or compromise between disputing people or groups, as aimed at by an intermediary MEDIATION, ARBITRATION, CONCILIATION
- agreement by which wages are raised after a certain increase in the cost of living THRESHOLD AGREEMENT
- agreement in certain features between things that are otherwise different ANALOGY
- agreement or contract COMPACT, COVENANT
- agreement or harmony among parts, claims, or the like CONSISTENCY, COORDINATION, CONFORMITY, CONCORD, CONGRUITY, CONSONANCE, COMPATIBILITY
- agreement or informal understanding between countries or powers ENTENTE CORDIALE
- agreement that is general and widespread, majority opinion CONSENSUS
- acceptance of an agreement or treaty ACCESSION
- affecting or undertaken by two parties, sometimes in different ways, as an agreement might be BIPARTITE, BILATERAL
- announce formally the rejection of an agreement DENOUNCE
- break an agreement, a contract, or the like INFRINGE, VIOLATE, RENEGE ON
- discuss terms in the attempt to reach an agreement NEGOTIATE
- person or party that signs and is bound to a treaty or other agreement SIGNATORY
- require or lay down as a condition in an agreement or contract STIPULATE
- summary or memorandum of a meeting or agreement, used as the basis of a fully detailed text AIDE-MÉMOIRE
- unspoken, implied, understood, as an informal agreement might be TACIT

agriculture See **farming**
aha!, exclamation of triumph on finding, solving, or discovering something EUREKA, VOILÀ
ahead of the times, pioneering AVANT-GARDE
aids or provisions, such as buildings and equipment, for a particular activity FACILITIES
aim, goal, desired objective, finishing point TERMINUS AD QUEM
- aim at or strive toward some goal, have an ambition ASPIRE

aimless, unsettled, drifting VAGABOND, VAGRANT
air - aerodynamics testing chamber for studying the effect of moving air speed on cars, aircraft, or the like WIND TUNNEL
- abnormal fear of fresh air AEROPHOBIA
- atmosphere of foul vapors or polluted air MIASMA
- bacterium or other organism that can live without air or free oxygen ANAEROBE
- bacterium or other organism that needs air or free oxygen to live AEROBE
- containing as much water vapor as possible, as humid air might SATURATED
- containing large amounts of water vapor, as moist air does, close, muggy HUMID
- death because of lack of air, suffocation ASPHYXIA
- exercise system increasing the intake of oxygen AEROBICS
- fresh and pure air, as at the seaside OZONE
- low in density, thin, as the air of the upper atmosphere is or a gas might be RAREFIED
- pass fresh air through a room, mine, or the like VENTILATE
- relating to the air or other gases PNEUMATIC
- release air or gas from something, such as a tire DEFLATE
- surrounding, in the immediate vicinity, as the air or temperature might be AMBIENT

air (combining form) AER-, AERO-, ATMO-, PNEUM-, PNEUMO-, PNEUMATO-
air bladder of a fish SOUND
air bubble BLEB
air conditioners - chemical used in refrigerators and air conditioners FREON
- air-conditioning channel DUCT

air cushion - support a severely burned patient on a cushion of air LEVITATE
air force See **military, services**
air freshener or fumigating substance in the form of a small cone of an aromatic preparation that is set alight PASTILLE
air mail PAR AVION
air raid or similar intensive attack BLITZ
air traffic - exclusive right of a country to assign internal air traffic to its own carriers CABOTAGE
air turbulence caused by an aircraft WASH
air vent SPIRACLE
aircraft See illustration, and also **jet engine**
- aircraft, such as a balloon or dirigible, that is lighter than air AEROSTAT
- aircraft, train, or the like traveling empty DEADHEAD
- aircraft attack on enemy ground troops, typically a low-flying machine-gun attack STRAFE
- aircraft fuselage or car body in which the stress is taken mainly by the casing MONOCOQUE
- aircraft-launching device, as on an aircraft carrier CATAPULT
- aircraft that is heavier than air AERODYNE
- aircraft that is propelled by flapping wings ORNITHOPTER, ORTHOPTER
- aircraft with both a horizontal rotor and conventional propellers AUTOGYRO, GYROPLANE
- aircraft that has its tailplane located in front of the main wings CANARD
- aircraft without a pilot, operated by remote control DRONE
- aircraft's cockpit that can be ejected as a unit in an emergency CAPSULE
- aircraft's course or direction, especially when guided by radio VECTOR
- aircraft's electronic recorder of technical details, used to establish the cause of a crash BLACK BOX, FLIGHT RECORDER
- aircraft's flight path, typically circular, when awaiting clearance to land HOLDING PATTERN
- aircraft's load of cargo, passengers, bombs, or the like PAYLOAD
- aircraft's wing, tailplane, flap, or other surface affecting lift or stability in flight AIRFOIL
- aerodynamics testing chamber for studying the effect of moving air speed on cars, aircraft, or the like WIND TUNNEL
- air deflector, as on an aircraft's wing or a racing car, to increase drag and reduce the tendency to lift SPOILER
- arched or upwardly curved surface, as of a road or aircraft's wing CAMBER

- circling an airport at different altitudes while waiting for landing clearance, as two or more aircraft might be STACKED
- explosive bang produced by the shock wave from an aircraft that is flying faster than the speed of sound SONIC BOOM
- fly an aircraft slightly into a crosswind to offset the drift it causes CRAB
- fly an aircraft very low, rising to avoid hedges, fences, and so on HEDGEHOP
- funnel-shaped target towed behind an aircraft DROGUE
- glide without power, as an aircraft might VOLPLANE
- instrument, as in an aircraft, for measuring altitude ALTIMETER
- land or run past the end of a runway, as an aircraft might OVERSHOOT
- land short of the runway, as an aircraft might UNDERSHOOT
- move slowly into position before takeoff or after landing, as aircraft do TAXI
- permission for an aircraft, ship, or the like to proceed, as after a weather check, customs inspection, traffic delay, or the like CLEARANCE
- referring to aircraft able to fly faster than the speed of sound SUPERSONIC
- referring to aircraft flying long distances without stopping LONG-HAUL
- seat in a military aircraft designed to hurl the pilot or crew member clear in an emergency EJECTION SEAT
- single raid or mission by a combat aircraft SORTIE
- spin or wobble in flight, as a missile or aircraft might YAW
- streamlined compartment, as for fuel or guns, on an aircraft POD
- take off quickly after an alert to intercept enemy aircraft SCRAMBLE
- tip or tilt sideways, as an aircraft does when turning BANK
- training device consisting of a model, machine, or system reproducing actual conditions, such as a model flight deck of an aircraft SIMULATOR
- transparent bubblelike cover of the cockpit of an aircraft CANOPY
- visible trail of condensed water vapor from the engine exhaust of an aircraft flying at high altitude VAPOR TRAIL, CONDENSATION TRAIL, CONTRAIL

airfield - tapering cloth tube fixed to a pole to indicate wind direction, as at airfields WINDSOCK, WIND CORE, WIND SLEEVE, AIR SOCK, DROGUE

airplane See **aircraft**

airport hall for passengers stopping temporarily, as for changing flights TRANSIT LOUNGE
- airport's forecourt for parked aircraft APRON
- building for parking aircraft HANGAR
- conveyer-belt apparatus in the baggage-claim section of an airport CAROUSEL
- open space for crowds, at an airport terminal, station, or other public place CONCOURSE
- rotating belt on corridor floors, as in an airport, for transporting pedestrians and their luggage MOVING SIDEWALK, WALKWAY, TRAVELATOR

airship of an early maneuverable kind DIRIGIBLE
- airship or balloon typically used as a barrage balloon BLIMP
- airship with a long oval body ZEPPELIN
- basket or cabin under a balloon or airship GONDOLA
- trailing rope on a balloon or airship, used for mooring or braking DRAGROPE

airstream behind a fast-moving aircraft or vehicle SLIPSTREAM

airtight, firmly sealed HERMETIC

airy, light as air ETHEREAL
- airy, unrealistic VISIONARY

aisle, cloister, or similar covered area for walking AMBULATORY

alarm signal, typically sounded on a bell TOCSIN

alchemist, alchemist's distilling flask, an early form of retort ALEMBIC, AMBIX

alchemy See chart, page 20

alcohol of the basic kind as found in wines and spirits ETHANOL, ETHYL ALCOHOL

Aircraft

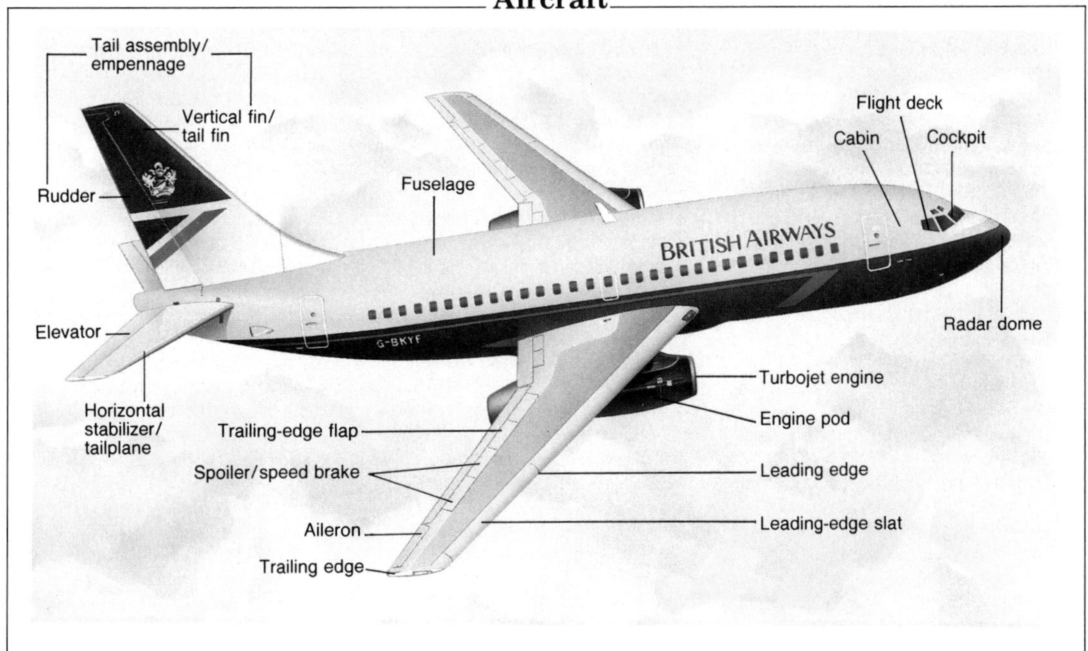

ALCHEMY TERMS

alembic/ ambix	apparatus for distillation
alkahest	universal solvent, dissolving all substances
almagest	medieval textbook of techniques
arcanum	Nature's great secret, sought by alchemists
azoth	mercury considered as the basis of all metals; universal remedy of Paracelsus
elixir	substance able to convert base metals into silver or gold; universal remedy; substance maintaining life indefinitely
iatrochemistry	alchemy devoted to medical purposes
kerotakis	apparatus for sublimation
luna	silver
magistery	transmuting substance, such as the philosophers' stone
panacea	universal remedy, cure-all
philosophers' stone	or philosopher's stone, lapis philosophorum; stone or similar substance able to convert base metals into silver or gold
prima materia	"first matter," out of which, it was thought, all physical objects could be made
spagyrist	alchemist
transmutation/ sublimation	conversion of base metals into silver or gold

- alcohol of a poisonous kind, used as an antifreeze METHANOL
- alcohol or drug addiction DEPENDENCE
- alcohol solution of a medicinal substance TINCTURE
- add alcohol secretly to a drink SPIKE, LACE
- ban on the making, selling, and consuming of alcoholic drinks, as in the United States from 1920 to 1933 PROHIBITION
- bar or informal shop for the illicit sale of alcoholic drinks, especially during the Prohibition era in the United States SPEAKEASY
- bar or informal shop for the illicit sale of alcoholic drinks, especially in Ireland or southern Africa SHEBEEN
- blend or dilute whiskey or other alcoholic spirits RECTIFY
- drink alcohol, whether in moderation or to excess INDULGE, IMBIBE
- leftover impure spirits from the distillation of alcoholic drinks, especially whiskey FAINTS, FEINTS
- licensed purveyor of alcoholic spirits VICTUALER
- lockable cagelike container for displaying decanters of alcoholic drinks TANTALUS
- make, sell, or transport goods illegally, especially alcohol during the Prohibition era in the United States BOOTLEG
- moderation in or shunning of the consumption of alcoholic drinks TEMPERANCE
- nausea-inducing substance added to methylated spirits or ethyl alcohol to make it unfit for drinking DENATURANT
- refraining from drinking alcohol ABSTAINING, ABSTINENCE, TEETOTALISM
- valved tap on an inverted bottle of alcoholic spirits, as in a bar or tavern, releasing an exact tot measure OPTIC

alcoholic See also **drunk**
- alcoholic, addicted to or characterized by alcoholic drink BIBULOUS

alcoholic drink See also **drink, wine**
- alcoholic drink INTOXICANT, LIBATION, TINCTURE
- small drink of alcoholic spirits SNIFTER, SNORT
- small measure for alcoholic drinks JIGGER
- someone's favorite or usual alcoholic drink TIPPLE

alcoholism, craving for alcoholic drink DIPSOMANIA, ALCOHOLOPHILIA
- abnormal aversion to alcohol DIPSOPHOBIA
- alcoholism treatment, a medical drug that causes nausea when one has an alcoholic drink ANTABUSE, DISULFIRAM
- device for testing drivers for alcohol intake BREATHALIZER
- drunkenness EBRIETY, INEBRIETY, INSOBRIETY
- liver disease or degeneration, typically irreversible, often resulting from alcoholism CIRRHOSIS
- severe mental disorder, sometimes accompanying alcoholism, involving tremors and hallucinations DELIRIUM TREMENS, D.T.'S

alert, watchful, on the lookout for danger VIGILANT, ON THE QUI VIVE, ARGUS-EYED
- take off quickly after an alert to intercept enemy aircraft SCRAMBLE

algae (combining form) PHYCO-

algebra - line drawn above two or more terms in algebra, linking them as a single unit VINCULUM
- algebraic system of symbolic logic BOOLEAN ALGEBRA

all (combining form) OMNI-, PAN-, PANTO-

all-embracing, as a view or survey might be PANOPTIC
- all-embracing, wide-ranging, liberal and broad-minded, as one's interests might be CATHOLIC

all-knowing OMNISCIENT

all-powerful OMNIPOTENT

all right, satisfactory, in good order HUNKY-DORY, OKEY-DOKE, KOSHER

all-rounder person who is learned in a variety of different subjects POLYMATH, POLYHISTOR, RENAISSANCE MAN, RENAISSANCE WOMAN

all the more so A FORTIORI

all together, as a whole, in a group EN BLOC, EN MASSE

allergy, allergy-induced skin rash, hives URTICARIA
- allergy test in which the allergens are applied to scratches made on the skin SCRATCH TEST
- allergy test in which the allergens are applied to the skin by means of a surgical pad PATCH TEST
- allergic response to a medicine, pollen, or some other substance REACTION
- compound released in allergic reactions HISTAMINE
- medical drug used in the treatment of allergies ANTIHISTAMINE
- protein mixture in wheat flour, an occasional source of allergy in chil-

dren GLUTEN
- sign, such as an allergy or dangerous side effect, that argues for the discontinuation of a medicine or treatment CONTRAINDICATION
- substance that induces an allergy, ALLERGEN

alliance or union, typically temporary, of political parties or other groups COALITION, CONSORTIUM

alligator - crocodile from tropical America, related to the alligator CAIMAN

allow, certify, or license something that meets a required standard ACCREDIT
- allow, enable, or permit AUTHORIZE, EMPOWER, WARRANT
- allow oneself, in a haughty way, to do something DEIGN, CONDESCEND
- allow oneself to satisfy a whim or craving INDULGE
- allow or tolerate COUNTENANCE, SANCTION

allowance, salary, or similar regular payment or grant STIPEND
- allowance for a day's expenses PER DIEM
- allowance of money to an employee to cover incidental expenses or as an advance on pay SUBSISTENCE ALLOWANCE
- anticipate and make allowance for something unwanted or dangerous DISCOUNT, LEGISLATE FOR

alloy See also **metal**
- alloy melted to fuse two metal parts SOLDER
- chief metal in an alloy MATRIX

ally, person associated in a profession COLLEAGUE
- people joined for a guilty purpose CONFEDERATES, ACCOMPLICES
- people working together ASSOCIATES

almond cookie MACAROON
- almond essence or flavoring RATAFIA
- almond-flavored Italian liqueur AMARETTO
- almond paste, sweetened and used for sweets or icing MARZIPAN
- adjective for an almond or almond tree AMYGDALOID, AMYGDALACEOUS
- loosen the skin of an almond by scalding BLANCH

almost or apparently, but not really QUASI

almshouse - formerly a man living in an almshouse BEADSMAN, BEDESMAN
- referring to alms or charity ELEEMOSYNARY

alone See also **lonely, unique**
- alone, cut off or remote from others of its kind ISOLATED, INSULATED, CLOISTERED, SEQUESTERED, INCOMMUNICADO
- alone, or preferring to remain alone SOLITARY, SECLUDED
- person who lives alone, withdrawn in solitude RECLUSE, HERMIT

alone (combining form) MON-, MONO, SOLI-, SOLO-, UNI-

alongside, next to ADJACENT, CONTIGUOUS, ABUTTING, JUXTAPOSED, TANGENTIAL

alphabet See chart, and also **Greek, script, typeface**
- alphabetic writing system ORTHOGRAPHY
- board displaying the alphabet, used in spiritualism sessions to register messages OUIJA BOARD
- code, as used by radio operators,

ALPHABETS AND WRITING SYSTEMS

boustrophedon	lines alternately written from left to right and right to left (an ancient system, now revived in computer printers)
cuneiform	ancient Middle Eastern script using wedge-shaped characters
Cyrillic	alphabet used in Russian and Bulgarian
demotics	a later hieroglyphic style
Devanagari	syllabic script used in Sanskrit texts and Hindi and other Indian languages
futhark	alphabet of runes
Glagolitic	early Slavonic alphabet
hieroglyphics	ancient Egyptian picture writing
ideography	system of symbolic characters to represent entire words or ideas, as in Chinese
International Phonetic Alphabet (IPA)	standard set of letters and symbols, as used in dictionaries, to represent the sounds of all languages
kana	either of two Japanese syllabic scripts, hiragana or katakana
kanji	Japanese syllabary based on Chinese characters
Kufic	early Arabic script or alphabet
Linear A	ancient Cretan script, still undeciphered
Linear B	ancient script used in Crete and mainland Greece, deciphered in 1952
ogham	ancient angular Celtic alphabet and script, used mainly in Ireland
pictography	system of pictures to represent entire words or phrases, as in hieroglyphics
Pinyin	new Chinese system of phonetic transcription
romaji	Roman alphabet as used to transliterate Japanese
Roman alphabet	standard alphabet of most Western and central European languages
Rosetta stone	basalt slab of 200 BC with the same text in hieroglyphics, demotic, and Greek characters, found in 1799
runes	ancient Germanic carved alphabetic script
syllabary	set of written characters, each representing a syllable
Wade-Giles	19th-century Chinese transcription system, replaced by Pinyin

for identifying letters of the alphabet, such as *Tango* standing for *T* PHONETIC ALPHABET
- series of notches cut into the front edge of a dictionary or other book, as for easy alphabetical reference THUMB INDEX
- write or spell in the letters of another alphabet TRANSLITERATE

alpine house or hut CHALET

Alps - sing in a voice wavering between normal and falsetto, as among folksingers in the Swiss Alps YODEL
- situated on, living on, or relating to the other side of the mountains, typically south of the Alps ULTRAMONTANE
- situated on, living on, or relating to this side of the mountains, typically north of the Alps CISMONTANE

also known as, under the assumed name of ALIAS, AKA

altar or chapel built especially for prayers or Mass for the benefactor's soul CHANTRY
- altar boy ACOLYTE, THURIFER
- altar's canopy, either of fabric or of stone BALDACHIN, TESTER
- altar's covering or pulpit cloth ANTEPENDIUM
- altar's decorative hanging or tapestry FRONTAL, DOSSAL
- altar's platform or shelf, or the decoration for it PREDELLA
- altar's surrounding area or sanctuary in the Eastern Orthodox church BEMA
- cover or canopy over a high altar, supported upon four pillars CIBORIUM
- shelf or ledge above an altar, for the cross, lights, flowers, or the like RETABLE
- tapestry, sculpture, or other decoration behind an altar REREDOS

altarpiece consisting of a painting or carving in three connected parts TRIPTYCH

alter See also **change**
- alter a document, accounts, or the like with the intent to deceive FALSIFY
- alter a female mammal through hysterectomy SPAY
- alteration or deliberate mutilation of a document so as to invalidate it SPOLIATION

alternate, proceed in a given order or sequence ROTATE

alternating back-and-forth movement RECIPROCATION

alternative medicine See **therapy**

alternatives - situation requiring a choice between two equal and typically undesirable alternatives DILEMMA, QUANDARY

aluminum - clayey mineral that is the chief ore of aluminum BAUXITE

always See **constant, permanent**

amateur - person whose interest in something, such as the arts, is amateurish or superficial DABBLER, DILETTANTE

amazed See **surprise**

ambassador See also **diplomat**
- ambassador from the Vatican NUNCIO
- ambassador or agent fully authorized to represent a foreign government PLENIPOTENTIARY
- document authorizing an ambassador or other diplomat to act on behalf of his government LETTER OF CREDENCE, LETTERS OF CREDENCE

ambiguity arising from loose grammar rather than from a word's meaning AMPHIBOLOGY
- ambiguity or multiple meaning in individual words POLYSEMY, DOUBLE ENTENDRE
- remove the ambiguity from, make clear DISAMBIGUATE

ambiguous or evasive, as an answer might be EQUIVOCAL
- ambiguous or evasive speech or behavior EQUIVOCATION, PREVARICATION, TEMPORIZING, TERGIVERSATION
- ambiguous or obscure, as though spoken by an oracle DELPHIC

ambition, desire or striving for success and recognition ASPIRATION
- ambition of an excessive kind, delusions of grandeur FOLIE DE GRANDEUR
- excessive and unjustified, as someone's ambition might be OVERWEENING
- ruin or thwart hopes, ambition, or the like BLIGHT

ambush AMBUSCADE
- ambush, lie in wait for and take by surprise WAYLAY

amendment, clause, or qualification added to a verdict, parliamentary bill, or the like RIDER

amends, atonement or reparation REDRESS, QUITTANCE, EXPIATION
- make amends, compensate or repay REIMBURSE, REQUITE, RECOUP, RECOMPENSE

America and Europe, and the West in general OCCIDENT

American black person considered subservient to whites UNCLE TOM
- American middle-class man, narrow-minded and self-satisfied BABBITT
- American nation or government personified UNCLE SAM
- American young woman fashionable around 1900 GIBSON GIRL

American Civil War - referring or relating to the period before the American Civil War ANTEBELLUM
- referring or relating to the period after the American Civil War POSTBELLUM

American Indian terms See chart

ammunition and weapons MUNITIONS, ORDNANCE
- ammunition box or horse-drawn vehicle formerly used to transport ammunition CAISSON

amoeba or similar tiny organism ANIMALCULE, ANIMALCULUM, PROTOZOAN

among (combining form) EPI-, INTER-

among other things INTER ALIA

amounting to, equivalent, equal in value or effect TANTAMOUNT

amphibian resembling a lizard in appearance SALAMANDER, AXOLOTL, NEWT
- study of amphibians and reptiles HERPETOLOGY

amphitheater - passageway to a bank of seats in a stadium or amphitheater, as in the Colosseum in Rome VOMITORY, VOMITORIUM

amputation, either surgical or accidental AVULSION
- amputation or surgical excision ABLATION
- illusory limb, still felt as the source of pain even though the real limb has been amputated PHANTOM LIMB

amuse oneself or occupy oneself in a pleasurable activity DISPORT
- amuse or give pleasure to, as by telling stories REGALE

amusement See also **entertainment**
- amusement, recreation DIVERSION, DISTRACTION

amusement-park attendant who attracts customers to a booth or sideshow by loud sales patter BARKER
- amusement-park performer who bites off the head of a live frog, mouse, chicken, snake, or the like GEEK
- amusement-park ride with small, rapidly direction-changing cars WHIP
- elevated railway at an amusement park, providing a fast exciting ride ROLLER COASTER
- small electric car driven and bumped into others at an amusement-park rink BUMPER CAR

amusing See **funny**

an or **a** in English grammar, introducing without strictly identifying the noun following it INDEFINITE ARTICLE

anal swelling and itching, piles HEMORRHOIDS

analysis of a complex project, based on comparing various combina-

tions of stages CRITICAL-PATH ANALYSIS
- analysis of complex information, plans, or the like into simpler units, especially in an unsophisticated and misleading way REDUCTIONISM
- analysis or critical explanation of a text, especially of the Bible EXEGESIS
- analysis or interpretation of a literary work, theory, or the like EXPLICATION, EXPOSITION
- analysis or review of a recent event, game, failure, or the like POSTMORTEM
- analysis or testing, especially of a precious metal ASSAY
- combining of separate elements into a coherent whole, the opposite process to analysis SYNTHESIS

analyze See also **examine, study**
- analyze or examine in fine detail DISSECT, ANATOMIZE
- analyze to sort the good from the bad SIFT, WINNOW

ancestor PROGENITOR, PROCREATOR, FOREBEAR
- ancestor or forefather, especially the first or earliest ancestor as of a people PRIMOGENITOR
- ancestor or forerunner PRECURSOR, PREDECESSOR, ANTECEDENT
- descended from the same ancestor, though by different lines COLLATERAL
- family tree, or the study of someone's ancestors GENEALOGY, LINEAGE
- group of plants or animals with a common ancestor CLADE
- influenced by or derived from one's ancestors HEREDITARY
- reappearance in a plant or animal of long absent features that had been characteristic of an ancestor generation ATAVISM

ancestry, line of descent LINEAGE, DERIVATION, PEDIGREE

anchor - anchor cable HAWSER
- anchor used for maneuvering a boat KEDGE
- anchor with several flukes, for mooring a small boat GRAPNEL
- lowest part of an anchor, where the arms are fixed CROWN
- opening in a ship's bow for the anchor cable HAWSE, HAWSEHOLE
- raise an anchor, as in preparation for sailing WEIGH, TRIP
- raised just clear of the bottom, as an anchor might be AWEIGH
- sea anchor DROGUE
- stone anchor KILLICK

anchovies - salad including chopped meat, anchovies, and eggs SALMAGUNDI

ancient, dating back to an earlier era ARCHAIC, ANCESTRAL
- ancient, going back beyond recorded history IMMEMORIAL
- ancient, no longer current, outmoded OBSOLETE, PASSÉ
- ancient, outmoded, or extremely old-fashioned ANTIQUATED
- ancient, primitive, prehistoric PRIMEVAL, PRISTINE
- ancient, stale, or unoriginal, as a joke might be HOARY, MUSTY
- ancient, stretching back to or as if back to the time before the biblical Flood ANTEDILUVIAN
- ancient and respected VENERABLE
- ancient Egyptian writing system using pictures HIEROGLYPHICS
- ancient Middle Eastern writing system using wedge-shaped characters CUNEIFORM
- ancient objects, as of a bygone civilization RELICS, ANTIQUITIES
- ancient times, history long ago ANTIQUITY
- relating to the civilization of ancient Greece and Rome, ancient China, or the like CLASSICAL

ancient (combining form) ARCHEO-, PALEO-

and - the sign *&* representing the word *and* AMPERSAND
- *and* or *but*, or similar conjunction joining words, phrases, or clauses of equal status in a sentence COORDINATING CONJUNCTION
- repetition of *and* or other conjunctions for stylistic effect, as in *blood and sweat and tears* POLYSYNDETON

anemia in which bone marrow produces too few blood cells or other components APLASTIC ANEMIA

anesthetic - injection of anesthetic into the lining of the spinal cord EPIDURAL
- gas commonly used as an anesthetic LAUGHING GAS, NITROUS OXIDE
- local anesthetic in common use NOVOCAIN, LIDOCAINE, LIGNOCAINE
- poisonous chemical extract used as premedication before a general anesthetic ATROPINE
- sedative given to a patient before a general anesthetic PREMEDICATION
- semiconsciousness or drowsy pain-free state produced by certain anesthetics TWILIGHT SLEEP
- volatile liquid formerly used as anesthetic CHLOROFORM, ETHER

angel See chart, page 24
- angel, chubby boy, or little cupid, as in paintings AMORETTO, PUTTO, CHERUB
- angel or similar nonphysical being INTELLIGENCE
- appearance of a ghost, spirit, angel, or the like VISITATION

anger See also **angry**

AMERICAN INDIAN TERMS

hogan	Navaho cabin of logs and mud
moccasin	soft leather shoe
papoose	baby or young child
potlatch	communal feast in northwest coastal regions, at which property is given away or destroyed
powwow	conference or ritual ceremony; medicine man
pueblo	communal residence or village in the southwestern U.S.
sachem, sagamore	tribal chief
squaw	woman or wife
tepee	cone-shaped tent
tomahawk	light ax
travois	sledgelike vehicle formerly used by the Plains Indians
wampum/peag	shell beads, used as money or decoration
wickiup	temporary hut of grass or reeds over a rough frame
wigwam	arching hut of branches, covered with bark, mats, or hides

ANGELS
the nine orders or choirs of angels (in descending order)
seraphim
cherubim
thrones
dominations/dominions
virtues
powers
principalities
archangels
angels

- anger moderately, irritate, vex IRK, PIQUE, RANKLE
- anger to the point of bitterness or estrangement ANTAGONIZE, ENVENOM, ALIENATE, EXACERBATE
- arousing strong feelings quickly, especially feelings of anger INFLAMMATORY
- calm or reduce someone's fear, anger, or the like ALLAY
- explode, burst out violently, as in anger ERUPT
- feeling of anger or distress arising from a sense of being injured or wronged GRIEVANCE
- feeling of anger or embarrassment because of disappointment or failure CHAGRIN
- feeling or display of anger, bitterness, or ill will ANIMOSITY, ACRIMONY, RANCOR
- fit or tantrum, as of anger PAROXYSM, CONNIPTION
- indignation or outrage, feeling of anger or resentment UMBRAGE, HACKLES, DUDGEON
- irritability, moderate anger, ill temper ASPERITY

angle See also **geometry**
- angle, as of a star, from a fixed reference, usually due south on the horizon, typically measured clockwise in degrees AZIMUTH
- angle added to another to produce a right angle COMPLEMENT
- angle at which light rays are first reflected by the surface of water, a glass lens, or the like CRITICAL ANGLE
- angle between a leafstalk and the stem, between a branch and the trunk, or the like AXIL
- angle between lines or surfaces other than a right angle, or such a line or surface BEVEL, CANT
- angle between two intersecting planes, specifically between an aircraft's wing and a horizontal line DIHEDRAL ANGLE
- angle or degree of slope GRADIENT, INCLINATION
- angle or fork formed by branches, steps, pants legs, or the like CROTCH
- angle or slope, as of a mast, theater's stage, aircraft's wings, or cutting edge of a tool RAKE
- define an arc or angle by cutting or ending the lines forming it SUBTEND
- instrument, used in navigation, for measuring the angles of stars and planets to determine the observer's position SEXTANT
- instrument used to measure and draw angles PROTRACTOR
- pointing or jutting outward, projecting, as an angle might SALIENT
- triangular sheet of wood, metal, or plastic, used to construct certain angles quickly in geometry or technical drawing SET SQUARE

angle (combining form) -CLIN-, CLINO-, -GON

Anglican EPISCOPAL

Anglo-Saxon See **medieval** and chart at **feudal system**

angry See also **anger**
- angry, or provoked IRATE, WRATHFUL, INDIGNANT, RILED
- angry criticism, expression of outrage FULMINATIONS, VITUPERATION, INVECTIVE
- angry in a snobbish way HOITY-TOITY
- angry mutual accusations RECRIMINATIONS
- angry or sulky frown SCOWL
- angry speech of denunciation HARANGUE, PHILIPPIC, JEREMIAD, TIRADE, DIATRIBE
- furious, intensely angry, seething, enraged APOPLECTIC, INCENSED, LIVID, RAMPAGEOUS
- gloomy, surly, dour, or readily angered CURMUDGEONLY, QUERULOUS
- irritable, easily angered, peevish TETCHY, CHOLERIC, BILIOUS, FRACTIOUS, DYSPEPTIC
- irritable, ill-tempered, easily provoked into becoming very angry SPLENETIC, CANTANKEROUS, IRASCIBLE, ATRABILIOUS
- moderately angry, displeased, crotchety DISGRUNTLED
- quick-tempered, easily angered or provoked VOLATILE, INFLAMMABLE
- unreasonably angry or discontented, snappish PETULANT

animal See chart, pages 25–26, and also **bird** and other entries at specific classes, orders, and species
- animal, such as a horse or ox, used for pulling heavy loads DRAFT ANIMAL
- animal form of a basic single-celled type, typically microscopic, such as an amoeba PROTOZOAN
- animal lover ZOOPHILE
- animal or plant bred from two different varieties or species HYBRID
- animal or plant established in a region though not indigenous to it DENIZEN
- animal or plant in a very early stage of its development EMBRYO
- animal skin or hide removed from the carcass PELT
- animal that kills and eats prey PREDATOR
- animal that moves from one region to another MIGRANT
- animal-transmitted disease such as rabies or malaria ZOONOSIS
- animals collectively, especially of a given region FAUNA
- active during the day rather than at night, as most animals are DIURNAL
- active during the night, as some animals are NOCTURNAL
- belt or band encircling something, such as a stripe of color on an animal's coat CINGULUM
- body of an animal, especially after being slaughtered and prepared for sale CARCASS
- book or collection, especially in medieval times, of moral fables based on animals BESTIARY
- cutting up or into the body of a living animal, especially for research VIVISECTION
- enclosure or tank for keeping or breeding animals or plants indoors VIVARIUM
- jaws and nose of an animal SNOUT, MUZZLE
- kill an animal, especially a weak one, as to reduce a herd CULL
- learning process in young animals IMPRINTING
- light or colored marking on an animal's coat FLASH
- plantlike animal ZOOPHYTE
- protective coloring of an animal by which it resembles an unrelated animal that is poisonous or unpalatable to predators BATESIAN MIMICRY
- relating to animal diseases or injuries and the treatment of them VETERINARY
- referring to animals inhabiting trees ARBOREAL
- referring to land-dwelling animals TERRESTRIAL
- referring to water-dwelling animals AQUATIC, MARINE
- reproduce or cause plants or animals to reproduce PROPAGATE
- small animals such as cockroaches or rats that are harmful or an-

ANIMAL TERMS						
ANIMAL	GROUP	MALE	FEMALE	YOUNG	RELATED ADJECTIVE	HOME OR MENAGERIE
ape	**shrewdness**				**simian, pongid**	
ass, donkey	**herd, drove, pace**	**jack, jackass dicky**	**jenny, she-ass**	**foal, colt (male), filly (female)**	**asinine**	
badger	**cete, colony**	**boar**	**sow**	**cub**	**meline**	**sett, set**
bear	**sloth**			**cub**	**ursine**	
boar	**sounder, herd, singular**	**boar**	**sow**	**piglet, squeaker, calf**	**porcine, suidian**	
cat	**clowder, cluster, glaring, dout/destruction (of wild cats), litter/kindle (of kittens)**	**tom, gib (usually castrated)**	**queen, tabby, puss, she-cat**	**kitten**	**feline**	**cattery, lair, den (wild cats)**
cattle	**herd, drove, team/yoke (oxen)**	**bull, ox, steer**	**cow**	**calf, stirk, bullock (male), heifer (female)**	**bovine, taurine (bulls)**	**barn, stable, pasture, byre**
deer	**herd, leash, parcel (hinds)**	**buck, stag, hart**	**doe, hind**	**fawn, calf, kid, pricket/brocket (male)**	**cervine**	
dog	**pack, kennel, litter**	**dog, hound**	**bitch**	**pup, whelp**	**canine**	**kennel**
elephant	**herd**	**bull**	**cow**	**calf**	**elephantine**	
ferret	**business, fesnying, cast**	**dog, buck, jack, hob**	**bitch, doe, jill**	**kit**	**musteline**	
fox	**skulk, lead**	**dog, vix**	**vixen**	**cub**	**vulpine**	**earth, lair**
frog	**army, colony**			**tadpole**	**ranine, batrachian, anuran, salientian**	
goat	**flock, herd, tribe**	**billy, buck**	**nanny, doe**	**kid, yearling**	**capric, hircine**	
hare	**drove, trace, down, husk, trip, leash**	**buck, jack**	**doe, puss**	**leveret**	**leporine**	**form**
horse	**herd, stable, harras, team, troop, race/rag/rake (of colts)**	**stallion, horse, sire, stud, gelding (castrated)**	**mare, dam**	**foal, colt (male), filly (female)**	**equine**	**stable, paddock, stall, stud**
kangaroo	**troop, herd, mob**	**buck, boomer**	**blue doe, blue flier**	**joey**	**macropine**	
leopard	**leap, lepe**	**leopard**	**leopardess**	**cub**	**pardine**	
lion	**pride, sault, troop**	**lion**	**lioness**	**cub**	**leonine**	**den**
mole	**labor, movement, company**				**talpine**	**burrow, fortress, tunnel**

continued

ANIMAL TERMS *continued*						
ANIMAL	GROUP	MALE	FEMALE	YOUNG	RELATED ADJECTIVE	HOME OR MENAGERIE
monkey	**troop, tribe, cartload**				**simian**	
mule	**barren, rake, pack, span**					
otter	**family, bevy**	**dog**	**bitch**	**cub**	**lutrine**	**holt, lodge**
pig	**herd, sounder, farrow (of piglets)**	**boar, hog, barrow (castrated)**	**sow, gilt**	**piglet, pigling, shoat, gilt (female)**	**porcine**	**pen, sty**
polecat	**chine**	**hob**	**jill**	**kit**	**mustelid, musteline**	
rabbit	**colony, bury, nest (of young)**	**buck**	**doe**	**nestling**	**oryctolagine**	**warren, burrow**
rat	**colony**	**buck**	**doe**	**nestling**	**murine**	
rhinoceros	**crash**	**bull**	**cow**	**calf**	**rhinocerotic**	
seal	**colony, crash, harem, bob, herd, pod, team**	**bull**	**cow**	**pup, cub**	**phocid, phocine**	
sheep	**flock, drove, trip, hurtle, down, fold**	**ram, wether (castrated), tup**	**ewe**	**lamb, hog, teg**	**ovine**	**fold**
snake	**den, pit, nest**				**anguine, ophidian**	**nest**
squirrel				**nestling**	**sciurine**	**drey**
tiger	**ambush**	**tiger**	**tigress**	**cub**	**tigrine**	**lair**
walrus	**herd, pod**	**bull**	**cow**	**calf**	**odobenid**	
whale	**school, herd, gam, pod**	**bull**	**cow**	**calf**	**cetacean**	
wolf	**pack, herd, rout**	**dog, he-wolf**	**bitch, she-wolf**	**cub, whelp**	**lupine**	**lair, den**
zebra	**herd**	**stallion**	**mare**	**foal, colt (male), filly (female)**	**zebrine**	

noying to humans VERMIN
- spots on the skin of an animal MACULATIONS
- study of animal behavior ETHOLOGY
- stuffing and preparing the skins of dead animals TAXIDERMY
- tame, train, or breed animals to live with and be of use to humans DOMESTICATE
- use of animal forms or symbols, as in art ZOOMORPHISM

animal (combining form) -ZO-, -ZOA, ZOO-, THERI-, THERIO-

ankle TARSUS
- ankle bone TALUS
- ankle covering of cloth or leather, worn over the shoe GAITER, SPAT
- bony bump at either side of the ankle MALLEOLUS
- metal fastening confining the wrists or ankles MANACLES, FETTERS, SHACKLES

annexation of Austria by Nazi Germany in 1938 ANSCHLUSS

anniversary See chart
- anniversary of a royal accession JUBILEE

announce, reveal, or disclose something private or secret DIVULGE
- announce official news PROCLAIM, HERALD
- announce or make known, often by subtle hints INTIMATE
- announce something publicly and officially, such as a law or doctrine PROMULGATE

announcement made officially to the press and public COMMUNIQUÉ, PROCLAMATION
- announcement of new information REVELATION, DISCLOSURE

annoy See also **anger, angry**
- annoying, irritating IRKSOME, VEXATIOUS, PESTIFEROUS, PESTILENTIAL

annual publication listing information such as tide patterns and weather statistics ALMANAC
- annual payment of an allowance, dividends, or the like ANNUITY

anointing for ritual or healing purposes UNCTION
- mixture of oil and balsam used in sacramental anointing CHRISM

anorexia - illness in which compulsive eating is often followed by bouts of self-induced vomiting BULIMIA, BULIMIA NERVOSA, BULMOREXIA

answer, pay back in kind, respond with a counterattack RETALIATE

- answer, reply, quick retaliatory action or retort RIPOSTE, REJOINDER, REPARTEE
- answer, response REPLICATION
- answer or response, such as a chorus of disagreement ANTIPHON
- answer or statement that is very short or curt, specifically one of a single syllable MONOSYLLABLE
- answering and anticipation of an argument or objection before it has been stated PROLEPSIS
- deliberately vague or noncommital as an answer might be EVASIVE
- witty answer or retort that occurs to one only when it is too late ESPRIT D'ESCALIER

ant PISMIRE
- ant-eating MYRMECOPHAGOUS
- antlike wood-eating insect TERMITE
- adjective for ants FORMIC
- practice among some species of ants of forcing ants from other species to do the work in their colony DULOSIS, HELOTISM
- study of ants MYRMECOLOGY
- swarm or teem, as if with ants, or creating such a sensation on the skin FORMICATE

ant (combining form) MYRMEC-, MYRMECO-

anteater of tropical Asia and Africa, having scales, a long tail, and a sticky tongue PANGOLIN

anthem of France MARSEILLAISE

anthill, or ant farm or colony kept in a glass box FORMICARY
- anthill-like nest built by a colony of termites TERMITARIUM

anthology, as of one author's works OMNIBUS
- anthology of literary extracts, as used for studying a foreign language CHRESTOMATHY
- anthology of varied writings MISCELLANY, COLLECTANEA

antiaircraft guns or fire ACK-ACK, FLAK

antibody - antibody's destruction of bacteria LYSIS

anticipate and thereby make unnecessary OBVIATE, PREEMPT
- anticipation and answering of an argument or objection before it has been started PROLEPSIS

anticlimax, disappointment, or failure following high expectations DAMP SQUIB
- anticlimax, especially from a high style to a low style BATHOS

anticommunist drive in the United States in the 1950's McCARTHYISM

antidote to poison obtained from the blood or tissue of immunized animals SERUM
- supposed antidote against all poisons MITHRIDATE

antiestablishment, attacking traditional ideas and institutions ICONOCLASTIC

antifreeze chemical ETHYLENE GLYCOL

anti-intellectual, hostile to cultural pursuits and values PHILISTINE
- anti-intellectual, opposed to inquiry, reform, or new knowledge OBSCURANTIST

antiknock - measure of gasoline's antiknock properties OCTANE NUMBER, OCTANE RATING

antiprogressive, conservative, as in art or politics REACTIONARY

antiques, curios, and objets d'art, or a cultivated liking for them VIRTU
- expert on antiques and other old objects ANTIQUARY
- relating to antiques and antiquities ANTIQUARIAN

antisocial and aggressive person PSYCHOPATH, SOCIOPATH

antivivisectionist ZOOPHILE

antler - antler's flat section PALM
- branch of a deer's antler TINE
- falling off or shed, as leaves or antlers might be DECIDUOUS

anus See also **rectum**
- area between the anus and genitals in the human body PERINEUM
- circular or ringlike muscle constricting or relaxing a body passage, as in the anus SPHINCTER
- surgical construction of an opening between the colon and the surface of the abdomen to serve as an artificial anus COLOSTOMY

anus (combining form) PROCT-, PROCTO-

anxiety, feeling of evil or disaster

ANNIVERSARIES

GENERAL ANNIVERSARY	CELEBRATING
triennial	3 years
quinquennial	5 years
centenary	100 years
bicentenary	200 years
tercentenary/tricentennial	300 years
quatercentenary/quadricentennial	400 years
quincentenary	500 years
millennium	1000 years

WEDDING ANNIVERSARY	CELEBRATING
cotton	1 year of marriage
paper	2
leather	3
flower/fruit	4
wood	5
iron/sugar candy	6
wool	7
bronze/electrical appliances	8
copper/pottery	9
tin	10
steel	11
silk and fine linen	12

WEDDING ANNIVERSARY	CELEBRATING
lace	13
ivory	14
crystal	15
china	20
silver	25
pearl	30
coral	35
ruby	40
sapphire	45
golden	50
emerald	55
diamond	60/65

FOREBODING, PREMONITION
- anxiety of a strong but unspecific kind ANGST
- anxiety or burden, such as a debt MILLSTONE
- free one's mind of a worry, grief, anxiety, guilt, or other burden DISBURDEN
- persistent or nagging, as a minor anxiety might be NIGGLING

anxious, concerned, or apprehensive SOLICITOUS
- anxious, fretful, very nervous or apprehensive OVERWROUGHT, PERTURBED, FRAUGHT, DISTRAUGHT
- anxious, tense, nervous, in suspense ON TENTERHOOKS

apart, separately, in pieces, item by item PIECEMEAL
- apart or into pieces, as one might tear something ASUNDER

apart (combining form) DIA-

apartment or room, especially near a city center, kept for occasional use by someone whose main home is elsewhere PIED-À-TERRE
- apartment on the roof or top floor of a large building PENTHOUSE
- apartment on three floors TRIPLEX
- apartment on two floors DUPLEX
- apartment on two floors, usually with its own outside door MAISONETTE
- apartment whose tenant is its owner but also an owner of the building including the building's common elements, such as the roof, the elevators, and the land, or the total property owned in this manner CONDOMINIUM, CONDO
- building that is owned and operated by its tenants, or an apartment in such a building COOPERATIVE, CO-OP

apathetic See **casual, indifferent**

ape, monkey, human, or related mammal PRIMATE
- ape, such as a gibbon or orangutan PONGID
- apelike in appearance or behavior ANTHROPOID, SIMIAN
- large ape such as a chimpanzee or gorilla TROGLODYTE
- troop of apes SHREWDNESS

apeman See **prehistoric humans**

aphrodisiac prepared from the crushed and dried bodies of a beetle CANTHARIDES, SPANISH FLY

Aphrodite - relating to the goddess Aphrodite PAPHIAN

apologetic, regretful DEPRECATORY
- apologetic, remorseful, self-reproaching CONTRITE, PENITENT, EXPIATORY
- apologetic or regretful, in a slightly cynical way, as a wry smile might be RUEFUL

apology - extremely humble, as an apology might be ABJECT

apparent, pretended, outward, as a given reason might be OSTENSIBLE
- apparent change in the position of an object when the observer changes position PARALLAX
- apparent focus of light rays, as in the image in a mirror VIRTUAL FOCUS
- apparent meaning PURPORT
- apparent rather than real, as a resemblance might be SUPERFICIAL

Arabic Alphabet

FORM	NAME	TRANSLITERATION
ا	'alif	'
ب	bā	b
ت	tā	t
ث	thā	th
ج	jīm	j
ح	ḥā	ḥ
خ	khā	kh
د	dāl	d
ذ	dhāl	dh
ر	rā	r
ز	zāy	z
س	sīn	s
ش	shīn	sh
ص	ṣād	ṣ
ض	ḍād	ḍ
ط	ṭā	ṭ
ظ	ẓā	ẓ
ع	'ayn	'
غ	ghayn	gh
ف	fā	f
ق	qāf	q
ك	kāf	k
ل	lām	·l
م	mīm	m
ن	nūn	n
ة	hā	h
و	wāw	w
ى	yā	y

apparently, supposedly REPUTEDLY
- apparently genuine or sound, but not really so SPECIOUS
- apparently or almost, but not really QUASI

appeal, attraction, or fascination ALLURE, CHARISMA
- appeal, aura of power or mystery MYSTIQUE
- appeal for, apply for, urge SOLICIT, INVOKE
- appeal or plead urgently, beg ENTREAT, BESEECH, ADJURE, IMPLORE, SUPPLICATE
- appeal to urgently or urge strongly EXHORT
- earnest appeal or passionate protest CRI DE COEUR
- person or party that appeals to a higher court to reverse a lower court's decision APPELLANT

appear or materialize, as a spirit might MANIFEST
- appear or claim to be or do something PURPORT, PROFESS
- appear or occur as an unexpected but important factor, as fate is said to do INTERVENE

appearance, especially a person's deceptive or suspect outward appearance FACADE
- appearance, expression, or manner MIEN, ASPECT, VISAGE
- appearance and character, as of a region PHYSIOGNOMY
- appearance of truth, likelihood VERISIMILITUDE
- appearance or aura acquired by age or association PATINA
- appearance or outward presentation SEMBLANCE, GUISE
- adopt or have the appearance of something else, often as a means of camouflage MIMIC, SIMULATE
- damaged in appearance, as by an accident or disease DEFORMED, MISSHAPEN, DISFIGURED
- give a deceptively acceptable or appealing appearance to GLOSS, VENEER

appearance (combining form) -PHANY

appendix VERMIFORM APPENDIX
- surgical removal of the appendix APPENDECTOMY

appetizer HORS D'OEUVRE, ANTIPASTO
- appetizer of a small open sandwich or spread biscuit CANAPÉ

appetizing or attractive SUCCULENT, TOOTHSOME
- appetizing or very appealing but unattainable TANTALIZING

appetite - appetite-arousing drink before a meal APERITIF
- appetite for unnatural food, such as mud or chalk PICA
- having a huge appetite RAVENOUS,

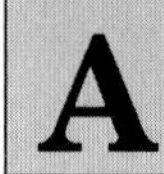

VORACIOUS
- increase appetite WHET
- indulge one's desires or appetites to the full SATE, SATIATE
- relating to the appetites ORECTIC
- unsatisfiable, as a desire or appetite might be INSATIABLE

applause See also **praise**
- applause or praise ACCLAIM, ACCOLADE
- applause that is prolonged and enthusiastic OVATION
- group of people hired, especially in former times, to applaud a play, concert, or the like CLAQUE
- reappearance on stage of a cast, choir, or the like, in acknowledgment of applause CURTAIN CALL

apple, pear, or related fleshy fruit whose seeds are in a large central capsule POME
- apple pulp remaining after the fruit has been crushed to extract the juice POMACE
- acid found in unripe fruit, especially apples MALIC ACID
- unripe apple CODLING

apple brandy CALVADOS

apple of one's eye, focus of attention, or beloved person CYNOSURE

applicable See **relevant**

application or practical side of a profession or field of study, as distinct from the theory PRAXIS

apply for, appeal for, urge SOLICIT, PETITION

appoint, choose for a task or position DESIGNATE, CONSTITUTE
- appoint as one's agent or representative DELEGATE, DEPUTE, COMMISSION
- appoint or elect a new member to a group by a decision of the existing group COOPT
- appoint to or recommend for an office or responsibility NOMINATE

appointment or meeting place, often secret RENDEZVOUS, ASSIGNATION, TRYST

apprentice - craftsman who is no longer apprenticed JOURNEYMAN

apprenticed, contracted as a trainee ARTICLED

approach, right to approach, or means of approaching ACCESS
- approach a problem, subject, or the like BROACH
- approach or come near or close to APPROXIMATE
- approach or intrude slowly on the property or rights of someone else, trespass ENCROACH
- approach or offer, as to initiate a relationship OVERTURE
- approach or stop in order to speak to ACCOST
- approach the same point from different directions CONVERGE
- based on trial and error, as an approach to solving a problem might be HEURISTIC

appropriate See also **suitable, relevant**

Arch

BASIC ROUND ARCH

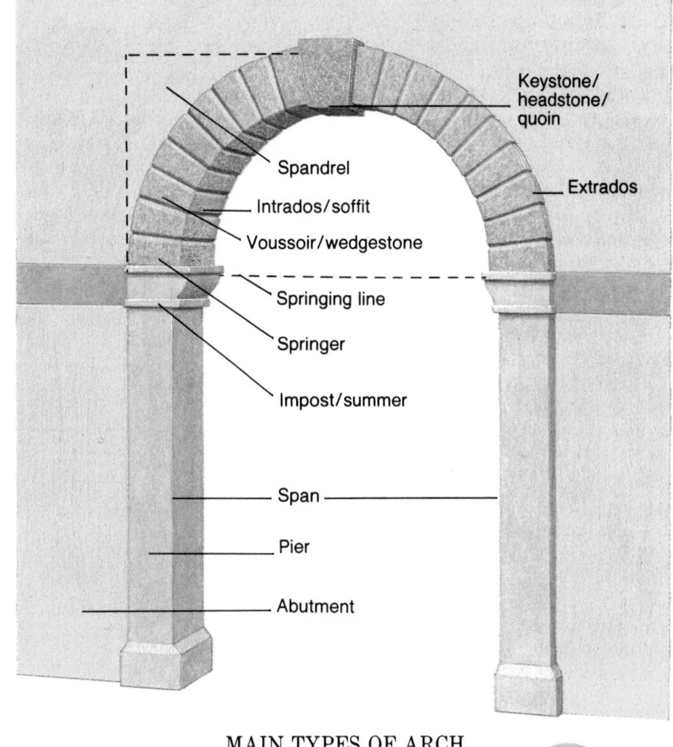

MAIN TYPES OF ARCH

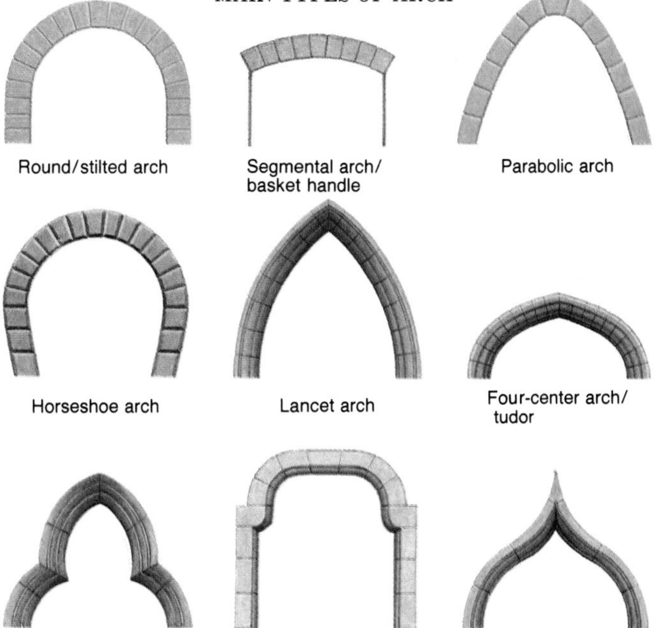

- appropriate, well-chosen, as a remark or compliment might be SEEMLY, OPPORTUNE, FELICITOUS

approval See also **praise**
- approval or praise, such as official endorsement COMMENDATION, PLAUDITS, APPROBATION, KUDOS
- official approval, as of a book, especially certified approval from a Roman Catholic censor NIHIL OBSTAT

approve See also **agree, allow**
- approve, agree, or assent to a belief, opinion, or the like SUBSCRIBE
- approve, support, or encourage COUNTENANCE
- approve or permit formally, confirm officially ENDORSE, RATIFY, SANCTION, VALIDATE

approximately or about, as written before an uncertain date CIRCA

apron - sleeveless garment worn as an apron or overdress PINAFORE

apse, gallery, or bishop's throne in a church TRIBUNE

aquarium - tiny crustacean used as food for aquarium fish DAPHNIA

Arab See also **Islam, clothes**
- Arab headdress of a shawl held in place by a cord headband KAFFIYEH
- Arab peasants or farmworkers FELLAHIN
- Arab prince, chieftain, or high official EMIR, SHEIKH, SHERIF
- Arab warrior or commando, especially against Israel FEDAYEE
- Arabian trading boat, typically with a large lateen sail DHOW
- covered market in an Arab or Muslim town SOUK
- long hooded Arab cloak BURNOOSE, JELLABA
- old quarter of an Arab town in North Africa CASBAH

Arabic See chart, page 28

arc of 90° QUADRANT
- draw a line, especially an arc or circle DESCRIBE

arch See illustration, page 29
- arch built to reinforce a structure RELIEVING ARCH

ARCHEOLOGY TERMS

barrow/tumulus	earth-covered burial mound
beehive tomb/ tholos	king's burial place, in the shape of a beehive
broch	round stone tower built in Scotland between 100 BC and AD 100
crannog	artificial island supporting buildings
cromlech	circle of upright stones
dendrochronology	method of dating past events by analysis of tree rings
denehole	vertical shaft that widens out into several chambers
dolmen	chamber or tomb formed by two or more vertical stones supporting a horizontal one
Eolithic	earliest period of human culture, preceding the Paleolithic
epigraphy	study of ancient inscriptions
henge	circle of wooden or stone uprights enclosed by a bank of earth or stone
kitchen midden/ midden	mound of kitchen refuse left by Stone Age people
ley lines	straight lines linking hilltops, tumuli, church sites, and other hallowed places, sometimes appearing to correspond with prehistoric tracks
lynchet	artificial terrace on a hillside resulting from cultivation, probably in the Iron Age
megalith	large stone used in construction
menhir	large free-standing stone or monolith
Mesolithic	Middle Stone Age
microlith	very small and delicately worked flint
monolith	single stone used as an upright in circles or avenues
Neolithic	New Stone Age, when the hunting economy changed to a farming one
obelisk	long, narrow shaft of stone
Paleolithic	Old Stone Age, which began two to three million years ago with the emergence of humans as toolmaking animals
paleontology	study of fossils and ancient forms of life
potsherd/sherd	fragment of broken pottery found in an excavation
radiocarbon dating/ carbon-14 dating	dating objects by measuring in dead organic matter the radioactive isotope carbon-14, which decays at a constant rate
sequence dating/ stratigraphy	relative dating of objects by determining the layers in which they lie, the deepest layer being assumed to be the oldest
stele	upright slab or pillar, usually with an inscription or decorative carving
trilithon	structure of two upright stones supporting a lintel stone

- arch or frame made of crisscrossing sticks, on which vines or creepers are trained to grow TRELLIS
- arch or stretch over, bridge SPAN
- arch's highest section or point CROWN
- front part of a theater stage, or the arch framing it PROSCENIUM
- referring to a broad arch whose rise is less than half its width SURBASED
- supported from a higher point on one side than on the other, as an arch might be RAMPANT
- wall, pillar, or the like between two windows, arches, or the like TRUMEAU

archbishop METROPOLITAN, PRIMATE
- adjective relating to an archbishop ARCHIEPISCOPAL

archdeacon - adjective relating to an archdeacon ARCHIDIACONAL
- title of respect for an Anglican archdeacon VENERABLE

arched, curved, as horns might be ARCUATE
- arched building or passage ARCADE
- arched ceiling or roof, typically of stone or masonry VAULT
- arched or upwardly curved surface, as of a road or airfoil CAMBER
- arched or vaulted structure, cave, room, or the like FORNIX
- arched recessed space, sometimes decorated with sculptures, above a doorway, as at the entrance of a medieval cathedral TYMPANUM

archeology See chart

archery contest, boxing match, or other competition MAIN
- archer or fan of archery TOXOPHILITE
- target in archery CLOUT

architecture See charts, pages 31 and 32, and also **arch, column, roof**
- architecture or other science of design ARCHITECTONICS
- architectural, relating to building or design or construction TECTONIC
- characteristic of a particular time or place, as local architecture would be VERNACULAR
- person skilled at drawing, especially of architectural or technical plans DRAFTSMAN, DRAFTSPERSON

arctic, northerly HYPERBOREAN
- arctic or subarctic region between the perpetual snow and the tree line TUNDRA

area See also **region**
- area entirely within a larger area ENCLAVE
- area of land, stretch of territory or terrain EXPANSE, TRACT
- area of landed property, or any district or stretch of territory DEMESNE
- area or place where some particular event occurred, or where a play or novel is set LOCALE
- area served by a particular school or hospital CATCHMENT AREA
- area under someone's control, or sphere of someone's influence FIEFDOM, DOMAIN, DOMINION, REALM, PARISH, BAILIWICK
- area where an animal or plant normally lives HABITAT

arena, as for horse shows HIPPODROME
- arena, as for tournaments of chivalric combat LISTS
- arena, sports hall, or the like with seating all the way round AMPHITHEATER
- combatant, typically with a sword, in an arena in ancient Rome GLADIATOR

arena (combining form) -DROME

Argentine cowboy GAUCHO

arguable, still in dispute, open to debate MOOT

argue, protest, or object, typically in order to dissuade REMONSTRATE, EXPOSTULATE
- argue, quarrel, wrangle BICKER
- argue against, dispute, contradict or deny GAINSAY, REPUDIATE, OPPUGN, CONTROVERT
- argue against and disprove REFUTE, REBUT
- argue back, counter RETORT
- argue or object needlessly, split hairs QUIBBLE, CAVIL

ARCHITECTURAL STYLES

Baroque	elaborate style developed in 17th-century Europe
Brutalism	stark modern style, without decoration
Byzantine	style marked by domes and minarets as in 5th-century Byzantium
Classical	formal, precise style based on Rome and Greece
Colonial	Georgian style of 17th- and 18th-century English settlements in North America
Decorated	14th-century English Gothic style, using decorative moldings and tracery
Early English	13th-century English Gothic style, with pointed arches and lancet windows
Flamboyant	15th- and 16th-century French Gothic style
Gothic	13th- to 15th-century style, with pointed windows and arches
Neoclassical	late-18th-century style reviving the precision and symmetry of Greece and Rome
Norman	late-11th- and -12th-century style, introduced to England from Normandy
Palladian	18th-century style based on the Italian architect Andrea Palladio
Perpendicular	late Gothic style in England, with emphasis on vertical lines
Regency	style of 1811-20, using stucco, tall windows, and delicate iron balconies
Renaissance	style reviving Greek and Roman ideals in the 15th to 17th centuries
Rococo	profusely elaborate style developed in 18th-century Europe
Romanesque	European 9th- to 12th-century style, represented by the Norman in Britain
Transitional	style of around 1100 in Europe, marked in Britain by a combination of Norman and Early English

ARCHITECTURE TERMS

arcade	roof supported by a series of arches
ashlar	masonry of smooth, squared stones
bargeboard	sloping board, often carved, along a gable roof
barrel vault	continuous semicircular arched vault
bay	space between windows or pillars
boss	carved projection at the intersection of ceiling ribs
buttress	brick or stone structure reinforcing a wall
campanile	detached bell tower
cartouche	decorative scrolled tablet, often bearing an inscription
caryatid	supporting column in the form of a female figure
coffer/ coffering	sunken panel in a ceiling or vault
corbel	carved stone block used as a supporting bracket
crocket	leaf-shaped ornament on Gothic pinnacles and gables
cruck	either of a pair of timbers joined to make a frame for a building
cupola	roof in the shape of a hemisphere
dado	lower part of an interior wall
engaged	partly sunk into a wall
entasis	bulge in a column, to counteract the optical illusion of concavity
exedra	alcove with a raised bench seat; apse or niche
facade	principal front of a building
fan vaulting	vaulting with curved ribs, resembling a fan
finial	ornament at the apex of a gable
flying buttress/ arc-boutant	arch carrying the thrust of a vault toward a buttress
gable	triangular section of the end wall of a house
gargoyle	spout, often grotesquely carved, to disperse rainwater
groin	curve formed at the intersection of two vaults
hammerbeam	bracket supporting the weight of a wooden arched roof
lantern	structure at the top of a building admitting light through open or glazed sides
lierne	supporting rib between the main ribs in a Gothic vault
loggia	roofed portico behind an open arcade
molding	ornamental shaped strip of stone or wood, sometimes elaborately carved
ogive	diagonal rib of a Gothic vault
piano nobile	principal floor of a building
pilaster	rectangular column set into a wall for ornament
podium	continuous base under a building
quatrefoil	four-lobed ornamental opening in Gothic stonework
quoin	dressed stone at the corner of a wall
rustication	heavy stonework with a rough surface, used to give Renaissance buildings an impression of strength
saucer dome	shallow dome in the form of an inverted saucer
stoa	ancient Greek colonnade
strapwork	Early English stone ornament resembling interlaced straps
string course	projecting course running along the face of a building
stucco	fine plaster used on interior and exterior walls
stylobate	platform supporting a classical colonnade
swag	festoon of ornamental fruit or flowers
trabeated	having beams or lintels, rather than arches
tracery	ornamental stonework in the upper part of a Gothic window
transom	crossbar of stone or wood in a window
vault	arched roof of stone, brick, or concrete

argument See also **dispute, logic, reasoning**
- argument, clinching remark, or hostile gesture made when leaving PARTHIAN SHOT
- argument, controversy, dispute, especially over a principle or belief POLEMIC
- argument, quarrel, heated disagreement ALTERCATION
- argument based less on reason than on references to one's opponent's personal affairs or qualities AD HOMINEM ARGUMENT
- argument in the form of an extended series of incomplete logical syllogisms SORITES
- argument of a spurious kind, put forward only to be knocked down at once MAN OF STRAW
- argument of a subtle philosophical or theological kind, as attempted by students QUODLIBET
- argument or confrontation CONTRETEMPS
- argument or document presented for consideration SUBMISSION
- argument or quarrel involving a noisy disturbance RUCTION
- argument or reasoning that is plausible but overly subtle, faulty, or deliberately deceptive CHOPLOGIC, CASUISTRY, SOPHISTRY
- argument or theme of a work, especially when used as the title LEMMA
- argument that is illogical or invalid, though not deliberately so PARALOGISM
- acknowledgment of a telling point, argument, or accusation made against one TOUCHÉ
- anticipation and answering of an argument or objection before it has been started PROLEPSIS
- arguing of an unfair or biased kind through selecting only certain favorable aspects SPECIAL PLEADING
- argumentation and logical disputing DIALECTIC
- base an argument on certain facts or suppositions PREDICATE
- based on reason and topical argument rather than on intuition DISCURSIVE
- disprove, weaken, or make ineffective an argument, claim, or the like INVALIDATE, NULLIFY, VOID, VITIATE
- intended as a trap, treacherous, as a sneaky argument might be INSIDIOUS
- involved in an argument, scandal, or the like EMBROILED
- long and indirect, as a roundabout journey or argument might be CIRCUITOUS
- person who puts forward a contrary or unpopular view, for the sake of argument or provocation DEVIL'S ADVOCATE
- plausible but really false, as an argument or excuse might be SPECIOUS
- powerful and convincing, as an argument might be COGENT, COMPELLING, INCISIVE, TRENCHANT
- produce or cite an example, argument, or reason as evidence or proof ADDUCE
- proposition on which an argument is based or from which a conclusion can be drawn PREMISE
- proposition on which an argument is based, using incorrect assumptions FALSE PREMISE
- put forward a proposition or idea for the sake of argument POSTULATE, POSIT
- reasonable, plausible, or maintainable against critical attack, as a philosophical argument might be TENABLE
- relating or given to argument, controversy, or logical dispute ERISTIC
- relating to argument from the general to the particular, from principles or causes to facts or effects DEDUCTIVE, A PRIORI, ANALYTICAL
- relating to argument from the particular to the general, from facts or effects to principles and causes EMPIRICAL, INDUCTIVE, A POSTERIORI, PEDAGOGICAL
- settle an argument decisively CLINCH
- settle an argument or differences COMPOSE, RECONCILE, ACCOMMODATE
- theory or proposition put forward and maintained by argument THESIS
- theory put forward for the sake of argument HYPOTHESIS, WORKING HYPOTHESIS
- undeniable, able to withstand attack, as a powerful argument might be IRREFUTABLE, INCONTROVERTIBLE, UNASSAILABLE
- unshakably strong, as an argument or legal case might be IRONCLAD, WATERTIGHT
- using the premise and conclusion to prove each other, as a faulty argument might CIRCULAR

aristocrat See **nobility**

aristocratic or dignified man GRAND SEIGNEUR, PATRICIAN

Aristotle - happiness or well-being, especially that produced, according to Aristotle's philosophy, by an active and rational life EUDEMONIA
- relating to Aristotle's philosophy, Aristotelian PERIPATETIC

arithmetic - solve problems or make calculations by the use of arithmetic CIPHER

arithmetical and conversion table READY RECKONER
- arithmetical procedure using a series of steps, such as long division ALGORITHM
- arithmetical skills, basic competence in counting and numerical calculations NUMERACY

ark of the covenant, ark of the covenant's chamber or shrine within the Temple in ancient Israel HOLY OF HOLIES, SANCTUM SANCTORUM, ORACLE

arm, armlike flexible projection near the mouth of an octopus, jellyfish, or the like TENTACLE
- arm or corresponding limb such as a flipper or wing BRACHIUM
- ancient measure of length, based on the length of the arm from fingertip to elbow CUBIT
- bind someone's arms to restrain him PINION
- relating to the arm, flipper, or wing BRACHIAL
- with hands on hips and elbows bent outward, as one's arms might be AKIMBO

armband of black material, worn as a sign of mourning CREPE
- armband or identifying badge worn on the upper arm BRASSARD

armchair FAUTEUIL
- coverlet for the top of the back of an armchair or sofa ANTIMACASSAR

armor See illustration, page 34
- armor, weapons, and full equipment of a warrior PANOPLY
- armor bearer, knight's squire ARMIGER
- armor for a horse's head CHAMFRON
- fastening consisting of a hook and loop, as formerly used on armor AGRAFFE
- short tunic worn by a knight over his armor, and typically bearing his coat of arms TABARD

armpit AXILLA, OXTER
- relating to the armpit AXILLARY, ALAR
- swelling and inflammation of a lymph gland, especially in the armpit or groin BUBO

arms See **weapons**

army See also **military, services**
- army canteen or shop PX
- army department in charge of food supplies and equipment COMMISSARIAT
- army officer responsible for provisions, clothing, and the like QUARTERMASTER

- army officers who help to plan and control operations GENERAL STAFF
- army of ordinary citizens rather than regular soldiers MILITIA
- army supplier in former times, often a camp follower selling provisions to soldiers SUTLER
- army's foot soldiers INFANTRY
- adjective for an army MILITARY, MARTIAL
- civilian, such as a peddler or prostitute, who follows an army unit to provide unofficial services CAMP FOLLOWER
- dismiss from the armed forces, impose a dishonorable discharge on CASHIER
- front position or troops of an advancing army VANGUARD
- government by the army STRATOCRACY
- novice, inexperienced person, as in the armed forces ROOKIE
- plundering, pillaging, as an advancing army might be RAPACIOUS
- recruit forcibly into the army or navy PRESS, PRESS-GANG, IMPRESS
- release or exempt from active duty, as in the army, on the grounds of disability INVALID
- remove the army, military equipment, or military control from an area DEMILITARIZE
- study of organizing army personnel and equipment, especially the transport of them LOGISTICS

around (combining form) AMPH-, AMPHI-, CIRCUM-, EPI-, PERI-

arouse by suggestive or suspenseful stimulation TITILLATE
- arouse or summon a memory, emotion, answer, or the like EVOKE
- arouse someone's curiosity, interest, or the like PIQUE
- arousal, incentive, stimulus, or excitement FILLIP
- aroused or provoked very easily

Armor

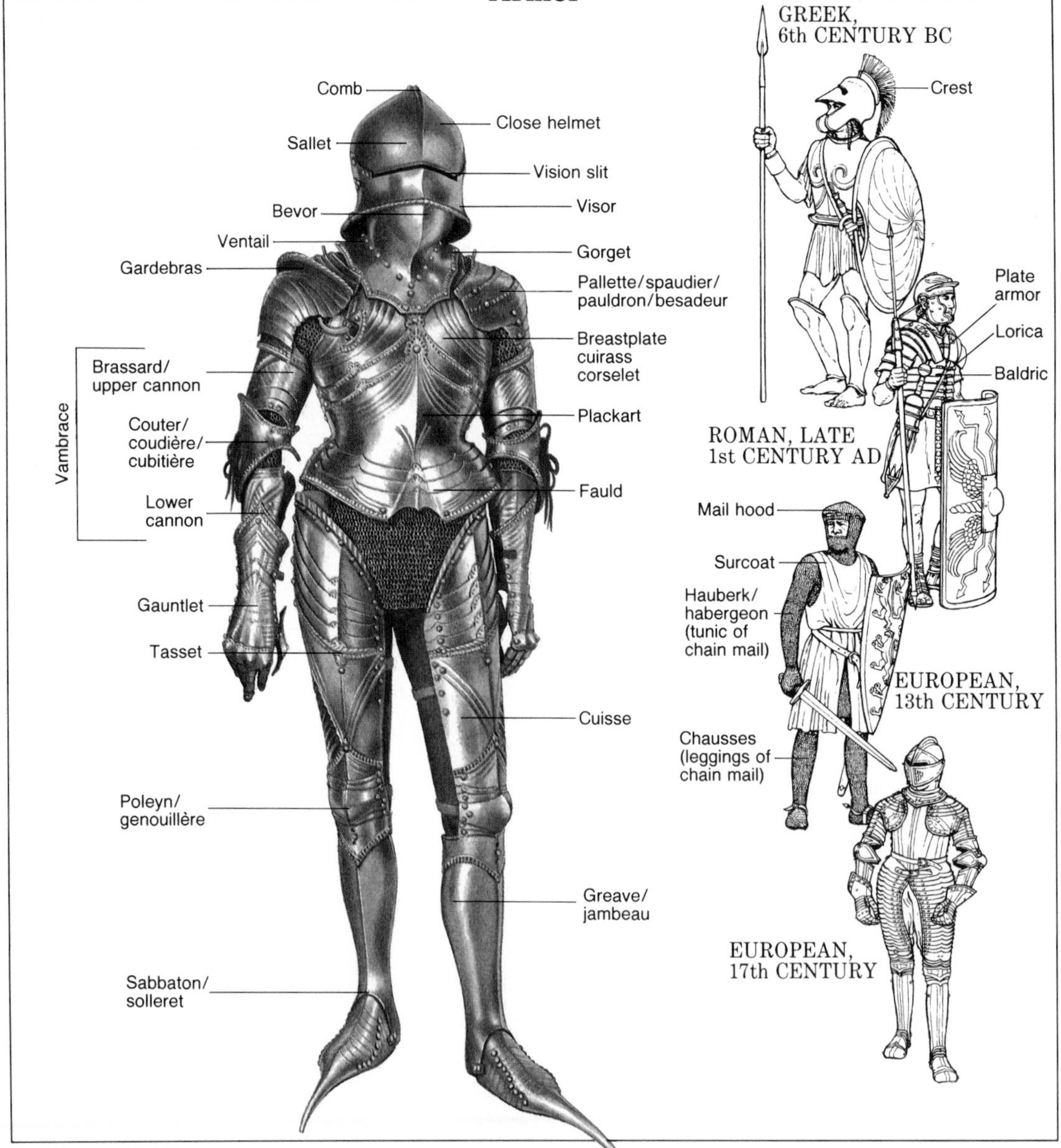

Comb
Close helmet
Sallet
Vision slit
Bevor
Visor
Ventail
Gorget
Gardebras
Pallette/spaudier/ pauldron/besadeur
Breastplate cuirass corselet
Vambrace
Brassard/ upper cannon
Couter/ coudière/ cubitière
Lower cannon
Plackart
Fauld
Gauntlet
Tasset
Cuisse
Poleyn/ genouillère
Greave/ jambeau
Sabbaton/ solleret

GREEK, 6th CENTURY BC
Crest
Plate armor
Lorica
Baldric
ROMAN, LATE 1st CENTURY AD
Mail hood
Surcoat
Hauberk/ habergeon (tunic of chain mail)
EUROPEAN, 13th CENTURY
Chausses (leggings of chain mail)
EUROPEAN, 17th CENTURY

HAIR-TRIGGER
- arousing anger, curiosity, lust, or the like PROVOCATIVE
- arousing strong feelings quickly, especially feelings of anger INFLAMMATORY

arrange, organize, or construct with some overall effect in mind ORCHESTRATE
- arrange, set in a particular order DISPOSE
- arrange in a corresponding or parallel relationship CORRELATE, COORDINATE
- arrange side by side, position together COLLOCATE
- arrange systematically DIGEST, CATALOG, CODIFY
- arrange things, such as computer data or pages of a book, in an appropriate layout or design FORMAT
- arranged, sponsored, or directed by UNDER THE AUSPICES OF, UNDER THE AEGIS OF
- arranging of any complicated project, especially one involving transport LOGISTICS

arrangement of parts CONFIGURATION, CONFORMATION, POSTURE
- arrangement or artistic organization of the elements in a poem, painting, building plan, or the like ORDONNANCE
- arrangement or orderly display, as of troops ARRAY
- arrangement or sequence according to rank or importance HIERARCHY
- arrangement to enable people with competing interests to continue working or living together MODUS VIVENDI
- lacking a planned order or arrangement RANDOM, HAPHAZARD, ARBITRARY

arrangement (combining form) TAX-, TAXO-, -TAXY, -TAXIS

arrest, seize, take into custody APPREHEND, COLLAR, BUST
- arrest or confiscate with the backing of legal authority ATTACH
- arrest warrant or writ CAPIAS
- detention, being held under arrest or under guard, as by the police CUSTODY
- immunity from arrest or punishment, as by taking refuge in a church or embassy SANCTUARY
- judicial writ authorizing a search, arrest, or the like WARRANT

arrival, coming ADVENT

arrogance, haughtiness, or proud attitude HAUTEUR
- arrogance, typically leading to downfall HUBRIS
- downfall or undoing, typically just retribution, as following arrogance NEMESIS

arrogant See also **pompous, cheeky**
- arrogant, boastful, and opinionated VAINGLORIOUS
- arrogant, disdainful or haughty, scornful SUPERCILIOUS
- arrogant, extremely forward or bold PRESUMPTUOUS
- arrogant, narrow-minded, and self-satisfied person PRIG
- arrogant, overbearing IMPERIOUS, DOMINEERING, OVERWEENING, PEREMPTORY
- arrogant, pushy, high-handed, self-assertive BUMPTIOUS
- arrogant or presumptuous person, especially a newcomer to his or her present higher social status UPSTART, NOUVEAU RICHE, PARVENU

arrow for a crossbow QUARREL
- arrow maker FLETCHER
- arrow that is blunt and lacks a barb BUTT SHAFT
- arrowlike, straight SAGITTAL
- arrow's feather VANE
- arrow's notch into which the bowstring fits NOCK
- barb or barbed head on an arrow, harpoon, or anchor arm FLUKE
- case for carrying arrows QUIVER
- feather or other flared tail giving stability to an arrow or dart FLIGHT
- fit an arrow with a feather FLEDGE, FLETCH
- simultaneous firing of a number of bullets, arrows, guns, or the like VOLLEY

arsonist INCENDIARY, PYROMANIAC, FIREBUG

art See chart, page 36, and also **arts, artist, painting, sculpture**
- art form or work in which many pieces of fabric, cloth, or the like are pasted on a surface COLLAGE
- art gallery or exhibition hall SALON
- art that is pretentious and vulgar KITSCH
- caretaker or keeper, as of an art collection CUSTODIAN, CURATOR
- category of art, movies, or the like GENRE
- damaging or malicious destruction of public property, artistic works, or the like VANDALISM
- excessive sentimentality, as in art and music SCHMALTZ
- expert in wine, art, or the like, or a person having refined tastes CONNOISSEUR
- forefront of, or early participants in, an artistic trend, political movement, or the like VANGUARD
- representation or conception of a work of art by a performance or adaptation of it INTERPRETATION

art exhibition covering many years of an artist's work RETROSPECTIVE

art lover, person who is sensitive to beauty AESTHETE
- art lover whose interest or knowledge is really amateurish or superficial DABBLER, DILETTANTE

artery just beneath the collarbone SUBCLAVIAN
- artery supplying blood to the head and neck CAROTID
- fatty deposit in an artery, restricting flow ATHEROMA
- hardening of the arteries SCLEROSIS
- main artery carrying blood from the heart AORTA

artichoke - core or center of an artichoke head, consisting of inedible hairs CHOKE

article or booklet on some specialist subject MONOGRAPH
- article or essay outlining the life and achievements of someone in the news PROFILE
- article printed separately, after first appearing in a journal or book OFFPRINT
- agency selling cartoons, articles, and the like for publication in numerous newspapers SYNDICATE
- line under the title of a magazine or newspaper article giving the writer's name BYLINE
- preliminary text or opening sentence or paragraph of a newspaper or magazine article LEAD
- reject an article or report, as an editor might SCRAP, SPIKE

artificial, human-made SIMULATED, SYNTHETIC
- artificial, not natural, strained, unspontaneous CONTRIVED, FACTITIOUS, STUDIED, MANNERED
- artificial, substitute, or imitation ERSATZ
- artificial and sudden development or device introduced to resolve a tricky situation or plot DEUS EX MACHINA
- artificial human being ANDROID, HUMANOID, GOLEM, AUTOMATON
- artificial leg, eye, tooth, or other body part PROSTHESIS
- artificial or conventional rather than realistic STYLIZED
- artificial sweetener, extracted from coal SACCHARIN
- artificial way of speaking, dressing, or behaving in order to impress others AFFECTATION, PRETENTIOUSNESS
- artificially prepared, cultivated, fertilized, or the like in a laboratory environment rather than in a living organism IN VITRO

artillery ORDNANCE

- artillery bombardment CANNONADE, STONK

artist - artist's complete works or output OEUVRE, CORPUS
- artist's studio ATELIER
- artists, writers, or other grouping whose aims or methods seem experimental, very daring, and ahead of their times AVANT-GARDE
- gathering of or reception for artists, celebrities, or the like SALON
- immature, early works of an artist or writer JUVENILIA

artistes in a group, especially a touring group TROUPE

artistic, literary, or cultural circle COTERIE, CLIQUE
- artistic incorruptibility, soundness of artistic values or standards INTEGRITY
- artistic or harmonious arrangement of parts, as in a painting COMPOSITION
- artistic or intellectual people, as

ART MOVEMENTS

Art Deco	decorative style of the 1920's and 1930's marked by bold geometric shapes and the use of plastic and steel
Art Nouveau	decorative style of the 1890's marked by tendrillike lines and swirling forms
Barbizon school	group of 19th-century French artists who delighted in landscape for its own sake
Baroque	ornate, dramatic style of the 17th and early 18th centuries
Bauhaus	20th-century German movement urging that the design of any object should be dictated by its function
Constructivism	form of nonrepresentational, geometric art developed in Russia around 1920
Cubism	early-20th-century movement that distorted perspective and introduced multiple viewpoints
Dada	early-20th-century art movement that rejected conventions in favor of the irrational
de Stijl	20th-century Dutch movement ("The Style") that took abstraction to an extreme
Expressionism	early-20th-century movement in painting that rejected naturalism in favor of direct expression of the artist's feelings
Fauvism	early-20th-century movement in painting marked by bright, vibrant colors and bold brushwork
Futurism	early-20th-century Italian movement seeking to depict the energy of the machine age
Impressionism	19th-century French movement that concentrated on the immediate visual impact of a subject
Mannerism	16th-century Italian style marked by the idealization of form and by extravagant effects
Neoclassicism	late-18th- and early-19th-century movement marked by a revival of classical proportion and restraint
Op Art	form of art that exploits optical effects to create an impression of movement
Pointillism	movement based on the use of closely spaced dots of primary color, blending from a distance to create a luminous quality
Pop Art	form of art that depicts everyday aspects of life, such as consumer goods and comic strips
Postimpressionism	movement in painting advancing from Impressionism toward compositions based on the arrangement of solid forms
Pre-Raphaelitism	English movement of the mid-19th century inspired by a romanticized vision of the Middle Ages and the style of painters before Raphael
Quattrocento	the 1400's, or 15th century, especially in Italian art
Realism	19th-century movement in many arts, directed or recording life objectively, with no idealization
Romanticism	early-19th-century movement in the arts, emphasizing individual emotions and free imagination
Surrealism	20th-century art movement that explored the world of fantasy, dreams, and the subconscious
Vorticism	English movement arising in 1914 marked by the expression of energy through abstract forms

a social class INTELLIGENTSIA
- artistic or literary person who lives in an unconventional way BOHEMIAN
- artistic rebirth or revival RENASCENCE, RENAISSANCE
- artistically impressive object, usually fairly small OBJET D'ART
- artistically impressive object that was not intended as a work of art OBJET TROUVÉ

artistry that displays outstanding technical ability, especially in playing a musical instrument VIRTUOSITY

arts or crafts, such as cabinetmaking or pottery, producing decorative objects or furniture DECORATIVE ARTS
- arts subjects and social sciences, as distinct from applied sciences and practical training LIBERAL ARTS, HUMANITIES
- arts such as movies, painting, and sculpture, dealing with the representation of three dimensions PLASTIC ARTS
- fine arts BEAUX ARTS

artwork illustrating a text GRAPHICS

as, in the role of QUA

as a whole, all together, in a group EN BLOC, EN MASSE

as good as, amounting to, equivalent in value or effect TANTAMOUNT

as such, in itself PER SE

ascribe See **assign**

asexual, developing or reproducing without sexual union and fertilization AGAMIC, AGAMOGENETIC, PARTHENOGENETIC

ash or debris left by burned coal or charcoal BREEZE
- consisting of ash, or resembling ash in texture or color CINEROUS
- glowing or smoldering cinders, left with ash after burning EMBERS
- larger pieces of residue, left with ash after burning CLINKER
- partly burned residue, left with ash after burning CINDERS

Ash Wednesday - recital of God's judgments on sinners, read in the Church of England on Ash Wednesday COMMINATION

ashamed or embarrassed ABASHED, OUT OF COUNTENANCE, DISCOMFITED
- ashamed or guilty-looking expression HANGDOG, SHAMEFACED, CRESTFALLEN
- deeply ashamed, humiliated MORTIFIED

ashes - place for keeping the ashes of a cremated body CINERARIUM
- vase, especially one used for storing the ashes of the dead after cremation URN
- vault with niches for urns containing the ashes of the dead COLUMBARIUM

Asia - rainy season in south and southeast Asia MONSOON
- Asian countries, and the East in general ORIENT

ask for or demand, often officially and in writing, needed supplies or equipment REQUISITION
- ask for or request humbly or urgently, apply for PETITION, SOLICIT, SUPPLICATE
- ask or appeal to urgently, plead with or implore BESEECH, ENTREAT, EXHORT, ADJURE
- ask or demand insistently, press, urge IMPORTUNE
- ask questions of in a probing way, examine thoroughly, interrogate CATECHIZE
- asked for or commanded by AT THE BEHEST OF
- asking, inquiring, always putting questions INQUISITIVE
- asking or begging humbly SUPPLIANT, SUPPLICANT

asleep, inactive, as during hibernation DORMANT

aspect or feature, as of someone's personality FACET

aspic, aspic-covered fish or meat dish, served cold GALANTINE

aspirin - aspirin poisoning SALICYLISM
- pain reliever that is a common alternative to aspirin ACETAMINOPHEN, PARACETAMOL, CODEINE

ass living wild in central Asia ONAGER

assemble See **gather**

assembly of churchmen for a conference SYNOD, CONVOCATION
- assembly of the people in an ancient Greek city, or the marketplace in which it met AGORA
- able to frame or alter a constitution, as a legislative assembly might be CONSTITUENT
- summon an assembly, call a meeting, or the like CONVOKE, CONVENE

assertion that is arbitrary and un-

ASTROLOGY TERMS

ascendant	section of the zodiac rising above the eastern horizon at a given moment
aspect	relative positioning of planets or stars to one another or to the subject
combust	star or planet too close to the sun to be visible
conjunction	overlapping or apparent meeting of two stars or planets
constellation	relative positioning of the planets or stars at the time of one's birth
cusp	division or transition between two houses or signs of the zodiac
descendant	point on the ecliptic opposite the ascendant
horoscope	relative positioning of the stars and planets at a given moment, or a diagram or forecast based on it
house/ mansion/sign	any of the 12 divisions of the heavens; sign of the zodiac in which a planet has its strongest influence
influence	ethereal force or fluid from the stars, affecting people's actions
nativity	horoscope based on the time of one's birth
quintile	relative positioning of two stars or planets 72° apart
trine	relative positioning of two stars or planets 120° apart
triplicity	group of three related signs of the zodiac
zodiac	imaginary band, representing the planets' paths, on the celestial sphere, divided into 12 sections or signs, each related to a constellation

supported by facts DOGMA, DICTUM, IPSE DIXIT

assertive, pushy, or insistent in manner STRIDENT

asset, such as a mine or oil well, whose value diminishes over the years WASTING ASSET
- assets easily convertible into cash LIQUID ASSETS
- convert property or assets into ready money REALIZE

assign or attach an error, guilt, or the like to some particular person or thing, credit with, pin or fasten on ASCRIBE, ATTRIBUTE, AFFIX, IMPUTE, PREDICATE
- assign or distribute, share out ALLOT, ALLOCATE, APPORTION
- assign work, duties, or powers to one's agent or subordinate DELEGATE, DEPUTE

assistance See also **help**
- assistance, especially financial support SUBVENTION
- assistance or relief in time of distress SUCCOR

assistant or employee doing a variety of work FACTOTUM
- assistant or fellow worker COADJUTANT, COADJUTOR, AIDE
- assistant or partner in some enterprise, especially a dubious scheme ACCOMPLICE, CONFEDERATE, COLLABORATOR
- assistant standing in temporarily for a superior, as in emergencies DEPUTY
- assistant to a general or other senior officer AIDE-DE-CAMP, ADC

assisting or supplementing, secondary SUBSIDIARY, AUXILIARY, ANCILLARY

associate or socialize with, mix with socially CONSORT, FRATERNIZE, HOBNOB

association See also **group**
- association or loose relationship or membership AFFILIATION
- associations and suggestions evoked by a word, rather than its literal meaning CONNOTATION
- living together of two organisms in close or dependent association, especially when beneficial to both SYMBIOSIS

assume, put forward a proposition or idea for the sake of argument POSTULATE, POSIT, PREMISE

assumed, hypothetical SUPPOSITITIOUS
- assumed, supposed, generally regarded as PUTATIVE

assumed name ALIAS
- in disguise or with an assumed name or appearance INCOGNITO

assurance, guarantee WARRANT, WARRANTY
- guarantee, certify, give personal assurance for VOUCH FOR, ATTEST TO

Astrological Signs

assured See **confident**

asterisks - printing symbol of three asterisks arranged in a triangle, ⁂ or ⁂, to alert the reader to the passage following ASTERISM

asthma - snoring or whistling sound from the chest, as in asthma, caused by partial blocking of the air channels RHONCHUS

astonished See **surprise**

astrologer, sorcerer, or soothsayer, especially of ancient times MAGUS, CHALDEAN

astrology See chart and illustration, pages 37 and 38, and also **zodiac**

astronaut from the U.S.S.R. COSMONAUT
- astronaut's activity, such as spacewalking, that takes place outside the spacecraft while away from earth EXTRAVEHICULAR ACTIVITY
- astronaut's supply line or tether to the spacecraft during a space walk UMBILICAL CORD

astronomy See chart

at first sight, based on a first impression PRIMA FACIE

at once, without hesitation or delay, instantly, immediately INSTANTANEOUSLY, INSTANTER

atheist, or unbeliever with regard to a particular religion INFIDEL
- atheist or polytheist, especially from a "primitive" nature-worshiping community HEATHEN, PAGAN
- atheist or skeptic who believes that humans control their own destiny HUMANIST
- atheist or skeptic who considers the existence of gods to be unknowable AGNOSTIC
- atheist or skeptic who rejects religion as being contrary to reason RATIONALIST
- person without beliefs, such as an atheist NULLIFIDIAN

athletes - artificial hormone increasing muscle and bone growth, sometimes used by athletes ANABOLIC STEROID
- portico used by athletes for exercise in ancient Greece XYST

athlete's foot, ringworm, or similar fungal skin disease TINEA, DERMATOPHYTOSIS

athletics event in which each contestant has to compete in ten specific disciplines, such as long jump and shot put DECATHLON

atmosphere See illustration, page 40
- atmosphere, thick or poisonous, as around a swamp MIASMA
- atmosphere based on feelings conveyed, often unconsciously, by one person or group to another

ASTRONOMY TERMS

aberration of starlight	apparent change in the position of a star
aphelion	point at which an object in solar orbit is farthest from the sun
apogee	point at which an orbiting object is farthest from the earth
armillary sphere	model with rings, used to show relationships between the circles on the celestial sphere
asteroid	minor planet in orbit around the Sun, 600 miles (1000 km) or less in diameter
astrolabe	medieval instrument consisting of a graduated vertical circle with a movable arm, used to determine the altitude of celestial bodies
azimuth	horizontal bearing of a celestial object measured clockwise from a given direction
big-bang theory	theory that the universe came into being as the result of a gigantic explosion
black hole	object in space whose gravitational pull is so great that nothing, not even light, can escape from it
celestial sphere	imaginary sphere around the earth on which celestial bodies are assumed to lie, for the purpose of finding or identifying their position
conjunction	occasion when two celestial bodies line up on the celestial sphere
Copernican theory/ heliocentric theory	former belief that the sun and not the earth is the center of the solar system
corona	faint halo of light around the sun and moon
cosmology	branch of astronomy that deals with the origin and evolution of the universe
declination	angular measure of a star's position, measured in degrees north and south of the celestial equator
double star/ binary	pair of stars linked by mutual gravitational attraction
ecliptic	great circle on the celestial sphere representing the apparent annual path of the sun relative to the stars
equinox	instant when the sun lies directly overhead at the equator
magnitude	measure of a celestial body's brightness, apparent or absolute
meteorite	chunk of rock or metal from space large enough to pass through the atmosphere of a planet without burning up and to reach the surface
nadir	point in the heavens diametrically opposite the zenith, or directly under an observer
nebula	cloud of dust and gas in a galaxy
nova	star that flares up suddenly in brightness to several times its normal magnitude
nutation	slight "nodding' of the earth's axis in space
orrery	mechanical model of the solar system
perigee	point at which an orbiting object is closest to the earth
perihelion	point at which an object in solar orbit is closest to the sun
Ptolemaic theory/ geocentric theory	view that the earth is the center of the universe
pulsar	rapidly rotating star that sends out a regular flash of radiation
quasar	intensely brilliant object that may be the energetic nucleus of a distant galaxy
red shift	lengthening of the wavelength of light from a receding celestial body
singularity	point in space-time where there is an infinite density of matter
solstice	farthest point north or south of the equator that the sun reaches each year
steady-state theory	theory that the universe has remained approximately the same throughout time
super nova	star exploding at the end of its life
syzygy	point in a celestial body's orbit at which it is either in opposition to or in conjunction with the sun
zenith	point in the heavens directly above an observer

Atmosphere

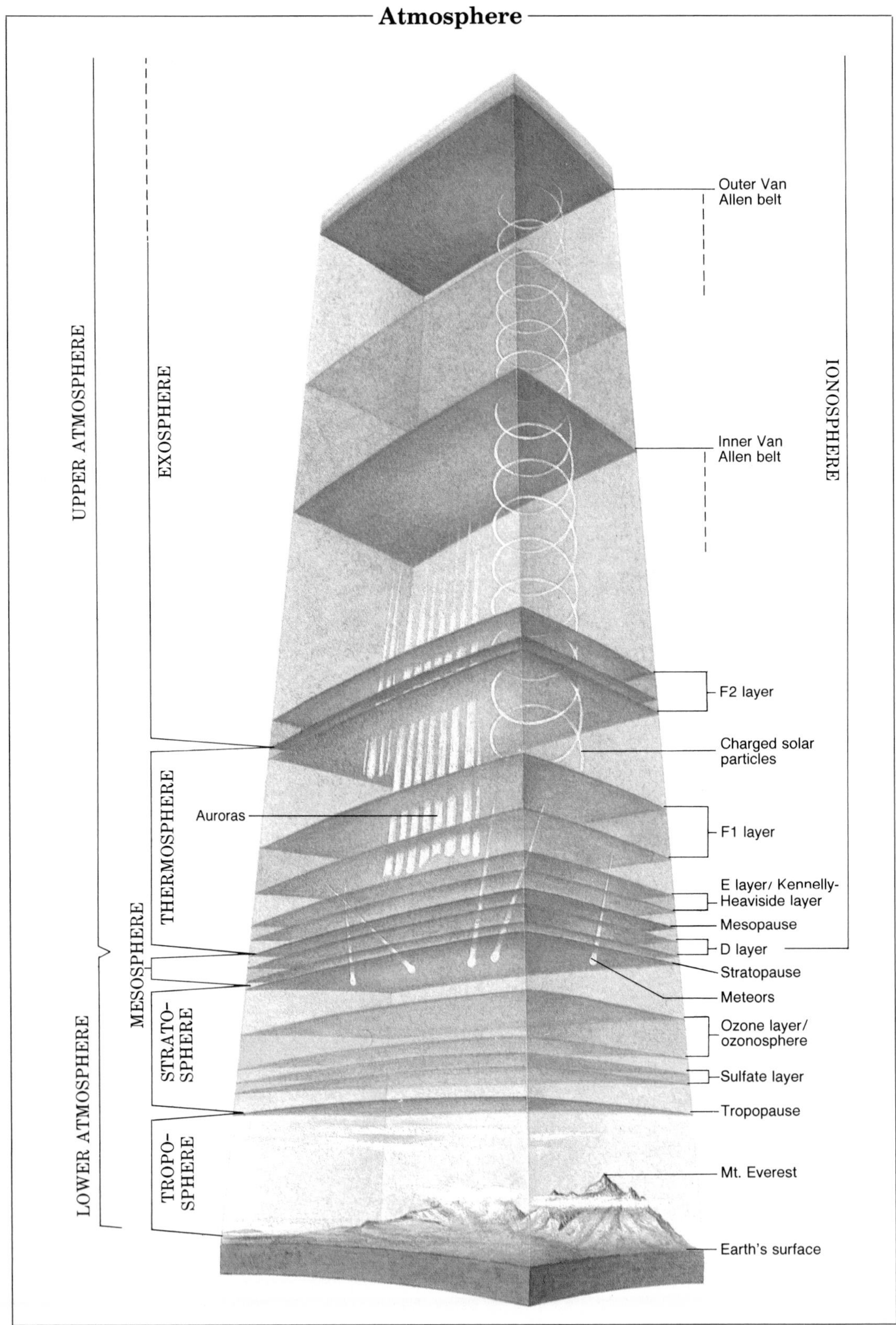
UPPER ATMOSPHERE
LOWER ATMOSPHERE
EXOSPHERE
THERMOSPHERE
MESOSPHERE
STRATO-SPHERE
TROPO-SPHERE
IONOSPHERE
Outer Van Allen belt
Inner Van Allen belt
F2 layer
Charged solar particles
Auroras
F1 layer
E layer/ Kennelly-Heaviside layer
Mesopause
D layer
Stratopause
Meteors
Ozone layer/ ozonosphere
Sulfate layer
Tropopause
Mt. Everest
Earth's surface

VIBES, WAVELENGTH
- atmosphere of awe MYSTIQUE
- atmosphere of gloom PALL
- atmosphere or quality, typically romantic or splendid, surrounding a person or thing AURA, NIMBUS
- atmospheric, suggestive, or arousing memories, as an idea or story might be EVOCATIVE
- cosy and cheerful, having a warm and friendly atmosphere GEMÜTLICH, CONGENIAL, AMIABLE
- heating of the earth's atmosphere through increased absorption of solar radiation GREENHOUSE EFFECT
- low in density, thin, as the air of the upper atmosphere is or a gas might be RAREFIED
- sociable or festive, as a party atmosphere might be CONVIVIAL

atmospheric pressure - instrument for measuring atmospheric pressure BAROMETER
- line on a weather map linking places with the same atmospheric pressure ISOBAR
- unit of atmospheric pressure MILLIBAR

atom See illustration, and also **subatomic particles, element**
- atom grouping of a chemical compound or element MOLECULE
- atom or group of atoms with one or more unpaired electrons RADICAL
- atom or group of atoms having an electric charge through gaining or losing one or more electrons ION
- atom with the same number of protons in its nucleus as another, but a different number of neutrons ISOTOPE
- atom's capacity to combine with other atoms VALENCE
- relating to atomic fusion at high temperatures, as in a hydrogen bomb THERMONUCLEAR
- splitting heavy atomic nuclei in a nuclear reaction FISSION
- union of atomic nuclei resulting in release of energy FUSION

atomic accelerator, producing high-energy beams of electrons BETATRON
- atomic clock based on radiation frequency and used in defining the second CESIUM CLOCK

atomizer - convert a liquid to a fine spray, as by an atomizer NEBULIZE

atonement, reparation or compensation made for some loss or injury caused REDRESS, AMENDS, EXPIATION, REDEMPTION
- making or needing penance and atonement, especially for sacrilege PIACULAR

attach See **join**

Atom

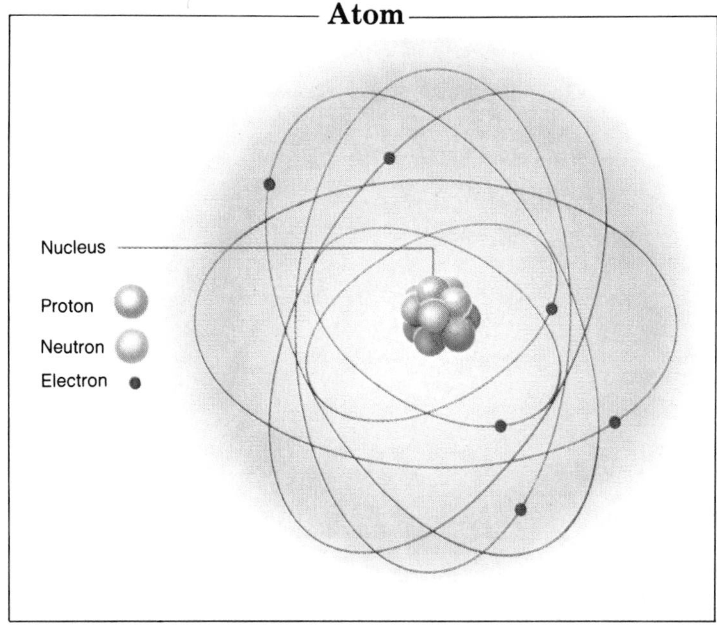

attached at the base, without a stalk, as a leaf or flower might be SESSILE

attachment, typically immature and neurotic, to a person or thing FIXATION

attack See also **criticize, insult**
- attack, military raid, or invasion INCURSION, IRRUPTION
- attack enemy ground troops with bombs or machine-gun fire from low-flying aircraft STRAFE
- attack from all sides, or besiege BESET, BELEAGUER
- attack in revenge REPRISAL, RETALIATION
- attack of rage, disease, or the like ACCESS
- attack on an enemy that takes them by surprise COUP DE MAIN
- attack on the opinions or beliefs of another POLEMIC
- attack or assault violently, as with blows to the body ASSAIL
- attack or burst of gunfire, rocket fire, or the like SALVO, FUSILLADE
- attack or raid by soldiers in a defensive position SORTIE, SALLY
- attack with gunfire from the side, raking the entire length of a troop formation or position ENFILADE
- face the impact or main force of a blow, shock, or attack BEAR THE BRUNT OF
- fierce or violent attack ONSLAUGHT
- harsh and scornful, as a criticism or verbal attack might be SCATHING, BLISTERING, WITHERING
- large-scale attack or assault, especially a military one OFFENSIVE
- sudden attack, raid, or military advance FORAY
- susceptible to danger, injury, or attack VULNERABLE

attack, seizure (combining form) -LEPSY

attend or visit a place regularly HAUNT, FREQUENT

attendant or servant of a magician or scholar in medieval times FAMULUS
- attendants following an important person RETINUE, CORTEGE

attention, public notice LIMELIGHT
- focusing of one's gaze or attention firmly on something FIXATION

attentive, alert, watchful VIGILANT, ON THE QUI VIVE
- attentive or careful in a very conscientious way, scrupulous SOLICITOUS

attic, room just under a pitched roof GARRET

attitude, point of view STANDPOINT
- attitude or posture of the body, characteristic way of standing or sitting BEARING, CARRIAGE, DEPORTMENT
- having a specified attitude or inclination toward something DISPOSED, ORIENTED, ORIENTATED
- offhand, disregarding the feelings of others, arrogant, as someone's attitude might be CAVALIER
- reversal or about-turn of attitude or policy VOLTE-FACE

attract, lure, tempt ENTICE

attraction, as between people or molecules AFFINITY
- move toward, as if drawn by an

irresistible attraction GRAVITATE

attraction to (combining form) PHIL-, -PHILIA

attractive, fascinating, almost bewitching BEGUILING, CAPTIVATING, ALLURING

- attractive in a delicate or dainty way MINION
- attractive in a modest or unspectacular way, pleasing and presentable PREPOSSESSING, PERSONABLE
- attractive in a quaint or strikingly unusual way PICTURESQUE
- attractive in a superficial or vulgar way GARISH, TINSELLY, MERETRICIOUS
- attractive or appetizing in a tempting way SUCCULENT, TOOTHSOME
- attractive or plausible in a superficial or artificial way GLOSSY, SPECIOUS

AUSTRALIAN TERMS

GENERAL	
backblocks/ outback	remote country areas
billabong	waterhole in a drying river
bludge	to shirk; to scrounge; an easy task; a period of idleness
bombora	submerged reef, or the turbulent water above it
boyla	aboriginal term for witch doctor
brumby	wild horse
bunyip	legendary aboriginal monster haunting swamps and waterholes
chunder	vomit
cobber	mate, friend
Coolgardie safe	dampened box or cupboard for keeping food cool
digger	Australian soldier; Australian
dilly bag	bag of woven grass or reed fiber
dinkum	genuine; honestly
drongo	fool; worthless or clumsy person
furphy	unfounded rumor
galah	fool, dunce
glory box	bottom drawer, trunk for a trousseau
gunyah	aboriginal term for shelter or hut
kelpie	sheepdog breed
larrikin	hooligan
lubra	aboriginal term for woman or wife
the mallee	bush country
ocker	unpolished Australian male
pavlova	meringue cake with fruit
sheila	woman
shiralee/ swag/bluey	tramp's bundle of belongings
skite	to boast
squatter/ pastoralist	large-scale sheep or cattle farmer
strine	broad Australian English
swagman	tramp, vagrant, or itinerant worker
tucker	food
waddy	club or stick
warrigal	dingo, or wild horse
wobble board	fiberboard sheet that booms when shaken, used as a musical instrument
wowser	puritan, killjoy, prude
PLANTS AND WILDLIFE	
bandicoot	ratlike marsupial
barramundi	long edible lungfish
cassowary	large flightless bird
coolabah	eucalyptus tree on river banks
dingo	wild dog
echidna	burrowing, egg-laying mammal, the spiny anteater
emu	large flightless bird
eucalyptus	gum tree
galah	pink and gray cockatoo
goanna	monitor lizard
kookaburra/ laughing jackass	raucous kingfisher
kurrajong	evergreen tree
lorikeet	small, brightly colored parrot
lyrebird	pheasantlike bird
platypus	egg-laying mammal with a broad bill and webbed feet
taipan	venomous snake
Tasmanian devil	small, fierce, flesh-eating marsupial
wombat	furry burrowing marsupial

- strong sensual attractiveness, powerful personal presence or "chemistry" ANIMAL MAGNETISM

attribute See **assign**

auburn color of hair, especially in a woman TITIAN, STRAWBERRY BLOND

auction bidder whose task is illicitly to bid up the price for the seller BY-BIDDER
- auction in which the asking price is progressively lowered until a buyer accepts DUTCH AUCTION
- auctioneer's hammer GAVEL
- collection of varied items sold as a single lot in an auction JOB LOT
- lowest price that the owner will accept at an auction RESERVE PRICE
- public sale or auction VENDUE

audience figures, and hence popularity, as estimated for a given radio or television program RATINGS

aura of power or mystery, glamour MYSTIQUE
- aura or atmosphere, typically romantic or splendid, surrounding a person or thing NIMBUS

Australia and New Zealand from the point of view of Europe ANTIPODES

Australian terms See chart

Austria - political union with Nazi Germany in 1938 ANSCHLUSS

author who writes a memoir or book on behalf of somebody else GHOST WRITER
- adjective for an author AUCTORIAL
- complete works or output of an author OEUVRE, CORPUS
- definitive list, as of an author's works CANON
- list of works by or about a particular author BIBLIOGRAPHY
- relating to an unnamed author, contributor, or the like ANONYMOUS
- share of the proceeds paid to an author from the sales of his or her work ROYALTY

authoritarian nondemocratic form of government, dictatorship or tyranny TOTALITARIANISM, DESPOTISM, ABSOLUTISM, AUTOCRACY, AUTARCHY
- authoritarian person, specifically an uncompromising military disciplinarian MARTINET

authoritative, commanding or controlling MAGISTERIAL
- authoritative, from the source of authority, as an official pronouncement might be EX CATHEDRA
- authoritative, reliable, and complete, as a history or biography might be DEFINITIVE
- authoritative but unsupported assertion DOGMA, DICTUM, IPSE DIXIT
- authoritative or arbitrary order from the czar or other autocrat UKASE

authority See also **power**
- authority, complete control or power SUPREMACY
- authority, or the legal and territorial extent of authority JURISDICTION
- authority, rule, control DOMINION, SOVEREIGNTY
- authority, ruling power, or influence of one state over another HEGEMONY
- authority exercised in a fatherly way, typically generous and concerned but restricting individual responsibility PATERNALISM
- authority or complete freedom to act as one thinks best CARTE BLANCHE
- authority or government that was formerly in power but has now been replaced ANCIEN RÉGIME
- area under someone's authority, or sphere of someone's influence FIEFDOM, DOMAIN, REALM, PARISH, BAILIWICK
- rod or staff carried as an emblem of authority or office VERGE
- transfer of power from central government to regional or local authorities DEVOLUTION

authorization, official permission FIAT
- authorization from the League of Nations for a country to administer a specific territory MANDATE

authorize, approve, permit, allow EMPOWER, WARRANT, SANCTION

authorized or officially recognized, having credentials that are acceptable ACCREDITED

authorship or origin PATERNITY
- of doubtful authorship or reliability, as a text or anecdote might be APOCRYPHAL

autobiography MEMOIRS

automatic, unthinking reaction KNEE-JERK REACTION
- automatic or predictable, as a reaction or response may be PAVLOVIAN

automatic doors - electronic device that reacts to changes in light intensity, as used in burglar alarms and automatic doors PHOTOELECTRIC CELL, PHOTOCELL, ELECTRIC EYE, MAGIC EYE

auxiliary (combining form) PARA-

available DISPOSABLE
- available or acquired with ease ACCESSIBLE
- invent or devise using available resources IMPROVISE

average See also **mediocre**
- average, middle value in a set of values MEDIAN
- average, sum total divided by the number of items in a set MEAN, ARITHMETIC MEAN
- average out, balance EQUATE

avoid, as by cunning or deceit EVADE
- avoid, ignore, or disregard BYPASS, CIRCUMVENT
- avoid, refuse, or be unwilling BALK, SHRINK, JIB
- avoid committing oneself, speak cautiously HEDGE
- avoid or abstain from ESCHEW
- avoid or escape capture, hunters, or the like, especially by cunning ELUDE
- avoid or stave off a disaster, evil, or the like AVERT
- avoiding of direct answers, evasiveness in discussion FENCING
- avoiding publicity INCONSPICUOUS, LOW-PROFILE, UNOBTRUSIVE, UNOSTENTATIOUS

awaiting confirmation or completion, still unfinished PENDING

award for work in the New York theater, the theatrical equivalent of an Oscar TONY
- award or honor, as for bravery COMMENDATION, CITATION
- propose for an honor or award NOMINATE

aware, conscious, responsive to stimuli SENTIENT
- aware, informed, having knowledge COGNIZANT, MINDFUL

away - carrying or conducting away from the brain, spinal cord, or other body part EFFERENT

awe - atmosphere of awe MYSTIQUE

awe-inspiring, exalted SUBLIME, AUGUST
- awe-inspiring NUMINOUS

awkward, bumbling, clumsy or ham-handed GAUCHE, MALADROIT, INEPT
- awkward, clumsy, gawky or lumbering, graceless in movement UNGAINLY, UNCOORDINATED, LUBBERLY
- awkward, difficult to move or use, as through being too heavy or unbalanced UNWIELDY, PONDEROUS, CUMBERSOME
- awkward or ill-at-ease teenager or young man or woman HOBBLEDEHOY

ax - bundle of rods with an ax, carried as a symbol of the magistrates' authority in ancient Rome FASCES
- groove or notch made in wood by an ax or saw KERF
- sacred double-headed ax in ancient Minoan culture LABYRIS

axle, axlelike spindle supporting wood on a lathe MANDREL
- axle pin holding the wheel in place LINCHPIN
- pivot of metal at the end of a wooden shaft or axle, as for a wheel to turn on GUDGEON

B

B.A. or other bachelor's degree BACCALAUREATE

baby See also **birth, childbirth, offspring,** and chart at **animal**
- baby born with a disorder of the red blood cells RHESUS BABY
- baby clothing and accessories LAYETTE
- baby of unknown parentage, found abandoned FOUNDLING
- baby or young animal that is still unweaned SUCKLING
- baby or young child, especially an Italian one BAMBINO, BAMBINA
- baby secretly substituted for another CHANGELING
- baby's bed usually made of basketwork and hooded BASSINET
- baby's nipple-shaped device to suck on PACIFIER
- baby's excrement expelled just after birth MECONIUM
- baby's pushchair STROLLER, BABY BUGGY
- be pregnant, carry unborn babies GESTATE
- blood and tissue discharged normally after the birth of a baby AFTERBIRTH, SECUNDINES, LOCHIA
- bounce a baby affectionately up and down, especially on one's knees DANDLE
- cord or tube linking the baby in the womb to the mother's placenta UMBILICAL CORD
- covering of fine downy hair, as on a newborn baby or fetus LANUGO
- delivery of a baby feet or buttocks first BREECH BIRTH, BREECH DELIVERY
- delivery of a baby with medical tongs FORCEPS DELIVERY
- formation of a close relationship, usually between mother and baby BONDING
- get a baby or young animal off mother's milk and on to solid food WEAN
- human embryo of advanced development, before its birth as a baby FETUS
- human product of conception during the first two months of pregnancy, before developing into the fetus and baby EMBRYO
- light wheeled frame supporting a baby learning to walk WALKER
- mass of tissue linking the unborn baby to the womb lining PLACENTA
- membrane surrounding an embryo, fetus, or unborn baby AMNION, CHORION
- Native American baby, especially one carried on its mother's back PAPOOSE
- nursery for babies or very young children, especially to enable parents to go to work DAY-CARE CENTER
- piece of the amniotic sac sometimes covering a baby's head at birth CAUL
- presence of two babies of different ages in the womb SUPERFETATION
- produce babies, reproduce PROCREATE
- producing many babies, very fertile PROLIFIC, PHILOPROGENITIVE
- referring to a baby born after the death of its father POSTHUMOUS
- relating to a baby less than one month old NEONATAL
- strips of cloth formerly wound around a newborn baby SWADDLING CLOTHES
- study of the causes and development of abnormalities in unborn babies TERATOLOGY
- surgical cut into the uterus to deliver a baby cesarean, cesarean section
- temperature-controlled container, as for premature babies INCUBATOR
- testing for the presence or position of a baby in the womb by prodding the uterus BALLOTTEMENT
- turning by hand the baby in the womb to aid delivery VERSION
- withdrawal by syringe of some of the fluid in a pregnant woman's womb, to monitor the health and determine the sex of the unborn baby AMNIOCENTESIS
- wrap a newborn baby tightly with clothes or narrow strips of cloth SWADDLE

baby (combining form) -LING

Babylonian temple tower shaped like a pyramid ZIGGURAT

Bacchus - staff, typically decorated with leaves and tipped with a pine cone, carried by Bacchus and his followers THYRSUS

bachelor who has at last decided to get married BENEDICT
- bachelor's degree, such as B.A. or B.Sc. BACCALAUREATE
- desirable and worthy for marriage, as a rich bachelor might be considered ELIGIBLE

back away, retreat from a particular point RECEDE
- back away or shrink back, as through fear or pain RECOIL, FLINCH, WINCE, BLENCH
- back gate or side gate POSTERN
- back of the head OCCIPUT
- back or corresponding part of an organ or limb, such as the back of the hand DORSUM
- back of the neck NAPE, NUCHA
- back or upper surface of a body segment, as of an insect or lobster TERGUM
- back pain LUMBAGO
- back up or confirm an opinion or statement, as with additional evidence CORROBORATE, SUBSTANTIATE, VALIDATE
- adjective for the back DORSAL
- get back, regain RETRIEVE
- lying on one's back SUPINE
- position of one's back when sitting or standing POSTURE
- referring to the lower back and sides, between the ribs and pelvis LUMBAR
- wrench, sprain, or strain one's back, ankle, or the like RICK

back (combining form) ANA-, DORS-, DORSI-, DORSO-, NOT-, NOTO-, RETR-, RETRO-

back again (combining form) RE-, PALIN-

back-and-forth movement ALTERNATION, RECIPROCATION
- send or pass back and forth SHUTTLECOCK

back country, remote rural areas, the bush HINTERLAND, BOONDOCKS, BACKBLOCKS, OUTBACK

backbone See also **spine, bone**
- backbone, spine, or a cut of meat containing it CHINE
- any animal whose embryo has a notochord or primitive backbone CHORDATE
- having a backbone or spinal column VERTEBRATE
- having no backbone or spinal column INVERTEBRATE

backfire, return to the originator with damaging effect BOOMERANG, REBOUND

backgammon, See chart and illustration
- backgammon or a variant form of it ACEY-DEUCY, SHESHBESH
- any of the 24 triangular partitions on a backgammon board POINT, FLÈCHE
- exposed single piece in backgammon BLOT
- win in backgammon achieved before the loser has borne off a single piece GAMMON, DOUBLE

background, conditions relating to and casting light on an event or statement CONTEXT
- background music accompanying a film or play INCIDENTAL MUSIC
- background music of a bland kind, as in waiting rooms MUZAK
- background of a design, as in lacework FOND
- background or early life of a person ANTECEDENTS
- forming part of the immediate background or environment, as the air temperature does AMBIENT
- in the background UNOBTRUSIVE, INCONSPICUOUS, LOW-PROFILE, UNOSTENTATIOUS

backless chair, as used by bishops FALDSTOOL

backward, mentally deficient RETARDED
- backward, reverse, unprogressive, going or bending backward RETROGRADE, REGRESSIVE, RECESSIVE, RETROGRESSIVE
- backward, to the rear, especially of a ship ASTERN
- backward flow of air or water, as from a propeller or a wave on the beach BACKWASH
- backward-looking, directed to the past RETROSPECTIVE
- backward pupils' lessons REMEDIAL CLASSES
- word or words reading the same backward as forward PALINDROME

backward (combining form) RETR-, RETRO-, PALIN-

backwoodsman or mountain dweller HILLBILLY

bacon See also **pork**
- bacon or pork fat roasted with game or lean meat to keep it moist BARD
- salted and cured side of bacon FLITCH
- stale, decomposing, smelling off, as old butter or bacon fat might be RANCID
- thin slice of bacon or ham RASHER

bacteria colony, or growth of other microorganisms, as for medical research CULTURE
- bacteria's breeding place, focus of an infection NIDUS
- bacterium of a cylindrical or rodlike shape BACILLUS
- bacterium of a spherical shape COCCUS
- bacterium of a spiral shape SPIRILLUM
- bacterium or other organism that can live without air or free oxygen ANAEROBE
- bacterium or other organism that needs air or free oxygen to live AEROBE
- any of an order of thin, twisting bacteria, such as the one causing syphilis SPIROCHETE
- capable of being decomposed by bacteria or by other biological processes as some packing materials are BIODEGRADABLE
- common bacterium, typically occurring clustered, often responsible for infection of wounds STAPHYLOCOCCUS
- common bacterium, typically occurring in chains, often responsible for throat and other infections STREPTOCOCCUS
- destruction of bacteria by an antibody LYSIS
- disease-producing bacteria, fungus, or the like PATHOGEN
- medicine for bacterial infection ANTIBIOTIC
- reflex movement, as by bacteria, in response to light or a similar stimulus TAXIS
- sewage tank in which solid waste is decomposed by bacteria SEPTIC TANK
- slimy bacterial mass, as formed in a sewage bed ZOOGLEA

bad See also **disgusting, disobedient, evil, horrible, immoral, mediocre, rotten, rude, spiteful**
- bad, blameworthy, as someone's behavior might be DISCREDITABLE, REPREHENSIBLE
- bad, contemptible, despicable, as a liar might be ABJECT
- bad, inappropriate, or improper, as a remark might be UNTIMELY, UNTOWARD, INFELICITOUS
- bad, off or bitter, as butter might be RANCID
- bad, rotten PUTRID
- bad, unwholesome, or undesirable atmosphere MALAISE
- bad and mean, base, as a betrayal might be SORDID, SQUALID, IGNOMINIOUS
- disappointingly bad, woefully weak or inadequate, feeble MEAGER, PALTRY
- extremely bad, appalling or disgraceful ATROCIOUS, ABOMINABLE, EXECRABLE, UNREDEEMABLE
- glaringly bad or wrong, outrageous FLAGRANT, EGREGIOUS

Backgammon

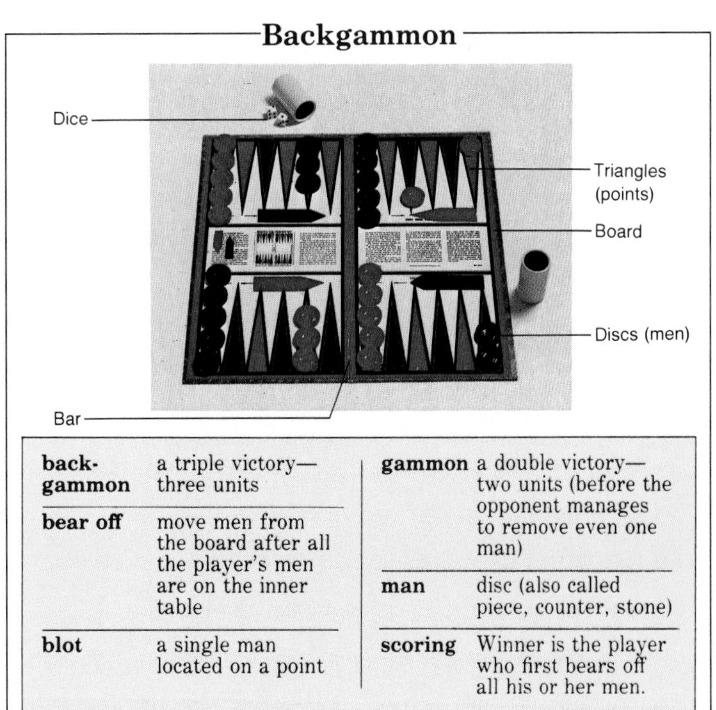

back-gammon	a triple victory—three units
bear off	move men from the board after all the player's men are on the inner table
blot	a single man located on a point
gammon	a double victory—two units (before the opponent manages to remove even one man)
man	disc (also called piece, counter, stone)
scoring	Winner is the player who first bears off all his or her men.

- inferior, of poor quality, very bad or shoddy, as a performance might be ABYSMAL, LAMENTABLE, EXCRUCIATING, DEPLORABLE
- seedy or shady, having a bad reputation, undesirable DISREPUTABLE, UNSAVORY, LOUCHE
- shockingly bad or evil, infamous DIABOLIC, FLAGITIOUS, HEINOUS, INIQUITOUS, NEFARIOUS, PERNICIOUS
- vile, extremely bad, hateful ODIOUS, OBNOXIOUS

bad (combining form) CACO-, DYS-, MAL-, MIS-

bad behavior, bad deeds, misconduct MISDEMEANORS, DELINQUENCY

bad breath HALITOSIS

bad check KITE

bad luck, misfortune MISADVENTURE, MISCHANCE, MISHAP
- person or thing supposedly bringing bad luck JINX, JONAH, HOODOO

bad-mannered See **rude**

bad news - person who causes trouble or seems to herald bad news STORMY PETREL

bad person, rascal, rogue CHARLATAN, RAPSCALLION, SCALLYWAG, SCAPEGRACE, REPROBATE
- bad person, villain, knave CAITIFF
- bad person, wretch or wrongdoer MISCREANT

bad taste in painting and other arts KITSCH

bad-tempered See **angry**

badge PLAQUE
- badges, emblems, or other official distinguishing symbols INSIGNIA

badger, or traditional name for a badger BROCK
- badger's burrow SETT
- group or colony of badgers CETE

badminton of an early style, or the racket used in playing it BATTLEDORE
- rounded cork with a cone of feathers used as the object of play in badminton SHUTTLECOCK

bag See also **case, handbag, suitcase**
- bag, often of canvas, with shoulder straps for carrying on the back RUCKSACK, HAVERSACK
- bag or basket of woven grass or bark in Australia DILLY BAG
- small bag, as for needle and thread, used by sailors DITTY BAG
- small bag, with a shoulder strap or straps, as used by schoolchildren for carrying books SATCHEL
- small bag or suitcase used as hand luggage VALISE

bagpipe music in the form of a series of martial or funeral variations PIBROCH
- bagpipe's bass drone BOURDON, BURDEN
- bagpipe's shrill piercing sound SKIRL
- pipe on a set of bagpipes on which the melody is played CHANTER
- pipe on a set of bagpipes producing a single note DRONE

bail - hold a suspect on bail, or return him to prison, to await trial REMAND

bailiff's area of jurisdiction BAILIWICK

baker's long-handled shovel used for moving bread, pies, pizza, or the like in and out of an oven PEEL

bakery specializing in cakes and pastries PATISSERIE

baking and serving dish for individual portions, especially of egg dishes COCOTTE
- baking dish, typically of earthenware, in which pâtés are cooked and served TERRINE
- baking form with a high rim that can be removed by releasing a clip SPRINGFORM MOLD, SPRINGFORM PAN

balance POISE
- balance, average out EQUATE
- balance, mix, or counteract and thereby make ineffective NEUTRALIZE
- balance in metabolism, or in a society or personality HOMEOSTASIS
- balance of forces, state of stability EQUILIBRIUM, EQUIPOISE, STASIS
- balance of the body, dependent on mechanisms in the inner ear EQUILIBRIUM
- balance or equality of validity or effect EQUIPOLLENCE
- balance or oppose with equal force, offset EQUIPONDERATE, COUNTERVAIL
- balance or scale consisting of a pivoted bar STEELYARD
- automatic movements and adjustments of the body to maintain balance COMPENSATION
- balanced and harmonious arrangement of parts SYMMETRY
- balanced very delicately, unstable PRECARIOUS
- set right, adjust, restore the balance REDRESS

balance (combining form) -STASIS

balcony in a theater MEZZANINE
- balcony or veranda along the outside of the upper level of a building LOGGIA
- balcony, window, or tower offering a wide view MIRADOR
- bracket or similar support, as for a balcony CANTILEVER

bald and smooth GLABROUS
- balding from the forehead backward RECEDING
- baldness, as caused by a skin disease ALOPECIA
- wig or hairpiece covering a bald spot TOUPEE

ball at which masks are worn MASQUERADE, MASQUE
- ball of iron with four spikes, formerly used to slow down enemy troops CALTROP, CROWFOOT
- ball of yarn or thread CLEW
- ball or formal dance PROMENADE
- ball-shaped CONGLOBATE
- curved flight path of a missile, ball, or the like TRAJECTORY
- electrostatic generator in which the electric charge accumulates on a large hollow metal ball VAN DE GRAAFF GENERATOR
- gain possession of the ball by cutting off the pass, as in soccer or hockey INTERCEPT
- produce or become covered with small balls of fiber, as a woollen sweater might PILL
- strike a ball before it bounces VOLLEY

ballad - book of popular ballads, poems, religious homilies, or the like CHAPBOOK

ballerina's very short skirt TUTU

ballet See chart
- balletlike body movements performed in a series as part of a Chinese form of exercise and mental training T'AI CHI
- ballet lover BALLETOMANE

balloon See also **airship**
- balloon, dirigible, or other lighter-than-air aircraft AEROSTAT
- balloon, filled with hydrogen, carrying weather-recording equipment into the upper atmosphere BALLOON SONDE, SOUNDING BALLOON
- balloon, often one of a series, holding up a cable or net that destroys or deters low-flying enemy aircraft BARRAGE BALLOON, BLIMP
- balloon-borne instrument used to collect and transmit information used for weather forecasting RADIOSONDE
- balloon pilot, or person flying in a lighter-than-air aircraft AERONAUT
- basket or cabin under a balloon or airship GONDOLA
- cord opening a panel on a balloon to release gas RIPCORD
- heavy material, such as sandbags, helping to stabilize a ship or balloon BALLAST
- system of ropes diverging from a single rope, as in the rigging of a balloon CROW'S-FOOT
- trailing rope on a balloon or airship, used for mooring or braking DRAGROPE

bamboo - Japanese martial art in which bamboo swords are used KENDO

ban See also **prevent, prohibit**
- ban, prohibit, suppress PROSCRIBE, INTERDICT
- ban, reject, shun, or exclude from participation DEBAR, EXCOMMUNICATE, OSTRACIZE, BLACKBALL

banana, bananalike starchy tropical fruit used in cooking PLANTAIN

band of black material, worn as a sign of mourning CREPE
- band of color on an insect or plant FASCIA
- band of decoration, as along the top of a wall in a room FRIEZE
- band of metal or strip of ribbon worn in the hair or round the neck FILLET
- band of musicians, especially jazz musicians COMBO
- band of musicians, group of dancers, or the like performing together ENSEMBLE
- band of musicians formerly playing at public processions or entertainments WAITS
- band of warriors, protesters, or the like COHORT
- bands of white cloth at the neck of some clerical or academic robes GENEVA BANDS

bandage, wrap, or bind SWATHE, SWADDLE
- bandage or ointment applied to produce warmth CALEFACIENT
- bandage tied in a figure-of-eight pattern as a means of immobilizing a limb SPICA
- bandagelike device wound tight to stanch heavy bleeding TOURNIQUET

bandit or robber BRIGAND

bang or explosive boom produced by the shock wave from an aircraft flying faster than the speed of sound SONIC BOOM

banish or exile DEPORT, PROSCRIBE
- banish or send to the country RUSTICATE
- banished, exiled, or living in a country other than one's homeland EXPATRIATE
- banishment, shunning, or exclusion from a social group OSTRACISM

banister - any of the supporting

BALLET TERMS

arabesque	pose on one leg, with the other leg stretched out behind
attitude	pose similar to an arabesque, but with the raised leg bent at a right angle
ballon	leap with a floating quality
barre	wall-mounted exercise rail, at hip level
battement	loosening-up exercises at the barre
batterie/battu	leap during which the dancer beats his or her calves together sharply
bourrée/pas de bourrée	small steps on toe points
brisé, pas de brisé	leap from one leg, beating the legs together before landing on both feet
capriole/ cabriole	leap during which the dancer beats one leg against the other in midair
chassé, pas chassé	step taken by sliding the foot without raising the heel
ciseaux, pas ciseaux	leap with the legs wide apart in midair
corps de ballet	group of supporting dancers
coryphée	senior member of the corps de ballet
divertissement	self-contained small dance, often within a ballet or an opera
écarté	with arm and leg extended on the same side of the body
élevation	technique by which a dancer remains airborne during a movement: the ability to leap high and gracefully
entrechat	vertical jump in which a dancer changes leg positions after beating his or her calves together
fish dive	move in which the ballerina dives to be caught by her partner, with her head and shoulders just clear of the floor
fouetté	pirouette in which a dancer throws his or her raised leg out and in while spinning
glissade	slow sliding movement with knees bent and feet brought together between steps
jeté	leap from one leg to the other
pas de deux	dance for two
pas de seul	solo dance
pirouette	spin on one foot with the other leg raised, straight or bent
plié	bending at the knees while standing
pointes, sur les pointes	dancing on the toes in blocked shoes
régisseur	director or producer of a ballet
répétiteur	person who coaches singers or ballet dancers
splits	move in which a dancer drops to the floor with the legs stretched to front and back in a straight line
stulchak	move in which a male dancer holds his partner above his head on one straight arm
tutu	classical ballet dress with hip-length bodice and short, frilled, net skirt

posts of a banister BALUSTER
- supporting post at either end of a banister NEWEL POST
bank alongside a drainage ditch DIKE
- bank annuities CONSOLS
- bank clerk TELLER
- bank of earth, as behind a trench, giving protection from the rear PARADOS
- bank of sand, stones, or the like, as a defense against enemy fire PARAPET, BULWARK, BREASTWORK
- bank or ridge bordering a river or irrigated field LEVEE
- banks' exchanging and canceling of checks, drafts, and the like, and the settling of remaining debts CLEARING
- drawing on one's bank account in excess of one's credit balance OVERDRAFT
- lowest rate of interest on bank loans PRIME RATE
- relating to or inhabiting a river bank RIPARIAN
banker or broker trading in shares or bonds for quick profits ARBITRAGEUR
banking and financial world in New York, including the Stock Exchange WALL STREET
- banking and financial world in Britain THE CITY, LOMBARD STREET
bankrupt INSOLVENT
- person appointed by a court to take over and manage the property of a bankrupt, minor, defendant, or the like RECEIVER
- settlement by which creditors accept partial payment from a debtor about to go bankrupt COMPOSITION
- sheriff's officer who carries out a court's orders such as confiscating a bankrupt's property BAILIFF
- wind up a bankrupt business or estate LIQUIDATE
banned because, or as if because, blasphemous or cursed TABOO
- banned goods, obtainable only by smuggling CONTRABAND
banner See **flag**
banquet - luxurious or elaborate, as a banquet might be LUCULLAN
- person who proposes toasts and introduces speakers at a banquet TOASTMASTER
- silver wine vessel, with handles, that is drunk from in turn, as by guests at a banquet LOVING CUP
banter, frivolous style, speech, or the like PERSIFLAGE
baptism, the Eucharist, or other church rite SACRAMENT
- baptism by pouring water on the head AFFUSION
- baptism by total submerging under the water IMMERSION
- mixture of oil and balsam used in sacramental anointing, as at baptism or confirmation CHRISM
- person, especially in the early days of Christianity, receiving instruction before baptism CATECHUMEN
- robe worn by a baby at baptism CHRISOM
- sprinkling of water, as at a baptism ASPERSION
- tank, font, building, or part of a church used for baptisms BAPTISTRY
bar in an inn or tavern TAPROOM
- bar inserted to fasten a loop or strap, or secure a knot TOGGLE
- bar of gold or other metal prepared for storage or transport INGOT
- bar of rolled steel with a U-shaped cross section CHANNEL BAR
- bar on a studio wall at hip height used for ballet practice BARRE
- bar or frame of steel strengthening a car roof in case of accident ROLL BAR
- bar or informal shop for the illicit sale of alcoholic drinks, especially during the Prohibition period in the United States SPEAKEASY
- bar or informal shop for the illicit sale of alcoholic drinks, especially in Ireland or southern Africa SHEBEEN
- bar or rod supporting or bracing a structure by taking pressure down its length STRUT
- bar or small shabby café, especially in France ESTAMINET
- bar serving food as well as drinks BRASSERIE
- comfortable bar or part of a bar SALOON, LOUNGE BAR
- small separate bar or private room in an English pub or inn SNUG
bar billiards BAGATELLE
bar diagram, as a statistical graph HISTOGRAM
barb or barbed head on an arrow, harpoon, or anchor arm FLUKE
barbecue of Japanese style, as used for cooking at table HIBACHI
- small brick of compressed charcoal or coal dust, used for fuel, as at barbecues BRIQUETTE
- South African term for a barbecue BRAAIVLEIS
barbed-wire fence or barrier of sharpened stakes FRAISE
- barrier of barbed wire, spikes, or sharpened stakes CHEVAL-DE-FRISE, FRAISE
barber - relating to barbering or hairdressing TONSORIAL
bard or minstrel in ancient Scandinavian SKALD
bare (combining form) NUDI-
barefist boxer PUGILIST
barefooted, referring to those orders of monks and nuns that wear sandals DISCALCED
barest trace, tiny amount SEMBLANCE, MODICUM
bargain or haggle CHAFFER, NEGOTIATE, HORSETRADE, DICKER, HUCKSTER, PALTER
- secure a bargain finally and decisively CLINCH
barge, especially for carrying coal KEEL
- barge used for dumping by a dredger HOPPER
bark, rind, husk, or similar outer layer CORTEX
- bark or tree from which quinine is derived CINCHONA
- cut a ring of bark from a tree trunk or branch in order to kill it or slow its growth RINGBARK, GIRDLE
- growing on or living in the bark of a tree CORTICOLOUS
barley - frame or floor on which barley is spread for malting COUCH
barn or cowshed BYRE
barnacles - immobile, rooted, fixed, as barnacles are SESSILE
barometer based on changes in slope of the lid of a partial-vacuum drum, according to variations in atmospheric pressure ANEROID BAROMETER
- vacuum formed at the top of an upright mercury-filled tube, as in a barometer TORRICELLIAN VACUUM
barracks or soldiers' quarters in a town, in former times CASERN
- barracks used in former times as temporary housing for slaves and convicts BARRACOON
barrel of large capacity, typically holding about 100 gallons PUNCHEON, PIPE, HOGSHEAD
- barrel of small size KILDERKIN, PIN
- barrel of small size, typically for storing butter or cheese FIRKIN
- barrel or cask of large capacity, especially for beer or wine TUN
- barrel's projecting rim or lip CHIME
- bulge of a barrel BILGE
- drawing off of beer or other liquid from a container such as a barrel, tapping DRAFT
- frame supporting a barrel that is lying on its side GANTRY
- front end of the barrel of a gun MUZZLE
- hole in a cask or barrel for the passage of liquid BUNGHOLE
- person who makes or repairs barrels COOPER, HOOPER
- pierce a cask, keg, or barrel in order to draw off the liquid inside

BASEBALL TERMS

ball	pitch outside the batter's strike zone and not swung at by the batter
base	each of the four corners of the baseball diamond
bat	wooden or aluminum device used to hit a pitched ball
batter	player who hits or tries to hit the ball with a bat
batter's box	rectangular area in which the batter must stand
box score	condensed statistical summary of a baseball game
bunt	ball that is intentionally batted softly into the infield
catcher	player stationed behind home plate to catch the ball
designated hitter	player designated before the game to bat in place of the pitcher
diamond	the baseball playing field
double	hit on which the batter reaches second base
doubleheader	two games held consecutively on the same day by the same teams
dugout	low shelter that contains the players' waiting bench
glove	padded leather hand covering used to protect the hand and to catch a ball
hit	batted ball that allows the batter to reach a base safely
home plate	rubber slab at which the batter stands, and which must be touched in scoring a run
home run	four-base hit on which the batter scores
infielder	defensive player at first, second, or third base or shortstop
inning	portion of a game with a turn at bat for each team
outfielder	defensive player beyond the infield perimeter
pitcher	player who throws the ball to the batter
pitcher's mound	elevated area from which the ball is pitched
shortstop	player position between second and third base
shutout	game in which the losing team does not score
stolen base	a runner's advancing from one base to the next while pitching is in progress
strike	pitched ball that is in the strike zone and not swung at or which is swung at and missed
walk/base on balls	advance to first base by a batter to whom four balls have been pitched

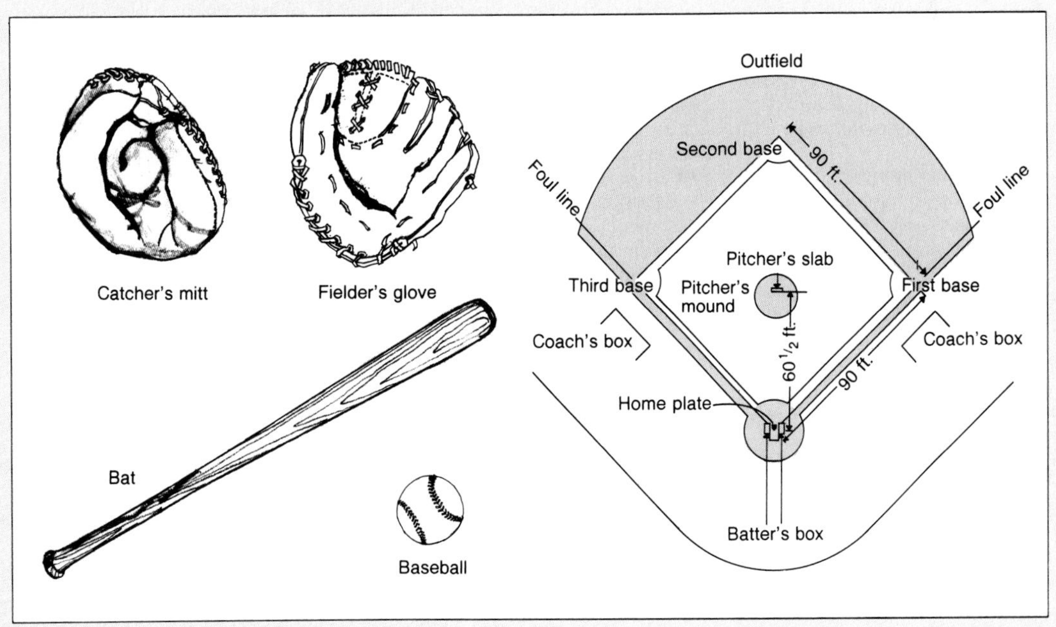

BROACH
- plug or bung in the vent of a cask or barrel SPIGOT, SPILE
- wooden block, cradle, or wedge used to stop a barrel, wheel, or boat from rolling or sliding CHOCK
- wooden strip or plank forming part of a barrel, ship's hull, or the like STAVE

barrel organ or similar mechanical musical instrument HURDY-GURDY

barren, incapable of further reproduction, as a plant or animal might be EFFETE

barrier See also **fortification**
- barrier, consisting of a frame with spikes or barbed wire, against enemy troops or horses CHEVAL-DE-FRISE
- barrier, such as a screen, curtain, or bank of earth TRAVERSE
- barrier floating on the water, as of logs or empty drums, to confine other logs, protect a harbor, or the like BOOM
- barrier of barbed wire or sharpened stakes FRAISE
- barrier or guarded line, as against a disease or hostile power CORDON SANITAIRE
- incapable of being overcome, as a barrier or obstacle might be INSUPERABLE, INSURMOUNTABLE

barrow - seller of food or goods from a barrow or market stall COSTERMONGER

base an argument on certain facts or suppositions PREDICATE
- base block or slab, as of a column, statue, vase, or trophy PLINTH, PEDESTAL

baseball See chart and illustration, page 49

based on or copied from an earlier example, unoriginal DERIVATIVE

basic See also **essence, essential, basis**
- basic nature or essence of something HYPOSTASIS, QUINTESSENCE
- basic or most important part of something ALPHA AND OMEGA
- basic principle believed to underlie a given thing QUINTESSENCE, ELIXIR
- basic principle or assumption, as in a philosophical argument AXIOM, PREMISE, POSTULATE
- basic principle or elementary stage of a skill or subject RUDIMENT
- basic support structure of society or an organization, including transport, electricity supply, education, and health care INFRASTRUCTURE

basic, primitive, or ancient (combining form) UR-

basin typically set in the wall of a church for draining away the water used in ceremonial washing PISCINA, SACRARIUM
- basin for holy water at the entrance of a church STOUP, FONT
- low bathroom basin, used for washing one's private parts BIDET

basis, foundation, underlying principle SUBSTRATUM, ANLAGE, BEDROCK
- basis or reason for an action, policy, or belief RATIONALE
- structure or conceptual system that is built on or developed from a basis or foundation SUPERSTRUCTURE

basket See illustration
- basket as used for a variety of farm work SKEP
- basket of food and drink, or for laundry HAMPER
- basket of wood or wickerwork, for garden produce or shopping TRUG
- basket or cabin under a balloon or airship GONDOLA
- basket or similar carrier, as on a pack animal or bicycle PANNIER
- basket or trap for fish, lobsters, or the like, made of wickerwork CREEL
- basket used for catching fish COOP
- carved architectural ornament in the form of a basket of fruit CORBEIL
- dried leaves, straw, or the like prepared for weaving or basketmaking CHIP
- fiber from palm leaves used for weaving baskets, mats, or the like RAFFIA
- plant shoots used to make baskets WICKER
- twig, or the willow bearing it, used in basketmaking OSIER

basketball See chart and illustration, page 52

bastard, born out of wedlock, born of unmarried parents ILLEGITIMATE, MISBEGOTTEN, SPURIOUS, NATURAL, SUPPOSITITIOUS
- in heraldry, a band crossing the shield diagonally from the top right, typically indicating a bastard line BEND SINISTER

bat See illustration, page 53
- bat of a small, common, insect-eating kind PIPISTRELLE
- bat or related flying mammal CHIROPTERAN
- adjective for a bat VESPERTILIAN
- establishing of the location of an object by means of high-frequency sound waves, as bats or dolphins do ECHOLOCATION
- winglike membrane between the fore and hind limb of a bat, flying squirrel, or the like PATAGIUM

bath of small size for sitting but not lying in HIPBATH, SITZ BATH
- bath or hot tub, with underwater jets for massage JACUZZI
- bathtub covered at one end SLIPPER BATH
- lie or roll lazily about in mud, a hot bath, or the like WALLOW
- public baths, especially in ancient Greece and Rome THERMAE
- room for taking hot baths in ancient Rome CALDARIUM
- spongelike, fibrous interior of the dishcloth gourd, used as a back scrubber in the bath LOOFAH
- steam bath of Finnish origin, or the room or building used for it SAUNA
- take delight or sensual pleasure, as in a bath LUXURIATE, BASK, REVEL, INDULGE ONESELF, LANGUISH

bathing area in India formed by a flight of steps beside a river GHAT
- bathing beach LIDO
- relating to baths or bathing BALNEAL

bathroom fixture in the form of a low basin, for washing one's private parts BIDET
- bathroom or lavatory facilities at a military base or camp LATRINE, ABLUTIONS

batik, batiklike dyeing technique in which parts of the cloth are tied tightly to produce a mottled effect TIE-DYE

battery - cables used to start a car by connecting its dead battery to another car's active battery JUMPER CABLES, JUMP LEADS
- condition of having two opposing physical properties at different points, as a magnet or battery has POLARITY
- conductor for the electric current into or out of the electrolyte in a battery ELECTRODE
- early batterylike device for the temporary storage of electric charge CAPACITOR, LEYDEN JAR
- ionizing substance such as an acid or paste that conducts electricity in a battery ELECTROLYTE
- referring to electric current produced by chemical action, as in a battery VOLTAIC, GALVANIC
- small projection for making connections at a battery terminal LUG

battery hens - hens kept in farmyards or fields, as distinct from battery hens FREE-RANGE HENS

battle formation of troops in close array PHALANX
- battle causing disaster and destruction ARMAGEDDON
- bravery, strength, or skill, as shown in battle PROWESS

- flag raised or waved on its pole as a rallying point for soldiers during a battle STANDARD
- minor or preliminary conflict, dispute, or battle SKIRMISH
- murderous, marked by widespread slaughter, as a bloody battle is INTERNECINE
- trial by combat or battle in medieval Britain WAGER OF BATTLE

battle cry, as formerly used by a Scottish clan SLOGAN

battlefield first-aid post DRESSING STATION

battlements See also **castle, fortifications**
- battlements, as on a castle CRENELLATIONS

bay, baylike body of sea water separated from the sea, as by coral reefs LAGOON
- bay or channel through which water flows inland ESTUARY
- bay or deep inlet from the sea SOUND
- bay or lake in Ireland LOUGH
- bay or lake in Scotland LOCH
- large expanse of sea partially enclosed by land, resembling a huge bay GULF
- small sheltered bay or inlet COVE
- wide bay, or the curve in the shoreline that forms it BIGHT

baying of the hounds when pursuing game QUESTING

bazaar or covered market in a Muslim country SOUK

be - verb such as *be* or *ring* that does not follow the usual pattern of inflections IRREGULAR VERB

beach or shore STRAND
- beach or shoreline covered with pebbles or stony gravel SHINGLE

bead at the end of each decade on the rosary, marking the point at which the Lord's prayer is said PATERNOSTER
- beadlike granules of cassava-root starch, used in milk puddings, as a thickener in soup, and the like TAPIOCA
- beads of shell formerly used as currency by North American Indians WAMPUM, PEAG
- string of beads, especially a small string of prayer beads CHAPLET
- string of beads used as an aid in counting prayers ROSARY

beak - bird's beak, insect's snout, projection at the front of a lobster's shell, or the like ROSTRUM
- either the upper or the lower part of a bird's beak MANDIBLE
- waxy swelling around the nostrils at the base of the upper beak in the parrot and some other birds CERE

Baskets

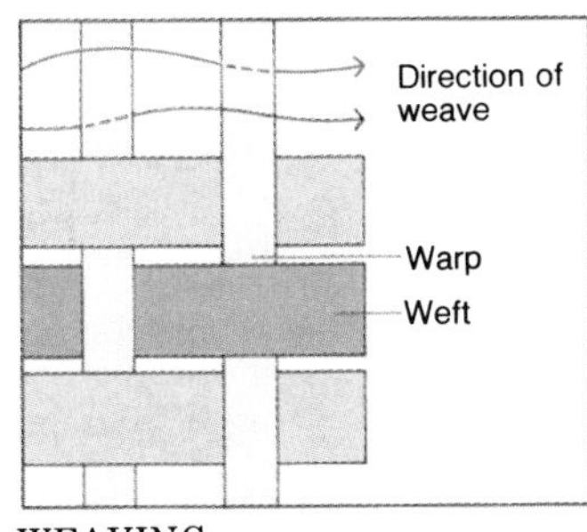

WEAVING

The basket maker produces this pattern, called "plain weave" or "tabby," by passing one strand of the warp over and under one strand of the weft for each row.

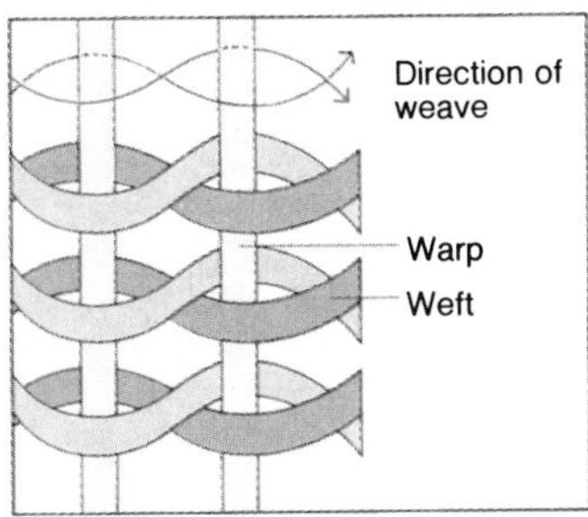

TWINING

In twining, the basket maker uses the warp strands in pairs. One strand is passed over a weft, and the other is carried under the same weft. In the completed basket, only the weft can be seen.

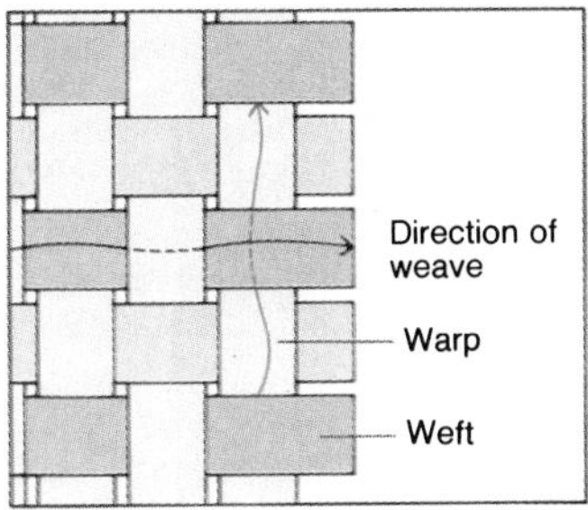

PLAITING

In plaiting, the warp and the weft are interwoven. As a result, it is often impossible to distinguish between the warp and weft strands in a finished basket.

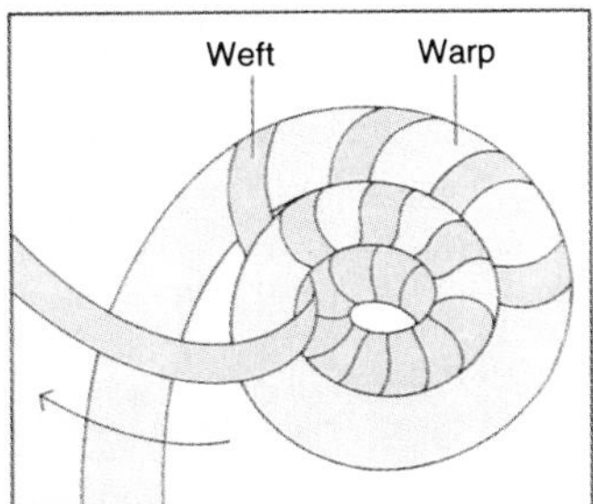

COILING

In coiling, the sides are made by winding coils of flexible material on top of each other and binding them together. The basket maker wraps each coil and binds it to the one before it.

beam, block, stone slab, or the like set horizontally in a wall to distribute pressure, as over a door frame TEMPLATE
- beam between walls supporting a ceiling or roof JOIST
- beam in the frame of a vaulted roof LAMELLA
- beam laid horizontally, as in building GIRDER
- beam or pillar, as of steel or concrete, driven into the ground, typically as part of a building's foundations PILE
- beam or similar projection fixed at only one end CANTILEVER
- beam or support along the top of a window or door frame LINTEL
- beam placed horizontally in a building, as for supporting a floor STRINGER, SUMMER
- hole or niche in a wall for supporting a beam COLUMBARIUM

bean, pea, or related pod-bearing plant LEGUME
- French bean or similar edible bean HARICOT, FLAGEOLET, FRIJOL

bean curd TOFU

bean sprouts - bean producing the bean sprouts used in salads and cooking MUNG BEAN

bear the impact or main force of a blow, shock, or attack BEAR THE BRUNT OF
- adjective for a bear URSINE
- group or family of bears SLOTH
- traditional name for a bear, as in children's stories BRUIN

bear, bearing (combining form) -FER-, -FEROUS

beard, beardlike whiskers down each side of the face SIDEBURNS, SIDEBOARDS, MUTTONCHOPS, DUNDREARIES
- Australian term for a beard ZIFF
- former term for a beard or bearded man BEAVER
- short pointed beard GOATEE, VANDYKE, LOUIS NAPOLEON BEARD
- tip of a pointed beard PEAK

bearded POGIONATE
- bearded, as a plant or animal might be BARBATE

bearer (combining form) -PHORE, -FER, -PHOROUS

bearing, manner, behavior DEMEANOR, MIEN, COMPORTMENT
- bearing, method of carrying or holding oneself when walking DEPORTMENT, GAIT
- bearing live young rather than laying eggs VIVIPAROUS
- bearing more than one offspring at a time MULTIPAROUS
- bearing young by means of eggs that hatch outside the body OVIPAROUS
- bearing young by means of eggs that hatch within the female's body, as with some fish and reptiles OVOVIVIPAROUS

bearings - finding one's bearings socially or spatially ORIENTATION
- having lost one's bearings, as when in an unfamiliar environment DISORIENTED, DISORIENTATED
- section of an axle or shaft covered or supported by a bearing JOURNAL

beast - adjective relating to a beast BESTIAL

beast (combining form) THERI-, THERIO-

beat See also **defeat**
- beat abnormally fast, as the heart might PALPITATE
- beat in a regular rhythm, throb, as the heart does PULSATE
- beat or buffet with or as if with a club BASTE, BLUDGEON, CUDGEL, FUSTIGATE
- beat or flog, typically with a whip, often as a form of self-chastisement SCOURGE, FLAGELLATE
- beat or hit repeatedly, especially

BASKETBALL TERMS

ball	spherical (leather, rubber, or synthetic) case with a rubber bladder; cirumference 75-78 cm, weight 600-650 g (about 29½–31″, 21–23 oz)
basket	net open at the bottom suspended in front of the backboard and constituting the goal, its rim ten feet above the ground
dribble	roll or bounce a ball and touch it again before another player does
dunk shot	ball thrown down into the basket by jumping high into the air
free throw	throw taken from the free-throw line after a foul
jump ball	initial ball thrown by the referee that the opposing centers jump for, trying to tap it to a teammate
scoring	making the ball enter the basket from above
teams	five players and five (sometimes seven) substitutes on each side
ten-second rule	team having the ball must move it to the front court within ten seconds
thirty-second rule	team must try for a goal within thirty seconds after getting the ball
three-second rule	player must not remain more than three seconds in a restricted area
time-out	brief suspension of the game for various reasons including a foul, a delay, or an injury

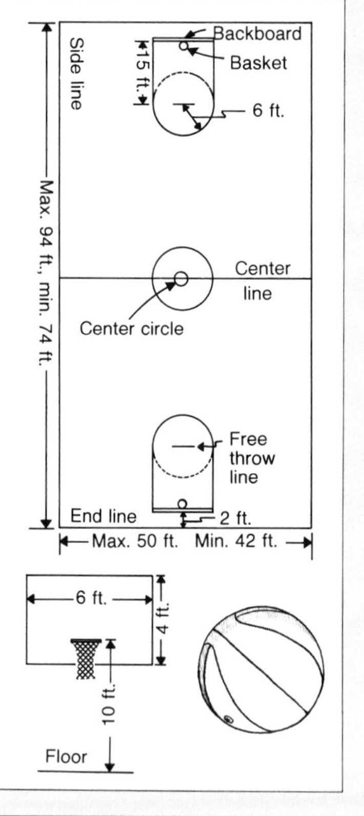

Bats

with the fists POMMEL, PUMMEL
- beat or strike heavily, as with the hand or a weapon SMITE
- beat or thrash with a stick DRUB, FLAIL, LAMBASTE
- beat with a whip to the point of stripping the skin from FLAY
- beating or striking of a surface, as by sound on the eardrum or by a stick on a drum PERCUSSION
- beating with a stick, especially on the soles of the feet, or the stick used BASTINADO
- punishment, as formerly in the army in which two lines of men beat an offender running between them GAUNTLET

beat about the bush, speak evasively, hedge EQUIVOCATE, TEMPORIZE, PREVARICATE

beautiful See also **attractive**
- beautiful, gorgeous RAVISHING
- beautiful in a powerful sensual way, luscious VOLUPTUOUS
- beautiful or dignified, especially when massive STATUESQUE
- beautiful young man APOLLO, ADONIS, DEMIGOD
- delicately beautiful EXQUISITE

beautify See **decorate**

beauty PULCHRITUDE
- beauty arising from harmonious arrangement of parts SYMMETRY
- beauty parlor, stylish fashion store, or the like SALON
- lover of beauty ESTHETE
- relating to beauty or good taste ESTHETIC
- womanly beauty of a dangerously bewitching kind CIRCEAN

beauty (combining form) CALLI-

beaver's den or burrow LODGE
- rise to the surface to breathe, as beavers and otters do VENT

beaver hat CASTOR

become or grow WAX

becoming (combining form) -ESCENT

bed of canvas or string suspended at both ends HAMMOCK
- bed on casters that is low enough to be stored under another bed TRUCKLE BED, TRUNDLE BED
- bed warmer of an early kind consisting of a covered metal pan filled with hot water or coals WARMING PAN
- canopy over a bed TESTER
- hard narrow bed, or straw-filled mattress PALLET, PALLIASSE
- reception held by a monarch just after getting out of bed LEVEE
- rest in bed for a woman just before or during childbirth CONFINEMENT, LYING-IN, ACCOUCHEMENT
- short decorative curtain hung along a shelf, edge of the bed, or the like VALANCE
- simple, stretcherlike bed widely used in India CHARPOY
- unsprung mattress of Japanese style, used as a bed FUTON

bedbug or related insect CIMEX

bedroom or private sitting room of a woman BOUDOIR, BOWER

bedsore DECUBITUS ULCER

bedspread, coverlet for a bed COUNTERPANE
- quilted bedspread COMFORTER, DUVET, CONTINENTAL QUILT

bee-eating, as some birds are APIVOROUS
- adjective for a bee APIAN
- having a sting, as a bee has ACULEATE
- male bee, doing no work except to fertilize the queen bee DRONE
- mixture of nectar and pollen fed by worker bees to the larvae BEEBREAD, AMBROSIA
- nourishing substance secreted by bees and fed to all larvae when very young ROYAL JELLY

beef See illustration, page 54, and also chart at **menu**
- cut or joint of beef consisting of a double sirloin BARON
- dried salted strips of meat, especially beef JERKY, CHARQUI, BILTONG
- streaks or mottling of fat on high-quality beef MARBLING

beehive or group of beehives APIARY
- beehive typically in the form of a straw dome SKEP

beekeeper APIARIST

beer barrel or wine cask of large capacity TUN
- beer mug, typically made of pottery and having a lid STEIN
- beer mug in the shape of a man wearing a three-cornered hat TOBY, TOBY JUG
- beer of a light, pale type with a strong flavor of hops PILSNER
- beer of a light, usually effervescent kind, typically brewed or stored for a relatively long time LAGER
- beer of poor quality SWIPES
- drink a large amount of beer without stopping CHUGALUG
- clarifying of wine, beer, or the like, as by adding isinglass FINING
- clear wine, beer, or cider of its dregs, typically by siphoning RACK
- drawing off of beer or other liquid from a container such as a barrel

DRAFT, TAP
- heat treatment of milk, beer, and other liquids to destroy germs and regulate fermentation PASTEURIZATION

beer brewing - fermentable pulp used in brewing beer MASH

beer hall or German restaurant, originally in the cellar of a town hall RATHSKELLER

beermats - collector of beermats TEGESTOLOGIST

beetle See also **insect**
- beetle of a family, including the dung beetles, that was treated as sacred in ancient Egypt SCARAB

beetroot of a large, yellowish variety MANGEL-WURZEL

before, prior, earlier PRECEDING, ANTECEDENT, ANTERIOR
- before birth PRENATAL, ANTENATAL
- before noon, in the morning ANTEMERIDIAN
- before or in preparation for, introductory PRELIMINARY, PRELATORY, PREPARATORY
- anticipation and answering of an argument or objection before it has been started PROLEPSIS
- feeling of having once before undergone an experience that one is now having for the first time DÉJÀ VU
- person or thing that comes before another in time FORERUNNER, PRECURSOR, HERALD, HARBINGER
- person who goes before another in time, as in a job PREDECESSOR
- suggest or indicate beforehand, especially in a sinister way PORTEND, FORESHADOW, PRESAGE

before (combining form) ANTE-, FORE-, PRE-, PRO-

beg, apply for, or request humbly or urgently PETITION, SOLICIT, SUPPLICATE
- beg or appeal to urgently, plead with or implore BESEECH, ENTREAT, EXHORT, ADJURE
- beg or demand insistently, press, urge SUE, IMPORTUNE
- beg or plead on behalf of another INTERCEDE
- relating to begging or entreaty PRECATORY, SUPPLICATORY
- beggarlike guest or visitor who expects or accepts too much hospitality or generosity FREELOADER, SPONGER, SCROUNGER, CADGER, LEECH
- relating to beggars or begging MENDICANT

begging the question, fallacy of assuming in the premise the very conclusion to be proved PETITIO PRINCIPII

begin, commence, set out on a venture EMBARK
- begin, introduce, or launch officially INAUGURATE
- begin, originate, institute USHER IN, INITIATE
- begin or develop something new, pioneer INNOVATE
- begin the development or production of, give rise to ENGENDER, GERMINATE
- begin the working of, implement, set in motion, trigger ACTUATE
- begin to discuss a subject BROACH

beginner, inexperienced person TENDERFOOT, GREENHORN, FLEDGLING, ROOKIE
- beginner, novice, or newcomer NEOPHYTE, TYRO
- beginner or learner, person still ignorant, specifically a pupil still learning the alphabet ABECEDARIAN
- beginner or novice, especially in a religious order NOVITIATE
- beginner's critical test in the form of a challenging problem PONS ASINORUM

beginning See also **origin, introduction**
- beginning, in a very early stage of development EMBRYONIC, INCHOATE, INCIPIENT
- beginning, just emerging or developing NASCENT
- beginning, origin, or creation of something GENESIS, CONCEPTION
- beginning, starting point, point of origin TERMINUS A QUO
- beginning of a course of action, career, or the like DEBUT
- beginning or emergence, as of a disease or problem ONSET
- beginning or initial stages of a project or period OUTSET, INCEPTION
- beginning or introduction of something new INNOVATION
- dating from or relating to the beginning of time or history PRIMORDIAL

beginning (combining form) -ESCENT

behave in a needlessly gracious way toward others, as though they were one's inferiors CONDESCEND, DEIGN, PATRONIZE
- behave in a way that departs from the norm or standard DEVIATE
- behave or conduct oneself in a specified way COMPORT ONESELF, DEPORT ONESELF, ACQUIT ONESELF
- behaving badly, out of control, disobeying orders, rebellious RESTIVE, UNRULY, INSUBORDINATE

behavior, conduct, manner DEMEANOR, DEPORTMENT, MIEN
- behavior in response to a stimulus that does not directly cause it but has come to be associated with it, as through training CONDITIONED RESPONSE
- behavior modification, training, or learning process through ad-

Beef Cuts

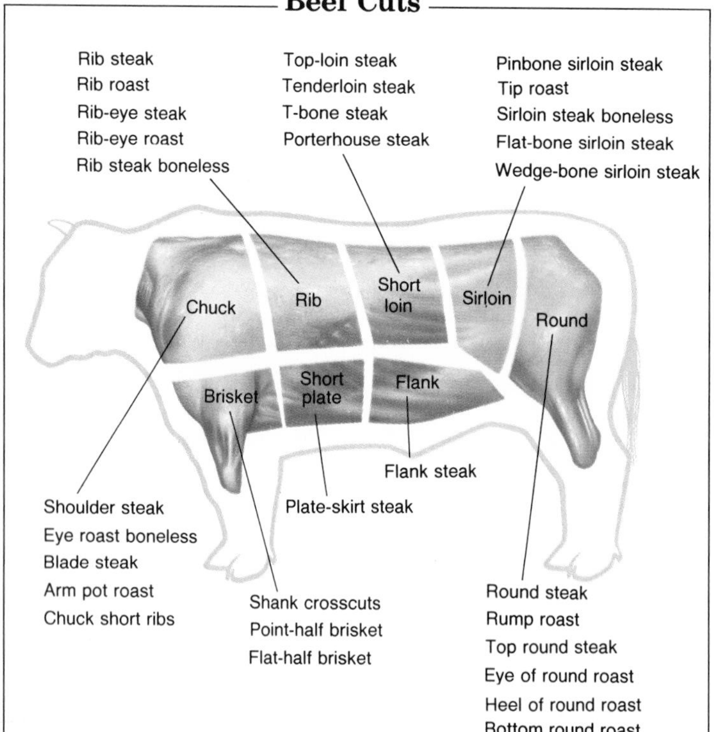

justment of stimuli CONDITIONING
- behavior of an exaggerated kind designed to conceal or make up for some defect or inadequacy COMPENSATION
- behavior of an overemotional type MELODRAMA
- behavior or mental activity directed toward change or action, including desire, striving, and so on CONATION
- behavior that is wild, intemperate, or overindulgent EXCESSES
- artificial behavior or way of speaking or dressing intended to impress others AFFECTATION, PRETENTIOUSNESS
- code of behavior, etiquette, especially among diplomats or rulers PROTOCOL
- distinctive item of behavior, peculiar trait or whim of a person IDIOSYNCRASY, ECCENTRICITY, FOIBLE, QUIRK, MANNERISM
- lapse or uncharacteristic piece of behavior or thinking ABERRATION, BRAINSTORM
- model of behavior, standard of acceptability, or the like NORM
- referring to bad or inappropriate behavior UNSEEMLY, INDECOROUS, UNBECOMING
- rough, noisy, and unrestrained, as children's behavior might be BOISTEROUS

behead, cut off the head of DECAPITATE
- device for beheading people, consisting of a heavy blade running between vertical posts GUILLOTINE

behind, at the rear POSTERIOR
- behind or to the rear of a ship ASTERN

behind (combining form) META-, POST-, RETR-, RETRO-

behind closed doors, as a court case might be IN CAMERA

being (combining form) ONTO-

belch or burp ERUCT

Belgian - Flemish-speaking Belgian FLEMING
- French-speaking Belgian WALLOON

belief See also **religion**
- belief, acceptance as true CREDENCE
- belief, especially in a religious or ideological system, of a strict, unquestioningly literal, or passionate kind FUNDAMENTALISM
- belief, religious principle, body of teachings, or the like DOCTRINE, CREED
- belief, religious principle, or doctrine held very firmly DOGMA, ARTICLE OF FAITH
- belief differing from the orthodox view HERESY, HETERODOXY
- belief in the virtues of hard work WORK ETHIC
- belief or confident opinion PERSUASION, CONVICTION
- belief or doctrine, as of a religious or professional group TENET
- belief or opinion that is mistaken or misleading DELUSION
- belief system and values of a society, especially as expressed in its arts MYTHOS
- beliefs or ideas as a system of thought IDEOLOGY
- assent to a belief, opinion, or the like SUBSCRIBE, ESPOUSE
- declare a belief in something, especially in a religion PROFESS
- defense or formal justification, as of one's beliefs APOLOGIA
- disbeliever, skeptic, person without faith or beliefs NULLIFIDIAN
- established, fixed, firmly settled, as beliefs might be ENTRENCHED
- express one's personal belief TESTIFY
- justification, as for a belief WARRANT
- neurotic or false belief, that one is ill, or likely to become ill HYPOCHONDRIA, VALETUDINARIANISM
- recognition of others' rights to dissenting beliefs, especially on religion TOLERATION
- relating to belief DOXASTIC
- statement of beliefs or principles CREDO, CREED, TESTAMENT

believable or persuasive though not necessarily truthful, as an excuse or politician might be PLAUSIBLE
- believable or reliable CREDIBLE

believe - unwilling to believe or accept something SKEPTICAL, INCREDULOUS

believer in or follower of a particular doctrine, religion, or the like ADHERENT

believing something too easily, without sufficient evidence CREDULOUS, GULLIBLE

belittle, criticize openly, make light of or represent as unimportant DISPARAGE, DECRY, DEPRECIATE, DEPRECATE, DERIDE

bell at Lloyd's of London rung to announce news of an insured ship that has been missing LUTINE BELL
- bell ringing, especially the art of musical ringing of church bells CAMPANOLOGY
- bell ringing using all possible variations or bobs CHANGE RINGING
- bell rung to indicate the time of the prayers commemorating the Annunciation ANGELUS
- bell-shaped, as some flowers are CAMPANULATE
- bell-shaped cover of plastic or glass, placed over young plants for protection CLOCHE
- bell tower, especially one that is freestanding rather than part of a church building CAMPANILE
- bell tower, or the part of it housing the church bells BELFRY
- bell used for sounding alarm signals TOCSIN
- bells, as in a tower, played in a set, or a tune on these bells CARILLON, PEAL
- official regulation requiring people to go home or be indoors by a certain hour of night, or the times of or bell signaling this restriction CURFEW
- ringing or jingling of bells TINTINNABULATION
- solemn ringing of a bell, as at a funeral KNELL, TOLLING
- swinging metal bar inside a bell TONGUE, CLAPPER
- wooden block from which a bell hangs STOCK

bellflower CAMPANULA

belly or abdomen of a mammal VENTER
- nerve network in the area of the belly, where one might be punched by an attacker SOLAR PLEXUS

belong as a necessary or rightful part PERTAIN, APPERTAIN
- belonging or existing as an essential part or characteristic INHERENT, INTRINSIC, INTEGRAL

belongings or personal property PARAPHERNALIA

below, under, especially beneath the earth's surface NETHER
- below or later in the text INFRA
- below the threshold of consciousness or perception SUBLIMINAL

below (combining form) HYPO-, INFRA-, SUB-

belt fitted with cartridge pockets, worn across the chest BANDOLEER
- belt or band encircling something, such as the ridge around the base of a tooth CINGULUM
- belt or girdle, as formerly worn by a bride CESTUS
- belt or sash crossing the chest from the shoulder, used for carrying a sword or bugle BALDRIC
- belt or sash worn round the waist, such as the cord on a monk's habit CINCTURE
- beltlike medical device worn to ease the pressure on a rupture TRUSS
- beltlike sash, wide and often pleated, worn with a dinner jacket CUMMERBUND
- continuous moving belt carrying

objects, as on a factory's assembly line CONVEYOR BELT
- military officer's wide belt supported by a diagonal strap passing over the right shoulder SAM BROWNE BELT
- ornamental belt presented as a trophy to a British boxing champion LONSDALE BELT
- put a belt around, or fasten with a belt GIRD

bench See also **furniture**
- high-backed wooden bench, typically with arms at the sides and a storage chest beneath SETTLE
- long upholstered bench against a wall BANQUETTE
- room, portico, or the like with a continuous bench, where people in ancient Greece and Rome would hold discussions EXEDRA

bend, curve, turn, or fold, as of a body part FLEXURE
- bend the knees, or kneel, as in worship GENUFLECT
- bending of a joint FLEXION
- bending or curving gracefully, as a winding road or the movements of a snake might be SINUOUS
- able to bend easily, or easy to bend SUPPLE, PLIANT, PLIABLE, FLEXIBLE, MALLEABLE, LITHE, LISSOM, LIMBER
- drive or travel successfully, as round a tight bend NEGOTIATE
- gentle bends in a river MEANDERS
- U-shaped bend in a river OXBOW
- warp, bend or crack, as a piece of wood might SPRING

bends, painful condition, as in deep-sea divers, following sudden change of pressure CAISSON DISEASE, DECOMPRESSION SICKNESS, AEROEMBOLISM

beneath (combining form) HYPO-, INFRA-, SUB-

beneath one's dignity INFRA DIG, INFRA DIGNITATEM

benefactor or sponsor PATRON

beneficial, improving, correcting, as advice might be SALUTARY

benefit See also **advantage**
- benefit or bonus from a favor or investment DIVIDEND
- benefit or extra privilege from one's employment over and above one's salary or wages PERK, PERQUISITE, FRINGE BENEFIT

bent or twisted out of shape, as a face might be CONTORTED, WRY

benzene - organic compound such as benzene, containing only hydrogen and carbon HYDROCARBON

bequest or trust, or the income derived from it ENDOWMENT

berry See also **fruit**
- berry-bearing BACCIFEROUS
- berry or fruit having a thick rind and segmented pulp, especially a citrus fruit HESPERIDIUM
- berrylike, having the form, flavor, or texture of a berry BACCATE
- berry's small segment or division ACINUS, DRUPE
- berries used to flavor gin JUNIPER BERRIES
- clustered, formed of tightly packed parts, as the raspberry and mulberry are AGGREGATE

beside, next to, alongside ADJACENT, CONTIGUOUS, TANGENTIAL, ABUTTING, JUXTAPOSED, ADJOINING

beside (combining form) PARA-

besiege BELEAGUER

best, richest, most powerful, or the like within a given group ELITE
- best, supreme, foremost PEERLESS, UNSURPASSED, PARAMOUNT, PREEMINENT, NONPAREIL, PAR EXCELLENCE
- best of the best, very best CRÈME DE LA CRÈME
- best or most favorable OPTIMUM, OPTIMAL
- best part or detail HIGHLIGHT
- typical of the best of its kind VINTAGE

bet See also **gambling, horse racing**
- bet, gamble WAGER, PLEDGE
- bet on four or more successive races, the winnings each time becoming the stake on the next PARLAY, ACCUMULATOR
- bet taker or card dealer at a gambling table CROUPIER
- betting system in which the winners receive a share of the total amount bet TOTALIZATOR, TOTE, PARI-MUTUEL
- betting technique of raising the stakes after each loss MARTINGALE
- bettor or gambler, especially on a horse race PUNTER
- balance a bet by taking other bets or precautions HEDGE

betray or slander TRADUCE

betrayal, breach of trust PERFIDY

better, outdo, be superior to or greater than EXCEED, EXCEL
- get better after an illness RECUPERATE, CONVALESCE

between, in the middle INTERMEDIATE, INTERVENING

between (combining form) INTER-

between ourselves, in confidence ENTRE NOUS

bewitching, dangerously attractive or charming CIRCEAN

beyond one's authority, outside one's legal powers ULTRA VIRES
- acting or speaking beyond the range of one's ability or expertise ULTRACREPIDARIAN
- beyond reasonable limits, excessive, unrestrained INORDINATE, IMMODERATE
- beyond the call of duty SUPEREROGATORY
- beyond the limits of ordinary experience TRANSCENDENT

beyond (combining form) EXO-, HYPER-, META-, PARA-, SUPER-, SUPRA-, SUR-, TRANS-, ULTRA-

bias See also **tendency**
- bias, prejudice, preformed judgment or preference PREDISPOSITION, PRECONCEPTION, PARTI PRIS

biased, favoring one particular view, especially a controversial one TENDENTIOUS
- biased, one-sided PARTIAL, PARTISAN
- biased or prejudiced in an intolerant way BIGOTED

Bible See illustration, and also **Scriptures**
- Bible, as found in hotel rooms, distributed by an international organization GIDEON BIBLE
- Bible in an English translation of 1611, the King James Bible AUTHORIZED VERSION
- Bible in an English translation of 1610 by Roman Catholic scholars DOUAY BIBLE
- Bible in its Latin version by Saint Jerome, authorized by the Roman Catholic Church VULGATE
- Bible or other book containing versions of a text in different languages POLYGLOT
- Bible's first five, six, or seven books respectively PENTATEUCH, HEXATEUCH, HEPTATEUCH
- biblical interpretation with a mystical emphasis, identifying spiritual symbols ANAGOGY
- critical analysis or explanation of a text, especially of the bible EXEGESIS
- disclosure of God's will or some religious truth, as through the bible REVELATION
- excessive reliance on the Bible as a guide, or excessively literal interpretation of it BIBLIOLATRY
- fourteen books of the Bible that are sometimes printed as an appendix to the Old Testament but which are excluded from the canon by Protestants APOCRYPHA
- God's promises to man, as revealed in the Bible COVENANT
- literal belief in the Bible as a divinely inspired and accurate historical account FUNDAMENTALISM
- officially recognized books of the Bible CANON
- referring to the first three biblical gospels SYNOPTIC
- study or methods of biblical interpretation HERMENEUTICS

- biblical founder or father of the human race or the Hebrew people PATRIARCH

bicycle See illustration, page 58
- bicycle for a small child, typically having two tiny extra supporting wheels at the back TRAINING BIKE
- bicyclelike vehicle with a single wheel UNICYCLE
- bicycle of an early design, propelled by pushing the feet along the ground VELOCIPEDE
- bicycle of an early kind with solid tires BONESHAKER
- bicycle or motorcycle with high handlebars CHOPPER
- bicycle or tricycle for two or more riders seated one behind the other TANDEM
- bicycle-racing arena, typically with a banked track VELODROME
- bicycle's basket or bag, usually attached in a pair PANNIER
- airstream behind a fast-moving vehicle, such as a bicycle, car, or aircraft SLIPSTREAM
- small stabilizing wheel attached to the back wheel of a child's bicycle TRAINING WHEEL, OUTRIDER

bid, offer to supply goods or labor at a specific rate or price TENDER

big See **large, huge**

big bang - hypothetical elemental matter, probably neutrons, according to the big-bang theory of the creation of the universe YLEM

big dipper, elevated railway at an amusement park, providing a fast exciting ride ROLLER COASTER, SWITCHBACK

big-headed, self-important, boastful EGOTISTIC, VAINGLORIOUS

big-hearted, forgiving, generous, noble MAGNANIMOUS

big toe HALLUX

big wheel, giant fairground wheel FERRIS WHEEL

bigoted or intolerant toward outsiders SECTARIAN

bikini bottom, topless swimming costume for a woman MONOKINI

bile (combining form) CHOLE-

bill, typically detailing the goods or services provided INVOICE, STATEMENT, CHECK
- added clause, amendment, or qualification to a verdict, legislative bill, or the like RIDER
- legislator who presents or supports a bill or motion SPONSOR
- list items one by one, as on a bill ITEMIZE, ENUMERATE
- presentation of a bill to legislators at various stages of its passage READING
- settling of a bill or account RECKONING
- submit a bill for payment RENDER

bind See also **join**
- bind a rope with a cord WHIP
- bind or fasten tightly by means of a coupling device SHACKLE, PINION
- bind, wrap, or bandage SWATHE, SWADDLE
- binding together LIGATURE

binding - set of printed pages, typically 16 or 32, folded from a single sheet, for binding with others to form a book SIGNATURE, GATHERING

bindweed or related plant CONVOLVULUS

bingo variant, especially as played by children LOTTO

biochemical catalyst in the form of a protein produced by living cells ENZYME

biography of saints HAGIOGRAPHY
- of one's own life AUTOBIOGRAPHY, MEMOIRS
- biography that is very short POTTED BIOGRAPHY
- biographical article or essay, as in a newspaper PROFILE

biology See also **classification, geology**
- biology of heredity in plants and animals GENETICS
- biological classification TAXONOMY
- biological degeneration, as opposed to evolution DEVOLUTION
- similarity of form or structure in biology ISOMORPHISM

biotechnology, study or application of biology and engineering in work ERGONOMICS

bird See illustration and chart, pages 60 and 61, and also **feather, wing**
- bird, such as the ostrich, emu, or kiwi, that cannot fly RATITE
- bird of prey RAPTOR

Books of the Bible

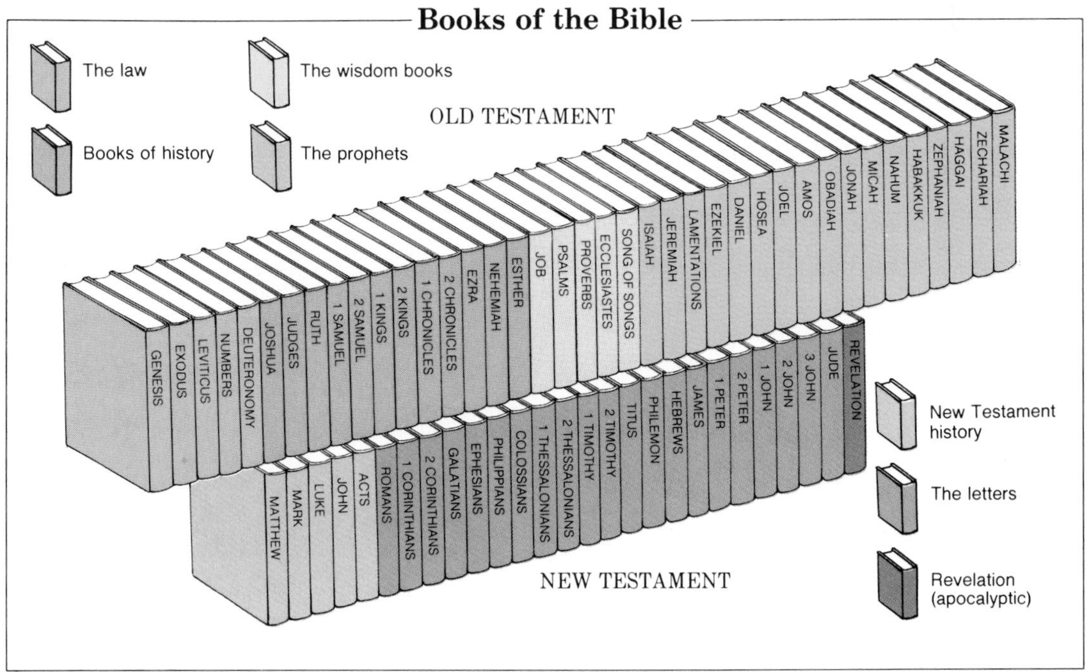

- bird of prey's claw POUNCE, TALON
- bird of prey's swooping down on its victim STOOP
- bird or other animal, live or artificial, used to lure others into shooting range or capture DECOY
- bird still too young to leave the nest NESTLING
- bird that has just grown the feathers necessary for flying FLEDGLING
- bird's feathers PLUMAGE
- bird's stomach area, often containing grit, for breaking down food GIZZARD, VENTRICULUS
- bird's vocal organ in the lower part of the windpipe SYRINX
- bird's wing, specifically the rear section holding the flight feathers PINION
- active at twilight or before dawn, as some birds or other creatures are CREPUSCULAR
- adapted for running, as some birds or bones are CURSORIAL
- adjective relating to birds AVIAN, ORNITHIC
- band or distinctive patch of color on the throat of a bird or other animal GORGET
- born blind and helpless, therefore requiring lengthy care in the nest, as some species of birds are NIDICOLOUS
- born fairly well-developed, and therefore able to leave the nest early, as some birds are NIDIFUGOUS
- clean the feathers with the beak, as a bird might PREEN
- dip lightly into the water, as a bird might DAP
- dry internal shell of a squidlike shellfish, used in polishes and as a mineral supplement for a cage bird's diet CUTTLEBONE
- enclosure, such as a large cage, for live birds AVIARY
- excrete, as birds do MUTE
- feed and care for a baby bird until it is ready to leave the nest FLEDGE
- fertilizer from coastal deposits of the dried dung of sea birds GUANO
- fledgling bird, especially a young pigeon SQUAB
- fold of skin hanging from the throat, as of some birds and lizards WATTLE
- huge and powerful bird of prey in Arabian legend ROC
- mass of undigested food, including bones, fur, and feathers, ejected by an owl or other bird of prey CAST, PELLET
- mythical bird that would burn itself every 500 years and rise rejuvenated from the ashes PHOENIX
- nonmigratory, resident in one area only, as some birds are SEDENTARY
- opening for the digestive and genital tracts in birds, fish, and reptiles CLOACA
- pouch in a bird's gullet for storing or predigesting food CROP, CRAW
- referring to a young bird still without flight feathers or not yet developed enough to fly CALLOW, UNFLEDGED
- referring to the largest order of birds, the perching songbirds PASSERINE
- referring to young birds that are naked and dependent when newly hatched ALTRICIAL
- scientific study of birds ORNITHOLOGY
- sticky substance spread on twigs or branches to trap birds LIME, BIRDLIME

bird (combining form) ORNITHO-

bird-of-paradise flower STRELITZIA

birdwatcher whose main interest is in sighting as many rare species as possible TWITCHER
- birdwatcher's tent or hiding place HIDE, BLIND

birth See also **childbirth**
- birth, as of an idea or project GENESIS
- birth, or the circumstances of one's birth NATIVITY

Bicycle

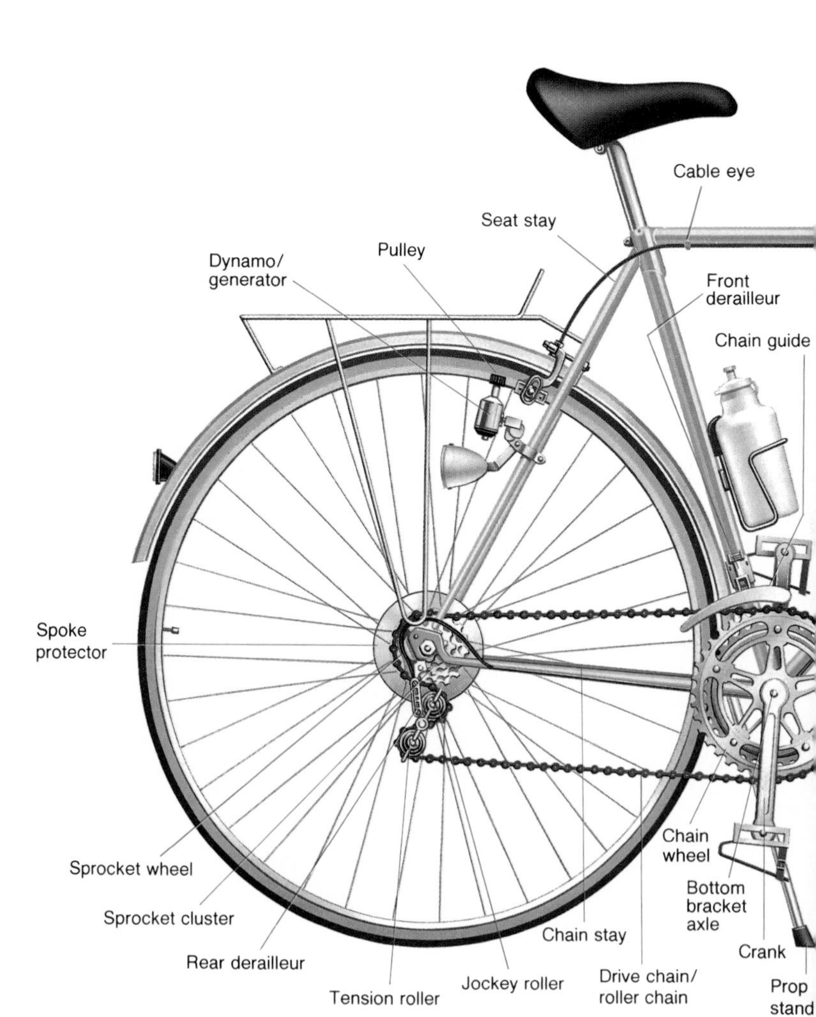

- birth or delivery of a baby feet or buttocks first BREECH BIRTH, BREECH DELIVERY
- birth or delivery of a baby requiring the use of medical tongs FORCEPS DELIVERY
- give birth, bear young, as sheep and goats do YEAN
- give birth to SPAWN, DROP
- give premature birth to a calf SLINK, SLIP
- giving birth by means of eggs that hatch outside the body OVIPAROUS
- giving birth by means of eggs that hatch within the female's body, as with some fish and reptiles OVOVIVIPAROUS
- giving birth to live offspring rather than laying eggs VIVIPAROUS
- membranes and placenta expelled from the mother's uterus after the birth of a baby AFTERBIRTH, SECUNDINES, LOCHIA
- period of confinement of a woman at the time of giving birth LYING-IN, ACCOUCHEMENT
- piece of the amniotic sac sometimes covering a baby's head at birth CAUL
- present from birth, as a character trait might be INNATE
- referring to a condition or abnormality existing from birth but not hereditary CONGENITAL
- relating or belonging to the place of one's birth NATIVE
- relating to a baby during the first month after birth NEONATAL
- relating to birth NATAL
- relating to the time before birth or during pregnancy PRENATAL, ANTENATAL
- relating to the time just after birth or after giving birth POSTNATAL, POSTPARTUM
- relating to the time just before or after birth PERINATAL

birth (combining form) -GEN, -GENESIS, -GENOUS, -PAROUS

birthmark, mole, or other congenital skin blemish or growth NEVUS
- birthmark, scar, spot, or rash on the skin STIGMA

biscuit See **cake**

bisexual, having both male and female sex organs or characteristics HERMAPHRODITE, ANDROGYNOUS

bishop, abbot, or clergymen of similar standing PRELATE
- bishop assisting or subordinate to another bishop SUFFRAGAN
- bishop of an Eastern Orthodox church EPARCH
- bishop of high rank METROPOLITAN
- bishop of senior rank in the early Christian Church, or the Roman Catholic Church or various Orthodox churches today PATRIARCH
- bishop of the highest rank in a region PRIMATE
- bishop or judge having direct judicial authority ORDINARY
- bishop's area of authority DIOCESE, SEE
- bishop's backless chair, as used when he is not on the throne FALDSTOOL
- bishop's chief administrative officer, dealing with legal secular matters in the diocese CHANCELLOR
- bishop's hat, symbolic of his office or authority MITER
- bishop's household helper or servant FAMILIAR
- bishop's junior or assistant bishop COADJUTOR
- bishop's letter to his diocese PASTORAL
- bishop's official chair or throne, or his office or diocese CATHEDRA
- bishop's official representative COMMISSARY
- bishop's permission for a clergyman to leave the diocese to work elsewhere EXEAT
- bishop's position, status, or term of office EPISCOPATE, EPISCOPACY
- bishop's staff, having a crook or cross at the top, carried as a symbol of office CROSIER

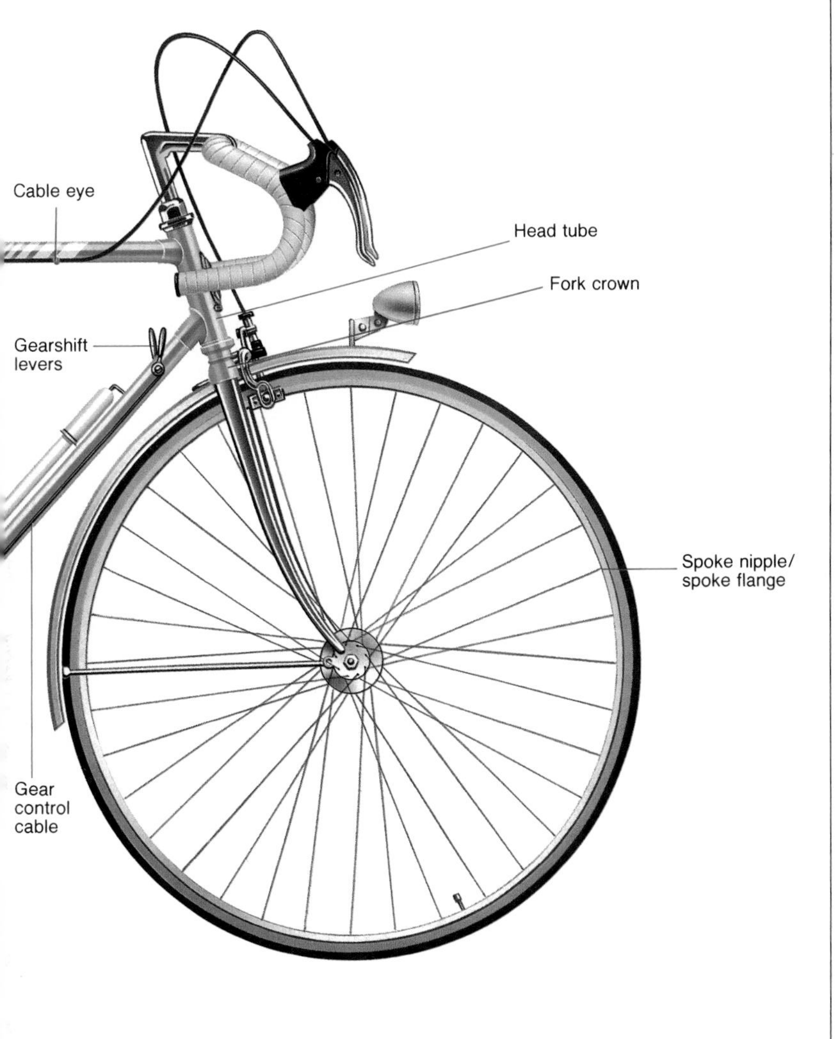

- bishop's throne in an apse TRIBUNE
- adjective for a bishop EPISCOPAL
- appoint someone as bishop or abbot MITER
- ordain a bishop CONSECRATE
- transfer a bishop to another diocese TRANSLATE

bit See illustration at **harness**
- bit, limited amount MODICUM
- bit, part, or portion SNIPPET, MOIETY
- bit, small or very modest amount DRIBLET, PITTANCE
- small bit or strand, such as a splinter or paring SLIVER
- tiny bit, barest trace, merest hint SEMBLANCE, SOUPÇON, TINCTURE, VESTIGE
- tiny bit, extremely small amount IOTA, SCINTILLA, SMIDGEN

bite - performer in a carnival or sideshow who bites off the head of a live frog, mouse, chicken, snake, or the like GEEK

biting or cutting, as wit can be CAUSTIC, MORDANT, PUNGENT, INCISIVE, ACERBIC

bits, fragments, splinters SMITHEREENS

bitter juice of grapes, apples, or the like, formerly used in cookery VERJUICE
- bitter orange, as used for making marmalade SEVILLE ORANGE
- bitter, tart, sour-tasting ACERBIC, ACETOUS, ACIDULOUS
- bitter or harsh to the taste or smell ACRID, ASTRINGENT
- bitter or sharp in attitude, speech, or manner, caustic ACRIMONIOUS, RANCOROUS
- bitterly critical or condemnatory SCATHING, CAUSTIC, VITRIOLIC, VITUPERATIVE, VIRULENT
- cynical or pessimistic in a bitter or sarcastic way SARDONIC, JAUNDICED
- hurtful and bitter mutual accusations RECRIMINATIONS
- resentful, piqued, embittered AGGRIEVED

bitterness or some distressing cause of it WORMWOOD
- cause irritation or bitterness over a lengthy period of time FESTER, RANKLE

bitters, bitter tonic mixture used to flavor drinks ANGOSTURA BITTERS

black See also **color**
- black American considered servile to whites UNCLE TOM
- black and white in blotches, as a horse might be PIEBALD, PINTO
- black cultural pride or racial self-esteem NEGRITUDE
- black formal evening jacket for men TUXEDO, DINNER JACKET
- black nationalist cult member, venerating the former Ethiopian emperor Haile Selassie RASTAFARIAN, RASTA
- black or colored township in South Africa LOCATION
- black or white, of neutral color ACHROMATIC, MONOCHROME
- blackish and glossy, pitchlike PICEOUS

black (combining form) MELAN-, MELANO-

black-and-white, as a photograph or television set might be MONOCHROME
- black-and-white portrait in the form of a shadow image or filled-in outline SILHOUETTE

black box, or electronic recorder of an aircraft's technical details, typically used to establish the cause of a crash FLIGHT RECORDER

black-currant syrup, cordial, or liqueur CASSIS

black hole, hyperdense region in space COLLAPSAR
- black hole's boundary EVENT HORIZON

black ice, thin coating of ice, as on a road GLAZE ICE

black magic based on worship of the dead NECROLATRY
- black magic or supernatural arts THE OCCULT, DIABOLISM
- man practicing sorcery or black magic, male witch WARLOCK

Black Sea - relating to the Black Sea PONTIC

blackberry, dog rose, or similar prickly shrub or plant BRAMBLE

blackbird MERLE

blackhead COMEDO

blacksmith's furnace FORGE
- blacksmith's hammer FULLER

bladder, especially the urinary bladder VESICA
- bladder-shaped AMPULLACEOUS

Bird

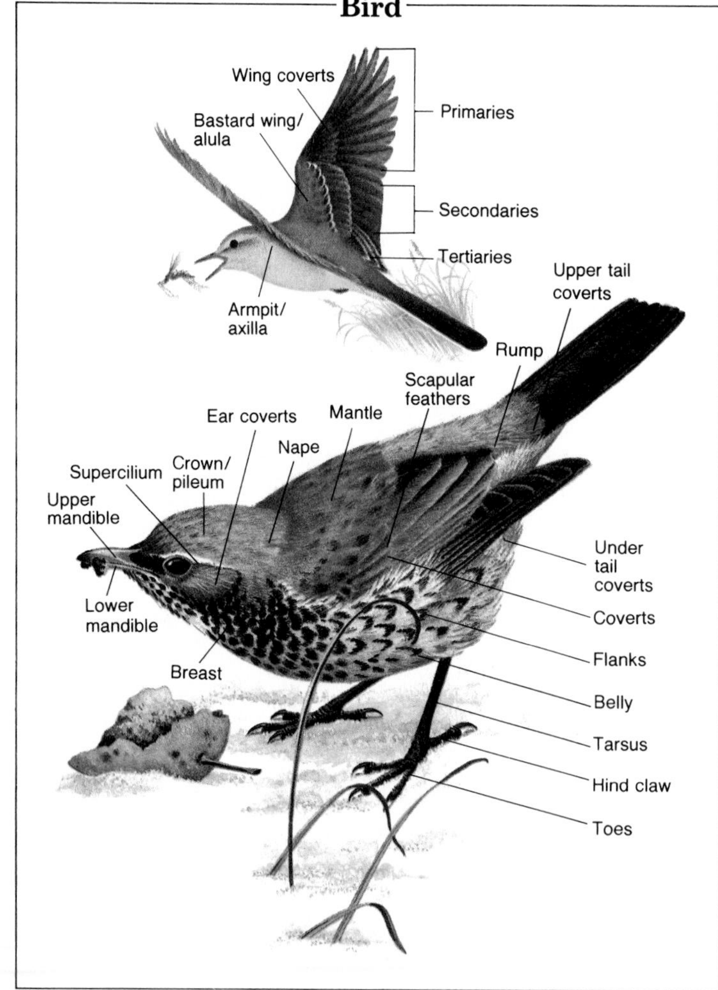

BIRD GROUPS

birds in general	**flock, flight, volley, congregation, bevy, pod, volary, dissimulation; plump (of wild fowl); brood (of chicks)**
bitterns, cranes, herons	**sedge, siege**
choughs	**chattering, clattering**
coots	**covert, raft**
crows	**murder, hover**
doves	**flight, dole, dule, prettying, pitying**
ducks	**flush, team, plump (in flight); dopping (diving); baddling (on water)**
eagles	**convocation**
falcons	**cast**
finches	**trimming, trembling**
geese	**gaggle, nide, flock; skein (in flight)**
goldfinches, humming-birds	**charm, drum, chattering, troubling**
grouse	**covey**
gulls	**colony**
hawks	**cast, leash**
jays	**band, party**
lapwings	**desert, deceit**
larks	**exaltation, bevy**
magpies	**tittering, tiding**
mallards	**sord, puddling (on water); flush, sute (on land)**
nightingales	**match, watch**
owls	**stare, parliament**
partridges	**covey**
peafowl	**muster, pride, ostentation**
penguins	**rookery, colony**
pheasants	**nye, bouquet**
pigeons	**flight, flock**
plovers	**congregation, wing, leash**
quails	**bevy, covey**
ravens	**unkindness**
rooks	**parliament, building, clamor**
snipe	**walk, wisp, whisper**
sparrows	**host, quarrel, tribe**
starlings	**murmuration**
swans	**herd, bevy, bank, wedge, game, squadron, whiteness**
teal	**spring, raft, coil, knob**
thrushes	**mutation**
turkeys	**flock, dole, dule, raft, raffle, rafter**
wigeon	**company, bunch, knob, coil**
woodcock	**fall, covey, plump**

- bladder stone or gallstone CYSTOLITH
- surgical removal of the gallbladder or part of the urinary bladder CYSTECTOMY

bladder (combining form) CYST-, CYSTO-

blade of a knife, or similar sharp part of a tool BIT
- blade of a leaf or petal LAMINA
- blade of a skate or sledge RUNNER
- blade of a turbine, propeller, windmill, or the like VANE
- blade of an oar or paddle PALM
- blade on the hull of a boat that raises it when speeding HYDROFOIL
- implement having a wide-tipped and flexible blade SPATULA

blame See also **criticize, scold**
- blame for or prove involvement in a crime INCRIMINATE, INCULPATE
- blame oneself or others REPROACH
- consider or pronounce free of blame or guilt, or from responsibility ABSOLVE, EXONERATE, EXCULPATE, VINDICATE
- person or group made to bear the blame for faults or distress of others SCAPEGOAT, WHIPPING BOY

blameless, beyond reproach or doubt UNIMPEACHABLE

blameworthy, deserving of criticism REPREHENSIBLE, DEPLORABLE, DISCREDITABLE, HEINOUS
- blameworthy, and punishable for wrongdoing CULPABLE
- represent or try to represent a crime, fault, or the like as less serious or blameworthy, as by making certain excuses EXTENUATE

blank cut or punched from a sheet of metal BURR
- blank metal disc made ready for stamping into a coin FLAN

blanket - blanketlike coat with a hole or slit in the middle for the head PONCHO
- woven with a loose, open texture, as a blanket might be CELLULAR

blasphemy - misuse, desecration, or blasphemously disrespectful treatment of something sacred or regarded as sacred SACRILEGE, PROFANATION

bleach - oxygen in the form of O_3, used in bleaching OZONE
- watery chemical solution used as a disinfectant and bleaching agent JAVELLE WATER

bleeding See also **blood**
- bleeding, as from a wound HEMORRHAGE
- hereditary disorder characterized by excessive or unstoppable bleeding HEMOPHILIA
- point on the body where an artery can be pressed shut to stop the bleeding of a wound further on PRESSURE POINT
- stopping or slowing down bleeding ASTRINGENT, STYPTIC, HEMOSTATIC

blend See also **mix**
- blend, word formed by fusing elements from two separate words PORTMANTEAU, PORTMANTEAU WORD

- blend or combine MELD
- blend or dilute whiskey or other alcoholic spirits RECTIFY

bless, make sacred or morally binding SANCTIFY, CONSECRATE, HALLOW

bless you - equivalent of "bless you!", of German origin, said to someone who has sneezed GESUNDHEIT

blessedness or a state of serene, joyful happiness BEATITUDE, NIRVANA

blessing, act of blessing, blessedness, or invocation of God's blessing BENEDICTION, BENISON
- blessing, benefit BOON
- blessing or grace, as before meals BENEDICITE

blind - reading or printing system for the blind BRAILLE

blind spot of the eye OPTIC DISC
- blindly committed to a theory, dogmatic DOCTRINAIRE
- very shortsighted or nearly blind PURBLIND

blinds or shutter with horizontal adjustable slats JALOUSIE
- blinds that can be raised and lowered, and whose slats can be angled VENETIAN BLIND

blink or wink, especially involuntarily and repeatedly PALPEBRATE
- blink or wink NICTITATE

bliss - relating to the state of marriage, marital, as bliss might be CONNUBIAL

blissful or delightful ELYSIAN
- blissful state of peace and freedom from care NIRVANA

blister BLEB, BULLA, VESICLE
- blister, boil, or inflammation in the body filled with pus ABSCESS, PUSTULE
- blistering agent, such as mustard gas VESICANT
- blisterlike sac or cavity in the body, normal or abnormal CYST
- clear watery fluid exuded by tissue, as in a blister SERUM

block See also **prevent, obstruct**
- block or ward off a blow, fencing thrust, or the like PARRY
- block or wedge placed under a wheel, log, or the like, to immobilize it on a slope SCOTCH
- blocked, overfull, clogged, as with blood or mucus CONGESTED
- blocking or deliberate exclusion of thoughts, desires, or the like from one's mind REPRESSION, SUPPRESSION

block of apartments or rented rooms, often in a slum area TENEMENT

blond and blue-eyed, and typically tall and long-headed in appearance, characteristic of northern Europeans NORDIC
- blond-haired TOWHEADED
- pale silvery-blond hair color PLATINUM BLOND

blood See chart, and also **heart, vein, artery, disease, bleeding**
- blood and tissue discharged normally after childbirth LOCHIA, AFTERBIRTH, SECUNDINES
- blood clot, air bubble, or the like drifting in the bloodstream before becoming lodged in a blood vessel EMBOLUS
- blood clot formed in a fixed position in a blood vessel or the heart THROMBUS
- blood from a wound, especially clotted blood GORE
- bloodletting by opening a vein PHLEBOTOMY, VENESECTION
- blood of the gods in mythology ICHOR
- blood poisoning PYEMIA, SEPTICEMIA, TOXEMIA
- blood purifying organ below the stomach SPLEEN
- blood relationship, or any close association CONSANGUINITY
- blood-sugar excess, as in diabetes HYPERGLYCEMIA
- blood-sugar shortage, as in diabetes HYPOGLYCEMIA
- bloodred INCARNADINE
- bloodthirsty, bloodstained, or bloody, characterized by blood or bloodshed SANGUINARY
- accumulation of blood in a body part, caused by poor circulation HYPOSTASIS
- adjective for blood HEMAL, HEMATIC, HEMIC
- artificial purifying of the blood, typically with a filtering machine, in cases of kidney failure HEMODIALYSIS, RENAL DIALYSIS
- bandage or similar device wound tight to stanch heavy bleeding TOURNIQUET
- be soaked in or covered with blood WELTER
- become a soft, solidified mass, clot or curdle, as blood, milk, or other liquids might COAGULATE

BLOOD CONSTITUENTS AND CHEMICALS

albumin/ albumen	protein found in blood serum and in milk, egg white, and the like
complement/ alexin	substance in blood serum combining with antibodies to destroy bacteria, foreign cells, and the like
corpuscle	free-moving blood cell
erythrocyte	red corpuscle, in which oxygen is transported to the body's tissues
gamma globulin	protein, often an antibody, helping immunity
hemoglobin	red iron-containing protein in the red corpuscles that transports oxygen to the body's tissues
insulin	protein hormone from the pancreas, controlling the level of sugar in the blood
leucocyte	any white corpuscle, with various defense and repair functions according to type
lymphocyte	common white corpuscle, with defense functions such as producing antibodies
phagocyte	cell, such as a white corpuscle, that envelops and digests bacteria, tissue debris, and the like
plasma	yellowish liquid base containing the cells and platelets
platelet/ thrombocyte	tiny disc helping blood clotting
Rh factor/ rhesus factor	substance on the surface of red blood cells that reacts adversely to cells lacking it
serum	purified plasma, from which clotting agents have been removed
transferrin	blood protein transferring iron in the body

- check or stop the flow of blood from a wound STANCH, STAUNCH
- fatty deposit on an artery wall, restricting the flow of blood ATHEROMA
- filled to excess with blood or other fluid ENGORGED
- former medical technique of attaching a glass cup to the skin by a partial vacuum, in order to draw blood to the surface CUPPING
- medical and scientific study of blood HEMATOLOGY
- oxygenate blood VENTILATE
- patient receiving blood, tissue, a transplanted organ, or the like from a donor RECIPIENT
- person who gives blood for transfusion DONOR
- presence of nitrogen bubbles in the blood, or the resulting illness, caused by an abrupt reduction in atmospheric pressure, as among sea divers AEROEMBOLISM, THE BENDS, DECOMPRESSION SICKNESS, CAISSON DISEASE
- referring to blood in the arteries ARTERIAL
- referring to blood in the veins VENOUS
- salt solution of similar concentration to that in the blood, as used in a medical drip SALINE
- soapy substance found in tissue, blood, and bile CHOLESTEROL
- stopping or slowing down the flow of blood ASTRINGENT, STYPTIC, HEMOSTATIC
- tissue death, or dead tissue, as caused by a blood clot INFARCTION
- transfer by injection of blood, plasma, or the like into the bloodstream TRANSFUSION
- unable to combine safely, as two types of blood in a transfusion might be INCOMPATIBLE

blood (combining form) EM-, HEM-, HEMO-, HEMATO-

blood clot (combining form) THROMB-, THROMBO-

blood feud, maintained by a cycle of revenge VENDETTA

blood pressure that is abnormally high HYPERTENSION
- blood pressure that is abnormally low HYPOTENSION
- instrument for measuring blood pressure, especially in the arteries SPHYGMOMANOMETER
- rotating cylinder on which a pen records changes in blood pressure, heartbeat, or the like KYMOGRAPH
- technique for regulating one's own heartbeat, blood pressure, or other apparently involuntary bodily functions BIOFEEDBACK

blood vessel of a very fine, thin-walled kind CAPILLARY
- blood vessel's outermost layer or covering ADVENTITIA
- air bubble, clot, or other foreign body blocking a blood vessel, EMBOLUS
- blocking of a blood vessel by a clot or air bubble EMBOLISM
- directed or conducting down or away from a center, as some nerves and blood vessels are DEFERENT, EFFERENT
- network of nerves and blood vessels PLEXUS
- sac, bulge, or pouch in the weakened wall of a blood vessel ANEURYSM

blood vessel (combining form) ANGIO-, VAS-, VASO-

bloodhound's fleshy drooping upper lip FLEWS

bloodshed and killing on a large scale, slaughter or massacre, especially in war CARNAGE
- place or scene of bloodshed, or great destruction SHAMBLES

blooming process or period in plants ANTHESIS
- blooming twice or more during a season REMONTANT

blossom, bud, sprout, begin to grow BURGEON
- blossoming, blooming, or the time of bursting into flower EFFLORESCENCE, FLORESCENCE

blouse See also chart at **clothes**
- frills down the front of a blouse or shirt JABOT, RUFFLE

blow - ward off a blow, fencing thrust, or the like PARRY

blowhole of a whale or related marine mammal SPIRACLE

blowing or whispering sound heard through a stethoscope, typically resulting from the flowing of the blood SOUFFLE

blown, dispersed as by wind, fanned WINNOWED

blue See **color**

blue dye, used by ancient Britons to color their skin WOAD

bluish, as bruised skin might be LIVID

blunder See also **mistake**
- blunder made in one's speech, slip of the tongue LAPSUS LINGUAE
- blunder or laughable mistake HOWLER, BONER
- blunder or social mistake, such as a gauche or tactless remark GAFFE, FAUX PAS

blunt See also **frank, rude**
- blunt or rounded at the tip, as a leaf or angle might be OBTUSE

blur, darken, make indistinct or dim OBFUSCATE
- blurred printed impressions, as caused by the paper's moving MACKLE

blushing or reddening of the skin ERUBESCENCE

board, typically heart-shaped and mounted on casters, that allegedly writes or spells out messages in spiritualism sessions PLANCHETTE
- board displaying the alphabet, used in spiritualism sessions to register messages OUIJA BOARD
- board forming the top rail of a fence or balustrade LEDGER BOARD
- board in an overlapping series, used especially to cover roofs or walls WEATHERBOARD, CLAPBOARD
- board made of thin sheets of wood glued together PLYWOOD
- board or boards laid to form a path over wet or muddy ground DUCKBOARD
- board or signboard above the door or window of a shop FASCIA
- either of two boards, typically for advertising, suspended from a person's shoulders SANDWICH BOARD

board and lodging, as in a small French hotel, or the hotel itself PENSION

boast, congratulate or plume oneself, take pride in oneself PREEN
- boast or brag about, describe in a boastful way, extol VAUNT, EMBLAZON
- boaster, braggart, swaggerer GASCON, ROISTERER, BLUSTERER
- boastful, bragging, swanking or strutting THRASONICAL
- boastful, conceited, self-important person COCKALORUM
- boastful, self-important EGOTISTIC, VAINGLORIOUS, VAPORING
- boastfulness, idle bluster, bravado BRAGGADOCIO, FANFARONADE, GASCONADE, RODOMONTADE
- boasting, boastful speech RODOMONTADE

boat See chart, page 64, and also **ship, sail**
- boat club's chairman COMMODORE
- boat race or series of races for boats REGATTA
- boat's float, attached parallel on each side for stabilization OUTRIGGER
- car tire or similar bumper on the side of a boat for protection against collision FENDER
- deep, wide, and safe enough for ships or boats to sail on or through NAVIGABLE
- dragging or carrying of boats overland from one waterway to another PORTAGE
- line or edge at which the bottom and side of a boat meet CHINE
- make a boat watertight by pack-

ing the seams, as with tar CAULK
- peg or pin, especially one used as a rowlock in the side of a boat THOLE
- person who steers a boat or directs those rowing it, as in a race COXSWAIN, COX
- plate or place on the stern of a ship or boat bearing the vessel's name ESCUTCHEON
- responsive, easily maneuverable, as a boat might be YARE
- seat extending across a rowing boat, typically for the oarsman THWART
- spaces at the front and back of a rowing boat SHEETS
- swiveling support for an oar on the side of a boat ROWLOCK
- upper edge of the side of a ship or boat GUNWALE, GUNNEL

body See also **corpse, digestion, reproduction,** and entries at various specific parts of the body
- body cavity, hollow, or channel, containing or conveying air, pus, blood, or the like SINUS
- body cavity, recess, sac, follicle, or the like CRYPT
- body cavity, tube, or pouch blocked at one end, such as the cecum CUL-DE-SAC
- body channel of very small size, as in a bone CANALICULUS
- body channel or vessel DUCT, VAS
- body fluid in ancient and medieval medicine HUMOR
- body movements performed very slowly and deliberately in a series as part of a Chinese form of exercise and mental training T'AI CHI
- body of a dead animal or bird CARCASS
- body of a dead person, corpse CADAVER
- body organs, especially those essential for maintaining life VITALS
- body part or organ, now degenerated or nonfunctioning, surviving as a remnant from an earlier stage of development or generation VESTIGE
- body processes and functions maintaining life METABOLISM
- body sense, awareness of one's body and its movements KINESTHESIA
- body's makeup as an indication of health and strength CONSTITUTION
- body's structure or appearance, based on shape, size, and muscular development PHYSIQUE
- abnormal rift or gap in a body part or organ DIASTEMA
- adjective for the body CORPORAL, SOMATIC
- affecting the entire body, as a disease or poison might SYSTEMIC
- bodily defect or crippled condition, such as a hunchback DEFORMITY, DISFIGUREMENT
- building or room in which the bodies or bones of the dead were stored in former times CHARNEL HOUSE
- corresponding in evolutionary origin but not in function, as body parts such as wings and arms are HOMOLOGOUS
- corresponding in function but not in evolutionary origin, as body parts such as gills and lungs are ANALOGOUS
- entertainer or acrobat who twists his limbs and body into abnormal positions CONTORTIONIST
- having bodily or human form INCARNATE
- having or referring to a heavy fat body or build, typically accompanied by an easygoing personality ENDOMORPHIC, PYKNIC
- having or referring to a strong and muscular body or build MESOMORPHIC
- having or referring to a thin weak body or build, typically accompanied by a nervous personality ECTOMORPHIC, LEPTOSOMIC
- lacking a body or lacking in reality INCORPOREAL, DISEMBODIED
- picture of the body, or a section of the body, without the skin, to illustrate the muscle structure ÉCORCHÉ
- rebirth in another body or form REINCARNATION
- relating to sexual and other desires and appetites of the body SENSUAL, CARNAL
- relating to the front or lower surface of the body, an aircraft, or the like VENTRAL
- representative in bodily human form of an ideal or model EMBODIMENT, INCARNATION, AVATAR
- rhythm of bodily processes or functions that have a regular 24-hour cycle CIRCADIAN RHYTHM
- section of the body between hip and neck, trunk TORSO
- side of the body or the thigh FLANK
- wasting away of the body caused by lengthy disease TABES

body (combining form) SOMAT-, SOMATO-, -SOME, -OME

body cavity (combining form) CEL-, COEL-, CELO-, COELO-

body language - study of body language, such as gesture and facial expression, as a form of communication KINESICS

bodybuilding or exercise through contracting the muscles without changing their length or moving the limbs ISOMETRIC EXERCISE, ISOMETRICS
- artificial hormone or drug, based on a ring of carbon atoms and increasing muscle and bone growth, sometimes used in bodybuilding ANABOLIC STEROID

bodyguard for the sovereign, drawn from retired army officers GENTLEMAN-AT-ARMS

bog, marsh, swamp, or mire SLOUGH, QUAGMIRE, MORASS

boil, evaporate, and condense a liquid repeatedly, as when extracting substances REFLUX
- boil down and concentrate a liquid, or extract an essence from a liquid by boiling DECOCT
- boil food briefly, as to remove bitter flavor or prepare for freezing BLANCH
- boil partially PARBOIL
- pierce or cut, make an incision, as into a boil LANCE
- pus-filled channel, as from a boil SINUS
- steep herbs, tea, or the like without boiling INFUSE
- technical name for a boil FU-

BOATS

POWERED BY OAR, PEDAL, OR PADDLE:

bumboat
caïque
coble
coracle/ currach
dinghy
felucca
gig
gondola
kayak
pedalo
pinnace
piragua/ pirogue
punt
randan
sampan
scull
shallop
shell
skiff
umiak
wherry

POWERED BY SAIL:

caïque
catamaran
coble
cutter
dhow
dinghy
felucca
gig
hoy
junk
lugger
nuggar
pink
pinnace
proa
sampan
shallop
skiff
sloop
smack
trimaran
wherry

POWERED BY MOTOR:

dory
drifter
gig
hydrofoil/ hydroplane
skiff
tender
trawler
vaporetto
vedette

RUNCLE

boiler - insulation material around a boiler LAGGING
- muddy deposit, as on a river bed or the inside of a boiler SLUDGE

bold See **brave, cheeky**

Bolsheviks' liberal opponents before and after the Russian Revolution MENSHEVIKS

bolt, revolving axle, or the like, as in a lock or between two door handles SPINDLE
- bolt tightened by a peglike crosspiece that serves as its nut TOGGLE BOLT
- edge plate of a lock into which the bolt slots SELVAGE

bomb See also **missile**
- bomb fragments produced by an explosion SHRAPNEL
- bomb or machine-gun enemy ground troops from low-flying aircraft STRAFE
- bombing, blows, gunfire, or the like of a heavy and sustained kind BARRAGE
- bomblike explosive device in a metal pipe, as for blasting a path through barbed wire BANGALORE TORPEDO
- aerial bomb scattering shrapnel widely CLUSTER BOMB, FRAGMENTATION BOMB
- atomic bomb produced by the splitting of atomic nuclei FISSION BOMB
- explode, as a bomb might, or cause to explode DETONATE
- extremely heavy concentration of bombing or other military force on an enemy target SATURATION
- firebomb, bomb designed to start a destructive fire INCENDIARY BOMB
- firebomb or inflammable substance used in ancient sea warfare GREEK FIRE
- firebomb that contains highly inflammable jellied petroleum NAPALM BOMB
- gasoline bomb or similar crude firebomb thrown by hand, typically a fuel-filled bottle stoppered with a rag wick MOLOTOV COCKTAIL
- guiding or stabilizing fin on a bomb or missile VANE
- hydrogen bomb or similar extremely powerful bomb produced by the fusion of light atomic nuclei FUSION BOMB, THERMONUCLEAR BOMB
- make a bomb inactive and harmless DEACTIVATE, DEFUSE
- nuclear bomb designed to kill people without destroying buildings, by releasing short-lived radiation NEUTRON BOMB, ENHANCED RADIATION BOMB
- section of a bomb, missile, or the like containing the actual explosive or toxic material WARHEAD
- simultaneous or rapid discharge or release of several bombs or missiles SALVO
- small bell-shaped bomb used in former times, as for breaching a castle wall PETARD

bombard or shell heavily CRUMP
- bombardment, as by artillery fire CANNONADE, STONK

bond, tie, connection or link VINCULUM, LIGATURE
- bond, typically long-term and unsecured, issued by a company or government organization DEBENTURE, DEBENTURE BOND

bone See illustration, page 66, and also **fracture**
- bone formation OSSIFICATION, OSTEOGENESIS
- bone of very small size, especially any of those in the inner ear OSSICLE
- bone or tooth decay CARIES
- bone surgery or bone grafting OSTEOPLASTY
- break a bone into many pieces COMMINUTE
- breaking of a bone in surgery in order to reset it or correct a deformity OSTEOCLASIS
- brittleness or weakening of the bones, especially in elderly people OSTEOPOROSIS
- building or room in which the bodies or bones of the dead were stored in former times CHARNEL HOUSE
- carved or engraved articles of ivory, whalebone, or the like, typically made by sailors SCRIMSHAW
- container of the bones of a corpse, such as an urn or vault OSSUARY
- containing or consisting of bone OSSEOUS
- creak, rattle, or crackle, as diseased lungs or broken bones might CREPITATE
- creaking or grating sound of the rubbing of the two ends of a broken bone CREPITUS
- cutting or removal of part of a bone in surgery OSTEOTOMY
- displace a limb or organ, or put a bone out of joint DISLOCATE
- end of a long bone, fused to the shaft only late in the growth process EPIPHYSIS
- expert in ancient forms of life, as through the study of old bones and fossils PALEONTOLOGIST
- having an enlarged headlike end, as some bones have CAPITATE
- headlike part, such as the end of a long bone or insect's antenna CAPITULUM
- hole or passageway in a bone through which nerves or blood vessels pass FORAMEN
- hollow or cavity in a bone, such as a sinus in the upper jawbone ANTRUM
- hollow or dimplelike pit in a bone or other body part FOSSA, FOVEA
- joining of broken bones, the edges of a wound, or the like COAPTATION
- knob on the end of a bone, as that fitting into a socket in a ball-and-socket joint CONDYLE
- medical specialist in bone diseases and disorders OSTEOLOGIST
- netlike, spongy, or porous in structure, as some bones are CANCELLATE
- relating to bone OSTEAL
- projection or bump, especially on the end of a bone for attaching a muscle or tendon TUBEROSITY
- remove the bones from a fish or cut of meat FILLET
- shaft of a long bone DIAPHYSIS
- surgeon specializing in bone and joint disorders ORTHOPEDIC SURGEON
- surgical instrument for scraping bones XYSTER
- technical term for a bone OS
- therapist skilled in manipulating bones, especially those of the spine OSTEOPATH
- thin ring or layer of bone LAMELLA, LAMINA
- tough band or strip of fibrous tissue connecting moving bones or cartilages, or supporting organs or muscles LIGAMENT
- tough tissue or gristle, as at the joints between bones CARTILAGE
- turn to bone, become hard or bony, as tissue or cartilage might OSSIFY

bone (combining form) OSTE-, OSTEO-

bone marrow (combining form) MYEL-, MYELO-

bonus, tip, or reward for services rendered GRATUITY
- bonus or added benefit from one's job, such as a company car or free telephone calls PERK, PERQUISITE, FRINGE BENEFIT
- bonus or benefit, as derived from a favor or investment DIVIDEND
- bonus or similar additional sum of money, as added to a regular price, salary, or the like PREMIUM

bony, hardened SCLEROUS

book See chart, page 68, and also **Scriptures**
- book, from surplus stock, sold off at a reduced price REMAINDER
- book, movie, or the like mixing fact and fiction FACTION
- book, movie, or the like dealing

with events earlier than those in the previous book, movie, or the like PREQUEL
- book, movie, or the like dealing with events following those in the previous book, movie, or the like SEQUEL
- book, movie, or the like that is well reviewed but fails to impress the public at large SUCCÈS D'ESTIME
- book, play, or the like written quickly and for money rather than intended as a serious work of art POTBOILER
- book, racehorse, or the like that achieves sudden success after an unpromising early phase SLEEPER
- book collection or catalog BIBLIOTHECA
- book collector or book lover BIBLIOPHILE
- book in which accounts are recorded in bookkeeping LEDGER
- book learning, knowledge of a formal, unimaginative, drily detailed kind PEDANTRY
- book or document in the author's handwriting HOLOGRAPH
- book that is weighty in size or seriousness TOME
- book's additional material, collected at the end APPENDIX
- books or magazines that are typically cheap and sensational or sentimental PULP
- book's size, shape, layout, or design FORMAT
- books still kept in print by a publisher even though published a considerable time in the past BACKLIST
- address a book or other work specifically to a person or group as a mark of respect or affection DEDICATE
- blank leaf at the front or back of a book FLYLEAF
- censor or alter a book or other text by removing objectionable or obscene passages EXPURGATE, BOWDLERIZE
- classification or shelf number of a book in a library CALL NUMBER
- company, writer, or editor producing books to be marketed by a separate publisher BOOK PRODUCER, PACKAGER
- concentrate intensely on a book PERUSE, PORE OVER
- decorative picture, vine-leaf de-

Bones

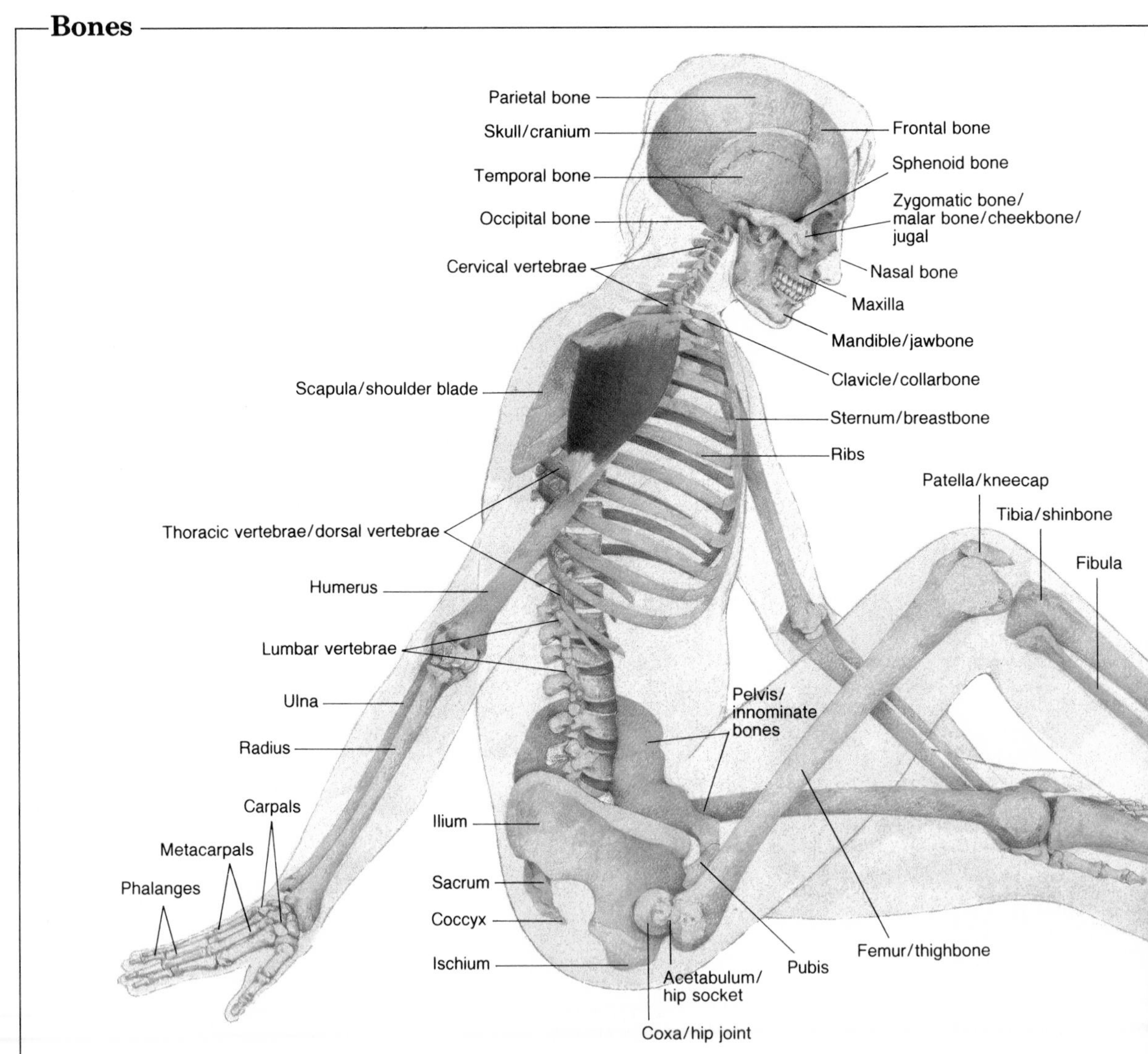

sign, or the like on a book's title page or at the beginning or end of a chapter VIGNETTE
- dedication written into a gift book INSCRIPTION
- description of the physical and technical features of a book COLLATION, SPECIFICATIONS, SPECS
- description or review for promotional purposes, as on the dust jacket of a book BLURB
- excessive interest in books BIBLIOLATRY
- extract the essentials of a book, report, or the like GUT
- hardbacked, as a book might be CASED, CASEBOUND
- hardbacked and cloth-covered, as a book might be CLOTHBOUND
- having the edges of the pages still unslit or untrimmed, as a book might UNCUT
- illustration at the front of a book, often opposite the title page FRONTISPIECE
- into the middle of things, straight into the narrative or plot, as a book or play might begin IN MEDIAS RES
- leaf rapidly through files, the pages of a book, or the like RIFFLE, SKIM
- left-hand, even-numbered page of a book VERSO
- library classification system for books and other publications DEWEY DECIMAL SYSTEM, LIBRARY OF CONGRESS CLASSIFICATION
- license for the publication of a book, as by a bishop or censor IMPRIMATUR, NIHIL OBSTAT
- list of corrections to a book, typically printed on a slip pasted at the front ERRATA, CORRIGENDA
- list of publishing details, such as dates and authorship, of editions of books BIBLIOGRAPHY
- material added to a book, article, or the like after the discovery of its omission ADDENDUM, ADDENDA
- narrow decorative line pressed into a book cover, or the wheel tool used to make it FILLET
- number assigned to a newly published book in keeping with an international book classification system ISBN
- passage copied from a book, speech, or the like, as for separate publication EXTRACT, EXCERPT
- produce the text of an anthology, dictionary, or other book by gathering the material from many sources COMPILE
- reading stand for supporting a book or notes, as in a church or lecture hall LECTERN
- referring to a book published after the writer's death POSTHUMOUS
- review or criticism of a book, movie, play, or the like CRITIQUE, COMPTE RENDU
- right-hand, odd-numbered page of a book RECTO
- scholarly comments, footnotes, variant readings, and so on in an edition of a book APPARATUS CRITICUS, CRITICAL APPARATUS
- section of a book, such as a dictionary, published separately FASCICLE, FASCICULE, FASCICULUS
- series of notches cut into the outer edge of a dictionary or other book, for easy alphabetical reference THUMB INDEX
- set of all the leaves of a book before binding QUIRE
- stained or discolored, as old books might be FOXED
- title, heading, or letter, typically illuminated in red in a manuscript or book RUBRIC
- white space between facing pages of a book, two postage stamps on a sheet, or the like GUTTER
- word used formerly to indicate the end of a book or manuscript EXPLICIT, FINIS

book (combining form) BIBLIO-

book of changes, ancient Chinese book of philosophy and forecasts I CHING

bookbinding See illustration, page 69
- bookbinding tool for applying gold leaf PALLET
- cardboard as used in bookbinding PASTEBOARD
- check and order the sections of a book before binding COLLATE
- fine parchment of calfskin, lambskin, or kidskin, as used in bookbinding VELLUM

bookcase with a double face, as in a library RANGE

bookish or scholarly people LITERATI

bookkeeping system in which all transactions are recorded as a debit in one account and a credit in another DOUBLE ENTRY
- book in which accounts are recorded in bookkeeping LEDGER

bookplates - inscription used on bookplates before the owner's name, meaning literally "from the library of" EX LIBRIS

bookseller - specializing in old and rare books, as a bookseller might be ANTIQUARIAN

boot - metal spikes fastened to a shoe or boot, as for mountaineering or walking on ice CRAMPONS
- large-headed nail protecting soles of boots HOBNAIL

booty, loot, spoils, stolen property PLUNDER, PILLAGE

border See also **boundary, trimming, edge**
- border, especially the area of floor bordering a carpet, doorway, or the like SURROUND
- border area or outskirts, furthermost parts PERIPHERY, PURLIEUS, PRECINCTS
- border or frontier areas MARCHLANDS, MARCHES
- border or border marker TERMINUS
- drapery forming a decorative border, as along the edge of a bed or shelf VALANCE
- narrow edge or border of a woven fabric to prevent unraveling SELVAGE

bordering, lying next to ADJACENT,

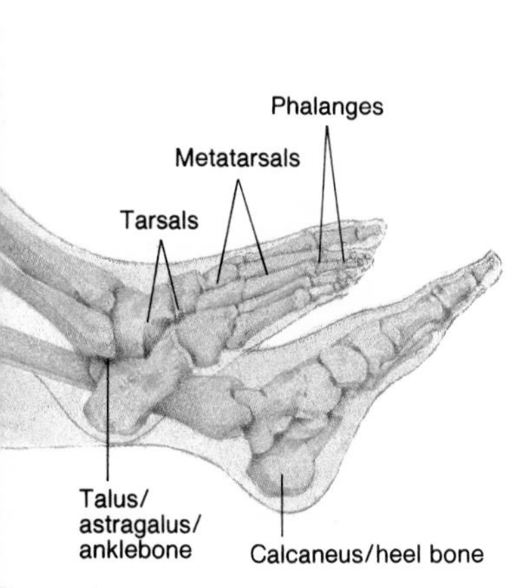

ADJOINING, CONTIGUOUS, JUXTAPOSED, ABUTTING, TANGENTIAL

bore, become tiresome PALL
- bore or drill a well, mine shaft or the like TREPAN
- boring or drilling tool AUGER, AWL

bored, uninterested or uncaring, indifferent APATHETIC
- bored or unenthusiastic because of overfamiliarity or overindulgence BLASÉ, JADED

boredom, depression, listlessness, or inactivity DOLDRUMS, ENNUI
- feeling of being tired of life, sense of desperate boredom TAEDIUM VITAE

boring See also **dull**
- boring, everyday or commonplace, as a dull routine existence is HUMDRUM
- boring, lacking all interest and spirit, colorless or lifeless, as a textbook might be ARID, DESICCATED
- boring, tiresome, or annoying, as petty rules or a long-winded speech might be IRKSOME
- boring or tiring work DRUDGERY
- boring periods of time or parts of a book, play, or movie LONGUEURS
- boring through being too long or slow, wearisome TEDIOUS
- boring through being unvaried or repetitious, dreary and drab MONOTONOUS
- boring to the point of almost putting one to sleep, deadly dull STULTIFYING, STUPEFYING

born - word meaning "born," used before the original surname when identifying a person who has changed name NÉ, NÉE
- born in wedlock, of married parents LEGITIMATE
- born out of wedlock, of unmarried parents, bastard ILLEGITIMATE,

BOOKS

almagest	medieval textbook, as on astronomy or alchemy
almanac	annual compilation of lists and charts of varied information
annals	records and reports of a learned society, field of study, or the like
anthology	collection of writings, as by a single author or on a particular theme
armorial	book listing or illustrating coats of arms
Baedeker	guidebook, specifically a 19th-century tourist guidebook
bestiary	medieval collection of animal fables
breviary	prayer book and hymnal for Roman Catholic clergymen
cambist	manual of exchange rates and conversion charts for weights and measures
catechism	instruction manual containing a series of questions and answers, especially on Christianity
chapbook	booklet or pamphlet of popular poems, ballads, religious homilies, or the like
commonplace book	personal journal containing ideas, reflections, and quoted extracts
concordance	index recording all the occurrences in context of the words in a text
festschrift	book of essays by scholars and compiled as a tribute to a learned colleague
formulary	book of prayers; book listing medical drugs, pharmaceutical formulas, and the like
herbal	textbook on plants, especially useful plants
hornbook	elementary textbook introducing a subject, primer
incunabulum	book printed before 1501
lectionary	book of scriptural lessons for reading at religious services
lexicon	dictionary, especially of an ancient language
missal	prayer book, specifically for the Roman Catholic Mass
monograph	booklet or pamphlet on some specialist subject
omnibus	book assembling any related studies, or many writings by a single author
pharmacopoeia/ dispensatory	official manual listing and describing medical drugs and preparations
primer	introductory textbook, especially a language-teaching book
psalter	book of psalms for use in religious services
thesaurus	book presenting a specialized vocabulary
vade mecum	ready-reference manual, typically carried about constantly
variorum	edition of a text with notes by several scholars

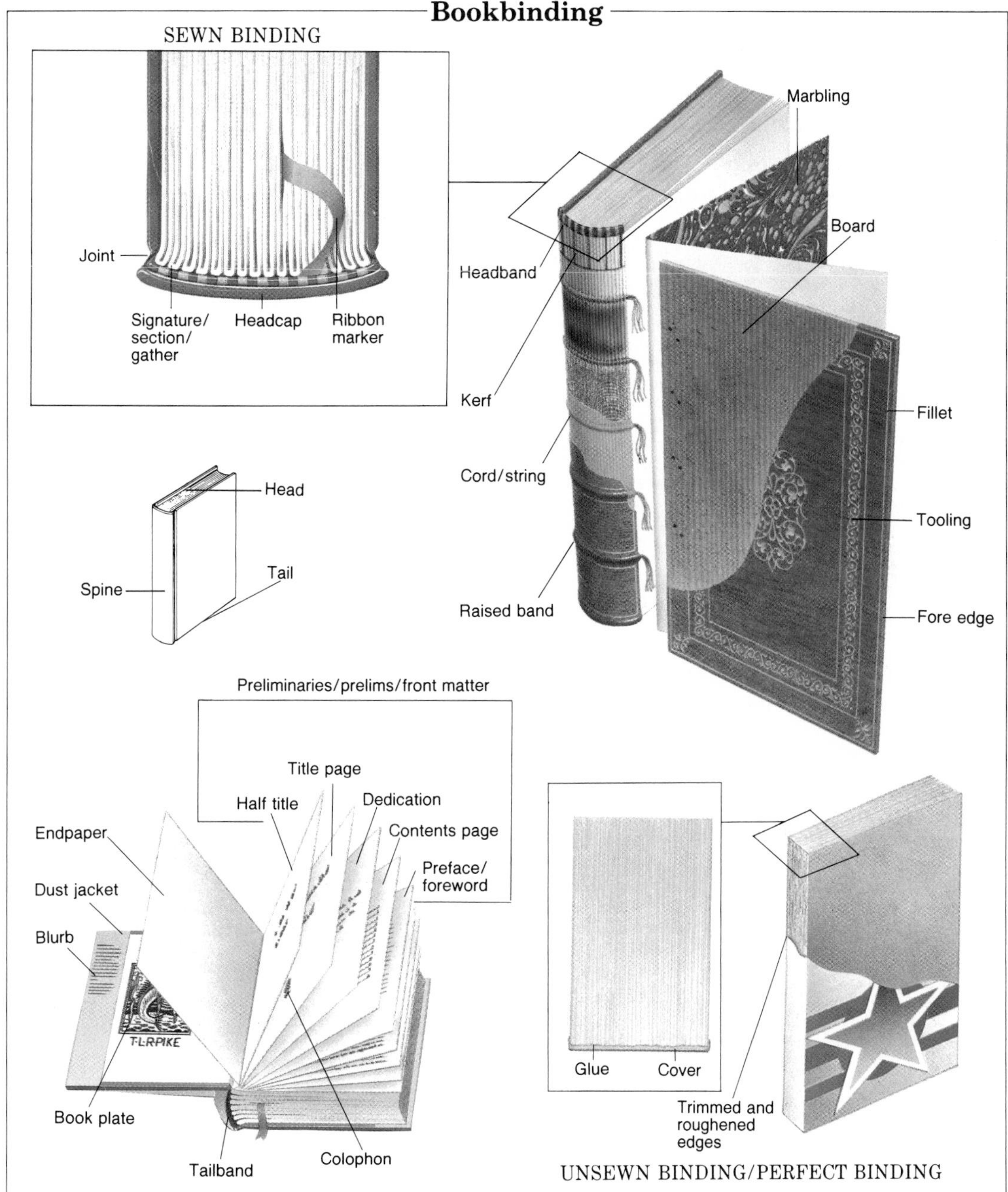

MISBEGOTTEN, SPURIOUS, NATURAL, SUPPOSITITIOUS
- just being born, beginning to develop, emerging NASCENT
- relating or belonging to the region where one was born NATIVE

borrowing of a word or phrase from another language by a literal translation of each element CALQUE, LOAN TRANSLATION
- borrowing or borrowed from a range of different sources ECLECTIC
- work, as of music, compiled by borrowing fragments or ideas from elsewhere PASTICCIO, PASTICHE

boss, employer, or word for "sir," as used in eastern Africa as a respectful form of address BWANA

bossy See **dominating**

botany, study of plants PHYTOLOGY

both (combining form) AMBI-, AMPH-, AMPHI-, BI-

both sides - place or be placed on both sides of a divide STRADDLE

bother, inconvenience, put out INCOMMODE

bottle See chart, page 70, and also **wine**
- bottle, often in a protective box or basket, for acids and other corrosive liquids CARBOY
- bottle for wine or water at table CARAFE, DECANTER
- bottle or small dispenser for oil or vinegar, as used at table CRUET
- bottle top, as on beer and cold-

drink bottles, with a crimped edge CROWN CAP
- bottle with more than one neck, used in a laboratory for bubbling gas through liquid WOULFE BOTTLE
- bottle with only one surface, used as a mathematical brainteaser KLEIN BOTTLE
- lockable cagelike container for displaying bottles or decanters of wine or spirits TANTALUS
- long narrow bottle or flask, sometimes covered in a straw casing DEMIJOHN
- narrow pitcher, or large bottle for wine or cider FLAGON
- small bottle, as for perfume, with a stopper FLACON
- small container, especially a tiny decorative bottle, for smelling salts VINAIGRETTE
- small container for medicine, poison, or other liquid, typically a tiny stoppered glass bottle VIAL, PHIAL
- squat two-handled bottle used in ancient Rome for storing wine, oil, or perfume AMPULLA

bottle gourd CALABASH

bottom layer SUBSTRATUM
- bottom part of a cycle, graph, or the like TROUGH

bounce or glance off a hard surface, as a bullet might RICOCHET
- bounce or jump back, as after a collision REBOUND, RECOIL
- bounce or skip, as over a stretch of water DAP
- pole, with a spring at the base, on which one can bounce along POGO STICK
- strike a ball before it bounces VOLLEY

boundary See also **border, trimming, edge**

BOTTLE SIZES

capacities expressed as multiples of the standard wine bottle holding 0.7 liter (1/5 gallon)

NAME	SIZE
magnum	2x
flagon	3x
jeroboam/ double magnum	4x or 6x
methuselah/ impériale	6x or 8x
salmanazar	12x
balthazar	16x
nebuchadnezzar	20x

- boundary, as of a geometric figure, sports field, or military position PERIMETER
- boundary, margin, or partition between the zones, distinct break DISCONTINUITY
- boundary, verge, or range COMPASS, CIRCUIT, BOURN, AMBIT
- boundary area, outskirts or outermost part PERIPHERY, PURLIEUS
- boundary between liquids, systems, phases, or the like INTERFACE
- boundary level above which something takes places or comes into effect THRESHOLD
- boundary line of an enclosed figure, especially a circle, or the length of it CIRCUMFERENCE
- boundary or boundary marker TERMINUS
- boundaries or limits, as of a budget or schedule PARAMETERS, CONSTRAINTS
- restrict, or establish the limits or boundaries of CIRCUMSCRIBE
- setting of boundaries between two areas, tasks, ideas, or the like DELIMITATION, DEMARCATION
- sharing a boundary, or having the same boundaries COTERMINOUS

bow, curtsy, or similar gesture of respect or submission OBEISANCE
- bow, kiss, or other gesture of greeting SALUTATION
- bow down or humble oneself, specifically by kneeling, as in worship GENUFLECT
- bow or lie down, as in worshiping or submission PROSTRATE
- bow very low, as in some Muslim societies, and touch one's forehead with the palm of one's right hand SALAAM
- bow very low, in traditional Chinese fashion, touching the ground with one's forehead KOWTOW
- gesture of greeting or respect, as in India, by placing one's hands together out in front of one and bowing NAMASTE
- groove at either end of the bow for holding the string NOCK
- reappearance on stage of an actor, cast, choir, or the like, as to take a bow CURTAIN CALL

bowels - bulky fiber-rich food, such as bran, assisting bowel regularity ROUGHAGE
- medicine or other substance that stimulates the bowels and relieves constipation LAXATIVE, CATHARTIC, PURGATIVE
- remove the bowels or internal organs of DISEMBOWEL, EVISCERATE, EXENTERATE

bowl in which something is ground with a pestle MORTAR
- bowl or small cup with a handle PORRINGER
- bowl-shaped pan, used in Chinese cooking, for stir-frying and the like WOK
- broad, deep bowl, as used for serving soup TUREEN

bowler hat DERBY

bowls, bowlslike game played in France, in which small metal balls are thrown at a target ball BOULES, PÉTANQUE
- ball rolled in bowls, a bowl WOOD
- characteristic of weight or shape that gives a bowl its swerve BIAS
- small white ball serving as the target in bowls JACK, MARK, KITTY
- uneven patch of the green in bowls RUB

box See also **container**
- box containing writing materials PAPETERIE
- box of large size and standard design for storing and transporting cargo CONTAINER, SKIP
- box or small chest for jewelry or other valuables CASKET
- box such as a chest or strongbox, typically for storing valuables COFFER
- box used by botanists or explorers for carrying plant specimens VASCULUM
- large box for ammunition CAISSON
- small box or can, especially for storing tea CADDY
- small box with a perforated lid, containing perfume POUNCET BOX

boxer, especially a professional boxer PUGILIST
- boxer who guards with his left hand and leads with his right SOUTHPAW
- boxer who is clumsy or unsuccessful PALOOKA

boxing glove or hand covering of leather loaded or studded with metal, worn by boxers in ancient Rome CESTUS
- code of rules in modern boxing QUEENSBERRY RULES
- lightest weight divisions in professional boxing FLYWEIGHT, BANTAMWEIGHT, FEATHERWEIGHT
- ornamental belt presented as a trophy to a British boxing champion LONSDALE BELT
- weight division just below heavyweight in boxing CRUISERWEIGHT
- wild swinging punch in boxing HAYMAKER

boy, especially a very young boy MANIKIN
- boy, lad, adolescent STRIPLING
- boy lover kept by a male homosexual CATAMITE
- boy or other person who gets the

blame for other people's faults SCAPEGOAT, WHIPPING BOY
- boy roaming the streets URCHIN, WAIF, GAMIN, RAGAMUFFIN, GUTTERSNIPE

boyfriend BEAU

bracelet - relating to a bracelet ARMILLARY

bracket, usually of stone or brick, supporting a cornice, balcony, arch, or the like CORBEL, TRUSS, CANTILEVER
- bracket on a wall for holding a candle, torch, or the like SCONCE
- brackets or round brackets in punctuation PARENTHESES
- brackets that are arrow-shaped, < > ANGLE BRACKETS
- ornamental bracket supporting a shelf or the like CONSOLE

braid, flat and narrow and forming zigzags, as used to trim clothing RICKRACK
- braid, metallic and plaited, as on the shoulder of a military uniform AIGUILLETTE
- braid, narrow and sometimes stiffened, used on clothes, curtains, and furniture GIMP, GUIMPE, GUIPURE
- braid or cord used for binding or trimming BOBBIN
- braid or looped cord used as a fastening, as formerly on military uniforms FROG
- braided cord on the left shoulder, as on a military uniform FOURRAGÈRE
- gold or silver wire or braid used as a trimming, as on military uniforms BULLION FRINGE

braille - reading and printing system for the blind, using raised letters, rather than dots as in braille MOON TYPE

brain See illustration
- brain operation in which one or more of the nerve tracts in the frontal lobe are severed LOBOTOMY, PREFRONTAL LEUCOTOMY
- brain surgeon NEUROSURGEON
- brain's electrical wave form typical of a normal waking state BETA WAVE
- brain's electrical wave form typical of a resting or drowsy state ALPHA RHYTHM
- adjective for the brain CEREBRAL
- application of biology to engineering and electronics, especially of brain functions to computers BIONICS
- disorder of the brain's normal functioning, involving brief attacks of dislocation, convulsions, or unconsciousness EPILEPSY
- either half of the brain along a lengthwise divide HEMISPHERE
- figure of a man modeled with limbs and organs proportional in size to the areas of the brain controlling them HOMUNCULUS
- instrument recording the electrical impulses in the brain, used for diagnosis ELECTROENCEPHALOGRAPH, EEG
- irregular ridge between grooves on the surface of the brain GYRUS, CONVOLUTION
- jarring of the brain, typically causing brief unconsciousness and loss of bearings CONCUSSION
- membranes surrounding the brain and spinal cord MENINGES
- stroke that is often followed by paralysis, resulting from the bursting or blocking of a blood vessel in the brain APOPLEXY, CERE-

Brain

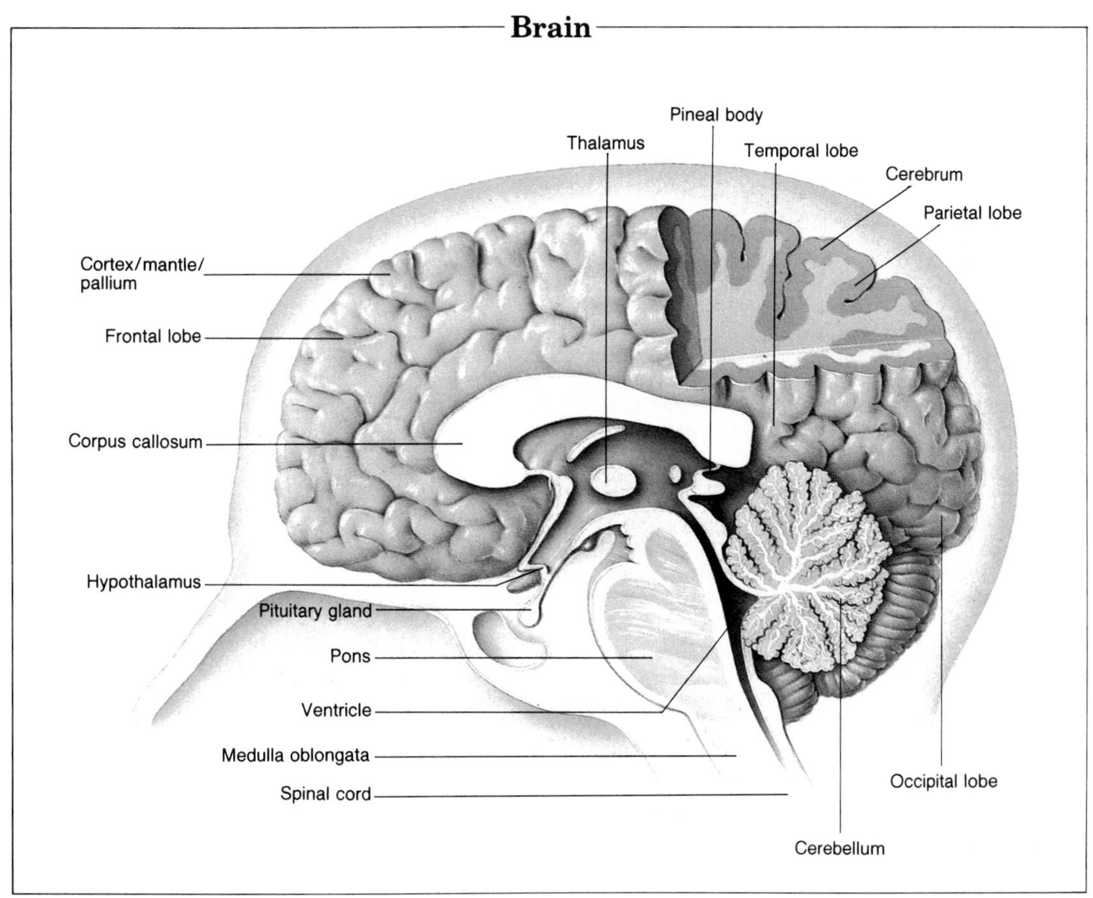

BRAL HEMORRHAGE
- technical name for a brain ENCEPHALON
- therapy for treating psychiatric patients in which an electric shock is administered to the brain ELECTROCONVULSIVE THERAPY, ECT
- tranquilizing or painkilling substance secreted by the brain ENDORPHIN

brain (combining form) ENCEPHAL-, ENCEPHALO-, CEREBR-, CEREBRO-, PHREN-, PHRENO-

brain fever ENCEPHALITIS

brainteaser in Zen Buddhism, designed to free the mind from the constraints of logic KOAN

brake flap on an airplane's wing DECELERON
- brake on a wagon or carriage DRAG
- brakes operated by compressed fluid HYDRAULIC BRAKES
- braking rocket, used to slow down or reverse a spacecraft or the like RETROROCKET, RETRO

bran or other fiber in the diet, assisting the regularity of bowel movement ROUGHAGE

branch, arrangement of branches, or branching process RAMIFICATION
- branch of knowledge, subject of study DISCIPLINE
- branching, forked FURCATE
- branching or repeated forking of a plant into two equal parts DICHOTOMY
- angle between a leafstalk and the stem, between a branch and the trunk, or the like AXIL
- bundle or cluster of leaves, branches, or the like FASCICLE, FASCICULE
- divide into several branches, as a plant stem might DELIQUESCE
- having branches RAMATE, RAMOSE
- having spread-out branches arranged in pairs, as some trees have BRACHIATE
- joint or branching point on a stem NODE
- spreading out widely, as branches might PATENT, PATULOUS
- stump remaining after a branch has broken off SNAG

brand mark as formerly on the skin of a slave or criminal STIGMA
- brand name or emblem MARQUE

brandy EAU-DE-VIE
- brandy, whiskey, or other strong spirits AQUA VITAE
- brandy distilled from the leftover pulp of pressed grapes MARC
- brandy from France COGNAC, ARMAGNAC

brass, a brass worker BRAZIER
- greenish coating forming on exposed copper, brass, or bronze objects PATINA, VERDIGRIS, VERD ANTIQUE, AERUGO

brass instruments See **wind instruments**

brave in a dashing and sometimes daredevil way, very bold or daring AUDACIOUS, VENTURESOME
- brave in an honorable way, chivalrous and courageous, heroic GALLANT, VALIANT, VALOROUS
- brave in a spirited way, plucky, game FEISTY, DOUGHTY, METTLESOME
- fearless, extremely brave DAUNTLESS, INTREPID
- unshakably brave, unshrinking, resolute in the face of intimidation STALWART, UNDAUNTED, UNFLINCHING

bravery, strength, or skill, as shown in battle PROWESS
- bravery and enterprise, nerve GUMPTION
- bravery involving endurance and strong will FORTITUDE, TENACITY
- bravery or daring spirit, especially in chivalric adventures DERRING-DO, EMPRISE
- bravery that is confident or swaggering but probably false BRAVADO, BLUSTER, BRAGGADOCIO
- award or honor, as for bravery COMMENDATION

bread See illustration
- bread of malted rye and wheat flour, containing wholemeal kernels GRANARY BREAD
- bread or biscuit formerly on sailing ships HARDTACK, SHIP'S BISCUIT
- bread or wafer consecrated in the Eucharist HOST
- bread soaked or dunked in gravy, soup, milk, or the like BREWIS, SOP
- baker's long-handled shovel used for moving bread, pies, pizza, or the like in and out of an oven PEEL
- crusty end of a loaf of bread HEEL
- flat Indian breads CHAPATTI, ROTI, NAN, PARATHA, PURI
- flat oval Greek or Middle Eastern bread PITTA
- long, thin Italian breadsticks GRISSINI
- made of dough without yeast or other fermentation agent, as Passover bread is UNLEAVENED
- protein mixture in bread, cakes, and the like, avoided in certain diets GLUTEN
- rich Welsh bread containing mixed fruit BARA BRITH
- rich yeast bread of German origin containing dried fruit and nuts STOLLEN
- substance added to dough to aid fermentation, as in breadmaking LEAVEN
- sweet Scottish bread containing dried fruit SELKIRK BANNOCK
- sweetened bread sliced and then crisped in an oven ZWIEBACK
- wedge of toast or fried bread, typically served as a garnish SIPPET

bread and wine consecrated and then consumed in commemoration of Jesus, or the Christian sacrament involved EUCHARIST
- conversion of the consecrated Communion bread and wine into the body and blood of Christ, as understood by Roman Catholics TRANSUBSTANTIATION
- coexistence of the consecrated Communion bread and wine with the body and blood of Christ, as understood by Protestants CONSUBSTANTIATION

breadbasket, nerve network in the stomach, where one might be punched and winded SOLAR PLEXUS

breadcrumbs - coated with breadcrumbs and sometimes cheese, and then grilled or browned, as cauliflower might be AU GRATIN

break See also **destroy, cancel, gap**
- break a code so as to translate its message, decode DECIPHER, DECRYPT
- break apart or into parts, sever or fracture SUNDER, REAVE
- break away from an alliance, organization, or the like SECEDE
- break by splitting CLEAVE, REND, RIFT
- break down into small or basic parts, crumble DECOMPOSE, DISINTEGRATE
- break down into tiny bits, reduce to a spray, powder, or the like ATOMIZE, VAPORIZE, PULVERIZE
- break in continuity, such as a gap or interruption LACUNA, HIATUS
- break in proceedings, such as a pause or interval RECESS, RESPITE, INTERMISSION
- break in the meter or rhythm within a single line of verse CAESURA
- break open, burst open RUPTURE
- break or smash inward, crush STAVE
- break out violently, explode, as in anger ERUPT
- break up a group or cease to function as a group DISBAND
- break up and loosen the surface of topsoil, a field, a road, or the like SCARIFY
- break up stone, especially with a hammer SPALL
- breaking of a law or regulation VIOLATION, BREACH, INFRINGEMENT, TRANSGRESSION, INFRACTION, CONTRAVENTION
- breaking the law, especially by a

public official MALFEASANCE, MALVERSATION
- person who breaks religious statues or sacred objects ICONOCLAST

break (combining form) FISSI-

breakable, brittle, fragile FRANGIBLE
- breakable, easily broken up or crumbled FRIABLE

breakfast food of cereals, nuts, raisins, and the like MUESLI

breakwater or jetty jutting into the sea to control erosion, protect a harbor, direct a current, or the like GROYNE, GROIN, SPUR, MOLE

breast, udder, or teat DUG
- breast examination by touch for a preliminary medical diagnosis PALPATION
- breast examination by X-rays MAMMOGRAM, MAMMOGRAPHY
- breast feeder of the child of another woman WET NURSE
- breast secretion of serum and white blood cells, lasting a few days after childbirth before the flow of milk begins COLOSTRUM
- abnormal enlargement of breasts in a man, as through hormone imbalance GYNECOMASTIA
- adjective for a breast MAMMARY
- chemical polymer used in breast implants and other cosmetic surgery SILICONE
- darkish area on a breast, surrounding the nipple AREOLA
- having or relating to full shapely breasts, busty PNEUMATIC
- line or hollow between a woman's breasts, as revealed by a low-cut dress CLEAVAGE
- produce milk, especially when breast-feeding LACTATE
- relating to the chest or breast PECTORAL
- surgical amputation of a breast MASTECTOMY
- surgical removal of a breast tumor without removing the whole breast LUMPECTOMY

breast (combining form) MAST-, MASTO-

breastbone STERNUM
- breastbone and its associated cartilages PLASTRON

breastplate as formerly worn under a coat of mail PLASTRON
- breastplate or item of armor protecting chest and back CUIRASS

breath that is bad-smelling HALITOSIS
- lozenge or pastille sucked in order to sweeten the breath CACHOU

breathe in INHALE
- breathe or sigh SUSPIRE
- breathe out EXHALE, EXPIRE

breathing RESPIRATION
- breathing at an abnormally decreased rate HYPOPNEA
- breathing at an abnormally increased rate, as after exercise HYPERPNEA, HYPERVENTILATION

Bread

- breathing difficulty, temporary inability to draw breath APNEA
- breathing hole, as in a beetle's exoskeleton or behind a shark's eye SPIRACLE
- breathing with or relating to a heavy snoring noise STERTOROUS
- done with difficulty, as breathing might be LABORED
- harsh vibrating sound in labored breathing STRIDOR
- person who breathes heavily and noisily GRAMPUS
- relating to breathing or suction ASPIRATORY
- surgical cut or opening through the throat to help breathing TRACHEOTOMY
- unconsciousness or death resulting from restricted breathing and lack of oxygen, suffocation ASPHYXIATION

breathing (combining form) PNEUM-, PNEUMO-, PNEUMATO-, SPIRO-

breathing apparatus for use under water including an air cylinder and oxygen mask AQUALUNG

breathing space, pause, or rest, typically in the middle of something unpleasant RESPITE

breed, or cause plants or animals to breed PROPAGATE
- breed from two different varieties or species HYBRID
- breed or reproduce PROCREATE
- breed rapidly PULLULATE
- breeding place, as for bacteria NIDUS
- breeding record or family tree of a thoroughbred horse, dog, or other animal PEDIGREE
- deliberate modification of the gene structure, as in breeding improved plant or animal strains GENETIC ENGINEERING
- horses or other domestic animals kept for breeding STUD
- study of or attempts at improving the human race by selective breeding EUGENICS

brewing - chemistry of fermentation in brewing ZYMURGY
- fermentable pulp used in brewing beer MASH

bribe or payment made in an illicit or underhand way to secure a favor BACKHANDER
- bribe or small tip DOUCEUR
- bribe or threaten someone into committing a wrongful act, especially perjury SUBORN
- bribe paid to preserve secrecy HUSH MONEY
- bribery, as of disc jockeys, to promote a product PAYOLA
- fund used for bribing and other corrupt activities SLUSH FUND
- open to or marked by bribery, corrupt VENAL

bric-a-brac, showy but cheap finery TRUMPERY

brick laid parallel to the line of a wall STRETCHER
- brick laid perpendicular to the line of a wall HEADER
- brick of sun-dried clay, as used in Mexico ADOBE
- brick or small block of charcoal, ice cream, or other substance BRIQUETTE
- brick tray, carried over the shoulder on a pole HOD
- bricks jutting out from a wall CORBELING
- cement or thin mortar for filling cracks or seams, as between bricks or tiles POINTING, GROUTING
- horizontal row or layer of bricks, tiles, or the like COURSE
- notch or groove in a brick to make it lighter FROG

bricklayer's work bench BANKER

brickwork See illustration
- brickwork foundation of a building STEREOBATE
- brickwork or masonry used to fill in a wooden framework NOGGING

bride's attendant who is herself married MATRON OF HONOR
- bride's money or property handed over to her husband on their marriage DOWRY
- bride's special wardrobe and household items assembled before her wedding TROUSSEAU

bridge See illustration, page 76
- bridge, extend over SPAN
- bridge, typically supported by a series of arches, carrying a road or railway, as over a valley VIADUCT
- bridge above a road OVERPASS
- bridge or roadway hinged near a weighted end so as to be raised or lowered BASCULE
- bridge that can be raised to prevent access or allow vessels to pass DRAWBRIDGE
- bridgelike arched structure supporting a canal or water channel AQUEDUCT
- bridge's supporting framework of beams, struts, or the like TRUSS, TRESTLE
- float for raising a sunken vessel or supporting a floating bridge PONTOON
- pillar or similar support at the meeting point of the spans of a bridge PIER
- relating to bridges PONTINE
- simple bridge, typically of stone slabs supported between piles of stones CLAPPER BRIDGE
- temporary steel bridge assembled from prefabricated parts BAILEY BRIDGE

bridge game - hand of 13 cards, especially in bridge or whist, in which no card is higher than a nine YARBOROUGH
- hand of 13 cards, especially in bridge or whist, in which no card is in trumps CHICANE
- match of three games in bridge or whist RUBBER
- trump a card in bridge or other card games RUFF

bridle See also **harness**
- bridle with an iron bit formerly used to silence scolding women BRANK

brief See also **concise, short-lived, summary**
- brief and mechanical, as a glance or smile might be PERFUNCTORY
- brief and superficial, as an inspection might be CURSORY
- brief and unsympathetic treatment, curt consideration and dismissal SHORT SHRIFT
- brief appearance, in a movie or play, of a famous actor or actress CAMEO ROLE
- brief or abrupt to the point of rudeness, very blunt or terse, curt BRUSQUE
- briefness, shortness BREVITY

briefcase for holding loose papers or official documents PORTFOLIO

bright See also **brilliant**
- bright, radiant, glossy or shiny LUSTROUS
- bright, striking, fresh, or lively VIVID
- bright in a dashing or showy way, glaring FLAMBOYANT
- bright through rubbing or polishing BURNISHED, FURBISHED
- brightened or beautified with colors, flowers, or the like EMBLAZONED
- unnaturally bright, flashy, gaudy GARISH, LURID

brilliance, as of a success or achievement ÉCLAT
- brilliance or outstanding technical ability, especially in playing a musical instrument VIRTUOSITY

brilliant, sparkling, glittering, as wit or a gemstone might be SCINTILLATING, CORUSCATING
- brilliant and successful act or decision MASTERSTROKE, COUP
- brilliant or dramatic display, as in a piano recital PYROTECHNICS
- brilliant or extremely successful person of very young age WHIZ KID, WUNDERKIND, CHILD PRODIGY
- glowing intensely, brilliantly bright INCANDESCENT
- shining brilliantly, radiantly illu-

minated, dazzling RESPLENDENT, EFFULGENT

bring back to life, raise from the dead RESURRECT

- bring back to life, revive or reactivate RESUSCITATE, REANIMATE, REVITALIZE, REVIVIFY, REGENERATE
- bring to light, draw out ELICIT
- bring up, train, foster NURTURE
- bring up or vomit partly digested food REGURGITATE

bristles - covered with tiny barbed hairs or bristles, as some plants and animals are BARBELLATE

bristling of the hair on the body, goose flesh PILOERECTION, HORRIPILATION

bristly (combining form) ECHINO-

Britain - poetic or old-fashioned term for Britain or England ALBION

British (combining form) ANGLO-

British Empire - former term for a large self-governing nation of the British Empire, such as Australia DOMINION

Britons - blue dye used by ancient Britons to color their skin WOAD

brittleness or weakening of the bones, especially in elderly people OSTEOPOROSIS

broad, inclusive, wide-ranging COMPREHENSIVE, COMPENDIOUS

- broad-minded, forgiving, unresentful MAGNANIMOUS
- broad-minded, tolerant, having wide sympathies, especially regarding religion LATITUDINARIAN
- broad-minded or tolerant, especially in matters of sexual conduct PERMISSIVE
- broad-tipped or splay-tipped, as fingers or leaves might be SPATULATE

broad bean FAVA BEAN

broadcast See also **radio, television**

- broadcast announcements or linking items designed to avoid breaks between programs CONTINUITY
- broadcast at the end of the day, typically a short religious program EPILOGUE
- broadcast covering a week's episodes of a series that have previously been broadcast separately OMNIBUS EDITION
- broadcast live a concert, speech, or the like via a transmitter RELAY
- broadcast of a program simultaneously on radio and television SIMULCAST
- broadcast that has been prerecorded TRANSCRIPTION
- broadcaster who coordinates

Brickword Bonds

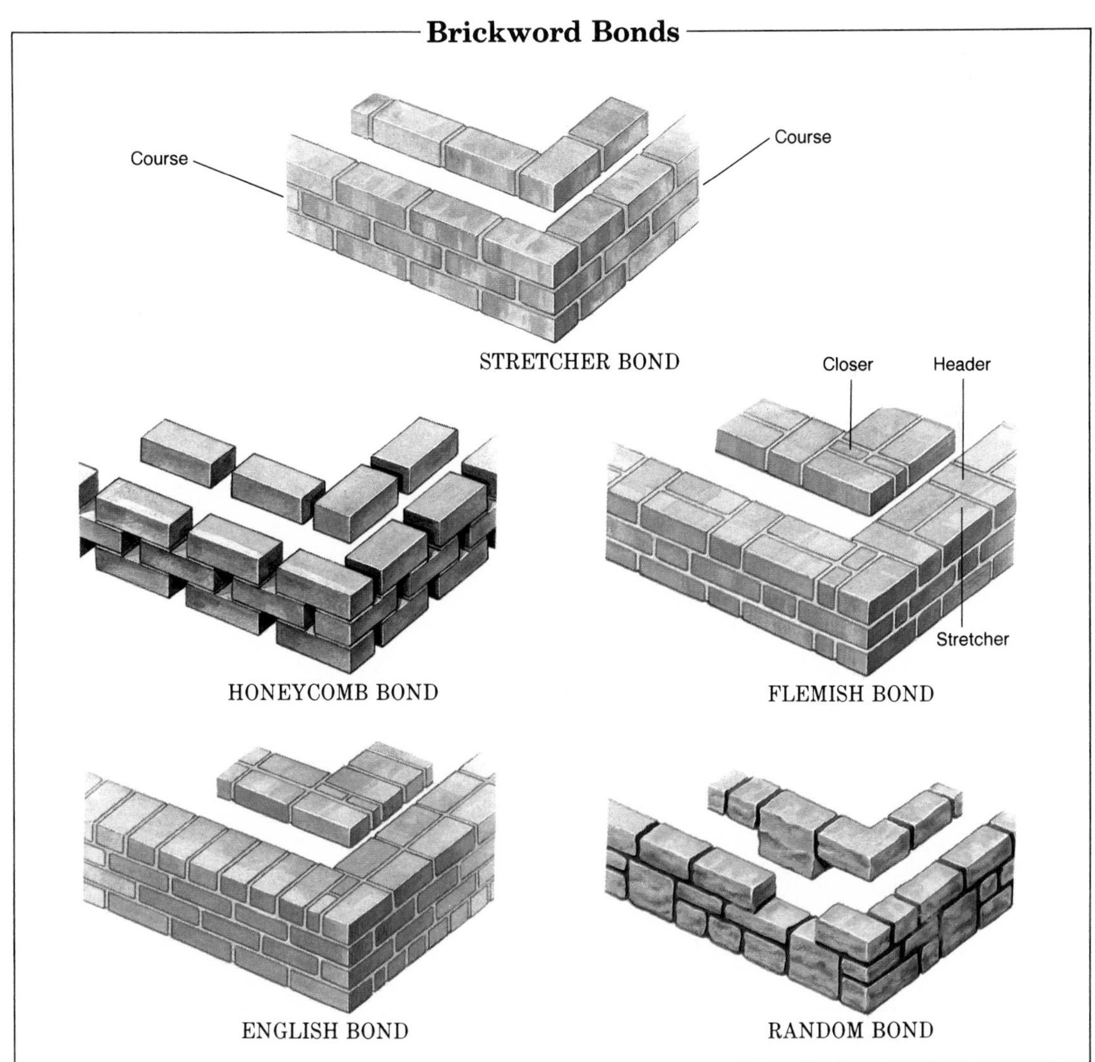

STRETCHER BOND

HONEYCOMB BOND

FLEMISH BOND

ENGLISH BOND

RANDOM BOND

many reports ANCHORMAN, ANCHORWOMAN, ANCHOR
- broadcasting network GRID
- relating to broadcasting in which members of the general public rather than professionals make the programs ACCESS

brochure from a university or other institution, detailing its main features PROSPECTUS

broken beyond repair, destroyed KAPUT
- broken bits, fragments, splinters SMITHEREENS
- broken down or worn out through age or overuse DECREPIT, DILAPIDATED
- broken fragments, scattered remains, rubble DEBRIS
- broken piece of glass, pottery, or other similarly brittle substance SHARD

broken leg - continuous stretching of a body part, as in treating a broken leg TRACTION

broker or banker trading in shares or bonds for quick profits ARBITRAGEUR
- brokerage of or speculation in stocks and shares AGIOTAGE, STOCK JOBBING

bronze - greenish coating forming on exposed copper, brass, or bronze objects VERDIGRIS, VERD ANTIQUE, AERUGO
- layer of oxide, usually green, forming naturally or artificially on a copper or bronze surface PATINA

bronze (combining form) CHALC-, CHALCO-

brooch, clasp, or other jeweled adornment in former times OUCH
- brooch, medal, or the like worn on the chest PECTORAL
- brooch worn as a membership badge PLAQUE
- medallion, on a brooch, ring, or the like, with a head in profile in raised relief CAMEO

broom of twigs BESOM

broth made in a casserole pot MARMITE

brothel BAGNIO, BAWDYHOUSE, BORDELLO
- brothel or other house where public order or decency is violated DISORDERLY HOUSE
- man who finds clients for a prostitute or brothel PIMP

brother or sister SIBLING
- murder of a brother FRATRICIDE

brotherhood, fellowship, community FRATERNITY, SODALITY

brotherly FRATERNAL

brow - draw in and wrinkle the brow or forehead PURSE, PUCKER

brown See also **color**
- brown-haired and dark-eyed woman BRUNETTE

brown coal LIGNITE

browning - metal plate heated for browning puddings or other food SALAMANDER

bruise CONTUSION
- bluish, as bruised skin might be LIVID

brush for grooming or currying a horse DANDY BRUSH

brutal, savage, beastlike BESTIAL
- brutally severe, extremely harsh, as repressive laws might be DRACONIAN

Bridges

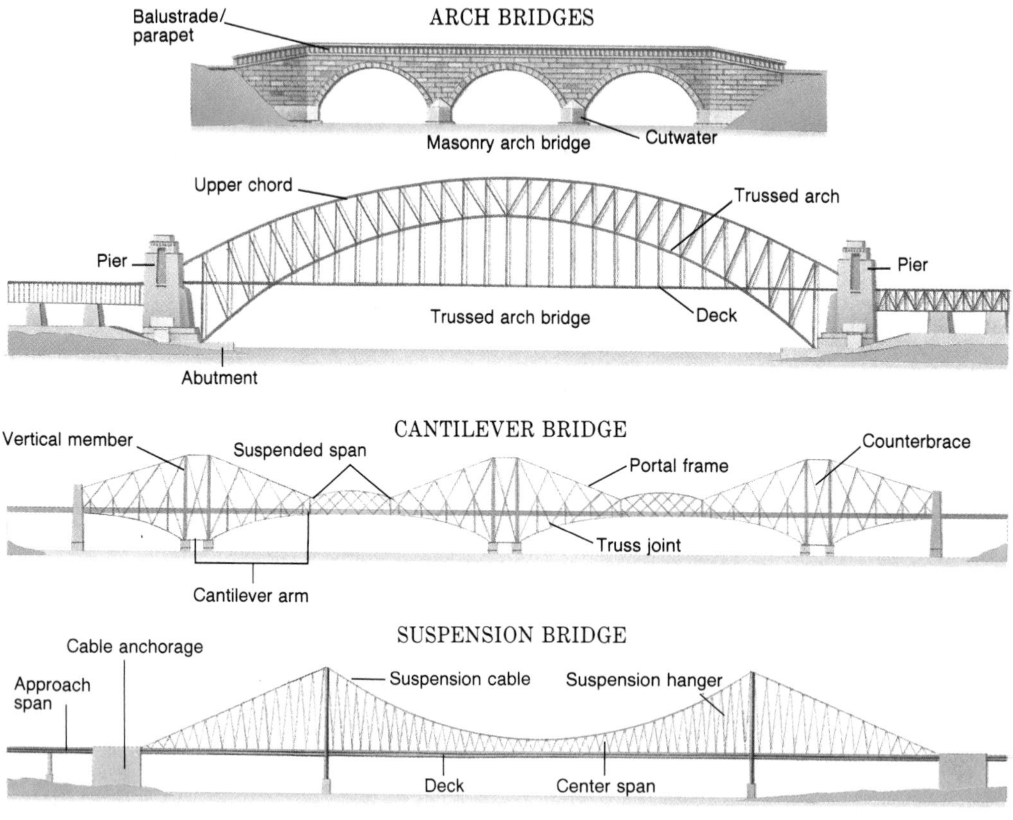

ARCH BRIDGES

CANTILEVER BRIDGE

SUSPENSION BRIDGE

brutish, without truly human understanding or feelings INSENSATE, INSENSIBLE
bubble of air surrounding some water-dwelling insects PLASTRON
bubbling, as a carbonated drink is EFFERVESCENT
- bubbling with excitement or enthusiasm, full of high spirits EBULLIENT, EXUBERANT
bucket, basin, or large mug STOUP
- bucket of wood with one stave extended above the rim as a handle PIGGIN, PIPKIN
- bucket used in wells or mine shafts KIBBLE
- handle of a bucket, in the form of a hooped rod BAIL
buckle - buckle's metal prong CHAPE
bud, sprout, or shoot, as a plant does BURGEON, PULLULATE
- bud of a plant embryo, developing into the shoot PLUMULE
- multiplying by means of buds, shoots, or small bulbs rather than by seeds VIVIPAROUS
bud (combining form) BLASTO-
Buddhism See chart
Buddhist monastery in Tibet LAMASERY
- Buddhist shrine or Hindu temple, typically a multistoried tapering tower PAGODA
- sacred language of Buddhists PALI
budget - limits or boundaries, as of a budget or schedule PARAMETERS, CONSTRAINTS
buffalo BISON
- hybrid cattle breed, a cross between a buffalo and domestic cow or bull CATTALO
buffet - buffet-style meal of Swedish origin SMORGASBORD
bugle call at sunset when the flag is lowered RETREAT
- bugle call first thing in the morning REVEILLE
- bugle call or drumbeat signaling soldiers to return to their quarters in the evening TATTOO
- bugle call sounded at military funerals or to signal lights out in a military camp TAPS, LAST POST
build See **body**
builder specializing in building with stone MASON
building See also **house, architecture, foundations, roof**
- building, especially one that is large and imposing EDIFICE
- building commemorating a nation's heroes PANTHEON
- building development, especially housing, along a road leading out of a town RIBBON DEVELOPMENT
- building of clay bricks or stone, typically of several floors, as a communal residence by Native Americans in the southwestern United States PUEBLO
- building of rented apartments, typically in a poor or slum area TENEMENT
- building of historical interest protected by law from alteration or demolition LANDMARK, LISTED BUILDING
- building or room in former times housing bones or dead bodies CHARNEL HOUSE
- building or room, such as a private library, set aside for reading ATHENAEUM
- building structure, such as a wall or pillar, between two windows, arches, or the like TRUMEAU
- building supervisor for maintenance and services SUPERINTENDENT, SUPER, JANITOR
- building with stone MASONRY
- building's basic framework of walls, floor, and roof FABRIC
- buildings, equipment, and other provisions for an activity FACILITIES
- buildings, land, and other immovable property REAL PROPERTY, REAL ESTATE, REALTY
- beam laid horizontally, as in building GIRDER
- broken down, falling to pieces, as a shabby old building is DILAPIDATED
- circular, often domed, building or room ROTUNDA
- declare a building, park, or the like open at a special ceremony DEDICATE
- demolish a building or city, destroy down to the ground RAZE
- deserted and falling into ruins, as

BUDDHIST TERMS

bonze	monk of the Mahayana school, active in China and Japan
bo tree/peepul	sacred fig tree, under which the Buddha attained enlightenment
Buddha	person who has achieved total spiritual enlightenment
Dalai Lama	traditional highest priest and ruler in Tibet and Mongolia
karma	sum of a person's total actions, determining his or her destiny in future lives; broadly, fate or destiny
lama	monk in Tibet or Mongolia
Mahayana	branch of Buddhism, as in Korea and Tibet, of a relatively liberal and evangelical kind
mandala	circular design symbolizing the universe
mantra	sacred word or formula repeated, sometimes in one's head, during prayer or meditation
nirvana	release from the cycle of reincarnations into a state of blessedness
prajna	wisdom or enlightenment sought through contemplation
prayer wheel	wheel or cylinder with written prayers on or in it
stupa/tope	Buddhist shrine, typically dome-shaped
sutra	scriptural text, especially any supposed discourse by the Buddha
tantra	any text from a group of later mystical writings
Theravada/ Hinayana	branch of Buddhism, as in Sri Lanka and southeast Asia, of a fundamentalist and monastic kind
Zen	Mahayana school or sect favoring meditation and intuition rather than scripture as a means to enlightenment

an old building might be DERELICT
- destruction of disused buildings DEMOLITION
- estimating of building costs and materials QUANTITY SURVEYING
- front or face of a building FACADE, FRONTISPIECE
- foundation of a stone building STEREOBATE
- large and striking building or complex of buildings PILE
- movable platform on the outside walls of a building, as used by window cleaners GONDOLA
- nonfunctional and usually whimsical building erected purely for decorative purposes FOLLY
- person who climbs the outside of buildings, as for a prank or bet STEGOPHILIST
- projecting wing or added section of or near to a building ANNEX, PAVILION
- ready-made standard unit used in constructing a building MODULE
- relating to building or construction TECTONIC
- restore a building to a former or better condition RENOVATE
- roundish building with tiers of seats surrounding an arena AMPHITHEATER
- sinking of the ground or of a building SUBSIDENCE
- structural inspection of a building, as to establish its value SURVEY, ASSESSMENT

building (combining form) -ARIUM, -ORIUM

building material, especially for flooring, made of stone chips set in polished concrete slabs or tiles TERRAZZO
- building material of interlaced sticks plastered with mud or clay WATTLE AND DAUB
- building material of large light blocks made of ash and cement BREEZE BLOCKS
- building material of overlapping boards used especially to cover roofs or walls WEATHERBOARDING, CLAPBOARDING
- building material of sun-dried clay bricks, as in Mexico ADOBE
- building material or stone, either a square block for walls or a thin slab for facings ASHLAR

buildup, slow increase through additions ACCRETION

built according to the buyer's specifications, as a car might be CUSTOM-BUILT
- built in sections in advance, before its assembly as cheap housing might be PREFABRICATED
- built shoddily and unreliably JERRY-BUILT

bulb, bulblike underground stem, as of the gladiolus CORM
- multiplying by means of buds, shoots, or small bulbs rather than by seeds VIVIPAROUS

bulging, swelling or protruding prominently outward PROTUBERANT, CONVEX
- bulging-eyed, specifically as a result of excess thyroid hormone EXOPHTHALMIC
- bulging or swollen TUMESCENT, TUMID, TURGID, TUBEROUS

bulky fiber-rich food, such as bran, assisting bowel regularity ROUGHAGE

bull - relating to a bull TAURINE

bull (combining form) TAUR-, TAURO-

bullet, shell, missile, rocket, or other object fired or hurled PROJECTILE
- bullet belt worn across the chest from the shoulder BANDOLEER
- bullet leaving a trail of smoke or light that allows its path to be monitored TRACER BULLET
- bullet with a soft or hollow nose that spreads on impact to produce a gaping wound DUMDUM BULLET, SPREAD-ON-IMPACT BULLET
- diameter of the inside of a tube, the bore of a gun, or a bullet or shell CALIBER
- groove, especially around a bullet CANNELURE
- main explosive charge or gunpowder content of a bullet PROPELLANT
- rebound from a hard surface, as a bullet might RICOCHET
- simultaneous firing of a number of bullets, arrows, guns, or the like VOLLEY
- small explosive cap in the base of a bullet that detonates the main charge PRIMER, DETONATOR CAP, PERCUSSION CAP
- study of guns and bullets, shells, and so on BALLISTICS

bullfighting See chart
- pierce or stab with a horn or tusk, as in bullfighting GORE

bull's-eye, center of a target BLANK
- bull's-eye of an archery target, or the target as a whole CLOUT

bully, oppress TYRANNIZE
- bully, punish unfairly, or discriminate against VICTIMIZE
- bully, threaten, or hector, as to persuade or discourage BROWBEAT
- bully or bulldoze into compliance DRAGOON, COERCE
- bully or frighten into submission INTIMIDATE
- bullying, overbearing IMPERIOUS, DOMINEERING, DESPOTIC
- bullying disciplinarian or authority MARTINET
- target of teasing, mockery, bullying, or the like BUTT

bump, bulge or similar projection PROTUBERANCE, PROTRUSION
- bump or knot on a tree or timber KNUR

BULLFIGHTING TERMS

aficionado	fan or devotee of bullfights
banderilla	large decorated dart thrust into the bull's neck or shoulder
banderillero	assistant who inserts the banderillas
corrida	bullfight
matador	principal bullfighter who kills the bull
moment of truth	point at which the matador is poised to make the final thrust of the sword to kill the bull
muleta	small cape on a stick, used by the matador for luring the bull during his final series of passes
pase/pass	presenting or flourishing of the cape by the matador to maneuver the bull
picador	horseman who wounds and weakens the bull with a lance during the early stages
toreador	bullfighter, especially one on a horse
torero	bullfighter, especially a matador
veronica	pass in which the stationary matador slowly swings the cape away from the charging bull

- bump or tiny rounded projection, as on the tongue or the root of a hair PAPILLA
- small knob, bump, swelling, or lump NODULE, NODE

bumper - bumper's upright attachment, fitted in pairs to prevent interlocking with another vehicle's bumper OVERRIDER

bunch of flowers, often used as a small gift POSY

bundle of rods with an ax, carried as a symbol of the magistrates' authority in ancient Rome FASCES
- bundle of twigs, branches, or sticks FAGGOT
- small bundle or cluster FASCICLE

bung, plug STOPPLE, SPIGOT, SPILE

burden, handicap, or hinder ENCUMBER
- burden, obstacle, or impediment ENCUMBRANCE
- burden of anxiety, such as a debt MILLSTONE
- burden or responsibility ONUS

burdensome, troublesome ONEROUS

bureaucracy or petty officialdom BEADLEDOM

bureaucrat or overzealous official APPARATCHIK
- bureaucratic jargon that is wordy and difficult to understand GOBBLEDYGOOK, OFFICIALESE

burglar - burglar's crowbar JIMMY
- electronic device that reacts to changes in light intensity, as used in burglar alarms and automatic doors PHOTOELECTRIC CELL, PHOTOCELL, ELECTRIC EYE, MAGIC EYE

burglary or large theft HEIST
- burglary or theft as formerly treated as a felony LARCENY

burial chamber, as beneath a church VAULT, CRYPT
- burial chamber or graveyard hidden underground CATACOMB, HYPOGEUM
- burial chamber, vault, or building in which the bones or bodies of the dead are stored CHARNEL HOUSE
- burial chamber or tomb, or an imposing building housing it MAUSOLEUM
- burial ground, especially a large and elaborate cemetery of an ancient city NECROPOLIS
- burial site or monument of standing stones from prehistoric times CROMLECH, DOLMEN
- burial vault, tomb, or grave SEPULCHER, REPOSITORY
- cloth used to wrap a body for burial SHROUD, WINDING SHEET
- heap of earth or stones covering an ancient burial site BARROW, MOUND, TUMULUS

burn a corpse to ashes CREMATE
- burn flesh or tissue with a corrosive chemical or a very hot or very cold instrument, as in treating wounds CAUTERIZE
- burn or cause to burn IGNITE, KINDLE
- burn or cause to burn fiercely or intensely DEFLAGRATE
- burn to ashes INCINERATE
- burn unevenly and drip wax down one side, as a candle might GUTTER
- burned or charred substance CINDER, CLINKER
- burning, as of fuel COMBUSTION
- burning of a heretic at the stake as ordered by the Inquisition AUTO-DA-FÉ
- burning of buildings or other property deliberately, for criminal purposes ARSON
- burning of leafy substance on the skin as a form of therapy of Asian origin MOXIBUSTION
- burning or dissolving, as some chemicals are CAUSTIC, CORROSIVE
- burning readily, or catching fire easily INFLAMMABLE, FLAMMABLE
- dummy or crude image of a person, intended as an object of scorn or hatred, and sometimes burned in public EFFIGY
- material that burns easily, such as twigs, used to get a fire going TINDER, KINDLING
- portable metal stand for burning coal or charcoal BRAZIER
- scab or layer of dead skin, as caused by a burn ESCHAR
- support a severely burned patient on a cushion of air LEVITATE

burn (combining form) PYRO-

burner producing a hot gas flame, used for laboratory experiments BUNSEN BURNER

burnt offering HOLOCAUST

burp or belch ERUCT

burst in violently IRRUPT
- burst of cheering, applause, or the like SALVO
- burst of gunfire FUSILLADE, BARRAGE
- burst or break open RUPTURE
- burst or quick discharge of oaths, or the like VOLLEY
- burst or split open along the seam, as some seed capsules do DEHISCE
- bursting forth, as if into bloom EFFLORESCENCE

bury, place in a grave INHUME, INTER
- bury or imprison in or as if in a tomb ENTOMB

bus station, or servicing area for buses or trains DEPOT

bush baby GALAGO

bushy mass, as of hair SHOCK

business See also chart at **economics**
- business agent FACTOR
- business asset, such as goodwill, that has a value but no physical existence INTANGIBLE
- business association of various interests formed for some joint enterprise CONSORTIUM, SYNDICATE
- business association or grouping of companies, especially an illegal one, to monopolize manufacture or control prices CARTEL
- business corporation made up of many wide-ranging companies CONGLOMERATE
- business costs such as rent and rates, spread across all departments OVERHEADS, BURDEN, ON-COST
- business deal TRANSACTION
- business or company controlling other businesses or companies HOLDING COMPANY
- business practice of buying a struggling company and selling off its assets bit by bit ASSET STRIPPING
- business records of an organization or society PROCEEDINGS
- business representative, as of a university SYNDIC
- business under another company's control SUBSIDIARY COMPANY
- business venture of a risky or daring kind FLIER
- businesslike and practical, dealing with or relating to facts and actual circumstances rather than theories or ideals PRAGMATIC
- business's most impressive or successful product FLAGSHIP
- business's owner or owner-manager PROPRIETOR
- authorization given by a business enterprise to dealers to use its name and products or formula FRANCHISE
- combining or uniting of separate businesses into a larger whole CONSOLIDATION
- exclusive control over some market or business activity MONOPOLY
- form a business into a registered company INCORPORATE
- "in or of the current month," as used in business correspondence INSTANT, INST.
- "in or of the next or following month," as used in business correspondence PROXIMO, PROX.
- "in or of the previous month," as used in business correspondence ULTIMO, ULT.
- launching or financing of a business venture by means of a share issue FLOTATION
- recruiting of business executives

for one firm from another firm HEADHUNTING
- rules, or the document containing them, required for registering a business ARTICLES OF ASSOCIATION
- trademark, symbol, or emblem of a business company LOGO
- undertake a variety of activities or investments, as a large business might DIVERSIFY

businessman or -woman of great wealth and influence MAGNATE, TYCOON
- businessman or -woman undertaking ventures requiring risk and initiative ENTREPRENEUR

bust - short pillar with a stone bust on top, used as a boundary marker or architectural ornament in ancient Rome TERM, TERMINUS

bustle - woman's fashionable forward-tilting posture in the late 19th century, often enhanced by a bustle GRECIAN BEND

busy and persevering in carrying out one's duty, industrious SEDULOUS, ASSIDUOUS, DILIGENT
- busy in a bustling, energetic way VIBRANT, DYNAMIC
- busy in a feverish way HECTIC, FRANTIC

busybody or gossip QUIDNUNC

but, *and*, or similar conjunction joining words, phrases, or clauses of equal status in a sentence COORDINATING CONJUNCTION
- *but*, *however*, or other word expressing contrast or opposition ADVERSATIVE, DISJUNCTIVE

Butterflies

Tiger swallowtail
Georgia satyr
Variegated fritillary
Banded hairstreak
Cabbage butterfly
Monarch
Tawny emperor
Orange sulfur

Throughout history, butterflies have appealed to the human imagination as symbols of ephemeral beauty.

Black swallowtail
American copper
Wood nymph
Red admiral
American tortoiseshell
Great-spangled fritillary
Great purple hairstreak
California tortoiseshell
Silver-spotted skipper

butcher's chopping knife CLEAVER
- butcher's frame from which animal carcasses are hung GAMBREL

butler or chief steward MAÎTRE D'HÔTEL, MAÎTRE D', MAJORDOMO

butter, lard, or oil, as used to make crumbly cookies or flaky pastry SHORTENING
- clarified butter from buffalo's milk, used in cooking in India GHEE
- purify butter or fat by gentle heating CLARIFY
- relating to, resembling, or containing butter BUTYRACEOUS
- stale, decomposing, as old butter or bacon fat might be RANCID

buttercup RANUNCULUS

butterfly See illustration, and also **caterpillar**
- butterfly, moth, or related insect LEPIDOPTERAN
- expert in or collector of butterflies and moths LEPIDOPTERIST
- pupa of a moth or butterfly, often cased in a cocoon CHRYSALIS
- transformation, as of a caterpillar into a butterfly METAMORPHOSIS

buttocks, rump, posterior BREECH, FUNDAMENT, HAUNCHES, HUNKERS, NATES, DERRIÈRE, KEISTER
- development of large fatty deposits in the buttocks, as among many Bushmen STEATOPYGIA
- having beautiful or elegantly shaped buttocks CALLIPYGIAN

buttonhole flower BOUTONNIERE

buyer, purchaser VENDEE
- principle that the buyer bears the risk CAVEAT EMPTOR

buying and selling of a commodity in a risky but potentially very profitable way SPECULATION
- buying of currencies, shares, bonds, or the like for quick resale at a higher price ARBITRAGE

buzzing or ringing in the ear as a medical condition TINNITUS
- buzzing toy instrument activated by the player's humming KAZOO

by airplane, by air mail PAR AVION

by chance, accidental, unplanned HAPHAZARD, FORTUITOUS, SERENDIPITOUS, COINCIDENTAL, HAPLY

by definition, by its very nature IPSO FACTO

by heart BY ROTE

by right, legally DE JURE

by the way, in passing APROPOS, INCIDENTALLY, EN PASSANT, PARENTHETICALLY, WHILE ON THE SUBJECT

C

cabbage salad, finely shredded with mayonnaise COLESLAW
- cabbage with tightly packed crinkled leaves SAVOY
- shredded or chopped cabbage, salted and fermented in its own juice SAUERKRAUT

cabin, especially a large and comfortable private cabin, on a ship STATEROOM
- cabin or hut, typically crudely built and run-down SHANTY

cabinet or low chest of drawers, typically on short legs and richly ornamented COMMODE
- reorganization of cabinet secretaries or ministers undertaken by the President or prime minister RESHUFFLE
- cabinet minister's post or duty in the government PORTFOLIO
- unofficial yet powerful advisers to a government who are not members of the official cabinet KITCHEN CABINET

cable, suspended from pylons, of an electric railway, streetcar, or the like CATENARY
- cable car, or transport system using such cars TELPHER
- cable car, ski-lift cabin, or the like GONDOLA
- cable or rope for anchoring or towing a ship HAWSER
- cable or rope supporting a mast, radio tower, or the like GUY, STAY
- cable railway FUNICULAR
- cables used to start a car by connecting its dead battery to another car's active battery JUMPER CABLES, JUMP LEADS
- rotating drum on the deck of a ship around which ropes or cables are wound CAPSTAN

cactus or other plant that thrives in a very dry environment XEROPHYTE
- cactus or similar plant with fleshy, sap-conserving stems or leaves SUCCULENT
- Mexican cactus yielding a hallucinatory drug MESCAL, PEYOTE

café or small shabby bar, especially in France ESTAMINET

cafeteria See **restaurant**
- cafeteria of a movie company or radio studio COMMISSARY

caffeine or other drug, food, or drink that temporarily increases activity or efficiency STIMULANT

cage for molting hawks MEW
- cage or container for small plants or animals TERRARIUM
- large cage for birds AVIARY

cake See chart, and also **dessert**
- cake decoration, consisting of the candied stem of an aromatic plant ANGELICA
- cakes, pastries, sweets, and other sweet items of prepared food CONFECTIONERY
- rich cakes and pastries, or a bakery selling them PATISSERIE

calculate and thereby ascertain COMPUTE, DETERMINE, CIPHER
- calculating device, as used in Asia, operated by moving beads on rods ABACUS
- calculating procedure using a series of steps ALGORITHM
- calculation of a rough-and-ready kind, based largely on guesswork DEAD RECKONING

calculations - aid to calculations, especially in the form of a table or list READY RECKONER

calculator - circuit in a calculator where figures are stored and computed ACCUMULATOR, MICROCHIP

calendar, with its system of leap years and new-style system of dates, introduced by Pope Gregory XIII GREGORIAN CALENDAR
- calendar in use before the current Gregorian calendar JULIAN CALENDAR
- calendar listing information such as tide patterns and weather statistics ALMANAC
- church calendar noting important religious events for each month MENOLOGY
- day falling roughly at the end of the first week of each month in the ancient Roman calendar NONES
- day falling roughly in the middle of each month in the ancient Roman calendar IDES
- first day of each month in the ancient Roman calendar CALENDS
- insertion of a day or days into the standard calendar to regularize it, as in leap years INTERCALATION, EMBOLISM

calf, especially a female calf, of about a year old STIRK
- calf or other baby domestic animal that is born prematurely SLINK
- hand-reared, as a calf might be CADE
- motherless calf DOGIE
- sterile female calf born as the twin of a male calf FREEMARTIN
- stomach lining of calves, or an extract of it used in cheesemaking RENNET

call, name, give a title or name to DESIGNATE, NOMINATE, STYLE, DUB
- call forth ELICIT, EVOKE
- call or address to an absent or dead person or personified thing APOSTROPHE
- call upon for help INVOKE
- ringing or inspiring, as a call to action might be CLARION

calling or strong inclination, as to a religious life VOCATION

calm, quiet, and passive SUBDUED, QUIESCENT
- calm, unemotional, expressionless IMPASSIVE, DISPASSIONATE
- calm and composed, self-possessed SEDATE
- calm and impassive in the endurance of pain or grief STOICAL
- calm and peaceful or quiet, typically in a dignified way TRANQUIL, SERENE
- calm and unexcitable in temperament or manner PLACID, IMPERTURBABLE
- calm and consistently even-tempered EQUABLE
- calm in the face of difficulties, accepting or resigned FATALISTIC, PHILOSOPHICAL
- calm or magically peaceful, as a childhood might be HALCYON
- calm state of restfulness, relaxation REPOSE
- calming, relaxing, soothing, as a medical drug might be SEDATIVE, ATARACTIC
- calming medicinal drug BROMIDE
- calmly detached, sober, and distant STAID, ALOOF
- calmly indifferent, unemotional PHLEGMATIC
- coolness, calm self-control or poise COMPOSURE
- even-temperedness, calm self-possession EQUANIMITY

CAKES, COOKIES, AND BISCUITS

LARGE CAKES	
angel cake	light almond sponge
Battenberg cake	striped, colored sponge layers covered in marzipan
Genoa cake	sponge cake, usually with cherries
kuchen	sugar-topped, yeast-dough coffee cake with fruit and nuts
lardy cake	sweet, breadlike cake with currants
panettone	Italian yeast cake
parkin	spiced, gingery cake
Sacher torte	rich, iced chocolate cake with a jam filling, of Austrian origin
savarin	rich, ring-shaped yeast cake
simnel	traditional Easter fruit cake
torte	rich layer cake
SMALL CAKES AND BUNS	
Banbury cake	pastry cake filled with raisins
brownies	flat chocolate squares with nuts
Chelsea bun	sugar-topped currant bun
drop scone/girdle cake/griddle cake	small, thick pancake
Eccles cake	sugar-topped, flaky pastry case with currant filling
frangipane	cream-filled, almond-flavored pastry
madeleine	small sponge cake with a jam or coconut coating
maid of honor	custard tart flavored with almond
napoleon/mille-feuille	small flaky pastry filled with cream and jam
petit four	tiny, decoratively iced cake
popover	very light muffin
queen cake	iced sponge cake with currants, often heart-shaped
rum baba	yeast-leavened, rum-flavored sponge cake
Sally Lunn	light tea cake
COOKIES AND BISCUITS	
Bath Oliver	large round unsweetened biscuit, often eaten with cheese
brandy snap	sweet, very thin cylindrical ginger cookie
farl	thin triangular Scottish biscuit, typically of oatmeal
florentine	rich flat cookie of nuts and dried fruit with a chocolate backing
garibaldi	thin cookie enclosing a layer of currants
gingersnap/gingernut	flat, brittle cookie spiced with ginger
hardtack/ship's biscuit	hard unflavored biscuit or bread formerly eaten by sailors
jumble/jumbal	light, crisp cake, typically with fruit or almonds and either ring-shaped or rolled up
langue de chat	long, thin, finger-shaped sweet biscuit
macaroon	small, light, almond or coconut cookie
oatcake	cake of baked oatmeal
pretzel	crisp, salted biscuit, typically shaped like a loose knot
ratafia	small macaroon
shortbread	cookie of flour, sugar, and butter

- imperturbable calm, unruffled temperament SANGFROID
- interval of calm LULL
- pacify or calm, as by making concessions MOLLIFY, PLACATE, APPEASE, CONCILIATE
- reconcile, or calm an offended person or power PROPITIATE
- slacken, calm down, or simmer down, as a temper or raging storm might SUBSIDE, ABATE
- soothe, calm, or relieve ASSUAGE
- soothe, dispel, or calm someone's fears ALLAY, QUELL

Calvinist - referring to a Calvinist or Zwinglian church REFORMED

camel See illustration, page 84
- camel of an Arabian breed, having a single hump DROMEDARY
- camel with two humps, originating in central Asia BACTRIAN CAMEL

cameo or other ornament or sculpture in low relief ANAGLYPH
- design cut into the surface of a hard material, as opposed to a cameo INTAGLIO

camera See also **lens, photography**
- camera movement sweeping over a scene or following a moving object or actor PAN
- camera or projector for cinematic films CINEMATOGRAPH

- camera stand or support with three legs TRIPOD
- camera support consisting of a one-legged stand MONOPOD
- camera that produces a print a few seconds after taking the photograph POLAROID
- camera using a single lens to direct the image both onto the film and into the viewfinder SINGLE-LENS REFLEX CAMERA, SLR
- button on a camera pressed to take a photograph SHUTTER RELEASE
- disc in a camera with an adjustable opening to control the amount of light admitted through the lens DIAPHRAGM, STOP
- five-sided prism in an SLR camera that deflects the image into the viewfinder PENTAPRISM
- focusing device in a camera based on bringing together the images produced from two different angles RANGE FINDER
- lens movement toward or away from the subject ZOOM
- lens or group of lenses producing the image in a camera or projector OBJECTIVE
- opening in a camera that is adjusted to limit the amount of light from the lense APERTURE
- short flexible syringe-operated wire used to operate a camera's shutter from a distance without shaking CABLE RELEASE, REMOTE CONTROL

camouflage - defense mechanism of a vulnerable animal, whereby it closely resembles a dangerous or unpalatable species and so deters predators PROTECTIVE COLORING, BATESIAN MIMICRY
- have a strong similarity or striking resemblance to something else, often as a means of camouflage MIMIC, SIMULATE
- referring or relating to the coloring of an animal that serves as camouflage APATETIC

camp - camp follower or army shopkeeper in former times, who sold provisions to soldiers SUTLER
- camp for ox-wagon travelers OUTSPAN
- camp for temporary accommodation, as for refugees or emigrants TRANSIT CAMP
- camp of a rough and temporary kind, as set up during a military operation or mountaineering expedition BIVOUAC
- camp or temporary buildings for quartering troops CANTONMENT
- campsite services building LODGE
- defensive camp, protected by wagons LAAGER
- small, portable camping stove, burning paraffin or oil PRIMUS

campaign for votes from people or a region in an election CANVASS
- campaign fervently in favor of a cause CRUSADE
- campaign of vindictive slander or obstructiveness VENDETTA
- campaigning for elections HUSTINGS
- catchphrase, motto, jingle, or the like used repeatedly, as in political campaigns SLOGAN, BANNER

Canada - financial center of Canada, or financial interests BAY STREET

canal, channel, or small dam, or the gate or valve holding back or regulating the water SLUICE
- artificial canal or water channel AQUEDUCT
- canal boat in Venice, propelled by a single oar at the stern GONDOLA
- dam in a river or canal to raise the water or regulate its flow WEIR
- path along a canal or river, as still sometimes used by horses pulling boats TOWPATH, BRIDLEPATH
- uninterrupted stretch of water on a river or canal REACH

cancel, deprive of force or validity, make useless or ineffective NULLIFY, INVALIDATE, VITIATE, ANNUL, ABROGATE
- cancel a claim, disown a belief, or the like RETRACT, RECANT, RENOUNCE, ABJURE, DISAVOW
- cancel a punishment REMIT
- cancel or abolish a law, ruling, or the like REPEAL, REVOKE, QUASH, ABROGATE
- cancel or erase, as by crossing through or obliterating DELETE, EFFACE, EXPUNGE
- cancel or reverse an order or command COUNTERMAND, RESCIND
- canceling of common factors in a fraction, or converting a fraction to a decimal REDUCTION

cancer - cancer-causing CARCINOGENIC
- cancer or malignant tumor CARCINOMA
- cancer treatment by means of drugs rather than radiation CHEMOTHERAPY
- cancer treatment by means of X-rays, injection of radioactive chemicals, and the like RADIOTHERAPY
- apparent decline in the severity of a disease such as cancer REMISSION
- cell used in cancer studies and biological research HE-LA CELL
- drug derived from peach pips, allegedly useful in cancer treatment VITAMIN B-17, LAETRILE
- fatal, certain to end in death, as an inoperable cancer is TERMINAL
- noncancerous, controlled or unthreatening to life, as a tumor might be BENIGN
- protein produced in response to a virus and inhibiting its spread, used experimentally in cancer treatment INTERFERON
- spread of cancer cells from one part of the body to another METASTASIS
- spreading uncontrolled, and resistant to treatment, as a cancer tumor is MALIGNANT
- test for cancer of the cervix in women PAP TEST, SMEAR TEST

cancer (combining form) -OMA

candid See **frank, honest**

candle consisting of a reed pith coated in tallow RUSHLIGHT
- candle holder of a large and branched design, usually hanging from the ceiling CHANDELIER
- candle lit and placed before a statue or shrine, especially in a Roman Catholic church VIGIL LIGHT
- candlemaker or candle seller CHANDLER

Camels

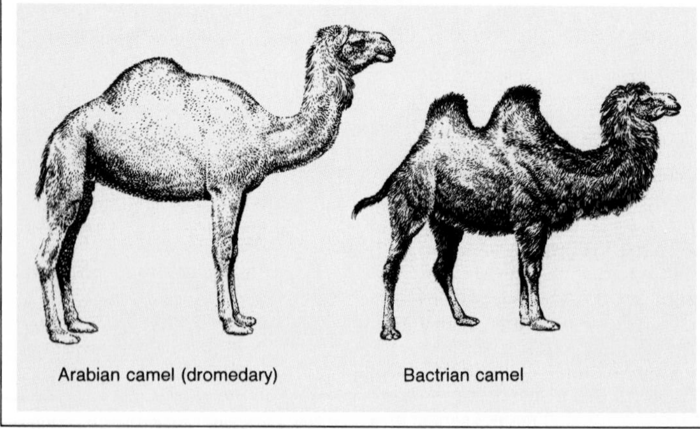

- candle of a small or thin kind TAPER
- burn unevenly and drip wax down one side, as a candle might GUTTER
- extinguish a candle or trim the charred end of its wick SNUFF
- hard fatty substance extracted from beef or lamb fat, used in making candles TALLOW
- put out a flame, candle, or the like DOUSE, EXTINGUISH

candlestick attached to a handle or a bracket SCONCE
- candlestick of a large and ornamental kind FLAMBEAU
- candlestick with a spike for keeping the candle upright, or the spike itself PRICKET
- candlestick with many branches, typically attached to a wall or mirror GIRANDOLE
- candlestick with several arms CANDELABRUM
- candelabrum of seven or nine arms in Jewish tradition MENORAH
- stand or table for supporting torches or candlesticks TORCHÈRE

cane, ruler, or the like for beating children, especially on the hand FERULE
- cane from a tropical Asian palm, as used for wickerwork furniture and walking sticks RATTAN
- cane made from the stem of the rattan palm MALACCA CANE
- cane or short stick carried by army officers SWAGGER STICK

cannabis HEMP, INDIAN HEMP, HASHISH, MARIJUANA

canned Norwegian herring SILD

cannibals ANTHROPOPHAGI
- human flesh as eaten by cannibals LONG PIG

cannon firing shells at a steep angle HOWITZER
- cannon or machine-gun emplacement in the form of a low round concrete building PILLBOX
- cluster of small projectiles fired from cannons GRAPESHOT
- harness strapped to a soldier for hauling cannons BRICOLE
- pin on either side of a cannon, container, or the like enabling it to be pivoted on a supporting frame TRUNNION
- platform or mound along the wall of a fort, from which cannons are fired BARBETTE
- plug or cover for the muzzle of a cannon when not in use TAMPION

canoe - canoe's float, attached parallel to one or both sides for stabilization OUTRIGGER
- Eskimo canoe KAYAK

canonical hours See chart

canopy or other covering, as for a boat or wagon TILT
- canopy over a bed, altar, or the like TESTER
- canopy placed over an altar or dais, or used in church processions BALDACHIN
- canvas canopy over the entrance to a theater, club, or the like MARQUEE

canvas bed, suspended at both ends HAMMOCK
- canvas cover, shaped like a tent, for temporary exhibitions or the like MARQUEE
- canvas used as a waterproof covering TARPAULIN

cap See also **hat**
- cap as used in a toy pistol or in an ancient firearm, that explodes when struck PERCUSSION CAP
- cloth flap at the back of a cap, against sunburn HAVELOCK
- types of cap worn by Roman Catholic clergymen BIRETTA, CALOTTE, ZUCCHETTO

capable See **able, expert**

capital or principal sum of money, value of an estate, or the like, as distinct from the interest or income CORPUS
- capital provided for new business enterprises VENTURE CAPITAL

capital letter MAJUSCULE, UPPERCASE LETTER
- letter of the alphabet that is not a capital letter MINUSCULE, LOWERCASE LETTER

capital punishment - person who urges or favors getting rid of capital punishment ABOLITIONIST
- person who urges or favors the retaining of capital punishment RETENTIONIST

captive of a kidnapper or hijacker HOSTAGE

CANONICAL HOURS

NAME OF PRAYER SERVICE	TIME ASSIGNED
matins, with lauds	dawn
prime	6 A.M.
terce	9 A.M.
sext	noon
none	3 P.M.
vespers	early evening
compline	just before bedtime

captivity, dependency, enslavement THRALL, THRALLDOM

captured weapons and other spoils of victory TROPHY

car See illustration, page 86, and also **vehicle**
- car body COACHWORK
- car body or aircraft fuselage in which the stress is taken mainly by the casing MONOCOQUE
- car made before 1905 VETERAN CAR
- car made between 1905 and 1919 EDWARDIAN CAR
- car made between 1919 and 1930 VINTAGE CAR
- car of a very long and luxurious design LIMOUSINE
- car of an early type with a folding roof over the rear seat LANDAU
- car or other possession or project, expensive and inefficient, requiring more trouble than it is worth WHITE ELEPHANT
- car or other vehicle that is old, noisy, and run-down BONESHAKER, JALOPY, RATTLETRAP
- car radio device used for private radio communication between drivers CITIZENS' BAND RADIO, CB, CELLULAR PHONE
- car that is old-fashioned, especially a Model T Ford TIN LIZZIE
- car whose roof can be folded back CONVERTIBLE, CABRIOLET
- car with a souped-up engine HOT ROD
- car with an upward-opening door at the rear HATCHBACK
- car with two doors COUPE, COUPÉ
- air deflector, as on an aircraft's wing or a racing car, to increase drag and reduce the tendency to lift SPOILER
- airstream behind a fast-moving car or bicycle SLIPSTREAM
- board on small wheels or casters, for lying on when working under a car CREEPER, CRADLE
- brand name of a car MARQUE
- built according to the buyer's specifications, as a car might be CUSTOM-BUILT
- canvas roof of a car that opens by folding back DROPHEAD
- closed car of a fairly large and standard design with two rows of seats SEDAN
- decorative line painted along the side of a car or other vehicle COACH LINE, CARRIAGE LINE
- degree of stability of a car, as on wet roads ROADHOLDING
- flashing of all the indicators on a car, as to warn other motorists during a breakdown HAZARD WARNING SIGNAL
- footboard at the side of some old

cars RUNNING BOARD
- framework of a car, to which the body is attached CHASSIS
- indicator, especially of an early kind in the form of a small arm, on the side of a car, that swung out and lit up TRAFFICATOR, DIRECTION INDICATOR
- indoor light of a car COURTESY LIGHT
- loss in value, as of a car, as through age or wear DEPRECIATION
- luggage compartment or folding seat at the rear of some early automobiles RUMBLE SEAT, DICKEY BOX
- metal bar or frame strengthening a car roof in case of accident ROLL BAR
- polish a car with wax SIMONIZE
- process of or mechanism for igniting the fuel in an engine, as for starting a car IGNITION
- procession of cars or other motor vehicles MOTORCADE
- remove useful parts from a car, machine, or the like for repairing a similar model CANNIBALIZE
- shock-reducing system in a car, including springs and shock absorbers SUSPENSION
- sports car or similar sleek high-speed car GRAN TURISMO, GT
- shafts, gears, and the like transmitting power from the engine to the car's wheels TRANSMISSION
- system of elastic cords joined at the center, used for strapping down loads, as on a car roof SPIDER, OCTOPUS

car (combining form) AUTO-

carbohydrate (combining form)-OSE

carbon - carbon used in lead pencils and as a lubricant GRAPHITE, PLUMBAGO
- producing coal or carbon CARBONIFEROUS
- referring to carbon compounds in chemistry ORGANIC

carbon (combining form) ORGANO-

carbon paper - transfer a drawing without carbon paper by loosely shading or coloring its reverse side, and then tracing it onto a surface or paper underneath CALK

carbonated, emitting small bubbles of gas, as with soda water or a sparkling cold drink EFFERVESCENT

carburetor - tube with a narrow throat, as in a carburetor, for providing suction VENTURI

card for brief display to an audience, especially as a visual aid in the classroom FLASHCARD
- card or disc that is spun or twirled to produce a merged image of the partial words or pictures on either side THAUMATROPE
- cards of a kind used in fortune-telling TAROT CARDS
- fortune-telling by means of a pack of tarot or playing cards CARTOMANCY

card games See chart, and also **gambling, bridge game, poker**
- arrange playing cards secretly in a favorable order STACK
- card dealer or bet taker at a gambling table CROUPIER
- card that is the only one of its suit in a hand dealt SINGLETON
- cards not dealt out at the beginning of a game TALON, STOCK
- jack, queen, or king of any suit in a pack of cards COURT CARD
- observer, as at a card game, who offers uninvited comments or advice KIBITZER

Car

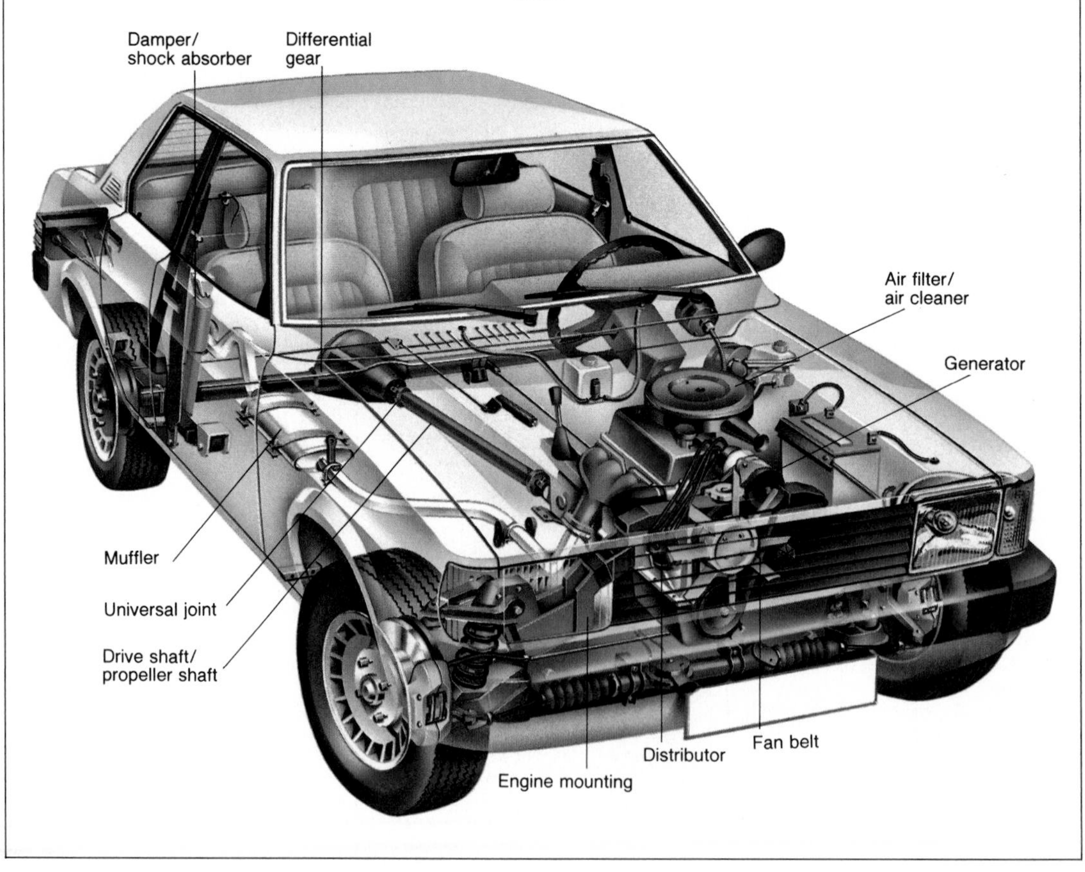

- play a trump in card games RUFF
- shuffle playing cards by flicking through two piles with the thumbs RIFFLE
- the highest cards, especially in trumps HONORS

cardboard as used in bookbinding PASTEBOARD
- cardboard to which a picture or photograph is pasted MOUNT

cardinal who handles the pope's financial affairs, papal treasurer CAMERLINGO
- assembly of cardinals, presided over by the pope CONSISTORY
- body or assembly of all the Roman Catholic cardinals, which elects and gives advice to the pope COLLEGE OF CARDINALS, SACRED COLLEGE

care, safekeeping, or guardianship, as of a minor CUSTODY, TUTELAGE
- careful in providing for one's own interests, especially in being thrifty PROVIDENT
- child, senile person, or the like under the legal care of a guardian or court of law WARD
- put into the care of someone ENTRUST, CONSIGN, COMMIT, COMMEND
- referring to spiritual care and guidance PASTORAL

care for, tend MINISTER

career, occupation, profession VOCATION, CALLING
- blossoming, emergence into prominence or success, as of a career EFFLORESCENCE
- person whose welfare is protected or whose career is advanced by an influential patron PROTÉGÉ
- summary of one's education and career, as for job applications CURRICULUM VITAE, RÉSUMÉ
- test identifying a person's skills and potential, often used as an aid in career guidance APTITUDE TEST

carefree, indifferent, easygoing, or unconcerned NONCHALANT, INSOUCIANT, DEBONAIR, BLITHE

careful in showing concern for others SOLICITOUS
- careful or alert, on one's guard or on the lookout VIGILANT
- careful or conscientious in a painstaking way, attentive to detail SCRUPULOUS, PUNCTILIOUS, DILIGENT, ASSIDUOUS, SEDULOUS
- careful or precise to a fault METICULOUS, FASTIDIOUS
- careful or tactful, showing caution or good judgment DISCREET, PRUDENT, JUDICIOUS, POLITIC
- careful or timid GINGERLY
- carefully assessing the possible consequences of an action, wary or chary CIRCUMSPECT
- carefully avoiding indicating any definite preference or purpose, as an evasive reply would NONCOMMITTAL

careless, showing insufficient judgment IMPROVIDENT, IMPRUDENT, INJUDICIOUS
- careless, untidy, slapdash SLOVENLY, SLIPSHOD
- careless and rash, reckless or impulsive IMPETUOUS, PRECIPITATE, HARUM-SCARUM
- careless in a clumsy or irresponsible way, heedless or lax REMISS, NEGLIGENT, FECKLESS
- careless through inattentiveness INADVERTENT

caretaker of a church in former times OSTIARY
- caretaker or doorman of a building, as of an apartment house or complex JANITOR, CONCIERGE, PORTER
- caretaker or keeper, as of an art collection CUSTODIAN, CURATOR, CONSERVATOR
- caretaker or porter of a building SUPERINTENDENT, SUPER, JANITOR
- caretaker's office LODGE

cargo list or inventory MANIFEST
- cargo or goods for delivery or disposal CONSIGNMENT
- cargo or wreckage remaining afloat after a ship has sunk FLOTSAM
- cargo thrown from a ship but marked by buoys for later recovery LAGAN
- cargo thrown overboard or washed ashore JETSAM
- large metal box of standard design for storing and transporting cargo CONTAINER
- load of cargo, passengers, bombs, or the like in an aircraft or spacecraft PAYLOAD
- stow cargo in a ship's hold STEEVE

caricature, crude and distorted imitation TRAVESTY

carnation, pink, or related flower DIANTHUS

carnival, holiday, feast, or celebration FIESTA
- carnival celebrations held on Shrove Tuesday MARDI GRAS
- carnival or lively celebration JAMBOREE

carol - carol singers WAITS
- carol sung at Christmas NOEL
- sing a part-song, such as a carol or round TROLL

carpentry See **joint**

carpet See also **rug**
- carpet of a flat-woven French type AUBUSSON
- carpet of English design or manufacture AXMINSTER, WILTON, KIDDERMINSTER
- coarse fabric or rough carpeting for covering a floor DRUGGET
- area bordering a carpet, doorway, or the like SURROUND
- edge, border, or fringe of a carpet, fabric, or the like finished so as to prevent unraveling SELVAGE
- long narrow carpet or tablecloth RUNNER
- long woolly nap, as on coarse cloth or a carpet SHAG
- soft raised velvety surface of a carpet PILE
- thick felt fabric laid under carpeting to increase insulation or resilience UNDERLAY

carriage, bearing, method of carrying or holding oneself when walking GAIT, DEPORTMENT

carriages See also chart at **horse-drawn vehicles**
- carriage entrance into the courtyard of a large house PORTE COCHERE
- carriage escort mounted on horseback OUTRIDER
- luggage compartment or folding seat at the rear of some carriages RUMBLE SEAT, DICKEY BOX

carrier, insect or other organism that transmits germs VECTOR

carry a sword or rifle diagonally across the body PORT
- carry lightly, as the wind carries the smell of flowers WAFT
- carrying or transportation, as of heavy supplies PORTAGE
- carrying something, such as

CARD GAMES

baccarat	**loo**
beggar-my-neighbor	**Michigan**
bezique	**monte**
blackjack/twenty-one/vingt-et-un	**nap, napoleon**
Black Maria	**old maid**
brag	**ombre**
bridge (auction, contract, duplicate)	**patience/solitaire**
canasta	**pinochle**
casino	**piquet**
chemin de fer	**poker (stud poker)**
concentration	**Pope Joan**
cribbage	**quadrille**
écarté	**racing demon**
euchre	**rouge et noir**
fantan	**rummy/gin rummy**
faro	**seven up**
five hundred	**skat**
gin/gin rummy	**snap**
hearts	**solo**
	speculation
	tarok
	war
	whist

nerve impulses, inward or toward a center, such as the brain AFFERENT
- carrying something, such as nerve impulses, outward or away from a center, such as the brain DEFERENT, EFFERENT

carry (combining form) -FER-

carry out a plan, operate IMPLEMENT, EXECUTE
- carry out or perform business TRANSACT

carrying (combining form) -PHORE, -PHOROUS

cart See also chart at **horse-drawn vehicles**
- open farm cart, or cart used during the French Revolution to transport condemned prisoners to the guillotine TUMBREL

Carthage - adjective for ancient Carthage PUNIC

cartilage(combining form) CHONDR-, CHONDRO-

cartoon portrait CARICATURE
- outline, roughly oval, for the printed words representing the speech or thoughts of a character in a cartoon strip BALLOON
- single scene in a cartoon strip FRAME

cartridge - former term for a cartridge, bullet, or box of cartridges CARTOUCHE

carved architectural ornament in the form of a basket of fruit CORBEIL
- carved or engraved articles of ivory, whalebone, or the like, typically made by sailors SCRIMSHAW

Casablanca - old quarter of a North African town such as Casablanca CASBAH

case See also **bag, suitcase**
- case for carrying papers BRIEFCASE, ATTACHÉ CASE
- case for holding loose papers or official documents PORTFOLIO, DISPATCH BOX
- action or decision in a law court used as an example or justification when treating a later case similarly PRECEDENT
- handbag or small case used by women for carrying cosmetics or toiletries VANITY CASE
- mention or list a case, example, or the like, as to support an argument CITE
- unshakably strong, without loopholes, as an argument or legal case might be IRONCLAD, WATERTIGHT

case history or full medical records of a patient ANAMNESIS

cash - having enough cash or assets to settle debts or run a business LIQUIDITY

cask See also **barrel**
- cask or small wooden barrel FIRKIN, KILDERKIN
- plug or bung in the vent of a cask SPIGOT, SPILE

casserole See also **food**
- casserole pot MARMITE

cast of characters in a play DRAMATIS PERSONAE
- cast off or molt a dead outer skin, as snakes do SLOUGH
- cast out evil spirits or demons, or free a possessed person from them EXORCISE
- casting a spell, summoning a spirit, or similar magic practice INCANTATION, INVOCATION, CONJUNCTION

caste See also chart at **Hinduism**
- member of the highest or priestly Hindu caste BRAHMAN
- untouchable, member of the lowest classes in Hindu society, technically outside the caste system HARIJAN

castle See illustration, and also **fortification**
- castle keeper or governor of a castle CASTELLAN, CHATELAIN, CHATELAINE, CONSTABLE
- castlelike, having turrets and battlements like a castle, or indentations resembling these CASTELLATED
- castle or manor house in France CHÂTEAU
- castle or stronghold protecting a town or city CITADEL
- back gate or door, as of a castle POSTERN
- embankment in front of a fort or castle, making attackers vulnerable to the defenders GLACIS, ESCARPMENT
- flat open area in front of a castle or other fortification, exposing the

Castle

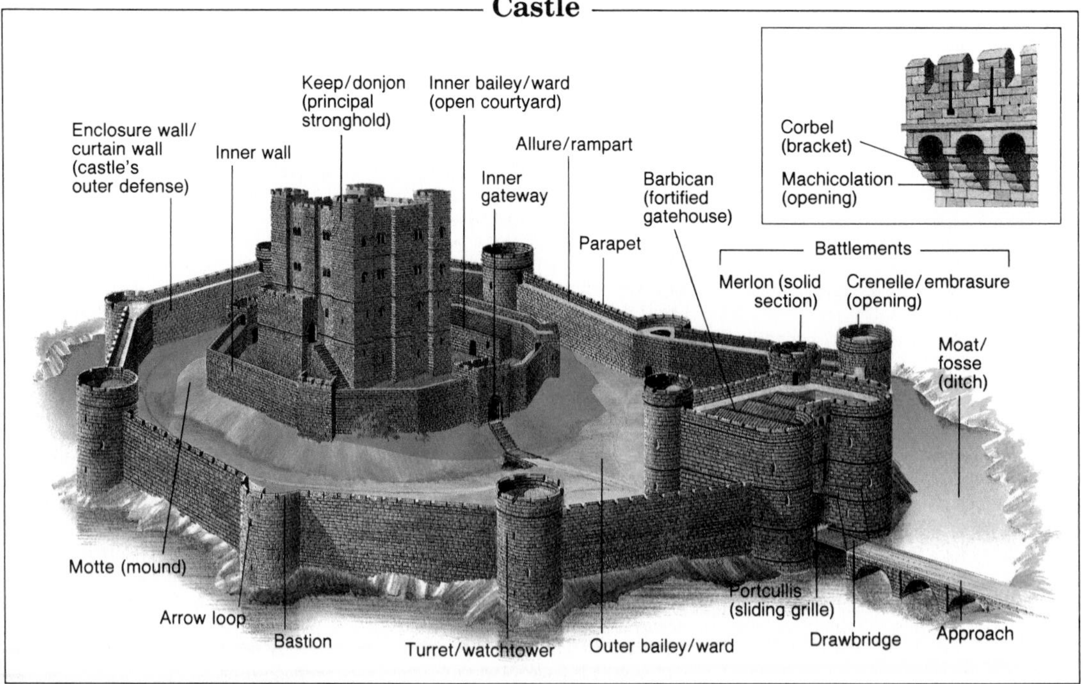

attackers to the defenders' fire ESPLANADE
- impossible to capture or enter forcibly, as a castle or fort might be IMPREGNABLE
- military governor or hereditary lord of a castle in medieval Germany BURGRAVE
- pathway between the moat and walls of a castle BERM
- slope formed, usually by rock debris, at the foot of a cliff, castle wall, or the like TALUS
- type or specific design of castle MOUND CASTLE, CONCENTRIC CASTLE, MOTTE-AND-BAILEY CASTLE

castrate, geld EMASCULATE, NEUTER
- castrated male chicken fattened for eating CAPON
- castrated male horse or other animal GELDING
- castrated male sheep WETHER
- castrated man, especially in former times, serving as a harem guard, court attendant, or the like EUNUCH
- pig castrated before reaching maturity BARROW
- pig or other male animal castrated after maturity STAG

casual, carefree, or unconcerned NONCHALANT, DEBONAIR, DÉGAGÉ, INSOUCIANT
- casual, disorganized HAPHAZARD, INDISCRIMINATE, LACKADAISICAL
- casual, offhand, or superficial, as a brief mechanical glance would be CURSORY, PERFUNCTORY
- casual, random, or unstructured, as a conversation might be DESULTORY
- casual, unimportant, or unplanned INCIDENTAL, UNPREMEDITATED
- chance, accidental, occurring casually or randomly CONTINGENT, ADVENTITIOUS, FORTUITOUS
- relating to or having casual sexual relationships with many partners PROMISCUOUS
- tendency to make casual finds of pleasing objects SERENDIPITY
- walk in a casual, leisurely, or aimless way, stroll SAUNTER, MEANDER, PROMENADE

casually, informally EN FAMILLE

cat See illustrations, pages 90 and 91
- cat, especially an old female cat, as in folk tales GRIMALKIN
- catlike mammal secreting a fluid used as a fixative in perfume making CIVET, ZIBET
- cat's whiskers or similar bristly hairs VIBRISSAE
- adjective for a cat FELINE
- brown or gray with darker streaks or spots, as a dog, cat, or cow might be BRINDLED
- informal term for a cat MOGGY
- shrill screech or cry, as of an excited cat CATERWAUL
- spotted forest cat of Central and South America OCELOT

catapult - catapultlike launcher of rocks or other heavy missiles, as used in ancient siege warfare BALLISTA, ONAGER, BRICOLE
- catapult or sling of large size, as used for hurling rocks, in medieval warfare TREBUCHET, MANGONEL

cataract - remove a cataract surgically by displacing the eye's lens downward COUCH

catastrophe, great destruction, or devastating battle or conflict ARMAGEDDON

catch, capture, or arrest APPREHEND
- catch a disease, become infected with CONTRACT
- catch or tangle in or as if in a net ENMESH
- catch or tear clothing on a nail, wooden stump, or the like SNAG
- catch or trap ENSNARE

catch fire IGNITE

catching, spreading, communicable, as a disease or laughter might be INFECTIOUS, CONTAGIOUS

catchphrase, motto, jingle, or the like used repeatedly, as in advertising or political campaigns SLOGAN, BANNER

category - title of a category or class RUBRIC

cater for someone's unworthy wishes PANDER

caterpillar See also **butterfly**
- creature resembling a caterpillar having two pairs of legs on each segment MILLIPEDE

cathedral or abbey in certain cities MINSTER
- cathedral surroundings or grounds PRECINCT, PURLIEU, CLOSE
- cathedral's canons as a group, or a meeting of them CHAPTER
- arched recess above a doorway, as at the entrance of a medieval cathedral TYMPANUM
- grotesque stone figure, as on a cathedral roof, often serving as a rainwater spout from a gutter GARGOYLE
- relating or belonging to a chapter of a cathedral CANONICAL

Catholic See **Roman Catholic**

cat's eye or similar twinkling gemstone CHATOYANT

cattle See also **ox**
- cattle dealer or driver DROVER
- cattle roundup, as for branding or counting RODEO, DRIFT
- cattle stall CRIB
- adjective for cattle BOVINE
- any of various hoofed, cud-chewing mammals, such as cattle, sheep, and deer RUMINANT
- drive cattle with a sharpened or electrified rod GOAD
- enclosure for cattle in southern Africa KRAAL
- enclosure for cattle or horses CORRAL
- flap of loose skin or hide hanging under the throat of cattle or dogs DEWLAP
- headlong rush, as of startled cattle or horses or of a panic-stricken crowd STAMPEDE
- infectious bacterial disease of cattle and sheep ANTHRAX
- infectious cattle disease of various severe kinds MURRAIN
- infectious viral disease of cattle, causing internal ulcers, literally "cattle plague" RINDERPEST
- rack or manger for fodder for cattle or other farm animals CRATCH

cauliflower - coated with breadcrumbs and sometimes cheese, and then grilled or browned, as cauliflower might be AU GRATIN

cause, as of a disease ETIOLOGY
- cause, bring about, devise, or produce ENCOMPASS, ENGENDER, PRECIPITATE
- cause, give rise to, prompt OCCASION, EFFECTUATE
- cause, provoke, stir up or promote INSTIGATE, FOMENT
- cause of a quarrel or war CASUS BELLI
- cause or principal source of some development MAINSPRING, FOUNTAINHEAD
- caused or developing outside the body or a body part EXOGENOUS
- caused or developing within the body or a body part ENDOGENOUS
- causing, promoting, contributing to, or favorable to a given result CONDUCIVE
- adopt or support a cause, faith, or ideal ESPOUSE
- belief or philosophy that everything follows inescapably from a cause or series of causes, and that there is no real free will DETERMINISM
- believer in or follower of a particular doctrine, cause, or the like ADHERENT
- defender or champion of a cause APOLOGIST
- energetically promoting a cause EVANGELISTIC
- person or thing that causes or provokes a change or event without itself being changed CATALYST
- self-generated, apparently uncaused SPONTANEOUS

Cats

SHORT-HAIRED BREEDS

Rex

Russian blue

Burmese

Havana brown

Korat

Siamese

Manx

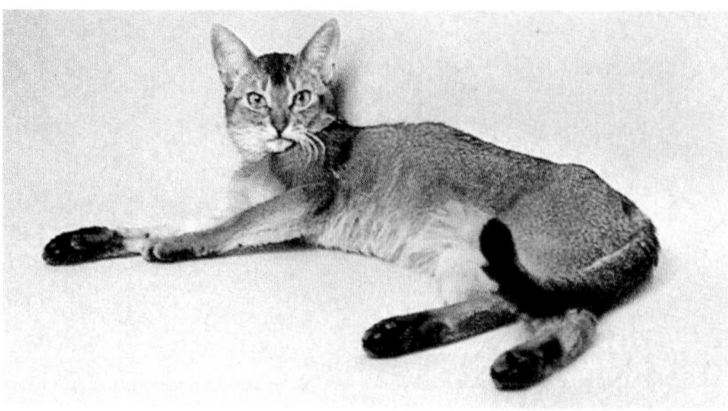
Abyssinian

LONG-HAIRED BREEDS

Maine coon

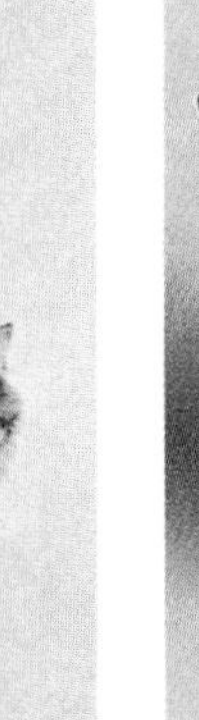

Birman

Persian

Balinese

Somali

Himalayan

Turkish Angora

cause (combining form) -GEN-, -GENESIS, -GENOUS
causing (combining form) -FACIENT, -FIC, -OTIC
cautious See **careful**
cavalry horse CHARGER
cavalryman having an ornate uniform of Hungarian design HUSSAR
cave drawing, rock painting, or other ancient or prehistoric drawing or painting PICTOGRAPH
- cave dweller or caveman TROGLODYTE
- cave of large size, or large chamber within a cave CAVERN
- cave or cavern, especially in a cliffside COVE
- iciclelike lime deposit hanging from the roof of a cave STALACTITE
- pillar or cone of lime deposit rising from the floor of a cave STALAGMITE
- small picturesque cave GROTTO
- study or exploration of caves SPELEOLOGY, SPELUNKING
caviar - caviar-producing fish STURGEON, BELUGA
cavity filled with gas or fluid, as in the body, plant tissue, or volcanic rock VESICLE
- cavity in the body, filled with fluid to reduce friction, as at joints BURSA
- cavity or blisterlike sac in the body, either normal or abnormal CYST
- pitted with small cells or cavities, honeycombed FAVEOLATE
cavity (combining form) -CEL-, COEL-, CELO-, COELO-
ceding or surrender of something, as of land, territory, or rights CESSION
ceiling, especially one decorated with paintings PLAFOND
- ceiling or roof or arched shape, typically of stone or masonry VAULT
- hanging sculpted ornament on a Gothic ceiling PENDANT
- inward curving surface between a ceiling and wall, or a concave molding COVE, COVING
- light fixture, large and branched, usually hanging from the ceiling, holding many bulbs or candles CHANDELIER
- ornamental sunken panel in a ceiling, dome, or the like COFFER, LACUNA, CAISSON
celebrate noisily ROISTER, REVEL
- celebrate or glorify splendidly and showily EMBLAZON
- celebrate riotously in public MAFFICK
celebration See also **party**
- celebration, as of a triumph JUBILANCE, JUBILATION, EXULTATION
- celebration of an anniversary JUBILEE
- celebration or festivity marked by heavy drinking and revelry WASSAIL, CAROUSAL, BACCHANAL
- celebration or pleasure outing, especially by public officials using public funds JUNKET
- noisy party or wild celebration SHINDIG
- solemn celebration or observance of an anniversary, such as a remembrance ceremony COMMEMORATION
- unrestrained licentious celebration, orgy, revelry SATURNALIA
celebrity or VIP PERSONAGE, DIGNITARY, LUMINARY
- treat someone as a celebrity LIONIZE
celestial bodies See chart at **astronomy**
cell biology CYTOLOGY
- cell division, as in a fertilized ovum CLEAVAGE, SEGMENTATION
- cell division in genetics MEIOSIS, MITOSIS
- cell tissue from which nails and teeth develop MATRIX
- cell used in cancer studies and biological research HE - LA CELL
- basic living matter in a plant or animal cell PROTOPLASM
- destruction or dissolving of a cell CYTOLYSIS
- fertilized egg or ovum, cell formed by the fusion of two reproductive cells ZYGOTE
- similarity of form or structure, as in different cells or crystals ISOMORPHISM
- sperm cell, male reproductive cell SPERMATOZOON
- sperm cell, ovum, or other cell that can combine to form a fertilized cell GAMETE
- splitting of a one-celled plant or animal as a means of reproduction FISSION
- tissue, typically a single layer of tightly packed cells, covering body organs and surfaces EPITHELIUM
- underground cell or dungeon whose door is in the ceiling OUBLIETTE
cell (combining form) CYT-, CYTO-, -CYTE, -BLAST, -PLAST
cell material (combining form) -PLASM
cell nucleus (combining form) KARY-, KARYO-
cellar - beer hall or German restaurant, originally in the cellar of a town hall RATHSKELLER
Celtic, relating to ancient Cornwall, Wales, Cumbria, and Brittany BRYTHONIC
- Celtic or Gaelic, or relating to a Gaelic speaker GOIDELIC
- Celtic people of the branch to which the Welsh, Cornish, and Bretons belong CYMRY
cement mixture or finish, as on a floor SCREED
- cement mixture or plaster used for coating walls PARGETING
- cement or mortar mixture for filling cracks or seams, as in brickwork or between tiles POINTING, GROUTING
- cement or other binding agent MATRIX
- cement that can set under water PORTLAND CEMENT
- tray, with a handle underneath, for carrying cement or plaster HAWK
- volcanic rock that can be ground for making cement TRASS
cemetery See also **burial**
- cemetery, burial place GOLGOTHA
- cemetery, especially a large and elaborate cemetery of an ancient city NECROPOLIS
censer THURIBLE
censor, remove from a text the parts considered indecent EXPURGATE, BOWDLERIZE
- censor or ban, prohibit, suppress PROSCRIBE, INTERDICT
- censor or edit out BLUE-PENCIL
- censor the press, free speech, or the like MUZZLE
- license for the publication of a book, as by a bishop or censor IMPRIMATUR, NIHIL OBSTAT
census - person who delivers and picks up census forms ENUMERATOR
center of a wheel or fan HUB
- center of attention, interest, or action FOCUS
- center of power, influence, or interest GANGLION
- center or fundamental part around which others are grouped or from which development takes place NUCLEUS
- central or key component or participant LINCHPIN
- direct away from or move outward and separate from a common center DIVERGE
- direct toward, move toward, or meet at a common center CONVERGE
- having a common center, as two circles of different sizes might CONCENTRIC
- having different or offset centers, as two overlapping circles would ECCENTRIC
- moving or growing inward, toward a center or axis CENTRIPETAL, AFFERENT

- moving or growing outward, away from a center or axis CENTRIFUGAL, EFFERENT
- stone at Delphi thought by the ancient Greeks to mark the center of the earth OMPHALOS

center (combining form) MES-, MESO-

centigrade CELSIUS

centipede - arthropod resembling a centipede having two pairs of legs on each segment MILLIPEDE

central heating - switching or controlling device for regulating temperature, as in a refrigerator or central-heating system THERMOSTAT

centralized, having or referring to a strongly centralized rather than federal government UNITARY

ceramics See **pottery**

cereal See also **wheat**
- cereal fungus or disease ERGOT
- cereal grass producing edible glossy grains and a syrup SORGHUM
- cereal grass widely cultivated for grain and fodder MILLET
- cereal or breakfast food containing nuts, raisins, and the like MUESLI
- beat harvested cereal to separate the grain from the chaff THRESH, FLAIL
- expose harvested cereal to a current of air to separate the grain from the chaff WINNOW

ceremony, custom, or ritual marking a change of status in a person's life RITE OF PASSAGE
- ceremony, formality, etiquette DECORUM, PROPRIETY
- ceremony at which a new monument, work of art, or the like, is formally displayed to the public for the first time UNVEILING
- ceremony conferring an office, award, or honor on a person INVESTITURE, INDUCTION
- ceremony or ritual of admission, as to membership of a group INITIATION
- ceremony or service honoring the memory of a person or event COMMEMORATION
- ceremonial military procession parading flags TROOPING THE COLOR
- ceremonial parade of horses or cars, or similar colorful procession CAVALCADE
- celebrate a marriage, perform a ceremony, or the like with formal or religious rites SOLEMNIZE
- formal opening ceremony, installation, or beginning INAUGURATION, DEDICATION, COMMENCEMENT
- garments worn by those officiating or assisting at a church service or ceremonial rite VESTMENTS

certain, absolute, without reservation or ambiguity, conclusive UNEQUIVOCAL, CATEGORICAL
- certain, incapable of failure or error INFALLIBLE
- certain, indisputable, without doubt INDUBITABLE, INCONTROVERTIBLE
- certain, proved beyond doubt, unquestionable APODICTIC
- certain, unyielding, refusing to budge ADAMANT
- certain means of accomplishing one's goal OPEN SESAME
- certain outcome, result that is definite or inevitable FOREGONE CONCLUSION
- certain to happen INEVITABLE

certainty, confident assurance CERTITUDE

certificate, voucher, or other formal document DOCKET
- certificate awarded for passing a course of study, or the course itself DIPLOMA
- certificate of entitlement, such as a share certificate SCRIP

certify, confirm, assure WARRANT
- certified or guaranteed as being up to a set standard ACCREDITED

Ceylonese, Sri Lankan belonging to the majority ethnic community SINGHALESE

chain, rope, or the like, as used for steadying a load or mooring an aerial GUY
- chain or clasp formerly worn by women at the waist, and used for holding keys, a handkerchief, or the like CHATELAINE
- chain together, link in a series CONCATENATE, CATENATE
- chains or confining bands around the ankles or wrists MANACLES, FETTERS, SHACKLES
- peg or crosspiece, attached to a rope, chain, or the like, used for fastening or to prevent slipping TOGGLE

chain of events - projected or possible chain of events SCENARIO

chain reaction DOMINO EFFECT

chair See also **furniture**
- chair, usually enclosed and carried on poles by a pair of footmen, used as a vehicle in former times SEDAN CHAIR
- chair to which wrongdoers or suspects were formerly tied, as for ducking or public mockery CUCKING STOOL
- crosspiece linking and securing the legs of a chair STAVE, SALTIRE, STRETCHER
- fabric, padding, springs, and so on, as used in making a soft covering for chairs UPHOLSTERY
- single wooden slat, often decorated, as in the middle of the back of a chair SPLAT
- small swiveling wheel on each leg of an armchair, sofa, or the like, for easy moving CASTER
- upright sidepiece forming part of the back of a chair STILE

chairperson of a meeting or synod MODERATOR
- chairperson's hammer GAVEL

chalk ground for use in paint, polish, or putty WHITING
- chalky, containing or resembling calcium carbonate CALCAREOUS
- chalky crayon PASTEL
- process of becoming chalky or stony through the action of calcium salts CALCIFICATION

challenge, as to a duel THROW DOWN THE GAUNTLET
- challenge, criticize, attack as false IMPUGN
- challenge and rejection by the defendant, without having to give reasons, of certain proposed members of the jury in a criminal trial PEREMPTORY CHALLENGE
- challenge, or object such as a glove formerly thrown down to issue a challenge GAGE
- challenging problem or critical test for beginners PONS ASINORUM

chamber pot - chair containing a concealed chamber pot COMMODE
- empty one's chamber pot as a morning routine in prison SLOP OUT
- warning cry in former times, especially in Edinburgh, when emptying a chamber pot or other slops into the street GARDYLOO

Chamberlain - Neville Chamberlain's policy of concessions to Hitler in the 1930's APPEASEMENT

chameleon See illustration, page 94

champagne - sweetish rather than very dry, as a champagne might be SEC
- very dry, as a wine, especially champagne, might be BRUT

champion, leading supporter, as of a cult or doctrine GURU
- champion, supporter, upholder, as of a doctrine or cause ADVOCATE, PROPONENT

chance, accidental, occurring randomly CONTINGENT, ADVENTITIOUS, FORTUITOUS, HAPHAZARD
- chance, unexpected and unplanned, incidental or accidental UNPREMEDITATED, INADVERTENT
- chance of buying something such as a house before it is offered to others FIRST REFUSAL
- changes of fortune occurring by chance VICISSITUDES
- depending on or happening by chance or luck, random ARBITRARY, ALEATORY

Chameleon

Flap-necked chameleon

- taking a chance, in the hope of success ON SPEC
- tendency to make fortunate finds by chance SERENDIPITY

chandelier, large and circular, hanging on a church ceiling CORONA
- chandelier, or any of its glass pendants LUSTER
- chandelier illuminated with gas lights GASOLIER

change, adjust, or tailor, as to improve or harmonize MODIFY, REGULATE
- change, convert, transform COMMUTE, MUTATE, TRANSMUTE
- change, vary, give variety to DIVERSIFY, VARIEGATE
- change in direction, attitude, policy, or results, as from bad to good TURNAROUND, ABOUT-TURN, VOLTE-FACE, U-TURN
- change of mind on an impulse CAPRICE, WHIM
- change or adapt to new circumstances, accustom or accommodate oneself to ACCLIMATIZE, ORIENTATE, ORIENT
- change or adjust delicately, temper carefully, fine-tune MODULATE
- change or advance of a discontinuous or sudden, dramatic, and vast kind QUANTUM LEAP
- change or alter the tone or pitch of the voice INFLECT
- change or passing from one form or state to another TRANSITION, METAMORPHOSIS
- change or reverse the ordering or relative position of two or more things TRANSPOSE
- change or swing, repeatedly or waveringly, from one state or action to another ALTERNATE, VACILLATE, FLUCTUATE, OSCILLATE
- change or switching of sounds or letters within a word, as in the development of *bird* from the earlier *brid* METATHESIS
- change or transformation of a spectacular kind TRANSFIGURATION, METAMORPHOSIS, TRANSMOGRIFICATION
- change or transformation of one substance into another, specifically of the Communion bread and wine into the body and blood of Christ TRANSUBSTANTIATION
- change or transition of an abrupt, discontinuous kind SALTATION
- change sides, defect, become a renegade TERGIVERSATE, APOSTATIZE
- change slowly by degrees GRADUATE
- change that results in something new INNOVATION
- change the order or sequence of PERMUTE
- changes and development by slow or natural means, as of species, art, or social systems EVOLUTION
- changes in society, nature, or personal affairs VICISSITUDES
- constant change, instability FLUX
- not changing or aging IMMUTABLE
- person or thing that provokes a change or event without itself being changed CATALYST
- sudden and violent disturbance, radical change UPHEAVAL
- sum of money used to provide change at the start of a business day FLOAT
- unprincipled person who changes his policies or opinions to serve his interests TRIMMER, TIMESERVER

change (combining form) TROP-, TROPO-, -TROPIC, -PLASIA, -PLASY

change of life, discontinuation of the menstrual cycle in women MENOPAUSE, CLIMACTERIC

changeable See **changing**

changeless, motionless, or producing no movement or change STATIC, IMMUTABLE

changes having been made as MUTATIS MUTANDIS

changing, constantly altering, liable to change MUTABLE, LABILE
- changing, variable, shifting in shape, form, character, or mood PROTEAN
- changing constantly and rapidly, unpredictable QUICKSILVER, MERCURIAL, VOLATILE
- changing continually, disturbed, unstable TURBULENT, VERTIGINOUS
- changing course in speech or thought TANGENTIAL, DIGRESSIVE
- changing easily to new conditions, adaptable PLIABLE
- changing in color, shimmering, as some fabrics do SHOT, IRIDESCENT, OPALESCENT, TAFFETA
- changing in luster, twinkling, as a cat's eye or similar gemstone does CHATOYANT
- changing or inconsistent in affections or aims FICKLE
- changing or unpredictable in behavior or attitude ERRATIC, SKITTISH, CAPRICIOUS, WHIMSICAL
- changing series or pattern of events KALEIDOSCOPE, CAVALCADE, CAROUSEL
- constant changing, unsteadiness, inconstancy LEVITY
- constantly changing or fickle person CHAMELEON, PROTEUS

changing (combining form) TRANS-

changing money - fee or premium paid when changing money AGIO

channel, hollow, or cavity in the body, containing or conveying air, pus, blood, or the like SINUS
- channel, trench, or groove, as for drainpipes or electric wires CHASE
- channel connecting two large bodies of water STRAIT
- channel for excess water, as round the side of a dam SPILLWAY
- channel of a strong current of water RACE
- channel of very small size in the body, as in a bone CANALICULUS
- channel or bay extending inland from the sea, as to the mouth of a river ESTUARY, FIRTH, FIORD
- channel or ditch cut in the ground by rainwater or a stream GULLY
- channel or opening in the body MEATUS
- channel or pipe, as for rainwater or an electric cable CULVERT, CONDUIT
- channel or vessel in the body DUCT, VAS

- artificial water channel or chute, as for transporting logs FLUME
- relating to or containing channels for conveying blood, sap, or other biological fluids VASCULAR

chant of the medieval Church PLAINSONG
- chant or liturgical plainsong in the Roman Catholic Church GREGORIAN CHANT
- chant or recite in a half-musical tone INTONE, CANTILLATE
- chanting of ritual sounds or magic spells INCANTATION

chapel for seamen, or a Nonconformist chapel BETHEL
- chapel or altar built specially for prayers or mass for the benefactor's soul CHANTRY

chaperone, especially an elderly woman DUENNA

chaplain or clergyman PADRE

character See also **personality**
- character, distinctive spirit, or value system of a particular culture, people, artistic movement, or the like ETHOS
- character or ability CALIBER
- character or personality, characteristic thought or behavior patterns of a person HUMOR, DISPOSITION, TEMPERAMENT
- character written or printed slightly above another, as in ab^2 SUPERSCRIPT, SUPERIOR
- character written or printed slightly below another, as in H_2O SUBSCRIPT
- characters in a novel, play, or other literary work PERSONAE, DRAMATIS PERSONAE

characteristic, feature of personality TRAIT
- characteristic that makes up or compensates for faults or deficiencies, saving grace REDEEMING FEATURE, MITIGATING FACTOR
- characteristics, marks, or features of a very distinctive or important kind LINEAMENTS

charcoal grill of Japanese style, as used for cooking at table HIBACHI
- charcoal stick or drawing FUSAIN
- portable metal stand for burning coal or charcoal BRAZIER
- small brick of compressed charcoal or coal dust, used for fuel, as at barbecues BRIQUETTE

charge See also **accusation**
- charge formally with an offense or crime INDICT, ARRAIGN
- charge less than a rival in order to secure a greater share of trade UNDERCUT
- additional charge or cost SURCHARGE
- clear of a charge or blame, declare innocent EXONERATE, EXCULPATE
- essential or most telling part of an accusation, charge, or complaint GRAVAMEN
- lay a charge against someone before a court PREFER
- obviously fabricated for base purposes, as a false charge or accusation might be TRUMPED-UP

charitable, concerned for others' welfare, humanitarian ALTRUISTIC, PHILANTHROPIC
- charitable, kindly, showing great goodwill BENEVOLENT, BENEFICENT
- charitable or generous in an ungrudging way BOUNTIFUL, MUNIFICENT
- charitable or religious gift or offering OBLATION, OFFERTORY

charity, Christian love, loving-kindness, as distinct from erotic love AGAPE
- charity, small bribe, or tip, given in Eastern countries BAKSHEESH
- charity contribution, handout, or gift DONATION
- charity contribution that is small but considered generous WIDOW'S MITE
- charity or giving help, or a charitable gift BENEFACTION
- contribute or pledge a sum of money, as to a charity or for a telephone service SUBSCRIBE
- distributor of charity, alms giver, as on behalf of a church or royal household ALMONER
- formal agreement or pledge, as to pay a specified sum each year to a charity COVENANT
- person who receives charity, a favor, money from a will, or the like BENEFICIARY
- relating to charity ELEEMOSYNARY
- support a person or group undertaking a challenge on behalf of a charity SPONSOR

Charlemagne - relating to the life or times of Charlemagne or his Frankish dynasty CAROLINGIAN, CARLOVINGIAN

Charles - relating to the life or times of kings Charles I and II of England CAROLINE
- supporter of Charles I in the English Civil War CAVALIER, ROYALIST

charm, fetish, or amulet used in magic religious rituals of African origin OBEAH, OBI
- charm, magic stone, or the like supposedly giving supernatural powers or protection TALISMAN, FETISH, JUJU
- charm, spell, or priest, used typically in a Haitian religion of African origin VOODOO
- charm, win the confidence or affection of DISARM
- charm carried, usually around the neck, as a protection against evil or misfortune AMULET, PERIAPT
- charm or talisman in ancient Egypt in the form of a stone or earthenware beetle SCARAB
- charmed, spellbound ENRAPTURED, ENTRANCED, ENCHANTED, TRANSPORTED, RAVISHED
- charms, attractions, inducements, or appeal ALLURE, ENTICEMENTS, BLANDISHMENTS
- fixed formula of words recited as a prayer or charm PATERNOSTER
- magnetic personal charm and power of influence or inspiration CHARISMA
- strong personal charm and sensual attractiveness ANIMAL MAGNETISM

charming, fascinating, almost bewitching ALLURING, BEGUILING, CAPTIVATING
- charming in an insincere, overly earnest way, currying favor UNCTUOUS, INGRATIATING
- charming or picturesque event or scene IDYLL
- charmingly simple and unsophisticated NAIVE, RUSTIC

chart or graph consisting of a series of bars whose lengths indicate quantities BAR GRAPH, BAR CHART
- chart or graph in the form of a circle with sectors of varying size representing the units PIE CHART

chatter, talk in an aimless, rambling, or incoherent manner PRATTLE, GIBBER, MAUNDER

cheap, priced at the manufacturer's bulk price, as distinct from retail WHOLESALE
- cheap and showy, and typically of poor quality, as imitation jewelry might be GAUDY, TAWDRY, BRUMMAGEM, GIMCRACK, CATCHPENNY
- cheap imitation, fake PINCHBECK
- cheaply sentimental MAUDLIN, MAWKISH

cheat, swindle, fleece, defraud COZEN, BEGUILE, BILK
- cheat, trick, dupe, or deceive HOODWINK, MULET, GULL, FLIMFLAM, GAMMON
- cheat by arranging playing cards secretly in a favorable order STACK
- cheat or betray by breaking an agreement DOUBLE-CROSS
- cheat or trickster, con man such as a quack MOUNTEBANK, CHARLATAN
- cheating, crafty scheming, or trickery JIGGERY-POKERY
- cheating or deception, especially the adoption of a false identity IMPOSTURE
- cheating or deception by trickery or lying DUPLICITY, CHICANERY

- achieve or acquire by trickery or cheating, wangle FINAGLE
- easily deceived, cheated, or duped CREDULOUS, GULLIBLE

check, keep tabs on, vet MONITOR
- check and confirm, prove correct or genuine VERIFY, VALIDATE, AUTHENTICATE, CORROBORATE, SUBSTANTIATE
- check off or tick off item by item TALLY
- check or stop a flow of blood or funds STANCH, STAUNCH
- check shape or design on textiles HOUND'S-TOOTH CHECK
- check stub or similar detachable record of a transaction, as on a receipt or postal order COUNTERFOIL
- checked pattern of colored lines forming squares against a plain background TATTERSALL
- date a check or other document earlier than the date of writing ANTEDATE
- date a check or other document later than the date of writing POSTDATE
- place one's signature on a document, the back of a check, or the like, as to indicate agreement, receipt, or transfer ENDORSE

checkered, mosaiclike TESSELLATED

cheek of a rude or defiant kind, insolence, nerve GALL, EFFRONTERY, AUDACITY, TEMERITY
- cheek of a saucy, shameless, rather engaging kind, impudence CHUTZPAH

cheekbone JUGAL, MALAR, ZYGOMA, ZYGOMATIC BONE

cheeks or jaws JOWLS
- having rutted or hollow cheeks, as through exhaustion HAGGARD
- relating to the mouth or cheeks BUCCAL

cheeky, bold, saucy, sassy PERT, MALAPERT, IMPUDENT
- cheeky and uncooperative or unruly OBSTREPEROUS
- cheeky in an arrogant and disrespectful way PRESUMPTUOUS, BUMPTIOUS, INSOLENT
- cheeky in a defiant and contemptuous way BRAZEN
- cheeky or naughty child or young man JACKANAPES, WHELP

cheerful, confident, or optimistic SANGUINE
- cheerful and cosy, having a warm and friendly atmosphere GEMÜTLICH, CONGENIAL

cheese See illustration
- cheeselike CASEOUS
- coated with breadcrumbs and sometimes cheese, and then grilled or browned, as cauliflower might be AU GRATIN
- container or frame used in cheesemaking CHESSEL
- dish of hot melted cheese and wine, eaten with pieces of bread or meat dipped into it FONDUE
- formation of cheese during the

Cheese

Many cheeses are instantly recognizable by their distinctive appearance.

Some of the more famous cheeses are illustrated here.

1 Provolone
2 Parmesan
3 Samsoe
4 Edam
5 Gouda
6 Mimolette
7 Blue Cheshire
8 Fontina (Danish)
9 Stilton
10 Cheddar (Canadian)
11 Gloucester
12 Cheddar (English)
13 White Wensleydale
14 Ricotta
15 Bleu de Bresse
16 Dunlop
17 Mozzarella
18 Jaalsberg
19 Danish blue
20 Caciocavallo
21 Leicester
22 Feta
23 Fontina (Italian)
24 Gruyère
25 Monterey Jack
26 Tome au raisin
27 Lancashire
28 Caerphilly
29 Edelpilzkäse
30 Limburger
31 St. Nectaire
32 New England Sage
33 Red Windsor
34 Brick
35 Port Salut
36 Gorgonzola
37 Vacherin
38 Epoisses
39 Emmenthal
40 Dolcelatte
41 Tilsiter
42 Pont l'Évèque
43 Livarot
44 Quargel
45 Roquefort
46 Banon
47 St. Marcellin
48 Camembert
49 Münster
50 Brie
51 Bel paese
52 Maroilles

coagulation of milk CASEATION
- milk protein that forms the basis of cheese CASEIN
- prepare, treat, or rectify something, such as cheese or photographic film, by a special method PROCESS
- stomach lining of calves, or an extract of it used in cheesemaking RENNET

chef of a very high standard or rank CORDON BLEU

chemical See chart, pages 98–99
- chemical dissolving or wearing away, especially of metals CORROSION
- chemical secretion from glands, modifying the workings of a tissue or organ HORMONE
- burning or dissolving, as some chemicals are CAUSTIC, CORROSIVE

chemical (combining form) CHEM-, CHEMO-

chemistry See chart, pages 98–99
- misguided form of chemistry in the Middle Ages, seeking a cure-all medicine and a means of turning base metal into gold ALCHEMY

cherry preserved in liqueur MARASCHINO CHERRY
- dark sour cherry MORELLO
- firm, sweet, heart-shaped cherry BIGARREAU
- pale sour cherry AMARELLE
- shiny sugar-coated cherry GLACÉ CHERRY
- sweet wild cherry GEAN, MAZZARD

cherry brandy KIRSCH

cherub or small boy in baroque paintings, sculptures, or reliefs PUTTO, AMORETTO

chess - drawn position in chess, in which any possible move by a player would place his king in check STALEMATE
- move or series of moves in chess, involving the sacrifice of a pawn or other piece for a positional advantage GAMBIT
- phrase used when touching a chesspiece to position it correctly rather than to make a move J'ADOUBE
- position in chess in which a player is forced to make a disadvantageous move ZUGZWANG
- referring to a chess piece exposed to capture EN PRISE
- warning given to the opposing chess player that his or her queen is threatened GARDEZ
- winning position in chess, in which the opponent's king cannot escape CHECKMATE

chest, area of the body between the neck and abdomen THORAX
- crackling sound in the chest, as of pneumonia patients CREPITUS
- feeling of tightness or pressure, as in the chest CONSTRICTION
- relating to the chest or breast PECTORAL
- strongbox or chest, typically for storing valuables COFFER

chest of drawers or low cabinet, typically on short legs and richly ornamented COMMODE

chestnuts preserved and coated in syrup MARRONS GLACÉS

chew, grind, or crush MASTICATE
- chew or munch impatiently or noisily CHAMP
- chew or nibble at repeatedly GNAW
- chew the cud RUMINATE
- chewing mixture in India, made of betel nuts and leaves PAN
- chewing muscle MASSETER
- chewing tobacco in a wad QUID
- basic ingredient of chewing gum, gum from the sapodilla tree CHICLE

chewy and firm through being lightly cooked, as spaghetti might be AL DENTE

chick, young of a domestic fowl, especially a turkey POULT

chicken See also **food** and chart at **menu**
- chicken fat used in cooking SCHMALTZ
- chicken-rearing system involving confinement to cages for fast fattening or high production of eggs BATTERY
- chicken that is dressed, split open, and fried or grilled soon after slaughter SPATCHCOCK
- chicken's edible offal GIBLETS
- adjective for the domestic fowl or chicken GALLINACEOUS
- castrated male chicken fattened for eating CAPON
- disc of dark meat in the pelvic bone of a cooked chicken OYSTER
- tie up or skewer the wings or legs of a chicken or other fowl before cooking TRUSS
- very young chicken bred for eating POUSSIN

chicken pox VARICELLA

chickpea GARBANZO
- chickpea fritters or spicy delicacy of Middle Eastern origin FELAFEL
- chickpea paste, of Middle Eastern origin HUMMUS
- chickpeas, mung beans, or other seeds used for food in India GRAM

chief See also **leader, main**
- chief, foremost, leading, supreme PARAMOUNT, PREDOMINANT, PREEMINENT, PREPONDERANT
- Native American chief SACHEM, SAGAMORE

chief (combining form) ARCH-

chief magistrate of a Scottish burgh PROVOST

child, especially a younger male child, in a family SCION
- child, grandchild, or more remote offspring DESCENDANT
- child, senile person, or the like under the legal protection of a guardian or court of law WARD
- child formerly thought to have been secretly exchanged for another by fairies CHANGELING
- child of unknown parentage, found abandoned FOUNDLING
- child or animal wandering about homeless WAIF
- child or baby, especially an Italian one BAMBINO
- child or worker who fails to achieve the results he or she is capable of UNDERACHIEVER
- child or young animal that is still unweaned SUCKLING
- child suffering from a mental illness involving a severe inability to relate to other people AUTISTIC CHILD
- child that is poor, dirty, and ragged, or mischievous and cheeky URCHIN, RAGAMUFFIN
- child with exceptional powers or talents CHILD PRODIGY, WUNDERKIND
- children and all the other descendants of a person POSTERITY, PROGENY, OFFSPRING
- bounce a child affectionately up and down, especially on one's knees DANDLE
- developing or maturing unusually early, as a clever or sophisticated child seems to do PRECOCIOUS
- guardianship, as of a minor child or a prisoner CUSTODY
- nursery for babies or very young children, especially to enable parents to go to work DAY-CARE CENTER, CRECHE
- produce children, reproduce PROCREATE
- producing many children PROLIFIC, PHILOPROGENITIVE
- referring to a child born after the death of the father POSTHUMOUS
- referring to a child in early adolescence, on the brink of sexual maturing PUBESCENT
- term called out by children to secure exemption from some undesirable task FEN, FAINS
- young child, youngster, young kid SHAVER, TYKE, NESTLING, NIPPER, SPROG

child (combining form) PED-, PAED-, PEDO-, PAEDO-

childbirth See also **birth**
- childbirth, act or process of giving birth PARTURITION
- blood and tissue discharged normally after childbirth AFTERBIRTH,

SECUNDINES, LOCHIA
- custom in some cultures in which it is the husband who takes to bed while his wife is in labor or giving birth COUVADE
- hasten the onset of labor or childbirth, especially by the use of medicinal drugs INDUCE
- inducing contractions to bring on childbirth, as some drugs might OXYTOCIC
- occurring at or relating to the time just before or after birth PERINATAL
- relating to childbirth PUERPERAL
- relating to the care of women during pregnancy or after childbirth OBSTETRIC
- rest in bed for a woman just before or during childbirth CONFINEMENT, LYING-IN, ACCOUCHEMENT
- shortening or tensing of a muscle or organ, either voluntary or, as in childbirth, involuntary CONTRACTION
- toxic condition in a woman, involving convulsions and sometimes coma, shortly before childbirth ECLAMPSIA

childbirth (combining form) -PAROUS, -PARA

childhood years important in one's development FORMATIVE YEARS

childish or immature, especially in being silly or impulsive PUERILE, JUVENILE, JEJUNE

chill or shivering attack, as preceding a fever RIGOR

chimney or similar opening for the escape of fumes, steam, or the like VENT
- hoodlike cover on a chimney to control ventilation COWL, BONNET
- pipe or duct for hot air, smoke, or the like, as in a boiler or chimney FLUE
- sloping surround, as of cement, for draining away water from a chimney, or the like FLANCH

chin divided into two sides by a vertical indentation CLEFT CHIN
- chin that is squarish and jutting LANTERN JAW
- adjective for the chin GENIAL, MENTAL
- having a prominent chin because of a jutting jaw PROGNATHOUS
- having correctly positioned jaws,

CHEMISTRY TERMS

alkali	soluble base, able to neutralize acids
allotrope	any of the different physical forms that an element may take, such as diamond and graphite in the case of carbon
amphoteric, amphiprotic	able to react as both an acid and a base
atomic number	number of protons in the atomic nucleus of an element
azeotropic mixture	mixture of liquids that cannot be separated by distillation
base	compound that reacts with an acid to form a salt
catalyst	substance that affects or speeds up a chemical reaction without itself being changed
chemical bond	force that holds atoms or ions together
colloid	mixture or suspension of very fine particles within a fluid, as with fog or paint
dopant	impurity added to a pure substance, such as a semiconductor, to alter its properties
efflorescence	process by which crystals are turned to powder by the loss of water
electrolysis	decomposition of a chemical compound by passing an electric current through it
electron	negatively charged particle orbiting the atomic nucleus
enzyme	protein of a kind produced by living cells and functioning as a biochemical catalyst
ester	organic compound, such as a fat, derived from the reaction of an acid with an alcohol
fractionation	separation of a mixture into its components on the basis of their different boiling points or different solubilities
halogen	any one of five nonmetallic elements—fluorine, chlorine, bromine, iodine, and astatine
hydrocarbon	organic compound of hydrogen and carbon, such as benzene (benzol)
hydrolysis	decomposition of a chemical compound by reaction with water
inert	chemically inactive, fully or almost fully unreactive, as some elements are
inhibitor	substance that slows down or stops a chemical reaction
inorganic	referring or relating to noncarbon compounds
ion	electrically charged atom, radical, or molecule
isomer	compound having the same elements and number of atoms as another, but with a different arrangement of the atoms and hence different properties
isotope	atom having the same number of protons in its nucleus as another atom of the same element, but a different number of neutrons

so that the chin is neither receding nor protruding ORTHOGNATHOUS

china See also **pottery**
- deliberate network of fine cracks in the glaze of a piece of pottery or china CRACKLING
- having a traditional blue-on-white pictorial design, as a china plate might WILLOW PATTERN

China - ancient or poetic name for China CATHAY
- study of the language, culture, and history of China SINOLOGY

Chinese See also chart at **menu**
- Chinese, Japanese, or person from any of various other East Asian countries ORIENTAL
- Chinese empire CELESTIAL EMPIRE
- Chinese form of exercise and mental training in which balletic body movements are performed slowly and deliberately T'AI CHI
- Chinese gambling game based on guessing the number of counters, beans or coins hidden under a bowl FAN-TAN
- Chinese idol JOSS
- Chinese or Japanese figurine, usually in a grotesque, crouched position MAGOT
- Chinese or other language that distinguishes words by their pitch or by their intonation TONE LANGUAGE
- Chinese place of worship JOSS HOUSE
- Chinese public official, in imperial times MANDARIN
- Chinese puzzle consisting of a set of simple shapes for reassembling into different figures TANGRAM
- Chinese-style bow of former times, touching the ground with one's forehead KOWTOW
- Chinese-style pottery, ornaments, and decorative design generally CHINOISERIE
- Chinese-style therapy in which needles are inserted into the skin or body at given points ACUPUNCTURE
- Chinese symbol or character that represents a thing or idea rather than indicating its sound IDEOGRAM
- Chinese writing system, or other writing system resembling it, in which each word is represented by

CHEMISTRY TERMS *continued*

latent heat	heat absorbed or released by a substance undergoing a change of state, as from ice to water	**radical**	atom or group of atoms with one or more unpaired electrons, acting as a unit in a compound
litmus paper	dyed paper that is turned red by acids but which remains blue or reverts to blue when treated with alkalis	**reagent**	substance used in analyzing, measuring, or synthesizing other substances in a chemical reaction
mass number	total number of protons and neutrons in the nucleus of an atom	**rectify**	refine, purify, or separate by means of distillation
molecule	group of atoms together as a stable entity	**reduction**	removal of oxygen from a compound or adding of hydrogen to it; reaction in which atoms, molecules, or the like gain electrons
noble gas	gas such as helium or neon that is almost inert or unreactive	**structural formula**	chemical formula detailing the arrangement of atoms and bonds within the molecule
neutron	electrically neutral particle in the atomic nucleus	**suspension**	mixture of undissolved particles within a fluid, as with muddy water
organic	referring or relating to carbon compounds	**syneresis**	slow release of the liquid from a gel, as in cheese making
osmosis	gradual passage of water or other solvent through a semipermeable membrane until there is an equal concentration of solutions on either side	**synthesis**	chemical reaction in which a compound is built up from simpler units
oxidation	adding of oxygen to a compound or removal of hydrogen from it; reaction in which atoms, molecules, or the like gain electrons	**systematic name**	name of a chemical compound that conveys details of its atomic structure
periodic table	table of the chemical elements, grouping them in columns according to their properties	**titration**	procedure for determining the concentration of a solution by adding a standard reagent
polymer	compound, such as starch or polyethylene, formed of chains of repeated units of molecules	**trivial name**	common name for a chemical compound, giving no information about its components
proton	positively charged particle in the atomic nucleus	**valency**	power of an atom or group of atoms to combine with other atoms, represented by a number

a single character or symbol LEXIGRAPHY
- active male force or principle in traditional Chinese philosophy YANG
- basic symbol or character, in Chinese or a similar writing system, that conveys a full meaning RADICAL
- bowl-shaped metal pan, as used in Chinese cooking for frying and the like WOK
- game of Chinese origin, played with small tiles bearing varied designs MAH-JONGG
- main Chinese dialect MANDARIN
- passive female force or principle in traditional Chinese philosophy YIN
- pronunciation of the sound /r/ as /l/, as by many Chinese people speaking English LALLATION
- strong colorless Chinese alcoholic drink distilled from grain MAO-TAI
- suit consisting of a loose jacket and trousers, as worn by Chinese women SAMFOO
- system of transcribing Chinese in the Roman alphabet PINYIN, YALE, WADE-GILES, POSTAL
- tight dress of Chinese design, with a slit skirt and high collar CHEONGSAM

Chinese (combining form) SINO-

Chinese restaurants - flavor enhancer, as used in Chinese restaurants MONOSODIUM GLUTAMATE, MSG

chip See also **microchip**
- chip, splinter, or break stone, especially with a hammer SPALL
- chip or counter used in gambling JETTON

chirp - shrill grating chirp produced by a cricket or grasshopper STRIDULATION

chisel used for rough dressing of stone DROVE
- handle of a chisel HELVE
- shape or dress stone roughly with a broad chisel BOAST
- sloping surface leading to the tip or cutting edge of a chisel, screwdriver, or other tool BEZEL

chivalrous man CHEVALIER
- chivalrously and excessively idealistic, and hence impractical or absentminded QUIXOTIC

chocolate - chocolatelike substance or flavoring, made from an edible pod CAROB
- chocolate strands used for sprinkling on cakes or desserts SPRINKLES, JIMMIES

choice, act or instance of choosing OPTION
- choice that is apparent rather than real, since there is no alternative HOBSON'S CHOICE
- arising from or relating to free choice or a choice of one's own free will VOLUNTARY
- optional, open to choice, as a course of study is ELECTIVE
- power of choice, deliberate decision VOLITION
- range of choices so wide as to make a decision very difficult EMBARRAS DE RICHESSES
- right to act, or judge, power of choice DISCRETION
- situation requiring a choice to be made between two equal and typically undesirable alternatives DILEMMA

choir, orchestra, or music society PHILHARMONIC
- choir gallery LOFT
- choir leader, especially in ancient Athens CHORAGUS
- choir leader, lead singer, or soloist in a church or synagogue CANTOR, PRECENTOR
- choir of four unaccompanied male voices BARBERSHOP QUARTET
- choir or chorus CHORALE
- choir or orchestra leader, as in 18th-century Germany KAPELLMEISTER
- choirboy or choir singer CHORISTER
- ledge on a choir-stall seat to lean against while standing MISERICORD
- procession of the choir and clergy out of the chancel at the end of a church service RECESSION
- situated on the north side of the choir in a church CANTORIAL
- small choir typically performing short light songs GLEE CLUB
- without instrumental accompaniment, as some choir music is A CAPPELLA

choke, gasp for breath GAG
- choke or strangle THROTTLE, ASPHYXIATE

choose as one's preference, single out, favor ELECT, PLUMP FOR
- choose between, distinguish, differentiate DISCRIMINATE
- choose from an assortment, pick out, select CULL
- choosing or chosen from a range of different sources ECLECTIC
- choosing or sorting by priority or to allocate scarce resources TRIAGE

chop - frilly paper covering adorning the end of a chop or cutlet PAPILLOTE, FRILL

chord played note by note in quick succession rather than simultaneously ARPEGGIO
- lowest note of a chord FUNDAMENTAL

chorus of a song or musical composition REFRAIN, BURDEN

chosen, optional, open to choice, as a course of study is ELECTIVE
- chosen freely rather than required or compelled VOLUNTARY
- chosen or choosing from a range of different sources ECLECTIC

Christ See also **Jesus**
- Christ's salvation of humans from sin REDEMPTION, DELIVERANCE

Christian See also **church, clergyman**
- Christian creed or profession of faith widely used in churches ATHENASIAN CREED, NICENE CREED
- Christian evangelizer full of enthusiasm HOT-GOSPELER
- Christian group having doctrines and rites in common DENOMINATION, COMMUNION, CONFESSION
- Christian love, charity, loving-kindness, as distinct from erotic love AGAPE
- Christian reform movement in 16th-century Europe that led to the emergence of the Protestant churches REFORMATION
- Christian sacrament commemorating the Last Supper by the consecration of bread and wine COMMUNION, EUCHARIST
- Christian studies THEOLOGY
- referring or relating to a person who has undergone a conversion to fervent Christianity BORN-AGAIN
- sacred Christian act, such as baptism, symbolizing a spiritual reality and conferring grace SACRAMENT
- unintelligible ecstatic speech, as in some evangelical Christian services GLOSSOLALIA, GIFT OF TONGUES

Christian era or A.D. as referred to by non-Christians COMMON ERA, C.E.

Christianity, Judaism, Islam, or other religion based on belief in a single God MONOTHEISM
- formal statement of religious beliefs, confession of faith, especially in Christianity CREED
- question-and-answer examinations or instruction book, particularly one on the basic principles of Christianity CATECHISM

Christmas carol singers WAITS
- Christmas festival or season YULE, NATIVITY, NOEL

church See illustration, and also **altar, Communion, clergyman, Christian, prayer,** and chart at **canonical hours**
- church assembly, especially when illegal and held in secret CONVENTICLE
- church authority's release of someone from a vow or rule, or the document certifying it DISPENSATION
- church caretaker, often acting as

bellringer and gravedigger as well SEXTON
- church conference or assembly of churchmen SYNOD, CONVOCATION
- church court or governing body, or a meeting of it CONSISTORY
- church endowment or estate of long standing PATRIMONY
- church land, typically granted to a clergyman as part of his benefice GLEBE
- church law or code of laws CANON
- church meeting of the parish committee or congregants VESTRY
- church of a monastery MINSTER
- church of any of various kinds, having more than one clergyman COLLEGIATE CHURCH
- church office or department dealing with legal matters, church records, and archives CHANCERY
- church officer in charge of the sacred vessels, vestments, and the like SACRISTAN
- church official in former times, with caretaking and ushering duties BEADLE
- church or cathedral used for special ceremonies among Roman Catholics BASILICA
- church or group having doctrines and rites in common DENOMINATION, COMMUNION, CONFESSION
- church or other place affording protection or refuge SANCTUARY
- church or place of prayer, especially a chapel in an institution or private home ORATORY
- church position, office, or job, together with its income LIVING, BENEFICE
- church position requiring little or no actual work in the parish SINECURE
- church service in the late afternoon or evening VESPERS
- church serving those living too far from the parish church CHAPEL OF EASE
- church surroundings or grounds, enclosed by a wall or other boundary PRECINCT
- church usher and attendant VERGER
- aisle down the east end of a church AMBULATORY
- alignment of a church so that the main altar is at the eastern end ORIENTATION
- any of various traditional, especially Eastern, churches ORTHODOX CHURCH
- anthem, biblical passage, or the

Church

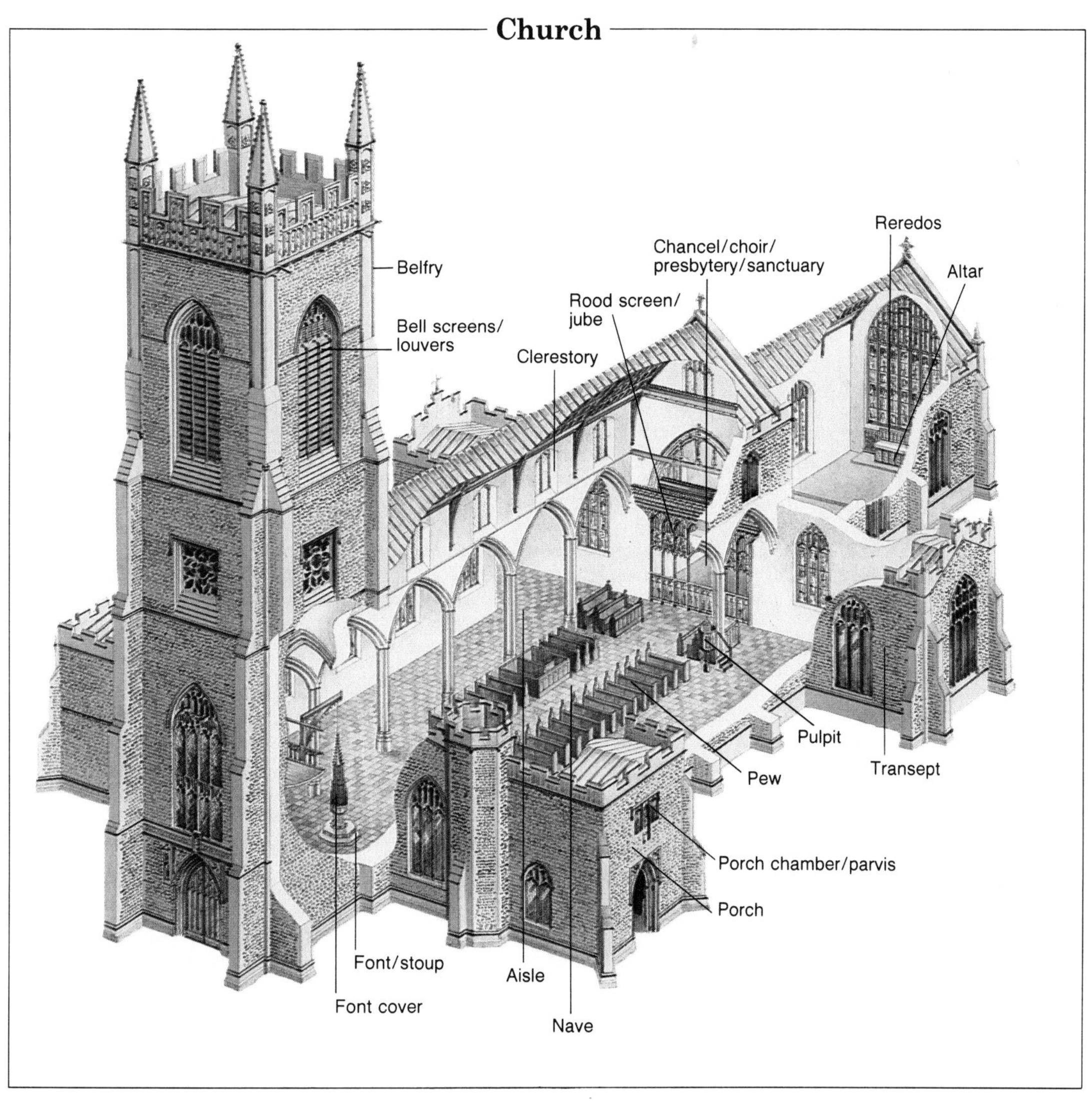

like recited or sung as a response during a church service ANTIPHON
- any place of worship that is not referred to as a church TABERNACLE
- area in a church where the nave and transept intersect CROSSING
- baptism, communion, or sometimes any of various other church rites SACRAMENT
- basin set in the wall of a church for draining away the water used in ceremonial washing PISCINA, SACRARIUM
- bell tower detached from the main church building CAMPANILE
- calling on God's blessing, as at the end of a church service BENEDICTION
- candle lit by a worshiper and placed before a shrine or statue in a church VIGIL LIGHT
- ceremonial garments worn by those officiating or assisting at a church service or rite VESTMENTS
- ceremony during a church service in which the priest washes his hands LAVABO
- chapel or porch at the entrance of a medieval church GALILEE
- chapel within a church, dedicated to the Virgin Mary LADY CHAPEL
- clergyman's salary or allowance paid by his church PREBEND
- corrupt buying and selling of church offices, relics, pardons, and the like SIMONY
- courtyard or colonnade in front of a church, palace, or Roman house PARVIS, ATRIUM
- cut off from membership of a church or religion EXCOMMUNICATE
- desk at which the litany is recited in an Anglican church FALDSTOOL
- entrance hall at the west end of a church NARTHEX
- form or system of church service or public worship as officially prescribed LITURGY
- gallery forming an upper floor of a church, as above the aisles TRIFORIUM
- governing body of elders and pastors in some Reformed churches CLASSIS
- grotesque stone figure, as on the roof of a Gothic church, often serving as a waterspout from a gutter GARGOYLE
- ledge on a church-stall seat to lean against while standing MISERICORD, MISERERE
- make or declare something sacred, such as a church DEDICATE, CONSECRATE, SANCTIFY
- make something, such as a church, unfit for religious or ceremonial use, as by blasphemy or vandalism PROFANE, DESECRATE, DEFILE
- narrow spire, usually of wood, as on a church roof FLÈCHE
- noncompliance with the doctrines of an established church NONCONFORMITY, DISSENT
- ordinary members of a church, as distinct from the clergy LAITY, LAYMEN, LAYPERSONS, LAY PEOPLE
- part of a church tower or steeple in which the bells are hung BELFRY
- platform or gallery in a church TRIBUNE
- prayer stool or kneeling bench in a church, with a shelf for elbows or books PRIE-DIEU
- procession of the choir and clergy out of the chancel at the end of a church service RECESSION
- promoting or relating to unity among the world's various churches ECUMENICAL
- rail or screen in a church, as for sectioning off a chapel PARCLOSE
- reading desk, as in a church for readings from the Bible LECTERN
- recess in the wall of a church, as for storing Communion vessels AMBRY, FENESTELLA
- relating to the church ECCLESIASTICAL
- room or annex in a church where the sacred objects and vestments are stored SACRISTY, VESTRY, SACRARIUM
- rule or custom, as for the conducting of a church ceremony RUBRIC
- semicircular projecting side of a church, usually vaulted, typically at the east end APSE, CHEVET
- situated on the north side of the choir in a church CANTORIAL
- situated on the south side of the choir in a church DECANAL
- splitting into opposing factions, as within a church SCHISM
- spoiling or destruction of the sacred quality of a church, graveyard, or the like, as by blasphemy or vandalism DESECRATION, PROFANATION, VIOLATION, SACRILEGE, DEFILEMENT
- study of the lives and writings of the fathers of the early Christian church PATRISTICS, PATROLOGY
- tenth of one's yearly income or production donated as a tax or voluntarily to the church or other good cause TITHE
- underground chamber, such as a church vault CRYPT, UNDERCROFT
- unvarying parts of the mass or church service ORDINARY, COMMON
- varying parts of the mass or church service, according to the time, day, or feast PROPER
- verse or phrase, to be followed by the response, sung or recited by the leader of a church service VERSICLE
- verse or phrase sung or recited by the choir or congregation as a reply to the leader during a church service RESPONSE
- vow of faith and support by members of a church COVENANT

churchwarden - churchwarden's assistant, especially the person who takes the collection SIDESMAN

churchyard - churchyard's roofed gate, where the coffin is traditionally rested at the start of the burial service LYCH-GATE

cider of a strong, rough brew, typically from southwestern England SCRUMPY

cigar, typically with both ends cut square CHEROOT
- cigar case in which the humidity can be kept constant HUMIDOR
- cheap thin cigar STOGY
- dark strong cigar MADURO
- large, high-quality Cuban cigar HAVANA
- large cigar tapered at both ends PERFECTO
- long tapering cigar with blunt ends CORONA
- long thin cigar PANATELLA
- tobacco leaf around a cigar WRAPPER

cigarette of Indian origin, consisting of a rolled leaf secured with thread BEEDI
- breathe in cigarette or other tobacco smoke INHALE
- peppermint-flavored, as some cigarettes are MENTHOLATED

cinema of an early kind, charging five cents for admission NICKELODEON
- film library or repertory cinema CINEMATHEQUE
- toy producing simple cinematic images, consisting of a picture-lined cylinder revolving past a viewing slit ZOETROPE

cinema (combining form) CINE-

cinnamon stick QUILL

circle See also **geometry**
- circle of stone or wooden pillars, from prehistoric cultures HENGE
- circle rolling, either inside or outside, round a larger circle EPICYCLE
- circle round a point or axis, spin GYRATE
- circles, typically overlapping, used as a diagram representing mathematical or logical relations VENN DIAGRAM, EULER DIAGRAM
- boundary line of an enclosed figure, especially a circle, or the length of it CIRCUMFERENCE

- draw a line, especially an arc or circle DESCRIBE
- draw a line or circle round CIRCUMSCRIBE
- having a common center, as two circles of different size might CONCENTRIC
- having different centers, as two overlapping circles would ECCENTRIC
- imaginary half-circle joining the poles on the earth's surface MERIDIAN
- shaped like a flattened or elongated circle ELLIPTICAL

circle (combining form) CYCL-, CYCLO-, CIRC-, ORB-

circuit - electronic circuit formed on a microchip INTEGRATED CIRCUIT

circular band, as around the base of a tooth CINGULUM
- circular or ring-shaped figure, space, marking, part, or object ANNULUS
- circular design symbolizing the universe, in Hindu and Buddhist art MANDALA
- circular painting, cameo, or medallion TONDO
- circular wall, especially one supporting a dome TAMBOUR

circular (combining form) GYRO-

circumference, as of a person's waist or a tree GIRTH

circumstances serving to make a crime, fault, or the like less serious or blameworthy EXTENUATING CIRCUMSTANCES, MITIGATING CIRCUMSTANCES

circus bar suspended from free-swinging ropes TRAPEZE
- circus horseback performer EQUESTRIAN, EQUESTRIENNE

citadel in ancient Greece ACROPOLIS

citizen, especially a middle-class citizen of a town in the Middle Ages BURGHER
- right of citizens to petition for a new law and get it voted on by the electorate INITIATIVE
- study of a citizen's rights and duties CIVICS

citizenship - foreigner having certain citizenship rights in his country of residence DENIZEN
- give voting rights or full citizenship rights to ENFRANCHISE
- grant citizenship to NATURALIZE

city See also **town**
- city, especially the chief city of a region METROPOLIS
- city, town, or other self-governing community MUNICIPALITY
- city area, inhabited by a poor or restricted group, typically a minority group GHETTO
- city area, often closed to traffic, set apart for pedestrians and shopping MALL, PRECINCT
- city of vast extent, group of towns fused into a single urban complex MEGALOPOLIS, CONURBATION
- city's electoral district, administrative division, or the like WARD
- adjective for a city CIVIC, MUNICIPAL, URBAN
- fortress or stronghold protecting a town or city CITADEL
- name of a city or other place used in a foreign language, such as *Florence* for *Firenze* EXONYM
- suburb or quarter of a city, especially a French-speaking city FAUBOURG

city-state in ancient Greece POLIS

civil servant of high rank and believed to have great political influence MANDARIN

civil war See also **American Civil War**
- mutually destructive or fatal, as civil war is INTERNECINE

civilian clothes, as distinct from military or other uniform MUFTI, CIVVIES

civilization - relating to the civilization of ancient Greece and Rome, or ancient China, or the like CLASSICAL

claim, usually false or unproven, to some right, title, skill, or the like PRETENSION
- claim as one's own without any right to do so APPROPRIATE, ARROGATE
- claim or appear to be or do something PURPORT, PROFESS
- claim or declare, confidently or forcefully AFFIRM, ASSERT, AVER, AVOUCH, AVOW
- claim or declare, formally or earnestly ASSEVERATE
- claim or declare, typically without proving, merely state or maintain ALLEGE
- claim or declare to be true or existing, assume or put forward, as for the state of argument POSTULATE, PREMISE
- claim or declare to belong to or be characteristic of someone or something PREDICATE
- disprove, weaken, or make ineffective an argument, claim, or the like INVALIDATE
- give up a claim or right voluntarily WAIVE, RELINQUISH
- having priority over, as one claim might have over another UNDERLIE, SUPERSEDE
- reject or deny a claim or accusation REPUDIATE

clairvoyance - alleged perception by means of a sixth sense, clairvoyance, telepathy, intuition, or the like EXTRASENSORY PERCEPTION, ESP, CRYPTESTHESIA

clamp or vice used to hold a tool or work piece, as in a drill or lathe CHUCK
- bent metal bar clamping stones or timber together, as in a wall CRAMP IRON, AGRAFFE

clan - group of related clans within a tribe PHRATRY

clarify a remark, idea, or the like by adding details AMPLIFY

clarinet - metal band securing the reed to the mouthpiece of a clarinet or saxophone LIGATURE

clasp or fastener hinged over a fixed staple, and typically secured with a padlock HASP

class given by a teacher to an individual student or a very small number of students TUTORIAL
- class in school, especially designed for slow learners REMEDIAL CLASS
- class of manual laborers or industrial wage-earners, the working class generally PROLETARIAT
- class or category of art, movies, or the like GENRE
- class-ridden, divided according to castes, classes, or the like, as a nation or society might be STRATIFIED
- class within society, especially any of the four major social divisions among Hindus CASTE
- belonging to a higher or larger class or level of generality, as opposed to subordinate SUPERORDINATE
- level, such as a class or caste, within a society or series STRATUM
- title of a category or class RUBRIC

classically elegant in style, as poetry or drama might be AUGUSTAN

classification See chart, page 104
- classification, especially of plants and animals TAXONOMY
- classification, separation into groups or categories DISTRIBUTION
- classification according to rank or importance HIERARCHY
- classification of diseases NOSOLOGY
- classification of plants and animals in groups according to shared ancestry CLADISTICS
- classification or name of a group DENOMINATION, DESIGNATION
- classification system, such as the standard system of names for plants or chemicals NOMENCLATURE
- classification system for animals or plants using two Latin names indicating the genus and then the species BINOMIAL NOMENCLATURE, LINNAEAN NOMENCLATURE
- classification system such as a scale or series, or a step or stage

within it GRADATION
- relating to a whole group, such as a genus in biological classification GENERIC
- species name as opposed to genus name in biological classification TRIVIAL NAME, SPECIFIC EPITHET

CLASSIFICATION

The main categories into which living things are divided, from the broadest to the most detailed

kingdom
phylum, division
class
order
(superfamily, stirps)
family
genus
species
(subspecies, stirps, variety, race, stock, strain, breed)
individual

(The following nonsense sentence is a memory device for the basic sequence in taxonomy: "King Philip Came Over For Ginger Snaps"—Kingdom, Phylum, Class, Order, Family, Genus, Species.)

classify, assign to a group or class CATEGORIZE, PIGEONHOLE
- classify or include in a wider category or under a general heading or principle SUBSUME
- classify systematically DIGEST, CODIFY, CATALOG

clause, amendment, or qualification added to a legal document, verdict, parliamentary bill, or the like RIDER
- clause of equal status or parallel structure to another in a sentence, as distinct from a subordinate clause COORDINATE CLAUSE
- linking of phrases or clauses by means of punctuation rather than conjunctions PARATAXIS
- referring to a subordinate clause within a sentence EMBEDDED
- subordination of a clause in grammar, typically by means of a conjunction HYPOTAXIS

claw, nail, hoof, or similar part UNGUIS
- claw of a bird of prey TALON, POUNCE
- claw of a lobster, crab, scorpion, or the like PINCER, CHELA

clay, or a sun-dried brick made from it, as in Mexico ADOBE
- clay as used in pottery ARGIL
- clay or brown earthy substance used as a pigment UMBER, SIENNA, BOLE
- clay used in filtering and decoloring FULLER'S EARTH
- brownish-red clay, or the pottery it is used to make TERRACOTTA
- china clay, used in ceramics and as a coating for paper KAOLIN, TERRA ALBA
- material made by firing clay or a similar substance, or an object made of such material CERAMIC
- moist clay used in making pottery or porcelain PASTE, PÂTE
- potter's wooden spatula used for mixing or molding clay PALLET
- rock particles finer than sand but coarser than clay SILT
- stiff whitish English clay CLUNCH
- thinned clay used by a potter for coating or decorating SLIP

clay-pigeon shooting TRAPSHOOTING
- clay-pigeon shooting in which the targets are thrown at varying speeds and angles from traps on either side of the range SKEET

clean, thoroughly hygienic, free of all germs and infection SANITARY, SANITIZED, DISINFECTED, ANTISEPTIC
- clean, repair, and restore something, such as a house REFURBISH
- cleaning or smoothing substance that scours and scrapes, such as pumice or emery ABRASIVE
- perfectly clean and pure, spotless and uncorrupted IMMACULATE, UNBLEMISHED, PRISTINE

clean slate, fresh start, need or chance to start again from scratch TABULA RASA

cleansing or purging, as of the digestive system CATHARTIC
- chemical-based cleansing substance as used for industrial and household cleaning DETERGENT
- cleansing or scouring, as a cleaning powder might be ABSTERGENT

clear, as water or a literary style might be LIMPID
- clear, forceful, and crisp, as a remark might be INCISIVE, TRENCHANT, COGENT
- clear, fully expressed, as directions might be EXPLICIT
- clear, obvious, plain to see EVIDENT, PATENT, PALPABLE, MANIFEST
- clear, plain, unambiguous, not open to doubt UNEQUIVOCAL
- clear, transparent CRYSTALLINE, DIAPHANOUS
- clear and unavoidable, as destiny might be MANIFEST
- clear of a charge or blame, declare innocent ACQUIT, EXONERATE, EXCULPATE, ABSOLVE, VINDICATE
- clear or conclusive, beyond dispute, as a clear-cut victory is DECISIVE
- clear the throat loudly HAWK
- clearly, especially, extremely SIGNALLY, CONSPICUOUSLY
- clearly described in vivid or exciting detail GRAPHIC
- clearly expressed, easily understandable LUCID, LUMINOUS, PELLUCID, PERSPICUOUS
- clearness CLARITY
- make clear or comprehensible CLARIFY, ELUCIDATE
- make clear, remove the ambiguity from, clarify DISAMBIGUATE

clear-cut, well-defined, distinct, as a difference between two options might be TRENCHANT

clearing or open space in a wood or forest GLADE

clergy See also **church**
- belonging to the congregation or general public as opposed to the clergy, as a preacher might be LAY, SECULAR
- ordinary members of a church, as distinct from the clergy LAITY, LAYMEN, LAYWOMEN, LAYPERSONS, LAY PEOPLE
- organization or grading according to rank or importance, as among the clergy HIERARCHY
- relating to clergymen or clergywomen CLERICAL

clergyman or clergywoman See chart, and also **church, priest,** and illustration at **clerical clothing**
- clergyman or clergywoman, priest ECCLESIASTIC
- clergyman or clergywoman holding a particular post INCUMBENT
- clergyman or clergywoman temporarily replacing the regular incumbent LOCUM, LOCUM TENENS
- clergyman or clergywoman who visits condemned convicts in the death cell ORDINARY
- clergyman's or clergywoman's acceptance into the ministry, or the ceremony of admission ORDINATION
- clergyman's or clergywoman's house, especially in Scotland MANSE
- clergyman's or clergywoman's salary or allowance, paid by the church PREBEND, STIPEND
- clergyman's permission from the bishop to leave the diocese to work elsewhere EXEAT
- clergyman's privilege in the Middle Ages to be tried by a church court rather than a secular court BENEFIT OF CLERGY
- appoint a clergyman or clergywoman to a benefice COLLATE
- authorize to be a clergyman or

clergywoman, invest into holy orders ORDAIN
- right to nominate a clergyman or clergywoman to a benefice PATRONAGE
- strip a clergyman of his status and rights in the church DEFROCK, UNFROCK
- strips of white cloth on clergyman's or clergywoman's robes GENEVA BANDS
- theological school, especially as a training school for clergymen or clergywomen SEMINARY

clerical clothing See illustration, page 106

clerk or official secretary SCRIBE, AMANUENSIS
- clerk or secretary in former times, especially one licensed to draft legal documents NOTARY

clever See also **skillful, sophisticated**
- clever, insightful, showing sensitive understanding or keen critical powers PERCEPTIVE, DISCERNING, PERCIPIENT, PENETRATING, PERSPICACIOUS
- clever, intelligent, quick at learning or at grasping new ideas RECEPTIVE, APT
- clever, tactful, and usually cautious, as in dealings with others PRUDENT, POLITIC, JUDICIOUS
- clever, wise, showing sound judgment SAPIENT, SAGACIOUS
- clever and witty person, displaying a fine mind BEL ESPRIT
- clever in an inventive or cunning way INGENIOUS
- clever or capable in practical things, especially in difficult circumstances RESOURCEFUL
- clever or extremely successful person of very young age WHIZ KID, WUNDERKIND, CHILD PRODIGY
- clever or shrewd, showing cunning and insight ASTUTE, CANNY
- clever or sophisticated beyond his or her years, as an advanced child seems to be PRECOCIOUS
- clever remark, witty saying BON MOT
- cleverness, insight, or good judgment ACUMEN
- cleverness, practical shrewdness, common sense GUMPTION
- cleverness of an imaginative or inventive kind INGENUITY

cliché, unoriginal and predictable remark, phrase, or thought PLATITUDE, COMMONPLACE, BROMIDE
- clichéd, especially pious formulas or the mindless repetition of them CANT
- clichéd, unoriginal and overused, threadbare and uninspiring HACKNEYED, TRITE, BANAL, SHOPWORN
- clichéd and widespread saying or belief SHIBBOLETH
- clichéd moral lesson, sermon, or proverb HOMILY
- clichéd statement of an obvious truth TRUISM
- pompous, moralizing, and typically cliché-ridden SENTENTIOUS

clicking wooden shells operated in the hand, as by Spanish dancers, in time to the music CASTANETS

cliff, steep river bank, headland, or the like BLUFF
- cliff or cliff face, or peak of rock CRAG, PRECIPICE, SCAR
- cliff or high stretch of land above the sea HEADLAND, PROMONTORY
- cliff or steep slope, typically resulting from erosion or faulting ESCARPMENT
- cliffs in a line, as overlooking a river PALISADES
- descend, as from a cliff top or helicopter, by means of a supporting rope around one's body ABSEIL
- rock debris at the foot of a cliff TALUS

climate - adjust to a new climate or surroundings ACCLIMATIZE
- having or referring to a mild climate TEMPERATE
- promoting or favorable to health or well-being, as a climate might be SALUBRIOUS
- referring to a climate having a relatively small range of temperature MARITIME, EQUABLE

climax, highest point CULMINATION
- climax of sexual excitement ORGASM

climb awkwardly, as up a rocky slope CLAMBER, SCRAMBLE
- climb or scale a castle wall, tower, or the like by means of a ladder,

CLERGYMEN AND CLERGYWOMEN

archdeacon	member of the clergy with administrative responsibilities within a diocese
canon	member of a cathedral chapter
chancellor	priest serving as a bishop, legal officer, or business manager
chaplain	member of the clergy who serves an individual or an institution, ship, regiment, college, or the like
curate	assistant to a parish priest
deacon	member of the clergy in the lowest stage of ordination, unqualified to perform certain sacraments
dean	cathedral administrator and head of the chapter of canons
metropolitan	bishop with authority over several dioceses; an archbishop or primate
padre	military chaplain
prebendary	canon, formerly having an endowed stipend
precentor	member of the clergy who directs choral services in a cathedral
prelate	high-ranking official such as a bishop or cardinal
primate	chief bishop or archbishop
prior	deputy head of a monastery, ranking below the abbot; head of any of various other religious communities
proctor	elected representative of the Anglican clergy in Convocation and the General Synod
provost	senior official in a cathedral of recent foundation
rural dean	member of the clergy with authority over a group of parishes
suffragan	assistant bishop in a diocese; bishop in relation to his archbishop

as during a military attack ESCALADE
- climb to the top of ASCEND, SURMOUNT
- person who climbs the outside of buildings, as for a prank or bet STEGOPHILIST

climbing plant or its stem BINE
- common climbing plant, typically with funnel-shaped flowers, twining around its support BINDWEED, CONVOLVULUS
- common woody climbing plant of tropical rain forests LIANA
- covered walk or arbor formed by a trellised roof carrying climbing plants PERGOLA
- twining shootlike part, serving to attach a climbing plant to its support TENDRIL

clinging, sticking, or holding firmly TENACIOUS
- clinging or dependent person, parasite LEECH, LIMPET
- persistently clinging person or thing BURR

cloak See **clothes**

clock made of imitation gold or gold-like alloy ORMOLU CLOCK
- clock mechanism, typically a ratchet system, for regulating the cogwheels and transmitting energy, as from the mainspring to the pendulum ESCAPEMENT
- clock of an ancient kind based on the dripping of water or mercury CLEPSYDRA
- clock of great accuracy, based on subatomic processes CESIUM CLOCK
- clock or watch of a very precise kind, especially one used at sea CHRONOMETER
- clock or watch that can be primed to strike the hour or quarter hour REPEATER
- clock's second hand SWEEP-SECOND HAND
- art of making watches or clocks, or the study of them HOROLOGY
- cone-shaped pulley or wheel with a spiraling groove, as in the mechanism of an early clock FUSEE
- device, as in a digital clock, that emits light when diodes are electrically stimulated LED
- display of symbols, as on a digital clock, produced by electrical stimulation of liquid crystals LCD
- glass or clear plastic cover over the face of a watch or clock CRYSTAL
- grandfather clock LONG-CASE CLOCK
- referring to a watch or clock with changing numbers to indicate the time, rather than moving hands on a dial DIGITAL
- referring to a watch or clock with traditional hands and dial to indicate the time ANALOG
- swinging body freely suspended, as used for regulating a grandfather clock PENDULUM

clockwise (combining form) DEXTR-, DEXTRO-

cloister, aisle, or similar covered area for walking AMBULATORY

close See also **end, stop**
- close at the end of a session, as the courts and congress do ADJOURN
- close of the action of a play, usually in the form of a poem or speech EPILOGUE
- close to or next to ADJACENT, ADJOINING, CONTIGUOUS, ABUTTING
- close together, placed side by side, as for contrast JUXTAPOSED, APPOSED
- closely associated, very familiar or friendly INTIMATE
- closely linked CHEEK BY JOWL
- closeness in time or position PROPINQUITY, PROXIMITY, VICINITY
- closest relative or relatives NEXT OF KIN
- closing section of a speech, article, or the like, typically a summing-up PERORATION
- closing section of a play or novel, unwinding or resolving the plot DENOUEMENT

close to (combining form) EPI-

close watch or observation, especially on someone or something suspicious SURVEILLANCE

cloth See also **fabric**
- cloth, fabric, material TEXTILE
- cloth, padding, springs, and the like, as used in making a soft covering for furniture UPHOLSTERY
- cloth dealer MERCER, DRAPER
- cloth left over after the rest of

Clerical Clothing

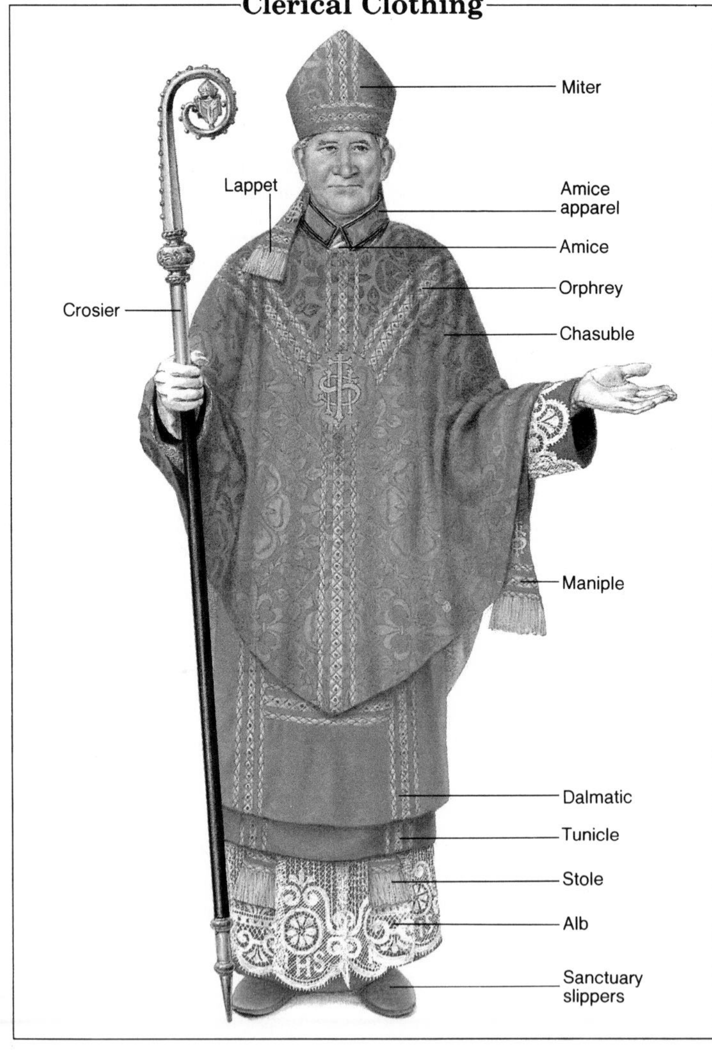

the roll has been sold REMNANT
- cloth or clothing arranged in folds, or a representation of it in sculpture or painting DRAPERY
- cloth scraps or fragments ODDMENTS, OFFCUTS
- cloth strip, brightly colored, used as a man's garment in western Africa KENTE
- cloth strip, brightly colored, used as a woman's garment in eastern Africa KANGA
- cloth strip, used as a flag or carrying a motto or slogan BANNER
- cloth strips or colorful streamers strung on a line for decoration BUNTING
- cloth strips, usually white, at the neck of some clerical or academic robes GENEVA BANDS
- cloth used to wrap a body for burial SHROUD, WINDING-SHEET
- cut cloth to form a deeply indented edging VANDYKE
- diagonal cut across the grain of a piece of cloth BIAS
- frame for drying or stretching cloth during manufacture TENTER
- gathered strip of cloth or pleated ruffle sewn to a garment or curtain FLOUNCE
- knot or lump in yarn or cloth BURL, SLUB
- make or press fluted folds in a piece of fabric, as for a ruff QUILL
- picture or scene, as viewed through a slit, formed by lights shining through a series of translucent cloth sheets DIORAMA
- piece of cloth sewn at the edge of a garment, as for decoration or to prevent fraying FACING, LIST, SELVAGE
- press through which paper or cloth is rolled for a smooth or glossy finish CALENDER
- roll of cloth BOLT
- sample piece of cloth SWATCH
- thicken cloth by shrinking it or bulking it up through moisture, heat, and pressing FULL
- triangle or wedge of cloth, as in a skirt, umbrella, or sail GORE, GUSSET

clothes See chart, pages 108-109, and also **collar, hat, shoe,** and illustration at **clerical clothing**
- clothes department or storeroom of a theater, royal household, or the like WARDROBE
- clothes model, whether a person or a life-size dummy MANNEQUIN
- clothes or accessories designed to be worn together COORDINATES
- clothes or personal belongings DUDS, TOGS
- clothes that are too expensive or fancy FRIPPERY, FROUFROU, FALLAL
- clothing, clothes, outfit APPAREL, ATTIRE, GARB, GARMENTS, RAIMENT, HABILIMENTS
- clothing and accessories for a newborn baby LAYETTE
- clothing and sewing materials HABERDASHERY
- clothing for a member of a religious order HABIT
- clothing of a very smart or expensive kind FINERY, ARRAY, CAPARISON, ADORNMENT, REGALIA
- clothing of high fashion HAUTE COUTURE
- clothing or cloth arranged in loose folds, or a representation of it in art DRAPERY
- clothing or distinctive outfit or uniform of a group of servants, guild members, or the like LIVERY
- civilian clothes rather than military uniform CIVVIES, MUFTI
- designer, maker, and seller of fashionable clothing for women COUTURIER, MODISTE
- made to order, as a suit of clothes might be BESPOKE
- man of fashion, whose chief interest is in clothes and manners BEAU, BEAU BRUMMELL, DANDY, FOP, COXCOMB
- matching set of clothes, outfit ENSEMBLE
- men's leather shorts with braces, as part of traditional Tyrolean or Bavarian clothing LEDERHOSEN
- mourning clothes WEEDS
- person who enjoys wearing clothes designed for the opposite sex TRANSVESTITE, CROSS-DRESSER
- priest's official clothing CANONICALS, VESTMENTS
- put on one's hat or clothes DON
- referring to clothes, hairstyles, or the like suitable for people of either sex UNISEX, EPICENE
- referring to clothing of an aggressive style, characterized by black leather, studs, and chains BONDAGE
- relating to clothing, especially smart men's clothing SARTORIAL
- shabby, untidy, or old-fashioned, as a woman or her clothes might be DOWDY, FRUMPY
- strip of something, such as clothes, rights, or property DIVEST
- supplementary or additional item to basic clothing ACCESSORY, PARAPHERNALIA
- take off one's hat or clothes DOFF
- tear or catch clothing on a nail, wooden stump, or the like SNAG

cloud See illustration, page 110
- cloud of dust or gas in outer space NEBULA
- cloud or obscure something, as fog might OBNUBILATE, OBFUSCATE
- clouds broken and driven by high winds RACK
- cloudy, misty, hazy NEBULOUS
- cloudy luminous aura surrounding a god or goddess when visiting earth NIMBUS
- cloudy with sediment, as river water might be TURBID
- covered with clouds, as the sky might be OVERCAST
- gathered in woolly masses, as clouds or dissolved particles might be FLOCCULENT
- sprinkle silver iodide or a similar chemical onto a cloud to produce rain SEED
- study of clouds NEPHOLOGY
- thin, wind-driven cloud SCUD

cloven, as a hoof might be, or having cloven hooves BISULCATE

clover leaf with four leaflets QUATREFOIL
- clover or similar plant whose leaves are made up of three leaflets TREFOIL, SHAMROCK
- three-leafed or with three leaflets, as the clover leaf TRIFOLIATE
- three-lobed ornamental figure, as in architecture, resembling a clover leaf TREFOIL

clown or fool in old comedies, especially one who mimics other characters ZANY
- amusing or irritating person given to clowning and ridiculous behavior BUFFOON
- professional clown or fool in former times JESTER
- traditional clown character, a boastful and cowardly Spanish nobleman SCARAMOUCHE
- traditional clown character, a fat hunchbacked man with a beaked nose on which the puppet Punch is based PUNCHINELLO
- traditional clown character, a foolish or lecherous and badly dressed old man PANTALOON
- traditional clown in a black mask and diamond-patterned tights HARLEQUIN
- traditional clown in Spanish comedy GRACIOSO
- traditional French clown with a whitened face and conical hat PIERROT
- whitened with cosmetic paint, as a clown might be FARDED

club or short stick used by a policeman TRUNCHEON, BILLY CLUB, NIGHTSTICK
- club or stick, or a beating with it, especially on the soles of the feet BASTINADO

CLOTHES

DAYWEAR	
Bermuda shorts	knee-length shorts
bolero	woman's very short jacket
chaps/ chaparejos	cowboy's seatless leather trousers
culottes	woman's flared trousers
dirndl	Tyrol-style dress with bodice and full skirt
dungarees	blue jeans, denim trousers, jeans
gilet	woman's waistcoat
guernsey	knitted sweater
guimpe	blouse under a jumper
halter	skimpy bodice tied behind the neck
jerkin	short jacket without sleeves or collar
jodhpurs	riding breeches, loose at the thighs
lederhosen	Austrian leather shorts with braces
leotard	tight sports garment from shoulder to thigh
muumuu	bright loose-fitting Hawaiian dress
Oxford bags	1920's-style baggy trousers
plus fours	men's baggy knickerbockers clasped below the knee
sloppy joe	long baggy sweater
trews	tight tartan trousers
zoot suit	1940's-style flashy suit with wide shoulders and narrow-cuffed pants
COATS AND CLOAKS	
anorak	padded waterproof jacket, parka
Burberry	worsted trench coat
cagoule	light hooded raincoat
capote	long cloak
chesterfield	overcoat, typically with concealed buttons and a velvet collar
dolman	woman's capelike cloak
domino	hooded robe worn at masked balls
duffle coat	short woollen coat, typically with a hood and toggles
Eton jacket	very short jacket with wide lapels
gaberdine	worsted raincoat
hacking jacket	riding jacket with slit sides or back
Inverness	loose overcoat with a removable cape
mantle	loose sleeveless cloak or overcoat
Norfolk jacket	man's jacket with a belt and box pleats
parka	hooded fur or cloth jacket
pelerine	woman's short cape
pelisse	long fur or fur-lined cloak
petersham	thick woollen overcoat
poncho	simple cloak of a large cloth with a hole for the head to pass through
raglan	coat or cloak with sleeves to the collar
reefer jacket	man's short double-breasted jacket
ulster	heavy overcoat, typically with a half-belt at the back
UNDERWEAR AND HOUSEWEAR	
camisole	short negligee, or sleeveless underbodice
chemise/ shift	woman's loose shirtlike undergarment
combinations	one-piece undergarment with sleeves and legs
corset, stays	tight supporting undergarment over the waist and hips
liberty bodice	buttoned sleeveless vest
negligee, peignoir	woman's light loose dressing gown
spencer	woman's short-sleeved jacket
ACCESSORIES	
bandanna	bright neckerchief or light scarf
boa	long stole or scarf, as of fur or feathers
cravat, ascot	man's small light knotted scarf
cummerbund	wide pleated sash for men, worn round the waist with a formal suit
dickey	biblike detachable shirt front
fichu	woman's light triangular scarf
mantilla	lace shawl, as worn over the head and shoulders by Spanish women
stock	long white neckerchief worn with formal riding dress

CLOTHES *continued*

CLERICAL AND RELIGIOUS	
alb	long white robe, as for Mass
amice	long white scarf tucked into the alb
cassock	long, close-fitting garment
chasuble	long sleeveless vestment
cope	long outer cloak
cotta	short surplice, often sleeveless
cowl, capuche	monk's hood or hooded robe
Geneva bands	pair of white cloth strips hanging from the collar
habit	dress or costume of a nun or friar
rochet	tight-sleeved white surplice, as worn by bishops
scapular	monk's sleeveless cloak
soutane	black cloak worn by Roman Catholic priests
surplice	loose-flowing white outer robe, sometimes worn over a cassock
tippet	long stole
wimple	cloth covering the head and neck, worn by some nuns
AFRICAN AND ARABIC	
burka	long hooded cloak worn by Muslim women
burnous	long hooded Arabic cloak
caftan	long Arabic tunic with a sash belt
dashiki	loose tunic, as worn by African men
djellaba	long, loose, hooded cloak, as worn by men in northern Africa
haik	Arab garment of a large cloth draped over the head and about the body
kanga	bright cotton cloth draped about the body by women in eastern Africa
kanzu	long white tunic worn by men in eastern Africa
kente	bright toga as worn in Ghana
yashmak	veil worn by Muslim women in public
ASIAN	
chador	garment worn by Muslim women covering the upper body and part of the face
cheongsam	tight Chinese dress with a high collar and slit skirt
choli	short-sleeved Indian blouse or bodice
dhoti	long shirtlike garment worn by Hindu men in India
khurta	long, loose, collarless Indian shirt
kimono	long, loose, formal Japanese robe, worn with a sash
lungi	loincloth, headdress, or scarf worn by Indian men
samfoo	loose Chinese suit for women
sari	garment worn by Hindu women, consisting of a long cloth wound about the body
sarong	skirtlike Malay garment formed by a long bright cloth
shalwar	baggy trousers as worn in Pakistan
sherwani	Indian men's high-collared coat
HISTORICAL	
balmoral	woollen petticoat showing below the skirt
chiton	loose woollen tunic worn by men and women in ancient Greece
chlamys	man's short cloak in ancient Greece
codpiece	pouch in the crotch of men's breeches, 15th-16th century
crinoline	stiff petticoat, or hooped skirt
doublet	man's tight jacket, 15th-17th century
farthingale	hoop supporting a skirt, 16th century
frock coat, surtout	man's formal overcoat with skirts to the knee, 19th century
galligaskins	long loose breeches, 16th-17th century
himation	long loose cloak worn by men and women in ancient Greece
hose	breeches fastened to a doublet
mantua	loose gown revealing an underskirt, 17th-18th century
paletot	woman's fitted jacket, 19th century
pallium, toga	cloak or robe in ancient Rome
peplos	woman's blouse or robe in ancient Greece

- club-shaped, thickened at one end CLAVATE, CLAVIFORM
- club with a spiked metal head used in medieval battles MACE

- hit or batter with or as if with a club BASTE, FUSTIGATE
- local branch of a club or society CHAPTER

- short heavy club CUDGEL, BLUDGEON, BLACKJACK
- small, weighted club for killing fish PRIEST

Clouds

Cirrus (bad weather coming)

Nimbostratus (rain imminent)

Cirrocumulus (unsettled weather)

Stratocumulus (dry but dull weather)

Cirrostratus (showers or rain soon)

Stratus (drizzle coming)

Altocumulus (sunny periods)

Cumulus/woolpack (sunny spells)

Altostratus (rain likely)

Cumulonimbus (showers and lightning)

- vote against or veto someone, especially to membership of a club BLACKBALL
- wooden bottle-shaped club thrown or swung about in juggling and gymnastics INDIAN CLUB
- wooden club used by Australian aborigines NULLA-NULLA, WADDY
- wooden club used in Ireland SHILLELAGH
- wooden club with a bulbous end used in southern Africa KNOBKERRIE

clump or tuft, as of grass or hair TUSSOCK, HASSOCK, TUFFET

clumsy, bumbling HAM-HANDED, HAM-FISTED, GAUCHE, INEPT, MALADROIT
- clumsy, jerky or graceless in movement, gawky or lumbering UNGAINLY, UNCOORDINATED, LUBBERLY, UNCOUTH
- clumsy and inelegant as a sentence might be CUMBERSOME, AWKWARD
- clumsy person, oaf or lout, duffer CLODHOPPER, GALOOT, LUBBER, SCHLEMIEL, KLUTZ, PALOOKA, STUMBLEBUM, LUMMOX

cluster, mass CONGLOMERATE
- cluster of fruit or flowers at the end of a stalk TRUSS

clutching or retentive, as a good memory is TENACIOUS

coach or large bus, as used for sightseeing CHARABANC
- rider of the left front horse of a coach POSTILION

coal dust or waste, or inferior coal from a mine CULM
- coal miner, or coal ship COLLIER
- coal of a hard and heavy kind that burns slowly with a hot, clear flame ANTHRACITE
- coal of a poor peaty quality LIGNITE, BROWN COAL
- coal of a soft and rich kind that burns with a smoky yellow flame BITUMINOUS COAL
- coal-producing CARBONIFEROUS
- coal that burns brightly and gives off much smoke CANNEL
- portable metal stand for burning coal or charcoal BRAZIER
- sloping channel or duct down which water, coal, parcels, or the like can be conveyed CHUTE
- small brick of compressed charcoal or coal dust, used for fuel, as at barbecues BRIQUETTE
- solid residue in ashes from burned coal CLINKER
- thin seam of coal lying above a larger seam in a mine RIDER

coal mine COLLIERY
- methane-based gas, explosive when mixed with air, formed in coal mines FIREDAMP
- waste rocks and minerals from a coal mine SLAG

coarse See **rude, vulgar**

coast See also **geography**
- coast road, often built into the side of a cliff CORNICHE
- adjective for a coast LITTORAL

coat See also **clothes**
- coat food with flour, sugar, or the like, as by sprinkling DREDGE
- coat or cover a surface with grease, plaster, or mud DAUB
- coat or covering, such as a seed's coat INTEGUMENT
- coat with plaster or cement RENDER, PARGET
- coating, cover, or surrounding layer MANTLE
- coating, filler, or glaze, as for paper or walls, made of wax, clay, glue, resin, or the like SIZE
- coating, insulation, or facing material on the outside of a building, pipe, tank, or the like CLADDING
- mammal's coat PELAGE
- powdery coating as on plums and new coins BLOOM
- thin coating of plastic, wood, or the like LAMINATE, VENEER
- thin coating of substance on the surface of a solid ADSORPTION
- thin outer cover or coating, such as a membrane or film PELLICLE

coat of arms See also **heraldry**
- ideal or principle stated by a word or maxim, as on a coat of arms MOTTO
- knight's tunic bearing his coat of arms TABARD
- person entitled to a coat of arms ARMIGER
- relating to heraldry or coats of arms ARMORIAL
- shield, as in heraldry, bearing a coat of arms ESCUTCHEON
- study, devising, or awarding of coats of arms HERALDRY
- title or inscription, as on a coin or coat of arms LEGEND

cobra - king cobra HAMADRYAD

cobweb film or mesh floating in the air or found on foliage GOSSAMER

cockfight MAIN, SPAR
- metal spur on a gamecock's leg in cockfighting GAFF

cockpit - transparent cover of the cockpit of an aircraft CANOPY

cocktails See **drink**

coconut cookies MACAROON
- coconut-husk fiber, as used for ropes and matting COIR
- coconut meat, dried and prepared for oil extraction COPRA
- dried and shredded or powdered, as preserved coconut is DESICCATED

cocoon - pupa of a moth or butterfly, often encased in a cocoon CHRYSALIS

cod - young cod, codling SPRAG

code, as among children, formed by regular rearrangements of spoken words, as in turning *dog* into *ogday* PIG LATIN
- code, as used by radio operators, for identifying letters of the alphabet, such as *Tango* standing for *T* PHONETIC ALPHABET
- code of a simple kind, in which letters are substituted according to a key CIPHER
- code of laws, especially a digest of Roman law PANDECTS
- code or signaling system based on the position of two flags, one held in each hand SEMAPHORE
- coded writing or message CRYPTOGRAM
- deciphering of codes, secret writings, and the like CRYPTANALYSIS
- in ordinary language, not put in code EN CLAIR
- interpret or clarify a code, decode DECIPHER, DECRYPT
- put a text into code ENCIPHER
- study of codes, or the technique or process of coding messages CRYPTOGRAPHY, CRYPTOLOGY

coffee, tea, or other drink, food, or drug that temporarily increases activity or efficiency STIMULANT
- coffee brewed by steam or hot water under pressure ESPRESSO
- coffee cup of small size, or the strong black coffee drunk from it DEMITASSE
- coffee house or smoking room in former times DIVAN
- coffee of high quality MOCHA
- coffee with frothed milk CAPPUCCINO
- coffee with most of the caffeine removed DECAFFEINATED COFFEE
- coffeepot in which hot water filters through ground coffee held in a small perforated tray PERCOLATOR
- dregs or sediment, lees, such as coffee grounds GROUTS
- root product used as a coffee additive or substitute CHICORY
- stimulant substance in tea and coffee CAFFEINE

coffin carrier or attendant at a funeral PALLBEARER
- coffin of stone, typically having a sculpture or inscription SARCOPHAGUS
- platform or stand for a corpse or coffin, before burial BIER
- raised platform or table on which a coffin or corpse lies, as during a state funeral CATAFALQUE
- roofed gate of a churchyard, where the coffin is traditionally rested at the start of the burial

service LYCH-GATE
cog - small cogwheel or gear wheel that engages with a larger gear wheel or toothed rack PINION
- toothed projection on a cogwheel or cylinder, designed to engage a moving post SPROCKET

coil of thread, wool, rope, or yarn SKEIN, HANK
- coil or whirl, as of a spiral shell VOLUTION
- coil of wire producing a magnetic field when carrying an electric current, as used for activating switches SOLENOID
- coiled or ring-shaped, as the frond of a young fern might be CIRCINATE
- coiled or rolled up CONVOLUTE, CONVOLUTED

coin See chart
- coin blank, plain metal disc ready for stamping as a coin PLANCHET, FLAN
- coin collector NUMISMATIST
- coinage, minted money SPECIE
- circular inscription on a coin or medal CIRCUMSCRIPTION
- engraved metal block for punching or pressing a design, as onto coins DIE
- face or side of a coin bearing the main design, "heads" OBVERSE
- face or side of a coin bearing the secondary design, "tails" VERSO, REVERSE
- government revenue from the minting of coins, after the cost of metal and production has been subtracted SEIGNIORAGE
- grade or unit in a classification system, such as a coin of a specified value DENOMINATION
- grooves or ridges round the edge of a coin MILLING, REEDING, FLUTING, ENGRAILING
- roll of coins wrapped in paper ROULEAU
- space beneath the main design on the reverse of a coin, as used for recording the date or place of minting EXERGUE
- study of coins, money, or medals NUMISMATICS
- title or inscription, as on a coin or coat of arms LEGEND

coincide, happen at the same time or place CONCUR
- coinciding, simultaneous occurrence CONJUNCTION
- coinciding or identical in range, size, meaning, or the like COTERMINOUS, COEXTENSIVE, CONGRUENT

coincidence of a supposedly significant kind, especially in Jungian philosophy SYNCHRONICITY

cold and clammy, as the skin of malaria patients is ALGID
- cold and sluggish in temperament SATURNINE
- cold-blooded, having a varying body temperature POIKILOTHERMIC
- cold drink with fizz CARBONATED DRINK
- cold remedy consisting of a hot sweet milk drink curdled with wine or beer POSSET
- coldly reserved ALOOF
- coldly simple, harsh or unadorned, austere, as furniture might be CLINICAL
- abnormally low body temperature, typically caused by exposure to the cold HYPOTHERMIA
- calmly indifferent, cold, stiff, unemotional IMPASSIVE, BLOODLESS, PHLEGMATIC
- cooling power of cold air based on wind speed and air temperature WINDCHILL FACTOR
- freezing cold, icy HYPERBOREAN

cold (combining form) CRYO-, PSYCHRO-

collaborating, in partnership with, especially in some dubious enterprise IN CAHOOTS, COLLUDING

collapse See also **break, fall**
- collapse, cave in, as the ground might SUBSIDE
- collapse, fail or break down com-

COINS

bezant	gold Byzantine coin; a solidus	**obol**	ancient Greek silver coin
bob	old British shilling	**rap**	counterfeit halfpenny in 18th-century Ireland
dandiprat	small 16th-century English coin	**real**	old silver coin of Spain and Spanish America
denarius	ancient Roman silver coin	**sequin/zecchino**	old coin of the Venetian Republic
dime	U.S. and Canadian ten-cent piece	**sesterce/as**	ancient Roman coin, of silver or bronze
doubloon	old Spanish gold coin	**solidus**	gold Byzantine coin
ducat	old European gold coin	**sou**	old French coin of low value
florin	old British two-shilling coin	**sovereign**	old British one-pound coin
groat	old British silver fourpenny coin	**stater**	ancient Greek coin
groschen	Austrian bronze coin, one-hundredth of a schilling; old silver German coin of varying value	**stiver**	old Dutch coin, one-twentieth of a guilder
Krugerrand	South African coin containing one ounce of pure gold	**taler/thaler**	old German, Swiss, or Austrian silver coin
louis d'or	old French gold coin	**tanner**	old British sixpence
moidore	old Portuguese gold coin	**tickey**	old South African threepenny piece
napoleon	old French gold coin		
nickel	U.S. and Canadian five-cent piece		
noble	old British gold coin, one-third of a pound		

pletely FOUNDER
- collapse in on itself, fold up TELESCOPE, CONCERTINA
- collapse inward, crumple under external pressure IMPLODE

collar - collarlike piece of armor protecting the throat GORGET
- collar of a high, stiff, round style MANDARIN STYLE
- collar of a high and often tight-fitting style CHOKER, STOCK
- collar of a wide, deeply indented design VANDYKE
- collar or necklace, typically of twisted metal, worn in ancient times TORQUE
- ring on a dog's collar for attaching a leash TERRET
- stiff, upright collar worn in the 17th century REBATO, RABATO
- wide collar, often of lace, covering the shoulders and neckline BERTHA
- wide decorative collar of lace or fine fabric, as worn in the 16th and 17th centuries RUFF
- wide linen or lace collar worn flat on the shoulders by men in the 17th century FALLING BAND

collarbone CLAVICLE

colleague See **partner**

collect See **gather**

collection See also **group, crowd**
- collection, as of games or useful hints, grouped together COMPENDIUM
- collection or hoard of various things ACCUMULATION, STOCKPILE, ASSEMBLAGE, CONGLOMERATION
- collection of assorted writings, compiled from the works of one or more authors CHRESTOMATHY, ANTHOLOGY, COLLECTANEA, POTPOURRI, OMNIBUS, MISCELLANY
- collection of complete writings, especially by a particular writer CORPUS, OEUVRE
- collection of unusual, foreign, or bizarre objects EXOTICA
- collection of varied items sold as a single lot JOB LOT
- collection or mixture of varied objects or elements CONGERIES, MOTLEY
- church collection, offerings by the congregation OFFERTORY
- churchwarden's assistant, especially the person who takes the collection SIDESMAN

collection (combining form) -ANA, -IANA

collective farm in Israel KIBBUTZ
- collective farm in the U.S.S.R. KOLKHOZ

collector or student of ancient art objects, pottery, jewelry, and the like ANTIQUARY
- collector of beer mats TEGESTOLOGIST
- collector of bookplates EX-LIBRIST
- collector of butterflies and moths LEPIDOPTERIST
- collector of coins, money, or medals NUMISMATIST
- collector of matchboxes, matchbox labels, and matchbooks PHILLUMENIST
- collector of postcards DELTIOLOGIST
- collector of stamps, postmarks, and the like PHILATELIST
- collector or lover of fine books BIBLIOPHILE
- collector's items such as antiques and curios, or a cultivated liking for them VIRTU

college See also **university**
- college dining room HALL, REFECTORY
- college official who has nominal rights of inspection and arbitration VISITOR
- college or university education TERTIARY EDUCATION
- college or university official in charge of finances BURSAR
- college principal or other administrative official WARDEN, RECTOR, PROVOST
- college steward who buys the provisions MANCIPLE
- first-year student at a college or university FRESHMAN
- referring to nonresident students or to studies or activities outside the normal courses of a university or college EXTRAMURAL

colony or county whose ruler formerly had royal powers PALATINATE
- colonial representative, as formerly in a protected Indian state RESIDENT
- colonist or settler in a new region in former times PLANTER

color See chart, page 114
- color belonging to any of various groups considered capable of generating all colors PRIMARY COLOR
- color-changing lizard CHAMELEON
- color of a light delicate tint PASTEL
- color or shade HUE, TINT, TINCTURE
- color parts of cloth with dye while tying other parts tightly, producing a mottled effect TIE-DYE
- color range, as of a painting or painter PALETTE
- colored too brightly, overornamented, flashy, loud GAUDY, TAWDRY, GARISH, TECHNICOLOR
- colors, such as yellow and blue, that can be mixed to produce white or gray COMPLEMENTARY COLORS
- band of color on an insect or plant FASCIA
- changing pattern of colors KALEIDOSCOPE
- distinction or variation of a very fine or subtle kind, as of tone, color, or meaning NUANCE
- having all the colors of the rainbow, multicolored PRISMATIC
- having different colors, especially blotches of black and white, as a horse might PIEBALD, PINTO
- having or displaying a variety of colors MOTLEY, PIED, PARTICOLORED, VARICOLORED, VARIEGATED, POLYCHROME
- maximum purity and vividness of a color SATURATION
- pale shade or tinge of color CAST
- range or image of the colors of the rainbow SPECTRUM
- relating to color or colors CHROMATIC
- scientific study of color CHROMATICS
- sensation of color evoked by a sound, or similar sensation of a sense different from the one stimulated SYNESTHESIA
- shimmering or changing in color, as some fabrics are SHOT, IRIDESCENT, OPALESCENT, TAFFETA
- spotted or streaked with different colors or tints MOTTLED
- spread across or through, as a color might SUFFUSE

color (combining form) CHROM-, CHROMO-

color blindness in which all colors are a single hue MONOCHROMATISM
- partial color blindness in which green and red are confused DALTONISM, PROTANOPIA
- partial color blindness in which blue cannot be distinguished TRITANOPIA

colorful or noisy display, designed to impress or advertise RAZZLE-DAZZLE, RAZZMATAZZ

coloring chemical in the skin, hair, and eye PIGMENT, MELANIN
- coloring matter, as for making paints or inks PIGMENT
- coloring or appearance that protects an animal by causing it to resemble an unrelated animal that is poisonous or unpalatable to predators BATESIAN MIMICRY
- coloring that protects or conceals an animal by camouflage CRYPTIC COLORING
- referring or relating to the coloring of an animal that serves as camouflage APATETIC
- referring to the coloring of an animal that warns off predators by suggesting that it is poisonous or bad-tasting APOSEMATIC

colorless, or of neutral color, such as black, white, or gray ACHROMATIC

colorless (combining form) LEUC-, LEUCO-, LEUKO-

Colosseum - aisle leading to seats in a stadium, as in the Colosseum in Rome VOMITORY
column See illustration, page 116, and also **pillar**
- column in classical architecture in the form of a statue of a man TELAMON, ATLAS
- column in classical architecture in the form of a statue of a woman CARYATID
- column width or page width in printing MEASURE
- arranged in a table of rows and columns TABULAR
- building whose roof rests on rows of columns HYPOSTYLE
- covered walk with columns on one or both sides, as in ancient Greek buildings STOA
- having a row of columns on all sides, as an ancient temple might PERIPTERAL
- presenting texts or data in columns side by side for comparison SYNOPTIC
- row of columns positioned at regular intervals COLONNADE
- row of columns surrounding a building or courtyard, or the area surrounded PERISTYLE
- slight bulge that makes a column appear straight when viewed from below ENTASIS
- style of classical architecture based on the type of column used ORDER
comb - comblike, having protrusions resembling the teeth of a comb, as a perch's scales have CTENOID
- comb of a cock or similar outgrowth, normal or abnormal, on an animal, seed, the skin, or the like CARUNCLE
- comb of steel for combing flax HACKLE
- comb the hair downward near the roots in order to bulk it up BACKCOMB, TEASE
combat arena, as for chivalric tournaments LISTS
- combat between knights, with lances on horseback JOUST, TILTING MATCH
- trial by combat in former times WAGER OF BATTLE
combatant, typically armed with a sword, in an ancient Roman arena GLADIATOR
- combatant armed with a net and trident in an ancient Roman arena RETIARIUS
combination See also **collection, group, mixture**
- combination of businesses or interests formed for some joint enterprise SYNDICATE, CONSORTIUM
- combination of experiences, such as those that make up a relationship GESTALT
- combination or possible variation of numbers, elements, or members PERMUTATION
combine See also **join, mix**
- combine or arrange in correct order COLLOCATE
- combine or blend into a single unit INCORPORATE, MELD
- combined, planned or performed together, as an effort might be CONCERTED, COORDINATED
- combined action, as of medicines or muscles, producing a greater effect than the sum of the individual effects SYNERGISM
- combining and uniting of separate things, such as small businesses, into a larger whole CONSOLIDATION, AMALGAMATION
- combining of parts or elements to form a whole, or the whole so produced SYNTHESIS
- combining property of an atom or chemical group VALENCE
come before in time or order

COLORS

REDDISH-PURPLE

amaranth
burgundy
cerise
magenta
maroon
mauve
puce

PURPLISH-BLUE OR VIOLET

amethyst
aubergine
heliotrope

BLUE

azure
cerulean
cyan
gentian
indigo
lapis lazuli
sapphire
saxe blue
ultramarine

GREENISH-BLUE

aquamarine
cobalt blue
ice blue
Nile blue
teal
turquoise

GREEN

celadon
eau de nile
emerald
jade
Kendal green
Lincoln green
loden
terre-verte

YELLOWISH-GREEN

chartreuse
luteous
reseda

YELLOW OR BROWNISH-YELLOW

barium yellow
chamois
champagne
citrine
citron
fallow/fawn
flax
fulvous
gamboge
jonquil
maize
nankeen
ochre
old gold
saffron
topaz

REDDISH-YELLOW OR ORANGE

amber
apricot
coral
flamingo
peach
salmon
tea rose

RED

cardinal
carmine/crimson/cochineal
cherry
cinnabar
old rose
rubious
solferino

REDDISH-BROWN

auburn
brick
chestnut
ginger
henna
mahogany
oxblood
roan
rust/rubiginous/ferruginous
russet/rufous
sienna/raw sienna
sorrel
terracotta
titian
vermilion/vermeil

BROWN

bay
beaver
beige
biscuit
café au lait
cinnamon
dun
mocha
nutmeg
sandalwood
sepia
taupe
tawny
tortoiseshell
umber
walnut

GRAY

battleship gray
charcoal gray
dove
nutria

BLACK

ebony
fuliginous
jet
raven
sable
subfusc

YELLOWISH-GRAY OR OFF-WHITE

alabaster
bisque
ecru
eggshell
oyster
putty

PRECEDE

come down, or behave as if coming down, to the level of others CONDESCEND, DEIGN, PATRONIZE

come out, issue from a source EMANATE

come to pass, turn out, happen EVENTUATE, TRANSPIRE

comedian, joker, or prankster FARCEUR, BUFFOON
- comedian's partner or foil who supplies openings or cues for jokes STRAIGHT MAN, STOOGE

comedy See also **satire, joke**
- comedy of an unsubtle, energetic, farcical kind SLAPSTICK

comet - bright dense central part of the head of a comet NUCLEUS
- cloud around the nucleus of a comet COMA
- point farthest from the sun in the orbit of a planet or comet APHELION
- point nearest to the sun in the orbit of a planet or comet PERIHELION

comfort See also **calm**
- comfort, sympathy, or reassurance SOLACE, CONSOLATION
- comforting, soothing, relaxing ANODYNE
- comforts, conveniences, pleasant and helpful features or services FACILITIES, AMENITIES
- relieve or reduce pain, grief, or the like in order to bring comfort ALLAY, ASSUAGE, ALLEVIATE, PALLIATE

comfortable, easy, as a job might be CUSHY
- comfortable and cozy, snug GEMÜTLICH
- comfortable and spacious COMMODIOUS
- comfortable enough to live in, adequate HABITABLE

comforter or sympathizer who causes only distress JOB'S COMFORTER

comic opera - male singer, usually bass singer, of comic opera roles BUFFO

coming, arrival ADVENT
- coming together, as of events CONFLUENCE, CONCOURSE

command See **order**

commanding, authoritative MAGISTERIAL

commandments - relating to Noah or his time, as the seven pre-Mosaic commandments are NOACHIAN

comment See also **remark**
- comment made in passing, incidental remark OBITER DICTUM
- comment on or discuss in detail EXPOUND, DESCANT, DISCOURSE
- comment or carefully considered observation, usually very critical ANIMADVERSION
- comments or notes written in the margin of a book ANNOTATIONS, MARGINALIA
- clear, crisp, and forceful, as a comment or argument might be TRENCHANT, COGENT
- cutting, penetrating, to the point, as a comment might be INCISIVE, MORDANT
- hurtfully indirect, cutting, as a comment might be BARBED
- throw in a comment by way of interruption INTERJECT, INTERPOSE

commentary, precise statement, detailed explanation EXPOSITION, EXEGESIS
- commentary on a text, note of criticism or explanation ANNOTATION, GLOSS, SCHOLIUM
- formal commentary or treatise on a subject DISQUISITION

commerce See also **company** and chart at **economics**
- adjective for trade or commerce MERCANTILE
- commercial activity, such as buying and selling, of a business TURNOVER

commit a crime, perform a hoax, make a blunder, or the like PERPETRATE
- commit oneself irrevocably to a particular course of action CROSS THE RUBICON
- commit oneself to a difficult task or risky project GRASP THE NETTLE

committed to and actively promoting a moral or political cause ENGAGÉ

committee set up for a particular purpose or occasion AD HOC COMMITTEE
- elect a new member to a committee or other group by a decision of the existing group CO-OPT
- number of persons required for a vote or other formal decision by a committee, assembly, or the like QUORUM

common, shared, joint MUTUAL, RECIPROCAL
- common, standard, or constantly needed commodity STAPLE
- common and typically unsophisticated opinion, taste, or group of people LOWEST COMMON DENOMINATOR
- common name, as of a plant or animal, by contrast with a technical Latin name TRIVIAL NAME
- common opinion, general agreement or attitude CONSENSUS
- common or crude, having vulgar tastes PLEBEIAN
- common or deeply rooted within a particular area or group ENDEMIC
- common or frequent, widespread PREVAILING, PREVALENT, PREDOMINANT, RIFE, REGNANT
- common or vulgar people, the masses or mob, rabble or riffraff HOI POLLOI, CANAILLE
- common people, especially lower-class working people PROLETARIAT
- common people of ancient Rome PLEBS
- common people or inhabitants COMMONALTY, POPULACE
- common speech of the people VERNACULAR, VULGATE, DEMOTIC
- commonest item in a numerical list MODE
- right to pasture animals on common land COMMONAGE

common (combining form) COEN-, COENO-

common sense practical shrewdness GUMPTION, NOUS
- rejection of commonsense observation in favor of abstract theory RATIONALISM

commonplace See also **cliché, dull**
- commonplace or familiar theme, idea, or image in literature TOPOS

Commonwealth - former term for a large self-governing nation of the Commonwealth DOMINION

communicate, make known, reveal IMPART, DISCLOSE, DIVULGE

communication between two minds by an alleged sixth sense TELEPATHY
- communication or contact, as between various sections of the armed forces LIAISON
- communication system sending telegrams through automatic exchanges TELEX
- characteristic way of thinking and feeling as a help or hindrance to communication with others WAVELENGTH
- referring to conversation, as about the weather, which expresses friendly feelings rather than to communicate ideas PHATIC
- study of gesture, facial expression, and the like as a form of communication KINESICS
- supplementing verbal communication, as voice qualities and gestures do PARALINGUISTIC
- unable to communicate with others INCOMMUNICADO

Communion given to a person in danger of death VIATICUM
- Communion service, especially in Eastern Churches LITURGY
- bell rung during the elevation of the Communion bread and wine in a Roman Catholic Church SACRING BELL
- bread or wafer consecrated in the Communion HOST, SACRAMENT, EUCHARIST

- breaking of the bread by the priest at Communion FRACTION
- calling on the Holy Spirit to consecrate the Communion bread and wine EPICLESIS
- consecrated bread and wine at Communion SPECIES
- container for storing the Communion bread and wine, typically an ornamental box TABERNACLE
- container for the consecrated Communion wafers CIBORIUM, PYX,

Columns

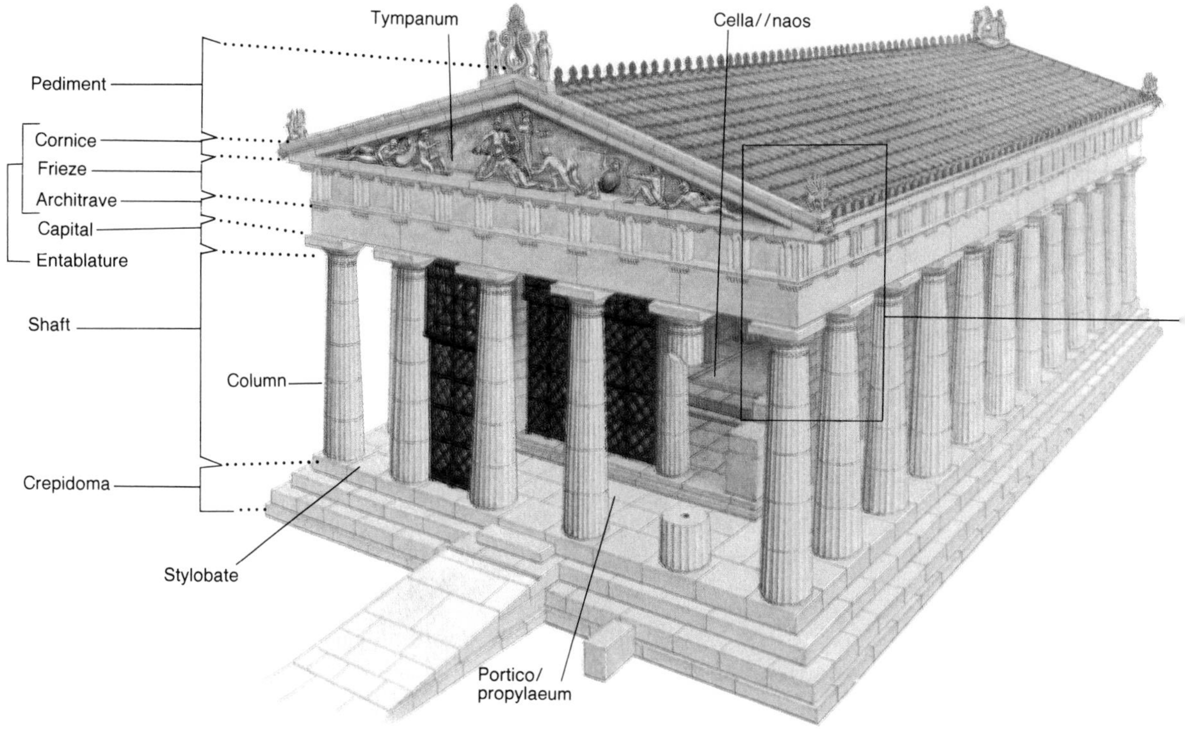

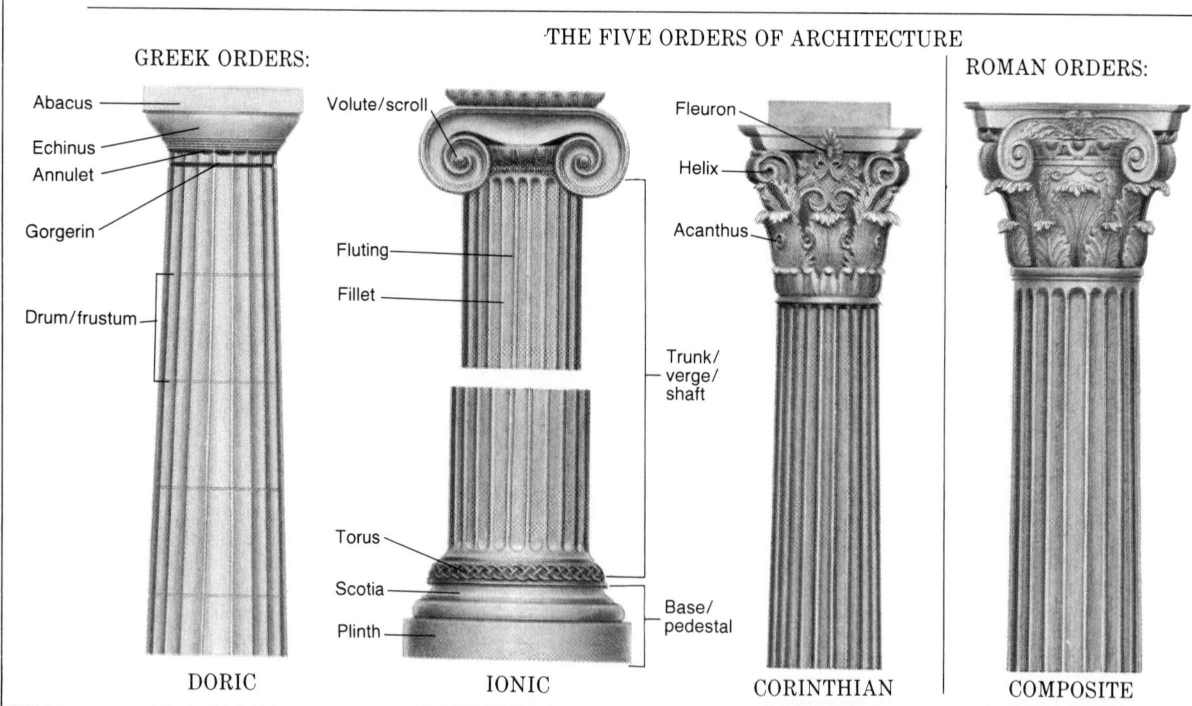

MONSTRANCE, OSTENSORY
- container for the water or wine at Communion CRUET, AMPULLA
- conversion of the consecrated Communion bread and wine into the body and blood of Christ TRANSUBSTANTIATION
- coexistence of the consecrated Communion bread and wine with the body and blood of Christ CONSUBSTANTIATION
- cup for the consecrated wine at Communion CHALICE
- kiss of peace at Communion, or the plate formerly used to convey it PAX
- lifting up of the Communion bread and wine for adoration by the congregation ELEVATION
- linen cloth for wiping the Communion chalice or the celebrant's lips PURIFICATOR
- linen square covering the Communion chalice PALL
- offering to God of the bread and wine of Communion OBLATION, OFFERTORY
- plate, typically of silver or gold, used for holding the bread at Communion PATEN
- priest officiating at Communion or some other religious ceremony or rite CELEBRANT, OFFICIANT
- table for the Communion bread and wine CREDENCE TABLE
- thin disc of unleavened bread used in Communion WAFER
- white linen cloth on which the bread and wine are placed for a Communion service CORPORAL

communist emblem HAMMER AND SICKLE
- communist or extreme radical BOLSHEVIK, BOLSHIE, RED
- Communist-party official in charge of political education and party loyalty COMMISSAR
- Communist-party supporter who is not actually a member of it FELLOW TRAVELER, PINKO
- Communist party's system of internal administration APPARAT
- persecution of suspected communist sympathizers in the United States in the 1950's McCARTHYISM, WITCH-HUNT

community, brotherhood, fellowship FRATERNITY, SODALITY
- relating to neighboring or rival communities SECTARIAN

companion, typically an older woman, for a young woman in public CHAPERON, DUENNA
- companion or friend who is affectionate, reliable, and usually lively BOON COMPANION
- sociable or festive, as a party atmosphere or drinking companion might be JOVIAL, CONVIVIAL

companionship, comradely or brotherly spirit ESPIRIT DE CORPS, CAMARADERIE, FRATERNITY

company grouping or business association, especially an illegal one, to monopolize manufacture or con-

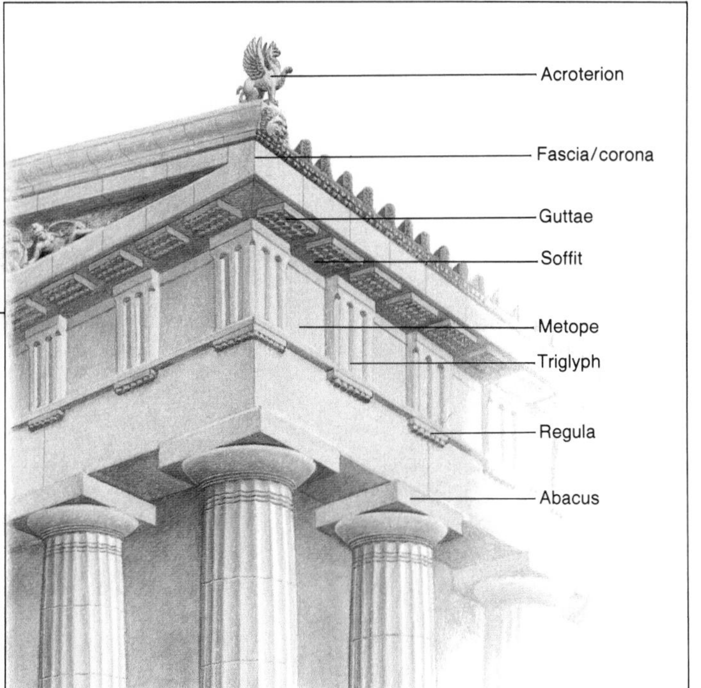

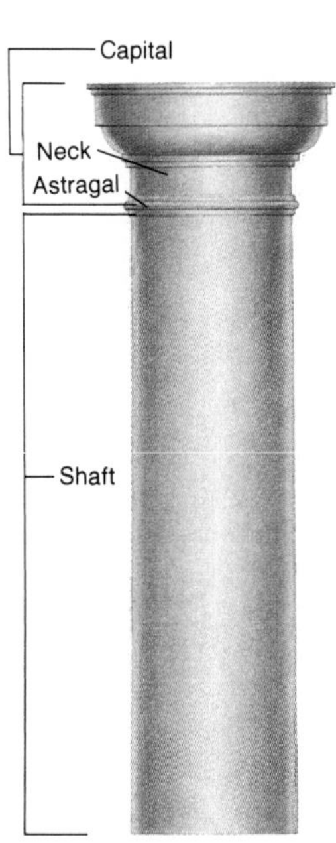

TUSCAN

FIGURES USED AS COLUMNS

Caryatid

Telamon/atlas

trol prices CARTEL, TRUST
- company of actors performing a variety of plays during a season REPERTORY COMPANY
- company or business having control of other businesses HOLDING COMPANY
- company producing books, TV movies, or the like for another company PRODUCER, PACKAGER
- company that is under another company's control SUBSIDIARY COMPANY
- company trademark, emblem, or symbol LOGO
- company's distinctive color scheme on its vehicles, aircraft, or the like LIVERY
- company's rules, or the document containing them, required for registration ARTICLES OF ASSOCIATION
- business association of various interests or companies formed for some joint enterprise CONSORTIUM, SYNDICATE
- business corporation made up of many wide-ranging companies CONGLOMERATE
- combining or uniting of separate businesses into a larger company CONSOLIDATION
- engage in a variety of activities or investments, as a large company might DIVERSIFY
- financing and launching of a company by means of a share issue FLOTATION
- form a business into a registered company INCORPORATE
- keep company or associate with in a friendly way CONSORT, FRATERNIZE, HOBNOB

compared to EQUATED WITH

compared with, in relation to, regarding VIS-À-VIS

comparison or metaphor of a witty, farfetched kind CONCEIT
- comparison showing the similarity between otherwise differing elements ANALOGY
- degrees of comparison of adjectives and adverbs POSITIVE, COMPARATIVE, SUPERLATIVE
- measure or standard used for comparison YARDSTICK
- placed side by side, as for comparison JUXTAPOSED
- so different or distinct that no comparison is possible DISPARATE, INCONGRUOUS
- standard of comparison in a statistical analysis or scientific experiment CONTROL
- unfair or offensive, as a discriminatory comparison would be INVIDIOUS

compass direction or course, as of an aircraft, especially when guided by radio VECTOR
- compass error resulting from variant local magnetic conditions DEVIATION
- compass stand on a ship BINNACLE
- circle, often decorated, printed on a map, showing the points of the compass COMPASS ROSE
- device to keep a compass horizontal at sea GIMBALS
- four main compass points CARDINAL POINTS

compasses - measuring instrument resembling a pair of compasses, used for measuring angular distance SECTOR
- instrument resembling a pair of compasses, used in draftsmanship for measuring or comparing lengths DIVIDERS
- pair of compasses for drawing large circles, or similar instrument for drawing ellipses TRAMMEL

compatible - make two apparently conflicting things consistent or compatible with each other RECONCILE

compensate for loss or damages INDEMNIFY, REIMBURSE, RECOMPENSE
- compensate for, offset, make up for COUNTERVAIL
- compensation, making good, repayment RESTITUTION, REPARATIONS, REDEMPTION, AMENDS, REDRESS

compete, struggle, or strive VIE, CONTEND
- compete with or rival, strive to equal or outdo EMULATE

competition See also **contest**
- competition, contest, or race in which the entire prize is awarded to the winner SWEEPSTAKES
- competition or tournament in which all the contestants compete against one another in turn, the league system ROUND ROBIN
- relating to competitions and competitors AGONISTIC

complain See also **protest, objection, criticize**
- complain, fret, be disheartened or depressed REPINE
- complain, protest, or object earnestly REMONSTRATE, EXPOSTULATE
- complain at or regret sadly, lament BEWAIL
- complain or grumble at petty things, nitpick, raise trivial objections CAVIL, CARP
- complain or grumble in a whining way YAMMER, KVETCH
- complaining in a whining way, fretful or peevish QUERULOUS
- complaining noisily VOCIFEROUS

complaint, protest, or statement, as in diplomatic matters or to the public authorities DEMARCHE
- complaint or protest, or the injustice giving rise to it GRIEVANCE
- complaint that is long and lamenting JEREMIAD
- complaints or appeals, as to an authority REPRESENTATIONS
- essential or most telling part of an accusation, charge, or complaint GRAVAMEN
- official investigating citizens' complaints into government incompetence or unfairness OMBUDSMAN
- register a complaint LODGE

complement, additional or matching part PENDANT
- complement or counterpart OBVERSE

complete See also **end, stop**
- complete, absolute, unlimited, as the surrender of a warring nation might be UNCONDITIONAL
- complete, detailed, thorough, as a report might be COMPREHENSIVE, CIRCUMSTANTIAL, EXHAUSTIVE
- complete, reliable, and authoritative, as a history or biography might be DEFINITIVE
- complete, utter, absolute RANK, OUTRIGHT, UNMITIGATED
- complete and impressive display, defense, or the like PANOPLY
- completeness, fullness PLENITUDE, PLENUM
- completeness, unity, undivided or unbroken condition INTEGRITY
- steps toward the completion of a task or process INROADS
- time required to complete a process, especially in manufacturing or transport TURNAROUND

complete (combining form) HOL-, HOLO-, TEL-, TELO-

completely (combining form) CATA-, PAN-

complex of unconscious emotions, in Freudian theory, affecting a young child, including sexual desire in the boy for his mother, and in the girl for her father OEDIPUS COMPLEX
- Oedipus complex in a girl ELECTRA COMPLEX

complexion - pale sickly yellowish in color or complexion SALLOW
- reddish in appearance or complexion, rosy, ruddy, or flushed FLORID
- referring to or having a reddish complexion SANGUINE

complicate, obscure, confuse OBFUSCATE

complicated See also **difficult**
- complicated, complex, having many interrelated or entangled elements INTRICATE, INVOLUTED,

RETICULAR
- complicated or devious, as intrigue often is LABYRINTHINE, BYZANTINE

complication, tangle, confusing factor CONVOLUTION
- complications, aftereffects, or condition following a disease SEQUELLA
- complications, unavoidable and usually undesirable consequences of an action or decision RAMIFICATIONS

compliment See **praise**

compliments, respects, courteous greetings DEVOIRS

composer's work, typically numbered in sequence OPUS
- classification and numbering (1 to 626) of Mozart's opus KÖCHEL LISTING
- share of the proceeds paid to a composer from sales or performances of his or her work ROYALTY

compound, made up of several parts COMPOSITE
- breaking down of a chemical compound into its constituents ANALYSIS
- forming of a chemical compound from its constituents SYNTHESIS

compressed air - filled with or run by compressed air, as most tires and some drills are PNEUMATIC

compromise, adapt oneself, or submit so as to fit in with current conditions as a way of gaining time TEMPORIZE
- compromise between people with competing interests, allowing them to get on together MODUS VIVENDI
- compromising or insincere person adapting his or her actions and opinions to those currently accepted TIMESERVER

compulsion or force, as by threatening DURESS, COERCION, CONSTRAINT
- compulsion to talk, sometimes caused by mental illness LOGORRHEA

compulsive, irrational and habitual, as a liar might be PATHOLOGICAL

compulsory, unavoidable, required OBLIGATORY, STATUTORY, MANDATORY, PREREQUISITE, IMPERATIVE
- compulsory, done or required against one's will INVOLUNTARY

computer See chart, page 120
- computer-aided study of information flow and control systems in electronics, mechanics, and biology CYBERNETICS
- computer chip, tiny electronic circuit based on a semiconductor wafer SILICON CHIP
- computerized mathematical representation of a problem, system, or situation SIMULATION
- application of biology to engineering and electronics, especially of brain functions to computers BIONICS
- capable of functioning together in an efficient way, as two linked computer parts should be COMPATIBLE

comradely feeling, trust, and understanding between people RAPPORT, CAMARADERIE

conceal See also **hidden, hide**
- conceal or cover up mistakes or wrongdoing WHITEWASH
- concealment of relevant information in order to mislead SUBREPTION
- steps taken to conceal misdeeds or actions in order to mislead SMOKE SCREEN

concentrate or thicken, as by boiling or evaporation INSPISSATE
- concentrated and exaggerated interest in a single idea or subject MONOMANIA, IDÉE FIXE
- concentrated extract or essence of something QUINTESSENCE
- concentrating intensely, deeply absorbed INTENT, ENGROSSED
- gradual evening out of differently concentrated solutions by transfer through the separating membrane OSMOSIS
- interruption, hindrance to concentration DISTRACTION
- measurement of the concentration of a solute by adding a chemical reagent to the solution TITRATION
- restore something to its natural state, such as dried food or concentrated lemon juice, as by adding water RECONSTITUTE

conception occurring in a female who has already conceived SUPERFETATION

concert building or theater in ancient Greece and Rome ODEUM
- concert performance by a solo musician RECITAL
- payment or order for an advance purchase, as of concert tickets or issues of a magazine over a period of time SUBSCRIPTION
- producer or organizer of stage shows, concerts, or the like IMPRESARIO

concise See also **brief, summary**
- concise, clearly, and economically expressed, unelaborated and to the point SUCCINCT, TERSE, PITHY, SUMMARY, COMPENDIOUS
- concise, often to the point of obscurity, as a literary style might be ELLIPTICAL
- concise and elegant, as a prose style might be LAPIDARY
- concise in a wry or offhand way LACONIC
- concisely and cleverly expressed, pointed, typically with a witty twist or puzzle EPIGRAMMATIC, APHORISTIC, GNOMIC
- conciseness, terseness, as of speech or writing BREVITY

conclude See **end, stop**

concluding part of a formal speech or written discourse, typically a rhetorical summing-up PERORATION
- concluding part of the action in a play or novel, resolving or unraveling the plot DENOUEMENT
- concluding poem or speech following the end of the action of a play EPILOGUE

conclusion based on strict logical reasoning DEDUCTION, INFERENCE
- conclusion on the basis of evidence that is not or cannot ever be exhaustive GENERALIZATION
- conclusion that is wrongly or illogically derived from the premises NON SEQUITUR
- proposition on which an argument is based or from which a conclusion can be drawn PREMISE
- reasonable or logical, as a conclusion might be LEGITIMATE

concrete See also **cement**
- concrete machine-gun emplacement PILLBOX
- concrete mixture or finish, as on a floor SCREED
- coarse gravel, sand, or stones, used in making concrete BALLAST, AGGREGATE
- slab of reinforced concrete laid on soft ground as part of a building's foundations RAFT

condemn See **criticize**

condense See also **summary**
- condense or thicken, as by boiling or evaporation INSPISSATE
- condenser used in distillation, as for purifying chemicals RECTIFIER

condescend to do something DEIGN
- condescend to, treat graciously as though dealing with a subordinate PATRONIZE
- condescending system of government or authority, typically caring but restricting individual responsibility PATERNALISM

condition See also **disease**
- condition of difficulty or distress PLIGHT, PREDICAMENT, QUANDARY, DILEMMA
- condition or restriction, as in an agreement or document PROVISO
- clause, typically beginning with *if* or *unless*, stating the condition in a conditional sentence or proposition PROTASIS, ANTECEDENT
- main clause, stating the conclu-

COMPUTER TERMS

ALGOL	Algorithmic Oriented Language—an arithmetical computer language
analog computer	former type of computer operating with numbers represented by corresponding voltages, rotations, etc.
BASIC	Beginner's All-purpose Symbolic Instruction Code—a computer language
binary system	number system, as used by computers, representing all numbers as combinations of the digits 0 and 1
bit	smallest unit in a computer's memory
boustrophedon	printing of lines alternately from left to right and right to left
bug	fault in a computer system or program
byte	standard unit, usually equivalent to eight bits, used to measure a computer's memory
COBOL	Common Business Oriented Language—a computer language
CPU	central processing unit—the core of a computer, performing the logical and arithmetical operations on the data
cursor	movable pointer on a VDU, typically a square of light, indicating a specific position
dedicated	referring to a computer, key on the keyboard, or program designed or set apart for a particular function
digital computer	computer operating with numbers represented by separate electronically expressed digits, typically in the binary system
disc	information storage device, consisting of a flat rotating circular disc with a magnetic coating
disc drive	device for "playing" a disc to transfer information to or from it
format	arrange data in a form that is usable by a computer
floppy disc/ diskette	thin flexible plastic disc, as typically used in home computers
FORTRAN	Formula Translation—an algebraic computer language
GIGO	garbage in, garbage out—a formula serving as a reminder that a computer is only as good as its users
hacker	person who gains unauthorized access to a computer system
hardware	actual machinery or physical parts of a computer
interface	item of hardware or software that connects two other items of computing equipment
K/kilobyte	about 1,000 bytes (actually, 1,024 bytes), a standard unit of measure for a computer's capacity
M/megabyte	about one million bytes (1,000 kilobytes), a higher standard unit of measure for a computer's capacity
mainframe	large powerful computer
modem	modulator-demodulator—device for transmitting computer data along telephone lines
mouse	small device rolled along a surface, used to move a cursor on a VDU
OCR	optical character reader—device for "reading" printed texts and converting them into an electronic form usable by a computer
peripheral	item of secondary hardware, such as a VDU or modem, or a disc drive that is not specifically part of the CPU
pixel	basic unit of a computer-graphics display on a VDU
program	set of directions or procedures that a computer follows to operate on data
RAM	random-access memory—set of data that may be changed or erased
ROM	read-only memory—set of data that cannot be changed or erased
scrolling	vertical movement of text on a VDU
software	set of programs, data, and the like essential to a computer system but not forming part of the actual machinery
user-friendly	easy for a person to handle
VDU/monitor	visual-display unit—the screen, such as a cathode-ray tube, displaying information from a computer

sion or consequence, in a conditional sentence or proposition APODOSIS, CONSEQUENT
- prior condition for something, necessity or requirement PREREQUISITE, PRESUPPOSITION
- require or lay down as a condition in an agreement or contract STIPULATE

condition (combining form) -OSIS, -TUDE

conditional, depending CONTINGENT

conditioning, in psychology, based on associating a response with a reinforcing reward OPERANT CONDITIONING, INSTRUMENTAL CONDITIONING
- conditioning, in psychology, based on associating two stimuli and thereby eliciting a response from an originally unrelated stimulus CLASSICAL CONDITIONING, PAVLOVIAN CONDITIONING

conduct See **behave**

conductor, music teacher, leading musician, orchestra conductor, or any artistic master MAESTRO
- conductor's stick for directing the orchestra BATON
- platform, as for a public speaker or music conductor ROSTRUM, DAIS, PODIUM

cone or cylinder with its top cut off at an angle UNGULA
- cone-shaped tied bundle, as of hay or straw COCK
- cone-shaped ornament or container CORNUCOPIA
- cone-shaped, resembling a cone on its tip TURBINATE
- cone-shaped roll of thread wound on a spindle COP
- cone-shaped starched headdress worn by women in the late Middle Ages CORNET
- base part or mid-section of a cone, pyramid, or other solid object FRUSTUM

conference of top officials SUMMIT
- conference or discussion, typically on a specialist academic or professional theme SYMPOSIUM, COLLOQUIUM
- conference or meeting for the exchange of information SEMINAR
- conference representative DELEGATE
- published records or transcripts of a conference, learned society's meetings, or the like PROCEEDINGS, TRANSACTIONS

confess, admit, acknowledge AVOW, CONCEDE
- confess or hear confession SHRIVE

confession heard or absolution granted by a priest SHRIFT
- confession of guilt, acknowledgment of wrongdoing or sin PECCAVI, MEA CULPA
- person who confesses his or her sins to a priest and submits to penance PENITENT

confetti - welcoming parade where paper strips are thrown like confetti TICKER-TAPE PARADE

confide or reveal one's thoughts or feelings UNBOSOM

confident, cheerful, or optimistic SANGUINE
- confident, poised, not embarrassed UNABASHED
- confident and optimistic attitude, as among soldiers MORALE
- confidence, self-assurance, poise APLOMB
- cause to lose confidence, discourage DISHEARTEN, DEMORALIZE
- lose confidence momentarily, hesitate WAVER, FALTER
- shy, lacking in confidence or self-assertiveness DIFFIDENT, HALTING
- strengthen or revive something, such as a person's confidence BOLSTER

confidentially, between ourselves, in confidence ENTRE NOUS

confine, as in jail INCARCERATE
- confine, shackle, make fast or secure PINION

confirm See also **strengthen**
- confirm, assure WARRANT
- confirm a law, ruling, or the like, approve officially RATIFY, SANCTION, VALIDATE
- confirm as genuine, prove, bear out VOUCH FOR, ATTEST, VERIFY, AUTHENTICATE
- confirm as valid or just, uphold something, such as an objection in a court of law SUSTAIN
- confirm or back up an opinion or statement, as with additional evidence CORROBORATE, SUBSTANTIATE

confirmation - mixture of oil and balsam used in sacramental anointing, as at baptism or confirmation CHRISM

confiscate or arrest with the backing of legal authority ATTACH
- confiscate or hold in custody IMPOUND, EMBARGO
- confiscate or seize for military use COMMANDEER
- confiscate or seize property temporarily, especially a debtor's goods SEQUESTRATE, LEVY
- confiscate or transfer the ownership of, especially for public use EXPROPRIATE
- sheriff's officer who carries out a court's orders, such as confiscating the property of a bankrupt BAILIFF

conflict See also **fight, hostile, dispute**
- conflict, inconsistency, lack of agreement, as between two claims DISPARITY, DISCREPANCY, DISSONANCE, INCONGRUITY
- conflict, strife, disharmony, infighting DISCORD, DISSENSION
- conflict between two rules or laws ANTINOMY
- conflict or argument within a larger dispute, often affecting outsiders CROSSFIRE
- conflict or disagreement within a group, nation, or the like FACTION
- belief or religion based on a conflict between the universal forces or principles, as of good and evil, or the light and the dark MANICHAEISM
- minor or preliminary conflict, dispute, or military encounter SKIRMISH
- referring to destructive conflict within a group INTERNECINE
- standstill in a conflict, resulting from equal strength or stubbornness STALEMATE, DEADLOCK

conflicting, differing, not in agreement, in dispute AT VARIANCE, AT LOGGERHEADS
- conflicting, inharmonious, incapable of working or living together INCOMPATIBLE, IRRECONCILABLE
- conflicting trend, tendency, or the like CROSSCURRENT

conformity - arbitrary standard that must be conformed to exactly PROCRUSTEAN BED

confront, accuse, or criticize TAX
- confront someone unexpectedly ACCOST, WAYLAY

confuse, embarrass, or fluster DISCONCERT, DISCOMFIT, DISCOUNTENANCE
- confuse, mistake one thing for another, treat two different things as the same CONFOUND
- confuse, obscure, complicate OBFUSCATE

confused, dazed, or dizzy WOOZY
- confused, disordered, or entangled, as a complicated state of affairs might be EMBROILED, TURBID
- confused, flustered, taken aback DISCOMBOBULATED
- confused, puzzled, mystified BEWILDERED, PERPLEXED, NONPLUSSED, FLUMMOXED, BEMUSED
- confused, stunned, or dazed, as by drink STUPEFIED, BEFUDDLED
- confused or disorganized, utterly chaotic HAYWIRE, ANARCHIC
- confused or entangled situation IMBROGLIO, PREDICAMENT, MORASS, QUAGMIRE
- confused or haphazard in structure, made up of a random mix of elements PROMISCUOUS
- confused or nonsensical speech

or writing RIGMAROLE
- confused or uneasy through having lost one's bearings DISORIENTED, DISORIENTATED
- confused use of a word through mistaking it for a similar-sounding word MALAPROPISM
- confusedly, haphazardly, in a disordered way HELTER-SKELTER

confusing, mazelike place or thing, such as a crowded neighborhood WARREN

confusion See also **mixture, nonsense**
- confusion, muddle, disorder HUGGER-MUGGER, HURLY-BURLY, SCHEMOZZLE
- confusion, stir, upheaval, fuss HULLABALOO, BROUHAHA, FUROR
- confusion, uproar, utter chaos BEDLAM, PANDEMONIUM, MAYHEM, HAVOC
- burst of excitement, or confused activity FLURRY
- dismay or amazement that throws everything into confusion CONSTERNATION
- noisy confusion or upheaval COMMOTION, HUBBUB, TUMULT
- scene of confusion or noisy disorder BABEL, BEAR GARDEN
- sense of dizziness and confusion, as through fear of heights VERTIGO
- situation of utter confusion, hopeless mess SNAFU, SHAMBLES
- state of agitation, unrest, or confusion FERMENT, TURBULENCE, TURMOIL, WELTER, PERTURBATION
- state of disorder or confusion DISARRAY, MAELSTROM
- sudden violent disturbance, disruption, or confusion UPHEAVAL

congratulate oneself on something, pride or plume oneself PIQUE, PREEN

congratulations FELICITATIONS

conjunction, such as *and* or *but*, joining words, phrases, or clauses of equal status in a sentence COORDINATING CONJUNCTION
- conjunction, such as *if* or *provided that*, introducing a supposition SUPPOSITIVE
- conjunction, such as *when* or *if*, joining clauses that are not of equal status in a sentence SUBORDINATING CONJUNCTION, SUBORDINATOR
- conjunctions, such as *neither* and *nor*, paired in a complementary grammatical relationship CORRELATIVE CONJUNCTIONS
- linking of phrases or clauses by means of punctuation rather than conjunctions PARATAXIS
- omission of conjunctions from a sentence ASYNDETON
- repetition of conjunctions for stylistic effect, as in *blood and sweat and tears* POLYSYNDETON
- subordination of a clause in grammar by means of a conjunction HYPOTAXIS

conjure up a spirit EVOKE

conjuring See **magician**

connect See also **join**
- connect, as two rooms might, through a shared door, passage, or the like COMMUNICATE
- connect, join, or fit neatly or harmoniously DOVETAIL
- connect in a series CONCATENATE, CATENATE
- connect with, be related to, belong to as a rightful part or function APPERTAIN
- connecting tie or bond LIGAMENT

connection or network of connections NEXUS

connoisseur, person appreciating fine food and wine, GOURMET, EPICURE, GASTRONOME, BON VIVANT
- connoisseur in the arts VIRTUOSO
- connoisseurs, experts in a particular subject or art COGNOSCENTI

conquer See also **defeat**
- conquer and subdue, force into subjection SUBJUGATE
- conquer or occupy territory, and incorporate it into another state or an empire ANNEX

conqueror, specifically any of the 16th-century Spanish conquerors of Mexico, Peru, and other regions in the New World CONQUISTADOR

conscience, guilty feeling, regret or remorse COMPUNCTION
- driven by conscience to rebuke oneself or others REPROACH
- pang of doubt, hesitation for reasons of conscience, principle, social unease, or the like MISGIVING, SCRUPLE, QUALM
- unscrupulous, not guided or restrained by conscience UNCONSCIONABLE

conscientious, active or industrious, persevering in one's duty SEDULOUS, ASSIDUOUS, DILIGENT
- conscientious in a rigorous, painstaking way SCRUPULOUS, PUNCTILIOUS, METICULOUS

conscious, aware, responsive to stimuli SENTIENT
- conscious, informed, having knowledge COGNIZANT
- conscious or sane period between bouts of coma or insanity LUCID MOMENT
- attempted suspension of normal consciousness by writers and artists to bring out submerged ideas AUTOMATISM
- below or beyond the threshold of consciousness or perception SUBLIMINAL

consequences See **result**

conservative, antiprogressive, as in art or politics REACTIONARY
- conservative and pompous man, especially an officer or bureaucrat COLONEL BLIMP
- conservative and powerful group of people, directing or influencing social trends, artistic activity, or the like ESTABLISHMENT
- conservative element as in a political party REARGUARD
- conservative or reactionary, as in politics HARD HAT
- extreme conservative, stubbornly opposed to change DIEHARD

consider See **think**

consist of, be composed of COMPRISE

consistent See also **agree, regular**
- consistent, corresponding, in a harmonious or matching relationship COORDINATED, CONGRUOUS, CONSONANT
- consistent, in agreement CONFORMABLE, IN UNISON
- consistent, unchanging, regular and reliable UNDEVIATING, UNSWERVING, UNFALTERING, UNWAVERING, STEADFAST
- consistent, uniform, or unchanging, as through habit or compulsion CHRONIC, INVETERATE, UNREGENERATE
- consistency or harmony, as between attitudes or claims CONCORD, CONCURRENCE
- fitting, living, or working together in a harmonious and consistent relationship COMPATIBLE
- make two apparently conflicting things consistent with each other RECONCILE

consolation, comfort, cheer SOLACE

conspicuous or exceptionally noticeable PROMINENT
- conspicuously or glaringly wrong or evil FLAGRANT, EGREGIOUS

conspiracy See also **plot**
- conspiracy or plot, or group of plotters CABAL, CONFEDERACY
- banded together in conspiracy IN CAHOOTS
- criminal conspiracy to cheat or injure a victim COVIN

constant See also **permanent**
- constant, continuing uninterruptedly, unceasing INCESSANT
- constant, long-lasting DURABLE, ABIDING, PERSISTENT
- constant, regular, even, unchanging INVARIABLE
- constant, unchanging, regular and reliable UNDEVIATING, STEADFAST, UNWAVERING, UNSWERVING, UNFALTERING
- constant, uniform, as through habit or compulsion CHRONIC, INVETERATE, UNREGENERATE
- constant, untiring, ceaseless UN-

FLAGGING, UNREMITTING
- constant or variable determining the form of a mathematical expression PARAMETER

constellation See chart, and also **zodiac**
- constellation or star cluster ASTERISM

constipated or causing constipation COSTIVE
- medicine or other substance that stimulates the bowels and relieves constipation LAXATIVE, CATHARTIC, PURGATIVE

constituency - manipulation of the boundaries of an electoral constituency for party advantage GERRYMANDERING

constitution or statement of aims CHARTER

consume, use up EXPEND

consumption TUBERCULOSIS, TB, PHTHISIS

contact - spread by physical contact, as a disease might be CONTAGIOUS, COMMUNICABLE

contain, include, consist of COMPRISE
- contain, take in, or include INCORPORATE, ENCOMPASS
- contain or enclose something considered sacred ENSHRINE
- contained within, forming an integral part of IMPLICIT, INHERENT

contain (combining form) -FER-

container See also **barrel, drink, jar, laboratory**
- container for holy water, oil, or wine AMPULLA, CRUSE
- container for molten metal CRUCIBLE
- container or cage for small plants or animals TERRARIUM
- container or chamber, as for a fluid RESERVOIR, RECEPTACLE, CISTERN
- container or shrine for sacred relics RELIQUARY
- container or small box, especially for tea CADDY
- flat metal or plastic container for carrying gasoline JERRICAN
- fuel container, such as a coal bin or gasoline tank BUNKER
- large cylindrical container for liquids, towed by a ship DRACONE
- metal container for gas, chemicals, or the like CANISTER
- pressurized steam-heated container AUTOCLAVE
- small bottle or container with a perforated top VINAIGRETTE
- small container, such as a jewelry case CASKET

contemplative, thoughtful, meditative RUMINANT

contemporary, of the same age or period COETANEOUS, COEVAL

contempt or hatred ODIUM
- contempt or scorn DISDAIN
- contemptuous behavior CONTUMACY
- show contempt or disrespect, belittle, slight DISPARAGE, DECRY, DEPRECIATE

contempt of court, as by failing to appear in court or disregarding a court order CONTUMACY

contest See also **competition**
- contest for superiority between two people, especially a hand-to-hand contest GRAPPLE
- competition, contest, lottery, or race in which the entry fees form the prize SWEEPSTAKES
- scratch from or fail to appear in a contest or match, thereby forfeiting it DEFAULT
- relating to contests AGONISTIC

context, network, or environment in which something develops MATRIX

continent - original single landmass that split up into the continents of today PANGAEA
- southern part of the earth's original landmass or supercontinent Pangaea GONDWANALAND
- northern part of the earth's original landmass or supercontinent Pangaea LAURASIA

continental quilt DUVET

continual See **constant**

continuation, development, something following SEQUEL
- continuation or uncontrollable repetition of an idea, spoken word, or the like PERSEVERATION

continue after a break RESUME
- continue despite discouragement, PERSIST, PERSEVERE
- continue in existence or manage to survive SUBSIST
- prolong, cause to continue PERPETUATE

continuous or unbroken belief, course of action, or the like PERSEVERANCE, STEADFASTNESSS
- continuous variation in form among members of a widespread species or population CLINE

contort the face into an expression of pain or disgust GRIMACE

contraceptive, especially referring to a condom PREVENTATIVE, PROPHYLACTIC
- internal temporary contraceptive device CERVICAL CAP, DIAPHRAGM
- semipermanent internal contraceptive device, such as the coil INTRAUTERINE DEVICE, IUD
- sex involving withdrawal before ejaculation as a means of contraception COITUS INTERRUPTUS
- surgical cutting of the sperm ducts of the testes, as permanent contraception VASECTOMY
- surgical tying of the fallopian tubes, as permanent contraception TUBAL LIGATION

contract, binding agreement, treaty COVENANT, COMPACT
- contract, money, or the like held by a third party until certain conditions are fulfilled ESCROW
- contract to repay a debt after the death of a person whose heir the debtor is POST-OBIT BOND
- amendment to a contract or other document ENDORSEMENT
- clause or amendment added to a contract or other document RIDER
- distinct section of a document, contract, law, or the like CLAUSE
- force or occurrence that unavoidably spoils one's plans or prevents the fulfillment of a contract FORCE MAJEURE
- make ineffective an argument, contract, or the like NULLIFY, INVALIDATE, VITIATE, VOID
- promise or action aimed at producing a legally binding contract CONSIDERATION
- require or lay down as a condition in a contract STIPULATE
- run out, as a contract or membership might EXPIRE
- spoken rather than written, as a contract might be ORAL, VERBAL

contracted as an apprentice or trainee ARTICLED
- contracted as a laborer for a specific period INDENTURED

contradict, dispute, or call into question OPPUGN
- contradict, prove false, give the lie to BELIE, NEGATE

contradiction between two equally

CONSTELLATIONS

Andromeda	**Draco/ Dragon**
Aquarius/ Water Bearer	**Gemini/ Twins**
Aquila/Eagle	**Leo/Lion**
Aries/Ram	**Libra/Scales**
Auriga/ Charioteer	**Orion**
Boötes/ Herdsman	**Pegasus/ Flying Horse**
Cancer/ Crab	**Perseus**
Capricornus/ Goat	**Pisces/Fish**
Cassiopeia	**Sagittarius/ Archer**
Cepheus	**Scorpius/ Scorpion**
Cetus	**Taurus/Bull**
Crux/ Southern Cross	**Ursa Major/ Great Bear**
Cygnus/ Swan	**Ursa Minor/ Little Bear**
	Virgo/Virgin

plausible statements PARADOX, ANTINOMY
- contradiction or incongruous phrase used as a figure of speech OXYMORON

contrary, opposing others' wishes or suggestions unreasonably PERVERSE, ADVERSE, FROWARD

contrast, as of color or shading, and the resulting emphasis RELIEF
- contrast as a literary or artistic technique CHIAROSCURO
- contrast or opposite ANTITHESIS
- contrasting person or thing FOIL
- placed side by side, as for contrast JUXTAPOSED

contribute or pledge a sum of money, as to a charity or for a telephone service SUBSCRIBE

contribution that is small but considered generous WIDOW'S MITE
- referring to a contribution made by an unknown or unnamed donor ANONYMOUS

control, direct, have or exercise authority PRESIDE
- control rule, power, or authority DOMINION, SOVEREIGNTY, JURISDICTION
- control and direct a force or energy HARNESS
- control events by careful manipulation STAGE-MANAGE
- control fully, dominate to the exclusion of all others MONOPOLIZE
- control operation or project, as to prevent further damage HOLDING OPERATION, HOLDING ACTION
- control or care, as granted by a court to a legal guardian of a child CUSTODY
- control or direct in keeping with the standard procedures or rules REGULATE
- control or self-restraint, such as sexual or urinary restraint CONTINENCE
- controlling and constricting force, as of custom TYRANNY, STRANGLEHOLD
- controlling or steering position, as in an organization or government TILLER, HELM
- controlling power over a dependent state, typically over its foreign affairs SUZERAINTY
- leading position of power, influence, or control DOMINANCE, PREEMINENCE, ASCENDANCY
- loss of bodily power or control PALSY
- subject to one's control by restraining or subduing SUBJUGATE, SUBORDINATE
- supervise, oversee, have control over SUPERINTEND

controversy See **argument, dispute**

convalescent home SANATORIUM

conveniences, comforts, pleasant and helpful features or services FACILITIES, AMENITIES

convenient, selfishly advantageous rather than fair or moral EXPEDIENT

convent, monastery, or other place of seclusion or retreat CLOISTER
- convent or monastery PRIORY
- head of a convent, abbey, or other religious community SUPERIOR

conventional, coldly formal, or traditional in approach to art or the like ACADEMIC
- conventional, unoriginal, and usually oversimplified image or opinion of someone or something STEREOTYPE
- conventional current, direction, or trend MAINSTREAM
- conventional medicine, as opposed to homeopathy ALLOPATHY
- conventional or artificial rather than realistic STYLIZED

conventions of a social group, defining it and its values MORES

conversation, especially between two people or groups DIALOGUE
- conversation, exchange of views DISCOURSE, CONFABULATION, PARLEY
- conversation in private between two people TÊTE-À-TÊTE
- conversation monopolized by one speaker MONOLOGUE
- conversation or formal dialogue or interview COLLOQUY
- conversation or gossipy meeting GABFEST, CAUSERIE
- conversation of a playful and joking nature BADINAGE, BANTER
- conversation with sharp and witty retorts BACKCHAT, REPARTEE
- jumping about, disconnected, as conversation might be DESULTORY
- observation, as in a conversation or speech, that departs briefly from the main subject DIGRESSION, ASIDE, PARENTHESIS, EXCURSION, EXCURSUS
- person taking part in a conversation or discussion INTERLOCUTOR, COLLOCUTOR
- person who excels in conversations at the dinner table DEIPNOSOPHIST
- referring to conversation, as about the weather, whose purpose is to express friendly feelings rather than to communicate ideas PHATIC

conversational, informal, characteristic of casual spoken language COLLOQUIAL

conversion and arithmetical table READY RECKONER
- conversion chart or manual for exchange rates or weights and measures CAMBIST

convert See also **change**
- convert, especially a new convert, to a religion or doctrine PROSELYTE, NEOPHYTE
- convert from Judaism to Christianity in medieval Spain or Portugal MARRANO
- convert or channel a sexual urge or other instinctual energy into a socially or culturally more acceptable activity SUBLIMATE
- convert or desert, become a renegade TERGIVERSATE, APOSTATIZE, RENEGE
- convert or transform something, such as base metal into gold COMMUTE

convict with special privileges, as for good behavior TRUSTY
- ship a convict in former times overseas to a penal colony TRANSPORT
- temporary barracks for convicts or slaves in former times BARRACOON

convincing See **persuasive**

cook food, especially eggs, in water at just below boiling point CODDLE

cookie See **cake**

cooking See charts, pages 125 and 126, and also chart at **menu** and entries at various types of food
- cooking, as of a particular style or region CUISINE, GASTRONOMY
- cooking of a high-class French style that cuts down on rich ingredients CUISINE MINCEUR
- cooking of high quality HAUTE CUISINE
- cooking stove of a large iron make, usually burning coal or wood, with one or more ovens RANGE
- cooking stove, small and portable, burning paraffin or kerosene PRIMUS
- metal stand or support, usually with three legs, especially for cooking pots or hot dishes TRIVET
- referring to food or cooking of a very high standard CORDON BLEU
- relating to cooking or the kitchen CULINARY

cool See **cold, calm**

cooling substance, as for operating a refrigerator or reducing a fever REFRIGERANT

coolness, calmness, self-possession, ability to remain unruffled when in danger or under stress SANGFROID

cooperate, act together, combine CONCUR
- cooperate secretly, conspire CONNIVE
- cooperate in a treasonous way with the enemy forces occupying

COOKING TERMS

al dente	referring to pasta that is cooked but firm to the bite	**hull**	remove the leaves and stems of soft fruit
à point	referring to medium-cooked meat	**infuse**	steep in water or other liquid
au bleu	referring to very rare meat	**jardiniere**	garnished with vegetables
bard	place fat or bacon on lean meat before roasting	**lard**	thread strips of fat through lean meat before roasting
bien cuit	referring to well-done meat	**liaison**	thickening agent such as cream, for sauces, soups, and the like
blanch	boil very briefly	**macedoine**	mixture of fruit or vegetables
bouchée	small puff-pastry case	**macerate**	soften by soaking in liquid
bouillon	stock or clear broth	**marinade**	blend of oil, wine or vinegar, herbs, and spices used to tenderize and flavor meat, game, or poultry
bouquet garni	bunch or small bag of herbs	**marinate**	steep in marinade
brûlé	glazed with a caramelized sugar	**medallion**	small circular cut of meat or fish
chine	separate backbone from ribs in a joint of meat	**parboil**	boil briefly to cook food slightly
coddle	simmer eggs slowly	**puree**	mash or pulp fruit or vegetables, as by long cooking or in a blender or food processor
crème fraîche	cream that is mature but not sour	**roux**	mixture of fat and flour, used as base for sauce
crimp	gash or score meat for crisper cooking	**saignant**	referring to underdone meat
deviling	grilling or roasting with highly seasoned ingredients	**sauté**	fry lightly in a little fat
dredge	coat with flour or sugar	**shirr**	bake eggs that have been removed from their shells
en croûte	in pastry	**soused**	pickled
farci	stuffed	**sweat**	cook vegetables or fruit slowly to release their juices
fines herbes	fresh, finely chopped mixture of parsley, chervil, tarragon, and chives	**zest**	outer, colored skin of citrus fruit
flambé	served or covered with flaming spirit		

one's country COLLABORATE

- cooperate with, indulge, or give in to a person's whims or wishes GRATIFY, PANDER TO
- cooperating, capable of living, working, or functioning together in a harmonious or efficient way COMPATIBLE
- cooperating, working in conjunction IN TANDEM
- cooperation or obedience of a token or insincere kind LIP SERVICE

cooperative, helpful, or considerate OBLIGING, COMPLIANT, COMPLAISANT, ACCOMMODATING

- cooperative, readily influenceable MALLEABLE, PLIABLE, FLEXIBLE
- cooperative, submissive, easily controlled AMENABLE, BIDDABLE, TRACTABLE, DOCILE
- cooperative action of two or more muscles, medicines, or the like to produce a greater joint effect SYNERGISM
- cooperative business relationship, trade policy, exchange of commercial favors and privileges, and the like RECIPROCITY
- cooperative farm or settlement in Israel KIBBUTZ
- cooperative farm or settlement in the U.S.S.R. KOLKHOZ
- cooperative or protective instinct or behavior among animals, serving to benefit the species as a whole ALTRUISM
- cooperative relationship or close beneficial association between two or more different plants or animals SYMBIOSIS
- cooperative settlement in Israel, consisting of a group of small farms MOSHAV

coordination - lack of coordination, movement disability, caused by brain damage or disease APRAXIA, ATAXIA

cope, contend with or struggle to overcome GRAPPLE

copper - greenish coating forming on exposed copper, brass, or bronze objects VERDIGRIS, VERD ANTIQUE, AERUGO

- thin layer of oxide, usually green, forming naturally or artificially on a copper or bronze surface PATINA

copper (combining form) CHALC-, CHALCO-, CUPR-, CUPRI-, CUPRO-

copy See also **imitate**

- copy, often on a smaller scale, especially of a work of art REPLICA, REPRODUCTION
- copy in writing or typescript of

court proceedings, a student's academic record, or the like TRANSCRIPT
- copy of a garment made up in cheap cloth as a basis for alterations TOILE
- copy or exact reproduction, as of a document FACSIMILE
- copy or forge something, especially money, for the purpose of fraud COUNTERFEIT
- copy someone else's ideas, writings, or the like and present them as one's own PLAGIARIZE
- copy or model in reduced size MINIATURE
- copy or reproduce four times QUADRUPLICATE
- copy or reproduce three times TRIPLICATE
- copy or reproduce twice DUPLICATE
- copied from or based on an earlier example, unoriginal DERIVATIVE
- copying process, as in some photocopying machines XEROGRAPHY, XEROX
- exact genetic copy or duplicate, or group of genetically identical organisms, such as plants produced from cuttings CLONE
- instrument for copying which transfers a diagram by means of a lever system when the original is traced over PANTOGRAPH
- machine for copying, typically one in which a stencil is stretched over a rotating inked drum DUPLICATOR, MIMEOGRAPH, CYCLOSTYLE
- make or be a copy of, reproduce REPLICATE, XEROGRAPH
- neat and clean copy of a revised and corrected document FAIR COPY
- person who copied manuscripts in former times SCRIBE, SCRIVENER, AMANUENSIS
- separate multiple copies, continuous stationery, or the like into individual documents COLLATE, DECOLLATE

copyright - unauthorized use of someone else's idea, patent, copyright material, or the like PIRACY, PLAGIARISM, INFRINGEMENT

coral, sea anemone, or related aquatic creature, typically tubelike and tentacled POLYP
- coral or rock reef, parallel to the coastline and often forming a lagoon BARRIER REEF
- coral reef or small coral island chain, typically circular and forming a lagoon ATOLL

cord, twine, or rope used for tying or binding LASHING
- cord or narrow braid used for binding or trimming BOBBIN
- cord or tube linking a fetus to the mother's placenta UMBILICAL CORD
- cord worn round an Arab headdress to hold it in place AGAL
- decoratively braided cord, worn on the left shoulder, as on a military uniform FOURRAGÈRE

cordial or flavoring of pomegranate or red-currant syrup GRENADINE

corduroy - rib or ridge on corduroy or a similar fabric, or the texture of such a fabric WALE

core of a speech, plot, or argument GIST, BURDEN, GRAVAMEN

cork, bung, plug STOPPLE
- cork or flat bung for a wide-mouthed bottle SHIVE
- corky, relating to or consisting of cork tissue SUBEROSE

corn, wart, or other small benign growth PAPILLOMA
- corn on the cob INDIAN CORN, MAIZE, MEALIE
- beat corn to separate the seed from the stems and husks THRESH, FLAIL
- gather leftover corn or other crops from a field after harvesting GLEAN
- treatment or care of the feet, as by cutting corns CHIROPODY

cornea (combining form) KERAT-, KERATO-

corner by a fireplace, often with seats facing each other INGLENOOK
- corner on the outside of a building CANT
- cut off the edge or corner of something BEVEL, CHAMFER

cornerstone of a building QUOIN, COIGN

coronation - cushioned stool for kneeling on during prayer, as by a sovereign at the coronation FALDSTOOL

coroner and public prosecutor in Scotland PROCURATOR FISCAL
- coroner's court finding of death without specifying the cause OPEN VERDICT
- coroner's investigation or inquiry into the cause of a death INQUEST

corpse, especially for medical research or dissection CADAVER
- corpse animated by a voodoo spell ZOMBIE
- corpse of an animal CARCASS
- building or room in which corpses are stored before autopsy, burial, or the like MORTUARY, MORGUE
- building or room in which corpses or bones were stored in former times CHARNEL HOUSE
- cloth used to wrap a corpse for burial SHROUD, WINDING-SHEET
- deep-freezing of a corpse, with the intention of reviving it in the future CRYONICS
- disposal of a corpse by burning it to ashes in a furnace CREMATION
- feeding on corpses or carrion NECROPHAGOUS

COOKING UTENSILS

bain-marie	double saucepan, or large pan of hot water in which smaller pans are placed
brochette	small spit or skewer
casserole	ovenproof dish with a close-fitting lid
cocotte	small ovenproof dish
coquille	shell-shaped ovenproof dish
Dutch oven	large, heavy iron pan with a lid; three-sided metal oven used in front of an open fire; oven that cooks by means of preheated bricks
griddle	flat cooking surface, as used for pancakes
mandoline	vegetable slicer in the form of a wooden board and adjustable blade, used for fine-slicing vegetables
olla	wide-mouthed earthenware pot or jar
ramekin	individual ovenproof dish
spatula	knife with a flat, blunt, pliable blade
terrine	earthenware pot
timbale	cup-shaped mold
wok	large, bowl-shaped metal pan used in Chinese cooking

- medical examination or dissection of a corpse, usually to establish the cause of death POSTMORTEM, AUTOPSY, NECROPSY
- platform or stand for a corpse or coffin, before burial BIER
- preserve a corpse from decay by chemical treatment EMBALM
- raised platform or table on which a coffin or corpse lies, as during a state funeral CATAFALQUE
- remove a corpse from a grave EXHUME, DISINTER
- slang term for a corpse STIFF
- wax-coated cloth in which corpses were formerly wrapped CERECLOTH, CEREMENT

corpse (combining form) NECR-, NECRO-

correct See also **improve, perfect, true, accurate**
- correct, proper, as it should be COMME IL FAUT
- correct someone, put someone right, rid someone of a mistaken idea DISABUSE
- correct, right and proper, acceptable or genuine PUKKA, KOSHER
- correct, set right, adjust RECTIFY, REMEDY, REDRESS
- correct all the time and in every case INFALLIBLE, UNERRING
- correct and improve a text by critical editing EMEND
- correct or applicable, as a sound argument is VALID
- capable of being corrected, or submitting to correction CORRIGIBLE
- confirm as existent, true, correct, or genuine ATTEST, CORROBORATE
- correcting, improving, beneficial, as advice might be SALUTARY
- correcting defects, faulty habits, or the like REMEDIAL

correct (combining form) ORTHO-

correction or allowance made for the variation in measurement or judgment stemming from human error PERSONAL EQUATION
- corrections and errors in a book, as listed separately, typically on an inserted sheet of paper CORRIGENDA, ERRATA
- word written to instruct a typesetter or printer to ignore a correction STET

corrective action or punishment DISCIPLINARY ACTION

correspond See also **agree**
- correspond, agree, match, be alike TALLY
- correspond to, agree or harmonize with CONFORM WITH, COMPORT WITH
- corresponding in amount, level, or degree, proportionate, as one's salary might be with one's qualifications COMMENSURATE
- corresponding in evolutionary origin but not in function, as a human arm and a bird's wing are HOMOLOGOUS
- corresponding in function but not in evolutionary origin, as gills and lungs are ANALOGOUS
- corresponding person in another team or organization COUNTERPART, OPPOSITE NUMBER, VIS-À-VIS
- corresponding with or agreeing with exactly COINCIDENT, COINCIDING

correspondence, parallelism, or mutual relationship between two things CORRELATION
- correspondence, rule associating the members of one set with those of another MAPPING
- correspondence or harmony among parts, claims, or the like CONSISTENCY, CONGRUITY, CONSONANCE
- relationship of correspondence, equivalence, or identity between systems or parts of a system SYMMETRY
- mathematical variable related to another in always having a corresponding value FUNCTION

corresponding (combining form) COUNTER-

corrupt See also **immoral**
- corrupt, debase, impair or taint VITIATE, DEFILE
- corrupt, open to or marked by bribery VENAL
- corrupt, pervert, or undermine SUBVERT
- corrupt, twist from what is correct or proper, warp PERVERT
- corrupt or dirty place or situation AUGEAN STABLE
- corrupt or seduce someone, especially someone young and innocent DEBAUCH
- corrupt someone into wrongdoing, specifically by bribing to commit perjury SUBORN
- corrupted or decaying, as in morals or culture DECADENT
- corrupting, damaging, harmful, or evil PERNICIOUS, PESTIFEROUS, PESTILENT, NOXIOUS

corruption, decay, or evil, especially when spreading rampantly CANKER
- corruption, private profit derived from a public office JOBBERY, GRAFT
- fund used for bribing public officials and for other corrupt activities SLUSH FUND
- moral corruption, pervertedness DEPRAVITY
- referring to a powerful and politically corrupt organization in a city or state government TAMMANY

corset stiffened with strips of bone, plastic, or metal STAYS
- confine or bind with a tight-fitting garment such as a corset or straitjacket TRUSS
- thin strip of wood, whalebone, or the like for stiffening a corset BUSK

cosmetics, makeup MAQUILLAGE
- black cosmetic powder used, especially in Asia, to darken the eyelids KOHL
- dark cosmetic preparation applied to the eyelashes MASCARA
- fat from sheep's wool used in cosmetics and ointments LANOLIN
- small case for needles, makeup, or the like ETUI

Cossack captain HETMAN, ATAMAN

cost - additional cost or charge SURCHARGE
- cut back on costs ECONOMIZE, RETRENCH
- pay, meet the costs or expenses DEFRAY

cost of living - pay agreement by which wages are raised after a certain increase in the cost of living THRESHOLD AGREEMENT, COST-OF-LIVING ALLOWANCE, COLA
- rising in keeping with the cost of living, as one's earnings or pension might INDEX-LINKED

costume ball at which masks are worn MASQUERADE
- costume department or storeroom of a theater, royal household, or the like WARDROBE

cottage that goes with a particular job TIED HOUSE
- farm worker or crofter in Scotland renting a cottage and smallholding COTTER

cotton or wool wadding used as stuffing for furniture or mattresses BATTING
- absorbent cotton ball or similar piece of absorbent material used for cleaning, applying a lotion, or the like SWAB
- open and clean raw cotton or wool fibers by means of a spiked drum WILLOW
- seed pod of cotton, flax, or similar plants BOLL
- strengthen and improve cotton thread by chemical treatment MERCERIZE

cotton candy, spun sugar CANDY FLOSS

couch See **furniture**

cough TUSSIS
- cough mixture that eases the production and expulsion of phlegm or sputum EXPECTORANT
- cough-relieving, as a drug might be ANTITUSSIVE
- cough syrup LINCTUS
- cough up and spit out EXPECTORATE

council appointed to advise the British king or queen PRIVY COUNCIL
- relating to a council, especially a church council CONCILIAR
- senior member of a town council ALDERMAN

count, reckon TALLY
- count off or list one by one ENUMERATE

counter, quick retaliatory action or retort RIPOSTE
- counter or turn aside a fencing thrust, hostile question, or the like PARRY

counteract and thereby make ineffective NEUTRALIZE

counteract (combining form) PARA-

counterclockwise WIDDERSHINS, WITHERSHINS

counterclockwise (combining form) LAEV-, LAEVO-, LEVO-

counterfeit See **fake**

counterpart, corresponding person VIS-À-VIS
- counterpart or complement OBVERSE

counterpoint, combination of two or more distinct melodic parts POLYPHONY
- counterpoint added above a basic musical theme DESCANT

counting individually, by head CAPITATION
- act or system of numbering or counting NUMERATION

country, usually small and neutral, lying between two powerful rival states BUFFER STATE
- country areas considered remote and undeveloped, the sticks, the bush HINTERLAND, BOONDOCKS, BACKVELD, BACKBLOCKS, OUTBACK, GRAMADOELAS, BUNDU
- country dweller, unfamiliar with city ways HILLBILLY, BUMPKIN, YOKEL, BUSHWHACKER, BACKWOODSMAN
- country economically or politically dependent on a more powerful country CLIENT STATE
- country gentleman in medieval England FRANKLIN
- country house in Russia DACHA
- country scene or event of simple charm IDYLL
- country's authority or power of jurisdiction beyond its borders, as over its citizens living abroad EXTRATERRITORIALITY
- countryman, typically owning a small farm in former times YEOMAN
- desert one's country, political party, or the like, especially to join its opponent DEFECT
- expel a foreigner from a country DEPORT
- narrow strip of land, as for allowing an inland country access to the sea CORRIDOR
- open level country, such as a stretch of plain CHAMPAIGN
- part of a country that is isolated within a foreign country's territory EXCLAVE
- part of a foreign country entirely within a country's territory ENCLAVE
- person from the same country as another person COMPATRIOT, LANDSMAN
- person who has left or been driven from his or her native country and now lives in another EXPATRIATE, EXILE, EMIGRANT, ÉMIGRÉ
- person who has lived or traveled in many countries and is free of national prejudices COSMOPOLITAN
- person who takes to the hills, living a primitive country life, to escape the effects of an expected nuclear war SURVIVALIST
- relating to country life, country people, or farming RURAL, RUSTIC, PASTORAL, BUCOLIC
- relating to open country or uncultivated fields CAMPESTRAL
- return someone or something to the country of origin REPATRIATE
- send or banish to the country RUSTICATE

county or colony whose ruler formerly had royal powers PALATINATE
- county-style in dress and manner TWEEDY
- officer of the Crown in an English or Welsh county SHERIFF

coupons - exchange coupons, vouchers, or the like for goods REDEEM

courage See also **brave, bravery**
- summon up courage MUSTER

course just before the main course, or the main course itself, of a meal ENTRÉE
- course of study CURRICULUM, SYLLABUS
- course of study offered by a university or college to part-time students EXTENSION COURSE
- course of study reacquainting and updating people already familiar with a subject REFRESHER COURSE
- course or dish served between the main courses of a meal ENTREMETS
- course or general direction, as of someone's life TENOR
- learning unit with a training course or educational syllabus MODULE
- optional, open to choice, as a course of study might be ELECTIVE

course of action - projected or possible course of action SCENARIO

court See also **trial**
- court case arousing great public interest CAUSE CÉLÈBRE
- court case debated as a training exercise by law students MOOT COURT
- court of appeal APPELLATE COURT
- court of justice, adjudicating board, or the like TRIBUNAL, FORUM
- court officer in former times who collected debts and pursued debtors BUM BAILIFF
- court officer MARSHAL
- court official's call for attention OYEZ
- court or legislative meeting, series of meetings, or period for meeting SESSION
- court or tribunal that is secretive and harsh STAR CHAMBER
- court order directed at some lower court, official body, or the like MANDAMUS
- court order directing the addressee to do or stop doing a specified act WRIT, INJUNCTION, RESTRAINING ORDER
- court order for the imprisonment of a person COMMITTAL, MITTIMUS
- court order prohibiting something INTERDICT
- court without legal jurisdiction, operated by a mob, prisoners, or the like KANGAROO COURT
- court's adviser on a case in which he or she is not directly involved AMICUS CURIAE
- court's powers, duties, or knowledge in a case COGNIZANCE
- applying or turning for help to a person or thing, such as the courts RECOURSE
- attempt to influence a court of law, as by bribes or threats EMBRACERY
- awaiting or undergoing a court hearing, in litigation IN CHANCERY
- break in proceedings or temporary ending of business, as between court sessions or during the legislative holiday RECESS
- bringing a lawsuit, pursuing a case in court LITIGATION
- child, senile person, or the like under the legal protection of a guardian or court of law WARD
- close at the end of a session, as the courts and parliament do ADJOURN
- courts of law and judges collectively JUDICATURE, JUDICIARY
- declare or give evidence under oath, as in a court of law TESTIFY
- deliberate giving of false evidence while under oath by a witness in court PERJURY
- doorkeeper in a court of law, legislative body, or the like USHER
- duty lawyer's consultation with

or hiring by the accused in the court building DOCK BRIEF
- evidence or declaration given in court by a witness under oath TESTIMONY
- failure to appear in court DEFAULT
- hold a suspect on bail, or return him to prison, as done by a court REMAND
- judge in a county court CIRCUIT JUDGE
- official summons to appear in court CITATION
- open central space in front of the judge's bench in a courtroom WELL
- person or group against whom a lawsuit or civil action is brought in court DEFENDANT
- person or group that sues another or brings a civil action in court PLAINTIFF
- privilege of clergymen in the Middle Ages to be tried by a church court rather than a secular court BENEFIT OF CLERGY
- promise or obligation, recorded in court, to appear in court, keep the peace, or the like BOND, RECOGNIZANCE
- question a witness who was called by the opposing side in a court case CROSS-EXAMINE, CROSS-QUESTION
- refer a case or decision to a lower court, committee, or the like REMIT
- refusal to appear in court or obey a court order, contempt of court CONTUMACY
- relating to a court hearing held in private, with the public excluded IN CAMERA
- relating to criminal law or to court cases FORENSIC
- relating to the principles of law guiding a court rather than to court rules or procedures SUBSTANTIVE
- relating to the rules or procedures of a court rather than to principles of law ADJECTIVE
- sessions of the law courts in English and Welsh counties in former times ASSIZES
- still before a judge or court, and therefore not to be discussed in public SUB JUDICE
- summary of a court case DOCKET
- writ summoning someone to appear in court SUBPOENA, SUMMONS

courteous, gentlemanly, especially toward women CHIVALROUS
- courteous and respectful DEFERENTIAL

courtesy, politeness CIVILITY, COMITY
- courtesies, polite social gestures AMENITIES, PLEASANTRIES

courtyard in front of a church or within an ancient Roman house ATRIUM
- courtyard or colonnade in front of a church or palace PARVIS
- courtyard surrounded by cloisters GARTH
- open-air courtyard within a house PATIO

cousin - first cousin COUSIN-GERMAN
- separated by a specified number of generations, as distant cousins might be REMOVED

cover of velvet for a coffin or tomb PALL
- cover or front man, apparently but not really in charge of a dubious scheme MAN OF STRAW
- cover or shelter from the wind LEE
- cover up mistakes or wrongdoing WHITEWASH
- cover with a thin sheet of plastic wood, or the like LAMINATE
- cover with fog or clouds OBNUBILATE
- bell-shaped cover of plastic or glass, placed over young plants for protection CLOCHE
- covered walk around a quadrangle CLOISTERS
- covered walk or arbor formed by a trellised roof carrying climbing plants PERGOLA
- covering, as of canvas, as for a boat or wagon TILT
- covering, such as a seed's coat or an animal's skin INTEGUMENT
- covering or ornamental awning, as above a throne CANOPY
- covering or outer layer, as of the brain PALLIUM, MANTLE, CORTEX
- covering that is dark and oppressive, as of smoke PALL

cover charge in a restaurant COUVERT

coverlet for the top of the back of an armchair or sofa ANTIMACASSAR

cow, sheep, deer, or related hoofed, cud-chewing mammal RUMINANT
- cow on the verge of giving birth SPRINGER
- cow or bullock between one or two years old, yearling STIRK
- cow that is young and not yet breeding HEIFER
- cow that yields milk for human use MILCH COW
- cow's first milk produced after giving birth BEESTINGS, COLOSTRUM
- cow shed or barn BYRE
- adjective for a cow BOVINE
- brown or gray with darker streaks or spots, as a dog, cat, or cow might be BRINDLED
- bushy tip of the tail of a cow or other animal SWITCH
- frame of two upright bars securing a cow round the neck in a stall STANCHION
- not pregnant or not calving in a particular year, as a cow might be FARROW

cow's stomachs See **stomach**

cowardly, base or weak-willed, spineless PUSILLANIMOUS, DASTARDLY, LILY-LIVERED, CRAVEN, RECREANT
- cowardly wretch POLTROON, CAITIFF

cowboy, especially one tending horses WRANGLER
- cowboy in South America GAUCHO
- cowboy or herdsman in the southwestern United States VAQUERO, BUCKEROO
- cowboy working far from the main group or camp OUTRIDER
- cowboy's heavy leather trousers, without a seat, worn over ordinary trousers to protect the legs CHAPS
- display or contest of cowboy skills, such as lassoing and bronco riding RODEO
- small toothed wheel on the end of a cowboy's spur ROWEL

cower See **draw back**

cowpox VACCINIA

cozy, informal, and private, as a small nightclub might be INTIMATE
- cozy and cheerful, having a warm and friendly atmosphere GEMÜTLICH, CONGENIAL

crab, lobster, prawn, or related creature having a segmented body, jointed limbs, and horny shell CRUSTACEAN
- crab, lobster, prawn, or related ten-legged crustacean DECAPOD
- crab family of crustaceans BRACHYURA
- crablike CANCROID
- crab's pincerlike claw CHELA

crack See also **break, gap**
- deep crack or chasm, as in a glacier CREVASSE
- having a network of fine cracks, as a piece of glazed pottery might CRAZED
- narrow crack or split, as in a rock face CLEFT, CREVICE, FISSURE
- network of fine cracks made deliberately in the glaze of a piece of pottery CRACKLING
- network of small cracks in the paint or varnish of an old painting CRAQUELURE

crack (combining form) FISSI-

cracker - joke, verse, or proverb on a slip of paper inside a paper cracker MOTTO

craftsman, skilled worker ARTISAN, ARTIFICER
- craftsman who is qualified but still employed by someone else JOURNEYMAN
- craftsman's work bench BANKER

crafty, scheming CALCULATING,

CONNIVING

cramp or rigid muscular contraction, as in a fever RIGOR

crane on a ship, typically paired with another, for hoisting lifeboats, cargo, or the like DAVIT
- crane or other lifting apparatus HOIST
- crane or spar for stowing cargo in a ship's hold STEEVE
- crane with boom and cables for lifting heavy objects DERRICK
- crane's moving hoist or similar lifting machine CRAB
- bridgelike frame supporting a traveling crane, railway signals, or the like GANTRY
- move the jib of a crane LUFF
- pivoting arm or spar on a crane or derrick, used to guide or steady the load BOOM

crater formed by the toppling or collapse of a volcano's cone CALDERA

craving for unnatural food, such as mud or chalk, occurring sometimes in hysteria or during pregnancy PICA

crawl or lie face downward, as in self-abasement or fear GROVEL

crayon made of chalky paste, or a picture made with such crayons PASTEL

craze or obsession MANIA

creak, rattle, or crackle, as diseased lungs or broken bones might CREPITATE

cream - rich, clotted cream DEVONSHIRE CREAM
- whipped cream, slightly sweetened CHANTILLY CREAM

crease, wrinkle, gather in folds, RUCK, PUCKER
- creased, ruffled RUMPLED

creation, as of an idea or project GENESIS, PROCREATION, INCEPTION

creative, original, or life-enhancing PROMETHEAN
- creative in a passionate and energetic way DIONYSIAC, DIONYSIAN
- creative inspiration, especially a poetic impulse AFFLATUS

credit See also **assign**
- have a specified effect, as to one's credit or advantage REDOUND

creditor - substitution of one person, especially a creditor, for another SUBROGATION

creed or profession of faith widely used in churches NICENE CREED, ATHANASIAN CREED

creeper See also **climbing plant**
- growing along the ground as a vine or creeper might PROSTRATE

cremation site for Hindus at the top of a flight of riverside steps BURNING GHAT
- place for keeping the ashes of a cremated body CINERARIUM
- wood pile prepared for a funeral fire on which to cremate a corpse PYRE

creole or dialect PATOIS
- simplified language of communication between two different language groups, sometimes developing into a creole or mother tongue PIDGIN

crescent-shaped BICORN, BICUSPID, LUNATE, LUNULAR, LUNULATE
- crescent-shaped mark at the base of a fingernail LUNULA
- crescent-shaped object or design MENISCUS
- crescent-shaped object or structure, such as the outwork of a fort DEMILUNE

crest (combining form) LOPHO-

crested, as some birds are PILEATED

crib death SUDDEN INFANT DEATH SYNDROME, SIDS

cricket See chart and illustration
- cricket's shrill grating chirp STRIDULATION

crime, misconduct, or wrongdoing, especially by an official MALFEASANCE
- crime, offense, or wrongful act of a serious kind FELONY
- crime, offense, or wrongful act of a minor kind MISDEMEANOR, DELINQUENCY, VIOLATION
- crime association SYNDICATE, MAFIA
- crime of concealing information about treason or some other serious offense MISPRISION
- crime of forcing money or favors from someone by blackmail, violence, or the like EXTORTION
- crime of fraudulently appropriating or misusing someone else's property or funds entrusted to one's care EMBEZZLEMENT, DEFALCATION, PECULATION
- crime of having sexual relations with a girl who is not yet of the age of consent STATUTORY RAPE
- crime of kidnapping ABDUCTION
- crime of marrying a person or persons while still married to someone else BIGAMY, POLYGAMY
- crime of passion, typically a murder provoked by sexual jealousy CRIME PASSIONNEL
- crime of setting fire deliberately to property ARSON
- crime of theft LARCENY
- crime of treason, or offense against the dignity of a ruler LÈSE MAJESTÉ, LESE MAJESTY
- crime of trying to influence a judge or jury outside the usual courtroom procedures, as by bribes or threats EMBRACERY
- crime or offense in former times of stirring up quarrels or bringing groundless lawsuits repeatedly BARRATRY
- crime or offense of contempt of court, as by failing to appear in court or disregarding a court order CONTUMACY
- crime or offense of giving false evidence, especially in court while under oath PERJURY
- crime or offense of homelessness combined with public nuisance VAGRANCY
- crime or offense of sexual intercourse between two close relatives INCEST
- crime or sin TRANSGRESSION
- accuse formally of an offense or crime INDICT
- agree not to prosecute a crime or felony, as in return for a bribe COMPOUND
- attribute a crime or fault to someone IMPUTE
- being an accomplice to a crime, cruel deed, or the like COMPLICITY
- civilian arrogating crime prevention and punitive powers to himself VIGILANTE
- clear someone of blame, a charge, or a crime, declare to be not guilty ACQUIT, EXONERATE, EXCULPATE, ABSOLVE, VINDICATE
- devise a dramatized version of a crime or historical event to gain a vivid idea of what actually took place RECONSTRUCT
- forgive or overlook an offense or crime CONDONE
- ignore or pretend ignorance of a crime, and thereby encourage it CONNIVE AT, WINK AT
- in the very act of committing a crime IN FLAGRANTE DELICTO, RED-HANDED
- involve in or prove involvement in a crime INCRIMINATE, INCULPATE
- law setting a time limit for prosecuting a crime or bringing a legal action STATUTE OF LIMITATIONS
- lessen or try to lessen the seriousness of a crime, by offering excuses EXTENUATE, MITIGATE
- monstrous or outrageous act, such as an abominable crime ENORMITY
- performing of a crime, sin, or the like COMMISSION, PERPETRATION
- person guilty of a crime or responsible for a mistake or accident CULPRIT
- person who encourages or helps another in the committing of a crime, either before or after, though not directly involved in it ACCESSORY, ACCESSARY

- person who helps another to commit a crime ACCOMPLICE
- plan or supervise a crime MASTERMIND

- plea that mental abnormality at the time of a crime reduces the culprit's responsibility DIMINISHED RESPONSIBILITY

- revealing of a scandal or crime, or the book, broadcast, or the like in which it is reported EXPOSÉ
- tendency of former prisoners to

CRICKET TERMS

the Ashes	trophy for which England and Australia compete, or Test series between them
body-line	fast bowling directed straight at the batsman, to intimidate him
bouncer	fast ball pitched short so that it bounces high, to intimidate the batsman
bye	run scored from a ball that passes the wicket without touching the bat or batsman
chinaman	off-break bowled by a left-handed bowler to a right-handed batsman
dolly catch/ sitter	easy catch
follow-on	forced start to a team's second innings immediately after its first innings
full toss	ball that reaches the batsman without bouncing
googly	off-break disguised to resemble a leg-break
grub	ball bowled underarm along the ground
hat-trick	bowler's feat of dismissing three batsmen with consecutive balls
hook	stroke that hits a ball from the off-side of the wicket to the on-side
leg-break	ball that turns from leg to off on pitching
long hop	poorly bowled short-pitched ball
maiden over	over in which no runs are conceded
night-watchman	nonspecialist batsman sent in to play out time
no-ball	an unlawfully delivered ball
off-break	ball that turns from off to leg on pitching
shooter	ball that does not rise as expected
yorker	ball that pitches directly at the batsman's feet

FIELDING POSITIONS

Long-off
Long-on
Boundary line
Deep extra cover
Mid-on
Mid-off
Batting crease
Umpire
Bowler
Extra cover
Right-handed batsman
Mid-wicket
Silly mid-off
Deep mid-wicket
Short extra cover
Silly mid-on
Cover point
Forward short-leg
Point
Deep square leg
Square leg
Silly point
Umpire
Gulley
Backward short-leg
Leg slip
Third slip
Second slip
Short third man
Stumps
First slip
Wicketkeeper
Deep third man
Deep fine leg
Long stop

revert to crime RECIDIVISM
- tricking or luring of someone as by the police, into crime, danger, or the like ENTRAPMENT
- wrongful act, other than a breach of contract, in civil law, in contrast to a crime TORT

criminal See also **evil, immoral**
- criminal, wrongdoer, or villain MISCREANT, MALEFACTOR, FELON
- criminal gangster, as in the Mafia MOBSTER
- criminal gangster or bandit, especially in mountainous country BRIGAND
- criminal gangster or hoodlum in Paris APACHE
- criminal or aggressive person with an antisocial-personality disorder PSYCHOPATH, SOCIOPATH
- criminal or suspect who is on the run FUGITIVE
- criminal who informs to the police, especially on his fellow criminals STOOL PIGEON, INFORMER
- criminal who is reckless and desperate DESPERADO
- conditional release of a criminal from jail before the end of his prison term PAROLE
- handing over a criminal, fugitive, or the like to the authority or country where he is wanted EXTRADITION
- help a criminal to adjust to a conventional job or role within society REHABILITATE
- legal term for criminal intent MENS REA
- kit or method for creating a picture of a wanted criminal IDENTIKIT, PHOTOFIT
- loss of civil rights in former times, suffered by a convicted traitor, outlaw, or criminal under sentence of death ATTAINDER
- person serving as a respectable cover for some secret or criminal activity FRONT MAN
- person working for or running criminal business operations RACKETEER
- person who hunts criminals or dangerous animals for a financial reward BOUNTY HUNTER
- secret agent who joins a political or criminal group and tries to entrap it into punishable or discrediting activities AGENT PROVOCATEUR
- study of the punishment and treatment of criminals, especially prison management PENOLOGY
- unscrupulous and often criminal politician, lawyer, or the like SHYSTER

crippled condition or bodily defect, such as a hunchback DEFORMITY, DISFIGUREMENT

crisis, fit, spasm, frenzy PAROXYSM, SEIZURE, APOPLEXY, CONVULSION
- negotiation or the art of gaining an advantage by pressing a dispute toward a crisis without backing down BRINKMANSHIP
- remove the tension or danger from a situation or crisis DEFUSE

crisscross pattern, as on a map or framework GRID
- crisscross pattern or design TRACERY
- crisscrossed strips of wood or metal, as in a screen or window LATTICE
- crisscrossing sticks forming a frame, as for climbing plants TRELLIS

criterion, test, standard, or measure used for judgment or comparison YARDSTICK, TOUCHSTONE

critical, disapproving, judgmental CENSORIOUS, DYSLOGISTIC
- critical edition or revision of a text, incorporating the most plausible variant readings RECENSION
- critical in a nitpicking way, faultfinding CARPING, CAPTIOUS
- critical interpretation or analysis of a literary work, philosophical theory, or the like EXPLICATION, EXPOSITION, EXEGESIS
- critical period, stage, or event CLIMACTERIC, WATERSHED
- critical point beyond which a tense situation will erupt into war or violence FLASHPOINT
- critical success but a failure with the public at large, as a book or film might be SUCCÈS D'ESTIME

criticism, disapproval STRICTURES, CENSURE, FLAK
- criticism or blunt critical remark BRICKBAT, BROADSIDE
- criticism or destruction of popular beliefs, cherished traditions, or the like ICONOCLASM
- criticism or fierce verbal attack launched maliciously HATCHET JOB
- criticism or rebuke for a misdeed or failing REPROOF
- criticism or review of a book, movie, play, or the like CRITIQUE, APPRAISAL
- criticism or short review, especially of a book COMPTE RENDU
- criticism or veiled accusation IMPUTATION, ANIMADVERSION
- criticism that is petty and trifling CAVIL
- bitter or abusive criticism, or a speech or text containing it INVECTIVE, DIATRIBE, POLEMIC
- easily withstanding attack, criticism, or the like INVULNERABLE, IMPREGNABLE
- harsh and extremely scornful, as a criticism or verbal attack might be SCATHING, BLISTERING, WITHERING, VITRIOLIC, CAUSTIC
- idea, custom, institution, or person unreasonably considered to be beyond criticism SACRED COW
- long passionate speech of criticism HARANGUE, TIRADE, PHILIPPIC
- open condemnation, strong or abusive criticism DENUNCIATION, EXECRATION, VITUPERATION, OBLOQUY
- undergo severe criticism RUN THE GAUNTLET

criticize See also **scold, insult**
- criticize, admonish, or explain in a priggish or preachy way MORALIZE, SERMONIZE
- criticize, attack verbally BELABOR, DECLAIM AGAINST
- criticize, challenge, attack as false IMPUGN
- criticize, punish, or scold severely CASTIGATE, CHASTISE
- criticize abusively or argue against passionately, rail against REVILE, VITUPERATE, INVEIGH AGAINST, EXCORIATE, FULMINATE AGAINST
- criticize in a belittling or dismissive way DECRY, DISPARAGE, DEPRECIATE, DEROGATE
- criticize mercilessly, pan, slate FLAY, CRUCIFY, PILLORY, SCARIFY
- criticize openly and earnestly, condemn CENSURE, REPREHEND
- criticize or disapprove of strongly DEPLORE, REPROBATE
- criticize vehemently, condemn strongly DENOUNCE, EXECRATE
- criticizing ignorantly, without the necessary knowledge or experience to warrant it ULTRACREPIDARIAN

critics - astonish someone or prove someone wrong, such as the critics CONFOUND

crocodile See illustration
- crocodile from tropical America, related to the alligator CAIMAN
- crocodilelike reptile with a narrow snout, found in India GAVIAL, GHARIAL

crop or commodity that is the major product of its kind grown in a region STAPLE
- crop or plant growing from seed that was not deliberately sown VOLUNTEER
- crop producing oil seed and fodder, with a distinctive yellow flower RAPE, COLZA
- cultivated soil, or its crop-bearing quality TILTH
- gather leftover corn or other crops from a field after harvesting GLEAN
- plant or grow crops in a fixed sequence ROTATE

crop spraying - fly very low when spraying crops, rising to avoid hedges, fences, and so on HEDGEHOP

croquet stick MALLET
- hit another player's ball with one's own in croquet, qualifying one to croquet it or drive it away ROQUET
- send another player's ball through a hoop in croquet PEEL
- small post in croquet that a ball must hit to end a game PEG

cross See illustration, page 134, and also **angry, anger**
- cross bearer, as in a religious procession CRUCIFER
- cross or crucifix representing the cross on which Jesus died ROOD, HOLY ROOD
- cross or divide a line or space INTERSECT
- cross or intersect to form an X DECUSSATE
- cross out or erase written or printed words DELETE
- cross-shaped CRUCIATE, CRUCIFORM
- crossbred, mixed in origin or makeup HYBRID
- crossing over of two structures in the body, such as the optic nerve fibers in the brain CHIASMA
- horizontal beam or crossbar, as on a gallows or cross TRANSOM
- taking down of Jesus from the cross, or a painting or sculpture of this DEPOSITION

crossbow bolt or arrow QUARREL
- crossbowlike launcher of rocks or other heavy missiles, as used in ancient siege warfare BALLISTA

cross-country motorcycle racing SCRAMBLING, MOTOCROSS
- cross-country racing involving use of a compass and map-reading skills ORIENTEERING
- cross-country runner HARRIER

crossing at which pedestrians themselves activate the traffic lights on the roadside PELICAN CROSSING

crosswise, diagonal, slanting CATERCORNER, OBLIQUE
- crosswise, lying across ATHWART, TRANSVERSE
- crosswise path, movement, line, building beam, or the like TRAVERSE

crow, both scavenging and predatory, with a black bill CARRION CROW
- adjective for a crow CORVINE

crowbar as used by burglars JIMMY

crowd, horde, or mob of people THRONG, MULTITUDE, CONCOURSE, RUCK
- crowd, large gathering or converging, as of people CONFLUENCE
- crowd together, assemble CONGREGATE
- crowded, containing a great multitude of inhabitants POPULOUS, TEEMING
- crowded, pressed together, tightly packed SERRIED
- crowds of moving people DROVES
- close-knit crowd of people PHALANX
- fear of crowds OCHLOPHOBIA, DEMOPHOBIA
- headlong rush, as of startled cattle or horses, or of a panic-stricken crowd STAMPEDE
- noisy and disorderly commotion of a crowd TUMULT
- overcrowded CONGESTED
- relating to a crowd, flock, or the like GREGARIOUS
- speech maker who rouses a crowd to violent passions or actions RABBLE-ROUSER, DEMAGOGUE

crown, typically light and jeweled DIADEM
- crown of small size, as worn by princes or noblemen as a sign of rank CORONET
- crown of the head PATE
- crown-shaped body part, such as the top of the head CORONA
- crowning of a king or queen CORONATION
- pope's beehive-shaped three-tiered crown or hat TIARA

crucial time or event WATERSHED

crucifix representing the cross on which Jesus died ROOD, HOLY ROOD

Crucifixion as represented in sculpture CALVARY
- sufferings of Jesus before and during the Crucifixion PASSION

crude See also **rude, vulgar**
- crude, primitive, unsophisticated, basic RUDIMENTARY
- crude or uncouth RUSTIC

cruel, aggressively harsh TRUCULENT
- cruel, insensitive, heartless CALLOUS, INDURATE
- cruel and greedy, in a wolflike way LUPINE
- cruel in a perverted way, relishing the inflicting of pain SADISTIC
- cruel oppression or ill-treatment

Crocodile

Estuarine crocodile

PERSECUTION
- cruel or frightful person OGRE
- cruel or greedy person HARPY
- cruel or extremely violent act, outrage ATROCITY, ENORMITY
- brutal, inhumanly cruel BESTIAL, FELL, FLAGITIOUS
- mercilessly cruel or grim, pitiless, unsparing REMORSELESS, IMPLACABLE, INEXORABLE

crumble, decay, turn to dust MOLDER AWAY
- crumbly, as soil might be FRIABLE

crumbs - coated with breadcrumbs and sometimes cheese, and then grilled or browned, as cauliflower might be AU GRATIN

Crusades - Muslim at the time of the Crusades SARACEN

crush, grind, or pound into powder or small particles TRITURATE, PULVERIZE, BRAY, COMMINUTE
- crush or put an end to something, such as a rumor or rebellion SCOTCH, SUPPRESS, SUBDUE, QUELL, QUASH, REPRESS
- crush or smash inward STAVE
- crushing, stamping, or grinding implement, as in a mill PESTLE

crust forming in bottles of old wine, especially port, or a wine containing this crust BEESWING

cry and sob noisily BLUBBER
- cry from the heart, earnest appeal CRI DE COEUR
- cry of praise to God HOSANNA
- cry or wail with a loud keening howl ULULATE
- cry or screech, as of an excited cat CATERWAUL
- cry or whimper repeatedly YAMMER
- cry out or shout loudly, especially in protest VOCIFERATE
- cry weakly or whimper MEWL
- crying continually LACHRYMOSE

crypt, vault, underground chamber UNDERCROFT

crystal, quill, bristle, or similar needle-shaped natural object or part ACICULA, ACULEUS
- crystal that produces electric polarity when subjected to pressure PIEZOELECTRIC CRYSTAL
- crystal that branches into a treelike structure DENDRITE
- add a crystal to a liquid to cause it to crystallize SEED
- any of the different physical forms, such as crystals, that an element may take ALLOTROPE
- between liquid and solid or crystal in structure or properties MESOMORPHIC, NEMATIC, SMECTIC
- capable of occurring in different forms, as crystals of a mineral

Crosses

Ankh/ansate
Avellan
Botonnée/preflée
Calvary
Cardinal's
Celtic
Constantinian/monogram
Crosslet
Fitchée
Fleury
Formée
Fourchée
Greek
Latin/passion
Lorraine
Maltese
Moline
Papal
Patriarchal
Pommée
Potent/Jerusalem
Quadrate
Russian
St. Andrew's/saltire
St. Anthony's/tau
St. Peter's
Swastika/fylfot/gammadion
Y cross

might be POLYMORPHIC
- instrument for measuring the angles of crystals GONIOMETER
- not possessing a distinct crystalline structure, as a rock or chemical might AMORPHOUS
- process by which crystals are turned to powder by loss of water EFFLORESCENCE
- regular geometric arrangement, as of the molecules in a crystal LATTICE
- rock cavity lined with crystals GEODE
- rock cavity or vein into which crystals project DRUSE
- similarity of form or structure, as in different cells or crystals ISOMORPHISM

crystal ball - see the future by gazing into a crystal ball SCRY

cube extended hypothetically into the fourth dimension TESSERACT

cuckold, man who tolerates his wife's infidelities WITTOL

cucumber - small cucumber, usually pickled GHERKIN

cud-chewing, hoofed mammal, such as a cow, sheep, or deer RUMINANT
- chew the cud RUMINATE

cue for an actor to speak or enter CATCHWORD

cult, aura of power or mystery MYSTIQUE, MYTHOS

cultivated, superior, and well-bred person PATRICIAN

cultivation of land for crops TILTH, TILLAGE
- cultivation of plants, especially flowers HORTICULTURE
- cultivation of plants without soil, using nutrients dissolved in water HYDROPONICS, AQUICULTURE

culture, including the classics and the arts, as distinct from the sciences HUMANITIES
- culture passed down over the generations HERITAGE
- change in culture through contact with another culture, usually more advanced ACCULTURATION
- declining or decaying, as in morals or culture DECADENT
- lacking in or hostile to cultural interests and values PHILISTINE
- place where different cultures meet and mix MELTING POT
- rebirth or revival of culture RENASCENCE, RENAISSANCE
- relating to a distinctive racial, religious, or cultural group within a society ETHNIC
- rootless, separated from one's homeland, social origins, familiar culture, or natural environment DERACINATED, DÉRACINÉ
- study of the culture of peoples, especially "primitive" peoples ETHNOLOGY

culture (combining form) ETHN-, ETHNO-

cultured, educated, or intellectual people INTELLIGENTSIA, COGNOSCENTI
- cultured or intellectual HIGHBROW

cunning, craftiness GUILE, WILES
- cunning, sly, or shrewd ARTFUL
- cunning in a shifty or calculating way DISINGENUOUS, DESIGNING
- cunning or opportunism in politics MACHIAVELLIANISM

cup, mug, or tankard STOUP
- cup for the consecrated wine at Mass CHALICE
- cup of small size, or the strong black coffee drunk from it DEMITASSE
- cup or platter used, according to medieval legend, by Jesus at the Last Supper GRAIL, HOLY GRAIL, SANGRAAL
- cup or small bowl with a handle PORRINGER
- cup or small can CANNIKIN
- cup or small metal pan PANNIKIN
- cup or small mug NOGGIN
- cup-shaped COTYLOID, CUPULATE
- cup-shaped flower CHALICE
- cup-shaped mold for jellies, small cakes, or the like DARIOLE

cupid, cherub, or small boy in baroque paintings, sculptures, or reliefs PUTTO, AMORETTO

curative, remedial THERAPEUTIC
- curative, restoring or promoting health SALUTARY

curdle CLABBER

curds - watery part of milk that can be separated from the solid curds WHEY, SERUM

cure, heal, treat medically PHYSIC
- cure-all, universal remedy, as sought by alchemists PANACEA, ELIXIR, CATHOLICON
- cure fish by smoking BLOAT
- cure in the form of a counteracting remedy, especially for poisoning ANTIDOTE
- cure or solution to a problem of doubtful effectiveness, quack remedy NOSTRUM
- curing, healing SANATIVE

curio or small trinket BIBELOT
- curios, antiques, and objets d'art, or a cultivated liking for them VIRTU

curiosity - arouse someone's curiosity, interest, or the like PIQUE

curious, prying, nosy INQUISITIVE
- impatient with curiosity AGOG

curl of hair or ringlet over the forehead LOVELOCK
- curly or spiral design or structure, as on a shell WHORL, VOLUTE
- pinch into tight curls, folds, or the like CRIMP

curling contest or game BONSPIEL
- broom or brush used in curling to smooth the path of the stone over the ice BESOM

currency See chart, page 136
- currency, money serving as a medium of exchange CIRCULATING MEDIUM, LEGAL TENDER
- currency equivalent, at the official rate of exchange PARITY
- currency exchanging or brokerage AGIOTAGE
- currency unit, or monetary unit used for purposes of accounting UNIT OF ACCOUNT
- allow a currency to find its real exchange value freely according to market forces FLOAT
- reduction by a government in the monetary or exchange value of a currency DEVALUATION
- referring to paper currency that is not backed by gold FIDUCIARY

current, conventional direction, or trend MAINSTREAM
- current, conventional, or widespread PREVAILING, PREVALENT
- current and interesting or important, as news might be TOPICAL
- current in an electrical circuit that changes direction continually ALTERNATING CURRENT, AC
- current in an electrical circuit that flows in a single direction DIRECT CURRENT, DC
- current of water RACE
- current or backward pull of receding waves after breaking on the shore UNDERTOW
- current or dangerous eddy in a narrow channel, caused by the tides MAELSTROM
- current or swirl moving against the main current, often creating a miniature whirlpool EDDY
- convert alternating current into direct current RECTIFY

current (combining form) RHEO-

curse EXECRATION, IMPRECATION
- curse of excommunication or damnation ANATHEMA
- curse or slanderous accusation MALEDICTION, DENUNCIATION, FULMINATION

curtain behind which women are screened, especially in India PURDAH
- curtain drawn up and outward to produce a draped effect, especially on a stage TABLEAU CURTAIN
- curtain hung over a doorway PORTIERE
- gathered strip of material or ornamental pleated ruffle sewn to a garment or curtain FLOUNCE
- length of board or fabric along

CURRENCY

Currency	Country
afghani (100 puls)	Afghanistan
austral	Argentina
baht (100 satang)	Thailand
balboa	Panama
birr	Ethiopia
bolivar	Venezuela
cedi (100 pesewas)	Ghana
colon	Costa Rica, El Salvador
cordoba	Nicaragua
cruzado	Brazil
deutsche mark (100 pfennigs)	Germany
dinar	Yugoslavia, Algeria, Kuwait, and others
dirham	Morocco, United Arab Emirates
dobra	Sao Tome and Principe
dong (10 hao)	Vietnam
drachma (100 lepta)	Greece
ekpwele	Equatorial Guinea
escudo	Cape Verde, Portugal
forint (100 fillér)	Hungary
franc	France, Switzerland, Senegal, and others
gourde	Haiti
guarani	Paraguay
gulden/guilder/florin	Netherlands, Suriname
inti	Peru
kina (100 toea)	Papua New Guinea
kip (100 at)	Laos
koruna (100 haleru)	Czechoslovakia
krona	Sweden, Iceland
krone	Denmark, Norway
kwacha (100 ngwee)	Malawi, Zambia
kwanza (100 lwei)	Angola
kyat (100 pyas)	Burma
lek (100 quindarkas)	Albania
lempira	Honduras
leone	Sierra Leone
leu (100 bani)	Romania
lev (100 stotinki)	Bulgaria
lira	Italy, Malta, Turkey
loti (100 licente)	Lesotho
markka (100 penniä)	Finland
metical	Mozambique
naira (100 kobo)	Nigeria
ngultrum (100 chetrums)	Bhutan
ouguiya (5 khoums)	Mauritania
pa'anga (100 seniti)	Tonga
peseta	Spain
peso	Philippines, Mexico, Chile, Cuba, and others
pula (100 thebe)	Botswana
quetzal	Guatemala
rand	South Africa
rial	Iran, Saudi Arabia, Yemen
riel (100 sen)	Cambodia
ringgit	Malaysia
riyal	Saudi Arabia, Qatar
ruble (100 kopecks)	U.S.S.R.
rupee	India, Pakistan, and others
rupiah (100 sen)	Indonesia
schilling (100 groschen)	Austria
shekel (100 agorot)	Israel
shilling	Kenya, Tanzania, and others
sucre	Ecuador
taka (100 paisa)	Bangladesh
tala (100 sene)	Western Samoa
tugrik (100 mongo)	Mongolia
vatu	Vanuatu
won	North Korea, South Korea
yen (100 sen)	Japan
yuan (100 fen)	China
zaire (100 makuta)	Zaire
zloty (100 groszy)	Poland

the top of a window, used to hide the curtain rod PELMET
- short decorative curtain hung along a pelmet, shelf, edge of the bed, or the like VALANCE

curtsy, bow, or similar gesture of respect or submission OBEISANCE

curve, bend, turn, or fold, as of a body part FLEXURE
- curve hypothetically formed by a uniform cable suspended from two points CATENARY
- curve on a geometric graph PARABOLA, HYPERBOLA
- curve or line enclosing a plane area in geometry PERIMETER
- curved surface, as of a road or airfoil CAMBER
- curved, arched, as horns might be ARCUATE
- curved, scimitar-shaped, as some leaves are ACINACIFORM
- curved flight path of a missile, ball, or the like TRAJECTORY
- curved molding, having an S-shape OGEE
- curved surface of a liquid MENISCUS
- curving gracefully, as a winding road or the movements of a snake might be SINUOUS
- curving inward, as a mirror or lens might CONCAVE
- curving outward, as a mirror or lens might CONVEX
- curving or turning line or shape, as of a whirlpool SPIRAL, HELIX, VOLUTE, WHORL
- draftsman's plastic stencil having many curves FRENCH CURVE
- line approaching a curve, as on a graph, such that they will meet only at infinity ASYMPTOTE
- point of intersection of two arcs of a geometrical curve CUSP, SPINODE
- touch, without intersecting, as two adjoining curves in geometry might OSCULATE

cushion, as of a sofa or car seat SQUAB
- cushion for kneeling on or resting feet on, especially in church HASSOCK
- cushion of a large firm kind, used as a seat POUFFE
- cushion or long, cylindrical pillow that is typically hard, stiff, and narrow BOLSTER
- cushioned stool for kneeling on during prayer, as by a sovereign at the coronation FALDSTOOL
- silky plant fiber used for stuffing cushions, for soundproofing, or the like KAPOK
- strong cloth used to cover a mattress or cushion TICKING

custard-filled puff-pastry slice NAPOLEON, MILLE-FEUILLE

custom, ceremony, or ritual marking a change of status in a person's life RITE OF PASSAGE
- custom, habit WONT, USAGE
- customs of a social group, defining it and its values MORES, PRAXIS

custom (combining form) NOMO-

customer buyer, reader, or the like PATRON
- customers or clients as a group, as of a restaurant or hairdresser CLIENTELE
- seek customers or support, especially in a forthright way TOUT

customs certificate authorizing repayment of duty DEBENTURE
- customs label or receipt DOCKET
- customs list of a ship's cargo MANIFEST
- customs permit for the temporary importing of a car or other vehicle CARNET
- customs union ZOLLVEREIN
- seize at customs CONFISCATE, IMPOUND, EMBARGO

cut, as in surgery INCISION
- cut a groove in FLUTE, CHAMFER, CHASE
- cut a surface into wood, a slope, or the like, to form an angle other than a right angle BEVEL
- cut from a text, delete EXCISE
- cut from a text the parts considered indecent EXPURGATE, BOWDLERIZE
- cut or divide a line or space, cross INTERSECT, TRANSECT, DECUSSATE
- cut or divide into two parts BISECT
- cut or lop top branches from a tree to promote lower and thicker growth POLLARD
- cut or scratch the skin slightly, as for vaccination SCARIFY
- cut or tear the flesh to form a jagged wound LACERATE
- cut or trim hair, grass, the edges of a photograph, or the like CROP
- cut small shavings from wood WHITTLE
- cut the hair, wool, or horns of POLL
- cut through an object, or the resulting piece or surface, revealing its inner structure CROSS SECTION
- cut to pieces DISMEMBER
- cut up or open, as in surgery or laboratory examination DISSECT
- cutting, splitting, dividing SCISSION
- pencillike stick containing a chemical for stopping the bleeding from small cuts STYPTIC PENCIL
- cutting up or into the body of a living animal, especially for research VIVISECTION

cut (combining form) TOM-, -TOME, -TOMY, -SECT

cut back on expenditure, economize RETRENCH, CURTAIL

cut off, seize, or stop something, such as a message, in its course INTERCEPT
- cut off from membership of a church or religion EXCOMMUNICATE
- cut off from outside influences CLOISTERED, HERMETIC, INSULATED, ISOLATED

cut short, abbreviate, or lop TRUNCATE

cutting, penetrating, to the point, as a remark might be INCISIVE, TRENCHANT, MORDANT, CAUSTIC
- cutting for planting or grafting SLIP, SCION

cuttings - tray of soil, usually covered, in which seeds or cuttings are grown PROPAGATOR

cycle of change in a system, involving a swing from one extreme to the other and then back OSCILLATION, PERIOD
- cycle or pattern of one's mental, physical, or emotional condition BIORHYTHM
- cycle-racing arena, typically with a banked track VELODROME
- cycling race in which two riders or teams try to overtake each other on a circular track PURSUIT

cylinder or cone with its top cut off at an angle UNGULA
- smooth worn-out engine cylinders by drilling, and fit slightly larger pistons REBORE

cymbals operated by a pedal in a pop or jazz group HIGH HAT

cynical, unidealistic DISILLUSIONED, DISENCHANTED, DISABUSED

D

daddy longlegs CRANEFLY, HARVESTMAN

daffodil or related flower NARCISSUS
- crown-shaped part of the daffodil or similar flower CORONA

dagger worn in the stocking of a person wearing traditional Scottish Highland dress SKEAN-DHU, DIRK

daily DIURNAL
- daily, occurring every day, as attacks of malaria might be QUOTIDIAN
- daily allowance for expenses PER DIEM

dainty in an affected, overrefined way MINCING

daisy, dandelion, or related plant having compound flower heads COMPOSITE
- flower cluster in the form of a dense disc, as in the daisy CAPITULUM
- tiny disc flower or ray flower, usually in a cluster, as in the head of a daisy or other composite flower FLORET

dam in a river or canal to raise the water or regulate its flow WEIR
- dam used for generating electricity HYDROELECTRIC DAM
- dam wall or similar obstruction across a waterway BARRAGE
- channel for excess water, as around the side of a dam SPILLWAY
- channel or small dam, or the gate or valve holding back or regulating the water SLUICE

damage, as caused by war HAVOC, DEVASTATION
- damage, harm, disadvantage DETRIMENT, DISSERVICE
- damage, weaken, or disable IMPAIR, MAR, INCAPACITATE
- damage extensively, spoil or destroy, as grief or fire might RAVAGE, DEVASTATE
- damage or destroy, as through neglect BLIGHT
- damage or destroy personal or public property wantonly and maliciously VANDALIZE
- damage or spoil, reduce to imperfection VITIATE
- damage severely or maim, as by removal of a limb or vital element MUTILATE
- damage the appearance or shape of DEFACE, DISFIGURE
- damage the reputation of, disgrace, dishonor DISCREDIT
- damage to a property caused by the tenant's neglect, or a list of the necessary repairs DILAPIDATIONS
- impossible to repair or make good, as devastating damage might be IRREPARABLE

damages - guilty party in a damages case TORTFEASOR
- fine or damages imposed by a court in former times AMERCEMENT
- succeed in a lawsuit, or gain compensation or damages through it RECOVER

damaging, harmful, or corrupting NOXIOUS, DELETERIOUS
- damaging or malicious destruction of public property, artistic works, or the like VANDALISM

damnation, hell PERDITION
- damnation curse ANATHEMA
- person doomed or predestined to damnation, in theology REPROBATE

damp, high in moisture content, as air might be HUMID

damper or mute for a musical instrument SORDINO

dance See chart, and also **ballet**
- dance of a rhythmical free-style kind, or a form of musical training using such movement EURHYTHMICS
- dance of death DANSE MACABRE
- dance popular in the 1920's and 1930's, held at teatime in the afternoon THÉ DANSANT
- dance step in ballroom dancing in which the couple are side by side FEATHER
- dance step in eastern European folk dancing, in which the legs are

DANCES

BALLROOM	HISTORICAL	FOLK	MODERN
beguine	**allemande**	**dashing white sergeant**	**body popping**
carioca	**bourrée**	**eightsome reel**	**boogie**
cha-cha	**chaconne**	**gigue/jig**	**bop**
foxtrot	**Charleston**	**Highland fling**	**break dancing**
Gay Gordons	**cotillion**	**hornpipe**	**frug**
hokey-cokey	**courante**	**morris dancing**	**go-go dancing**
Lambeth walk	**écossaise**	**Sir Roger de Coverley**	**hustle**
lancers	**galliard**	**square dance (hoedown)**	**jitterbug**
mambo	**gavotte**	**strathspey**	**jive**
merengue	**minuet**	**strip the willow**	**rock 'n' roll**
paso doble	**passacaglia**	**sword dance**	**salsa**
Paul Jones	**passepied**		**shuffle**
polka	**pavane**		**twist**
quickstep	**quadrille**		
rumba	**rigadoon**		
samba	**sarabande**		
shimmy	**schottische**		
tango	**turkey trot**		
waltz	**volta**		

NATIONAL

bolero - Spanish	**habanera** - Cuban	**maxixe** - Brazilian
bossa nova - Brazilian	**haka** - Maori	**mazurka** - Polish
cachucha - Spanish	**hora** - Romanian/Israeli	**nautch** - Indian
czardas - Hungarian	**hula** - Polynesian	**polonaise** - Polish
fandango - Spanish	**kazatzka** - Russian	**saltarello** - Italian
farandole - French	**ländler** - Austrian	**seguidilla** - Spanish
flamenco - Spanish	**limbo** - Caribbean	**tambourin** - French
galop/galopade - German/French	**malaguena** - Spanish	**tarantella** - Italian
		zapateado - Spanish

kicked out alternately from a squatting position PRISIADKA
- dance step or series of dance steps PAS
- dancing or ballet as an art CHOREOGRAPHY
- figure in country dancing in which couples join hands and circle one another POUSSETTE
- figure in square or country dancing in which two dancers pass each other and then circle back to back DO-SI-DO
- marching sequence during a square or country dance PROMENADE
- relating to dancing TERPSICHOREAN
- teenager or woman who is seldom invited to partner a man at a dance WALLFLOWER

dancer employed by a nightclub or dance hall to dance with the patrons for a fee each time TAXI DANCER
- dancer's close-fitting garment LEOTARD
- supple and lithe, as the movements of a ballet dancer might be SINUOUS

dandelion, daisy, or related plant having compound flower heads COMPOSITE
- dandelion's tuft of fluff, helping to disperse the seeds PAPPUS

dandruff or similar scaling of the skin SCURF, FURFURES

dandy FOP, COXCOMB

danger, threat, risk MENACE
- danger or risk associated with one's job or a specified activity OCCUPATIONAL HAZARD
- hidden danger or difficulty PITFALL
- in great danger, distress, or need IN EXTREMITY
- open to danger, attack, or criticism VULNERABLE, EXPOSED, SUSCEPTIBLE
- prevent or ward off danger, disaster, or the like AVERT
- put in danger IMPERIL, JEOPARDIZE
- risk taking of a foolhardy kind, disregard of danger TEMERITY

dangerous, corrupting, evil PERNICIOUS, PESTIFEROUS, PESTILENT
- dangerous, risky HAZARDOUS, PERILOUS
- dangerous and uncertain PARLOUS
- dangerous in a subtle or treacherous way INSIDIOUS
- dangerous or risky project, such as a new business undertaking, or the like VENTURE
- dangerous or threatening FORBIDDING
- dangerous or worrying experience, of short duration MAUVAIS QUART D'HEURE
- dangerous trouble spot or explosive situation TINDERBOX, POWDER KEG
- dangerous venture of a suicidally risky kind RUSSIAN ROULETTE
- dangerously attractive or charming, bewitching CIRCEAN
- dangerously positioned, insecure, liable to failure or disaster PRECARIOUS
- caught between two equally dangerous alternatives BETWEEN SCYLLA AND CHARYBDIS, BETWEEN A ROCK AND A HARD PLACE
- glass box in which dangerous radioactive or toxic substances can be handled with protective gloves sealed into the side GLOVE BOX

dare, risk, gamble, expose to danger HAZARD, VENTURE, BRAVE

daredevil, adventurous, flamboyant SWASHBUCKLING

dark, dim, gloomy, murky SOMBER, TENEBROUS, FUNEREAL, CALIGINOUS
- dark, drab, dull, SUBFUSC
- dark, very gloomy CIMMERIAN, STYGIAN
- dark area, especially the darkest part of a shadow UMBRA
- dark-skinned or sunburned in appearance SWARTHY
- darkish area, as during an eclipse, between areas of full shadow and full illumination PENUMBRA

dark (combining form) MELAN-, MELANO-, NYCT-, NYCTI-, NYCTO-

dark chamber in which the image of an outside view is projected onto a surface by a lens above or opposite CAMERA OBSCURA

darken, as with fog or clouds OBNUBILATE
- darken, blur, make indistinct or dim OBFUSCATE
- darkening or changing color when exposed to light, as the glass or plastic in some sunglasses PHOTOCHROMIC

dart or steel missile dropped from an aircraft, as in the First World War FLÉCHETTE
- feather or other flared tail giving stability to an arrow or dart FLIGHT
- line from which a darts player throws darts at the board OCHE

Darwin - theory of the gradual and natural development of species EVOLUTIONISM
- survival of the fittest, as in the theory of Charles Darwin NATURAL SELECTION
- theory, going against strict Darwinian ideas of evolution, that acquired characteristics can be inherited LAMARCKISM, LYSENKOISM

date a check or other document earlier than the date of writing ANTEDATE
- date a check or other document later than the date of writing POSTDATE
- about or approximately, as written before an uncertain date CIRCA
- calculation of the dates of past events, or ordering of events according to their dates, or a list of such events CHRONOLOGY
- outmoded system of reckoning dates, replaced by the Gregorian calendar JULIAN CALENDAR
- present system of reckoning dates, on the basis of the Gregorian calendar NEW STYLE

dating, as of wood samples or of archeological specimens, by measuring their radioactive carbon-14 content RADIOCARBON DATING, CARBON DATING
- dating method for rocks and minerals up to 1,000 million years old RUBIDIUM-STRONTIUM DATING

daughter - adjective for a son or daughter FILIAL

dawn - poem, song, or tune suited to or dealing with dawn or the early morning AUBADE

day beginning a new season or payment quarter QUARTER DAY
- days of fine weather, tranquillity, or prosperity HALCYON DAYS
- days of summer, hot and lazy, from mid-July to September DOG DAYS
- active during the day rather than at night, as most animals are DIURNAL
- either of the two times during the year when day and night are of equal length all over the earth EQUINOX
- either the longest or the shortest day of the year SOLSTICE
- relating to biological processes that have a regular cycle of a 24-hour day CIRCADIAN
- weekday that is not a feast day FERIA

daybreak, spring, or similar early part or beginning of something PRIME

daydream REVERIE
- daydreamer, typically a person who indulges in fantasies to compensate for his own inadequacies WALTER MITTY
- daydreaming, absentmindedness WOOLGATHERING

dazed, confused, or dizzy WOOZY, STUPEFIED, GROGGY
- dazed, hypnotic, or dreamlike state TRANCE

de, *von*, or similar preposition accompanying a title or surname, indicating noble rank NOBILIARY

PARTICLE

deacon - office or status, or deacons collectively DIACONATE
- adjective for a deacon DIACONAL

dead See also **death**
- dead, invalid, or inoperative DEFUNCT
- dead, lifeless, not living INANIMATE
- dead as a species, having died out EXTINCT
- dead person THE DECEASED, DECEDENT, LOVED ONE
- conjuring up of the spirits of the dead as a supposed means of predicting or influencing the future NECROMANCY
- hymn, service, or piece of music for a dead person REQUIEM
- list of dead people, especially those who have died recently NECROLOGY
- pretend to be dead, asleep, or ignorant PLAY POSSUM
- speech or poem of praise or a written tribute, as for someone recently dead EULOGY, ELEGY
- speech or written obituary commemorating a dead person EPITAPH

dead (combining form) NECR-, NECRO-, MORT-

dead animal - body of a dead animal CARCASS
- flesh of a dead animal CARRION
- hyena, vulture, insect, or the like that feeds on dead animals, rotting meat, or other decaying organic matter SCAVENGER
- stuffing and preparing the skins of dead animals for exhibiting TAXIDERMY

dead body See **corpse**

dead end CUL-DE-SAC
- dead end, deadlock IMPASSE
- dead end, road blocked at one end CLOSE

dead matter (combining form) SAPR-, SAPRO-

deaden, dull PETRIFY

deadlock, drawn contest, or unresolvable difficulty, blocking progress IMPASSE, STALEMATE

deadly, destructive LETHAL, FATAL, BANEFUL, PERNICIOUS, PESTILENT

deaf - sign language with the hands, as used by deaf and dumb people DACTYLOLOGY

dealer (combining form) -MONGER

dean - adjective for a dean DECANAL

Dear Sir or similar conventional opening words of a letter SALUTATION

death See also **dead**
- death DEMISE, DECEASE, EXPIRATION, DEPARTURE, PASSING
- death, decay, or disintegration DISSOLUTION
- death as a relief or release from life QUIETUS
- death as personified in Greek mythology, or death wish in Freudian theory THANATOS
- death notice, as in a newspaper, often with a short biography of the deceased OBITUARY
- death of body tissue NECROSIS, GANGRENE, MORTIFICATION
- death of many people, specifically one million MEGADEATH
- death or an accident or occurrence causing death FATALITY
- death through accident rather than crime MISADVENTURE
- Death viewed as Father Time with his scythe GRIM REAPER
- deathlike or temporary dormant state of a living organism SUSPENDED ANIMATION
- apparition of a person supposedly appearing just before his death WRAITH
- at the point of death IN EXTREMIS, MORIBUND
- causing, able to cause, or relating to death LETHAL, FATAL
- deliberate causing of a painless death in order to relieve suffering, as from an incurable illness EUTHANASIA
- deprived or desolated, as by the death of a loved one BEREAVED, BEREFT
- fascinated by or preoccupied with death MORBID
- fatal, certain to end in death, as an inoperable cancer may be TERMINAL
- hospital specializing in care for those near to death HOSPICE
- medical specialist and public official conducting inquests with a jury into deaths that may not have been the result of natural causes CORONER
- medical specialist who conducts postmortem examinations to establish the cause of death PATHOLOGIST
- occurring after death POSTMORTEM
- painful spasms, as on approaching death PANGS, THROES
- person excessively fascinated by death GHOUL
- premature, before the proper or allotted time, as an early death is UNTIMELY
- relating to death MORTAL, MORTUARY
- relating to the time after a person's death POSTHUMOUS, POST-OBIT
- reminder of inescapable death, such as a skull MEMENTO MORI
- reminiscent of death and its horrors MACABRE
- signal or omen of disaster or death KNELL
- starvation or exhaustion as a cause of death INANITION
- temporary rigidity, caused by chemical changes, of the muscles and joints of a dead body RIGOR MORTIS

death (combining form) NECR-, NECRO-, MORT-

death penalty - cancellation or postponement of a punishment, such as the death penalty REPRIEVE, RESPITE, PARDON
- person who urges or favors the ending of the death penalty ABOLITIONIST
- person who urges or favors the retaining of the death penalty RETENTIONIST

deathly, ghastly SEPULCHRAL, CHARNEL
- deathly pale, ill-looking CADAVEROUS

debate, discuss, or negotiate PARLEY
- debate, especially a formal and learned debate DISPUTATION
- debate on a legal topic conducted by law students MOOT COURT
- ending of a debate, as in legislating, and the immediate voting on the motion CLOSURE, CLOTURE

debauched man, rake, especially an aging one ROUÉ

debt, financial obligation LIABILITY
- debt, such as rent, that remains unpaid ARREARS
- debt as recorded in the left-hand side of an account or bookkeeping ledger DEBIT
- debt collector, or his insistent demand for payment DUN
- debt collector and court officer who pursued debtors in former times BUM BAILIFF
- adjust a debt and settle for a smaller amount than the claim COMPOUND
- bond or contract to repay a debt after the death of a person whose heir the debtor is POST-OBIT
- certificate or voucher acknowledging a debt DEBENTURE
- discharge, as from duty or debt QUIETUS, QUITTANCE
- fail to carry out a task, promise, or duty, especially to pay a debt DEFAULT, WELSH
- in debt and unable to pay it off INSOLVENT, BANKRUPT
- in debt to, owing thanks to OBLIGED, INDEBTED, BEHOLDEN
- part payment of a debt made as part of a series INSTALLMENT
- pay off a debt or mortgage by installments AMORTIZE
- postponement or suspension of debt payments MORATORIUM
- reduce or revise a debt, payment,

or the like COMMUTE
- refuse to acknowledge a debt REPUDIATE
- run away, especially when leaving unpaid debts behind LEVANT
- run up a debt INCUR, CONTRACT
- settle a debt, in law EXTINGUISH
- settle a debt or claim LIQUIDATE
- value of a property or business once all debts are taken into account EQUITY
- withhold the pay or seize the property of a debtor GARNISHEE, SEQUESTER, LEVY

debtor - legal right to a debtor's property until he or she settles the debt LIEN
- sheriff's officer in medieval times who arrested debtors CATCHPOLE

decanters - lockable cagelike container for displaying decanters of wine or spirits TANTALUS

decay, crumble away, turn to dust MOLDER
- decay, evil, or corruption, especially when spreading rampantly CANKER
- decay and death of body tissue, limbs, or the like, typically through a failure of blood supply GANGRENE, NECROSIS, MORTIFICATION
- decay of teeth or bones CARIES
- decay or rot DECOMPOSE, FESTER, PUTREFY
- decay or waste away, as through disuse ATROPHY
- decayed organic matter that enriches the soil HUMUS
- decaying, falling to pieces, broken down, as a shabby old house is DILAPIDATED, DECREPIT
- decaying flesh of a dead animal CARRION
- decaying or rotting smell, as from a swamp or rubbish heap EFFLUVIUM
- hyena, vulture, insect, or the like that feeds on dead animals, rotting meat, or other decaying organic matter SCAVENGER

decaying matter (combining form) SAPR-, SAPRO-

deceive See also **cheat**
- deceive, pretend to be something or someone that one is not MASQUERADE, DISSEMBLE
- deceive or flatter with smooth, charming talk BLARNEY
- easily deceived, fooled, or duped CREDULOUS, GULLIBLE

deception, cheating, fraud DUPLICITY, CHICANERY
- deception, crafty scheme, or the like, as to conceal, escape, or evade something SUBTERFUGE
- deception or clever trickery SLEIGHT OF HAND, LEGERDEMAIN
- deception or fraud, as by assuming a false identity IMPOSTURE
- deceptions, tricks WILES

deceptive, apparently attractive, genuine, or sound, but not really so SPECIOUS
- deceptive, misleading, or imaginary ILLUSORY, FALLACIOUS
- deceptive or evasive, as an ambiguous reply might be EQUIVOCAL
- deceptive person or thing WILL-O'-THE-WISP, IGNIS FATUUS
- deceptive three-dimensional painting technique that makes the objects look like real ones TROMPE L'OEIL
- deceptively attractive or superficially impressive outward appearance VENEER, GLOSS
- deceptively luxurious or abundant, sham or counterfeit, as a feast might be BARMECIDAL

decide See also **choose**
- decide when mediating, act as judge ARBITRATE, ADJUDICATE
- decided in advance PREDETERMINED

deciduous trees See illustration, page 142

decimal fraction with a repeated and neverending pattern REPEATING DECIMAL, RECURRING DECIMAL, CIRCULATING DECIMAL
- decimal point RADIX POINT
- decimal system of numbers ALGORISM

decipher See also **code**
- deciphering of codes, secret writings, and the like CRYPTANALYSIS

decision, deliberate choice VOLITION
- decision, legal judgment, or the like used as an example or standard justification when treating later cases similarly PRECEDENT
- decision already taken, preconceived opinion, prejudice PARTI PRIS
- decision taken on a particular occasion or issue rather than as general policy AD HOC DECISION
- agree to, support, or subscribe to a decision UNDERWRITE
- analysis of the efficiency of a work force, machine system, or the like, as an aid to decision making OPERATIONAL RESEARCH
- backward, unprogressive, as a step or decision might be RETROGRADE
- coming to a decision according to one's own judgment rather than according to a set of rules DISCRETIONARY
- disallow or reverse something, such as a decision OVERRULE, RESCIND, INVALIDATE, OVERTURN, QUASH
- impossible to change, reverse, or take back, as a decision might be IRREVOCABLE
- overhasty or sudden, as a decision might be IMPETUOUS, IMPULSIVE, PRECIPITATE
- settle a dispute by an authoritative decision DETERMINE

decisive, definite, conclusive, as a refusal or victory might be CATEGORICAL, UNEQUIVOCAL
- decisive factor, telling argument or strategy TRUMP CARD, CLINCHER
- decisive vote cast by the chairperson or presiding officer when the votes in an assembly are tied CASTING VOTE

deck above the main deck near the back of a ship POOP DECK
- deck or section of the upper deck, near the front of a ship FORECASTLE, FO'C'S'LE
- part of a ship's structure situated above the main deck SUPERSTRUCTURE
- stairway from a ship's upper deck to the cabins or deck below COMPANIONWAY

declaration in writing that is made under oath AFFIDAVIT
- make a declaration or state formally ENUNCIATE

declare See **claim**

decline See also **lessen**
- decline or regress after apparently recovering from illness RELAPSE
- declining or decaying, as in culture or morals DECADENT

decode, interpret or clarify a code DECIPHER, DECRYPT

decompose - capable of being decomposed by bacteria or by other biological processes, as some materials are BIODEGRADABLE

decorate a surface by embedding ornamental pieces in it INLAY
- decorate food, as with cress or a slice of lemon GARNISH
- decorate in a gaudy or vulgar way BEDAUB, BEDIZEN
- decorate lavishly, as in luxurious clothing, deck out, adorn ARRAY, BEDECK, CAPARISON
- decorate metal by engraving or embossing CHASE, ENCHASE
- decorate metal by etching or inlaying wavy patterns DAMASCENE, DAMASK
- decorate splendidly, typically in bright colors EMBLAZON

decoration, such as a trill added by a musician EMBELLISHMENT
- decoration formed by fastening small pieces of one material onto the surface of another material, such as wooden cuttings onto metal APPLIQUÉ
- decoration in the form of a chain or garland of flowers, ribbons, or the like suspended in a loop

FESTOON
- decoration of colored cloth strips or streamers strung on a line BUNTING
- decoration of thin bright threads or strips, as on a Christmas tree TINSEL
- decoration or ornamentation, as of buildings or clothing TRIM
- decorations and furniture of a place, or the style of decoration DECOR
- delicate and intricate decoration, especially ornamental work of gold or silver wire FILIGREE

decoy, informer, or police spy STOOL PIGEON

decrease See also **lessen**
- decrease, deterioration, or deviation from a standard, custom, or the like DECLENSION, DECLINATION
- decrease, or the amount lost or wasted in a decrease DECREMENT, DIMINUTION
- decreasing output or reward, after a certain point, for each increase in input, effort, or production DIMINISHING RETURNS

decree, arbitrary command, or order FIAT
- taking effect, as a divorce decree might, on a specified date unless the court is shown cause why it should not NISI

deduce, infer, work out, or prove by reasoning DERIVE
- deduce, or guess at from known information EXTRAPOLATE

deduction from a sum of money to be paid REBATE, DISCOUNT
- deductive reasoning, logical deduction SYNTHESIS
- inference of general truths from particular instances, as distinct from strict logical deduction INDUCTION
- pattern of deduction in which two premises generate a conclusion SYLLOGISM

deed or adventure, especially a noble or heroic one EXPLOIT, GEST
- deed showing right of ownership of a property TITLE DEED

deep, at or from a great depth PROFOUND
- deep, dark, and empty CAVERNOUS
- deep, wide, and safe enough for

Deciduous Trees

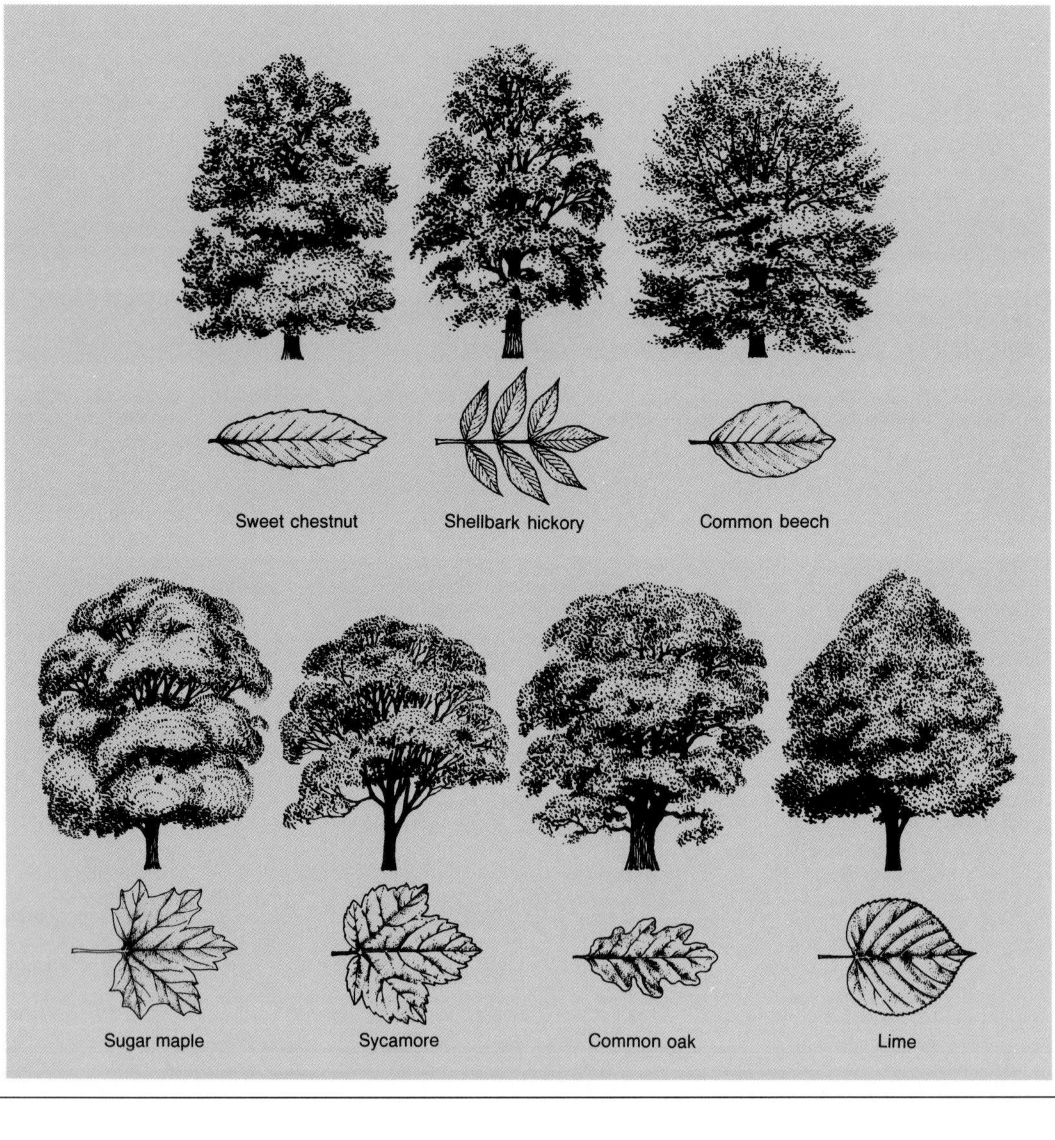

Sweet chestnut
Shellbark hickory
Common beech
Sugar maple
Sycamore
Common oak
Lime

ships or boats to sail on or through NAVIGABLE
- deep-rooted, persistent, long-established, as a tendency might be INVETERATE
- deep-seated and hard to remove, as dirt or vices may be INGRAINED
- deepest, lowest, farthest down NETHERMOST
- deepest or lowest point, as of one's fortunes or of depression NADIR
- deeply rooted or common within a particular area or group ENDEMIC
- period or state of deep thought BROWN STUDY, REVERIE
- extremely or immeasurably deep FATHOMLESS

deep (combining form) BATH-, BATHY-, BATHO-

deer, cow, or other hoofed mammal, having two or four toes on each foot ARTIODACTYL
- deerlike African forest mammal, related to the giraffe OKAPI
- deer's flesh used as food VENISON
- deer's offal, as formerly given as food to hunt attendants UMBLES, NUMBLES
- deer's track or trail SLOT
- adjective relating to a deer CERVINE
- young male deer with unbranched antlers PRICKET

defeat, outperform, outshine, as in a competition ECLIPSE, EXCEL, SURPASS
- defeat oneself by being too ambitious OVERREACH
- defeat or overcome, as in battle VANQUISH
- defeat overwhelmingly, crush, trounce ANNIHILATE, DEVASTATE, PULVERIZE, ROUT, CRUCIFY
- bring under control or force into submission, as after a defeat SUBJUGATE, SUBDUE

defect, as in a machine MALFUNCTION
- defect, change sides, become a renegade TERGIVERSATE, APOSTATIZE

defendant in a divorce action RESPONDENT

defender of the faith, one of the titles of the British sovereign FIDEI DEFENSOR

defense See also **protection, fortification**
- defense of any kind, as against oppression BULWARK, BASTION, OUTPOST, STRONGHOLD
- defense of life and property to be undertaken by civilians in time of war or natural disaster CIVIL DEFENSE
- defense or formal justification, as of one's beliefs APOLOGIA
- defense or fortification against enemy fire or observation DEFILADE
- defense or protection, specifically the embankment and walls of a fortification RAMPART
- defense policy or weapons, such as nuclear warheads, designed to discourage enemy attack DETERRENT
- defender or champion of a cause APOLOGIST

defensible or maintainable, as a military or philosophical position might be TENABLE

defensive, jealously protective TERRITORIAL
- defensive bank, as behind a trench, giving protection from the rear PARADOS
- defensive bank of sand, stones, or the like, protecting against enemy fire PARAPET, BULWARK, BREASTWORK
- defensive barrier, such as a bank of earth, in front of a trench or rampart TRAVERSE
- defensive barrier or fortress made of upright posts or stakes STOCKADE
- defensive obstacle, consisting of a frame with spikes or barbed wire, against enemy troops or horses CHEVAL-DE-FRISE
- defensive shelter underground with a bank or gun emplacements above ground BUNKER
- defensive stronghold, usually a small and temporary fortification REDOUBT
- defensive trench or wall, within outer walls or fortifications RETRENCHMENT
- defensive wall or barricade for protection against explosions REVETMENT
- defensive wall surrounding a castle, town, or the like, or the area protected by it ENCEINTE

define, set the limits or boundaries of DELIMIT, DEMARCATE, CIRCUMSCRIBE
- defining or limiting factor, as of a budget or schedule PARAMETERS, CONSTRAINTS

definite, particular, individual SPECIFIC

definition by means of a direct example of the term defined OSTENSIVE DEFINITION
- by definition, by its very nature IPSO FACTO

degree awarded "with great praise" MAGNA CUM LAUDE
- degree awarded "with greatest praise" SUMMA CUM LAUDE
- degree awarded "with praise" CUM LAUDE
- degree conferred on a student who was too ill to sit exams at the time AEGROTAT
- degree ranking below a doctorate in some European universities LICENTIATE
- awarded as an honor, as a degree might be HONORARY, HONORIS CAUSA
- present or bestow a degree or honor CONFER
- referring to a degree awarded even though the graduate is absent IN ABSENTIA
- research report, especially for a higher academic degree THESIS, DISSERTATION
- student about to receive a degree GRADUAND

degrees of comparison of adjectives and adverbs POSITIVE, COMPARATIVE, SUPERLATIVE

deity, saint, or other protecting power TUTELARY

delay See also **postpone**
- delay PROCRASTINATION, CUNCTATION
- delay, hinder, or obstruct as a deliberate strategy, as in legislative debate STONEWALL
- delay, lag, be late or slow in doing something TARRY, LOITER
- delay by holding back or preventing the departure of DETAIN
- delay decisions or draw out discussions as a way of gaining time TEMPORIZE
- delay or block legislation, voting, or the like by means of lengthy speeches or other obstructive tactics FILIBUSTER
- delay or slow down the development or progress of something RETARD
- delayed, late in arriving TARDY
- delaying, wasting time, dawdling DILATORY
- cause a delay by being indecisive or disorganized DITHER, DILLY-DALLY, VACILLATE, SHILLY-SHALLY
- granted delay or postponement, as of payments MORATORIUM
- temporary delay, relief, or postponement, such as a stay of execution RESPITE, REPRIEVE

delegate or representative, as of the pope LEGATE, EMISSARY

delete, erase, or obliterate something, such as a word EXPUNGE
- delete a passage from a text EXCISE
- delete words, passages, or the like from a text considered to be improper, objectionable, or obscene EXPURGATE, BOWDLERIZE

deliberate, planned beforehand, as a murder might be PREMEDITATED
- deliberate decision, choice VOLITION

delicacy, precision, subtlety, as in negotiations NICETY
- delicacy or sensitivity, as in one's dealings with other people TACT

- delicacy or subtlety, as of painting style, negotiation technique, or tennis strokes FINESSE

delicate, light, insubstantial GOSSAMER
- delicate, sensitive, capable of or based on fine distinctions SUBTLE, EXQUISITE
- delicate, very refined ETHEREAL
- delicate or dainty in an affected way MINCING, NIMINY-PIMINY

delicious, especially when sweet and juicy LUSCIOUS
- delicious, tempting TOOTHSOME
- delicious drink NECTAR
- delicious food AMBROSIA
- delicious or delightful DELECTABLE, SCRUMPTIOUS

delight, great joy ECSTASY, RAPTURE, TRANSPORT, JUBILATION, EXULTATION, ELATION
- delight, please, afford satisfaction to GRATIFY
- delight in or satisfaction at others' misfortunes GLOATING, SCHADENFREUDE
- regard with cruel or smug delight GLOAT

delightful See also **attractive, charming**
- delightful or blissful ELYSIAN, IDYLLIC
- delightful or delicious DELECTABLE, SCRUMPTIOUS

delivery See also **birth, childbirth**
- delivery of a baby requiring the use of medical tongs FORCEPS DELIVERY

Delphi - prophecy, shrine, or priest of a prophetic god, as in ancient Delphi ORACLE

delusion, or wishful thinking MARE'S NEST
- delusions of grandeur FOLIE DE GRANDEUR
- delusions of grandeur or persecution PARANOIA

demand, require or lay down as a condition in an agreement or contract STIPULATE
- demand or request, often in writing and official, for needed supplies or equipment REQUISITION
- demand persistently IMPORTUNE, HECTOR

demanding, exacting, pressing, urgent EXIGENT
- demanding, exacting, requiring painstaking work or one's detailed attention NIGGLING
- demanding, strict, rigorous STRINGENT
- demanding, tiring, requiring great effort TAXING
- demanding and determined person, insisting on obedience, tidiness, accuracy, or the like STICKLER
- referring to or making insistent demands STRIDENT

demolish a building or city, destroy down to the ground RAZE

demon or evil spirit reputed to have sex with a sleeping man SUCCUBUS
- demon or evil spirit reputed to have sex with a sleeping woman INCUBUS
- demon that preys on corpses, in Muslim legend GHOUL
- drive out demons or evil spirits, or free a possessed person from them, as by religious rites EXORCISE
- person supposedly possessed by a demon DEMONIAC, ENERGUMEN
- summon a demon or spirit by means of a magic spell CONJURE

demonstrate See also **prove**
- demonstrate, indicate, signify BESPEAK, BETOKEN
- demonstrate or reveal, make evident MANIFEST, EVINCE
- demonstrated beyond doubt, indisputably certain APODICTIC
- demonstrating or showing directly, pointing out OSTENSIVE, DEICTIC

demonstration, political protest rally MANIFESTATION
- demonstration or protest outside a place of work, typically during a strike, as to discourage other workers or customers from entering PICKET
- placard or message-bearing cloth strip carried in a demonstration or procession BANNER

demonstrative emotionally GUSHING, EFFUSIVE

denial of an allegation in a lawsuit TRAVERSE
- absolute, without reservation, as a denial might be CATEGORICAL

dental filling, as of gold or porcelain, cemented into a cavity INLAY
- dental plate with a false tooth or teeth permanently fixed to natural teeth BRIDGE, BRIDGEWORK
- mercury alloy, as used for dental fillings AMALGAM

dentist specializing in correcting the positioning of teeth ORTHODONTIST
- dentist's colleague specializing in scaling and polishing the teeth DENTAL HYGIENIST

dentistry concerned with diseases of the tissues and supporting structures surrounding the teeth PERIODONTICS
- rubbery latex substance used in electrical insulation and dentistry GUTTA-PERCHA

deny and disprove REFUTE, REBUT
- deny or contradict NEGATE, CONTROVERT, GAINSAY
- deny or reject without necessarily disproving REPUDIATE
- deny or withdraw a former statement or belief RECANT, RETRACT, RENOUNCE, FORSWEAR, ABJURE
- deny responsibility for or connection with DISAVOW, DISCLAIM, DISOWN

depart hastily, run away, or flee SKEDADDLE, SCARPER, VAMOOSE
- depart or flee secretly, as after committing a theft ABSCOND, DECAMP, ABSQUATULATE, HIGHTAIL
- depart or flee secretly with a lover, typically to get married ELOPE
- depart or withdraw, as from a dangerous area EVACUATE, VACATE
- departure, especially of a large number of people EXODUS
- departure from a convention, norm, standard, set path, or the like DIVERGENCE, DEVIATION
- departure or absence that is without permission or notification AWOL, FRENCH LEAVE

department - administrative department of a large public or international organization such as the United Nations SECRETARIAT

department store or large retail shop selling a wide range of goods EMPORIUM

dependency, captivity, enslavement THRALL, THRALLDOM
- value or thing in a relationship of dependency with or close correspondence to another FUNCTION

dependent clinging person, parasite LEECH, LIMPET
- dependent, hinging on, conditional CONTINGENT, PROVISIONAL
- dependent relationship, typically that of living together, of two organisms, especially when beneficial to both SYMBIOSIS

deposit money EARNEST
- deposit of fine sandy sediment in or from a river SILT, ALLUVIUM
- deposit of rock fragments or similar debris left by wind, water, or glaciers SEDIMENT
- deposit of sediment in a river's tidal estuary WARP
- deposit or pledge given as security GAGE

depot or warehouse ENTREPÔT

depression MELANCHOLIA
- depression, boredom, or inactivity DOLDRUMS, ENNUI
- depression, state of deep despair SLOUGH OF DESPOND
- depression or hysteria, supposed in former times to be caused by gases produced within the body THE VAPORS
- depression or unease MALAISE
- depression or withdrawn condition accompanying a nervous breakdown NEURASTHENIA

deprive of meaning, importance, or

an essential part EVISCERATE
- deprive or strip of something, such as clothes, rights, or property DIVEST, DENUDE, DESPOIL
- deprive someone of something, seize or appropriate, as by way of punishment or in an emergency EXPROPRIATE, CONFISCATE, COMMANDEER

depth, as of feeling, meaning, or thinking PROFUNDITY, PROFOUNDNESS
- depth appearance of various objects in different spatial relationships PERSPECTIVE
- establishing the depth of water by high-frequency sound waves ECHO SOUNDING, SONAR, ASDIC
- instrument for measuring the depth of water BATHOMETER
- measure the depth of, as with a weighted line SOUND, FATHOM, PLUMB

depth (combining form) BATH-, BATHO-, BATHY-

deputy See also **agent, substitute**
- deputy, representative of a superior official LIEUTENANT
- deputy, substitute, or stand-in VICAR, SURROGATE
- deputy administrative officer assisting a king, magistrate, or the like VICEGERENT
- deputy who does someone else's dirty work HATCHET MAN

derived from (combining form) AP-, APO-

Descartes - relating to Descartes or his philosophy, mathematics, or methods CARTESIAN

descend - descended from the same ancestor, though by different lines, as branches of a family might be COLLATERAL
- descended in a direct line from a particular ancestor LINEAL
- descended through the male line, related on the father's side AGNATE
- descending slope or downward tendency DECLENSION, DECLINATION, DECLINE, DECLIVITY
- descent, source, or origin DERIVATION
- relating to the female line of descent MATRILINEAL
- family tree or lineage, or study of descent and ancestors GENEALOGY
- relating to the male line of descent PATRILINEAL

descendant or offspring, especially male SCION
- descendants of a particular ancestor LINEAGE, POSTERITY

describe or draw, either in broad or in precise detail DELINEATE, DEPICT
- describe or portray, characterize LIMN
- difficult to describe, lacking distinct individual features, uninteresting NONDESCRIPT

description - brief description or account of someone, as in a magazine article PROFILE, POTTED BIOGRAPHY, THUMBNAIL SKETCH, PEN PICTURE
- precise description, list of components or details, plan, or proposal SPECIFICATION

desert, wilderness WASTE, WASTELAND
- desert area with eroded ridges and gullies BADLANDS
- desert one's country, political party, or the like, especially to join its opponent DEFECT
- desert or convert, become a renegade TERGIVERSATE, APOSTATIZE
- desert rat JERBOA
- deserted, uninhabited DESOLATE
- deserter of a religion or cause RENEGADE, APOSTATE
- dry and infertile, as desert land might be ARID
- fertile area in a desert OASIS
- illusion or image of a nonpresent object, such as an oasis in a desert MIRAGE
- relating to an extremely dry habitat such as a desert XERIC
- travelers in a group or convoy, as through a desert CARAVAN

deserved and appropriate, as a punishment might be CONDIGN

design See also **pattern**
- design, typically stamped or gilded, on books or leather TOOLING
- design, usually circular, symbolizing the universe, in Hindu and Buddhist art MANDALA
- design consisting of superimposed letters, as for an emblem MONOGRAM, CIPHER
- design made up of many other designs or pictures overlapping or stuck side by side MONTAGE, COLLAGE
- design of modern style using industrial materials HIGH-TECH
- design or painting on a wall or ceiling MURAL
- design or picture made up of many small pieces of stone, tile, or glass MOSAIC
- design or purpose in Nature, or the study of or belief in it TELEOLOGY
- design or structure, as in architecture or music ARCHITECTONICS
- design or symbol, as on a flag or embroidery DEVICE, EMBLEM
- design produced by superimposing one pattern on another MOIRÉ PATTERN
- designed for esthetic rather than realistic effect STYLIZED
- designer, craftsman, or craftswoman who is highly skilled ARTIFICER
- background for a design, as in lacework FOND
- basic design or layout, as of a broadcast or diagram FORMAT
- make a design or pattern by embedding decorative pieces in a surface INLAY
- original design or model, on which later versions are based PROTOTYPE, ARCHETYPE
- repeated shape or theme in a design or composition LEITMOTIV, MOTIF
- simplified, abstract, stylized, as a painting or design might be CONVENTIONALIZED

desirable but frustratingly inaccessible TANTALIZING

desire See also **tendency**
- desire or look forward to eagerly RELISH
- desire or slight tendency, without any action taken to fulfill it VELLEITY
- desire something that belongs to someone else COVET
- desire that is compulsive and harmful, mania CACOËTHES
- desire to achieve or succeed at something ASPIRATION
- behavior or mental activity directed toward change or action CONATION
- deep or intense desire, longing, yearning, craving HANKERING, YEN
- exclusion or deliberate blocking of thoughts, desires, or the like from one's mind SUPPRESSION, REPRESSION
- frenzy of frustrated desire for something unattainable NYMPHOLEPSY
- indulge one's desires or appetites to the full SATE, SATIATE
- indulge or yield to a whim, desire, or the like GRATIFY
- natural desire, tendency, or attraction APPETENCE
- relating to the desires ORECTIC
- something wished for, needed, or desired DESIDERATUM
- strong desire, especially sexual desire CONCUPISCENCE
- strong desire or greed, especially for money or material things CUPIDITY
- unsatisfiable, as an appetite or desire might be INSATIABLE

desire (combining form) -MANIA

desk See also **furniture**
- desk at which a person may kneel to pray PRIE-DIEU
- desk or panel containing the controls of a computer, lighting system, or the like CONSOLE
- rolltop desk's sliding front of wooden strips TAMBOUR
- set of drawers supporting a desk top PEDESTAL

despair, state of deep depression

SLOUGH OF DESPOND
- despair or spiritual lethargy ACEDIA, ACCIDIE

despise See **dislike, insult**
- despise or scorn DISDAIN, CONTEMN

despot See also **dictator**
- despot or absolute ruler who is moderate, enlightened, and well-disposed toward his subjects BENEVOLENT DESPOT

dessert See chart, and also **cake**

destination, purpose, goal, finishing point TERMINUS AD QUEM
- destination or goal BOURN

destine, decree ORDAIN

destiny See **fate**
- clear and unavoidable, as destiny might be MANIFEST

destroy, get rid of, or put an end to rules, practices, or the like ABOLISH
- destroy, ruin, or damage something, such as a plan SCUPPER, SCUTTLE
- destroy by taking to pieces DISMANTLE
- destroy completely, snuff out ANNIHILATE, EXTINGUISH, SPIFLICATE
- destroy a building or city, tear down to the ground DEMOLISH, RAZE
- destroy gradually, wear away CORRODE, ERODE
- destroy or eliminate something completely, such as vermin EXTERMINATE
- destroy or get rid of completely, stamp out ERADICATE, OBLITERATE, EXTIRPATE, EXPUNGE
- destroy or kill a large proportion of DECIMATE
- destroy or make ineffective an argument, contract, or the like ANNUL, NULLIFY, VOID, INVALIDATE, VITIATE
- destroy or obscure something, such as a memory EFFACE
- destroy the inside or power of GUT
- destroyed or completely ruined FORDONE
- explode or be destroyed, either automatically or following a signal, as a misfired missile might SELF-DESTRUCT

destroy (combining form) PHAG-, PHAGO-, -PHAGOUS

destruction, as caused by a war HAVOC, DEVASTATION
- destruction and plunder DEPREDATION
- destruction by breaking up DISINTEGRATION, PULVERIZATION, DISSOLUTION
- destruction by fire HOLOCAUST
- destruction of bacteria by an antibody LYSIS
- destruction of sacred objects or

DESSERTS AND PUDDINGS

baked Alaska	ice cream covered with baked meringue
Bakewell tart	open tart with almond-flavored sponge over a layer of jam
baklava	paper-thin pastry with chopped nuts and honey
Bavarian cream	fruit-flavored or chocolate-flavored egg custard with whipped cream
bombe	molded ice cream
cassata	Neapolitan ice cream with candied fruit and nuts
charlotte	sponge cake or bread mold filled with fruit
compote	dish of fresh or dried fruit cooked in syrup
coupe	garnished ice cream
crème brûlée	dish of cream or custard with a caramelized sugar top
crepe suzette	thin pancake with orange sauce, served with flaming spirit sauce
Eve's pudding	baked sponge pudding with a fruit base
flummery	custard, blancmange, or similar soft, bland dessert
fool	cold pudding of crushed fruit mixed with cream or custard
frappé	fruit-flavored water ice
frumenty	sweetened and spiced milk pudding of boiled wheat
granita	coarse-grained sherbet
halvah	sweetmeat of ground sesame seed or semolina and chopped nuts, in syrup, lemon juice, or the like
junket	sweetened milk set with rennet
mela stregata	ball of ice cream flavored with Strega liqueur, and coated with chocolate
Nesselrode	frozen pudding with preserved fruit and chestnut puree
pandowdy	dessert of baked apple slices with a sweet crust
parfait	frozen pudding of cream, eggs, sugar, and flavoring
profiteroles	small, cream-filled light pastry rolls, usually with a chocolate sauce
sorbet	water ice of fruit juice or fruit puree
strudel	baked pastry consisting of fruit rolled in wafer-thin sheets of dough
sundae	ice cream with various toppings
syllabub	sweetened, thickened cream flavored with sherry or wine and fruit juice
vacherin	meringue with cream and fresh fruit
zabaglione	beaten egg yolks with marsala wine and sugar
zuppa inglese	Italian dessert cake with rum and candied fruits

traditions ICONOCLASM
- destruction or attempted undermining, by secret activity, of a government or political system SUBVERSION
- destruction or damaging of property, as by enemy agents or dissatisfied workers SABOTAGE
- destruction or failure of some magnificent project or person GÖTTERDÄMMERUNG
- destruction or injury of a wanton or widespread kind MAYHEM
- destruction or just retribution, or an agent of it NEMESIS
- destruction or malicious damaging of public property, artistic works, or the like VANDALISM
- random, willful, unprovoked, as mindless destruction is WANTON, GRATUITOUS
- sudden and violent change, upheaval, or destruction CATACLYSM

destructive, deadly, harmful LETHAL, FATAL, BANEFUL, PERNICIOUS, PESTILENT
- destructive, especially through plundering or robbery PREDATORY
- destructive, frenzied, or violent in behavior RAMPAGING, ON THE RAMPAGE
- destructive effects, damage RAVAGES
- destructiveness of an unselective all-embracing kind NIHILISM

detach someone from old habits and pastimes and thereby encourage his or her independence WEAN

detail, individual item PARTICULAR
- detail, subtle point, fine distinction NICETY
- detail that is important only to a specialist, or that arises only from a strict ruling TECHNICALITY
- detail that is trivial, needless, or oversubtle QUIBBLE, NIGGLE
- detailed, complete, thorough, as a report might be COMPREHENSIVE, DEFINITIVE, CIRCUMSTANTIAL
- detailed analysis or criticism DISSECTION
- detailed and clearly expressed, as directions might be EXPLICIT
- details, particulars SPECIFICS, SPECIFICATIONS, SPECS
- details that are precise or sometimes needlessly fussy MINUTIAE, TRIVIA
- clearly described in vivid or exciting detail GRAPHIC
- excessive attention to small details of knowledge at the expense of deeper insight and understanding PEDANTRY
- improve or enliven a report or story by adding colorful, often false or unnecessary, details EMBELLISH, EMBROIDER
- overconcerned with details NITPICKING, HAIRSPLITTING, METICULOUS
- overfussy detail, as of etiquette or protocol PUNCTILIO
- talk or write at length and in detail on a subject ELABORATE, EXPATIATE, ENLARGE, DILATE

detain or imprison, especially in wartime INTERN

detective, private eye SLEUTH, SHAMUS, GUMSHOE, PI

detention, being held under arrest or under guard, as by the police CUSTODY

determined, fussy, or insistent person, making demands in the face of difficulties STICKLER
- determined, gritty, stubbornly persevering DOGGED, TENACIOUS
- determined, single-mindedly firm of purpose, staunch and unwavering RESOLUTE, STALWART, STEADFAST
- determined, unshakable, unyielding INDOMITABLE

detour for traffic DIVERSION

devastate, afflict severely SCOURGE

develop, help to grow, encourage the advancement of NURTURE, FOSTER
- develop, enlarge, or expand a statement, speech, idea, or the like AMPLIFY, ELABORATE
- develop, reproduce, breed PROPAGATE
- develop, stir up, or provoke troubles, or the like FOMENT
- develop buds or sprouts, or breed rapidly PULLULATE
- develop or grow rapidly FLOURISH, BURGEON
- develop slowly or gradually, or cause to develop GERMINATE, INCUBATE, GESTATE

develop (combining form) -GEN, -GENESIS, -GENY

developing, just beginning or emerging NASCENT
- developing or caused outside the body or a body part EXOGENOUS
- developing or caused within the body or a body part ENDOGENOUS
- developing or maturing unusually early, as a bright, clever, or sophisticated child seems to be PRECOCIOUS
- developing or shaping one's personality FORMATIVE

developing (combining form) -PLASTIC

development by slow or natural means, as of species, art, or social systems EVOLUTION
- development or evolution of a species, genus, language, custom, or the like PHYLOGENY
- development or evolution of an individual ONTOGENY
- in the earliest stage of growth or development EMBRYONIC, SEMINAL, GERMINAL
- something that nourishes or promotes growth or development NUTRIMENT

deviate briefly from the correct course, as a ship or aircraft might YAW

device adopted for an urgent purpose EXPEDIENT
- referring to any device or technique that encourages the learning process through independent investigation HEURISTIC

devil See also **demon**
- devil worship, black magic, witchcraft, or the like DIABOLISM

devilish, hellish, demonic DIABOLIC, FIENDISH, SATANIC, INFERNAL

devil's advocate - official name in the Roman Catholic Church for the devil's advocate PROMOTER OF THE FAITH, FIDEI DEFENSOR

devise or perform a poem, play, melody, or the like, composing as one goes IMPROVISE

devote one's life or time fully to a specified cause or purpose CONSECRATE, DEDICATE
- devoted or dutiful, especially in one's religious observances, pious DEVOUT
- devoted to one's wife, especially in an excessive or fawning way UXORIOUS
- devotion, great respect, awe, as shown to God REVERENCE, VENERATION
- devotion or excessive admiration IDOLATRY, HERO WORSHIP

diabetes - abnormally high sugar level in the blood, as in diabetes HYPERGLYCEMIA
- abnormally low sugar level in the blood, as in diabetes HYPOGLYCEMIA
- hormone regulating the blood-sugar level, deficiency of which results in diabetes INSULIN

diacritical marks See **punctuation**

diagnosis by means of tapping the chest, back, or the like and assessing the sound produced PERCUSSION
- diagnostic sign identifying a disease STIGMA
- dye, radioactive substance, or the like, whose course can be monitored through a system, as used in medical diagnosis TRACER
- listening to body sounds, as through a stethoscope, for purposes of diagnosis AUSCULTATION

diagonal, crosswise CATERCORNER
- diagonal or crosswise route across a slope, as in skiing TRAVERSE

- diagonal punctuation mark, slash, as in *and/or* SLASH, SLANT, SOLIDUS, VIRGULE, OBLIQUE, SHILLING MARK

diagram explaining a series of operations, as in a computer program or industrial process FLOW CHART
- diagram in the form of a circle divided into sectors, showing the proportions of the various parts PIE CHART
- diagram or illustration of a machine or structure showing its parts separately EXPLODED VIEW
- diagram or model, as of an engine or building, with part of the wall or casing omitted or cut away to reveal the interior CUTAWAY
- diagram showing the relationships within an industrial process, electronic system, or the like by means of lines linking labeled rectangles BLOCK DIAGRAM

dial - referring to a watch, clock, or meter indicating readings by changing numbers rather than by moving hands on a dial DIGITAL
- referring to a watch, clock, or meter indicating readings by moving hands on a dial rather than by changing numbers ANALOG

dialect, especially a provincial dialect PATOIS
- line on a dialect map linking places using the same distinctive word or pronunciation ISOGLOSS

dialectic - final stage in the dialectical reasoning process of Hegel, through combining thesis and antithesis SYNTHESIS

dialogue, as in ancient Greek drama, in which alternate lines of verse are spoken by different characters STICHOMYTHIA
- dialogue in a literary composition COLLOQUY
- person taking part in a dialogue or discussion INTERLOCUTOR

diameter of the inside of a tube, the bore of a gun, or a bullet or shell CALIBER

diamond See also **gemstone**
- diamond-bearing rock KIMBERLITE
- diamond of poor quality, used for industrial purposes BORT, BORTZ
- diamond or other gemstone set by itself, as in a ring SOLITAIRE
- diamond that is unflawed and very large PARAGON
- diamondlike in brilliance or hardness ADAMANTINE
- diamondlike mineral used as a gemstone ZIRCON
- diamondlike shape or geometrical figure LOZENGE, RHOMBUS
- any of the different physical forms that an element may take, such as diamond or graphite as forms of carbon ALLOTROPE
- artificial diamond made of paste or quartz RHINESTONE
- decorated with glass, sequins, or artificial jewels to produce a diamondlike glitter DIAMANTÉ
- headband or semicircle, typically decorated with diamonds or other jewels, worn by a woman on formal occasions TIARA
- brilliance of a diamond WATER
- relating to or resembling diamonds DIAMANTINE

diaphragm (combining form) PHREN-, PHRENO-

diarrhea as experienced by tourists in hot countries, especially Mexico MONTEZUMA'S REVENGE
- discharge of body fluids in abnormally large quantities, as of watery feces in diarrhoea FLUX
- inflammation of the lining of the stomach and intestines, causing diarrhea GASTROENTERITIS

dice throw MAIN
- dice throw producing the lowest score, especially a throw of two with a pair of dice CRABS, AMBSACE
- group or setting of five objects arranged in a rectangle with one in the middle, as with the five on dice QUINCUNX

dictation - secretary or scribe who takes dictation or makes neat copies of documents AMANUENSIS

dictator See also **ruler, bully**
- dictator or authoritarian ruler DESPOT, TYRANT, führer, duce, autocrat, autarch
- dictator, usually a military leader, in Spanish-speaking countries CAUDILLO
- dictator who is moderate, enlightened, and well-disposed toward his subjects BENEVOLENT DESPOT
- dictatorial person, specifically an authoritarian and uncompromising military disciplinarian MARTINET
- group of military officers ruling a country in a dictatorial way, especially after a coup d'état JUNTA
- dictatorial system aiming at total control TOTALITARIANISM, ABSOLUTISM
- subordinate dictator SATRAP

dictionary classifying synonyms and sometimes antonyms systematically THESAURUS
- dictionary compiler, editor, or expert LEXICOGRAPHER
- dictionary definition or explanation of a headword DEFINIENS
- dictionary headword that is the subject of the definition DEFINIENDUM
- dictionary of a small specialized kind, as for reference in a textbook LEXICON, GLOSSARY, VOCABULARY
- dictionary or listing of geographic names GAZETTEER
- produce the text of an anthology, dictionary, or other book by gathering the material from many sources COMPILE
- quotation or reference used as an authority, as for a dictionary or legal argument CITATION
- series of notches cut into the outer edge of the pages of a dictionary or other book, for easy alphabetical reference THUMB INDEX
- word at the top of a page of a dictionary, telephone directory, or the like, indicating the alphabetical entries of that page GUIDE WORD, CATCHWORD, RUNNING HEAD
- word or phrase forming a main heading and explained or defined in a dictionary HEADWORD

die See also **dead, death**
- die, breathe one's last EXPIRE, PERISH
- "he died" or "she died," formal term used before the date of death OBIIT

diesel engine COMPRESSION-IGNITION ENGINE
- diesel fuel's performance rating CETANE NUMBER
- diesel oil used as fuel for road vehicles DERV

diet system based on cereals and organically grown vegetables MACROBIOTICS
- preparation taken to balance or improve the diet SUPPLEMENT
- protein mixture in wheat flour, avoided in certain diets GLUTEN
- study of the intake, assimilation, and value of food, especially in the human diet NUTRITION
- system of exercise, therapy, diet, or the like REGIMEN

difference See also **change, dispute, disagreement**
- difference, contrast, or opposite ANTITHESIS
- difference, variation, departure from the norm DEVIATION, DIVERGENCE, ECCENTRICITY
- difference in brightness, as of separate areas of a photograph or television picture CONTRAST
- difference or alteration of a very fine or subtle kind, such as a shade of meaning NUANCE
- difference or inconsistency, as in results, claims, reports, or the like DISCREPANCY

different, completely dissimilar, so distinct that no comparison is possible DISPARATE
- different, numerous and assorted, various SUNDRY, MISCELLANEOUS,

DIVERSE, MANIFOLD
- different in an unexpected or inharmonious way HETEROGENEOUS, INCONGRUOUS
- having or displaying a variety of different colors MOTLEY, PIED, PARTICOLORED, VARIEGATED, POLYCHROME
- slightly different from the standard form, spelling, pronunciation, or the like VARIANT

different (combining form) ALLO-, ANISO-, HETER-, HETERO-, VARI-, VARIO-, XENO-

different direction (combining form) DIA-

differentiate, distinguish, tell apart DISCRIMINATE
- differentiating, indicating or serving as a difference or distinction DIACRITICAL

difficult, mysterious, or secret, as sacred rites might be ARCANE, OCCULT, ESOTERIC
- difficult and painful route or course of action VIA DOLOROSA
- difficult or demanding, burdensome, as a task might be ONEROUS, EXIGENT, EXACTING
- difficult or very straining, as a task might be HERCULEAN
- difficult to accomplish, backbreaking, taking great effort ARDUOUS, STRENUOUS
- difficult to deal with or defeat, as a problem or opponent might be FORMIDABLE
- difficult to follow or unravel, extremely complicated or devious, as intrigue might be BYZANTINE, LABYRINTHINE, TORTUOUS
- difficult to hold, catch, remember, or the like ELUSIVE
- difficult to interpret, obscure or ambiguous, as a warning might be DELPHIC, ORACULAR
- difficult to solve or deal with, as a knotty problem would be INTRACTABLE, SCABROUS
- difficult to understand or disentangle, knotty, highly complicated INTRICATE, CONVOLUTED
- difficult to understand, complex ABSTRUSE, RECONDITE, IMPALPABLE
- impossibly difficult to follow, baffling, beyond understanding INCOMPREHENSIBLE, UNINTELLIGIBLE, UNFATHOMABLE, OPAQUE

difficult (combining form) DYS-

difficulty, minor obstacle SNAG
- add to or aggravate an error or difficulty COMPOUND
- in very serious difficulty IN EXTREMIS
- overcome a difficulty or obstacle SURMOUNT
- painful difficulty, trying or distressing situation or experience

Digestive System

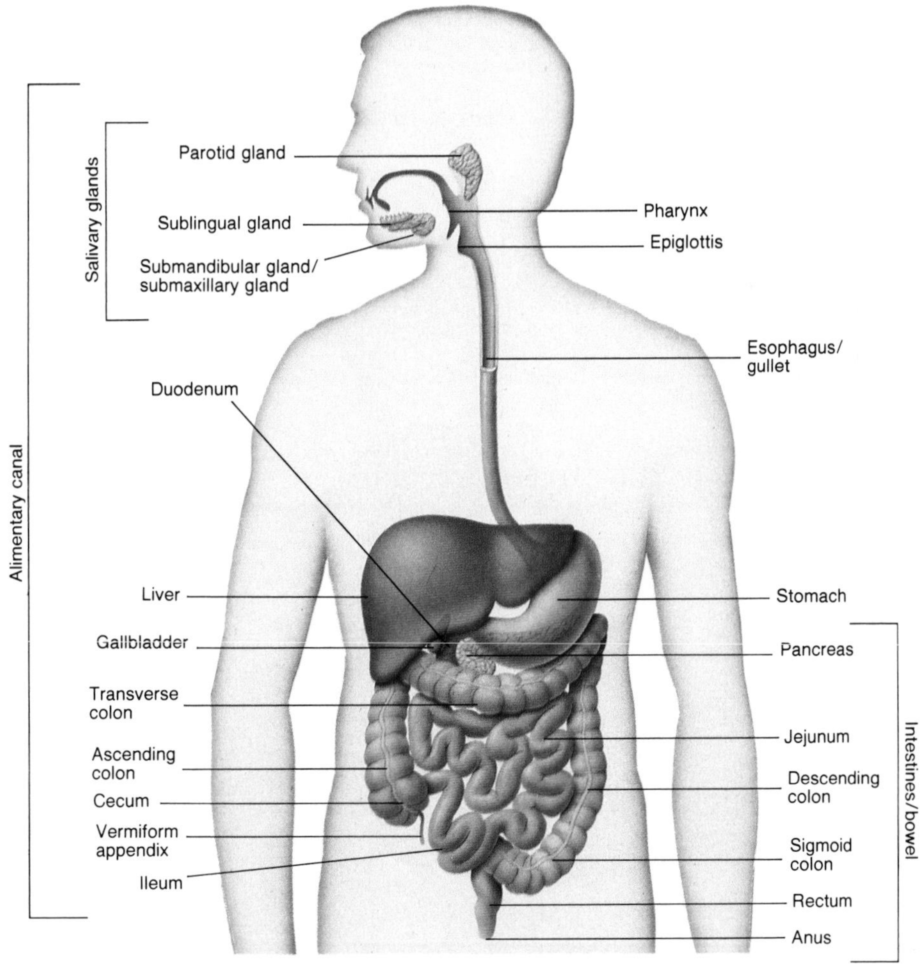

ORDEAL, TRIBULATION
- serious difficulty or distress PLIGHT, PREDICAMENT, QUANDARY, STRAITS

dig, hollow out, as to make a hole or tunnel EXCAVATE
- dig up and remove a dead body from a grave EXHUME, DISINTER

digest, absorb, or incorporate something, such as food or facts ASSIMILATE

digestion See illustration, page 149
- milky fluid formed in the small intestine during digestion CHYLE
- relating to digestion PEPTIC
- relating to food, nutrition, or digestion ALIMENTARY

digital display of symbols, as on a watch, produced by electrical stimulation of liquid crystals LCD

dignified or aristocratic man GRAND SEIGNEUR
- dignified or beautiful, especially when formal, or massive STATUESQUE
- dignified or noble in appearance DISTINGUÉ

dignity - beneath one's dignity INFRA DIG, INFRA DIGNITATEM
- challenge, attack, or spoil someone's dignity, honor, or the like IMPUGN
- do something below one's dignity DEIGN, CONDESCEND
- snobbishly standing on one's dignity HOITY-TOITY

digressive, changing course in speech or thought, as a comment might be TANGENTIAL

dike - stretch of low-lying land, especially in Holland, reclaimed from the sea and protected by dikes POLDER

dilemma, situation of unresolvable conflict DOUBLE BIND
- dilemma or predicament QUANDARY

dilute, thin, or weaken a solution or other substance ATTENUATE
- dilute or add impurities to milk, wine, or the like ADULTERATE

dim, make faded, EFFACE
- dim or faint, as a weak light is WAN

diminish See **lessen**

dinghy or service boat towed or carried by a yacht, launch, or small ship TENDER

dining hall in a monastery REFECTORY, FRATER

dinner - just after dinner POSTPRANDIAL
- relating to dinner PRANDIAL

dinner jacket TUXEDO

dinner table - person who excels in conversations at the dinner table DEIPNOSOPHIST

dinosaur See illustration
- extinct dinosaurlike flying reptile PTERODACTYL
- heavy three-horned dinosaur of North America, with a large skull, bony collar, and powerful tail TRICERATOPS
- huge long-necked dinosaur once inhabiting all the continents APATOSAURUS, BRONTOSAURUS

diocese, bishop's area of authority and jurisdiction SEE

Dionysus - staff, typically decorated with leaves and tipped with a pine cone, carried by Dionysus and his followers THYRSUS

dip lightly into the water, as a bird might DAP

diplomat of high rank, just beneath ambassador MINISTER

Dinosaurs

- diplomat of senior rank COUNSELOR
- diplomat fully authorized to represent a foreign government PLENIPOTENTIARY
- diplomat representing a country's commercial interests and assisting its citizens abroad CONSUL
- diplomat standing in for an ambassador or minister CHARGÉ D'AFFAIRES
- diplomat who is unacceptable to a foreign government PERSONA NON GRATA
- diplomatic agent sent on a special mission ENVOY, EMISSARY
- diplomat's document of authorization and introduction to a foreign government LETTERS OF CREDENCE
- diplomats' code of etiquette and official formalities PROTOCOL
- chief secretary of a diplomatic mission CHANCELLOR
- officially authorized, having acceptable credentials, as a diplomat might be ACCREDITED
- senior diplomatic representative in a protected state in former times RESIDENT
- senior diplomatic representative of one Commonwealth country serving in another HIGH COMMISSIONER
- technical expert assigned to a diplomatic mission ATTACHÉ

diplomatic immunity or similar exemption from the jurisdiction of one's country of residence EXTRATERRITORIALITY
- diplomatic in one's dealings with others, tactful and cautious PRUDENT, DISCREET, JUDICIOUS
- diplomatic initiative or step DEMARCHE
- diplomatic mission ranking below an embassy in status LEGATION
- political section of a diplomatic mission CHANCELLERY, CHANCERY

direction, as of a ship or aircraft BEARING
- direction, conventional current, or trend MAINSTREAM
- direction, supervision, sponsorship AUSPICES, AEGIS
- direction or course, especially when guided by radio VECTOR
- direction or general movement, as of someone's life TENOR
- directional tendency of a plant's growth TROPISM
- approach from several different directions to meet at a point CONVERGE
- having lost one's sense of direction or bearings DISORIENTED, DISORIENTATED
- separate and move in different directions from a point DIVERGE

direction (combining form) TROP-, TROPO-, -TROPIC, -WARD, -WISE

director of a ballet or other theatrical work REGISSEUR
- director of a museum or public art gallery CURATOR

dirt - deep-seated, hard to remove, as dirt may be INGRAINED

dirty, run-down house or hut HOVEL
- dirty, soil, or spoil, as through adding impurities CONTAMINATE, POLLUTE, ADULTERATE
- dirty, spattered, or smudged SPLODGED
- dirty, taint, stain, or corrupt DEFILE, SULLY, TARNISH
- dirty all over, thoroughly soiled, covered or smeared with grime BEDAUBED, BEFOULED, BEMIRED, BESMIRCHED
- dirty and disgusting place CESSPOOL
- dirty and untidily dressed child RAGAMUFFIN
- dirty and untidy, as after being caught in the rain BEDRAGGLED
- dirty or corrupt place or situation AUGEAN STABLE
- dirty or seedy, as through neglect SQUALID, SLEAZY, SORDID
- extremely dirty, filthy, soiled by or as if by excrement FECULENT

disadvantage, disability, handicap, hindrance LIABILITY, DRAWBACK
- disadvantage, harm, damage DETRIMENT

disagreement See also **dispute**
- disagreement, as of political opinions DISSIDENCE, DISSENT
- disagreement, difference of opinion DISSENSION, VARIANCE
- disagreement or disharmony among parts, claims, statements, or the like INCONSISTENCY, DISCREPANCY, IRRECONCILABILITY, DISPARITY, DISSONANCE, DISCORD, INCOMPATIBILITY, INCONGRUITY
- preposition used to acknowledge someone when disagreeing with his or her opinion, "with due respect to" PACE

disappear, by or as if by losing bodily form DEMATERIALIZE
- disappear after breaking up or scattering DISPERSE, DISSIPATE
- disappear or fade, as hopes might WITHER
- disappear slowly, as mist might EVANESCE
- disappearance of a heavenly body during an eclipse OCCULTATION

disappointed, discontented, dissatisfied DISILLUSIONED, DISENCHANTED, DISABUSED

disappointing, unimpressive, failing to come up to expectations UNDERWHELMING
- disappointing outcome, failure, or anticlimax following high expectations ANTICLIMAX, BATHOS

disapprove See also **complain, criticize**
- disapprove of, discourage, protest against DEPRECATE, LOOK ASKANCE AT, DISCOUNTENANCE
- disapproval DISAPPROBATION
- disapprove of strongly, condemn DEPLORE, REPREHEND, REPROBATE
- disapproving or unfavorable, as a particular sense or use of a word might be PEJORATIVE, DISPARAGING, DEPRECIATORY
- puritanically disapproving, self-righteous and usually hypocritical PHARISAICAL

disarmament - involving a single nation or faction operating on its own, as disarmament might UNILATERAL
- involving several nations or factions, as disarmament might MULTILATERAL

disaster, appalling mishap or destruction DEVASTATION, CALAMITY, CATASTROPHE
- disaster, event involving enormous destruction or disruption APOCALYPSE, CATACLYSM
- disaster, great destruction, or terrible battle or conflict ARMAGEDDON
- disaster about to happen, or the constant threat of disaster SWORD OF DAMOCLES
- disastrous collapse, failure, or defeat ROUT, DEBACLE, FIASCO
- prevent or ward off danger, disaster, or the like AVERT

disbelief - feeling or expressing disbelief, doubting INCREDULOUS, SKEPTICAL

disbelieve or cast doubt on DISCREDIT
- disbeliever, skeptic, person without faith or beliefs NULLIFIDIAN

disc of metal PATEN, PLANCHET
- disc of shiny metal or plastic, used to ornament clothing, handbags, or the like SEQUIN
- disc of silicon or other semiconductor material, as used for integrated circuits WAFER
- disc or card that is spun or twirled to produce a merged image of the partial words or pictures on either side THAUMATROPE
- disc or wheel whose axis is off-center and which converts rotary motion to reciprocating motion ECCENTRIC
- disc used as an ornament in architecture BEZANT

discharge, as from duty QUIETUS
- discharge of body fluids in abnor-

mally large quantities, as of watery feces in diarrhea FLUX

discharge (combining form) -RRHEA, -RRHAGIA

disciple, imitator, or follower who is markedly inferior to his master EPIGONE

- disciple or pupil of a guru CHELA

discipline one's body by self-denial or punishment MORTIFY

- discipline or punish in order to improve CHASTEN

- strict disciplinarian or person in authority MARTINET

discomfort, feeling of unease or anxiety DISQUIETUDE

disconnected, disordered, incoherent, as a report or story might be DISJOINTED

- disconnected, jumping about, as conversation might be DESULTORY

- abrupt, distinct, disconnected, and jerky in sound STACCATO

discontented, disappointed, and dissatisfied DISILLUSIONED, DISENCHANTED

- discontented, no longer feeling affection or loyalty ALIENATED, DISAFFECTED

- discontented, rebellious person MALCONTENT

discontinue a legislative or a similar body, without dissolving it PROROGUE

discontinuous, irregular, periodic INTERMITTENT

discount or partial refund, as on a bulk purchase REBATE

discourage, cause to lose confidence, morale, or hope DISPIRIT, DISHEARTEN, DEMORALIZE, DAUNT

- discourage, disapprove of, dis-

DISEASES, DISORDERS, AND CONDITIONS

BLOOD, HEART, OR CIRCULATION

anemia
aneurism
angina
atheroma
Buerger's disease
decompression sickness/caisson disease/bends
edema/dropsy
hemophilia
hypertension/high blood pressure
hypotension/low blood pressure
leukemia
pericarditis
phlebitis
Raynaud's syndrome
septicemia/blood poisoning
tachycardia
toxemia/blood poisoning

BONES OR JOINTS

bursitis/housemaid's knee
bursitis/tennis elbow
fibrositis
osteoarthritis
osteomyelitis
Paget's disease
Perthes' disease
scoliosis
synovitis

BRAIN AND NERVOUS SYSTEM

Alzheimer's disease
Bell's palsy
catalepsy
catatonia
delirium tremens (DTs)
dementia
Down's syndrome/mongolism
dyslexia
encephalitis
hydrocephalus/water on the brain
meningitis
motor-neuron disease
multiple sclerosis
muscular dystrophy
myasthenia gravis
narcolepsy
Parkinson's disease
porphyria
rabies/hydrophobia
spina bifida
Sydenham's chorea/Saint Vitus' dance
trigeminal neuralgia/tic douloureux

DIGESTIVE OR URINARY SYSTEM

celiac disease
cirrhosis
colitis
cystic fibrosis
diverticulitis
hepatitis
nephritis/Bright's disease
peritonitis
regional ileitis/Crohn's disease
schistosomiasis/bilharziasis
strangury
trichinosis
typhoid/enteric fever

EARS, EYES, OR MOUTH

blepharitis
chorioretinitis
conjunctivitis
gingivitis
glaucoma
labyrinthitis
mastoiditis
Ménière's disease
nystagmus
otitis
pyorrhea
tinnitus
trachoma
vascular occlusion

GLANDS OR CELLS

Addison's disease
carcinoma/cancer
Cushing's disease or syndrome
Hodgkin's disease
scrofula/king's evil
thyrotoxicosis/Graves' disease/exophthalmic goiter

INFECTIOUS, VIRAL, OR PARASITIC DISEASES

AIDS (Acquired Immune-Deficiency Syndrome)
anthrax
brucellosis
dengue fever
diphtheria
gonorrhea
Lassa fever
leishmaniasis/Dum-dum fever/kala-azar
poliomyelitis/infantile paralysis
Q fever
rubella/German measles
rubeola/measles
tetanus/lockjaw
trypanosomiasis/sleeping sickness
variola/smallpox
yaws

MEN'S DISORDERS

balanitis
hydrocele
orchitis
prostatis

PSYCHIATRIC DISORDERS

amnesia
anorexia nervosa
autism
bulimia nervosa
fetishism
paranoia
pica
schizophrenia
zoophilia

RESPIRATORY SYSTEM

emphysema
Legionnaires' disease
mononucleosis/glandular fever
pleurisy
pneumoconiosis
psittacosis/parrot fever
quinsy
silicosis
tuberculosis/consumption/phthisis

SKIN

candidiasis/moniliasis/thrush
dermatitis
eczema
erysipelas/Saint Anthony's fire
herpes zoster/shingles
ichthyosis
impetigo
lupus
miliaria rubra/prickly heat
myxedema
psoriasis
rosacea
scabies
seborrhea
tinea/ringworm
urticaria/nettle rash/hives

VITAMIN DEFICIENCY

beriberi
kwashiorkor
pellagra
rachitis/rickets
scurvy

WOMEN'S DISORDERS

amenorrhea
eclampsia
endometriosis
mastitis
puerperal fever
salpingitis

suade DEPRECATE
- discourage or prevent someone from doing something, as by threatening DETER

discover or bring to light by careful searching or research FERRET OUT, UNEARTH
- discover or detect after conscientious effort DESCRY
- discover or prove definitely ASCERTAIN
- discover the meaning or secret of FATHOM
- exclamation of triumph on finding, solving, or discovering something EUREKA

discovery, or bright new idea TROUVAILLE
- helping or encouraging the process of learning or discovery HEURISTIC
- tendency to make lucky discoveries by accident SERENDIPITY

discriminate against, bully, or punish unfairly VICTIMIZE

discus, discus thrower or statue of one in ancient Greece and Rome DISCOBOLUS

discuss, exchange views, or consult PARLEY, CONFER, DISCOURSE
- discuss and investigate a subject thoroughly CANVASS
- discuss an issue freely, express openly, examine publicly VENTILATE
- discuss or comment on something at length DESCANT
- discuss or consider seriously and in detail DELIBERATE, MOOT
- discuss or converse earnestly CONFABULATE
- discuss terms, such as a contract, in the attempt to reach an agreement NEGOTIATE
- avoid or evade direct answers, refuse to discuss seriously FENCE, PREVARICATE, TEMPORIZE, EQUIVOCATE
- begin to discuss a subject BROACH

discussion, as at a public meeting or in a magazine column FORUM
- discussion and logical disputing DIALECTIC
- discussion between two people, private conversation TÊTE-À-TÊTE
- discussion group or social clique CENACLE
- discussion or conference, as among rival interest groups PALAVER, POWWOW, INDABA
- discussion or conference, typically on a specialist academic or professional theme SYMPOSIUM, COLLOQUIUM
- discussion or exchange of views DIALOGUE
- informal chat or discussion CAUSERIE
- person taking part in a conversation or discussion INTERLOCUTOR, COLLOCUTER

disdainful, haughty, scornful SUPERCILIOUS

disease See chart
- disease, illness AILMENT, MALADY
- disease, such as tuberculosis, that weakens, decays, or emaciates the body WASTING DISEASE
- disease-causing agent, germ PATHOGEN
- disease in which no organic change or cause is observable FUNCTIONAL DISEASE
- disease in which the structure of a body part or organ is affected ORGANIC DISEASE
- disease of a serious infectious kind, such as cholera or tuberculosis, that has to be reported to the health authorities NOTIFIABLE DISEASE
- disease resulting from one's job OCCUPATIONAL DISEASE
- disease that develops slowly or lasts a long time CHRONIC DISEASE
- disease that is sudden and severe, or that lasts only a short time ACUTE DISEASE
- disease that is very widespread EPIDEMIC, PANDEMIC
- disease transmitted by an animal, such as rabies or malaria ZOONOSIS
- affecting the entire body, as a disease or poison might SYSTEMIC
- aftereffects, complications, or condition following a disease SEQUELLA
- branch of medicine dealing with classification of diseases NOSOLOGY
- catch a disease CONTRACT
- cause or origin of a disease, or study of such ETIOLOGY
- caused or developing outside the body or a body part, as some diseases are EXOGENOUS
- caused or developing within the body or a body part, as some diseases are ENDOGENOUS
- decline in the severity of a disease REMISSION
- decline in the severity of the symptoms of a disease over a long period LYSIS
- detention or isolation of a sick or possibly sick person or animal, to prevent the spread of disease QUARANTINE
- diseased or infectious PESTIFEROUS, PESTILENT
- dormant or inactive, as a disease might be QUIESCENT, LATENT
- forecast of the developmnt of a disease PROGNOSIS
- hospital for treating contagious diseases in former times LAZARET, LAZARETTO
- identification of a disease, injury, or problem DIAGNOSIS
- indication, especially as expressed by the patient, of a disease or disorder SYMPTOM
- insect or other organism that transmits disease-causing microorganisms VECTOR, CARRIER
- localized, restricted to a particular area or group, as a disease might be ENDEMIC
- medical testing for potential sufferers from a disease, carried out on a wide range of the population SCREENING
- preventing or protecting against something, especially disease PROPHYLACTIC
- protect against disease, as by injecting a vaccine INOCULATE, VACCINATE
- recurrence of a disease after a period of inactivity or improvement RELAPSE, RECRUDESCENCE
- referring to a disease or abnormality existing from birth but not hereditary CONGENITAL
- referring to a disease that strikes suddenly and fiercely FOUDROYANT
- referring to disease MORBID, PATHOLOGICAL
- referring to physical diseases or disorders caused or aggravated by psychological factors, such as stress PSYCHOSOMATIC
- referring to the early stage of an infection or disease before symptoms have been revealed SUBCLINICAL
- scientific study of disease PATHOLOGY
- spread of a disease from one part of the body to another METASTASIS
- spreading or progressing almost unnoticed, as a disease might be INSIDIOUS
- spreading uncontrolled, as a life-threatening disease might MALIGNANT, VIRULENT
- symptoms or signs jointly indicating or characterizing a disease, abnormality, or the like SYNDROME
- tendency to contract a particular disease PREDISPOSITION
- tending to be affected by something adverse, such as a disease SUSCEPTIBLE, AT RISK
- transmittable, liable to be passed on, as many diseases are INFECTIOUS, COMMUNICABLE
- transmitted by physical contact, as a disease might be CONTAGIOUS
- unresponsive to treatment, as a disease might be REFRACTORY

disease (combining form) NOS-, NOSO-, -PATH-, PATHO-, -PATHY, -OSIS

diseased (combining form)DYS-, -OTIC

disembowel, remove the internal organs of EVISCERATE, EXENTERATE
disentangle, untangle, unravel UNSNARL
disgrace, as by deprivation of rank, status, office, or the like DEGRADATION
- disgrace, dishonor, bad reputation DISREPUTE, OBLOQUY
- disgrace, dishonor, damage the reputation of DISCREDIT
- disgrace of an extreme kind resulting especially from wickedness INFAMY, ODIUM
- disgrace or dishonor, shame or humiliation IGNOMINY, OPPROBIUM
- mark or sign of shame or disgrace STIGMA
- shun or banish a person in disgrace OSTRACIZE
disguise oneself as someone else IMPERSONATE
- disguise or hide something, such as one's fear, feelings, or intentions DISSIMULATE, DISSEMBLE
- disguised enemy or threat within one's own ranks TROJAN HORSE, FIFTH COLUMN
- disguised or under a false name INCOGNITO
disgust, feeling of sheer loathing or distaste REVULSION
- disgust, sicken, or infuriate NAUSEATE, MAKE SOMEONE'S STOMACH TURN
- disgust or extreme dislike, or the person or thing causing it AVERSION
- draw back, as in fear or disgust RECOIL, BLENCH
disgusting, appalling, horribly distasteful ABHORRENT
- disgusting, extremely distasteful or offensive, detestable REPULSIVE, REPUGNANT
- disgusting, offensive, foul, loathsome ABOMINABLE, ODIOUS
- disgusting, offensive to good taste FULSOME
- disgusting, sickening, gross NAUSEATING, REVOLTING
- disgusting or forbidding, repellent or fearsome REBARBATIVE
- disgusting or offensive, as a foul smell is NOISOME
- disgustingly base, despicable, morally degraded SCURVY, SCROFULOUS
- disgustingly dirty or corrupt place CESSPOOL
- disgustingly often, regularly or repeatedly to a tiresome extent AD NAUSEAM
dish See also **cooking, plate,** and chart at **menu**
- dish, typically of glass or plastic and fitted with a loose cover, as used in laboratories for growing bacteria cultures PETRI DISH
- dish just before the main dish, or the main dish itself, of a meal ENTRÉE
- dish or course served between the main courses of a meal ENTREMETS
- dish set on a hotplate or warmer, used to cook food or keep it warm CHAFING DISH
- dish that forms the main part of a meal PIÈCE DE RÉSISTANCE
dishonest, false, lying, deliberately misleading DECEITFUL, MENDACIOUS
- dishonest dealings, trickery or deception, sharp practice CHICANERY
- dishonestly or hypocritically appearing simple or naive, deceptively candid or sincere DISINGENUOUS
- dishonesty, deliberate deception, double-dealing DUPLICITY
- speak or act in an evasive or dishonest way, so as to obscure the truth EQUIVOCATE, PREVARICATE
dishonor See **disgrace**
- dishonorable discharge, specifically from the armed forces CASHIERING
dishwashing - room off or recess in a kitchen for dishwashing, vegetable peeling, and the like SCULLERY
disillusioned or disappointed DISABUSED, DISENCHANTED
disinfect - fill a room or building with poisonous smoke to disinfect it, exterminate insects, and so on FUMIGATE
- watery chemical solution used as a disinfectant and bleaching agent JAVELLE WATER
disintegrate, separate, or soften by means of soaking MACERATE
dislike See also **hatred**
- dislike intensely, loathe ABHOR, ABOMINATE, EXECRATE
- dislike or displeasure DISTASTE
- arousing dislike or resentment, offensive INVIDIOUS
- extreme dislike or intense feeling of hostility or repulsion AVERSION, ANTIPATHY, REVULSION, REPUGNANCE
- indicating dislike or hostility, cold and unfriendly INIMICAL
- person or thing that one has a particular dislike of BÊTE NOIRE
- strong dislike or bitter enmity ANIMOSITY, ANIMUS
disloyal, unfaithful, characteristic of a deserter RECREANT, RENEGADE
- disloyalty, faithlessness, treachery PERFIDY, INFIDELITY
dismay or amazement that throws everything into confusion CONSTERNATION
dismissal, permission or order to leave NUNC DIMITTIS
- dismissal from a job CONGÉ, HEAVE-HO
- dishonorable dismissal from the armed forces CASHIERING
disobedient toward central authority, rebellious or divisive DISSENTING, FACTIOUS
- conscientiously disobedient, refusing to submit to established authority RECUSANT
- openly disobedient toward lawful authority, rebellious MUTINOUS
- persistently disobedient or unruly, uncontrollable, resisting authority INSUBORDINATE, REFRACTORY, RESTIVE, TURBULENT
- stubbornly disobedient, or challenging or ignoring authority repeatedly DEFIANT, RECALCITRANT, CONTUMACIOUS
- stubbornly disobedient or uncooperative, firmly fixed in attitude or behavior INTRANSIGENT
- tending to be disobedient or uncooperative CONTRARY, PERVERSE, FROWARD, WAYWARD
disobey a rule, break a law, defy a code or practice, or the like INFRINGE, VIOLATE, CONTRAVENE, TRANSGRESS
- disobey a ruling contemptuously, openly defy a convention, or the like FLOUT
- disobey or confront a person or authority boldly and unwaveringly OUTFACE
disorder See **confusion, disease**
disorganized See **confused**
disown or cast off a wife, husband, lover, or relative REPUDIATE
dispensary PHARMACY
displace a limb or organ, or put a bone out of joint DISLOCATE
display in a showy way BRANDISH
- display of symbols, as on a digital watch, produced by electrical stimulation of liquid crystals LCD
- display or symbol that is colorful, dramatic, or showy BLAZON, FLOURISH
- display stand or exhibition hall PAVILION
dispose of, make unnecessary OBVIATE
- disposable, unnecessary, inessential EXPENDABLE
disprove, show to be false or invalid CONFUTE, REFUTE, REBUT
- disprove, weaken, or make ineffective an argument, claim, or the like INVALIDATE
- reject or deny without actually disproving REPUDIATE
dispute, contradict, deny, or call into question OPPUGN, GAINSAY, REPUDIATE, CONTROVERT
- dispute, controversy, argument, especially over a principle or belief

POLEMIC
- dispute, difference of opinion DISSENSION, VARIANCE
- dispute, quarrel, heated disagreement CONTRETEMPS, ALTERCATION
- dispute or quarrel involving a noisy disturbance RUCTION
- causing disputes DIVISIVE
- come forward to mediate in a dispute INTERCEDE
- committee investigating or arbitrating a dispute, or the place where this is done TRIBUNAL
- go-between or judge in a dispute ARBITRATOR, MEDIATOR, HONEST BROKER, MODERATOR, INTERMEDIARY
- involved in a dispute, scandal, or the like EMBROILED
- minor or preliminary conflict, dispute, or military encounter SKIRMISH
- mutually destructive dispute INTERNECINE
- settle a dispute or difference between parties RECONCILE, COMPOSE, DETERMINE
- settle or attempt to settle a dispute between other people or groups MEDIATE, ARBITRATE, CONCILIATE
- settlement of a dispute by an impartial third party ARBITRATION, ADJUDICATION

disregard See **ignore**

disreputable, seedy or squalid, as a nightclub or café might be SORDID, SLEAZY
- disreputable, shady or shifty UNSAVORY, LOUCHE

disrespectful - treat disrespectfully, mess about TRIFLE WITH

dissatisfied, disappointed, stripped of one's illusions DISILLUSIONED, DISENCHANTED
- dissatisfied, peeved DISGRUNTLED
- dissatisfied, no longer feeling affection or loyalty ALIENATED, DISAFFECTED

dissidents - elimination of political opponents or dissidents PURGE

dissolve gradually, as some chemicals do, by absorbing water vapor from the air DELIQUESCE
- dissolve away soluble part, as from soil LEACH
- capable of being dissolved SOLUBLE
- containing as much dissolved substance as possible, as a solution might SATURATED
- impossible to solve or resolve a problem or dissolve a substance INSOLUBLE
- liquid in which a substance dissolves SOLVENT
- mixture of solid particles dispersed in but not dissolved in a liquid SUSPENSION, COLLOID
- substance that dissolves in a liquid SOLUTE

dissolving (combining form) LYS-, LYSO-, -LYSIS

distance See also chart at **weights and measures**
- distance, division, unbridgeable gap GULF
- distance around the edge of a shape CIRCUMFERENCE
- distance or time between limits SPAN
- report or official communication sent over a distance DISPATCH

distance (combining form) TEL-, TELE-

distant See also **shy, stiff**
- distant and inaccessible place, or a fortified place or stronghold FASTNESS
- distant country areas, the sticks, the bush HINTERLAND, BOONDOCKS, BACKBLOCKS, OUTBACK, BUNDU
- distant region, goal, or ideal ULTIMA THULE
- fairly distant or remote from the center OUTLYING

distillation, crystallization, or other means of separating a mixture of chemicals into its components FRACTIONATION
- distillation flask as used by alchemists ALEMBIC
- distillation flask with a long neck, formerly used in chemistry MATRASS
- glass vessel with a long, bent-over neck, as used in a laboratory for distillation RETORT
- refine, separate, or purify in chemistry, usually by distillation RECTIFY

distinct, individual DIVERSE
- distinct, separate, unconnected, individual DISCRETE
- make or become distinct DIFFERENTIATE

distinction, detail, or variation of a very fine or subtle kind, such as a shade of meaning NUANCE, NICETY, SUBTLETY
- making needless or oversubtle distinctions HAIRSPLITTING, QUIBBLING

distinctive quality or pattern of a piece of music, historical period, or the like TEXTURE

distinguishing, indicating or serving as a difference or distinction DIACRITICAL

distress call MAYDAY, SOS
- distress or cause of distress WORMWOOD
- distress, or great or prolonged suffering, especially from persecution TRIBULATION
- distressing or affecting the emotions POIGNANT

distribute in shares, assign proportionally, parcel out ALLOCATE, ADMEASURE, APPORTION, PRORATE
- distribute or deal out something, especially justice or punishment METE OUT, ALLOT, ADMINISTER, DISPENSE
- distribute throughout a speech, text, or the like, interlace INTERLARD, INTERSPERSE
- distribute widely, scatter or strew, spread over a wide area DISPERSE, DIFFUSE, DISSEMINATE, PROPAGATE

disturb See also **confusion**
- disturb, confuse, embarrass, or unsettle DISCONCERT, DISCOMFIT
- disturb, inconvenience, annoy DISCOMMODE
- disturb, stir up ROIL, AGITATE
- disturb or interrupt the peace, someone's privacy, or the like VIOLATE
- disturb the serenity of, make anxious, or uneasy DISQUIET, DISCOMPOSE
- disturbed, agitated, as rushing water is TURBULENT
- disturbing, annoying, causing a nuisance VEXATIOUS
- make trouble, cause an uproar or disturbance RAISE CAIN
- sudden and violent disturbance, radical change UPHEAVAL

disuse, state of being out of use or practice DESUETUDE

ditch, as for drainage, typically with a raised bank alongside DIKE
- ditch or channel cut in the ground by rainwater or a stream GULLY
- ditch or defensive moat FOSSE
- ditch or moat as a barrier, as in a garden HA-HA, SUNK FENCE

dive down quickly and deep, as a whale or large fish might SOUND
- dive in which the diver bends double at the hips and then straightens out before entering the water JACKKNIFE
- dive in which the diver's back is arched and arms spread outward SWALLOW DIVE
- dive involving a forward leap followed by a backward somersault GAINER
- diving position in which the body is bent double at the hips PIKE
- diving vessel for manned scientific observation in deep water at sea BATHYSCAPHE, BATHYSPHERE

diver or underwater researcher AQUANAUT
- diver using a compressed-air breathing apparatus SCUBA DIVER
- diver's breathing apparatus, including an air cylinder and oxygen mask AQUALUNG
- diver's supply line or tether to the vessel UMBILICAL CORD
- painful condition, as in deep-sea

divers, following sudden change of pressure THE BENDS, CAISSON DISEASE, DECOMPRESSION SICKNESS, AEROEMBOLISM

diverging from the point, changing course in speech or thought TANGENTIAL, DIGRESSIVE

divide See also **cut, separate, division**
- divide a territory into small warring states BALKANIZE
- divide into steps or intervals, as for making measurements GRADUATE
- divide into two extreme and opposing positions or groups POLARIZE
- divide or cut into two equal parts BISECT
- divide or separate into different classes, categories, sections, or the like COMPARTMENTALIZE, PIGEONHOLE
- divide up, separate into sections PARTITION, DISMEMBER, SEGMENT, FRAGMENT
- divided, separated, split CLEFT, ASUNDER
- divided according to castes, classes, or the like, as a nation or society might be STRATIFIED
- divided along racial or sectarian lines SEGREGATED
- divided into two streams or parts, forked, branched BIFURCATE
- dividing an exact number of times, without remainder, into a larger quantity ALIQUOT
- number or a quantity by which another is divided DIVISOR, DENOMINATOR
- number or a quantity that is divided by another DIVIDEND, NUMERATOR

divide (combining form) -SECT-

dividing (combining form) -KINESIS

divination See **fortunetelling**
- divining for water, ore, or the like by means of a rod or wand DOWSING, RHABDOMANCY

divination (combining form) -MANCY

divine, filled with a sense of divine influence or energy NUMINOUS
- divine manifestation, appearance of a deity to a human THEOPHANY
- divine manifestation or revelation EPIPHANY
- divine word, God's self-revealing thought and will LOGOS
- communion with the divine, or meditation designed to achieve it MYSTICISM

division See also **divide, classification, boundary**
- division, partition, or membrane separating tissues or cavities, as between the nostrils SEPTUM
- division, separation, disconnection DISJUNCTION, PARTITION
- division, splitting, or cutting SCISSION, RUPTURE
- division into opposing factions, as within a church SCHISM
- division of cells in genetics MEIOSIS, MITOSIS
- division of overhead among various departments of a business ALLOCATION
- division or classification into two parts, such as conflicting opinions DICHOTOMY
- division or group, as within a political party, typically dissenting from the larger group FACTION
- quantity or total produced by dividing one number by another QUOTIENT

division (combining form) SCHIZ-, SCHIZO-

divorce - final court ruling granting a divorce DECREE ABSOLUTE
- financial support given by one former spouse to the other after a divorce ALIMONY, MAINTENANCE
- financial support given to a lover after separation, analogous to maintenance after divorce PALIMONY
- person against whom a divorce action is brought RESPONDENT
- person bringing a divorce action APPLICANT
- person cited in a divorce case as having committed adultery with the partner being sued CORESPONDENT
- preliminary and provisional court ruling, especially that in a divorce case DECREE NISI
- right of access to the children by a divorced or separated parent VISITATION RIGHTS

dizzy, confused, groggy, or dazed WOOZY
- dizziness, giddiness VERTIGO

DNA molecule's twin spiral structure DOUBLE HELIX

do-re-mi - use of the *do-re-mi* syllables to correspond to notes of the scale, as for voice training TONIC SOL-FA, SOLFEGGIO, SOLMIZATION

do without, avoid FORGO, FORBEAR, REFRAIN, ABSTAIN

dock worker LONGSHOREMAN
- dock worker who boards ships to load and unload them STEVEDORE
- docking platform, pier, or the like at which ships can moor for loading or unloading WHARF
- docks for small boats MARINA

doctor, especially one who is not a surgeon PHYSICIAN
- doctor, psychologist, or psychiatrist practicing or studying the treatment of patients CLINICIAN
- doctor doing a term of specialized training RESIDENT
- doctor of the highest rank in a hospital ATTENDING PHYSICIAN
- doctor of the second highest rank in hospital RESIDENT
- doctor or other professional person pursuing his or her occupation PRACTITIONER
- doctor qualified as a specialist DIPLOMATE
- doctor specializing in heart diseases CARDIOLOGIST
- doctor temporarily replacing another LOCUM, LOCUM TENENS
- doctor's instrument for listening to sounds produced in the body STETHOSCOPE
- doctor's medical equipment and supplies ARMAMENTARIUM
- doctor's negligence or misconduct MALPRACTICE
- doctor's oath to observe professional ethics HIPPOCRATIC OATH
- doctor's small, portable radio receiver sounding a coded alert signal BEEPER, BLEEPER
- caused by the doctor or his treatment, as an illness might be IATROGENIC
- family doctor GENERAL PRACTITIONER, G.P.
- junior doctor undergoing hospital training INTERN
- specialist in children's ailments PEDIATRICIAN
- symbol, associated with doctors, of a winged staff with one or two snakes twined around it CADUCEUS

doctrine See also **philosophy**
- doctrine or principle, as of a religious or professional group TENET

document authorizing a diplomat to act on behalf of his or her government LETTERS OF CREDENCE
- document certifying a contract or transfer of property DEED
- document in writing, warranted under oath as true AFFIDAVIT
- document of entitlement, such as a share certificate SCRIP
- document or argument presented for consideration SUBMISSION
- document or book in the author's handwriting HOLOGRAPH
- document in the form of a roll of parchment or paper SCROLL
- document or image sent or produced telegraphically as a facsimile FAX
- document or pamphlet containing a forceful declaration or rallying call TRACT
- document showing right of ownership of a property TITLE DEED
- document such as an official voucher or certificate DOCKET

- document in former times under a sovereign's seal, authorizing imprisonment without trial LETTRE DE CACHET
- document's introductory statement or explanation PREAMBLE
- added clause, amendment, or qualification to a legal document, verdict, or the like RIDER
- addition to a document APPENDIX, ADDENDUM, ANNEX, SUPPLEMENT, POSTSCRIPT, CODICIL
- alter a document, accounts, evidence, or the like in order to deceive FALSIFY, FORGE
- amendment to, draft for, or supplement to a treaty or other such document PROTOCOL
- clean copy of a revised and corrected document FAIR COPY
- deliberate alteration or mutilation of a document so as to make it invalid SPOLIATION
- exact copy or reproduction, as of a document FACSIMILE
- file of documents on a particular person or subject DOSSIER
- formal document or statement, such as a deed of conveyance PRESENTS
- legally enforced revealing of relevant documents by a party in a civil action DISCOVERY
- public document or deed CHARTER
- reservation or proviso, as in a legal document SALVO
- sign or endorse a document UNDERWRITE
- study of ancient or historical documents DIPLOMATICS
- transfer ownership of or sell documents, shares, or the like NEGOTIATE

doer (combining form) -TOR, -TRESS, -TRIX

dog See illustration, pages 158-159
- dog, especially a mongrel, with a vicious nature CUR
- dog placed in a treadmill in former times to turn a roasting spit TURNSPIT
- dog's snout, or the small basket of wire or leather fitted over the snout of a dog or other animal to restrain it MUZZLE
- adjective for a dog CANINE
- brown or gray with darker streaks or spots, as a dog, cat, or cow might be BRINDLED
- disease affecting young dogs, a contagious viral fever DISTEMPER
- fear of dogs CYNOPHOBIA
- flap of a dog's ear LEATHER
- fleshy drooping upper lip of the bloodhound or similar dog FLEWS
- free a dog, hawk, or the like from restraint SLIP
- functionless rudimentary inner claw on a dog's foot DEWCLAW
- give birth to a dog, wolf, or other canine WHELP
- group of dogs PACK, KENNEL
- half-wild or stray dog in Asia PYE-DOG, PARIAH DOG
- highest point on the back of a horse or dog, between the shoulders WITHERS
- hindquarters or rump of a horse or dog CROUP
- knee joint in the hind leg of a horse or dog STIFLE
- long hair on the legs or tail of some horses or dogs FEATHERS
- loose fold of skin under the throat of a dog, ox, or the like DEWLAP
- section of the body of a horse or dog between the forequarters and hindquarters COUPLING
- three-headed dog in Greek myth that guards the entrance to the underworld CERBERUS

dogmatic, pedantic, excessively precise or subtle SCHOLASTIC
- dogmatic, self-assured, arrogant, overbearing PEREMPTORY, IMPERIOUS
- dogmatic and unduly fussy about details PEDANTIC
- dogmatic and unsupported assertion DICTUM, IPSE DIXIT
- dogmatically and blindly committed to a theory, impractical DOCTRINAIRE
- speak in a pompous, dogmatic, or overconfident way PONTIFICATE, DOGMATIZE

dogsled journey MUSH

doll - magic intended to achieve an effect by some imitative ceremony or symbolic object, as in sticking pins into a doll SYMPATHETIC MAGIC

dolphin - dolphinlike sea mammal with a blunt snout GRAMPUS
- dolphin or related mammal with a beaklike snout BOTTLENOSE

dome formed of interlocking polygons GEODESIC DOME
- dome-shaped Buddhist shrine STUPA, TOPE
- dome-shaped roof or ceiling, or dome on a roof or larger dome CUPOLA
- dome-shaped room or building for projecting images of the stars and planets PLANETARIUM
- circular, often domed, building or room ROTUNDA
- circular or crescent-shaped opening in a domed roof LUNETTE
- circular wall, especially one supporting a dome TAMBOUR
- ornamental sunken panel in a ceiling, dome, or the like COFFER, LACUNA, CAISSON

domestic or unskilled work MENIAL WORK

dominate See also **bully, dictator**
- dominate or discourage by threats or bullying BROWBEAT
- dominate or force into submission by means of threats or by violence INTIMIDATE
- dominate to the exclusion of all others, control fully MONOPOLIZE
- dominated by a nagging or willful wife HENPECKED
- domination or mastery, as in the political or economic sphere PREEMINENCE, SUPREMACY, ASCENDANCY
- domination of one group or country over another HEGEMONY

dominating in an arrogantly assured way, lordly, overbearing IMPERIOUS, MAGISTERIAL, OVERWEENING, DOMINEERING

dominion or power over a dependent state, typically over its foreign affairs SUZERAINTY

donation that provides a source of income ENDOWMENT

done - something that is already done and unalterable, an unchangeable fact FAIT ACCOMPLI

donkey, especially one used as a pack animal BURRO

doom - prophet of doom whose warnings are ignored CASSANDRA

door, entrance, or gateway, typically large or impressive PORTAL
- door hinge consisting of two metal flaps linked with a stout pin BUTT HINGE
- door or window with slats LOUVER
- door-to-door seller of goods HAWKER, PEDDLER
- doorway or entrance, or the plank or stone lying under a door THRESHOLD
- arched recess above a doorway, as at the entrance of a medieval cathedral TYMPANUM
- axle, revolving bolt, or the like, as in a lock or between two door handles SPINDLE
- back door or gate POSTERN
- central vertical strip separating the panels in a door MUNTIN
- crescent-shaped window or recess above a door LUNETTE
- decorative molded frame around a door or window ARCHITRAVE
- decorative triangular recess or projection of stone or masonry above a door or window PEDIMENT, FRONTISPIECE, GABLE
- glass door, typically occurring in pairs, opening onto a garden or balcony FRENCH DOOR, FRENCH WINDOW
- horizontal beam or crossbar over a door LINTEL, TEMPLATE, TRANSOM
- one-way viewing hole or tiny win-

Dogs

SPORTING DOGS
Cocker spaniel
Pointer
TOY DOGS
Miniature pinscher
Smooth-coat chihuahua
Long-coat chihuahua

HOUNDS
Borzoi
Long-haired dachshund
Miniature long-haired dachshund
Miniature smooth-haired dachshund
NONSPORTING DOGS
Bulldog
Standard poodle

TERRIERS

HERDING DOGS

WORKING DOGS

MONGRELS
(Crossbreeds, mixed breeds)

dow in a door, for identifying visitors PEEPHOLE, JUDAS
- opening in a wall, wider inside than out, for a door or window EMBRASURE
- shieldlike plate covering a keyhole, surrounding a door handle, protecting a light switch, or the like ESCUTCHEON
- sloping or beveled recess wall, as at a door or window SPLAY
- small door or gate, often forming part of a larger one WICKET
- upright post or strut of a door frame, window sash, or the like JAMB, STILE

doorkeeper in a court of law, legislative assembly, or the like USHER

doorman or caretaker of a building JANITOR, SUPERINTENDENT, SUPER, CONCIERGE, PORTER

dormant or inactive, as a disease might be QUIESCENT, LATENT

dot-dot-dot or series of asterisks indicating the omission of words or letters in a text ELLIPSIS

dots, usually regularly arranged, on a patterned fabric POLKA DOTS
- dots placed above a vowel, as in *gemütlich* DIERESIS, UMLAUT
- dotted, spotted, pockmarked, or the like PUNCTATE
- dotted or flecked, as with paint or natural colors STIPPLED

double, twofold DIPLOID, DUAL
- double, twofold, having two separate parts BINARY
- double or ghostly counterpart, sometimes haunting a person in legend DOPPELGÄNGER
- double vowel, speech sound in which a vowel changes in quality during the syllable, such as the sound of *i* in *sigh* DIPHTHONG
- doubled, forming a pair GEMINATE

double (combining form) AMPH-, AMPHI-, DI-, DIPL-, DIPLO-, ZYG-, ZYGO-

doubt or cast doubt on DISCREDIT
- doubt or worry leading to the withholding of full support or approval RESERVATION, QUALIFICATION
- doubting, disbelieving SKEPTICAL, INCREDULOUS
- doubts and uncertainties that discourage a projected action SCRUPLES
- express doubts or reluctance,

DRAMA TERMS

Term	Definition	Term	Definition
absurd—theater of the absurd	modern drama emphasizing the cruelty and futility of modern life	**curtain call**	reappearance on stage of an actor, cast, choir, or the like, to acknowledge applause
alienation effect	deliberate effect, as in the plays of Brecht, of reducing the audience's involvement with the action of the play, as when an actor addresses them directly	**denouement, catastrophe**	solution, climax, or unraveling of a plot
		deus ex machina	god brought in to resolve a tricky situation in the plot in classical drama
anagnorisis	moment of recognition of the truth by the hero in classical tragedy, which leads to the denouement	**dramatic irony**	drama in which the meaning of the words are understood by the audience but not the characters
black comedy	comedy with an underlying pessimism, typically dealing with grim or grotesque subjects	**dramatis personae**	list of a play's characters
		dry	to forget one's lines while on stage, as a nervous actor might
business	various incidental actions by an actor, as during a pause	**duologue**	play or scene in which only two actors have speaking parts
catharsis	drama that figuratively cleanses the emotions of the audience	**ensemble**	entire cast of a play; specifically, the supporting actors
comedy of manners	play that satirizes the faults of society	**epilogue**	concluding poem or speech after the end of the action of a play
commedia dell'arte	comedy of a type developed in 16th-century Italy, placing stock characters in an improvised plot	**epitasis**	part of a play, especially a Greek tragedy, in which the plot moves toward its climax
corpse	to laugh on stage inappropriately, as an actor might when something goes wrong	**extra**	minor character without a speaking role
		Grand Guignol	short, horrifying, macabre play, or the style based on it
coup de theatre	sudden turn of events in a play; brilliant or astonishing piece of stagecraft	**interlude, entr'acte, divertissement**	short entertainment between the acts of a play

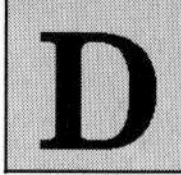

protest or object DEMUR
- pang of doubt, a feeling of conscience or mistrust, or the like MISGIVING, QUALM
- persistent or nagging, as minor doubts might be NIGGLING
- state of doubt, perplexity or the like DILEMMA, QUANDARY

doubtful, hesitant, or uncertain WAVERING, IRRESOLUTE, INDECISIVE, VACILLATING
- doubtful, insecure, not certain to succeed PRECARIOUS
- doubtful, suspiciously vague, and possibly insincere EQUIVOCAL, AMBIGUOUS
- doubtful, uncertain, or uncommitted AGNOSTIC
- of doubtful accuracy or authenticity, as a farfetched or fanciful anecdote is APOCRYPHAL
- of doubtful quality, legality, or the like, or causing suspicions DUBIOUS, SUSPECT

dough - substance added to dough to aid fermentation, as in bread making LEAVEN

doughnut - shape of a doughnut TORUS

dove - adjective for a dove COLUMBINE
- dovecote COLUMBARIUM

down feather PLUMULE

downfall or undoing, typically just retribution, as following pride or overconfidence NEMESIS

downward slope or tendency DECLINATION, DECLENSION
- downward stroke of the pen in handwriting MINIM

downward (combining form) CATA-

dowry, woman's marriage portion DOT
- money or goods given, as a kind of reverse dowry in some societies, by the bridegroom's family to the bride's BRIDE-PRICE, LOBOLA

drab, dusky, dull in color SUBFUSC

dragon with wings and a serpent's tail, as in heraldry WYVERN
- adjective for a dragon DRACONIC

drain a body cavity of fluid by means of a suction device, as in surgery ASPIRATE
- drain or sewer, as under a road CULVERT, CONDUIT
- drainage pit, as in a mine SUMP
- kitchen utensil for rinsing or

DRAMA TERMS *continued*

Kabuki	elaborate Japanese drama with music and dancing, in which all parts are played by men
kitchen-sink drama	modern drama representing sordid domestic life
legitimate	referring to serious plays, as opposed to satirical revues, musicals, and the like
masque	spectacular entertainment of dance, music, and drama, based on a mythical or allegorical theme, popular at English courts in the 16th and 17th centuries
melodrama	play characterized by sensational and highly emotional episodes and exaggerated vice and virtue, popular in the 19th century
method	type of acting, developed by Stanislavski, emphasizing identification with the character
mime	play or scene acted out with gestures but no speech
miracle play, mystery play	medieval dramatization of events from the Bible or the lives of the saints
mise en scène	stage setting, or the props and scenery used for it
monologue	long speech by a single actor
morality play	allegorical play of the 15th and 16th centuries, such as *Everyman*, in which the characters represent abstract virtues and vices
mummer	actor in a traditional folk drama or mime dealing with death and resurrection
No, Noh	classical Japanese drama, developed in the 14th century, representing legends and Buddhist themes with dance and song
peripeteia	sudden change in the course of events in a play; a twist in the plot
prologue	speech introducing the action of a play, or the character or actor delivering it
protagonist	principal character in a traditional play
protasis	introductory section of a play, especially a classical tragedy, introducing and developing the plot
repertory	presentation by a theater company of a succession of plays, typically alternating, in a single season
soliloquy	monologue typically representing the character's unspoken thoughts
stichomythia	dialogue in Greek drama in which alternate lines of verse are spoken by different characters
tableau	stage scene in which the actors freeze briefly
tetralogy	group of four related dramas, especially a series of three tragedies and one satire in ancient Greece
unities	three principles of composition—unity of action, time, and place—requiring that a classical drama limit itself to a single plot line, day, and location

draining, consisting of a perforated bowl COLANDER
- pit or hole for sewage or waste from household drains CESSPOOL
- rubber suction cup with a long handle, used for clearing blocked drains and pipes PLUNGER, PLUMBER'S HELPER

drama See chart, pages 160-161, and also **theater**

dramatic, relating to drama or acting THESPIAN
- dramatic or brilliant display, as in a piano recital PYROTECHNICS
- dramatic or overemotional behavior HISTRIONICS
- dramatic situation at the end of an episode of a serialized movie, play, or the like CLIFFHANGER

drapery - ornamental loop of drapery, flowers, or the like FESTOON, SWAG
- short decorative skirt of drapery hung along a shelf, edge of the bed, or the like VALANCE

draw a line, especially a circle or arc DESCRIBE
- draw, tie, or deadlock, especially in a sports event STANDOFF
- draw attention away from, steal the show from UPSTAGE
- draw or derive pleasure, interest, or the like from a seemingly unpromising source EXTRACT
- draw or describe, either in broad or in precise detail DELINEATE
- draw or paint a picture of LIMN
- draw out, bring to light ELICIT
- drawing of lots SORTITION
- drawn contest, deadlocked situation STALEMATE
- game, match, or the like played between two drawn or tied contestants to find a winner PLAY-OFF

draw back, as from pain or in fear, shy away WINCE, FLINCH, SHRINK, QUAIL, BLENCH, RECOIL, COWER
- draw back, as the tide might RECEDE
- draw back something, as a snail might draw in its horns RETRACT

drawer - set of drawers supporting a desk top PEDESTAL
- supporting strut along which a drawer slides RUNNER

drawing made to scale PROTRACTION
- drawing or diagram of a machine or structure showing its parts separately EXPLODED VIEW
- drawing or model, as of an engine or building, with part of the wall or casing omitted or cut away to reveal the interior CUTAWAY
- drawing or preliminary sketch, often full-size, for a tapestry, painting, mosaic, or the like CARTOON
- drawing to scale of an outside face of a building or structure ELEVATION
- drawings or writings, often witty or obscene, scribbled typically on walls in public places GRAFFITI
- art of drawing, as in architecture or engineering, according to mathematical rules of projection, technical drawing GRAPHICS
- person skilled at drawing, especially of architectural or technical plans DRAFTSPERSON, DRAFTSMAN, DRAFTSWOMAN
- shading of a drawing with intersecting sets of parallel lines CROSSHATCHING
- shading of fine lines in a drawing HATCHING
- sheet of wood, metal, or plastic, usually triangular, used to construct certain angles and lines quickly in technical drawing SET SQUARE
- sheet of wood, metal, or plastic with the outlines of various curves on it, used for drawing curves in technical drawing FRENCH CURVE
- shortening of lines in drawing or painting a scene, for apparent depth or distance FORESHORTENING, PERSPECTIVE
- transfer a drawing by loosely shading or coloring its reverse side, and then tracing it onto a surface or paper underneath CALK

drawing (combining form) -GRAM, -GRAPH

drawing room, as in a large French house, for receiving guests SALON

dream - dreamlike, dazed, or hypnotic state TRANCE
- dream world, impractical realm of fantasy and imagination CLOUD-CUCKOO-LAND
- dreamlike, distorted or irrational in a bizarre way SURREAL
- dreamlike false perception or illusion HALLUCINATION
- dreamlike succession of confusing images, as experienced in a fever PHANTASMAGORIA
- dreamy, lost in thought, moony and absentminded ABSTRACTED, PREOCCUPIED
- adjective for dreams ONEIRIC
- movement of the eyeballs behind closed lids during the dreaming phase of sleep RAPID EYE MOVEMENT, REM
- relating to dreams VISIONARY
- referring to dreams or hallucinations that are proved true by subsequent events or revelations VERIDICAL

dream (combining form) ONEIR-, ONEIRO-

dregs or other matter that settles at the bottom of a liquid SEDIMENT
- dregs or sediment, such as coffee grounds GROUTS
- dregs or sediment of wine, cider, or the like LEES
- clear wine, beer, or cider of its dregs, usually by siphoning RACK

dress See also **clothes**
- dress in or put on one's hat or clothes DON
- dress made up in cheap cloth as a basis for alterations or copies TOILE
- dress or tidy oneself very neatly PRIMP, PREEN, PRINK
- dressed or equipped in a specified way ACCOUTRED
- adoption of female dress and behavior by a man EONISM, TRANSVESTISM
- gather fabric into decorative rows, as on a dress, often using elastic thread SHIRR
- insert or fill-in at the front of a low-cut dress GUIMPE
- low revealing neckline, or a dress or blouse with such a neckline DÉCOLLETAGE
- part of a dress or gown trailing behind the wearer TRAIN
- part of a dress or other garment that has been gathered into a puff POUFFE
- state of being undressed or partially dressed DISHABILLE, DESHABILLE
- waist or bodice of a dress CORSAGE

dress shirt's false front DICKEY, PLASTRON

dressing, as of moist bread or meal heated and spread on a cloth, then applied to ease pain or inflammation POULTICE, CATAPLASM

dressing gown, light and loose-fitting, for a woman NEGLIGEE, PEIGNOIR

dressing room, bedroom, or private sitting room of a woman BOUDOIR, BOWER

dressmaking or designing of high quality for women of fashion COUTURE, HAUTE COUTURE

dribble saliva from the mouth SLOBBER, DROOL, SLAVER

dried, cured, and salted strips of meat, especially beef JERKY, CHARQUI, BILTONG
- dried, demoisturized, as some preserved food is DEHYDRATED, DESICCATED
- dried up, shriveled and wrinkled, as an old person's face might be WIZENED
- restore something to its natural state, such as dried food or concentrated lemon juice, as by adding

water RECONSTITUTE
- traditional Native American food of cakes of pounded dried meat PEMMICAN

drift or float gently, as the smell of flowers does in the wind WAFT

drill-like tool, as used in mining TREPAN
- drill worked by hand BRACE AND BIT
- drilling or boring tool AUGER, AWL, WIMBLE
- drill's handle or brace, into which the bit is fixed BITSTOCK
- drill's socket in which the bit is held POD
- equipment for a specified purpose, as for drilling or for extracting oil from a well RIG
- filled with or run by compressed air, as some drills are PNEUMATIC
- vise or clamp used to hold a tool or workpiece, as in a drill CHUCK

drink See chart, and also **alcohol, wine, tea**
- drink, apart from water BEVERAGE
- drink, as of beer, taken after spirits CHASER
- drink, food, or drug, such as caffeine, that temporarily increases activity or efficiency STIMULANT
- drink, or the act of drinking POTATION
- drink heavily, go on a drinking spree CAROUSE
- drink of the gods in Greek and Roman mythology NECTAR
- drink or swallow eagerly, gulp SWIG, SWILL, QUAFF
- drink someone's health or engage in riotous festive drinking WASSAIL
- drink something, especially alcohol IMBIBE
- drinks machine or other vending device DISPENSER
- add alcohol secretly to a drink SPIKE
- refraining from alcoholic drink TEETOTALISM, ABSTINENCE, TEMPERANCE
- sliver of citrus peel to decorate or flavor a drink TWIST
- small drink of alcoholic spirits SNIFTER, SNORT, SHOT
- small mat or disc placed under a drink to protect the table top COASTER
- small thin stick for stirring or removing bubbles from a drink SWIZZLE STICK

drinkable and nonpoisonous POTABLE

drinker, especially an excessive drinker, as of wine BIBBER, TIPPLER, TOPER
- heavy drinker, drunkard LUSH, SOAK, SOT, SOUSE, TOSSPOT

drinking fountain or, formerly, a water cask on a ship SCUTTLEBUTT
- drinking or act of swallowing, or the amount taken in DRAFT
- drinking partly in ancient Greece, typically with music and conversation SYMPOSIUM
- drinking spree RAZZLE
- drinking vessel, especially for wine, with a stem GOBLET
- drinking vessel filled to the brim, as for a toast BUMPER
- drinking vessel holding two quarts POTTLE
- drinking vessel such as a flat leather flask formerly carried attached to one's belt COSTREL
- beer mug with a lid STEIN
- flask as used by soldiers for carrying drinking water CANTEEN
- glass drinking vessel, typically with a rounded bottom inside TUMBLER
- horn-shaped drinking vessel in ancient Greece RHYTON
- large cuplike drinking vessel with a wide mouth BEAKER
- large drinking bowl, typically of wood, in former times MAZER
- large drinking glass, usually with a short stem RUMMER
- large drinking glass for sherry or port, or large glass for beer SCHOONER
- leather drinking vessel treated with tar or wax BLACKJACK
- large drinking vessel with a handle, used especially for beer TANKARD, POT
- small can or cup for drinking CANNIKIN
- treatment for drinking problems, a drug that causes nausea when one has an alcoholic drink ANTABUSE, DISULFIRAM

drip - dripping in or into a vein, as an injection or feeding drip might be INTRAVENOUS
- salt solution used in a medical drip SALINE

drive away or dispel a crowd, meeting, or the like DISPERSE, DISSIPATE, ROUT
- drive away or expel a person from his or her homeland BANISH, EXILE, EXPATRIATE
- drive away or expel someone foreign from a country DEPORT
- drive back or repel an attack REBUFF, REPULSE
- drive dangerously closely behind

DRINKS

BEERS, CIDERS, AND OTHER FERMENTED DRINKS

barley wine
bock
dortmunder
kumiss
kvass
mead
metheglin
münchener
perry
pilsener
pombe
porter
scrumpy

BEVERAGES AND SOFT DRINKS

camomile tea
float
grenadine/ grenadine red
infusion
julep
maté/ Paraguay tea/yerba maté
root beer
saloop
sarsaparilla
seltzer
tiger's milk
tisane

COCKTAILS AND LONG DRINKS

Bacardi
black velvet
Bloody Mary
Bronx
buck's fizz
caudle
cobbler
daiquiri
eggnog
frappé
gimlet
gin sling
glühwein
Harvey Wallbanger
highball
kir
manhattan
margarita
martini
mint julep
negus
old-fashioned
orgeat
piña colada
planter's punch
posset
rickey
sangria
screwdriver
shandy
shrub
sidecar
snowball
stinger
syllabub/ sillabub
Tom Collins
wassail
whiskey sour
white satin

SPIRITS AND LIQUEURS

absinthe
advocaat
amaretto
anisette
applejack
aqua vitae
aquavit
armagnac
arrack/arak
bourbon
calvados
crème de cacao
crème de cassis
crème de menthe
crème de noyau
curaçao
fine champagne
fior dell'alpi
galliano
grappa
Hollands/ geneva
kirsch/ kirschwasser
kümmel
mao-tai
maraschino
marc
mastic
mescal
mirabelle
negra
ouzo
pastis
poteau
pousse-café
raki
ratafia
redeye
sake
sambucca
schnapps
slivovitz
steinhager
strega
tequila
Tia Maria
van der Hum

another vehicle TAILGATE
- drive or instinctive interest MOTIVATION
- drive or prod cattle with a sharpened or electrified rod GOAD
- drive or travel successfully, as around a tight bend NEGOTIATE
- drive out, throw out, force out, expel EJECT, OUST
- drive out an evil spirit, or free a possessed person from evil spirits, as by religious rites EXORCISE
- drive out or expel a tenant or squatter from a property EVICT
- driving or pushing forward PROPULSION
- irresistible and often irrational drive to perform a certain action COMPULSION

driving away (combining form) -FUGE, -FUGAL

drone of bagpipes BURDEN

droop from heat or exhaustion WILT
- drooping, as some flowers and buds are CERNUOUS
- drooping limply, flabby, lacking firmness FLACCID

drop See also **fall**
- drop of liquid, or very small amount DRIBLET
- droplike or having drops GUTTATE

droplet of liquid GLOBULE

droppings, animal dung, especially that of animals being trailed or hunted SCATS

dropsy EDEMA

drug See chart, and also **medicine, medical**
- drug, food, or drink, such as coffee, that temporarily increases activity or efficiency STIMULANT
- drug, often addictive and illegal, that typically dulls the senses or induces a deep sleep NARCOTIC
- drug, potion, or technique for forgetting pains and sorrows NEPENTHE
- drug, such as LSD, producing hallucinations or sensory distortion HALLUCINOGENIC, PSYCHEDELIC DRUG
- drug addiction, or a drugged state NARCOTISM
- drug dealer PUSHER, PEDDLER
- drug-induced illusion HALLUCINATION
- drug-induced stupor or unconsciousness NARCOSIS
- drug or alcohol addiction DEPENDENCE
- drug or hormone, based on a ring of carbon atoms, sometimes used by bodybuilders and athletes STEROID, ANABOLIC STEROID
- drug slipped into a drink to make the drinker unconscious or defenseless MICKEY FINN, KNOCKOUT DROPS
- drug that neutralizes or counteracts the effects of another drug ANTAGONIST
- drugging, narcotic STUPEFACIENT
- drugs collectively, as used in the preparation of medicine PHARMACOPOEIA
- effect, especially an adverse one produced by a drug REACTION
- effective, powerful, or still active, as drugs or medicines might be POTENT
- inject illegal drugs directly into a vein MAINLINE
- painful effects of giving up drugs WITHDRAWAL SYMPTOMS
- painful method of curing drug addiction by sudden and complete disuse COLD TURKEY
- person delivering messages, parcels, smuggled drugs, or the like on behalf of another COURIER, MULE
- plant with a forked root, formerly used as a narcotic drug MANDRAKE
- pleasant, relaxed feeling, as from a drug BUZZ, HIGH, RUSH, FLASH

drug (combining form) PHARMACO-

Druid circle of stone or wooden pillars HENGE

DRUGS OF ABUSE

HALLUCINOGENS

LSD/acid
magic mushroom/sacred mushroom
mescal/peyote
mescaline
STP

STIMULANTS

amphetamine/Benzedrine/benny/blue/purple heart/speed
amyl nitrite/popper
anabolic steroid
coca/cocaine/coke/crack/snow/speedball
cubeb
doll/pop pill
methamphetamine/crystal
upper

SEDATIVES OR NARCOTICS

barbiturate/doll/goofball
betel
bhang/cannabis/dagga/ganja/grass/hashish/Indian hemp/marijuana/pot/weed
diacetylmorphine/heroin
downer
laudanum
morphine
opiate
opium
truth drug/Pentothal Sodium

drum TAMBOUR
- drum, cymbal, xylophone, or related instrument that is struck to produce the sound PERCUSSION INSTRUMENT
- drum major's or majorette's stick that is spun and thrown into the air BATON
- drumhead, skin of a drum TYMPAN, VELLUM
- drummer in an orchestra, especially one who plays the kettledrums TYMPANIST
- any of the strings stretched over the lower skin of a small drum to produce a rattling sound SNARE
- deaden the sound of a drum MUFFLE
- narrow cylindrical drum beaten with the hands in Latin American music BONGO DRUM, CONGA DRUM, TIMBAL
- pair of small Indian drums that are beaten with the hands TABLA
- small drum played to accompany the fife TABOR

drumbeat DUB
- drumbeat in a regular, even rhythm TATTOO
- low and continuous drumbeat that is softer than a drumroll RUFFLE

drunk INTOXICATED, INEBRIATED, PIXILATED, SHICKERED
- drunk and confused or stupefied BEFUDDLED, BESOTTED
- drunk and tearfully sentimental MAUDLIN
- drunken, or addicted to alcohol BIBULOUS
- drunken, or having a hangover as a result of drunkenness CRAPULENT
- drunken party, noisy festivity BACCHANAL, REVEL, CAROUSAL, WASSAIL, BACCHANALIA, RAZZLE
- slightly drunk, tiddly TIPSY, MELLOW, SQUIFFY
- tending to cause drunkenness HEADY, INTOXICATING

drunkard, heavy drinker LUSH, SOAK, SOT, SOUSE, TOPER, TOSSPOT, BIBBER
- habitual drunkard, alcoholic DIPSOMANIAC

dry See also **dried, dull**
- dry, as a wine might be SEC
- dry, as champagne might be BRUT
- dry, deprived of water or moisture DEHYDRATED
- dry, withered, shriveled, as a dead leaf would be SERE
- dry or parched, as land might be ARID
- dry and overprecise, pedantic or dogmatic SCHOLASTIC
- dry by heating PARCH
- dry out, remove moisture from,

as for preserving DESICCATE
- dry scrubland vegetation MAQUIS, CHAPARRAL
- dry up, as parched flowers might SHRIVEL, WITHER, SEAR
- drying device, squeezing water from wet laundry by pressing it between rollers WRINGER
- drying substance added to paints, inks, some medicines, and the like SICCATIVE
- of or relating to an extremely dry habitat XERIC

dry (combining form) XERO-

dry land, solid ground TERRA FIRMA

duck that feeds near the surface of the water or on land rather than deep underwater DABBLER
- bright colored patch on a duck's wing SPECULUM
- flock of geese or wild ducks in flight SKEIN
- webbed, as a duck's feet are PALMATE
- wild duck MALLARD, WIGEON

ducking stool to which wrongdoers or suspects were formerly tied, as for ducking or public mockery CUCKING STOOL

duct, bodily vessel or channel VAS

duel between knights, with lances on horseback JOUST, TILTING MATCH
- duel over a point of honor AFFAIRE D'HONNEUR

duffel coat - peg or crosspiece, such as a duffel coat's button, used for fastening TOGGLE

duke - adjective for a duke DUCAL
- dukedom, territory ruled by a duke or duchess DUCHY

dull, boring periods of time or parts of a book, play, or movie LONGUEURS
- dull, conventional, everyday, lacking in any striking features NONDESCRIPT, FACELESS, STEREOTYPED, BANAL
- dull, laborious, stodgy, plodding, as a speech might be PONDEROUS, PEDESTRIAN
- dull, lifeless, colorless, sterile, as a textbook might be ARID, PALLID, DESICCATED, LACKLUSTER
- dull, narrow-minded, limited in outlook, unimaginative PAROCHIAL
- dull, ordinary, unoriginal, as a person's imagination or conversation might be MUNDANE, HUMDRUM, BANAL, PROSAIC
- dull, trite, or obvious remark PLATITUDE, COMMONPLACE, BROMIDE, TRUISM
- dull, unadventurous, lacking in zest or flavor, as a comedy might be INSIPID, BLAND, VAPID, ANODYNE
- dull and inactive, sluggish or stale STAGNANT
- dull and indistinct rather than acute, as a pain might be OBTUSE
- dull finish or surface, as of a nonglossy paint MAT
- dull in color, drab SUBFUSC
- dull or mindless, as the expression on someone's face might be VACUOUS
- dull or purposeless task or way of life SQUIRREL CAGE
- dull or tiring routine work DRUDGERY
- dull to the point of almost sending one to sleep, extremely boring STULTIFYING, STUPEFYING, SOPORIFIC
- dully austere, lacking in liveliness or decoration, as a room or report might be CLINICAL, ASEPTIC
- dully mechanical, purely functional or materialistic BANAUSIC
- dully routine, drearily repetitious TEDIOUS, MONOTONOUS
- lead a dull, passive life VEGETATE, STAGNATE

dumb or speechless because shy, embarrassed, or astonished TONGUE-TIED

dummy or crude image of a person, intended as an object of scorn or hatred, and sometimes burned in public EFFIGY
- jointed dummy of a human figure, used as an artists' model LAY FIGURE, MANNEQUIN
- voice production, especially by an entertainer, giving the impression that the sound originates in a dummy VENTRILOQUISM

dung See also **excrement**
- dung, excrement ORDURE
- dung-eating, as some beetles and flies are COPROPHAGOUS, SCATOPHAGOUS
- dung of sea birds, collected from dried deposits along the coast for use as a fertilizer GUANO
- dung or droppings, especially of animals being trailed or hunted SCATS
- containing or relating to dung STERCORACEOUS
- dunghill or rubbish heap MIDDEN

dung (combining form) COPRO-

dung beetle SCARAB

dungeon whose door is in the ceiling OUBLIETTE

duplicating machine typically based on a wax stencil stretched over a rotating inked cylinder MIMEOGRAPH, RONEO, CYCLOSTYLE

during (combining form) DIA-, INTRA-

dust speck MOTE
- crumble, decay, turn to dust MOLDER AWAY

dutiful, loyal, or enthusiastic to an excessive, foolish, uncritical, or dangerous degree GUNG HO
- dutiful, working attentively or applying oneself conscientiously to a task DILIGENT, ASSIDUOUS, SEDULOUS
- dutiful or conscientious in a very rigorous, careful, or painstaking way SCRUPULOUS, PUNCTILIOUS, METICULOUS
- dutiful or devoted, especially in religious observance, pious, DEVOUT

DYES AND PIGMENTS

RED

alkanet
brazilin
carmine
carotene
chrome red
cinnabar
cochineal
Congo red
crocein
fuchsin/magenta
henna
jewelers' rouge
kermes
lake
madder
orcein
red arsenic
red lead/minium
red ocher
rhodamine
ruddle/reddle/raddle
vermilion/mercuric sulfide

BLUE/VIOLET

anil
cobalt blue
cyanine
gentian violet
indigo
mauveine/Perkin's purple
orchil/cudbear
Prussian blue/iron blue
Tyrian purple
ultramarine
woad

YELLOW AND ORANGE

annatto
bister
cadmium yellow
chrome yellow
flavin
fustic
Indian yellow
phosphine/chrysaniline yellow
safflower/dyer's thistle
saffron
weld/dyer's rocket
yellow ocher

GREEN

chrome green
sumac
terre-verte
viridian

BROWN

bister
brown ocher
butternut
catechu/cachou/cutch
sienna
tannin/tannic acid
umber

BLACK

black iron oxide
boneblack
carbon black
lampblack
nigrosine

WHITE

Chinese white/zinc white
titanium white
white lead

DYNASTIES

Abbasids	Arabic, 8th–13th century	**Mogul/ Moghul/ Mughal**	Indian, 16th–19th century
Achaemenid	Persian, 6th–4th century BC	**Nasrid**	Moorish (Granada), 13th–15th century
Almoravides	Berber, 11th–12th century	**O'Neill/Uí Néill**	Irish, 8th–10th century
Angevin	English, 12th–13th century	**Orange**	Netherlands, from 19th century
Árpád	Hungarian, 9th–14th century	**Ottoman**	Turkish, 14th–20th century
Aviz	Portuguese, 14th–16th century	**Pahlavi**	Iranian, 20th century
Bourbon	Franco-Spanish, from 16th century	**Plantagenet**	English, 12th–15th century
Bragança	Portuguese, 17th–20th century	**Ptolemaic**	Egyptian, 4th–1st century BC
Capetian	French, 10th–14th century	**Qâjar**	Persian, 18th–20th century
Carolingian/ Carlovingian	Frankish, 8th–10th century	**Romanov**	Russian, 17th–20th century
Chakkri	Siamese (Thai), from 18th century	**Safawid**	Persian, 16th–18th century
Ch'in/Qin	Chinese, 3rd century BC	**Savoy**	Italian, 19th–20th century
Ch'ing/Qing	Chinese 17th–20th century	**Seleucid**	Hellenic, 4th–1st century BC
Chou	Chinese, 11th–3rd century BC	**Seljuk**	Turkish, 11th–13th century
Fatimids	North African, 10th–12th century	**Shang**	Chinese, about 16th century BC
Franconian/ Salian	German, 11th–12th century	**Stewart/Stuart**	Scottish, 14th–18th century
Habsburg/ Hapsburg	Holy Roman Empire and Austro-Hungarian Empire, 13th–20th century	**Sung**	Chinese, 10th–13th century
Han	Chinese, 3rd century BC to 3rd century AD	**Tang**	Chinese, 7th–10th century
Hanoverian	Germano-British, 17th–20th century	**Tudor**	English, 15th–17th century
Hohenstaufen	German, 12th–13th century	**Umayyad/ Ommiad**	Arabian, 8th–11th century
Hohenzollern	Brandenburg-Prussian, 15th–20th century	**Valois**	French, 14th–16th century
Hyksos	Egyptian, 17th–16th century BC	**Varangian**	Russo-Scandinavian, 9th century
Lancaster	English, 15th century	**Windsor**	British, 20th century
Mameluke/ Mamluk	Egyptian, 13th–16th century	**Wittelsbach**	German, 14th–20th century
Merovingian	Frankish, 6th–8th century	**York**	English, 15th century
Ming	Chinese, 14th–17th century	**Yuan**	Mongol, 13th century
		Zand	Persian, 18th century

- dutiful or respectful, especially to one's elders and betters DEFERENTIAL
- dutifulness, devotion, or loyalty, especially toward one's parents and family PIETY

duty, honor, or respect, granted to someone or to a belief or cause HOMAGE
- duty, promise, contract, or the like demanding a certain course of action OBLIGATION
- duty or loyalty owed by a vassal to his feudal lord FEALTY
- duty or responsibility DEVOIR
- duty or responsibility, burdensome task, as to prove one's allegations ONUS
- duty or task that one has been specifically set to perform ASSIGNMENT
- duty payment, tax, or levy IMPOST
- duty schedule or system of taxes, especially on imports TARIFF
- duty to which a soldier may be specially assigned DETAIL
- assign work, duties, or powers to one's agent or subordinate DELEGATE, DEPUTE
- beyond the call of duty SUPEREROGATORY
- discharge, as from duty or debt QUIETUS

- failure or neglect in the performing of one's duty NEGLIGENCE, DERELICTION, DELINQUENCY
- financial or moral duty or obligation COMMITMENT
- free from responsibility, a duty, or the like EXONERATE, EXEMPT
- in proportion to the value of the goods, as a tax or duty might be AD VALOREM
- list of duties or register of the people to perform them ROSTER, ROTA
- perform official duties on a formal occasion, as a host or priest would OFFICIATE
- period or fixed amount of work or duty STINT
- period or shift of duty on guard or on shipboard WATCH, TRICK
- person, such as an actor or actress, able and ready to take on the duties of another in an emergency UNDERSTUDY
- referring to rights, duties, and similar ethical concepts DEONTIC
- referring to the duty or respect owed by sons and daughters to their parents FILIAL
- referring to the religious duties of spiritual care and guidance PASTORAL
- release from guard duty, through the arrival of a replacement guard RELIEF
- required as a duty INCUMBENT, OBLIGATORY
- shirk work or duty MALINGER, GOLDBRICK, GOOF OFF, SKIVE

dwarf See also **gnome**
- dwarf, in Greek mythology PYGMY
- dwarf tree or shrub produced by rigorous pruning, or the traditional Japanese art of producing such plants BONSAI
- bone condition that causes dwarfism ACHONDROPLASIA

dye See chart, page 165
- dye, radioactive substance, or the like, whose course can be monitored through a system, as used in medical diagnosis TRACER
- dye of a kind made fast by being oxidized once within the fiber to an insoluble form VAT DYE
- dye of red ocher, used for marking sheep RUDDLE
- dye parts of cloth while tying other parts tightly, producing a mottled effect TIE-DYE
- dye produced synthetically, especially from coal-tar compounds ANILINE DYE
- dye used by ancient Britons to color their skin blue WOAD
- dyeing chemical, acting as a fixative MORDANT
- dyeing technique involving the use of wax to keep areas of the cloth undyed BATIK
- referring to a dye or color that needs no fixative SUBSTANTIVE

dying See also **dead, death**
- dying, on the brink of death MORIBUND, IN EXTREMIS
- hospital specializing in care for the dying HOSPICE

dynasty See chart

E

each other - felt, owed, given, or done by two people or groups about or to each other MUTUAL, RECIPROCAL

eager See also **enthusiastic, emotional**
- eager, hopeful, looking forward to EXPECTANT
- eager and willing SOLICITOUS
- eager or impatient with curiosity AGOG
- eager to please, cooperative COMPLIANT, COMPLAISANT, OBLIGING
- eager to please or obey in a fawning or excessive way SERVILE, OBSEQUIOUS
- be eager for or excited at something SALIVATE

eagle - eaglelike, relating to an eagle AQUILINE
- eagle's nest built on a cliff or other high place AERIE, EYRIE

ear See illustration
- ear, nose, and throat specialist OTORHINOLARYNGOLOGIST
- ear-shaped AURICULATE
- ear-shaped part or extension on a body organ AURICLE
- buzzing or ringing in the ear as a medical condition TINNITUS
- clip part of an animal's ear, especially for identification CROP
- having drooping ears, as beagles might LOP-EARED
- relating to or hearing with both ears BINAURAL
- relating to or hearing with only one ear MONAURAL
- relating to the ear AURAL, AURICULAR, OTIC
- simple small metal ring worn in a pierced ear to prevent the hole from sealing up when earrings are not being worn SLEEPER
- small chamber in the inner ear important for bodily balance and coordination UTRICLE, SACCULE
- small structure in the inner ear that converts sound into nerve impulses to be transmitted to the brain ORGAN OF CORTI

ear (combining form) -OT-, OTO-

eardrum, resonating membrane in the ear TYMPANIC MEMBRANE, TYMPANUM

earlier, previous, being before in time, rank, order, or the like PRECEDING, ANTECEDENT, ANTERIOR
- come earlier in time, precede ANTEDATE
- scene or passage in a novel, movie, or the like that interrupts the main story line to revert to earlier events FLASHBACK

earlier (combining form) PRE-

earliest, first, or original PRIMEVAL, PRIMITIVE, PRIMAL, ARCHETYPAL,
- earliest example or model, on which copies or later developments are based PROTOTYPE, ARCHETYPE
- relating to the earliest time or condition PRISTINE, PRIMORDIAL

earliest (combining form) PROTO-, UR-

early, immature works of a composer, writer, or the like JUVENILIA
- early, in the morning MATUTINAL
- early in development, in the earliest stage of growth EMBRYONIC, SEMINAL, GERMINAL, NASCENT
- early in development, just beginning INCHOATE, INCIPIENT
- act, use, pay, or produce too early, before the appropriate time ANTICIPATE
- developing or maturing unusually early, especially in intellectual ability PRECOCIOUS
- occurring too early PREMATURE, PREVIOUS, UNTIMELY

early (combining form) EO-

early show, as of a play MATINEE

earn or obtain money in dubious ways HUSTLE

earring with a large stone surrounded by smaller ones GIRANDOLE

earth See illustration, page 170, and also **atmosphere**
- heating of the earth's atmosphere because of increased absorption of solar radiation GREENHOUSE EFFECT
- imaginary half-circle joining the poles on the earth's surface MERIDIAN
- point in its orbit when the moon or a satellite is farthest from the earth APOGEE
- point in its orbit when the moon or a satellite is nearest to the earth PERIGEE
- regarding the earth as the center of the universe, as in early astronomy GEOCENTRIC
- relating to the earth, earthly TERRESTRIAL, PLANETARY, TELLURIC
- relating to the earth, earthly existence, or everyday life, as opposed to higher or more spiritual concerns MUNDANE, SUBLUNARY, TEMPORAL
- sail or fly completely around something, such as the earth CIRCUMNAVIGATE
- spherical but flattened at the poles, as the earth is OBLATE
- spin or turn on an axis, as the earth does ROTATE
- study of the earth's crust on the theory that it consists of giant sliding plates PLATE TECTONICS
- zone on the earth's surface lying between the tropics TORRID ZONE
- zones on the earth's surface lying between the polar regions and the tropics TEMPERATE ZONES
- zones on the earth's surface lying within the polar regions FRIGID ZONES

earth (combining form) GEO-, AGR-, AGRI-, AGRO-

earthquake or series of tremors that follows the main shock of a large earthquake AFTERSHOCK
- area on the earth's surface directly above the point of origin of an earthquake EPICENTER
- energy of an earthquake at its source, as measured on the Richter scale MAGNITUDE
- instrument for detecting and measuring tremors of the earth's crust as caused by earthquakes or explosions SEISMOGRAPH
- preliminary tremor of an earthquake FORESHOCK
- relating to an earthquake, large explosion, or other vibration of the earth's crust SEISMIC
- scale registering the magnitude of an earthquake RICHTER SCALE
- study of earthquakes and other vibrations of the earth's crust or mantle SEISMOLOGY

earthquake (combining form) SEISM-, SEISMO-

earthworm, leech, or other similarly segmented worm ANNELID
- coil of earth excreted by an earthworm CAST, CASTING

earwax CERUMEN

ease, help to bring about FACILITATE
- ease of action or performance FACILITY
- easing of tension, as between nations DÉTENTE

Easter - adjective for Easter or Passover PASCHAL

eastern Mediterranean countries LEVANT
- eastern temple or shrine, typically a multistoried tapering tower PAGODA
- Far Eastern countries or regions ORIENT

Ear

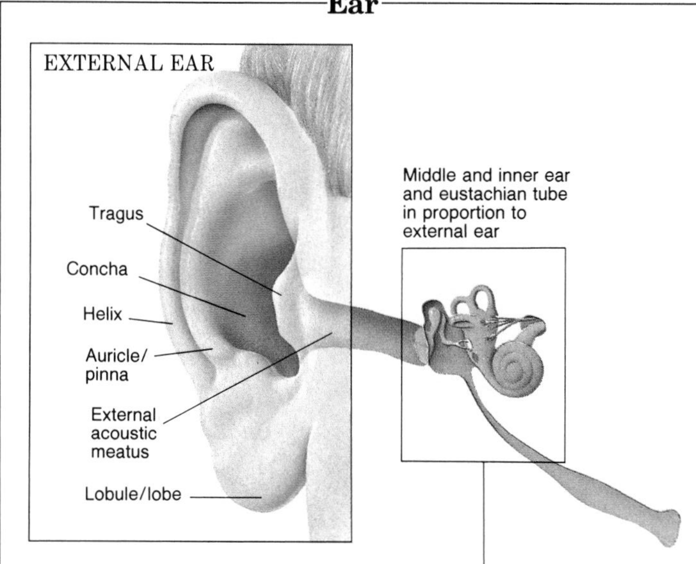

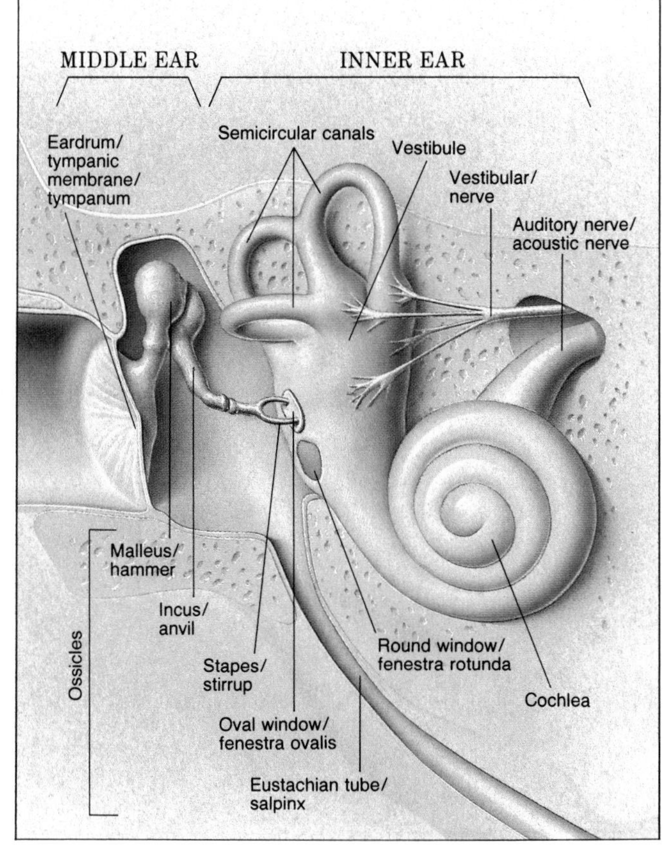

Eastern Orthodox abbot, head of an Eastern Orthodox monastery HEGUMEN, ARCHIMANDRITE
- Eastern Orthodox bishop, or governor of an Eastern Orthodox diocese EPARCH
- Eastern Orthodox monk CALOYER
- Eastern Orthodox Churches' liturgical language OLD CHURCH SLAVONIC

easy, simple, relating to basic knowledge, elementary RUDIMENTARY
- easy but very profitable work GRAVY TRAIN
- easy to obtain or to understand ACCESSIBLE
- easy to understand, clearly expressed PERSPICUOUS, LUCID, TRANSPARENT
- easy-to-beat opponent or easily accomplished task PUSHOVER
- something easy to achieve, or a certainty CINCH

eat See also **feeding**
- eat gluttonously or greedily, gorge GORMANDIZE
- eat or swallow greedily and hastily DEVOUR
- eat or take in by swallowing INGEST
- eatable, fit to eat EDIBLE, COMESTIBLE, ESCULENT
- eating abundantly, having a huge appetite RAVENOUS, VORACIOUS
- eating all kinds of food, both meat and plant foods OMNIVOROUS
- eating and drinking excessively, overindulgent, gluttonous INTEMPERATE, CRAPULENT
- eating meat occasionally or eating only meat, as lions and some other animals do CARNIVOROUS
- eating plants only, as many animals do HERBIVOROUS
- art of good eating or cooking GASTRONOMY
- full or overfull after eating SATIATED, SATED, GLUTTED
- person who enjoys food and eats abundantly TRENCHERMAN
- person who enjoys fine cooking or eating GOURMET
- person who enjoys good or excessive eating GOURMAND

eat (combining form) -PHAG-, PHAGO-, -PHAGOUS, -VOROUS

ebb, flowing back REFLUX

eccentric gesture, quaint idea, or the like WHIMSY

echo, echolike sound, as heard by a

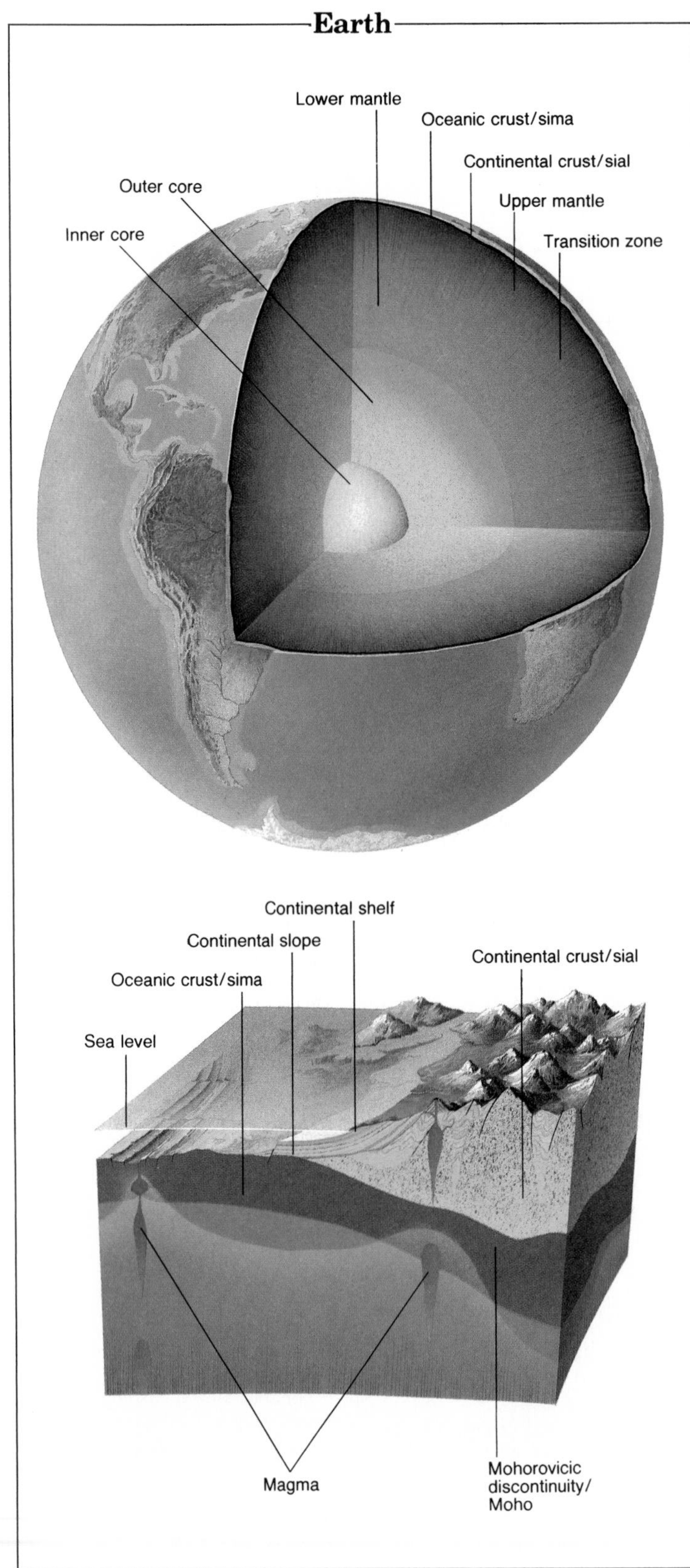

doctor tapping a patient's chest RESONANCE
- echo or ring with noise RESOUND, REVERBERATE
- echo sounder, used for detecting enemy submarines SONAR, ASDIC

eclipse, or disappearance of a heavenly body during an eclipse OCCULTATION
- eclipse in which a ring of the sun remains visible around the silhouetted moon ANNULAR ECLIPSE
- arrangement of three celestial bodies in a straight line, as of the earth, sun, and moon during an eclipse SYZYGY
- close approach, but without eclipse, of two celestial bodies APPULSE
- huge column of burning gas rising from the sun, visible during a total eclipse PROMINENCE
- partial shadow, as during an eclipse, between areas of full shadow and full illumination PENUMBRA
- region of full shadow cast on the earth's surface during a total eclipse UMBRA

economic See also **thrifty**
- economic independence from the need for imports or aid AUTARKY
- economic system in Europe after the feudal system, based on increased foreign trade MERCANTILE SYSTEM, MERCANTILISM
- economical use of resources HUSBANDRY, CONSERVATION

economics See chart, pages 171-172
- relating to the economics of large and complex systems, such as a whole country or region MACROECONOMICS

economize, cut back on expenses RETRENCH

ecstatic, highly enthusiastic or elated RHAPSODIC
- ecstatic, irrational DIONYSIAC, DIONYSIAN
- ecstatic and usually unintelligible or nonsensical speech, as in some religious services, "gift of tongues" GLOSSOLALIA
- become enraptured or ecstatic SWOON

edge See also **border, boundary, trimming**
- edge, border, or fringe of a fabric, carpet, or the like finished so as to prevent unraveling SELVAGE
- edge, end, farthest point or part EXTREMITY
- edge, fringe, or boundary, as of a social group PERIPHERY
- edge or outer limits, as of one's authority or hearing PERIMETER
- edge or protecting rim, as on a wheel or beam, for strengthening,

attaching, or the like FLANGE
- edging of tiny loops, as on ribbon or lace PICOTS
- edging or trimming, as for upholstery, consisting of a narrow tube of folded cloth, that often envelops a cord PIPING
- cut cloth to form a deeply indented edging VANDYKE
- cut off the edge or corner of BEVEL, CHAMFER
- drapery forming a decorative border, as along the edge of a bed or shelf VALANCE
- ornamental border or edging, as on a violin or building PURFLE
- ornamental strip of wood, metal, or the like, typically for edging BEADING

edible, suitable for eating ESCULENT, COMESTIBLE

ECONOMICS AND FINANCE TERMS

AMEX	American Stock Exchange
arbitrage	buying of shares, currencies, and commodities for quick resale at a higher price
arbitrageur	speculator who buys up shares in companies threatened by takeover bids, to resell at a profit if the bid succeeds
asset stripping	commercial practice of taking over a company and selling off its assets for a quick profit
bear	speculator who anticipates falling prices, and sells securities hoping to rebuy them later at a lower price
black economy	unofficial and technically illegal production and sale of goods and services, evading the tax system
blue chip	share considered safe and profitable through having a long record of reliability
bull	speculator who anticipates rising prices, and buys securities hoping to sell them later at a profit
cartel	agreement between producers or manufacturers to control output, prices, and the like, often resulting in an illegal monopoly
collateral	property pledged as security for a loan
conglomerate	business corporation made up of many wide-ranging companies
consolidation	combining or uniting of separate businesses into a larger whole
consols/ consolidated stock	interest-bearing British government stock, without a fixed redemption date
consortium/ syndicate	business association of various interests formed for some joint enterprise
dawn raid	surprise attempt by a person or group to buy a large shareholding in a company, often at an inflated price, typically before a takeover bid
debenture bond, loan stock	fixed-interest security, typically long-term and guaranteed, issued by a company or government organization
deflation	reduction in the level of prices and general economic activity, especially through a government policy of restricting the money supply
discount rate	rate of interest deducted in advance, as on a treasury bill
Dow Jones Index	daily average of prices on the New York Stock Exchange, based on the average price of a selected group of ordinary shares
equity security/ common stock	ordinary shares, as distinct from fixed-interest securities such as preferred stock
fiscal year	accounting period of 12 months, such as the government's tax year
floating	referring to a currency whose exchange rate is determined solely by the forces of supply and demand, without government intervention
flotation	launching or financing of a business venture by means of a share issue
futures	commodities or securities bought or sold at an agreed price for future delivery
gilts/gilt-edged securities	low-risk fixed-interest securities issued by the government
gross domestic product/GDP	total value of the goods and services produced in a country in one year, excluding income from investments abroad
gross national product/GNP	total value of the goods and services produced in a country in one year, including the net income from investments abroad

continued

edit, correct, or revise, especially by censoring or editing out some of the material BLUE-PENCIL
- edit or revise a text for publication REDACT

edition of a writer's works, together with accumulated notes and comments by many scholars VARIORUM
- edition or critical revision of a text, incorporating the most plausible variant readings RECENSION

educate, train, foster NURTURE
- educated, cultured, or intellectual people as a group or social class INTELLIGENTSIA, LITERATI, CLERISY
- educated, learned, scholarly LITERATE

education and the world of scholarship and universities ACADEMIA
- education at university or college

ECONOMICS AND FINANCE TERMS *continued*

intangible	business asset, such as goodwill, that has a value but no physical existence
laissez-faire	policy or practice of non-intervention by a government in economic activity
letter of credit	written authorization by a banker for a named person to draw a stated sum from the addressee
minimum lending rate/ MLR	rate of interest at which a central bank lends money to the rest of the banking system
monetarism	doctrine that a country's economy is best managed by keeping close control over the amount of money in circulation
mutual fund	finance and investment company that buys a variety of shares and sells units from the combined portfolio to the public
NYSE	New York Stock Echange
par value/ nominal value	face value of a security
portfolio	investor's entire set of securities
preferred stock	fixed-interest security, with dividends payable before any are assigned to ordinary shares
promissory note/note of hand	written IOU or promise to repay a loan at a given time or on demand
recession	reduction in economic activity, less severe than a depression, at a generally prosperous time
reflation	increase in general economic activity, especially through a government policy of easing the money supply
restrictive practices	trading agreements considered unfair to competitors or generally against the public interest
revaluation	increase in the official value or exchange rate of a country's currency, based on a formal government decision
rights issue	issue of new shares to current shareholders, normally at a discount price and in proportion to their existing shareholdings
securities	stock certificates, bonds, or similar salable evidence of ownership or entitlement used to guarantee an obligation; investments generally in the form of stock, shares, and bonds
the Snake	system agreed to by members of the European Economic Community (EC) to keep fluctuations in exchange rates within certain limits
stagflation	combination of static or falling production and employment with inflation in an economy
stock split	issuing of a number of shares for each share of stock now outstanding
supply-side	referring to an economic doctrine that encourages tax reductions as a means of boosting investment and productivity
tontine	finance or insurance scheme in which a member's shares or benefits pass on to the other members of the group when he or she dies or defaults
treasury bill	an obligation of the treasury maturing within one year and bearing no interest but sold at a discount
underwriter	person or company that guarantees the success of a share issue by undertaking to buy any securities left over
valorize	raise or maintain artificially the value or price of a commodity, especially by deliberate government action
white knight	person or group that acts to rescue a company threatened by closure or takeover

level TERTIARY EDUCATION
- education technique based on questioning assumptions and drawing out supposedly inborn knowledge SOCRATIC METHOD
- education technique for young children, based on play, self-expression, and initiative rather than discipline and control MONTESSORI METHOD
- relating to a method in education in which the learner is allowed or encouraged to discover things for himself or herself HEURISTIC
- report or summary of a person's education and career, as for job applications CURRICULUM VITAE, VITA, RÉSUMÉ

eel of a large sea-dwelling species or family CONGER, CONGER EEL
- eel that is split and then grilled or fried SPITCHCOCK
- eellike creature with a jawless sucking mouth LAMPREY
- eellike fish of a brightly colored, tropical, sea-dwelling species MORAY
- eelshaped ANGUILLIFORM
- young or undeveloped eel ELVER, GLASS EEL, LEPTOCEPHALUS

effect See also **result**
- have a favorable or unfavorable effect REDOUND
- positive effect on a patient's condition of an inactive substance taken by him or her in the belief that it is a medicine PLACEBO EFFECT

effective, sound, or acceptable, as an argument, title, or passport might be VALID
- effective or penetrating, as an argument might be TRENCHANT, INCISIVE, COGENT

effeminate or intersexual EPICENE

efficiency - analysis of the efficiency of a workforce, machine system, or the like, as an aid to policy making OPERATIONAL RESEARCH
- modernize an industry, process, or the like, and increase its efficiency RATIONALIZE
- plan or use with maximum efficiency OPTIMIZE

effort, hard work, and conscientious attention to duty or tasks DILIGENCE, ASSIDUITY, SEDULOUSNESS, APPLICATION
- effort, labor, strenuous physical or mental endeavors TRAVAIL, EXERTIONS
- planned or performed together, combined, as an effort might be CONCERTED, COORDINATED
- requiring a great deal of effort ARDUOUS, STRENUOUS

effortless, flowing, or graceful FLUENT
- effortless, fluent FACILE

egg See illustration
- egg cell, unfertilized reproductive cell in female animals OVUM
- egg-laying mammal such as the platypus MONOTREME
- egg-laying tube in most insects and some fish OVIPOSITOR
- egg-producing gland OVARY
- egg-shaped OVAL, OVATE
- egg with a tough shell, typical of birds, insects, and reptiles CLEIDOIC EGG
- eggs of a fish, frog, or the like SPAWN
- bake eggs that have been removed from their shells SHIRR
- chicken-rearing system involving confinement to cages for fast fattening or high production of eggs BATTERY
- cook food, especially eggs, in water at just below boiling point CODDLE
- dish of fried or poached eggs with spinach EGGS FLORENTINE
- fertilization of an egg cell by sperm, the beginning of pregnancy CONCEPTION, IMPREGNATION
- fertilized egg or ovum ZYGOTE
- fluffy baked egg dish, either savory or sweet SOUFFLÉ
- full of eggs or roe GRAVID
- keep eggs warm before hatching INCUBATE, BROOD
- mature, unfertilized female egg cell or male sperm GAMETE
- organism in a very early stage of its development, such as a fertilized egg EMBRYO
- ornamental jeweled egg made by a famous Russian goldsmith FABERGÉ EGG
- produce an egg cell or ovum OVULATE
- producing only one egg or offspring at a time UNIPAROUS
- rotten, as an egg might be ADDLED

Egg

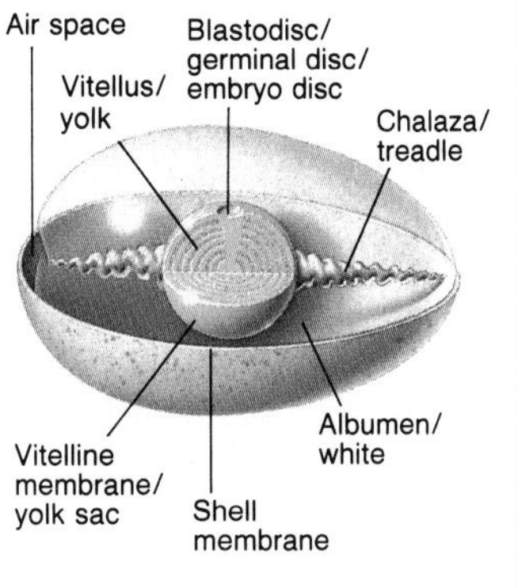

- small dish for baking and serving individual portions, especially of egg dishes COCOTTE

egg (combining form) -OO-, -OV-, OVI-, OVO-

egg white ALBUMEN

egg yolk VITELLUS, PARABLAST

egocentric, self-regarding, or in love with oneself NARCISSISTIC

Egypt - ancient water-raising device, as used in Egypt, consisting of a pivoted pole with a bucket and a counterweight SHADOOF
- building with columns supporting the roof, as in ancient Egyptian architecture HYPOSTYLE
- Egyptian Christian Church COPTIC CHURCH
- beetle of a family including the dung beetles, treated as sacred in ancient Egypt SCARAB
- jar used in ancient Egypt for holding a mummy's entrails CANOPIC JAR
- Ottoman viceroy in Egypt in former times KHEDIVE
- ruling caste in Egypt between the 13th and 16th centuries MAMELUKE
- script or hieroglyphics of a complex rounded form used by priests in ancient Egypt HIERATIC
- script or hieroglyphics of a simplified form, used by literate laymen in ancient Egypt DEMOTIC
- stone tablet providing the key to ancient Egyptian hieroglyphics ROSETTA STONE
- tapering four-sided stone pillar with a pyramidal top, of a kind used as a monument in ancient Egypt OBELISK
- tomb in ancient Egypt, of oblong shape with sloping sides and a flat roof MASTABA
- writing system using pictures in ancient Egypt HIEROGLYPHICS

eight-note pitch interval between the notes of music OCTAVE
- eight-sided figure OCTAGON
- eight singers or musicians, or a composition for such a group OCTET

eight (combining form) OCT-, OCTO-

eighty-year-old, or a person aged between 80 and 89 OCTOGENARIAN

elaborate See **highfalutin, showy, complicated, decorate**

elastic, extendable without breaking, stretchable EXTENSILE, DUCTILE

elbow one's way in a crowd JOSTLE

eldest or senior member of a group, society, diplomatic circle, or the like DOYEN, DOYENNE
- state of being the eldest child, or his right to inherit the title or entire estate PRIMOGENITURE

elect or appoint a new member to a group by a decision of the existing group CO-OPT

election See also **vote**

- election campaigning HUSTINGS
- election in which members of a political party or voters in a region choose their delegates or candidates PRIMARY
- election majority in which the winner fails to secure more than half of the total votes or seats RELATIVE MAJORITY, PLURALITY
- election majority in which the winner secures more than half of the total votes or seats ABSOLUTE MAJORITY
- admit defeat in an election CONCEDE
- campaign for votes from people or a region in an election campaign CANVASS
- catchphrase, motto, jingle, or the like used repeatedly, as in advertising or elections SLOGAN
- list of people entitled to vote in an election ELECTORAL ROLL, ELECTORAL REGISTER
- political party's declaration of its policies, as before an election PLATFORM, MANIFESTO
- poll taken in a cross section of society, especially to forecast election results GALLUP POLL
- representation of parties in an elective body according to the proportion of votes that they win in an election PROPORTIONAL REPRESENTATION
- study of elections and electoral systems PSEPHOLOGY
- support for a government's policies, as considered given by an election victory MANDATE

electioneering by touring rural areas and making speeches there BARNSTORMING

- electioneering tour in which a politician briefly visits a series of small towns WHISTLE-STOP TOUR

electoral district, or the group of voters within it CONSTITUENCY

- electoral district in a town or city WARD, PRECINCT
- manipulation of the boundaries of an electoral district for party advantage GERRYMANDERING

electricity See chart

- electric cables' supporting tower PYLON
- electrical coil that can be placed in a cup or other container to heat

ELECTRICITY AND ELECTRONICS TERMS

alternating current/AC	current that changes direction continually
alternator	generator producing alternating current
ammeter	instrument that measures electric current
ampere/amp	unit of electric current
anode	positive electrode, as in a battery
armature	rotor, wound with wire coils, of an electric motor or generator; vibrating part of a loudspeaker, electric bell, or other electromagnetic device
band-pass filter	filter that blocks all signals except those within a selected frequency range
capacitance	ability to store electric charge; measure of this ability, the ratio of induced charge to potential difference
capacitor, condenser	circuit element used to store charge temporarily
cathode	negative electrode, as in a battery
cathode-ray tube	vacuum tube for focusing an electron beam onto a fluorescent screen, as in television sets and oscilloscopes
commutator	device, as on an electric motor or generator, for reversing the direction of a current, or converting alternating current into direct current
conductance, conductivity	property of transferring, or measure of the ability to transfer, electric current in a circuit
coulomb	unit of electric charge
dielectric	nonconductor of electric current, insulator
diode	component with two terminals, typically allowing current to flow in only one direction
Dolby	system in a tape recorder, cassette player, or the like for reducing hiss and other unwanted noise
dynamo	generator, especially for direct current
electrode	conductor for an electric current, as in a battery or valve
electrolyte	solution that conducts electricity, as in a battery
farad	unit of electric capacitance
faraday cage	screen used to insulate apparatus from outside electric interference
galvanic, voltaic	relating or referring to electric current produced by chemical action, as in a battery
galvanometer	instrument for detecting or measuring small electric currents
henry	unit of electric inductance
impedance, reactance, resistance	property of opposing, or measure of the opposition to, the flow of current, especially alternating current, in a circuit
inductance	property of a circuit allowing electric induction

water or other liquids IMMERSION HEATER
- electrical glow seen on a ship's mast, church spire, or the like during stormy weather SAINT ELMO'S FIRE, CORPOSANT
- electrical plug connecting one or more other plugs to a socket ADAPTER
- electrical sparks or crackling, as produced by friction STATIC
- electricity connection point, such as a wall socket OUTLET
- electricity produced from the energy of running water HYDROELECTRICITY
- electricity-supply failure OUTAGE
- frame on the roof of an electric train engine, streetcar, or trolleybus, collecting current from an overhead wire PANTOGRAPH
- network of power stations and cables for distributing electricity over a wide area GRID
- pipe or channel for electric wires or cables DUCT, CONDUIT
- prevent or reduce the transfer of electricity, sound, or heat INSULATE
- rubbery latex substance used in electrical insulation and dentistry GUTTA-PERCHA
- sudden increase in electric current SURGE
- therapy for treating psychiatric patients, in which an electric shock is administered to the brain ELECTROCONVULSIVE TREATMENT, ECT, ELECTROSHOCK THERAPY, EST

electron - atom or group of atoms having an electric charge through gaining or losing one or more electrons ION

electronics See chart
- electronic keyboard instrument capable of imitating various instruments and producing a wide range of musical sounds MOOG SYNTHESIZER
- electronic keyboard instrument producing eerie musical sounds by means of varying frequencies in an oscillator ONDES MARTENOT
- electronic keyboard instrument using tape loops to imitate various orchestral instruments MELLOTRON

elegant, refined, exquisite, especially in an affected or pretentious way RECHERCHÉ
- elegant, sophisticated, or well-

ELECTRICITY AND ELECTRONICS TERMS *continued*

induction	generation of electric charge or other form of energy in an object, typically by the use of a magnetic field set up by another object nearby
integrated circuit	electronic circuit with components connected in a single small package, as on a silicon chip
inverter	device for converting direct current into alternating current
joule	unit of work or energy
modulation	superimposing or combining of two waves, so that their frequency, amplitude, or the like vary in unison, as for transmitting a sound signal by means of a radio wave, such as frequency modulation (FM)
ohm	unit of resistance
oscilloscope	instrument presenting varying signals in visible form as a graph or trace on the screen of a cathode-ray tube
piezoelectricity	electricity generated by crystals subjected to pressure
polarity	property of having either a positive or negative electric charge
potential difference	energy needed to move a unit quantity of electricity from one point to another
rectifier	device, such as a diode, for converting alternating current into direct current
resistor	component with a known resistance to electric current
rheostat	continuously variable resistor, typically with a sliding contact, used to regulate current, as in a lighting system
semiconductor	solid crystalline substance, such as silicon, with medium conductivity
siemens	unit of electric conductance
solenoid	coil of wire producing a magnetic field when electrically charged, as used for activating switches
solid-state	based on semiconductors or microchips, as many modern appliances are
superconductor	substance that, typically at low temperatures, has almost no electric resistance
transformer	device for changing the voltage of an alternating current without alteration of the frequency
tweeter	loudspeaker in a hi-fi system for reproducing chiefly high-pitched sounds
Van de Graaff generator	generator of high-voltage static electricity that accumulates on a large hollow metal ball
volt	unit of electric potential
watt	unit of power
Wheatstone bridge	instrument used to measure resistance
woofer	loudspeaker for reproducing chiefly low-pitched sounds

Elements

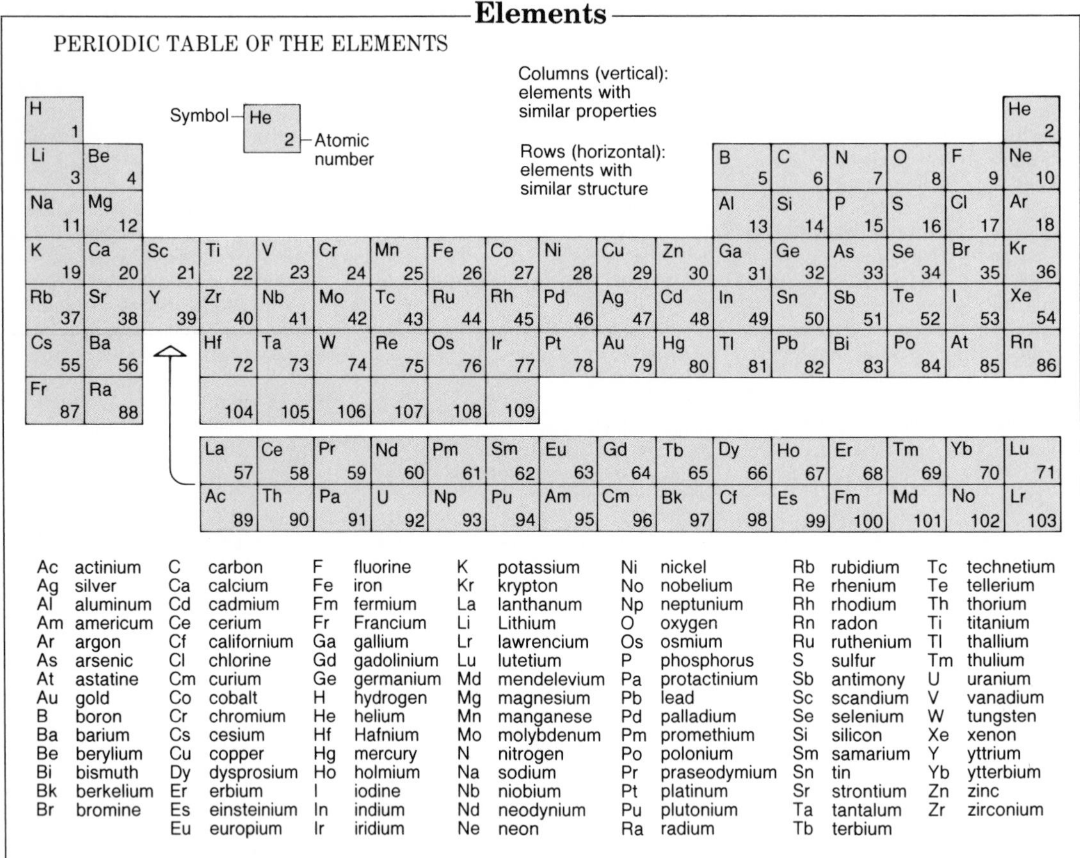

groomed, polished SOIGNÉ
- elegant and concise, as a prose style might be LAPIDARY
- elegant in an affected, over-refined way MINCING
- elegant or refined feature NICETY
- elegant or refined in manner, courtly, polished URBANE, GENTEEL
- luxurious and grand, extravagantly elegant LAVISH, SUMPTUOUS
- majestic, grand, elegantly formal STATELY, STATUESQUE

element See illustration
- element, part of a whole COMPONENT, CONSTITUENT
- element, such as zinc, present in tiny quantities in an organism and essential for its full functioning or development TRACE ELEMENT
- any of the different physical forms, such as crystals, that an element may take ALLOTROPE
- gaseous chemical element, such as helium or neon, formerly considered incapable of chemical reaction INERT GAS, NOBLE GAS, RARE GAS
- table of the chemical elements arranged according to their atomic number and other properties PERIODIC TABLE

elementary, relating to basic knowledge, simple, basic RUDIMENTARY

elephant, hippopotamus, or similar thick-skinned mammal PACHYDERM
- elephant driver and keeper in India or the East Indies MAHOUT
- elephant or wild boar with impressive tusks TUSKER
- elephant's trunk or similar long flexible snout PROBOSCIS
- extinct prehistoric mammal resembling an elephant or mammoth MASTODON
- frenzied sexual excitement in male elephants and other large mammals MUSTH, MUST
- seat with a canopy on an elephant's back HOWDAH

eleven (combining form) HENDECA-

elf or fairy FAY
- mischievous elf, in Irish folklore, typically a cobbler with buried treasure LEPRECHAUN

eliminate, destroy, wipe out, erase EXPUNGE
- eliminate or exclude after careful sorting, sift out WINNOW OUT

elk WAPITI

ellipse - instrument used for drawing ellipses TRAMMEL

elusive or slippery LUBRICOUS
- elusive person or thing WILL-O'-THE-WISP, IGNIS FATUUS

embankment with two faces forming an outward-projecting angle in front of a fortification RAVELIN

embarrass cruelly, shame HUMILIATE, MORTIFY
- embarrass in a humbling or belittling way, put down or degrade DEMEAN, DEFLATE
- embarrass or annoy CHAGRIN, DISCOMFIT
- embarrassed or ashamed ABASHED, DISCOUNTENANCED, OUT OF COUNTENANCE
- embarrassing or awkward situation or occurrence CONTRETEMPS

embassy See also **diplomat**
- diplomatic mission ranking below an embassy in status LEGATION
- political section of an embassy CHANCELLERY, CHANCERY

embezzle, misuse or misappropriate funds DEFALCATE, PECULATE

emblem, symbol, or trademark of a company LOGO
- emblems, badges, or other official distinguishing symbols INSIGNIA

embodied, having bodily or human form INCARNATE
- embodiment or incarnation of an idea or model AVATAR

embrace CLINCH

embroidery See illustration, page 178, and also **sewing**
- embroidery, needlework, or other decoration consisting of different materials pasted or sewn together APPLIQUÉ
- embroidery border adorning clerical vestments ORPHREY
- embroidery frame in the form of two concentric wooden hoops between which the fabric is locked TAMBOUR
- embroidery in which cloth is gathered and stitched into decorative rows SMOCKING
- embroidery in which heavy thread is sewn to a backing with tiny stitches COUCHING
- embroidery of an open pattern done on white cotton or fine linen BRODERIE ANGLAISE
- embroidery or lace edging PURL
- decorative piece of embroidery in which many different stitches are used, often with pictures and mottoes SAMPLER

embryo See **egg, baby**

embryo (combining form) -BLAST-, BLASTO-

emergency, state of urgent need EXIGENCY
- emergency or critical point beyond which a tense situation will erupt into war or violence FLASHPOINT
- adopted temporarily, often as an emergency measure MAKESHIFT, STOPGAP, EXPEDIENT
- provision for some possible though unlikely future occurrence or emergency, as a fund or plan might CONTINGENCY

emotion of great joy, delight ECSTASY, RAPTURE, TRANSPORT
- assigning of human emotions or characteristics to natural or inanimate objects, as in poetic metaphors PATHETIC FALLACY
- express or release an emotion VENT
- range of emotions, musical notes, or other repertoire or series GAMUT
- relating to emotions and their arousal, rather than to thoughts and ideas AFFECTIVE
- showing or feeling no emotion IMPASSIVE
- sudden rush of emotion SURGE
- understanding of another that is so deep that one seems to enter into or share his or her emotions EMPATHY

emotional and intellectual affinity, sympathetic relationship RAPPORT
- emotional and spontaneous rather than rational and deliberate DIONYSIAC, DIONYSIAN
- emotional behavior of a wild, neurotic kind HYSTERIA
- emotional fit or outburst, as of rage PAROXYSM
- emotional in an excessive, theatrical way HISTRIONIC
- emotional or nervous disorder, revealed in phobias, obsessions, or the like, that induces anxiety and is mildly disabling NEUROSIS
- emotional or sentimental when drunk MAUDLIN
- emotional outpouring in speech or writing EFFUSION
- emotional poetry, rather than dramatic or narrative poetry LYRIC POETRY
- emotional purification through pity and fear, as when watching a tragic drama CATHARSIS
- emotional reaction of an exaggerated kind to a situation MELODRAMA
- emotional shock, typically having long-lasting psychological effects TRAUMA
- emotionally affecting or distressing POIGNANT
- emotionally charged speech or writing, as in a tribute or literary work RHAPSODY
- emotionally detached and unbiased DISPASSIONATE, OBJECTIVE
- emotionally insecure, oversensitive VULNERABLE
- emotionally sensitive, easily affected SUSCEPTIBLE
- emotionally upset or extremely agitated DISTRAUGHT
- excessively excited, strained, or emotionally worked up OVERWROUGHT
- excessively or unrestrainedly emotional GUSHING, EFFUSIVE
- openly emotional, expressing one's feelings readily DEMONSTRATIVE

emotional state (combining form) -THYMIA

emperor of Germany in former times, or of the Holy Roman Empire KAISER
- emperor of Japan MIKADO, TENNO
- emperor of Russia in former times CZAR, TSAR
- like an emperor IMPERIAL

emphasis through contrast, as of color or shading RELIEF

emphasize, stress, or intensify, draw attention to something emphatically ACCENTUATE, UNDERSCORE
- emphasize a point by constantly repeating it, dwell on, hammer home BELABOR
- emphasize or bring to people's attention HIGHLIGHT

emphatic, passionate, or intense VEHEMENT
- emphatically and unmistakably noticeable, bold or striking PROMINENT, CONSPICUOUS, SALIENT, GLARING
- state emphatically ASSEVERATE

empire See chart at **dynasty**
- adjective for an empire or emperor IMPERIAL

employ more workers than needed, as under a union rule or safety statute FEATHERBED

employee in a large organization, underling MINION
- employee or assistant doing a variety of work FACTOTUM
- employee's extra benefit, in addition to his wages or salary FRINGE BENEFIT
- reduction in the number of employees through redundancy RETRENCHMENT
- reduction in the number of employees through retirement or resignation ATTRITION

empty, clear out, remove the contents or air from EVACUATE, VOID
- empty space, emptiness VOID, VACUITY

enamel or glossy black lacquer JAPAN
- technique or style of enameling different colored panels between strips of metal, or enamelware made in this way CLOISONNÉ
- enameled, glazed pottery, brightly decorated, of a 16th-century Italian style MAJOLICA
- silver or other metal ornament or object decorated by the insertion of colored enamel into cut grooves CHAMPLEVÉ

encircling a body part, as nerves, blood vessels, or the like are CORONARY

enclosed building or grounds, as of a church PRECINCT

encourage, give renewed cheer to HEARTEN, REASSURE, BUOY UP
- encourage, help forward, or cultivate something, such as someone's career FOSTER, ADVANCE, NURTURE
- encourage, revive, inspire with renewed strength or determination ANIMATE, EMBOLDEN, INSPIRIT, INVIGORATE
- encourage, support, or give approval for COUNTENANCE, SANCTION, ENDORSE
- encourage or assist, especially in some wrongdoing, be an accessory to ABET, CONNIVE
- encourage or support a cause AD-

VOCATE, CHAMPION, PROMOTE
- encourage strongly or appeal to urgently EXHORT

encouragement, influence, goad or spur to action INCENTIVE, INDUCEMENT, INCITEMENT, MOTIVATION, STIMULUS
- encouragement of a wrongful act, such as one's spouse's adultery, by ignoring it CONNIVANCE
- encouragement or active support PATRONAGE, CHAMPIONSHIP

encouraging, urging HORTATORY, HORTATIVE

encroach or trespass on INFRINGE

end See also **stop**
- end, edge, farthest point or part EXTREMITY
- end, last part or element of something OMEGA
- end, run out, cease to be effective EXPIRE
- end in a climax, reach a conclusion CULMINATE
- end or conclude something successfully, such as a conflict RESOLVE
- end or crush something firmly, such as a rumor or rebellion SCOTCH, QUASH
- ending of a play with the unwinding or solution of the plot DENOUEMENT
- ending or failure DEMISE
- ending that fails ludicrously after a promising start ANTICLIMAX, BATHOS
- add or attach at the end APPEND, SUFFIX, ANNEX
- complete successfully, reach the end of, fulfill ACCOMPLISH, CONSUMMATE, CROWN
- directed or tending toward a specific end or purpose TELIC

end, purpose (combining form) TEL-, TELE-

end, tip (combining form) ACRO-

end of the world - branch of theology dealing with the end of the world ESCHATOLOGY
- relating to, prophesying, resembling, or suggesting the end of the world APOCALYPTIC
- setting of the final battle between the forces of good and evil that will herald, according to the Bible, the end of the world ARMAGEDDON

endanger, put at risk IMPERIL, JEOPARDIZE

endless, tediously long INTERMINABLE

endurance, capacity of enduring or withstanding something unpleasant TOLERANCE
- powers of endurance, staying power STAMINA

endure, survive a crisis, danger, or the like WEATHER

enema for washing out the bowels COLONIC
- former term for an enema CLYSTER

enemy, opponent, or rival ADVERSARY, ANTAGONIST
- enemy territory secured by advance troops as a foothold or protection for the main attacking force BRIDGEHEAD, BEACHHEAD, SALIENT
- enemy within, hostile or subversive element within a country at war or an organization FIFTH COLUMN, TROJAN HORSE
- adjective for an enemy INIMICAL
- barrier of buffer states guarding a country from potential enemy at-

Embroidery Stitches

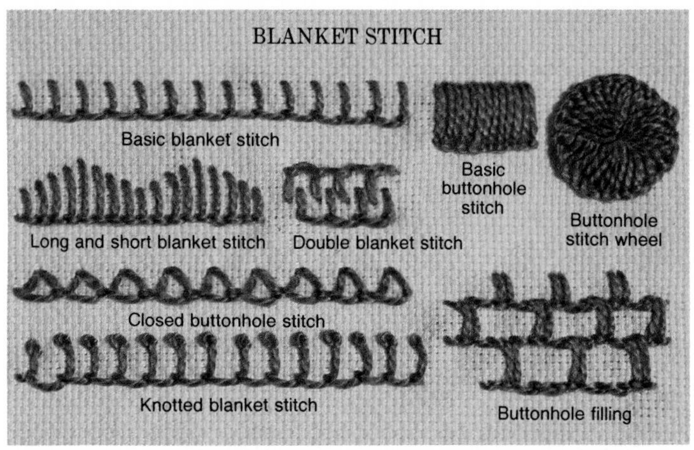

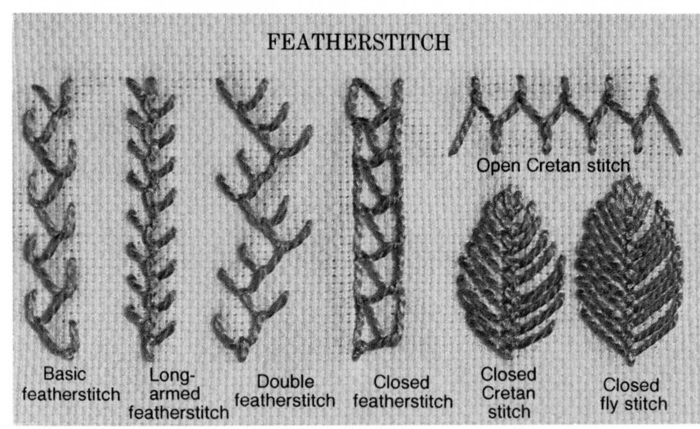

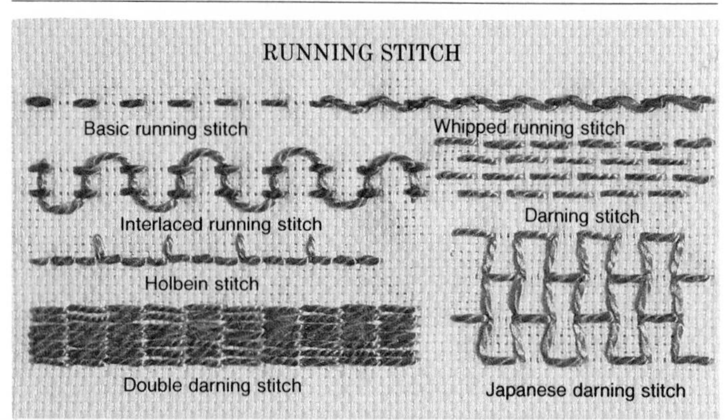

tack CORDON SANITAIRE
- distraction or deception of an enemy, such as a pretended attack DIVERSION, DECOY
- mixing socially with the people of an occupied or enemy country FRATERNIZATION
- policy of agreeing to the demands of a potential enemy for the sake of maintaining peace APPEASEMENT
- preventing of enemy forces or nations from extending their territory or influence CONTAINMENT
- victor's decree or settlement imposed on a defeated enemy DIKTAT

energetic See also **enthusiastic**
- energetic, forceful, vigorous VITAL, VIBRANT, VIRILE
- energetic, hardworking, or forceful person DYNAMO
- energetic, inspiring, and emotional person FIREBALL, FIREBRAND
- energetic and passionate in a creative way DIONYSIAC, DIONYSIAN
- energetic or vigorous, even though elderly SPRY, SPRIGHTLY
- energetic resourcefulness, enterprise INITIATIVE

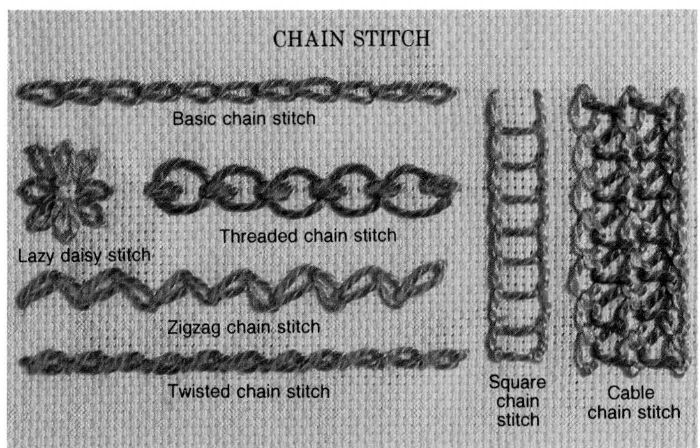

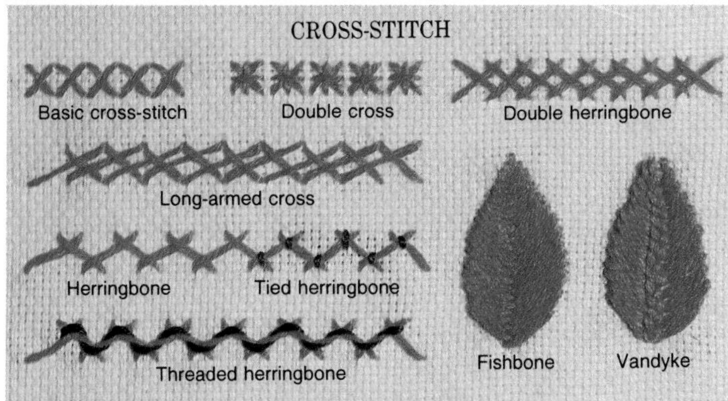

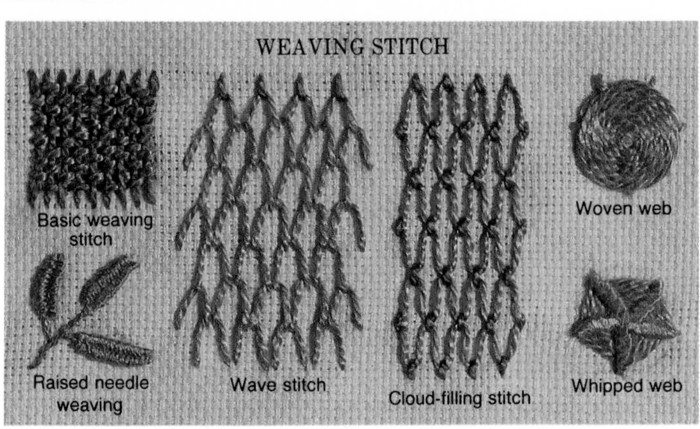

energy See also **enthusiasm**
- energy, vigor, verve, zest ÉLAN, BRIO, VITALITY, PIZZAZZ
- energy of a system or body based on its actual motion KINETIC ENERGY
- energy of a system or body based on its position rather than its motion POTENTIAL ENERGY
- energy or divine spirit supposedly inhabiting and guiding a person NUMEN
- energy or powers of endurance enabling one to resist fatigue or hardship STAMINA
- energy released in a nuclear explosion, expressed in terms of weight of TNT YIELD
- energy unit of the smallest possible size in physics QUANTUM
- channel or transform a sexual impulse or other instinctual energy into a socially or culturally more acceptable activity SUBLIMATE
- control or direct energy HARNESS
- focusing of psychic or emotional energy on a person, thing, or idea CATHEXIS
- means of displaying or releasing one's talents, energies, or creative ability OUTLET
- referring to an energy source considered never-ending RENEWABLE
- referring to energy derived from heat in the earth's interior GEOTHERMAL
- requiring or involving great effort or energy STRENUOUS
- running down of the energy in the universe or any other closed system ENTROPY

engaged to be married BETROTHED, AFFIANCED

engine See chart, page 180, and also **car, motor, jet engine,** and illustration at **internal-combustion engine**
- engine, usually detachable, fitted externally at the stern of a boat OUTBOARD MOTOR
- engine valve regulating the flow of steam or vaporized fuel to the cylinders THROTTLE
- chamber in which vaporized fuel burns, as in the cylinders of an in-

ternal-combustion engine COMBUSTION CHAMBER
- clean an engine of its carbon deposits DECARBONIZE, DECARBURIZE
- cooling system, as in a car engine, through which water or other coolant flows RADIATOR
- device for conveying electric current to the spark plugs in an engine DISTRIBUTOR
- device in the exhaust of an engine, as in a car, for burning off or neutralizing harmful fumes AFTERBURNER
- electrical coil used as a relay or

ENGINES AND MOTORS

aeolipile	ancient steam engine or simple turbine, consisting of a rotating metal sphere powered by exhaust jets
beam engine	large early steam engine in which a beam or lever transferred the motion from piston rod to crankshaft, as used for pumping out mines
booster	engine or rocket that supplements the main power system of a jet or spacecraft, often as the first stage of a multistage rocket
bypass engine	jet engine or gas turbine in which some of the compressed air is diverted around the combustion zone to join the exhaust gases directly for extra thrust
donkey engine	small auxiliary steam engine used for hoisting or pumping
fuel-injection engine	internal-combustion engine with a system for spraying vaporized fuel into the cylinders without carburetors
induction motor	electric motor whose rotation is induced by the interaction of magnetic fields
internal-combustion engine	standard modern engine in which the fuel is burned internally, rather than externally as in a steam engine
ion engine/ion rocket	rocket engine producing thrust by expelling a high-speed beam of ions
Lenoir's engine	first successful gas-fired, two-stroke internal-combustion engine, built in 1860
Newcomen atmospheric engine	early beam engine, invented in 1712
plasma engine	hypothetical engine for use in space, producing thrust by expelling a jet of plasma—or highly ionized gas
radial engine	internal-combustion engine with cylinders arranged around the crankshaft like the spokes of a wheel, as formerly used in propeller-driven aircraft
ramjet/athodyd	jet engine with a special duct for air intake and compression, operating only at speed
retrorocket	rocket engine for braking or reversing
sustainer	small rocket motor that sustains the speed of a spacecraft after the booster is jettisoned
synchronous motor	electric motor with a speed directly proportional to the frequency of the current driving it
thermomotor	engine operated by the expansion of heated gas
thruster	small rocket engine for controlling altitude in a spacecraft or aircraft
turbine	rotary engine with a vaned shaft rotated by the pressure of steam, water, exhaust gases, or the like
turbojet	jet engine with a turbine-powered compressor feeding compressed air to the combustion chamber
turboprop/prop-jet	turbojet engine used to drive an external propeller
V-engine	engine with cylinders arranged in the shape of a V
vernier rocket/vernier engine	small secondary rocket engine used for making fine adjustments in speed or direction
Wankel engine	internal-combustion engine without pistons, having a triangular rotor forming combustion chambers as it turns

switch connecting the battery to the starter motor of an engine SOLENOID
- electrical contact, as in the distributor of a car engine POINTS
- fan or compressor used to increase the air intake in an internal-combustion engine SUPERCHARGER, BOOSTER, BLOWER
- make sharp popping noises, as a poorly tuned engine might KNOCK
- smooth worn-out engine cylinders by drilling, and fit slightly larger pistons REBORE
- start an engine, as of an early car, by vigorously turning a handle inserted into it CRANK
- system for setting the vaporized fuel burning in an internal-combustion engine IGNITION

engineering - application of biology to engineering and electronics, especially of brain functions to computers BIONICS
- deliberate modification or engineering of the gene structure, as in breeding improved plant or animal strains GENETIC ENGINEERING
- study or application of biology and engineering in work and the workplace ERGONOMICS, BIOTECHNOLOGY

England - area in northeast England under Danish law in Anglo-Saxon times DANELAW
- former or literary name for England ANGLIA
- poetic or old-fashioned term for Britain or England ALBION

English of a plain, straightforward, blunt kind, sometimes using swear words ANGLO-SAXON
- English of a simplified spoken form, including elements from other languages, used for basic communication PIDGIN ENGLISH
- English-speaking ANGLOPHONE
- English word, phrase, or idiom occurring in another language ANGLICISM
- in English, translated into English ANGLICE
- make English in style, form, or the like ANGLICIZE

English (combining form) ANGLO-

engraving in relief, typically with the raised design of a different color from the background CAMEO
- engraving or etching with a sharp pointed instrument STYLOGRAPHY
- engraving or incising to produce a sunken rather than raised design, as for a signet ring INTAGLIO
- engraver's style or technique, or sharp chisellike tool used in engraving BURIN
- decorate metal by engraving or embossing CHASE, ENCHASE
- relating to carving or engraving, especially on gemstones GLYPTIC

enjoy greatly, take pleasure in, delight in RELISH
- enjoy in an appreciative or leisurely way SAVOR

enjoyable, delightful, or delicious DELECTABLE
- enjoyable, pleasing, satisfying GRATIFYING

enjoyment, delight, great pleasure DELECTATION
- enjoyment, zest, or vitality GUSTO
- enjoyment of life JOIE DE VIVRE
- enjoyment or merrymaking of a wild uninhibited kind HILARITY

enlarge See **increase**

enlightened people ILLUMINATI

enlightenment, in Buddhism or Hinduism NIRVANA

enliven, give life or liveliness to ANIMATE, VIVIFY

enormous See **huge**

enslavement, slavery THRALL, THRALDOM

enter a town, country, or the like to conquer it INVADE
- enter gradually or penetrate secretly an enemy country or territory, criminal organization, or the like INFILTRATE
- enter illegally or unwarrantedly ENCROACH, TRESPASS, IMPINGE, INFRINGE, INTRUDE
- enter suddenly and violently, burst in IRRUPT

enterprise, adventure, or project EXPLOIT, UNDERTAKING
- enterprise, energetic resourcefulness INITIATIVE
- enterprise, initiative, pluck GUMPTION
- enterprising businessman undertaking new and risky ventures ENTREPRENEUR

entertain or give pleasure to, as by telling stories REGALE
- entertaining, amusing, or distracting DIVERTING

entertainer, as at an amusement park, who bites off the head of a live frog, mouse, chicken, snake, or the like GEEK
- entertainer or acrobat who twists his or her limbs and body into abnormal positions CONTORTIONIST
- entertainer who breaks free from chains, escapes from locked boxes, and the like ESCAPOLOGIST
- entertainer who "throws his voice," giving the impression that it originates elsewhere, especially in a dummy VENTRILOQUIST
- entertainers in a group, especially a touring group TROUPE

entertainment, literary work, or the like that is elaborate, fanciful, or spectacular EXTRAVAGANZA
- entertainment given at night, typically outdoors, using sound and light effects in presenting the history of the site SON-ET-LUMIÈRE
- entertainment hall, athletics or sports stadium, large arena, or the like COLISEUM
- entertainment on stage during the interval of an opera or play DIVERTISSEMENT

enthusiasm combined with style and vigor, zest, flair ÉLAN, VIVACITY, BRIO
- enthusiasm of a passionate, burning kind ARDOR, FERVOR
- enthusiasm or devotion that is extreme and often excessive or irrational FANATICISM
- arouse or inspire passion, enthusiasm, or the like KINDLE

enthusiastic See also **emotional**
- enthusiastic, extremely keen and devoted AVID, ARDENT, FERVENT, PERFERVID
- enthusiastic, loyal, or dutiful to an excessive, foolish, or dangerous degree GUNG HO
- enthusiastic enjoyment or vitality GUSTO
- extremely enthusiastic and zealous in promoting a cause EVANGELISTIC
- extremely enthusiastic or excited, full of high spirits EXUBERANT, EBULLIENT, EFFERVESCENT
- passionately enthusiastic, highly delighted, ecstatic RHAPSODIC

entice, lure, or incite, especially into a sinful or illegal act SOLICIT

entire, whole INTEGRAL

entirely (combining form) PAN-

entrails See also **digestion**
- entrails, internal bodily organs VISCERA, INNARDS
- entrails of a chicken or other fowl GIBLETS
- entrails of a deer as formerly used for food NUMBLES, UMBLES
- priest in ancient Rome who looked into the future by inspecting animals' entrails HARUSPEX

entrance, right to enter, or means of entering ACCESS, INGRESS
- entrance hall, waiting room, or reception area FOYER, LOBBY
- entrance hall or room leading into a larger room ANTECHAMBER, VESTIBULE, ANTEROOM
- entrance or doorway THRESHOLD
- entrance stairway or porch at a house door STOOP
- entrance to a building, with a roof often supported by columns PORTICO

- entrance to or porch of a temple PROPYLAEUM
- canopy marking the entrance to a theater, club, or the like MARQUEE
- outside stairway or platform at the entrance of a building PERRON

entry, admittance, right of access ENTRÉE
- certain means of gaining entry or success OPEN SESAME
- impossible to capture or enter forcibly, as a castle might be IMPREGNABLE

envelop, wrap closely, as in furs SWATHE

environment, network, or context in which something develops MATRIX
- environment for an animal or plant HABITAT
- environment or surroundings MILIEU, AMBIENCE
- adjust to a new environment ACCLIMATIZE
- capable of living under more than one set of environmental conditions, as some microorganisms are FACULTATIVE
- characteristics transmitted by genetic means as opposed to those arising from environmental influences HEREDITY
- environmental influences on the development of an organism, as distinguished from genetic influences NURTURE
- having lost one's bearings, as when in an unfamiliar environment DISORIENTED, DISORIENTATED
- protection and preservation of the natural environment CONSERVATION
- relationship between people, plants, or animals and their environment ECOLOGY
- theory, opposed by strict Darwinian ideas of evolution, that new characteristics produced environmentally can be inherited LAMARCKISM, LYSENKOISM

environment (combining form) ECO-

envy and desire to own something owned by someone else COVET
- envy someone for his or her possessions, or envy the possessions BEGRUDGE

enzyme (combining form) -ASE

epic poem, or part of one used for recitation, in ancient Greece RHAPSODY

epidemic and deadly disease, especially bubonic plague PESTILENCE
- epidemic over a very wide area PANDEMIC

epilepsy or epileptic fit of a severe kind GRAND MAL
- epilepsy or epileptic fit of a mild kind PETIT MAL
- noise, flashing of light, or other sensation occurring just before an attack of epilepsy or severe migraine AURA

episode of a serial INSTALLMENT
- dramatic situation at the end of an episode of a serialized movie, radio or television play, or the like CLIFFHANGER

epitaph - "in memory of," as used in epitaphs IN MEMORIAM

equal, person having the same status or ability as another person PEER, COMPEER
- equal in size, range, or duration COMMENSURATE, COTERMINOUS, COEXTENSIVE
- equal in value or effect, amounting to, equivalent TANTAMOUNT, CONSTITUTING
- "equal quantities of," referring to ingredients in a prescription ANA
- equality or equivalence, as of amount or status PARITY
- relating to or supporting equality, as of political and legal rights EGALITARIAN
- make or treat as equal or equivalent EQUATE

equal (combining form) EQUI-, IS-, ISO-

equation containing an unknown term raised to the power of two QUADRATIC EQUATION

equipment, buildings, and other provisions for an activity FACILITIES
- equipment, clothing, or other distinctive trappings ACCOUTREMENTS
- equipment, furniture, or fittings APPOINTMENTS
- equipment or machinery for a specified purpose, as for drilling or for extracting oil from a well RIG
- equipment or gear needed for an activity PARAPHERNALIA, APPURTENANCES
- equipment or requirements for effectiveness in one's profession or pursuits STOCK-IN-TRADE
- referring to teaching aids or equipment, such as films, that conveys information to both hearing and sight AUDIOVISUAL

equipped properly, well-furnished WELL-APPOINTED

equivalence, idea of balance or equality EQUATION
- correspondence, equivalence, or identity between systems or parts of a system SYMMETRY

equivalent, equal in value or effect, amounting to TANTAMOUNT
- equivalent or corresponding person in another team, organization, or group COUNTERPART, OPPOSITE NUMBER
- item or favor of equivalent value given in exchange or compensation for another QUID PRO QUO

era, historical period EPOCH

erase, rub out, wipe out permanently EFFACE, EXPUNGE
- erase words, computer data, tape recordings, or the like DELETE

erosion - area badly eroded into ridges and gullies BADLANDS
- low wall or fence jutting into the sea to control erosion of a beach GROYNE

erratic or peculiar action or notion WHIM, CAPRICE, VAGARY

erring, liable to err FALLIBLE

error See also **mistake**
- error based on the apparent change in the position of an object when the observer changes position PARALLAX ERROR
- error-free, perfect IMMACULATE, IMPECCABLE
- error in logic or reasoning that invalidates the conclusion FALLACY
- error in printing, typing, or writing TYPOGRAPHICAL ERROR, TYPO
- error of grammar or pronunciation, such as *between you and I*, produced by avoiding an imaginary error HYPERCORRECTION
- error or variation in a measurement, judgment, or the like because of human differences or prejudices PERSONAL EQUATION
- errors and corrections in a book, as listed on an inserted sheet of paper CORRIGENDA, ERRATA
- add to or aggravate an error or difficulty COMPOUND
- glaringly or offensively obvious, as a lie or error might be BLATANT
- supposed source of problems, errors, or mischief GREMLIN

escalator - escalatorlike device, consisting of a horizontal rotating belt on corridor floors, for transporting pedestrians MOVING SIDEWALK, TRAVELATOR, WALKWAY

escape See also **depart**
- escape or avoid capture, hunters, or the like, especially by cunning ELUDE, EVADE, BILK
- escaped or fleeing criminal, runaway FUGITIVE
- entertainer who breaks free from chains, escapes from locked boxes, and the like ESCAPOLOGIST
- means of escape, way out of a difficult situation BOLT-HOLE
- person who escapes from war or suppression REFUGEE

escapist or sheltered intellectual retreat from everyday life, as a university is sometimes considered to be IVORY TOWER

escort, accompany troops, ships, or vehicles for protection CONVOY

- escort, gentlemanly companion GALLANT, CAVALIER
- escort, guide, or attendant, especially when riding a horse or motorcycle OUTRIDER
- escort, lead, or conduct USHER
- escort or companion for someone, especially a young unmarried woman, for protection and propriety CHAPERON, DUENNA
- escort ship CONSORT
- escort typically paid for by an older woman GIGOLO

Eskimo INUIT
- Eskimo boat made of animal skins over a wooden frame UMIAK
- Eskimo boot of sealskin or reindeer hide MUKLUK
- Eskimo canoe KAYAK
- Eskimo from the islands off Alaska ALEUT
- Eskimo sledge dog HUSKY, MALAMUTE
- Eskimo's ice house IGLOO

especially, extremely, clearly, remarkably SIGNALLY, EMINENTLY, CONSPICUOUSLY

essays and poetry considered as art rather than for their educational or moral value BELLES LETTRES
- volume of essays by academics or scholars compiled as a tribute to a learned colleague FESTSCHRIFT

essence, embodiment, typical or perfect example of its kind EPITOME, PERSONIFICATION
- essence, foundation, underlying principle SUBSTRATUM, ANLAGE
- essence, fundamental factor, starting point BEDROCK
- essence, or concentrated or pure form of something DISTILLATE
- essence of a speech, plot, or argument, crux, nub, gist TENOR, BURDEN, GRAVAMEN
- essence or basic nature of something HYPOSTASIS, QUINTESSENCE, ELIXIR, QUIDDITY
- essence produced by boiling down a liquid DECOCTION

essential, basic, underlying, fundamental CONSTITUTIVE, SUBSTANTIVE
- essential, inseparable, forming a vital constituent INTEGRAL, INTRINSIC, INHERENT
- essential, required by law or demanded by custom COMPULSORY, STATUTORY, MANDATORY, DE RIGUEUR
- essential as a duty, inescapable, binding INCUMBENT, OBLIGATORY, IMPERATIVE, IRREMISSIBLE
- essential details, basic facts, the quick or core, brass tacks NITTY-GRITTY
- essential element, core, gist PITH
- essential or central component or participant LINCHPIN, CORNERSTONE, ALPHA AND OMEGA
- essential or primary, of basic or underlying importance RUDIMENTARY, PRIMORDIAL
- essential or vital, impossible to leave out, absolutely necessary INDISPENSABLE
- essential thing or condition, a factor without which something cannot occur PREREQUISITE, SINE QUA NON

establish the answer, as by calculating DETERMINE
- establish an argument on certain facts or suppositions PREDICATE

established, firm, inherent, underlying SUBSTANTIVE
- established, fixed, firmly and immovably settled, as opinions or troops might be ENTRENCHED
- established or settled firmly or securely in position ENSCONCED
- person or thing long established and regarded as permanent in a given place or position FIXTURE

estate See also **land, property**
- estate, domain, or house of a feudal lord MANOR
- estate or large landed property DEMESNE
- estate or plantation of a Spanish type HACIENDA
- estate owner in Scotland LAIRD
- estate returning to a lessor or grantor after the agreed term, or the right to this estate REVERSION
- estate that cannot be disposed of except for a permitted period, or this limitation on it PERPETUITY
- agent legally entitled to control or administer the estate or other property of someone else TRUSTEE
- agent who runs a landowner's estate STEWARD, BAILIFF
- large landed estate, especially in Latin America or ancient Rome LATIFUNDIUM
- limit the inheritance of an estate to a particular line of heirs ENTAIL

estimate of costs or prices, as for a building job QUOTATION
- estimate or assess the value of EVALUATE, APPRAISE, ASSAY
- rough estimate or calculation APPROXIMATION

etch or inlay metal bearing wavy decorative patterns DAMASCENE, DAMASK
- etching or engraving with a sharp pointed instrument STYLOGRAPHY
- etching technique producing varied tones, or an etching produced by this technique AQUATINT

eternal See also **permanent, constant**
- eternal damnation, hell PERDITION

eternity, endlessness PERPETUITY

ethics - relating to rights, duties, and similar ethical concepts DEONTIC

etiquette - code of behavior, especially among diplomats or rulers PROTOCOL
- mistake or improper usage, especially in grammar or etiquette SOLECISM
- overfussy detail, as of etiquette or protocol PUNCTILIO

Eucharist See **Communion**

euphemism - unpleasant or offensive word or phrase substituted for a neutral or favorable one, the reverse of a euphemism DYSPHEMISM

Europe and America, and the West in general OCCIDENT

European woman in India, especially the wife of a British official during the Raj MEMSAHIB

euthanasia in the form of withholding treatment that would prolong the patient's life PASSIVE EUTHANASIA

evaporating readily at normal temperatures and pressure VOLATILE
- thicken or condense, as by boiling or evaporating INSPISSATE

evasive, avoiding indicating any definite preference or purpose, as by a cautious reply NONCOMMITTAL
- evasiveness, shiftiness, or ambiguous speech or behavior, as to gain time EQUIVOCATION, TEMPORIZING, TERGIVERSATION, PREVARICATION

even temper, psychological stability EQUILIBRIUM, EQUANIMITY

even-tempered See **calm**

evening party or reception SOIREE
- evening prayers VESPERS, COMPLINE, VIGILS
- love song, typically sung outside a woman's house in the evening SERENADE
- relating to, appearing in, or occurring in the evening VESPERTINE, CREPUSCULAR

event marking an important stage in history or in one's life MILESTONE, LANDMARK
- projected or possible chain of events SCENARIO

everybody agreeing, of one mind, as in a vote UNANIMOUS

evergreen See illustration, page 185
- cone-bearing tree, such as a pine or fir CONIFER

everlasting, permanent, perpetual PERENNIAL
- everlasting plant, which keeps its color when dried IMMORTELLE

everyday, uninspired, ordinary, commonplace HUMDRUM, MUNDANE, PEDESTRIAN, BANAL, TRITE
- everyday speech of the people VERNACULAR, VULGATE, DEMOTIC

everything (combining form) PAN-, PANTO-
everywhere, at any one time UBIQUITOUS, OMNIPRESENT
everywhere (combining form) OMNI-
evidence, often relating to medical or scientific facts, used in legal cases FORENSIC EVIDENCE
- evidence, proof, demonstration TESTIMONY, TESTAMENT
- evidence based on what others have said HEARSAY
- evidence given on oath DEPOSITION
- evidence or indication of a disease, social condition, or the like SIGN, SYMPTOM
- evidence that is indirect, requiring an inference rather than relating directly to the case CIRCUMSTANTIAL EVIDENCE
- evidence that would be considered strong or reliable unless challenged PRIMA-FACIE EVIDENCE
- alter a document, accounts, evidence, or the like in order to deceive FALSIFY
- clearly understandable, substantial, as concrete evidence is TANGIBLE, SUBSTANTIVE
- confirm or back up an opinion or statement, as with additional evidence CORROBORATE, SUBSTANTIATE
- deliberate giving of false evidence by a witness under oath PERJURY
- document, weapon, or other object formally used as evidence in court EXHIBIT
- from a different source, from somewhere else, as evidence might be ALIUNDE
- give evidence of or a reference for, bear witness to ATTEST, TESTIFY
- indisputable, undeniable, certain, as an overwhelmingly powerful argument or piece of evidence would be INCONTROVERTIBLE
- record or report in detail, and support with evidence DOCUMENT
- supporting, as evidence might be CORROBORATIVE, COLLATERAL
evil See also **immoral**
- evil, decay, or corruption, especially when spreading rampantly CANKER
- evil, wicked, infamous, as a sinful plot or notorious murderer is NEFARIOUS
- evil, wickedness, baseness, sinfulness INIQUITY, DEPRAVITY, TURPITUDE
- evil in influence or effect, or foreshadowing evil BALEFUL
- evil or evil deed, outrage, monstrous act ENORMITY
- evil or harmful in intention or influence MALEVOLENT, MALICIOUS, MALIGN, MALEFICENT, MALIGNANT, PERNICIOUS
- anxiety, feeling that evil or disaster is to come FOREBODING
- designed to ward off evil, as a ritual ceremony might be APOTROPAIC
- extremely evil, shockingly wicked, vile INFAMOUS, HEINOUS, FLAGITIOUS
evil spirit reputed to have sex with a sleeping man SUCCUBUS
- evil spirit reputed to have sex with a sleeping woman INCUBUS
- drive out an evil spirit, or free a possessed person from evil spirits, as by religious rites EXORCISE
- person supposedly possessed by an evil spirit DEMONIAC, ENERGUMEN
evolution of a species into several different species adapted to different environments ADAPTIVE RADIATION
- evolution or development of a species, genus, race, or the like PHYLOGENY
- evolution or development of an individual ONTOGENY
- theory, opposed by strict Darwinian ideas of evolution, that acquired characteristics can be inherited LAMARCKISM, LYSENKOISM
- theory or classification system based on the view that shared characteristics indicate species' evolution from a common ancestor CLADISTICS
exact See also **precise**
- exact description, list of details, plan, or proposal SPECIFICATION, SPECS
- contained an exact number of times in a larger quantity, as a fraction or part might be ALIQUOT
exaggerate, improve, or enliven a report or story by adding colorful details EMBELLISH, EMBROIDER
- exaggerate one's illness, as to get off work MALINGER
- exaggerated, overstated, or theatrical, as a display of a person's emotions might be HISTRIONIC, MELODRAMATIC
- exaggerated or affected habit or trait IDIOSYNCRASY, ECCENTRICITY, ABERRATION, MANNERISM
- exaggeration AGGRANDIZEMENT, HYPERBOLE
exalted, awe-inspiring SUBLIME
examination in the form of an interview rather than written answers ORAL, VIVA VOCE
- examination of a dead body, usually to establish the cause of death POSTMORTEM, AUTOPSY, NECROPSY
- examination of one's feelings or motives SOUL-SEARCHING, HEART-SEARCHING, INTROSPECTION
- examination of tissue from a living body, used in diagnosing disease BIOPSY
- examination or instruction book, particularly one on the basic principles of Christianity CATECHISM
- examination or investigation, such as a judicial inquiry, into a matter of concern INQUISITION
- certificate, pass, or degree awarded when a university student misses part of an examination through illness AEGROTAT
- instructions printed at the head of an examination paper RUBRIC
- outline of a course of study or examination requirements SYLLABUS, CURRICULUM
- study intensely at the last minute for an examination CRAM
- supervise and keep watch over students at an examination MONITOR, PROCTOR, INVIGILATE
examination (combining form) -OPSY
examine See also **test**
- examine accounts, claims, or records as to correct or approve them AUDIT
- examine by touching for the purpose of a preliminary medical diagnosis PALPATE
- examine in order to sort the good from the bad, sift through WINNOW
- examine or analyze in fine detail DISSECT, ANATOMIZE
- examine or investigate thoroughly, probe PLUMB
- examine or question intensely INTERROGATE, CROSS-EXAMINE
- examine or study in detail, pore over PERUSE, SCRUTINIZE, TRAVERSE
- examine something to assess its value or quality ASSESS, APPRAISE
example, or perfect or typical representative or embodiment, of an idea or ideal EXEMPLAR, ARCHETYPE, AVATAR, EPITOME, PERSONIFICATION, INCARNATION, TYPE
- example, typical or representative, of a class or quality BYWORD
- example from a classic or standard text that is considered authoritative LOCUS CLASSICUS
- example or model serving as a standard for others PARADIGM
- action or decision used as an example or justification when treating later cases similarly PRECEDENT
- be a typical example or symbol of, exemplify EMBODY, EPITOMIZE, TYPIFY
- produce or cite an example, argument, or reason as evidence or proof ADDUCE
- serve as an example of, or demonstrate by example EXEMPLIFY
- "that is", "namely", term introducing examples VIDELICET, VIZ

Evergreens

DIFFERENT WAYS OF IDENTIFYING CONIFERS

Telling one conifer from another is simply a matter of narrowing down the many possibilities. First decide whether or not a particular tree is indeed a conifer. All conifers have needle-shaped or scalelike leaves. Look at the needles to discover the major group (such as a pine). Tree shape may provide some clues. A cone by itself, away from the tree that produced it, is often difficult to identify as to species.

GUIDE TO NEEDLES OR SCALES

Needles are the easiest way to identify a conifer. Compare them with the ones shown here, which represent the major groups. A field guide will help you to determine the precise species.

LARCHES
(Tamarack)

Larches have bristling clusters of 12 to 20 short needles, which fall from the tree in autumn.

PINES
(Scotch pine)

All pines grow needles in bundles, wrapped together at the base. Some kinds have two needles per group, other species have more.

FIRS
(Balsam fir)

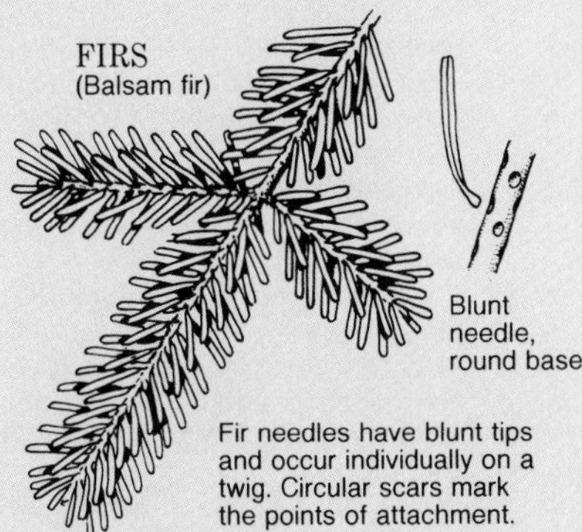

Fir needles have blunt tips and occur individually on a twig. Circular scars mark the points of attachment.

SPRUCES
(Norway spruce)

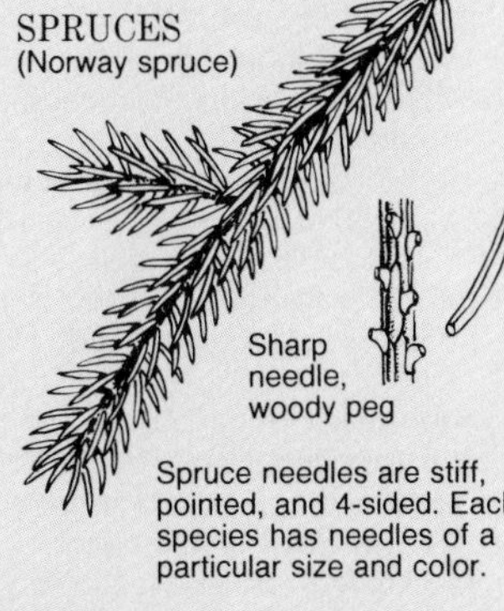

Spruce needles are stiff, pointed, and 4-sided. Each species has needles of a particular size and color.

CEDARS AND JUNIPERS
(Northern white cedar)

Small, flat, and scalelike leaves (not the needles of other conifers) make cedars and junipers distinctive.

HEMLOCKS
(Eastern hemlock)

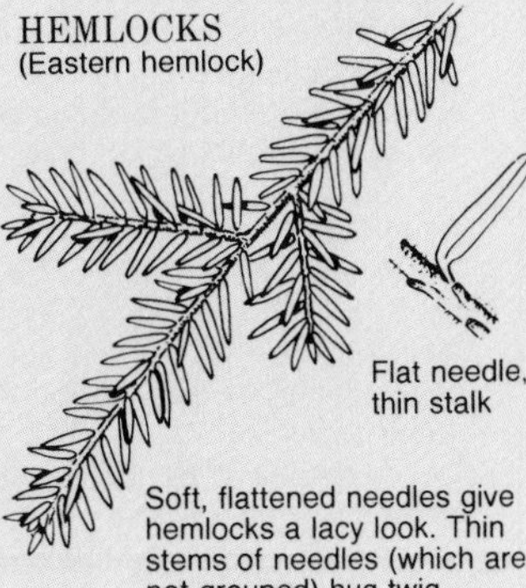

Soft, flattened needles give hemlocks a lacy look. Thin stems of needles (which are not grouped) hug twig.

THE SHAPE OF A CONIFER

Experts can often identify conifers, such as spruces, by shape—the density and arrangement of branches. But individual trees vary greatly. For beginners, shape may be less helpful than needles in tree identification.

CONES CONFIRM A TREE'S IDENTITY

Each kind of conifer produces cones of a unique size and shape. The selection of cones below shows the tremendous diversity within one group—the pines. The cones have been drawn to scale, each at about half its natural size.

Knobcone pine

Shortleaf pine

exceed, as in quantity or degree SURPASS, PREPONDERATE
exceeding (combining form) SUPER-, ULTRA-, TRANS-
excellent See also **perfect**
- excellent, incomparable, unequaled or unsurpassed PEERLESS, MATCHLESS, UNPARALLELED, UNRIVALED
- excellent, of outstanding quality or reputation BLUE-CHIP
- excellent, outstanding, superior to all others SUPERLATIVE
- excellent, serving as an example or model for others of its kind EXEMPLARY, COPYBOOK
- excellent, wonderful, stunning STUPENDOUS, SUBLIME
- excellent or perfect example or representative EXEMPLAR, PARAGON
- excellent person or thing, a marvel HUMDINGER
- excellent person or thing, without equal NONPAREIL, NONESUCH

excelling others, outstanding PREEMINENT, TRANSCENDENT
exceptional, remarkable, extraordinary SURPASSING
excess, overabundance, or surplus GLUT, PLETHORA, SUPERFLUITY, SURFEIT
- excess or redundancy NIMIETY

excessive, beyond the required or regular number SUPERNUMERARY, SUPERFLUOUS, REDUNDANT, SUPEREROGATORY
- excessive, extravagant, unreasonable, as prices or demands might be EXORBITANT, EXTORTIONATE
- excessive, unrestrained, beyond reasonable limits INTEMPERATE, IMMODERATE, DISPROPORTIONATE, UNCONSCIONABLE
- excessive or exaggerated, as ambition might be OVERWEENING, INORDINATE
- excessive or indulgent act, as of violence, drinking, or crime ORGY, RAMPAGE, FRENZY
- excessive or insincere, as overlavish praise might be FULSOME
- excessive praise, emotion, or the like SCHMALTZ
- excessive response to a problem or challenge OVERREACTION, OVERKILL
- excessive talking, sometimes caused by mental illness LOGORRHEA
- excessively, overly UNDULY
- excessively and monotonously sweet-tasting, devoted, or the like CLOYING
- excessively eager to help or advise OFFICIOUS
- excessively revered object or activity FETISH
- excessively worried, fussy, sensitive, or the like NEUROTIC

excessive (combining form) HYPER-, SUPER-, POLY-
excessive discharge (combining form) -RRHAGIA
exchange, interchange, give or take mutually RECIPROCATE
- exchange, marketplace, trading center RIALTO, FORUM
- exchange goods or services directly, without using money BARTER
- exchange of one thing for something equivalent QUID PRO QUO
- exchange or central distribution point for banking transactions, commodities, information, or the like CLEARING HOUSE
- exchange or substitute COMMUTE

excite, stimulate, stir up, or provoke GALVANIZE, ELECTRIFY, ENERGIZE, INVIGORATE
- excite by suggestive or suspenseful stimulation TITILLATE
- excite or arouse someone's curiosity, interest, or the like PIQUE
- excitable or nervous, fidgety and restless SKITTISH
- excited or agitated uncontrollably DELIRIOUS, FRENZIED
- excitedly active, bustling HECTIC
- excitedly nervous and flustered ATWITTER
- be eager for or excited at something SALIVATE
- extremely excited or enthusiastic, full of high spirits EXUBERANT, EBULLIENT, EFFERVESCENT
- wildly or uncontrollably excited, frenzied FRANTIC, FRENETIC

excitement, arousal, incentive, or stimulus FILLIP
- feeling of prickling or stinging, as from excitement TINGLING
- substance that supposedly produces a surge of excitement or nervousness ADRENALINE, EPINEPHRINE

excitement (combining form) -MANIA
exciting, colorful, or noisy display, designed to impress or advertise RAZZLE-DAZZLE, RAZZMATAZZ
- exciting, stimulating, invigorating HEADY, EXHILARATING
- clearly described in vivid or exciting detail GRAPHIC

exclamation, sudden emphatic utterance INTERJECTION, EJACULATION
- exclamation of praise, joy, or surprise HALLELUJAH
- exclamation of praise to God HOSANNA
- exclamation of triumph on finding, solving, or discovering something EUREKA
- exclamation or oath, especially a swearword or profanity EXPLETIVE

exclamation mark combined with a question mark into a single punctuation mark INTERROBANG
- informal term for an exclamation mark SCREAMER, BANG

exclude See also **prevent**
- exclude, cast out, or banish from a group RELEGATE
- exclude, shut out, or prohibit, DEBAR
- exclude from all business dealings, refuse to trade or associate with, typically as a protest BOYCOTT, BLACKLIST
- exclude from membership of a club or society by vetoing or voting against BLACKBALL
- exclude from one's community or social circle, shun OSTRACIZE
- exclude officially from religious rights and privileges, membership of a church, or the like EXCOMMUNICATE
- exclude or eliminate after careful sorting, sift out WINNOW OUT
- excluded because, or as if because, blasphemous or cursed TABOO

exclusion, shunning, or banishment from a social group OSTRACISM, PURDAH
- exclusion or deliberate blocking of thoughts, desires, or the like from one's mind REPRESSION, SUPPRESSION

exclusive, restricted to a small group SELECT, ESOTERIC, RAREFIED
- exclusive circle of friends or colleagues CLIQUE
- exclusive control or rights, dominance to the exclusion of all others MONOPOLY
- exclusive right or possession, or something claimed to be one PERQUISITE
- exclusiveness and standoffishness ELITISM
- divided into separate and exclusive racial groupings, as a community or country might be SEGREGATED

excommunication - formal pronouncement of excommunication, damning curse ANATHEMA
excrement, dung FECES, DEJECTA, EXCRETA, EGESTA, ORDURE
- excrement-eating, feeding on dung, as some insects are COPROPHAGOUS, SCATOPHAGOUS
- excrement of a newborn baby MECONIUM
- excrement of insects FRASS
- excrement or droppings of animals, especially those being hunted or trailed SCATS
- excrement or dung of sea birds, as used for fertilizer GUANO
- containing or relating to excrement STERCORACEOUS
- fossilized excrement, as found in

archeological sites COPROLITE
- human excrement for use as a fertilizer NIGHT SOIL
- medical or archeological study of excrement SCATOLOGY
- soiled with or as if with excrement, extremely dirty FECULENT

excrement (combining form) COPRO-, SCATO-

excrete DEFECATE, EVACUATE
- excrete, as birds do MUTE
- coil of earth excreted by an earthworm CAST, CASTING

excusable, easily pardoned or forgiven VENIAL

excuse See also **forgive, pardon**
- excuse, specifically a claim that one was somewhere else than at the scene of the crime ALIBI
- excuse, uphold, or justify by means of arguments, evidence, or proof VINDICATE
- excuse or expedient, face-saver SALVO
- excuse or free from responsibility, a duty, or the like EXONERATE, EXEMPT, ACQUIT
- believable or persuasive, as an excuse or politician might be PLAUSIBLE
- lessen or try to lessen the seriousness of a crime, guilt, or the like, as by offering certain excuses EXTENUATE, MITIGATE
- make up or invent an excuse, story, or the like CONCOCT
- pretended or false excuse PRETEXT
- self-deceiving excuse or explanation for one's actions, giving likely reasons but ignoring deeper motives RATIONALIZATION

execution by means of strangling or breaking the neck with an iron collar GARROTE
- device for executing people by beheading, consisting of a heavy blade running between vertical posts GUILLOTINE
- platform or raised wooden framework, as for executing criminals SCAFFOLD

exempt, free or excuse from responsibility, blame, or the like EXONERATE

exemption or immunity, as for foreign diplomats, from the jurisdiction of one's country of residence EXTRATERRITORIALITY
- exemption or release from a rule, law, obligation, or the like DISPENSATION

exercise system, based on Hindu principles, for physical and mental well-being YOGA, HATHA YOGA
- exercise and stretch, as before beginning a race LIMBER UP
- exercise that stimulates the breathing and blood circulation AEROBICS
- exercise through contracting the muscles without changing their length or moving the limbs ISOMETRIC EXERCISE
- exercises of a simple physical kind done for fitness and muscle tone CALLISTHENICS
- heavy ball used for physical exercise MEDICINE BALL
- system of exercise, therapy, diet, or the like REGIMEN
- wooden bottle-shaped club swung about for physical exercise INDIAN CLUB

exhaust pipe's attachment, purifying the engine's exhaust gases CATALYTIC CONVERTER
- something that is given off, such as radiation or exhaust fumes EMISSION

exhausted, deprived of one's natural force and vitality, as through inbreeding or overindulgence EFFETE
- exhausted, severely weakened, drained or enfeebled DEBILITATED, DEPLETED, ENERVATED

exhaustion, as through starvation INANITION

exhibit or three-dimensional scene, as in museums, with models of figures set against a background DIORAMA
- exhibit or parade ostentatiously, show off FLAUNT

exhibition, especially a large industrial exhibition EXPO, EXPOSITION
- exhibition covering many years of an artist's work RETROSPECTIVE
- exhibition hall or display stand PAVILION

exile, banish, forbid, or outlaw PROSCRIBE
- exile or banish DEPORT
- exiled, banished, or living in a country other than one's homeland EXPATRIATE

exist, be current, remain in force, as a custom might PREVAIL, OBTAIN
- exist, continue in existence, or manage to exist SUBSIST
- existing in the real world independently of the mind OBJECTIVE
- existing state of affairs STATUS QUO
- existing still, surviving, not lost or extinct or destroyed EXTANT
- existing thing or notion, independent of other things or notions ENTITY

existence - regard a concept or idea as having a real concrete existence HYPOSTATIZE, REIFY

existence (combining form) ONTO-

exit, outlet, means of escape VENT
- exit, way out EGRESS
- stage direction indicating the exit of all the characters EXEUNT OMNES

expand See **increase**
- expand and clarify a remark, idea, or the like by adding details AMPLIFY, ELABORATE, DILATE, EXPATIATE
- expand range of activities or interests DIVERSIFY

expect, look forward to ANTICIPATE

expectations, chances or hopes of success, outlook PROSPECTS
- go against expectations CONFOUND

expedition or military advance ANABASIS

expel See **drive**

expelling (combining form) -FUGE

expenditure, money or funds paid out DISBURSEMENT

expenses - referring to expenses that are minor and not essential INCIDENTAL

expensive and inefficient gift, project, or possession, requiring more trouble than it is worth WHITE ELEPHANT
- extremely expensive, extravagantly or excessively priced, ruinous EXORBITANT, EXTORTIONATE, PROHIBITIVE

experience in and confident knowledge of society, tact in social situations SAVOIR FAIRE
- experience involving great effort or suffering ORDEAL
- changes in fortune, experience, or the like VICISSITUDES
- doctrine that all knowledge derives from experience, especially from sense perceptions EMPIRICISM
- relating to intuitive knowledge or supernatural experience TRANSCENDENTAL
- unpleasant or dangerous experience, of short duration MAUVAIS QUART D'HEURE

experienced, sophisticated, even cynical WORLDLY-WISE, WORLDLY
- experienced in, acquainted or familiar with CONVERSANT, AU FAIT
- experienced or enjoyed through the actions or achievements of someone else, as pleasure might be VICARIOUS
- experienced person, as through long service in the army VETERAN
- experienced worker, performer, or the like TROUPER

experiment - experimenting or operating on the body of a living animal, especially for research VIVISECTION
- referring or relating to an experiment in which neither the subjects nor the testers know which test items are real or active and which are just controls DOUBLE-BLIND
- referring to arguments or rea-

soning based on experiment or experience rather than on theory or internal consistency EMPIRICAL, INDUCTIVE, A POSTERIORI

experimental, incompletely developed, or provisional, as a plan might be TENTATIVE

expert See also **able, skillful**
- expert, especially a master chef CORDON BLEU
- expert, person skilled and experienced at a specified pursuit PAST MASTER, MAVEN
- expert adviser CONSULTANT
- expert in fine food and drink GOURMET, CONNOISSEUR
- expert or authority in any field PUNDIT
- expert or master in any of the arts, especially music MAESTRO
- expert source of information, whether human or written AUTHORITY
- experts with specialized knowledge or superior tastes COGNOSCENTI
- group of experts who give unofficial advice to government or industry BRAIN TRUST

expertise - acting or speaking out of turn, beyond the range of one's ability or expertise ULTRACREPIDARIAN
- pretended expertise or knowledge, veneer of scholarship SCIOLISM

expiation See **atonement**

explain, make clear, or interpret EXPOUND, EXPLICATE, ELUCIDATE
- explain in a reasonable or apparently reasonable way, often to suit one's convenience RATIONALIZE
- explain in lengthy detail, enlarge on DILATE, ELABORATE, AMPLIFY, EXPATIATE
- explainable EXPLICABLE
- explaining, interpreting EXPONENT

explanation EXPLICATION, EXPOSITION
- explanation, as in science, that awaits proof HYPOTHESIS, WORKING HYPOTHESIS, THEORY
- explanation or critical analysis of a text, especially of the Bible EXEGESIS
- explanation or interpretation of a statement or action CONSTRUCTION
- explanation that is more difficult to understand than the problem IGNOTUM PER IGNOTIUS
- principle that the best explanation for something is the simplest one OCCAM'S RAZOR

explanatory note, translation, or commentary, as in the margin of a manuscript or text GLOSS
- explanatory phrase or remark within a sentence PARENTHESIS

explode, as a bomb might, or cause to explode DETONATE
- explode, as a mine does when set off SPRING
- explode, burst out violently, as in anger ERUPT

exploration, investigation, or survey, as of a stretch of enemy territory RECONNAISSANCE, RECCE

explore an area for gold or other minerals PROSPECT

explorer who travels by ship NAVIGATOR

explosion See also **bomb**
- energy released in a nuclear explosion, expressed in terms of weight of TNT YIELD
- relating to an earthquake, large explosion, or other vibration of the earth's crust SEISMIC
- sudden and violent inward collapse, the opposite process to an explosion IMPLOSION

explosive, unstable VOLATILE
- explosive cap, as used either in a toy pistol or in a firearm PERCUSSION CAP
- explosive charge, rocket fuel, or the like, generating thrust PROPELLANT
- explosive charge in a missile's warhead PAYLOAD
- explosive liquid used in the manufacture of dynamite and gelignite NITROGLYCERIN
- explosive mixture of methane and air, in coal mines FIREDAMP
- explosive place, situation, or person TINDERBOX, POWDER KEG
- explosive powder, as for bullets and shells CORDITE
- explosive power equivalent to one million tons of TNT MEGATON
- explosives, or destruction by explosives, as by military engineers DEMOLITIONS
- cellulose nitrate in a form used as an explosive GUNCOTTON
- potassium nitrate, used in making explosives and preserving meat SALTPETER

expose See **reveal**

exposures - apparatus giving brief exposures of visual images, as for experiments in memory or perception TACHISTOSCOPE

express a thought or idea in words of a particular style COUCH
- express an emotion or idea in words ARTICULATE, VERBALIZE, ENUNCIATE
- express openly, discuss freely, examine publicly VENTILATE
- express or display something clearly, such as surprise EVINCE, MANIFEST
- express or release an emotion VENT

expression See also **emotion, figure of speech, style, phrase**
- expression, bearing, or manner MIEN
- expression in the voice, use of stress and pitch to convey meaning MODULATION
- expression of a feeling, or the form it takes MANIFESTATION
- expression of an indirect, roundabout kind CIRCUMLOCUTION, PERIPHRASIS
- expression of sulkiness POUT, MOUE
- expression of sulkiness or threat, frown SCOWL
- expression or sign of intentions or feelings GESTURE
- expression that is simple, clear, and elegant ATTICISM
- expressions of great delight ECSTASIES, RAPTURES, TRANSPORTS
- choice of words, mode of expression, as of a particular person or group PARLANCE, PHRASEOLOGY
- choice of words or manner of expressing oneself in speech or writing DICTION
- contorted facial expression, as of pain or disgust GRIMACE
- cowardly, ashamed, or downcast, as someone's expression might be SHEEPISH, HANGDOG
- distinctive word, phrase, or expression, especially when typical of a regional or cultural style LOCUTION
- informal word or expression, as used in everyday speech COLLOQUIALISM
- phrase or expression used as a figure of speech TROPE
- showing distaste or cynicism, as one's expression might WRY
- uninterpretable, as a facial expression might be INSCRUTABLE, UNFATHOMABLE, DEADPAN, ENIGMATIC

expression (combining form) -LOGY

expressionless, unemotional, showing no distinctive attitude or response VACUOUS, IMPASSIVE

expressive, expressing emotions or one's feelings openly DEMONSTRATIVE
- expressive or emotional, as a poem might be EVOCATIVE
- expressive or moving, especially in use of language ELOQUENT

exquisite, elegant, refined, especially in an affected or pretentious way RECHERCHÉ

extend, prolong, cause to continue PERPETUATE
- extend over, bridge SPAN
- extend range of activities or interests DIVERSIFY

extent, range, or scope, as of a law or one's outlook PURVIEW

exterminate - fill a room or building with poisonous smoke to disinfect it, exterminate insects, and so on FUMIGATE

extermination of a social or religious group GENOCIDE

external angle of a wall QUOIN, COIGN
- coming from outside, of foreign or external origin EXTRANEOUS, EXTRINSIC, EXOGENOUS

external (combining form) EXO-

extinct See also **dinosaur**
- extinct ox, probably the forebear of today's domestic cattle AUROCH, URUS
- extinct prehistoric bird still retaining some reptile features such as teeth and a long tail ARCHAEOPTERYX
- extinct prehistoric flying reptile PTERODACTYL
- extinct prehistoric horselike mammal EOHIPPUS
- extinct mammal resembling the elephant or mammoth MASTODON
- flightless bird from Mauritius, extinct since the 17th century DODO
- flightless bird from New Zealand, extinct since the 19th century MOA
- still in existence, surviving, not lost or extinct EXTANT
- zebralike mammal from southern Africa, extinct since the 19th century QUAGGA

extra actor who has a nonspeaking role, as in a play or movie SUPERNUMARY
- extra, additional SUPPLEMENTARY, SUPERVENIENT
- extra, exceeding the required or regular number, excessive or redundant SUPERFLUOUS, SUPEREROGATORY
- extra charge or cost SURCHARGE
- extra information, added at the end of a book, message, or the like AFTERTHOUGHT, POSTSCRIPT, APPENDIX, ANNEX, SUPPLEMENT, ADDENDUM
- extra profit or benefit from one's employment over and above one's salary or wages PERK, PERQUISITE, FRINGE BENEFIT
- extra soldiers or supplies sent to support those that are already in use REINFORCEMENTS
- extramarital sex, sexual unfaithfulness INFIDELITY, ADULTERY

extract an essence from a liquid by boiling DECOCT
- extract from a text, snippet GOBBET
- extract or concentrated essence of something QUINTESSENCE
- extract or selected passage or scene from a book, movie, or the like EXCERPT
- extract or separate an essence, idea, or the like DISTILL
- extract something with difficulty, such as information PRY OUT
- extract the essentials of a book, report, or the like GUT
- extraction of useful substances from waste material RECOVERY, RECYCLING
- evaporate and condense a liquid repeatedly by boiling, as when extracting substances REFLUX

extraordinary, exceptional, remarkable SURPASSING, SINGULAR
- extraordinary, or wonderful PRODIGIOUS

extrasensory perception, such as clairvoyance CRYPTESTHESIA, TELESTHESIA

extravagant or generous LAVISH
- extravagant or wasteful PRODIGAL

extreme in political attitudes, favoring basic and far-reaching social and economic changes RADICAL
- extreme or excessive in one's devotion to a cause, irrationally enthusiastic or furious FANATICAL, RABID
- extreme or uncompromising, as in one's political stance INTRANSIGENT
- extreme point or perfect state NE PLUS ULTRA
- divide into two extreme and hostile positions or groups POLARIZE

extreme (combining form) ULTRA-

extremely, especially, clearly, remarkably SIGNALLY, EMINENTLY, CONSPICUOUSLY

extremist, radical, or revolutionary in politics SANSCULOTTE, JACOBIN
- extremist and uncompromising revolutionary MAXIMALIST
- extremist revolutionary advocating the destruction of all existing social and political institutions ANARCHIST, NIHILIST

eye See illustration
- eye, as of most insects, made up of many separate light-sensitive elements COMPOUND EYE
- eye-bearing stalk, as of a snail or crab OMMATOPHORE

Eye

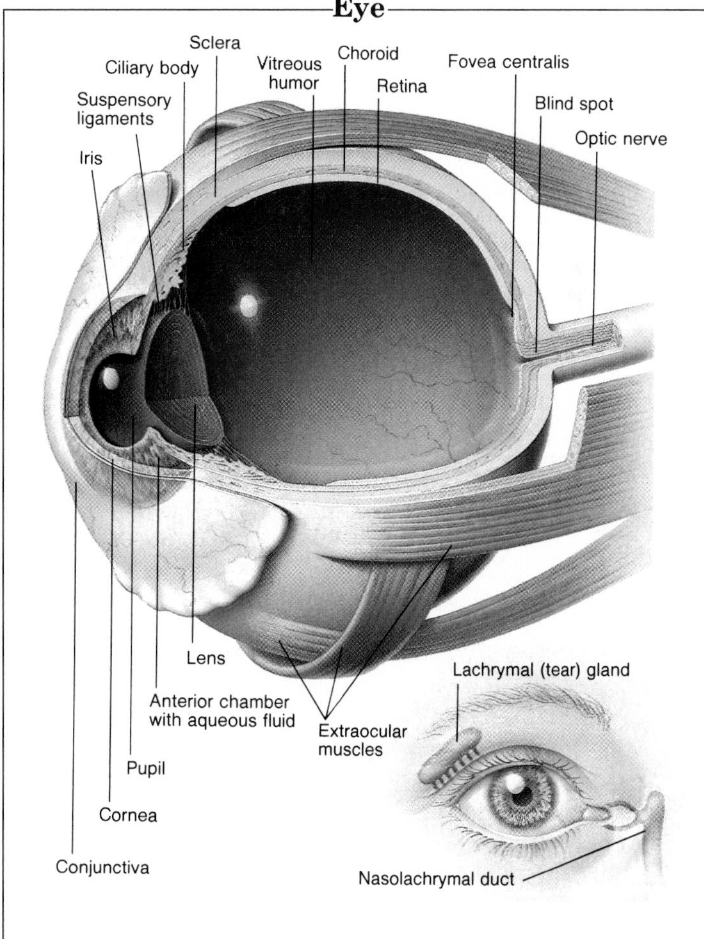

- eye-for-an-eye law or punishment, or the system or principle of making the punishment fit the crime TALION, LEX TALIONIS
- eye of an elementary kind, as in some insects, or eyelike marking, as on a peacock's tail OCELLUS
- eye socket ORBIT
- eye specialist, medical expert in eye diseases OCULIST, OPHTHALMOLOGIST
- eye specialist, prescribing glasses but not medical treatment OPTOMETRIST, OPHTHALMIC OPTICIAN
- eye with a whitish iris, or an outward-turning squint WALLEYE
- eye's ability to focus by changing the direction of incoming light rays REFRACTION
- adjective for the eye OCULAR, OPHTHALMIC, OPTICAL
- any of the lenses in a compound eye as of an insect FACET
- clouding of the lens of the eye CATARACT
- corner of the eye, meeting point of the eyelids CANTHUS, COMMISSURE
- focusing defect caused by an imbalance in the eye muscles, squint STRABISMUS
- focusing of one's eyes or attention firmly on something FIXATION
- fold of skin descending over the inner corner of the eye, Mongolian fold EPICANTHIC FOLD
- having bulging eyes, specifically as a result of excess thyroid hormone EXOPHTHALMIC
- having eyes dulled by tears or tiredness BLEARY-EYED
- having very dark blue eyes, or slanted eyes SLOE-EYED
- mucous discharge from the eyes RHEUM
- poisonous chemical extract used to dilate the pupil of the eye ATROPINE
- red light-sensitive pigment in the retinal rods of the eye RHODOPSIN
- relating to one eye rather than two MONOCULAR
- relating to the use of both eyes, specifically to their focusing on a single object at one time BINOCULAR
- spots before the eyes, specks or threads in one's vision caused by defects or impurities in the eyes MUSCAE VOLITANTES
- turn away one's eyes, gaze, or the like AVERT
- turning inward of the eyes to focus on a nearer object CONVERGENCE
- uncontrolled movement of the eyeball NYSTAGMUS
- violet light-sensitive pigment in the retinal cones of the eye IODOPSIN
- white opaque narrow circle around the cornea of the eye, as found sometimes in elderly people ARCUS SENILIS
- white opaque patch or tissue on the cornea of the eye LEUCOMA
- widen or expand, as the pupil of the eye does in the dark DILATE
- wrinkles at the outer corner of the eye CROW'S-FEET

eye (combining form) OPHTHALMO-, OCUL-

eye condition (combining form) -OPIA, -OPY, -OPSIA, -OPSY

eye lotion, eyewash COLLYRIUM

eye shadow, as used in Eastern countries KOHL

eye tooth CANINE

eyebrow - relating to or positioned above the eyebrow SUPERCILIARY
- having bushy and prominently projecting eyebrows BEETLE-BROWED

eyelashes CILIA
- eyelash makeup MASCARA

eyelet or ring, as of rope or rubber, for securing a sail, protecting a wire from chafing, or the like GROMMET

eyelid - adjective for the eyelids PALPEBRAL
- having eyelids PALPEBRATE
- inflammation of a sebaceous gland in the eyelid STY
- membrane forming an inner eyelid, as in reptiles, birds, and cats NICTITATING MEMBRANE

eyesight See also **color blindness**
- eyesight on the outer edge of the normal field of vision PERIPHERAL VISION
- eyesight that is perfect EMMETROPIA, TWENTY-TWENTY VISION
- eyesight that is satisfactory straight ahead but poor or limited on either side TUNNEL VISION
- eyesight that is weak in dim light NYCTALOPIA
- eye exercises as a method of improving eyesight ORTHOPTICS
- farsightedness, longsightedness HYPEROPIA, HYPERMETROPIA
- relating to eyesight OPTICAL, VISUAL, OCULAR
- sharpness of eyesight, hearing, or mind ACUITY
- shortsightedness, defective distance vision MYOPIA
- very shortsighted or nearly blind PURBLIND

eyesight (combining form) -OPIA, -OPY, -OPSIA, -OPSY

F

fable, moral story, or picture in which the characters or scenes symbolize abstractions or ideas and convey a deeper meaning ALLEGORY
- fable or moral story, as used in medieval sermons EXEMPLUM
- fable with a moral message APOLOGUE
- collection, especially in medieval times, of moral fables based on animals BESTIARY
- writer of fables or fantasies FABULIST

fabric See chart, page 192, and also **cloth**
- fabric, cloth, material TEXTILE
- fabrics with a wrinkled or crinkly texture CREPE, PLISSÉ, SEERSUCKER
- shimmering or changing in color, as some fabrics are SHOT, IRIDESCENT
- thin, light, and translucent, as some fine fabrics are SHEER, DIAPHANOUS

face, or expression on a face COUNTENANCE, VISAGE
- face downward, lying face downward PRONE, PROSTRATE
- face or front of a building FACADE
- face or turn in a specified direction, specifically eastward as with a church ORIENT, ORIENTATE
- face that is long, gaunt, and sharp-featured HATCHET FACE
- face that reveals nothing about one's thoughts or feelings, an inscrutable face POKER FACE
- face to face, opposite VIS-À-VIS
- contort the face into an expression of pain, contempt, or disgust GRIMACE
- keeping a straight face or being apparently serious, as when telling a joke DEADPAN
- kit or method for creating a picture of a wanted suspect's face IDENTIKIT, PHOTOFIT
- pale face, or pale-faced person WHEY-FACE
- twitch or spasm, especially in the face TIC
- uninterpretable, as a facial expression might be INSCRUTABLE, UNFATHOMABLE, DEADPAN, ENIGMATIC

face (combining form) -HEDRON

face value, value printed on the face of a share certificate or bond, for assessing dividends PAR VALUE

facelift or similar surgery designed to improve one's physical appearance COSMETIC SURGERY

facial features, especially when regarded as indicating character PHYSIOGNOMY
- facial features or shape LINEAMENTS, COUNTENANCE
- facial pain caused by the fifth cranial nerve TRIGEMINAL NEURALGIA, TIC DOLOUREUX

facilities, conveniences, pleasant and helpful features or services AMENITIES

facing, opposite VIS-À-VIS
- facing the observer OBVERSE

facing (combining form) -WARD, -WARDS

fact - by the fact itself, by its very nature, by definition IPSO FACTO
- facts of a case, accepted as evidence in court RES GESTAE
- practical, dealing with or relating to facts and circumstances rather than to theories or ideals PRAGMATIC
- repeat or reproduce facts in an unthinking way REGURGITATE
- something that is already done and unalterable, an unchangeable fact FAIT ACCOMPLI

factor that makes up or compensates for faults or deficiencies REDEEMING CHARACTERISTIC, MITIGATING FACTOR
- factor that shares in the responsibility for something CONTRIBUTORY FACTOR

factory, farm, or business owned collectively by the workers or users COOPERATIVE
- factory, workshop, or the like where pay and working conditions are very poor SWEATSHOP
- continuous moving belt carrying objects, as on a factory's assembly line CONVEYOR BELT
- deliberate disruption of normal functioning or industrial procedures, as in a factory SABOTAGE
- enclosure, especially in the East, for a factory, rich housing, or the like COMPOUND
- line of workers and equipment operating step by step on a product in a factory ASSEMBLY LINE, PRODUCTION LINE

factual, actual, existing in the real world independently of the mind OBJECTIVE

fade from sight, disappear slowly EVANESCE
- faded or blanched, as grass becomes when shielded constantly from sunlight ETIOLATED

fail, go wrong MISCARRY, FOUNDER
- fail to honor one's debts, keep one's promises, or the like WELSH, DEFAULT
- complete and usually embarrassing failure, utter disaster FIASCO

failed, unsuccessful, would-be, unfulfilled MANQUÉ
- failed through lacking complete development ABORTIVE

failure, disappointment, or anticlimax after high expectations DAMP SQUIB
- failure, ending, or death DEMISE
- failure or destruction of some magnificent project or person GÖTTERDÄMMERUNG

faint SWOON
- fainting, temporary loss of consciousness SYNCOPE

fair, evenhanded, just and reasonable EQUITABLE
- fair, unbiased, and emotionally detached DISPASSIONATE
- fair, unbiased, unprejudiced IMPARTIAL, DISINTERESTED
- fair-haired and fair-skinned XANTHOCHROID
- fair-skinned, "white" person CAUCASIAN
- charity fair or bazaar, typically held outdoors FETE
- large public exhibition, such as a trade fair EXPOSITION

fair play - rules of fair play, specifically those applied in boxing QUEENSBERRY RULES

fairground See **amusement park**

fairness, justice EQUITY

fairy See also **gnome, spirit**
- fairy, elf, or pixie FAY
- beautiful fairylike creature, originally in Persian folklore PERI
- mischievous fairy or elf, in Irish folklore, typically a cobbler with buried treasure LEPRECHAUN

faith - adopt or support a cause, faith, or ideal ESPOUSE
- complete and unquestioning, as

strong faith is IMPLICIT
- creed or profession of faith widely used in churches Athanasian Creed, Nicene Creed
- disbeliever, skeptic, person without faith or beliefs NULLIFIDIAN, AGNOSTIC
- formal statement of religious beliefs, confession of faith, especially in Christianity CREED
- profess one's faith openly TESTIFY

faithful See also **loyal**
- faithfulness or loyalty, as to one's spouse, the facts, or one's duty FIDELITY

faithlessness, disloyalty, treachery PERFIDY

fake, cheap imitation, as flashy jewelry might be PINCHBECK, GIMCRACK, BRUMMAGEM
- fake, contrived or insincere, as an emotion might be FACTITIOUS
- fake, forged, as a coin might be SNIDE
- fake, forged, fraudulently imitative, as a document or emotion might be COUNTERFEIT, SPURIOUS
- fake, imitation, artificial, as a synthetic flavoring would be SIMULATED, ERSATZ
- fake, invisibly spoiled or cheapened by deliberate dilution or adding of impurities ADULTERATED
- fake, not genuine, sham BOGUS
- fake, pretend, or falsely display something, such as relief FEIGN, SIMULATE, DISSEMBLE
- fake, substituted fraudulently SUPPOSITITIOUS
- fake identity or similar deception IMPOSTURE

falcon See also **hawk**
- falcon of a small and dark-feathered species MERLIN
- falcon of a small, fast, common species, popular in falconry in former times PEREGRINE FALCON
- falcon or hawk that is still young enough to be trained for falconry EYAS
- falcons released by a falconer in a pair to pursue quarry as a team CAST
- male hawk or falcon TIERCEL
- stitch closing the eyes of a falcon to quiet or tame it SEEL

fall See also **lessen**
- fall, as in a series from one level to the next CASCADE
- fall, sink, or settle down GRAVITATE, SUBSIDE
- fall, trip, sprawl on the ground MEASURE ONE'S LENGTH
- fall behind or stray STRAGGLE
- fall in the pitch of the voice, as at the end of a sentence, falling intonation CADENCE
- fall out of place PROLAPSE
- fall straight down and suddenly, hurtle PLUMMET, PRECIPITATE
- fall to someone, be passed on to or conferred on DEVOLVE ON
- fall to the ground, or sprawl or grovel GRABBLE
- falling down, badly built or maintained, shaky, as an old house might be RICKETY, RAMSHACKLE, DILAPIDATED
- falling off or shed at a point of time or growth, as leaves or antlers might be DECIDUOUS

fallacy of assuming in the premise the very conclusion to be proved, begging the question PETITIO PRINCIPII, HYSTERON PROTERON
- fallacy of assuming that an event or situation that follows another in time must also be the result of it POST HOC, ERGO PROPTER HOC
- fallacy of proving or disproving an irrelevant point and assuming that the proposition at issue has been proven or disproven IGNORATIO ELENCHI
- fallacy or invalid argument, especially when it is unintended PARALOGISM

fallopian tube SALPINX

fallow - year in which farm land is left to lie fallow, observed every seventh year by the ancient and some modern Israeli Jews SABBATICAL YEAR

false See also **fake, lie**
- false, made-up, concocted, as a charge or accusation might be TRUMPED-UP
- false, sham, artificial or inauthentic SPURIOUS, POSTICHE
- false, sham, or artificial outward appearance FACADE
- false appearance, feigning, pretense SIMULATION, GUISE
- false conclusion, faulty argument, or invalid reasoning, especially when unintended PARALOGISM
- false evidence used to incriminate an innocent party FRAME-UP
- false idea or misleading conclusion, based on misinformation or faulty reasoning FALLACY
- false interpretation or incorrect explanation, misunderstanding MISCONSTRUCTION
- false opinion or faulty understanding MISCONCEPTION, MISAPPREHENSION

FABRICS

COTTON OR LINEN

baize
buckram
bunting
calico
cambric
candlewick
cheesecloth
chintz
corduroy
cretonne
denim
dimity
drill
duck
flannel
flannelette
gingham
lawn
lisle
madras
moleskin
muslin
nainsook
nankeen
percale
sailcloth
sateen
scrim
terry cloth
ticking
tiffany
velveteen

WOOLEN OR WOOL-LIKE

alpaca
angora
baize
camel hair
cashmere
Duffel
flannel
grogram
Harris tweed
Kendal green
kersey
lawn
loden
melton
merino
mohair
paisley
petersham
serge
tweed
vicuna
whipcord
worsted

SILK

crepe de chine
gossamer
grogram
marocain
moiré
organzine
shantung
tiffany

MIXED FIBER

barathea
bombazine
grogram
linsey-woolsey
merino

JUTE OR HEMP

burlap/hessian
canvas
gunny
hopsack
sackcloth

SYNTHETIC OR SILK

chiffon
grosgrain
ninon
organza
taffeta
tulle

SYNTHETIC

acetate
acrylic
Courtelle
Crimplene
Dacron
Lurex
nylon
polyester
rayon
spandex

SPECIAL WEAVES AND FINISHES

astrakhan
batiste
bombazine
bouclé
brocade
challis
chenille
ciré
foulard
gabardine
gauze
georgette
lamé
moquette
mousseline
organdy
poplin
rep
satin
seersucker
suede
twill
velour
velvet
voile

- false or deceptive speech or behavior, deliberate misleading of someone DUPLICITY
- false or insincere claim to have certain feelings or beliefs HYPOCRISY
- false or highly questionable, as a story might be APOCRYPHAL
- false or lying MENDACIOUS
- false or superficial likeness or image of something SIMULACRUM
- false perception MIRAGE, ILLUSION, DELUSION, HALLUCINATION
- false report or accusation, intended as a slighting criticism ASPERSION
- false statement, forgery, or similar deliberately contrived deception FABRICATION
- false statement or charge made knowingly that injures someone's reputation SLANDER, DEFAMATION, LIBEL, CALUMNY
- false story or report, unfounded rumor CANARD
- false though plausible, as an ingenious argument might be SOPHISTIC, SPECIOUS
- falsely, showily attractive MERETRICIOUS
- falsely reasoned, logically inconsistent, as a conclusion might be INVALID
- apparent or outward, but often false or pretended, as someone's stated reason for an action might be OSTENSIBLE
- deliberate giving of false evidence by a witness under oath PERJURY
- display something falsely, fake or pretend something, such as relief FEIGN, SIMULATE, DISSEMBLE
- prove an argument or statement false CONFUTE, REFUTE, REBUT
- put someone right, rid someone of a mistake or false notion DISABUSE
- represent falsely or show to be false BELIE

false (combining form) PSEUD-, PSEUDO-

false identity - person who assumes a false identity IMPOSTOR

false teeth - dental plate with a false tooth or teeth permanently fixed to natural teeth BRIDGE, BRIDGEWORK
- plate or set of false teeth DENTURE

fame, reputation STATURE
- fame or award resulting from some achievement KUDOS
- fame or great success LUSTER, ÉCLAT
- fame or high status, typically coupled with considerable influence PRESTIGE

familiar, closely associated, very friendly INTIMATE
- familiar or acquainted with, knowledgeable CONVERSANT, AU FAIT
- familiar theme, idea, or image in literature TOPOS

familiarize, adapt, adjust to new circumstances ORIENT, ORIENTATE

family, relatives KIN, KINSMEN
- family name, surname COGNOMEN
- family of rulers over successive generations DYNASTY
- family unit consisting of parents and children and sometimes grandparents NUCLEAR FAMILY
- family unit including grandparents, cousins, and the like all living together or nearby EXTENDED FAMILY
- family's female side or maternal line DISTAFF SIDE, SPINDLE SIDE
- family's male side or paternal line SPEAR SIDE
- descended from the same ancestor, though by different lines, as branches of a family might be COLLATERAL
- within or with one's family EN FAMILLE

family tree, list of ancestors PEDIGREE
- family tree or history, or study of one's ancestors GENEALOGY, LINEAGE

famous, widely known or admired by the public CELEBRATED, NOTED, RENOWNED, ACCLAIMED, ILLUSTRIOUS
- famous for a particular and usually unfavorable quality NOTORIOUS, INFAMOUS
- famous or greatly respected and honored, especially when old VENERABLE, AUGUST
- famous or highly regarded for outstanding qualities or contributions EMINENT, DISTINGUISHED, PROMINENT
- famous person or VIP, often famous chiefly for being famous CELEBRITY, LUMINARY
- famous to the point of becoming a historical hero, legendary FABLED, STORIED
- be famous, achieve wide publicity RESOUND

fan, as in India, in the form of a large cloth or leaf waved to and fro PUNKAH
- fan, vent, or vacuum device for drawing out gas or stale air from a room EXTRACTOR, VENTILATOR
- fan or enthusiastic follower of a specified sport or pastime, buff DEVOTEE, AFICIONADO
- fan-shaped FLABELLATE
- fan used in religious ceremonies FLABELLUM
- fan whose blades form the outer edge of a cylinder SQUIRREL CAGE
- any of the ribs of a fan BRIN

fanatic, extremist ZEALOT, ENERGUMEN

fanciful idea, often combined with mildly eccentric behavior WHIMSY

fanfare on a trumpet TUCKET
- fanfare or blast on a horn or trumpet TANTARA, TANTIVY
- fanfare or similar dramatic musical passage FLOURISH

fantasy, notion typically credited to imagination FIGMENT
- fantasy land of luxury and idleness COCKAIGNE
- fantasy of a playful kind WHIMSY
- fantasy world, impractical realm of the imagination and dreams CLOUD-CUCKOO-LAND
- person who indulges in fantasies to compensate for his inadequacies WALTER MITTY
- relating to dreams or fantasies VISIONARY
- writer or teller of fables or fantasies FABULIST

far away, fairly distant or remote from the center OUTLYING
- far away, and difficult to reach INACCESSIBLE
- far from the joint, center, or the like, as a bone or limb might be DISTAL

Far Eastern countries or regions ORIENT

faraway or remote region, goal, or ideal ULTIMA THULE

farewell, good-bye, act of leave-taking VALEDICTION, CONGÉ
- farewell or final appearance, act, work, or statement SWAN SONG

farm, factory, or business owned collectively by the workers or users COOPERATIVE
- farm of very small size SMALLHOLDING
- farm or farm buildings GRANGE
- farm or farmhouse of a Spanish type HACIENDA
- farm or settlement collectively administered in Israel KIBBUTZ
- farm or settlement collectively administered in the U.S.S.R. KOLKHOZ
- farm worker bound to a feudal lord or estate SERF, VILLEIN
- farm worker during the U.S. depression who was impoverished and uprooted OKIE
- farm worker in Scotland renting a cottage and smallholding COTTER
- farm workers or peasants in an Arab country FELLAHIN
- farmhouse and adjoining buildings and land HOMESTEAD
- farming cooperative in Israel, consisting of a group of small farms MOSHAV
- farming estate, especially in Latin America or ancient Rome LATI-

FUNDIUM
- large farm for sheep or cattle in Australia STATION
farmer, especially a tenant farmer, who pays rent in the form of crops SHARECROPPER
- farmer holding his or her own land YEOMAN
- farmer of a smallholding, especially in Scotland CROFTER
- farmer or rancher rearing livestock on grazing land RANCHER, GRAZIER
- farmer who rents his or her land from another rather than owning it himself or herself TENANT FARMER
- large-scale sheep or cattle farmer in Australia PASTORALIST, SQUATTER
farming AGRICULTURE, HUSBANDRY
- farming of a kind in which the farmer and family consume most of the produce, with little surplus for marketing SUBSISTENCE FARMING
- referring to farming based on large amounts of capital and labor rather than on large stretches of land INTENSIVE
- referring to farming of large stretches of land with little labor or capital expense EXTENSIVE
- referring to farming or farming land AGRARIAN, AGRICULTURAL
- referring to the farming of corn or other crops ARABLE
- referring to the farming of livestock, particularly sheep PASTORAL
farming (combining form) AGR-, AGRI-, AGRO-
farsighted, prudent PROVIDENT
- farsightedness, longsightedness, defective close vision HYPEROPIA, HYPERMETROPIA
farthest See also **furthest**
- farthest down, deepest, lowest NETHERMOST
- farthest point or part, end, edge EXTREMITY
fascinating, tempting, attractive ALLURING
Fascism - bundle of rods with a projecting axhead, a symbol of Italian Fascism FASCES
fashion - fashion-conscious man, whose chief interest is in clothes and manners BEAU, DANDY, FOP, SWELL
- fashion or popularity VOGUE
- designer, maker, and seller of fashionable clothing for women COUTURIER, MODISTE
- forefront of, or early participants in, an artistic fashion, political movement, or the like VANGUARD
- high fashion, or fashionable clothes HAUTE COUTURE
- latest fashion DERNIER CRI
- person who starts or popularizes a fashion or fad TRENDSETTER
fashionable, elegant, or sophisticated CHIC, SOIGNÉ
- fashionable, in keeping with current style À LA MODE
- fashionable gathering of or a reception for intellectuals, celebrities, or the like SALON
- fashionable man widely seen in public, man-about-town BOULEVARDIER
- fashionable or pretty in a pretentious or affected way CHICHI
- fashionable society BEAU MONDE
- relating to clothing, especially fashionable men's clothing SARTORIAL
fast See also **quick**
- fast observed by Muslims during the ninth month of their calendar, or the month itself RAMADAN
fast (combining form) TACH-, TACHY-, TACHEO-
fasten See **join**
fastener or clasp hinged over a fixed staple, and typically secured with a padlock HASP
- fastener or metal pin with two flexible arms, as for securing a wheel to an axle SPLIT PIN, COTTER PIN
- fastening device, such as a strap or grommet, for securing ropes, spars, or oars on a boat or ship BECKET
- fastening device consisting of a bolt tightened by a peglike crosspiece TOGGLE BOLT
- fastening device consisting of two strips of fabric with minute interlocking nylon hooks and loops VELCRO
- bent metal bar fastening stones or timbers together, as in a wall CRAMP IRON, AGRAFE
- clamp, beam, or the like for fastening or steadying something in position BRACE
- double-headed bolt or pin, typically used for fastening metal plates together RIVET
fat See also **fatty**
- fat, bulky yet typically sleek-looking CORPULENT, PORTLY, ROTUND, SONSY
- fat, especially chicken fat, used in cooking SCHMALTZ
- fat, such as butter or lard, as used to make crumbly cookies or flaky pastry SHORTENING
- fat, well-fed appearance, plumpness, stoutness EMBONPOINT
- fat belly PAUNCH, CORPORATION
- fat in its hard or solidified form STEARIN
- fat in living cells LIPID
- fat of a whale, forming in a layer beneath its skin BLUBBER
- fat streaks or mottling of fat on high-quality beef MARBLING
- acid found in solid fat, used in making soap and candles STEARIC ACID
- extremely fat, dangerously overweight OBESE, BLOATED
- hard fatty substance extracted from beef or mutton fat, as used in making candles TALLOW
- melt, extract, or convert fat by heating RENDER
- purify butter or fat by gentle heating CLARIFY
- short fat person SQUAB, DUMPLING
- slightly fat in an attractive way, as a plump shapely woman is BUXOM
- stale, decomposing, smelling off, as old butter or bacon fat might be RANCID
fat (combining form) LIPO-, SEBI-, SEBO-, STEAT-, STEATO-
fate, certain outcome DESTINY, LOT, PORTION
- fate or destiny, especially in Hinduism and Buddhism KARMA
- fate or destiny, in Eastern or Muslim countries KISMET
- fated, certain to happen, as if decreed in advance by providence PREDESTINED, FOREORDAINED, PREDETERMINED, FOREDOOMED
- appear or occur as an unexpected but important factor, as fate is said to do INTERVENE
- inescapable, unavoidable, as one's fate is INELUCTABLE
- unpredictable action or twist, as of fate QUIRK
Fates in Roman mythology PARCAE
father, be the parent of BEGET, SIRE
- father, term of address for a Roman Catholic priest or military chaplain PADRE
- father of a family, viewed as the head of the household PATERFAMILIAS
- father or founder of a tribe, tradition, or the like PATRIARCH
- adjective for a father PATERNAL
- informal or mock formal term for a father PATER
- murder of one's father PATRICIDE
- name based on one's father's name PATRONYMIC
- referring to descent traced through the father PATRILINEAL
- reputed or commonly considered, as a child's supposed father might be PUTATIVE
father (combining form) PATR-, PATRI-
Father Time - Death viewed as Father Time with his scythe GRIM REAPER
fatherhood, or origin or descent from a father PATERNITY

fatty, oily, greasy PINGUID, SEBACEOUS, UNCTUOUS, OLEAGINOUS
- fatty, relating to animal fat ADIPOSE
- fatty material, as on the thighs and buttocks CELLULITE
- fatty substance formed from oils in a whale's head, used for cosmetics, ointments, and candles SPERMACETI
- fatty substance produced by the skin glands SEBUM, SMEGMA

fault - faultfinding, critical in a petty, nitpicking way CARPING, CAPTIOUS, CAVILING, NIGGLING
- fault in the earth's surface DISLOCATION
- fault or impairment, as in a body organ DYSFUNCTION
- fault or sin considered petty or trifling PECCADILLO
- minor personal fault or shortcoming, character flaw or demerit FOIBLE
- person given to petty criticism, quibbler, faultfinder MOMUS, PETTIFOGGER
- technical fault, mechanical breakdown, malfunction GLITCH

faultless, flawless, unblemished IMMACULATE, UNIMPEACHABLE, IMPECCABLE

faulty (combining form) DYS-

favor or an equivalent-value item given in exchange or compensation for another QUID PRO QUO
- favor or service for which the recipient is indebted OBLIGATION
- ask favors persistently IMPORTUNE, HECTOR
- curry favor for oneself with others, as by flattery INGRATIATE, FAWN, KOWTOW, TRUCKLE
- given as a favor rather than out of legal obligation, as a payment might be EX GRATIA
- restore oneself to favor REDEEM ONESELF
- trying to gain favor by excessive flattery, humility, or obligingness INGRATIATING, TOADYING, SYCOPHANTIC, SERVILE, FAWNING, UNCTUOUS, OBSEQUIOUS

favorable, advantageous, healthy BENEFICIAL, BENIGN, BENIGNANT
- favorable, promising AUSPICIOUS, PROPITIOUS
- favorable or "cosmetic" presentation of awkward facts or policies, as by their careful selection WINDOW DRESSING

favoring one particular view, especially a controversial one, biased TENDENTIOUS
- favoring or supporting a single cause or party in a prejudiced way PARTISAN

favoring (combining form) PRO-

favorite, darling MINION
- favorite place to visit HAUNT

favoritism, such as the giving of political appointments or promotions to relatives, by those in positions of power NEPOTISM

fear See also **scared** and chart at **phobias**
- fear of or anxiety over the future APPREHENSION
- feared or respected as awesome or very impressive FORMIDABLE, REDOUBTABLE
- back or shy away in fear COWER, CRINGE, FLINCH, WINCE, RECOIL, QUAIL, BLENCH
- calm or reduce someone's fear, anger, or the like ALLAY, LULL
- disguise or hide something, such as one's fear DISSEMBLE
- dispel or lay to rest someone's fears QUELL
- exaggerated, psychologically unhealthy, as a fear might be MORBID
- feeling or situation of sudden dismay, fear, and confusion CONSTERNATION
- irrational, uncontrollable fear or hatred of some particular thing PHOBIA
- object or thought causing persistent but often needless fear BUGBEAR, BUGABOO, BOGEY, CHIMERA, HOBGOBLIN
- shiver or thrill of fear or excitement FRISSON
- state of nervous fear, dread, alarm TREPIDATION
- state of fear or panic FUNK
- sudden feeling of anxiety or fear, misgiving QUALM
- tremble or shake, as with fear PALPITATE
- unconscious, as secret fears or painful memories might be REPRESSED

fear (combining form) -PHOBE, -PHOBIA, -PHOBIC

feast See also **holiday**
- feast, holiday, carnival, or celebration FIESTA
- feast that is plentiful or luxurious, but only in appearance or by report BARMECIDAL FEAST
- luxurious or elaborate, as a feast might be LUCULLAN
- relating to a feast, festival, or festivity, especially a joyous one FESTAL
- weekday that is not a feast day on a church calendar FERIA

Feast of Lights, Feast of Dedication, in the Jewish calendar HANUKKAH, CHANUKAH

feat of outstanding skill or strength TOUR DE FORCE
- feat or exploit of note GEST

feather, ribbon, or rosette worn on the hat, especially by soldiers COCKADE
- feather, specifically a flight feather PINION
- feather, wing, fin, or similar projecting body part PINNA
- feather on an arrow VANE
- feather or plume on a helmet or hat PANACHE
- feather or trimming of feathers, as formerly used on women's hats OSPREY
- feather-shaped PINNATE
- feathered cork used in badminton SHUTTLECOCK
- feathered or winged PINNATE
- flat side section of a feather VANE, VEXILLUM, WEB
- hollow main shaft of a feather

Feather

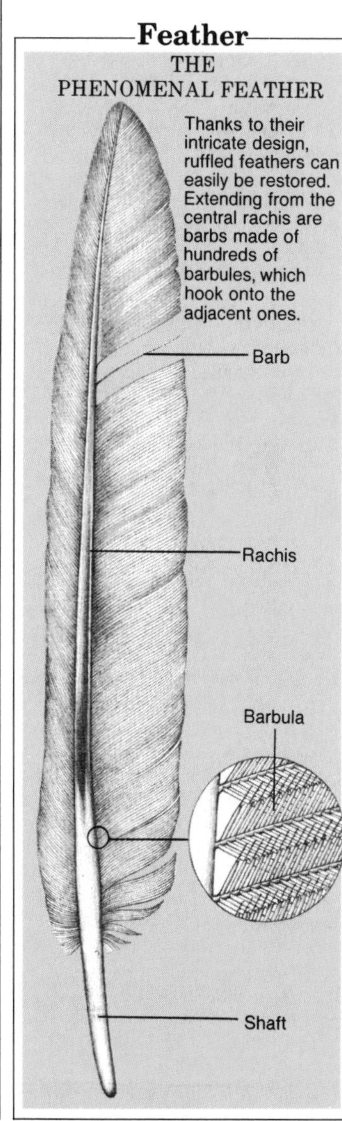

QUILL, CALAMUS, RACHIS, BARREL, SCAPE
- opening or small hole in the shaft of a feather UMBILICUS
- small parallel filaments, attached to the shaft, forming the flat sides of a feather BARBS

feather (combining form) PTERO-

feathers See illustration, page 195, and also **bird**
- feathers PLUMAGE
- feathers, especially an egret's tail feathers, used for a plume, as on a hat AIGRETTE
- feathers in or around a bird's ears, as on the owl AURICULARS
- feathers of a bird's back and wings when of a different color from the other feathers MANTLE
- feathers or hair projecting from an animal's neck FRILL, RUFF
- feathers or hairs on the back of an animal's neck HACKLES
- any of the large curving feathers on a rooster's tail SICKLE FEATHER
- any of the large visible feathers on a bird's plumage, as opposed to the down feathers PINNA
- any of the small feathers clustered at the base of a main feather on a bird's wing or tail TECTRIX, COVERT
- any of the stiff flight feathers on a bird's wing REMEX
- any of the stiff main feathers, regulating flight, in a bird's tail RECTRIX
- bristly feathers near the beak of an insect-eating bird VIBRISSAE
- clean the feathers with the beak PREEN
- cover with, or develop feathers FLEDGE
- erect the feathers RUFFLE
- outer feathers on a bird's body, determining its characteristic shape CONTOUR FEATHERS
- shed feathers or fur, as many animals do MOLT
- still without feathers, as a young bird might be CALLOW, UNFLEDGED

feature or aspect, as of someone's personality FACET
- feature that makes up or compensates for faults or deficiencies REDEEMING FEATURE, MITIGATING FACTOR

features, marks, or characteristics of a very distinctive or important kind LINEAMENTS
- bent or twisted out of shape, as a person's features might be CONTORTED

feces See **excrement**

fee, as paid initially to a lawyer, or regularly to a consultant RETAINER
- fee, usually small, paid for a service that is technically free HONORARIUM
- fee, wages, or other form of profit from one's job or office EMOLUMENT
- fee or percentage paid to a salesman or agent for successfully completed services COMMISSION
- fee paid for instruction TUITION

feed, nourish NURTURE

feeding by means of a tube down the throat, especially force-feeding GAVAGE
- feeding on all kinds of food, both meat and plant foods OMNIVOROUS
- feeding on ants, as anteaters are MYRMECOPHAGOUS
- feeding on corpses or carrion NECROPHAGOUS
- feeding on dung, as some beetles and flies are COPROPHAGOUS, SCATOPHAGOUS
- feeding on fish PISCIVOROUS
- feeding on fruit, as some bats are FRUGIVOROUS, CARPOPHAGOUS
- feeding on grasses, seeds, or grains GRAMINIVOROUS, GRANIVOROUS
- feeding on insects, as some birds and mammals are ENTOMOPHAGOUS, INSECTIVOROUS
- feeding on leaves, as some insects are PHYLLOPHAGOUS
- feeding on meat from time to time, or feeding exclusively on meat CARNIVOROUS
- feeding on many kinds of food POLYPHAGOUS
- feeding on plants, as an insect might PHYTOPHAGOUS
- feeding on plants only, as many animals are HERBIVOROUS
- feeding on wood, as some insects are XYLOPHAGOUS
- feeding trough in a stable or barn MANGER

feeding on (combining form) -VOROUS, PHAGO-, -PHAGOUS, -PHAGE, -PHAGY

feel and return the same emotion as someone feels toward oneself RECIPROCATE
- feel around for or scratch about with the hands, grope GRABBLE
- sensitive to emotion or suffering, able to feel, or sympathize PASSIBLE

feelers on the head of an insect, crustacean, or the like ANTENNAE
- feelers or sensory organs near the mouth, as in some insects and shellfish PALPS, PALPI

feeling See also **emotional**
- feeling, as distinct from thought or perception SENTIENCE
- feeling for language, an "ear" for what is correct or appropriate SPRACHGEFÜHL
- feeling of doubt, social unease, troubled conscience, or the like MISGIVING, SCRUPLE, QUALM
- feeling of great happiness, joy, or delight ECSTASY, RAPTURE, TRANSPORT
- feeling of having undergone previously an experience that one is now having for the first time DÉJÀ VU, DÉJÀ VECU, DÉJÀ ENTENDU, DÉJÀ RACONTÉ, DÉJÀ PENSÉ
- feeling of illness, unease, or depression MALAISE
- feeling of impending disaster or evil FOREBODING
- feeling or emotion usually associated with a particular idea or thought, in psychology AFFECT
- feeling or sense of something about to happen FOREBODING, PREMONITION, PRESENTIMENT
- feeling or showing no emotion IMPASSIVE
- feelings conveyed, often unconsciously, by one person or group to another VIBES
- assigning of human feelings or characteristics to inanimate or natural objects, as in poetic metaphors PATHETIC FALLACY
- depth, as of feeling, meaning, or thinking PROFUNDITY
- examine a part of the body by feeling it with the hands, for a preliminary medical diagnosis PALPATE
- expressing emotions or one's feelings openly DEMONSTRATIVE
- fine feeling, keen power of perception, sensitive openness to emotional influences SENSIBILITY, SUSCEPTIBILITY
- have specific feelings ENTERTAIN, NOURISH, HARBOR
- hide one's true feelings or intentions by pretending DISSIMULATE
- understanding of another that is so deep that one seems to enter into or share his or her feelings EMPATHY
- used for feeling and touching, as an insect's antenna is TACTILE
- vague feeling or intuition, hint, inkling INTIMATION
- wound or hurt someone's feelings, as by severe criticism SCARIFY

feeling (combining form) PATH-, -PATHY

feet See also **foot**
- feet or hands EXTREMITIES
- beating with a stick, especially on the soles of the feet BASTINADO
- care of or treatment for the feet and toenails PEDICURE, PODIATRY, CHIROPODY
- chains or bands around the ankles or feet FETTERS, SHACKLES
- fettered iron bar, formerly used for shackling prisoners' feet BILBOES
- turned outward, as feet might be SPLAY

feet (combining form) PEDI-, -PEDE,

-POD, -PODE

feign See **pretend**

fellow countryman, person from the same country as another person COMPATRIOT
- fellow worker in a joint effort CO-ADJUTANT, COADJUTOR, COLLABORATOR

fellowship, brotherhood, community of feeling or interests FRATERNITY, SODALITY, FREEMASONRY

female behavior and dress adopted by a man EONISM, TRANSVESTISM
- female club or social group, as at a university SORORITY
- female demon supposed to have sexual intercourse with a sleeping man SUCCUBUS
- female hormone ESTROGEN
- female principle or personality in a man's unconscious, in Jungian psychology ANIMA
- female side or maternal line of a family DISTAFF SIDE, SPINDLE SIDE
- related through the female line of a family, especially having the same mother but different fathers UTERINE
- relating to the female line of descent MATRILINEAL

female (combining form) GYN-, GYNO-, -ESS, -TRESS, -TRIX, PARTHENO

femininity or womanhood MULIEBRITY

feminist symbol or emblem, in the form of a double-headed ax LABRYS

fence, hedge, or row of trees designed to break the force of the wind WINDBREAK
- fence, line, or the like protecting or marking the boundary of an area PERIMETER
- fence-making material of poles interlaced with reeds, sticks, or the like WATTLE
- fence of barbed wire or sharpened stakes FRAISE
- fence of pointed upright stakes PICKET FENCE, PALING
- fence of wood temporarily surrounding a construction site or the like HOARDING
- fence of wooden stakes serving as a fortification PALISADE, STOCKADE
- board forming the top rail of a fence or balustrade LEDGER BOARD

fenced enclosure for cattle or horses CORRAL
- fenced enclosure for cattle or sheep in South Africa KRAAL
- fenced-in field, as for horses and other farm animals PADDOCK

fencing See chart, and also **sword**
- types of sword used in modern fencing competitions SABER, FOIL, ÉPÉE

fermentation - chemistry of fermentation in brewing ZYMURGY
- fermenting grape juice MUST, STUM

fermentation (combining form) ZYMO-

fern leaf FROND
- feathery fern with fan-shaped leaves MAIDENHAIR
- hooked or coiled tip of a young fern frond CROSIER
- large, coarse fern BRACKEN
- primitive seed-bearing plant, resembling a palm, but having fern-like leaves and seed cones CYCAD
- reproductive cell or organ in nonflowering plants such as mosses and ferns and in fungi SPORE
- stalk, as of a mushroom or a frond of fern or seaweed STIPE

ferret, weasel, badger, otter, or related animal MUSTELINE

ferryboat, steamer taking a regular route PACKET

fertile, capable of reproduction PROGENITIVE
- fertile area in a desert OASIS
- fertile or productive, producing many offspring, crops, creative works, or the like FECUND, PROLIFIC

fertilization of a plant by its own pollen, self-fertilization AUTOGAMY
- fertilization of one plant by another, cross-pollination XENOGAMY
- referring to fertilization induced in an artificial laboratory environment rather than occurring naturally in the womb IN VITRO

fertilize an egg IMPREGNATE
- fertilize by pollen POLLINATE
- fertilize or make pregnant FECUNDATE
- fertilized egg or ovum ZYGOTE
- sperm cell, ovum, or other cell that can combine to form a fertilized cell GAMETE

fertilizer, lime, or the like added to improve soil DRESSING
- fertilizer consisting of human ex-

FENCING TERMS

appel	stamping of the foot as a feint
balestra	attacking movement in the form of a short jump forward
barrage	deciding heat in the event of a draw
coquille	guard at the end of the blade, protecting the hand
en garde	term warning a fencer to take the starting position for a bout
épée	sword with a triangular, fluted, blunt blade and a bell-shaped guard
feint	false attack, intended to create an opening for a final thrust
flèche	running attack, a short quick run forward
foible	weaker half of the blade, nearer the point
foil	light thrust sword, with a slim, very flexible blade and a blunt point
forte	stronger half of the blade, nearer the handle
parry/ parade	defensive action, deflecting the attacker's blade
piste	long rectangular area in which bouts take place
plastron	protective quilted covering for the upper body and armpit
remise	renewed attack, made without returning to the en garde position
reprise	renewed attack, made after returning to the en garde position
riposte	attacking movement following a successful parry
saber	cut-and-thrust sword, with a slightly flattened blade and a half-circular guard
touché	word used to acknowledge a hit by one's opponent
volt	sudden movement made to dodge a thrust

crement NIGHT SOIL
- fertilizer from coastal deposits of the dried dung of sea birds GUANO
- fertilizer or protective humus for young plants MULCH
- chemical compounds commonly used in fertilizers PHOSPHATE, POTASH, NITRATE
- conversion of nitrogen in the air into a fertilizer or other compound FIXATION, NITROGEN FIXATION
- decayed organic matter that fertilizes the soil HUMUS

festival See also **holiday**
- festival or religious celebration, as on a saint's day, especially in a Spanish-speaking country FIESTA
- festival parade or costumed procession PAGEANT, CAVALCADE

festival (combining form) -MAS

fetch, carry back RETRIEVE

fetus See **baby**

feud, maintained by a cycle of revenge VENDETTA

feudal system See chart

fever See also **disease**
- fever AGUE, PYREXIA
- fever, especially a mild tropical fever CALENTURE
- fever or extremely high body temperature HYPERPYREXIA, HYPERTHERMIA
- fever-reducing, as a drug might be ANTIPYRETIC
- chill or shivering attack, as preceding a fever RIGOR
- mentally confused or agitated, as during a high fever DELIRIOUS
- recurring daily, as attacks of a fever might be QUOTIDIAN
- relating to inflammation and fever PHLOGISTIC
- subsiding or ending of a fever, inflammation, or disease RESOLUTION

fever (combining form) FEBRI-, PYR-

feverish, bustling HECTIC
- feverish or relating to fever FEBRILE, PYRETIC

few (combining form) OLIGO-

fewness or scarcity PAUCITY

fiancé or fiancée BETHROTHED

fiber, thin wire, thread, or the like FILAMENT
- fiber from coconut husks, as used for ropes and matting COIR
- fiber from palm leaves used for weaving baskets, mats, or the like RAFFIA
- fiber from which linen is made, or the plant producing it FLAX
- fiber in the diet ROUGHAGE
- fiber of hemp or jute, often treated with tar, used for sealing pipe points and caulking the seams in wooden ships OAKUM
- fiber used in making ropes, or the tropical plant whose leaves yield the fiber SISAL
- fiber used in pillows, for soundproofing, or the like KAPOK
- fiber used in sacking HEMP, JUTE
- fibers, typically in a silky mass, as from cotton, maize, or silkworm cocoons FLOSS
- hard fiber used for making twine MAGUEY, CANTALA
- short, broken fiber, as of flax or hemp, used for yarn, stuffing, or the like TOW
- synthetic fiber ACRYLIC, ORLON
- thin, flexible fiber for transmission of light and telecommunications messages, as around corners OPTICAL FIBER
- tough tropical fiber, as used for making rope and paper ABACA, MANILA HEMP

fickle, changing constantly or liable to change LABILE
- fickleness, unsteadiness, inconstancy LEVITY

fictional place or imaginary world or land where things are better than in real life UTOPIA, COCKAIGNE, SHANGRI-LA
- fictional place or imaginary world or land where things are worse than in real life DYSTOPIA, CACOTOPIA

fictitious, imaginary MYTHICAL, CHIMERIC

field, plot of land held by a parson as part of his benefice GLEBE
- field of study, academic subject or speciality DISCIPLINE
- field or province of activity, sphere of operation or expertise PRESERVE, DOMAIN, BAILIWICK
- field or range of possible activity, scope, reach AMBIT, ORBIT, COMPASS
- enclosed field or pasture CROFT
- grassy field or meadow LEA
- plowed but left unseeded for a season, as a field might be, to regain fertility FALLOW
- relating to open country or uncultivated fields CAMPESTRAL
- ridge or bank bordering a river or irrigated field LEVEE

field (combining form) AGR-, AGRI-, AGRO-, -DROME

fifth QUINARY
- fifth anniversary QUINQUENNIAL

fifty-year-old, or a person who is aged between 50 and 59 inclusive QUINQUAGENARIAN

fig, fruit of the fig tree SYCONIUM

fight See also **attack, dispute, hostile**
- fight back, attack in revenge RETALIATE
- fight or argument, within a larger conflict, in which outsiders often get caught up CROSSFIRE
- fight or campaign in favor of a cause CRUSADE
- fight or combat between two mounted knights armed with lances JOUST, TILTING MATCH
- fight or oppose TILT AT
- fighting imaginary enemies, shadow boxing SCIAMACHY
- angry conflict or disagreement, often with bitter fighting STRIFE, FRICTION, DISSENSION
- angry quarrel or fight, clash ALTERCATION, CONTRETEMPS
- brawl, scuffle, disorderly fight or free-for-all FRAY, SHINDY, MELEE, TUSSLE
- deeply involved in a fight, scandal, or the like EMBROILED
- engaged in a fight or running argument, seriously in dispute AT LOGGERHEADS
- given to fighting, easily provoked or antagonized FRACTIOUS, TRUCULENT, PUGNACIOUS
- hostile encounter, fight or conflict CONFRONTATION
- minor fight or conflict, sometimes preliminary to a major battle SKIRMISH
- noisy fight or quarrel, rowdy brawl AFFRAY, BROIL, DONNYBROOK, FRACAS
- petty fight or quarrel TIFF, SPAT
- referring to destructive fighting or conflict within a group INTERNECINE
- stir into a fighting mood MAKE ONE'S HACKLES RISE

fighter See **soldier**

figure - shapely and narrow-waisted, as a woman's figure might be HOURGLASS

figure of speech See chart, pages 200–201
- figure of speech, or figurative use of language, as for rhetorical effect TROPE
- based on or using figures of speech, metaphorical FIGURATIVE
- clever and elaborate figure of speech, especially an ingenious metaphor CONCEIT

figurine, usually crouched and grotesque, of Chinese or Japanese carving MAGOT

file, grate, or scrape RASP
- file for wood- or metalworking that is long, thin, and cylindrical RATTAIL
- file or collection of papers giving information on a particular person or subject DOSSIER
- file or similar scraping tool with a curved face RIFFLER
- file with metal rings for holding loose leaves RING BINDER
- shape or enlarge a hole, as in

FEUDAL AND MEDIEVAL TERMS

allodium	land held in absolute ownership, rather than subject to feudal restrictions
attainder	forfeiture of land and civil rights imposed upon outlaws and condemned felons
benevolences	"voluntary" payments made to earn the goodwill of the king
ceorl/churl	lowest-ranking freeman
chamberlain	principal financial officer of the king's household
commonage	right of pasture on common land
constable	chief military officer of the king's household
corvée	day's unpaid labor owed by a vassal to his lord
cotter	villein granted a cottage and land in return for work
demesne	lands kept by a feudal lord for his own use
droit de seigneur	mythical right (it never existed) of a feudal lord to have sexual intercourse with a vassal's new bride
ealderman/ alderman	chief officer of a shire
escheat	return of lands to a feudal lord, as when the tenant has no heir
esne	Anglo-Saxon person of the lower classes
esquire/ squire	candidate for knighthood in the service of a knight
fealty	allegiance owed by a vassal or tenant to his feudal lord
fee/feoff/fief/ feud	feudal land granted by a lord to a vassal in return for homage and service
franklin	landowning commoner, country gentleman
frankpledge	joint responsibility among members of a tithing for the good conduct of the others
geld	tax or tribute paid to the Crown
glebe	land endowed to a parish church
grange	farm building in which grain paid as tithes was stored
hide	amount of land adequate to support a peasant family
homage	formal acknowledgment of allegiance by a vassal to a feudal lord
hue and cry	pursuit of a felon with shouts and cries; legal duty to join such pursuit
liege	lord to whom feudal service is due; vassal, liegeman owing allegiance to a lord
marshal	senior member of the king's household, especially a judicial adviser
mesne lord	feudal lord holding land from a superior
moot/gemot	meeting, assembly, or court
murage	tax levied to maintain or build city walls
pannage/ panage	right of a villein to pasture his pigs in woodland; rent paid for this right
pardoner	layman commissioned to sell ecclesiastical indulgences
quitrent	rent paid by a freeman in lieu of various feudal services
reeve	high-ranking local administrative officer; bailiff or steward
scutage	tax paid in lieu of doing military service
seneschal	steward, official in charge of servants and domestic arrangements in a noble household
serf	peasant bound to the land and its lord in a slavelike condition
socage	holding of land by a tenant in return for payment or services
suzerain/ seigneur	feudal lord or overlord
thane/thegn	freeman ranking above a churl but below a noble
tithe	annual tax of one tenth of a person's income and produce, paid to support the Church
tithing	group of ten householders bound together by a system of mutual responsibility for good conduct
vassal	liegeman or feudal tenant owing allegiance to a lord
vavasor/ vavasour	knightly vassal ranking just below a baron, and having other vassals subject to him
villein	semifreeman, owing some rents and services to his lord, but not in bondage
witan/ witenagemot	national assembly in Anglo-Saxon England, consisting of noblemen advising the king

wood, with a special cylindrical file REAM

fill, spread widely, or permeate with something damaging RIDDLE
- fill or resupply something, such as a larder REPLENISH
- fill someone with or feed into someone knowledge, principles, or the like IMBUE, PERMEATE, PERVADE, INCULCATE, INSTILL
- fill something with a substance or introduce it into something, as by soaking IMPREGNATE, INFUSE, SATURATE, SUFFUSE
- filled, as with food or drink, satisfied to the point of excess SATED, SATIATED, REPLETE, GLUTTED, GORGED
- filled to excess with blood or other fluid ENGORGED
- overfilled or overcrowded, as a room might be CONGESTED

filler, glaze, or coating, as for paper or walls, made of wax, clay, glue, resin, or the like SIZE

filling - mercury alloy, such as that used by dentists as a filling for teeth AMALGAM

film See chart, page 202
- film, book, or the like dealing with events earlier than those in the previous one PREQUEL
- film, book, or the like dealing with events following those in the previous one SEQUEL
- film, book, or the like, mixing fact and fiction FACTION
- film buff, cinema enthusiast, creative filmmaker or critic CINEAST
- film camera or projector CINEMATOGRAPH
- film library or repertory cinema CINEMATHEQUE
- film or television program intended as an accurate history or analysis but using actors and dramatic reconstructions DOCUDRAMA
- film or television program presented as a nonfictional analysis or history DOCUMENTARY
- film projector of an early type BIOSCOPE
- filmmaking as an art or technique CINEMATOGRAPHY
- accumulation of a thin film of a substance on the surface of a solid ADSORPTION
- blank length of tape, used for threading, at the beginning or end of a reel of film or tape LEADER
- brief scene in a film, book, or play

FIGURES OF SPEECH AND RHETORICAL DEVICES

alliteration	use of words starting with or containing the same letter of sound, especially the same consonant: *The furrow followed free*
anacoluthon	grammatically inconsistent sentence or phrase, with a shift of construction midway: *My advice is, since time is running out, shouldn't you get started at once?*
anadiplosis	repetition of a word or group of words at the end of one phrase and beginning of the next one, for rhetorical effect: *waited for the dawn—the dawn that would restore hope*
anastrophe	rhetorical inversion of the normal order of words: *Full many a glorious morning have I seen*
antiphrasis	ironic or playful use of words in a sense opposite or contradictory to the accepted sense: *eighty years young*
antithesis	expression in which contrasting ideas are carefully balanced: *more haste, less speed*
antonomasia	use of a personal name or proper noun to refer to anyone belonging to a class: *an Einstein* to refer to a brilliantly intelligent person
apostrophe	direct address to an absent or dead person or personified thing: *O Freedom! hear my call!*
assonance	repetition of vowel sounds, producing a half-rhyme effect: *Slowly blowing over the cold plateau*
asyndeton	omission of conjunctions: *I came, I saw, I conquered*
ellipsis/ aposiopesis	omission of words, or sudden breaking off in midsentence, for dramatic effect: *The door opened, and ...*
euphemism	use of an inoffensive expression to stand in for a sharper or more explicit one: *passed away* for *died*
hendiadys	use of two nouns joined by *and* to express an idea that would normally be expressed by an adjective and noun; or a similarly expanded phrase: *through storm and weather* instead of *through stormy weather*
hypallage	switching of the syntactic roles of two terms: *joy is lost to her* and *she is lost to joy*
hyperbole	exaggeration or overstatement for emphasis: *I could eat a horse*
irony	use of word or words to convey something markedly different from the literal meaning: *I don't suppose you'd be interested to hear that you've just won the jackpot*
litotes/meiosis	understatement in which an idea is tellingly conveyed, typically by contradicting its opposite: *He's not exactly sober*
malapropism	word misused through confusion with a similar-sounding word, sometimes deliberately for comic effect: *He's being used as a prawn in the game*

VIGNETTE
- category of literature, films, or the like GENRE
- early or afternoon screening of a film MATINEE
- extract or selected passage or scene from a book, film, or the like EXCERPT
- first public presentation of a film, play, or the like PREMIERE
- join two strips of film, rope, or the like at the ends SPLICE
- place something over or on top of something else, such as one film sequence on another SUPERIMPOSE
- pornographic film for a male audience STAG FILM
- prepare, treat, or rectify something, such as a film or cheese, by a special method PROCESS
- review or criticism of a book, film, play, or the like CRITIQUE
- scene or passage in a film, novel, or the like that interrupts the main story line to revert to previous events FLASHBACK
- single exposure on a strip of film FRAME
- toy producing simple filmlike images, consisting of a picture-lined cylinder revolving past a viewing slit ZOETROPE
- vegetable matter used in making paper, rayon, and photographic film CELLULOSE

film (combining form) CINE-, PELLI-

filter or sift PERCOLATE
- clay used in filtering FULLER'S EARTH
- technique for filtering impurities from the blood of patients with kidney failure DIALYSIS
- pass through a filter or filterlike obstruction INFILTRATE

filthy See **dirty**

fin See also **fish**
- fin, wing, feather, or similar projecting body part PINNA
- fin on a bomb or missile for guiding or stabilizing it VANE
- bony spines supporting a fish's fin RAYS

final and decisive, allowing of no refusal or argument, as a command might be PEREMPTORY
- final or farewell appearance, act, work, or statement SWAN SONG
- final or highest point CULMINATION, CLIMAX
- final part of a formal speech or

FIGURES OF SPEECH AND RHETORICAL DEVICES *continued*

metaphor	description of one thing in terms of another that is related to it by analogy: *She sailed across the room*
metonymy	use of an associated word rather than the literal word; for example, *the sword* to refer to war
onomatopoeia	use of words whose sound suggests their meaning: *sizzle; splash; Ping-Pong*
oxymoron	linking of incongruous or contradictory terms: *The wisest fool in Christendom*
pathetic fallacy	assigning of human feelings or characteristics to natural or inanimate objects: *The trees groaned*
personification	representation of an object or idea as human: *The jovial moon smiling benignly down at us*
pleonasm	use of superfluous or redundant words: *The plane descended downward.*
polysyndeton	repetition of conjunctions for rhetorical effect: *We went to Florence and Venice and Rome and Naples*
prosopopoeia	making an imaginary, absent, or dead person appear to be speaking
rhetorical question/ erotema	question asked for effect or to convey information, or used as a social formula, rather than to elicit an answer: *Isn't it a lovely day?; How do you do?*
simile	comparison of two unlike ideas or objects, using the word *like* or *as* to make it explicit: *lips like rosebuds*
syllepsis	use of a single word to apply to two others, in different ways: *He held his tongue and my hand*
synecdoche	use of a narrower term for a wider term, or vice versa: *fifty sail* to refer to fifty ships, or *copper* to refer to a penny
tautology	repetition of an idea by needless or emphatic use of words: *Do a U-turn and face the other way*
tmesis	separation of the parts of a word by the insertion of another word: *what person soever* for "whatsoever person"
transferred epithet	deliberate misapplication of an adjective to a noun, for a compact or dramatic effect: *a sleepless night; the poisoned cup; the condemned cell*
zeugma	use of a single word to apply to two others, especially when it is appropriate to only one; a faulty syllepsis: *He held his tongue and his promise*

FILMS AND FILMING TERMS

animation	art or process of filming a series of static drawings to give the impression of movement, as for cartoon films
back projection	projection of a film onto the reverse side of a screen, often as a background for filming in front of it
best boy	assistant to the gaffer
biopic	biographical film
cameo role	brief but dramatic appearance of a well-known actor
cinema-verité	films or filming intended to represent life very realistically
clapper board	hinged boards bearing the take number clapped in front of the camera, to synchronize sound and picture prints
commissary	cafeteria in a film studio
compilation film	film using some real-life documentary sequences
continuity	detailed script for ensuring consistency from scene to scene
credits	list of performers and workers in the making of a film
cut-in	inserted shot, typically a still close-up, interrupting a running sequence of film
dissolve	change of scenes, in which one scene fades out as the next appears
dolly	low platform on castors or wheels for moving a camera about the set
dub	add a new soundtrack, especially a translation of the dialogue
fade-in, fade-out	gradual appearance or disappearance of an image or sound
film à clef	apparently fictional film based on facts, but with the names of places and characters changed
footage	sequence or portion of film
freeze frame	repeated single frame, producing the impression of a static picture
gaffer	electrician or lighting technician on a production crew
grip	member of a production crew who adjusts the set and shifts the camera equipment
intercut/ crosscut	insert a shot or scene into a sequence, as for dramatic contrast
klieg light	carbon-arc lamp producing intense light
location	site for filming that is outside the studio
montage	sequence of shots or short scenes depicting the same theme or event in different ways
new wave/ nouvelle vague	French cinema movement of the 1960s that cut down on standard narrative and filming techniques in favor of improvisation, simple settings, and symbolism
opticals	trick techniques such as wipes and dissolves
outtake	series of frames discarded in the editing process of a film
pan	swing the camera sideways, across a scene, to follow a moving object or produce a panoramic effect
rush	first, unedited print of a scene
scenario/ screenplay	script that includes camera directions and scene descriptions
shooting script	script giving details of camera work and the order of shooting
split-screen	referring to the technique in which two or more images appear simultaneously on different parts of the same screen
take	uninterrupted filming of a scene; filmed scene produced in this way, often reshot several times
time-lapse	referring to the technique of photographing a scene at intervals to give a continuous, accelerated view of a slow process, such as a flower opening
track	move the camera, usually on rails, to follow the action
treatment	full and detailed narrative version of a script
voice-over	commentary of an unseen narrator, or representation on the sound track of a character's unspoken thoughts
wipe	change of scenes in which a line moves across to obliterate the old scene and bring in the new
zoom	quick increase or decrease in the size of the image of an object, by means of a special lens

written discourse, typically a summing-up PERORATION
- final part of the action in a play or novel, resolving or unraveling the plot DENOUEMENT
- final part or element of something OMEGA
- final poem or speech after the end of a play EPILOGUE
- final section, often an afterthought or addition, of a novel, piece of music, or the like CODA
- final terms offered in negotiating, to be accepted "or else" ULTIMATUM
- final touch, finishing act COUP DE GRACE
- make something decided or final, such as an argument or bargain CLINCH

final (combining form) TEL-, TELEO-, TERM-, EPI-

finance See also chart at **economics**
- finance, guarantee against financial failure UNDERWRITE
- finance a project, support an institution, or the like by means of a grant of money SUBSIDIZE
- finance office of a college or university BURSARY, TREASURY
- relating to finances, especially those of a country or government department FISCAL

financial center or powerful financial interests in the U.S. economy WALL STREET
- financial center or powerful financial interests in the British economy THE CITY, LOMBARD STREET
- financial center or powerful financial interests in the Canadian economy BAY STREET
- financial director COMPTROLLER
- financial grant, such as an endowment SUBVENTION
- financial obligation LIABILITY
- financial supporter or promoter of a project, sportsman, cultural activity, sport, or the like SPONSOR, PATRON, ANGEL
- financially in a position to meet all debts SOLVENT
- financially restrictive, characterized by a scarcity of loan money STRINGENT

finch, sparrow, or related bird FRINGILLID

find, bring to light, dig up, root out UNEARTH
- find or discover by painstaking research or observation DESCRY
- find out the meaning of, come to understand FATHOM
- find out with difficulty PRY OUT, WINKLE OUT
- finding one's bearings, socially or spatially ORIENTATION
- exclamation of triumph on finding, solving, or discovering something EUREKA
- tendency to make fortunate finds by chance SERENDIPITY

fine distinction or subtle point or detail NICETY
- fine or damages imposed by a court in former times AMERCEMENT
- fine or similar penalty MULCT
- impose or collect a tax, fine, membership fee, or the like LEVY

fine arts BEAUX ARTS

finger See also **hand, thumb**
- finger, toe, or corresponding part of an animal DIGIT, DACTYL
- finger bones or toe bones PHALANGES
- finger of a glove, or protective sheath for an injured finger or toe STALL
- broad-tipped, as fingers or leaves might be SPATULATE
- fleshy underpart of the top joint of a finger or toe PAD
- flicking of the finger after holding it back with the thumb FILLIP

finger (combining form) DACTYL-, DACTYLO-

finger hole as on a flute VENTAGE

fingernail - crescent-shaped mark at the base of a fingernail LUNULA
- strip of hardened skin at the base of a fingernail CUTICLE

fingerprint See also **hand**
- basic patterns for classifying and identifying fingerprints LOOP, ARCH, WHORL
- informal term for a fingerprint DAB
- scientific study of fingerprints as a technique of identification DACTYLOGRAPHY
- technical term for a fingerprint DACTYLOGRAM

finish See **end, stop**
- finish off, dispose of, complete efficiently DISPATCH
- finishing or surface layer, as of fine wood VENEER

finishing point, destination, objective, goal TERMINUS AD QUEM

finishing touch, final action COUP DE GRACE

Finnish steam-bath treatment or recreation, typically followed by a cold plunge SAUNA

fir, pine, or related cone-bearing tree CONIFER

fire blazing furiously with hellish flames INFERNO
- fire of a large-scale and destructive kind CONFLAGRATION, HOLOCAUST
- fire sensor that activates an extinguisher or alarm PYROSTAT
- able to cause fire or catch fire INCENDIARY
- attack enemy ground troops with bombs or machine-gun fire from low-flying aircraft STRAFE
- attack or burst of gunfire, rocket fire, or the like SALVO, FUSILLADE
- attack with gunfire from the side, raking the entire length of a troop formation or position ENFILADE
- burning readily, catching fire easily INFLAMMABLE, FLAMMABLE
- catch fire, or set fire to IGNITE
- catching fire without external ignition, as in coal dust or hay self-heated through oxidation SPONTANEOUS COMBUSTION
- cooking pot or large kettle with a hooped handle for hanging over an open fire CALDRON
- cover a fire with ashes or fresh fuel to keep it burning low BANK
- form of legal trial in the Middle Ages, in which God's judgment was allegedly secured through exposing the accused to fire, immersion in water, or the like ORDEAL
- glowing or smoldering coal or wood, as in a dying fire EMBERS
- great destruction by or as if by fire HOLOCAUST
- hypothetical substance or principle formerly thought to exist in combustible matter and be released in a fire PHLOGISTON
- lizardlike creature, in myth, that lived in or withstood fire SALAMANDER
- mentally disturbed person who starts fires PYROMANIAC
- person who sets fire to property illegally ARSONIST, INCENDIARY
- put out a fire or flame, extinguish QUENCH, DOUSE
- relating to or resembling fire IGNEOUS
- setting fire to buildings or other property deliberately, for criminal purposes ARSON
- strip or destroy the inside of, as fire might destroy the inside of a building GUT
- three-legged metal stand, as for supporting pots over a fire TRIVET
- twigs, decayed wood, or similar combustible material used to get a fire going TINDER, KINDLING, TOUCHWOOD, SPUNK, PUNK
- twist of paper or sliver of wood for lighting a fire SPILL
- wood pile prepared for a funeral fire on which to cremate a corpse PYRE

fire (combining form) PYRO-

fire bomb, bomb designed to start a destructive fire INCENDIARY BOMB
- fire bomb containing highly inflammable jellied gasoline NAPALM BOMB

- fire bomb or inflammable substance used in ancient sea warfare GREEK FIRE
- crude fire bomb thrown by hand, typically a fuel-filled bottle stoppered with a rag wick MOLOTOV COCKTAIL

fire hose - sidewalk water pipe for fire hoses HYDRANT

firearm See **gun**

fireball or meteor that is unusually large and bright, and may burn out or explode BOLIDE

fireplace HEARTH
- fireplace frame, often decorated MANTEL
- fireplace rack or stand, as for keeping dishes warm FOOTMAN
- fireplace shelf, as for keeping food warm HOB
- chimney corner by a fireplace, often with seats facing each other INGLENOOK
- fireguard, metal grid keeping coals or embers within the fireplace FENDER
- metal stand, used in pairs, for logs in a fireplace ANDIRON, FIREDOG
- screen or decorative iron plate at the back of a fireplace REREDOS
- solid residue from a coal-fired furnace or fireplace CLINKER

firework rocket that flies in a winding or spiral path TOURBILLION
- firework that makes a hissing or fizzing sound FIZGIG
- fireworks display or manufacture PYROTECHNICS
- fireworks or jets of water that appear to rotate GIRANDOLE
- loud exploding firework PETARD
- paper casing for the powder in some fireworks CARTOUCHE
- small firework that hisses and then explodes with a bang SQUIB
- smoldering substance, such as knotted rags, used to light fireworks PUNK

firing of guns in a rapid burst FUSILLADE, BARRAGE
- firing platform behind a parapet or in a trench BANQUETTE
- firing simultaneously of all the guns along one side of a warship BROADSIDE
- object for firing or throwing, such as a bullet or missile PROJECTILE
- platform or mound along the wall of a fort, from which cannons are fired over the parapet BARBETTE

firm, established, inherent, or essential SUBSTANTIVE
- firm, loyal, steadfast STAUNCH
- firm, tough, resolute TENACIOUS
- firmly and immovably settled, as opinions or troops might be ENTRENCHED
- firmly fixed or established in position, impossible to release or dislodge INEXTRICABLE

firmness, texture, as of a pudding CONSISTENCY

first, earliest, original PRIMARY, INITIAL, PRIMAL, ARCHETYPAL, PRIMEVAL
- first, second, third, and so on ORDINAL NUMBERS
- first example or model, on which copies or later developments are based PROTOTYPE, ARCHETYPE
- first experience of or exposure to a painful ordeal, especially on the battlefield BAPTISM OF FIRE
- first principle or elementary stage of a skill or subject RUDIMENT
- first public appearance, as of an actor, musician, or the like DEBUT
- first public displaying of a monument, work of art, or the like UNVEILING
- first public presentation of a movie, play, or the like PREMIERE
- first success or foothold that opens the way to further achievements BEACHHEAD, BRIDGEHEAD, SALIENT
- ability to take the first step of a plan or project INITIATIVE
- condition of being first PRIMACY
- just beginning to develop, in the first stages of growth EMBRYONIC, SEMINAL, GERMINAL, NASCENT, INCIPIENT, INCHOATE

first (combining form) FORE-, PROTO-, UR-

first-aid station near a battlefield DRESSING STATION

first among equals PRIMUS INTER PARES

first cousin COUSIN-GERMAN

first-year student of a high school, college, or university FRESHMAN

firstborn - state of being the firstborn child, or firstborn right to in-

FISH DISHES

Arbroath smokie	small whole haddock hot smoked to a brown color
bloater	dried, salted, and smoked whole herring
Bombay duck	dried and salted bummalo, an Indian fish, eaten with curry
bouillabaisse	strongly seasoned French stew of several kinds of fish and shellfish
calamari	squid, often served deep-fried
coquilles Saint Jacques	scallops prepared and served in their own shells
coulibiac	traditional Russian fish pie
gefilte fish	seasoned fish cakes or balls bound with meal, and boiled in fish stock
goujons	strips of catfish or sole, crumbed and fried
gravadlax	Scandinavian pickled salmon
kedgeree	flaked fish mixed with rice, and sometimes eggs and cream
matelote	French fish stew with wine
rissoles	small balls or cakes of minced cooked fish or meat, covered with pastry
rollmops	pickled herring, wrapped around an onion or gherkin and skewered
sole bonne femme	fillets of sole served with a white wine and button mushroom sauce
sole meunière	sole lightly fried in butter, then sprinkled with lemon juice and herbs

herit the entire estate or monarchy PRIMOGENITURE

fish See illustration and chart
- fish, such as sharks and rays, whose skeleton is entirely of cartilage rather than hard bone CARTILAGINOUS FISH
- fish, turtles, and other free-swimming animals, in a lake, the sea, or other body of water NEKTON
- fish-eating, feeding on fish PISCIVOROUS
- fish eggs, frog eggs, or the like SPAWN
- fish pen, turtle enclosure, or the like CRAWL
- fish sperm or testis MILT
- fish tank AQUARIUM
- air bladder of a fish SOUND
- catch or attempt to catch fish with one's hands GUDDLE
- dive down quickly and deep, as a large fish or whale might SOUND
- gash or score raw meat or fish for crisper cooking CRIMP
- group or school of fish SHOAL, RUN
- having spawned recently, as a food fish might have done, and so of less value as food SHOTTEN
- opening for the eliminative and genital tracts in fish, birds, and reptiles CLOACA
- relating to or resembling a fish PISCINE
- steak cut from the side of a halibut or other fish FLITCH
- very small fish TIDDLER
- young or undeveloped fish FRY, FINGERLING

fish (combining form) ICHTHY-, ICHTHYO-, PISC-, PISCI-

fishing See chart, page 206
- fishing equipment TACKLE
- fishing spear or set of hooks for impaling fish GIG
- fishing spear with three prongs LEISTER
- baggy middle section of a fishing net or square sail BUNT
- relating to fishing or fishermen PISCATORIAL
- remove the hook from a fish after catching it DISGORGE
- time of year when hunting, fishing, shooting of game, or the like is permitted OPEN SEASON
- time of year when hunting, fishing, shooting of game, or the like is prohibited CLOSED SEASON

fit, join, or connect comfortably or harmoniously DOVETAIL
- fit, stroke, or brainstorm ICTUS
- fit, sudden attack, spasm, frenzy PAROXYSM, SEIZURE, APOPLEXY, CONVULSION
- fit of resentment or temper, as from a blow to one's pride PIQUE

Fish

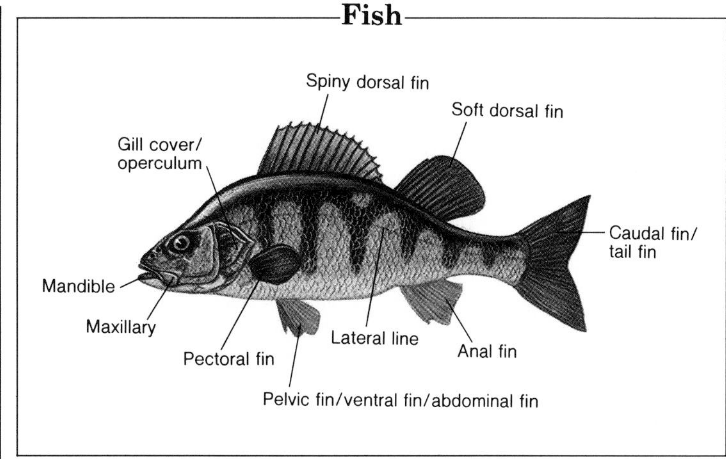

- fit or accord comfortably, harmonize MESH
- fit or frenzy of frustrated desire for something unattainable NYMPHOLEPSY

fit, seizure (combining form) -LEPSY

fits and starts - happening in fits and starts, intermittent SPASMODIC

fitted and permanent appliance, item of furnishings, or the like FIXTURE

five children or young born at one birth QUINTUPLETS
- five-lined light humorous verse, rhyming *aabba* LIMERICK
- five-pointed star, formed by five straight lines, sometimes credited with magic powers PENTACLE, PENTANGLE, PENTAGRAM
- five-sided figure PENTAGON
- five-year period QUINQUENNIUM
- group or series of five elements PENTAD
- group or setting of five objects arranged in a rectangle with one in the middle, as with the five on dice QUINCUNX
- multiply by five QUINTUPLE
- the number five, in cards or dice CINQUE

five (combining form) PENT-, PENTA-, QUIN-, QUINQU-

five-hundredth anniversary QUINCENTENARY

five-lobed - plant with five-lobed compound leaves CINQUEFOIL

fix See **repair, join**

fixed, established, firmly and immovably settled, as opinions, or troops on a battlefield, might be ENTRENCHED
- fixed, rooted, immovable, as barnacles are SESSILE
- fixed firmly, impossible to eliminate, as incorrigible vices are INERADICABLE
- fixed firmly, impossible to release or to move EMBEDDED, INEXTRICABLE
- fixed idea, preoccupation to the exclusion of everything else OBSESSION, IDÉE FIXE
- fixed or impressed firmly, as in the memory ENGRAVED
- fixed-price meal, typically offering a narrow range of choices, served in a restaurant or hotel TABLE D'HÔTE, PRIX FIXE

fizzy drink CARBONATED DRINK
- fizzy mineral water, either natural or artificially aerated SELTZER WATER

flabby and limp, drooping, lacking firmness FLACCID
- flabby flesh under the jaw JOWL, DEWLAP

flag See illustration, page 207
- flag, typically triangular or forked, flown from the mast of a ship or yacht BURGEE
- flag, especially one of small size, on the bow of a ship to indicate its nationality JACK
- flag or banner, as of a military unit ENSIGN, ANCIENT, STANDARD
- flag or banner, especially on a horizontal bar, as used in church parades GONFALON
- flags, especially those of a boat, or the light cloth used in making them BUNTING
- flags grouped to make a signal HOIST
- ceremonial military parading of flags TROOPING THE COLOR
- inspiring flag or other symbol, modeled on a traditional red royal French flag ORIFLAMME
- long, narrow flag, often forked, as attached to a knight's lance BANDEROLE, BANNEROL, PENCEL, STREAMER, PENNONCEL
- long, narrow flag, often triangular, as used for signaling PENNANT, PENNON

FISHING TERMS

coop	basket used for trapping or landing fish
creel	wickerwork basket used for trapping or carrying fish
dapping	bobbing a fly or baited hook gently on the surface of the water
disgorger	instrument for removing hook from fish
drail	lead-weighted hook dragged through the water
fancy fly	artificial fly that does not resemble a living fly
gaff	hooked pole for hauling large fish aboard or ashore
gag	instrument for holding open the jaws of a fish while hooks are extracted
gang hook	compound fishhook made of several hooks joined shank to shank
ground bait	unattached bait thrown into the river, sea, or pool to attract fish
guddle	catch or try to catch fish with one's hands
hackle fly	artificial fly with a rufflike tuft, as of feathers
jig	metal lure with one or more hooks that is jerked up and down or pulled through the water
keep net	net placed in the water, into which caught fish are put to keep them alive
ledger bait	bait fixed in position, typically on the bottom
lure	spinning bait or artificial fly that does not resemble any natural fly
paternoster line	weighted fishing line with a row of shorter lines carrying hooks
priest	small weighted club for killing fish after landing
seine	net hanging upright in the water
skittering	skipping or skimming a lure or hook lightly over the water
spinning	winding back the bait after casting, to simulate a swimming fish
spoon	shiny concave lure that spins when drawn through the water
tag	colorful piece of feather or other material surrounding the shank of the hook in a fishing fly
trace	connecting line, often of wire, between the hook and the main line
trammel	net of three layers, set upright in the water
trawl	bag-shaped net towed underwater
trolling	fishing with a baited hook trailing behind a boat
trotting	angling in fast-moving water, using a float and line that holds the bait near the bottom

- lower a mast, sail, or flag STRIKE
- relating to flags or ensigns VEXILLARY
- roll up a flag or umbrella FURL
- rope used for hoisting or lowering a flag HALYARD
- side of a flag nearest the flagpole HOIST
- small flag carried as the standard of a military unit GUIDON
- small flag for signaling or indicating wind direction WAFT, WAIF
- study of flags VEXILLOLOGY
- unroll or open out something, such as a flag UNFURL
- wave or flutter proudly, as a flag does FLAUNT

flame See also **fire**
- flame hovering over marshy ground WILL-O'-THE-WISP, JACK-O'-LANTERN, IGNIS FATUUS, FRIAR'S LANTERN
- extinguish a lamp, candle, flame, or the like, typically by smothering it SNUFF
- flaming torch FLAMBEAU
- flicker or be on the point of going out, as a candle flame might GUTTER
- flickering or glowing gently, as a flame might be LAMBENT
- gas burner producing a hot flame, used for laboratory experiments BUNSEN BURNER
- gas mixture used for the high-temperature flame in welding OXY-ACETYLENE
- put out a flame, candle, or the like, extinguish DOUSE, QUENCH
- ring of hot gas around a flame MANTLE

flap, as a sail might when losing wind LUFF
- flap of cloth at the back of a cap, to protect the neck from sunburn HAVELOCK

flare fired from a special pistol, used as a signal or for illumination, especially at sea VERY LIGHT

flash, glitter, sparkle, as a gemstone might CORUSCATE, SCINTILLATE, FULGURATE

flashy See **showy**

flask with a long near-horizontal neck, formerly used for distilling in chemistry MATRASS, ALEMBIC

flat, having a broad plane surface TABULAR
- flat, level, parallel to the horizon HORIZONTAL
- flat, turned-out foot SPLAYFOOT
- flat and raised stretch of land PLATEAU
- flat or even, as two neatly fitting edges are FLUSH

- flat shelf cut, usually in a series, into the side of a slope, for cultivation, preventing erosion, or the like TERRACE
- flat stretch of ground for walking along, especially along a seashore ESPLANADE
- flat-topped hill, with steep sides, as in the arid areas of southwestern United States MESA
- lying down flat PROSTRATE, RECUMBENT
- lying flat on one's back SUPINE
- lying flat on one's front PRONE
- lying flat with one's arms and legs spread out SPREAD-EAGLED

flat (combining form) PLAN-, PLANO-, PLATY-

flatter See also **praise**
- flatter or deceive with smooth, charming talk BLARNEY
- flatter with undue respect or admiration, treat as a VIP LIONIZE
- flatterer or toady, buttering up influential people as a means of self-advancement SYCOPHANT
- flatterers or self-interested followers of an influential patron CLAQUE
- flattering, temptations, urging or wheedling BLANDISHMENTS
- flattering or cooperating overeagerly, slavishly submissive or yielding, overeager to please SERVILE, OBSEQUIOUS
- flattering and overhumble underling, a groveler, toady, or bootlicker APPLE-POLISHER, LICKSPITTLE
- coax or persuade, as by means of flattery CAJOLE
- curry favor, as by flattery or excessive humility FAWN, KOWTOW, TRUCKLE
- gushing or excessively demonstrative, as flattering compliments might be EFFUSIVE
- smoothly flattering or obliging in a suspiciously humble way, oily, smarmy UNCTUOUS
- submissive self-humbling follower, flattering and dancing attendance on his patron FLUNKY, LACKEY, MINION, COURTIER, MYRMIDON

flavor, taste RELISH, SAPOR
- flavor enhancer, as used in many Chinese restaurants MONOSODIUM GLUTAMATE, MSG
- sharp flavor, taste, or smell TANG

flavoring for drinks in the form of a bitter tonic ANGOSTURA BITTERS
- flavoring of orange and almond, as used in cocktails ORGEAT
- flavoring of pomegranate or redcurrant syrup GRENADINE

flavorless, dull, unexciting INSIPID

flavorsome, tasty, or agreeable to eat PALATABLE

flawless, faultless IMMACULATE, IMPECCABLE

flax - steel comb for combing flax HACKLE

flecked or dotted, as with paint or natural colors STIPPLED

flee, run away or depart hastily SKEDADDLE, SCARPER, VAMOOSE
- flee secretly, as after committing a theft ABSCOND, ABSQUATULATE, DECAMP, HIGHTAIL
- flee secretly with a lover, typically to get married ELOPE
- fleeing person or escaped criminal FUGITIVE
- emigrant, specifically one who has fled his homeland for political reasons ÉMIGRÉ
- person who flees from war or suppression REFUGEE

fleecy or fluffy mass FLOCCULUS

fleet of merchant ships ARGOSY
- fleet of small ships, or small fleet of ships FLOTILLA
- fleet of warships ARMADA

flesh - "flesh"-colored INCARNADINE
- flesh-eating or insect-eating, as lions, dogs, vultures, and pitcher plants are CARNIVOROUS, CREOPHAGOUS
- flesh of a dead and rotting animal CARRION
- discipline one's fleshly appetites and desires by punishment or self-denial MORTIFY
- tear the flesh, as with a knife or whip LACERATE

flesh (combining form) SARC-, SARCO-, CARN-, CARNI-

flexible, easily drawn out into threads DUCTILE
- flexible, easily molded or shaped

Flags

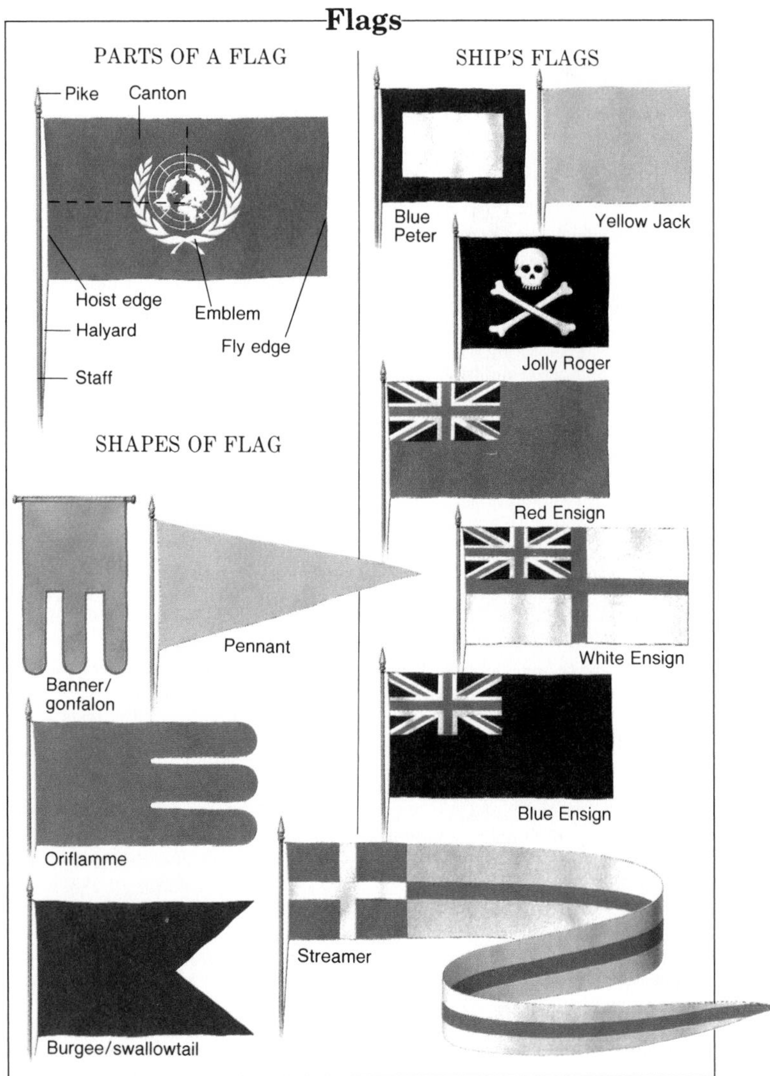

MALLEABLE, PLIABLE
- flexible, supple, nimble, or agile LITHE, LIMBER, LISSOM

flick of the finger FILLIP

flicker or be on the point of going out, as a candle flame might GUTTER
- flickering or glowing gently, as a flame might be LAMBENT

flight from danger HEGIRA, EXODUS
- flight path, often circular, of an aircraft awaiting clearance to land HOLDING PATTERN
- flight path, typically curved, of a missile, ball, or the like TRAJECTORY
- referring to flights over long distances LONG-HAUL

flightless, as the ostrich and related birds are STRUTHIOUS
- flightless bird such as the ostrich, emu, or kiwi RATITE

flint tool with a chisellike head, from prehistoric times BURIN

flirt, or engage in casual love affairs PHILANDER
- flirt, tease, or toy with TRIFLE, DALLY, COQUET
- flirt or socialize, especially while wandering about GAD ABOUT, GALLIVANT
- flirtation, loveplay DALLIANCE
- flirtatious woman COQUETTE

float attached parallel on one or both sides of a canoe to stabilize it OUTRIGGER
- float filled with air for raising sunken ships CAISSON, CAMEL
- float for raising sunken ships or supporting a floating bridge PONTOON
- float in the air, apparently in defiance of gravity LEVITATE
- float in the air, or fly without changing position HOVER
- float or drift gently, as the smell of flowers does in the wind WAFT
- floating or swimming NATANT
- floating wreckage or cargo after a ship has sunk FLOTSAM, JETSAM
- tendency or ability to float BUOYANCY

flock of geese or other wildfowl in flight SKEIN
- flock or herd of animals being driven together DROVE
- living or migrating in a herd, pack, flock, or the like GREGARIOUS

flog, whip, as for religious discipline or sexual gratification FLAGELLATE, SCOURGE

flood, downpour DELUGE
- flood, earthquake, or other sudden, ruinous disaster CATACLYSM
- flood, overwhelm INUNDATE
- flood barrier in the form of an embankment DIKE
- flood barrier in the form of an embankment along a river LEVEE
- flood or sudden, violent torrent after heavy rains FLASH FLOOD
- flood that is typically sudden and violent SPATE, DEBACLE
- flooding INUNDATION, ALLUVION
- existing or occurring before the biblical Flood ANTEDILUVIAN
- relating to a flood DILUVIAL
- unrestrained flood of water, passion, or the like TORRENT

floor covering of mosaic wood blocks or strips PARQUET
- floor of a building lying between the first floor and second floor MEZZANINE, ENTRESOL
- concrete mixture or finish, as on a floor SCREED
- principal floor of a building PIANO NOBILE
- horizontal beam supporting a floor or ceiling JOIST

Florence - Italian dialect spoken in Florence TUSCAN

flour from a cereal grain FARINA
- floury or starchy FARINACEOUS
- coat food with flour, sugar, or the like, as by sprinkling DREDGE
- protein mixture in wheat flour, used in glues GLUTEN
- whole-wheat flour GRAHAM FLOUR
- whole-wheat flour mix, with malted wheat and rye, used for bread GRANARY FLOUR

flourish, as in music or handwriting QUIRK
- "flourished," term indicating the most active or creative period of someone whose birth and death dates are uncertain FLORUIT
- flourishing, rich, as vegetation might be VERDANT, VERDUROUS, LUSH, LUXURIANT
- "may it flourish," motto used with the name of a place or institution FLOREAT

flow See also **flowing**
- flow of water, passion, or the like that is turbulent and unrestrained TORRENT
- flow or stream of people or things coming in INFLUX
- flow out of a valley, as a river might DEBOUCH
- flow out or discharge at the mouth of a river DISEMBOGUE
- flow toward, as of blood to the head AFFLUX
- instrument for measuring the speed and direction of wind ANEMOMETER

flow (combining form) RHEO-

flower See illustration
- flower cluster, in which each flower has its own stem attached to a larger branch THYRSUS
- flower cluster developing outward, with the central stem and all side stems bearing a single flower CYME
- flower cluster in the form of a compacted head, as in a daisy or thistle GLOMERULE
- flower cluster or flower-bearing stalk, or the arrangement of the flowers on it INFLORESCENCE
- flower cluster or spike, typically dense and drooping, as of the birch or alder CATKIN, AMENT
- flower gardening or cultivation HORTICULTURE
- flower or fruit cluster at the end of a stalk TRUSS
- flower or fruit of a cultivated rather than natural variety CULTIVAR
- flower or plant bred from two different varieties or species HYBRID
- flower or plant that turns to keep facing the sun HELIOTROPE
- flower or small posy of flowers, as pinned to a woman's dress CORSAGE
- flower support, such as a spiked board or pierced sponge in a vase FROG
- flower that never fades or dies, according to legend AMARANTH
- flower that keeps its color when dried IMMORTELLE
- flowering plant ANGIOSPERM
- flowering plant living for three or more years PERENNIAL
- flowering plant that develops and dies within a single year ANNUAL
- flowers arranged in a ring, as for decoration or as a memorial WREATH
- flowers cut and arranged in a cluster POSY, BOUQUET, NOSEGAY
- adjective for a flower FLORAL
- attached directly at the base, without a stalk, as a flower might be SESSILE
- bell-shaped, as some flowers are CAMPANULATE
- circular series of leaflike scales below a flower, fruit, or flower cluster INVOLUCRE
- clustered, formed of tightly packed parts, as a fruit or flower might be AGGREGATE
- crownlike or bell-shaped part of a daffodil or similar flower CORONA
- cut the dead flowers from a plant DEADHEAD
- decorative chain or garland of flowers, ribbons, or the like suspended in a loop FESTOON
- drooping, as some flowers and buds are CERNUOUS
- gather or collect something, such as flowers CULL
- go limp, droop, as a flower

might WILT
- having both male and female flowers on the same stalk, as some plants are ANDROGYNOUS
- head-shaped, as some flowers or flower clusters are CAPITATE
- leaflike plant part just beneath a flower or cluster of flowers BRACT
- open during the day and closed at night, as many flowers are DIURNAL
- opening in the evening, as some flowers are VESPERTINE
- outer part of a flower, the petals and sepals collectively FLORAL ENVELOPE, PERIANTH
- plant that flowers continuously through the growing season PERPETUAL
- pollinated by insects, as some flowers are ENTOMOPHILOUS
- pollinated by wind-blown pollen, as grass flowers are ANEMOPHILOUS
- relating to flowers and other plants BOTANICAL
- remaining attached to the plant even after withering, as some leaves and flowers are PERSISTENT
- short-lived, dying or falling quickly, as flowers might be FUGACIOUS
- spike of tiny close-packed flowers, as in the cuckoopint SPADIX
- stem supporting a flower, fruit, or flower cluster PEDUNCLE
- sweet liquid secreted by flowers, and gathered by bees for making honey NECTAR
- tiny disc flower or ray flower, usually in a cluster, as in the head of a daisy or other composite flower FLORET
- wreath or crown of flowers worn on the head GARLAND, CHAPLET, CORONAL
- wreath or garland of flowers, worn around the neck in Polynesia, especially in Hawaii LEI

flower (combining form) ANTHO-, -ANTHOUS, FLOR-

flower arranging as an art, of Japanese origin IKEBANA

flower garden designed with an ornamental pattern of paths between the flowerbeds PARTERRE

flowerbed, typically of perennial plants HERBACEOUS BORDER

flowering, bursting into bloom, blossoming, or the time of flowering FLORESCENCE, EFFLORESCENCE
- flowering process or period in plants ANTHESIS

flowery, fussy, pretentious or overelaborate in style FLORID, CHICHI, CHINTZY, PRECIOUS

flowing, effortless, or graceful FLUENT
- flowing out or something that flows out EFFLUENCE, EFFLUX
- flowing together or meeting point of two or more rivers CONFLUENCE

flowing (combining form) -RRHEA, -RRHAGIA

flu - former term for flu GRIPPE

fluent, effortless FACILE
- fluent or effortless, as in speaking or writing, but typically shallow and insincere FACILE, GLIB

fluffy mass FLOCCULUS
- fluffy or downy matter, as gather-

Flowers

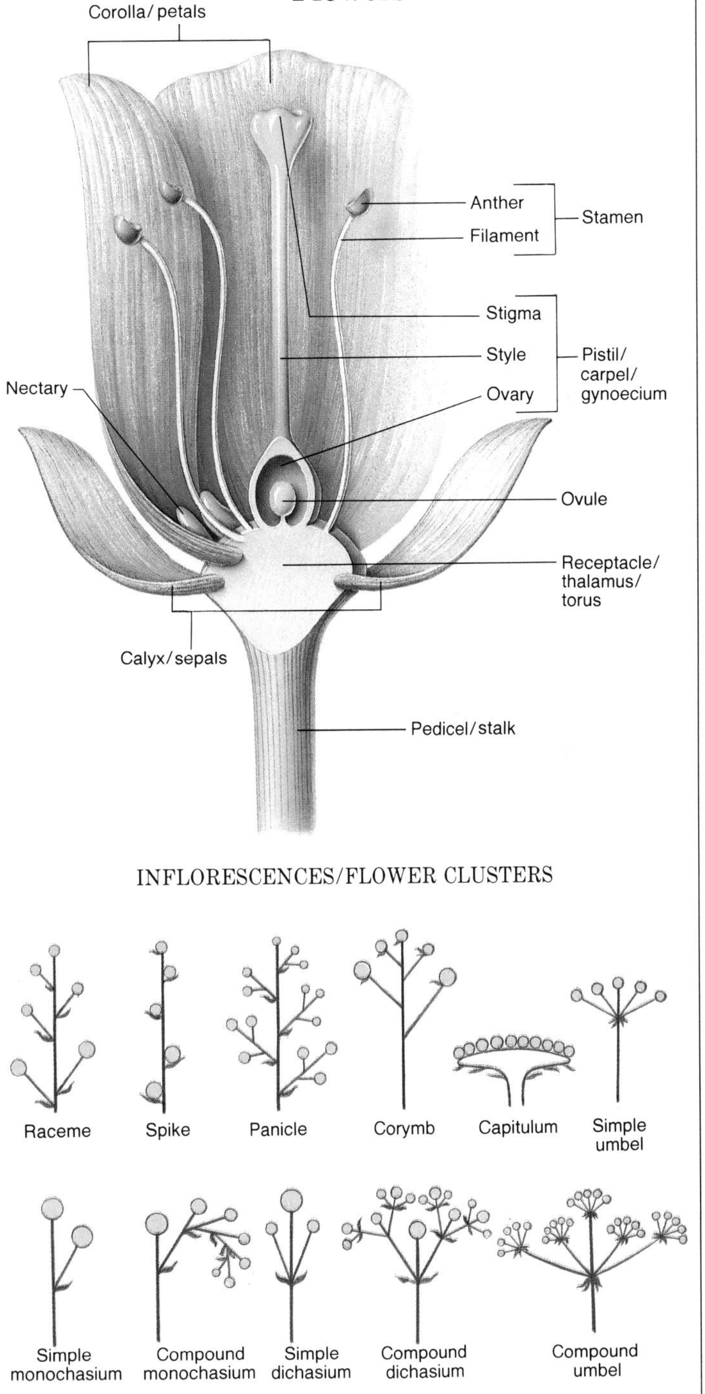

ing on fur or a new carpet FLUE

fluid, clear and thick, secreted by membranes in joints, tendon sheaths, and so on SINOVIA
- fluid-containing cavity or sac in the body CISTERNA, CISTERN
- fluid in the body, according to ancient and medieval medicine, determining the personality and health HUMOR
- fluid surrounding the embryo or fetus, as in the womb AMNIOTIC FLUID
- device to slow down or regulate the flow of a fluid BAFFLE
- operated by or involving fluid pressure HYDRAULIC
- pouch or baglike part, often filled with fluid, in a plant or animal SAC
- swelling caused by a buildup of fluid in the tissues EDEMA

fluke, parasitic flatworm TREMATODE

fluorescent lamps - gas used in fluorescent lamps KRYPTON

flute-like instrument, egg-shaped with fingerholes OCARINA
- flute player FLUTIST, FLAUTIST
- finger hole, as on a flute VENTAGE
- referring to the modern flute, with its mouthpiece on the side TRANSVERSE
- trilling of a flute or other wind instrument by a rapid vibration of the tongue FLUTTER TONGUING

fly an aircraft very low, not far above hedges, fences, and so on HEDGEHOP
- fly for fishing, with a tuft of feathers HACKLE FLY
- fly or move rapidly away, as flushed gamebirds do SKIRR
- fly or sail completely around something, such as the earth or the moon CIRCUMNAVIGATE
- fly whisk, as used in East Africa MGWISHO
- fly without changing position HOVER
- flying and navigating by visual observation of beacons and landmarks CONTACT FLYING
- flying or able to fly VOLANT, VOLITANT
- adjective for a fly, especially a housefly MUSCID
- art, science, profession, or pastime of flying aircraft AVIATION
- bloodsucking fly from Africa, transmitting sleeping sickness TSETSE FLY
- disturbed mental and body rhythms resulting from long flights across time zones JET LAG
- still without flight feathers, not yet developed enough to fly UNFLEDGED
- tour the countryside to give theatrical or stunt-flying performances or make election speeches BARNSTORM

flying buttress ARC-BOUTANT

flying saucer or similar mysterious flying object UNIDENTIFIED FLYING OBJECT, UFO

foam gathering at the surface of fermenting beer BARM
- foam occurring during fermentation, as of vinegar or cider WORK
- foam or froth, especially on or from the sea SPUME
- foamy light white synthetic solid substance used as packing and insulating material POLYSTYRENE

focus - apparent focus of light rays, as in the image in a mirror VIRTUAL FOCUS

focus of attention, especially an admired or beloved person CYNOSURE

focusing ability of the eye through changing the direction of incoming light rays REFRACTION
- focusing disability resulting from faulty curvature of the lens of the eye ASTIGMATISM

fodder, as made of clover STOVER
- fodder, such as hay, fed to livestock PROVENDER
- fodder of fermented grass, corn, or the like prepared in a pit or silo SILAGE
- fodder trough or rack CRIB, MANGER, CRATCH
- residue of oilseed, used as animal fodder EXPELLERS, EXTRACTIONS
- tall fodder plant with cloverlike leaves ALFALFA, LUCERNE
- yellow-flowering crop grown for oilseed and fodder RAPE, COLZA
- yellowish beet used for fodder MANGEL-WURZEL

fog - foglike polar weather condition producing very low visibility WHITEOUT

foil - hammer metal into foil, or coat glass with metal foil FOLIATE

fold, wrinkle, or crease, as when pursing one's lips PUCKER
- fold or curl something tightly, such as hair or dress material CRIMP
- fold or ridge of skin, shell, or the like PLICA
- fold up or collapse in on itself CONCERTINA
- folds of the brain surface CONVOLUTIONS, GYRI, SULCI
- make or press fluted folds in a piece of fabric, as for a ruff QUILL

folded into a series of long parallel ridges, as land or an iron sheet might be CORRUGATED
- folded page or insert in a book or magazine that is larger than other pages GATEFOLD, FOLDOUT

folk song of a melancholy kind sung in Portuguese FADO

folksy, quaint ETHNIC

folktales, fairy-tales MÄRCHEN

follow a trail, fox, or the like, as hunting hounds do DRAG
- follow directly, come immediately after, often as a direct result SUPERVENE, ENSUE
- follow directly in a job or the like, take over from SUCCEED
- follow persistently HOUND
- development, continuation, something that follows SEQUEL

follower, imitator, or disciple who is markedly inferior to his master EPIGONE
- follower of or devoted believer in a religion, political leader, or the like VOTARY
- follower of the doctrines of a philosopher, teacher, intellectual movement, or the like DISCIPLE, ACOLYTE, ADHERENT
- follower or companion who is overeager to please SYCOPHANT, MINION, TOADY
- follower or fan, as of a specified sport or pastime DEVOTEE, AFICIONADO
- follower or trusted supporter, ready to lend physical as well as moral support HENCHMAN, MYRMIDON
- followers or attendants, as of a nobleman RETAINERS, ENTOURAGE, RETINUE
- followers or devoted admirers, typically self-interested and fawning toadies CLAQUE

following, coming after in time SUBSEQUENT
- following as an effect or conclusion, resulting CONSEQUENTIAL
- following in order, as of officeholders or monarchs SUCCESSION
- following in order, successive SEQUENTIAL, CONSECUTIVE, SERIAL
- following in sequence, item by item in series SERIATIM

fond (combining form) PHIL-, -PHILE

fondly devoted to one's wife, especially in an excessive or fawning way UXORIOUS

fondness, loving feelings TENDRESSE

font, basin for holy water at the entrance of a church STOUP

food See also **cooking**, chart at **menu**, and entries at various types of food
- food COMESTIBLES, VICTUALS, VIANDS
- food, nourishment NURTURE, SUSTENANCE, ALIMENT
- food, or food for thought, typically of an insipid and easily digested kind PABULUM, PAB
- food, packaged and processed, re-

quiring little preparation before serving FAST FOOD
- food additive or flavor enhancer, as used in Chinese restaurants MONOSODIUM GLUTAMATE, MSG
- food basket HAMPER
- food for animals, especially pigs, consisting of kitchen scraps and liquid SWILL, SLOPS
- food in its partly digested fluid form in the stomach CHYME
- food of the gods, in mythology AMBROSIA, AMRIT
- food preparation, or the food prepared, of a particular style CUISINE
- food seasoning, such as salt, mustard, or spices CONDIMENT
- food seller or provider, such as a wholesale grocer PROVISIONER, PURVEYOR
- food stand or cart placed next to a dining table DUMBWAITER
- food storage room PANTRY, BUTTERY
- food store, specializing in fine, often prepared, foods DELICATESSEN
- food that is soft or mashed, as for a baby PAP
- concentrated preparation or essence of a food or other substance, as for flavoring EXTRACT
- craving for unnatural food, such as mud or chalk PICA
- decorate food, as with cress or a slice of lemon GARNISH
- digest, absorb, or incorporate something, such as food or facts ASSIMILATE
- eating all kinds of food, both meat and plant foods OMNIVOROUS
- expertise in good food or cooking GASTRONOMY
- full to excess, as of food REPLETE, SATIATED, SATED, GLUTTED, GORGED
- item of food, something edible ESCULENT
- liking for good food or abundant eating GOURMANDISE
- nourishing substance, as in food or in the solution absorbed by plant roots NUTRIENT
- officer of a ship, airplane, or the like supervising the food and provisions STEWARD
- person who appreciates or is an expert in fine food and drink GOURMET, CONNOISSEUR, EPICURE, GASTRONOME
- person who enjoys food and eats abundantly GOURMAND, TRENCHERMAN
- referring to food, nutrition, or digestion ALIMENTARY
- referring to food, such as pork, considered impure and forbidden according to Jewish law TREF
- referring to food considered pure according to Jewish law KOSHER
- referring to food intake DIETARY
- referring to food or cooking of a very high standard CORDON BLEU
- search through refuse for food or useful objects SCAVENGE
- small, soft lump of matter, particularly of chewed food BOLUS
- study of the intake, assimilation, and value of food, especially in the human diet NUTRITION
- substance added to a food to preserve, flavor, color, or enrich it ADDITIVE
- take in food by or as if by swallowing INGEST
- vomit or bring up partly digested food REGURGITATE

food poisoning PTOMAINE POISONING
- food poisoning caused by a bacterial toxin found in badly tinned or smoked food BOTULISM
- food poisoning caused by rod-shaped bacteria of a kind often found in inadequately cooked meat and eggs SALMONELLA POISONING, SALMONELLOSIS

fool See also **clown, cheat, victim**
- fool, blockhead, dull-brained person DUNDERHEAD, NUMSKULL, NINCOMPOOP, CRETIN
- fool, blunderer, person who tends to get things wrong DUFFER, SCHLEMIEL
- fool, dim-witted and usually clumsy person, dolt BOOBY, IMBECILE, NUDNICK, ZOMBIE
- fool, simpleton, silly person who is forgetful and easily confused ADDLEPATE, NINNY, MOONCALF
- fool, very talkative scatterbrain BLATHERSKITE, FLIBBERTIGIBBET
- multicolored clothing of a court jester or fool MOTLEY
- playing the fool BUFFOONERY
- red cap of a court jester or fool COXCOMB

foolhardiness, reckless disregard of danger TEMERITY

foolish See **stupid, silly**

fool's gold IRON PYRITES, PYRITE

foot See also **feet**
- foot, especially a pig's foot, used as food TROTTER
- foot misshapen from birth CLUBFOOT, TALIPES
- foot-operated lever for driving a sewing machine, potter's wheel, or the like TREADLE
- foot soldiers INFANTRY
- foot that is abnormally flat and turned outward SPLAYFOOT
- on or relating to the sole of the foot PLANTAR
- relating to the sole of the foot VOLAR
- sole of the foot THENAR

foot (combining form) PEDI-, -PEDE, -POD, -PODE

football See chart and illustration, page 212

foothold of a temporary or uncertain kind TOEHOLD
- foothold or early success that makes possible further achievements BEACHHEAD, BRIDGEHEAD
- military foothold or front-line position projecting into enemy-held territory SALIENT

footlights in a theater FLOATS

footnote See also **reference**
- footnotes, references, lists of variants, and the like, as in a literary text APPARATUS CRITICUS, CRITICAL APPARATUS
- cross-shaped printing symbol, †, as for indicating footnotes DAGGER, OBELISK
- double cross-shaped printing symbol, ‡, as for indicating footnotes DOUBLE DAGGER, DIESIS
- star-shaped printing symbol, *, indicating footnotes ASTERISK

footprint See illustration, page 213
- footprints, tracks, trail SPOOR
- mold, as taken for evidence in court MOULAGE

foot specialist, expert in the treatment of feet and toenails PODIATRIST, CHIROPODIST, PEDICURE

footstool - padded cushion used as a footstool or leg rest, or for kneeling on in church HASSOCK

for (combining form) PRO-

for example, e.g. EXEMPLI GRATIA

for one's country PRO PATRIA

for the present, for the time being, temporarily FOR THE NONCE, PRO TEM, PRO TEMPORE

forbid See **prohibit, prevent**

forbidden, prohibited VERBOTEN
- forbidden as food to Jews, nonkosher, as pork is TREF
- forbidden or shunned because, or as if because, blasphemous or cursed TABOO

force, speed, or other quantity having both magnitude and direction VECTOR
- force acting inward on a rotating or revolving body, toward the center or axis CENTRIPETAL FORCE
- force acting outward on a rotating or revolving body, away from the center or axis CENTRIFUGAL FORCE
- force driving or moving a person or thing onward PROPULSION
- force-feeding, by means of a tube down the throat GAVAGE
- force or bully someone into a course of action, as by bluster, threats, or violence BLUDGEON, BULLDOZE, STRONG-ARM
- force or compulsion DURESS, COERCION, CONSTRAINT

- force or drive someone to action, spur or goad, incite or prompt IMPEL, ACTUATE
- force or impose a person or thing on someone FOIST, OBTRUDE
- force or occurrence that unavoidably spoils one's plans or prevents the fulfillment of a contract FORCE MAJEURE, ACT OF GOD
- force or power, especially as a result of continuing movement MOMENTUM, IMPETUS
- force or pressure someone into doing something against his or her will DRAGOON, PRESS-GANG, RAILROAD
- force or trick someone into an undesirable action or situation SHANGHAI
- force out, push, or squeeze EXTRUDE
- force out, remove from office, power, the throne, or the like DEPOSE, OUST
- force out and provide a substitute for SUPPLANT
- force out from a fixed position, hiding place, dwelling, or the like DISLODGE
- force payment, tribute, or the like EXACT, EXTORT
- force produced by lowered pressure SUCTION
- force that overpowers and destroys, or demands self-sacrifice JUGGERNAUT
- force to leave, dismiss, expel, as from a building or rented property EJECT, EVICT
- force under one's control, or crush or put down by force SUPPRESS, SUBDUE, SUBJUGATE, REPRESS
- seize by force and hold illegally the power, rights, throne, or the like of another USURP
- seize or wrench something by force, such as power WREST
- stability, balance of forces EQUILIBRIUM
- tendency of a body to remain at rest or in unchanged motion until it is affected by an external force INERTIA
- twisting force or the technical measurement of it TORQUE

FOOTBALL TERMS

downs	the four segments given to the offensive team to move the ball 10 yards toward the other team's goal line
end zone	section at either end of the field, each 30 feet deep by 160 feet wide
extra points	points scored by a kick, run, or pass after scoring a touchdown
field goal	ball clearing the crossbar of the opposition's goal and staying between the uprights, to score three points
forward pass	a backfield player receiving the ball behind the line and throwing it to a teammate down-field
interception	forward pass caught by the opposition
kickoff	place-kicking the ball from the kicking team's 35-yard line or from just behind it
lateral pass	a player throwing the ball to a teammate who is not in front of the player
line of scrimmage	line at which the forward motion of the ball stopped on the previous play, and where the next play begins
period of play	division of the game into halves and again into quarters
tackling	use of hands or arms trying to hold the runner or throw him to the ground
touchdown	moving the ball into the other team's end zone: a six-point score

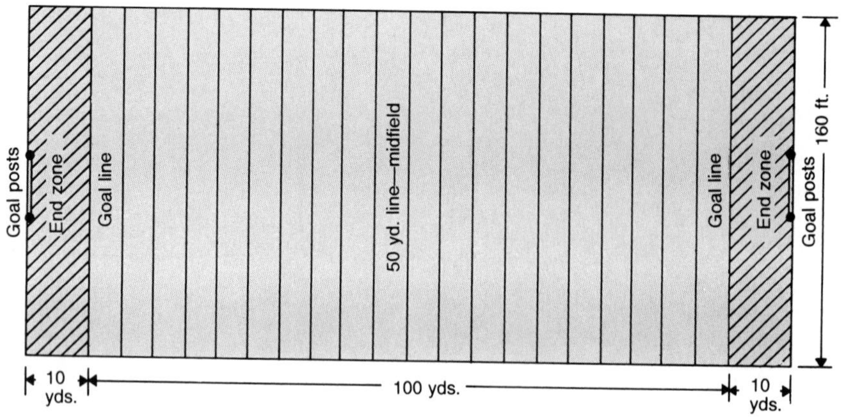

A regulation football field is marked off with white lines at five-yard intervals, making it look like a cooking griddle. Hence the term gridiron.

forced, artificial, stiff and unspontaneous CONTRIVED, MANNERED, STILTED, RECHERCHÉ
- forced, done or required against one's will INVOLUNTARY
- forced, embarrassed, or inhibited manner, situation, or the like CONSTRAINT
- forced, striving for effect, strained AGONISTIC, VOULU
- forced labor and imprisonment PENAL SERVITUDE

forceful, aggressively confident, stating and enforcing one's rights and wishes boldly ASSERTIVE
- forceful, clear, and crisp, as a remark or argument might be INCISIVE, TRENCHANT, COMPELLING, COGENT
- forceful, vigorous, possessing great energy POTENT, VIRILE
- forceful, hardworking, and energetic person DYNAMO
- forceful, passionate, or emphatic VEHEMENT
- forceful in an irresponsibly bullying or overbearing way, dictatorial, tyrannical IMPERIOUS, DOMINEERING
- forceful seizing of property, as in wartime PILLAGE, RAPINE

forecast See also **fortune-telling**
- forecast based on the relative positions of planets and signs of the zodiac at a given time HOROSCOPE
- forecast or predict on the basis of signs or symptoms PROGNOSTICATE
- forecast or prediction, especially of the development of a disease PROGNOSIS
- scientific study of the weather, especially for the purpose of making forecasts METEOROLOGY

forefather or ancestor, especially the first or earliest ancestor as of a people PRIMOGENITOR
- forefather or forebear, direct ancestor PROGENITOR
- forefathers, ancestors ANTECEDENTS, FOREBEARS

forefront of, or early participants in, an artistic fashion, political movement, or the like VANGUARD

forehead of a bird or animal FRONTLET
- relating to or of the forehead FRONTAL, METOPIC
- slope backward, as one's forehead might RECEDE

foreign, coming from outside, of external origin EXTRANEOUS, EXTRINSIC
- foreign, from another part of the world EXOTIC, PEREGRINE
- foreign, growing or living in a new or temporary environment, as a weed might be ADVENTIVE
- foreign resident of a country ALIEN

foreign (combining form) XENO-

foreign language - alleged ability of clairvoyants or mediums to speak a foreign language they do not know XENOGLOSSIA

foreign policy based on revenge or regaining of territory REVANCHISM
- foreign policy based uncompromisingly on national self-interest rather than on moral considerations REALPOLITIK

Footprints

IDENTIFYING MAMMAL PRINTS

From foxes to finches to frogs, most animals make tracks. Mammal prints are the easiest to identify. First learn the similarities among the species, and then the differences.

HOW TO TELL CATS FROM DOGS

Cat and dog tracks have large heel pads and four toes. House cats make miniature versions of tiger prints. Because cats usually keep their claws retracted, claws do not show in their tracks. Most prints from members of the dog family have toenails.

SOME HOOFPRINTS ARE SPLIT IN TWO

Hoofed animals, called ungulates, have toes enclosed in horny sheaths. Most ungulates—deer, antelope, goats, cattle—have two toes on each foot. When these animals run or jump, their tracks show the pair of toes spread apart. Single-toed ungulates include horses and zebras.

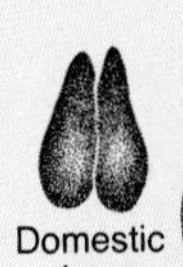

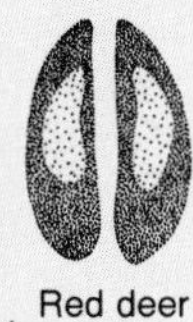

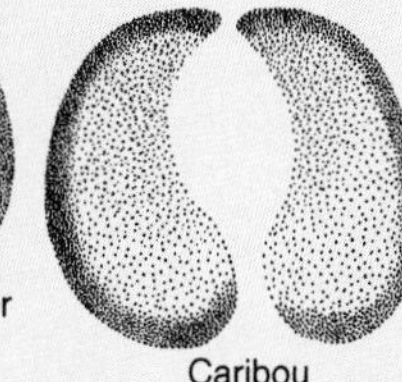

TRACKS IN DRY SOIL DIFFER FROM THOSE IN MUD

Tracks made by the same animal vary greatly, depending on the material in which they are left. But some distinguishing feature, such as the tail line of a white-footed (deer) mouse, may identify the animal.

COMPARE THE SHAPES AND SIZES

The shape and size of a track reveals much about an animal. Handlike prints, such as those made by squirrels, raccoons, and opossums, indicate an inquisitive, dexterous creature.

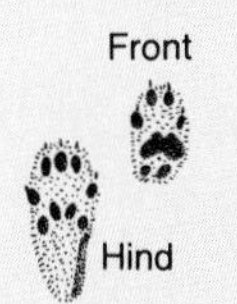

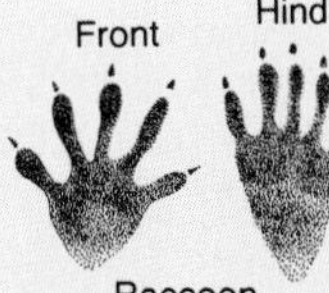

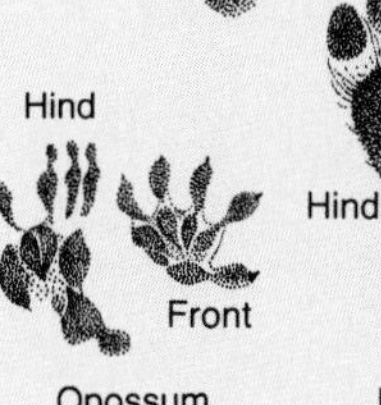

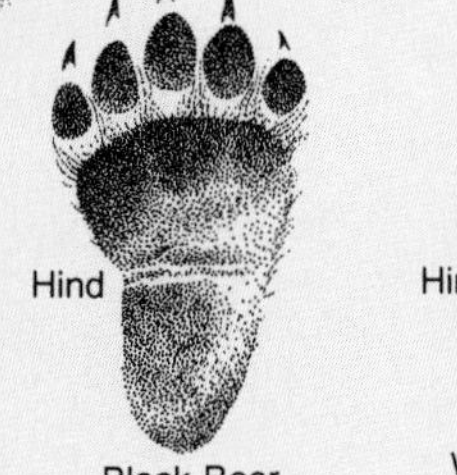

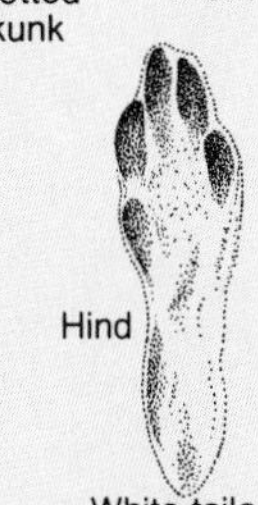

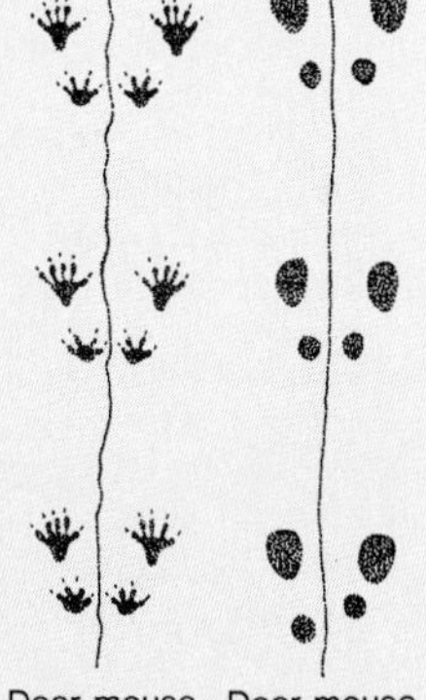

foreigner having certain citizenship rights in his or her country of residence DENIZEN
- expel a foreigner from a country DEPORT
- hostility to or fear of foreign people and ideas XENOPHOBIA

forerunner, person or thing signaling the arrival of something HARBINGER, PRESAGER, HERALD
- forerunner, person or thing that came before, such as a previous occupant of a position PREDECESSOR, ANTECEDENT, PRECURSOR

foresee, think of as a future possibility ENVISAGE, ENVISION

foresight - having foresight or great imagination VISIONARY

foreskin PREPUCE
- removal of the foreskin CIRCUMCISION

forest clearing, open space in a wood GLADE
- forest from prehistoric times, "turned to stone" by the action of mineral-rich water PETRIFIED FOREST
- forest's outskirts or perimeter area PURLIEU
- forests or trees of a particular region SILVA
- officer in charge of the royal forests in former times VERDERER
- relating to forests SYLVAN
- top layer, consisting of dead leaves, of a forest floor LITTER

forestry, care and cultivation of trees in forests SILVICULTURE

foretell See also **prophetic, fortune-telling**
- foretell or forecast on the basis of signs or symptoms PROGNOSTICATE
- foretell or indicate, be a sign or omen of, point to the future occurrence of FORESHADOW, PREFIGURE, BODE, PRESAGE, BESPEAK, BETOKEN, ADUMBRATE
- foretell or indicate some unfavorable event, serve as a warning sign or omen PORTEND, FOREBODE
- foretell or predict on the basis of signs and omens, prophesy AUGUR, VATICINATE
- foretelling events or revealing hidden information, as by observing omens or drawing on supernatural help DIVINATION, SOOTHSAYING
- foretelling things just before they happen, having an advance sense of events PRESENTIENT
- power of foretelling events, extrasensory advance knowledge, accurate foresight CLAIRVOYANCE, PRECOGNITION, PRESCIENCE

forever See **permanent**

forge something, especially banknotes, for the purpose of fraud COUNTERFEIT
- forged, fake, counterfeit SPURIOUS
- put forged money into circulation UTTER

forget - forgetful, absentminded, and unaware of one's surroundings OBLIVIOUS, ABSTRACTED, PREOCCUPIED
- forgetfulness, loss of memory OBLIVION, LETHE
- forgetting of one's past, loss of memory, as caused by shock or brain damage AMNESIA
- drug, potion, or technique for forgetting pains and sorrows NEPENTHE

forget-me-not MYOSOTIS

forgivable, easily excused or pardoned VENIAL

forgive See also **excuse, pardon**
- forgive or overlook an offense readily CONDONE
- forgiveness for sins, or release from punishment or guilt ABSOLUTION, REMISSION
- forgiving attitude, mildness or mercifulness CLEMENCY, LENIENCY, INDULGENCE

forgotten or neglected state, oblivion LIMBO

fork - forklike bone or body part, such as a chicken's wishbone FURCULA, FOURCHETTE
- fork or branch into two as a road might BISECT
- fork or spear with three prongs, as used by gladiators or carried by Neptune TRIDENT
- prong of a fork or fork-shaped tool TINE
- forked, branching FURCATE
- forked, branching, divided into two streams or parts BIFURCATE

forklift - platform supporting cargo or stored goods, typically moved by a forklift truck PALLET, SKID

form, shape, or outline CONFIGURATION, CONTOUR, CONFORMATION
- form or structure, as of a plant or animal organism MORPHOLOGY
- form that a god, idea, feeling, or the like may take MANIFESTATION
- capable of occurring in different forms, as crystals of a mineral or insects of a single species might be POLYMORPHIC
- give a definite shape or form to something, such as an idea CRYSTALLIZE

form (combining form) -GEN, -GENIC, -GENOUS, -MORPH-, MORPHO-, -MORPHIC, -FY

formal See also **stiff, old-fashioned**
- formal, traditional, or coldly conventional approach to art ACADEMICISM, ACADEMISM
- formal and appropriate behavior, propriety, etiquette CONVENANCE
- formal approval, official confirmation RATIFICATION, SANCTION, VALIDATION
- formal black evening jacket for men TUXEDO, TUX, DINNER JACKET
- formal or extremely polite and proper DECOROUS, CEREMONIOUS
- formal rules of behavior, code of ceremonial conduct PROTOCOL

formation, as of soldiers or ships, in stepped or offset parallel rows ECHELON
- formation of troops in close array PHALANX

former, one-time ERSTWHILE, QUONDAM, WHILOM

former (combining form) EX-

formidable, awesome, very impressive REDOUBTABLE

formless, lacking shape APLASTIC, AMORPHOUS

formula in chemistry detailing the arrangement of atoms and bonds within the molecule STRUCTURAL FORMULA

fort See also **castle**
- fortress or stronghold protecting a town or city CITADEL

forthright See **frank**

fortification See also **castle**
- fortification of concrete or wood, with loopholes for observation or weapons BLOCKHOUSE
- fortification, such as a trench, within outer walls or defenses RETRENCHMENT
- fortification, typically of a temporary kind, of two walls joined at an angle LUNETTE, REDAN
- fortification, usually small and temporary, sometimes within a permanent fortress REDOUBT
- fortification against enemy fire or observation DEFILADE
- fortification in the form of a fence of wooden stakes PALISADE, STOCKADE
- fortification or parapet built hastily to about chest height BREASTWORK
- fortified or well-defended place BASTION, FASTNESS, STRONGHOLD
- fortified shelter underground with a bank or gun emplacements above ground BUNKER
- fortified wall or bank, as behind a trench, giving protection from the rear PARADOS
- fortified wall or barricade for protection against explosions REVETMENT
- fortified wall or barrier, such as a bank of earth, in front of a trench or rampart TRAVERSE
- fortified wall about a castle, town, or the like, or the area protected by it ENCEINTE

- defense or protection, specifically the walls of a fortification RAMPART, BULWARK
- embankment in front of a fortification or castle, making attackers vulnerable to the defenders GLACIS
- flat open area in front of a fortification, exposing the attackers to the defenders' fire ESPLANADE
- half-moon or crescent-shaped object or structure, such as the outwork of a fortification DEMILUNE
- inner side of a ditch in a fortification SCARP
- opening in fortifications for the passage of troops DÉBOUCHÉ
- outer side of a ditch in a fortification COUNTERSCARP
- part of a fortification, trench system, line of defense, or the like that projects toward the enemy SALIENT
- passage into an outwork of a fort or fortification GORGE
- platform in a trench or behind the parapet of a fortification, from which firing takes place BANQUETTE
- platform or mound along the wall of a fortification, from which firing takes place over the parapet BARBETTE
- pointed wall or parapet of a fortification projecting outward toward the enemy FLÈCHE
- small overhanging turret, as on the tower of a fortification BARTIZAN
- two-faced embankment that projects outward in front of a fortification RAVELIN

fortune See **fate, luck, rich**
- accidental developments, such as changes of fortune VICISSITUDES

fortune-telling, telling the future, or revealing hidden information, as by means of visions CLAIRVOYANCE
- fortune-telling based on an ancient Chinese book containing 64 symbolic diagrams I CHING
- fortune-telling based on the pattern of lines in the palm of the hand PALMISTRY, CHIROMANCY
- fortune-telling based on the relative positions of planets and signs of the zodiac at a given time HOROSCOPE
- fortune-telling by means of casting or drawing lots SORTILEGE
- fortune-telling by means of consulting ghosts SCIOMANCY
- fortune-telling by means of communication with the spirits of the dead NECROMANCY
- fortune-telling by means of examining a pack of tarot or playing cards CARTOMANCY
- fortune-telling by means of inspecting the entrails of animals, as practiced by priests in ancient Rome HARUSPICATION
- fortune-telling by means of interpreting dreams ONEIROMANCY
- fortune-telling by means of interpreting lines or figures drawn randomly or patterns in the dust GEOMANCY
- fortune-telling by means of interpreting passages chosen at random from the Bible or some other book BIBLIOMANCY
- fortune-telling by means of observing fire or flames PYROMANCY
- fortune-telling by means of observing the feeding or flying patterns of birds AUSPICE, ORNITHOSCOPY
- fortune-telling or revealing hidden information, as by observing omens or drawing on supernatural help DIVINATION, AUGURY, SOOTHSAYING
- fortune-telling or revealing hidden information by gazing into a crystal ball SCRYING
- playing cards of a kind used in fortune-telling TAROT CARDS

forty-five-degree arc OCTANT

forward (combining form) PRO-

fossil - fossilized excrement COPROLITE
- fossilized shell of a type of extinct mollusk AMMONITE
- fine-grained rock material in which fossils are found MATRIX
- scientific study of fossils PALEONTOLOGY

foul-smelling, smelly MALODOROUS, FETID, RANCID

foundation, basis, underlying principle SUBSTRATUM
- foundation of a building, typically a solid brickwork platform STEREOBATE
- foundation post or pillar for a building PILE
- row of large concrete wedges or pillars used as foundations or stilts for a building PILOTIS
- slab of reinforced concrete laid on soft ground as part of a building's foundations RAFT

founder of a tradition, tribe, trend, or the like PROGENITOR, PRECURSOR, PATRIARCH
- founder or leader of a movement PATRON SAINT

founding member of an organization CHARTER MEMBER

fountain with rotating jets GIRANDOLE

four children or young born at one birth QUADRUPLETS
- four-dimensional extension of a cube, as a hypothetical mathematical construct TESSERACT
- four-dimensional space in mathematics HYPERSPACE
- four-legged animal QUADRUPED, TETRAPOD
- four-lined stanza or verse of poetry QUATRAIN
- four-sided closed figure QUADRILATERAL, TETRAGON
- four-year period QUADRENNIUM
- multiply by four QUADRUPLE

four (combining form) TETR-, TETRA-, QUADR-, QUADRI-, QUADRU-

four-hundredth anniversary QUADRICENTENNIAL, QUATERCENTENARY

fowl See **chicken**

fox, as named in folk tales and fables REYNARD
- fox's lair EARTH
- fox's tail BRUSH, BUSH
- adjective for a fox VULPINE
- female fox VIXEN

fox hunter - fox hunter's scarlet coat PINK

fox hunting See **huntsman**

foxglove or related plant DIGITALIS

fraction in which both the numerator and denominator are whole numbers, simple fraction, common fraction VULGAR FRACTION
- based on the number ten, as a fraction, number system, or currency might be DECIMAL
- canceling of common factors in a fraction, or converting a fraction to a decimal REDUCTION
- number or expression positioned above the line in a fraction NUMERATOR, DIVIDEND
- number or expression positioned below the line in a fraction DENOMINATOR, DIVISOR
- related inversely to each other, as fractions might be RECIPROCAL
- simple fraction equal to greater than one IMPROPER FRACTION
- simple fraction that is less than one PROPER FRACTION

fracture See illustration, page 216
- fracture of a bone in surgery in order to reset it or correct a deformity OSTEOCLASIS
- fracture that is very thin and clean HAIRLINE FRACTURE

fragment or chip of stone SPALL
- fragment or splinter of glass, pottery, or other brittle substance SHARD
- fragments, scattered remains, or the like of something broken RUBBLE, DEBRIS, DETRITUS
- fragments, splinters, broken pieces SMITHEREENS
- fragments from a shell, bomb, or mine produced by an explosion SHRAPNEL

fragrant or smelly ODOROUS, ODOR-

Fractures

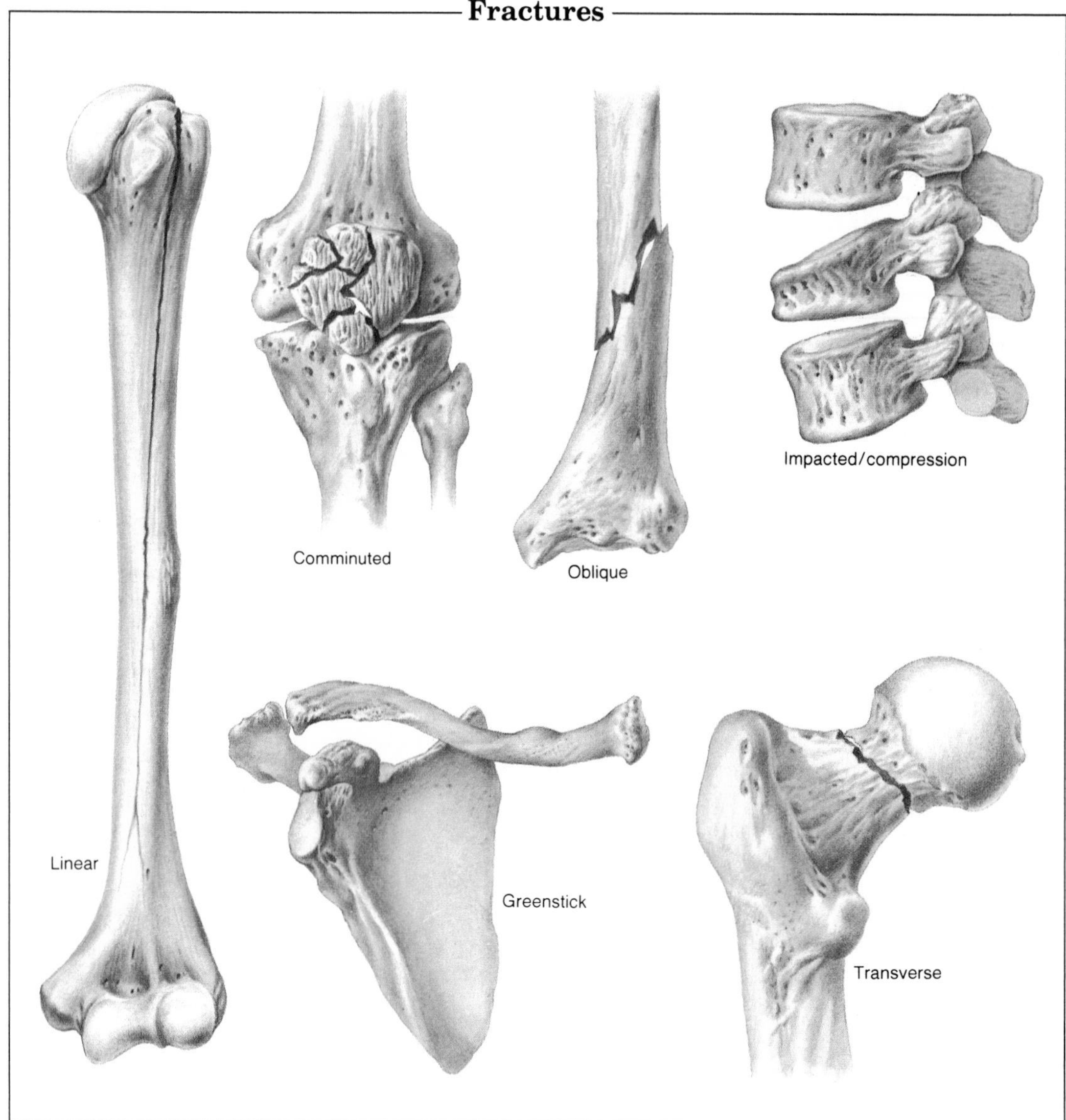

IFEROUS

frame for drying or stretching cloth during manufacture TENTER

- frame of two upright bars securing cattle round the neck in a stall, or upright of a goalpost in sports STANCHION

- frame or arch, typically made of crisscrossing sticks, on which vines or creepers are trained to grow TRELLIS

framework, structure, or basic pattern FABRIC

- framework of crisscrossed strips of wood or metal, as in a screen or window LATTICE

- framework of guidelines or limits, as of a budget or schedule PARAMETERS, CONSTRAINTS

- framework supporting a traveling crane, railway signals, or the like GANTRY

France (combining form) FRANCO-, GALLO-, GALLIC-

Franco's title as dictator of Spain CAUDILLO

frank, honest and open, straightforward CANDID

- frank, simple, or naive GUILELESS, ARTLESS, INGENUOUS

- frank and forthright, blunt, nononsense BLUFF, FOURSQUARE

- frank and open, communicative, informative FORTHCOMING

- frank and unreserved, direct, down-to-earth UP-FRONT, EXPLICIT, OUTSPOKEN, UNCONSTRAINED

- abrupt and gruff, blunt or frank CURT, BRUSQUE

fraud See also **trick**

- fraud, cheating, deception DUPLICITY

- fraud, trickster CHARLATAN, MOUNTEBANK

- fraud or deception, as by assuming a false identity IMPOSTURE

- fraudulent or worthless discovery MARE'S NEST

- fraudulent taking or using for oneself money or property entrusted to one EMBEZZLEMENT, DEFALCATION, PECULATION

- fraudulently substituted SUPPOSITITIOUS, SPURIOUS

- inflate the value of something fraudulently SALT

freak, monster LUSUS NATURAE

freckle LENTIGO
- freckle of large size developing on the skin LIVER SPOT
- freckle, spot, or similar discoloration of the skin MACULA

free See also **release**
- free, or set loose, as from prison or slavery ENLARGE, SET AT LARGE
- free, release, especially from foreign domination LIBERATE
- free a captive by making a payment REDEEM, RANSOM
- free a prisoner without bail, on certain conditions RELEASE SOMEONE ON HIS OR HER OWN RECOGNIZANCE
- free a prisoner provisionally before the completion of his or her sentence PAROLE
- free and unrestricted, unimpeded or unchained UNFETTERED, UNSHACKLED, UNTRAMMELED
- free from or relieve of a problem or burden DISEMBARRASS, DISENCUMBER
- free from slavery, duties, obligations, or the like ENFRANCHISE, AFFRANCHISE
- free from slavery or oppression EMANCIPATE, MANUMIT
- free hand, freedom to act as one thinks best CARTE BLANCHE
- free of charge GRATIS, GRATUITOUS
- free or excuse from responsibility, a duty, or the like EXEMPT, EXONERATE
- free or reduced goods or similar offer, used as an incentive to purchase PREMIUM
- free or release from difficulties, unfasten or disentangle EXTRICATE
- free to do whatever one likes, FOOTLOOSE, UNENCUMBERED
- freeing or rescuing DELIVERANCE
- freely or spontaneously, without preparation AD LIB
- freely or willingly given, generous UNSTINTED, UNGRUDGING

free trade, noninterference by governments in commercial activity LAISSEZ-FAIRE

free verse VERS LIBRE

free will, free choice VOLITION
- arising from or relating to free choice or an action of one's own free will VOLUNTARY
- attitude of submissiveness to fate, as though lacking free will FATALISM
- belief or philosophy that everything follows inescapably from a cause, and that there is no real free will DETERMINISM

freedom, especially from imperialist rule in Africa UHURU
- freedom, lack of controls LAISSEZ-ALLER
- freedom of speech, assembly, and so on CIVIL LIBERTY
- freedom of thought or action, allowing room for movement LATITUDE, LEEWAY

freehold farmer in former times YEOMAN

freeing (combining form) -LYS-, LYSO-, -LYSIS

freemasons' secrets MYSTERIES

freeze See also **frozen**
- freeze, solidify, or jell CONGEAL, COAGULATE
- freezing, solidification through cooling GELATION
- freezing of a corpse, with the intention of reviving it in the future CRYONICS

freezing (combining form) CRYO-

French See chart, page 218, and also chart at **menu**
- French, relating to France or ancient Gaul GALLIC
- French borough or small administrative district ARRONDISSEMENT
- French café or small shabby bar ESTAMINET
- French containing many English words and elements FRANGLAIS
- French main geographic administrative unit DÉPARTEMENT
- French courtly poet-musician in the Middles Ages TROUBADOUR, TROUVÈRE
- French king's eldest son in former times DAUPHIN
- French national anthem MARSEILLAISE
- French policeman GENDARME, FLIC
- French Protestant of the 16th and 17th centuries HUGUENOT
- French-speaking FRANCOPHONE
- French word, phrase, or idiom in another language GALLICISM
- any of the French provincial dialects PATOIS
- pronunciation of a final consonant that is normally silent, especially in French, when the next word begins with a vowel sound LIAISON
- French academic secondary school LYCÉE

French (combining form) FRANCO-, GALLO-, GALLIC-

French bean HARICOT

French Revolution - extreme radical republican in the French Revolution SANSCULOTTE
- old French government and social system that was swept away by the French Revolution in 1789 ANCIEN RÉGIME
- Parisian women who would knit unconcernedly while watching guillotinings during the French Revolution TRICOTEUSES

frenzy of frustrated desire for something unattainable NYMPHOLEPSY
- frenzied, behaving violently or destructively RAMPAGING, ON THE RAMPAGE

frequency of occurrence INCIDENCE
- frequency distribution in statistics OGIVE
- units of measurement of frequency FRESNEL, HERTZ

frequent, common, normal PREVAILING, PREVALENT, PREDOMINANT
- frequent, repeated, continuous PERSISTENT, RECURRENT, HABITUAL
- frequent visitor HABITUÉ

fresh, healthy, and vigorous condition VERDURE
- fresh, striking, bright, or lively VIVID, VIBRANT
- fresh and youthful, springlike VERNAL
- fresh start, clean slate, need or chance to start again from scratch TABULA RASA
- freshness, originality, newness NOVELTY

Freudian See also **complex**
- death wish or instinct for self-destruction, in Freudian psychology THANATOS
- Freudian theories, or the practice of psychological treatment based on them PSYCHOANALYSIS
- life-enhancing drive and self-preserving instinct, in Freudian psychology EROS
- mental and emotional energy and sexual drive derived from deep biological urges, in Freudian psychology LIBIDO

friar belonging to an order living on charity MENDICANT FRIAR

friction, as of wheels on a road TRACTION
- oil, grease, or other substance used to reduce friction LUBRICANT
- rubbing down or wearing away, through friction, as by wind-blown sand ATTRITION
- study of friction and lubrication TRIBOLOGY

friction (combining form) TRIBO-

fried lightly in butter or fat SAUTÉED

friend or acquaintance with whom one discusses private personal matters CONFIDANT, CONFIDANTE
- friend or companion who is affectionate, reliable, and usually lively BOON COMPANION
- friends extremely devoted to each other DAMON AND PYTHIAS
- exclusive circle of friends or colleagues CLIQUE
- close friend, associate, or hanger-

FRENCH TERMS

à la mode	in fashion
amour propre	self-esteem
au fait	familiar or conversant with
avant-garde	ahead of the times, pioneering
beau monde	fashionable society
beaux arts	fine arts
belle époque	the era preceding World War II ("beautiful period")
belles lettres	sophisticated literature
bête noire	especially disliked person or thing
billet-doux	love letter
bon mot	pithy witticism
bonne bouche	delectable tidbit or item
bon vivant	person who enjoys luxurious living
carte blanche	free hand, unconditional authorization
cause célèbre	interesting and controversial public issue
c'est la vie	that's life!
comme il faut	proper, in keeping with accepted standards
cordon sanitaire	buffer zone
coup de grâce	conclusive stroke; death blow
coup d'état	sudden overthrow of government
cri de coeur	heartfelt cry or appeal
crime passionnel	crime provoked by sexual jealousy
déjà vu	sense of having undergone before something being experienced for the first time now
démodé	out-of-fashion, out-of-date
de rigueur	required by fashion or social custom
dernier cri	latest fashion
de trop	unwanted, getting in the way
éminence grise	influential person behind the scenes
enfant terrible	provokingly unconventional person
en passant	by the way
entente cordiale	informal friendly understanding between nations
entre nous	in confidence, between us
esprit de corps	group spirit, morale
fait accompli	irreversible fact
faute de mieux	for want of anything better
faux pas	blunder
haute couture	high fashion
haute cuisine	high-class cooking
hors de combat	out of action
idée fixe	obsession
idée recue	conventional opinion
je ne sais quoi	an indefinable but distinctive quality
jeu d'esprit	witty comment
jeunesse dorée	wealthy, fashionable young people
joie de vivre	high spirits
laissez-faire	noninterference
laissez-passer	entry permit, pass
mauvais quart d'heure	brief, nasty experience
mot juste	the exactly appropriate expression
noblesse oblige	obligations imposed by honor or rank
nouveau riche	newly and ostentatiously rich person
par excellence	to the highest degree
parti pris	prejudice
passé	out of date or fashion
pièce de résistance	outstanding item, showpiece
pied-à-terre	temporary or secondary residence
pis aller	desperate course of action, last resort
plat du jour	dish of the day
porte-cochère	covered entrance to a building
raison d'être	justification for existence
réchauffé	a rehash
recherché	in great demand, mannered, affected
risqué	indelicate or suggestive, saucy
sangfroid	calm self-control, self-possession
savoir faire	knowledge of appropriate behavior
soi-disant	self-styled, so-called
tant mieux	so much the better
tant pis	so much the worse
tête-à-tête	intimate conversation, in private
tour de force	outstanding feat
tout court	plainly and simply
trahison des clercs	betrayal of a cause by intellectuals
vis-à-vis	in relation to, compared with
volte-face	about-face, policy reversal

on CRONY, SIDEKICK, FAMILIAR
- extremely close friend, constant companion INTIMATE, ALTER EGO
- loyal friend, faithful companion ACHATES

friendly, sympathetic, sharing one's tastes CONGENIAL, SIMPATICO
- friendly, easy to get along with AFFABLE, CORDIAL, DEBONAIR
- friendly, enjoying the company of others, sociable GREGARIOUS, EXPANSIVE, CONVIVIAL, JOVIAL
- friendly, good-natured AMIABLE
- friendly, kindly, or well-disposed in an unclelike way AVUNCULAR
- friendly, lively, hearty, especially in a facile or gushing way HAIL-FELLOW-WELL-MET
- friendly, outgoing, lively person EXTROVERT
- friendly good nature BONHOMIE, GENIALITY
- friendly in tone, characterized by good will AMICABLE
- friendly social relations, as with the people of an occupied or an enemy country FRATERNIZATION
- friendly understanding and trust RAPPORT, CAMARADERIE
- friendly understanding or informal agreement between countries or powers ENTENTE CORDIALE
- be friendly and associated socially HOBNOB
- bubbling with excitement, enthusiasm, or friendliness EBULLIENT, EXUBERANT, EFFERVESCENT
- having a friendly and cosy atmosphere GEMÜTLICH

friendship, peaceful relations, especially between countries AMITY
- referring to love or close friendship between two people that is free of sexual desire PLATONIC
- restore friendship, marital harmony, or the like between people in conflict RECONCILE

frighten or dismay into losing confidence UNNERVE, DISCOMFIT
- frighten so as to silence or deter INTIMIDATE, COW
- frighten to the point of paralysis PETRIFY, GORGONIZE

frightened See **scared, cowardly**

frightening, fearsome, formidable REDOUBTABLE
- frightening, forbidding or repelling REBARBATIVE
- frightening and discouraging, disheartening DAUNTING

frill of lace or fabric, used as a trimming RUCHE, RUFFLE
- frill or ruff of lace or linen formerly worn by women around the neck or shoulders TUCKER
- frills down the front of a blouse or shirt JABOT
- frilly paper adorning the end of a chop, cutlet, or drumstick PAPILLOTE

fringe, border, or edge of a fabric, carpet, or the like finished so as to prevent unraveling SELVAGE
- fringe, edge, or boundary, as of a social group PERIPHERY

frivolity of manner, especially when inappropriate LEVITY

frog See illustration
- frog, newt, or related animal developing in water but living or able to live on land AMPHIBIAN
- adjective for a frog or toad ANURAN, SALIENTIAN, BATRACHIAN, RANINE

from (combining form) EX-, DE-, AB-

from the beginning AB INITIO, AB OVO

front of a building FACADE, FRONTISPIECE
- front position or troops of an advancing army VANGUARD
- front side of a leaf of printed paper RECTO
- relating to the head end or front part of something ANTERIOR

front (combining form) FORE-

front man or cover, apparently but not really in charge of a dubious scheme MAN OF STRAW

frontier See also **border, boundary**
- frontier settlement OUTPOST

frost, as formed on the windward side of trees, twigs, telegraph wires, and the like RIME
- frost of small white ice crystals HOARFROST

frost (combining form) CRYO-

frosted glass - allowing the passage of light, as frosted glass does, but only in a diffused form unlike transparent glass TRANSLUCENT

froth See **foam**

frown, look angry, menacing, or sulky SCOWL, LOWER, GLOWER

frozen See also **freeze**
- frozen ground, where subsoil is permanently frozen PERMAFROST
- frozen-subsoil region between the Arctic's perpetual snow and the tree line TUNDRA

frugal, austere, simple SPARTAN, THRIFTY, PARSIMONIOUS

fruit See chart, page 220
- fruit-bearing FRUCTIFEROUS
- fruit-eating, as some bats are CARPOPHAGOUS, FRUGIVOROUS
- fruit having a single hard stone enclosing the seed DRUPE
- fruit produced by the fusing of several flowers or flower ovaries MULTIPLE FRUIT, AGGREGATE FRUIT, COLLECTIVE FRUIT
- fruit or flower of a cultivated rather than natural variety CULTIVAR
- fruit salad finely diced and sometimes in jelly MACÉDOINE
- fruit stewed and served hot or cold in a syrup COMPOTE
- fruit such as oranges, lemons, and grapefruit CITRUS FRUIT
- fruit that has fallen in the wind WINDFALL
- fruit tree or shrub trained to lie flat against a wall, trellis, or the like ESPALIER
- fruit whose seeds are in a large central capsule POME
- fruit whose stone or pit does not separate easily from the flesh CLINGSTONE
- fruit whose stone or pit separates easily from the flesh FREESTONE
- bear fruit, or make something fruitful or productive FRUCTIFY
- fleshy fruit, or the flesh of such

Frogs

a fruit SARCOCARP
- gel-forming substance found in ripe fruit and used as a setting agent in jams PECTIN
- open tart filled with fruit or cheese FLAN
- person who eats only fruit FRUITARIAN
- pulp remaining after apples, pears, or other fruits have been crushed in order to extract the juice POMACE, MARC
- scientific study and cultivation of fruit POMOLOGY
- split or burst open along a seam, as a pod or fruit might, to release seeds or pollen DEHISCE
- sugar-coated, as preserved fruit might be CRYSTALLIZED

fruit (combining form) CARP-, -CARPY, -FRUCT-, -FRUG-, FRUCTI-, FRUGI-

frustrate and annoy EXASPERATE
- frustrate or torment by parading but withholding something desirable TANTALIZE
- frenzy of frustrated desire for something unattainable NYMPHOLEPSY

fry lightly in butter or fat SAUTÉ

fuel, such as coal or petroleum, found in the earth's crust, and formed from decomposed living matter FOSSIL FUEL
- fuel in a rocket, explosive charge, or similar agent generating thrust PROPELLANT
- hydrocarbon gas used in fuels such as those in gas canisters BUTANE, PROPANE

fulfill a promise, pledge, or the like REDEEM

full See also **fill**
- full, abounding, swarming TEEMING
- full, as of food or drink, satisfied to the point of excess SATED, SATIATED, REPLETE, GLUTTED, GORGED
- full, as of liquid or happiness BRIMMING
- full amount, number, or the like COMPLEMENT
- full-length, not shortened or condensed UNABRIDGED
- full of emotion, danger, tension, or the like CHARGED, FRAUGHT
- full to excess, blocked or clogged, as the nasal passages might be CONGESTED
- fullness, completeness PLENITUDE, PLENUM

full (combining form) -ULENT

full moon that follows the harvest moon HUNTER'S MOON

fully and clearly expressed, as directions might be EXPLICIT
- fully attended or open to all, as a session of a conference might be PLENARY

fumigation chamber for killing insects or fungi FUMATORIUM

fun or merrymaking of a wild, noisy, and uninhibited kind HILARITY, REVELRY

function, correspondence, rule associating the members of one set with those of another MAPPING
- functioning properly, in working order OPERATIONAL, OPERATIVE
- functions or processes maintaining life METABOLISM

fund used for bribing and other corrupt activities SLUSH FUND
- providing for some possible though not expected future occurrence or emergency, as a fund or plan might CONTINGENCY

fundamental See **basic, essential**

funds - appeal for or request something earnestly, such as votes or funds SOLICIT
- misuse or theft of property or funds entrusted to one MISAPPROPRIATION, EMBEZZLEMENT, DEFALCATION, PECULATION

funeral, or funeral ceremonies and rites OBSEQUIES, EXEQUIES
- funeral director UNDERTAKER, MORTICIAN
- funeral hymn, lament DIRGE
- funeral procession or other formal or ceremonial procession CORTEGE

FRUIT

EXOTIC FRUIT		HARD FRUIT	SOFT FRUIT
breadfruit	kumquat	bullace	bilberry
cantaloupe	mandarin	crab apple	blackberry
cherimoya	naartje	damson	blueberry
durian	ortanique	greengage	boysenberry
granadilla	satsuma	medlar	cranberry
guava	shaddock/pomelo	nectarine	loganberry
kiwifruit/Chinese gooseberry	tangelo/ugli	quince	mulberry
litchi		sloe	whortleberry
longan			
loquat			
mangosteen			
naseberry/sapodilla			
papaw			
papaya			
passion fruit			
persimmon			
pomegranate			
rambutan			
spanspek			
star apple			
tamarind			
CITRUS FRUIT			
citron			
clementine			

- funeral speech of praise EULOGY
- funeral watch or festivity before burial WAKE
- bugle call sounded at military funerals or to signal lights out in a military camp TAPS, LAST POST
- church gate with a roof, at which the coffin is rested before funerals or burials LYCH-GATE
- person who carries or accompanies the coffin at a funeral PALLBEARER
- raised platform or table on which a coffin or corpse lies, as during a state funeral CATAFALQUE
- vehicle for carrying a coffin to a funeral HEARSE
- wood pile prepared for a funeral fire on which to cremate a corpse PYRE

fungus See also **mushroom**
- fungus, as in plant diseases or on damp walls MILDEW, MOLD
- fungus growing underground and considered a delicacy TRUFFLE
- fungus producing a disease in cereals ERGOT
- fungous skin disease, such as athlete's foot or ringworm TINEA, DERMATOPHYTOSIS
- chemical that destroys fungi FUNGICIDE
- hornlike substance occurring in some fungi and shells CHITIN
- reproductive cell or organ in fungi and in nonflowering plants such as mosses and ferns SPORE

fungus (combining form) MYC-, MYCO-, -MYCETE

funnel - funnel-shaped, as some plant parts are INFUNDIBULIFORM
- funnel-shaped device, such as a sea anchor or a target towed behind an aircraft DROGUE
- slope backward, as a ship's mast or funnel might RAKE

funny See also **humorous**
- funny, good-humored, given to joking JOCULAR, JOCOSE, WAGGISH
- funny in a bizarre or clownish way ZANY
- funny in a coarse way, vulgarly humorous BAWDY, RABELAISIAN
- funny in a peculiar, whimsical, or wry way DROLL
- funny in an unintentional way, laughable, ridiculous LUDICROUS, RISIBLE, COMICAL
- extremely funny, sidesplitting, priceless, hysterical HILARIOUS, RIOTOUS, UPROARIOUS
- jesting or lack of earnestness at the wrong time, inappropriate attempt at being funny LEVITY, FRIVOLITY, FLIPPANCY, INAPPROPRIATE AFFECT
- mildly funny, pleasantly amusing or entertaining DIVERTING

funny bone OLECRANON
- long bone of the upper arm, ending near the funny bone on the elbow HUMERUS

fur, wool, or soft hair PILE
- fur-trimmed cloak PELISSE
- white fur of the stoat, as used to trim peers' or judges' robes ERMINE
- white or light gray fur used to trim medieval robes MINIVER

Furies in Greek mythology EUMENIDES, ERINYES

furnace, as for burning rubbish INCINERATOR
- furnace, as for smelting iron, in which the coke is ignited by a blast of hot air BLAST FURNACE
- furnace, as in a smithy FORGE
- furnace for smelting metal, using reflected heat on the ore REVERBERATORY
- furnace or oven for drying or hardening, as in a pottery KILN
- furnace's waste material after smelting or refining SLAG, SINTER, CINDER, SCORIA
- bottom part of a furnace HEARTH
- container in a furnace that receives the molten metal CRUCIBLE
- heat-resistant material, such as

FURNITURE

armoire	large ornate cabinet or wardrobe
chaise longue	reclining chair with a long padded seat resembling a settee
chesterfield	large padded sofa, often with button upholstery
cheval glass	long mirror mounted on swivels in a frame
chiffonier	high and narrow chest of drawers; ornamental cabinet with drawers or shelves
club chair	deep, thickly upholstered easy chair with heavy arms and sides, and often a low back
commode	low cabinet or chest of drawers, usually on legs or short feet
console table	table supported by decorative brackets fixed to a wall
credenza	cupboard or sideboard, typically without legs
davenport	small writing desk with side drawers; large upholstered sofa
dos-à-dos	sofa that accommodates two people seated back to back
escritoire	writing desk, typically with a hinged top closing over small drawers
étagère/ whatnot	lightweight stand with three or more open shelves
farthingale chair	armless chair with a high seat and low straight back
fauteuil	upholstered armchair
love seat	large chair or small sofa that seats two people
morris chair	large easy chair with an adjustable back and big loose cushions
ottoman	long upholstered seat, with or without a back
pier table	table designed to stand against a wall between two windows
pouf	large firm cushion used as a seat; low, soft, backless couch
secretary/ secretaire	drop-front desk, sometimes with drawers below and a bookcase above
taboret	low cylindrical stool or cabinet
tallboy	double chest of drawers, with one section standing on top of the other
teapoy	small tea table, typically with three legs
tête-à-tête/ conversation chair	S-shaped sofa allowing two people to face each other when seated
torchère	slender decorative candle stand or lamp, often with a tripod base
triclinium	couch or set of couches surrounding three sides of a table
Windsor chair	comfortable wooden chair with arms, a spoked back, and splayed legs
FURNITURE STYLES	
Adam	delicate 18th-century English neoclassic style developed by Robert Adam
Biedermeier	conventional 19th-century style developed in Germany
boulle/buhl/ boule	style developed by the French cabinetmaker André Charles Boulle, using inlays of metal and tortoiseshell
Chippendale	elegant and ornate mid-18th-century English style developed by Thomas Chippendale
Queen Anne	early-18th-century English style characterized by fine upholstery and wood inlays
Regency	decorative early-19th-century English style
Second Empire	ornate 19th-century French style
Sheraton	late-18th-century English style developed by Thomas Sheraton, characterized by graceful proportions

alumina or fireclay, as used to line furnaces REFRACTORY
- metal residue or slag remaining in a furnace SALAMANDER
- movable plate adjusting the airflow in a stove or furnace flue DAMPER
- nozzle or duct through which the air is blown into a blast furnace TUYERE

furnished properly, well-equipped WELL-APPOINTED

furniture See chart, page 221
- furniture, equipment, or fittings APPOINTMENTS
- furniture, ornaments, curios, and the like, displayed and valued as rare or quaint BRIC-A-BRAC
- furniture leg of an 18th-century style, curving outward near the top, and inward to an ornamental foot CABRIOLE
- aged artificially, as some furniture or leather is DISTRESSED
- cane from a tropical Asian palm, as used for wickerwork furniture and walking sticks RATTAN
- fabric, padding, springs, as used in making a soft covering for furniture UPHOLSTERY
- item of furniture or fittings that can be moved about FITMENT
- item of furniture or fittings that is fixed in place and cannot be moved about FIXTURE
- made of rough branches, as some furniture is RUSTIC
- modern style of furniture, typically using metal piping HIGH-TECH
- narrow fabric trimming, used on clothes, curtains, and furniture GIMP, GUIMPE, GUIPURE
- narrow tube of folded material, often enveloping a cord, as used for edging upholstered furniture PIPING
- patterns of inlaid wood, ivory, and the like, as used in decorating furniture MARQUETRY
- ready-made standard unit used in constructing furniture MODULE
- small swiveling wheellike device on each leg of an item of furniture, for easy moving CASTOR

furrow or narrow groove, as on a plant stem or the surface of the brain SULCUS

furthest See also **farthest**
- furthest possible stage, greatest possible degree NE PLUS ULTRA

fuse See **join**
- fuse, grow together, merge COALESCE
- fuse consisting of a line of gunpowder laid to explode a charge TRAIN
- fuse metals using heat WELD
- fuse or blend MELD

fusion (combining form) ZYG-, ZYGO-, JUNC-

fusion bomb, such as a hydrogen bomb THERMONUCLEAR BOMB

fuss, ado, showy display or stir FANFARE
- fuss or bother, needlessly complicated procedure PALAVER
- fuss or fret over petty details NIGGLE
- fuss over nothing, pointless argument or to-do PRODUCTION, HOO-HA

fussy, choosy, picky CHARY, FADDISH
- fussy, determined, or insistent person, perfectionist PRECISIAN, STICKLER
- fussy, needlessly concerned with minute details, nit-picking PERSNICKETY, QUIBBLING, PETTIFOGGING
- fussy attention to small details of knowledge, especially when at the expense of deeper insight and understanding PEDANTRY
- fussy in one's tastes or habits, selective or refined DISCERNING, DISCRIMINATING
- fussy or precise to a fault, painstakingly conscientious or dutiful METICULOUS, FASTIDIOUS, FINICKY, FINICAL
- fussily proper or refined, overnice PRECIOUS, EXQUISITE, PRISSY
- conscientious, attentive to duty or detail, precise, appropriately fussy PUNCTILIOUS, SCRUPULOUS

future See also **fortune-telling, foretell**
- future or future generations POSTERITY
- future time of happiness and prosperity expected or desired MILLENNIUM
- about to happen, due to take place in the very near future, looming IMMINENT, IMPENDING
- advance sense or intuition of something that is to happen in the near future PREMONITION, PRESENTIMENT
- advance sign or intuition of something, especially something evil or dangerous, that is to happen in the near future PORTENT, FOREBODING
- announcer or announcement of a future event HERALD, HARBINGER, PRECURSOR, CASSANDRA
- impression or overall view of historical events, the future, or the like VISTA, PROSPECT
- likely to happen in the future, probably forthcoming PROSPECTIVE
- possible future occurrence or situation EVENTUALITY, CONTINGENCY
- think of as a future possibility, foresee ENVISAGE, ENVISION

future, forecast (combining form) -MANCY

G

gable roof with steplike projections or cuts near the top CORBIE GABLE
Gaelic or Celtic, specifically from Ireland or Scotland GOIDELIC
gain an advantage over OUTFLANK
galaxy other than the Milky Way NEBULA
gall, bitterness WORMWOOD
gall (combining form) CHOLE-
gallant, chivalrous man CHEVALIER
gallbladder - surgical removal of the gallbladder or part of the urinary bladder CYSTECTOMY
gallery or veranda along the outside of the upper level of a building LOGGIA
galloping at full speed TANTIVY
gallows GIBBET, SCAFFOLD
- gallows trapdoor DROP
- horizontal beam or crossbar, on a gallows or cross TRANSOM
gallstone, kidney stone, or similar solid mass formed in a body cavity or tissue CALCULUS, CONCRETION, CYSTOLITH
gambling See also **horse racing, bet, poker, roulette**
- gambling chip JETON
- gambling game where winning tickets are picked from a revolving container TOMBOLA
- gambling place CASINO
- gambling technique of raising or doubling the stakes after each loss MARTINGALE
- gamble, risk, expose to danger HAZARD, VENTURE, BRAVE
- gambler on the dealer's right, or the dealer's opponent in two-handed card games PONE
- gambler or bettor, especially on a horse race PUNTER
- gambler who cannot refrain from gambling COMPULSIVE GAMBLER
- box from which cards are dealt in gambling SHOE, SABOT
- card dealer or bet taker at a gambling table CROUPIER
game, match, or the like between two drawn or tied contestants to determine a winner PLAY-OFF
- game animal or animals, prey of hunters QUARRY
- game killed during a day's hunting or shooting BAG
- game or hunting preserve, privately owned but unfenced CHASE
- store and ripen game such as venison or pheasant HANG
gamekeeper WARRENER
games See **sports, card games**
- games or sports festival in ancient Greece AGON
- collection, as of games or useful hints COMPENDIUM
gammon See **bacon**
Gandhi's policy of nonviolent resistance in India to press for political reform SATYAGRAHA
gang of young noblemen in 18th-century London, engaging in muggings and vandalism MOHOCKS
- Mafia-like criminal gang in Naples CAMORRA
gangplank - rope handrail on a ship's gangplank or ladder MANROPE
gangrene NECROSIS, MORTIFICATION
gap See also **hole**
- gap between the teeth, especially one that is abnormally wide DIASTEMA
- gap or break caused by splitting, cutting, or the like CLEAVAGE, DISCONTINUITY, VOID
- gap or break in proceedings, such as an interval RECESS, RESPITE, ADJOURNMENT, INTERMISSION
- gap or missing part, interruption, break in continuity HIATUS, LACUNA
- gap or opening in a bone, membrane, or other part of the body FORAMEN
- gap or oversight, as in a law or contract, making evasion possible LOOPHOLE
- gap or point between two nerve cells across which a nerve impulse is transmitted SYNAPSE
- deep gap in the earth's surface or on a mountain, gorge or gulf ABYSS, CHASM
- narrow gap or gorge, as gouged out by a river or floodwaters CANYON, RAVINE, COULOIR, GULLY, GULCH, WADI
- narrow gap or pass, as through mountains DEFILE
- small gap or opening, as in a wall or rock CRANNY, FISSURE, RIFT, CLEFT, CREVICE
- small space, opening, or gap, as between the strands of a net INTERSTICE
garden arch or frame made of criss-crossing sticks, on which climbing plants are trained to grow TRELLIS
- garden designed with an ornamental pattern of paths between the flowerbeds PARTERRE
- garden of formal design, with detailed patterns of flowerbeds KNOT GARDEN
- garden party, picnic, or other outdoor meal or entertainment FÊTE CHAMPÊTRE
- garden pavilion or summerhouse, usually having a fine view GAZEBO, BELVEDERE
- garden shelter, often made of trellising BOWER, ARBOR
- garden walk or tree-lined terrace in ancient Rome XYST
- garden's summerhouse, bower, or other secluded spot ALCOVE
- improved by contouring and planting, as large grounds or gardens might be LANDSCAPED
garden predators See illustration, page 224
gardening, especially flower growing HORTICULTURE
- gardening tool for making holes in the soil, as for bulbs or seedlings DIBBER, DIBBLE
- ornamental gardening in which trees or hedges are clipped into designs TOPIARY
garland or wreath CORONAL
garlic, onion, leek, or related plant ALLIUM
- smelling or tasting of onions or garlic ALLIACEOUS
garlic mayonnaise AIOLI
garment, especially a ceremonial robe VESTMENT
- garment made up in cheap cloth as a basis for alterations or copies TOILE
- triangular insert of material for enlarging or reinforcing a garment, bag, or the like GUSSET
garnish of diced, cooked vegetables JARDINIERE
gas See chart, page 225
- gas, smoke, or vapor blown or breathed out EXHALATION
- gas, such as helium or neon, formerly considered incapable of chemical reaction INERT GAS, NOBLE GAS, RARE GAS

- gas build-up in the digestive tract, causing breaking of wind FLATULENCE
- gas built up in the digestive tract, causing breaking of wind FLATUS
- gas burner producing a hot flame, used for laboratory experiments BUNSEN BURNER
- gas of a poisonous or bad-smelling kind rising from the ground MEPHITIS
- gas or vapor, as rising from a swamp or rubbish heap, smelly and invisible EFFLUVIUM
- gas produced in radioactive decay EMANATION
- gas used in aerosol sprays PROPELLANT
- gas well or oil well with an abundant natural flow GUSHER
- gaslike matter of enormously high temperature, as in stars and fusion reactors PLASMA
- abdominal pain caused by gas in the intestines COLIC
- able to absorb gas or liquid PERMEABLE, POROUS
- adjective for a gas GASEOUS
- convert into a gas VAPORIZE
- expelling or reducing gas in the stomach or intestines, relieving flatulence CARMINATIVE
- hypothetical gaslike substance formerly thought to fill all space and sustain light waves ETHER
- low in density, thin, as the air of the upper atmosphere is or a gas might be RAREFIED
- release air or gas from something, such as a tire DEFLATE
- resistant to liquids or gases IMPERMEABLE, IMPERVIOUS
- send out or give off something, such as gas or radiation EMIT
- turn directly from a gas into a solid or vice versa without becoming a liquid SUBLIMATE

gas (combining form) AER-, AERO-, ATMO-, PNEUM-, PNEUMO-, PNEUMATO-

gas mask - covering for the mouth and nose, resembling a gas mask, to purify or warm the air before breathing RESPIRATOR

gasoline - jellied gasoline used in firebombs and flamethrowers NAPALM
- bottle filled with gasoline or other flammable liquid and stoppered with a rag wick, thrown by hand as a crude fire bomb MOLOTOV COCKTAIL
- measure of gasoline's antiknock properties OCTANE NUMBER

gate - churchyard's roofed gate, where the coffin is traditionally rested at the start of the burial LYCH-GATE
- defensive tower or fortification, such as the gate of a castle or town BARBICAN
- revolving door or gate TURNSTILE
- side or back gate POSTERN

gather, collect, store up ACCUMULATE, AMASS
- gather, crowd together, assemble CONGREGATE, FORGATHER
- gather and store, as in a granary GARNER
- gather data, poems, or other items from several sources, for use in a book or survey COMPILE
- gather grain or crops left in a field after harvesting GLEAN
- gather into a mass or whole, come or bring together AGGREGATE, CONGLOMERATE
- gather or bring together helpers, arguments, or the like MARSHAL, MUSTER, MOBILIZE, ENLIST, RALLY
- gather or collect something, such as flowers CULL
- gather or summon, as for a formal meeting or public assembly CONVENE, CONVOKE

Garden Predators

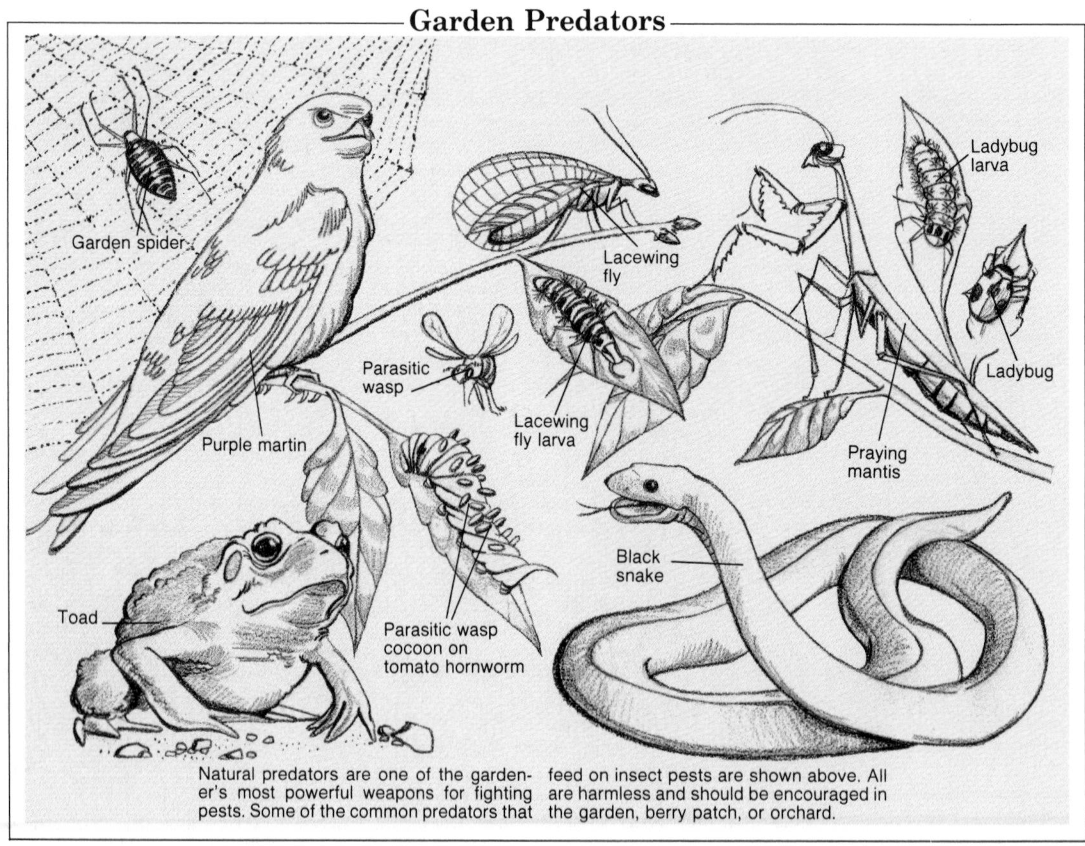

Natural predators are one of the gardener's most powerful weapons for fighting pests. Some of the common predators that feed on insect pests are shown above. All are harmless and should be encouraged in the garden, berry patch, or orchard.

gathering See also **meeting, crowd**
- gathering or contracting, as of the brows PURSING, PUCKERING
- gathering and stitching of cloth into tucked patterns SMOCKING
- gathering or pleating of fabric into a frilled trimming or decoration RUFFLING, RUCHE
- gather fabric into decorative rows, as on a dress SHIRR

gaudy, vulgar, tasteless and showy, cheap-looking TAWDRY, GIMCRACK

gauge - metal strip of known thickness used to gauge a narrow gap between two parts FEELER GAGE

gear enabling the driving wheels to turn at different rates, as when cornering DIFFERENTIAL GEAR
- gear higher than the normal range OVERDRIVE
- gear system in which one or more wheels move around the outside or inside of a fixed-axis wheel EPICYCLIC TRAIN
- gear system synchronizing the speeds of the moving parts SYNCHROMESH
- gears, clutch, or shaft by which power passes from an engine or pedals to the axle TRANSMISSION
- change gear by pausing in neutral to declutch and pressing the accelerator briefly DOUBLE-DECLUTCH
- conical gear meshing with another to transmit power between shafts at an angle to each other but in the same plane BEVEL GEAR
- device for changing gear on a bicycle, transferring the chain between sprockets DERAILLEUR
- engage or interlock, as gear teeth might MESH
- smaller gear wheel PINION
- toothed bar that meshes with a gear wheel RACK
- toothed gear wheel or bar allowing movement in one direction only RATCHET
- toothlike projection, as on a gear wheel DENT, DENTATION, DENTICLE

geese - adjective for geese ANSERINE
- flock of geese on land GAGGLE
- flock of geese or other wildfowl in flight SKEIN

gel-forming substance used as a setting agent in jams PECTIN

gelatin made from the air bladders of certain freshwater fish ISINGLASS

gelatin (combining form) COLLO-

gemstone See illustration, page 226, and also **jewelry** and chart at **precious stones**
- gemstone, shell, or the like engraved with a raised design CAMEO
- gemstone associated with people born during a given month BIRTHSTONE
- gemstone set by itself, as in a ring SOLITAIRE
- gemstone with a changing luster or twinkling surface, such as a cat's eye CHATOYANT
- art of carving or engraving on gemstones GLYPTOGRAPHY
- artificial gemstone of quartz or fine glass RHINESTONE
- degree of shine or transparency of a gemstone LUSTER, WATER
- deep red, rounded, uncut gemstone CARBUNCLE
- fake gemstone, typically consisting of colored glass with a face of real gemstone DOUBLET
- fine hard glass used in making artificial gemstones PASTE, STRASS
- groove, rim, ring, or the like for

GASES

acetylene	used for producing a hot flame for welding and cutting metal
ammonia	used in making fertilizers and synthetic fibers, and as a refrigerant
blackdamp/ chokedamp	mixture high in carbon dioxide, found in coal mines after a fire or explosion
butane	used in cigarette lighters and domestic fuels
carbon dioxide	used as a refrigerant and in fizzy drinks and aerosols
carbon monoxide	formed by incomplete burning of coal, gasoline, or the like; known as white damp or afterdamp in coal mines
cyanogen	used for pest control, as a chemical weapon, and as a rocket propellant
ether/diethyl ether	used as an anesthetic and in many industrial processes
ethylene/ethene	made from natural gas or petroleum, used in making plastics
helium	used in fluorescent lighting tubes, lasers, and balloons
hydrogen sulfide	used in chemical analyses (smell of rotten eggs)
krypton	used in light bulbs, and in high-speed photography
methane/marsh gas/firedamp	main constituent of natural gas, and found in coal mines, marshlands, and the like; used in making chloroform and methyl alcohol
mustard gas/ yperite	dichlorodiethyl sulfide, used in chemical warfare, to produce burns and eye irritation
neon	used in lasers and illuminated signs, glowing pink or red
nitrous oxide/ laughing gas	used as a mild anesthetic
ozone	unstable form of oxygen, common in the upper atmosphere; used in bleaches, air-conditioning systems, and purification processes
propane	often found in natural gas and petroleum, used as a fuel and refrigerant
radon	formed by the radioactive decay of radium, used in radiotherapy and atomic research
tear gas/ lacrimator	used in riot control
xenon	used in thermionic valves, lamps, and lasers

Gemstones

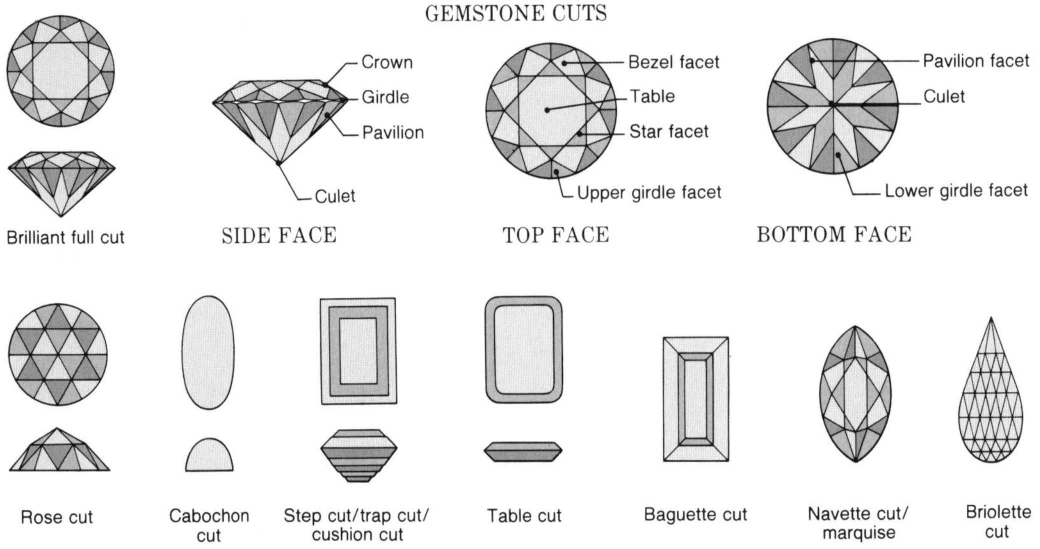

GEMSTONE CUTS
Crown
Girdle
Pavilion
Culet
Bezel facet
Table
Star facet
Upper girdle facet
Pavilion facet
Culet
Lower girdle facet
Brilliant full cut
SIDE FACE
TOP FACE
BOTTOM FACE
Rose cut
Cabochon cut
Step cut/trap cut/ cushion cut
Table cut
Baguette cut
Navette cut/ marquise
Briolette cut

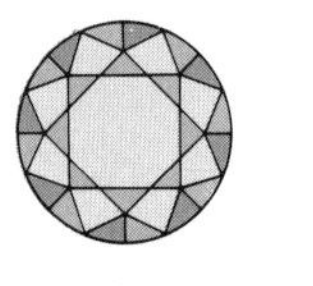

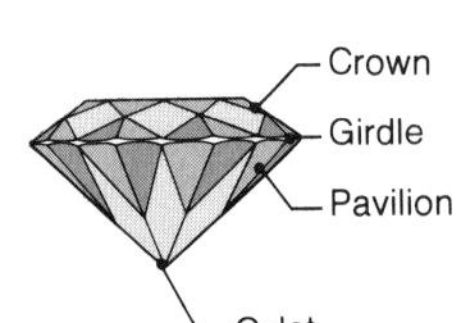

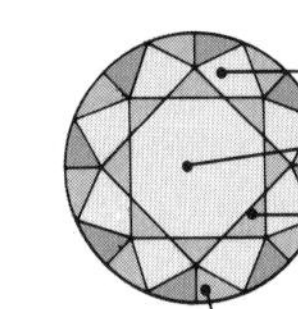

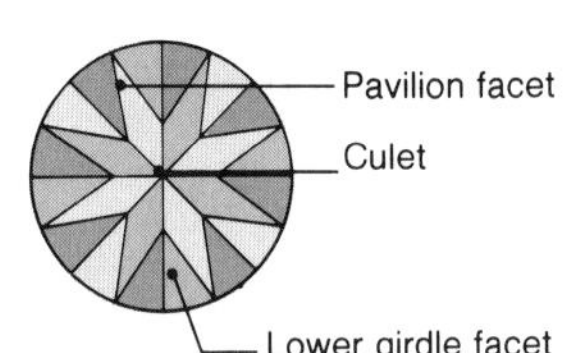

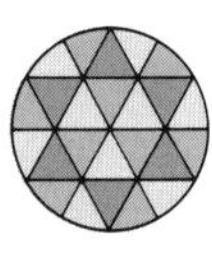

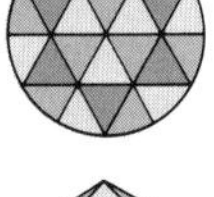

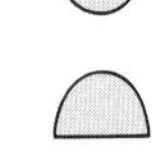

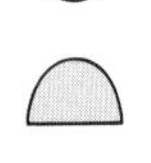

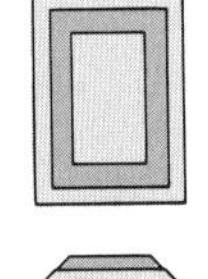

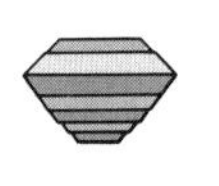

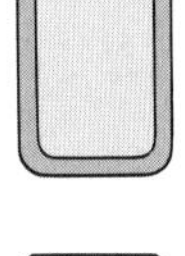

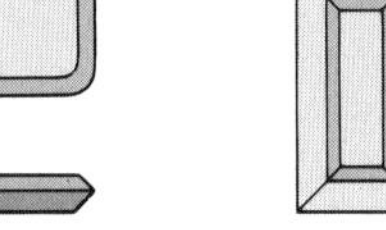

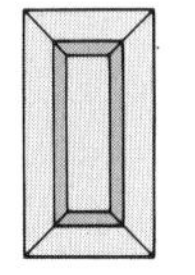

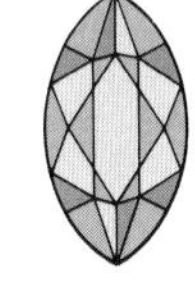

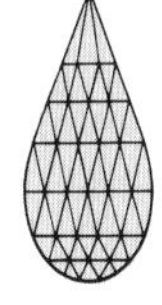

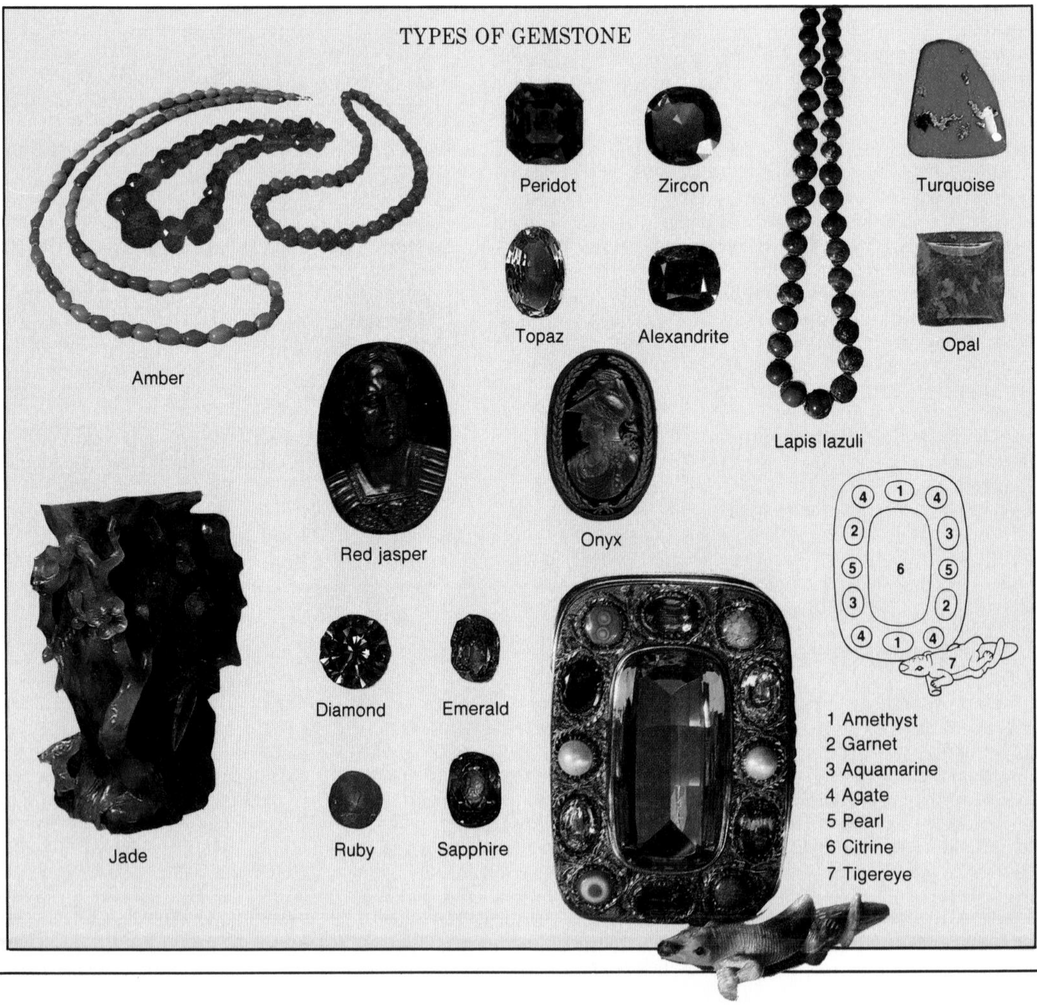

TYPES OF GEMSTONE
Amber
Peridot
Zircon
Turquoise
Topaz
Alexandrite
Opal
Lapis lazuli
Red jasper
Onyx
Jade
Diamond
Emerald
Ruby
Sapphire
1 Amethyst
2 Garnet
3 Aquamarine
4 Agate
5 Pearl
6 Citrine
7 Tigereye

clamping a gemstone or watch crystal BEZEL
- metal leaf fixed under a gemstone for added brilliance FOIL
- person who cuts and polishes gemstones LAPIDARY
- relating to carving or engraving, especially on gemstones GLYPTIC
- revolving drum in which gemstones are smoothed and polished by abrasives TUMBLING BARREL, TUMBLER, RUMBLE
- rim securing a gemstone in a piece of jewelry COLLET
- setting for a gemstone OUCH
- support or backing, as for a gemstone MOUNTING

gender, as of *child* or *lawyer*, that may be either masculine or feminine in reference COMMON GENDER
- neither masculine nor feminine in gender NEUTER, EPICENE

gene See **genetics**

general, universal, sweeping, all-embracing CATHOLIC
- general, universal, very widespread, prevalent, EPIDEMIC, PANDEMIC, ENDEMIC
- general, wide-ranging, comprehensive, giving or having a broad view SYNOPTIC, PANORAMIC, MACROSCOPIC
- general agreement CONSENSUS
- general assembly, meeting with all members present PLENUM, PLENARY SESSION
- general assistant or employee doing a variety of work FACTOTUM
- general direction or movement, as of someone's life TENOR
- general idea, or word referring to a general idea rather than to a specific thing ABSTRACTION
- general impression, survey, or description OVERVIEW, CONSPECTUS
- generally or widely applicable, talented, or the like VERSATILE
- belonging to a higher or larger class or level of generality SUPERORDINATE
- classify or include in a wider category or under a general heading or principle SUBSUME

generalness, or generalization GENERALITY

generator, especially of direct current DYNAMO
- generator in the ignition system of some engines MAGNETO
- device, as on an electric motor or generator, for reversing the direction of a current, or converting alternating current into direct current COMMUTATOR
- electrostatic generator in which the charge accumulates on a hollow metal ball VAN DE GRAAFF GENERATOR
- rotating part of a generator or electric motor ARMATURE

generosity shown in the form of gifts of money or favors LARGESSE

generous, or willingly given UNSTINTED, UNGRUDGING, BOUNTEOUS
- generous and charitable, selfless PHILANTHROPIC, ALTRUISTIC
- generous in forgiving, bighearted, noble MAGNANIMOUS
- generous or extravagant LAVISH, PRODIGAL, PROFUSE
- generous with gifts, hospitality, or the like, openhanded MUNIFICENT, BOUNTIFUL, LIBERAL
- obligation on noble or noble-minded people to be generous and honorable NOBLESSE OBLIGE

genetics See also **cell**
- genetically deviant organism MUTANT, SPORT
- gene that can produce a particular characteristic in an organism when paired with an identical or dissimilar gene DOMINANT GENE
- gene that can produce a particular characteristic only when it is paired with an identical gene RECESSIVE GENE
- laws of genetics, the basic principles of heredity MENDEL'S LAWS
- plant, animal, or cell genetically identical to another through asexual descent from a common ancestor CLONE
- plant or animal that is a genetic mix CHIMERA
- thread of RNA, DNA, and protein in a cell nucleus, carrying genes with genetic code and responsible for transmitting hereditary characteristics CHROMOSOME
- transference of genetic information from DNA to RNA TRANSCRIPTION

genie, spirit taking human form, in Muslim legend JINNI

genitals See also **sex**
- genital, relating to the region around the sex organs PUBIC
- genital area CROTCH, CRUTCH
- genital area in males GROIN
- genital sore or growth, hard and red, indicating syphilis CHANCRE
- genital sore or growth that is soft and nonsyphilitic CHANCROID
- area between the anus and genitals in the human body PERINEUM
- external genital organs, especially a woman's PUDENDA
- opening for the digestive and genital tracts in birds, fish, and reptiles CLOACA
- relating to sex or the genital organs VENEREAL

gentleman, such as an able horseman or a courtly escort CAVALIER
- gentleman in Spanish-speaking countries CABALLERO
- gentlemanly, courteous, especially toward women CHIVALROUS

gentleness, mildness of manner MANSUETUDE

genuine, real, not imaginary or apparent SUBSTANTIVE, VERITABLE
- genuine, real, true, reliable AUTHENTIC, BONA FIDE, ECHT, SIMON-PURE, KOSHER
- genuine, right and proper PUKKA
- genuine or true, in accordance with the facts VERIDICAL
- attractive or plausible but not really true or genuine SPECIOUS
- superficially similar but not corresponding or genuine SPURIOUS

genus - adjective for a genus or similar classification GENERIC

geography See chart, page 228, and also **earth, glacier, volcano, map, atmosphere**
- geographical features of a region, as on a map TOPOGRAPHY
- geographical mistake, placement error, positioning something in the wrong locality ANACHORISM

geology See also **earth, earthquake, glacier, volcano, rock, mountain, continent, time**
- geological accumulation of rock debris SCREE, TALUS
- geological deposit of dust laid down by the wind LOESS
- geological downfold of rock layers SYNCLINE
- geological fracture along which rock displacement occurs FAULT
- geological mountain-building episode OROGENY
- geological upfold of rock layers ANTICLINE
- geological uplift or subsidence of continental landmasses without folding EPEIROGENY
- divisions of geological time ERA, PERIOD, EPOCH, AGE, AEON
- highland between two parallel geological faults HORST
- in geology, a mass of calcite projecting from the floor of a cave STALAGMITE
- in geology, an iciclelike mass of calcite hanging from the roof of a cave STALACTITE
- replacement of geological organic matter by minerals, as in fossils PETRIFACTION
- study of rocks in geology PETROLOGY
- trough in the earth's crust whose floor is subsiding under geological sediments GEOSYNCLINE
- valley between two parallel geological faults GRABEN, RIFT VALLEY

geometry See illustration, page 230, and also **mathematics, graph, curve, line**
- geometric figure, line, or angle, as used in solving a problem or proving a theorem CONSTRUCTION
- geometrical measurement MENSURATION
- geometrical puzzle consisting of a one-sided surface made by forming a twisted strip into a ring MÖBIUS STRIP
- instrument used to draw circles, as in geometry COMPASSES
- instrument used to measure and draw angles, as in geometry PROTRACTOR
- problem or supplementary rule arising from a theorem, as in geometry RIDER

geranium PELARGONIUM

germ See also **bacteria, virus**
- germ, disease-causing agent PATHOGEN
- germ, poison, or any other harmful substance that prompts the body's immune system to produce antibodies ANTIGEN
- blood protein that is produced to counteract germs or other invading substances ANTIBODY
- insect or other organism that transmits germs VECTOR, CARRIER

germ (combining form) -BLAST-

German See chart, page 232
- German academic secondary school GYMNASIUM
- German as spoken in northern Germany in a variety of dialects PLATTDEUTSCH
- German chief minister CHANCELLOR, KANZLER
- German prisoner-of-war camp for captured Allied soldiers during World War II STALAG
- German restaurant, originally in the cellars of a town hall RATHSKELLER
- German town hall RATHAUS
- Germany's annexation of Austria in 1938 ANSCHLUSS
- derogatory term for a German KRAUT, BOCHE
- member of German guild formed to promote music and poetry MEISTERSINGER
- Rhine siren of German legend LORELEI

German measles RUBELLA

germinate or sprout PULLULATE

germination See **seed**

germination (combining form) BLASTO-

gesture of greeting SALUTATION
- gesture of greeting or respect, as in India, by placing one's hands out together in front of one and bowing slightly NAMASTE
- gesture of greeting or respect, as

GEOGRAPHICAL FEATURES

archipelago	cluster of islands in the sea
atoll	circular coral reef enclosing a lagoon
barrier reef	coral reef running parallel to the coast
butte	small, prominent, flat-topped hill rising abruptly from the surrounding desert
campo	large, grassy plain with small trees in South America
cay	low islet of coral or sand
erg/reg	area of shifting sand dunes, typically in North Africa
fjord	deep and long inlet of the sea
guyot	flat-topped mountain on the sea-bed
inselberg	isolated domed hill in arid regions
isthmus	strip of land connecting two much larger pieces of land
kopje	small prominent hill in southern Africa
llano	treeless grassland in northern South America
massif	large highland region with well-defined boundaries
mesa	flat-topped highland with clifflike sides in arid regions
oxbow/oxbow lake/mortlake	bow-shaped lake formed when a river cuts across the neck of a U-shaped bend
pamir	high grassland in central Asia
pampa	grasslands in Argentina and Uruguay
playa/salt pan/salina	flat basin that may periodically become a shallow salt lake
polder	area of low-lying reclaimed land, typically in the Netherlands
prairie	treeless grassland in North America
ria	indentation where the sea has drowned the lower part of a river valley
savanna	grassland with scattered trees in tropical and subtropical regions
sierra	high range of mountains with jagged peaks
strath	steep-sided, broad, flat-floored valley, typically in Scotland
tundra	land between the area of permanent snow and the tree line in Arctic regions
veld/bushveld	grassland with low trees in parts of southern Africa
wadi/donga	rocky desert ravine occasionally carrying a torrent after heavy rain
wasserschicht	layer or stratum of water

in many Muslim societies, by bowing and touching the forehead with the right hand SALAAM
- gesture of humility, as formerly in China, by prostrating oneself or kneeling and touching the ground with one's forehead KOWTOW
- gesture of humility or reverence, by bending or kneeling briefly on one knee GENUFLECTION
- gesture of minimal compliance with a law or custom TOKENISM
- gesture of respect or submission, such as a bow or curtsy OBEISANCE
- gesture of scorn made by thumbing the nose SNOOK
- gesture or action that is noble in appearance, though sometimes empty in effect BEAU GESTE
- gesture vigorously, as to reinforce speech GESTICULATE
- gestures, posture, and similar nonverbal and unconscious communication BODY LANGUAGE
- hostile gesture made when leaving PARTHIAN SHOT
- study of movement, gesture, and expression KINESICS
- supplementing verbal communication, as voice qualities and gestures are PARALINGUISTIC

get, obtain, receive, gain ACQUIRE, SECURE, PROCURE, GARNER

get rid of See also **destroy, exclude**
- get rid of, cancel, or withdraw officially a law, decree, or the like REPEAL, REVOKE, RESCIND
- get rid of, put an end to, abolish, or lessen something ABATE
- get rid of, reject, or disown a wife, child, or the like REPUDIATE
- get rid of or abolish formally a law, treaty, or the like ABROGATE, ANNUL, NULLIFY
- get rid of or manage without DISPENSE WITH
- get rid of or throw away something unwanted DISPOSE OF, DISCARD, JETTISON, SLOUGH OFF

geyser - expel hot water and steam forcefully and abundantly, as a geyser does ERUPT

ghost See also **spirit, demon**
- ghost, supernatural being, spirit from another world VISITANT
- ghost or ghostly figure, phantom SPECTER, APPARITION, PHANTASM, PRESENCE, EIDOLON
- ghost or spirit, someone returned from the dead in ghostly form SHADE, WRAITH, REVENANT
- ghost or spirit in Caribbean folklore DUPPY
- ghostlike substance supposedly emerging from a spiritualist medium during a seance ECTOPLASM
- ghostly counterpart or double DOPPELGÄNGER
- ghosts or spirits of the dead in ancient Rome MANES, LEMURES
- appearance of a ghost, spirit, angel, or the like VISITATION
- forecasting or divination by consulting ghosts SCIOMANCY
- noisy or mischievous ghost or spirit POLTERGEIST
- person who is believed to be dead and reanimated, but without a soul, the converse of a ghost ZOMBIE
- take bodily form, become visible, as a ghost is said to do MATERIALIZE

giant See also **monster**
- giant TITAN, COLOSSUS
- giant or gnome in Scandinavian folklore TROLL
- giant or humanlike monster OGRE

gift, payment, or other expression of respect, submission, homage, or the like TRIBUTE, FAVOR
- gift, possession, or project requiring more trouble than it is worth WHITE ELEPHANT
- gift or grant, as to a charity CONTRIBUTION, DONATION
- gift or payment in return for a service or favor CONSIDERATION, RECOMPENSE
- gift or small favor offered to appease or bribe SOP
- gift that serves to remind one of the giver KEEPSAKE, MEMENTO
- gifts, money, or favors distributed generously LARGESSE
- small gift or bonus, tip PERK, PERQUISITE

gift of tongues, emotional or ecstatic and largely unintelligible speech GLOSSOLALIA

gifts of the Magi - perfumed resins, among the gifts of the Magi MYRRH, FRANKINCENSE

gilded silver, bronze, or copper VERMEIL

gill - gill cover on a fish OPERCULUM

gills (combining form) BRANCH-

gin, as sold in stone bottles HOLLANDS, HOLLAND GIN, GENEVA
- berries used to flavor gin JUNIPER BERRIES

giraffe - African forest mammal, related to the giraffe OKAPI
- former term for a giraffe CAMELOPARD

girder supporting the timbers of a floor STRINGER, SUMMER

girl, maiden, young woman DAMSEL
- girl of the streets URCHIN, WAIF
- girl or young woman, slim and attractive in a boyish way GAMINE
- girls' or women's club, as at a college SORORITY
- beautiful girl or young woman NYMPH
- group of girls, larks, quail, or roe deer BEVY
- ideal fashionable girl or young woman around 1900 GIBSON GIRL
- innocent and naive girl or young women INGENUE
- Irish term for a girl or young woman COLLEEN
- small, slim, dainty as a girl or young woman might be PETITE

Girl Guides - senior member of the Girl Guides RANGER

Girl Scouts - senior member of the Girl Scouts SENIOR

give away or sell DISPOSE OF
- give back as much as one has received RECIPROCATE
- give off or discharge slowly or conspicuously EXUDE
- give off something, such as radiation EMIT, EMANATE, EXHALE
- give or apply medication, assistance, or the like ADMINISTER
- give or commit something permanently CONSIGN
- give or contribute DONATE
- give or convey something, such as greetings or respectability EXTEND, IMPART
- give or grant something, such as a favor or nod, in a patronizing way VOUCHSAFE
- give or grant something, such as an honor or blessing BESTOW, CONFER, ACCORD
- give or provide something, such as assistance or a view AFFORD, FURNISH, RENDER
- give or spend generously and unsparingly, dole out LAVISH
- give or yield formally CEDE
- give out or distribute something, in portions or shares DISPENSE, ALLOCATE, ALLOT, APPORTION
- give reluctantly DISGORGE
- give rise to ELICIT, EVOKE
- give to, provide with, equip or entrust with INVEST WITH, ENDOW WITH, ENDUE WITH
- keep offering or giving something to PLY
- person who gives money for charity or the like DONOR

give in See also **yield**
- give in to or indulge a whim, desire, or the like GRATIFY

give up See also **stop, surrender**
- give up a claim or right voluntarily WAIVE
- give up or abandon something desirable FORSAKE, RELINQUISH, ABNEGATE, ABJURE
- give up or abstain from something desirable or promising, such as an opportunity FORGO
- give up or lose something by way

Geometric Shapes

SOLIDS

POLYHEDRA/PLATONIC SOLIDS

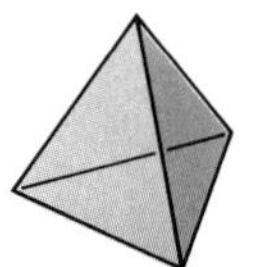
Tetrahedron

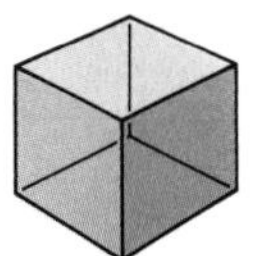
Cube: 6 faces

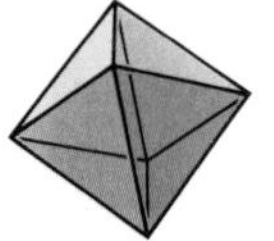
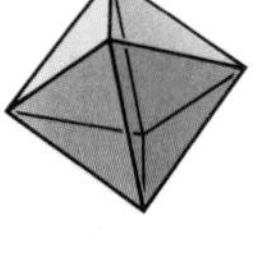
Octahedron: 8 faces

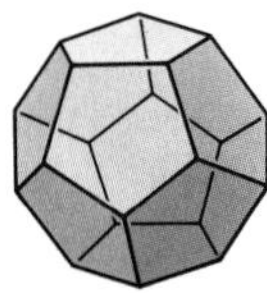
Dodecahedron: 12 faces

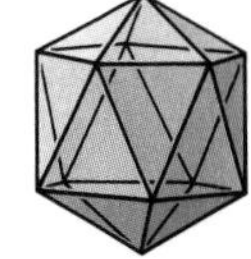
Icosahedron: 20 faces

OTHER SOLIDS

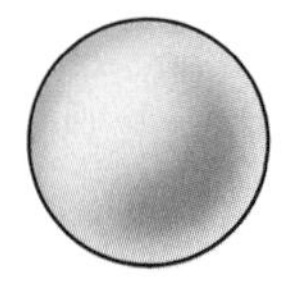
Sphere

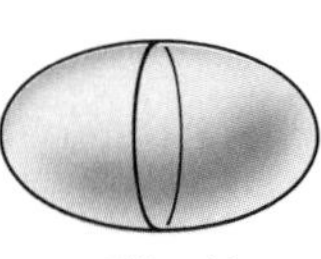
Ellipsoid

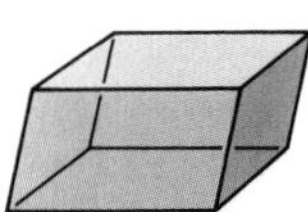
Parallelepiped

Truncated cone

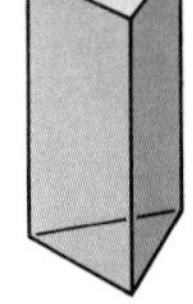
Triangular prism

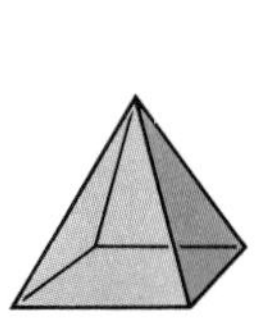
Quadrilateral pyramid

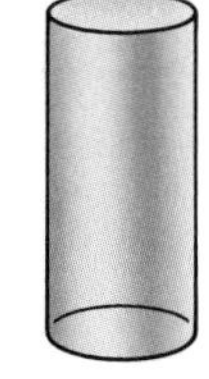
Cylinder

POLYGONS

TRIANGLES

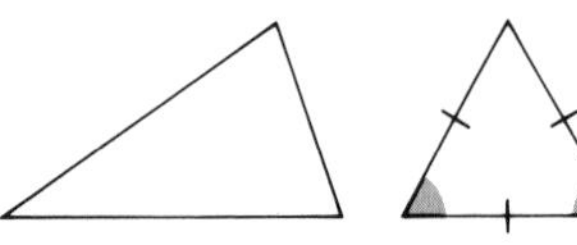
Acute

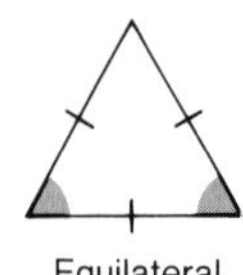
Equilateral

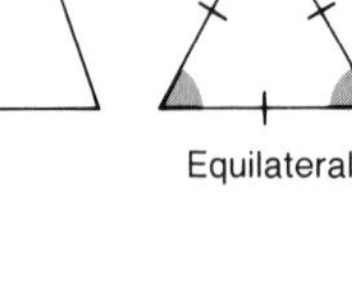

Isosceles

Right-angled

Scalene

Obtuse

QUADRILATERALS

PARALLELOGRAMS

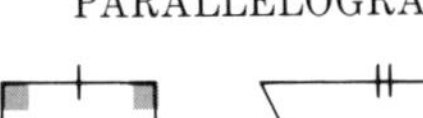
Square

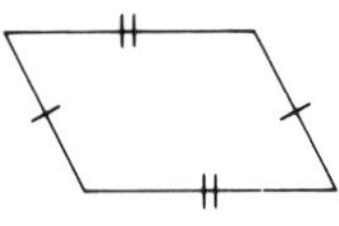
Rhomboid

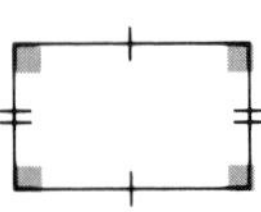
Rectangle

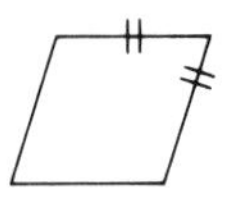
Rhombus

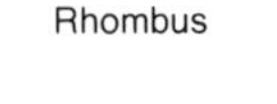

OTHER QUADRILATERALS

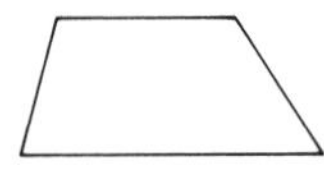
Trapezium

Kite

PENTAGON

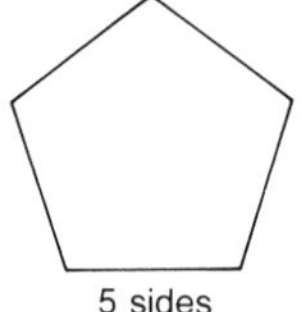
5 sides

HEXAGON

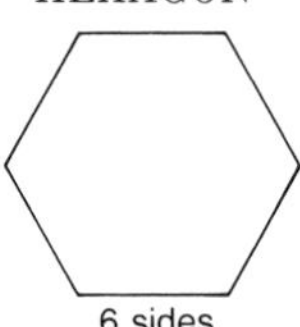
6 sides

HEPTAGON

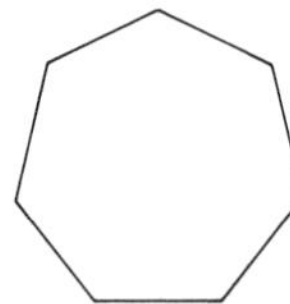
7 sides

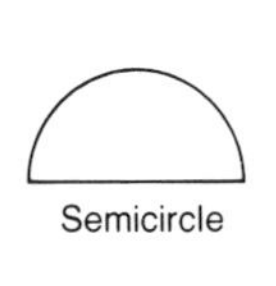
Semicircle

Ellipse

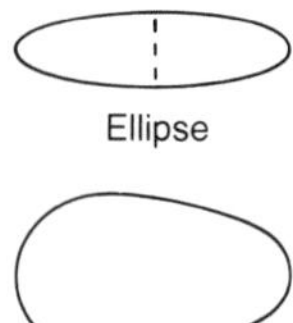
Oval

CIRCLES

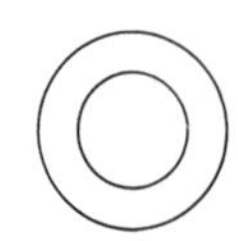
Concentric circles

Inscribed circle

PARTS OF A CIRCLE

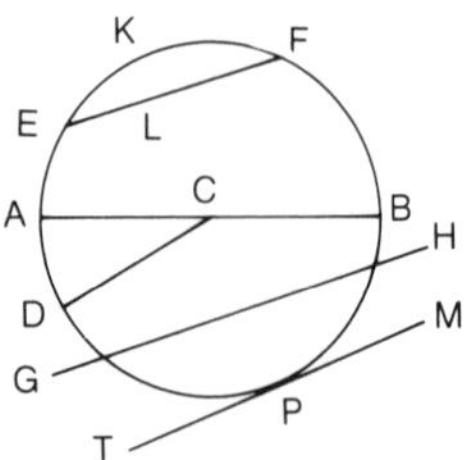

AB diameter. C center. CD, CA, CB radii. EKF arc on EF chord. EFKL (area) segment on EF chord. ACD (area) sector. GH secant. TPM tangent. EKFBPDA circumference

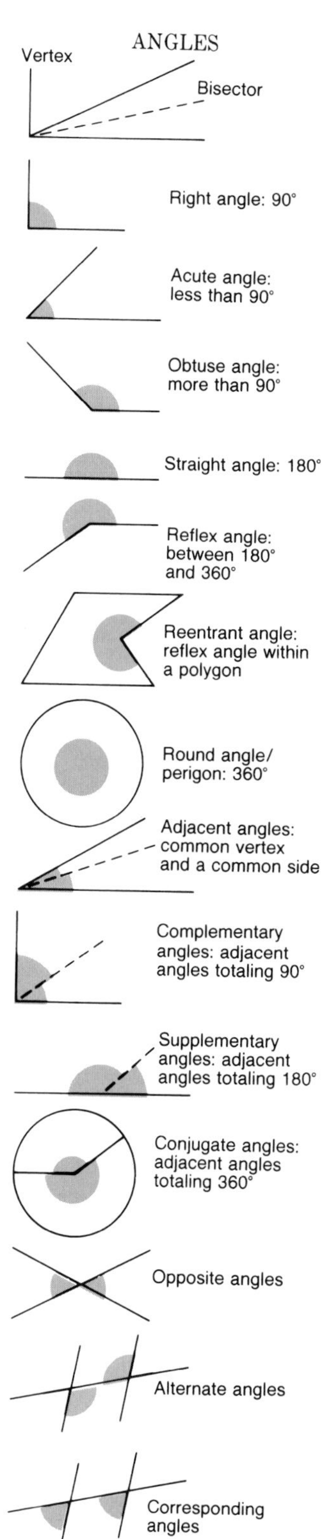

of a fine or penalty FORFEIT
- give up or reject all claims to or connection with, disown RENOUNCE, DISCLAIM, REPUDIATE, FORSWEAR
- give up power ABDICATE

given or done in return or exchange RECIPROCAL
- given willingly, unsparing UNSTINTED, UNGRUDGING

giving up or surrender of something, as of land or rights CESSION

glacier See illustration, page 233
- ridge of debris deposited by a melting glacier or ice sheet KAME
- streamlined hill formed by glacial deposits DRUMLIN
- wearing away of a glacier, as by melting ABLATION

gladiator, in ancient Rome, armed with a net and trident RETIARIUS
- gladiator's three-pronged spear TRIDENT

glamour, aura of mystery MYSTIQUE

glance, quick inspection COUP D'OEIL

gland See chart, page 234
- chemical secretion from glands, modifying the workings of a tissue or organ HORMONE
- oily substance produced by glands SEBUM, SMEGMA
- relating to glands ADENOIDAL
- study of glands ENDOCRINOLOGY
- swelling and inflammation of a lymph gland BUBO

gland (combining form) ADEN-, ADENO-

glandular fever INFECTIOUS MONONUCLEOSIS

glare - glare-reducing plastic, as used in some sunglasses POLAROID
- glare shield fitted at the top of a car's windscreen VISOR

glaringly or outrageously wrong or evil FLAGRANT, EGREGIOUS
- glaringly bright in color GARISH, LURID

glass, goblet, tankard, or the like filled to the brim BUMPER
- glass cover for a watch face LUNETTE
- glass for drinking, especially one having a rounded bottom inside TUMBLER
- glass in a heated lump, ready for molding or blowing PARISON
- glass of a decorative multicolored type, as used in lamps and ornaments in the early 1900s FAVRILE GLASS, TIFFANY GLASS
- glass of a heat-resistant type, used for ovenware PYREX
- glass of a pale-whitish, semi-transparent or shimmering type OPALINE
- glass or transparent plastic block, triangular in cross section, as in cameras, for reflecting, refracting, or dispersing light PRISM
- glass tile or disc set in a pavement, deck, or the like to admit light BULL'S-EYE
- glass tube, open at both ends, into which liquid is sucked to be measured or transferred PIPETTE
- glass vessel with a long drooping neck, as used for distilling RETORT
- glassware decorated with pieces of colored metal or glass MURRHINE GLASS
- allowing the passage of light diffusely, as frosted glass does TRANSLUCENT
- allowing the passage of light freely, as clear glass does, so that objects on the other side are fully visible TRANSPARENT
- chemical compound used in glass and concrete manufacture SILICA, SILICON DIOXIDE, QUARTZ
- clarifying of molten glass by removing gas bubbles FINING
- clear acrylic plastic used as a substitute for glass PERSPEX
- dark glass containing sparkling metal particles AVENTURINE
- darkening or changing color if exposed to light, as some glass or plastic is PHOTOCHROMIC
- fine hard glass of varying kinds used in making lenses OPTICAL GLASS, CROWN GLASS, FLINT GLASS
- fine hard glass used in making artificial gems PASTE, STRASS
- fine Irish glassware with a bluish tinge WATERFORD GLASS
- former medical technique of attaching a glass cup to the skin by a partial vacuum, in order to draw blood to the surface CUPPING
- heat and then cool glass or metal to strengthen it TEMPER, ANNEAL
- iron rod used for finishing in glassmaking PUNTY, PONTIL
- large drinking glass, usually with a short stem RUMMER
- large glass for sherry or port, or large beer glass SCHOONER
- person who installs window glass GLAZIER
- process discarded glass, paper, water, and so on for reuse RECYCLE
- referring to glass that is ground and polished on both sides PATENT
- safety glass containing thin layers of plastic or wire LAMINATED GLASS
- small glass used for serving or measuring spirits JIGGER
- small mat or disc placed under a bottle or glass to protect the table top COASTER
- soluble fusible white mineral used in making glass and pottery BORAX
- turn into glass, as by heating or

melting VITRIFY
- window glass of former times, with a circular shape and a lump in the center from the worker's rod CROWN GLASS

glass (combining form) HYAL-, HYALO-, VITR-, VITRO-

glass fiber, thin and flexible, for transmission of light and telecommunications messages, as around corners OPTICAL FIBER

glasses or pair of opera glasses supported in position by a small handle LORGNETTE, LORGNON

GERMAN TERMS

angst	anxiety	**lebensraum**	living space for an expanding population
auf Wiedersehen	good-bye	**lederhosen**	man's leather shorts
bierstube	(beer) tavern	**lied**	song, art song
bildungsroman	novel dealing with the early life of one person	**luftwaffe**	German air force
blitzkrieg	lightning attack	**panzer**	army tank
doppelgänger	ghostly double	**putsch**	sudden attempt to overthrow a government
ersatz	inferior substitute	**rathskeller**	basement tavern
festschrift	homage volume	**realpolitik**	harsh policy of national self-interest
gasthaus	inn, hotel	**reich**	nation, empire
gauleiter	Nazi district governor; petty tyrant	**schadenfreude**	gloating (over a disadvantage or misfortunes)
gemütlich	comfortable; snug	**schmalz**	excessive sentimentality
gesundheit!	bless you!	**stein**	earthenware tankard
Gymnasium	German academic secondary school	**Sturm und Drang**	late-18th-century German romantic literary movement
hausfrau	housewife	**weltanschauung**	world view, philosophy of life
herrenvolk	master race	**weltschmerz**	sentimental sadness or pessimism, world weariness
Junker	former Prussian aristocrat	**zeitgeist**	the spirit of the times
kaiser	emperor		
kapellmeister	director of a choir or orchestra		
kaput	broken, out of order, useless		
kitsch	sentimentally bad taste in the arts		

- glasses with compound lenses, correcting for both near and distant vision BIFOCALS
- glasses without sidepieces, held in place by being clipped to the bridge of the nose PINCE-NEZ
- maker and seller of glasses OPTICIAN
- referring to glasses with frames of horn, tortoiseshell, or plastic HORN-RIMMED, TORTOISESHELL
- single glass lens, often on a handle or ribbon, serving as half of a pair of glasses MONOCLE, QUIZZING GLASS

glasshouse see **greenhouse**

glassy, or relating to or consisting of glass VITREOUS
- glassy rock, black and shiny, of volcanic origin OBSIDIAN

glaze of a shiny metallic kind on pottery LUSTER
- glazed fish or meat dish, served cold GALANTINE

glide, skim, or skip lightly, as over the surface of water SKITTER
- glide or move smoothly, as clouds might SCUD
- glide without power, as an aircraft might VOLPLANE

glider in the form of a single large cloth wing from which the pilot hangs in a harness HANG GLIDER

glitter, sparkle, flash, as a gemstone might CORUSCATE, SPANGLE, SCINTILLATE, FULGURATE
- glitter gently, gleam GLISTEN, SHIMMER
- glitter or sheen LUSTER
- glitter or shine producing a variety of colors IRIDESCENCE
- glittering, as with sequins CLINQUANT
- glittering, decorated with powdered glass, sequins, or artificial jewels to produce a diamondlike effect DIAMANTÉ
- glittering decoration of thin threads or strips, as on a Christmas tree TINSEL
- glittering fabric containing silver or golden threads LAMÉ

gloomy, tomblike SEPULCHRAL
- gloomy in temper, or cold and sluggish in temperament SATURNINE

glorification of someone or something by or as if by elevation to the status of a god EXALTATION, DEIFICATION, APOTHEOSIS, TRANSLATION

glorify, exalt TRANSFIGURE

glory, honor LAURELS
- glory, prestige, or award resulting from some achievement KUDOS

glove, as on a suit of armor or for certain sports GAUNTLET
- glove or other object formerly

thrown down to issue a challenge GAGE
- glove with one section for four fingers and one section for the thumb MITTEN, MITT
- finger of a glove, or protective sheath for an injured finger or toe STALL

glowing, as with self-generated light LUMINOUS
- glowing coals or wood, burning without flame CINDER, EMBERS
- glowing electrical discharge seen on a ship's mast, church spire, or the like during stormy weather SAINT ELMO'S FIRE, CORPOSANT
- glowing emitted by some fungi on rotting wood FOX FIRE
- glowing or shimmering with a rainbowlike range of colors OPALESCENT
- glowing produced at low temperatures, as through radioactivity LUMINESCENCE
- glowing produced by high temperature, as in a light bulb INCANDESCENCE
- glowing produced by or in living organisms, such as fireflies, some fish, and some fungi BIOLUMINESCENCE
- glowing produced during stimulation by radiation, as in a neon light FLUORESCENCE
- glowing that continues after stimulation by radiation PHOSPHORESCENCE
- glowing or flickering gently, as a flame might LAMBENT

glucose (combining form) GLYC-, GLYCO-

glue, paste, or other substance for sticking something to a surface ADHESIVE, MUCILAGE
- resin of a tough synthetic kind used in coatings and glues EPOXY
- spatula or similar device for applying glue, ointment, or the like to a surface APPLICATOR

glue (combining form) COLLO-

glue sniffing SOLVENT ABUSE

gluey, gummy, sticky, as some thick liquids are GLUTINOUS, VISCOUS, VISCID

gluttony, excessive eating GOURMANDISM
- eat gluttonously or greedily, gorge GORMANDIZE, GOURMANDIZE

gnawing mammal, such as the rat or squirrel RODENT

gnome or goblin in German folklore, who lives either underground or secretly in human households KOBOLD
- gnome or giant in Scandinavian folklore, living in caves or on mountains TROLL

gnu WILDEBEEST

go See **depart, move, walk**
- go one's way WEND

go along with someone's wishes or ideas HUMOR, INDULGE

go back on one's promise or commitment RENEGE
- go back to an earlier condition RELAPSE, REVERT, REGRESS

go-between, agent or means mediating between people or things, as in a dispute INTERMEDIARY, ARBITRATOR, BROKER
- go-between in a sexual relationship PIMP, PANDER, PANDERER, PROCURER

go off, as a bomb might, or cause to go off DETONATE

goal, aim, desired end, finishing point TERMINUS AD QUEM
- goal, aim, intention OBJECTIVE
- goal of a person's strivings MECCA, ZION
- goal or destination BOURN
- goal or intention, or the fulfillment of it CONSUMMATION
- belief that Nature is directed to-

Glacier

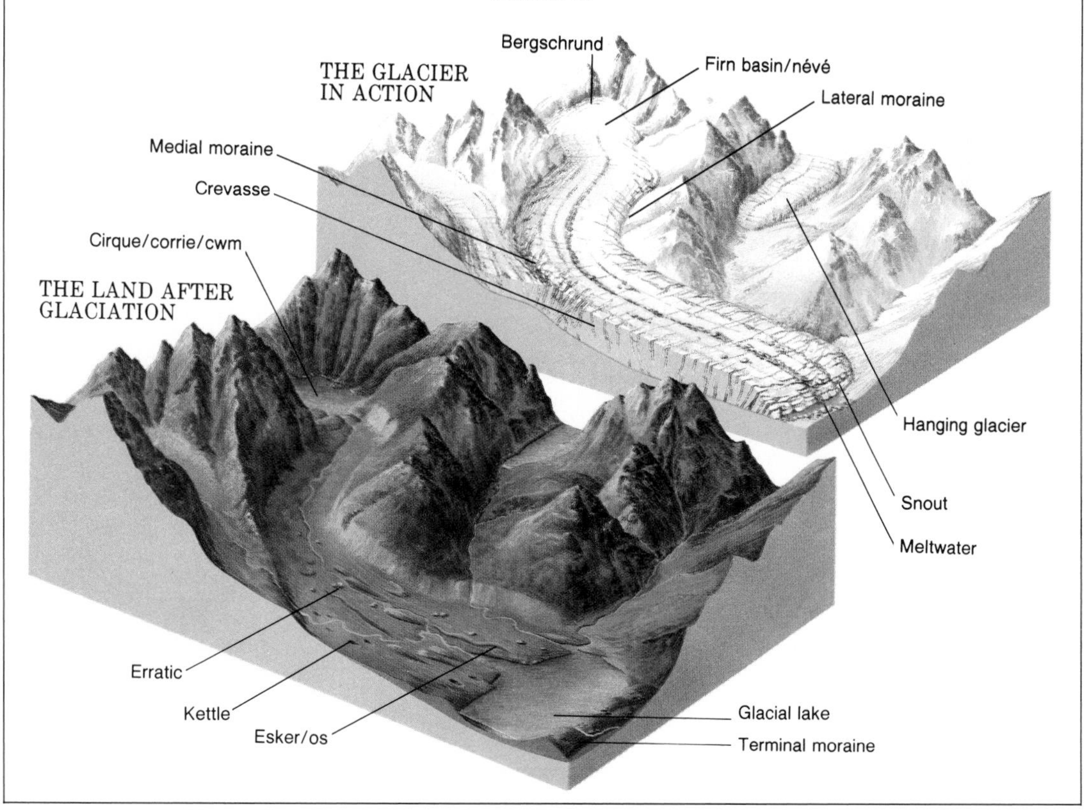

ward goals or is determined by a purpose TELEOLOGY
- directed or tending toward a specific goal or purpose TELIC
- upright pole or support, such as a goalpost STANCHION

goat - adjective for a goat CAPRINE, HIRCINE
- bear young, as sheep and goats do YEAN
- female goat NANNY GOAT
- male goat BILLY GOAT
- rural deity in mythology, part man and part goat in form FAUN, SATYR
- skin of a young goat, or the leather made from it CHEVRETTE
- young goat, kid YEANLING

goat hair as used in fabrics ANGORA, MOHAIR

goatskin or sheepskin treated for writing or painting on PARCHMENT

goblin - goblinlike creature supposedly causing mechanical failures, as in aircraft GREMLIN
- goblin or gnome in German folklore, living either underground or secretly in human households KOBOLD

god - godlike or godly DIVINE
- god of minor rank, or mythological being who is half mortal and half divine DEMIGOD
- god or goddess DEITY, DIVINITY
- belief in or worship of a single god MONOTHEISM
- belief in or worship of two or more gods POLYTHEISM
- blood of the gods in mythology ICHOR
- drink of the gods in mythology NECTAR
- food of the gods in mythology AMBROSIA
- guardian spirit or protective god of a particular person or place TUTELARY
- group of all the gods, or a temple dedicated to them PANTHEON
- household gods in ancient Rome LARES, PENATES
- idol, image, or idea of a Chinese god JOSS
- killing or killer of a god DEICIDE
- luminous cloud surrounding a god or goddess when visiting earth NIMBUS
- minor woodland god or demon, half man and half goat, in classical mythology SATYR, FAUN
- offering to a god, designed to appease PROPITIATION, HOLOCAUST
- prophecy, shrine, or priest, of a prophetic god, as in ancient Greece ORACLE
- raise to the rank of a god, glorify EXALT, DEIFY, APOTHEOSIZE, TRANSLATE
- relating to the Greek gods OLYMPIAN
- representation of gods in the form of animals ZOOMORPHISM
- representation of gods in the form of humans ANTHROPOMORPHISM
- "twilight of the gods," destruction of the ancient gods in their battle with the forces of evil GÖTTERDÄMMERUNG

God - Godlike being in ancient philosophy who created or regulates the universe DEMIURGE, PRIME MOVER, PRIMUM MOBILE

GLANDS

adrenal glands/ suprarenal glands	glands located above the kidneys that secrete epinephrine (adrenaline) and corticosteroid hormones into the bloodstream
apocrine glands	glands, such as mammary glands, in which part of the secreting cell itself goes into the secretion
eccrine glands	glands that secrete externally, specifically the sweat glands
endocrine glands/ductless glands	glands, such as the thyroid and pituitary, that secrete hormones directly into the bloodstream
exocrine glands	glands, such as salivary or sweat glands, that secrete through a duct
holocrine glands	glands, such as sebaceous glands, in which cells disintegrate entirely to form the secretion
lachrymal glands	tear glands, beneath the upper eyelids
lymph nodes/ lymph glands	glandlike masses of tissue throughout the body that supply certain white blood cells, absorb bacteria, and purify the lymph for the bloodstream
mammary glands	milk-producing glands in female mammals
merocrine glands	glands, such as sweat glands, in which the secreting cells remain intact
ovaries	female reproductive glands
pancreas	gland near the stomach, secreting digestive juices into the duodenum, and containing the insulin-producing islets of Langerhans
parathyroid glands	glands that secrete hormones that raise the level of calcium in the blood
parotid glands	largest of the salivary glands, below each ear
pineal body/ pineal gland	glandlike structure in the brain of vertebrates, about whose function little is known
pituitary gland/ pituitary body/ hypophysis	master endocrine gland at the base of the brain, producing hormones that regulate other glands and stimulate bone growth
prostate gland	gland in male mammals, secreting a liquid that forms part of the semen
sebaceous glands	skin glands that secrete an oily substance into the hair follicles and onto the skin
testes	male reproductive glands, the testicles
thymus	glandlike structure behind the breastbone, producing some white blood cells during early childhood
thyroid gland	gland in the neck, producing hormones that regulate metabolism and growth

- God's name, as assigned at various times or places ANCIENT OF DAYS, ADONAI, ELOHIM, YAHWEH, JEHOVAH, LORD, LORD OF HOSTS, LORD OF SABAOTH, THE OMNIPOTENT, DOMINUS, ALLAH
- God's ordering of earthly life and events DISPENSATION, PROVIDENCE
- God's self-revealing thought and will LOGOS
- appearance or manifestation to humans of God or a god or divine influence EPIPHANY, AVATAR, THEOPHANY
- belief in God as being present throughout the world, or identical with the world PANTHEISM
- belief in God as including the world as part of his being PANENTHEISM
- belief in God as the creator who no longer intervenes in the world DEISM
- belief in God or a god as the creator who at once transcends and yet is present in the world THEISM
- contemptuous or disrespectful toward God, religion, or sacred things BLASPHEMOUS, PROFANE
- devotion, great respect, awe, as shown to God or a god REVERENCE, VENERATION
- disclosure or realization of God's will or some religious truth REVELATION
- independent of and outside the created universe, as God is said to be in some views TRANSCENDENT
- philosophical doctrine seeing belief or disbelief in God as moot or of secondary importance, and elevating human values instead HUMANISM
- philosophical doctrine seeing belief or disbelief in God as moot or of secondary importance, and elevating scientific values instead RATIONALISM
- philosophical doctrine that says one cannot know whether God exists or not AGNOSTICISM
- philosophical doctrine that asserts that there is no God, denial of God's existence ATHEISM
- present throughout the universe, and within nature and people's souls, as God is said to be in some views IMMANENT
- set of four Hebrew letters, corresponding to YHWH, that represents God's name in the Old Testament TETRAGRAMMATON
- study of the nature of God and religious truth THEOLOGY

God, god (combining form) DE-, DEO-, THE-, THEO-

God willing DEO VOLENTE

godliness, saintliness SANCTITY

godparent SPONSOR

going away, especially of a large number of people EXODUS
- going out, or the right to go out EGRESS

gold, silver, or other metal that resists corrosion NOBLE METAL
- gold bar or similarly convenient block of metal INGOT
- gold-bearing, as gravel or rocks might be AURIFEROUS
- gold-bearing fragmentary rock found in South Africa BANKET

GOLF TERMS

apron	section of the fairway leading on to the green
birdie	score of one stroke under par for the hole
bogey	score of one stroke over par for the hole
brassie	formerly, a wooden-headed club equivalent to a modern No. 2 wood
caddie	person who carries a player's clubs during play
carry	distance a ball struck from the tee travels through the air until it touches the ground
divot	clump of turf gouged out by a golf club
dormie	in match play, referring to the player or side leading by as many holes as there are holes left to play
double eagle	score of three strokes under par for the hole
eagle	score of two strokes under par for the hole
fade	veer; cause the ball to veer
fore	warning cry to people in the line of play
golden ferret	holing of a ball directly from a sand trap
handicap	allowance corresponding to the number of strokes by which a player is expected to exceed par in a round of golf
links	golf course
mashie	formerly, a club for lifting the ball high, especially a No. 5 iron
match play	match or competition decided by the number of holes won by each player or side
niblick	a club producing a great deal of lift, specifically a No. 8 or No. 9 iron
par	number of strokes set as a testing standard for each hole
slope	undulations of a green, which have to be taken into account when putting
stableford	system of scoring that awards points for each hole rather than counting the total number of strokes
stroke play	match or competition decided by the total number of strokes taken by each player or side
stymie	obstruction of an opponent's ball on the green
wedge	club with a very wide angled face, specifically a No. 10 iron, as used for sand-trap shots

- gold or silver in bulk BULLION
- gold or silver thread used in embroidery PURL
- gold or silver wire or cord used as a trimming, as on military uniforms BULLION FRINGE
- gold-plated silver, bronze, or copper, as used in jewelry ROLLED GOLD, VERMEIL
- goldlike, or covered in gold leaf GILT, GILDED, AUREATE
- alchemists' alleged conversion of base metals into silver or gold TRANSMUTATION
- alloy of copper and zinc used in jewelry as imitation gold PINCHBECK
- alloy with gold color, made of copper and zinc, used in decorating furniture, clocks, and the like ORMOLU
- chemical analysis, as of the gold content of a metal object ASSAY
- convert or transform something, such as base metal into gold COMMUTE, TRANSMUTE
- cover with a thin layer of gold or gold leaf, gold-plate GILD
- explore an area for gold or other minerals PROSPECT
- fabric decorated with gold or silver thread LAMÉ
- lump, especially of natural gold NUGGET
- mark stamped on gold or silver objects indicating the purity of the metal HALLMARK, PLATE MARK
- ornamental work of twisted wire, especially of gold or silver FILIGREE
- precursor to science in the Middle Ages, seeking a cure-all medicine and a means of turning base metal into gold ALCHEMY
- search for gold, as in rivers or waste dumps FOSSICK
- separate gold from earth or sand by washing PAN
- substance or stone believed by alchemists to have the power of turning base metals into gold PHILOSOPHERS' STONE, ELIXIR
- tinsel or imitation gold leaf CLINQUANT
- tool for applying gold leaf in bookbinding PALLET
- trough of a long and sloping design, as for washing gold ore SLUICE
- weighing system for gold, other precious metals, and gems, using a 12-ounce pound TROY WEIGHT

gold (combining form) CHRYS-, CHRYSO-, AURI-

golden GILDED, AUREATE

golden age, looked forward to in the distant future MILLENNIUM
- belief in the imminent arrival of a golden age or era of peace MESSIANISM

golf See chart, page 235

gondolier's song having a rhythm of rowing BARCAROLE

good See also **excellent, perfect**
- good, admirable, deserving praise or respect COMMENDABLE, LAUDABLE, ESTIMABLE, CREDITABLE, MERITORIOUS
- good, helpful, promoting good results ADVANTAGEOUS, BENEFICIAL
- good, reliable, honorable REPUTABLE, STERLING
- good, typical or reminiscent of the best from the past VINTAGE
- good, very well-behaved ANGELIC, IRREPROACHABLE, DOCILE
- good for the health, promoting well-being SALUTARY, SALUBRIOUS
- extremely good or pleasing, champion, capital BONZER, BRAW, COPACETIC, CRACKERJACK, SPIFFING, TOP-NOTCH

good (combining form) BON-, EU-

good appetite, eat well, enjoy your meal BON APPETIT, GUTEN APPETIT

good-bye, farewell, leave-taking VALEDICTION
- good-bye, as borrowed from various other languages ADIEU, AU REVOIR, ARRIVEDERCI, CIAO, AUF WIEDERSEHEN, ADIOS, HASTA LA VISTA, SAYONARA, ALOHA

good faith, honest intention BONA FIDES

good-luck object, animal, or person, as adopted by a team MASCOT

good-natured, friendly, likable AFFABLE, AMIABLE, CONVIVIAL, GENIAL, CORDIAL
- good-natured, kind or generous, good-hearted BENIGN, HUMANE, BENEFICIENT
- good-natured friendliness BONHOMIE

goodness, virtue, moral uprightness RECTITUDE, INTEGRITY, PROBITY

goods, such as furniture and household appliances, that are long-lasting, seldom needing to be replaced DURABLES
- goods or cargo for delivery or disposal CONSIGNMENT
- goods or property in one's personal possession CHATTELS, CHOSES
- goods or total stock on hand INVENTORY
- anything commercially useful, such as a farm product, mined metal, or any tradable goods or services COMMODITY
- unrequested, without being ordered or asked for, as some goods delivered by mail might be UNSOLICITED

goodwill, love of one's fellow humans and promotion of their welfare PHILANTHROPY, ALTRUISM
- goodwill or similar business asset that has a value but no physical existence INTANGIBLE

goose - gooselike, resembling or characteristic of a goose ANSERINE
- goose-liver paste, typically with truffles PÂTÉ DE FOIE GRAS

gooseflesh HORRIPILATION, PILOERECTION

gorge, narrow pass DEFILE
- gorge or narrow ravine with a stream flowing through it FLUME
- gorge or ravine, as gouged out by a river or flood waters CANYON, COULOIR, GULLY, GULCH, WADI

gospels - referring to the first three gospels SYNOPTIC

gossip HEARSAY, ON-DIT
- gossip or busybody QUIDNUNC
- gossipy conversation or meeting GABFEST
- pass or toss something back and forth, such as a person's name in a gossipy conversation, or the like BANDY

Gothic typeface BLACK LETTER

gourd CALABASH

gourmet, connoisseur, person who appreciates fine food and wine EPICURE, GASTRONOME

gout, especially as affecting the big toe PODAGRA
- natural acid in the body that can cause gout when unregulated URIC ACID

governess, chaperon, or elderly female companion of the daughters in a Spanish or Portuguese family DUENNA

governing, ruling, in authority DOMINANT
- governing itself, relatively independent of outside rule or domination AUTONOMOUS
- governing strictly, or favoring strict authority and obedience AUTHORITARIAN

government See chart, and also **leader** and chart at **feudal system**
- government action taken to regulate economic factors such as the exchange rate INTERVENTION
- government advisers forming an unofficial yet influential group KITCHEN CABINET
- government grant, as of property or exploration rights CONCESSION
- government in which the laws and political principles limit the powers of the rulers CONSTITUTIONALISM
- government made up of a group of officers after a military takeover JUNTA
- government or authority exer-

cised in a fatherly way, typically generous and concerned but restricting individual responsibility PATERNALISM
- government or authority that was formerly in power but has now been replaced ANCIEN RÉGIME
- government or rule, especially when authoritarian or military REGIME
- government policy, especially foreign policy, based uncompromisingly on national self-interest rather than on moral considerations REALPOLITIK
- government-sponsored organization that is independent of government control QUANGO
- government structure of a nation, church, or the like POLITY
- opponent of a government, especially in a one-party state DISSIDENT
- overthrow or attempt to destroy something, especially a government or political system, by means of secret undermining SUBVERT
- period of time between two successive reigns, governments, or the like INTERREGNUM
- power of government, influence, or authority of one state over another HEGEMONY, SUZERAINTY
- power of government, rule, control, authority DOMINION, SOVEREIGNTY, SUPREMACY, JURISDICTION
- power to appoint people to government jobs PATRONAGE
- referring to a form of government or a country in which power is divided between a central authority and various regions FEDERAL
- support for a government's policies, as considered given by an election victory MANDATE
- transfer of power from central government to regional or local authorities DEVOLUTION

government (combining form) -CRACY, -OCRACY, -NOMY, -ARCHY

governor See also **leader**
- governor of a colony or country ruling in the name of the sovereign VICEROY
- governor of a country while the king or queen is incapable of ruling REGENT
- referring to a governor, as to a state governor GUBERNATORIAL

grace or blessing, as before meals BENEDICITE

grace note in music, usually just above the main note APPOGGIATURA
- grace note in music, usually just below the main note ACCIACCATURA

graceful and slim, as a racehorse or elegant woman might be WILLOWY
- graceful or effortless, as a dancer's movements might be FLUENT
- graceful or agile, supple and nimble LITHE, LIMBER, LISSOM
- graceful or sleek, as cats are SLINKY
- graceful, persuasive, or moving in use of language, expression, or the like ELOQUENT

gracious, refined in manner, courtly, polished URBANE, GENTEEL, SUAVE

graded series according to rank or importance HIERARCHY
- graded series of slight differences, as of form or intensity CONTINUUM, CLINE

gradual absorption or acquisition, as of knowledge OSMOSIS
- gradual development, slow, natural or historical process of change EVOLUTION
- gradual progression, series of tiny stages, as in the change from one color to another GRADATION
- gradually, bit by bit PIECEMEAL

graduate or former student of a school, college, or university ALUMNUS, ALUMNA
- graduates of a university, or an assembly or conference of them CONVOCATION

graduation ceremony at high schools, colleges, and universities COMMENCEMENT

graft - budded shoot or twig detached and joined to a stock for grafting SCION

grain, especially oats, that is coarsely ground GRITS, GROATS
- grain due for grinding or having been ground GRIST
- grain-eating GRAMINIVOROUS, GRANIVOROUS
- grain fungus or disease ERGOT
- amount of liquid, grain, or the like that evaporates or leaks from a container ULLAGE

GOVERNMENT SYSTEMS

absolutism	all-powerful monarch or dictator
aristocracy	hereditary ruling class or privileged minority
autarchy/ autocracy/ monocracy	all-powerful individual ruler
despotism	all-powerful ruling person or group
duumvirate	two rulers or officials jointly
dyarchy	two rulers or ruling bodies jointly
gerontocracy	elderly ruling persons
hierocracy	priests or clergymen
matriarchy	women
meritocracy	people who have proven skill or intellect
monarchy	king, queen, or similar hereditary ruler
ochlocracy/ mobocracy	the mob
oligarchy	small faction of people or families
pantisocracy	all members of a community equally
patriarchy	men, to the exclusion of women
pentarchy	five rulers or officials jointly
plutocracy	the wealthy
stratocracy	the army
technocracy	scientific and technical experts
theocracy	a dominating religion; priesthood representing God or a deity
timocracy	citizens possessing property
totalitarianism	all-powerful dictator or political party
triumvirate	three rulers or officials jointly

GRAMMAR AND LINGUISTIC TERMS

ablative	case of a noun expressing direction from or cause
ablaut/ gradation	change of vowels in verb forms, typically indicating different tenses: *sing, sang, sung*
accidence	part of grammar that deals with word inflections
accusative	case of a noun that is the direct object of a verb or preposition
amelioration/ elevation	process by which a word acquires a more favorable meaning or tone: the development of *shrewd* from its earlier sense of "wicked" or "cruel"
apposition	relationship of two nouns or noun phrases set side by side, the one explaining the other: *Socrates, the philosopher, died after drinking hemlock*
auxiliary verb	verb such as *may* or *will* that accompanies a main verb to form a mood, tense, or the like
back-formation	formation of a new word by mistakenly assuming that is the form from which an existing word derives: *burgle,* from *burglar*
case	form of a word indicating its relation to other words in a sentence
clipping	shortening of a word in such a way that the new word is used with the same meaning: *prof* from *professor* (back-clipping, preferred by adults), *fessor* from *professor* (front-clipping, preferred by children)
complement	noun, noun phrase, or clause that follows a verb to complete the predicate
conjugation	inflections of a verb
dangling participle/ misrelated participle	participle that has no clear connection with the word it modifies grammatically: *Walking home from work, it started to rain*
dative	case of a noun that is the indirect object of a verb
declension	inflections of a noun, pronoun, or adjective
deep structure	grammatical relationship inherent in the words of a sentence which is not immediately apparent from the formal order of the words alone (that is, the meaning of a sentence), as distinct from surface structure
deterioration/ pejoration	process by which a word acquires a less favorable meaning or tone: the development of *surly* from its earlier sense of "masterful"
determiner	word such as *the* or *my* that qualifies a noun or noun phrase and is positioned in front of any other adjective
diachronic	referring to study of languages or a language developing over time
genitive	case of a noun expressing possession, measurement, or source
gerund	verb form, ending in *-ing* in English, that can be used as a noun: *I hate jogging*
grammar	the distinctive features and structural principles of a language, especially the construction of words (morphology) and sentences (syntax)
grapheme	letter or combination of letters that represents one sound; minimum distinctive unit of a writing system: *g* or *ph* in *grapheme*
homographs	words that are identical in spelling but different in origin and meaning, whether pronounced the same or not: *flag* (cloth) and *flag* (hang loose), *tear* /tair/ and *tear* /teer/
homonyms	words that are both homographs and homophones, that is, words that are spelled and pronounced alike but are different in meaning: *flag* (cloth) and *flag* (hang loose), *lie* (untruth) and *lie* (recline)
homophones	words that are identical in pronunciation but different in meaning, whether spelled the same or not: *flag* (cloth) and *flag* (hang loose), *some* and *sum*
imperative	construction or form of a verb expressing a command
indicative	construction or form of a verb indicating something is a fact
infinitive	basic uninflected form of a verb, often preceded by the infinitive particle *to* in English: *to be*
inflection	change in the form of a word to indicate tense, number, and so on, as in *sounds, sounding, sounded*
interrogative	construction expressing a question

GRAMMAR AND LINGUISTIC TERMS *continued*

intransitive	referring to a verb that has no direct object: *The King triumphed*
langue	language regarded as an abstract system available to all speakers
lexicography	science and art of compiling dictionaries; applied lexicology
lexicology	study of the meaning of words and their idiomatic combinations
linguistics	study of speech habits and of languages and their structures, including phonology, grammar (morphology, syntax), lexicology, phonetics, and semantics
metalanguage	language or set of symbols used to describe another language or set of symbols
morpheme	minimum unit of grammar that distinguishes one word from another, or that cannot be further divided without losing its meaning: *time* and *-ly* in *timely*
morphology	study of inflection, derivation, and composition of words
nominative	case of a noun that is the subject of a verb
parole	language as actually used by individual speakers
participle	form of a verb, typically ending in *-ed* or *-ing* in English, used in forming tenses or as an adjective
phoneme	minimum unit of speech that distinguishes one utterance from another: /b/ and /p/ distinguish *bitch* from *pitch*, /ee/ and /i/ distinguish *bay leaf* from *bailiff*
phonetics	study of speech processes, of the production, perception, and transcription of speech sounds
phonics	method of teaching reading based on the sounds of the letters in a word rather than on the word as a unit
phonology	sound system of a language
predicate	the part of a sentence or clause that expresses something about the subject of the sentence or clause, often consisting of a verb and object
preterit	form of a verb expressing a past or completed action: *walked, ran*
reflexive	referring to a verb or pronoun in a construction expressing an action or relationship affecting the subject itself: *prides himself on his strength*
semantics	study or science of meaning in language
source language	language of the learner of a foreign language, or language from which a translation is made
structuralism	study of the internal structure of a language rather than its history or its resemblances to other languages
subjunctive	form of a verb expressing a supposition, purpose, wish, condition, or doubt: *unless I be mistaken*
substantive	word or phrase serving as a noun
surface structure	the merely formal or grammatically consistent relationship between the words of a sentence, as distinct from deep structure
synchronic	referring to the study of languages at any one time rather than developing over time
syntax	rules for the combination of words into grammatical sentences; the way words are combined in this manner
target language	foreign language that is being taught, or language into which a translation is made
tokens	in word-frequency studies, the number of words in a text, regardless of repetition, as distinct from types: *She understood, and she left* has five tokens (but only four types)
transformational grammar	grammar that studies the ways in which elements of one sentence can be rearranged to produce other, usually more complex, sentences
transitive	referring to a verb that needs a direct object: *The king defeated his enemy*
types	in word-frequency studies, the number of different words in a text, as distinct from tokens: *She understood, and she left* has four types (out of five tokens)
vocative	case of a noun used in addressing a person or thing directly

- funnel for dispensing fuel or grain HOPPER
- gather leftover grain or other crops after harvesting GLEAN
- particle, pellet or small grain GRANULE
- pile of corn or sheaves of grain gathered in a field to dry STOOK, SHOCK
- resembling or made of grain, especially wheat FRUMENTACEOUS
- separate chaff from grain or seed by means of a wind WINNOW
- separate chaff from grain or seed by means of beating THRESH, FLAIL
- storage tower or pit for grain or fodder SILO, ELEVATOR
- storehouse for grain, or region producing grain GRANARY

grain (combining form) GRANI-

grainy in texture or appearance GRANULAR

grammar See chart, pages 238–239
- grammatical correctness, or the adherence to traditional rules of grammar PURISM
- grammatical error or improper usage SOLECISM
- grammatical error produced by avoiding an imaginary error, as in the faulty phrase *between you and I* HYPERCORRECTION
- analyze the grammatical structure of a sentence CONSTRUE, PARSE
- any of two or more varying realizations of the same grammatical form VARIANT

grand See also **famous, highfalutin, large**
- grand, high, majestic as a literary style or social circle might be RAREFIED
- grand, high-ranking, or honored, especially when elderly AUGUST, VENERABLE
- grand, impressively large or noble, majestic or monumental EXALTED, LOFTY, IMPOSING, SUBLIME
- grand, luxurious, extravagant LAVISH, SUMPTUOUS, EXPANSIVE
- grand, majestically elegant or dignified STATELY, STATUESQUE
- grand, superbly confident or skillful, authoritative MAGISTERIAL
- grand in a showy or pretentious way OSTENTATIOUS

Grand Lama of Tibet DALAI LAMA, PANCHEN LAMA, TASHI LAMA

grandfather clock LONG-CASE CLOCK

grandstand in the open air BLEACHERS

granite, basalt, or other rock formed directly from cooled molten rock IGNEOUS ROCK

grant by a government, as of property, or exploration or prospecting rights CONCESSION
- grant of money to support some person or institution, finance a project, or the like SUBSIDY
- grant or gift, as to a charity CONTRIBUTION, DONATION

grape cultivation, especially for winemaking VITICULTURE, VINICULTURE
- grape harvest or yield VINTAGE
- grape juice fermenting into wine MUST, STUM
- grape pip or seed, or bunch of grapes ACINUS
- grape skins, pips, and stems left over after the juice has been extracted for winemaking RAPE
- destructive insect, very harmful to grape crops PHYLLOXERA
- fungus on grape skins producing a sweeter grape, as for dessert wines NOBLE ROT
- having the shape of a bunch of grapes or a raspberry ACINIFORM
- pulp left after pressing fruit, especially grapes, to extract the juice MARC

grapefruit or grapefruitlike citrus fruit SHADDOCK, POMELO

graph See also **geometry, statistics, mathematics**
- graph of a cumulative frequency distribution in statistics OGIVE
- graph or chart in the form of a circle with sectors of varying size representing the units PIE CHART
- graph or chart in the form of a series of columns whose lengths are proportional to the sizes of the quantities concerned BAR GRAPH, BAR CHART
- flattish section of a graph PLATEAU
- line approaching a curve, as on a graph, such that they will meet only at infinity ASYMPTOTE
- loop on a graph or diagram LOBE
- set of numbers or measurements that pinpoint a position, as on a map or graph COORDINATES
- set of values in statistics, often represented by a graph FREQUENCY DISTRIBUTION

graphite PLUMBAGO

grappling irons CRAMPONS

grass See illustration
- grass-eating, feeding on grasses, seeds, or grains GRAMINIVOROUS
- grasslike marsh plant SEDGE
- grasslike nylon and vinyl surfacing material, as used on sports grounds ASTROTURF
- grasslike or relating to grass GRAMINEOUS
- grass of a Spanish or Algerian species yielding a fiber used in making rope, paper, and the like ESPARTO
- grass of a genus widely cultivated and used for lawns and pasturage FESCUE
- grass or hay cut by a scythe or mower SWATH
- grass or other vegetation eaten by grazing livestock PASTURE, PASTURAGE, HERBAGE
- grass stem that is hollow and jointed CULM
- circle more luxuriant than the surrounding grass, typically caused by fungal growth underground FAIRY RING
- clump of thick grass TUSSOCK, HASSOCK, TUFFET
- clump of turf dug from a grass surface, as by a golf club or horse's hoof DIVOT
- cut or graze on grass CROP
- field plant that is not a grass FORB
- second crop of grass or hay in a single season AFTERMATH, ROWEN
- whitened through lack of sunlight, as grass or other green plants might become ETIOLATED

grasshopper with long horns, and a high-pitched song in the males KATYDID
- grasshopper's shrill grating chirp STRIDULATION

grassland, meadow LEA
- grassland or open country in South Africa VELD
- grassland with scattered shrubs and trees in drier tropical and subtropical regions SAVANNA
- grassland in natural, uncultivated state, as in the Mississippi valley PRAIRIE
- grasslands as in South America LLANOS, PAMPAS
- vast plain of semiarid grassland, especially in southern Siberia and European U.S.S.R. STEPPE

grassy lawn or meadow SWARD

grate, file, or scrape RASP
- grating chirp of a cricket or grasshopper STRIDULATION

grateful, thankful OBLIGED, INDEBTED, BEHOLDEN

gratitude - expression of gratitude or appreciation TRIBUTE, TESTIMONIAL

grave See also **burial**
- grave, tomb, or burial vault SEPULCHER, REPOSITORY
- grave mound of ancient times TUMULUS, BARROW
- grave robber GHOUL
- dig up or remove from a grave or tomb DISINTER, EXHUME
- gravestone inscription meaning "here lies" HIC JACET
- inscription on a gravestone, tombstone, or monument commemorating the person buried there EPITAPH
- stone slab, as set over a grave

LEDGER

graveyard or burial chamber underground CATACOMB, HYPOGEUM

gravity - rise and float in the air, supposedly in defiance of gravity LEVITATE

gravy - gravy-soaked piece of bread or toast SIPPET, SOP, BREWIS
- served in its own gravy or juices, as a roast might be AU JUS

gray-haired GRIZZLED
- gray or white, as through old age HOARY
- design, painting, or style of painting using various shades of gray GRISAILLE

Grasses

Orchard grass
Meadow grass
Timothy
Perennial ryegrass
Side view
Italian ryegrass
Side view
Wild oats
Slender foxtail
Alternative form
Canary grass
Alternative form
Reed grass

graze or rub the skin from something, especially one's shin BARK

grazing land, or the grass or other vegetation on it that is eaten by livestock PASTURE, PASTURAGE, HERBAGE

grease, oil, graphite, or other substance used to reduce friction LUBRICANT

greasy, oily, fatty, or slippery PINGUID, SEBACEOUS, UNCTUOUS

great See also **famous, large, huge**
- great work of scholarship, research, or artistic creation MAGNUM OPUS
- "greatest happiness for the greatest number is the greatest good" as an ethical theory UTILITARIANISM

greater than (combining form) SUPRA-

greatness, fame STATURE, EMINENCE

Greece See **Greek**

greed, powerful desire, especially for money CUPIDITY, AVARICE, MAMMONISM

greed or gluttony GULOSITY

greedy, especially for money or material possessions MERCENARY, ACQUISITIVE
- greedy, excessively demanding, whimsical, self-pitying, or the like SELF-INDULGENT
- greedy, grasping, or hungry to an extreme degree RAVENOUS, VORACIOUS, INSATIABLE, RAPACIOUS
- greedy, hungry, or gluttonous EDACIOUS, ESURIENT
- greedy or grasping person, glutton or moneygrubber CORMORANT
- eat gluttonously or greedily, gorge GORMANDIZE

Greek See chart, page 242, and also **column, Eastern Orthodox**, and charts at **menu, drama**
- Greek, characteristic of ancient or modern Greece, Greeks, or the Greek language HELLENIC
- Greek and Latin literature CLASSICS
- Greek and Roman culture as a subject of study HUMANITIES
- Greek artistic style, cultural spirit, idiom, or the like GRECISM
- Greek city-state in ancient times POLIS
- Greek dialect used as a lingua franca that became the standard form, and gave rise to later stages of Greek KOINE
- Greek dialects in ancient times ATTIC-IONIC, ARCADO-CYPRIAN, AEOLIC, DORIC
- Greek drinking party in ancient times, typically with music and in-

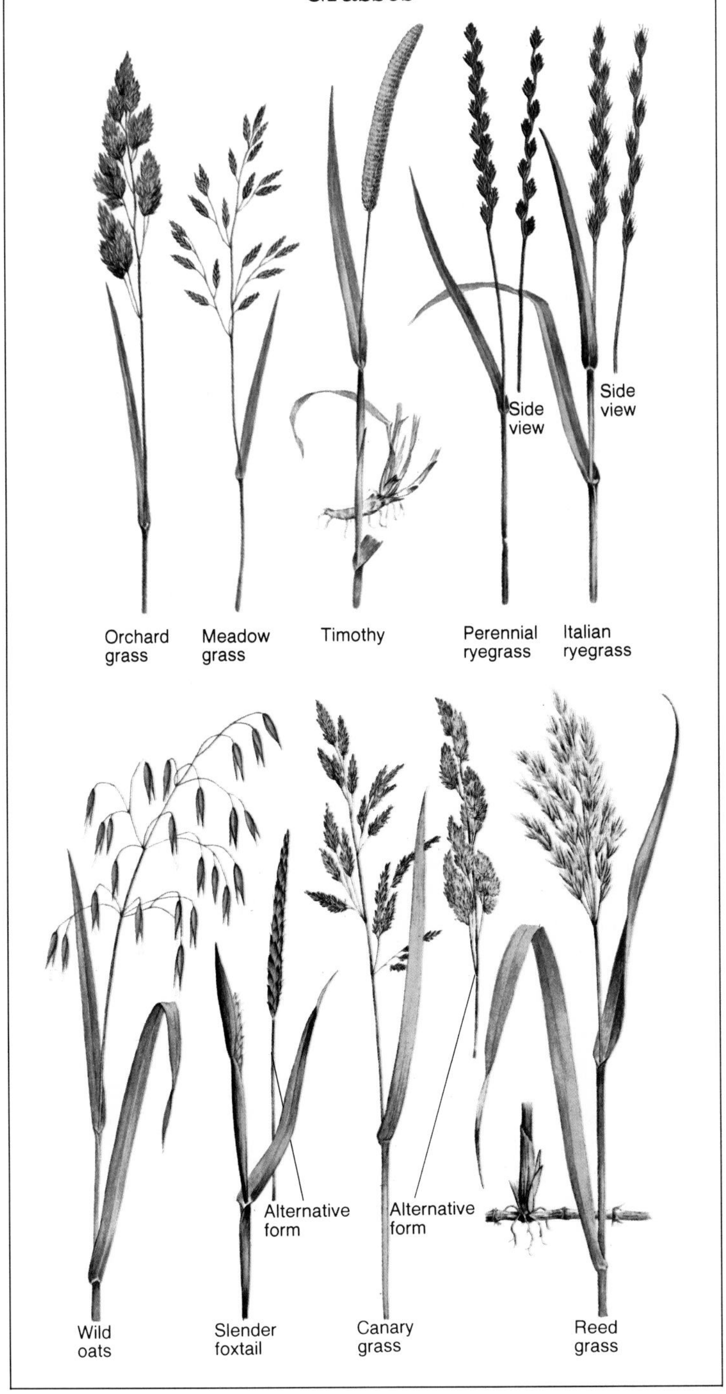

tellectual conversation SYMPOSIUM
- Greek kinship grouping, civic class, or tribal subdivision in ancient times PHYLE, PHRATRY
- Greek person in ancient times ARGIVE, ACHAEAN
- Greek restaurant TAVERNA
- Greek string instrument similar to the mandolin BOUZOUKI
- Greek wine flavored with resin RETSINA
- admirer or student of classical Greek culture HELLENIST
- assembly of citizens in an ancient Greek state ECCLESIA
- banishment of a citizen, by popular vote, from an ancient Greek city OSTRACISM
- citadel of an ancient Greek city ACROPOLIS
- foreign resident of an ancient Greek city, enjoying some rights of citizenship METIC
- heavily armed foot soldier in ancient Greece HOPLITE
- marketplace in ancient Greece, used for meetings of the people's assembly AGORA
- modern Greek in its everyday colloquial form DEMOTIC
- modern Greek in its literary and official form, patterned on classical usage KATHAREVUSA, PURISTIC
- prostitute, courtesan, or concubine in ancient Greece HETAERA
- referring or relating to ancient Greek or Roman civilization CLASSICAL
- religious festival held in the spring in ancient Greece ELEUSINIAN MYSTERIES
- serf in ancient Greece, especially Sparta, ranking between a slave and free man HELOT
- short white skirt worn by Greek men at folk festivals and ceremonial occasions FUSTANELLA

Greek (combining form) GRECO-, GRAECO-, HELLEN-

Greek tragedy See **tragedy** and chart at **drama**

green See also **color**
- green, especially as growing plants are, or covered with vegetation VIRID, VERDANT
- green mineral, used for jewelry and ornaments VERDITER, MALACHITE
- green pigment in leaves that traps energy from sunlight for photosynthesis CHLOROPHYLL
- green vegetation VERDURE
- green woolen fabric used on top of pool or billiard tables BAIZE
- greenish crust that forms on exposed copper, brass, or bronze objects VERDIGRIS, AERUGO, VERD ANTIQUE
- thin green layer of oxide forming naturally or artificially on a copper or bronze surface PATINA

green (combining form) CHLOR-, CHLORO-, VERD-

greenhouse ORANGERY
- greenhouse, typically attached to a house CONSERVATORY

greeting SALUTATION
- greetings, respects, compliments DEVOIRS
- greetings of a formal kind, as on an official letter COMPLIMENTS

greyhound racing - boxlike stall from which a greyhound is released at the start of a race TRAP

grief or sorrow DOLOR
- enduring pain and grief with unemotional resignation STOICAL
- free one's mind of a worry, grief, anxiety, guilt, or other burden DISBURDEN
- public show of grief or repentance SACKCLOTH AND ASHES
- reduce the severity of pain, grief, or the like ALLAY, ALLEVIATE, ASSUAGE
- waste away, as with grief PINE

grievance - valid or reasonable, as a grievance might be LEGITIMATE

grill, expose to direct heat BROIL
- grilling frame of parallel metal bars GRIDIRON

grin, unnatural gaping expression or smile RICTUS
- grinlike fixed facial expression, as from muscular contraction in tetanus cases RISUS SARDONICUS

grind, crush, or pound into powder or small particles TRITURATE, PULVERIZE, BRAY, COMMINUTE
- grind the teeth, as in anger GNASH
- bowl in which a pestle is used to grind something MORTAR

grindstone made of or containing the abrasive mineral aluminum oxide CORUNDUM STONE
- type of silicon carbide, as used in grindstones and the like CARBORUNDUM

grip or stance adopted when shifting or securing something PURCHASE
- any of the ridges on a handle or object to make it easier to grip KNURL
- gripping, sticking, or clinging firmly TENACIOUS
- gripping or grasping device, especially a grapnel GRAPPLE

gristle, tough tissue, as at the joints between bones CARTILAGE

groggy, dazed STUPEFIED, WOOZY

groin - relating to or located in the groin INGUINAL

groove, especially around a bullet CANNELURE
- groove, notch, slot, or decorate by engraving CHASE
- groove or indentation, as in a stone column or pleated ruffle FLUTE
- groove or narrow furrow, as on a plant stem or the surface of the brain SULCUS
- groove or notch, as in a piece of wood CHAMFER
- groove or notch made in wood by chopping or sawing KERF
- groove or notch, or a series of them INDENTATION
- groove or notch that houses an inserted part in a joint or hinge MORTISE, GAIN, RABBET
- groove or ridge linking two planks, shafts, or the like SPLINE
- groove running vertically from the nose to the upper lip PHILTRUM
- grooved, streaked, or ridged STRIATE, STRIGOSE
- grooved beam of wood in which

Greek Alphabet

FORM	NAME	TRANSLITERATION
Αα	alpha	a
Ββ	beta	b
Γγ	gamma	g
Δδ	delta	d
Εε	epsilon	e
Ζζ	zēta	z
Ηη	ēta	ē
Θθ	thēta	th
Ιι	iota	i
Κκ	kappa	k
Λλ	lambda	l
Μμ	mu	m
Νν	nu	n
Ξξ	xi	x
Οο	omicron	o
Ππ	pi	p
Ρρ	rhō	r, rh
Σσ	sigma	s
Ττ	tau	t
Υυ	upsilon	u
Φφ	phi	ph
Χχ	chi khi	kh
Ψψ	psi	ps
Ωω	ōmega	ō

a sliding frame or panel is fitted COULISSE
- grooved or indented like a castle's battlements, as a ridge of hills might be CASTELLATED
- grooves or ridges around the edge of a coin MILLING, FLUTING
- grooves or teeth in a series, as on a saw or the edge of a leaf SERRATION
- square notches or grooves, as on a molding CRENELLATIONS
- strip or wedge of wood fitting into a groove to make a joint FEATHER, TENON
- vertical groove, as in a decorative band on a Doric column GLYPH

grope, scratch about or feel around for with the hands GRABBLE

grotesque stone figure, as on a cathedral roof, that often serves as a rainwater spout from a gutter GARGOYLE

ground or land, especially in respect of its physical characteristics TERRAIN
- collapse, cave in, as the ground might SUBSIDE
- level at or below which the ground is saturated with water WATER TABLE
- physical features of ground or land TOPOGRAPHY

grounds - improved by contouring and planting, as large grounds or gardens might be LANDSCAPED

group See also **classification, animal, bird, services**
- group, as within a religion or political party, typically dissenting from the larger group FACTION, CAUCUS, ENCLAVE, SECT
- group of armed men temporarily given law-enforcement powers, as for capturing criminals POSSE
- group of artistic or intellectual people who meet frequently COTERIE
- group of artists, writers, or the like using the most modern or experimental methods or ideas AVANT-GARDE
- group of attendants or assistants accompanying a VIP RETINUE
- group of cars, ships, or the like traveling together CONVOY
- group of girls BEVY
- group of individual items massed together AGGREGATE, CONGERIES, ASSEMBLAGE, CONGLOMERATION
- group of jazz musicians, small band COMBO
- group of people, nations, political parties, or the like cooperating in a common cause ALLIANCE, COALITION, BLOC, ALIGNMENT, CONFEDERACY, LEAGUE
- group of people gathered in response to a summons CONVOCATION
- group of people living in the same area or having interests in common COMMUNITY
- group of people living together and sharing their property COMMUNE
- group of people of the same age COEVALS
- group of people of the same age and status PEER GROUP
- group of people picturesquely arranged TABLEAU
- group of people with common aims or interests CLIQUE, CORPS, GUILD, LOBBY, COHORT
- group of people with common political aims, usually subversive CABAL, JUNTO, CELL
- group of representatives, such as a group of workers having discussions with the management DELEGATION, DEPUTATION
- group of similar or related items intended for use together BATTERY, SUITE, COMPENDIUM, ENSEMBLE
- group of songs, plays, or the like that an artiste or company can perform REPERTOIRE
- group of undesirable or disreputable people GALÈRE, ROGUE'S GALLERY
- group of voters, supporters, or people whose interests have to be considered CONSTITUENCY
- group or company of touring actors, dancers, or the like TROUPE
- group or society of men, brotherhood FRATERNITY, SODALITY
- group or society of women, sisterhood SORORITY
- group pride or loyalty, fellowship ESPRIT DE CORPS
- group together or arrange in correct order, classify COORDINATE, CODIFY, TABULATE, CATALOG, COLLOCATE, COLLATE
- group unity, fellow feeling and mutual support within a group, especially in the face of opposition SOLIDARITY
- grouping of business interests formed for some joint enterprise CONSORTIUM, SYNDICATE
- grouping of businesses or industries, especially an illegal one, that operates to monopolize manufacture or control prices CARTEL, TRUST
- grouping of citizens or clans, as in ancient Greece PHRATRY, PHYLE
- break up a group or cease to function as a group DISBAND
- large group of people crowded together DROVE, CONCOURSE, RUCK, CONFLUENCE, PHALANX
- large group of people or things BATTALION, HORDE, THRONG, MULTITUDE
- referring to a group, crowd, flock, or the like, or liking to be in a group GREGARIOUS
- referring to a whole group or category, such as a genus in biological classification GENERIC
- referring to all the members of a group jointly, shared, common, as a name or decision might COLLECTIVE, COMMUNAL
- separation into divided ethnic or religious groups SEGREGATION
- small central group of experts or founder members, as in a political movement, forming the nucleus of a larger organization CADRE
- small group of people or things COVEY
- social coexistence of several ethnic or religious groups PLURALISM

grouse - large Old World wood grouse CAPERCAILLIE
- mountain-dwelling grouse of a species that turns white in winter PTARMIGAN

grove or small thicket of trees COPSE, SPINNEY

grow See also **increase**
- grow, sprout, as seeds do GERMINATE
- grow buds or sprouts, or breed rapidly PULLULATE
- grow crops in a fixed sequence ROTATE
- grow or develop rapidly FLOURISH, BURGEON
- grow or reproduce rapidly PROLIFERATE
- grow or spread abnormally, with fleshy outgrowths, as warts and some tumors do VEGETATE
- grow slowly or gradually, as an idea might, or cause to grow INCUBATE, GESTATE
- grow together, merge, fuse COALESCE, AMALGAMATE, ACCRETE
- develop, help to grow, encourage the advancement of NURTURE, FOSTER
- develop, reproduce, breed, cause to grow PROPAGATE

growing along the ground as a vine or creeper might PROSTRATE
- growing old SENESCENCE
- growing or mounting up by a series of steps or additions CUMULATIVE
- growing or spread out in an untidy, irregular way STRAGGLY
- growing together, fusion, as of plant parts or body organs CONCRESCENCE, CONCRETION, COALESCENCE
- growing vegetation VERDURE
- growing vigorously and widely, as weeds might RANK
- growing wild, especially on cultivated land, as wild flowers or

weeds might AGRESTAL
growing (combining form) -PLASTIC, -TROPE, -TROPIC, CRESC-
growth, small swelling, or wartlike projection NODULE, TUBERCLE
- growth of a population that is optimal and therefore accelerating EXPONENTIAL GROWTH
- growth on or under a mucous membrane, as in the nose POLYP
- growth or abnormal projection on the body EXCRESCENCE
- growth or evolution of a species, genus, language, custom, or the like PHYLOGENY
- growth or expansion, increase INCREMENT
- growth or increase, as of public feeling or opinion GROUNDSWELL
- growth through slow additions, buildup ACCRETION
- in the earliest stage of growth or development EMBRYONIC, SEMINAL, GERMINAL, NASCENT
- something that nourishes or promotes growth or development NUTRIMENT
growth (combining form) -BLAST-, BLASTO-, NASC-, TROPH-, TROPHO-, -TROPHIC, -TROPHY, -PLASIA, -PLASY
grub - grublike young hatched from the egg of an insect LARVA
grudge - bear a grudge HARBOR
grumble See **complain**
guarantee, assurance, promise WARRANT, WARRANTY, UNDERTAKING, COVENANT
- guarantee, give personal assurance for VOUCH FOR
- guarantee, token, pledge, or promise EARNEST
- guarantee against financial failure UNDERWRITE
- guarantee or guarantor against loss or damage SURETY
- guarantee or promise UNDERTAKING
- guarantee or safeguard of society PALLADIUM
guard, sentry SENTINEL
- guard duty WATCH
- guard of the Roman emperors PRAETORIAN GUARD
- guard or watch kept during the hours of sleep VIGIL
- guard or watch stationed as a defense against surprise attack, or in an industrial dispute PICKET
- release from guard duty, through the arrival of a replacement RELIEF
guardian of a minor in Roman law TUTOR
- guardian spirit of a place GENIUS, GENIUS LOCI
- guardian spirit or guiding genius DAEMON
- relating to or acting as a guardian TUTELARY
guardianship, as of an orphan or prisoner CUSTODY
- guardianship or tutorship, or subjection to it TUTELAGE
guerrilla fighting behind enemy lines or in territory occupied by the enemy PARTISAN
- deliberate damaging or destruction of property, as by guerrillas or dissatisfied workers SABOTAGE
- military action taken by the authorities against rebels or guerrillas COUNTERINSURGENCY, PACIFICATION, REPRESSION
guess, opinion based on incomplete evidence SPECULATION, SURMISE, CONJECTURE
- guess or deduce from known information EXTRAPOLATE, INFER
- guess or know by intuition, or predict DIVINE
- guesswork, calculation of a rough-and-ready kind DEAD RECKONING
- offer a guess HAZARD, VENTURE
guest, visitor, or the like who expects or accepts too much hospitality or generosity FREELOADER, SPONGER, SCROUNGER, CADGER, BLUDGER
- frequent guest, as at a club HABITUÉ, FREQUENTER
guide, escort, or attendant, especially when riding a horse or motorcycle OUTRIDER
- guide, warning, or sign BEACON
- guide a pilot, aircraft, missile, or the like by radio instructions VECTOR
- guide for tourists on sightseeing expeditions CICERONE
- guide or interpreter in the Middle East in former times DRAGOMAN
- guide or plot the course of a ship, aircraft, or other vehicle NAVIGATE
- guide or wise personal teacher MENTOR, GURU
- guide to conduct, in the form of a short phrase MOTTO, MAXIM
guidebook for tourists BAEDEKER
- guidebook or ready-reference manual VADE MECUM
- guiding, helping the learning process HEURISTIC
- guiding principle, belief, or doctrine GOSPEL
- guiding principle, objective, or standard LODESTAR, POLESTAR
- guiding spirit, guardian genius DAEMON
guidelines or limiting factors, as of a budget or schedule PARAMETERS, CONSTRAINTS
guillotine - guillotinelike frame used in 16th- and 17th-century Scotland for executions MAIDEN
- cart that carried prisoners off to the guillotine during the French Revolution TUMBREL
- Parisian women who would knit unconcernedly while attending guillotinings as spectators during the French Revolution TRICOTEUSES
guilt - clear of guilt or blame EXCULPATE, EXONERATE
- consider or pronounce free of blame or guilt, or from responsibility or punishment ABSOLVE
- free one's mind of a worry, grief, anxiety, guilt, or other burden DISBURDEN
- lessen or try to lessen the seriousness of a crime, guilt, or the like, as by offering certain excuses EXTENUATE, MITIGATE
- suggest the guilt of someone INCRIMINATE, INCULPATE
guilty feeling, regret or remorse COMPUNCTION

GUNS

HANDGUNS AND PISTOLS

Beretta
bulldog
Colt
derringer
Luger
magnum
Mauser
six-shooter
Smith and Wesson
Walther
Webley and Scott
zip gun

MACHINE GUNS

Breda
Bren gun
Browning gun
Gatling gun
Hotchkiss gun
Lanchester gun
Lewis gun
Maxim
mitrailleuse
Sten gun
Sterling gun
Thompson gun/tommy gun
Uzi
Vickers gun

SHOTGUNS AND RIFLES

Armalite
blunderbuss
Browning automatic
carbine
chokebore
Enfield/Lee-Enfield
flintlock
FN rifle
fowling piece
fusil
Garand rifle
harquebus/arquebus
jingal
Kalashnikov/AK 47
matchlock
musket
petronel
pump gun
punt gun
Springfield
wheel lock
Winchester

ARTILLERY

ack-ack gun
basilisk
bazooka
Big Bertha
Bofors gun
bombard
carronade
culverin
howitzer
Long Tom
mortar
pom-pom
serpentine
stern chaser/bow chaser
swivel gun

- guilty-looking or ashamed HANGDOG, SHAMEFACED
- guilty of sin PECCANT
- guilty party in a damages case TORT-FEASOR
- negotiations between the defense and prosecution before a criminal trial, aimed at exchanging a guilty plea in court for a reduced charge PLEA BARGAINING
- person guilty of a crime or responsible for a mistake or accident CULPRIT

guinea pig or related South American rodent CAVY

guitar that does not use electric amplification ACOUSTIC GUITAR
- movable bar clamped to the fingerboard of a guitar, lute, or the like to raise the pitch of all the strings CAPO
- placing of the forefinger over some or all of the strings of a guitar, lute, or the like to raise their pitch BARRÉ
- small thin disc or plate, as of plastic, used for plucking the strings of a guitar, lute, or related instrument PLECTRUM, PICK

gullet ESOPHAGUS

gullible person, sucker GREENHORN, DUPE, GULL

gully See **gorge**

gulp, drink or swallow eagerly SWIG, SWILL

gum from the sap of the sapodilla tree, used as the main ingredient of chewing gum CHICLE
- gum in which our teeth are lodged GINGIVA
- gum inflammation, often causing loosening of the teeth PYORRHEA, GINGIVITIS
- gum obtained from some plants RESIN, MUCILAGE
- gum or resin used in making perfume MYRRH
- gum or resin used in incense FRANKINCENSE, OLIBANUM
- gum or resin used in varnish MASTIC

gummy, gluey, sticky, as some thick liquids are GLUTINOUS, VISCOUS, VISCID

gun See illustration and chart
- gun opening in a wall, tank, or the like PORT
- gun or cannon firing shells at a steep angle HOWITZER
- check the range of a gun CALIBRATE
- guns, ammunition, and other equipment of an army, as distinct from personnel MATÉRIEL
- guns, especially heavy guns, of a military unit ARTILLERY, ORDNANCE
- guns along one side of a warship, or their combined firing simultaneously BROADSIDE
- guns or heavy artillery, as on a warship BATTERY
- guns or missiles grouped in an emplacement NEST
- low, round concrete building serving as a small fort for guns and gunners PILLBOX
- plug or cover for the muzzle of a gun when not in use TAMPION
- position, such as a platform or mounting, specially prepared for a gun or other weapon EMPLACEMENT
- revolving armored dome or drum on a tank or warship in which guns are mounted TURRET
- rod for cleaning a rifle or inserting the charge into a muzzle-loading gun RAMROD
- spring back, as a gun does when fired RECOIL
- sighting lines, at right angles to each other, in the sights of a gun, theodolite, or the like CROSS WIRES, CROSS HAIRS
- study of guns, bullets, shells, or

Gun

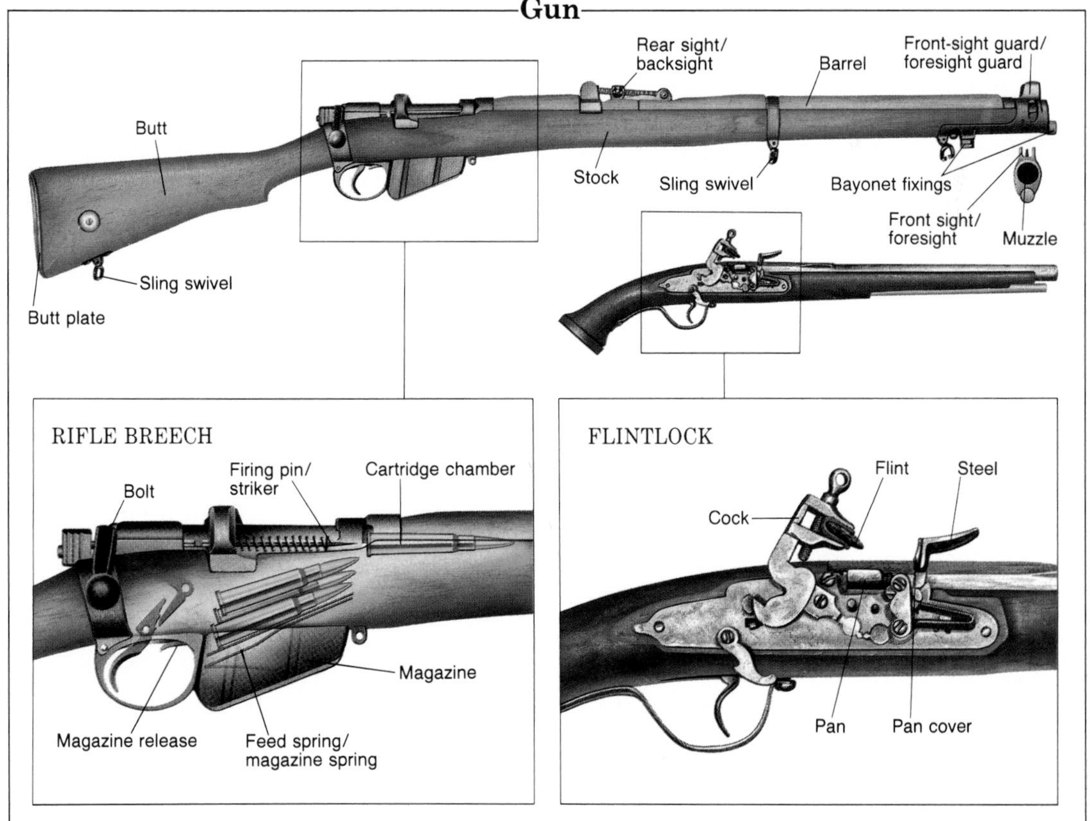

the like BALLISTICS

gunfire, blows, bombing, or the like of a heavy and sustained kind BARRAGE

- gunfire in a rapid burst FUSILLADE, VOLLEY, SALVO

- abrupt, jerky, and distinct in sound, as gunfire might be STACCATO

- troop formation or position subject to gunfire along its entire length ENFILADE

gunman or marksman shooting, typically at long range and from a well-concealed position, at exposed individuals SNIPER

gunpowder-filled cap, as used either in a toy pistol or in a firearm, that explodes when struck PERCUSSION CAP

- line of gunpowder laid as a fuse to explode a charge TRAIN

- potassium nitrate, as used in making gunpowder and preserving meat SALTPETER

guru, spiritual leader or teacher in Hinduism MAHARISHI, MAHATMA

- guru's pupil or disciple CHELA

gushing, emotionally demonstrative EFFUSIVE, DEMONSTRATIVE, EMOTIVE, GOOEY

gut feeling - instinctive or intuitive, as a gut feeling is, rather than rational VISCERAL

gutter CLOACA, FLUME

- gutter on a roof CULLIS

gymnastics - gymnast or acrobat specializing in turning somersaults or cartwheels TUMBLER

- gymnastic exercises designed to improve physical fitness and muscle tone CALLISTHENICS, FLOOR EXERCISES

- apparatus in gymnastics exercises and competitions POMMEL HORSE, PARALLEL BARS, ASYMMETRIC BARS, RINGS, BEAM, VAULTING HORSE

- back handspring in gymnastics, a key tumbling move FLICFLAC

- handspring vault in gymnastics involving a cartwheel onto the horse and a back somersault in the flight-off TSUKAHARA

- handspring vault in gymnastics involving a tight tucked position in the flight-off from the horse YAMASHITA

- near-horizontal position of a gymnast when supporting himself or herself on hands and arms alone PLANCHE

- position on the rings in gymnastics in which the body is held upright and the arms stretched out horizontally CROSS, CRUCIFIX

- somersault in gymnastics, taking off from the feet and landing on the feet SALTO

- wooden bottle-shaped club thrown or swung about in juggling and gymnastics INDIAN CLUB

gynecological smear test PAP TEST

Gypsy, especially an Italian Gypsy ZINGARO

- Gypsy, especially one from Hungary TZIGANE

- Gypsy man or gentleman ROM, RYE

- Gypsy man or woman, or the Gypsy language ROMANY

- person who is not a Gypsy, as referred to by Gypsies GORGIO

h - breathy speech sound represented in English by the letter *h* ASPIRATE

habit, custom WONT, USAGE
- habits of a social group, defining it and its values MORES
- exaggerated or affected habit or trait IDIOSYNCRASY, ECCENTRICITY, ABERRATION, MANNERISM

habitual, confirmed, regular, as a persistent liar might be INVETERATE, CHRONIC
- habitual tendency or inclination DISPOSITION
- habitual through irrational compulsion, as a liar might be PATHOLOGICAL

had - past perfect tense of a verb, as in *had climbed* PLUPERFECT

haddock - smoked haddock FINNAN HADDOCK, FINNAN HADDIE

hair See also **hairstyle**
- hair dye or tint of a reddish color HENNA
- hair in a detached tress, worked into a person's own hair in certain hairstyles SWITCH
- hair in the region of the genital organs PUBIC HAIR
- hair loss or baldness, as caused by a skin disease ALOPECIA
- hair of artificial fiber, used for makeup in the theater CREPE HAIR
- hair or feathers projecting from an animal's neck FRILL, RUFF
- hair-removing lotion DEPILATORY
- hairlike, very slender CAPILLARY
- hairlike projection, as on moss or in the small intestine VILLUS
- hairlike threads on a cell or microscopic organism, whose waving produces locomotion CILIA
- hairs in a tuft on the seed coat of some seeds COMA
- hairs or feathers on the back of an animal's neck HACKLES
- arrange a woman's hair COIF
- auburn or reddish gold color of a person's hair TITIAN, STRAWBERRY BLOND
- bleach used to make hair blond PEROXIDE
- bristling of the hair on the body HORRIPILATION, PILOERECTION, GOOSEFLESH
- cavity in the skin from which a hair grows FOLLICLE
- comb the hair downward near the roots to bulk it up BACKCOMB, TEASE
- covered with fine grayish hairs or down HOARY
- covered with gray hair GRIZZLED
- covered with tiny barbed hairs or bristles, as some plants and animals are BARBELLATE
- covered with woolly hairs, as leaves might be LANATE
- curl the hair tightly, as with curling irons CRIMP
- destruction of hair roots or other living tissue by means of an electric current ELECTROLYSIS
- having fair hair and skin XANTHOCHROID
- having tightly curled hair on the head, as most black Africans have ULOTRICHOUS
- light streak in the hair HIGHLIGHT
- lock or tuft of hair across or rising from the forehead COWLICK
- long, flat, and limp, as some hair is LANK
- narrow band, ribbon, velvet strip, or the like, as worn in a woman's hair FILLET, BANDEAU
- natural brown pigment coloring the skin and hair MELANIN
- pale yellow, as hair might be FLAXEN
- remove the hair from DEPILATE
- shear, trim, or cut the hair, wool, or horns of POLL
- shed hair, feathers, or fur, as many animals do MOLT
- short, fine, downy hair, as on a fetus LANUGO
- single curl of hair RINGLET
- small cap or pouch, typically of netting, holding a woman's hair in place at the back SNOOD
- study of hair and its diseases, especially baldness TRICHOLOGY
- tangled mass, as of matted hair SHAG
- taper, thin, and trim the hair by cutting FEATHER
- thick bushy mass, as of hair SHOCK
- tiny lump on the root of a hair PAPILLA, FOLLICLE BULB
- tough protein substance forming the outer layer of hair, nails, horns, and the like KERATIN
- tuft of hair, as on a dog's tail FEATHER
- uncombed or untidy, as hair might be UNKEMPT, DISHEVELED, UNGROOMED, RUMPLED, TOUSLED
- whiskers or sensitive hairs, as on either side of a cat's mouth VIBRISSAE
- woman's thick, long, flowing locks of hair TRESSES

hair (combining form) PIL-, PILI-, PILO-, TRICH-, TRICHO-, -TRICHOUS

hair clip with clamped ends BOBBY PIN

hair oil, perfumed and sometimes thickened into a gel BRILLIANTINE
- hair oil, or cream for the hair, usually perfumed POMADE, POMATUM

haircut - massage of perfumed lotion into the scalp, as after a haircut FRICTION

hairdresser COIFFEUR, COIFFEUSE

hairdressing or beauty parlor, stylish fashion store, or the like SALON
- relating to barbering or hairdressing TONSORIAL

hairless and smooth GLABROUS

hairline forming a V-shape in the center of the forehead WIDOW'S PEAK
- hairline of a balding man that is moving back increasingly from the forehead RECEDING HAIRLINE

hairpiece covering and hiding a bald spot TOUPEE

hairsplitting, needless arguing or drawing of distinctions QUIBBLING, PEDANTRY
- hairsplitting, quibbling, dogmatic SCHOLASTIC, SOPHISTIC

hairstyle See chart, page 248
- hairstyle, especially of a woman COIFFURE

hairy, having long or thick hair HIRSUTE
- hairy, covered with fine soft hair PILOSE, CRINITE, LANATE
- hairy, relating to or consisting of hair PILEOUS
- hairy or resembling a tuft of hairs COMATE

Haiti's irregular police force under "Papa Doc" Duvalier TONTON-MACOUTES
- Haitian religion blending Catholicism and African rituals VOODOO

half a sphere, globe, or the earth HEMISPHERE
- half-line of verse HEMISTICH
- half or portion MOIETY

- halfway, in the middle, in between INTERMEDIATE, MIDPOINT
- referring to half-brothers or half-sisters having the same mother but a different father UTERINE

half (combining form) SEMI-, DEMI-, HEMI-, BI-, BIS-, DICH-, DICHO-

half-hearted See also **mix**
- half-hearted, unenthusiastic TEPID, LUKEWARM

hall in which an audience sits, as for a meeting or play AUDITORIUM

hall of fame of a particular group or field of endeavor PANTHEON

Halloween lantern made from a pumpkin JACK-O'-LANTERN

hallucination-producing or relating to hallucinations PSYCHEDELIC
- severe mental disorder, as in some alcoholics, involving tremors and hallucinations DELIRIUM TREMENS, THE D.T.'S

halo - halolike area of light, in medieval paintings, surrounding a holy figure MANDORLA, AUREOLE, VESICA PISCIS
- halolike radiance or similar sign of sanctity above or behind the head of God, a saint, or a monarch in art NIMBUS, GLORIA, GLORIOLE, GLORY
- halolike ring of faint light, as around the moon when viewed through a haze CORONA

ham See also **bacon, pork**
- ham cured and spiced in a traditional Italian style PROSCIUTTO

hammer, long and heavy, for driving in stakes or pegs MAUL
- hammer having a fork at one end of the head for removing nails CLAW HAMMER
- hammer used by a judge, auctioneer, or chairman, for making a rapping noise GAVEL
- hammer with small rubber head used for testing reflexes and tapping the chest for purposes of diagnosis PLEXOR
- blunt or broad end of a hammer, ax, or the like POLL
- break up stone, especially with a hammer SPALL
- handle of a hammer HELVE
- heavy forge hammer levered up and then dropped TILT HAMMER
- wedge- or ball-shaped head opposite the flat surface of a hammer PEEN

hammock - cords supporting a hammock CLEWS

hand See illustration, and also **bone**
- hand, paw, claw, hoof, or the like MANUS
- hand-shaped PALMATE
- hand warmer consisting of a large fur or cloth ring MUFF
- hands or feet EXTREMITIES
- able to use both hands equally expertly AMBIDEXTROUS
- adjective for the hands MANUAL
- distance between the tips of the thumb and little finger of a spread hand SPAN
- fleshy base of the thumb THENAR
- gesture of greeting or respect, as in India, by placing one's hands together out in front of one and bowing slightly NAMASTE
- pad of muscle on the hand below the thumb HEEL
- skillful or clever, especially with one's hands DEXTEROUS, DEFT, ADROIT
- skill or speed of hand movements, as used in conjuring tricks SLEIGHT OF HAND, PRESTIDIGITATION, LEGERDEMAIN

hand (combining form) CHIRO-, MANU-

hand down or pass on to one's children or successors BEQUEATH
- something handed down from the past LEGACY, BEQUEST

hand grenade - powerful oval-shaped hand grenade MILLS BOMB

hand over goods for transporting, delivery, disposal, or the like CONSIGN
- handing over a criminal, fugitive, or the like to the authority or country where he or she is wanted EXTRADITION

handbag, pouch, or purse, in former times RETICULE

HAIRSTYLES

Afro	bushy and frizzy
bangs	fringe cut straight across the forehead
beehive	piled up by backcombing
bob	short even cut all around the head
bouffant	puffed out through backcombing
chignon	long hair rolled into a knot or bun at the back
cornrows	tight parallel braids set close to the head, popular with African and Afro-American women
crew cut/en brosse	cut short and standing stiffly upright
crimps	tight curls or waves
dreadlocks	long twisted locks, typically worn by Rastafarian men
ducktail	hair backswept at the sides with a high tuft and a curl at the back, resembling a duck's tail, popular among young men in the 1950s
Eton crop/ shingle	cropped short in the manner of a schoolboy, popular with women in the 1920s
French pleat/ French roll	cylindrical roll gathered at the back
frizette	curled fringe across the forehead
marcel wave	regular, tight waves set close to the head
Mohawk/ Mohican	spiky sweep of hair down the center of an otherwise shaved head
page boy	straight hair with the ends curled gently inward, typically shoulder-length
pompadour	brushed up from the forehead and turned back over a pad, as worn by women in the early 18th century
pouf	piled high in rolled puffs, as worn by women in the 18th century

Hand

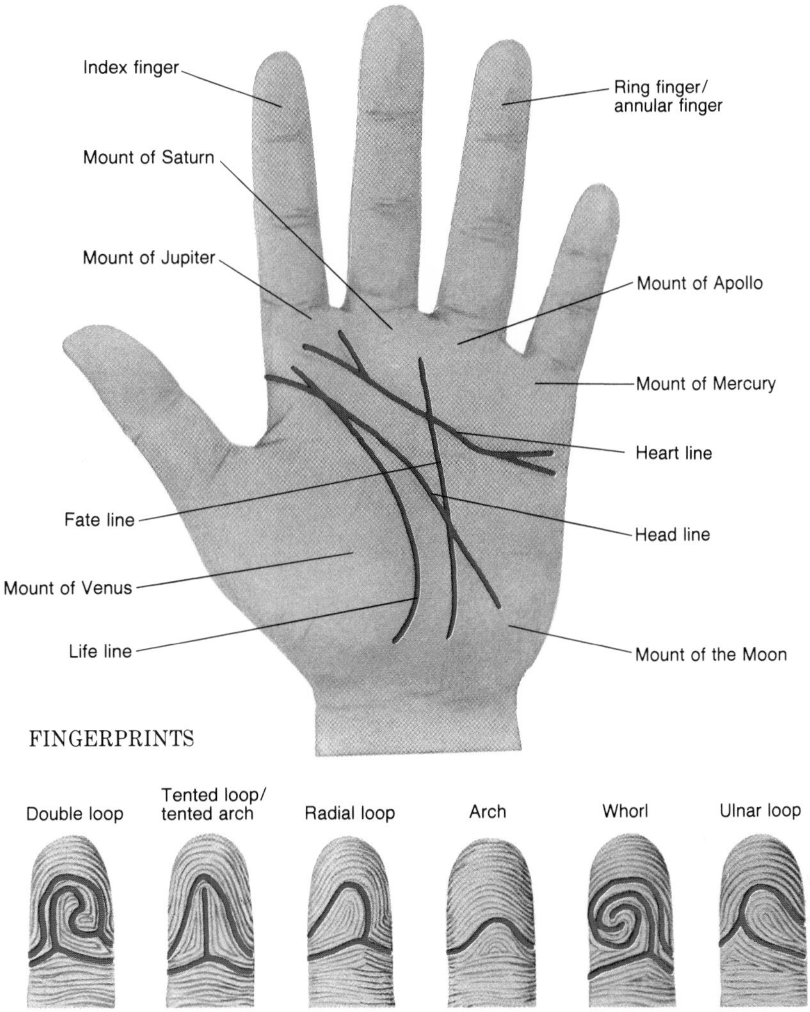

Index finger
Ring finger/ annular finger
Mount of Saturn
Mount of Jupiter
Mount of Apollo
Mount of Mercury
Heart line
Fate line
Head line
Mount of Venus
Life line
Mount of the Moon

FINGERPRINTS

Double loop
Tented loop/ tented arch
Radial loop
Arch
Whorl
Ulnar loop

handcuffs or similar metal fastening confining the hands and arms or the feet MANACLES, FETTERS, SHACKLES, IRONS
- fettered iron bar, a counterpart of handcuffs, formerly used for shackling prisoners' feet BILBO

handicap, burden, or hinder ENCUMBER
- handicap, disadvantage, hindrance LIABILITY
- handicap, put at a disadvantage PENALIZE
- handicap weight that a racehorse must carry IMPOST

handkerchief, large and usually brightly colored, used as a scarf BANDANNA, NECKERCHIEF

handle in the form of a hooped rod, as of a bucket or kettle BAIL
- handle of a sword, knife, or the like HILT, HAFT
- handle of an ax, hammer, or the like HELVE
- handle or butt of a whip, fishing rod, or the like STOCK
- any of the ridges on an object to make it easier to grip KNURL
- ear-shaped handle on a machine, jug, or the like LUG
- having a handle or similar extension ANSATE

handrail's supporting post BALUSTER

handsome in a modest and unspectacular way, pleasing and presentable PERSONABLE, PREPOSSESSING
- handsome young man APOLLO, ADONIS, DEMIGOD

handwriting See also **writing** and illustration at **script**
- handwriting, or a handwritten document MANUSCRIPT
- handwriting, or a manuscript in the author's own handwriting AUTOGRAPH
- handwriting or penmanship that is very neat, elegant, or artistic CALLIGRAPHY, CHIROGRAPHY
- handwriting style based on capital letters MAJUSCULE
- handwriting style based on small joined letters, as in medieval manuscripts MINUSCULE
- handwriting style using joined letters, as distinct from block printing CURSIVE
- handwriting style using large, rounded, separated capital letters, as in early medieval Greek and Roman manuscripts UNCIAL

- handwriting that is poor or illegible, scrawl HIEROGLYPHICS, CACOGRAPHY
- handwriting using full spelling, as distinct from shorthand LONGHAND
- difficult to read, as a cramped handwriting might be CRABBED
- downward stroke of the pen in handwriting MINIM
- readable, as handwriting might be LEGIBLE
- secretary or scribe who takes dictation or makes neat copies of documents in handwriting AMANUENSIS
- showy decoration in handwriting, especially in a signature FLOURISH, QUIRK
- study of handwriting, as for psychological analysis or detection of forgery GRAPHOLOGY
- trembling or caused by trembling, as shaky handwriting might be TREMULOUS

hanger-on, sponger, person living off another PARASITE, FREELOADER, LEECH, SCROUNGER

hanging, dangling, suspended from above PENDENT, PENDULOUS
- hanging limply, drooping FLACCID
- hanging sculpted ornament on a Gothic ceiling, or hanging item of jewelry PENDANT
- part of a garment hanging down or out, such as a sleeve, hood, or cape TIPPET
- platform or raised wooden framework, as used for hanging or beheading criminals SCAFFOLD
- post for displaying the bodies of hanged criminals GIBBET
- rope for securing a horse or cow, or for a noose in hanging HALTER

hangover remedy of a raw egg usually immersed in Worcestershire sauce or vinegar PRAIRIE OYSTER
- having a hangover as a result of drunkenness CRAPULOUS, CRAPULENT

happen, occur, take place, come to pass TRANSPIRE
- happen as a result, follow ENSUE, EVENTUATE
- happen as something unexpected, irrelevant, or unnecessary SUPERVENE
- happen at the same time, cause to be simultaneous SYNCHRONIZE
- develop into reality, become fact, actually happen MATERIALIZE

happening at the same time or place, simultaneously, as two prison sentences might be CONCURRENT
- happening in fits and starts, intermittent SPASMODIC

happiness, joy FELICITY
- happiness or well-being, especially that produced, according to Aristotle's philosophy, by an active and rational life EUDEMONIA
- continual happiness and optimism, enjoyment of life JOIE DE VIVRE
- place or state of perfect happiness ELYSIUM
- state of supreme or blessed happiness BEATITUDE

happy, cheerful, and carefree BLITHE, BUOYANT, DEBONAIR, JAUNTY
- enchanted, extremely happy or delighted ENRAPTURED, TRANSPORTED, RAPTUROUS
- excitedly happy, filled with joy, as after a triumph or success ELATED, EXHILARATED, EXULTANT
- extremely happy, often in a dangerously exaggerated or complacent way EUPHORIC
- extremely happy or pleased, overwhelmed with delight, overjoyed ECSTATIC, DELIRIOUS
- pleased, satisfied, happy and contented GRATIFIED
- supremely and serenely happy, as if blessed BEATIFIC
- very happy, delighted, in high spirits JUBILANT, COCK-A-HOOP, EXUBERANT

happy-go-lucky See **casual**

harass in a bullying way HECTOR, BADGER
- harass or jeer at a speaker with repeated critical comments HECKLE

harbor protected by a massive stone breakwater, or the breakwater itself MOLE
- clean or deepen a harbor, channel, or the like by means of a scooping machine DREDGE
- pier or breakwater to protect a harbor or shore JETTY
- platform or dockside in a harbor for mooring, loading, and unloading ships WHARF, QUAY

hard See also **difficult**
- hard and apparently unbreakable stone or other substance ADAMANT
- hard coating or shell, as of some insects TEST
- hard or unyielding as stone FLINTY, GRANITE

hard (combining form) DUR-, SCLER-, SCLERO-

hard coal ANTHRACITE

hard work, effort, or attention to duty APPLICATION

hardback and cloth-covered, as a book might be CLOTHBOUND, CASED, CASEBOUND

harden, solidify, curdle, or clot, as exposed blood does CONGEAL, COAGULATE
- harden, toughen, or make callous INDURATE
- harden or strengthen rubber by heat-treating with sulfur compounds VULCANIZE
- harden or toughen glass, steel, or the like, as by alternate heating and cooling TEMPER, ANNEAL
- hardened, bony SCLEROUS
- hardened emotionally CASE-HARDENED, CALLOUS
- hardening of the arteries SCLEROSIS
- hardening of tissue or other substance through the action of calcium salts CALCIFICATION

hardness - index of the hardness of a metal BRINELL HARDNESS
- scale of hardness of minerals, based on resistance to scratching by a diamond or other mineral MOHS' SCALE

hardworking, dedicated, conscientious, and persevering ASSIDUOUS, DILIGENT, SEDULOUS
- hardworking, energetic, and forceful person DYNAMO

hare - adjective for a hare LEPORINE
- sport of hunting game, such as hares, with hounds relying on sight rather than scent COURSING
- young hare, especially one in its first year of life LEVERET

harem SERAGLIO
- harem concubine or woman slave ODALISQUE
- harem room ODA

harm See also **damage**
- harm, damage, disadvantage DETRIMENT, DISSERVICE
- harm, harmful effects, damage RAVAGES
- harm, injury, or wound LESION, TRAUMA
- harm the originator, as a hurtful policy might REBOUND, RECOIL, REDOUND

harmful, damaging, poisonous, or corrupting NOXIOUS
- harmful, extremely infectious, or very rapid in effect, as a disease or poison might be VIRULENT
- harmful in a stealthy or secretive way, treacherous INSIDIOUS
- harmful or damaging INJURIOUS, DELETERIOUS, DETRIMENTAL
- harmful or evil in intention or influence MALEVOLENT, MALICIOUS, MALIGN, MALEFICENT, PESTILENT, MISCHIEVOUS, BALEFUL, MALIGNANT, PERNICIOUS
- harmful to something or someone ADVERSE, INIMICAL

harmless or unobjectionable INOFFENSIVE, INNOCUOUS

harmony See also **agree**
- harmony of musical notes CHORD, CONCORD, CONSONANCE
- harmony or correspondence among parts, claims, or the like,

consistency COMPATIBILITY, CONGRUENCE, CONCURRENCE
- harmony or order COSMOS
- harmonious, in agreement, corresponding CONFORMABLE, IN UNISON
- harmonious and balanced arrangement of parts SYMMETRY
- harmonious and effective interaction COORDINATION

harness See illustration

harpsichord - plucking device or plectrum for the strings of a harpsichord or related instrument QUILL

harsh See also **cruel, bitter, strict**
- harsh, demanding, or severe, as laws or standards might be RIGOROUS, STRINGENT, DRACONIAN, DRACONIC
- harsh, dissonant, discordant, or out-of-tune sound, as of a faulty violin or specially tuned piano WOLF
- harsh and persistent, relentless or pitiless, unyielding IMPLACABLE, INEXORABLE, UNREMITTING
- harsh or abrupt in manner or speech GRUFF, CURT, BRUSQUE
- harsh or grim, as a bleak, barren landscape is STARK, DESOLATE
- harsh or severe, as a very strict upbringing is SPARTAN, AUSTERE
- harsh-sounding or shrill or hoarse-sounding, grating RAUCOUS, STRIDENT

Harvard - referring to eight old and famous universities, including Harvard and Yale IVY LEAGUE

harvesting machine that cuts, threshes, and cleans a crop of grain COMBINE HARVESTER

hasty, rash IMPETUOUS, IMPULSIVE, PRECIPITATE, CURSORY

hat See illustration, page 252
- hat with a high crown and wide brim, popular in the western United States STETSON
- black academic hat consisting of a tight cap topped by a stiff square and sometimes a tassel MORTARBOARD, TRENCHER, TRENCHER CAP

Harness

COLLAR HARNESS OF A DRAFT HORSE

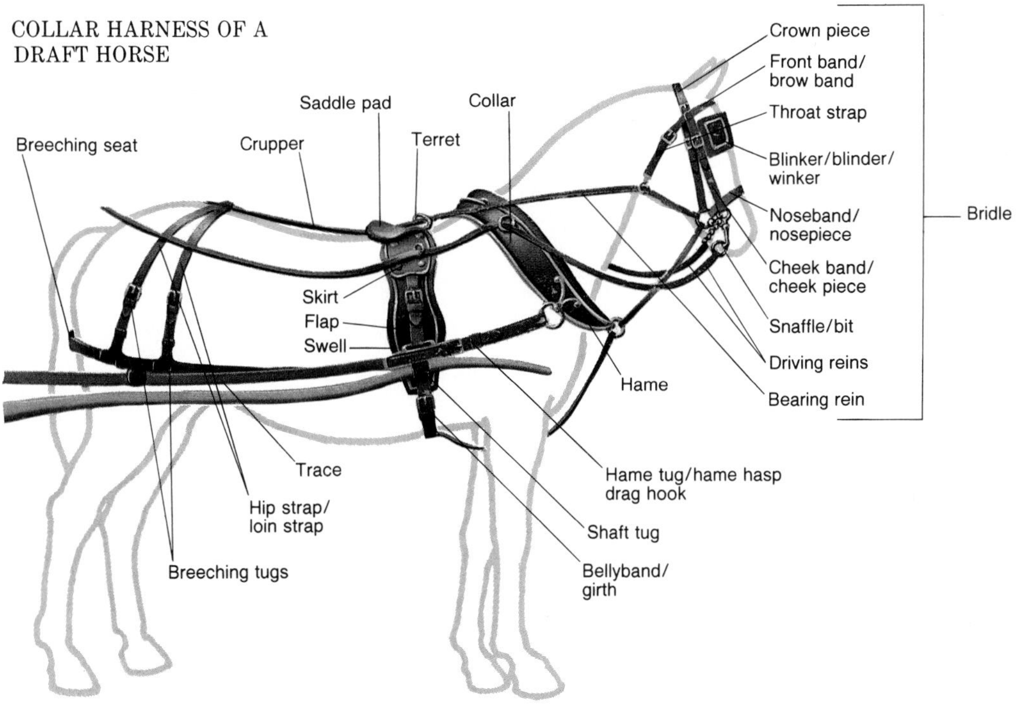

Crown piece
Front band/ brow band
Throat strap
Blinker/blinder/ winker
Noseband/ nosepiece
Cheek band/ cheek piece
Snaffle/bit
Driving reins
Bearing rein
Bridle
Saddle pad
Collar
Terret
Breeching seat
Crupper
Skirt
Flap
Swell
Hame
Trace
Hip strap/ loin strap
Breeching tugs
Hame tug/hame hasp drag hook
Shaft tug
Bellyband/ girth

COMMON TYPES OF BIT

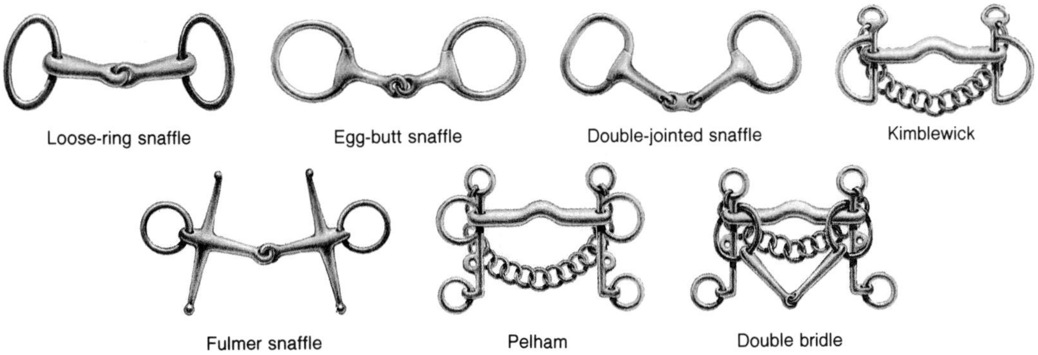

Loose-ring snaffle
Egg-butt snaffle
Double-jointed snaffle
Kimblewick
Fulmer snaffle
Pelham
Double bridle

- derby hat BOWLER
- hats for women MILLINERY
- feather, ribbon, or rosette worn on the hat, especially by soldiers COCKADE
- huntsman's hat in the form of a round cap with earflaps MONTERO
- low brimless Scottish hat or cap, often having a pompom on top TAM-O'-SHANTER
- low-crowned hat with a broad brim projecting at the front, as formerly worn by some clergymen SHOVEL HAT
- maker or seller of women's hats MILLINER
- man's felt hat with a narrow brim and dented crown TRILBY, HOMBURG
- put on one's hat or clothes DON
- small, stiff round hat for a woman PILLBOX
- soft cloth hat with peaks at front and back, and earflaps typically tied on top DEERSTALKER
- stiff straw hat with a low crown BOATER
- take off one's hat or clothes DOFF
- top hat BEAVER, CASTOR
- trimming of twisted ribbon or cord for a hat TORSADE
- waterproof hat, as worn by sailors, with a broad brim at the back SOU'WESTER
- wide-brimmed hat made of tropical leaves, as worn in Latin America PANAMA
- wide-brimmed Spanish or Mexican hat of felt or straw SOMBRERO

hatch - keep eggs warm before hatching INCUBATE, BROOD

hatchway, hinged porthole, or the like on a ship SCUTTLE

hate intensely, loathe, ABOMINATE, EXECRATE, ABHOR

hate, hatred (combining form) MIS-, MISO-, -PHOBE, -PHOBIA, -PHOBIC

hated person or thing ANATHEMA

hateful, vile, or appallingly wicked ABOMINABLE, ODIOUS, HEINOUS, FLAGITIOUS

hatred, ill will MALIGNITY, MALICE
- hatred of men MISANDRY
- hatred of people MISANTHROPY
- hatred of women MISOGYNY
- hatred or bitter enmity ANIMUS, ANIMOSITY
- hatred or contempt ODIUM
- hatred or intense feeling of hostility or repulsion AVERSION, ANTIPATHY, REVULSION, REPUGNANCE
- bitterness, deep hostility, feeling of hatred or ill will RANCOR
- feelings of or remarks indicating intense hatred VITRIOL
- irrational and uncontrollable fear or hatred of something PHOBIA

haughty, disdainful SUPERCILIOUS,

Hats

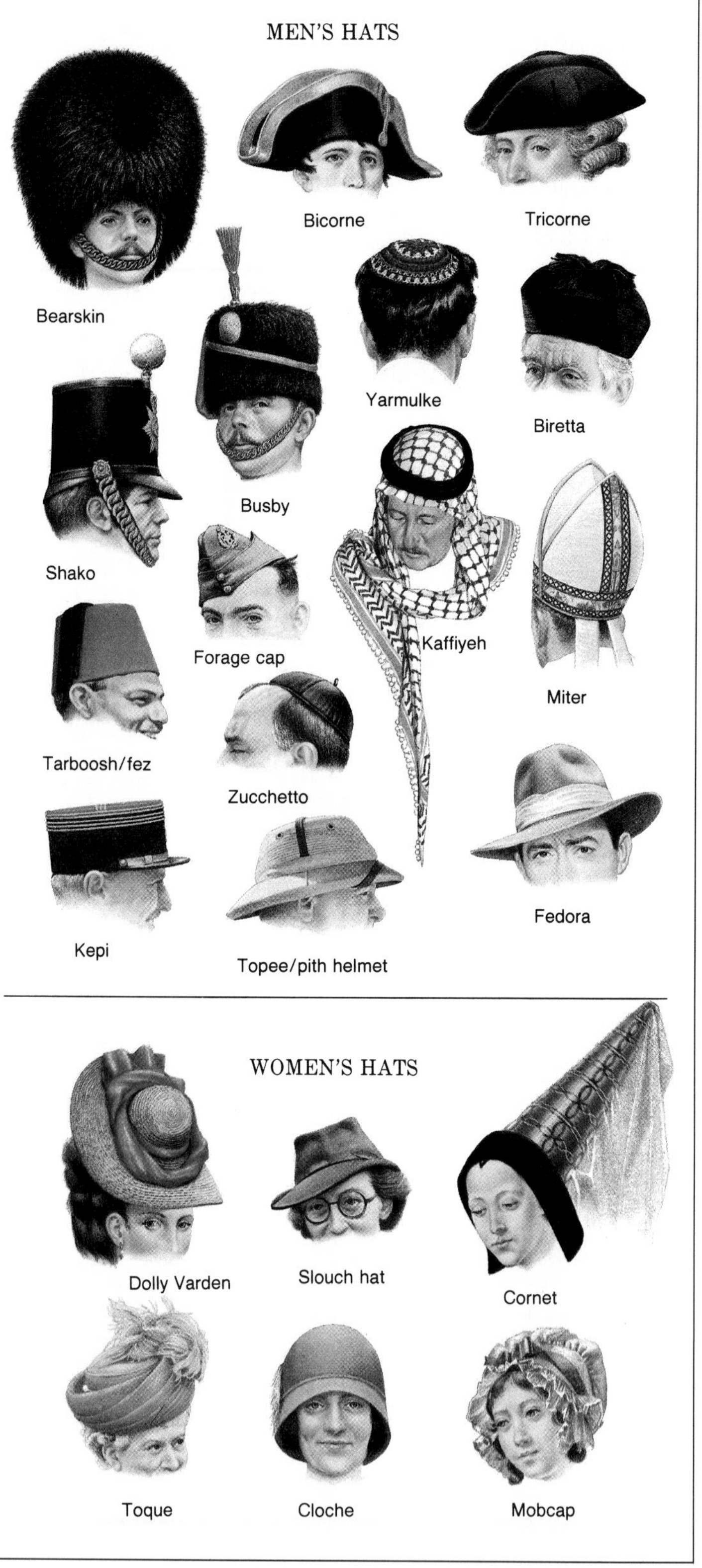

MEN'S HATS

Bearskin
Bicorne
Tricorne
Yarmulke
Biretta
Busby
Shako
Forage cap
Kaffiyeh
Miter
Tarboosh/fez
Zucchetto
Kepi
Topee/pith helmet
Fedora

WOMEN'S HATS

Dolly Varden
Slouch hat
Cornet
Toque
Cloche
Mobcap

CONDESCENDING, PATRONIZING, CONTEMPTUOUS
- haughtiness, arrogance HAUTEUR

hauling machine, typically a rope-wound drum WINDLASS, CAPSTAN

haven, refuge, or relief OASIS

having (combining form) -OSE

havoc - cause havoc WREAK HAVOC

Hawaiian dress of a loose, brightly colored style MUUMUU
- Hawaiian feast LUAU
- Hawaiian greeting or farewell ALOHA
- Hawaiian wreath or garland of flowers, typically worn around the neck LEI

hawk of various kinds, including the sparrowhawk and goshawk ACCIPITER
- hawk or falcon still young enough to be trained for falconry EYAS
- bunch of feathers, sometimes with a bait of meat, attached to a long cord, used by a falconer to recall a hawk LURE
- cage for hawks, especially one to molt in MEW
- feeding rack for a hawk HACK
- female hawk, especially one used in falconry FORMEL
- free a dog, hawk, or the like from its leash or other restraint SLIP
- group of hawks CAST, LEASH
- hawks released by a falconer in a pair to pursue quarry as a team CAST
- jump about and struggle to escape, as a leashed hawk might BATE
- leather strap or leash tied to the leg of a hawk JESS
- male hawk, especially one used in falconry TERCEL
- stitch up the eyes of a hawk or falcon to quieten or tame it SEEL
- untamed adult hawk HAGGARD

hawker, seller of small items who typically roves the streets PEDDLER

hay, grass, or the like for pasturing HERBAGE
- hay or grass cut by a scythe or mower SWATH
- hay or other dry fodder fed to livestock PROVENDER
- rack for hay or other food for farm animals CRATCH, CRIB
- second crop of grass or hay in a single season AFTERMATH, ROWEN

hay fever remedy, reducing the symptoms of allergies ANTIHISTAMINE

haystack, pile of straw, or the like in the open air RICK
- haystack of a small cone-shaped kind COCK, HAYCOCK

hazelnut FILBERT

hazy, misty, cloudy NEBULOUS

head See also **bone, skull**
- head, especially the hairy top of the head POLL
- head, or crown of the head PATE
- head cloth framing the face, as worn by some nuns WIMPLE
- head-shaped, as some flowers or flower-clusters are CAPITATE
- head swelling caused by a build-up of cerebrospinal fluid HYDROCEPHALUS
- head to foot CAP-A-PIE
- headlike part, such as the end of a long bone or insect's antenna CAPITULUM
- back of the head, rear skull OCCIPUT
- cut the head off, behead DECAPITATE
- front of the head, upper forward part of the skull SINCIPUT
- having a broad, roundish head, relatively short from front to back BRACHYCEPHALIC
- having a long head, with the length of the skull front to back considerably greater than its breadth DOLICHOCEPHALIC
- having a medium-shaped head, neither markedly long nor markedly broad MESOCEPHALIC
- having an enlarged headlike end, as some bones have CAPITATE
- having two heads BICEPHALOUS
- jerking of the head, causing injury to the neck, as in a car accident WHIPLASH
- medallion, on a brooch, ring, or the like, with a head in profile in raised relief CAMEO
- outermost, slightly protruding point at the back of the head INION
- relating to the head end or front part of animals, leaves, or the like ANTERIOR
- relating to the head or the skull CEPHALIC
- shaven head, especially of a monk or priest TONSURE
- system for classifying people or "races" according to the shape of the skull or head CEPHALIC INDEX
- top of the head, highest point of the skull VERTEX
- top of the head, or other crown-shaped body part CORONA
- wreath or crown of flowers worn on the head GARLAND, CHAPLET

head (combining form) CEPHAL-, CEPHALO-, CAP-, CAPIT-, CAPUT-

head cold CORYZA

head waiter MAJORDOMO, MAÎTRE D'HÔTEL, MAÎTRE D'

headache that changes its site, often accompanied by nausea and blurred vision MIGRAINE

headband as worn by desert Arabs to hold the kaffiyeh or headdress in place AGAL
- headband, usually decorated FRONTLET
- headband of a narrow strip of metal, ribbon, or the like worn around the forehead FILLET
- headband or semicircle, typically decorated with diamonds or other jewels, worn by a woman on formal occasions TIARA

headed writing paper, or the heading on it LETTERHEAD

heading or introduction LEMMA
- heading or title under which something is classed RUBRIC
- classify or include in a wider category or under a general heading or principle SUBSUME

headline or title on every page or every other page of a book or magazine RUNNING HEAD
- headline running across the whole page of a newspaper BANNER HEADLINE, STREAMER

headquarters - group of senior officers responsible for planning at military headquarters GENERAL STAFF

heads face of a coin OBVERSE

headscarf as worn by Russian peasant women BABUSHKA

heal, cure, treat medically PHYSIC
- heal by forming a scar CICATRIZE

healing, curing, remedial THERAPEUTIC, SANATIVE
- healing or soothing substance, person, or influence SALVE
- formation of small beads of new tissue on the surface of a wound during healing GRANULATION
- medical, relating to healing AESCULAPIAN

health-obsessed person HYPOCHONDRIAC, VALETUDINARIAN
- health-promoting, favorable to well-being SALUBRIOUS, BENEFICIAL
- health-promoting or -preserving, free from infection SANITARY
- general state of health or state of mind CONSTITUTION
- recover strongly, improve quickly, as one's health or spirits might RALLY
- regain one's health or strength, as after an illness RECUPERATE, CONVALESCE
- restoration of one's health through therapy REHABILITATION
- restoring or promoting health, curative SALUTARY

healthy SALUBRIOUS, WHOLESOME, SALUTARY
- healthy, active, and vigorous, typically in spite of being old SPRY, SPRIGHTLY
- healthy, fresh, and vigorous con-

dition VERDURE
- healthy, robust HALE
- healthy and nourishing, as good food is NUTRITIOUS

heap of earth or stones covering an ancient burial site BARROW, MOUND, TUMULUS

hear ye, call for attention by town crier or court official OYEZ

hearing of allegedly superhuman perception or telepathic sensitivity CLAIRAUDIENCE
- perceptible to hearing, loud enough to be heard AUDIBLE
- relating to sound or hearing ACOUSTIC
- relating to the sense or organs of hearing AUDITORY, AURICULAR

hearing (combining form) AUDI-, AUDIO-, AUSCULT-

heart See illustration
- heart attack or condition caused by a blood clot in the coronary artery CORONARY THROMBOSIS
- heart murmur or other abnormal body sound BRUIT
- heart muscle, muscle tissue of the heart MYOCARDIUM
- heart specialist CARDIOLOGIST
- heart-shaped, as a shell or leaf might be CORDATE, CORDIFORM
- heart wall PARIES
- beat abnormally fast, as the heart might PALPITATE
- beat in a regular rhythm, as the heart does PULSATE
- death of an organ or part of an organ, such as the heart, as due to a blood clot INFARCTION
- instrument recording the electrical impulses in the heart ELECTROCARDIOGRAPH, ECG, EKG
- machine used to start the heart beating again, by administering an electric shock DEFIBRILLATOR
- relating to the heart CORONARY, CARDIAC, CORDIAL
- rhythmic contraction of the heart, pumping the blood into the aorta and pulmonary arteries SYSTOLE
- rhythmic relaxation of the heart, drawing blood into its chambers DIASTOLE
- soapy substance found in body tissue, fat, and bile, which may be involved in heart disease CHOLESTEROL
- study of the heart CARDIOLOGY
- twitching of the heart muscle, affecting the normal rhythm of contractions FIBRILLATION

heart (combining form) CARDI-, COR-, CORD-

heartbeat irregularity ARRHYTHMIA
- heartbeat regulator, either natural tissue or a small implanted device PACEMAKER
- heartbeat that is abnormally slow BRADYCARDIA
- heartbeat that is abnormally fast TACHYCARDIA
- heartbeat that is irregular or abnormally fast PALPITATION
- rotating cylinder on which a pen records changes in pressure, heartbeat, or the like KYMOGRAPH
- technique for regulating one's own heartbeat, blood pressure, or other apparently involuntary body functions BIOFEEDBACK

heartburn PYROSIS
- hearty eater TRENCHERMAN

heat, period of sexual excitement in some female mammals ESTRUS, RUT
- heat and spice wine or ale MULL
- heat given out or absorbed by a substance when it changes state, as during melting LATENT HEAT
- heat-producing CALEFACIENT
- heat treatment of milk, beer, and other consumable liquids to destroy germs and regulate fermentation PASTEURIZATION
- heatproof, soundproof, or protect from electricity INSULATE
- measurement of heat, as in chemical reactions CALORIMETRY
- relating to heat THERMAL
- relating to heat from the earth's interior GEOTHERMAL
- relating to the measuring of heat or calories CALORIC, CALORIFIC
- transfer of heat along or through a static body CONDUCTION
- transfer of heat by rays from a hot object RADIATION
- transfer of heat through the movement of air or other fluid between areas of different temperatures and densities CONVECTION

heat (combining form) THERM-, THERMO-, -THERMY, CALE-, CALOR-, PYRO-

heat shield of a spacecraft ABLATOR

heated passion or burning enthusiasm ARDOR

heater essentially consisting of a series of pipes through which hot water or steam flows RADIATOR
- heater typically consisting of an electric element from which warm air gently circulates CONVECTOR

heating channel under the floor in an ancient Roman house HYPOCAUST
- heating element or coil in a drinking cup or hot-water tank IMMERSION HEATER
- heating of the earth's atmosphere through increased absorption of solar radiation GREENHOUSE EFFECT

heaven See also **paradise**
- heaven, arching vault of the sky WELKIN, FIRMAMENT
- heavenlike abode of the gods in Greek mythology OLYMPUS
- heavenly, relating to the sky or heavens, sublime SUPERNAL, CELESTIAL, ETHEREAL, EMPYREAL

Heart

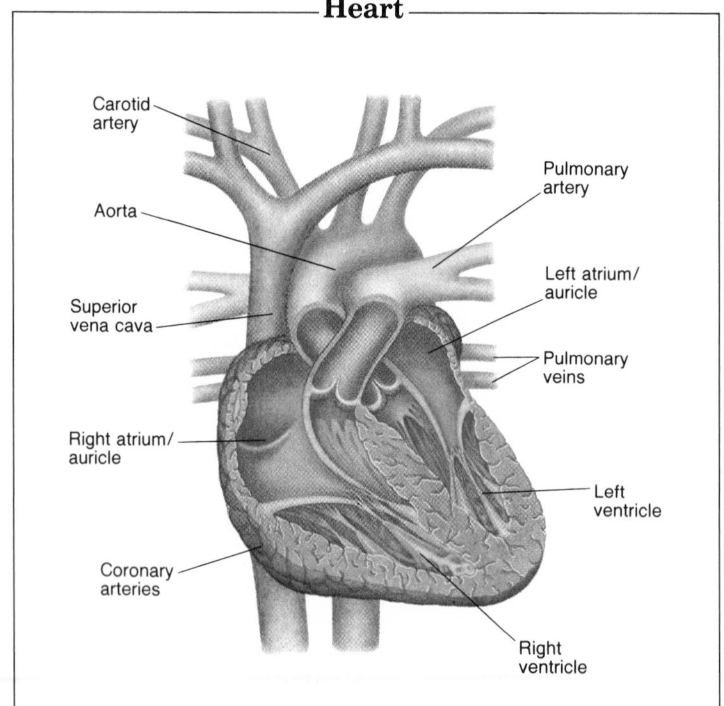

- heavenly kingdom ZION
- heavens, the skies, space beyond the earth's atmosphere, according to Greek myth ETHER
- abode of just souls barred from heaven, as through not having been baptized LIMBO
- branch of theology dealing with last things, such as heaven and hell ESCHATOLOGY
- highest level of heaven, formerly thought to be the realm of pure fire or of God and the angels EMPYREAN
- relating to the joys of heaven or sainthood BEATIFIC
- taking up of the Virgin Mary into heaven ASSUMPTION
- transporting to heaven of someone who has not yet died TRANSLATION, ASCENSION, APOTHEOSIS

heavens (combining form) URAN-, URANO-, CELEST-

heavy See also **huge, fat**
- heavy, as breathing might be LABORED
- heavy, starchy, as thick porridge or similar food is STODGY
- heavy and awkward, bulky or lumbering, ungainly PONDEROUS
- heavy hydrogen DEUTERIUM
- heavy water DEUTERIUM OXIDE
- difficult to handle, awkward or unwieldy, as through being too heavy CUMBERSOME
- imposing heavy burdens or responsibilities, oppressive, as a task might be ONEROUS

Hebrew See chart
- Hebrew scholar HEBRAIST
- secret or mystical philosophy, specifically an occult philosophy based on the Hebrew scriptures CABALA

hedge, fence, or row of trees designed to break the force of the wind WINDBREAK
- hedge of plants or cuttings individually planted QUICKSET
- hedged pathways in a puzzling pattern MAZE
- plait or weave branches or bark in making a hedge or arbor PLASH, PLEACH
- trimming of trees or hedges into ornamental shapes TOPIARY

hedgehog's or porcupine's spines QUILLS
- adjective for a hedgehog ERINACEOUS

heel bone CALCANEUS
- high, tapering, pointed heel on a woman's shoe STILETTO
- solid tapering heel joined to the sole of a shoe to form a single surface WEDGE HEEL, WEDGIE
- weakness or flaw, as small and apparently unimportant as one's heel, but fatally vulnerable ACHILLES' HEEL

heel (combining form) CALC-

Hegel - final stage in the dialectical reasoning process of Hegel, through combining thesis and antithesis SYNTHESIS
- process of reaching truth, as in Hegel, by examining and exploiting contradictions DIALECTIC

height, especially of a person when standing upright STATURE
- height, width, or length DIMENSION
- dizziness or sense of confusion, as experienced when looking down from a height VERTIGO
- fear of heights ACROPHOBIA, HYPSOPHOBIA, CREMNOPHOBIA
- instrument measuring the height of an aircraft above the ground ALTIMETER

Hebrew Alphabet

FORM	NAME	TRANS-LITERATION
א	'aleph, 'alef	'
ב	bēth	b(bh)
ג	gimel	g(gh)
ד	dāleth	d(dh)
ה	hē	h
ו	vav waw	w
ז	zayin	z
ח	ḥeth	ḥ
ט	ṭeth	ṭ
י	yod, yodh	y
ך כ	kāph	k(kh)
ל	lāmedth	l
מ ם	mēm	m
נ ן	nūn	n
ס	samekh	s
ע	'ayin	'
ף פ	pē	p(ph)
ץ צ	sade, ṣadhe	ṣ
ק	qōph	q
ר	rēsh	r
שׂ	sin	s
שׁ	shin	sh
ת	tāv, tāw	t(th)

- instrument measuring height of land above sea level OROMETER

height (combining form) ACRO-, HYPS-, HYPSO-, ALT-

heir or offspring SCION
- heir sharing equally with another PARCENER, COPARCENER
- assured and unchallengeable heir HEIR APPARENT
- current and provisional heir, whose claims would be canceled by the birth of someone with a prior right HEIR PRESUMPTIVE
- deprive an heir of his or her inheritance, as by cutting him or her out of one's will DISINHERIT
- passing or transmitted to an heir HEREDITARY

helicopter CHOPPER, WHIRLYBIRD
- helicopter's control lever that adjusts the angle of attack of all the rotor blades at once, regulating vertical movement COLLECTIVE PITCH LEVER
- helicopter's control lever that adjusts the angle of attack of individual rotor blades, regulating horizontal movement CYCLIC PITCH LEVER
- descend, as from a cliff top or helicopter, by means of a supporting rope fastened around one's body ABSEIL
- runners or struts beneath a helicopter, on which it stands or lands SKIDS
- system of blades supporting a helicopter or similar aircraft in flight ROTOR

helium, neon, or other gaseous element formerly considered incapable of chemical reaction INERT GAS, NOBLE GAS, RARE GAS

hell, eternal damnation PERDITION
- hell, place of punishment for the wicked after death GEHENNA, SHEOL
- hell or the underworld in Greek mythology HADES, ORCUS, TARTARUS
- hell, or a blazing fire suggestive of hell INFERNO, HOLOCAUST
- region or state in the afterlife between heaven and hell, in which venial sinners can atone PURGATORY
- relating to hell or the abode of the dead INFERNAL

helmet See also **armor**
- helmet, or helmetlike covering or knob, as on the bill of a hornbill CASQUE
- helmet, or the ridge or plume on it CREST
- helmet of light steel used in medieval times, often with a visor BASINET
- hinged front part of an armored helmet, covering the eyes and nose VISOR, BEAVER
- light 15th-century helmet with a

neck guard at the rear SALLET
- movable lower front part of a medieval helmet VENTAIL
- plume on a helmet PANACHE
- scarf or cloth covering a helmet in medieval times LAMBREQUIN

help, especially financial assistance SUBVENTION, SUBSIDY
- help or be of value AVAIL
- help another by begging or pleading on his or her behalf INTERCEDE
- help or encourage, especially in wrongdoing ABET, CONNIVE
- help or relief in time of distress SUCCOR
- help or service MINISTRATIONS
- help or support by a grant of money SUBSIDIZE
- help to bring about, ease FACILITATE, EXPEDITE
- applying or turning for help to a person or thing, such as the courts RECOURSE
- call upon or appeal to for help INVOKE
- give something, such as help or assistance RENDER

helper, especially one who gives financial assistance BENEFACTOR, BENEFACTRESS
- helper offering services willingly and for free VOLUNTEER
- helper or fellow worker COADJUTANT, COADJUTOR

helping, assisting, supplementing, or supporting AUXILIARY, ADJUVANT, ADJUNCT, SUBSIDIARY, ANCILLARY
- helping, cooperative, or considerate OBLIGING
- helping, promoting, contributing to, or favorable to a given result CONDUCIVE

hen, especially when less than a year old PULLET
- hen kept in farmyards or fields rather than batteries FREE-RANGE HEN
- hen that has been spayed and fattened for eating POULARDE

henchman or follower MYRMIDON
- henchman who does somebody else's dirty work HATCHET MAN

heraldry See illustration and chart, pages 257 and 258
- relating to heraldry ARMORIAL

herb having medicinal properties SIMPLE

herb tea INFUSION, TISANE

herbs See illustration and chart, pages 259 and 260

Hercules - snakelike monster with multiplying heads, killed by Hercules HYDRA

herd or flock of animals being driven together DROVE
- herding of cattle, horses, or the like DRIFT
- living or migrating in a herd, or the like GREGARIOUS

"here lies", a Latin inscription on gravestones HIC JACET

hereditary, as some diseases are GENETIC
- hereditary unit in a chromosome that determines an individual's characteristics GENE
- referring to a condition or abnormality existing from birth but not hereditary CONGENITAL

heredity laws in genetics MENDEL'S LAWS

heresy of various kinds in the early Christian church ARIANISM, GNOSTICISM, PELAGIANISM
- heresy of various kinds in the medieval Christian church ALBIGENSIANISM, CATHARISM
- heresy, or doctrines and movement considered heretical, in the Roman Catholic church in the 17th century JANSENISM
- heretical, different from orthodox beliefs HETERODOX
- burning of a heretic at the stake, as ordered by the Inquisition AUTO-DA-FÉ
- investigation or tribunal of the Roman Catholic Church, as for trying suspected witches or heretics in former times INQUISITION

heritage, legacy PATRIMONY

hermit, solitary person, living alone in seclusion RECLUSE
- hermit in early Christian times who lived on top of a high pillar STYLITE
- hermit or recluse, person who has gone into seclusion for religious reasons ANCHORITE, ANCHORESS, EREMITE

hernia in which part of the stomach pushes through the diaphragm HIATUS HERNIA
- beltlike medical device worn to keep a hernia from protruding TRUSS

hero or leading character in a play, novel, or other literary work PROTAGONIST
- heroes or list of heroes of a particular group or field of endeavor PANTHEON
- referring to the person, fictional hero, or the like, from whom a word is derived, or after whom a city, novel, or the like is named EPONYMOUS
- unhonored and usually unknown, as obscure heroes often are UNSUNG

heroic knightly or chivalrous hero PALADIN
- heroic deed or exploit GEST

heroin - inject heroin or other drugs directly into a vein MAINLINE

herring, especially from Norway, typically canned like sardines SILD, BRISLING
- herring fillet that is marinated and rolled up ROLLMOPS
- herring or mackerel salted in brine and lightly smoked BLOATER
- herring that is smoked and eaten as a delicacy BUCKLING
- having spawned recently, as a herring might have, and so of less value as food SHOTTEN
- young herring or similar fish BRIT, SPRAT, BRISLING

hesitant, undecided VACILLATING, WAVERING, IRRESOLUTE
- hesitant or jerky, as uncertain speech is HALTING

hesitate, be undecided VACILLATE, WAVER, HOVER
- hesitate, dither, avoid committing oneself HAVER, SHILLY-SHALLY, PUSSYFOOT
- hesitate and postpone, delay or put off PROCRASTINATE
- hesitate for reasons of conscience or principle SCRUPLE
- hesitate in speech, walking, operation, or the like FALTER

hi-fi See **stereo**

hibernation - sleep or dormancy through the summer, rather than through the winter as in hibernation ESTIVATION

hiccup SINGULTUS

hidden, present but not visible or active, as a tendency might be LATENT
- hidden, remote, shut away from the world SECLUDED, CLOISTERED
- hidden, secret, operating unseen SUBTERRANEAN
- hidden, secret, or secluded places RECESSES
- hidden and secret, often for an illicit purpose CLANDESTINE, FURTIVE, COVERT, SURREPTITIOUS
- hidden or secluded place, hideaway HERMITAGE, RETREAT
- hidden or secret, as mystical knowledge might be OCCULT, ESOTERIC, ARCANE
- hidden store of money, drugs, or the like, or its hiding place STASH
- hidden store of stolen goods, arms, or the like, or its hiding place CACHE
- obscured or half-hidden, scarcely visible UNOBTRUSIVE, INDISTINCT, IMPERCEPTIBLE

hidden (combining form) CRYPT-, CRYPTO-

hide of an animal, removed from the carcass PELT, FELL
- hide of an animal, tanned and entire CROP
- hide on board a departing ship,

Heraldry

POSITIONS

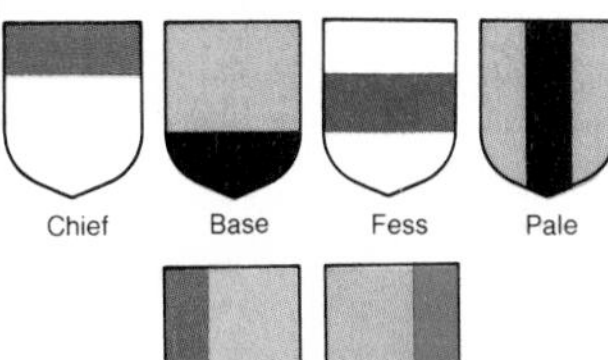

Chief Base Fess Pale

Dexter Sinister

CHARGES

Lion rampant · Lion passant reguardant · Leopard passant guardant · Boar passant

Talbot sejant · Stag's head cabossed · Unicorn statant · Eagle displayed

DIFFERENCING MARKS

Label (eldest son) · Crescent (second son) · Mullet (third son) · Martlet (fourth son)

Annulet (fifth son) · Fleur-de-lis (sixth son) · Rose (seventh son) · Cross moline (eighth son)

QUARTERINGS

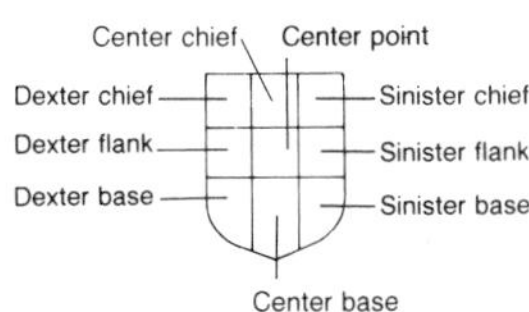

PARTITION LINES

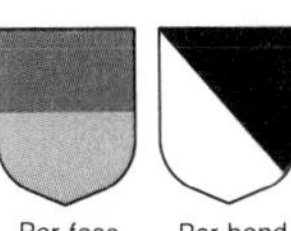
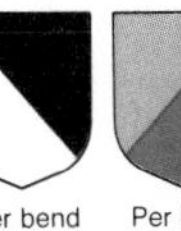
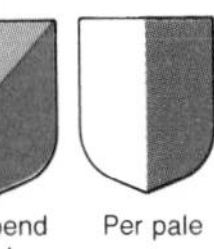

Per fess · Per bend · Per bend sinister · Per pale

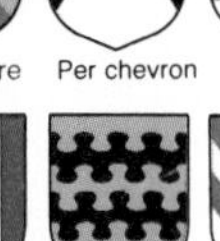

Per saltire · Per chevron · Barry · Quarterly

Paly · Barry nebuly · Bendy · Chevronny

ARMS OF A WOMAN

Lozenge · Impaling · Escutcheon of pretense

TINCTURES

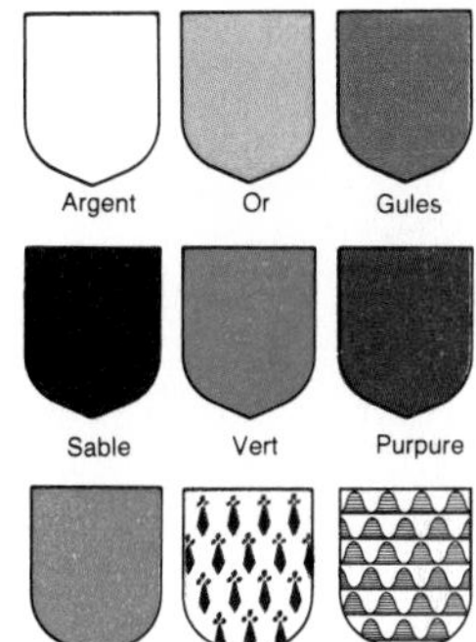

Argent · Or · Gules

Sable · Vert · Purpure

Azure · Ermine · Vair

CANTING ARMS

Bower · Shakespeare · Cockburn · Trumpington

ORDINARIES

Bend · Chevron · Pile · Pall

Cross · Saltire · Annulet · Quarter

Orle · Bordure · Gyronny · Flaunches

ACHIEVEMENT OF ARMS

train, or the like for a free journey STOWAWAY
- hide or cover, as if by draping with a cloth MANTLE, ENSHROUD
- hide or disguise something, such as one's fear DISSEMBLE
- hide or mask something, typically a woman's face VEIL
- hide or lie in wait, typically for a sinister purpose SKULK, LURK
- hide or shut away safely, as for private discussions CLOSET, ENSCONCE
- person who hides away or lives in solitude RECLUSE, HERMIT

hideaway, place for seclusion or withdrawal HERMITAGE, RETREAT
- hideaway, shelter, hiding place, or disguise COVERT

hieroglyphics of a kind used by priests in ancient Egypt HIERATIC
- hieroglyphics of a simplified form, used by literate laymen in ancient Egypt DEMOTIC
- oblong frame around names of gods, kings, or queens in Egyptian hieroglyphics CARTOUCHE
- stone tablet providing the key to ancient Egyptian hieroglyphics ROSETTA STONE

high, inaccessible place, fortress, or the like AERIE
- high and impressive, as a tall building or cliff might be IMPOSING, TOWERING, COMMANDING, SOARING
- high-pitched or shrill, as a voice might be REEDY, CLARION, TREBLE
- high-pitched or squeaky, as a boy's voice might be FALSETTO
- high-ranking or important person DIGNITARY
- high-ranking or noble-looking person MAGNIFICO, GRANDEE
- high up in altitude, rank, intellectual level, or the like ELEVATED, LOFTY

high (combining form) ACRO-, ALTI-

high point, final development or achievement, peak ACME, APEX, PINNACLE, ZENITH, MERIDIAN, SUMMIT, APOGEE, VERTEX
- high point, furthest possible stage or degree NE PLUS ULTRA
- high point, time or point of greatest intensity, as of a series of events, story, play, or the like CLIMAX, CULMINATION

HERALDRY TERMS

addorsed	back to back
ambulant	walking
attires	deer's antlers
bearing/ device/charge	emblem or figure on a shield
bezant	gold roundel
blazon	written description of armorial bearing
camelopard	giraffelike creature with horns
canting arms/ armes parlantes	punning shield or emblem
canton	small square division on a shield
cinquefoil	five-petaled flower
clarion	horn or trumpet
cockatrice	cockerel with a dragon's wings and tail
cognizance	crest or badge
College of Arms	ruling body of heraldry in England
couchant	lying, with head raised
Court of the Lord Lyon	ruling body of heraldry in Scotland
dormant	lying, with head on paws
embattled	with battlements
ensigned	with official headgear, such as a coronet or miter, set above the shield
escutcheon	shield
field	surface of a shield
gouttes	droplets
griffin	beast with the front parts of an eagle and the back parts of a lion
hatchment/ achievement	diamond-shaped display of a dead person's coat of arms
herald	senior heraldic officer
issuant	emerging
lambrequin/ mantling	scarf over a helmet
mound	ball or orb of gold
nowed	knotted
phoenix	eaglelike bird arising from flames
pursuivant	junior heraldic officer
quatrefoil	four-petaled flower
roundel	circular design or symbol
salient	leaping, jumping, or rearing
semé	scattered with small figures
splendor	human-faced sun surrounded by rays
tierced	divided into three
undé/undy	wavy
urdée	pointed
urinant	(water animal) with head bowed
voided	with center empty or cut out
volant	flying
wyvern	two-legged winged dragon

Herbs

Dill.
Aniseed flavor in leaves and seeds

Fennel.
Aniseed-flavored leaves and seeds

Bay.
Sweetly aromatic leaves

Tarragon.
Sweet leaves

Mint.
Spearmint flavor

Chervil.
Flavor similar to parsley but sweeter

Thyme.
Sweetly spicy leaves

Parsley.
Fresh peppery flavor

Rosemary.
Strongly lavender-flavored leaves

Borage.
Cucumber-flavored leaves

Marjoram.
Spicy leaves similar in flavor to thyme

Coriander.
Dried seeds for spicy flavor

Horseradish.
Hot-pepper-flavored root

Garlic.
Onion-flavored bulb

Basil.
Sweet clove-flavored leaves

Chives.
Mild onion-flavored leaves

Angelica.
Slight musky flavor in candied stems

Sage.
Leaves with strong, rather bitter flavor

- high point or essence, final development or distillation APOTHEOSIS

high-pressure area ANTICYCLONE

high priest in ancient Rome PONTIFEX MAXIMUS

high relief ALTO-RELIEVO

high spirits, mischief, lively prankishness SHENANIGANS, HIGH JINKS

- high spirits, zest for life, enjoyment of living JOIE DE VIVRE

high-wire walker or other performer of balancing feats EQUILIBRIST

higher in status, rank, or value, superior SUPERORDINATE

higher, higher than (combining form) SUPER-, SUPRA-

higher education TERTIARY EDUCATION

highest in pitch ALTISSIMO

- highest or final point CULMINATION, PINNACLE, MERIDIAN

highest (combining form) ARCH-, ULTIM-

highfalutin, exaggeratedly rich or elegant in style, as purple prose is FLORID, TUMID, AUREATE, ROCOCO

- highfalutin, full of windy style or padding but lacking in real content FUSTIAN, FLATULENT, TURGID

- highfalutin or lofty in style and vocabulary SONOROUS, LATINATE, SESQUIPEDALIAN, MANDARIN

- highfalutin, pompous and inflated, inappropriately grand, as a speaker or a speech might be BOMBASTIC, GRANDILOQUENT, ROTUND, MAGNILOQUENT, OROTUND

- highfalutin, speechifying, trying to impress and manipulate rather than inform RHETORICAL, ORATORICAL, DECLAMATORY

- highfalutin and artificially stylish in expression, using very long words and extravagant figures of speech EUPHUISTIC, GONGORISTIC

hijack captive HOSTAGE

hill in North America with a flat top and steep sides MESA, BUTTE

- hill or high ground, rise EMINENCE, ELEVATION

- hill or outcrop that is high, rocky, and bare TOR

- hill or ridge formed by glacial deposits DRUMLIN, KAME, ESKER, OS

HERBS AND SPICES

allspice	spice with a flavor of cinnamon, clove, and nutmeg, used in baked fruit
aniseed	licorice-flavored spice used in pie fillings
asafetida	yellow-brown resinous spice used in oriental cooking
balm	lemon-scented leaves used in omelettes and fruit drinks
basil	clove-flavored herb used with poultry
bay leaf	herb used to flavor sauces and as part of a bouquet garni
borage	cucumber-flavored leaves used in salads and cold drinks
bouquet garni	mix of herbs tied or wrapped together, as used to flavor soups or stews
caraway	seeds of a parsleylike plant used to flavor bread and cakes
cardamom	spice with a flavor similar to eucalyptus, either pods as used in curries, or seeds as used in custards and baked fruits
cayenne	hot spice used in chutneys and cheese dishes
chervil	delicate, parsley-flavored herb used in soups
chili	hot spice used in dishes such as chili con carne
chives	mild onion-flavored leaves used to season salads
cinnamon	pungent sweet spice used to flavor cakes and stewed fruit
cloves	pungent spice used whole with baked fruits, and ground in milk puddings
coriander seeds	seeds with a flavor of orange peel used in chutneys and cheeses
cumin	seeds used in curries
dill	spice with a mild aniseed flavor used in fish dishes, salads, and sauces
fennel	herb with an aniseed flavor used to counteract the richness of oily fish in sauces
fenugreek	pungent, aromatic seed used in curries
garam masala	mix of spices used in Indian cooking
lovage	strongly flavored, celerylike leaves used to flavor soups, stews, and sauces
mace	the husk of nutmeg, used whole or ground
marjoram	spicy leaves similar in flavor to thyme, used in stuffings and meat dishes
nutmeg	spice used ground for sweet or savory flavoring
oregano	mint herb used in Greek and Italian dishes
paprika	mild, sweet pepper for spicy meat dishes such as goulash
rosemary	strongly flavored leaves used with lamb
saffron	vivid yellow spice for coloring rice and fish dishes
sage	strong bitter leaves used in stuffings
tarragon	herb with sweet leaves used in vinegar and mayonnaise
thyme	herb used in stuffings and meat dishes
turmeric	spice with vivid yellow color, used in curries for coloring rice

- hill or ridge with steep eroded sides HOGBACK
- hill that is small, rounded, and often grassy or wooded KNOLL, HUMMOCK, HOLT
- hilly ridge or crest of land CHINE
- heap of rock fragments at the foot of a cliff or hill TALUS, SCREE
- rocky hill standing solitary on a plain KOPJE, INSELBERG

hillock or mound TUFFET

hinder See also **prevent, prohibit, limit**
- hinder, burden, or handicap ENCUMBER
- hinder, disrupt someone's plans, thwart the efforts or aims of FOIL, FRUSTRATE, DISCOMFIT, BAFFLE, STYMIE
- hinder, obstruct, or delay as a deliberate strategy, as in legislative debate STONEWALL
- hinder, obstruct, or delay the progress of a lesgislative debate by the use of unnecessarily long speeches FILIBUSTER
- hinder, obstruct, restrict IMPEDE, HAMPER, STIFLE, STRAITJACKET, TRAMMEL, HAMSTRING, HAMSHACKLE
- hinder or prevent FORECLOSE
- hinder the progress of, delay, slow down RETARD
- hindering rather than helping as intended COUNTERPRODUCTIVE

Hindi - script, syllabic rather than alphabetic, in which Sanskrit and Hindi are written DEVANAGARI

hindquarters of a horse or other domestic animal RUMP, CROUP, HAUNCHES, CRUPPER

hindrance, disadvantage, handicap LIABILITY
- hindrance, obstruction IMPEDIMENT, TRAMMEL, STUMBLING BLOCK

Hinduism See chart, page 262

hinge joining a door to a door frame, consisting of two metal flaps linked with a stout pin BUTT HINGE
- cylindrical edge of a hinge in which the pin is fitted KNUCKLE
- notch or groove that houses an inserted part in a joint or hinge MORTISE, GAIN
- socket, as for a rudder or the pin of a hinge GUDGEON

hinged metal clamp for lifting heavy objects such as building materials GRAPPLING IRONS, CRAMPONS
- measuring instrument consisting of a pair of graduated arms hinged at one end, as used in geometry SECTOR

hint, make known indirectly or subtly INTIMATE
- hint, vague notion, or unconfirmed suspicion INKLING, INTIMATION
- hint at, outline ADUMBRATE
- hint or oblique reference, passing mention ALLUSION
- hint or suggestion of a veiled and typically offensive kind INNUENDO, ASPERSION, INSINUATION, IMPUTATION
- hint or vague suggestion of something about to happen STRAW IN THE WIND
- hint slyly INSINUATE
- indefinable quality, distinctive feature that can only be hinted at JE NE SAIS QUOI
- tiny amount, trace, or hint of something SMACK, SOUPÇON

hip bone INNOMINATE BONE
- hip bone or joint COXA
- hip of an animal HAUNCH, HUCKLE
- hips and pelvic region LOINS
- socket of the hip bone, into which the thigh bone fits ACETABULUM

hippopotamus, elephant, or similar thick-skinned mammal PACHYDERM
- hippopotamus or similar large animal mentioned in the book of Job BEHEMOTH

hissing sound such as /s/ or /z/ SIBILANT

historian - community bard or oral historian in an African community GRIOT

historical, relating to the development of something through time DIACHRONIC
- historical development of a language, custom, or the like PHYLOGENY
- historical period or era EPOCH
- historical records of events over the years CHRONICLE, ANNALS
- historical records of an institution, group of people, or the like ARCHIVES
- historical turning point LANDMARK
- devise a dramatized version of a crime or historical event to gain a vivid idea of what actually took place RECONSTRUCT

history long ago, ancient times ANTIQUITY
- history that is very short and simplified POTTED HISTORY
- calculation of the dates of historical events, or ordering of events according to their dates, or a list of such events CHRONOLOGY
- complete, reliable, and authoritative, as a history or biography might be DEFINITIVE
- relating to the beginning of time or history PRIMORDIAL
- use of statistics in the study of history CLIOMETRICS

hit See **beat**

Hitler's title as Nazi dictator of Germany FÜHRER

hives, nettle rash URTICARIA, UREDO

hoarse and often emotional in sound HUSKY

hoax or worthless discovery MARE'S NEST
- rumor or news report that is false or a deliberate hoax CANARD

hobby, leisure activity AVOCATION
- person who has a specified hobby, such as breeding plants or animals FANCIER

hockey See chart and illustration, page 263
- hockey or ice hockey of an early form BANDY

hodgepodge, mixture of widely varying elements MISCELLANY, POTPOURRI, SALMAGUNDI

hoe - hoelike farming or gardening tool MATTOCK

hoist or raise, especially by machine WINCH

hold someone around the arms to restrain him or her PINION
- holding, sticking, or clinging firmly, clasping, TENACIOUS
- holding or grasping device, especially a grapnel GRAPPLE
- firm hold or grip, as when pushing, climbing, or the like PURCHASE

hole See also **gap**
- hole, slit, or opening, such as the adjustable opening in a camera lens controlling the entry of light APERTURE
- hole cut with a special tool into a metal sheet, skull bone, or the like TREPAN, TREPHINE
- hole or cavity, such as a honeycomb cell or a tooth socket in the jawbone ALVEOLUS
- hole or opening for fumes, air, or liquids to pass through VENT
- hole or opening for the digestive and genital tracts in birds, fish, and reptiles CLOACA
- hole or rectangular slot into which the matching tenon is fitted when joining two pieces of wood, stone, or metal MORTISE
- hole or series of holes made in something PERFORATION
- breathing hole near an insect's neck, blowhole of a whale, or the like SPIRACLE
- hollow or dig out, as to make a hole or tunnel EXCAVATE
- gardening tool for making holes in the soil, as for bulbs or seedlings DIBBER, DIBBLE
- make a hole or row of holes PERFORATE
- make or enlarge a hole by means of a gimlet or similar tool BROACH
- pierce with many holes RIDDLE
- shape or enlarge a hole, as in wood, with a special cylindrical file REAM
- small body hole or opening, espe-

cially any of those in a bone through which blood vessels and nerves pass FORAMEN
- small body hole or opening, especially that between the middle and inner ear FENESTRA
- small hole, as for a shoelace or hook fastening EYELET
- small mouthlike hole, especially any of those in a sponge OSCULUM

holiday See chart, page 264, and also **vacation**

holier-than-thou SANCTIMONIOUS, PIETISTIC, UNCTUOUS, PHARISAICAL, PECKSNIFFIAN, HYPOCRITICAL

holiness, saintliness SANCTITY

Holland - stretch of low-lying land reclaimed from the sea, especially in Holland POLDER

hollow, area or place sunk below the surrounding ground DEPRESSION
- hollow, cavity, or channel in the body, containing or conveying air, pus, blood, or the like SINUS
- hollow filled with mud SLOUGH
- hollow or dig out, as to make a hole or tunnel EXCAVATE

HINDUISM TERMS

ashram	holy man's hermitage; religious retreat or meeting place
atman	individual essence; universal soul
avatar	descent to earth of a deity; any of the incarnations of the god Vishnu
Bhagavad Gita	religious text in the Mahabharata
bhakti	devotion to a particular god as a means of achieving salvation
Brahma	creator god of the divine trinity
Brahman	member of the highest caste, originally composed of priests
chela	pupil or disciple of a guru
deva	god or divinity
dharma	ultimate principle of all things, cosmic or natural law; behavior or duty in keeping with this
fakir/sadhu	wandering religious ascetic or preacher
guru	spiritual teacher or leader
harijan	lower-class Hindu, an "untouchable," technically outside the caste system
Juggernaut	form of the god Krishna, or an idol of him drawn on a huge wagon at an annual festival
Kama Sutra	4th-century text on erotic love
karma	fate; force produced by one's deeds, affecting one's destiny in the next existence
Krishna	main avatar or incarnation of the god Vishnu
Mahabharata/ Ramayana	ancient epic Sanskrit poems
maharishi	wise man or great spiritual teacher
mahatma	person revered for his wisdom and virtue, specifically a Brahman sage
mandala	symbol representing the universe, as used in meditation
mandir	Hindu temple
mantra	sacred sound or formula used in prayer and meditation
maya	illusion; the world regarded as unreal or illusory
mudra	set of ritual hand movements and body postures used in sacred dancing
nirvana	state of blessedness or enlightenment, involving release from the cycle of reincarnation, leading to reabsorption into Brahma
pandit	learned Brahman
Rig-Veda	ancient collection of religious poems
samsara	repeated cycle of birth, suffering, death, and rebirth
sannyasi	holy Brahman beggar in his final incarnation, who will not return to earth again
Sanskrit	ancient language of Hinduism
Siva/Shiva	destroyer god of the divine trinity
suttee	former practice of willing self-cremation by a widow on her husband's funeral pyre; widow who cremates herself in this way
swami	term of address for a religious teacher or ascetic
tantras	various mystical religious texts
Upanishads	various philosophical and theological texts elaborating upon the Vedas
Vedanta	philosophical system dealing with the singleness of reality and the believer's duty of self-transcendence
Vedas	various ancient sacred writings
Vishnu	preserver god of the divine trinity

- hollow or indented space, as set back from the main surface of a wall RECESS, ALCOVE

hollow (combining form) COEL-, COELO-, -CELE

hollyhock ALTHAEA

holy, extremely sacred SACROSANCT, INVIOLABLE
- holy, deeply religious, pious DEVOUT, REVERENT
- Holy Communion given to a person in danger of death VIATICUM
- holy in a hypocritical or self-satisfied way, pretending to be pious SANCTIMONIOUS, UNCTUOUS, PIETISTIC
- holy place associated with a saint or other revered person SHRINE
- holy place, or the holiest part of a sacred place SANCTUARY
- authorize to be a clergyman, invest with holy orders ORDAIN
- beggar, often a holy beggar wandering from place to place MENDICANT
- Hindu holy man, preacher, or ascetic SADHU
- Hindu or Muslim holy man or ascetic, often wandering and begging from place to place FAKIR
- make or declare something holy, such as a church CONSECRATE, SANCTIFY
- make or treat as holy REVERE, HALLOW, VENERATE
- Muslim holy man or ascetic DERVISH, CALENDER
- shrine or container for holy relics RELIQUARY
- spoiling or destruction of the holy quality of a church, graveyard, or other consecrated place, as by blasphemy or vandalism DESECRATION, PROFANATION, VIOLATION, SACRILEGE

holy (combining form) HIER-, HIERO-, SACR-

holy books See **Scriptures**

Holy Ghost in the role of comforter, supporter, or counselor PARACLETE

holy of holies in the Temple in ancient Israel SANCTUM SANCTORUM, ORACLE

holy place (combining form) HAGI-, HAGIO-

holy war conducted by Muslims as a religious duty JIHAD
- holy war or expedition, especially any of those conducted by Christians in the Holy Land in the Middle Ages CRUSADE

holy water - basin for holy water at the entrance of a church STOUP, FONT, ASPERSORIUM
- sprinkler for holy water, such as a brush or perforated spoon ASPERGILLUM

home, legal dwelling place or country of residence DOMICILE
- home, one's place of living ABODE
- occasional home, typically a small apartment near a city center, kept by someone whose main home is elsewhere PIED-À-TERRE

homeland person from the same homeland as another person COMPATRIOT
- person who has left or been driven from his or her homeland and now lives in another country EXPATRIATE, EXILE, EMIGRANT
- return someone to his or her homeland REPATRIATE

homeopathy - conventional medical treatment, as opposed to homeopathy ALLOPATHY

homesickness NOSTALGIA

homosexual INVERT
- homosexual man's boy lover CATAMITE
- homosexual relations, especially between a man and a boy PEDERASTY
- attracted to persons of the opposite sex, as distinct from homosexual HETEROSEXUAL

honest See also **frank**
- honest, constantly truthful VERACIOUS

honesty, moral soundness INTEGRITY, PROBITY, RECTITUDE, VERACITY

honey as used in medicines MEL
- honey-based alcoholic drink, common in the Middle Ages MEAD
- honeycomb cell or similar deep cavity ALVEOLUS
- honeycombed, pitted with small, deep indentations ALVEOLATE, FAVEOLATE
- sweet liquid secreted by flowers and gathered by bees for making honey NECTAR
- sweetmeat made of honey and

FIELD-HOCKEY TERMS

ball	white ball of cork and twine covered with leather; 5 1/2 to 5 3/4 oz.
dribble	propelling the ball along in front with a series of quick hits and taps
drive	hard shot trying to get the ball past an opponent or into the goal
flick	quick pass to a player on the right or left by lifting the ball slightly off the ground
push	short pass, usually to a player on the right
stick	stick with a flat face on its left-hand side; 12-28 oz. for men, max. of 23 oz. for women
sticks	penalty for raising the stick above shoulder height
stop	holding the stick perpendicular to the ground to stop the ball before shooting
team	11 players: 5 forwards, 3 halfbacks, 2 fullbacks, and the goalkeeper

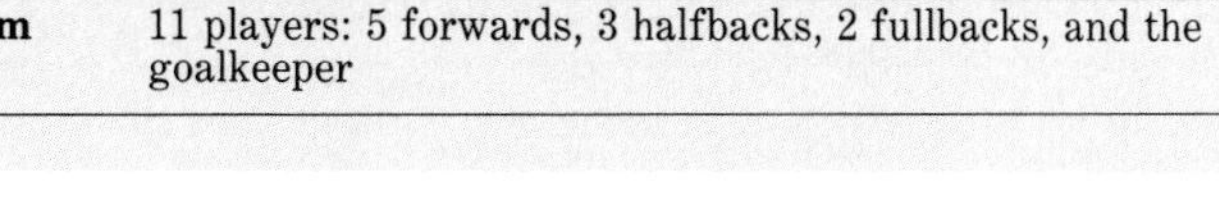

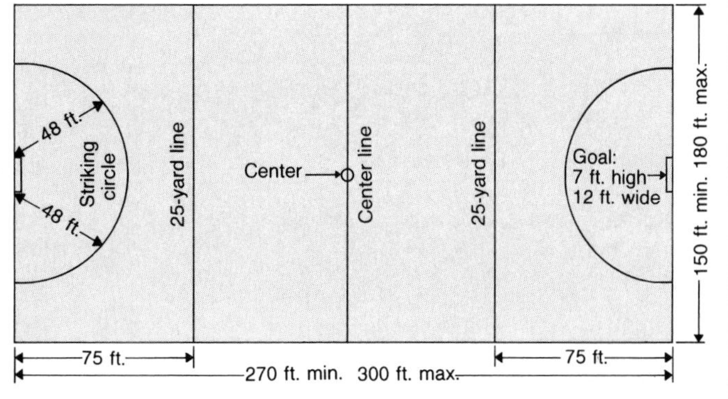

HOLIDAYS AND FESTIVALS

ANZAC Day	April 25, a holiday in Australia and New Zealand commemorating the landing at Gallipoli in 1915
Ascension Day	fortieth day after Easter, a Christian Church feast commemorating the ascension of Christ into heaven
Ash Wednesday	seventh Wednesday before Easter, a day of penitence in the Roman Catholic Church
Assumption Day	August 15, Christian Church feast celebrating the taking up of the Virgin Mary into heaven
Bairam	either of two Muslim festivals, one at the end of Ramadan and the other 70 days later
Bastille Day	July 14, a holiday in France commemorating the storming of the Bastille in 1789
Bon/Feast of Lanterns	in July, a Buddhist festival held in Japan, honoring ancestral spirits
Candlemas	February 2, a Christian Church feast commemorating the purification of the Virgin Mary and the presentation of the infant Christ in the temple
Columbus Day	October 12, a holiday in the U.S. commemorating the discovery of the Bahamas by Columbus in 1492
Corpus Christi	ten or 14 days after Pentecost, a Roman Catholic festival in honor of the Eucharist
Day of the Vow	December 16, a holiday in South Africa celebrating the victory of the Boers over a Zulu army at Blood River in 1838
Dominion Day/Canada Day	July 1, a holiday in Canada celebrating the anniversary of the founding of the Dominion of Canada in 1867
Halloween/ All Hallows' Eve	October 31, the eve of All Saints' Day, when ghosts, witches, and fairies are supposed to walk abroad
Hanukkah/ Chanukkah/ Feast of Lights	usually in December, an eight-day Jewish festival commemorating the victory of the Maccabees over the Syrians in 165 BC
Independence Day	July 4, a holiday in the U.S. commemorating the signing of the Declaration of Independence in 1776
Karneval/ Fasching	November 11 to Ash Wednesday, pre-Lenten carnivals and feasts in many German and Austrian towns
Labor Day	first Monday in September, a holiday in the U.S. and Canada
Lady Day	March 25, a Christian Church feast commemorating the Annunciation
Mardi Gras	last day before Lent, celebrated by carnivals, especially in New Orleans
Martinmas	November 11, a Christian Church festival celebrating Saint Martin's Day
Maundy Thursday	Thursday before Easter, a commemoration of the Last Supper, on which in England the Sovereign gives specially minted coins to selected poor people
Muharram	in July or August, a Muslim festival held during the first 10 days of the Muslim year
Orangeman's Day	July 12, a public holiday in Northern Ireland celebrated by Protestants—"Orangemen," after William, Prince of Orange—as the anniversary of the Battle of the Boyne in 1690
Passover/ Pesach	in March or April, an eight-day Jewish festival commemorating the escape of the Jews from Egypt
Pentecost/ Whit Sunday	the seventh Sunday after Easter, a Christian Church festival commemorating the descent of the Holy Ghost on the followers of Jesus; Jewish Feast of the Weeks, 50 days after the second day of Passover
Ramadan	in March and April, 30 days' fast from sunrise to sunset, observed by Muslims
Rosh Hashanah	Jewish New Year, between late September and early October
Saint John's Eve	June 23, the eve of the feast of Saint John the Baptist, a holiday in Portugal
Shrove Tuesday	last day before Lent, seven weeks before Easter, the day when pancakes are traditionally eaten
Tet	Vietnamese New Year, in January or February
Thanksgiving Day	fourth Thursday of November, a holiday in the U.S. commemorating the first harvest of the Pilgrim Fathers in 1621
Twelfth Night/ Epiphany	January 6, the twelfth night after Christmas, celebrating the manifestation of the divine nature of Christ to the Magi, the three Wise Men
Waitangi Day	February 6, a national holiday in New Zealand on the anniversary of the Treaty of Waitangi, between the British Government and Maori tribes in 1840
Walpurgis Night	the eve of May Day, in Germany the supposed occasion of a witches' Sabbath
Yom Kippur/ Day of Atonement	in September or October, a Jewish day of fasting, to pray for the atonement of sins

crushed sesame seeds HALVAH

honor See also **praise**
- honor, duty, or respect, granted to someone or to a belief or cause HOMAGE, REVERE, REVERENCE, TRIBUTE
- honor, expression of gratitude or appreciation, a written or spoken tribute TESTIMONIAL
- honor, glory, or a mark of honor, originally a wreath or crown of laurel or bay leaves LAURELS, BAYS
- honor, moral soundness, virtue INTEGRITY, PROBITY, RECTITUDE
- honor generously or flatteringly, treat as a hero or celebrity FETE, LIONIZE
- honor or award, such as a medal or honorary degree ACCOLADE
- honor or glorify above all others VENERATE, BEATIFY, HALLOW, REVERENCE, EXALT
- honor the memory, as of a person or event, by means of a ceremony COMMEMORATE
- challenge, attack, or spoil someone's dignity, honor, integrity, or the like IMPUGN, IMPEACH, DISCREDIT
- obligation on noble or noble-minded people to be generous and honorable NOBLESSE OBLIGE
- poet, Nobel prize winner, or other eminent person in the arts or sciences who receives a special honor LAUREATE
- present or bestow a degree or honor CONFER

honorable, chivalrous or gallant man GALAHAD, CHEVALIER

honorary, awarded as a mark of honor, as a degree might be HONORIS CAUSA

hood-shaped or hooded CUCULLATE

hoof, claw, nail, or similar part UNGUIS
- hoofed mammal, such as a horse, pig, or deer UNGULATE
- divided into two, as an animal's or devil's hoof might be CLEFT, CLOVEN, BISULCATE
- horny wedge in the sole of a horse's hoof FROG

hook on a drying or stretching frame for cloth during manufacture TENTERHOOK
- hook or small hooklike device CROTCHET
- hook-shaped UNCIFORM
- iron device with hooks, attached to a rope, thrown onto a wall, nearby ship, or the like to grip it and create a connection GRAPNEL, GRAPPLING IRON
- remove the hook from a fish after catching it DISGORGE

hooked or coiled tip of a young fern frond CROSIER
- hooked or curved, resembling an eagle's beak, as one's nose might be AQUILINE
- hooked pole used for hauling large fish aboard GAFF

hoop of plastic, swung around the body by hip movements HULA HOOP
- hoop or series of hoops formerly worn under a skirt to support it, or the skirt itself FARTHINGALE

hope or wish that is fanciful and unrealistic PIPE DREAM
- deprived, as of hope or comfort BEREFT
- ruin or thwart hopes, ambition, or the like BLIGHT

hopeful, cheerful, confident SANGUINE, BUOYANT
- hopeful or optimistic, especially about economic prospects and stock-exchange prices BULLISH

hopeless, beyond remedy IRREDEEMABLE
- hopeless, in an awkward or helpless position IN CHANCERY
- hopeless enterprise FORLORN HOPE

horizontal beam or crossbar, as in a window or over a door TRANSOM, LINTEL
- horizontal timber beam in a building, as for supporting a floor STRINGER, SUMMER

hormone or drug, based on a ring of carbon atoms, sometimes used by bodybuilders and athletes STEROID, ANABOLIC STEROID
- hormone secreted by the pancreas and regulating the level of blood sugar INSULIN
- hormone secreted during times of stress, and increasing pulse rate and blood pressure EPINEPHRINE, ADRENALINE
- hormone used in the treatment of allergies and rheumatoid arthritis CORTISONE
- female hormone, regulating ovulation and promoting feminine characteristics such as developed breasts ESTROGEN
- male hormones, promoting masculine characteristics such as facial hair ANDROGEN, TESTOSTERONE

horn - hornlike in shape or texture CERATOID
- horn of plenty, goat's horn overflowing with fruit and vegetables, symbolizing abundance, in paintings and sculptures CORNUCOPIA
- horn on old cars KLAXON
- horn-shaped or having horns CORNUTE
- hornlike or horn-shaped body part CORNU
- hornlike or horny CORNEOUS
- hornlike substance occurring in some fungi and in the shell of a lobster, crab, or the like CHITIN
- arched, curved, as horns might be FORNICATE, ARCUATE
- fanfare or blast on a horn or trumpet TANTARA, TANTIVY
- having hollow horns rather than antlers CAVICORN
- having horns or hornlike projections CORNICULATE
- hornless goat, ox, sheep, or other usually horned animal POLLARD
- pierce or stab with a horn or tusk, as in bullfighting GORE

hornet's nest, or colony of wasps or hornets VESPIARY

horny tissue (combining form) KERAT-, KERATO-

horrible, dreadful, grim, as a ghastly sight of bloodshed is GRISLY, GRUESOME
- horrible, hideous, terrifyingly hateful LOATHSOME, ABOMINABLE, HORRENDOUS, UNSPEAKABLE
- horrible, sensational, or bloodcurdling, often in a deliberately artificial way GRAND GUIGNOL
- horrible, very upsetting, as an appalling ordeal is HARROWING
- horrible, weird, dealing or obsessed with death, LURID, MORBID, MACABRE

horror - draw back, as in fear or horror RECOIL

hors d'oeuvre, appetizer ANTIPASTO

horse See illustration, page 266, and also **harness, horse racing, saddle**
- horse, pig, deer, or other hoofed mammal UNGULATE
- horse or the like regarded as the mother of another DAM
- horse that is old or worn out HACK, NAG, JADE
- horses harnessed one behind the other in a team, or a two-wheeled carriage drawn by such a team TANDEM
- adjective for a horse EQUINE
- attendant for horses at an inn, stableman OSTLER
- brownish, golden-colored horse SORREL
- brownish horse with a cream-colored mane and tail PALOMINO
- castrated male horse GELDING
- enclosure for horses CORRAL, PADDOCK
- extinct horselike mammal of prehistoric times EOHIPPUS
- groom a horse CURRY
- having different colors, especially blotches of black and white, as a horse might PIEBALD, PINTO
- herding of horses DRIFT
- horny wedge in the sole of a horse's hoof FROG
- hybrid animal from a female don-

Horse

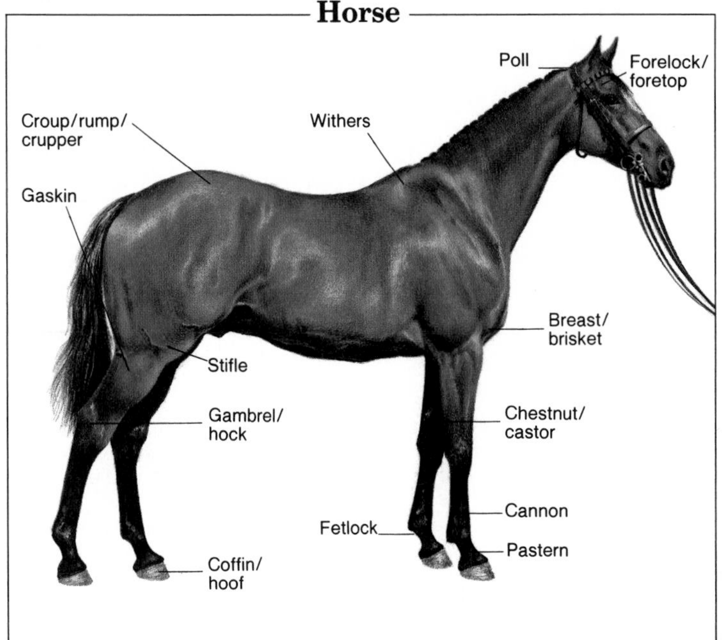

key and male horse HINNY
- infectious bacterial disease in horses, causing ulcers in the lungs and skin GLANDERS, FARCY
- ironsmith who made spurs and bits for horses LORIMER
- laming inflammation of the sensitive tissue in a horse's hoof LAMINITIS, FOUNDER
- laming swelling or growth on a horse's hock or lower leg SPAVIN
- long hair on the legs or tail of some horses or dogs FEATHERS
- marked with white or gray, brown, or reddish spots, as some horses are SKEWBALD
- monster in Greek mythology having a man's torso, and a horse's body or legs CENTAUR
- ornamental armor or covering for a horse BARD
- ornamental covering and harness for a horse CAPARISON, TRAPPINGS
- person who shoes horses or treats them for disorders FARRIER
- racehorse, book, or the like that achieves sudden success after an unpromising early phase SLEEPER, DARK HORSE
- reddish horse with a sprinkling of grayish hairs on its coat ROAN
- refuse, stop short, as a horse might at a jump JIB, BALK, SHY
- restrict or prevent a horse's straying, by means of a rope hampering leg movements HOBBLE, HAMSHACKLE
- rider of the left front horse of a coach POSTILION
- rising and falling of the rider in the saddle in time with a horse's trot POST
- rope, chain, or halter restricting a horse to a small range of movement or grazing area TETHER
- saddle or seat for a second rider, as on a horse or motorcycle PILLION
- section of the body of a horse or dog between the forequarters and hindquarters COUPLING
- short-legged, extremely stocky horse SHETLAND PONY, SHELTY
- short-legged, stocky, compact horse COB
- stable for boarding horses or letting out horses and carriages LIVERY STABLE
- strap or rope to secure a horse by the neck HALTER
- strap that ties a saddle, blanket, pack, or the like around a horse SURCINGLE
- strike a hind foot against a forefoot, as a horse might OVERREACH
- stumble and go lame, as a horse might FOUNDER
- swelling on a horse's back, typically causing stiffness SPAVIN
- thoroughbred horses, especially racehorses BLOODSTOCK
- troops on horses CAVALRY
- uncastrated male horse STALLION, ENTIRE
- urine of horses STALE
- white horse of a breed used in the Spanish Riding School in Vienna LIPIZZANER
- white spot on a horse's forehead BLAZE, STAR
- wild horse of the U.S. plains MUSTANG
- wild or untamed horse, as used in rodeos BRONCO
- woman's riding horse in former times PALFREY

horse (combining form) HIPPO-, EQUIN-

horse-drawn vehicles See chart

horse racing See chart
- horse race across open country, or over artificial jumps STEEPLECHASE
- horse race or other contest in which the entire prize is awarded to the winner SWEEPSTAKE
- horse-race track HIPPODROME
- horse race with only one starter, which wins by walking or running over the course WALKOVER

horseman in former times, especially an armed and mounted gentleman or knight CAVALIER
- horseback rider or performer EQUESTRIAN, EQUESTRIENNE

horsemanship See chart
- relating to horsemanship or mounted troops EQUESTRIAN

horseshoe - stud on a horseshoe or shoe to prevent slipping CALK

hospital attendant ORDERLY
- hospital formerly for treating contagious diseases LAZARETTO
- hospital or clinic INFIRMARY
- hospital specializing in care for

HORSE-DRAWN VEHICLES

TWO-WHEELED	FOUR-WHEELED
buggy	**barouche**
cabriolet	**berlin**
curricle	**brougham**
désobligeante	**buckboard**
dogcart	**calash**
gig	**clarence/growler**
hansom	**Conestoga wagon**
jaunting car	**coupé**
quadriga	**diligence**
stanhope	**dos-à-dos**
sulky	**droshky**
tilbury	**fiacre**
tonga	**fly**
trap	**four-in-hand**
tumbrel	**hackney carriage**
VARYING NUMBERS OF WHEELS	**landau**
break/brake	**phaeton**
chaise	**post chaise**
dray	**surrey**
gharry	**victoria**
troika	**vis-à-vis**
	wain

HORSE-RACING AND HORSEMANSHIP TERMS

HORSE-RACING TERMS

accumulator/ parlay	cumulative bet in which winnings from one race form the stake on the next
antepost bet	bet placed at any time up to the day before a race
blind bet	bet made by bookmaker to divert attention from a favorite
double	bet on the winners of two races
each way	bet on a horse to win or be placed
forecast/ perfecta/ exacta	bet on the first and second finishers in the correct order
handicap	race in which extra weight is carried by some horses to even out the abilities of the field
lay off/ hedge	bookmaker's placing of a bet on a horse against which he has accepted many bets, to reduce his losses if the horse wins
long odds	odds offered on a horse considered unlikely to win
maiden	horse that has never won a race
nap	tipster's most fancied horse of the day
nursery stakes	race for two-year-olds
odds on	odds offered on a horse extremely likely to win
pari-mutuel	betting system, used by the tote, in which all bets are pooled and the pool is divided among the winners
place	finishing position of a horse, varying from the first two to the first four according to the total number of runners
point-to-point	cross-country race around a course marked by flags
pulling	illegal holding back of a horse by its jockey to stop it winning or doing well
ringer	horse entered in a race under the name of another, usually inferior, horse
short odds	odds offered on a horse considered to have a good chance of winning
show	be placed third, or fourth, in a handicap race with more than 16 runners
silks	jockey's cap and shirt bearing the colors of his or her horse's owner or stable
starting price	final odds offered at the start of a race
steward	racecourse official
string	group of horses belonging to one owner
ticktack	bookmakers' system of hand signals used to communicate at racecourses
totalizator/ tote	organized system of pari-mutuel betting; computer used to record bets and calculate winnings
yankee	stake adding up to 11 bets, laid on four horses each running in a different race

HORSEMANSHIP TERMS

capriole	upward jump in dressage, in which the horse kicks back its hind legs
caracole	half-turn movement in dressage
cavaletto	rail for training horses in jumping
cavesson	noseband with a lunging rein, used in training
curvet/ gambado	low prancing jump in dressage, launched from the hind legs
dressage	movements performed by a horse responding to the rider's indications
hacking	leisurely riding, usually for pleasure
hand	measure, equal to four inches, of a horse's height
haute école	stiff classical style of riding
jib/balk	shy or refuse at a jump or obstacle
levade	dressage movement in which the horse balances on its hind legs
lunging rein	long rein used for exercising and training horses
manège	training of riders and horses in dressage techniques; riding school
martingale	strap linking the bit or noseband and the girth, as used in training a horse to keep its head lowered
oxer	obstacle consisting of a hedge and rails, and sometimes a ditch
passage	high-stepping trot in dressage
piaffe	trot very slowly, in dressage, sometimes on the spot
pirouette	turn on the haunches, in dressage
puissance	show-jumping competition involving large obstacles
rack/single-foot	fast, showy walking step in dressage
tittup	prance or caper
volt	movement tracing a six-meter circle, in dressage

the dying HOSPICE
- hospital unit for the gravely ill INTENSIVE-CARE UNIT
- hospital's medical equipment and supplies ARMAMENTARIUM
- formerly, a hospital social worker or charity worker ALMONER
- place, such as a hospital office, from which medicines and medical supplies are given out DISPENSARY

hostage's tendency to help or fall in love with his or her captor STOCKHOLM SYNDROME

hostile, full of hate or spite, doing or wishing evil to others MALEVOLENT, RANCOROUS
- hostile, quarrelsome, or unruly TRUCULENT
- hostile, ready or eager to argue or fight AGGRESSIVE, COMBATIVE, BELLIGERENT, BELLICOSE
- hostile, uncompromisingly opposed IRRECONCILABLE, IMPLACABLE
- hostile or opposed to something or someone ANTAGONISTIC, INIMICAL, AVERSE, ANTIPATHETIC, OPPUGNANT
- hostile or subversive element within an organization or country at war FIFTH COLUMN
- hostile reaction, as to an apparent social threat BACKLASH
- divide into two extreme and hostile positions or groups POLARIZE
- very bitter or hostile VIRULENT
- extremely hostile, chilling GLACIAL

hostility, open opposition ANTAGONISM
- become liable or subject to something such as debts or someone's hostility INCUR
- deep hostility, intense dislike, enmity ANIMUS, ANIMOSITY
- feeling of intense hostility, dislike, or revulsion ANTIPATHY, AVERSION
- lay to rest the hostility of, win the friendship of DISARM

hot, relating to heat or hot springs THERMAL
- hot and humid, sweltering, as tropical weather can be TORRID, SULTRY, MUGGY

hot (combining form) PYRO-, THERM-, THERMO-, CALD-

hot spring THERMAL SPRING
- hot spring throwing up column of water and steam GEYSER

hotel providing water-based therapy SPA
- hotel in Spain PARADOR
- hotel or inn, with a courtyard, for groups of travelers in the East CARAVANSARY
- boarding house or small hotel, as in France PENSION
- entrance hall of a hotel or other public building LOBBY, VESTIBULE
- half board, as at a hotel DEMI-PENSION

hothouse ORANGERY

hounds' baying when pursuing game QUESTING
- hunting of game, such as hares, with hounds relying on sight rather than scent COURSING
- pack of hounds CRY

hour - adjective for an hour HORARY

house, such as a brothel, where public order or decency is violated DISORDERLY HOUSE
- house for a clergyman VICARAGE, RECTORY, MANSE
- house on a Spanish or Latin American ranch or large estate, or the estate as a whole HACIENDA
- house or hut that is run-down and dirty HOVEL
- house or lodge a soldier, especially in a civilian residence BILLET
- badly built or maintained, shaky, as an old house might be RICKETY, RAMSHACKLE, DILAPIDATED
- built in sections in advance, before its assembly, as cheap housing might be PREFABRICATED
- built shoddily and unreliably, as houses sometimes are JERRY-BUILT
- country house or farmhouse with its outbuildings GRANGE
- country house or summer villa in Russia DACHA
- Eskimo house, typically domed and made of ice IGLOO
- irregular and spread-out in design, as a large house might be SPRAWLING, RAMBLING
- repair something, such as a house REFURBISH, RENOVATE
- round house, cottage, or hut with a conical roof, in South Africa RONDAVEL

household MÉNAGE
- household gods in ancient Rome LARES, PENATES
- household implement, especially one used in the kitchen UTENSIL
- father, viewed as head of the household PATERFAMILIAS
- master and mistress of a castle, or a large household CHATELAIN, CHATELAINE
- valued household possessions LARES AND PENATES

housing - enclosure, especially in the East, for a factory, rich housing, or the like COMPOUND

howl or wail, as if lamenting ULULATE

hub of a wheel NAVE
- hub of a propeller BOSS

huge, immense, as someone's appetite might be GARGANTUAN
- huge, immense GIGANTIC, COLOSSAL, BROBDIGNAGIAN
- huge, overwhelmingly or abnormally large or imposing PRODIGIOUS, TITANIC, HERCULEAN
- huge, vast, limitless, incalculable BOUNDLESS, IMMEASURABLE
- huge animal or object LEVIATHAN, BEHEMOTH
- huge column of burning gas rising from the sun, visible during a total eclipse PROMINENCE
- huge statue, or extremely large or important person or object COLOSSUS

huge (combining form) MEGA-, MEGALO-, MACRO-

human, ape, monkey, or related mammal PRIMATE
- human being, regarded as a thinking animal HOMO SAPIENS
- human being identical to another CLONE
- human flesh as eaten by cannibals LONG PIG
- human in form or nature INCARNATE, EMBODIED, PERSONIFIED
- human in shape or appearance ANTHROPOID, ANTHROPOMORPHIC
- human of very small proportions HOMUNCULUS, MANIKIN, PYGMY
- human or humanlike extinct mammal HOMINID
- attributing of human form or behavior to gods, animals, nonliving objects, and so on ANTHROPOMORPHISM, PERSONIFICATION
- crediting of human qualities, as in poetry, to things in nature PATHETIC FALLACY
- representative, in human form, of an ideal, god, or model EMBODIMENT, INCARNATION, AVATAR
- study of or attempts at improving the human race by selective breeding EUGENICS

human (combining form) ANTHROP-, ANTHROPO-

humanitarian work or feelings, charity PHILANTHROPY

human nature - rational, orderly, and sober, as one side of human nature is, in Nietzsche's terminology APOLLONIAN
- spontaneous, irrational, passionate, and creative, as one side of human nature is, in Nietzsche's terminology DIONYSIAN, DIONYSIAC

humble See also **flatter, modest, humiliate**
- humble oneself, cringe, bow and scrape GROVEL, TRUCKLE
- humble oneself or make oneself inconspicuous EFFACE
- humbled, subdued, or restrained, as by punishment CHASTENED
- humbly asking or begging SUPPLIANT, SUPPLICANT
- very humble or respectful, as an apology might be ABJECT

- extremely humble or submissive in attitude or behavior SERVILE

humbug - full of humbug about benevolence and high moral standards SANCTIMONIOUS, PECKSNIFFIAN, PIETISTIC

humid - containing as much water vapor as possible, as humid as can be SATURATED

humidity - instrument for measuring relative humidity HYGROMETER, PSYCHROMETER

humiliate See also **insult, disgrace**
- humiliate or belittle, as by contemptuous remarks DENIGRATE, DISPARAGE, DEROGATE
- humiliated, disgraced, or dishonored DEGRADED, DEBASED
- humiliated by the puncturing of one's self-esteem or boasting, as through a rebuff or put-down DEFLATED, CHASTENED
- humiliated or ashamed, as by a failure MORTIFIED
- humiliating of oneself, as through a sense of guilt or inferiority SELF-ABASEMENT

humor See also **humors**
- humor based on the use of words or expressions that seem to have a second, typically saucy meaning DOUBLE ENTENDRE
- humor oneself or someone else by yielding to wishes INDULGE
- something used to soothe or humor someone PLACEBO

humorous See also **funny**
- humorous action or remark PLEASANTRY
- humorous but disguised so as to appear as if intended seriously TONGUE-IN-CHEEK
- humorous in a coarse, earthy, and robust way RABELAISIAN
- humorous in a dry way WRY
- humorous in a mocking or cynical way SARDONIC
- humorous or mildly sarcastic use of words to express something markedly different from or opposite to their literal sense IRONY
- keeping a straight face as a humorous person might DEADPAN

humors - character of a person, according to medieval physiology, based on the dominance of one of the four humors TEMPERAMENT
- characterized by one of the four humors in medieval physiology SANGUINE, CHOLERIC, PHLEGMATIC, MELANCHOLIC
- the four humors in medieval physiology BLOOD, YELLOW BILE (CHOLER), PHLEGM, BLACK BILE

humus forming in soil MULL

hunchback or other visible bodily defect DEFORMITY
- hunchbacked GIBBOUS

hundred (combining form) CENT-, CENTI-, HECT-, HECTO-

hundred-year-old, or a person aged 100 or more CENTENARIAN

hundredth anniversary CENTENARY, CENTENNIAL

Hungarian cavalryman HUSSAR
- Hungarian Gypsy TZIGANE
- Hungarian person or language MAGYAR
- stew of a traditional Hungarian style, seasoned with paprika GOULASH

hunger - satisfy or appease someone's hunger, longings, or the like ASSUAGE
- sharp feelings of hunger PANGS

hungry or greedy to an extreme degree RAVENOUS, VORACIOUS, INSATIABLE
- starving, in an extremely hungry state FAMISHED

hunter of dangerous animals or criminals on the offer of a reward BOUNTY HUNTER
- hunter who is extremely keen and skilled NIMROD

hunting See illustration, page 270
- hunting as an art or hobby VENERY
- hunting of game, such as hares, with hounds relying on sight rather than scent COURSING
- hunting or game preserve, privately owned but unfenced CHASE
- animal pursued in hunting, or anything pursued in a conscientious way QUARRY
- relating to hunting VENATIC
- scented bag used in hunting to lay on artificial trail DRAG
- time of year when hunting, fishing, shooting of game, or the like is permitted OPEN SEASON
- time of year when hunting, fishing, shooting of game, or the like is prohibited CLOSED SEASON

huntsman CHASSEUR
- huntsman's assistant who controls the hounds WHIPPER-IN
- huntsman's scarlet coat PINK
- call to the huntsman that a fox has been sighted VIEW HALLOO
- chief huntsman of a fox hunt MASTER OF FOXHOUNDS, MFH

hurry, nag, harass CHIVY
- hurry along the progress of something such as a business matter EXPEDITE
- hurry away or flee SKEDADDLE, SCARPER, HOTFOOT, VAMOOSE
- hurry or make a quick escape HIGHTAIL, DECAMP
- hurry the occurrence of something, bring about quickly or prematurely PRECIPITATE

hurt, distressed, or offended by an apparent injustice AGGRIEVED
- hurt or offend, cause a sympathetic or friendly person to become indifferent or hostile ALIENATE, ANTAGONIZE, ESTRANGE
- hurt someone's feelings, as by severe criticism SCARIFY

husband of a woman who has committed adultery CUCKOLD
- husband or wife of a monarch CONSORT
- custom or state of having only one husband at a time MONANDRY
- custom or state of having two husband or wives at a time BIGAMY
- custom or state of having two or more husbands at a time POLYANDRY
- custom or state of having two or more husbands or wives at a time POLYGAMY
- excessively devoted to one's wife, as an attentive husband might be UXORIOUS
- legal right to the help, company, and affection of one's husband or wife CONSORTIUM

husband (combining form) -ANDR-

hut - hutlike shelter of arched corrugated iron sheets NISSEN HUT
- hut or shack, typically crudely built and run-down SHANTY
- hut that is run-down and dirty HOVEL
- hut used by hunters, skiers, or the like LODGE

hybrid animal, from a female donkey and male horse HINNY

hydrogen isotope, with atomic mass 1 PROTIUM
- hydrogen isotope, with atomic mass 2 DEUTERIUM
- chemical removal of oxygen from a compound or adding of hydrogen to it REDUCTION

hydrogen bomb or similar extremely powerful bomb produced by the fusion of light atomic nuclei FUSION BOMB, THERMONUCLEAR BOMB

hyena, vulture, insect, or the like that feeds on dead animals, rotting meat, or other decaying organic matter SCAVENGER

hygienic, free of infection SANITARY

hymn See also **prayer**
- hymn, service, or piece of music in honor of a dead person REQUIEM
- hymn, verse, or formula praising God in the liturgy DOXOLOGY
- hymn and frenzied dance for a chorus in ancient Greece, in honor of Dionysus DITHYRAMB
- hymn of praise or adoration sung during the Communion service SANCTUS
- hymn or piece of music at the beginning of a church service, while

Evolution of Hunting Skills

Time			TOOLS	ANIMALS
PRE-STONE AGE	1 million - 4 million years ago	*Australopithecus* INDIVIDUAL HUNTING Small animals Stone throwing Clubbing with stones and sticks Stabbing with sticks Scavenging	Pebble chopper tools Pebble tools Digging sticks Stabbing sticks Clubs	Baby antelope Lizards Rodents Birds Bush baby Insects
OLD STONE AGE	1 million - 1.5 million years ago	EARLY *Homo erectus* COOPERATIVE AND INDIVIDUAL HUNTING Big game Ambush Scavenging	Chopping tools Clubs Fire-hardened wooden spears Hand axes Fire	Wolf Aurochs Horse Red deer Hare Merck's rhinoceros
	35,000-100,000 years ago	MIDDLE NEANDERTHAL MAN *Homo sapiens* COOPERATIVE AND INDIVIDUAL HUNTING Big game Ambush Stampede	Point Hide scraper Wooden spearhead Core and flint tools Handleless axes Sharp bones Wooden spears Fire	Wolf Bison Horse Ibex Reindeer Cave bear Woolly rhinoceros
	35,000-40,000 years ago	LATE CRO-MAGNON MAN *Homo sapiens sapiens* COOPERATIVE AND INDIVIDUAL HUNTING Big game Fishing Trapping Ambush Stampede Wolf domesticated for hunting	Flint blades Harpoons Bow and arrow Flint blades Spearheads in bone and ivory Harpoons Throwing sticks Fire	Bison Wild boar Aurochs Horse Red deer Eurasian elk Mammoth Fish
MIDDLE STONE AGE	8,000-11,000 years ago	PRE-AGRICULTURE MODERN MAN *Homo sapiens sapiens* DIVERSIFIED, COOPERATIVE AND INDIVIDUAL HUNTING Hunting with dogs Fishing from canoes Trapping Seashore gathering	Mattock of elk bone Bone hooks Spearhead slotted for flints Flake axes Variety of spears Fishing nets Bolas Canoes Traps Bow and arrow	Wolf Wild boar Aurochs Red deer Roe deer Seal Wildfowl Fish Shellfish

the choir and clergy are entering PROCESSIONAL
- hymn or piece of music at the end of a church service, while the choir and clergy are leaving RECESSIONAL
- hymn or psalm sung at the beginning of a service INTROIT
- hymn or psalm sung with responses, in alternating parts ANTIPHON
- hymn or religious song or poem CANTICLE
- hymn or song of praise LAUD, MAGNIFICAT
- hymn tune, as for singing or for the organ CHORALE
- medieval Latin hymn commemorating the Virgin Mary's grief at the Crucifixion STABAT MATER
- medieval Latin hymn describing the Last Judgment, used in the Mass for the dead DIES IRAE

hypnotic, dazed, or dreamlike state TRANCE

hypnotize MESMERIZE

hypochondriac, health-obsessed person VALETUDINARIAN

hypocrisy, pretending HUMBUG

hypocrite, especially a pious hypocrite WHITED SEPULCHER, PLASTER SAINT, PHARISEE

hypocritical, affecting benevolence and high moral standards SANCTIMONIOUS, PECKSNIFFIAN, PIETISTIC
- hypocritical, insincere, sly rather than forthright DISINGENUOUS
- hypocritical, insincere, or moralizing speech or writing CANT
- hypocritically self-righteous, puritanically disapproving PHARISAICAL

hypothesis or premise put forward without proof THESIS
- hypothesis meant to help find an answer or do a task WORKING HYPOTHESIS

hypothetical, assumed SUPPOSITITIOUS, CONJECTURAL, NOTIONAL

hysteria-induced symptoms of a nonpresent disease MIMESIS
- hysteria or depression, supposed in former times to be caused by gases produced within the body THE VAPORS

hysterical or overemotional in behavior MELODRAMATIC, HYSTERIFORM, HISTRIONIC

I

ice coating rock, roads, or the like in a thin film VERGLAS
- ice covering a road or path in a thin, transparent layer BLACK ICE, GLAZE ICE
- ice floating in small harmless pieces in the sea DRIFT ICE
- ice hole used by whales, seals, and so on for taking breath BLOWHOLE
- ice mass or other obstruction blocking a narrow passage GORGE
- ice masses, often jammed together, floating in polar seas PACK ICE
- ice sheet or slab floating in the sea FLOE
- breaking up of the ice on the surface of a river, often causing flooding DEBACLE
- drink, usually alcoholic, poured over crushed ice FRAPPÉ
- house built of ice, as of an Eskimo IGLOO
- mass of porous ice formed from snow, but not yet turned into glacier ice FIRN, NÉVÉ
- metal spikes or spiked plate fastened to a shoe or boot, as for mountaineering or walking across ice CRAMPONS, CLAMPER
- river of ice formed of snow and moving very slowly GLACIER
- slushy ice, as forming on the surface of the sea SLUDGE
- water ice made from fruit SORBET

ice-cream or other delicacy containing candied or fresh diced fruits TUTTI-FRUTTI
- dessert or delicacy of frozen syrup or fruit puree, resembling ice cream, water ice SORBET
- Italian ice cream of various kinds, typically containing nuts and candied fruit CASSATA, SPUMONI
- served with ice cream, as apple pie might be À LA MODE
- small brick or block of ice cream, charcoal, or other substance BRIQUETTE

ice hockey - hard rubber disc used in ice hockey PUCK
- pass of the puck in ice hockey that enables a teammate to score ASSIST

ice skating See also **skating**
- jumps of various kinds in ice skating, taking off on one skate, spinning in the air, and landing on the other skate AXEL, LUTZ, SALCHOW
- turn from one edge of one skate to the other edge of the other skate in ice skating CHOCTAW

iceberg - small iceberg, presenting a danger to shipping GROWLER

icicle - lime deposit, resembling an icicle, hanging from the roof of a cave STALACTITE

icing in thin tubelike strands squeezed through a nozzle PIPING
- icing of sweet almond paste, as on wedding cakes MARZIPAN
- coated with icing or sugar, as cherries might be GLACÉ

idea, custom, institution, or person considered unreasonably to be beyond criticism SACRED COW
- idea based on extracting the qualities from various specific things or examples GENERALIZATION, ABSTRACTION
- idea or deduction based on scanty evidence SURMISE, CONJECTURE
- idea or feeling that dominates all others OBSESSION, PREOCCUPATION, IDÉE FIXE, FIXATION
- idea or hint that is unconfirmed or still not fully formed INKLING, HUNCH, INTUITION, INTIMATION
- idea or logical invention forming part of a theory CONSTRUCT, WORKING HYPOTHESIS
- idea or opinion based on convention rather than real belief IDÉE REÇUE
- idea or proposition put forward as the basis on which an argument or theory can be built AXIOM, POSTULATE, PREMISE
- idea that derives from the collective unconscious, in Jungian psychology ARCHETYPE
- based on convention rather than belief, as an idea or practice might be RECEIVED
- develop slowly in the mind, as an idea might do GESTATE
- discussion in which thoughts are swapped or analyzed intensely as a means of solving problems or creating new ideas BRAINSTORMING
- existing only as an idea, not in reality HYPOTHETICAL, NOTIONAL
- general idea, opinion, or understanding CONCEPT, NOTION, APPREHENSION
- give a definite shape or form to something, such as an idea CRYSTALLIZE
- medium, such as a play, for conveying ideas, expressing talents, or the like VEHICLE
- mix up or confuse ideas, elements, or the like CONFOUND
- odd, fanciful, or impulsive idea or wish WHIM, CAPRICE
- odd or eccentric idea, flight of fancy VAGARY
- person or group whose reactions serve as a test for new ideas or opinions SOUNDING BOARD
- put one's ideas into words FORMULATE, ARTICULATE
- referring to an idea or concept inherent in the mind rather than learned INNATE
- separation of or difference between ideas, opinions, or the like DIVERGENCE
- similarity of ideas, opinions, or the like CONVERGENCE
- treat an idea or abstraction as a real or concrete thing REIFY
- undeveloped though promising, as an idea might be FALLOW, LATENT

idea (combining form) IDEO-

ideal, model, or original that is copied or worth copying, PROTOTYPE, ARCHETYPE, EXEMPLAR
- ideal example or typical representative of a specified virtue or vice PERSONIFICATION, EMBODIMENT, INCARNATION
- ideal or principle expressed by a word or maxim, as on a coat of arms MOTTO

idealize, exalt, treat with awe DEIFY
- idealized image formed in childhood IMAGO

idealist with impractical ambitions DON QUIXOTE

idealistic, unrealistic, and impractical, especially in wishing to reform society UTOPIAN, VISIONARY
- idealistic in an excessively romantic way, and hence impractical or absentminded QUIXOTIC
- idealistic belief in the imminent arrival of a golden age of peace MESSIANISM, MILLENARIANISM

identical See **same, equal**
- identical twins MONOZYGOTIC TWINS

- genetically identical organism or group of organisms CLONE
- person almost identical in appearance to another RINGER
- twins that are not identical FRATERNAL TWINS

identical (combining form) TAUT-, TAUTO-, SYNON-, HOMO-

identification of a disease, injury, or problem DIAGNOSIS
- close emotional identification with another EMPATHY
- system or equipment for creating a picture of a face, as for police identification, by combining drawings of features IDENTIKIT
- system or equipment for creating a picture of a face, as for police identification, by combining photographs of features PHOTOFIT

identifying sign, as of a current or former disease STIGMA

identity or social role that a person adopts, especially when in public PERSONA
- person who takes another's identity IMPERSONATOR, IMPOSTOR
- sense of rootlessness, confusion, and loss of personal identity, in the absence of a supportive community ALIENATION, ANOMIE

ideology - influence someone into accepting an ideology, belief, or point of view uncritically INDOCTRINATE, BRAINWASH

idiom, way of talking PARLANCE
- idiom of a trade, profession, or other specialized group JARGON, CANT, ARGOT, VERNACULAR

idiot See **fool, stupid**

idler, aimless loafer FLANEUR, FAINÉANT

idol worship, or strong and uncritical admiration IDOLATRY

if, *provided that*, or other conjunction introducing a supposition SUPPOSITIVE
- clause, typically beginning with *if* or *unless*, stating the condition in a conditional sentence PROTASIS, CONDITIONAL CLAUSE
- main clause in an *if* or conditional sentence APODOSIS
- proposition or premise in the *if*-part of a conditional sentence ANTECEDENT

igloo See illustration

ignorance - vast and deeply bad, as ignorance might be ABYSMAL

ignorant See also **stupid**
- ignorant, unaware UNWITTING
- ignorant, uninformed in moral or cultural matters, unenlightened BENIGHTED, NESCIENT
- ignorant of reading and writing ILLITERATE, UNLETTERED
- ignorant yet behaving as if knowledgeable ULTRACREPIDARIAN

ignore, avoid BYPASS, CIRCUMVENT
- ignore, neglect, overlook, or omit PRETERMIT
- ignore or disregard something as irrelevant or unreliable DISCOUNT
- ignore or pretend ignorance of a wrongful act, and thereby encourage it CONNIVE AT, WINK AT
- ignore or snub abruptly or disdainfully REBUFF

ill, unwell, poorly, under the weather AILING, INDISPOSED
- ill-looking, deathly pale CADAVEROUS
- chronically ill person INVALID
- person who is constantly worrying about his or her health or constantly believes to be ill HYPOCHONDRIAC, VALETUDINARIAN
- pretend to be ill, as to get off work MALINGER

ill will, bitterness, hostility ACRIMONY, ANIMOSITY, ANIMUS, RANCOR, MALEFICENCE
- ill will, feeling of resentment GRUDGE
- full of ill will, MALICIOUS, MALEVOLENT
- offensive, liable to cause ill will or resentment INVIDIOUS

illegal See **crime**
- illegal, unlawful ILLEGITIMATE, ILLICIT, UNCONSTITUTIONAL
- illegal act, especially by a public official MALFEASANCE, MALVERSATION

illegitimate, bastard MISBEGOTTEN, SPURIOUS
- heraldic sign or suggestion of illegitimate birth BAR SINISTER
- referring to an illegitimate child, or one falsely represented as the genuine heir SUPPOSITITIOUS, SUPPOSITIOUS

illicit whiskey, especially in the Southern states MOONSHINE, MOUNTAIN DEW

illiterate or uneducated UNLETTERED
- unable to deal with numbers, as different from illiterate INNUMERATE

illness See also **disease**
- illness, disease AILMENT, COMPLAINT, AFFLICTION, MALADY
- illness and its attendant weakness and failing powers INFIRMITY
- illness or fear of illness that is imaginary or self-induced HYPOCHONDRIA
- caused by the doctor or his or her treatment, as an illness might be IATROGENIC
- decline or regress after apparent-

Igloo

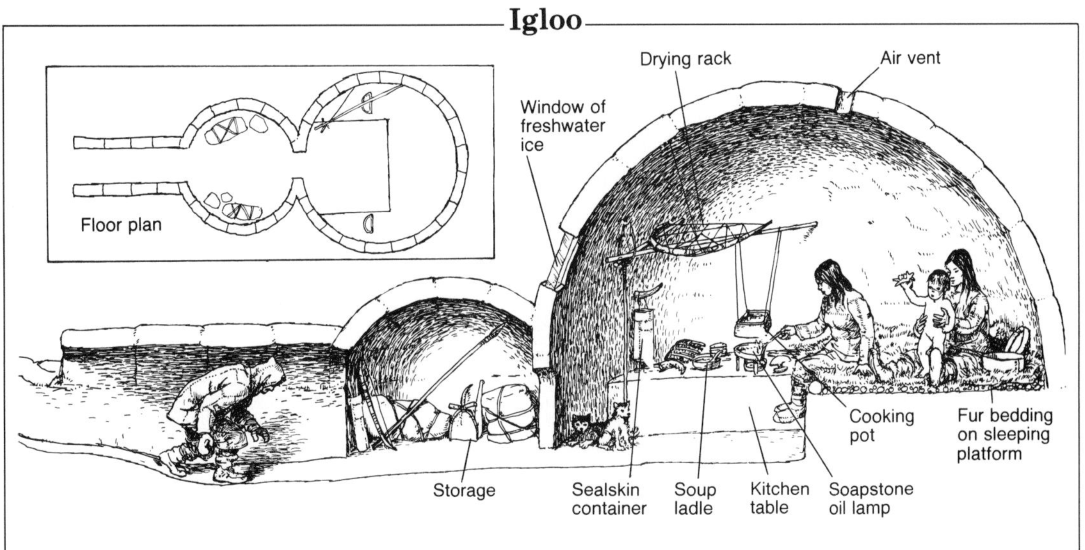

ly recovering from an illness RELAPSE
- gradual return to health after an illness, especially by resting CONVALESCENCE
- referring to illness brought on by stress or other psychological factors PSYCHOSOMATIC
- regain one's health or strength, as after an illness RECUPERATE, CONVALESCE
- sudden fit or attack of illness ICTUS

illogical, against reason IRRATIONAL
- illogical or irrelevant conclusion or statement NON SEQUITUR
- illogical reasoning or argument, though not deliberately so PARALOGISM
- illogical reasoning or argument that is knowingly invalid and deliberately misleading SOPHISM
- illogical reasoning or faulty argument that invalidates the conclusion FALLACY

illuminated title, heading, or letter, standing out from the rest of the text in a manuscript or book RUBRIC

illumination, such as a small picture or ornamental letter, in a manuscript MINIATURE

illusion, apparent object that is not real PHANTASM, HALLUCINATION
- illusion or image of an object, such as an oasis MIRAGE
- illusion produced by a disturbed mind, overactive imagination, or the like ABERRATION, CHIMERA, SPECTER

illusory image, especially mirage FATA MORGANA
- illusory or unrealistic hope or wish PIPE DREAM, FAIRY GOLD
- illusory, seemingly plentiful or lavish BARMECIDAL
- visual illusion, deceptive impression presented to the eyes OPTICAL ILLUSION

illustration See also **picture**
- illustration at the front of a book, often opposite the title page FRONTISPIECE
- illustration or diagram of a machine or structure showing its parts separately EXPLODED VIEW
- illustration or model, as of an engine or building, with part of the wall or casing omitted or cut away to reveal the interior CUTAWAY
- illustrations accompanying a text GRAPHICS

image, representation, or likeness of something, sometimes misleading or superficial SIMULACRUM
- image or opinion of someone or something that is conventional, unthinking and usually oversimplified STEREOTYPE
- image or symbol ICON
- image that is familiar and recurrent in literature TOPOS, MOTIF
- apparatus giving brief exposures of visual images, as for experiments in memory or perception TACHISTOSCOPE
- apparent image formed by reflected or refracted light rays, such as the image in a mirror VIRTUAL IMAGE
- referring to very vivid yet unreal visual images, as experienced in childhood EIDETIC

imaginary, fictitious, misleading, deceiving ILLUSORY
- imaginary fear, pure fantasy, or the like CHIMERA, SPECTER
- imaginary land of luxury and idleness COCKAIGNE
- imaginary or self-induced illness or suffering HYPOCHONDRIA
- imaginary or theoretical rather than actual NOTIONAL, HYPOTHETICAL
- imaginary or unreal thing NONENTITY, CHIMERA
- imaginary place, as in fiction, where things are worse than in real life DYSTOPIA, CACOTOPIA
- imaginary place or condition of perfect justice, ideal happiness, or the like UTOPIA, SHANGRI-LA

imagination of a lively kind, often combined with mildly eccentric behavior WHIMSY
- having foresight or great imagination VISIONARY
- inventive cleverness, showing imagination INGENUITY
- notion, fantasy, or invention, typically credited to the imagination FIGMENT
- state of being lost in thought or living briefly in one's imagination REVERIE

imagine, bring to the mind's eye CONJURE UP, FANTASIZE
- imagine, form a mental image or vision of VISUALIZE, ENVISAGE

imbalance between parts ASYMMETRY
- imbalance or instability DISEQUILIBRIUM

imitate See also **copy**
- imitate another person's voice or mannerisms in a mocking way MIME, MIMIC, APE
- imitate in order to equal or outperform EMULATE
- imitate or pass oneself off as someone else IMPERSONATE
- imitate the form, appearance, or sound of, often in order to deceive SIMULATE
- unique, impossible to imitate successfully MATCHLESS, INIMITABLE

imitation, fake, substitute, or artificial SYNTHETIC, ERSATZ, PINCHBECK, SPURIOUS
- imitation or representation of nature or human nature in literature and art MIMESIS
- imitation or representation that is crudely distorted TRAVESTY, MOCKERY, PARODY
- mocking imitation, satire, or caricature SPOOF, BURLESQUE, LAMPOON
- satirical imitation of a literary, musical, or other artistic work PARODY, PASTICHE

imitator, follower, or disciple who is markedly inferior to his or her master EPIGONE

immature, underdeveloped, basic, in an early stage RUDIMENTARY, INCHOATE
- immature, young, childish, unsophisticated JUVENILE, ADOLESCENT, PUERILE, JEJUNE
- immature early works of a composer, writer, artist, or the like JUVENILIA
- immature or inexperienced, unsophisticated CALLOW, VERDANT
- immature or inexperienced person GREENHORN

immaturity NONAGE

immediately, instantly, without hesitation or delay INSTANTANEOUSLY, FORTHWITH, INSTANTER

immigrant group's adjustment to or adoption of a dominant culture ASSIMILATION
- limited or specified quantity or number, as of imports, immigrants, or the like QUOTA
- process of immigrants' thorough asssimilation MELTING POT
- relating to a distinctive racial, religious, or cultural group, such as an immigrant group, within a society ETHNIC

immoral, corrupt, debased DEGENERATE, REPROBATE
- immoral, utterly abandoned or unprincipled, shameless DISSOLUTE, LIBERTINE, LICENTIOUS, PROFLIGATE, WANTON
- immoral and debauched man, rake, especially an aging one ROUÉ, CORINTHIAN
- immoral behavior of a base and vile kind DEPRAVITY, TURPITUDE
- immoral overindulgence in sensual pleasures DISSIPATION, INTEMPERANCE, DEBAUCHERY
- immorally luxurious place or situation BABYLON

immovable and impersonal, as inflexible bureaucracy might be MONOLITHIC

immune to attack, damage, or the like INVULNERABLE

immunize against a disease, dangerous opinion, or the like INOCULATE

immunity from consequences, such as regret or punishment IMPUNITY
- immunity from prosecution, or a period of immunity, enabling offenders to confess without fear AMNESTY
- immunity or exemption, as for foreign diplomats, from the jurisdiction of one's country of residence EXTRATERRITORIALITY
- blood protein produced to counteract germs or other invading substances, and so promote immunity against infection ANTIBODY
- noncongenital, life-threatening lack of the body's immunity system ACQUIRED IMMUNE-DEFICIENCY SYNDROME, AIDS

impatient, fidgety, on edge, behaving badly RESTIVE
- impatient or restless, as to go traveling FOOTLOOSE
- impatient with curiosity AGOG

imperfect or unsatisfactory item that is thrown out REJECT, DISCARD

impersonal and immovable, as an inflexible bureaucracy might be MONOLITHIC

imply, involve, have as a necessary consequence ENTAIL
- imply slyly INSINUATE
- implied, unspoken, understood, as an informal agreement might be TACIT

import duty TARIFF
- limited or specified quantity or number, as of imports QUOTA

importance in rank or status, relative greatness MAGNITUDE
- increase in power, importance, or the like AGGRANDIZEMENT
- play down, minimize the importance of SOFT-PEDAL
- right of priority, first choice, or the like, as by virtue of greater importance or urgency PRECEDENCE

important, extremely significant, as historic discovery might be EARTHSHAKING, EPOCH-MAKING, EPOCHAL, MOMENTOUS, MONUMENTAL
- important, influential, high-ranking CONSEQUENTIAL, CONSIDERABLE, PROMINENT, EXALTED, FORMIDABLE, REDOUBTABLE
- important and genuine, as some issues of concern are SUBSTANTIVE
- important and wealthy man NABOB, MAGNATE, GRANDEE, MAGNIFICO
- important for long-term policy STRATEGIC
- important or high-ranking person DIGNITARY, NAME TO CONJURE WITH, EMINENCE, VIP
- important person or personality, leading light CELEBRITY, WORTHY, LUMINARY
- extremely important, crucial, vital PIVOTAL, CARDINAL, SEMINAL, SIGNAL
- extremely important, urgently essential IMPERATIVE
- extremely large or important person or thing COLOSSUS
- having important and far-reaching consequences FATEFUL, MOMENTOUS, PORTENTOUS
- most important, more necessary or urgent than anything else PARAMOUNT, OVERRIDING
- most important or common, basic or customary STAPLE
- most important or striking, as the main point of a talk is SALIENT
- most important or powerful, leading, foremost PREDOMINANT, PREPONDERANT
- most important part, core or essence ALPHA AND OMEGA
- most important work of scholarship or literature MAGNUM OPUS

impose or collect a tax, fine, membership fee, or the like LEVY

impractical, excessively idealistic or romantic QUIXOTIC
- impractical and absentminded, daydreaming OTHERWORLDLY
- impractical and idealistic, especially in wishing to reform society radically UTOPIAN, VISIONARY
- impractical idealist, romantic dreamer DON QUIXOTE
- impractically committed to a theory, dogmatic DOCTRINAIRE

impregnate or fertilize FECUNDATE
- impregnate with semen INSEMINATE

impression, suspicion, hint INKLING, INTIMATION, HUNCH, INTUITION
- impression or overall view of a series of historical events, the future, or the like VISTA
- person who shows off in an attempt to make an impression on others POSEUR
- unforgettable or enduring, as an impression might be INDELIBLE

impressive, respected FORMIDABLE, REDOUBTABLE
- impressive and complete display, defense, or the like PANOPLY
- impressive and dignified, commanding or elegant STATELY, LOFTY, BARONIAL

imprison, jail INCARCERATE
- imprison, shut up within walls IMMURE
- imprison or detain, especially in wartime INTERN

imprisonment DURANCE, CONFINEMENT, DURESS
- imprisonment and forced labor PENAL SERVITUDE
- imprisonment or temporary custody DETENTION
- document in former times under a sovereign's seal, typically authorizing imprisonment without trial LETTRE DE CACHET
- legal writ for release from unlawful imprisonment HABEAS CORPUS

improper or distasteful UNSEEMLY, UNBECOMING, INDECOROUS, INDELICATE
- improper usage, especially in grammar or etiquette SOLECISM

improve, become or make better AMELIORATE, MELIORATE, AMEND
- improve, make reparation, or atone for REDRESS, MAKE AMENDS, MAKE RESTITUTION
- improve, reform, revitalize or restore RECLAIM, REGENERATE, REHABILITATE
- improve as much as possible OPTIMIZE
- improve by a spectacular change of appearance, attitude, or the like TRANSFORM, TRANSFIGURE
- improve by cleaning or repairing, restore to good condition RENOVATE, REFURBISH, REVAMP
- improve in health after an illness RECUPERATE, CONVALESCE
- improve or enliven a story by adding colorful, often false, details EMBELLISH, EMBROIDER, GARNISH
- improve or increase the value or quality of ENHANCE
- improve the appearance of, usually deceptively GILD, GLOSS
- improvement, instruction, or enlightenment, especially when morally uplifting EDIFICATION

improving, correcting, beneficial, as advice might be SALUTARY

improvised, makeshift, temporary EXTEMPORANEOUS
- improvised, unrehearsed, off-the-cuff, as a speech might be IMPROMPTU, EXTEMPORE

imprudent, ill-advised or incautious, as a rash remark might be INJUDICIOUS, INDISCREET, IMPOLITIC

impudent See **cheeky**

impulsive See **rash, reckless**

impure blemished MACULATE
- impure, tainted, CONTAMINATED, POLLUTED, DEFILED
- add impurities to a substance, such as milk or wine ADULTERATE

in (combining form) END-, ENDO-, ENTO-, INTRA-, INTRO-

in accordance with PURSUANT TO

in bad faith MALA FIDE

in confidence, just between us ENTRE NOUS

in consequence of PURSUANT TO

in fact, in reality, actually DE FACTO

in front, at the head ANTERIOR

in front (combining form) PROS-

in front of (combining form)

ANTE-, PRE-
in itself, as such PER SE
in labor, about to give birth PARTURIENT
in love ENAMORED
- passionately in love in an intense but often immature or superficial way INFATUATED, BESOTTED
in memory of, as used in epitaphs IN MEMORIAM
in name only, not actual NOMINAL
in order, proper, acceptable KOSHER
- in order, all right HUNKY-DORY
- in order, working OPERATIONAL, OPERATIVE, FUNCTIONAL
in passing, by the way EN PASSANT
in person, live IN PROPRIA PERSONA
in proportion PRO RATA
in relation to, regarding, compared with VIS-À-VIS
in suspense, anxious, tense, nervous ON TENTERHOOKS
in the act RED-HANDED, IN FLAGRANTE DELICTO
in the red OVERDRAWN
in the same place, used as a footnote formula IBIDEM, IBID.
in the way, unwanted SUPERFLUOUS, DE TROP
in two minds, having conflicting feelings or views AMBIVALENT
in vain, useless, futile UNAVAILING, TO NO AVAIL, BOOTLESS
inability to carry out some duty or task INCAPACITY
inactive, chemically unreactive, as some elements are INERT
- inactive, unlikely to erupt, as a volcano might be EXTINCT
- inactive, sluggish TORPID, LETHARGIC
- inactive but capable of being aroused LATENT, DORMANT
- inactive or dormant, as a disease might be QUIESCENT
- temporarily inactive IN ABEYANCE
inactivity, depression, or boredom DOLDRUMS, ENNUI
inadequate, See **mediocre**
- inadequate, scanty, sparse or skimpy MEAGER, JEJUNE, LENTEN, EXIGUOUS
inanimate, without human understanding or feelings, as a block of wood is INSENSATE, INSENSIBLE
inappropriate, inconvenient, unsuitable, or badly timed INOPPORTUNE, UNSEASONABLE, UNTIMELY
- inappropriate, out of place, as a saucy joke might be INAPPOSITE, MALAPROPOS, INDECOROUS
- inappropriate, strange, out of place INCONGRUOUS
- inappropriate, unsuitable, or unbecoming, as a rash remark might be UNTOWARD, INFELICITOUS
inattentive, absentminded, or distracted DISTRAIT
inborn INNATE
Inca wind instrument, egg-shaped OCARINA
incarnation or embodiment of an idea, model, or god AVATAR
incense container, especially one that is swung at festivals CENSER, THURIBLE
- resin used in incense FRANKINCENSE, OLIBANUM
- stick of perfumed substance, burned as incense JOSS STICK
incessant See **constant**
incidental, added in a secondary or helping role rather than essential AUXILIARY, ANCILLARY, ADJUNCT, ADSCITITIOUS
- incidental, not intended or inherent ADVENTITIOUS, CONTINGENT, FORTUITOUS
- incidental, not relevant MARGINAL, PERIPHERAL, TANGENTIAL
- incidental, of secondary importance, serving a subordinate function ACCESSORY, SUPPLEMENTARY, SUBSIDIARY, ANCILLARY
- incidental remark, comment made in passing OBITER DICTUM
- something that is incidental to something else CONTINGENCY
incidentally, by the way EN PASSANT, PARENTHETICALLY, APROPOS
incite, entice, or lure, especially into a sinful or illegal act SOLICIT, SUBORN, SEDUCE
- secret agent who joins a political or criminal group and tries to incite it into punishable or discrediting activities AGENT PROVOCATEUR
inciter (combining form) -AGOGUE, -MONGER
inclination See **tendency**
include, contain, consist of COMPRISE
- include, take in EMBRACE, COMPREHEND, SUBSUME
- include or contain INCORPORATE, EMBODY, EMBED, ENCOMPASS
- including many things, aspects, or examples OMNIBUS, COMPENDIOUS
income, as from a bequest or trust, or the source of it ENDOWMENT
- income, especially that of a government REVENUE
- income level that is the minimum for providing the necessities of life SUBSISTENCE LEVEL
- income or standard of living that is adequate but modest SUFFICIENCY, COMPETENCE
- income remaining for use after taxes have been deducted, net income DISPOSABLE INCOME
- income remaining for use after the necessities have been taken care of DISCRETIONARY INCOME
incompatible, as two people or ideas might be IRRECONCILABLE
- incompatible, jarring INCONGRUOUS, DISCORDANT, DISSONANT
incompetence - principle that people tend to get promoted until they reach a position in which they are incompetent PETER PRINCIPLE
incomplete or insufficient DEFICIENT
incomprehensible or inscrutable UNFATHOMABLE
inconsistency or disagreement, as in results, claims, or reports DISCREPANCY, VARIANCE, DISPARITY
inconsistent or apparently self-contradictory phrase, such as *joyous grief*, used as a figure of speech OXYMORON
- inconsistent or apparently self-contradictory statement, often used for effect PARADOX
- inconsistent or clashing, jarring or divergent DISSONANT, DISCORDANT, INCONGRUOUS
- inconsistent or conflicting, as two opposed logical propositions might be INCOMPATIBLE, IRRECONCILABLE
inconspicuous, attracting little attention LOW-PROFILE, UNOBTRUSIVE, UNOSTENTATIOUS
inconvenience, disturb INCOMMODE
inconvenient, inappropriate, or badly timed INOPPORTUNE, UNSEASONABLE, UNTIMELY
incorrect See also **mistake**
- incorrect, making or based on a mistake ERRONEOUS
- incorrect, out of proper order, off course, off beam ADRIFT, AMISS, AWRY
- incorrect conclusion, faulty argument, or invalid reasoning, especially when unintended PARALOGISM
- incorrect idea or misleading opinion, based on misinformation or faulty reasoning FALLACY
- incorrect interpretation or explanation, misunderstanding MISCONSTRUCTION
- incorrect opinion or faulty understanding MISCONCEPTION, MISAPPREHENSION
- incorrect or illogical though plausible, as an argument might be SPECIOUS, SOPHISTIC
- incorrect or inappropriate name MISNOMER
- incorrect use of a word, such as *flaunt* in a context requiring *flout* CATACHRESIS
- incorrect use of words, grammatical error SOLECISM
- prove a statement of argument incorrect REFUTE, REBUT, CONFUTE
- word used incorrectly in place of one that is similar in sound or spelling MALAPROPISM
incorrect (combining form) CACO-, MAL- MIS-

increase, as capital does by the addition of interest ACCRUE
- increase, extend, enlarge, expand AMPLIFY, AUGMENT, WAX
- increase as much as possible MAXIMIZE
- increase dramatically, as an animal population might in favorable conditions IRRUPT
- increase greatly or intensify energetically one's efforts REDOUBLE
- increase in intensity or scope, as a war or quarrel might ESCALATE, FLARE UP, INFLAME, SPIRAL
- increase in loudness, as of a passage of music CRESCENDO
- increase in size, swell, expand DILATE, INFLATE, DISTEND
- increase or addition, as to one's salary INCREMENT
- increase or growth, as of public feeling or opinion GROUNDSWELL
- increase or spread, as by reproduction PROPAGATION
- increase or spread rapidly PROLIFERATE, BURGEON
- increase or stimulate, as one's appetite WHET
- increase suddenly, as electric current might SURGE
- increase the intensity or severity of a pain, problem, or the like AGGRAVATE, EXACERBATE
- increase the power, influence, or reputation of ENHANCE, ELEVATE, EXALT, AGGRANDIZE
- increase the time or length of, extend PROTRACT
- increase through slow additions ACCUMULATION, ACCRETION
- increasing or mounting by a series of steps or additions CUMULATIVE

incurable, beyond remedy, hopeless IRREDEEMABLE
- incurable optimist MICAWBER, POLLYANNA

indecent See also **rude**
- indecent, outrageously indelicate or rude SCABROUS

indecisive, hesitant, lacking in confidence or commitment FALTERING
- indecisive, in two minds AMBIVALENT
- indecisive, uncertain, in two minds WAVERING, VACILLATING

indefinable but distinctive characteristic JE NE SAIS QUOI

indefinitely, without a date being set for resumption SINE DIE

indentation See **groove, notch**

indented space or hollow, niche, as set back from the main surface of a wall RECESS, ALCOVE

independence, self-government SOVEREIGNTY, AUTONOMY

independent, existing or functioning in its own right rather than as subordinate to something else SUBSTANTIVE
- independent, self-governing, or self-sufficient AUTONOMOUS, SOVEREIGN
- independent-minded politician MUGWUMP
- independent-minded or unorthodox thinker or group member, individualist MAVERICK
- independent of the order of the terms, as an operation such as multiplication is COMMUTATIVE

indescribable, unspeakable INEFFABLE

index in which the keyword is listed with its context KWIC INDEX
- index of all the words in a text, such as the Bible or the works of Shakespeare, listing every occurrence of each word CONCORDANCE

Indian terms See chart, page 278, and also charts at **Hinduism, menu, clothes, American Indian terms**

indicate, point out DESIGNATE, SPECIFY, PARTICULARIZE
- indicate, reveal, disclose MANIFEST, EVINCE, EVIDENCE
- indicate, signify, signal, mean DENOTE, BESPEAK, BETOKEN
- indicate, show, exhibit REGISTER
- indicate or signal the approach of something HERALD, HARBINGER, PRESAGE

indication, sign, token INDEX
- indication or evidence of a disease, social condition, or the like SYMPTOM, SIGN
- indication or evidence that one possesses a specified quality PATENT

indifferent, lukewarm, especially in politics or religion LAODICEAN
- indifferent, unexcitable, not caring greatly NONCHALANT, INSOUCIANT

indigestion DYSPEPSIA
- buildup of gas in the digestive tract, or the feeling of indigestion caused by it FLATULENCE

indirect, evasive, not straightforward OBLIQUE, ABSTRUSE
- indirect, roundabout expression CIRCUMLOCUTION, PERIPHRASIS
- indirect or roundabout route or road DETOUR
- indirect or secondhand, as pleasure is when gained through someone else's achievements or actions VICARIOUS

indispensable or essential thing or condition SINE QUA NON

indisputable, undeniable, certain, as an overwhelmingly powerful argument or evidence would be INCONTROVERTIBLE, IRREFUTABLE

individual, definite, particular, explicit SPECIFIC
- individual, unconnected, separate, distinct DISCRETE, DIVERSE
- individual born singly rather than as a twin or in a litter SINGLETON
- individual detail PARTICULAR
- individual speech pattern of a person IDIOLECT
- relating to or arising from the individual self or mind rather than observable external reality SUBJECTIVE

individual (combining form) IDIO-

individually, singly, in the order stated RESPECTIVELY

inducing contractions to bring on childbirth, as some drugs are OXYTOCIC

indulge one's lust, appetites, or the like to the full SATE, SATIATE
- indulge oneself in pleasures, extravagant emotions, or the like LUXURIATE, REVEL, WALLOW
- indulge or yield to a whim, desire, or the like GRATIFY

indulgence in sensual or immoral pursuits DISSIPATION, INTEMPERANCE, DEBAUCHERY, DEPRAVITY, DISSOLUTENESS

indulgent or excessive act, as of violence, drinking, or crime ORGY, RAMPAGE, FRENZY

industrial diamond BORT
- industrial exhibition EXPOSITION, EXPO
- industrial workers or the working class generally PROLETARIAT
- industrial worker, such as a welder or riveter, in heavy industries such as shipbuilding and the like BOILERMAKER

industrial dispute - deliberate disruption of normal functioning, as in a factory during an industrial dispute SABOTAGE
- harrassment of employers by the workers in industrial disputes in India GHERAO
- settlement of an industrial dispute by negotiating through a third party CONCILIATION, MEDIATION
- settlement of an industrial dispute by submitting to the judgment of a third party ARBITRATION, ADJUDICATION

industrialist or businessman of great power and influence MAGNATE, TYCOON

industrious, painstaking, persevering SEDULOUS, ASSIDUOUS, DILIGENT

industry - modernize an industry, process, or the like, and make it more efficient RATIONALIZE
- return a nationalized industry to private ownership DENATIONALIZE,

INDIAN TERMS

ahimsa	doctrine of nonviolence toward all living creatures	**nizam**	title of the rulers of the former state of Hyderabad
beedi	hand-rolled cigarette, typically a single rolled leaf tied with thread	**pan**	leaf of the betel palm; preparation of this leaf with betel nuts and lime for chewing
bhishti	water-carrier in former times	**punka**	ceiling fan made of a cloth or palm leaf
chapati/roti/ nan/puri/ paratha	flat bread of various kinds	**purdah**	curtain concealing women from public view, or the social system requiring this
charka	spinning wheel	**raga**	conventional music pattern forming the basis of a composition of interpretation
charpoy	light bedstead	**raj**	dominion/sovereignty
crore	ten million	**rajah/ maharajah**	prince, chief, or ruler
dacoit	member of an armed robber band	**rani/maharani**	wife of a rajah, princess in her own right
dak	mail or post	**sahib**	form of address, as formerly used to colonial Europeans, equivalent to *sir* or *master*
dak bungalow	house providing accommodation for travelers	**satyagraha**	Gandhi's policy of nonviolent resistance to British rule
dhobi/dhobi-wallah	man who washes clothes	**sepoy**	Indian soldier serving under the British in India
dooly	stretcher or litter for carrying a person or goods	**shikaree**	hunter, or guide for big-game hunters
durbar	state reception; reception hall of an Indian prince	**sitar/vina/ tamboura/sarod**	stringed musical instruments of various kinds
gharry	small horse-drawn carriage	**syce**	stableman or groom
ghat	mountain pass; flight of steps down to a river	**tabla**	pair of small drums
ghee	clarified butter, as from buffalo milk, used in Indian cooking	**tiffin**	light lunch or snack
lakh	hundred thousand, especially when referring to rupees	**tonga**	light, two-wheeled horse-drawn vehicle
mahout	keeper and driver of an elephant	**wallah**	a person who does a particular type of work, such as a dhobi-wallah
maidan	open space in or near a town, used for sports or displays		
nautch	dance performed by girls		
nawab/nabob	governor of a province or state of the Mogul Empire		

PRIVATIZE

ineffective or powerless as a result of counterbalancing NEUTRALIZED
- make ineffective or invalid an argument, contract, or the like NULLIFY, INVALIDATE, VITIATE, VOID

inequality (combining form) ANISO-

inescapable, inevitable INELUCTABLE

inessential, suitable for throwing away if necessary EXPENDABLE
- inessential, supplementary, not inherent EXTRANEOUS, EXTRINSIC

inevitable, not to be eluded or escaped INELUCTABLE

inexperienced or immature, unsophisticated CALLOW, UNFLEDGED, VERDANT
- inexperienced person, relative newcomer, beginner ROOKIE, TENDERFOOT, NOVICE, GREENHORN, TYRO, NEOPHYTE

infallible judgment or utterance ORACLE

infamous, well-known for a particular and usually unfavorable quality NOTORIOUS

infection - blood protein produced to counteract germs or other invading substances, and so promote immunity against infection ANTIBODY
- development or spread of infection, or of an infectious disease ZYMOSIS
- main site of an infection FOCUS, NIDUS

infectious, as a disease might be COMMUNICABLE, TRANSMITTED, TRANSMISSIBLE
- infectious, extremely harmful, or very rapid in effect, as a disease or poison might be VIRULENT
- infectious, spreading disease PESTIFEROUS, PESTILENT
- spread by physical contact, as an infectious disease might be CONTAGIOUS

infer or guess with only scanty evi-

dence to go on SURMISE, CONJECTURE
- infer or work out from given evidence DEDUCE, EXTRAPOLATE

inference of general truths from particular instances, as distinct from strict logical deduction INDUCTION

inferior (combining form) INFRA-, SUB-

infidel - a Christian or other non-Muslim regarded as an infidel by a Muslim GIAOUR
- a non-Jew regarded as an infidel by a Jew GOY
- a non-Jew regarded as an infidel by a Jew, or a Jew or other non-Mormon regarded as an infidel by a Mormon GENTILE

infidelity - man who tolerates his wife's infidelities WITTOL

inflammation - reducing inflammation, as a drug might be ANTIPHLOGISTIC
- relating to inflammation and fever PHLOGISTIC

inflammation (combining form) -ITIS

inflation in which an increase in demand or in money supply causes prices to rise DEMAND-PULL INFLATION
- inflation in which wage increases and other increased production costs cause prices to rise COST-PUSH INFLATION
- means of protection, as against inflation HEDGE
- official price index issued each month, used as a guide to inflation RETAIL PRICE INDEX

inflexibility, unadaptability PERSEVERATION

influence, drive, or force VECTOR
- influence, motivation, encouragement INCENTIVE, INCITEMENT, STIMULUS
- influence, power of affecting others' decisions or behavior, pulling strings, LEVERAGE, MANIPULATION, CLOUT
- influence, serve as evidence, or affect MILITATE
- influence, such as a moral principle, that determines an action or decision SANCTION
- influence or urge legislators to adopt a certain policy LOBBY
- influence someone into accepting something uncritically, as by biased education INDOCTRINATE, BRAINWASH
- influenced, guided, or driven by some motive or force ACTUATED, IMPELLED, INSTIGATED
- easily influenced, readily affected, prone to something SUSCEPTIBLE
- easily led, persuaded, or influenced, cooperative FLEXIBLE, DUCTILE, TRACTABLE, MALLEABLE, PLIABLE, BIDDABLE, DOCILE
- leading position of power, influence, or control DOMINANCE, PREEMINENCE, ASCENDANCY
- magnetic personal charm and power of influence or inspiration CHARISMA
- person exerting or trying to exert a sinister influence over another's will SVENGALI

influential and powerful person, typically a rich industrialist MAGNATE, TYCOON
- influential but unofficial group of advisers to a head of government or other leader KITCHEN CABINET
- influential or inspiring person LUMINARY
- influential person wielding power behind the scenes ÉMINENCE GRISE

inform against or accuse DENOUNCE
- inform or advise someone of something, keep someone posted NOTIFY, ALERT, ACQUAINT, APPRISE, FAMILIARIZE

informal See also **casual**
- informal, conversational, characteristic of casual spoken language COLLOQUIAL
- informally, casually EN FAMILLE

information, news, reports INTELLIGENCE, TIDINGS
- information, often dubious, spread publicly to further a cause PROPAGANDA
- information added at the end of a book, message, or the like AFTERTHOUGHT, POSTSCRIPT, APPENDIX
- information from other people HEARSAY
- information in response to an inquiry, experiment, program, or the like FEEDBACK
- information or mental stimulation, usually of a dull and pointless kind PABULUM
- information or news as communicated informally LOWDOWN, SCOOP
- information store, as for a computer DATA BASE
- announcement of some new information, item of news REVELATION, DISCLOSURE
- exchange or central distribution point for banking transactions, commodities, information, or the like CLEARING HOUSE
- file or collection of papers giving information on a particular person or subject DOSSIER
- gather information or knowledge bit by bit GLEAN
- official announcement of information for public attention COMMUNIQUÉ, BULLETIN
- reveal or relate information IMPART, DIVULGE
- secret, as official information might be CLASSIFIED
- study of information flow and control systems in electronics, mechanics, and biology CYBERNETICS
- supply someone with background information BRIEF, PRIME

informed, conscious, having knowledge COGNIZANT

informer, decoy, or police spy STOOL PIGEON, STOOLIE

-ing - verb form functioning as a noun, ending in *-ing* in English, as in *They enjoy sailing* GERUND
- verb form used as an adjective or in indicating various tenses, typically ending in *-ing* or *-ed* in English, as in *She was running* or *an invented expression* PARTICIPLE

inhabit or occupy a place TENANT

inhabitant of a place going back to the earliest times ABORIGINAL, AUTOCHTHON
- inhabitant or resident of a place or region DENIZEN

inhabiting (combining form) -COLOUS

inherent in the very structure of the economy, society, or the like, as unemployment might be STRUCTURAL

inheritance, or the right to it or sequence of it, of a title, property, throne, or the like SUCCESSION
- inheritance from one's father or ancestor PATRIMONY
- inheritance or heirship shared by two or more beneficiaries PARCENARY, COPARCENARY
- inheritance or legacy BEQUEST
- laws of inheritance in genetics MENDEL'S LAWS
- legal limitation on the inheritance or use of an estate, interest, or the like to a specific person or persons TAIL
- limit the inheritance of property to a particular line of heirs ENTAIL
- owned through or passing down by inheritance HEREDITARY
- right of the eldest son to inherit the entire estate, the kingship, or the like PRIMOGENITURE
- right to or expectation of an inheritance REVERSION
- theory, opposed by orthodox genetics, that acquired characteristics can be inherited LAMARCKISM, LYSENKOISM

inherited, as some diseases are GENETIC, HEREDITARY
- inherited article of value, kept within a family HEIRLOOM
- inherited traditions, customs, or the like HERITAGE

inhuman, without truly human understanding or feelings INSENSATE, INSENSIBLE

initial letter - repeated occurrence of a letter or sound, especially the initial letter, in writing or speech ALLITERATION
initials - design, often of one's initials, as for an emblem MONOGRAM
initiation ceremony or similar ritual marking a change of status in a person's life RITE OF PASSAGE
- initiation into or first experience of a painful ordeal, especially on the battlefield BAPTISM OF FIRE
- initiation or introduction, as into a ritual or profession INDUCTION
initiative, enterprise, pluck GUMPTION
- initiative or step, as in diplomatic matters DEMARCHE
inject heroin or other drugs directly into a vein MAINLINE
injection - adjective for an injection made just beneath the skin SUBCUTANEOUS, HYPODERMIC
- injection of blood, plasma, or the like into the bloodstream TRANSFUSION
- injection of liquid into the rectum for medication or purging the bowels ENEMA, COLONIC, CLYSTER
- injection of vaccine following the main dose to increase or sustain its effectiveness BOOSTER
- administration of a medicine by slow injection INFUSION
- given or taken by injection rather than by mouth, as a medical drug might be PARENTERAL
- in or into a vein, as an injection might be INTRAVENOUS
- puncturing of a vein, as in injecting medicine VENIPUNCTURE
- small glass bottle, especially a sealed one containing liquid for injections AMPOULE, AMPUL
injure or wound very severely, causing serious disfigurement or disability MAIM, MUTILATE
- injured or seriously weakened or disabled INCAPACITATED
- anger arising from being injured or wronged GRIEVANCE
injury, wound, or harm LESION, TRAUMA
- injury or destruction of a wanton or widespread kind MAYHEM
- injury or wound, as caused by an accident or surgery TRAUMA
- injury to the neck, caused by a sudden jerk WHIPLASH
- susceptible to danger, injury, or attack VULNERABLE
injustice resulting from inconsistencies, bias, or unfairness, as in a law INEQUITY
- injustice or supposed injustice GRIEVANCE
- outrageous or glaringly wrong, as an injustice might be FLAGRANT
ink that cannot be washed off or erased INDELIBLE INK
- dark brown ink or pigment originally obtained from the inky secretion of the cuttlefish SEPIA
inkblot test, personality test based on the subject's interpretations of various abstract inkblot designs RORSCHACH TEST
inland, without access to the sea, as some countries are LANDLOCKED
- inland region HINTERLAND
inlay, pave, or decorate with a mosaic of tiny tiles TESSELLATE
- inlay or etch metal with wavy decorative patterns DAMASCENE, DAMASK
- inlaid furniture decoration, or an item of furniture so decorated BOULLE, BUHL
- inlaid woodwork, as used in decorating furniture MARQUETRY
inn or hostel in Eastern countries, typically built around a large courtyard, for groups of travelers CARAVANSARY, KHAN
- inn or pub HOSTELRY
- inn or shelter for the needy or travelers HOSPICE
- inn keeper VICTUALLER
- servant caring for guests' horses at an inn HOSTLER, OSTLER
innocent, unsophisticated, simple NAIVE, ARTLESS, GUILELESS, INGENUOUS
- innocent and naive young woman INGENUE
- clear of blame, declare innocent EXONERATE, EXCULPATE
- person, typically innocent, who is involved in an incident merely by being present BYSTANDER
Inquisition - burning of a heretic at the stake, as ordered by the Inquisition AUTO-DA-FÉ
inquisitive person, busybody or gossip QUIDNUNC
insane See also **mad**
- prove someone to be insane and therefore not legally responsible or liable STULTIFY
insanity See **madness**
inscription or title LEGEND
- scroll-shaped ornamental tablet sometimes bearing an inscription CARTOUCHE
inscriptions - study of ancient inscriptions EPIGRAPHY
insect See illustration
- insect-eating, feeding on insects INSECTIVOROUS, ENTOMOPHAGOUS
- insect-eating plant having juglike leaves that attract and trap the insects PITCHER PLANT
- insect-eating plant trapping its prey between hinged leaf blades VENUS'S-FLYTRAP
- insect excrement FRASS
- insect in the adult stage IMAGO
- insect in the nonmobile stage between larva and adult PUPA, CHRYSALIS
- insect larva, as of the mayfly or dragonfly, that develops directly into the adult rather than going through the pupal stage NYMPH
- insect larva of the mayfly or similar insect, living in water NAIAD
- insect of a kind found in hot countries, producing a high-pitched droning sound CICADA
- insect of a kind that feeds on plant juices, often causing serious damage to grape crops PHYLLOXERA
- insect of a kind that feeds on plant juices, often being a serious garden pest APHID
- insect or other organism that transmits germs VECTOR, CARRIER
- insect that rests in a "praying"

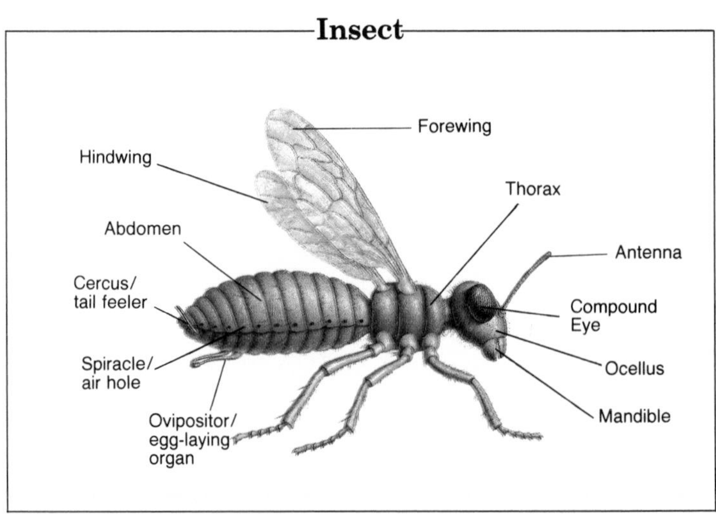

position MANTIS
- insects, spiders, lobsters, and other animals having jointed limbs, a horny shell, and a segmented body ARTHROPODS
- air bubble surrounding some water-dwelling insects PLASTRON
- back or upper surface of a body segment, as of an insect or lobster TERGUM
- fear of insects ENTOMOPHOBIA
- fumigation chamber for killing insects or fungi FUMATORIUM
- headlike part at the end of an insect's antenna CAPITULUM
- lotion or other substance that keeps insects away REPELLENT
- nest of an insect NIDUS
- projecting or secondary part of a plant or lower animal, such as an insect's leg or feeler APPENDAGE
- shed skin of an insect CAST, CASTING
- sting or egg-laying tube of an insect ACULEUS
- student of insects ENTOMOLOGIST
- study of insects ENTOMOLOGY
- transformation of an insect's structure and properties METAMORPHOSIS
- tubelike feeding structure on some insects PROBOSCIS

insect (combining form) ENTOMO-

insecure, risky, or unstable PRECARIOUS
- insecure, susceptible to danger, injury, or attack VULNERABLE

inseparable, part and parcel, forming an essential part of the whole INTEGRAL, INTRINSIC, INHERENT
- inseparably linked, connected closely and in many complex ways INEXTRICABLY LINKED

insert or introduce between other elements, layers, or the like INTERCALATE, INTERPOLATE, INTERPOSE

inside, existing within as an essence or force IMMANENT, IMPLICIT, INHERENT, INTRINSIC

inside (combining form) END-, ENDO-, ENTO-, INTRA-

inside out or upside down INVERTED
- turn a body part or organ inside out EVAGINATE, EVERT

insight INTUITION
- insightful remark or observation APERÇU

insignificant, worthless, trifling NUGATORY, PALTRY
- insignificant person or thing NONENTITY

insincere, hypocritical, or moralizing speech or writing CANT
- insincere, pretended claims to have certain feelings or beliefs HYPOCRISY
- insincere, not candid, pretending to be ignorant DISINGENUOUS
- insincere person adapting his or her actions and opinions to those currently accepted OPPORTUNIST, TIMESERVER, TEMPORIZER, VICAR OF BRAY
- effortless or fluent, as in speaking or writing, but typically shallow and insincere GLIB, PAT, FACILE
- insincerely or overearnestly charming, or flattering, fawning UNCTUOUS, INGRATIATING

insistent, assertive, or pushy in manner STRIDENT, IMPORTUNATE

inspect See **examine, study, test**

inspection of the structural state of a building, as to establish its value SURVEY
- preliminary inspection of a region, as to assess the terrain or study enemy positions RECONNAISSANCE, RECONNOITER

inspiration, especially a poetic impulse AFFLATUS
- magnetic personal charm and power of influence or inspiration CHARISMA

inspire with ideas, principles, or the like IMBUE, PERMEATE, PERVADE
- inspired new idea or discovery TROUVAILLE
- inspiring or ringing, as a call to action might be CLARION

instability, constant change FLUX
- instability or imbalance DISEQUILIBRIUM

install or introduce, especially

INSURANCE TERMS

actuary	statistician whose calculations of risk are the basis of insurance premiums
annuity	fixed annual payment in return for a lump sum, or premiums over a number of years
comprehensive	providing wide-ranging insurance cover, especially for a motor vehicle
endorsement	amendment to a policy
endowment policy	life-insurance policy that matures on the death of the insured or at a set date, whichever is the earlier
loading	extra charge or payment on top of a premium to cover special risks or expenses
maturity	time at which the proceeds of a policy are due to be paid
moral hazard	risk to the insurer resulting from the possible dishonesty or carelessness of the insured
mortality table	table used by insurers to calculate risk, showing life expectancies and death rates of people of varying age and status
personal liability	risk of a person causing death, injury, or loss to other persons by his or her action
pluvious insurance	insurance against bad weather taken out by organizers of outdoor events
reversion	sum of money paid on the death of the holder of a life-insurance policy
surrender value	value of a policy when it is discontinued voluntarily before its maturity
term insurance	insurance for a specified period only, and without surrender value
third party	providing cover against liability for accidents to other people or their property
tontine	insurance scheme in which a member's shares or benefits pass to the other members when he or she dies or defaults
underwriter	company or agent that accepts part of an insurance risk

through a formal procedure INDUCT, INVEST, INAUGURATE, INSTATE

installments - pay off a debt or mortgage by installments AMORTIZE

instant, moment, very short period of time TRICE

instead of IN LIEU OF

instinct for self-destruction, death wish in Freudian theory THANATOS
- instinct for self-preservation and pleasure, life instinct and sexual drive in Freudian theory EROS
- channel or transform a sexual or other instinctual impulse into a socially or culturally more acceptable activity SUBLIMATE
- instinctive drive to achieve, in human or animal behavior MOTIVATION
- instinctive knowledge INTUITION
- instinctive or intuitive, as a gut feeling is, rather than rational VISCERAL
- emotional and mental energy and sexual drive derived from the basic life instinct in Freudian theory LIBIDO

institution, custom, idea, or person considered unreasonably to be beyond criticism SACRED COW
- member of the supervisory board of an institution TRUSTEE
- someone confined in an institution, such as a mental hospital or a prison INMATE

instruction See also **order**
- instruction, enlightenment, or improvement, especially when morally uplifting EDIFICATION
- instruction by question and answer, especially on the basic principles of Christianity CATECHISM, CATECHESIS
- instruction or teaching TUITION

instrument See **laboratory, measuring instrument, medical, percussion, wind instruments, electronics, string instruments, tool,** and chart at **keyboard instruments**

insufficient or incomplete, lacking a necessary quality DEFICIENT

insulation, coating, or facing material on the outside of a building, pipe, tank, or the like CLADDING, LAGGING
- insulation or seedbed material in the form of lightweight fragments of mica-derived material VERMICULITE
- rubbery latex substance used in electrical insulation and dentistry GUTTA-PERCHA

insult, address in a rude and contemptuous way ABUSE, REVILE, BLACKGUARD
- insult, taunt, scoff at, sneer at, or despise FLEER, TWIT, FLOUT

Internal-Combustion Engine

OVERHEAD-VALVE (OHV) ENGINE

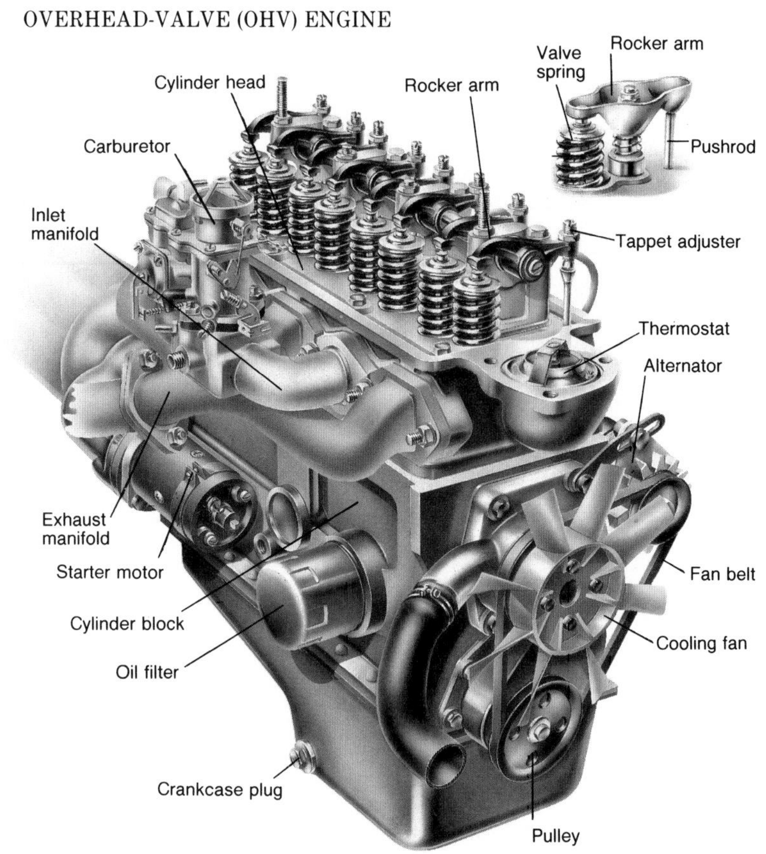

- insult, tease, or ridicule repeatedly, torment BAIT
- insult, typically in the form of a false charge, that injures someone's reputation LIBEL, SMEAR, SLANDER, DEFAMATION, CALUMNY, ASPERSION, SLUR, CHARACTER ASSASSINATION
- insult in a slanderous way, describe or accuse in a false and demeaning way MALIGN, CALUMNIATE, VILIFY, TRADUCE, STIGMATIZE
- insult or contempt directed at God, religion, or anything sacred BLASPHEMY, PROFANITY, SACRILEGE
- insult or criticize with passionate scorn, curse heartily, DENOUNCE, EXECRATE, ANATHEMATIZE, VITUPERATE, INVEIGH AGAINST
- insult or slander someone in his or her absence BACKBITE
- insult to someone's dignity or authority, overstepping the mark LÈSE MAJESTÉ
- insulting, rude, or contemptuous behavior or remark CONTUMELY
- insulting in a deliberate way, intended to offend or belittle DEROGATORY, DISPARAGING
- insulting language, abuse or obscenities BILLINGSGATE
- insulting or offensive statement or act OUTRAGE
- insultingly haughty or contemptuous DISDAINFUL, SUPERCILIOUS
- abusive in a personal way, as an insult of an opponent might be AD HOMINEM
- criticize in an insulting or diminishing way, belittle and despise DENIGRATE, DISPARAGE, DERIDE, DECRY, DEPRECIATE, DEROGATE, VILIPEND, CONTEMN
- disgrace or disrepute after being subjected to insult and abuse OBLOQUY, IGNOMINY
- offend someone, as by a direct insult or rebuff AFFRONT
- offend someone, as by an unintended insult PIQUE
- passionate criticism, accusation, or insulting curse INVECTIVE, DENUNCIATION, VITUPERATION
- resentment, offense, feeling of anger at some supposed insult

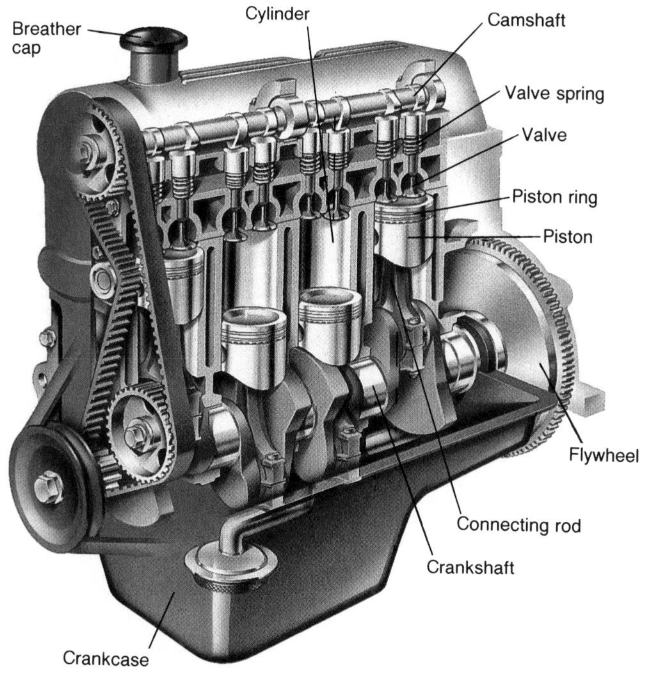

UMBRAGE

insurance See chart, page 281

insure against loss or legal responsibility INDEMNIFY, UNDERWRITE

integrity - challenge or attack someone's honor or integrity IMPEACH, DISCREDIT

intellectual or artistic people regarded as a social class INTELLIGENTSIA
- intellectual or bookish people LITERATI
- intellectual or cultured HIGHBROW
- intellectual or cultivated person, sage, especially if old or conservative MANDARIN
- intellectual or scholarly woman, especially an austere and unappealing one BLUESTOCKING
- intellectual rather than emotional and instinctual CEREBRAL, APOLLONIAN
- gathering of or reception for intellectuals, celebrities, or the like SALON

intended, planned PROJECTED, CONTEMPLATED, PURPOSED
- intended or certain, as if planned by fate DESTINED, PREDESTINED

intense, passionate, or emphatic as a denial might be VEHEMENT

intention, aim, goal OBJECTIVE
- intention, purpose, or motive ANIMUS, IMPULSION
- intention or goal, or the fulfillment of it CONSUMMATION
- intention or purpose that is concealed, especially so as to deceive ULTERIOR MOTIVE, HIDDEN AGENDA, ARRIÈRE-PENSÉE
- test, sample, or probe opinions or intentions SOUND

interchange, exchange, give or take mutually RECIPROCATE

interest greatly, fascinate, rivet the attention of OBSESS, INTRIGUE, PREOCCUPY, HAUNT
- interest in or concern for social institutions, economic policies, or the like that one derives personal benefit from VESTED INTEREST
- interest of an all-absorbing kind FIXATION, IDÉE FIXE
- interest paid on both the principal and the accumulating interest COMPOUND INTEREST, CUMULATIVE INTEREST
- increase, as capital does by the addition of interest ACCRUE
- lowest rate of interest on bank loans PRIME RATE
- play at some pursuit, take a casual interest in something DABBLE
- similarity, as of people's interests COMMUNITY
- wide-ranging, all-embracing, liberal and broad-minded, as one's interests might be CATHOLIC

interested by and deeply engaged in an activity, to the point of losing contact with one's surroundings ABSORBED, IMMERSED, ENGROSSED, INTENT, RAPT, PREOCCUPIED

interesting, colorful, or thought-provoking CHALLENGING, ROUSING, STIMULATING
- interesting or attractive in a slightly disturbing or provocative way PIQUANT, TANTALIZING
- extremely interesting, gripping the attention, as through suspense or cleverness ENTHRALLING, RIVETING, SPELLBINDING, MESMERIZING, COMPELLING, ARRESTING
- extremely interesting and very appealing, as through charm or attractiveness BEWITCHING, CAPTIVATING, BEGUILING, ENTRANCING, ENCHANTING, ENGAGING

interfere, as in a nation's internal affairs or the free economic market INTERVENE
- interfere, participate or meddle inappropriately, as in a conversation INTRUDE

interfering, overattentive, excessively eager to help or advise OFFICIOUS, SOLICITOUS
- interfering person or intruder INTERLOPER
- warning against touching or interfering NOLI ME TANGERE

interference, unwanted electric signals producing random noise in a radio or a speckled television picture STATIC
- interference in a legal action by someone not directly involved in it MAINTENANCE

intermediate course of action, factor, or the like when there are supposed to be only two TERTIUM QUID
- intermediate place or condition, such as an unsatisfactory state of waiting LIMBO

intermittent, irregular, occasional, periodic SPORADIC, FITFUL, EPISODIC, SPASMODIC

internal in origin, as a body organ might be ENDOGENOUS
- internal or inside, existing within as an essence or force IMPLICIT, IM-

MANENT, INHERENT, INTRINSIC
- internal to a given institution, as a private inquiry or training course might be INTRAMURAL
internal-combustion engine See illustration, pages 282–283, and also **jet engine, engine**
internal organs See **intestines, digestion, entrails**
international agreement, such as a peace agreement PACT, TREATY
- international conference of top officials SUMMIT
- international language of the sea, used by naval and maritime officers for communication, based on simple English SEASPEAK
- international artificial languages of various kinds, based typically on common roots from several European languages ESPERANTO, IDO, INTERGLOSSA, INTERLINGUA, NOVIAL, VOLAPÜK
- international negotiation aimed at gaining an advantage, by pressing a dispute toward a crisis without backing down BRINKMANSHIP
- international or multicultural, as a city might be COSMOPOLITAN
- international relations, or skill in conducting them DIPLOMACY
interpret in a reasonable or apparently reasonable way, often to suit one's convenience RATIONALIZE
- interpret or clarify a code, obscure text, mystery, or the like DECIPHER, DECRYPT
- interpret or explain EXPOUND, ELUCIDATE, CONSTRUE
interpretation, as of the Scriptures, with a mystical emphasis, identifying spiritual symbols ANAGOGE, ANAGOGY
- interpretation or analysis of a literary work, philosophical theory, or the like EXPLICATION, EXPOSITION
- interpretation or critical analysis of a text, especially of the Bible EXEGESIS
- interpretation or explanation of a statement or action CONSTRUCTION
- interpretation or explanation that is convenient but often misleading GLOSS
- open to two or more interpretations AMBIGUOUS
- permitting or admitting of something, such as an interpretation SUSCEPTIBLE
- study or methods of interpretation, especially of the Bible HERMENEUTICS
interpreter, person who explains a theory, cause, or the like EXPONENT
- interpreter or guide in the Middle East in former times DRAGOMAN
interrupt, hinder, or throw into disorder DISRUPT
- interrupt, seize, or stop something, such as a message, in its course INTERCEPT
- interrupt at regular intervals PUNCTUATE
- interrupt by throwing in a comment INTERJECT, INTERPOSE
- interrupt or disturb the peace, someone's privacy, or the like VIOLATE
- interrupt some intended course of action SUPERVENE, INTERVENE
- interrupt with jeering or critical comments HECKLE
interruption, hindrance to concentration DISTRACTION
interval, intervening period or event INTERLUDE
- interval, pause, temporary stop INTERMISSION
- interval, time between two periods or events INTERIM
- interval of peace or inactivity LULL, RESPITE
- interval or discontinuity between two successive reigns or governments INTERREGNUM
- interval or interval performance in a theater, such as a short play or dance INTERMEZZO, ENTR'ACTE
- referring to an interval in music that is decreased by a semitone DIMINISHED
- referring to an interval in music that is increased by a semitone AUGMENTED
intervention by an intermediary between disputing people or groups MEDIATION, INTERCESSION, CONCILIATION
intestines See also **digestion, entrails**
- intestines, or the internal organs generally VISCERA, ENTRAILS
- intestines, usually of a pig, prepared as a food CHITTERLINGS
- intestinal pains GRIPES, COLIC
- milky fluid formed in the small intestine during digestion CHYLE
- muscular contractions in the intestine or similar tubelike organ that force the contents onward PERISTALSIS, VERMICULATION
- sac or pouch formed in the weakened wall of a hollow body part, especially the intestines DIVERTICULUM
- tiny hairlike projection, as on moss or in the small intestine VILLUS
intestine (combining form) ENTER-, ENTERO-
into (combining form) INTRO-
intolerable, unbearable, unendurable INSUFFERABLE, INSUPPORTABLE
intolerant and prejudiced person, fanatic BIGOT, ZEALOT
- intolerant toward or discriminating against outsiders SECTARIAN
intrigue or plot, or group of plotters CONSPIRACY, CABAL
- devious or complicated, as intrigue often is LABYRINTHINE, BYZANTINE
introduce See also **begin**
- introduce or begin something new, in an inventive way INNOVATE
- introduce or gain acceptance for gradually or cunningly INSINUATE
- introduce or insert between other elements, layers, or the like INTERCALATE, INTERPOSE, INTERPOLATE
- introduce or install, especially through a formal procedure INDUCT, INVEST
- introduce or precede something, or signal its approach HERALD, INAUGURATE, USHER IN, HARBINGER, PRESAGE
- introduce someone into participation in an activity or to new knowledge INITIATE
introduction of themes, intentions, or the like, as in an argument or artistic work EXPOSITION
- introduction or heading LEMMA
- introduction or prior event, period, or the like PRELUDE
- introduction to a book, speech, or the like PREFACE, FOREWORD, PROLOGUE, PROEM
- introduction to a scholarly text or more detailed study PROLEGOMENON, PROLUSION
- introductory, preliminary, or preparing for something to come PREPARATORY, PRECURSORY, PREFATORY
- introductory course to a new setting, as for novice university students FAMILIARIZATION, ORIENTATION, INDUCTION
- introductory event, entertainment, or the like, as before the main sports match or play CURTAIN RAISER
- introductory or explanatory commentary or instructions RUBRIC
- introductory part of a classical drama PROTASIS
- introductory piece of music to an opera, play, or the like OVERTURE
- introductory statement or explanation, as to a formal document, treatise, or speech EXORDIUM, PREAMBLE
introductory (combining form) FORE-, PRO-, PRE-
intrude on someone's property, privacy, or rights TRESPASS, INFRINGE
- intruder or interfering person INTERLOPER
intuition - alleged perception by means of a sixth sense, supernatural powers, intuition, or the like ESP, EXTRASENSORY PERCEPTION, CRYP-

TESTHESIA

invader in search of loot MARAUDER, PLUNDERER, PILLAGER

invalid, chronically weak and sickly person, especially a hypochondriac VALETUDINARIAN

- invalid, inauthentic, false SPURIOUS
- invalid, inoperative, or powerless, as a disregarded law or regulation is NUGATORY
- make invalid, useless or ineffective, deprive of force NULLIFY

invasion of people or things INFLUX

invent or develop something, such as a new machine or technique EVOLVE, PIONEER

- invent or make up a story, deception, or the like FABRICATE, CONCOCT
- invent or produce something using available resources IMPROVISE
- invent or plan DEVISE, CONTRIVE, EXCOGITATE, ORIGINATE

invention or something new INNOVATION

- inventor's right to the exclusive use and development of his or her invention, or the document granting such a right PATENT
- share of the proceeds paid to an inventor for the use or development of his or her invention ROYALTY

inventiveness, imagination INGENUITY

inversion of left and right, as in an image seen in a mirror LATERAL INVERSION

investigate, probe SOUND

investigation of a formal or official kind, as into the cause of a death INQUEST, INQUIRY

investigator or questioner, especially one appointed to root out supposed evil INQUISITOR

investment company buying a variety of shares and selling publicly the units from the combined portfolio MUTUAL FUND

- investment in a government stock GILT, GILT-EDGED SECURITY
- investment of a risky but potentially very profitable kind SPECULATION
- investments and other assets, in a detailed list PORTFOLIO
- investments in the form of stocks, shares, or bonds SECURITIES
- person whose income is derived chiefly from rents or investments RENTIER

invisible, impossible to see IMPERCEPTIBLE, INDISCERNIBLE

- invisible radiation with a wavelength between those of light and microwaves INFRARED
- invisible radiation with a wavelength between those of light and X-rays ULTRAVIOLET

invitation or offer OVERTURE

invite or approach a potential customer, as a prostitute might IMPORTUNE, SOLICIT, ACCOST

- invite someone in return RECIPROCATE

involuntary, automatic, unstudied, unrehearsed SPONTANEOUS

- involuntary, mechanical, or unconscious, as sneezes, knee jerks, or similar responses are REFLEX

involve, imply, have as a necessary consequence ENTAIL

involved, as in a robbery IMPLICATED

IRISH TERMS

acushla	"O pulse (of my heart)": a term of endearment
banshee	female spirit whose wailing warns of an impending death
céad míle fáilte	"a hundred thousand welcomes"
ceilidh	social gathering
colleen	girl, young woman
coronach	Gaelic funeral dirge
Gaeltacht	region where Gaelic is usually spoken
Garda	the police force
gombeen-man	village moneylender
gossoon	young lad
leprechaun	mischievous elf
machree/ mochree	"my heart": a term of endearment
mavourneen	"my darling"
pishogue	witchcraft or black magic
poteen	illicitly distilled whiskey
shebeen	illegal drinking house
shillelagh	club or cudgel
spalpeen	rascal or young lad

- involved, entangled ENMESHED
- involved in an argument, scandal, or the like EMBROILED

inward-moving or inward-growing CENTRIPETAL

- inward-tending, especially toward the brain or spinal cord, as some nerves are AFFERENT
- inward-positioning of the front wheels in relation to the rear wheels, to improve steering TOE-IN
- having feet that turn inward PIGEON-TOED

inward (combining form) INTRO-

ion with a negative charge ANION

- ion with a positive charge CATION

IOU, certificate or voucher acknowledging a debt DEBENTURE

- IOU note, a written promise to pay a specified sum on a specified date or else on demand PROMISSORY NOTE
- IOU or bond guaranteeing the repayment of a debt after the death of a person whose heir the debtor is POST-OBIT

Iran - garment of a long cloth, usually black, worn by some Muslim women, especially in Iran, to cover the head and shoulders and part of the face CHADOR

- religious leader of the highest rank among Shiite Muslims, as in Iran AYATOLLAH

Ireland See chart

- adjective for Ireland MILESIAN, GAELIC, HIBERNIAN
- Irish accent BROGUE
- Irish Gaelic, the Celtic language of Ireland ERSE
- Irish person, especially an Irish speaker GAEL
- national emblem of Ireland, a clover or similar plant with compound leaves of three leaflets SHAMROCK
- poetic name for Ireland HIBERNIA
- supporter of the republican cause in Northern Ireland FENIAN

iris, especially a white-flowered variety FLEUR-DE-LIS

- iris with a fragrant rootstock ORRIS

iron or steel sheet, as for roofing, folded into a series of parallel ridges and furrows CORRUGATED IRON

- iron ore PYRITE, HEMATITE, MAGNETITE, LIMONITE
- bundle or load of scrap iron, or the iron box holding it FAGOT
- coat or rustproof iron with zinc GALVANIZE
- containing iron salts, or tasting of iron, as some waters are CHALYBEATE
- crude iron cast in oblong blocks PIG IRON

ISLAMIC TERMS

Allah	God, Supreme Being
ayatollah	Shiite religious leader
azan	summons to prayer, made by the muezzin five times daily
begum	Muslim princess or lady of high rank, especially in India
cadi	judge, intepreting the Muslim law
calender	member of a wandering mystical sect, as in Turkey and India, supported by charity
dervish	member of various ascetic Muslim orders, some of which perform whirling dances to attain ecstasy
emir	Muslim prince, chieftain, governor, or head of state
ghazi	Muslim warrior fighting against infidels in former times
giaour	infidel, non-Muslim, especially a Christian, and especially as formerly referred to by the Turks
hafiz	Muslim who knows the Koran by heart
hajj	pilgrimage to Mecca, undertaken as a religious duty
hajji	person who has made the hajj
hakim	ruler, governor, or judge
halal	killing animals in accordance with Muslim law; meat from such animals
Hegira	the Muslim era, dating from AD 622; Muhammad's flight from Mecca to Medina in that year
houri	nymph or virgin attending the blessed in paradise
ihram	white robes worn by pilgrims to Mecca
imam	prayer leader in a mosque; scholar or legal expert; ruler, caliph
Imam	Shiite leader considered to be a divinely appointed successor of Muhammad
Ismaili	small Shiite sect, led by the Aga Khan; member of this sect
jihad	holy war or crusade, waged as a religious duty
Juma	Islamic Sabbath, falling on Friday
Kaaba	shrine in Mecca, the goal of Muslim pilgrimage, toward which Muslims turn in praying
Koran/ Alcoran/ Qur'an	Muslim sacred book, containing Allah's revelations to Muhammad
Mahdi	Muslim messiah, and a leader claiming to be the messiah
marabout	Muslim holy man in North Africa, or a shrine marking his grave
mihrab/qibla	niche in the wall of a mosque, indicating the direction of Mecca toward which the faithful pray
minaret	tall slender tower of a mosque, from which the faithful are summoned to prayer
moolvi	title of respect, especially in India, for a Muslim scholar, teacher, or legal authority
mosque/masjid	house of worship
muezzin	official who summons the faithful to prayer at five fixed times every day, from the minaret or door of the mosque
mufti	expert in and adviser on the laws of the Koran; community leader during the Ottoman Empire
mullah	scholar or teacher of holy law
Ramadan	holy month, during which the faithful fast from dawn to dusk; the fast itself
sherif/sharif	title of respect for a Muslim ruler; governor of Mecca; person claiming descent from Muhammad
Shiite/Shiah	member of the smaller of the two main branches of Islam, believing in a line of succession of spiritual authority from Muhammad's cousin and son-in-law Ali
Sufi	member of a mystical Muslim sect, associated chiefly with Iran
Sunni/Sunnite	member of the larger of the two main branches of Islam, stressing the authority of traditional Islamic law
sura	chapter of the Koran
ulema	group of religious scholars or leaders, or a member of this group
Wahhabi	member of a puritanical sect, observing strictly the wording of the Koran, based mainly in Saudi Arabia

- made by hammering or shaping with tools rather than by casting, as iron railings might be WROUGHT
- press pleats or ridges into material, especially with a heated iron GOFFER
- relating to or containing iron FERRIC, FERROUS
- undersurface of an iron that presses the cloth or clothes SOLEPLATE

iron (combining form) FERR-, FERRI-, FERRO-, SIDER-, SIDERO-

ironic in tone, meant humorously, not seriously TONGUE-IN-CHEEK
- ironic or joking at the wrong time or in an inappropriate way FACETIOUS
- ironic use of a word in a very different sense from its usual one ANTIPHRASIS
- bitingly or cruelly ironic SARCASTIC, CAUSTIC, MORDANT
- ironically mocking or disdainful SARDONIC
- ironically or drily humorous WRY

ironsmith who made spurs and bits for horses LORIMER

irrational, distorted or dreamlike in a bizarre way SURREAL
- irrational, uncontrollable fear or hatred of something specified PHOBIA
- irrational and habitual, compulsive, as an inveterate liar might be PATHOLOGICAL
- irrational or extreme devotion, excessive enthusiasm FANATICISM
- relating to irrational, mystical, or supernatural experience TRANSCENDENTAL

irregular, departing from the normal or expected DEVIANT, ABERRANT, ANOMALOUS
- irregular, discontinuous, occasional, periodic INTERMITTENT, SPORADIC, FITFUL, EPISODIC, SPASMODIC
- irregular, inconsistent, or unconventional ERRATIC, ECCENTRIC
- irregular, unsystematic, rambling, as a conversation might be DESULTORY
- irregular in design, unbalanced ASYMMETRICAL
- rough-edged, having an irregular or indented surface, jagged SERRATED, CORRUGATED
- irregularly spread out STRAGGLY

irregularity, abnormality ANOMALY, ABERRATION

irrelevant, not of central importance, nonessential MARGINAL, PERIPHERAL, TANGENTIAL, INCIDENTAL
- irrelevant, unimportant, inapplicable IMMATERIAL, IMPERTINENT, EXTRANEOUS

irreligious or extremely disrespectful treatment of something sacred or considered sacred SACRILEGE

irresponsible, dangerously unthinking IMPETUOUS, IMPULSIVE, HARUM-SCARUM, RECKLESS

irreversible, impossible to change or take back, as a decision might be IRREVOCABLE

ITALIAN TERMS

aggiornamento	modernization
al fresco/ alfresco	in the open air
arrivederci	good-bye
autostrada	turnpike
carabiniere	policeman
che sarà sarà	what will be, will be
ciao	informal greeting or good-bye
cicerone	guide who shows visitors round a place
cognoscente	connoisseur
condottieri	mercenary soldiers
dolce far niente	enjoyable idleness
gran turismo	high performance touring car
la dolce vita	the good life
opera buffa	comic opera
padrone	proprietor of an inn or restaurant
palazzo	mansion or palace
piazza	public square; courtyard with a colonnade
prima donna	leading female singer in an opera; temperamental performer
sotto voce	in an undertone
trattoria	restaurant

irrigation device, as along the Nile, consisting of a bucket on a counterweighted pivoted pole SHADOOF
- irrigation device consisting of a wheel rimmed with buckets that dip into a stream or pool NORIA

irritable, easily angered, peevish TETCHY, CHOLERIC, BILIOUS, FRACTIOUS, DYSPEPTIC
- irritable, ill-tempered, easily provoked SPLENETIC, CANTANKEROUS, IRASCIBLE, ATRABILIOUS
- irritable, surly, or gloomy CURMUDGEONLY, QUERULOUS
- irritable or fussy behavior FANTOD
- irritability, harsh temper ASPERITY
- unreasonably irritable, snappish, PETULANT

irritate See also **anger, angry**
- irritate persistently, badger, HECTOR, HARASS, HARRY, BAIT
- irritated in a snobbish way HOITY-TOITY
- irritating, annoying IRKSOME, VEXATIOUS, PESTIFEROUS, GALLING
- irritating person, pest, nuisance GADFLY
- cause irritation or bitterness over a long period of time FESTER, RANKLE

Islam See chart, and also **clothes**

island - adjective for an island INSULAR
- group of islands, or sea containing such groups ARCHIPELAGO
- ring of coral islands enclosing a lagoon ATOLL
- small low island, typically of coral and sand CAY, KEY
- small rocky island, as off the coast of Scotland SKERRY

-isms See **philosophy**

isolated, scattered, or occasional SPORADIC
- isolated, withdrawn into seclusion SEQUESTERED

isolation, remoteness, or aloneness SOLITUDE
- isolation of a sick or possibly sick person or animal to prevent the spread of disease QUARANTINE

Israel - political movement to establish or consolidate Israel as the Jewish national state ZIONISM

Israeli communal farm KIBBUTZ
- Israeli cooperative settlement, consisting of a group of small farms MOSHAV
- native-born Israeli SABRA

Israelites' tent or sanctuary for the Ark of the Covenant during the Exodus TABERNACLE

issue or originate from a source EMANATE
- genuine and important, as some issues of concern are SUBSTANTIVE
- in honor of the memory of a per-

son or event, as an issue of stamps might be COMMEMORATIVE

Italian See chart, page 287, and also **pasta** and chart at **menu**
- Italian dialect spoken in Florence TUSCAN

itch to write CACOËTHES SCRIBENDI
- itching of the skin PRURITUS
- itching or stinging sensation, typically accompanied by weals on the skin URTICATION
- itching sensation, as though ants were crawling over one's skin FORMICATION

item, individual detail PARTICULAR

ivory - carved or engraved articles of ivory, whalebone, or the like SCRIMSHAW

J

jacket See **clothes**
jade, the less valuable variety, as distinct from jadeite NEPHRITE
jagged, as a coastline might be INDENTED
jail See **prison, imprison**
jailer, prison guard WARDER, WARDEN
- jailer who keeps the keys to an old-style prison TURNKEY
jam - gel-forming substance found in ripe fruit and used as a setting agent in jams PECTIN
Jamaican Creole PATOIS
Japanese See chart, page 290, and also chart at **menu**
- Japanese, Chinese, or person from any of various other East Asian countries ORIENTAL
- Japanese name for Japan NIPPON
- Japanese or Chinese figurine, usually in a grotesque, crouched position MAGOT
jar lined inside and out with tin foil, forming an early type of storage device for an electrical charge LEYDEN JAR
- jar or urn used in ancient Egypt for holding a mummy's entrails CANOPIC JAR
- jar with two handles and a narrow neck, used for wine or oil in ancient Greece and Rome AMPHORA
- large earthenware jar or pot with a wide mouth OLLA
- small ceramic jar formerly used for ointments or medicines GALLIPOT
jargon, specialized language of a group CANT, PATOIS, ARGOT
jarring, inconsistent, discordant INCONGRUOUS
jaundice ICTERUS
- liver disease producing jaundice HEPATITIS
- yellow compound in the bile, causing the yellowish skin in jaundice sufferers BILIRUBIN
Java - orchestra, as in Java, based on chimes and other percussion instruments GAMELAN
jaw, lower jaw, or either part of a beak MANDIBLE
- jaw or cheek of a pig, used as food CHAP
- jaw that is squarish and jutting LANTERN JAW
- jaws, as of a shark or lion MAW
- jaws, or fleshy flaps under the jaw JOWLS
- adjective for the jaw GNATHIC
- corner point on either side of the lower jaw GONION
- having a jutting jaw or jaws PROGNATHOUS
- having correctly positioned jaws ORTHOGNATHOUS
- paralysis of the jaw muscles LOCKJAW, TETANUS, TRISMUS
- referring to a lower jaw that projects beyond the upper jaw UNDERHUNG, UNDERSHOT
- referring to an upper jaw that projects too far beyond the lower jaw OVERSHOT
jaw (combining form) GNATH-, -GNATHOUS
jazz based on a traditional New Orleans style, but with more regular melody and rhythm DIXIELAND
- jazz group or other small group of musicians COMBO
- jazz of an early style, involving energetic improvisations BARRELHOUSE
- jazz player or fan HEPCAT
jealously defensive or possessive TERRITORIAL
jeer at, harass and interrupt a public speaker or performer with repeated critical comments or questions HECKLE
Jehovah - set of four Hebrew letters, corresponding to YHWH and often said to stand for Jehovah or Yahweh, representing one of God's names in the Old Testament TETRAGRAMMATON
jelly-covered fish or meat dish, served cold GALANTINE
- jelly made from meat or fish stock, used as a garnish or mold ASPIC
- jellylike and thick VISCOUS, GELATINOUS
- becoming liquid when stirred or shaken, as emulsion paint and some other jellylike substances are THIXOTROPIC
jellyfish MEDUSA, MEDUSOID
- jellyfishlike sea creature with long stinging tentacles PORTUGUESE MAN-OF-WAR
jerk - move in a jolting way, jerk along JOUNCE, LURCH
- shake up and down, jerk about JIGGLE, JOGGLE
- uncontrollable muscular jerks or spasms CONVULSIONS, PAROXYSM, SEIZURES
jerky, happening in fits and starts, periodic, occasional INTERMITTENT, SPORADIC, SPASMODIC, FITFUL, EPISODIC
- jerky or hesitant, as uncertain speech is HALTING
jester's cap COXCOMB, COCKSCOMB
- jester's multicolored clothing MOTLEY
- jester's scepter, in the form of a stick with a carved head BAUBLE
Jesus See also **Christ**
- Jesus's birth, or a painting, play, or any other representation of it NATIVITY
- Jesus's name or title, as assigned at various times and places THE NAZARENE, PASCHAL LAMB, SACRED HEART, THE REDEEMER, GREAT PHYSICIAN
- Jesus's route from Pilate's judgment hall to the hill of Calvary VIA DOLOROSA
- Jesus's sayings that do not appear in the Gospels AGRAPHA
- Jesus's sufferings before and during the Crucifixion PASSION
- family tree showing Jesus's ancestry JESSE TREE
- image of Jesus's face, as on a cloth or badge VERONICA
- picture or sculpture of Jesus wearing the crown of thorns ECCE HOMO
- Semitic language that was spoken by Jesus ARAMAIC
- sores or marks corresponding to the locations of Jesus's crucifixion wounds, developing spontaneously as a hysterical or conversion reaction or, supposedly, in saintly persons STIGMATA
- tableau, as at Christmas, of Jesus's Nativity CRÈCHE, CRIB
- taking down of Jesus from the cross, or a painting or sculpture of this DEPOSITION
jet engine See illustration, page 291, and also **engine**
- device in a jet engine for burning unburned gas to provide extra power AFTERBURNER
- widening duct in a wind tunnel or

jet engine that slows down the flow DIFFUSER

jetty jutting into the sea to control erosion, direct a current, or the like GROIN, SPUR, BREAKWATER

- jetty or breakwater of stone, protecting a harbor MOLE

Jew See also chart at **Judaism**

- Jew converted nominally to Christianity in medieval Spain or Portugal MARRANO, CONVERSO
- Jew in Biblical times, such as Samson, committed by vows to a life of austerity NAZIRITE
- adjective for Jews or Jewish culture JUDAIC
- among Jews, a person who is not a Jew GENTILE, GOY
- homeland of the Jews, symbolic of Jewish aspirations ZION
- hostile toward or prejudiced against Jews ANTI-SEMITIC
- in Nazi doctrine, a Caucasian, especially Nordic, person of non-Jewish descent ARYAN
- Jewish books, art objects, and the like JUDAICA
- mass killing of Jews by the Nazis THE HOLOCAUST
- massacre, typically organized in former times with official backing, as of Jews in Eastern Europe POGROM
- quarter in European cities inhabited by Jews in former times GHETTO
- temple of the Jews in ancient times TABERNACLE

Jew, Jewish (combining form) JUDEO-

jeweler's eyepiece or magnifying glass LOUPE

- jewelers' weighing system for

JAPANESE TERMS

aikido	martial art, similar to judo
Ainu	aboriginal inhabitant of northern Japan
banzai	"10,000 years," battle cry, or greeting to the emperor
bonsai	cultivation of miniature trees
bunraku	traditional puppet theater
bushido	Samurai code of ethics
daimyo	prince or noble
futon	padded mattress laid on the floor, used as a bed
geisha	young woman trained as a professional entertainer and companion for men
geta	wooden sandal
haiku	three-line poem with 17 syllables
hara-kiri/ seppuku	ritual suicide by disemboweling
hibachi	portable charcoal grill
ikebana	art of flower arranging
inro	lacquered box for carrying medicine, fastened to the belt by a netsuke
jujitsu	art of unarmed self-defense from which judo developed
Kabuki	popular traditional stylized theater, developed from the Noh theater
kamikaze	suicide pilot or plane of World War II
kendo	fencing with bamboo poles or sticks
kimono	long loose robe secured with a wide sash
mikado	Japanese emperor, as referred to by foreigners
netsuke	carved wooden or ivory toggle, as used for fastening a pouch to a kimono sash
No/Noh	stylized classical drama, including music, dancing, and elaborate costumes
obi	wide sash securing a kimono, typically with a large flat bow at the back
origami	art of folding paper into decorative shapes and designs
sake/saki	alcoholic beverage from rice
samisen	three-stringed musical instrument
samurai	knight or aristocratic warrior in feudal Japan
sayonara	good-bye
Shinto	Japanese religion involving veneration of nature spirits and ancestors
shogun	hereditary commander in chief of the Japanese army until 1867
shoji	translucent sliding door or screen made of paper
sumo	elaborate and ritualized form of wrestling
tanka/uta	five-line poem of 31 syllables
tenno	Japanese emperor, especially as considered the divinely appointed religious leader
tatami	straw mat or floor covering
torii	gateway of a Shinto temple, essentially two uprights with a crosspiece
zaibatsu	powerful business enterprise or association, in the control of a few leading families

Jet Engine

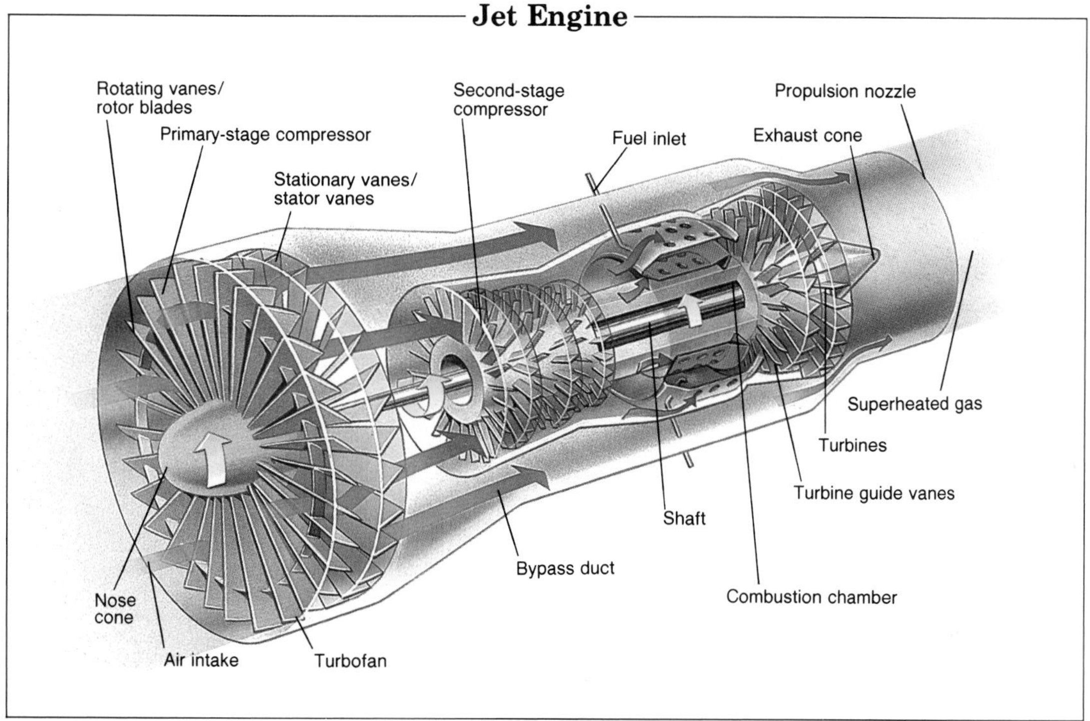

gems, using a 12-ounce pound TROY WEIGHT

jewelry See chart, page 292, and also **gemstone**
- jewelry carried, usually around the neck, as a charm against evil or misfortune AMULET
- jewelry chest or similar small box for valuables CASKET
- jewelry of a delicately worked kind, or a collection of it BIJOUTERIE
- jewelry, especially imitation jewelry, or other goods that are small, cheap, and gaudy BRUMMAGEM, TRINKETS, GEWGAWS, BAUBLES
- circular rim securing the gemstone in a ring or other piece of jewelry COLLET
- richly decorated, as with jewels ENCRUSTED

jigsaw - jigsawlike Chinese puzzle of simple shapes for reassembling into different figures TANGRAM

job, position, or activity particularly suited to a person NICHE
- job at which one is skilled and happy, profession MÉTIER
- job or office that requires little or no work even though providing an income SINECURE, GRAVY TRAIN
- demanding and difficult, as a job might be EXACTING
- easy, comfortable, as a job might be CUSHY
- involving a great deal of sitting, as a job might SEDENTARY
- loss of jobs through the elimination of them rather than through dismissal REDUNDANCY, RETRENCHMENT, ATTRITION
- recruiting of executive personnel from other firms for jobs in a particular firm HEADHUNTING
- report or summary of a person's education and career, as for job applications CURRICULUM VITAE, RÉSUMÉ

jockey's identifying cap and shirt, typically in bright colors SILKS

join, connect, or fit neatly, tightly, or harmoniously DOVETAIL, FAY
- join, grow or run together, fuse or unify, form a single mass or single unit ACCRETE, AGGLOMERATE, AGGLUTINATE, AGGREGATE, CONGLOMERATE, COALESCE
- join, link, or connect COUPLE
- join, unite, combine, as in business MERGE, AMALGAMATE, CONSOLIDATE, INCORPORATE
- join at a point after approaching from different directions CONVERGE
- join by tying together COLLIGATE, LASH
- join one object to another one, attach, fasten AFFIX, APPOSE
- join or attach by means of a joint or hinge ARTICULATE
- join or attach to something that is larger or more important ANNEX, APPEND
- join or bind together, clamp or connect YOKE, TETHER
- join or blend the versions of a text into a single version CONFLATE
- join or fasten firmly by or as if by bolting together RIVET
- join or hold together, stick or cling COHERE
- join or link into a single group or cluster CONSTELLATE
- join the parts of something together, build up ASSEMBLE
- join two strips of film, wire, rope, or the like together at the ends SPLICE
- joined or grouped together as a pair CONJUGATE, CONJOINT, CONJUNCT
- joined or united into an alliance or league CONFEDERATE
- joined to or associated with a larger grouping or organization AFFILIATED
- joined-up writing CURSIVE
- joining, touching, positioned next to, side by side ABUTTING, CONTIGUOUS, ADJACENT, JUXTAPOSED
- made up of several different components joined together COMPOUND, COMPOSITE, INTEGRATED, SYNTHESIZED

joint, consisting of a notch and projection, between items of building material DOWEL, JOGGLE
- joint, formed by a groove, between two pieces of wood, or the groove itself RABBET, REBATE
- joint between two beveled edges, typically forming a right-angled corner MITER JOINT

- joint between two surfaces lying flush against each other BUTT JOINT, CARVEL JOINT
- joint in which a rounded edge or knob moves freely within a socket BALL-AND-SOCKET JOINT
- joint in which a strip on the edge of one board fits into a corresponding groove in another TONGUE-AND-GROOVE JOINT
- joint in woodwork, including a wedge-shaped tenon, or the tenon itself DOVETAIL
- joint or branching point on the stem of a plant NODE
- jointed or segmented ARTICULATE
- bending of a joint or limb FLEXION
- clear thick liquid secreted by membranes in joints, tendon sheaths, and similar points in the body SINOVIA, SINOVIAL FLUID
- inflammation of the body's joints, resulting in pain and stiffness ARTHRITIS
- length of tube or bushing for making a pipe joint FERRULE
- notch or groove that houses an inserted part in a joint or hinge MORTISE, GAIN
- projecting end, strip, or wedge on a piece of wood fitting into a corresponding mortise in another piece to form a joint TENON, COG, FEATHER
- small cavity in the body, filled with fluid to reduce friction, as at joints BURSA
- tough fibrous tissue in the joints between bones, gristle CARTILAGE

joint (combining form) ARTHR-, ARTHRO-, ARTIC-

jointly (combining form) CO-, COM-

joke or drawn-out anecdote whose supposed humor lies in the irrelevance or anticlimax of the punch line SHAGGY-DOG STORY
- joke or humorous antic PLEASANTRY
- joke or teasing remark at someone's expense, taunt GIBE
- joke or prank, gag, jest JAPE
- joking and playful conversation BADINAGE, BANTER, REPARTEE
- joking with levity and in an inappropriate way FACETIOUS
- clever, subtle remark WITTICISM
- clever retort or taunting joke, quip WISECRACK, SALLY
- given to joking, good-humored, jolly JOCOSE, JOCUND
- intended as a joke, meant in jest JOCULAR
- keeping a straight face or being apparently serious, as when telling a joke DEADPAN
- range or stock of jokes, pieces of music, or the like available to a performer REPERTOIRE
- verging on the indelicate or improper, as a joke might be RISQUÉ

jolly See **friendly, happy**

journal article printed alone as a separate pamphlet OFFPRINT
- journal or periodical recording the meetings of a learned society, developments in an academic field, or the like ANNALS

journalist, typically one covering the local news in an area, working on a part-time basis STRINGER
- journalist, writer, artist, or the like, who is self-employed and tends to undertake only short-term projects FREE LANCE, FREELANCER
- journalist doing routine or mediocre work HACK

journey, often by foot, that is long and far PEREGRINATION
- journey or short outing, often at a special low fare EXCURSION
- journey that is long and eventful ODYSSEY
- journey's destination or goal BOURN, MECCA
- long and indirect, as a journey or argument might be CIRCUITOUS
- planned route for a journey ITINERARY
- provisions or allowance for a journey VIATICUM
- requiring a great deal of effort or endurance, as a journey might ARDUOUS, STRENUOUS

joust - aim or thrust a lance in a joust TILT

joy See **delight**

Judaism See chart, and also **Jew**

judge in a county court CIRCUIT JUDGE
- judge in a court of law, or the judge's seat or official position BENCH
- judge or bishop having direct judicial authority ORDINARY
- judge, interpret, or make statements in a priggish or preachy

JEWELRY

aigrette	spray of gemstones in the form of a tuft of feathers
cameo	engraved gemstone with a design in relief; medallion with a silhouetted head in relief
carcanet	jeweled necklace or collar, in former times
circlet	ornamental band worn around the head
coronet	crown-shaped headband of precious metal, set with jewels
diadem	royal crown or headband
diamanté	jewelry made from paste, or artificial gemstones, designed to glitter like diamonds
girandole	earring, brooch, or the like with a large gemstone surrounded by smaller ones
intaglio	engraved gemstone with a sunken design
labret	item of jewelry, ornament, or gemstone set into the lip
locket	small, hinged case holding a picture or keepsake, usually worn on a chain around the neck
ouch	jeweled brooch or clasp, in former times
pendant/ lavaliere	single ornament, medallion, or item of jewelry worn on a chain around the neck
rivière	necklace of diamonds or other precious stones, typically in a single strand
signet ring	ring bearing a seal or set of initials
solitaire ring	ring with a single gemstone, such as a diamond
tiara	formal semicircular headband of precious metal set with jewels
torque	necklace or collar, typically of twisted metal, in former times

way MORALIZE, SERMONIZE
- judge or referee in a dispute ARBITER, ARBITRATOR, ADJUDICATOR, MEDIATOR, MODERATOR
- judge's expert assistant or adviser ASSESSOR
- judge's hammer GAVEL
- judge's incidental comment during a case, that is not directly relevant or binding OBITER DICTUM
- judge's minority opinion in a court of law or tribunal DISSENTING OPINION
- judge's order compelling or prohibiting a party from a particular action INJUNCTION
- judge's room for hearing minor cases or conducting private consultations CHAMBERS
- judge's summing-up and address to the jury once all the evidence has been presented in court CHARGE, INSTRUCTION
- judges and law courts collectively JUDICATURE, JUDICIARY
- adjective for judges or justice JUDICIAL, JUDICIARY
- attempt to influence a judge or jury, as by bribes or threats EMBRACERY

JUDAISM AND JEWISH TERMS

Ashkenazi	Jew of Central or Eastern European descent
bar mitzvah	boy of 13, considered an adult; ceremony marking his attaining adult status
cabala	mystical philosophy based on interpretations of the Old Testament
Chassidim/ Hassidim	sect of extremely orthodox Jews of a mystical tradition
chazan	cantor, chief singer in a synagogue
chutzpah	cheek, effrontery
Diaspora	Jews or Jewish communities living outside Israel; dispersion of the Jews in ancient times
dybbuk	in folklore, evil spirit that enters and controls the body
golem	in folklore, artificial human figure brought to life
goy	gentile, non-Jew
Kaddish	ancient prayer praising God, recited especially by those in mourning
kosher	referring to ritually pure food, prepared and served according to Jewish dietary laws
matzo	unleavened bread, as eaten during Passover
menorah	ceremonial seven-branched candelabrum, symbolizing the seven days of the Creation
mezuzah	tiny scroll of parchment inscribed with biblical passages and fixed to doorposts in the homes of observing Jews
minyan	quorum of 10 male Jews needed for a fully formal religious service
mitzvah	command imposed by the scriptures; good deed
parve	referring to foods prepared without meat or milk products, so suitable for any meal
phylacteries/ tefillin	small leather boxes containing parchments inscribed with biblical passages which are tied by leather straps to the head and left arm by devout Jewish men during their morning prayers
Sanhedrin	ancient Jewish high court and council
schlemiel	clumsy, unlucky, or long-suffering person
schmaltz	syrupy sentimentality
schnook	foolish or stupid person; person who is easily duped
schnorrer	beggar; sponger
Sephardi	Jew of Spanish or Portuguese descent
shiksa/ shikse	non-Jewish girl; Jewish girl not keeping to Jewish traditions
shofar	ram's horn blown like a trumpet on various holy days
tabernacle	portable sanctuary or tent in which the Ark of the Covenant was carried through the desert by the ancient Jews
tallith	fringed prayer shawl worn by Jewish men
Talmud	collection of ancient writings forming the basis of Jewish traditional law and teachings
Torah	the first five books of the Old Testament, the Pentateuch; scroll or parchment containing this text
tref	referring to food considered impure, not in keeping with Jewish dietary laws
yarmulke	skullcap worn by observing Jewish men
yeshiva	school for religious or rabbinical studies
Yiddish	High German dialect , with Hebrew, Slavic, and other elements and written in Hebrew characters, a common language mainly of Central and Eastern European Jews

- challenge, object to, or reject a judge or juror RECUSE
- experienced lawyer serving as a part-time judge RECORDER
- Muslim judge, or interpreter of Islamic law QADI, CADI
- office, status, or dignity of a judge, king, or nobleman ERMINE
- referring to a judicial system in which the judge in a criminal trial also acts as prosecutor INQUISITORIAL
- referring to a judicial system in which the judge in a criminal trial only considers the case that is argued by a prosecutor ACCUSATORIAL
- still before a judge or court and therefore not to be discussed in public, as a legal case might be SUB JUDICE
- traveling from place to place, as some circuit judges or preacher are ITINERANT

judgment, good sense DISCRETION
- judgment, legal decision, or the like used as an example or standard justification when treating later cases similarly PRECEDENT
- judgment, opinion ESTIMATION, ASSESSMENT, EVALUATION, VERDICT, APPRAISAL
- adjective for judgment JUDICIAL, JUDICIARY
- having good judgment in practical matters and social situations, tactful DISCREET, PRUDENT, POLITIC, JUDICIOUS
- having good judgment or perception, shrewd or quick-witted ASTUTE, SAGACIOUS
- having good taste or judgment DISCERNING, DISCRIMINATING
- measure or standard used when making a judgment YARDSTICK, CRITERION
- overturning or cancellation as of a law or judgment ANNULMENT, ABROGATION, CASSATION
- place for making judgments, or group who judge or decide TRIBUNAL
- severe in judgment, going strictly by the letter of the law LEGALISTIC, RHADAMANTHINE

judo, karate, kung fu, and similar self-defense techniques or sports MARTIAL ARTS
- judo expert or one who competes JUDOKA
- judo suit, as worn during contests JUDOGI
- any of the 12 proficiency grades in judo at black-belt level DAN
- full scoring point in a judo bout, resulting in victory directly IPPON
- room or mat for judo practice DOJO

jug, specifically a large two-handled jug PITCHER
- jug, typically large and with a wide mouth EWER

juggling - bottle-shaped wooden club thrown or swung about by persons engaged in juggling and gymnastics INDIAN CLUB

juice of grapes or other fruit before fermentation MUST
- juice of unripe grapes, sour apples, or the like, used in cookery VERJUICE
- squeeze or press out juice or milk EXPRESS, EXTRACT

juicy and usually delicious SUCCULENT, LUSCIOUS, LUSH

jukebox or player piano NICKELODEON

jump about, move about playfully FRISK, GAMBOL, FROLIC, ROMP, SPORT, ROLLICK, CAPER, CAVORT
- jump in a sequence, as in a series of logical arguments SALTUS
- jump or bounce back, as after a collision REBOUND
- jumping, leaping, or dancing SALTATION
- jumping, moving by means of leaping, as frogs and toads usually do SALIENT
- jumping about, disconnected, as conversation might be DESULTORY
- jumping movement of various kinds in ballet ENTRECHAT, JETÉ
- jumping movement of various kinds performed by a horse in dressage CURVET, CAPRIOLE, GAMBADO
- lively jumping movement, as of a spirited horse PRANCE, CAPER, TITTUP
- pole, with a spring at the base, on which one can bounce or jump along POGO STICK
- relating to or adapted for jumping SALTATORIAL
- springy nylon or canvas sheet used for recreational jumping, acrobatic displays, or the like TRAMPOLINE

Jung - in Jungian psychology, an inherited idea or cast of mind deriving from the collective unconscious ARCHETYPE
- in Jungian psychology, the masculine side of the female personality ANIMUS
- in Jungian psychology, the social mask or front adopted by a person in keeping with his or her outward role in life PERSONA
- in Jungian psychology, the true inner self, or the feminine side of the male personality ANIMA

junior employee in a big organization MINION

junk, odds and ends, discarded or miscellaneous objects FLOTSAM, JETSAM, BRIC-A-BRAC

Jupiter - adjective for Jupiter JOVIAN

jury jury that is unable to agree on a verdict HUNG JURY
- jury's verdict or similar formal pronouncement DELIVERANCE
- attempt to influence a judge or jury, as by bribes or threats EMBRACERY
- bribe or threaten a jury into reaching a particular verdict SUBORN
- defendant's right to reject a certain number of proposed jurors in a criminal trial without giving a reason PEREMPTORY CHALLENGE
- fill a jury, committee, or the like with one's supporters PACK

justice, fairness IMPARTIALITY, EQUITY
- adjective for judges or justice JUDICIAL, JUDICIARY
- deliver or administer justice or the law DISPENSE, RENDER
- distribute or deal out something, especially justice METE OUT, ALLOT
- failure or misapplication of justice MISCARRIAGE
- place or court of justice, or group who judge TRIBUNAL
- power or right to administer laws and justice JURISDICTION
- pretense, caricature, or crudely distorted imitation of something, such as justice TRAVESTY
- the legal system of administering justice JUDICATURE, JUDICIARY

justification, as for a belief WARRANT
- justification, typically a formal defense, as of one's beliefs APOLOGIA, APOLOGY

justify, authorize, accept, or permit as rightful LEGITIMATE
- justify, uphold, or excuse by means of arguments, evidence, or proof VINDICATE
- justify in a reasonable or apparently reasonable way, often to suit one's convenience RATIONALIZE

jut out, project or overhang PROTRUDE, BEETLE, EXTRUDE

K

kangaroo See illustration
- kangaroo or other pouch-bearing mammal MARSUPIAL
- kangaroo's pouch MARSUPIUM
- female kangaroo DOE, BLUE FLIER
- male kangaroo BUCK, BOOMER
- young or baby kangaroo JOEY

Kant - thing as it appears, according to Kantian philosophy, as experienced by the senses rather than as understood by reason or intuition PHENOMENON
- thing-in-itself, according to Kantian philosophy, as understood by reason or intuition rather than as it appears to the senses NOUMENON
- universally applicable moral law, according to Kantian philosophy, that is derived from reason CATEGORICAL IMPERATIVE

karate, kung fu, judo, and similar self-defense techniques or sports MARTIAL ARTS

keel, as on a yacht, that can be raised or lowered CHEESECUTTER, DAGGER BOARD

keen See **eager, enthusiastic**
- keen and willing, eager SOLICITOUS
- keenness or sharpness of the senses or the mind ACUITY

keep back, hold on to RETAIN
- keep back, keep in good condition, or preserve something, such as food or one's strength CONSERVE
- keep or set aside for future use in long-lasting storage, shelve indefinitely MOTHBALL
- keep safe or secure, protect, as from danger or attack SAFEGUARD
- keeper of a magnet ARMATURE
- keeper or caretaker, as of an art collection CUSTODIAN, CURATOR
- keeping, guarding, protection, or imprisonment CUSTODY
- kept temporarily inoperative, set aside, or suspended, as a law might be IN ABEYANCE

kettle's handle, in the form of a hooped rod BAIL

kettledrum TIMBAL
- percussionist in an orchestra, especially one who plays the kettledrums TIMPANIST
- set of kettledrums TIMPANI

key explaining the symbols used in a map, chart, or the like LEGEND
- key on the keyboard of a piano, organ, or other keyboard instrument DIGITAL
- key or central component or participant LINCHPIN
- key that fits a variety of locks PASSE-PARTOUT, SKELETON KEY, PASSKEY, MASTER KEY
- key to a simple form of secret code CIPHER
- looped end of a key BOW
- ridge in a lock or keyhole, or corresponding notch on a key WARD
- shieldlike plate covering a keyhole, surrounding a door handle, protecting a light switch, or the like ESCUTCHEON
- write or play a musical composition in a different key TRANSPOSE

keyboard instruments See chart, page 296

kidnap NOBBLE, ABDUCT
- kidnap and press-gang a man, typically after making him drunk or drugging him, for service on a ship SHANGHAI
- tendency of a kidnap victim or other hostage to help or fall in love with his or her captor STOCKHOLM SYNDROME

kidney machine HEMODIALYZER, DIALYZER
- kidney pain NEPHRALGIA
- kidney stone, gallstone, or similar solid mass formed in a body cavity or tissue CALCULUS, CONCRETION
- kidney-shaped RENIFORM
- kidneys, liver, and other organs of an animal, especially when regarded as edible OFFAL
- relating to the kidneys RENAL, NEPHRITIC

kidney (combining form) REN-, RENI-, RENO-

kill, get rid of or destroy utterly, wipe out ANNIHILATE, EXTIRPATE, EXTERMINATE, LIQUIDATE
- kill a prominent politician or public figure ASSASSINATE
- kill an animal, especially a weak one, as to reduce a herd CULL
- kill as a sacrifice, as by burning IMMOLATE
- kill by beheading DECAPITATE
- kill by cutting off the supply of air, strangle, stifle, smother, or

Kangaroo

Red kangaroo

suffocate ASPHYXIATE
- kill by strangling, wring the neck of, manhandle SCRAG
- kill or killing by strangulation or by breaking the neck with an iron collar, as used formerly for executions in Spain GARROTTE
- kill or destroy a large proportion of DECIMATE
- kill secretively, especially by stifling BURKE
- kill summarily, dispose of promptly DISPATCH
- kill without trial, as an impassioned mob might kill an alleged offender LYNCH
- killed, ruined, or exhausted FORDONE
- agent or power that kills, suppresses, or eliminates QUIETUS

killer or killing of one's brother or sister FRATRICIDE
- killer or killing of one's father PATRICIDE
- killer or killing of a god or goddess DEICIDE
- killer or killing of a human being HOMICIDE
- killer or killing of a king or sovereign REGICIDE
- killer or killing of one's mother MATRICIDE
- killer or killing of one's parent or other close relative PARRICIDE
- killer or killing of a prophet VATICIDE
- killer or killing of one's sister SORORICIDE
- killer or killing of one's wife UXORICIDE
- hired killer HATCHET MAN
- person who kills himself or herself SUICIDE

killer (combining form) -CIDE

killing, violence, or bloody fighting, as in movies or on television GORE
- killing of a person, as through negligence, that is unlawful though not necessarily murder CULPABLE HOMICIDE
- killing of a person or animal already seriously wounded, as in battle, duel or a bullfight COUP DE GRACE
- killing of a whole racial or social group GENOCIDE
- killing of oneself, or a person who does this SUICIDE
- killing on a huge scale, slaughter, especially in war CARNAGE, MASSACRE, HOLOCAUST
- killing that is unlawful though not deliberate MANSLAUGHTER
- action by one person that provokes another into killing him or her PROVOCATION
- mercy killing EUTHANASIA
- mutually destructive, within a group and ruinous to both sides, as killings within a family or nation are INTERNECINE
- random, willful, unprovoked, as vandalism or mindless killing is WANTON, GRATUITOUS
- violent, frenzied, and destructive action or behavior, often involving indiscriminate and wide-scale killing RAMPAGE
- wide-scale killing, typically organized with official backing, as of Jewish communities in Eastern Europe in former times POGROM

killing (combining form) -CIDE

kiln for drying hops or malt OAST

kilt worn by Scottish Highlanders FILLEBEG
- dagger worn in the stocking of a person dressed in a kilt SKEAN DHU, DIRK
- furry pouch worn in front of the kilt in traditional Highland dress SPORRAN

kimono - wide sash securing a kimo-

KEYBOARD INSTRUMENTS

accordion	portable instrument with metal reeds controlled by a small keyboard and sounded by a rush of air produced by a pleated bellows
carillon	set of bells, often housed in a tower, still sometimes operated by manual and pedal keyboards
celesta	small, pianolike instrument with a bell-like sound produced by hammers striking metal bars
clavicembalo/ cembalo	keyed dulcimer, or harpsichord
clavichord	soft-sounding instrument with horizontal strings struck by brass pins
clavier/ klavier	"keyboard," any of various keyboard instruments, such as a piano or harpsichord
Hammond organ	trademark for an electronic organ that sounds like a pipe organ
harmonium	small organ powered by bellows forcing air through the reeds
harpsichord	pianolike instrument with strings plucked by quills or leather plectrums
pedal piano	piano with a pedal keyboard in addition to a manual keyboard, as used for practicing the organ
piano accordion	accordionlike instrument with a keyboard for the right hand
player piano/ Pianola	piano that plays automatically by means of a mechanism guided by a perforated roll of paper
portative organ	portable medieval organ
regal	small, portable organ of the 16th and 17th centuries
spinet	wing-shaped instrument like a small harpsichord
square piano	boxlike piano with horizontal strings
synthesizer/ Moog synthesizer	electronic keyboard instrument that can produce a wide range of musical and electronic sounds
virginal	small harpsichordlike instrument
Wurlitzer	trademark for an organ formerly widely used in movie theaters

Kites

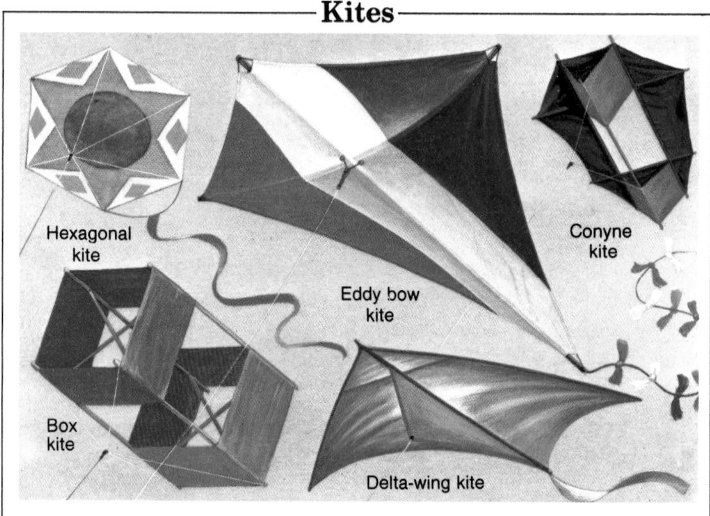

no, tied in a large flat bow at the back OBI

kind, charitable, acting or done for the good of others, particularly the poor or distressed ALTRUISTIC, PHILANTHROPIC, ELEEMOSYNARY
- kind and benevolent, as an uncle might be AVUNCULAR
- kind, friendly, good-natured, pleasant to be with AFFABLE, AMIABLE, CORDIAL, GENIAL, WELL-DISPOSED
- kind, generous or charitable, full of goodwill BENEVOLENT, BENEFICENT, BOUNTEOUS
- kind, gentle, mild BENIGN
- kind, sympathetic, agreeable CONGENIAL, SIMPATICO
- kind, sympathetic, merciful, forgiving, full of pity COMPASSIONATE, HUMANE, HUMANITARIAN, MAGNANIMOUS
- kind to a fault, overlenient, spoiling INDULGENT

kindling in the form of decayed wood or similar dry material TOUCHWOOD, PUNK, TINDER

king's assistant or officer who manages the royal household CHAMBERLAIN
- King's evil, tuberculosis of the lymph nodes SCROFULA
- king's wife or queen's husband CONSORT
- attain or ascend the throne, as when a prince becomes king ACCEDE
- attendants or companions of a king or queen RETINUE
- defender of the faith, one of the titles of the British king or queen FIDEI DEFENSOR
- give up or relinquish the throne formally, as a king or queen might ABDICATE
- killer or killing of a king REGICIDE
- land or other means of support given by a king to a relative, typically a younger son APPANAGE
- office, status, or dignity of a judge, king, or nobleman ERMINE
- relating to a king or queen ROYAL, REGAL
- replacement ruler for a king during his illness, minority, or the like REGENT
- ruling by hereditary right, as a king might be LEGITIMATE
- staff carried by a king or queen as a sign of authority SCEPTER
- title of a king, as used in documents REX

king cobra HAMADRYAD

kingdom REALM

kingfisher in mythology HALCYON

kiss OSCULATE
- kiss, bow, or other gesture of greeting SALUTATION, OSCULATION
- kiss of peace at Communion, or the plate used to convey it PAX
- kissing disease GLANDULAR FEVER, INFECTIOUS MONONUCLEOSIS
- routine, mechanical, as a kiss might be PERFUNCTORY

kitchen See also **cooking**
- kitchen implement or container UTENSIL
- kitchen on a ship, boat, or aircraft GALLEY
- kitchen on the deck of a ship CABOOSE
- kitchen scraps or rubbish SWILL
- menial kitchen servant SCULLION
- relating to cooking or the kitchen CULINARY
- room off or recess in a kitchen for dishwashing, vegetable peeling, and the like SCULLERY

kite See illustration
- kitelike glider in the form of a single large cloth wing from which the pilot hangs HANG GLIDER

kitsch - fashionable in an affected or slightly kitschy way CHICHI

kittens - litter or group of kittens KINDLE

kiwi APTERYX

knave - notorious, as a knave is said to be ARRANT

knee jerk or similar response performed involuntarily rather than by conscious choice REFLEX, AUTOMATISM
- bounce a child affectionately up and down, especially on one's knees DANDLE
- housemaid's knee BURSITIS
- joint corresponding to the knee in the hind leg of a horse or other four-legged mammal STIFLE

kneecap PATELLA

kneel or bend the knees as in worship GENUFLECT
- cushion for kneeling on, especially in church HASSOCK
- cushioned stool for kneeling on during prayer, as by a sovereign at the coronation FALDSTOOL

knickknack, trinket, or small curio or item of bric-a-brac BIBELOT

knife See chart
- knife blade, cutting part of a plane, or similar sharp part of a tool BIT
- knife handle, hilt HAFT
- knife seller, maker, or repairer CUTLER
- knife sharpener HONE, WHETSTONE
- knives, forks, and spoons CUTLERY, SILVERWARE, FLATWARE
- former term for a dagger or similar knife BODKIN
- sharpen a knife or other cutting

KNIVES

WORKING KNIVES

bistoury
cleaver
drawknife
lancet
machete
palette knife
panga
scalpel
Stanley knife
Swiss army knife

WEAPONS

anlace
bayonet
bolo
bowie knife
dagger
dirk
dudgeon
kirpan
kris
kukri
misericord
poniard
shiv
skean
skean dhu
snickersnee
stiletto
switchblade/ flick knife
trench knife

tool WHET, HONE
- tongue or prong at the foot of the blade of a knife, tool, or the like for embedding into the handle SHANK, TANG

knight, mounted soldier, or military cadet in France in former times CHEVALIER
- knight commanding men in battle

Knots

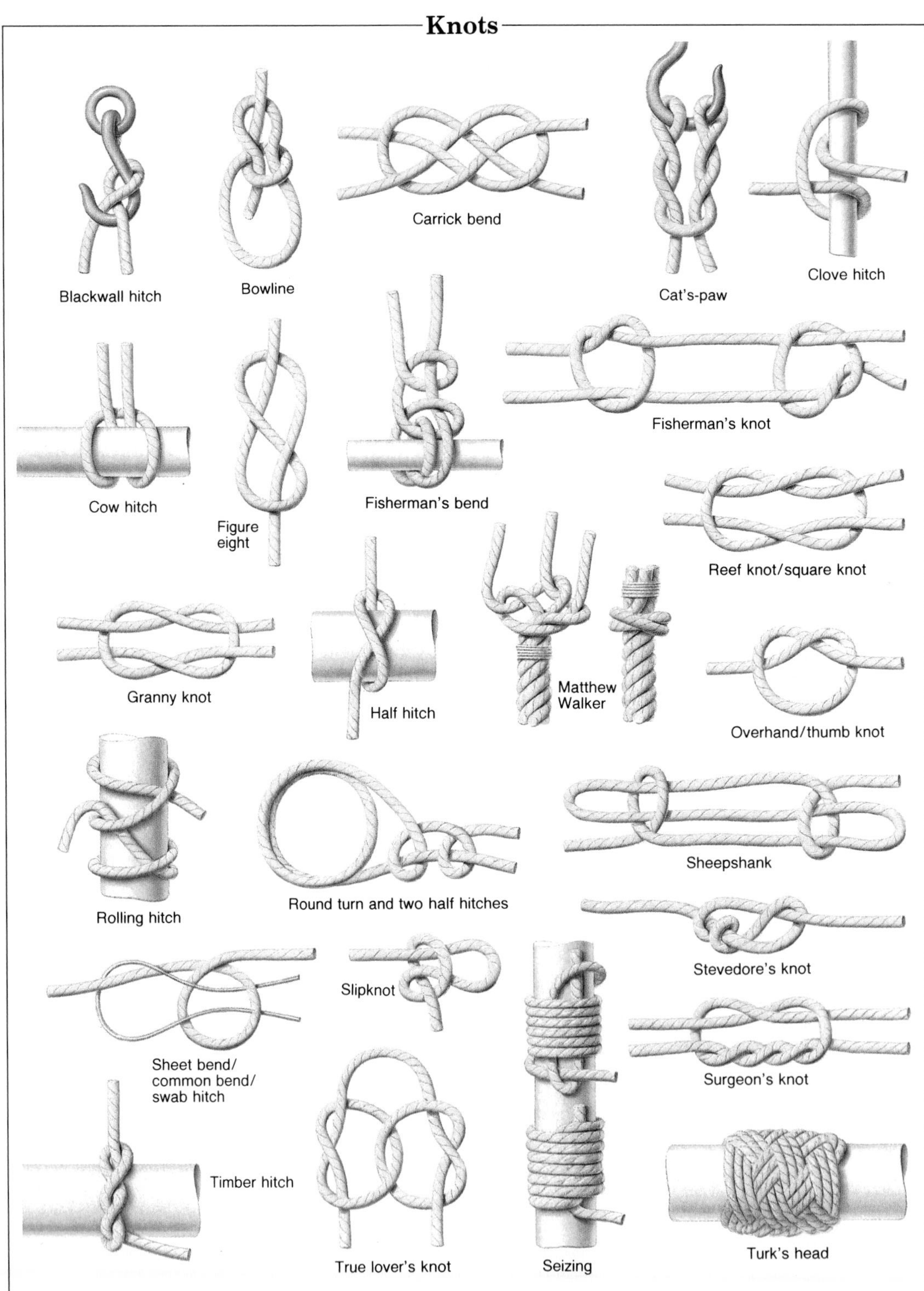

under his own standard or banner BANNERET
- knight of lowest rank in some orders of knighthood COMPANION
- knight wandering about in search of chivalric adventures KNIGHT ERRANT
- knight's expedition, as in search of the Holy Grail QUEST
- knight's page VARLET
- knight's tunic, often bearing his coat of arms and worn over his armor TABARD, SURCOAT
- knights' tournament, involving horse races and riding displays CAROUSEL
- area set aside for knights to joust LISTS
- attendant and armor bearer of a knight in medieval times, typically a candidate for knighthood ESQUIRE, ARMIGER
- charge by knights in a medieval tournament COURSE
- duel between knights with lances on horseback JOUST, TILTING MATCH
- perfect, chivalrous, and heroic knight PALADIN, GALAHAD

knighthood as a medieval institution, or the qualities of a knight, such as courtesy, honesty, and gallantry CHIVALRY
- ceremonial conferring of knighthood, as by a touch of a sword on the shoulder ACCOLADE
- confer knighthood on by ceremonially tapping on the shoulder with a sword DUB

knitted with two kinds of wool, one in the front and one at the back PLATED

knitting See also **sewing, embroidery**
- knitting or weaving pattern of diamond shapes in two or more colors ARGYLE
- knitting stitch made by inverting a plain stitch PURL STITCH
- knitting technique for using several differently colored yarns to produce complex stocking-stitch designs, as for sweaters FAIR ISLE
- knitting technique for using several yarns on the needle at once to produce designs of large stocking-stitch colored patches INTARSIA
- Parisian women who would continue knitting unconcernedly while attending guillotinings as spectators during the French Revolution TRICOTEUSES
- measure of fineness or density in knitting, as based on the thickness of wool, the number of loops per inch, or the like TENSION, GAUGE

knob, as on a shield or ceiling BOSS
- knob, knotty projection, swelling NODE, NODULE
- knob or bump, especially any of the ridges on a handle or object to make it easier to grip KNURL
- knob or headlike part, such as the end of a long bone or insect's antenna CAPITULUM
- knoblike growth or projection, as on a legume's root, the skin, or a bone TUBERCLE
- knoblike protuberance, as in the center of a shield or on a mushroom's cap UMBO

knobbly - small lump in a yarn or in fabric, sometimes made deliberately to produce a knobbly appearance SLUB

knock-knees VARUS

knot See illustration
- knot or bump on a tree or timber KNUR
- knot or lump in wool or cloth BURL
- knotted string patterned into ornamental lacework MACRAMÉ
- pin inserted into a knot to stop it slipping TOGGLE

knotty and twisted, as the trunk or branches of a tree might be GNARLED
- knotty problem that can be resolved only by bold or drastic action GORDIAN KNOT
- knotty projection, knob, swelling NODE, NODULE

know See also **foretell**
- come to light, become known TRANSPIRE
- know by intuition DIVINE

know-all WISEACRE, WISE GUY

knowledge, or the mental processes used in acquiring it COGNITION
- knowledge after the event HINDSIGHT
- knowledge of a deep or scholarly kind ERUDITION
- knowledge of a formal, unimaginative, dryly detailed kind, book learning PEDANTRY
- knowledge of an instinctive kind INTUITION
- knowledge of appropriate behavior, especially in social situations SAVOIR FAIRE
- knowledge of everything OMNISCIENCE
- knowledge of something allegedly before it actually happens PRECOGNITION
- knowledge or learning, as encouraged or represented by the Renaissance HUMANISM
- knowledge or perception allegedly by means of a sixth sense, supernatural powers, intuition, telepathy, or the like CLAIRVOYANCE, EXTRASENSORY PERCEPTION, ESP, CRYPTESTHESIA
- doctrine that all knowledge derives from experience, especially from sense perceptions EMPIRICISM
- doctrine that all knowledge derives from the exercise of reason rather than from experience or perception RATIONALISM
- gather information or knowledge bit by bit GLEAN
- gradual absorption or acquisition, as of knowledge OSMOSIS
- having a deep knowledge of or close acquaintance with INTIMATE
- pretended learning or knowledge, veneer of scholarship SCIOLISM
- relating to intuitive knowledge or supernatural experience TRANSCENDENTAL
- secret, hidden from the uninitiated, as knowledge or understanding of a cult may be ARCANE, OCCULT, ESOTERIC
- slight and fragmented knowledge, as of a foreign language SMATTERING
- spread something widely, such as news or knowledge DISSEMINATE, DIFFUSE, DISPERSE, PROMULGATE
- theory of knowledge, or the philosophical study of the nature of knowledge EPISTEMOLOGY
- traditional knowledge and beliefs LORE

knowledge (combining form) -GNOSIS, -NOMY, -SOPHY

knowledgeable, expert or skillful VERSED, WELL-VERSED, PROFICIENT, AU FAIT
- knowledgeable, made aware, free from prejudice or superstition ENLIGHTENED
- knowledgeable about, or acquainted with CONVERSANT WITH
- knowledgeable person, especially an expert in a particular field of study SAVANT
- conscious, aware, informed, knowledgeable COGNIZANT
- person knowledgeable in many subjects POLYMATH, POLYHISTOR

Koran - one of the 114 chapters of the Koran SURA
- Muslim who has memorized the entire Koran HAFIZ

kosher - forbidden as food in Judaism, nonkosher, as pork is TREF
- laws concerning kosher food, or the state of being kosher KASHRUTH
- Muslim equivalent of kosher HALAL

kung fu, karate, judo, and similar self-defense techniques or sports MARTIAL ARTS

L

label or ticket, as fixed on or attached to a parcel DOCKET
labor, toil, strenuous physical or mental effort TRAVAIL
- producing contractions to bring on childbirth, as some labor-inducing medical drugs are OXYTOCIC
- hasten the onset of labor or childbirth, especially by the use of medical drugs INDUCE
- in labor, about to give birth PARTURIENT

laboratory See chart
- laboratory used in establishing scientific or medical facts to become evidence in legal cases FORENSIC LABORATORY

laborer, as on a building site NAVVY
- laborer bound by a contract for a specified period INDENTURED LABORER
- laborer in a slavelike condition, bound to a feudal lord or estate SERF

laborious, troublesome ONEROUS
labor-union federation AFL-CIO
- labor-union member elected by fellow workers, typically in a factory, as their spokesperson and representative SHOP STEWARD
- labor union open to all the different types of workers in an industry INDUSTRIAL UNION, VERTICAL UNION
- labor union restricted to people engaged in the same trade or work CRAFT UNION, HORIZONTAL UNION
- business or factory contracted to employ only members of a particular labor union CLOSED SHOP
- business or factory employing workers without regard to labor-union membership OPEN SHOP
- business or factory whose employees are required to join a specific labor union after being hired UNION SHOP
- clearly defined separation of the tasks done by various labor-union members DEMARCATION
- employee who works on while his or her labor union has ordered a strike SCAB

labyrinth - monster slain by Theseus in the labyrinth, in Greek mythology MINOTAUR

lace - lacelike ornamental metalwork FILIGREE
- lace made by looping a single thread by means of a small hand shuttle TATTING
- lace made by winding thread around pins stuck into a small cushion in a set pattern BOBBIN LACE, PILLOW LACE
- lace made with a needle on a pattern NEEDLEPOINT, POINT LACE
- lace of a heavy, large-patterned kind on a backing of fabric rather than netting GUIPURE
- lace or embroidery edging PURL
- lace or linen formerly worn in a frill by women around the neck or shoulders TUCKER
- lacelike or crisscross pattern or design TRACERY
- background of a design, as in lacework FOND
- background pattern or mesh used in lacemaking RESEAU
- coarse lace with a simple geometric pattern TORCHON LACE
- edging of tiny loops, as on ribbon or lace PICOTS
- lacework of knotted string MACRAMÉ
- fine ornamental lace of various kinds BRUSSELS LACE, DUCHESSE LACE, CHANTILLY LACE, MALINES, MECHLIN, HONITON, MIGNONETTE, VALENCIENNES
- metal or plastic tip on a ribbon, shoelace, or the like AGLET
- pleated or gathered strip of lace or fabric, used as a trimming RUCHE, RUFFLE
- thread or loop joining sections of a lace pattern or needlework pattern BRIDE, BAR

lack, insufficiency, shortage, scarcity SPARSITY, DEARTH, PAUCITY, DEFICIENCY
- lack, need, fault, or failure to perform some duty DEFAULT
- lack or loss of basic comforts or of the essentials of life PRIVATION
- extreme poverty, lack of all comforts and essentials PENURY, DESTITUTION

lack (combining form) DIS-, MIS-
lacking, incomplete, or insufficient DEFICIENT
- completely lacking, entirely without DESTITUTE OF, DEVOID OF

lacking (combining form) AP-, APO-, UN-
lacquer or glossy black varnish JAPAN
- lacquer or similar preservative applied to a drawing, as to prevent smudging FIXATIVE

lacrosse stick, consisting of a racketlike staff bearing a shallow net CROSSE
- keep the ball in the net of the stick in lacrosse while running CRADLE

lad, adolescent boy STRIPLING
ladder on a ship, usually of rope but with rigid rungs JACOB'S LADDER
- ladder or portable staircase on the side of a ship ACCOMMODATION LADDER
- ladder with rope sides and two or three rungs of metal or wood, used in mountaineering ÉTRIER
- any of the rungs of a ladder SPOKE, STAVE
- scaling, by ladders, of a castle wall, rampart, or the like, as during a military attack ESCALADE
- upright post or strut of a ladder, door frame, window sash, or the like STILE

ladybird or related beetle having club-shaped antennae CLAVICORN
lag, fall behind or stray STRAGGLE
lake in a hollow in the mountains TARN
- lake in the area formed by a loop in a river OXBOW LAKE
- lake or bay in Ireland LOUGH
- lake or bay in Scotland LOCH
- lake or pond MERE
- adjective for a lake LACUSTRINE
- scientific study of lakes and other bodies of fresh water LIMNOLOGY

Lama - Grand Lama of Tibet DALAI LAMA, PANCHEN LAMA, TASHI LAMA
lamb See illustration, page 302
- lamb reared as a pet COSSET
- leg of lamb GIGOT

Lamb of God, picture of a lamb representing Christ AGNUS DEI
lame or limping HALTING
- lameness, limp CLAUDICATION

lament, funeral hymn, or poem of mourning on the occasion of someone's death DIRGE, ELEGY, THRENODY, MONODY
- lament, poem of grief, usually

over lost love COMPLAINT
- lament or mourn for the dead KEEN
- lamentation or elaborate complaint JEREMIAD

lamp See also **light**
- lamp drum or dome that increases the light of a gas lamp when heated MANTLE

lance - aim or thrust a lance in a joust TILT
- duel between mounted knights, with lances JOUST, TILTING MATCH
- lower a lance to the attacking position, as in a joust COUCH

land See also **estate, property**
- land, buildings, and other immovable property REAL PROPERTY, REAL ESTATE, REALTY
- land belonging to a church, and typically granted to a clergyman as part of his benefice GLEBE
- land formation, especially by the deposit of sediment from a river ALLUVION
- land in border areas MARCHLANDS, MARCHES

LABORATORY EQUIPMENT

alembic	distilling flask or retort used by alchemists in former times
autoclave	chamber for heating substances under high pressure, as in sterilizing and cooking
bell jar	bell-shaped cover used to protect delicate instruments or to maintain a controlled environment
Büchner funnel	device for filtering by suction
Bunsen burner	small burner that uses a mixture of gas and air, producing a single concentrated flame
burette	graduated glass tube with a stopcock, used for dispensing known volumes of liquid
centrifuge	machine that separates particles from a suspension by means of high-speed rotation
condenser	device for converting vapors into liquid during distillation
crucible	small ceramic cup used for calcining and melting substances at high temperatures
desiccator	drying chamber, containing chemicals that readily take up water or water vapor
diffusion pump/ condensation pump	pump for producing a high vacuum
fractionating column	condenser used to collect the components of a mixture as they boil off at different temperatures
glove box	chamber with protective gloves sealed into the side, in which dangerous radioactive or toxic substances can be handled
Kipp's apparatus/Kipp generator	arrangement of three linked glass vessels used for the controlled production of a gas such as hydrogen sulfide by the action of a liquid on a solid
Leyden jar	glass jar whose lower walls are lined inside and outside with tin foil to form an electrostatic capacitator
Liebig condenser	device for condensing a vapor by passing it through a tube inside another tube through which a coolant, usually water, passes
Nicol prism	two prisms cut and cemented together in such a way that waves of light passing through them vibrate in a single plane
Petri dish	shallow, flat, round glass dish with a lid, used especially for culturing microorganisms
pipette	glass tube of known capacity, used for transferring liquids
rectifier	condenser for separating or purifying a liquid
retort	round flask with a bent-over, narrow neck, used especially for distillation
wash bottle	sealed container with two outlet tubes, from which liquid is dispensed by blowing down one tube
Wimshurst machine	demonstration apparatus generating static electricity by the rotation of its two insulating discs in opposite directions
Winchester/ Winchester quart	cylindrical, narrow-necked glass bottle with a capacity of about 2 liters (or 3 1/2 pints), used for storing and carrying liquids
Woulff bottle/ Woulfe bottle	glass container with two or more necks, used for passing a gas through a liquid

Lamb Cuts

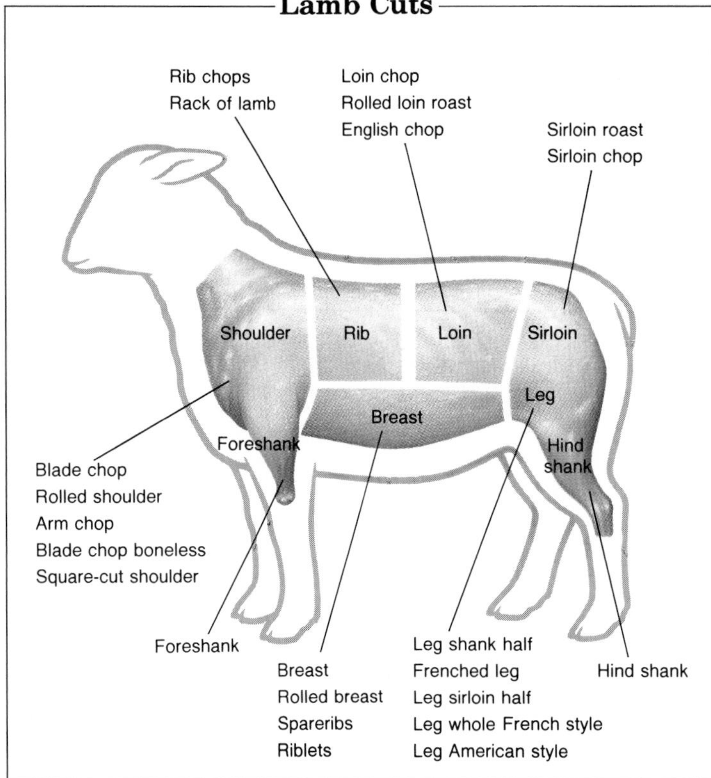

- northern part of the earth's hypothetical original landmass or supercontinent Pangaea LAURASIA
- not touching, adjoining, or positioned next to, as pieces of land might be OUTLYING
- outline or shape, as of a stretch of land CONTOUR
- ownership of land, as by churches, that is fixed forever, preventing sale or transfer MORTMAIN, DEAD HAND
- physical features of land or a region TOPOGRAPHY
- plowable, and suitable for cultivating crops, as land might be ARABLE
- plowed but left unseeded, as farming land might be, to regain fertility for a season FALLOW
- policy of regaining land that is historically or culturally connected to one's nation but now under foreign control IRREDENTISM
- qualified ownership of inherited land, restricting its disposal to a specified heir or heirs FEE TAIL
- relating to land, farming, or the country AGRARIAN
- relating to or living on dry land TERRESTRIAL
- return of land, in former times, to the Crown or a feudal lord in the absence of legal heirs ESCHEAT
- right of use over another person's land or property for specific purposes SERVITUDE
- right of way or similar legal right over another person's land EASEMENT
- share of the proceeds paid to a landowner for the use or development of his or her property ROYALTY
- small triangular piece of land GORE
- southern part of the earth's hypothetical original landmass or supercontinent Pangaea GONDWANALAND
- stretch of land TRACT
- take away a person's private property or land, especially for public ownership EXPROPRIATE
- touching, adjoining, be positioned next to, as pieces of land might be ABUTTING, ADJACENT, CONTIGUOUS
- turning desert, marshes, submerged land, or the like into useful land fit for living on or farming RECLAMATION
- use and possession of one's own land, in law DEMESNE
- wide, open stretch of land, sea, or sky EXPANSE
- year in which farm land is left to lie fallow, observed every seventh

- land of luxury and idleness in medieval legend COCKAIGNE
- land of perfect peace and happiness, utopia SHANGRI-LA
- land of plenty and contentment GOSHEN
- land or ground, especially in respect of its physical characteristics TERRAIN
- land or other means of support given by a king to a relative, typically a younger son APPANAGE
- land or settlement that is reserved for a minority community, such as the Native Americans RESERVATION
- land owned or the ownership of it DOMAIN
- land reclaimed from the sea or a lake and protected by dikes, especially in Holland POLDER
- land that is gained from the sea, a river, or a lake, as by natural tide changes DERELICTION
- land used for camping or grazing animals by ox-wagon travelers OUTSPAN
- absolute ownership of inherited land, allowing the owner to dispose of it as he or she wishes FEE SIMPLE
- appropriation of land, especially common land, by fencing it in ENCLOSURE
- come in to land past the end of the runway, as an aircraft might OVERSHOOT
- come in to land short of the runway, as an aircraft might UNDERSHOOT
- divide land or property into several small units COMMINUTE
- dry, as land might be ARID
- flood land for irrigation purposes FLOAT
- government's right to take over private land or property for public use, compensation usually being paid EMINENT DOMAIN
- inspect or survey a stretch of land, an enemy's positions, or the like RECONNOITER, RECCE, RECCO
- leveling of land, as by erosion or deposition GRADATION
- measure, or measure and map, the heights and distances of an area of land SURVEY
- narrow strip of land, as for allowing an inland country access to the sea CORRIDOR
- narrow strip of land extending into the sea or a lake from the mainland PENINSULA
- narrow strip of land from one territory, state, or the like projecting into another PANHANDLE

year by the ancient Jews SABBATICAL YEAR

landed gentry class, or government by it SQUIREARCHY

landlord or landlady, person letting property under a lease LESSOR
- landlord or other person whose income is derived chiefly from rents or investments RENTIER

landowner in Scotland LAIRD
- landowning gentleman in medieval England FRANKLIN

language See illustration, page 304, and also **grammar, style**
- language, such as Chinese or Swedish, that distinguishes words by their pitch or intonation TONE LANGUAGE
- language, typically extinct and reconstructed by scholars, that is the parent language of a group of later languages URSPRACHE
- language as actually used, rather than as an abstract system PAROLE
- language as an abstract system shared by a speech community LANGUE
- language based on a two or more languages that has developed into a mother tongue CREOLE
- language based on a simplified mix of two or more languages and used for basic communication PIDGIN
- language element, word or part of a word, with a fixed meaning and not divisible into smaller elements MORPHEME
- language expert, a speaker of several languages, or person who studies language LINGUIST
- language family to which English belongs, embracing most European languages and many Indian and Iranian languages INDO-EUROPEAN
- language group or subfamily descended from Latin, including French, Italian, and Spanish ROMANCE
- language of a literary, persuasive, or oratorical kind, or the study of its structure and effects RHETORIC
- language of an earlier stage of development, no longer in everyday use ARCHAISM
- language of an obscene kind BAWDRY
- language of the people, informal everyday speech COLLOQUIAL, VERNACULAR, VULGATE
- language or speech exclusive to a profession or other group JARGON, CANT, ARGOT
- language or speech pattern of an individual person IDIOLECT
- language or speech pattern of a particular regional or social group DIALECT
- language spoken between people who have different mother tongues LINGUA FRANCA, KOINE
- language study based on analysis of actual usage rather than on standards of correctness DESCRIPTIVISM
- language study based on ideas of correctness rather than on actual usage PRESCRIPTIVISM, NORMATIVE GRAMMAR
- language style appropriate to a particular social setting or use REGISTER
- language teaching using very little of the pupils' mother tongue or the formal grammar DIRECT METHOD
- language that is ambiguous or deliberately distorted for propaganda purposes NEWSPEAK
- language that is long-winded, indirect, or evasive CIRCUMLOCUTION, PERIPHRASIS, PROLIXITY
- language that is pompous and showy FUSTIAN, BOMBAST, EUPHUISM, GRANDILOQUENCE
- language used in a graceful, moving, or effective way ELOQUENCE
- ability to use and understand spoken language ORACY
- actual forms of expression in a language USAGE
- adherence to traditional standards or rules, as in the use of language PURISM
- adjective for language or languages LINGUISTIC
- adopt a foreign term fully into the language NATURALIZE
- ancient Semitic language that was spoken by Jesus ARAMAIC
- bureaucratic language or official jargon that is wordy and difficult to understand GOBBLEDYGOOK, OFFICIALESE, BUREAUCRATESE
- collection of texts in a language used for grammatical analysis, compiling dictionaries, and the like CORPUS, TOKENS
- commonly used, popular, as the ordinary form of a language is DEMOTIC, VERNACULAR
- conversational, informal, characteristic of casual spoken language COLLOQUIAL
- feeling for language, an ear for what is correct or appropriate SPRACHGEFÜHL
- gradual change in a language DRIFT
- international language of the sea, used by naval and maritime officers for communication, based on simple English SEASPEAK
- international, synthetic language of various kinds, based typically on common roots from several European languages ESPERANTO, IDO, INTERGLOSSA, INTERLINGUA, NOVIAL, VOLAPÜK
- line on a language map linking places using the same distinctive word or pronunciation ISOGLOSS
- perfect or effortless, as one's use of a foreign language might be FLUENT
- referring to a language such as English or Chinese using word order or function words rather than inflections to indicate grammatical structure ISOLATING, ANALYTICAL
- referring to a language such as Latin, German, or Russian using inflections rather than word order or function words to indicate grammatical structure SYNTHETIC
- referring to a language such as Turkish or Swahili in which complex words are formed by the regular addition of unchanging component units AGGLUTINATIVE
- referring to a mix of languages, as in some witty verse MACARONIC
- referring to events or phenomena, such as language usage, at a given point in time without regard to the historical background SYNCHRONIC
- referring to events or phenomena, such as language usage, viewed as a process of historical development DIACHRONIC
- relating to meaning in language SEMANTIC
- slight and fragmented knowledge, as of a foreign language SMATTERING
- speaking, knowing, or involving only one language MONOLINGUAL, MONOGLOT
- speaking, knowing, or involving several languages MULTILINGUAL, POLYGLOT
- speaking, knowing, or involving two languages BILINGUAL
- statistical study of the historical relationship between different languages GLOTTOCHRONOLOGY
- study or science of grammar in language, or the grammar of a sentence, phrase, or the like SYNTAX
- study or science of language LINGUISTICS, PHILOLOGY
- study or science of language meaning SEMANTICS
- study or science of language sounds PHONETICS, PHONOLOGY, PHONEMICS
- study or science of language use, including contexts, behavior of speakers, and the like PRAGMATICS

- style of expressing oneself in language, way of putting things PHRASEOLOGY, DICTION
- text used by linguists for analyzing features of language beyond the level of single sentences DISCOURSE
- using language clearly and effectively ARTICULATE

language (combining form) LINGU-, LINGUA-, GLOSS-, -GLOT

language speaker (combining form) -PHONE

lantern made from a pumpkin JACK-O'-LANTERN
- lantern with a thick glass lens BULL'S-EYE

lapel, turned-back cuff, or other part of clothing showing the reverse side REVERS

lapse, uncharacteristic piece of behavior or thinking ABERRATION, BRAINSTORM

large See also **huge, fat**

Indo-European Languages

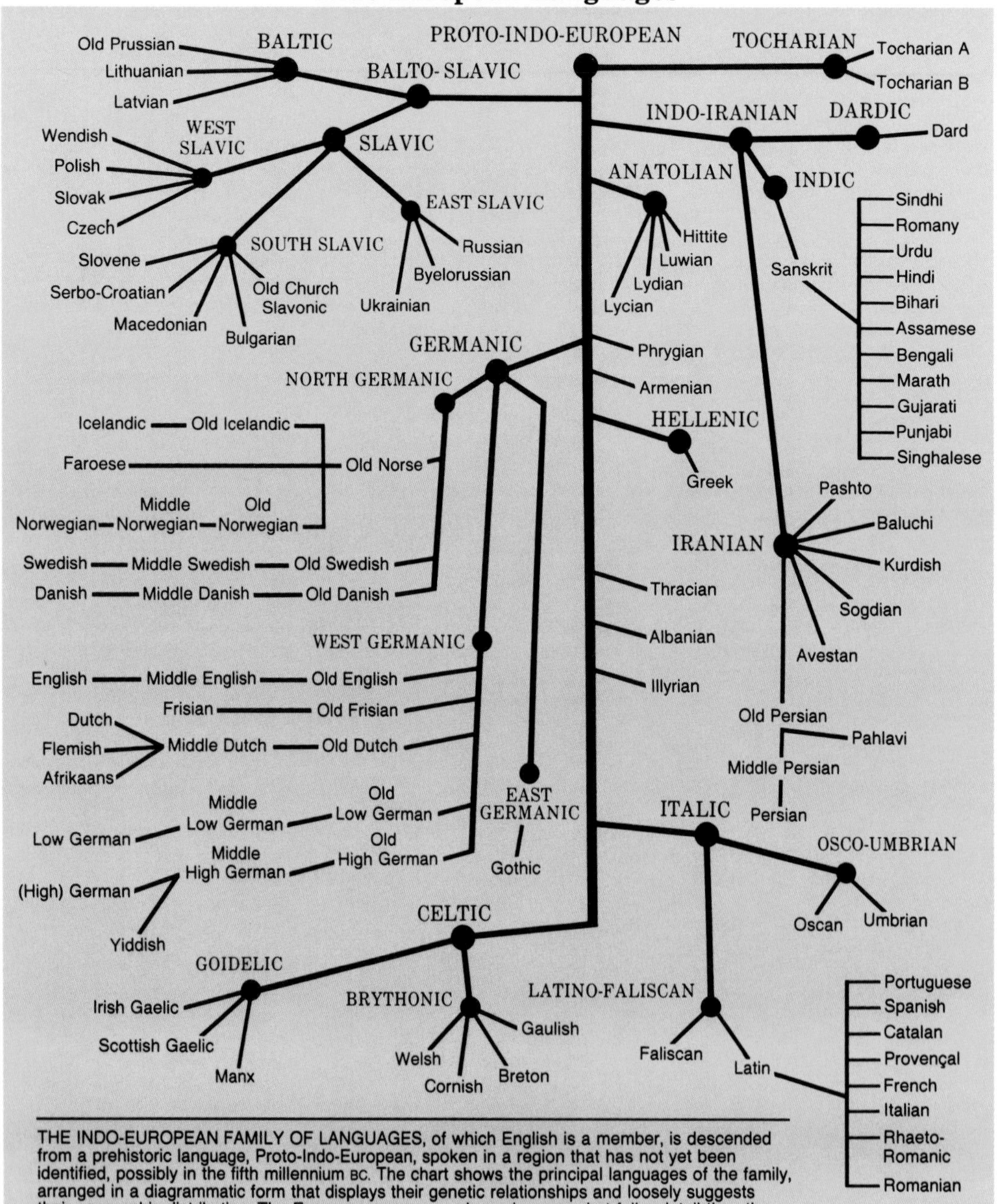

PROTO-INDO-EUROPEAN

BALTO-SLAVIC
BALTIC
Old Prussian
Lithuanian
Latvian
SLAVIC
WEST SLAVIC
Wendish
Polish
Slovak
Czech
EAST SLAVIC
Russian
Byelorussian
Ukrainian
SOUTH SLAVIC
Slovene
Serbo-Croatian
Macedonian
Bulgarian
Old Church Slavonic

TOCHARIAN
Tocharian A
Tocharian B

INDO-IRANIAN
DARDIC
Dard
INDIC
Sanskrit
Sindhi
Romany
Urdu
Hindi
Bihari
Assamese
Bengali
Marath
Gujarati
Punjabi
Singhalese
IRANIAN
Pashto
Baluchi
Kurdish
Sogdian
Avestan
Old Persian
Pahlavi
Middle Persian
Persian

ANATOLIAN
Hittite
Luwian
Lydian
Lycian

Phrygian
Armenian
HELLENIC
Greek
Thracian
Albanian
Illyrian

GERMANIC
NORTH GERMANIC
Icelandic — Old Icelandic
Faroese
Old Norse
Norwegian — Middle Norwegian — Old Norwegian
Swedish — Middle Swedish — Old Swedish
Danish — Middle Danish — Old Danish
WEST GERMANIC
English — Middle English — Old English
Frisian — Old Frisian
Dutch, Flemish, Afrikaans — Middle Dutch — Old Dutch
Low German — Middle Low German — Old Low German
(High) German, Yiddish — Middle High German — Old High German
EAST GERMANIC
Gothic

ITALIC
OSCO-UMBRIAN
Oscan
Umbrian
LATINO-FALISCAN
Faliscan
Latin
Portuguese
Spanish
Catalan
Provençal
French
Italian
Rhaeto-Romanic
Romanian

CELTIC
GOIDELIC
Irish Gaelic
Scottish Gaelic
Manx
BRYTHONIC
Gaulish
Welsh
Cornish
Breton

THE INDO-EUROPEAN FAMILY OF LANGUAGES, of which English is a member, is descended from a prehistoric language, Proto-Indo-European, spoken in a region that has not yet been identified, possibly in the fifth millennium BC. The chart shows the principal languages of the family, arranged in a diagrammatic form that displays their genetic relationships and loosely suggests their geographic distribution. The European groups are shown in somewhat fuller detail than the Asian groups, and in the Germanic group, to which English belongs, the intermediate historical phases of the languages are also shown.

- large, bulky, ungainly and heavy PONDEROUS, HULKING, UNWIELDY
- large, considerable, as in size or number AMPLE, SUBSTANTIAL
- large, grand, impressive IMPOSING, MONUMENTAL, GRANDIOSE
- large, spacious, roomy, extensive COMMODIOUS, CAPACIOUS, VOLUMINOUS
- large, sturdy and thickset BURLY
- large or long, and disorganized, as a house or speech might be RAMBLING
- large-scale and indiscriminate, as slaughter might be WHOLESALE

large (combining form) MACRO-, MAXI-, MEGA-, MEGALO-

larger (combining form) SUPER-

larks - flock of larks EXALTATION

larva See also **insect**
- larva, as of the mayfly or dragonfly, that develops directly into the adult rather than going through the pupal stage NYMPH
- larva of an oyster or other bivalve mollusk SPAT
- larva of the mayfly or similar insect, living in water NAIAD

laser-produced three-dimensional photo or pattern HOLOGRAM

lasso - lassolike device of a rope with weights attached, used in South America for catching cattle or game by snaring the legs BOLA
- lasso used for catching livestock LARIAT

last, final, concluding ULTIMATE
- last but one, second to last PENULTIMATE
- last but two, third from last ANTEPENULTIMATE
- last part of something, the end OMEGA

last resort, expedient adopted for want of any alternative PIS ALLER, FAUTE DE MIEUX
- last resort, of unsuspected power or effectiveness TRUMP CARD
- as a last resort, if all else fails IN EXTREMIS

Last Supper - cup or platter used, according to medieval legend, by Jesus at the Last Supper GRAIL, HOLY GRAIL, SANGREAL
- room in which the Last Supper took place CENACLE

last things - branch of theology dealing with last things, such as heaven and hell ESCHATOLOGY

lastborn - right of the lastborn son to inherit the estate ULTIMOGENITURE, BOROUGH ENGLISH

lasting only a short time, short-lived, fleeting EPHEMERAL, TRANSITORY
- lasting throughout the year, as high snows might PERENNIAL

late, after the appropriate time, as thanks or a gift might be BELATED
- late, past the due time of arrival or return, as a train or library book might be OVERDUE
- late-blooming period of contentment or tranquil success, as in the autumn of one's life INDIAN SUMMER
- late in acting, tending to postpone or delay DILATORY, PROCRASTINATING
- late in arriving, unpunctual, or slow and reluctant TARDY
- late in paying rent or some other debt IN ARREARS
- delay, be late or slow in doing something TARRY
- delay, put off a duty or the like till later PROCRASTINATE

later SUBSEQUENTLY

later (combining form) META-, POST-

latest fashion DERNIER CRI

lathe with a swiveling attachment holding a number of tools for successive operations CAPSTAN LATHE, TURRET LATHE
- rotating shaft, as in a lathe or other machine tool ARBOR, SPINDLE, MANDREL
- vice or clamp used to hold a tool or workpiece, as in a drill or lathe CHUCK

Latin See chart, pages 306–307, and also **legal**
- Latin and Greek literature THE CLASSICS
- Latin as spoken by the common people in ancient Rome, from which the Romance languages developed VULGAR LATIN
- Latin version of the Bible by Saint Jerome, authorized by the Roman Catholic Church VULGATE
- relating to writings mixing a modern language with Latin or mock-Latin MACARONIC

Latin America - adjective for Spain and Latin America except Brazil HISPANIC
- large farming estate, as in Latin America or ancient Rome LATIFUNDIUM
- ranch or ranch house in Spain or in Latin America HACIENDA

laugh See also **mock**
- laugh, giggle, or smile in a silly, coy, and affected way SIMPER
- laugh in a snide, malicious, or slightly stifled way SNIGGER, SNICKER, TITTER
- laugh loudly, make belly laughs GUFFAW, CACHINNATE
- laugh with a throaty chuckle CHORTLE
- loud, unrestrained or coarse laugh HORSE LAUGH, BELLY LAUGH

laughable, absurd LUDICROUS
- laughable, relating to laughter, or inclined to laugh RISIBLE
- laughably inadequate, insultingly small or mean, as a proposed pay increase might be DERISORY

laughing jackass KOOKABURRA

laughter or enjoyment MIRTH, GLEE
- laughter that is loud and uninhibited HILARITY
- fit of uncontrollable laughter CONVULSIONS
- spreading from one person to another easily, as laughter or enthusiasm might be INFECTIOUS, CONTAGIOUS

laundry - device for squeezing water from wet laundry by pressing it between rollers WRINGER, MANGLE
- laundry basket HAMPER
- laundryman in India DHOBI

lava in a solidified sheet COULÉE
- lava rock of a glassy black type OBSIDIAN, BASALT
- molten rock material that flows out as lava on the surface MAGMA
- referring to rocks formed from solidified lava IGNEOUS
- solid lava fragments from a volcano SCORIAE, CINDERS, SLAG

lavatory, especially one in an outhouse PRIVY
- lavatory in which matter is later covered with earth EARTH CLOSET
- lavatory at a military base or camp LATRINE
- lavatory or privy behind a dormitory in an abbey or monastery RERE-DORTER
- lavatory tank, water tank in the roof, or similar container CISTERN
- communal lavatories and bathroom facilities at a military base or camp ABLUTIONS
- device controlling water levels, as in a lavatory cistern, based on a floating ball connected to a valve BALL COCK
- euphemistic term for a lavatory RESTROOM, COMFORT STATION, TOILET
- old term for a lavatory JAKES
- pipe carrying sewage from a lavatory SOIL PIPE
- ship's lavatory HEAD

law See also **legal, court, trial**
- law, or order that has the force of law DECREE, EDICT, PROCLAMATION, RESCRIPT, FIAT, UKASE
- law, rule, or code of laws CANON
- law as relating to practice and procedure rather than legal principles ADJECTIVE LAW
- law as relating to rights, duties, and legal principles rather than practice and procedure SUBSTANTIVE LAW
- law based on custom and court decisions rather than written codes COMMON LAW

- law based on judgments in earlier cases rather than strictly on statutes CASE LAW
- law courts and judges collectively JUDICATURE, JUDICIARY
- law-enforcement officer in a county SHERIFF
- law formally enacted and recorded STATUTE
- law giving special powers to a government department or the like ENABLING ACT
- law or principle of all things, cosmic or natural law in Hindu philosophy DHARMA
- law or rule no longer enforced though still officially valid DEAD-LETTER LAW
- law setting a time limit for enforcing a right or bringing a legal action STATUTE OF LIMITATIONS
- laws framed into a complete system PANDECTS, CODE, CANON
- laws of genetic inheritance MENDEL'S LAWS
- lawful, legal, in accordance with the law LEGITIMATE, LICIT
- lawmaking, or a law or laws made by means of drafting and enacting LEGISLATION
- administer justice or the law DISPENSE
- against the law ILLEGITIMATE, ILLICIT, ILLEGAL
- applying to the past, or taking effect as from a date in the past, as a law might be RETROACTIVE, RETROSPECTIVE, EX POST FACTO
- body of legal rules based on natural justice and fairness, supplementing and moderating common and statute law EQUITY
- branch of government authorized to make laws LEGISLATURE
- branch of government responsible for carrying out the laws EXECUTIVE, ADMINISTRATION
- breaking of a law or regulation VIOLATION, BREACH, INFRINGEMENT, TRANSGRESSION, INFRACTION, CONTRAVENTION, FLOUTING

LATIN WORDS AND PHRASES

a fortiori	all the more so, with even greater reason
a priori	self-evident, known independently of experience; from the general to the particular, as deductive reasoning is
ab ovo	"from the egg": from the beginning
ad hoc	"for this thing": for a particular purpose or occasion, as a committee might be
ad hominem	"to the person": directed at someone personally, as criticism might be
ad lib/ad libitum	"at pleasure": freely, unscripted, improvised
ad nauseam	to the point of disgust
aegrotat	"he is ill": sickness certificate
alma mater	"nourishing mother": one's old school, college, or university
alumnus	"foster child": former student, as of an alma mater
annus mirabilis	year of wonders, great achievements or disasters, or the like
bona fide	"in good faith": genuine or sincere
casus belli	"cause of war": justification or cause of a dispute
cave	"beware": look out, be careful
caveat emptor	"let the buyer beware": the principle that a purchaser cannot assume that his or her purchase will be exactly as hoped
compos mentis	"of sound mind": sane
cum laude	"with praise": referring to a good examination result or degree
curriculum vitae	"course of life": outline or résumé, as on a job application, of one's qualifications and career
de facto	"in reality": regardless of legal status
de jure	in accordance with the law, by right, legally
de profundis	"from the depths": in deep despair
deo volente/d.v.	"God willing"
deus ex machina	"god out of a machine": person or thing that suddenly resolves a problem; device providing a contrived resolution in a play
ex gratia	"out of goodness": referring to a payment made as a favor, not an obligation
ex libris	"from the books": phrase used before the owner's name on bookplates
felo-de-se	"felon of himself": suicide
festina lente	"hasten slowly": more haste, less speed
genius loci	"spirit of the place": atmosphere of a place and its influence on visitors
in loco parentis	"in the place of a parent": having the responsibilities or role of a parent
in medias res	"into the midst of things": the way a story or play might begin

- breaking or violation of civil law, other than breach of contract TORT
- bring a law into operation by official publication of it PROMULGATE
- bringing a lawsuit, pursuing a case in court LITIGATION
- by right, legally, according to law DE JURE
- cancel or invalidate a law RESCIND, REVOKE, REPEAL, ANNUL, QUASH
- civilian who arrogates law-enforcement and punitive powers to himself or herself VIGILANTE
- collect and arrange laws, rules, principles, or the like into a comprehensive system CODIFY
- confirm a law, ruling, or the like RATIFY, SANCTION
- court case debated as a training exercise by law students MOOT
- draft and enact laws LEGISLATE
- exemption or release from a rule, law, obligation, or the like DISPENSATION
- expert on the law or legal principles JURIST
- full listing of laws or court rulings DIGEST
- gap or oversight, as in a law or contract, making evasion possible LOOPHOLE
- implying or setting standards of acceptability, as a strict law or a prescriptive grammar is NORMATIVE
- in force, as laws might be OPERATIVE
- injustice resulting from inconsistencies, bias, or unfairness, as in a law INEQUITY
- invalid, inoperative, or powerless, as a disregarded law or regulation is NUGATORY
- making or relating to rules or laws PRESCRIPTIVE
- official doorkeeper in a court of law or the like USHER, SERGEANT AT ARMS
- overturning or cancellation, as of a law or judgment ANNULMENT, ABROGATION, CASSATION
- person or group that is sued by

LATIN WORDS AND PHRASES *continued*

in toto	completely, "as a whole," totally
infra dig/infra dignitatem	"beneath (one's) dignity"
inter alia	"among other things"
ipso facto	"by that fact": as an immediate consequence of that fact or act
magnum opus	"great work": major work of a writer, composer, or the like
mea culpa	"my fault": acknowledging one's guilt
mirabile dictu	"wonderful to relate": amazingly
modus operandi	"way of working": method of proceeding with a task
modus vivendi	"way of living": compromise or living arrangement between people or parties of differing interests
mutatis mutandis	with the necessary or appropriate changes having been made
ne plus ultra	"no more beyond": the limit; perfection
nil desperandum	"nothing to be despaired of": don't despair; never say die
non sequitur	"it does not follow": an illogical remark or inapplicable statement
obiter dictum	"said by the way": an incidental remark
pace	"by leave of": as used in front of someone's name as an apology when contradicting him or her
per capita	measured "by head" of the population, per person
per se	"by itself," in itself, as such, intrinsically
persona non grata	"unacceptable person": person, especially a diplomat, whose presence is not welcome
pons asinorum	"bridge of donkeys": test for beginners; problem that the slow-witted cannot solve
prima facie	"at first sight": on the face of it
pro rata	"in proportion"
quid pro quo	"something in return for something else": a favor in return, a substitution or fair exchange
quod erat demonstrandum/ Q.E.D.	"which was to be demonstrated": as added to the end of a proof to show that the point has been made
rara avis	"rare bird": unusual or exceptional person or thing
sine die	"without a day": at no set date, indefinitely
sine qua non	"without which not": a necessity, something indispensable
status quo	the present position, the "existing state" of affairs
sub rosa	"under the rose": secretly, confidentially, privately
sui generis	"of its own kind": unique
victor ludorum	"winner of the games": sports champion
vox populi	"the voice of the people": public opinion

another, party against which a lawsuit is brought DEFENDANT
- person or group that sues another, party initiating a lawsuit PLAINTIFF
- philosophy or the science of law JURISPRUDENCE
- power or right to administer laws and justice JURISDICTION
- relating to criminal law and court cases FORENSIC
- relating to, permitted, or enforced by the law LEGAL
- sessions of the law courts in English and Welsh counties in former times ASSIZES
- severe and literal in interpreting the law LEGALISTIC, RHADAMANTHINE
- very harsh, as laws or punishments might be DRACONIAN

law (combining form) NOM-, NOMO-, -NOMY, JUR-

lawn or grassy meadow SWARD

lawyer See also **legal**
- lawyer giving legal advice in a court case COUNSEL
- lawyer representing a client ATTORNEY
- lawyer who pleads a case on behalf of a client in court ADVOCATE
- lawyer who uses unscrupulous and dubious methods PETTIFOGGER
- British lawyer at a lower court SOLICITOR
- British lawyer at a superior court BARRISTER
- government lawyer who argues the case against the accused in a criminal trial PUBLIC PROSECUTOR
- seeking of or meeting for advice, as from a doctor or lawyer CONSULTATION

laxative, bowel stimulant CATHARTIC, EVACUANT, PHYSIC, PURGATIVE, APERIENT
- medicinal salts used as a vigorous laxative and for reducing inflammation EPSOM SALTS

lay down as a condition in an agreement or contract STIPULATE

layer, as of folded cloth or paper PLY
- layer, as of rock, archeological remains, or skin cells STRATUM
- layer of green oxide forming on a copper or bronze surface PATINA, VERDIGRIS, AERUGO
- layer on or near the outside, as of a root or stem, or brain or kidney CORTEX
- layer or thin plate or scale of plant or animal tissue LAMELLA, LAMINA
- having concentric layers such as those of the onion TUNICATE
- split or beat into thin layers, or join several layers together LAMINATE

layered (combining form) -FOLIATE

layout or design of a book or magazine FORMAT

laziness IDLENESS, INDOLENCE
- laziness, aversion to work or effort SLOTH, ACCIDIE, ACEDIA
- laziness, dullness of mind, indifference, lack of emotion or interest APATHY, HEBETUDE
- laziness, indifference, sluggishness LETHARGY
- laziness, torpor, exhaustion LANGUOR, LASSITUDE

lazy IDLE, INDOLENT
- lazy, careless, unconcerned or slack LAX, REMISS, LACKADAISICAL, INSOUCIANT
- lazy, dull, or sluggish COSTIVE, BOVINE
- lazy, good-for-nothing, habitually avoiding work or commitment SHIFTLESS, WORK-SHY
- lazy, idle, useless, or superfluous OTIOSE
- lazy, incompetent, or ungainly person SLOUCH, SCHLEPPER
- lazy, lacking energy, will, or vitality, sluggish LISTLESS, LETHARGIC, TORPID, LANGUID
- lazy, neglectful, shirking TRUANT
- lazy, sluggish, difficult to arouse, resisting motion or activity INERT
- lazy, torpid, sleepy COMATOSE
- lazy and self-indulgent person devoted to pleasure and luxury LOTUS-EATER, SYBARITE, VOLUPTUARY
- lazy by nature, unemotional in temperament, calm, unexcitable PHLEGMATIC, LYMPHATIC
- lazy in a carefree or irresponsible way FAINÉANT
- lazy man who idles away his time in fashionable places LOUNGE LIZARD
- lazy or inactive period of one's life DOG DAYS
- lazy person, addicted to inactive amusements such as watching television COUCH POTATO
- lazy person, aimless idler, loafer FLANEUR, WASTREL
- lazy person, idler SLUGGARD
- lazy person, lagging behind LAGGARD, DAWDLER
- be lazy, avoid work, neglect one's duties SHIRK, MALINGER

lead See also **order, begin**
- lead, arrange, guide, set in order MARSHAL
- lead, conduct, and escort, or precede and introduce USHER
- lead, direct, have authority over a meeting, committee, or the like PRESIDE
- lead, escort and protect on a journey CONVOY
- lead, first step or action, initial impulse THE INITIATIVE
- lead an attack, drive, or the like SPEARHEAD
- leading, foremost, chief, supreme PARAMOUNT, PREDOMINANT, PREEMINENT, PREPONDERANT
- leading character, as in a play, novel, or other literary work PROTAGONIST
- leading position of power, influence, or control DOMINANCE, PREEMINENCE, ASCENDANCY, PRIMACY, SUPREMACY

lead oxide, red lead, as used formerly in paint MINIUM, CINNABAR
- lead poisoning PLUMBISM, SATURNISM
- lead weight hanging on a cord or line, as used in fishing, depth-sounding, or for determining a truly vertical line PLUMB
- dark gray allotropic form of carbon used for pencil leads and as a lubricant GRAPHITE, PLUMBAGO

lead (combining form) PLUMB-, PLUMBO-

leader See chart
- leader in name only, without any real power or true responsibility FIGUREHEAD, FRONT MAN
- leader or founder of a movement PATRON SAINT
- leader or initiator in any field of endeavor TRAILBLAZER, PIONEER, INNOVATOR, GROUNDBREAKER, TRENDSETTER, PACEMAKER
- leader or representative of a faithful or closely knit group BELLWETHER
- leaders or those in the most advanced position of a military advance, artistic movement, or the like VANGUARD
- idealistic or visionary, promising deliverance or prosperity, as a charismatic leader might MESSIANIC
- spiritual teacher or leader, as among Hindus or Sikhs GURU

leader (combining form) -GOGUE, -ARCH

leaf See illustration, page 310
- leaf-eating, feeding on leaves PHYLLOPHAGOUS
- leaf made up of three leaflets TREFOIL
- leaf of a fern or palm FROND
- leaf-patterned carving on the capital of a Corinthian column ACANTHUS
- leaflike plant part growing in pairs at the base of some leaves STIPULE
- leaflike plant part just beneath a flower or cluster of flowers BRACT
- leaflike sheath that encloses a flower spike, as on the cuckoopint SPATHE
- leaves FOLIAGE
- leaves or petals in a radiating pattern WHORL
- angle between a leafstalk and the

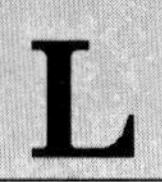

LEADERS AND RULERS

aga	high-ranking official of the Ottoman Empire
ashantehene	paramount chief of the Ashanti people, of Ghana
ataman/ hetman	Cossack chief
ayatollah	highest ranking religious leader of the Shiite branch of Islam
bey/beg	provincial governor or other high official in the Ottoman Empire
cacique	chief of a Native American tribe in Latin America; local political boss in Latin America
Caesar	Roman emperor; any powerful or dictatorial leader
caliph	ruler of a Muslim state
capo	divisional leader in the Mafia
caudillo	Spanish military dictator
chogyal	ruler of Sikkim
collector	chief administrative officer of a district of India during British rule
consul	chief official or magistrate in ancient Rome, ruling in a pair
czar	emperor of Russia in former times
Dalai Lama	Buddhist leader of Tibet (now in exile)
dey	Turkish governor or commander in Algeria in former times
doge	chief magistrate of the old republics of Venice and of Genoa
duce	leader in Italy (especially Mussolini)
emir	Muslim prince, chieftain, or governor in the Middle East
fugleman	political leader; formerly, a leader or demonstrator in military drill
führer	leader in Germany (especially Hitler)
gauleiter	district governor in Nazi Germany
kabaka	former ruler of the Baganda people of Uganda
kaiser	Holy Roman emperor, Austro-Hungarian emperor, or German emperor
khan/cham	medieval emperor or ruler in China or central Asia
khedive	viceroy in Egypt during the period of Ottoman control
mandarin	senior civil servant in imperial China; any powerful and relatively independent official
mikado/tenno	emperor of Japan
nawab	Muslim prince or ruler in India in former times
nizam	former ruler of Hyderabad
pasha	former provincial governor in the Ottoman Empire
sachem/ sagamore	Native American tribal chief
satrap	provincial governor in ancient Persia; any dictatorial minor ruler
sheikh	leader of an Arab tribe or village; Muslim religious leader
shogun	Japanese military commander, especially any of those who effectively ruled Japan in former times
stadholder	chief magistrate or provincial governor in the Netherlands in former times
sultan	ruler of a Muslim state, especially in the Ottoman Empire
suzerain	feudal lord
taoiseach	prime minister of the Irish Republic
tetrarch	any of four joint rulers, or ruler of a quarter of a region; prince enjoying limited power in the Roman Empire
tuchun	military governor of a Chinese province in former times
viceroy	governor of a country, colony, or the like, ruling in the name of his sovereign or government
vizier	high-ranking official, such as a provincial governor or chief minister, in Muslim countries, especially in the Ottoman Empire

stem, between a branch and the trunk, or the like AXIL
- arrangement of leaves on a stem PHYLLOTAXY
- attached at the base, without a stalk, as a leaf might be SESSILE
- blade of a leaf or petal LAMINA
- blistered or wrinkled in appearance, as some leaves are BULLATE

- clover or similar plant with compound leaves of three leaflets SHAMROCK
- cluster of leaves. branches, and the like FASCICLE, FASCICULE
- covered with a sticky substance, as some leaves are VISCID
- covered with stiff bristly hairs, as some leaves are STRIGOSE
- covered with very fine, small, or woolly hairs, as some leaves are LANATE, CILIATE, VILLOUS
- curved like a scimitar, as some leaves are ACINACIFORM
- dry, withered, shriveled, as a dead leaf would be SERE
- falling off or shed at a point of time or growth, as leaves or antlers might be DECIDUOUS
- green pigment in leaves that traps energy from sunlight for photosynthesis CHLOROPHYLL
- having wavy edges, as some leaves are CRENATE, CRENULATE, SINUATE, REPAND
- lose or give off water vapor through pores, as from the surface of a leaf TRANSPIRE
- main axis or stem, as of a flower cluster, compound leaf, or feather RACHIS
- notch or hollow between the lobes of a leaf, petal, or the like SINUS
- plant's use of light energy, absorbed by chlorophyll in the leaves and other plant tissues PHOTOSYNTHESIS
- pointed, tapering to a tip, as some leaves are ACUMINATE, APICULATE, CUSPIDATE
- pore on the surface of a leaf for the passage of gases and water vapor STOMA
- ridged or wrinkled in appearance, as some leaves are RUGOSE
- relating to or resembling a leaf or leaves FOLIACEOUS, FOLIATE
- remaining attached to the plant even after withering, as some leaves and flowers are PERSISTENT
- rounded projecting part, as on the ear or a leaf LOBE
- stalk attaching a leaf to a stem PETIOLE
- strip a tree or other plant of leaves, as by means of a chemical spray in a war zone DEFOLIATE
- tiny leaf or leaflet, as on a fern frond PINNA
- vein or rib of a leaf NERVURE
- veins, or the arrangement of veins, on a leaf, insect's wing, or the like VENATION

leaf (combining form) -PHYLL, PHYLLO-, FOLI-, FOLIO-

leaflet, advertisement, or notice distributed widely CIRCULAR, FLIER
- leaflet distributed by hand, handout HANDBILL

leafy retreat ARBOR, BOWER

leakage, oozing SEEPAGE
- amount of liquid, grain, or the like that evaporates or leaks from a container ULLAGE

lean back or lie down RECLINE
- lean or tip over to one side, as a ship or boat might LIST, HEEL OVER, KEEL OVER, CAREEN
- leaning or resting against related tissue, as a body organ might be RECUMBENT

leap See **jump**

leap year BISSEXTILE YEAR
- year with an extra day or month inserted, such as a leap year INTERCALARY YEAR

learn, determine, or discover by ex-

Leaf Shapes

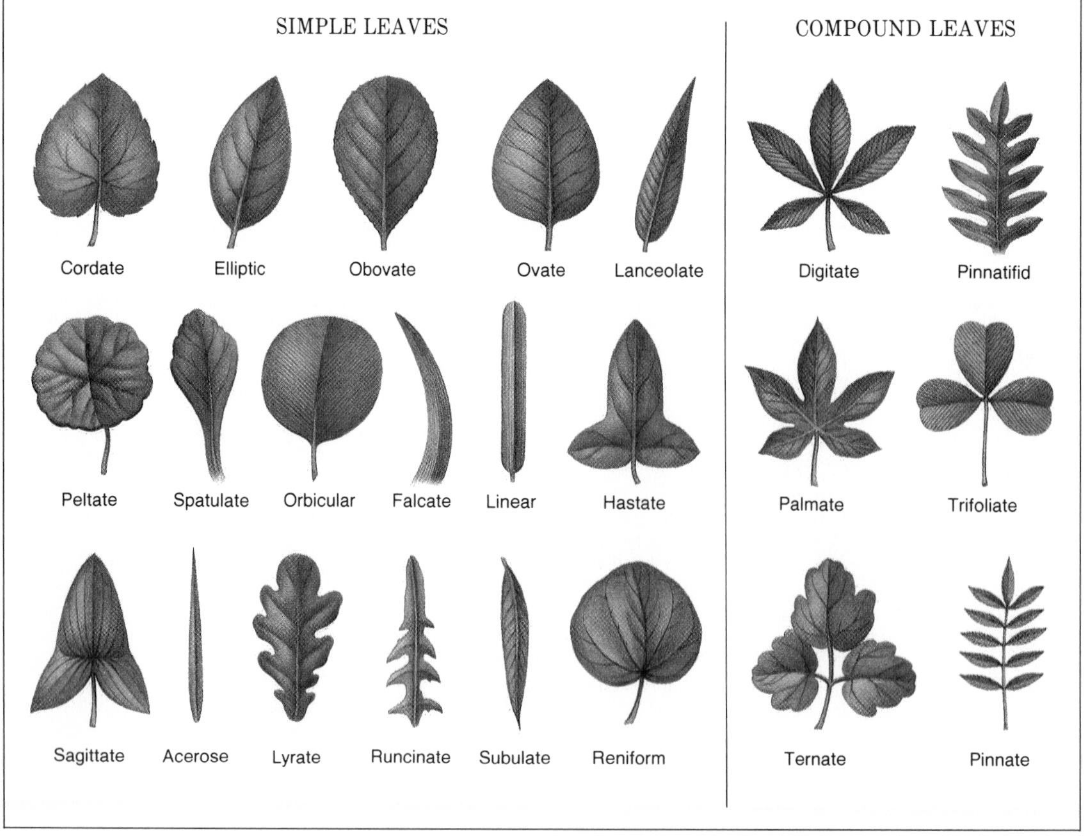

SIMPLE LEAVES

Cordate, Elliptic, Obovate, Ovate, Lanceolate

Peltate, Spatulate, Orbicular, Falcate, Linear, Hastate

Sagittate, Acerose, Lyrate, Runcinate, Subulate, Reniform

COMPOUND LEAVES

Digitate, Pinnatifid

Palmate, Trifoliate

Ternate, Pinnate

LEATHERS AND HIDES

box calf	calfskin tanned black, with square-shaped markings
buff	thick, soft, undyed leather, cream to light brown in color, typically made from buffalo, ox, or elk hide
cabretta	soft leather made from the skins of African or South American sheep
capeskin	soft leather made from the skins of lambs or sheep with hairlike wool
chamois	soft leather, as for garments or for polishing, originally from a mountain antelope, now commonly from flesh side of deerskin or sheepskin
chevrette	leather made from the skin of a young goat
cordovan	fine leather, usually from horsehide, originally made from goatskin in Cordoba, Spain
glacé kid	soft shoe leather with a glossy finish
levant/ levant morocco	morocco leather patterned with irregular creases
mocha	soft goatskin or sheepskin with a suede finish, used for gloves
morocco/ morocco leather/ morocco goat	fine, soft leather made from goatskin treated with sumac, originally made in Morocco, and used mainly for bookbinding and shoes
nappa	soft leather made from kid, lambskin, or sheepskin, used for gloves and garments
patent leather	leather or imitation leather lacquered to give a hard, glossy finish
rawhide	untanned hide
roan	soft, flexible leather with a close, tough grain, made from sheepskin
shagreen	rough, grainy leather; untreated sharkskins, or ray skins, used as abrasives
skiver	soft, thin leather made from hair side of sheepskin
slink/hair calf	skin of a prematurely born calf
washleather	soft split leather dressed with oil in imitation of chamois

amination or experimentation ASCERTAIN
- learn, grasp mentally, understand APPREHEND
- learn and understand something thoroughly ASSIMILATE, DIGEST
- learn by heart, memorize LEARN BY ROTE, CON
- learn or collect information or the like bit by bit GLEAN

learned, scholarly ERUDITE
- learned in a showy way, as deliberately "literary" terms are INKHORN
- learned person, especially an expert in a particular field of study SAVANT
- learned person who is knowledgeable in many subjects POLYMATH, POLYHISTOR
- learned written study on a particular subject TREATISE

learning, culture HUMANISM
- learning, scholarly knowledge ERUDITION
- learning based on step-by-step instruction from a book or computer rather than by classroom lessons PROGRAMMED LEARNING
- learning of a formal, unimaginative, dryly detailed kind PEDANTRY
- learning or remembering by repetition rather than through understanding ROTE-LEARNING
- learning or teaching by means of lessons heard during sleep HYPNOPEDIA
- learning process in young animals IMPRINTING
- learning process, training, or behavior modification through adjustment of stimuli CONDITIONING
- helping or encouraging the process of learning or discovery HEURISTIC
- institution for the advancement of learning ATHENAEUM
- strengthening of learning by means of rewards or punishments REINFORCEMENT

lease - a person who grants a lease LESSOR

leaseholder LESSEE

leash - free a dog, hawk, or the like from its leash or any other form of restraint SLIP
- ring on a dog's collar for attaching a leash TERRET

leather See chart
- leather, goatskin, or sheepskin treated for writing or painting on PARCHMENT
- leather or canvas strip for sharpening a straight razor STROP
- leather strap split into strips at the end, used for beating prisoners or children CAT-O'-NINE-TAILS, TAWS
- leather strip THONG
- leatherlike, tough CORIACEOUS
- aged artificially, as some furniture or leather is DISTRESSED
- bend leather, as in shoemaking CRIMP
- decorate leather or a similar material with a pattern of tiny holes PINK
- dress leather by rubbing DUB
- grainy or crinkled surface, as on leather or paper PEBBLE
- grease of tallow and oil used for waterproofing leather DUBBIN
- person who softens, dyes, or prepares tanned leather CURRIER
- pointed instrument for making holes in leather or cloth AWL, BODKIN
- soften, dye, or prepare tanned leather CURRY
- stamped or gilded ornamenting on books or leather TOOLING
- tan hides, as with alum or salt, especially to produce pale leather TAW

leave See also **depart**

- leave behind, abandon, desert or give up FORSAKE, RELINQUISH
- leave granted, as to a soldier, for reasons of personal distress, such as a death in the family COMPASSIONATE LEAVE
- leave of absence, as from school EXEAT
- leave of absence in the armed forces FURLOUGH
- absence without leave AWOL, FRENCH LEAVE

leave-taking, farewell, good-bye VALEDICTION

leaves See **leaf**

Lebanese Christian MARONITE

lecherous man SATYR

lecture made by a recently installed professor, president, or the like INAUGURAL LECTURE
- lecture of a boring, moralizing kind HOMILY
- lecture or treatise on or formal study of a subject DISQUISITION

lecturer in certain universities LECTOR, DOCENT

leech, earthworm, or other similarly segmented worm ANNELID

leek, onion, garlic, or related plant ALLIUM

leer, stare at lustfully OGLE

left-hand page in a book VERSO
- left-handed, on the left, or relating to the left side SINISTRAL
- left-hander, specifically a ballplayer or boxer adopting a left-handed stance SOUTHPAW
- left side of a ship PORT, LARBOARD
- left-winger or extreme radical BOLSHEVIK, BOLSHIE
- both left-handed and right-handed, able to use both hands equally expertly AMBIDEXTROUS

left, leftward (combining form) LEV-, LEVO-

left over, surviving, remaining, continuing RESIDUAL
- leftover food, scrap ORT
- leftover part, inferior remnant RUMP
- leftovers or remains of something destroyed REMNANTS, VESTIGES, WRACK
- referring to leftover food that is warmed up before serving RÉCHAUFFÉ

leg, especially the lower leg between knee and foot SHANK, CRUS
- leg coverings, either a long cloth strip for winding or a wide canvas strip for buckling around the leg PUTTEE
- leg coverings, of cloth or leather, buttoned from knee to ankle and strapped under the foot GAITER, LEGGING
- leg covering, of leather, as formerly worn to protect against splashes when riding SPATTERDASH
- leg covering or gaiter, as on the leg of a rider GAMBADO
- leg coverings of leather, worn over the trousers, as by cowboys CHAPS, CHAPARAJOS
- leg of an item of furniture, curving outward near the top, and then inward to an ornamental foot CABRIOLE
- leg of lamb GIGOT
- leg support consisting of metal rods with straps CALIPER, CALIPER SPLINT
- angle or fork formed by steps, trouser legs, or the like CROTCH
- relating to the leg, shank, or thigh CRURAL
- tendon on the leg, above and behind the knee HAMSTRING
- vein, especially in the legs, that has become abnormally knotted and swollen VARICOSE VEIN, VARIX

legacy, heritage PATRIMONY
- legacy or inheritance BEQUEST

legal See chart, and also **law, court, trial**
- legal, proper, conforming with the requirements CANONICAL
- legal authorization to act as another's agent, or the document conveying it POWER OF ATTORNEY, PROCURATION
- legal case arousing great public interest CAUSE CÉLÈBRE
- legal document, analyzing a case and detailing instructions BRIEF
- legal document certifying a contract or transfer of property DEED
- legal means of ensuring justice REMEDY
- legal philosophy JURISPRUDENCE
- legal right DROIT
- legally acceptable, binding, or in force, as a title or passport might be VALID
- legally qualified ADMISSIBLE, COMPETENT, ELIGIBLE
- legally required LIABLE
- bringing a legal action, pursuing a case in court LITIGATION
- heading in or section of a legal code RUBRIC

leisure activity, hobby AVOCATION

lemon or orange rind used as flavoring ZEST
- sliver of lemon to decorate or flavor a drink TWIST

length, height, or width DIMENSION
- length of time for which something continues or lasts DURATION
- ancient measure of length, based on the length of the arm from fingertip to elbow CUBIT
- relating to length LONGITUDINAL

lenient and unwilling to impose discipline on others INDULGENT, PERMISSIVE

lens, as though from a pair of glasses, for just one eye MONOCLE
- lens covering a watch face LUNETTE
- lens defect or the blurred pear-shaped image it causes COMA
- lens of a compound or twofold prescription, correcting for both near and distant vision BIFOCAL LENS
- lens or group of lenses forming the image in a camera or projector OBJECTIVE LENS
- lens or lens-shaped surface MENISCUS
- lens or mirror that concentrates light CONDENSER
- lens system on a camera allowing rapid changes in the degree of magnification while retaining the sharpness of an image ZOOM LENS
- adjustable opening controlling the amount of light entering a lens APERTURE
- curved inward, as a mirror or lens might be CONCAVE
- curved outward, as a mirror or lens might be CONVEX
- defect in a lens ABERRATION
- faulty image, as caused by an imperfect lens DISTORTION
- irregularity in the lens of the eye, or the faulty vision resulting from it ASTIGMATISM
- network of lines or fine wires, as on a lens, used for measuring or locating the observed objects RETICLE, RETICULE, GRATICULE

leopard's spots MACULATIONS

leprosy HANSEN'S DISEASE
- hospital for treating leprosy, plague, or other contagious diseases in former times LAZARETTO
- person afflicted with leprosy, leper LAZAR

lesbian SAPPHIC
- lesbian woman TRIBADE
- lesbian symbol or emblem, of a double-headed ax LABYRIS

lessen, decrease, reduce, or decline DIMINISH
- lessen in size or significance MINIFY
- lessen in size or volume, make or become smaller CONDENSE, COMPRESS
- lessen or cut back on expenditure, size of the work force, or the like RETRENCH
- lessen or decline dramatically in number or value, fall uncontrollably PLUMMET, SLUMP
- lessen or decline gradually in amount or intensity, wind down, as if coming to an end ABATE, SUBSIDE, TAPER OFF
- lessen or decline gradually in

LEGAL TERMS

affidavit	"he has sworn": a sworn, written statement
ancient lights	right to unobstructed light; windows protected by this right
bind over	order a person to do something, such as keep the peace, or refrain from some action
codicil	supplement or afterthought added to a will
corpus delicti	"body of the crime": material evidence or substance of a crime, such as a corpse
delict	wrongful act, for which the injured party is entitled to compensation
deposition	written statement made under oath, presented as evidence in court
distrain	seize goods as redress or compensation
easement	right of a house owner or landowner over another's property, as for access
entail	settling of the inheritance of an estate beyond one generation, so that it may not be disposed of by an individual heir
equity	body of legal rules based on natural justice and fairness, supplementing and moderating common and statute law
escrow	goods, money, a contract, or the like that is put in the safekeeping of a third party, to be handed over only when certain conditions are met
estovers	articles such as fallen timber that tenants are legally permitted to remove from their landlord's estate
ex parte	"on behalf of": referring to a court application or injunction made on behalf of one side only
garnishment	court order requiring a trustee or third party holding property of a debtor either to withhold it from the debtor or to hand it over to the creditor
habeas corpus	"you may have the body": writ requiring that a detainee be produced before a court and reasons be given for the detention
in camera	"in the chamber": referring to proceedings that a judge hears with the public excluded from the court
indemnity	legal exemption from penalties or liabilities one may incur or has incurred
indictment	written accusation, read out to the accused at a trial
in flagrante delicto	in the very act of committing a crime; red-handed
injunction/ restraining order	court order to carry out or refrain from an act, such as visiting a person or place
laches	negligence or unreasonable delay in pursuing a legal claim
lien	right to take or hold another's property as security for a debt
malice aforethought/ malice prepense	premeditation, plan or conscious intention to commit a crime, especially a murder or a violent crime leading to death
mens rea	criminal intent
nolle prosequi	"to be unwilling to pursue": an entry in court records showing that a case was not proceeded with
parole	"word (of honor)": release of a prisoner, before the end of a sentence, on condition of good behavior
piscary	rights of fishing in another's waters
probate	establishing of the validity of a will; document certifying the validity of a will
recognizance	undertaking by a person to pay a debt or return to court on a specific day; money pledged as security for this
sequestration	seizure of goods or assets until conditions laid down in a decree have been met
sub judice	"under a judge": under deliberation by the courts, and therefore not open to public comment or discussion
subpoena	writ requiring a person to appear and give evidence in court
tort	breach or violation of civil law, other than breach of contract
ultra vires	beyond the legal powers of a person or institution
usufruct	right to use and benefit from another's property, so long as it remains undamaged

size, number, or strength, usually gradually DWINDLE, WANE, EBB
- lessen or decline in size or number, shrink CONTRACT
- lessen or ease a hardship, pain, fear, or the like, relieve ALLAY, ALLEVIATE, PALLIATE, ASSUAGE
- lessen or limit the scope or freedom of CONSTRICT

- lessen or reduce significantly in amount or number DEPLETE, DECIMATE
- lessen or reduce the dignity, importance, or apparent worth of a person or thing BELITTLE, DEBASE, DEMEAN, DISPARAGE, DEPRECIATE, MINIMIZE, DEVALUE, DETRACT FROM, DEROGATE
- lessen or reduce the size of a herd or flock by killing selected animals CULL
- lessen or relax the intensity, pace, or the like REMIT, SLACKEN
- lessen or wear down gradually, as if by cutting away with a knife PARE DOWN, WHITTLE DOWN
- lessen or withdraw, usually gradually, as hair might RECEDE
- lessen the apparent severity of a crime or fault, partially excuse EXTENUATE, MITIGATE
- negative or contemptuous, serving to lessen someone's reputation or dignity DEROGATORY, DISPARAGING, PEJORATIVE
- reduce, cut short, lessen the time or extent of ABBREVIATE, CURTAIL, TRUNCATE
- shorten, lessen the time or length of, as by making cuts from a book ABRIDGE
- weaken or thin down, lessen in strength, force, or purity DILUTE, ATTENUATE

lesson or Bible passage to be read during a church service LECTION
- drive home a lesson, as by repetition INSTILL, INCULCATE

let See also **allow**
- "let it stand," instruction to a typesetter or printer to ignore a correction STET, SIC
- "let the buyer beware," principle that the buyer bears the risk CAVEAT EMPTOR

letdown, disappointing ending after a promising buildup ANTICLIMAX, BATHOS

letter See also **script, type, post**
- letter, especially a long, formal, or official letter EPISTLE, MISSIVE
- letter, for airmail delivery, without an envelope AIR LETTER, AEROGRAM
- letter, symbol, or group of characters that can represent more than one sound, such as the English *g* in *gin* and *gain* POLYPHONE
- letter, usually anonymous, containing abuse, warnings, or the like POISON-PEN LETTER
- letter, written þ, representing the sounds /th/ and /th/, as used in Old and Middle English THORN
- letter, written ð, representing the /th/ sound as in *this*, in old Germanic languages and in modern Icelandic EDH, ETH
- letter, written ȝ, representing various sounds similar to /y/ or the /kh/ of *loch*, as used in Old and Middle English YOGH
- letter, written æ, representing various vowel sounds including /a/ as in *hat*, used in Old English, modern Icelandic, and other old Germanic languages ASH
- letter from the pope to bishops in all countries ENCYCLICAL
- letter of a decorative italic design SWASH LETTER
- letter of an early medieval Germanic alphabet, typically used in carved inscriptions RUNE
- letter of recommendation, a reference TESTIMONIAL
- letter of the alphabet or symbol representing an entire word or phrase LOGOGRAM, LOGOGRAPH
- letter of the alphabet that is a capital letter MAJUSCULE, UPPERCASE LETTER
- letter of the alphabet that is not a capital letter MINUSCULE, LOWERCASE LETTER
- letter officially recorded and insured REGISTERED LETTER
- letter or number printed at the foot of some pages in a book, specifying the sequence for binding the sections SIGNATURE
- letter or number written or printed slightly above another, as in ab^2 SUPERSCRIPT, SUPERIOR
- letter or number written or printed slightly below another, as in H_2O SUBSCRIPT
- letter or symbol ŋ, used in dictionaries to represent the /ng/ sound, as in *long* AGMA, ENG
- letter or symbol /ə/, used in dictionaries to represent the unstressed central vowel sound, as in the first syllable of *about* SCHWA
- letter sent by a woman breaking off her relationship with her male friend or fiancé DEAR JOHN LETTER
- letter that each recipient in turn is meant to copy and send to several further addresses CHAIN LETTER
- letters A to G of the alphabet, applied to the Sundays in a given year to determine the church calendar DOMINICAL LETTERS
- letters run together, such as *œ*, or paired to represent a single speech sound, such as /th/ DIGRAPH
- "Dear Sir" or similar conventional opening words of a letter SALUTATION
- design consisting of superimposed letters, as for an emblem MONOGRAM, CIPHER
- humorous term for a love letter BILLET-DOUX
- loss or cutting off of a letter, syllable, or sound at the beginning of a word APHAERESIS, APHESIS, FRONT-CLIPPING
- loss or cutting off of a letter, syllable, or sound from the end of a word APOCOPE, BACK-CLIPPING
- loss or cutting off of a letter, syllable, or sound in a word or group of words ELISION
- loss or cutting off of a letter, syllable, or sound in the middle of a word SYNCOPE
- mark or stamp a letter or parcel to indicate payment of postage FRANK
- message or afterthought at the end of a letter, after the writer's signature POSTSCRIPT, PS
- old-fashioned term for an official letter or business letter FAVOR
- part of a small letter, such as *q* or *y*, reaching below the "body" size (of, for example, letter *a*), or such a letter DESCENDER
- part of a small letter, such as *b* or *k*, rising above the "body" size, or such a letter ASCENDER
- phrase used in the address on a letter that is to be kept at a particular post office for collection by the addressee GENERAL DELIVERY, POSTE RESTANTE
- raised part of a piece of printer's type, bearing the letter or character to be printed KERN
- relating to letters or letter writing, or consisting of letters, as some novels are EPISTOLARY
- repeated occurrence of a letter or sound, especially at the start of words, in writing or speech ALLITERATION
- short ornamental line finishing the stroke of a printed letter SERIF
- sign or mark, such as a cedilla or circumflex, added to a letter usually to indicate a special pronunciation DIACRITIC
- typed or printed character of two or more letters joined together, such as *fi* LIGATURE
- upright stroke of a typeface or letter or musical note STEM
- write or spell in the letters of another alphabet TRANSLITERATE

level See also **flat**
- level, as of anxiety QUOTIENT
- level, flat, parallel to the horizon HORIZONTAL
- level, such as a class or caste, within a society or series STRATUM
- level at or below which the ground is saturated with water WATER TABLE
- level of authority or responsibili-

ty in a hierarchical organization ECHELON
- level of income that is the minimum for providing the necessities of life SUBSISTENCE LEVEL
- level or condition, as of economic activity, that is relatively stable PLATEAU
- level or flat, having a broad plane surface TABULAR
- level or flat and even, as two neatly fitting edges are FLUSH
- level or row, as of seating in a theater or stadium, in a rising series TIER, TERRACE
- level stretch of ground for walking along, especially along a seashore ESPLANADE
- leveling of land, as by erosion or deposition GRADATION
- instrument using an air bubble in a tube of liquid to test if a surface is level LEVEL, SPIRIT LEVEL

lever - hinge, support, or turning point of a lever FULCRUM

lewd, arousing or appealing to sexual lust SALACIOUS, PRURIENT

liability - person who assumes liability for the debts or obligations of another SURETY, GUARANTOR

liable or tending to err FALLIBLE
- liable to be affected by something adverse, such as an illness SUSCEPTIBLE, PRONE, VULNERABLE, EXPOSED, SUBJECT
- liable to or allowing of testing, criticism, or judgment ACCESSIBLE, AMENABLE
- become liable or subject to something such as debts or someone's wrath INCUR

liar See **lie**

liberal, especially in matters of religion LATITUDINARIAN

liberal arts HUMANITIES
- higher division, with four subjects, of the liberal arts studied at a medieval university QUADRIVIUM
- lower or earlier division, with three subjects, of the liberal arts studied at a medieval university TRIVIUM

library book or similar addition to a collection ACCESSION
- library classification system for cataloging books DEWEY DECIMAL SYSTEM, LIBRARY OF CONGRESS CLASSIFICATION
- library or catalog of books BIBLIOTHECA
- library reading room, as in an academy ATHENAEUM
- author's right to a fee when his or her books are borrowed from public libraries PUBLIC-LENDING RIGHT, PLR
- classification or shelf number of a book in a library CALL NUMBER
- run out, come to an end, as the loan period of a library book might EXPIRE
- section of shelving, as in a library, usually separated from other shelves by vertical dividing walls STACK
- sheet of microfilm, as used for the pages of library catalogs MICROFICHE, FICHE
- small cubicle in a library for private study CARREL

lice-infestation PEDICULOSIS, PHTHIRIASIS
- relating to lice PEDICULAR

license fee for certain pursuits, such as sports promotions and operating a casino EXCISE
- license or authorization given by a business enterprise to dealers to use its name and products FRANCHISE
- licensed purveyor of alcoholic spirits VICTUALLER

license plates specially designed by the vehicle's owner, often including his or her initials VANITY PLATES

licorice-flavored seed of the anise plant, used as a flavoring or medicine ANISEED

lie See also **lying**
- lie, falsehood, evasion of the truth, deceptive speech or action PREVARICATION, EQUIVOCATION, MENDACITY
- lie, misrepresentation, or deliberate concealment of relevant information SUBREPTION
- lie, or act ambiguously or evasively TERGIVERSATE, EQUIVOCATE, TEMPORIZE, PREVARICATE, FUDGE, PALTER
- lie about in a relaxed or apathetic way LANGUISH
- lie before a court, on oath, or the like PERJURE ONESELF
- lie in and enjoy something, such as a bath or favorable publicity BASK
- lie or crawl face downward, as in self-abasement or fear GROVEL
- glaringly or offensively obvious, as a lie or error might be BLATANT
- habitual or regular, especially in an uncontrolled way, as a persistent liar might be INVETERATE, CHRONIC
- invent or devise evidence, a story, or the like, typically embellished with lies FABRICATE
- shameless or despicable, as a liar might be ABJECT

lie detector, or any instrument recording changes in pulse, blood pressure, breathing rate, and the like POLYGRAPH

lie down and rest REPOSE
- lie down or lean back RECLINE

lie in wait for and take by surprise WAYLAY, AMBUSH

life See also **living**
- life-enhancing, original, or creative PROMETHEAN, DIONYSIAN
- life-expectancy chart as used by insurance companies MORTALITY TABLE
- life-form of a basic single-celled type, typically microscopic, such as an amoeba PROTOZOAN
- life history, story of a person's life, as written by another person BIOGRAPHY
- life instinct, self-preserving instincts and life-enhancing drive in Freudian theory EROS
- life-supporting regions of the earth or universe ECOSPHERE
- life-sustaining agent, especially food SUSTENANCE
- lifelike, true to life, as a novel or painting would be NATURALISTIC, REALISTIC
- adjective for life VITAL
- functions or processes maintaining life METABOLISM
- give life or liveliness to ANIMATE, VIVIFY, ENLIVEN
- give new life and energy to REVIVIFY
- hypothetical emergence of life or living organisms from nonliving matter SPONTANEOUS GENERATION, ABIOGENESIS
- length of life LONGEVITY
- liquid mixture of organic chemicals in early times from which life may have developed PRIMORDIAL SOUP, PRIMORDIAL CLAY
- restore to life or consciousness RESUSCITATE, RESURRECT
- return to life after apparent death RESUSCITATION, ANABIOSIS
- reverence for all life, as in some Indian religions, often with a belief in nonviolence and reincarnation AHIMSA
- study of the life processes and the functioning of living matter PHYSIOLOGY
- substance sought by alchemists for prolonging life indefinitely ELIXIR, ELIXIR OF LIFE

life (combining form) BIO-, VIV-, VIT-

life jacket MAE WEST

lifeboat - ship's crane, typically paired with another, for hoisting lifeboats, cargo, or the like DAVIT

lifting machine, such as the moving hoist on a crane CRAB
- lifting machine, typically a rope-wound drum WINDLASS
- lifting mechanism consisting of open platforms on a continuous chain, moving up on one side and

down on the other very slowly without stopping (used like an elevator) PATERNOSTER
- crane with boom and cables for lifting heavy objects DERRICK

light See also **shine**
- light, extremely delicate, almost insubstantial GOSSAMER, CHIFFON, ETHEREAL
- light and delicate, translucent, as fine silk is DIAPHANOUS
- light and shade in drawing and painting CHIAROSCURO
- light emission at low temperatures, through chemical or atomic processes LUMINESCENCE, FLUORESCENCE, PHOSPHORESCENCE
- light emitted, through a biochemical process, by fireflies, fish, fungi, or other living organisms BIOLUMINESCENCE
- light emitted as a result of heating INCANDESCENCE
- light emitted in quick intense flashes, producing a jerky or stationary image of moving objects STROBE LIGHT
- light fitting suspended from the ceiling PENDANT
- light fixture, usually hanging from the ceiling, holding many bulbs or candles CHANDELIER
- light fixture's frosted covering, matt reflector, or the like, designed to reduce glare DIFFUSER
- light hovering over marshy ground, probably produced by flaming methane gas WILL-O'-THE-WISP, IGNIS FATUUS, JACK-O'-LANTERN, FRIAR'S LANTERN
- light inside a car COURTESY LIGHT
- light meal COLLATION
- light of great intensity, produced by an electric arc crossing a gap ARC LIGHT
- light or halo, as in a painting, around the head or body of a saint, deity, or the like AUREOLE, NIMBUS
- light produced by heating lime, as formerly used in theaters LIMELIGHT, CALCIUM LIGHT
- light allegedly given off by and surrounding a person and visible to clairvoyants AURA
- light that shines brilliantly, sparkle RADIANCE, LUSTER, SCINTILLATION
- lights seen flashing in the night sky, especially in polar regions AURORA
- lights used in navigation, either on shore as a guide to ships, or on the masts of ships for identification purposes RANGE LIGHTS
- adjusting of light or other radiation into a particular pattern, especially restricting its vibrations to a single plane POLARIZATION
- allowing the passage of light, as frosted glass is, but only in a diffused form TRANSLUCENT
- allowing the passage of light freely, as clear glass is, so that objects on the other side are fully visible TRANSPARENT
- allowing the passage of no light at all, not transmitting light, or not reflecting light OPAQUE
- apparatus that produces a beam of intensely pure light LASER
- apparent movement of a stationary light, such as a candle flame, when observed in a darkened room AUTOKINETIC PHENOMENON
- breaking up of light into the colors of the rainbow, as by a glass surface DIFFRACTION
- bright carbon-arc light used in making films KLIEG LIGHT
- change in direction of a light or sound wave as it changes speed between mediums REFRACTION
- colors of the rainbow, or an image of them, as when a light beam is split up SPECTRUM
- dazzling or harsh, as artificial light might be GARISH
- device, as in a digital clock, that gives off light when electrically stimulated LED
- device launched into the air to produce a bright light, as for illuminating a search area at night or as a distress signal FLARE
- dim or faint, as a weak light is WAN
- electronic device that reacts to changes in light intensity, as used in light meters, burglar alarms, and automatic doors PHOTOELECTRIC CELL, PHOTOCELL, ELECTRIC EYE, MAGIC EYE
- emitting self-generated light, glowing LUMINOUS, FLUORESCENT, PHOSPHORESCENT
- flickering or glowing with a gentle light LAMBENT
- give out heat, light, or the like RADIATE
- having waves of the same frequency or related phases, as light is COHERENT
- lacking light, or relating to the absence of light APHOTIC
- lamp or light bulb producing light from a heated element or filament INCANDESCENT LAMP
- neon light or similar lamp based on the stimulation of atoms or molecules into emitting light FLUORESCENT LAMP
- plant's use of light energy, absorbed by chlorophyll, for forming organic compounds from carbon dioxide and water PHOTOSYNTHESIS
- put out a light or fire EXTINGUISH, DOUSE, SNUFF, QUENCH
- radiation with wavelengths between those of visible light and radio waves INFRARED
- radiation with wavelengths between those of visible light and X-rays ULTRAVIOLET
- relating to light PHOTIC
- ring or disc of faint light, as around the moon when viewed through a haze CORONA, AUREOLE
- scientific study of vision and light OPTICS
- separate light or other radiation into parts with different wavelengths DISPERSE
- signal flare used in former times, burning with a bright blue light BENGAL LIGHT
- signal or lighting flare fired from a special pistol VERY LIGHT
- substance that emits light when stimulated by radiation PHOSPHOR
- theory that light consists of a stream of tiny particles rather than of waves CORPUSCULAR THEORY
- theory that light consists of forward-moving waves rather than of a stream of particles WAVE THEORY
- triangle of light seen in the sky near sunrise or sunset ZODIACAL LIGHT

light (combining form) LUMIN-, PHOTO-, -PHOT-, -PHOS-

light and dark - belief or religion based on a conflict between the universal forces or principles, as of good and evil, or light and dark MANICHAEISM

light-bulb fitting in which pins fasten into slots BAYONET FITTING
- fine wire in a light bulb, heated by electric current to emit light FILAMENT
- hard metallic element used in light-bulb filaments TUNGSTEN

light-hearted, high-spirited literary work JEU D'ESPRIT

lighten or liven up something dull or humorless LEAVEN

lighthouse PHAROS

lighting technician or electrician on a film or television crew GAFFER
- assistant lighting technician or electrician on a film or television crew BEST BOY

lightness or frivolity of manner, especially when it is inappropriate LEVITY

lightning See illustration
- lightning in the form of a single well-defined electrical discharge STREAK LIGHTNING
- lightning that appears as a broad sheetlike flicker, resulting from reflection by clouds SHEET LIGHTNING

- discharge of ball lightning FIREBALL
- flash with or like lightning FULGURATE
- old word for lightning LEVIN

lights out - bugle call sounded at military funerals or to signal lights out in a military camp TAPS, LAST POST

likable, agreeable to one's tastes CONGENIAL

like, similar to, or resembling but not really being QUASI
- like, want, or be fond of in a limited way FANCY
- like and enjoy, or look forward to eagerly RELISH
- like or display a preference for FAVOR, AFFECT
- like or enjoy something very much, such as praise or glory REVEL IN, BASK IN
- like too much, be foolishly, excessively, and indulgently fond of DOTE ON
- like with a warm and caring affection, hold dear CHERISH

like (combining form) HOMEO-, HOMO-, PARA-, -ESQUE, -OID, -OSE

like it or not WILLY-NILLY, NOLENS VOLENS

likely, believable, possible FEASIBLE
- likely, seemingly true, as an excuse might be PLAUSIBLE
- likely to become someone or something specified, in the offing PROSPECTIVE

likeness, representation, or image of something, sometimes misleading or superficial SIMULACRUM

liking See also **tendency, love**
- natural personal liking or attraction, affection AFFINITY
- special liking, often for something unusual PARTIALITY, PREDILECTION
- strong and continued liking or inclination PENCHANT

liking (combining form) PHIL-, -PHILE

lilt, rise and fall of the pitch of the voice INTONATION

lily or related water plant LOTUS
- water lily NENUPHAR

limb - cut or pull off a limb or body part of a person or animal MUTILATE, MAIM, DISMEMBER
- displace a limb or organ, or put a bone out of joint DISLOCATE
- illusory limb, still felt as the source of pain even though the real limb has been amputated PHANTOM LIMB
- replacement of a limb by tissue growth, as of a lizard's tail REGENERATION
- ripping away or sudden amputation of a limb or other body part, either surgically or in an accident AVULSION

lime - pillar or cone of lime deposit hanging from the roof of a cave STALACTITE
- pillar or cone of lime deposit rising from the floor of a cave STALAGMITE

lime (combining form) CALC-, CALCI-

limestone - chalky, containing or resembling limestone or calcium carbonate CALCAREOUS

limit, or establish the limits or boundaries of CIRCUMSCRIBE, DEMARCATE, DELIMIT
- limit, moderate, restrain TEMPER, QUALIFY, CHASTEN
- limit, outermost boundary, outer surface, or the like PERIPHERY
- limit, restraint, restriction STRICTURE
- limit or boundary level above which something takes place or comes into effect THRESHOLD
- limit or confine something, such as an outbreak of disease to a restricted area LOCALIZE
- limit or outer edge, as of the range of one's authority or hearing PERIMETER
- limit or turning point, beyond which there is no going back RUBICON
- limit the amount given, begrudge, be miserly with STINT
- limit the movement or freedom of, as by strict rules or physical restraint STRAITJACKET, TETHER
- limitation or condition, as in an agreement or document PROVISO
- limited or specified quantity or number, as of imports, members of a group, or the like QUOTA
- limited amount or fixed allowance allocated to a person, as during a shortage RATION
- limited in number or amount, liable to end or run out FINITE
- limited in size, growth, or development, as through insufficient food or stimulation STUNTED
- limited severely by rules or prejudices HIDEBOUND, INFLEXIBLE

Lightning

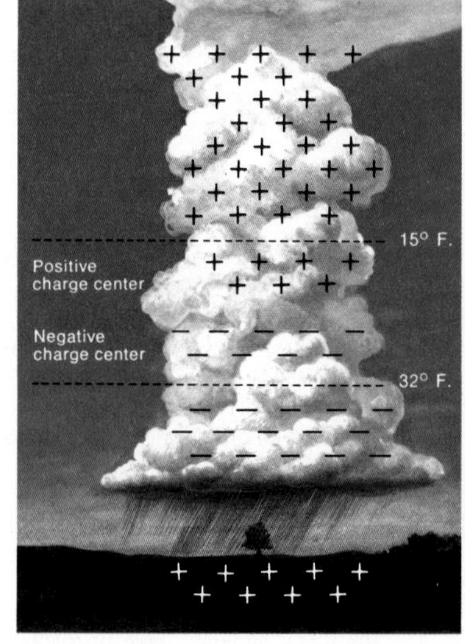

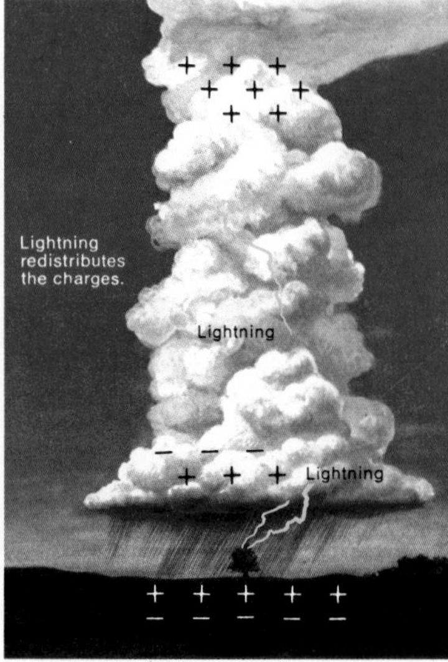

LIGHTNING CORRECTS AN ELECTRICAL IMBALANCE

The positive and negative charges in a thundercloud are attracted to each other. They are prevented from coming together by air, which acts as an insulator.

When charges in thunderclouds and on the ground become strong enough, they overcome the insulating barrier of the air. The charges connect in the effect we call lightning.

- limited to a small group, restricted EXCLUSIVE, SELECT, ESOTERIC, RAREFIED
- limits of one's knowledge or experience HORIZONS
- limits or boundaries, as of a budget or schedule PARAMETERS, CONSTRAINTS
- limits or boundaries, as of a restricted space or strict set of rules CONFINES
- degree of variation from a standard without going beyond the limit TOLERANCE, LEEWAY, PLAY
- go beyond a limit TRANSGRESS
- law setting a time limit for enforcing a right or bringing a legal action STATUTE OF LIMITATIONS
- regulation limiting people's movements, especially after a set hour at night CURFEW
- rise above or extend beyond the limits of TRANSCEND

limp, drooping, flabby, lacking firmness FLACCID
- limp, lameness CLAUDICATION
- limp or walk awkwardly HOBBLE
- limping or lame HALTING

line, as of ships or police, surrounding or guarding an area CORDON
- line, curve, or surface touching but not intersecting another TANGENT
- line approaching a curve, as on a graph, such that they will meet only at infinity ASYMPTOTE
- line at the top of a page, stating the title of the chapter, page number, or the like RUNNING HEAD
- line of latitude PARALLEL
- line of longitude MERIDIAN
- line of poetry STICH
- line or cord with a weight on the end, as for determining depth or the true vertical PLUMB LINE
- line or curve enclosing a plane area in geometry PERIMETER
- line or set of lines marked on the side of a cargo ship showing its legal load level in various conditions PLIMSOLL MARK
- line that is very thin, as in a fracture or typeface HAIRLINE
- line up, arrange in rows ALIGN
- line up in straight ranks, as soldiers do on parade DRESS
- line used for reference, as on a graph or technical drawing AXIS
- lines, as of a poem, in which some letters, usually the first, spell out a name or message ACROSTIC
- lines intersecting to form a pattern or design TRACERY
- lines of fine wire, at right angles to each other, used for sighting on a rifle, theodolite, or the like CROSS WIRES, CROSS HAIRS
- lines or grid of fine wires, as on a lens, used for measuring or locating the objects under observation RETICLE, RETICULE, GRATICULE
- adjective for a line, relating to lines LINEAR
- code of lines and numbers, as on a library book or item of shipping, typically read by a laser optical scanner BAR CODE, UNIVERSAL PRODUCT CODE, UPC
- cut or divide a line or space, cross INTERSECT
- dialogue, as in ancient Greek drama, in which alternate lines of verse are spoken by different characters STICHOMYTHIA
- distance east or west of the prime meridian at Greenwich, measured in degrees and represented typically by vertical lines on a map LONGITUDE
- distance north or south of the equator, measured in degrees and represented by horizontal lines on a map LATITUDE
- fine lines forming the shading in a drawing HATCHING
- having lines written alternately from left to right and from right to left BOUSTROPHEDONIC
- lying on the same straight line, as various points might be COLLINEAR, COAXIAL
- meeting at or approaching a common point, as intersecting lines are CONCURRENT, CONVERGENT
- pattern of colored lines forming squares against a plain background TATTERSALL
- point at which lines intersect or diverge NODE, CUSP
- referring to lines of verse that pause at the end, typically with a punctuation mark END-STOPPED
- referring to lines of verse that run over into the following line without any pause produced by a sense break or punctuation ENJAMBED
- referring to straight lines RECTILINEAR
- short ornamental line finishing off a stroke of a printed letter SERIF

line (combining form) -STICH, -STICHOUS

linguistics See **language, grammar**
- linguistics, language study PHILOLOGY
- linguistics using a historical approach, studying a language through its development through time DIACHRONIC LINGUISTICS
- linguistics using a nonhistorical approach, studying a language at one particular point in time SYNCHRONIC LINGUISTICS

lining of a lapel, cuff, or other folded part of clothing REVERS

lining up, as of color plates in printing color pictures REGISTER
- lining up three celestial bodies, as of the earth, sun, and moon at full moon or new moon SYZYGY

link, bond, or tie VINCULUM
- link in a series CONCATENATE, CATENATE
- link or bond, or network of connections NEXUS
- linked tightly, in many complex ways INEXTRICABLY LINKED
- linking groove or ridge between two planks, shafts or the like SPLINE

lion, as named in children's stories LEO, SIMBA
- adjective for a lion LEONINE
- group or family of lions PRIDE

lip - adjective for the lips LABIAL
- congenital split in the upper lip, associated with cleft palate HARELIP
- draw in the lips to a tight wrinkled shape PURSE, PUCKER
- ring or ornament inserted in the lip LABRET
- shallow groove running vertically from the nose to the upper lip PHILTRUM
- sulky expression in which lips are pushed outward POUT

lips (combining form) LABI-, LABIO-

liqueur See **drink**

liquid of a kind in between a fine suspension and a solution, containing particles that are larger than molecules COLLOID, COLLOIDAL SOLUTION
- liquid or sauce in which meat or fish is left to soak before cooking MARINADE
- liquid poured out as part of a religious ritual LIBATION
- liquid suspension, in pharmacology MAGMA
- liquid waste, as from a factory or sewage works EFFLUENT
- able to absorb or admit gas or liquid POROUS, PERMEABLE
- amount of liquid, grain, or the like that evaporates or leaks from a container ULLAGE
- become a soft, solidified mass, as blood, milk, or other liquids might COAGULATE, CLOT, CURDLE
- becoming liquid when stirred or shaken THIXOTROPIC
- change from a liquid into a gas or vapor EVAPORATE
- change from a vapor or gaseous state to a liquid CONDENSE
- clear, thick liquid, secreted by membranes in joints, tendon sheaths, and so on SINOVIA, SINO-

VIAL FLUID
- clear-to-whitish, watery liquid from the body tissues LYMPH
- device to slow down or regulate the flow of a liquid BAFFLE
- essence produced by boiling down a liquid DECOCTION
- gluey, thick, and sticky, as some liquids are VISCID, VISCOUS
- injection of liquid into the rectum, as for medication ENEMA
- make a liquid cloudy or muddy by stirring up sediment ROIL
- mixture of solid particles dispersed but not dissolved in a liquid SUSPENSION
- movement of a liquid through a semipermeable membrane such as a cell wall OSMOSIS
- operated by or involving liquid pressure HYDRAULIC
- property of liquids of appearing to form a film across their surface SURFACE TENSION
- raising or lowering of the surface of a liquid in contact with a solid, as a result of surface tension CAPILLARITY, CAPILLARY ACTION
- resistant to liquids or gases IMPERMEABLE, IMPERVIOUS
- sediment or residue at the bottom of liquid LEES, DREGS
- surface forming the boundary between liquids INTERFACE
- surface of a liquid, curved like a lens MENISCUS
- suspension of globules of one liquid inside another EMULSION
- thin layer of liquid LAMELLA, LAMINA
- thin liquid mixture of cement, manure, mud, or the like SLURRY
- unable to blend or mix, as two liquids might be IMMISCIBLE
- watery, yellowish liquid discharged from an ulcer or wound PUS, ICHOR

liquid (combining form) HYDR-, HYDRO-

liquid crystal, between liquid and solid or crystal in structure or properties MESOMORPHIC

list, or the items listed INVENTORY
- list items one by one, as on a bill ITEMIZE, ENUMERATE, TALLY, DETAIL
- list of dead people NECROLOGY
- list of duties or of the people to perform them ROSTER, ROTA
- list of items to be dealt with at a meeting AGENDA
- list of people to be murdered, projects to be axed, or the like HIT LIST
- list of plays, skills, or the like that a drama group, or the like can draw on REPERTOIRE
- list of procedures that is pointlessly complicated RIGMAROLE
- list of requirements, described and detailed SPECIFICATIONS, SPECS
- list or note in detail PARTICULARIZE, SPECIFY
- arrange in lists, tables, or the like TABULATE, CODIFY
- definitive list, as of church laws or an author's works CANON
- ordered list of people, goods, or the like DIRECTORY, CATALOG
- put someone's name on a list to join a club, class, or the like ENROLL, REGISTER
- reading out of a list of names of those supposed to be present, as in the army ROLL CALL, MUSTER

listen closely HEARKEN
- listen secretly to a conversation between others EAVESDROP
- listener AUDITOR
- listening, especially when attempting a diagnosis by means of a stethoscope AUSCULTATION
- listening instrument used by doctors to study sounds produced in the body STETHOSCOPE
- call to attention, as when a town crier makes an announcement, "listen!" OYEZ

literacy - ability to use and understand language, though not necessarily to read and write it as in literacy ORACY
- basic skill in arithmetic or competence in numerical calculations, regarded as the counterpart of literacy NUMERACY

literal and unduly fussy about details PEDANTIC
- metaphorical, based on or using figures of speech, not literal FIGURATIVE

literary See chart, page 320, and also **poetry, highfalutin**, and chart at **drama**
- literary, artistic, or cultural circle COTERIE, CLIQUE, CENACLE, SALON
- literary characters, as in a novel or play PERSONAE
- "literary" in a showy way INKHORN
- literary or scientific institution ATHENAEUM
- literary selections from a larger work or group of works DIGEST, ANTHOLOGY, ANALECTS
- literary theft, passing off as one's own the writings or ideas of another PLAGIARISM
- literary work, entertainment, or the like that is elaborate, fanciful, or spectacular EXTRAVAGANZA
- literary work in a lighthearted, high-spirited vein JEU D'ESPRIT
- note of critical commentary or explanation, as on a literary text ANNOTATION, GLOSS
- short literary work, dramatic sketch, or the like CAMEO
- contrast as a literary or artistic technique CHIAROSCURO
- overrefined, excessively rich or precious, as a literary style might be DECADENT
- references, footnotes, and so on in a scholarly edition of a literary text APPARATUS CRITICUS, CRITICAL APPARATUS

literature ancient works of literature still admired CLASSICS
- bookish people who parade their knowledge of literature and writers LITERATI
- category of literature, films, or the like GENRE
- fine literature BELLES LETTRES
- great work of literature OEUVRE
- relating to literature that is refined and classically elegant in style AUGUSTAN
- repeated theme in a work of literature, art or music MOTIF, LEITMOTIV
- selection of passages from literature, used as a text when studying a foreign or ancient language CHRESTOMATHY

litter of piglets FARROW

little See **lack, mediocre, small**

live See also **living**
- live, continue in existence, or manage to survive SUBSIST
- live, in person IN PROPRIA PERSONA
- live a dull, passive life VEGETATE, STAGNATE
- area where an animal or plant normally lives HABITAT
- place where one lives, legal place of residence DOMICILE

liveliness, spirit, wit ESPIRIT

lively, active, and vigorous SPRY, SPRIGHTLY
- lively, mischievous SKITTISH
- lively, noisy, unruly RAMBUNCTIOUS, RUMBUSTIOUS, BOISTEROUS
- lively, sociable, friendly person EXTROVERT
- lively, sparkling, or spirited ANIMATED, VIVACIOUS, EFFERVESCENT, EXUBERANT
- lively, stimulating, or cheering INVIGORATING, EXHILARATING
- lively spirits, enjoyment of life JOIE DE VIVRE

liven up or lighten something dull or humorless LEAVEN

liver, kidneys, and so on of an animal OFFAL
- liver degeneration, often because of alcoholism CIRRHOSIS
- liver disease or inflammation, typically producing jaundice HEPATITIS
- adjective for the liver HEPATIC
- savory paste of goose liver PÂTÉ

LITERARY TERMS

allegory	work in which the characters or events have symbolic meaning and illustrate a moral or spiritual theme
antinovel	work of fiction that rejects the conventional structure and elements of a novel
bathos	sudden descent from the exalted to the ridiculous
belles lettres	literature considered as art rather than for its educational or moral value
bildungsroman	novel relating the early development and education of the hero
epigram	short, pithy, and memorable saying making a pointed observation
epistolary novel	novel in the form of a series of letters
euphuism	high-flown rhetorical style of writing
gothic novel	novel popular in the 18th-19th century (and again currently), characterized by exotic or medieval settings, and macabre or supernatural incidents
leitmotiv	recurring theme, as in a novel
mimesis	imitation or realistic representation in literature of nature or human nature
naturalism	true-to-life style of writing
novella	structured short narrative or novel
passus	section of a story, poem, or the like, especially in medieval literature
pastiche	literary work, often satirical, imitating the style of another writer
pathetic fallacy	representation of inanimate objects in nature as having human qualities and feelings
picaresque novel	episodic novel, popular in the 18th century, relating the adventures of an amiable wandering rogue
roman à clef	novel representing real people, places, and events in a thinly disguised fictional form
roman-fleuve	very long novel, or a series of novels, such as a family saga, chronicling a social group over many years
stream of consciousness/ interior monologue	technique of depicting a character's thoughts and feelings as a flow of disjointed or ungrammatical reflections
Sturm und Drang	"storm and yearning," late-18th-century German literary movement, highly romantic and inspirational in spirit, often dealing with an individual person's struggle against society or nature
textual criticism	in-depth study and analysis of a text; examination of a literary work, the Bible, or the like in the attempt to establish the original text
topos	stock theme or idea, often forming the basis of early narratives
trilogy	set of three related works by the same author

DE FOIE GRAS

liver (combining form) HEPAT-, HEPATO-

living See also **live, life**
- living, or resembling a living organism, as society or poetry might be considered ORGANIC
- living or able to live both on land and in water AMPHIBIOUS
- living plant or animal ORGANISM
- living together without being legally married COHABITATION, CONCUBINAGE, POSSLQ'ING
- living together of two organisms in association, often beneficial to at least one, never parasitic COMMENSALISM
- living together of two organisms in close or dependent association, especially when beneficial to both SYMBIOSIS
- capable of living or surviving independently VIABLE
- capable of living, working, or functioning together in a harmonious or efficient way COMPATIBLE
- cutting up or into the body of a living animal, especially when done for research VIVISECTION
- deathlike or temporary dormant state of a living organism SUSPENDED ANIMATION

living (combining form) -BIOSIS

living matter (combining form) -PLAST

living on (combining form) -COLOUS

lizard with the ability to change color as a means of camouflage CHAMELEON
- lizardlike SAURIAN
- lizardlike creature in myth, living in or capable of withstanding fire SALAMANDER
- Australian monitor lizard GOANNA
- fold of skin hanging from the throat, as of some lizards and birds WATTLE
- insect-eating lizard with adhesive footpads, often seen on walls and ceilings in warm countries GECKO
- large tropical American lizard with a spiny ridge along its back IGUANA
- replacement of a limb by tissue growth, as of a lizard's tail REGENERATION
- shedding of a body part, such as a lizard's tail, as a means of protection when attacked AUTOTOMY
- tropical lizard with very short legs and a scaly body SKINK

lizard (combining form) SAURO-, -SAUR-, -SAURUS

llama - South American mammals that are closely related to and very similar to the llama GUANACO, ALPACA, VICUÑA

loan agency or moneylender that accepts trade debts as security FACTOR
- loan guaranteed by the pledge of property as security COLLATERAL LOAN
- loan repayable immediately on demand CALL LOAN, DEMAND LOAN
- pay off a loan, promissory note, mortgage, or the like REDEEM
- temporary or conditional transfer of title deeds of property as security for a loan MORTGAGE

loan translation, word or phrase translated element by element from another language CALQUE

lobster, crab, prawn, or related ten-legged creature DECAPOD
- lobster, crab, shrimp, or related creature having a segmented body, jointed limbs, and horny shell CRUSTACEAN
- lobster trap or fish basket of wickerwork CREEL
- lobster's claw PINCER, CHELA
- lobster's liver, sometimes regarded as a delicacy TOMALLEY
- lobster's shell MAIL
- roe of a lobster or crab, pink when cooked CORAL

local, native, restricted to a particular area or group, as a disease might be ENDEMIC
- local, native to or originating in a particular region INDIGENOUS, ABORIGINAL, AUTOCHTHONOUS
- local, on or for a particular place, as the application of a medicinal cream might be TOPICAL
- local language or dialect of a particular region VERNACULAR

lock of the kind almost wholly contained within a cavity in the edge of the door MORTISE LOCK
- lock of the kind having a revolving barrel or cylinder operated by a flat, serrated key YALE LOCK
- lock whose bolt can be drawn back only by means of a key DEADLOCK
- axle, revolving bolt, or the like, as in a lock or between two door handles SPINDLE
- clasp or fastener hinged over a fixed staple, and typically secured with a padlock HASP
- edge of a lock's bolt against which the key presses to drive it home TALON
- edge plate of a lock into which the bolt slots SELVAGE
- metal plate surrounding or covering the keyhole on a lock ESCUTCHEON
- ridge on a lock, or keyhole, or corresponding notch in a key WARD
- section of a lock that obstructs the bolt until moved away by the key TUMBLER

lockjaw TETANUS, TRISMUS

locomotive - frame on the roof of a streetcar, locomotive, or the like collecting electric current from an overhead wire as it slides along it PANTOGRAPH
- steam-powered locomotive, as for dragging heavy equipment over roads or fields TRACTION ENGINE
- steam-powered locomotive, that carries its own water and coal rather than using a separate tender TANK LOCOMOTIVE

log - channel for transporting logs SLUICE
- floating barrier, as of logs or empty drums, to confine other logs, protect a harbor, or the like BOOM
- logrolling BIRLING
- metal stand, used in pairs, for logs in a fireplace ANDIRON, FIREDOG
- pole with an adjustable hook used for moving logs PEAVEY, CANT HOOK
- wedge or block placed under a wheel, log, or the like, to immobilize it on a slope SCOTCH, CHOCK

logarithm - decimal part of a logarithm MANTISSA
- integer part of a logarithm CHARACTERISTIC, ARGUMENT

logic See also **argument, reasoning, fallacy, philosophy**
- logic or study of necessity, possibility, and so on MODAL LOGIC
- logic system or method based on deductions using syllogisms ARISTOTELIAN LOGIC
- logic system using mathematical symbols and relationships BOOLEAN ALGEBRA
- logical, based on or showing reason RATIONAL
- logical argument in the form of an extended series of incomplete syllogisms SORITES
- logical coherence or compatibility CONSISTENCY
- logical disproof of a proposition by showing that the inevitable consequences of it are absurd REDUCTIO AD ABSURDUM
- logical element or invented idea forming part of a theory CONSTRUCT
- logical error or faulty argument that invalidates the conclusion FALLACY
- logical or reasonable, as a conclusion might be LEGITIMATE
- logical pattern of deduction in which two premises generate a conclusion SYLLOGISM
- logical reasoning that is based on moving from general premises to particular conclusions that follow from them necessarily DEDUCTION, SYNTHESIS
- logical reasoning RATIOCINATION
- logical reasoning by inferring general truths from particular instances, as distinct from strict logical deduction INDUCTION
- logically inconsistent or conflicting, as two opposed propositions might be INCOMPATIBLE, DILEMMATIC
- logically inconsistent or false, as a conclusion might be INVALID
- logically obvious or self-evident, true by the very nature of its wording or logical form ANALYTIC, TAUTOLOGOUS, A PRIORI, APODICTIC
- logically organized, consistent, and comprehensible COHERENT
- argument that presents two or more equally conclusive alternatives DILEMMA
- characteristic or attribute that is affirmed or denied of something in a proposition in logic PREDICATE
- conclusion that is faulty by failing to follow logically from the premises NON SEQUITUR
- diagram of overlapping circles, as for representing relations between the terms of a proposition in logic VENN DIAGRAM, EULER DIAGRAM
- minor proposition, taken as valid or self-evidently true, and used in proving another proposition LEMMA
- proposition in logic, forming either of the first two parts of a syllogism, from which the conclusion can be deduced PREMISE
- proposition in logic containing two simple statements joined by the word *or* DISJUNCTION
- refuting of an argument in logic by proving that the contrary of its conclusion is true ELENCHUS, SYLLOGISTIC REFUTATION
- shortened syllogism in logic, in which one of the premises is left unstated ENTHYMEME
- sudden jump in a sequence, as of logical arguments SALTUS
- thinking of an imaginative and free-ranging rather than strictly logical mode, often producing unexpected solutions to problems LATERAL THINKING

London's banking and financial world LOMBARD STREET, THE CITY

lonely See also **alone**
- lonely, remote, isolated, solitary, as a place or a life might be SECLUDED
- lonely or miserable through the loss or desertion of a companion or loved one BEREFT, FORLORN, FORSAKEN, DESOLATE
- lonely through being an outcast,

withdrawing from society, or losing the sympathy of others ESTRANGED, ALIENATED
- person who is lonely or alone through living independently of society OUTSIDER, LONER
- state of being alone, lonely, or secluded SOLITUDE

long, drawn-out, extended in time, as applause might be PROLONGED, PROTRACTED, SUSTAINED
- long, lengthened, extended, stretched ELONGATED
- long and indirect, as a journey or argument might be CIRCUITOUS
- long and tedious, seemingly endless INTERMINABLE, MARATHON
- long-established, persistent, or deep-rooted, as a tendency might be INVETERATE
- long for something intensely, yearn PINE, HANKER
- long life, age LONGEVITY
- long period of time, specifically a billion (a thousand million) years AEON
- long-range overall view, as in military combat STRATEGY

long ago, in the old days LANG SYNE

long division or other calculating procedure using a series of steps ALGORITHM

long-lasting See also **constant, permanent**
- long-lasting, continuing, or regularly recurring, as an illness might be PERSISTENT, CHRONIC
- long-lasting, resistant to decay ABIDING, DURABLE, RESILIENT, ENDURING
- long-lasting in its effect, as poetry might be RESONANT

long-winded, roundabout, or evasive speech or writing CIRCUMLOCUTION, PROLIXITY, PERIPHRASIS
- long-winded, talkative, chattering in an aimless or boring way GARRULOUS, LOQUACIOUS, MAUNDERING
- long-winded, tedious, or very strained, as a political speech might be LABORED
- long-winded, wordy in a boring way PROLIX, VERBOSE, DIFFUSE
- long-winded or glib speech, sales talk, or the like SPIEL, PATTER

longing, yearning, sadly reflective over something unobtainable WISTFUL
- longing or sentimental yearning for the past NOSTALGIA

longitude - line of longitude MERIDIAN

longsightedness, defective close-up vision HYPEROPIA, HYPERMETROPIA
- longsightedness caused by advancing age and the hardening of the lens PRESBYOPIA

look See also **search, see**
- look at someone, especially in a lustful way LEER, OGLE
- look at fixedly and wide-eyed, stare GAPE, GOGGLE
- look down on from a height, overlook, tower above DOMINATE
- look for, scratch about, or feel around for with the hands, grope GRABBLE
- look forward to, expect ANTICIPATE
- look or stare angrily or frowningly GLOWER, SCOWL
- look through, grub about, ferret RUMMAGE
- belittling, causing embarrassment, as sarcasm or a disapproving look might WITHERING
- invite foolishly or unwittingly look for trouble COURT DISASTER
- suspiciously or disapprovingly, the way one might look at a person or suggestion ASKANCE
- take a look, make a preliminary investigation, as of enemy positions RECONNOITER, RECCE, RECCO

look-alike, person bearing a striking resemblance to another RINGER

looking back HINDSIGHT, RETROSPECT

loom, of the early 19th century, for mechanical weaving of intricately patterned cloth JACQUARD LOOM

loop on a graph or diagram LOBE
- loop or coil, as of rope HANK
- loops forming an edging on ribbon, lace, or the like PICOTS
- decorative chain or garland of flowers, ribbons, or the like suspended in a loop FESTOON, SWAG
- uncut loop in the pile of toweling or a similar fabric TERRY

loose, sagging, or flabby FLACCID
- loose, supple, nimble, or agile LITHE, LISSOM, LIMBER
- loose, unconnected DETACHED

loosen or slacken a rope or cable SURGE, PAY

loosening (combining form) -LYS-, LYSO-, -LYSIS

loot, booty, stolen property PLUNDER, SWAG, HAUL
- raider in search of loot PLUNDERER, MARAUDER, PILLAGER

lord of the manor in Scotland LAIRD
- lord or vassal in feudal times LIEGE
- lord's estate, domain, or house in feudal times MANOR, DEMESNE

Lord See also **God**
- "Lord, have mercy," the Christian prayer or the musical setting for it KYRIE ELEISON
- Lord's prayer, especially in its Latin version PATERNOSTER

lose MISLAY, MISPLACE
- lose a legal case, sports competition, or the like through failure to appear DEFAULT
- lose confidence momentarily, hesitate WAVER, FALTER
- lose or surrender as punishment for a crime or the like FORFEIT
- lose resistance, yield, submit, or give in to SUCCUMB

loser - likely loser in an election, fight, or other contest UNDERDOG

loss, as through evaporation or leakage, of a substance in a container ULLAGE
- loss, damage, disadvantage DETRIMENT
- loss in value, as of a car, as through age or wear DEPRECIATION
- loss or death of a loved one BEREAVEMENT
- make amends for a loss or injury, as by a payment COMPENSATE
- make good one's losses RECOUP

lost, missing ASTRAY
- lost in thought ABSTRACTED, PREOCCUPIED, ABSORBED
- having lost one's bearings or sense of place DISORIENTED

lotion for soothing and softening the skin EMOLLIENT
- lotion with soothing or healing properties, rubbed into the skin LINIMENT, EMBROCATION

lots See also **many, plenty**
- lots, many, a multitude LEGIONS
- lots, many, loads, tons SLEWS
- lots, much, loads OODLES, REAMS, SLATHERS, SLEWS

lottery game where winning tickets are picked from a revolving container TOMBOLA
- lottery in which the entire prize is awarded to the winner SWEEPSTAKE

loud See also **noisy**
- loud, booming, deep, and rich in sound SONOROUS, RESONANT
- loud, deep, and resonant, as the sound of waves crashing on the shore is PLANGENT
- loud, harsh or shrill STRIDENT, EAR-PIERCING, BLARING
- loud, having an extremely loud voice STENTORIAN
- loud, resonant, sustained or repeated noise, din CLANGOR
- loud and insistent, especially in protest VOCIFEROUS
- loud enough to be heard AUDIBLE
- loud pedal on a piano SUSTAINING PEDAL, REVERBERATION PEDAL

loudly, especially in music FORTE, FORTISSIMO

loudness - gradual decrease in loudness, as of a passage of music DECRESCENDO, DIMINUENDO
- gradual increase in loudness, as of a passage of music CRESCENDO
- unit of loudness DECIBEL

loudspeaker reproducing bass fre-

quencies WOOFER
- loudspeaker reproducing high-pitched frequencies TWEETER
- loudspeaker system for public announcements, especially in a large building PUBLIC-ADDRESS SYSTEM, PA SYSTEM
- sound-regulating device, as in a microphone, loudspeaker, or the like BAFFLE, DIFFUSER

Louisiana - member of a community in Louisiana descended from 18th-century Canadian immigrants, or their French dialect CAJUN

louse See **lice**

love See also **like, friendly, sex**
- love affair, especially a secret or illicit one AMOUR, LIAISON
- love feast, meal commemorating the Last Supper, in the early Christian Church AGAPE
- love letter BILLET-DOUX
- love of great intensity, ecstatic love RAPTURE, ARDOR
- love or passion, typically foolish and short-lived INFATUATION
- love play or flirtation DALLIANCE
- love potion PHILTER
- love produced or feigned for the sake of some selfish benefit CUPBOARD LOVE
- love song, especially about unrequited love TORCH SONG
- love song, typically sung outside a woman's house in the evening SERENADE
- love too much, adore, be excessively fond of IDOLIZE, DOTE ON
- loving devotion, awe, as shown to God REVERENCE, VENERATION
- Christian love, charity, as distinct from erotic love AGAPE
- loving feelings, fondness TENDRESSE
- loving word, gesture, or the like ENDEARMENT
- engage in casual love affairs PHILANDER
- excessive love, praise, or flattery, worship ADULATION
- in love ENAMORED, SMITTEN
- not returned or reciprocated, as love might be UNREQUITED
- referring to love, especially sexual love AMOROUS, AMATORY, EROTIC
- referring to love between two unrelated people that is free of sexual desire PLATONIC
- return someone's love REQUITE, RECIPROCATE

love (combining form) -PHIL-, PHILO-

lovely See **beautiful, attractive**

lovemaking in the form of kissing and cuddling NECKING

lover, sweetheart PARAMOUR, LEMAN
- lover kept by an older woman GIGOLO
- lover of a promiscuous kind, playboy RAKE, LADYKILLER, DON JUAN
- lover of his own creation, as an artist might be PYGMALION
- lovers' meeting, or the appointment for it RENDEZVOUS, TRYST, ASSIGNATION
- abandon a lover cruelly JILT
- female lover, mistress, or girlfriend, especially a disreputable one MOLL, FLOOZY, DOXY
- female lover, regular or live-in mistress, or secondary wife CONCUBINE
- male lover or escort of a married woman, especially in 18th-century Italy CICISBEO
- male suitor, lover, or sweetheart SWAIN, BEAU, INAMORATO
- mistress, lover, or secondary wife of a married man SIDE-GIRL
- run away secretly with a lover, especially to marry ELOPE
- self-lover, person in love with himself or herself NARCISSUS

low-cut, as a dress or blouse might be, or dressed in such a garment DÉCOLLETÉ
- low part of a cycle, graph, or the like TROUGH

low (combining form) HYPO-

lower See **lessen, insult**
- lower in rank or status, subordinate, secondary SUBALTERN
- lower or downgrade in status DEMOTE, RELEGATE, DEGRADE

lower (combining form) BASI-, CATA-, INFRA-

lower class or working class, especially the class of industrial wage earners PROLETARIAT
- lower-class person PLEBEIAN, PLEB
- lower classes, considered by Marxists to be uninterested in social change LUMPENPROLETARIAT

lower jaw MANDIBLE
- referring to a lower jaw that projects beyond the upper jaw HYPAGNATHOUS, UNDERSHOT, UNDERHUNG
- referring to an upper jaw that projects beyond the lower jaw OVERSHOT

lowest, deepest NETHERMOST
- lowest layer or level BEDROCK
- lowest point, as of one's fortunes or of depression NADIR

lowland Scots dialect, especially as developed as a literary language LALLANS

loyal, firm, steadfast STAUNCH
- loyal colleague, advisor, or friend TROUPER
- loyal follower or supporter LIEGEMAN
- loyal or supportive in a passionate, often mindless way PARTISAN, CHAUVINISTIC
- blindly and unthinkingly loyal or imitative of SLAVISH
- loyalty, faithfulness, or steadfastness, as to a spouse, the facts, or one's duty FIDELITY, CONSTANCY
- loyalty, or the duties it demands, to one's country, king, or cause ALLEGIANCE
- loyalty or dutifulness, especially toward one's parents PIETY
- loyalty or fidelity to a party, cause, or set of rules ADHERENCE
- loyalty to and pride in one's group, fellowship ESPRIT DE CORPS
- constant and changeless, as unwavering loyalty is UNSWERVING
- entitled to loyalty, as a lord might be, or bound to give loyalty, as a subject might be LIEGE
- oath or public expression of loyalty by a vassal to his feudal lord HOMAGE, FEALTY

lozenge of a medicated preparation for chewing or sucking PASTILLE, TROCHE

LSD or similar drug producing hallucinations or sensory distortion HALLUCINOGENIC DRUG, PSYCHEDELIC DRUG

lubrication - study of friction and lubrication TRIBOLOGY

luck See also **fate**
- accidental developments, such as changes of luck VICISSITUDES
- depending on or happening by chance or luck ALEATORY
- source of great wealth or luck BONANZA
- tendency to make pleasant discoveries by accident or good luck SERENDIPITY
- unexpected piece of good luck WINDFALL, GODSEND

lucky, boding well, as a day or sign might be considered AUSPICIOUS, PROPITIOUS
- lucky, by a happy accident, by chance FORTUITOUS
- lucky, opportune, happening as if by a miracle PROVIDENTIAL
- lucky accident FLUKE
- lucky charm, magic stone, or the like supposedly with supernatural powers of protection TALISMAN
- lucky charm or piece of jewelry carried about for protection AMULET, PERIAPT
- lucky object, animal, or person, as adopted by a team MASCOT

luggage compartment or folding seat at the rear of a carriage or early automobile RUMBLE SEAT, DICKEY
- conveyer-belt apparatus in the baggage-claims section of an airport CAROUSEL

lukewarm TEPID
- lukewarm, especially in politics or religion LAODICEAN

lullaby or cradlesong BERCEUSE

luminous glow of fungus on rotting wood FOX FIRE

lump, bump, bulge, or similar rounded projection PROTUBERANCE, PROTRUSION
- lump, especially of natural gold NUGGET
- lump in a yarn of fabric, sometimes made deliberately to produce a knobbly appearance SLUB
- lump of soft matter, particularly of chewed food BOLUS
- lump or chunk, as of raw meat GOBBET
- small knob, lump, bump, or swelling NODULE, NODE

lung disease of an infectious bacterial type, characterized by small swellings or lesions TUBERCULOSIS, TB, CONSUMPTION, PHTHISIS
- lung disorder, caused by swelling of the air sacs, involving wheezing and breathlessness EMPHYSEMA
- lungs of a slaughtered pig, sheep, or the like, used especially for pet food LIGHTS
- crackling sound of diseased or fluid-filled lungs RALE
- creak, rattle, or crackle, as diseased lungs or broken bones might CREPITATE
- membrane lining the chest cavity and encasing the lungs PLEURA
- pooling of blood or fluid in the lungs or other organ because of bad circulation HYPOSTASIS
- relating to the lungs PULMONARY, PNEUMONIC
- small cavity or pit, such as a honeycomb cell or any of the tiny air cells in a lung where oxygen is absorbed by the blood ALVEOLUS
- thick-walled tubes linking the windpipe to the lungs BRONCHI

lung (combining form) PNEUM-, PNEUMO-

lure, entice, or incite, especially into a sinful or illegal act SOLICIT
- lure, tempt, attract ENTICE
- bird or other animal, artificial or live, used to lure others into shooting range or capture DECOY

lust See also **sex**
- arousing or appealing to sexual lust, lewd SALACIOUS, PRURIENT, LUBRICIOUS
- indulge one's lust, appetites, or the like to the full SATE, SATIATE
- unsatisfiable, as thirst or lust might be INSATIABLE
- lustful, given to or arousing excessive and uncontrolled lust or sexual desire LASCIVIOUS, LECHEROUS, LIBERTINE, LIBIDINOUS, CONCUPISCENT, RUTTISH
- lustful as a goat HIRCINE
- lustful man, lecher SATYR, FAUN
- lustful or knowing look LEER

lusty, robust, or coarsely humorous RABELAISIAN

luxurious, grand or ornate, as plush furnishings might be LAVISH, OPULENT, SUMPTUOUS
- luxurious, gratifying to the senses VOLUPTUOUS
- luxurious or elaborate, as a feast might be LUCULLAN
- luxurious or immoral place or situation BABYLON
- luxurious or plentiful only in appearance or by report, as an illusory feast might be BARMECIDAL
- luxuriously sensual or self-indulgent living FLESHPOTS
- indulge oneself luxuriously, as in sensual pleasures or self-pity REVEL, WALLOW

luxury-loving person, devoted to sensual pleasures SYBARITE, VOLUPTUARY, HEDONIST, EPICUREAN
- luxury-loving, spendthrift, or wasteful person PRODIGAL, PROFLIGATE
- land of luxury and idleness in medieval legend COCKAIGNE
- living in wasteful or immoral luxury CORINTHIAN
- person who enjoys luxurious living BON VIVANT

lying See also **lie**
- lying down, especially face down, as in submission or grief PROSTRATE
- lying down flat RECLINING, DECUMBENT, RECUMBENT
- lying face downward PRONE
- lying face upward on one's back SUPINE
- lying next to or alongside ADJACENT, CONTIGUOUS, MARGINAL, TANGENTIAL
- lying or false MENDACIOUS
- lying stretched out on the ground, with arms and legs spread out SPREAD-EAGLED

lying-in, confinement during childbirth ACCOUCHEMENT

lymph vessel (combining form) ANGIO-

lynch mob POSSE

M

machine See also charts at **scientific instruments, measuring instrument, laboratory, medical**
- machine or device, especially an irregular or makeshift one CONTRAPTION
- machinelike person, behaving as though not under his or her own control AUTOMATON, ROBOT, ZOMBIE
- person opposed to the introduction of machinery or technical advance LUDDITE
- remove parts from a car, machine, or the like and use them for repairing a similar model CANNIBALIZE
- working model or device reproducing the conditions of a real environment, machine, or the like, used for training or experiment SIMULATOR

machine-gun emplacement in the form of a low round concrete building PILLBOX
- machine-gun or bomb enemy ground troops from low-flying aircraft STRAFE
- machine guns, missiles, or the like grouped in an emplacement NEST

mackerel or herring salted in brine and lightly smoked BLOATER
- small young mackerel not over six inches long SPIKE

mad, crazy, insane CERTIFIABLE
- mad, frantic, or unbalanced, as through anxiety or grief DEMENTED, DERANGED, DISTRACTED, DISTRAUGHT, UNHINGED
- mad, out of one's mind, and thus not responsible for one's actions NON COMPOS MENTIS
- mad or uncontrollable because of an overpowering emotion or the alleged influence of evil spirits POSSESSED
- mad woman in a frenzied and ecstatic state MAENAD
- act with mad, destructive, or frantic violence GO BERSERK, RUN AMOK
- madly enthusiastic, extreme, possessed by excessive or irrational zeal FANATICAL, OBSESSED
- foreign terms for mad LOCO, PAZZO, FOU, FOLLE, MESHUGA
- odd, cranky, sometimes appearing a little mad ECCENTRIC, IDIOSYNCRATIC, QUIRKY

mad dog - fatal illness caused by the bite of a mad dog RABIES, HYDROPHOBIA

made-to-order, custom-made, as a suit of clothes might be BESPOKE

made-up, false, fabricated, as a charge or accusation might be TRUMPED-UP

madman - aggressive, violent madman, typically subject to wildly fluctuating moods PSYCHOPATH

madness - mental disorder characterized by delusions of persecution or grandeur and similar signs of apparent madness PARANOIA
- mental illness characterized by emotional instability, delusions, and withdrawal from reality SCHIZOPHRENIA
- mental illness or apparent madness occurring simultaneously in a married couple or pair of close relatives FOLIE À DEUX
- mental or emotional deterioration to the point of apparent madness DEMENTIA
- fit of madness that is characterized by irrational enthusiasm, rapidly changing ideas, or violence MANIA
- psychological disorder characterized by deep obsessions, hallucinations, severe confusion PSYCHOSIS
- temporary madness characterized by confusion, raving, tremors, or the like, as caused by fever, intoxication, or shock DELIRIUM
- wild, violent madness, or a fit of such madness FRENZY

magazine, review, or periodical with short or summarized articles and reports DIGEST
- magazine for those with a particular hobby or interest, especially a science-fiction or fantasy magazine FANZINE
- magazine's listing of its owner and staff, often printed prominently on the front page FLAG, MASTHEAD
- magazine's size, shape, layout, or design FORMAT
- magazines or books that are typically cheap and sensational or sentimental PULP
- expensively produced magazine, usually with many color photographs, on shiny paper GLOSSY
- number of copies distributed or sold of a newspaper or magazine CIRCULATION
- payment or order for an advance purchase, as of concert tickets or issues of a magazine over a period of time SUBSCRIPTION
- small stall, as for selling magazines KIOSK

Magi - names of the three Magi, according to tradition CASPAR, MELCHIOR, BALTHAZAR
- perfumed resins among the gifts of the Magi MYRRH, FRANKINCENSE

magic See also **black magic**
- magic, sorcery SORTILEGE
- magic intended to achieve an effect by some imitative ceremony or symbolic object, as in sticking pins into a doll SYMPATHETIC MAGIC
- magic or supernatural arts and happenings THE OCCULT, RELIGIOUS RITES
- magic potion believed to arouse love or desire PHILTER
- magic spell cast through ritual chanting INCANTATION
- magic symbol, inscription, or the like RUNE
- object believed to have magical powers AMULET, CHARM, TALISMAN, RABBIT'S FOOT, WISHBONE, RELIC, FETISH, JUJU, LUCKY PIECE

magician CONJURER
- magician, astrologer, or soothsayer CHALDEAN
- magician or astrologer of ancient times MAGUS
- magician or miracle worker THAUMATURGIST, ENCHANTER
- magician or ventriloquist ILLUSIONIST
- magician or wizard SORCERER
- magician's or scholar's attendant in medieval times FAMULUS
- magician's talk HOCUS-POCUS
- great magician or chief wizard ARCHIMAGE
- skill or speed of hand movements, as used in a magician's conjuring tricks SLEIGHT OF HAND, LEGERDEMAIN, PRESTIDIGITATION

magistrate in a Scottish town in former times BAILIE

- magistrate of high rank in ancient Rome PRAETOR
- magistrate's court, or a sitting of it PETTY SESSIONS
- chief magistrate of a Scottish burgh PROVOST
- relating to a master or magistrate MAGISTERIAL

magnet - condition of having two opposing physical properties at different points, as a magnet or battery has POLARITY
- soft iron bar linking the two poles of a horseshoe magnet KEEPER, ARMATURE

magnetic force driving two bodies apart REPULSION
- magnetic mineral, used in early compasses LODESTONE
- magnetic personal charm and power of inspiration CHARISMA
- neutralize the magnetic field of something, especially of a ship's hull DEGAUSS
- pair of closely positioned magnetic poles or electric charges that are equal but opposite DIPOLE
- state of maximum magnetization of a metal SATURATION

magnificent in appearance, splendid RESPLENDENT, DAZZLING

magnifying glass in a jeweler's eyepiece LOUPE

maharajah's wife MAHARANI, RANI

mahogany wood ACAJOU

maid, nanny, or nursemaid in India AYAH
- young woman, especially a flirtatious lady's maid, in a comic opera SOUBRETTE

maiden name - "born," used before the maiden name of a married woman when identifying her NÉE

maidenhead HYMEN

mail See **letter, post**

main See also **important**
- main, chief, foremost, supreme PARAMOUNT, PREDOMINANT, PREEMINENT, PREPONDERANT
- main axis or stem, as of a flower cluster or feather RACHIS
- main dish of a meal PIÈCE DE RÉSISTANCE
- main part of something, such as a body organ CORPUS
- main part or ingredient STAPLE
- main point of a speech or argument GIST, BURDEN, GRAVAMEN
- main route bearing traffic, messages, or the like ARTERY

main (combining form) ARCH-, PRIM-

maintenance payment made to a lover after separation PALIMONY

majority, the greater part THE GENERALITY
- majority in an election in which the winner fails to secure more than half of the votes or seats RELATIVE MAJORITY, PLURALITY
- majority in an election in which the winner secures more than half of the total votes or seats ABSOLUTE MAJORITY

make, accomplish, produce according to a prescribed plan EXECUTE
- make, cause to become RENDER
- make, construct, or put together from separate parts ASSEMBLE
- make, invent, or prepare something artificial or dubious, cook up CONCOCT, FABRICATE
- make, put together, prepare CONFECT
- make, produce, or invent something using whatever resources are available IMPROVISE
- make again in the original form RECONSTITUTE, RECONSTRUCT
- make by careful planning or inventiveness CONTRIVE, DEVISE, EXCOGITATE
- make by giving shape to FORGE, MOLD, FASHION
- make industrially MANUFACTURE
- make or introduce by developing or inventing PIONEER, ORIGINATE, INNOVATE
- make or invent by gradual development EVOLVE

make (combining form) -FY

make good one's losses RECOUP
- making good, compensation, repayment RESTITUTION, AMENDS, REPARATIONS, REDRESS
- making good, release from debt or sin, atonement REDEMPTION, QUITTANCE, EXPIATION, REQUITAL

make up for or counterbalance something OFFSET, COMPENSATE, COUNTERVAIL

makeshift, improvised, temporary EXTEMPORANEOUS
- makeshift, substitute STOPGAP

makeup See **cosmetics**
- makeup used by actors GREASEPAINT
- covered with makeup, as a clown might be FARDED

making (combing form) -FACIENT, -FIC, -POIESIS

malaria PALUDISM
- malaria-infested PALUDAL
- malaria or other disease transmitted by animals ZOONOSIS
- malaria or similar fever involving chills and shivering AGUE
- malaria treatment, drug derived from the bark of a South American tree QUININE, CINCHONA, CINCHONINE
- mosquito of the kind that carries malaria ANOPHELES
- recurring daily, as attacks of malaria might be QUOTIDIAN

Malay village or compound KAMPONG
- Malay garment in the form of a colored cloth wrapped around the waist SARONG
- Malay sword or large knife with a wavy double-edged blade KRIS
- Malayan form of polite address, equivalent to "Mr." or "Sir" TUAN
- Malaysian who is an indigenous ethnic Malay BUMIPUTRA

male club or social group FRATERNITY
- male-dominated society PATRIARCHY
- male hormone ANDROGEN, TESTOSTERONE
- male menopause MALE CLIMACTERIC
- male pride of a swaggering, exaggerated kind, aggressive masculinity MACHISMO
- male principle or personality in a woman's unconscious, in Jungian philosophy ANIMUS
- abnormal development of male characteristics in a woman VIRILISM
- active male force or principle in Eastern philosophy YANG
- having the qualities of an adult male VIRILE
- relating to the male line of descent PATRILINEAL
- sex chromosome associated with male characteristics Y CHROMOSOME
- weaken, deprive of initiative and other qualities traditionally regarded as male EMASCULATE

male (combining form) ANDR-, ANDRO-, VIR-

malicious, random, unprovoked, as vandalism or willful destruction is WANTON, GRATUITOUS
- malicious, spiteful, hate-filled VIRULENT

malnutrition disease, as among African children, resulting from lack of protein KWASHIORKOR
- malnutrition disease resulting from lack of vitamin B BERIBERI
- malnutrition disease resulting from lack of vitamin C SCURVY

malt vinegar ALEGAR
- frame or floor on which barley is spread for malting COUCH
- kiln for drying hops or malt OAST

mammal with a very thick skin, especially the elephant, rhinoceros, and hippopotamus PACHYDERM
- mammal of the group that has hooves, including horses and cattle UNGULATE
- mammal of the order that has an even number of toes, including cattle, antelope, deer, and pigs ARTIODACTYL
- mammal of the order that has an odd number of toes, including horses and rhinoceroses PERISSODACTYL
- mammal of the order that has in-

cisor teeth especially adapted for gnawing, including rats and squirrels RODENT
- mammal of the suborder that has four stomachs and chews the cud, including cattle, sheep, and deer RUMINANT
- having a backbone or spinal column, as fish, birds, and mammals do VERTEBRATE

man See also **human**
- having the qualities of a grown man VIRILE

man (combining form) ANDR-, ANDRO-, -ANTHROP-, ANTHROPO-

man-about-town, man of fashion BOULEVARDIER

man-made, human-made ARTIFICIAL, SYNTHETIC

man of fashion whose chief interest is in clothes and manners BEAU, BEAU BRUMMELL, DANDY, FOP, POPINJAY

manage, supervise, or control ADMINISTER, REGULATE, SUPERINTEND
- manage to do something, especially by means of a trick ENGINEER, CONTRIVE
- manage without or get rid of DISPENSE WITH, FORGO

manager of property, finances, social arrangements, or the like STEWARD

-mancy See **fortune-telling**

maneuver around an enemy unit OUTFLANK

maneuverable, steerable DIRIGIBLE
- maneuver for position or advantage JOCKEY
- maneuver in which deception or surprise is used to outwit the enemy STRATAGEM

manhood, masculine vigor VIRILITY

mania See chart
- compulsive and harmful mania, desire, or urging CACOËTHES

manifestation, appearance (combining form) -PHANY

manipulate the boundaries of an electoral constituency for party advantage GERRYMANDER
- manipulating the bones, as a form of therapy OSTEOPATHY
- person or group manipulated to further the purposes of another PAWN

manner of behaving or conducting oneself DEMEANOR, DEPORTMENT
- affected, fussily overelegant as someone's manner or speech might be PRECIOUS
- harsh or curt in speech or manner BRUSQUE, ABRASIVE

manner (combining form) -WISE

manners, code of proper behavior within a given group or society, good form ETIQUETTE, PROTOCOL, RUBRIC
- manners of a smooth or perfect kind, polish FINISH

MANIAS

OBSESSION WITH, OR ADDICTION TO:	
alcohol	**dipsomania**
books	**bibliomania**
bridges	**gephyromania**
cats	**ailuromania**
crowds	**demomania/ ochlomania**
dead bodies	**necromania**
death	**thanatomania**
dogs	**cynomania**
drugs	**narcomania**
eating	**phagomania/ sitomania**
fire, arson	**pyromania**
flowers	**anthomania**
horses	**hippomania**
lying and exaggerating	**mythomania**
oneself	**egomania**
personal cleanliness	**ablutomania**
pleasure	**hedonomania**
power	**megalomania**
religion	**entheomania/ theomania**
riches	**plutomania/ chrematomania**
sex	**erotomania/ nymphomania/ satyromania**
single idea or thing	**monomania**
stealing	**kleptomania**
surgery or undergoing surgery	**tomomania**
talking	**logomania/ verbomania**
traveling	**dromomania/ hodomania/ poriomania**
work	**ergomania**

- act, usually unintended, of bad manners or improper behavior SOLECISM
- good manners or correct behavior, propriety DECORUM
- overfussy detail, as of manners or protocol PUNCTILIO

manor of a feudal lord SEIGNIORY, DEMESNE

manual worker who is skilled at a craft ARTISAN
- relating to manual wage earners BLUE-COLLAR

manufacturer, industrialist, or powerful business person TYCOON, MAGNATE

manuscript adorned with painted designs and lettering ILLUMINATED MANUSCRIPT
- manuscript illumination, such as a small picture or ornamental letter MINIATURE
- manuscript in the author's handwriting AUTOGRAPH, HOLOGRAPH
- manuscript with more than one layer of text, or one from which an earlier text has been erased PALIMPSEST
- compare manuscripts or other texts to see where they differ COLLATE
- containing errors or changes, as the text of a copied manuscript might be CORRUPT
- copyist of manuscripts in ancient and medieval times SCRIBE
- correct and style a manuscript in preparation for typesetting COPYEDIT
- room in a monastery in which scribes could copy records or manuscripts SCRIPTORIUM
- space or missing part in a manuscript LACUNA
- style of script or handwriting in medieval manuscripts MINUSCULE, UNCIAL
- title, heading, or letter, typically illuminated in red in a manuscript or book RUBRIC
- treated sheepskin or goatskin on which ancient manuscripts are written PARCHMENT
- volume of ancient manuscripts, as of the Scriptures CODEX

Manx emblem of three limbs radiating from a center TRISKELION

many See also **lots, excessive, plenty**
- many, several, varied MULTIPLE, MANIFOLD, DIVERSE, SUNDRY, NUMEROUS, MULTIPLEX
- made of many parts or kinds, having great variety MULTIFARIOUS
- very many, countless INNUMERABLE, MYRIAD, MULTITUDINOUS, UMPTEEN, LEGION

many (combining form) PLURI-, MULTI-, POLY-
many-headed monster killed by Hercules HYDRA
many-sided, as a problem might be HYDRA-HEADED
Maori See chart
map See illustration
- map projection of the earth producing straight parallel lines for both latitude and longitude, similar to Mercator's projection GALL'S PROJECTION
- map projection of the earth showing the various continents in correct proportion to their real size HOMOLOGRAPHIC PROJECTION, HAMMER'S PROJECTION, PETERS PROJECTION
- map showing different altitudes of the land CONTOUR MAP, RELIEF MAP
- map the heights and distances of an area of land by measuring and calculating SURVEY
- mapping of a region, as a skill or technique CHOROGRAPHY
- mapping system, especially the representation of the earth on a flat surface PROJECTION
- circle, often decorated, printed on a map, showing the points of the compass COMPASS ROSE
- crisscross pattern, as on a map GRID
- description or display of a place's geographical features, as on a map TOPOGRAPHY
- distance east or west of the prime meridian at Greenwich, measured in degrees and often represented by vertical lines on a map LONGITUDE
- distance north or south of the equator, measured in degrees and often represented by horizontal lines on a map LATITUDE
- key explaining the symbols used in a map or chart LEGEND
- line on a language map linking places using the same distinctive word or pronunciation ISOGLOSS
- line on a weather map linking places of equal atmospheric pressure ISOBAR
- numbers or measurements that pinpoint a position, as on a map or graph COORDINATES

mapmaking or chart making CARTOGRAPHY
marathon runners' physical or psychological difficulties often arising after about 20 miles THE WALL
marble, of a fine white variety, as used in ancient statues PARIAN MARBLE
- marble of high quality used in sculpture CARRARA MARBLE
- marble of Italian origin having greenish streaks CIPOLIN
- marble or similar stone with greenish veins or mottles, as used for interior decoration VERD ANTIQUE
- marble tomb or stone coffin SARCOPHAGUS
- marblelike ornamental stone ALABASTER, ONYX MARBLE
- marblelike stone that has a glassy finish PURBECK MARBLE
- adjective for marble MARMOREAL

MAORI TERMS

Aotearoa	"land of the long white cloud": New Zealand
haeremai	"welcome!
haka	war dance accompanied by chanting
kia ora	"good luck!," "good health!": a greeting
kit/ kite	basket, usually of woven flax
mahi	work
mana	magical power; charismatic personality
marae	meeting place
moko	tattoo pattern
pa/pah	village, originally fortified
pakeha	white person, as opposed to a Maori
rangatira	chief or noble
taiaha	long, spearlike weapon
tama	youth, boy
tangata	man or husband
tangi	"weeping": mourning, or a funeral
tiki/hei-tiki	stone figurine of an ancestor, strung on flax and worn around the neck as a talisman
wahine	Polynesian or Maori woman or wife

- area or pit from which marble is extracted QUARRY

marbles as a game, or a large marble, or the line from which a marble player shoots TAW
- large playing marble ALLEY

march in single file, as troops might DEFILE
- marching step, as in some countries' military parades, in which the legs are kept straight and swung high GOOSE STEP

March 15 in the Roman calendar, or a corresponding day in other months IDES
margarine - referring to natural oils, as used in healthy margarines, with many double or triple chemical bonds POLYUNSATURATED
margin, as of variation or error LEEWAY, LATITUDE
- margin set in at the beginning of a paragraph INDENTATION
- marginal explanatory note, as in the Bible POSTIL
- having printed lines set flush with the margins JUSTIFIED
- set lines of type or print against a specified margin RANGE

marines See **services**
mark of quality or identification, impressed faintly onto paper and visible when held up to the light WATERMARK
- mark or sign of shame or disgrace STIGMA
- mark something, such as a passage in a book, with a tab, symbol, or the like FLAG
- mark stamped on gold or silver objects indicating the purity of the metal HALLMARK, PLATEMARK
- marks, features, or characteristics of a very distinctive or important kind LINEAMENTS

market or covered bazaar in a Muslim country SOUK
- market quarter of a North African town CASBAH
- maximum possible supply of a commodity within a market SATURATION

marketing and transport of commercial goods DISTRIBUTION
- marketing rights for a particular product in a given area CONCESSION, FRANCHISE

marketplace, exchange, trading center RIALTO
- marketplace in an ancient Greek city AGORA
- marketplace in ancient Rome FORUM

marksman, marksperson shooting, typically at long range, at exposed individuals or victims SNIPER
marriage, in keeping with Old Tes-

tament law, to the widow of one's brother LEVIRATE
- marriage announcement, as read out in church on the three Sundays before the wedding BANNS
- marriage between a royal or noble person and a partner of lower rank, with strict limitations on rights of inheritance MORGANATIC MARRIAGE
- marriage between people of different tribes, clans, or castes EXOGAMY, OUTBREEDING
- marriage by a man to two or more sisters successively SORORATE
- marriage officer in a registry office REGISTRAR
- marriage or sexual relations between people considered to be of different "races" MISCEGENATION
- marriage performed by a justice of the peace or other qualified civil official rather than by a member of the clergy CIVIL MARRIAGE
- marriage song or poem EPITHALAMIUM, PROTHALAMION, HYMENEAL
- marriage state or ceremony MATRIMONY
- marriage that is considered unsuitable or which is unsuccessful MISALLIANCE
- marriage with someone considered to be socially inferior MÉSALLIANCE
- marriage within one's own tribe, clan, or caste ENDOGAMY
- marriagelike relationship, often recognized as a marriage in law, of a couple who have lived together for several years COMMON-LAW MARRIAGE
- married SPLICED, YOKED
- married or engaged ESPOUSED, BETROTHED
- born in wedlock, of married parents LEGITIMATE
- bride's money or property handed over to her husband on their marriage DOWRY
- capable of living together harmoniously, as the partners in a marriage should be COMPATIBLE
- celebrate a marriage, perform a ceremony, or the like with formal or religious rites SOLEMNIZE
- clothing, linen, and the like collected by a woman for use after her marriage TROUSSEAU
- crime or custom of being married to two or more people at any one time BIGAMY
- custom or practice of being married to more than one man at a time POLYANDRY
- custom or practice of having more than one marriage partner, especially more than one wife, at a time POLYGAMY
- custom or practice of having only one marriage partner at a time MONOGAMY
- desirable, marriageable, as an attractive young woman is said to be NUBILE
- desirable and worthy for marriage, as a rich bachelor might be considered ELIGIBLE
- end or cancel a legal bond such as marriage ANNUL, DISSOLVE
- in reaction to or during recovery from disappointment, as a marriage might be ON THE REBOUND
- legal completion of a marriage by an act of sexual intercourse CON-

Map Projections

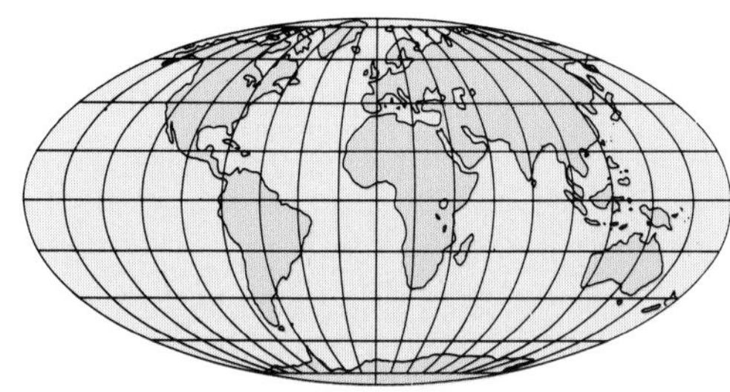

Mollweide's homolographic projection:
continents in correct proportion to their actual size

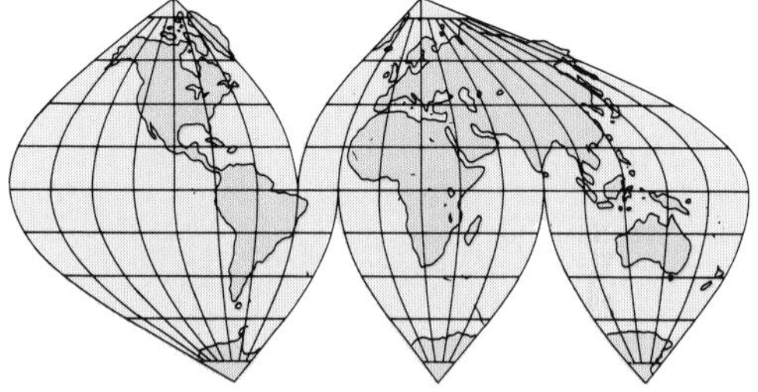

Interrupted projection:
distortion reduced by division into segments

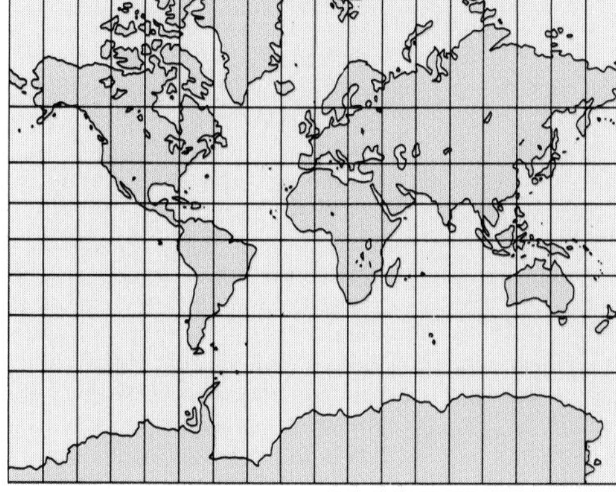

Mercator's projection:
shapes and bearings accurate: high-latitude areas distorted

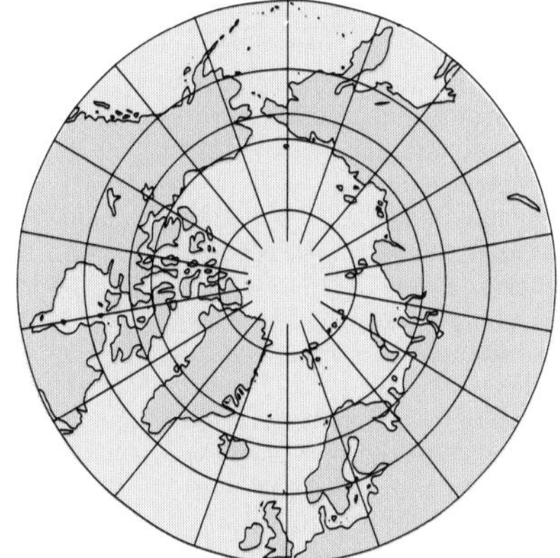

Polar zenithal projection:
compass bearings accurate from a central point

SUMMATION
- legal right to the help, company, and affection of one's marriage partner CONSORTIUM
- living together and having a sexual relationship without being formally married COHABITATION
- persistent conflict and disharmony in a marriage INCOMPATIBILITY
- person who tries to bring a pair together for marriage MATCHMAKER
- real or fictitious drawer for a trousseau saved by a young woman for use after her marriage, or the goods themselves BOTTOM DRAWER, HOPE CHEST, GLORY BOX
- referring to a spouse's sexual relationship outside marriage EXTRAMARITAL, ADULTEROUS, ILLICIT, OFFSHORE
- relating to marriage MARITAL, MATRIMONIAL, HYMENEAL, NUPTIAL, CONJUGAL, CONNUBIAL
- restoration of harmony or mutual acceptance between the partners in a marriage RECONCILIATION
- run away secretly with a lover, especially to get married ELOPE

marriage (combining form) -GAM-

marrow of a bone or pith of a stem MEDULLA

marrow (combining form) MYEL-, MYELO-

Mars - "sea" or dark patch on Mars or the Moon MARE

marsh, swamp, mire or bog QUAGMIRE, SLOUGH, FEN, MUSKEG
- marsh gas METHANE
- marsh plant related to the grass family SEDGE
- marshy stretch of land WASH, MORASS, OOZE, SWALE, VLEI
- marshy tributary of a river or lake, especially in Louisiana BAYOU
- adjective for a marsh or swamp PALUDAL
- atmosphere of a marsh, swamp, or the like MIASMA
- light hovering over marshy ground, probably produced by flaming methane gas WILL-O'-THE-WISP, IGNIS FATUUS, JACK-O'-LANTERN, FRIAR'S LANTERN
- smelly and invisible vapor or gas, as rising from a marsh or rubbish dump EFFLUVIUM

martial arts See **sports**

marvel, outstanding person or thing HUMDINGER
- marvel or extraordinary event, thing, or action PRODIGY, PORTENT

Marxist theory of reality in which historical change occurs through the resolving of successive contradictions DIALECTICAL MATERIALISM

masculine See **male**

mash or sieve boiled food to produce a pulpy consistency PUREE

mask, or the hooded robe worn with it, at a masquerade DOMINO
- mask for shielding the eyes, as worn by welders VISOR
- mask over the mouth and nose to purify or warm the air before breathing RESPIRATOR
- masked actor in an old-fashioned masque or mime MUMMER
- masked ball MASQUERADE

masonry See **brickwork**

Mass See also **Communion, church**
- Mass of a traditional Latin form used from 1570 to Vatican II TRIDENTINE MASS
- Mass that is optional or special, as for a wedding, rather than the prescribed Mass of the day VOTIVE MASS
- endowment for the saying of prayers or Mass, usually for the soul of the benefactor CHANTRY
- prayer book for the Roman Catholic Mass MISSAL

mass See **lump, pile, join**
- thick bushy mass, as of hair SHOCK

mass (combining form) -OME, -OMA

massacre, typically organized with official backing, as of Jews in Eastern Europe POGROM

massage, remedial exercises, and similar forms of medical treatment PHYSIOTHERAPY
- massage of perfumed lotion into the scalp, as after a haircut FRICTION
- massage therapy for relieving emotional and muscular tension and adjusting the body to benefit from gravity ROLFING
- person who gives massages MASSEUR, MASSEUSE

masses See **common**

mast - crossbeam attached to a mast and supporting a sail YARD
- crosstree on a masthead JACK
- iron rod buttressing a ship's mast FUTTOCK SHROUD
- lower a mast, sail, or flag STRIKE
- lower end of a mast HEEL
- pole used as a mast or boom SPAR
- rope or cable supporting a mast on a ship or boat SHROUD, GUY, STAY
- slope backward, as a ship's mast or funnel might RAKE
- support frame on deck for a pivoting mast TABERNACLE
- tub-shaped lookout platform near the top of a ship's mast CROW'S NEST

master of an art, especially a leading musician MAESTRO, VIRTUOSO
- adjective for a master MAGISTERIAL
- title of respect in East Africa, as used for a master or boss BWANA
- title of respect in colonial India, roughly equivalent to "Master" or "Sir" SAHIB

master key or skeleton key PASSKEY, PASSE-PARTOUT

master of ceremonies, as on a television or radio show MC
- master of ceremonies at a celebration or banquet who proposes toasts and presents speakers TOASTMASTER

masterpiece CHEF D'OEUVRE, TOUR DE FORCE

masturbation MANUSTUPRATION, ONANISM, MALTHUSIANISM

mat of lace, paper, or the like, as placed on plates DOILY
- mat of straw used as a floor covering in a Japanese home TATAMI
- mat on the upper part of a chair to protect the fabric from hair oil ANTIMACASSAR
- coconut-husk fiber, as used for ropes and matting COIR

match See also **agree**
- match, correspond TALLY
- match, game, or the like played between tied contestants to determine a winner PLAY-OFF
- match formerly used for lighting cigars VESUVIAN
- match that ignites when struck against any rough surface FRICTION MATCH, LUCIFER
- match with a large head, remaining alight in the wind FUSEE
- chemical element used in safety matches PHOSPHORUS
- short friction match, typically with a wax-coated stick VESTA

matchbox- or matchbook-label collector PHILLUMENIST

matching clothes or accessories designed to be worn together COORDINATES
- matching partner, complementary part PENDANT

mate - habit of having only one female mate, as with many male animals MONOGYNY
- habit of having only one male mate, as with many female animals MONANDRY
- habit of having only one mate at a time, as with many animals MONOGAMY
- habit of having several different mates during a single breeding season, as with some animals POLYGAMY
- habit of mating with several different females during a single breeding season, as with some male animals POLYGYNY
- habit of mating with several different males during a single breeding season, as with some female animals POLYANDRY

material See also **cloth, fabric**

- material, physical, or actual rather than conceptual or imaginary OBJECTIVE
- material, such as reinforced concrete, made of two or more distinct materials COMPOSITE
- trimming or decoration consisting of different materials pasted or sewn together APPLIQUÉ

materialistic, interested chiefly or only in money and possessions MERCENARY
- materialistic and nonintellectual, purely functional or mechanical BANAUSIC

mathematics See charts, pages 331 and 332, and also **geometry, graph, statistics**
- mathematical representation of a problem, system, or situation SIMULATION
- mathematical study of information flow and control systems in electronics, mechanics, and biology CYBERNETICS
- familiar with mathematical principles or a scientific approach NUMERATE

matter (combining form) HYL-, HYLO-, PLASM-

Matthew, Mark, Luke, or John, as author of one of the Christian Gospels EVANGELIST
- Gospels of Matthew, Mark, and Luke SYNOPTIC GOSPELS

mattress - hard mattress, typically filled with straw PALLET, PALLIASSE
- strong cloth used to cover a mattress or pillow TICKING
- unsprung mattress of Japanese style FUTON

mature and dignified MELLOW
- maturing or developing unusually early, as a clever or sophisticated child seems to be PRECOCIOUS
- phase in maturing during early adolescence, in which adult reproductive characteristics develop PUBERTY

maximum, as of magnetization, strength of a solution, or supply in a market SATURATION
- maximum possible speed of a missile, falling object, aircraft, or the like, as determined by such factors as air resistance TERMINAL VELOCITY

mayfly or related short-lived insect EPHEMERID

mayonnaise flavored with garlic AIOLI

maze, confusing network of paths or passages LABYRINTH
- mazelike place or thing, such as a crowded neighborhood WARREN

mead, especially spiced mead as drunk in former times METHEGLIN

meadow, grassland LEA
- meadow, lawn, or similar grassy stretch of land SWARD

meal See also **cooking**, chart at **menu**, and entries at various types of food
- meal, or the food eaten at a meal REPAST
- meal eaten late in the morning as a combination of breakfast and lunch BRUNCH
- meal in which diners help themselves from dishes of food placed on a counter or table BUFFET

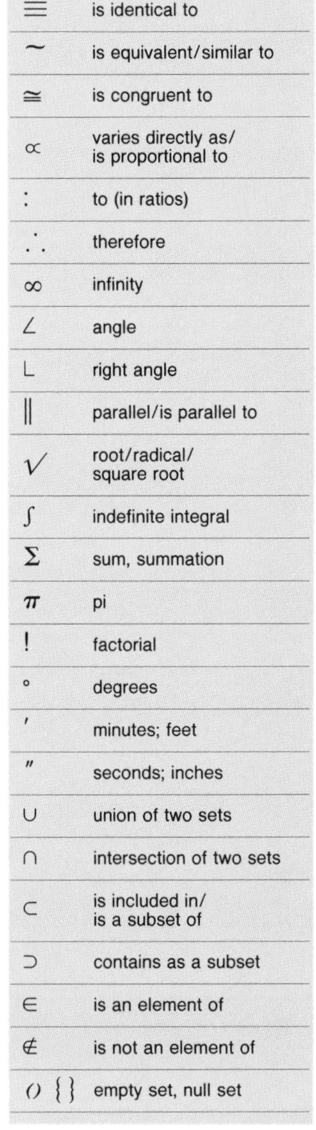

Mathematical Symbols

≈	is approximately equal to
≡	is identical to
~	is equivalent/similar to
≅	is congruent to
∝	varies directly as/ is proportional to
:	to (in ratios)
∴	therefore
∞	infinity
∠	angle
∟	right angle
∥	parallel/is parallel to
√	root/radical/ square root
∫	indefinite integral
Σ	sum, summation
π	pi
!	factorial
°	degrees
′	minutes; feet
″	seconds; inches
∪	union of two sets
∩	intersection of two sets
⊂	is included in/ is a subset of
⊃	contains as a subset
∈	is an element of
∉	is not an element of
∅ { }	empty set, null set

- dish or course served between the main courses of a meal ENTREMETS
- first course of a meal, or appetizer HORS D'OEUVRE
- just after a meal, especially dinner POSTPRANDIAL
- light meal COLLATION
- main course, or course just before the main course, of a meal ENTRÉE
- outdoors, in the open air, as a meal might be ALFRESCO
- referring to a meal, especially dinner PRANDIAL
- referring to a meal, typically with a narrow range of choices, offered at a fixed price in a restaurant or hotel TABLE D'HÔTE, PRIX FIXE
- referring to a meal of separately priced dishes in a restaurant or hotel À LA CARTE
- snack or light meal TIFFIN

mean See also **stingy**
- mean, claim, present an appearance of PROFESS, PURPORT
- mean, imply, represent, give a sign or portent of BETOKEN, SIGNIFY
- mean, indicate, refer to directly, stand for, or specify DENOTE, DESIGNATE, DENOMINATE
- mean, suggest, imply, involve as a consequence or condition CONNOTE

meaning, aim, purpose INTENT
- meaning, sense, general direction PURPORT, TENOR
- meaning, significance IMPORT
- meaning implied by a word's associations, rather than literal meaning CONNOTATION
- meaning or explicit reference of a word DENOTATION
- meaning or message that is implied but not directly expressed, as in a speech or play SUBTEXT
- accepted or usual meaning or sense of a word or phrase ACCEPTATION
- deduce or interpret the meaning of CONSTRUE
- depth of feeling, meaning, or thinking PROFUNDITY
- general meaning or drift, main point, as of a speech GIST, BURDEN, GRAVAMEN
- having a hidden or mysterious meaning CRYPTIC, ENIGMATIC
- having only one meaning UNIVOCAL
- having several different meanings POLYSEMOUS
- having two or more meanings AMBIGUOUS
- object of meaning, the idea or thing referred to by a word, phrase, or sign REFERENT

MATHEMATICS TERMS

algorithm	method of calculation by the use of a detailed step-by-step procedure
arithmetic progression	sequence in which each number differs from the preceding one by a constant amount, such as *2, 5, 8, 11, 14 ...*
binary	relating to a system of numbers having 2 as its base
calculus	branch of mathematics dealing with continuously changing quantities; method of calculation in which symbols are used
coefficient	numerical factor in an elementary algebraic term, such as 3 in the term $3x$
congruent	referring to geometrical figures that coincide exactly in shape and size
constant	quantity retaining a fixed value throughout a series of calculations
coordinates	set of numbers used to determine the position of a point, line, or curve
denominator/ divisor	quantity that is divided into another; quantity below the division line in a fraction
equation	mathematical statement in which two expressions or numbers are connected by an equal sign, such as $3x + 2y = 17$
exponent/ index/power	symbol indicating the number of times a quantity is to be multiplied by itself, such as the ^{3} in $2^3 = 8$
factor	any of the quantities that can be divided into a given quantity exactly: 7 and 5 are factors of 35
factorial	product of all the whole numbers from a given number down to 1: 4 factorial is $4 \times 3 \times 2 \times 1 = 24$
Fibonacci sequence	infinite series of numbers, each of which is the sum of the preceding two
function	variable connected with another variable in such a way that a change in one produces a corresponding change in the other
geometrical progression	sequence of numbers in which each term is obtained by multiplying the preceding term by a constant factor, such as *2, 6, 18, 54, 162 ...*
integer	any whole number, positive or negative, together with zero
locus	path traced by a point, line, or surface that moves under stated conditions
logarithm/ log	any one of a system of figures used in calculations, based on the number of times a base number, such as 10, has to be multiplied by itself to produce a given number
multiple	any of the quantities that a given number can be divided into exactly: 21, 35, 49, and so on are all multiples of 7
numerator/ dividend	quantity into which another is divided; quantity above the division line in a fraction
permutation	ordered arrangement of the quantities in a set into any of various possible groups
product	result of multiplying one quantity by another
Pythagorean theorem	theorem relating to the length of the sides of a right-angled triangle
quotient	result of dividing one quantity by another
rational number	number that can be expressed as a real whole number, or as a fraction involving two whole numbers
reciprocal/ inverse	number obtained when another number is divided into 1
recurring decimal	decimal number ending in a pattern of one or more digits repeated indefinitely, as *0.878787...*
secant	straight line intersecting a curve at two or more points
tangent	line, curve, or surface touching but not cutting another
topology	geometry studying the properties of a figure or solid that remain unaffected even when the figure or solid is stretched or twisted
trigonometry	study and application of the relationships involving the sides and angles of triangles, as used in surveying and navigation
variable	quantity that can assume any of various possible values
variance	in statistics, a measure of the spread of a source of numbers or measurements
vertex	point at which two lines or planes meet to form an angle

- referring to a word having full lexical meaning rather than just grammatical function NOTIONAL
- referring to meaning, as of words, gestures, or symbols SEMANTIC
- shade of meaning, subtle distinction NUANCE
- speech or writing surrounding a specified word or passage and refining its meaning CONTEXT
- twist the meaning of, misinterpret PERVERT, DISTORT, MISCONSTRUE
- word meaning the same or nearly the same as another in the same language SYNONYM
- word meaning the opposite or nearly the opposite of another in the same language ANTONYM
- word or phrase that seems to have a second, typically saucy, meaning DOUBLE ENTENDRE

means or medium, such as a play, for conveying ideas, expressing talents, or the like VEHICLE
- means to an end, or device adopted for an urgent purpose EXPEDIENT

meanwhile, in the meantime IN THE INTERIM

measles RUBEOLA, MORBILLI
- German measles RUBELLA
- red skin rash, as in measles ROSEOLA

measurable by the same units or standard COMMENSURABLE, COMMENSURATE

measure See also chart at **weights and measures**
- measure, test, or standard used for judgment or comparison YARDSTICK, CRITERION
- measure or basic property in physics DIMENSION, CONSTANT
- measure or map an area of land SURVEY
- measure the depth of, as with a weighted line SOUND, FATHOM
- adjective for measures or measurement MENSURAL, METRICAL

measurement, as in geometry MENSURATION
- measurement around a person's waist or a tree GIRTH

measurement (combining form) METR-, -METRY

measuring instrument See chart, page 334
- measuring instrument consisting of a pair of arms hinged at one end, as used in geometry SECTOR, DIVIDERS
- finely adjusted or graduated scale supplementing the main scale of a measuring instrument VERNIER
- mark, adjust, or check the scale of a measuring instrument CALIBRATE

meat See also **bacon, pork, beef, lamb, cooking,** and chart at **menu**
- meat-eating, feeding on meat or flesh CARNIVOROUS, CREOPHAGOUS, ZOOPHAGOUS
- meat tenderizer consisting of a papaya-derived enzyme PAPAIN
- meatless, as a diet might be, or certain days of religious abstinence MAIGRE
- brown meat by quick frying at high temperature SEAR
- cooking appliance fitted with a rotating spit for roasting meat ROTISSERIE
- highly seasoned smoked meat, prepared from breast or shoulder of beef PASTRAMI
- gash or score raw meat or fish for crisper cooking CRIMP
- lump or chunk, as of raw meat GOBBET
- referring to meat slaughtered in accordance with Jewish law KOSHER
- referring to meat slaughtered in accordance with Muslim law HALAL
- referring to meat that is medium-cooked À POINT
- referring to meat that is underdone SAIGNANT
- referring to meat that is very rare AU BLEU
- referring to meat that is well done BIEN CUIT
- refraining from eating meat, as an act of penance, especially as formerly among Roman Catholics ABSTINENCE
- sausage, ham, and other cold cooked meats CHARCUTERIE
- spicy minced meat or poultry used for stuffing FORCEMEAT
- thin slice of meat, especially veal, typically fried in breadcrumbs ESCALOPE, ESCALLOP, SCALLOP

Mecca - Muslim pilgrimage made to Mecca HAJJ

mechanical, involuntary, or unconscious, as sneezes, knee jerks, or similar responses are REFLEX
- mechanical, routine, indifferent, as a glance or smile might be PERFUNCTORY
- mechanical or electrical device or element forming part of a machine or circuit COMPONENT
- mechanical repetition, unthinking routine ROTE

medal, badge, or similar item awarded as an honor DECORATION
- medal, brooch, or the like worn on the chest PECTORAL
- medal or military decoration awarded to those wounded in action PURPLE HEART
- back of a coin or medal, "tails" VERSO, REVERSE
- front of a coin or medal, "heads" OBVERSE
- small metal tag, bar, or insignia on a medal ribbon, indicating either a second award or details of the award CLASP
- study of coins, money, or medals NUMISMATICS

mediation in a dispute INTERCESSION

mediator in a dispute between two parties ARBITRATOR, GO-BETWEEN, INTERMEDIARY, OMBUDSMAN, HONEST BROKER

medical See charts, pages 335 and 336, and also **therapy**
- medical, relating to healing AESCULAPIAN
- medical equipment and supplies of a doctor or hospital ARMAMENTARIUM
- medical implement inserted into the rectum, urethra, or other body canal for dilation, medication, or the like BOUGIE
- medical pad, as of gauze, used to stop bleeding or to reduce pain or inflammation COMPRESS
- medical records or preliminary case history of a patient ANAMNESIS
- medical social worker in former times ALMONER
- medical specialist DIPLOMATE
- medical testing for potential sufferers from a disease, carried out on a wide range of the population SCREENING
- combining inefficiently or dangerously, as different medical drugs might be INCOMPATIBLE, ANTAGONISTIC, INTERACTING
- referring to medical drugs used to prevent rejection of a transplanted organ IMMUNOSUPPRESSIVE
- referring to medical staff, such as therapists, who are not trained doctors PARAMEDICAL
- symbol of the medical profession, a winged staff with two snakes twined around it CADUCEUS

medical (combining form) IATRO-, -IATR-, -ATRICS, -IATRY

medical drug (combining form) PHARMACO-

medical examination (combining form) -OPSY

medical student having an MD degree but still undergoing supervised hospital training INTERN
- junior doctor undergoing advanced training in a medical specialty RESIDENT

medical treatment See also **therapy**
- medical treatment, of Chinese origin, in which fine, wirelike needles

MEASURING INSTRUMENTS

Instrument	Measures
actinometer	intensity of radiation
almucantar	bearing and altitude of celestial bodies
altimeter	height of an aircraft above the ground
anemometer	wind speed; flow rate of a fluid
atmometer/ evaporometer	rate of evaporation
baroscope	atmospheric pressure
bathometer	depth of water in the sea
Beckmann thermometer	small temperature changes
calipers	diameters of rods or tubes
calorimeter	heat
cathetometer	distances between fluid levels in vertical tubes
chronometer	precise time
clinometer	angle of an incline
colorimeter	colors; concentration of solutions, by comparison of colors
Crookes radiometer	intensity of radiated light
cryometer	extremely low temperatures
cyclometer	distance traveled by a wheel
densimeter	density
densitometer	optical density, degree of transparency
dilatometer	volume expansion of liquids with temperature
electrometer	potential difference and charge
electroscope	presence of an electric charge
gaussmeter	magnetic flux, density
Geiger counter	radiation
goniometer	angles, as of crystals
gravimeter	gravitational field
hydrometer	relative density of liquids
hygrometer	humidity
hypsometer	land elevations
interferometer	wavelengths of light
Machmeter	speeds at and beyond the speed of sound
magnetometer	strengths of magnetic fields
manometer	pressures of gases and liquids
micrometer	precise dimensions of small distances or angles
octant	altitude of celestial bodies
ondometer	frequency of radio waves
optometer	refraction of the eye
orometer	height above sea level
pedometer	distance traveled by a walking person
photometer	light intensity
piezometer	high pressures, compressibility
planimeter	surface area of a plane figure
pluviometer	rainfall
polarimeter	optical rotation of polarized light
potentiometer	voltages or potential differences
protractor	angles
psychrometer	humidity
pycnometer	relative density of liquids and solids
pyrheliometer	solar radiation
pyrometer	high temperatures
radio-micrometer	heat radiation
saccharometer	sugar content in a solution
salimeter	salt in a solution
scintillation counter	ionizing radiation
sclerometer	hardness of material
seismograph	earth tremors
sextant	altitude of celestial bodies (angles)
spectrometer	optical spectra
spherometer	curvature of a sphere or cylinder
steelyard	weight of objects
tachometer/ rev counter	speed of rotation of a shaft
tachymeter/ tacheometer	distance, elevations, and bearings
tellurometer	distances (through radio signals)
tensiometer	tensile strength, stretchability
theodolite	vertical and horizontal angles, and hence distances and elevations
variometer	rate of climb or descent of an aircraft
velocimeter	velocity or speed
vinometer	alcohol content of wine
voltameter	quantity of electricity (volts)

are inserted into the skin at given points ACUPUNCTURE
- medical treatment, type of therapy MODALITY
- medical treatment based on giving tiny doses of a substance that in larger doses would induce symptoms similar to those of the disease HOMEOPATHY
- medical treatment based on inducing a condition different from the symptoms of the disease, conventional medicine ALLOPATHY
- medical treatment of an unorthodox kind, opposed to mainstream Western medical techniques ALTERNATIVE MEDICINE
- medical treatment of bone and muscle disorders ORTHOPEDICS
- medical treatment of children's diseases PEDIATRICS
- medical treatment of disorders of the nervous system NEUROLOGY
- medical treatment using massage and infrared or ultraviolet rays PHYSIOTHERAPY
- medical treatment of skin diseases DERMATOLOGY
- medical treatment of blood disorders HEMATOLOGY
- medical treatment of disorders of the bladder UROLOGY
- medical treatment of women's diseases GYNECOLOGY
- based on practical experience rather than theory or proof, as medical treatment might be EMPIRICAL
- restoration of one's health through medical treatment REHABILITATION

medical treatment (combining form) -PATH-, -PATHY

medication in solid form designed to be inserted into a body cavity, especially the rectum or vagina SUPPOSITORY

medicinal, remedial THERAPEUTIC
- medicinal drug PHARMACEUTICAL
- medicinal plant, especially an herb SIMPLE

MEDICAL AND SURGICAL INSTRUMENTS

aspirator	removing liquids from a body cavity	**kymograph**	recording variations in blood pressure
audiometer	measuring sharpness of hearing	**lancet**	making incisions, in surgery
bistoury	making small surgical incisions	**ophthalmoscope**	examining the interior of the eye
cannula	draining or injecting fluids	**osteoclast**	fracturing a bone, as for resetting to correct a deformity
CAT scanner	creating a three-dimensional image of body tissues by X-ray recordings	**otoscope**	examining the inner ear
colposcope	examining the cervix and vagina	**polygraph**	recording changes in heartbeat, breathing rate, and blood pressure
defibrillator	restoring heart rhythm by electric shock	**raspatory**	scraping bones
dermatome	cutting skin for grafting	**retinoscope**	examining light refraction in the eye
écraseur	removing tumors by tightening a wire loop	**retractor**	holding open a surgical incision
electrocardiograph	recording heartbeats	**scalpel**	making incisions
electroencephalograph	recording brain activity	**snare**	removing tumors and polyps
electromyograph	recording muscle activity	**speculum**	opening a body passage for inspection
endoscope	examining hollow organs such as the bowel	**sphygmomanometer**	measuring blood pressure
forceps	delivering babies	**sphygmometer**	measuring pulse strength
fiberscope	examining inner tissues and organs	**stethoscope**	listening to body sounds
gastroscope	examining the interior of the stomach	**tenaculum**	lifting and holding blood vessels
gorget	removing stones from the bladder	**trephine/trepan**	removing discs of bone from the skull
iron lung	providing artificial respiration	**xyster**	scraping bones

- medicinal preparation or drug, especially a laxative PHYSIC
- medicinal sweet LOZENGE, PASTILLE, TROCHE
- medicinal tablet or pill of large size BOLUS

medicine See chart
- medicine, medicinal remedy MEDICAMENT
- medicine, method, or device designed to protect against disease PROPHYLACTIC
- medicine as used in establishing facts for evidence in legal cases FORENSIC MEDICINE
- medicine boasting of secret ingredients, typically a quack remedy NOSTRUM
- medicine or remedy claimed to befor all ailments PANACEA
- medicine intended for a particular disease or disorder SPECIFIC
- medicine or drug that revives or restores one's health or strength RESTORATIVE
- medicine protected by a trademark and typically available without prescription PATENT MEDICINE
- capsule or wafer of an early kind for containing an unpleasant-tasting medicine CACHET
- drugs collectively, as used in the preparation of medicine PHARMACOPOEIA
- effect, especially an adverse effect, of a medicine or drug REACTION
- effective, powerful, or still active, as drugs or medicines might be POTENT
- give out in portions, distribute something such as medicines as a pharmacist does DISPENSE
- given or taken by injection rather than by mouth, as a medicine might be PARENTERAL
- inactive substance administered as a medicine, as for humoring a patient or for comparisons in an experiment PLACEBO
- mix medicinal drugs according to a prescription COMPOUND
- oil or other inert medium used for bulking up an active medicine VEHICLE
- place, such as a hospital office, from which medicines and medical supplies are given out DISPENSARY
- referring to a medicine or drug available without prescription OVER-THE-COUNTER, OFFICINAL
- referring to a medicine or drug prepared according to a specific prescription MAGISTRAL
- referring to a medicine or drug sold under a trademark PROPRIETARY

MEDICINES

GROUP OF MEDICINES	WHAT THEY TREAT
analgesic	pain
antacid	stomach and gullet ulcers
anthelmintic/ vermifuge	intestinal worms
antibiotic	bacterial infections
anti-coagulant	blood clotting
anti-convulsant	convulsions, epilepsy
anti-histamine	hay fever and other allergies
antipyretic	fever
antiscorbutic	scurvy
antitussive	coughs
beta blocker	anxiety, hypertension
broncho-dilator	asthma and other breathing difficulties
cathartic	constipation
cytotoxin	tumors
decongestant	blocked nasal passages
demulcent	mouth ulcers
diuretic	urine retention
emetic	poisoning, by causing vomiting
expectorant	phlegm in the air passages
hypnotic/ soporific	insomnia
laxative	constipation
paregoric	intestinal pain, diarrhea
purgative	constipation
sedative	anxiety, tension, insomnia
tetracycline/ sulfonamide	bacterial infections
tranquilizer	anxiety, stress, insomnia
vasodilator	angina

SPECIFIC MEDICINE	WHAT IT TREATS
amitryptiline	depression
amoxycillin	bacterial infections
atropine	peptic ulcers, spasms
calamine	skin inflammation
chloral hydrate	insomnia
codeine	pain, coughing, insomnia
cortisone	arthritis, rheumatism, skin disorders
curare	tetanus
diazepam/ Valium	anxiety, tension
digitalis/ digoxin	heart disorders
dill water	babies' colic
Dimotane	allergies
disulfiram	alcoholism
gentian violet/ crystal violet	skin infections
Glauber's salt	constipation
heparin	blood clotting
insulin	diabetes
L-dopa	Parkinson's disease
nitrazepam	insomnia
norepi-nephrine/ noradrenaline	shock
paracetamol	pain, fever
pentobarbi-tone sodium/ Nembutal	insomnia
pethidine	pain
phenacetin	pain
phenelzine	depression
quinine	malaria
valerian	anxiety, tension
warfarin	blood clotting

- referring to a prescription medicine or drug ETHICAL
- sign, such as an allergy or dangerous side effect, that argues for the discontinuation of a medicine or treatment CONTRAINDICATION
- small container for medicine, poison, or other liquid, typically a tiny stoppered glass bottle VIAL, PHIAL
- starch or other inactive substance added to a medical drug to make it more suitable for administering EXCIPIENT
- syrup or similar preparation added to an unpleasant-tasting medicine ELIXIR
- syrupy drink to which medicine can be added JULEP

medicine man or similar priest endowed with apparent magic powers SHAMAN

medieval See also chart at **feudal system**
- medieval church music, traditionally chanted unaccompanied PLAINSONG
- medieval European social system in which vassals exchanged homage and service for land and protection from a lord FEUDALISM, FEUDAL SYSTEM
- medieval romance in prose or verse GEST
- medieval tournament, in which knights took part in horse races and riding displays CAROUSEL
- medieval town, largely self-governing COMMUNE
- medieval trade and mutual-aid association of merchants or craftsmen GUILD, COMPANY
- medieval wandering minstrel JONGLEUR, TROUBADOUR
- higher division, with four subjects, of the liberal arts studied at a medieval university QUADRIVIUM
- lower division, with three subjects, of the liberal arts studied at a medieval university TRIVIUM

mediocre, acceptable, reasonable, merely satisfactory or competent ADEQUATE, PASSABLE, PRESENTABLE, TOLERABLE, SERVICEABLE
- mediocre, average, or uneven in quality MIDDLING, PATCHY
- mediocre, fairly bad, disappointing INDIFFERENT
- mediocre, lacking distinctive character, uninspiring BLAND, INSIPID
- mediocre, ordinary, everyday, uninspired RUN-OF-THE-MILL, UNDISTINGUISHED, UNEXCEPTIONAL, WORKMANLIKE

meditation of a simple westernized form TRANSCENDENTAL MEDITATION, T.M.
- meditation or religious contemplation as a means of experiencing communion with the divine MYSTICISM
- sitting position, with crossed legs and hands resting on knees, as used in yoga and meditation LOTUS POSITION
- word or formula repeated, silently or aloud, in meditation MANTRA

Mediterranean - referring to countries bordering the eastern Mediterranean LEVANT

medium or means, such as a play, for conveying ideas, expressing talents, or the like VEHICLE

meek, submissive, and excessively eager to please SERVILE, FAWNING, SYCOPHANTIC
- behave meekly and submissively, yield weakly to someone TRUCKLE, KOWTOW, FAWN

meet and confront or attack someone unexpectedly ACCOST, WAYLAY

meeting, typically casual and unplanned ENCOUNTER
- meeting attended by heads of government or other very senior politicians SUMMIT
- meeting between lovers or with one's fate, or the appointment for it TRYST, ASSIGNATION
- meeting for a discussion, typically on a specialist academic or professional theme SYMPOSIUM, COLLOQUIUM, CONVENTION, SEMINAR
- meeting for a public discussion FORUM
- meeting in which thoughts are swapped or discussed intensely as a means of solving problems or creating new ideas BRAINSTORMING
- meeting of the members of a local political party to decide policy or select candidates for office CAUCUS
- meeting or assembly of a shire's freemen in Anglo-Saxon times MOOT
- meeting or assembly of the clergy to discuss policy CONSISTORY
- meeting or assembly with all members present PLENUM
- meeting or council, especially of church officials SYNOD
- meeting or interview for exchanging views or securing advice CONFERENCE, CONSULTATION, POWWOW
- meeting or local court in Anglo-Saxon England GEMOT
- meeting or meeting place agreed on beforehand RENDEZVOUS
- meeting or reception held by a monarch or VIP when getting up in the morning LEVEE
- meeting or seminar in which problems in a given field are discussed CLINIC, WORKSHOP
- meeting or social gathering, especially for discussion of the arts CONVERSAZIONE
- meeting point or boundary at which two different theories, groups, or systems communicate or interact INTERFACE
- chairperson or presiding officer of a meeting MODERATOR, CONVENER
- decision or statement discussed and voted on at a meeting RESOLUTION, MOTION, BILL
- end and dismiss a meeting, lawmaking body, or the like DISSOLVE
- formal meeting or assembly of representatives or delegates, as to decide policy CONGRESS, CONVENTION
- formal meeting or conference with a VIP, such as the pope or a monarch AUDIENCE
- interrupt or postpone a meeting until a later time ADJOURN
- minimum number of persons required for a committee meeting, assembly, or the like QUORUM
- public meeting or assembly, usually for a political or religious cause RALLY
- published records or transcripts of a conference, learned society's meetings, or the like PROCEEDINGS, TRANSACTIONS
- record of the points of a meeting MINUTES
- secret meeting, specifically the meeting of cardinals to elect a new pope CONCLAVE
- secret religious meeting, as among dissenters in 17th-century England CONVENTICLE
- summary or memorandum of a meeting or agreement AIDE-MÉMOIRE
- summon an assembly, call a meeting, or the like CONVOKE, CONVENE

melody added as counterpoint above a basic melody DESCANT
- combination of two or more distinct melodic parts COUNTERPOINT, POLYPHONY

melon, squash, pumpkin, or related pulpy fruit or vegetable PEPO
- melon with a fragrant orange flesh MUSKMELON, CANTALOUPE, SPANSPEK
- melon with a sweet green flesh HONEYDEW MELON

melt or extract fat from meat by heating RENDER
- melt gradually DELIQUESCE
- extract metal from ore by melting it SMELT
- vessel in which metals are melted CRUCIBLE

member - acquire new members, soldiers, or the like RECRUIT, ENLIST, ENROLL

- member of a lawmaking body LEGISLATOR
- member of a lawmaking body who supervises attendance and voting of his party's delegates WHIP
- member of parliament formerly representing a borough, town, or university BURGESS
- member of parliament in France and some other countries DEPUTY
- member of parliament who is committed neither to the government nor to the opposition CROSSBENCHER
- member of parliament who is not a minister or shadow minister BACKBENCHER
- elect or appoint a new member to a group by a decision of the existing group CO-OPT
- original or founding member of an organization CHARTER MEMBER
- person represented by a member of a lawmaking body CONSTITUENT
- senior lawmaking member who serves as chairperson during debates SPEAKER

membership - ceremony of admission, as to membership of a group INITIATION
- come to an end, as a contract or membership might EXPIRE
- trial period, as for membership of a profession or religious order PROBATION

membrane, partition, or division separating tissues or cavities, as between the nostrils SEPTUM
- membrane, such as the peritoneum, lining a closed body cavity SEROUS MEMBRANE, SEROSA
- membrane forming an inner eyelid NICTITATING MEMBRANE
- membrane initially blocking the entrance to the vagina HYMEN
- membrane lining the abdominal cavity and covering most of the organs PERITONEUM
- membrane or similar thin partition DIAPHRAGM
- membrane surrounding an embryo or fetus AMNION, CHORION
- gradual evening out of differently concentrated solutions by transfer through the separating membrane OSMOSIS
- separation of different types of molecule in a solution by means of a membrane DIALYSIS

memorable or long-lasting in its effect, as poetry might be RESONANT

memorandum or summary of a meeting or agreement AIDE-MÉMOIRE

memorial, monument honoring dead people buried elsewhere CENOTAPH

memorial tablet, nameplate, or the like, as mounted on a wall or monument PLAQUE

memorize - memorizing by repetition rather than through understanding ROTE
- arouse or summon a memory, answer, or the like EVOKE
- fixed firmly, as in the memory INSCRIBED, ENGRAVED
- preserve the memory of EMBALM
- referring to a very strong visual memory that retains perfect or vivid images EIDETIC
- reinforcement, as of a memory CONSOLIDATION
- retentive, as a good memory is TENACIOUS
- unconscious, as secret fears or painful memories might be REPRESSED

memory, power of remembering RETENTION, RECALL, RETRIEVAL
- memory aid, such as a jingle or formula MNEMONIC DEVICE, MNEMONIC
- memory disorder in which dreams and fantasies are confused with reality PARAMNESIA
- memory loss OBLIVION, LETHE
- memory loss, as through shock or brain damage AMNESIA, FUGUE
- memory of an event REMINISCENCE, RECOLLECTION, ANAMNESIS
- push painful memories or thoughts into the unconscious REPRESS

men-only party, held just before a wedding STAG PARTY
- hatred of men MISANDRY
- rule by men PATRIARCHY

mend See **repair**

menopause CLIMACTERIC

menstruation on its first occurrence in a young woman MENARCHE
- menstrual blood MENSES
- abnormal absence of menstruation AMENORRHEA
- discontinuation of the menstrual cycle in women MENOPAUSE, CLIMACTERIC, CHANGE OF LIFE
- mucous membrane lining the uterus, shed during menstruation or childbirth DECIDUA

mental See also **mad, madness**
- mental or illusory image of an object PHANTASM
- mental lapse, sudden eccentric thought or lapse of thought BRAINSTORM, ABERRATION
- mentally confused or agitated, as during a high fever DELIRIOUS
- mentally deficient, backward RETARDED, IMBECILIC, CRETINOUS
- official sending of a person to prison or a mental hospital COMMITTAL

mental (combining form) PSYCH-, PSYCHO-, PHREN-, PHRENO-, CEREBR-, RATIO-, INTELL-, CONCEPT-, LOG-, COGNIT-, COGIT-, NOO-

mentality that is rigid, narrow, unsympathetic, and defensive BUNKER MENTALITY, LAAGER MENTALITY, MONOLITHIC MENTALITY

mention, list, or record by way of example, proof, or the like CITE
- mention individually, single out PARTICULARIZE, SPECIFY
- mention or refer to indirectly ALLUDE TO

menu See chart, and also **cooking** and entries for various foods
- menu TARIFF, BILL OF FARE

merchant ship, especially a richly laden one ARGOSY
- trade and mutual-aid association, especially of merchants or craftsmen in medieval times GUILD, COMPANY

mercury QUICKSILVER
- mercury as used in alchemy AZOTH
- reddish mineral that is the principal ore of mercury CINNABAR, VERMILION

Mercury's staff, with wings and two twining snakes, serving as a symbol of the medical profession CADUCEUS

mercy, mild treatment, or merciful attitude CLEMENCY, LENIENCY
- mercy, pity COMPASSION
- mercy killing EUTHANASIA
- mercy killing by withholding treatment that would prolong the patient's life PASSIVE EUTHANASIA

merry See **happy, lively, friendly**

merry-go-round CAROUSEL

merrymaking See also **party, celebration**
- merrymaking or noisy celebration or festivity ROISTERING, REVELRY, JOLLIFICATION, CAROUSAL

mesmerize, paralyze, or stupefy, as with fear GORGONIZE, PETRIFY

mess See also **confusion, mixture, untidy**
- mess about, treat disrespectfully TRIFLE WITH

message or meaning that is implied but not directly expressed, as in a speech or play SUBTEXT
- interrupt, seize, or stop something, such as a message, in its course INTERCEPT
- pass on a message RELAY

messenger, as for a parcel delivery service, diplomatic service, or spy ring COURIER
- messenger or agent sent on a mission ENVOY, EMISSARY
- messenger or envoy delivering news HERALD

messiah in Islam MAHDI

MENU TERMS

CENTRAL AND EAST EUROPEAN	
blinis	buckwheat pancakes, served with sour cream or caviar
kasha	boiled or baked buckwheat
knish	ball of dough stuffed with meat or vegetables and baked or fried
piroshki/ pirogi	pastry with a savory filling
CHINESE	
dim sum	small sweet or savory snacks
foo yong	omelet filled with green pepper, bean sprouts, and onion
lo mein/wo mein	egg noodles in meat sauce, with vegetables, prawns, or crab
wonton	deep-fried spicy chicken or pork dumplings
FRENCH	
à la carte	referring to separately priced dishes, as distinct from a set meal
à la grecque	cooked in olive oil, with herbs, lemon juice, or vinegar
à la normande	cooked with cider and cream
au gratin/ gratiné	browned with bread crumbs or cheese, butter, and sometimes cream
blanquette	casserole of white meat in a creamy sauce
bouchée	puff pastry case with a savory or sweet filling
bourguignonne	cooked with red wine
canapé	small piece of bread or toast with a savory topping
carbonade	beef stew made with beer
cassoulet	stew of meat or poultry, with haricots (beans)
coq au vin	casserole of chicken in red wine
daube	stew of braised meat and vegetables
en brochette	cut into chunks, and broiled on a skewer
en croûte	encased in pastry, as beef Wellington is
en papillote	baked in a greased paper case
entrée	main dish; in an elaborate meal, the course after the fish course
filet mignon	small fillet steak
forestière	garnished with mushrooms, bacon, and tiny potatoes
fricandeau	veal braised or roasted with vegetables
fricassee	chicken or veal in a light gravy
galantine	cold, boned stuffed meat set in jelly
goujon	small strip of fish, usually deep-fried
julienne	garnish of matchstick-thin strips of vegetables
lyonnaise	garnished or cooked with onions
marinière	referring to fish cooked in white wine
meunière	referring to fish cooked in butter and herbs
navarin	lamb or mutton stew, with root vegetables
niçoise	cooked with tomatoes, onions, garlic, and black olives
noisette	small, round piece of meat; made with hazel nuts; nut-sized piece of potato
parmentier	cooked or garnished with potatoes
pâté de foie gras	pâté made from goose or duck liver
paupiette	small, thin slice of meat rolled around a savory filling
prix fixe	set price for any of a variety of set meals
provençale	cooked with garlic and tomatoes
quenelles	dumplings of fish or meat
roulade	piece of meat or pastry rolled around a filling
servis compris	service charge included in the price
tournedos	thick, round steak cut from a fillet of beef
Véronique	garnished with white grapes
GREEK	
baklava	dessert made from paper-thin layers of pastry, with chopped nuts and honey
moussaka	pie of ground lamb and eggplants, topped with béchamel or cheese sauce
souvlakia/ shish kebab	skewers of meat, often with vegetable chunks, cooked over charcoal
stifado	veal or hare stewed with shallots and spices
taramasalata	puree of gray mullet roe or cod roe
tzatziki	cucumber and yogurt salad or dip with oil, vinegar, and garlic

continued

MENU TERMS *continued*

INDIAN	
bhindi	okra
biryani	highly spiced meat, fish, or vegetables mixed with rice and colored with saffron or turmeric
chapati	thin, flat cake of unleavened wholemeal bread
dhal/dal	chickpea purée
garam masala	mixture of spices
ghee	clarified butter
jalebis/gulab jaman	syrupy fried dumpling
khorma	cooked dry in curd, with spices and vegetables
koftas	spiced balls of meat, fish, or vegetables
mulligatawny	curried meat soup
nan	leavened bread, usually cooked in a clay oven
paratha	puffed wholemeal bread
pilau/pulao	seasoned rice with added meat and vegetables
poppadom/ poppadum	thin crisp-fried pancake made of pulse flour
samosa	deep-fried pastry case with a sweet or savory filling
tandoori	cooked in a clay oven
vindaloo	cooked in curry sauce with ginger and chili
INDONESIAN	
bami goreng	savory spiced dish based on fried noodles
nasi goreng	savory spiced dish based on fried rice
rijstafel	meal based on rice served with numerous side dishes of meat and vegetables, with sauces and condiments
satay	grilled marinated meat kebab with peanut sauce
ITALIAN	
antipasto	hors d'oeuvre
gnocchi	small dumplings served with a sauce
lasagna	dish of wide flat noodles layered with spiced ground meat
napolitana	cooked with tomatoes and basil
osso bucco	shin of veal cooked with wine and tomatoes
parmigiana	prepared with grated cheese from Parma
pizzaiola	cooked in oil with chopped tomatoes, garlic, and herbs
prosciutto	raw, smoked ham
ravioli	small savory-filled pasta envelopes, served with a sauce
saltimbocca	rolls of veal and ham, cooked in wine
scaloppe/ scaloppine	veal escalope
tournedos Rossini	fillet steak served with a coating of pâté
JAPANESE	
sukiyaki	thin slices of meat, fried with vegetables and seasoning
sushi	small snacks of raw fish and cold rice
tempura	deep-fried pieces of fish and vegetables
teriyaki	skewered and grilled slices of marinated meat or shellfish
MIDDLE EASTERN	
dolmas	vine leaves with a savory filling
doner kebab	thin lamb slices, flavored with garlic and herbs, cut from a revolving spit
halvah	confection of honey and crushed sesame seeds
hummus	dip made from pureed chickpeas
pita	flat, unleavened bread
shashlik	skewer of grilled mutton chunks, with vegetables and peppers
tahina/tahini	sesame paste, as used in hummus and other dips
SPANISH AND LATIN AMERICAN	
enchilada	fried tortilla served with a hot chili sauce
paella	seasoned rice dish with chicken, shellfish, and often vegetables
taco	tortilla with a meat or cheese filling
tamale	dish of spicy fried ground meat and crushed corn
tapas	hors d'oeuvres or savory snacks of sausage, seafood, or the like
tortilla	thin cornmeal pancake, usually served hot with a savory filling

- referring to a messiah MESSIANIC

metal See also **steel**
- metal, such as gold or silver, that resists corrosion NOBLE METAL
- metal alloy, chiefly of iron and nickel, that hardly expands or contracts, used for measuring rods and the like INVAR
- metal alloy of copper and tin, polished for use in mirrors, reflectors, and the like SPECULUM
- metal alloy of gold and brass, as used for jewelry TALMI GOLD
- metal alloy of gold or nickel and silver, as used for jewelry ELECTRUM
- metal alloy of gold or silver with a base metal such as copper, used for making coins BILLON
- metal alloy of tin and lead, used for making tableware, drinking vessels, and the like PEWTER
- metal bar or block prepared for storage or transport INGOT
- metal-casting factory or workshop FOUNDRY
- metal consisting of a mix of two or more metals, or of metal with other elements such as carbon ALLOY
- metal disc PATEN
- metal filings or shavings removed by a cutting tool SWARF
- metal foil released in strips into the air to thwart an enemy's radar system CHAFF, WINDOW
- metal fragments from a shell, bomb, or mine SHRAPNEL
- metal mesh, as used for reinforcing glass EXPANDED METAL
- metal or alloy, especially brass, produced in thin sheets LATTEN
- metal or mineral deposit in rock VEIN, LODE
- metal plate for reinforcing a corner joist GUSSET
- metal strip used to measure or set a narrow gap between two parts FEELER GAUGE, FEELER
- metal that is not a precious metal BASE METAL
- metal tool, machine part, stamp, or the like, for cutting, punching, or folding objects DIE
- alloy melted to fuse two metal parts SOLDER
- alloy of various metals, producing very little friction, used in bearings BABBITT METAL
- capable of being drawn or pulled out, stretchable as some metals are TRACTILE, DUCTILE, TENSILE
- capable of being shaped by pressure or blows, workable, as some metals are MALLEABLE
- chemical analysis, as of a sample of metal ASSAY
- chief metal in an alloy MATRIX
- decorate metal by engraving or embossing CHASE, ENCHASE
- dissolving or wearing away, especially of metals CORROSION
- etch or inlay metal with wavy decorative patterns DAMASCENE, DAMASK
- gold-colored metal alloy of copper, zinc, and sometimes tin used for jewelry, clocks, furniture ornamentation, and the like ORMOLU
- gold-colored metal alloy of copper and zinc, used in cheap jewelry PINCHBECK
- hammer or cut metal into thin foil FOLIATE
- heat and beat metal into shape FORGE
- heat and then cool metal or glass to strengthen it TEMPER, ANNEAL
- impurities formed on molten metal during smelting DROSS
- join or fuse metals using heat WELD
- made by hammering or shaping rather than by casting, as a metal object might be WROUGHT
- maker of metal accessories, such as bits and spurs, for horses in former times LORIMER
- produce wire, metal or plastic sheeting, or the like by pressing through a nozzle or die EXTRUDE
- refuse from smelted ore or crude metal SLAG, SCORIA
- study of metals, or the extraction and refinement of them METALLURGY
- vessel for heating or melting metals, or floor of a furnace for collecting molten metal CRUCIBLE
- weakness in metal or other solid material caused by stress FATIGUE

metamorphosis See illustration, page 342
- metamorphosis TRANSFORMATION, TRANSUBSTANTIATION, TRANSFIGURATION, TRANSLATION, TRANSMUTATION, TRANSMOGRIFICATION, METAPLASIA, MUTATION, PERMUTATION, MODIFICATION, CONVERSION, REFORMATION, RECRUDESCENCE, REGENERATION

metaphor or image of a witty, far-fetched kind CONCEIT
- metaphor replacing a common term in Old Norse and Old English poetry KENNING
- metaphors and symbols, as in poetry IMAGERY
- based on or using figures of speech METAPHORICAL, FIGURATIVE
- image in which the meaning of a metaphor is embodied VEHICLE
- meaning or general drift of a metaphor TENOR

meteor shower's apparent point of origin in the sky RADIANT
- meteor that is large, bright and may explode FIREBALL, BOLIDE

meteorite or stone from a meteorite CHONDRITE

meteorology See **weather**

meter See also **poetry**
- analysis of the metrical or rhythm patterns of verse SCANSION
- referring to a watch, clock, or meter indicating readings by changing numbers rather than by moving hands on a dial DIGITAL
- referring to a watch, clock, or meter indicating readings by moving hands on a dial ANALOG
- unit of poetic meter, somewhat analogous to a bar in music FOOT

methane - organic compound such as methane, containing only hydrogen and carbon HYDROCARBON

method of operation, way of working MODUS OPERANDI
- method of teaching reading based on the sounds of the letters rather than on the word as a unit PHONICS
- method or approach, especially a mode of therapy MODALITY
- method or plan based on a long-range or overall view of things STRATEGY
- method or prescribed procedure of operating REGIMEN
- method or style MODE
- methods or plans designed to achieve short-term, local, or immediate objectives TACTICS
- based on or relating to scientific observation or experiment, as a method of investigation might be EMPIRICAL
- referring to the educational method based on problem solving and trial and error HEURISTIC

Mexican-American CHICANO
- Mexican cowboy or herdsman VAQUERO
- Mexican hors d'oeuvre or dip of pureed avocado GUACAMOLE
- Mexican sun-dried brick ADOBE

Mexico - Spanish invader of Mexico and Peru in the 16th century CONQUISTADOR

mice fear of mice MUSOPHOBIA

microchip, tiny electronic circuit based on a semiconductor wafer SILICON CHIP
- electronic circuit formed on a microchip INTEGRATED CIRCUIT
- relating to semiconductors, as in microchips SOLID-STATE

microfilm sheet, as used for library catalogs MICROFICHE, FICHE

microphone - long movable metal arm supporting an overhead microphone BOOM
- return into a system or process of

a part of its output, such as microphone noise FEEDBACK
- sound-regulating device, as in a microphone or loudspeaker BAFFLE
- thin disc, as in a telephone or microphone, whose vibrations convert sound to electronic signals or vice versa DIAPHRAGM

microscope in which the specimen is side-lighted to show the particles as bright spots against a dark background DARK-FIELD MICROSCOPE, ULTRAMICROSCOPE
- eyepiece of a microscope OCULAR
- having fine threads for use in measuring, as the eyepiece of a microscope might be FILAR
- lens or set of lenses, nearest to the object being viewed, in a microscope or telescope OBJECTIVE
- place a specimen on a slide for a microscope MOUNT
- thin slice or specimen, as of tissue, for examination by microscope SECTION
- visible to the naked eye, without a microscope MACROSCOPIC

microscopic organism, invisible to the naked eye ANIMALCULE
- microscopic single-celled organism PROTOZOAN

microwaves - device producing microwaves RESONATOR
- electronic valve helping to generate high-power microwaves, as in radar systems MAGNETRON

middle See also **mediocre**
- middle, between extremes INTERMEDIATE
- middle course of action, factor, or the like when there should be only two TERTIUM QUID
- middle ear TYMPANUM
- middle in position, quality, or extent, average MEAN
- middle item or value in an ordered list of numbers MEDIAN
- middle way, policy, or course of action that avoids extremes VIA MEDIA
- adjective for the middle MEDIAL, MEDIAN
- "into the middle of things," straight into the narrative or plot, as a book or play might begin IN MEDIAS RES

middle (combining form) MEDI-, MEDIO-, MES-, MESO-

Middle Ages See **medieval** and chart at **feudal system**
- adjective for the Middle Ages MEDIEVAL

middle-class BOURGEOIS
- middle-class American man, narrow-minded and self-satisfied BABBITT
- change a working-class area into a middle-class one GENTRIFY

middleman or agent in a business transaction BROKER, FACTOR, JOBBER

middling in quality MEDIOCRE

midsummer or midwinter position of the sun in relation to the earth, at its apparently farthest point from the equator SOLSTICE

midwife ACCOUCHEUSE
- male counterpart to a midwife ACCOUCHEUR

migrate - nonmigratory, resident in one area only, as some birds are SEDENTARY

mild in climate TEMPERATE

mildness of manner, gentleness MANSUETUDE

mile - nautical miles per hour KNOT

military See chart, and also **services, soldier, troops**
- military attack or campaign that is quick and intensive BLITZKRIEG
- military attack or maneuver to draw an enemy away from the planned main attack DIVERSION
- military attack or raid INCURSION
- military barracks or quarters, especially in a town, in former times CASERN
- military base's shops for personnel and families POST EXCHANGE, PX
- military communications to maintain contact LIAISON
- military court, or a trial conducted by it COURT-MARTIAL
- military demand or request for needed supplies or equipment REQUISITION
- military department in charge of food supplies and equipment COMMISSARIAT
- military detachment protecting the front of an army unit VANGUARD
- military detachment protecting the rear of an army unit, as in retreat REARGUARD
- military disciplinarian or authority demanding strict obedience MARTINET
- military display presented outdoors, usually in the evening TATTOO
- military encampment set up temporarily, as during an expedition BIVOUAC
- military expedition ANABASIS
- military forces or supplies sent to support those already in use REINFORCEMENTS
- military formation, in ancient Greece, of foot soldiers with overlapping shields and long spears PHALANX
- military formation or siege device in ancient Rome, typically of a screen of overlapping shields held above the heads of soldiers approaching the walls TESTUDO, TORTOISE
- military leader of a royal household in the Middle Ages CONSTABLE
- military leave FURLOUGH
- military maneuver in which deception or surprise is used to out-

Metamorphosis

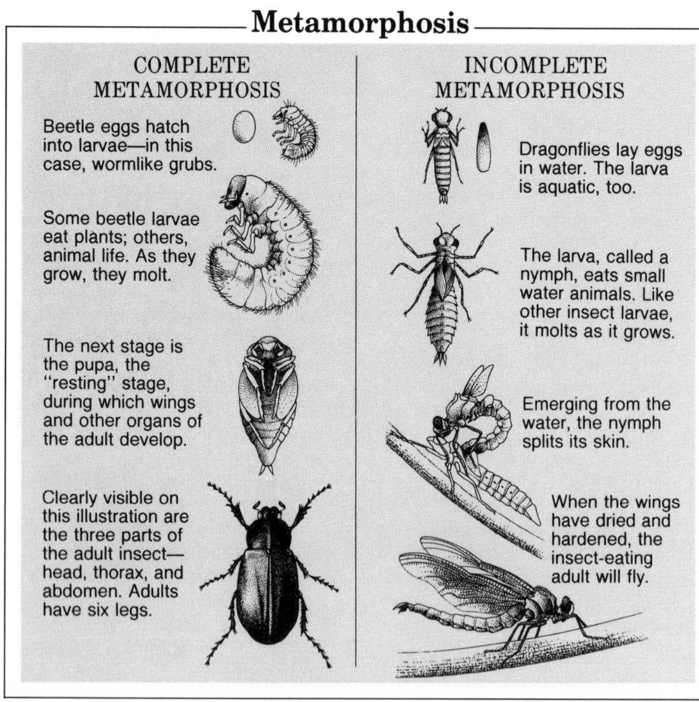

wit the enemy STRATAGEM
- military maneuver of attacking an enemy force or position on two flanks PINCER MOVEMENT
- military officer or official of high rank BRASS HAT
- military officer responsible for provisions, clothing, and the like QUARTERMASTER
- military officer serving as assistant to the general or other senior officer AIDE-DE-CAMP, ADC
- military officer who assists a senior officer in administrative work ADJUTANT
- military officer with a second-lieutenant or higher rank COMMISSIONED OFFICER
- military officer's honorary promotion to a higher rank, without the corresponding rise in pay or authority BREVET
- military officers who help to plan and control battle operations GENERAL STAFF
- military operations or techniques designed to achieve short-term, local, or immediate objectives TACTICS
- military or diplomatic planning as an art or science STRATEGY
- military or naval subdivision ECHELON
- military or political grouping that forms the core of a potentially larger unit CADRE
- military parade first thing in the morning REVEILLE
- military persecution, subjection to soldiers DRAGOONING
- military planning, specifically of organizing and transporting personnel and equipment LOGISTICS
- military policy of burning or destroying all crops, food, and anything else likely to be of use to an advancing enemy SCORCHED-EARTH POLICY
- military position or foothold established in enemy territory by advance troops BRIDGEHEAD, SALIENT, AIRHEAD
- military position set up on an enemy's shoreline in advance of the main invading force BEACHHEAD
- military post, or the soldiers stationed there GARRISON
- military regiment's permanent base and training center DEPOT
- military unit, squadron of ships, or the like selected from a larger unit for a special mission DETACHMENT, TASK FORCE
- military unit in ancient Rome consisting of 3,000 to 6,000 troops LEGION
- military unit in ancient Rome forming one tenth of a legion COHORT
- military unit in ancient Rome forming one fiftieth of a legion MANIPLE
- military unit or post far from the main body of the army OUTPOST
- military weapons, ammunition, and related equipment ORDNANCE,

MILITARY RANKS

COMMISSIONED OFFICERS

ARMY	NAVY
general of the Army	**fleet admiral**
AIR FORCE, ARMY, AND MARINE CORPS	NAVY
general	**admiral**
lieutenant general	**vice admiral**
major general	**rear admiral**
brigadier general	**commodore**
colonel	**captain**
lieutenant colonel	**commander**
major	**lieutenant commander**
captain	**lieutenant**
first lieutenant	**lieutenant (junior grade)**
second lieutenant	**ensign**

WARRANT OFFICERS—ARMY, MARINE CORPS, AND NAVY

chief warrant officer 2, 3, and 4

warrant officer

ENLISTED PERSONNEL

AIR FORCE	ARMY	MARINE CORPS	NAVY
chief master sergeant	**sergeant major**	**sergeant major; gunnery sergeant**	**master chief petty officer**
senior master sergeant	**first sergeant; master sergeant**	**first sergeant; master sergeant**	**senior chief petty officer**
master sergeant	**sergeant first class; specialist 7**	**gunnery sergeant**	**chief petty officer**
technical sergeant	**staff sergeant; specialist 6**	**staff sergeant**	**petty officer first class**
staff sergeant	**sergeant; specialist 5**	**sergeant**	**petty officer second class**
sergeant	**corporal; specialist 4**	**corporal**	**petty officer third class**
airman first class	**private first class**	**lance corporal**	**seaman**
airman	**private**	**private first class**	**seaman apprentice**
airman basic	**recruit**	**private**	**seaman recruit**

MUNITIONS
- acquire new members for military service by force of law CONSCRIPT, LEVY, DRAFT
- acquire new members, sign men on for military service, or the like RECRUIT, ENLIST, ENROLL
- assign accommodation to military officers or troops, as in civilian buildings BILLET, QUARTER, CANTON
- braided cord on the left shoulder, as on a military uniform FOURRAGÈRE
- commanding officer of a military post, organization, or the like COMMANDANT, CO
- discharge from military service DEMOBILIZE
- dismiss from a military unit, impose a dishonorable discharge on CASHIER
- equipment used in a military operation or by a military unit MATÉRIEL
- extremely heavy concentration of bombing or other military force on an enemy target SATURATION
- force into military service, draft or recruit by violence or threats COMMANDEER, PRESS-GANG, PRESS, IMPRESS, CRIMP, SHANGHAI
- government by the military STRATOCRACY
- lieutenant or other British military officer below the rank of captain SUBALTERN
- member of a military force, such as a sergeant, having certain leadership functions but without an official appointment as an officer NONCOMMISSIONED OFFICER, NCO
- menial work in a military camp or barracks, often imposed as punishment FATIGUE
- minor or preliminary conflict or military encounter SKIRMISH
- move military forces to a new area REDEPLOY
- official commendation or public statement, as for bravery or outstanding military service CITATION
- part of or group within a conference, military force, or the like CONTINGENT
- people involved in a military operation or employed by a military force PERSONNEL
- person who is not employed in military service CIVILIAN
- person who signs up for military service of his or her own free will VOLUNTEER
- reduction or removal of military forces and weapons DISARMAMENT
- referring to an unofficial or auxiliary military group PARAMILITARY
- referring to ordinary public life or work, as distinct from the military or ecclesiastical CIVIL
- release or exempt from military service, active duty, or the like, on the grounds of illness or disability INVALID
- remove troops, military equipment, or military control from an area DEMILITARIZE
- report sent over a distance, as by a newspaper correspondent or military field officer DISPATCH
- ruling group of officers after a military takeover JUNTA
- section of a military force consisting of foot soldiers fighting with small arms INFANTRY
- section of a military force consisting of troops mounted on horseback CAVALRY
- section of a military force consisting of troops serving on both land and sea MARINES
- section of a military force consisting of troops trained for parachute missions PARATROOPS
- section of a military force consisting of troops using heavy guns ARTILLERY
- small military unit or fighting force specializing in quick destructive raids COMMANDO
- smallest military unit or formation, as for drilling or patrol SQUAD
- supreme U.S. military headquarters PENTAGON
- trainee officer in the police or military forces CADET
- withdraw military forces from active conflict DISENGAGE

milk containing bacteria that survive in acids, used in treating digestive disorders ACIDOPHILUS MILK
- milk drink, heated, spiced, and sweetened, and curdled with wine or beer POSSET
- milk protein that forms the basis of cheese CASEIN
- milk sugar LACTOSE
- milk that has been concentrated but not sweetened EVAPORATED MILK
- milk that is sour and curdled CLABBER
- milk that is the first produced by a cow or similar mammal directly after giving birth BEASTINGS, COLOSTRUM
- milk that is uniform in consistency, through the emulsification of the fat HOMOGENIZED MILK
- milk's watery part that can be separated from the solid curds WHEY, SERUM
- adjective for milk LACTEAL, LACTIC
- become a soft, solidified mass, as blood, milk, or other liquids might COAGULATE, CLOT, CURDLE
- dilute or add impurities to a substance, such as milk ADULTERATE
- get a baby or young animal off mother's milk and on to solid food WEAN
- heat treatment of milk, beer, and other liquids to destroy germs and regulate fermentation PASTEURIZATION
- produce milk, especially when breast-feeding LACTATE
- squeeze or press out juice or milk EXPRESS

milk (combining form) GALACT-, GALACTO-, LACT-, LACTO-

milky liquid EMULSION

mill driven by water flowing over the top of the waterwheel OVERSHOT MILL
- mill driven by water flowing under the base of the waterwheel UNDERSHOT MILL
- mill for grinding grain, turned by hand QUERN
- watercourse directing water into a mill, turbine, or waterwheel HEADRACE

million (combining form) MEGA-

million million, trillion (combining form) TERA-

million million million, quintillion EXA-

million million millionth, quintillionth (combining form) ATTO-

million millionth, trillionth (combining form) PICO-

millionth (combining form) MICRO-

mime artist or actor in an oldfasioned masque MUMMER

mimicry, mocking and satirical, as of a writer's or composer's work PARODY, PASTICHE
- mimicry of one animal by another for protection MIMESIS

mincemeat - spicy mincemeat used for stuffing FORCEMEAT

mind, especially considered in relation to the body PSYCHE
- mind or reason, especially as the governing principle in the universe NOUS, LOGOS
- mind reading or other alleged form of extrasensory perception CRYPTESTHESIA, TELEPATHY
- mind regarded as a clean slate, before being formed by outside impressions TABULA RASA
- "of sound mind," sane COMPOS MENTIS
- relating to diseases, disorders, or the like based on an interaction of mind and body PSYCHOSOMATIC

mind (combining form) -PHREN-, PHRENO-, PSYCH-, PSYCHO-, CEREB-, RATIO-, INTELL-, CONCEPT-, LOG-, COGNIT-, COGIT-, NOO-

mindless, random, unprovoked, as

vandalism or willful destruction is WANTON, GRATUITOUS

mine See also **bomb**

- mine, oil well, or similar asset whose value diminishes over the years WASTING ASSET
- mine attached to a wall, vehicle, or the like LIMPET MINE
- mine or other source of great wealth GOLCONDA
- mine wagon or basket in former times CORF
- mines connected into a single explosive sequence GIRANDOLE
- mining by means of surface excavation rather than shafts OPEN-CAST MINING, STRIP MINING
- coal mine COLLIERY
- cut or channel, as for access in mining or excavating GULLET
- drainage pit or pool, as in a mine SUMP, SINK
- excavation in a mine, typically like a set of steps, formed as the ore is extracted from a vein STOPE
- explode a mine SPRING
- explore an area for gold or other minerals worth mining PROSPECT
- horizontal, or almost horizontal shaft into a mine, for access or drainage ADIT
- horizontal passage into a mine, following a mineral vein DRIFT
- introduce valuable ore fraudulently into a mine to inflate its value SALT
- lifting equipment and framework built above a mine shaft HEADGEAR
- methane-based gas, explosive when mixed with air, formed in coal mines FIREDAMP
- poisonous gas in a mine after an explosion or fire AFTERDAMP, BLACKDAMP, CHOKEDAMP
- prop supporting the roof of a tunnel in a mine SPRAG, GIB
- rock-boring tool, as used in mining TREPAN
- safety lamp formerly used by coal miners DAVY LAMP
- sawing device at the front edge of a minesweeper used to cut mine cables PARAVANE
- screen of wood or cloth used to control ventilation in a mine BRATTICE
- sloping or vertical shaft in a mine, as for ventilation between levels WINZE
- thin seam of coal or mineral ore lying above a larger seam in a mine RIDER
- ventilation shaft in a mine DOWNCAST, UPCAST

mineral See also **rock**

- mineral deposit in rock VEIN, LODE, REEF, SEAM
- mineral- or water-divining attempted by means of a stick or wand RHABDOMANCY
- mineral spring SPA
- mineral water, either natural or artificially aerated SELTZER WATER

miniature man HOMUNCULUS, MANIKIN, PYGMY

- miniature representation of the whole universe, as a single person, group, or system might be MICROCOSM
- miniature tree or shrub produced by rigorous pruning, or the traditional Japanese art of producing such plants BONSAI

minimal compliance with a law or a custom through a small gesture TOKENISM

minimize the importance of, play down SOFT-PEDAL

minimum level of intensity for registering or tolerating something, such as pain THRESHOLD

- minimum number of persons required for a committee meeting, assembly, or the like QUORUM
- minimum of food, shelter, or the like necessary to sustain life SUBSISTENCE

minister's or cabinet member's post or duty in the government PORTFOLIO

- reorganization or reassignment of cabinet members or ministers RESHUFFLE

ministry - clergyman's acceptance into the ministry, or the ceremony of admission ORDINATION

minor, insignificant, as differences might be SUPERFICIAL, TRIVIAL

- minor, unimportant INCIDENTAL
- minor god DEMIGOD

minor (combining form) DEMI-, SUB-

minority, period of being legally under age NONAGE

- minority group's adjustment to or adoption of the dominant culture ASSIMILATION
- referring to a distinctive racial, religious, or cultural group, typically a minority group, within a society ETHNIC

minstrel, specifically a medieval poet-musician of northern France TROUVÈRE

- minstrel, specifically a medieval poet-musician writing in Provençal TROUBADOUR
- minstrel traveling about in medieval times JONGLEUR

mint flavoring MENTHOL

- box at the government mint in which new coins are kept for testing PYX
- fee charged by the mint for turning bullion into coins SEIGNIORAGE

minutes or business records of an organization or society PROCEEDINGS

miracle worker or magician THAUMATURGIST

mirage, false or illusory image FATA MORGANA

mirror or lens that concentrates light CONDENSER

- mirror or reflector in some optical instruments SPECULUM
- curved inward, as a mirror or lens might be CONCAVE
- curved outward, as a mirror or lens might be CONVEX
- defect in a mirror ABERRATION
- full-length mirror, hinged to swivel in its frame CHEVAL GLASS
- image apparently formed by reflected or refracted light rays, such as the image in a mirror VIRTUAL IMAGE
- inversion of left and right, as in an image seen in a mirror LATERAL INVERSION
- metal coating behind the glass of a mirror FOIL, TAIN
- relating to mirrors and reflections CATOPTRIC
- signal or signaling device based on mirror-reflected flashes of sunlight HELIOGRAPH
- similarity, balance, mirror-image relationship, or the like between structures or parts of a system SYMMETRY
- tall mirror, especially one hung between two windows PIER GLASS

misbehavior, misdeed, or minor offense DELINQUENCY

miscarriage SPONTANEOUS ABORTION

mischief, high spirits, hanky-panky SHENANIGANS

- supposed source of problems, errors, or mischief GREMLIN

mischievous, elflike PUCKISH

- mischievous or wild adventure, caper, prank ESCAPADE

misconduct by someone acting in a professional capacity or as a public official MALVERSATION, MALFEASANCE

miserable or wretched ABJECT

miserly See also **stingy**

- miserly or sour-tempered person CURMUDGEON
- miserly, stingy, and grasping person SKINFLINT, NIGGARD, PINCHPENNY, PENNY-PINCHER, TIGHTWAD

misery, lonely wretchedness DESOLATION

misfortune, bad luck AMBSACE

misinterpret, twist the meaning of PERVERT, DISTORT, MISCONSTRUE

mislead See also **deceive, deceptive**

- mislead or surprise someone and force him or her into an embarrassing position WRONG-FOOT

- misleading, deceiving, ILLUSORY, FACTITIOUS
- misleading, especially as a result of deliberate misrepresentation DISTORTED, GARBLED
- misleading or evasive, as an answer might be EQUIVOCAL
- misleading person or thing WILL-O'-THE-WISP, IGNIS FATUUS

misprint or misspelling LITERAL

mispronunciation CACOEPY
- mispronunciation of a word by omission of a syllable HAPLOLOGY

missile See also **bomb**
- missile guidance by means of instructions radioed to it during its flight COMMAND GUIDANCE
- missile in the form of a shot-filled cylinder or shrapnel shell fired from a cannon CANISTER
- missile or other object that is fired or hurled PROJECTILE
- missile system in which a single rocket launches several warheads MIRV
- missile that is powered on its ascent but unpowered and unguided on its descent BALLISTIC MISSILE
- missile's sideways deviation from its intended course AZIMUTH
- missile's warhead or explosive charge PAYLOAD
- bullet-filled or pellet-filled antipersonnel missile exploding above enemy positions SHRAPNEL
- cigar-shaped self-powered underwater missile TORPEDO
- curved flight path of a missile, ball, or the like TRAJECTORY
- explosive long-range German missile bombarding London in World War II BUZZ BOMB, V-1, ROBOT BOMB
- guided missile tracing the path of a microwave beam BEAM-RIDER
- guiding or stabilizing fin on a bomb or missile VANE
- long-range low-flying nuclear missile CRUISE MISSILE
- section of a bomb, missile, or the like containing the actual explosive or toxic material WARHEAD
- simultaneous or rapid discharge or release of several bombs or missiles SALVO
- spin or wobble in flight, as a missile or aircraft might YAW
- surface-to-air missile SAM
- underground shelter for housing guided missiles SILO

missing part in a manuscript LACUNA
- missing part or gap in a series HIATUS

mission - messenger or agent sent on a mission, typically by a government or head of state EMISSARY
- report by or questioning of a spy, astronaut, diplomat, or the like on his return from a mission DEBRIEFING
- representative, messenger, or agent sent on a mission ENVOY

missionary work, devoted spreading of the gospel EVANGELISM

misspelling CACOGRAPHY
- misspelling or misprint LITERAL, TYPO

mist, paint, or other suspension of very fine particles in a consistent medium COLLOID
- mistlike polar weather condition producing very low visibility WHITEOUT
- misty, cloudy, hazy NEBULOUS
- disappear slowly, as mist might EVANESCE

mistake See also **error**
- mistake, such as a slip of the tongue, that discloses someone's real feelings or unconscious thoughts FREUDIAN SLIP
- mistake made in one's speech, slip of the tongue LAPSUS LINGUAE
- mistake of spelling or typing in a printed text LITERAL, TYPO
- mistake one thing for another, treat two different things as the same, confuse CONFOUND
- mistake or improper usage in grammar or etiquette SOLECISM
- mistaken, incorrect, off beam ADRIFT, AMISS, AWRY
- mistaken interpretation or explanation, misunderstanding MISCONSTRUCTION
- mistaken interpretation or faulty understanding, delusion MISCONCEPTION, MISAPPREHENSION
- mistaken or faulty reasoning, illogical argument, or invalid conclusion, especially when unintended PARALOGISM
- mistaken or misleading idea or opinion, based on misinformation or faulty reasoning FALLACY
- mistaken though plausible, as a cunning but illogical argument might be SPECIOUS, SOPHISTIC
- mistaken use of a word, such as *flaunt* in a context requiring *flout* CATACHRESIS
- embarrassing mistake or laughable blunder HOWLER, BONER, CLANGER, PRATFALL
- "let it stand," instruction to retain a passage as written or typeset and to disregard a requested change STET
- liable or tending to make mistakes FALLIBLE
- person guilty of a crime or responsible for a mistake or accident CULPRIT
- prove a statement or argument to be mistaken REFUTE, REBUT, CONFUTE
- put someone right, rid someone of a mistaken idea DISABUSE
- "so," "thus," term used in a text to indicate the deliberate reproduction of a mistaken or surprising wording or fact being quoted SIC
- social mistake or blunder, such as a gauche or tactless remark GAFFE, FAUX PAS
- word used by mistake in place of a similar one, such as *pineapple* for *pinnacle* MALAPROPISM

mistress of a high-ranking man, or a fashionable prostitute COURTESAN
- mistress or sexually promiscuous woman consigned to the fringes of respectable society, as in the 19th century DEMIMONDAINE

mistrusting, disbelieving SKEPTICAL

misunderstand or misinterpret MISCONSTRUE
- misunderstanding, mistaken assumption MISAPPREHENSION, MISCONCEPTION
- misunderstanding, or opposing aims CROSS-PURPOSES

misuse, use for an improper or incorrect purpose PERVERT
- misuse of a word through confusion with a similar-sounding word MALAPROPISM

mite, tick, or similar related creature ACARID
- infestation of the skin or hair with mites or ticks ACARIASIS
- mix a speech, article, or the like with jokes or other extraneous matter INTERLARD, INTERSPERSE
- mix and combine to form a new, complex product or whole SYNTHESIZE, HOMOLOGIZE
- mix into a crowd or other larger entity so as to become inconspicuous MERGE, BLEND, MINGLE
- mix or combine BLEND, MELD

mix or counteract and thereby make ineffective NEUTRALIZE
- mix socially, come to participate in the life of a group or community INTEGRATE, ASSIMILATE
- mix to an even consistency, make the same in all parts HOMOGENIZE
- mix up or confuse ideas, elements, or the like CONFOUND
- mixed, confused, and unruly crowd MELEE
- mixed and varied in ingredients, characteristics, or subject matter MISCELLANEOUS
- mixed in origin or makeup, crossed HYBRID, MONGREL
- mixing socially with the people of an occupied or enemy country FRATERNIZATION
- mixing two reagents in solution

so as to measure the concentration of a solute TITRATION
- containing deliberately mixed or usefully varied parts DIVERSIFIED
- having mixed, dissimilar, or unmatching parts HETEROGENEOUS, PROMISCUOUS, MULTIFARIOUS, OMNIFARIOUS, DIFFUSE
- part or element mixed in, ingredient ADMIXTURE
- unable to blend or mix, as two liquids might be IMMISCIBLE

mixed feelings, conflicting views AMBIVALENCE

mixture, assembly, collection, choice ASSORTMENT, CONGLOMERATION
- mixture of disparate parts or elements, especially an unsuitable or confused one HODGEPODGE, JUMBLE, FARRAGO, GALLIMAUFRY, MOTLEY, MÉLANGE, MISHMASH, PATCHWORK, OMNIUM-GATHERUM, HYBRID
- mixture of elements chemically combined COMPOUND
- mixture of many assorted parts POTPOURRI, HODGEPODGE, OLLA PODRIDA, OLIO, PASTICCIO, SALMAGUNDI, PASTICHE
- mixture of many widely varying elements MISCELLANY, MEDLEY
- mixture of various kinds, based on fine particles dispersed but not dissolved in a liquid to form a consistent medium COLLOID, EMULSION, SUSPENSION
- mixture or combination of varied but usefully integrated parts ALLOY, AMALGAM
- mixture such as plaster or mortar COMPO
- book, performance, or the like containing a mixture or collection of connected works OMNIBUS, ANTHOLOGY

moat or defensive ditch FOSSE
- moat or protective ditch, as in a garden HA-HA, SUNK FENCE

mob, the masses, common people HOI POLLOI, PLEBS, CANAILLE
- mob rule OCHLOCRACY, MOBOCRACY
- seize and kill without trial an alleged offender, as an impassioned mob might LYNCH

mock, ridicule, make scornful comments at JEER, TWIT, DERIDE, FLEER, SNEER, SCOFF AT, DEROGATE
- mock or criticize bitterly and mercilessly PILLORY
- mock or make fun of by imitating MIMIC, APE, PARODY
- mock to expose and ridicule pretensions DEBUNK
- mockery DERISION, RIDICULE
- mocking, light, flippant chat or repartee, teasing BANTER, BADINAGE, PERSIFLAGE, RAILLERY
- mocking and bitingly critical piece of writing SATIRE, LAMPOON, PASQUINADE
- mocking and derisive or hurtful remark GIBE, TAUNT
- mocking imitation of a literary or other artistic work BURLESQUE, PARODY, PASTICHE, SPOOF, TRAVESTY, CARICATURE
- mocking in a disdainful, cynical way SARDONIC
- harsh, shrill call or whistle, indicating disapproval or mockery CATCALL
- ignore someone's authority or wishes to the point of mockery or contempt FLOUT
- interrupt a speaker with mocking comments HECKLE
- rude and contemptuous mockery CONTUMELY

mock trial or legal debate conducted by law students MOOT

model for clothes, whether a woman or a life-size dummy MANNEQUIN
- model of a personal quality or abstract concept AVATAR
- model of excellence, perfect representative EXEMPLAR, PARAGON
- model of behavior, standard of acceptability, or the like NORM
- model of the celestial sphere, consisting of solid rings, used by early astronomers ARMILLARY SPHERE
- model of the solar system, used in studying astronomy ORRERY
- model or copy in reduced size MINIATURE
- model or illustration, as of an engine or building, with part of the wall or casing omitted to reveal the interior CUTAWAY
- model or original pattern on which other versions or copies are based ARCHETYPE, PROTOTYPE, BLUEPRINT
- jointed dummy of a human figure, used as an artists' model and by medical students LAY FIGURE, MANNEQUIN, MANIKIN
- person or thing valued as a guide or model LODESTAR
- rough model for a sculpture MAQUETTE, BOZZETTO
- system or item regarded as a model of a larger system of which it is a part MICROCOSM
- three-dimensional scene or tableau, as in museums, with models of figures exhibited against a background DIORAMA

moderation or restraint, especially in drinking alcohol TEMPERANCE
- path of moderation VIA MEDIA

modern, ahead of one's times, with it AVANT-GARDE
- modern, up to date CONTEMPORARY
- modern, using the latest technology or theories STATE-OF-THE-ART
- modern design or style using industrial materials HIGH-TECH
- modern in an extreme or unnecessary way NEWFANGLED
- modern or recent LATTER-DAY
- extremely modern, in advance of current fashion FUTURISTIC
- traditional and conventional in the arts and sciences, as opposed to modern and experimental CLASSICAL

modernizing or updating of ideas, especially in the Roman Catholic Church AGGIORNAMENTO

modest See also **mediocre, humble, shy**
- modest, avoiding all boasting or showiness UNASSUMING
- modest, reserved, sometimes in an affected way DEMURE
- modest and discreet, staying in the background UNOBTRUSIVE, SELF-EFFACING, UNPRETENTIOUS
- modest but adequate income or standard of living SUFFICIENCY
- modest or prim to an excessive degree, especially in sexual matters PRUDISH
- modest or shy, lacking in confidence DIFFIDENT
- modestly playing down one's own achievements or qualities SELF-DEPRECATING
- modestly putting aside one's own claims, rights, or interests SELF-ABNEGATING

mogul governor in India NABOB

mohair ANGORA

moist (combining form) HYGRO-

moisture - containing as much moisture as possible SATURATED
- deprived of water or moisture, dry DEHYDRATED
- helping to retain moisture, as glycerine is HUMECTANT

mold MUST, MILDEW
- mold, typically reusable, in which objects are cast DIE
- mold taken, especially from a footprint, as for evidence in court MOULAGE
- moldy-smelling FUSTY, MUSTY
- clay mold around a wax model of a sculpture MANTLE
- hole or channel through which molten material is introduced into a mold SPRUE
- small cup-shaped mold, for jellies, cakes, or the like DARIOLE

molding See also **column**
- molding around or above a doorway, window frame, or the like ARCHITRAVE
- molding in the form of a narrow, protruding, half-cylindrical piping BAGUETTE
- molding projecting beyond an ad-

jacent panel or frame BOLECTION
- molding with a zigzag pattern CHEVRON, DANCETTE
- concave molding CAVETTO, CONGÉ, COVE
- continuous ornamental molding along a wall STRINGCOURSE, TABLE, CORNICE
- double-curved molding CYMA, OGEE, TALON
- groove running lengthwise along an architectural molding QUIRK
- narrow convex molding BAGUETTE, BEADING, REEDING
- narrow convex molding, sometimes resembling a string of beads ASTRAGAL, CHAPLET

mole's burrow FORTRESS
- adjective for a mole TALPINE
- mole, birthmark, or other congenital skin blemish or growth NEVUS
- group or family of moles LABOR, MOVEMENT, COMPANY

molecule moleculelike group of atoms or atom having an electric charge through gaining or losing one or more electrons ION
- compound formed of chains of repeated units of molecules POLYMER
- twin spiral structure of a DNA molecule DOUBLE HELIX

molten rock LAVA, MAGMA

moment, instant, very short period of time TRICE
- moment of sanity or normal consciousness between bouts of coma or insanity LUCID MOMENT

momentary See **short-lived**

Monaco - person born or living in Monaco MONEGASQUE, MONACAN

monarch See **king**

monastery See also **monk, abbey**
- monastery, convent, or other place of seclusion CLOISTER
- monastery belonging to the Carthusian order CHARTERHOUSE
- monastery church MINSTER
- monastery inn or shelter for the needy or travelers HOSPICE
- monastery or convent PRIORY
- Buddhist monastery LAMASERY
- deputy head of a monastery in former times PROVOST
- dining hall of a monastery REFECTORY, FRATER
- head of a monastery ABBOT
- head of a monastic community SUPERIOR, CUSTOS
- head of a monastery in the Eastern Orthodox Church ARCHIMANDRITE, HEGUMEN
- latrine behind a dormitory in an abbey or monastery REREDORTER
- layperson living a religious life in a monastery without having taken formal vows OBLATE
- room in a monastery in which scribes could copy records or manuscripts SCRIPTORIUM

money See also **currency, coin**
- money, contract, or the like held by a third party until certain conditions are fulfilled ESCROW
- money, currency serving as a legally authorized medium of exchange or payment CIRCULATING MEDIUM, LEGAL TENDER
- money, profits, especially as a temptation to sin LUCRE
- money, wealth as a corrupting influence MAMMON
- money bestowed as a gift, especially to an inferior LARGESSE
- money deposited as security or guarantee, as against damage, debt, or nonpayment CAUTION MONEY, EARNEST, BOND
- money earned for or spent on nonessential items PIN MONEY

MONSTERS AND MYTHOLOGICAL CREATURES

abominable snowman/yeti	large, hairy humanlike animal said to live in the Himalayas
afreet/efreet	powerful evil demon of Arab mythology
basilisk	serpent, lizard, or dragon reputed to kill by its breath or look
behemoth	hippopotamuslike beast described in the Book of Job
bunyip	monster said to live in the swamps and lagoons of central Australia
centaur	creature of Greek mythology having the head, trunk, and arms of a man, and two legs (or the trunk and four legs) of a horse
Cerberus	three-headed watchdog of Hades, the Greek underworld
Chimera/ Chimaera	fire-breathing monster of classical mythology, having a lion's head, a she-goat's body, and a serpent's tail
cockatrice	creature of classical mythology, hatched from a cock's egg and having a death-dealing glance
Cyclops	any of the giants with a single eye in midforehead encountered by Odysseus
dryad/ hamadryad	wood nymph of classical mythology
Fafnir	dragon slain by Siegfried, in German mythology
Furies/ Eumenides/ Erinyes	three winged goddesses of classical mythology, with serpents for hair, who punished evildoers
Gigantes	giants with a man's torso, and legs in the form of serpents, defeated by the gods and Hercules
golem	artificial humanlike creature of Jewish legend
Gorgons	winged female creatures of classical mythology, having serpents for hair
griffin/ gryphon	creature of classical mythology having an eagle's head and wings, and a lion's body
Harpies	ravenous, slimy monsters of classical mythology, having women's heads and birds' bodies
hippocampus	sea horse with a horse's forelegs and the tail of a fish or dolphin, ridden by Neptune
hippogriff/ hippogryph	creature of classical mythology having the head, claws, and wings of a griffin and the body of a horse

- money given as a tip or reward POURBOIRE, GRATUITY
- money as coinage SPECIE
- money-market dealer, speculator, or specialist CAMBIST
- money-mindedness MATERIALISM
- money or income REVENUE
- money or other resources required for a particular purpose WHEREWITHAL
- money or property left in a will LEGACY, BEQUEST
- money or wealth, especially if acquired in a dubious way PELF
- money order or bill of exchange DRAFT
- money paid as a bribe to preserve secrecy HUSH MONEY
- money paid by an employer as a compensation to an employee who has lost his job SEVERANCE PAY, GOLDEN HANDSHAKE
- money paid out, expenditure DISBURSEMENT
- money raised by a charity campaign or sale PROCEEDS
- money set aside for a specific purpose APPROPRIATION
- money store, funds, treasury COFFERS, EXCHEQUER
- money used to provide change at the start of a business day FLOAT
- money voted by the British parliament for the running of the royal household PRIVY PURSE
- money withdrawn from one's bank account in excess of one's credit balance OVERDRAFT
- amount by which an actual amount, as of money, is lower than the expected or required amount SHORTFALL, DEFICIT
- beads and polished shells formerly used by Native Americans as money WAMPUM, PEAG
- circulate counterfeit money UTTER
- colloquial term for money DOUGH, BREAD, LOLLY, MOOLA, GELT, MAZUMA
- conceal the dubious or illegal origin of a sum of money LAUNDER
- convert property or assets into ready money REALIZE, LIQUIDATE
- devoted to gaining money or material possessions MATERIALISTIC, MERCENARY
- economic doctrine that a country's economy is best controlled by means of careful regulation of the money supply MONETARISM
- forge something, especially money COUNTERFEIT
- having money in hand, able to meet all debts SOLVENT
- misuse or steal money that one has control of MISAPPROPRIATE, EMBEZZLE
- obtain money, promises, or the like by threats EXTORT, BLACKMAIL
- principal or capital sum of money, value of an estate, or the like, as distinct from the interest or income CORPUS
- producing much money, profitable REMUNERATIVE, LUCRATIVE
- profitable job requiring little work, or similar easy source of money GRAVY TRAIN, MILCH COW, SINECURE
- reduction by a government in the monetary or exchange value of a currency DEVALUATION
- referring to money MONETARY, PECUNIARY
- referring to money, coins, or currency NUMISMATIC
- referring to paper money not backed by gold FIDUCIARY
- return of part of the money paid REBATE

MONSTERS AND MYTHOLOGICAL CREATURES *continued*

Hydra	nine-headed water snake, which sprouted two heads where one was struck off
kelpie	Scottish water spirit, usually a horse that drowned its riders
kraken	sea monster of Norwegian waters
lamia	creature of classical mythology having the head and breasts of a woman and the body of a serpent
leviathan	fiery, scaled, seven-headed sea serpent described in the Book of Job
Lilith	Biblical female demon living in deserted places, said to assault children
Minotaur	eater of human flesh, half man and half bull, confined to the Cretan Labyrinth and killed by Theseus
naiad	freshwater nymph of classical mythology
nereid	sea nymph of classical mythology
orc	monstrous creature of classical mythology
oread	mountain nymph of classical mythology
Pegasus	winged horse, the offspring of the Gorgon Medusa, and the mount of Perseus and Bellerophon
Phoenix	fabulous bird of classical mythology which from time to time destroyed itself on a burning altar, a new bird emerging from the ashes
roc	bird of enormous size and strength in Arabian legend
salamander	lizard or other reptilian monster; creature able to live in fire
satyr/faun	spirit of field and woodland of classical mythology, having a human torso, the hindquarters of a goat, and horns, noted for lechery
Sphinx	creature of classical mythology, having the head of a woman and the body of a lion, that killed all those unable to solve its riddle
unicorn	white, horselike animal with a long, single horn, able to outwit all captors except virgins
werewolf	monster alternating between the forms of a human being and a wolf
wyvern/ wivern	winged dragon of European mythology, having bird's feet and a serpent's tail

- seizure of money or property as security against legal claims SEQUESTRATION, LEVY
- slang term for small amounts of money PEANUTS, DIBS
- tiny, token, insignificant, as a sum of money might be NOMINAL
- trade through direct exchange of goods and services, without using money BARTER
- transfer money REMIT
- unexpected piece of good fortune, especially the sudden acquiring of money WINDFALL
- unit of money used for purposes of accounting UNIT OF ACCOUNT
- very small amount of money, such as a tiny salary PITTANCE

moneylender, especially one who charges an exorbitant rate of interest USURER
- moneylender or loan agency that accepts trade debts as security FACTOR

mongolism CONGENITAL ACROMICRIA, DOWN'S SYNDROME, LANGDON DOWN'S DISEASE, AUTOSOMAL TRISOMY OF GROUP G

monk See also **monastery**
- monk in the Greek Orthodox Church CALOYER
- monk of a Cistercian order noted for its austerity and vow of silence TRAPPIST
- monk or friar of various orders BENEDICTINE, CARTHUSIAN, CAPUCHIN, CISTERCIAN, DOMINICAN, FRANCISCAN
- monk or nun VOTARY
- monk or nun holding a subordinate office OBEDIENTIARY
- monk or other member of a communal order CENOBITE
- monk wandering about in former times PALMER
- monk's garment consisting of a long band of cloth hanging at the front and back from the shoulders SCAPULAR
- monk's hood or hooded cloak or habit COWL, CAPUCHE
- monk's shaven head TONSURE
- Buddhist monk in Tibet or Mongolia LAMA
- candidate monk or nun POSTULANT, NOVICE, NEOPHYTE
- referring to a clergyman who is not a monk SECULAR

monkey, ape, human, or related mammal PRIMATE
- relating to an ape or monkey SIMIAN
- small Indian macaque monkey widely used in medical research RHESUS MONKEY

monocle QUIZZING GLASS

monopoly - association, often unofficial or illegal, of independent businesses combining to secure a monopoly in a market and control prices CARTEL, TRUST
- regulating business monopolies to ensure fair competition ANTITRUST

monotonous task, routine TREADMILL

monster See chart, pages 348-349
- monster, freak LUSUS NATURAE
- monsterlike creation or scheme dangerous even to its creator FRANKENSTEIN'S MONSTER
- story or book about monsters or mythical creatures TERATOLOGY

monster (combining form) TERAT-, TERATO-, THERI-, THERO-

monstrous deed or behavior, outrage ENORMITY
- monstrously large animal or thing LEVIATHAN, BEHEMOTH

month - "in or during the next month," as used in business correspondence PROXIMO, PROX.
- "in or during the previous month," as used in business correspondence ULTIMO, ULT.
- "of the current month", as used in business correspondence INSTANT, INST.
- per month, monthly PER MENSEM

monument, as in ancient Egypt, in the form of a tapering four-sided stone pillar with a pyramidal top OBELISK
- monument commemorating a nation's heroes PANTHEON
- monument honoring soldiers killed in battle or other dead people buried elsewhere CENOTAPH
- ceremony at which a new monument, work of art, or the like is formally displayed to the public for the first time UNVEILING
- sculpture or painting of a person, as on a monument EFFIGY
- wording carved on a statue, monument, or building EPIGRAPH, INSCRIPTION

mood, frame of mind HUMOR, DISPOSITION, TEMPERAMENT
- suffering from extreme shifts of mood, from overexcitement to deep depression MANIC-DEPRESSIVE

moody See **irritable**

moon See illustration
- moon as personified in poetry CYNTHIA, DIANA, PHOEBE, SELENE
- moon when between half and full GIBBOUS MOON
- moon's orbit of the earth, or similar orbit in which the same face of the satellite is always pointing to the primary CAPTURED ROTATION, SYNCHRONOUS ROTATION
- adjective for the moon LUNAR, SELENIAN
- any of several long channels or valleys on the moon RILL
- arrangement of three celestial bodies in a straight line, as of the earth, sun, and moon at new moon or during an eclipse SYZYGY
- concave shape, as of a sickle or the moon in its first or last quarter CRESCENT
- decrease in apparent size or illumination, as the moon does when approaching new moon WANE
- decreasing, as the waning moon is DECRESCENT
- either pointed end of a crescent moon CUSP
- full moon nearest to the autumn equinox HARVEST MOON
- full moon that follows the harvest moon HUNTER'S MOON
- half-moon or crescent-shaped object or structure, such as the outwork of a fort DEMILUNE
- having two points, horns, or cusps, as a crescent moon is BICUSPID
- increase in apparent size or illumination, as the moon does when approaching full moon WAX
- increasing, as the waxing moon is INCRESCENT
- period between the old and new moon during which the moon is invisible INTERLUNATION
- point at which a spacecraft in lunar orbit is closest to the moon PERICYNTHION, PERILUNE
- point at which a spacecraft in lunar orbit is farthest from the moon APOCYNTHION, APOLUNE, APOSELENE
- point in its orbit when the moon or a satellite is farthest from the earth APOGEE
- point in its orbit when the moon or a satellite is nearest the earth PERIGEE
- ring of faint light, as around the moon when viewed through a haze CORONA, AUREOLE
- scientific study or geography of the moon SELENOGRAPHY
- "sea" or dark patch on Mars or the moon MARE

moon (combining form) SELEN-, SELENO-, LUN-

Moonies UNIFICATION CHURCH

mooring post on a quay or deck for a ship's ropes or cables BOLLARD

moral baseness or vileness DEPRAVITY, TURPITUDE
- moral considerations or doubts SCRUPLES
- moral customs and conventions of a group MORES
- moral disapproval of an excessive kind, narrow-minded propriety GRUNDYISM

- moral duty, promise, contract, or the like OBLIGATION
- moral lesson HOMILY
- moral or intellectual instruction or enlightenment EDIFICATION
- moral philosophy ETHICS
- moral principles allowing different behavior in one person or group from that expected of another DOUBLE STANDARD
- moral principle for everyone, in Kant's terminology CATEGORICAL IMPERATIVE
- Moral Rearmament BUCHMANISM, OXFORD GROUP
- moral soundness, honesty INTEGRITY, PROBITY, RECTITUDE
- moral story or fable, as used in medieval sermons EXEMPLUM
- moralizing in a pompous way, especially by means of proverbs and platitudes SENTENTIOUS
- morally corrupting or evil PERNICIOUS, PESTIFEROUS, PESTILENT, NOXIOUS
- morally instructive, designed to convey a moral lesson DIDACTIC
- morally unrestrained DISSOLUTE, LIBERTINE, LICENTIOUS
- absence of clear moral guidelines in a person or society ANOMIE
- declining or decaying in morale DECADENT
- philosophy of moral duty or responsibility DEONTOLOGY
- rejection of all moral and social values NIHILISM, ANARCHISM
- relating to rights, duties, and similar moral concepts DEONTIC
- unable to distinguish between moral and immoral AMORAL

morale, group spirit ESPRIT DE CORPS

more (combining form) PLEO-, PLEIO-, PLIO-, SUPER-, PLURI-, MULTI-

Mormons LATTER-DAY SAINTS
- Mormon priest of high rank PATRIARCH, EVANGELIST
- person who is not a Mormon, as referred to by Mormons GENTILE

morning prayer MATINS
- adjective for the early morning MATUTINAL
- in the morning ANTEMERIDIAN
- poem, song, or tune suited to or dealing with dawn or the early morning AUBADE

morse-code signal or signaling device based on mirror flashes of sunlight HELIOGRAPH

mortar - mortarlike cannon firing shells at a steep angle HOWITZER
- mortar or cement for filling cracks or seams POINTING
- crush to a powder, as in a mortar BRAY
- small club-shaped implement for crushing or grinding substances in a mortar PESTLE
- thin mortar, as used between tiles GROUT

mortgage or other charge or claim on a property ENCUMBRANCE
- mortgage or pledge something as security HYPOTHECATE
- pay off a debt or mortgage by installments AMORTIZE
- repossess mortgaged property FORECLOSE

mortise - projecting end of a piece of wood fitting into a corresponding mortise in another piece to form a joint TENON

mosaic of inlaid wood INTARSIA
- inlay, pave, or decorate with a mosaic of tiny tiles TESSELLATE
- tiny square tile used in making a mosaic TESSERA

Moscow - person born or living in Moscow MUSCOVITE

Moslem See **Muslim, Islam**

mosque in an Arab country MASJID

Moon

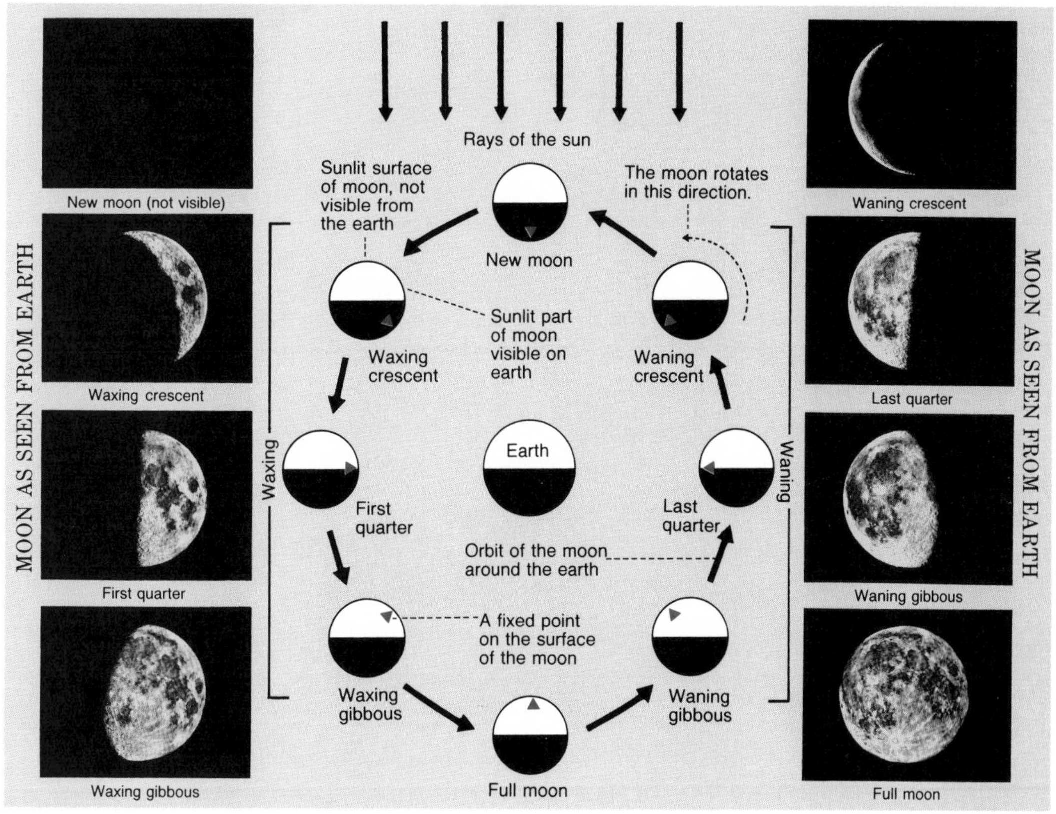

- mosque official who summons the faithful to prayer MUEZZIN
- niche in a mosque to show the direction of Mecca MIHRAB
- narrow tower of a mosque, from which the faithful are summoned to prayer MINARET
- pulpit in a mosque MINBAR

mosquito of the kind that transmits malaria ANOPHELES
- mosquito of the kind that transmits yellow fever AËDES
- mosquito or other organism that transmits germs VECTOR, CARRIER
- mosquito or related insect CULICID
- common house mosquito CULEX, CULICINE
- fabric used as mosquito netting MARQUISETTE
- lotion or other substance that keeps mosquitoes away REPELLENT

moss of the kind that forms peat when decomposed SPHAGNUM
- reproductive cell or organ, in nonflowering plants such as mosses and ferns and in fungi SPORE
- study of mosses BRYOLOGY
- tiny hairlike projection, as on moss or in the intestines VILLUS

moss(combining form) BRYO-

moth, butterfly, or related insect LEPIDOPTERAN
- pupa of a moth or butterfly, often encased in a cocoon CHRYSALIS

mothballs - sharp-smelling hydrocarbon substance used in mothballs, dyes, and explosives NAPHTHALENE

mother of a family, as the head of the household MATERFAMILIAS
- mother or bearer of a child on behalf of another, usually infertile, woman SURROGATE MOTHER
- mother or founder of a tribe, tradition, or the like MATRIARCH
- adjective for a mother or motherhood MATERNAL
- complex of a boy's unconscious emotions that include sexual desire for his mother, in Freudian theory OEDIPUS COMPLEX
- female sheep, horse, or the like as the mother of another DAM
- having the same mother but a different father UTERINE
- legal term for the womb of a mother VENTER
- mock-formal term for a mother MATER
- murder of one's mother MATRICIDE
- name based on one's mother's name, or that of a female ancestor METRONYMIC, MATRONYMIC
- referring to descent traced through the mother rather than the father MATRILINEAL

mother (combining form) MATRI-

motherhood MATERNITY

mother-of-pearl NACRE
- large shellfish providing mother-of-pearl ABALONE
- New Zealand shellfish with a shimmering green shell like mother-of-pearl PAUA

motion - random motion of microscopic particles suspended in liquid or gas BROWNIAN MOTION
- referring to motion KINETIC
- tendency of a physical body to remain at rest or in unchanged motion unless acted on by external forces INERTIA

motionless, unchanging, or producing no movement or change STATIC, INERT

motivation, encouragement, influence INCENTIVE, INCITEMENT, STIMULUS, INDUCEMENT

motive kept concealed so as to deceive ULTERIOR MOTIVE

motiveless, random, unprovoked, as vandalism or willful destruction is WANTON, GRATUITOUS

motor See also **engine, car, jet engine**, and chart at **internal-combustion engine**
- motor, usually detachable, fitted externally at the stern of a boat OUTBOARD MOTOR
- motor-racing assembly area for the cars PADDOCK
- motor-racing over a rough grass track AUTOCROSS
- rotor of an induction motor, having copper bars arranged to form the outer edge of a cylinder SQUIRREL CAGE
- series of tight bends, or a barrier used in forming them, on a motor-racing circuit CHICANE
- stationary part of an electric motor or generator STATOR
- turning or rotating part of an electric motor or generator ROTOR

motorboat that skims the surface

Mouth, Nose, and Throat

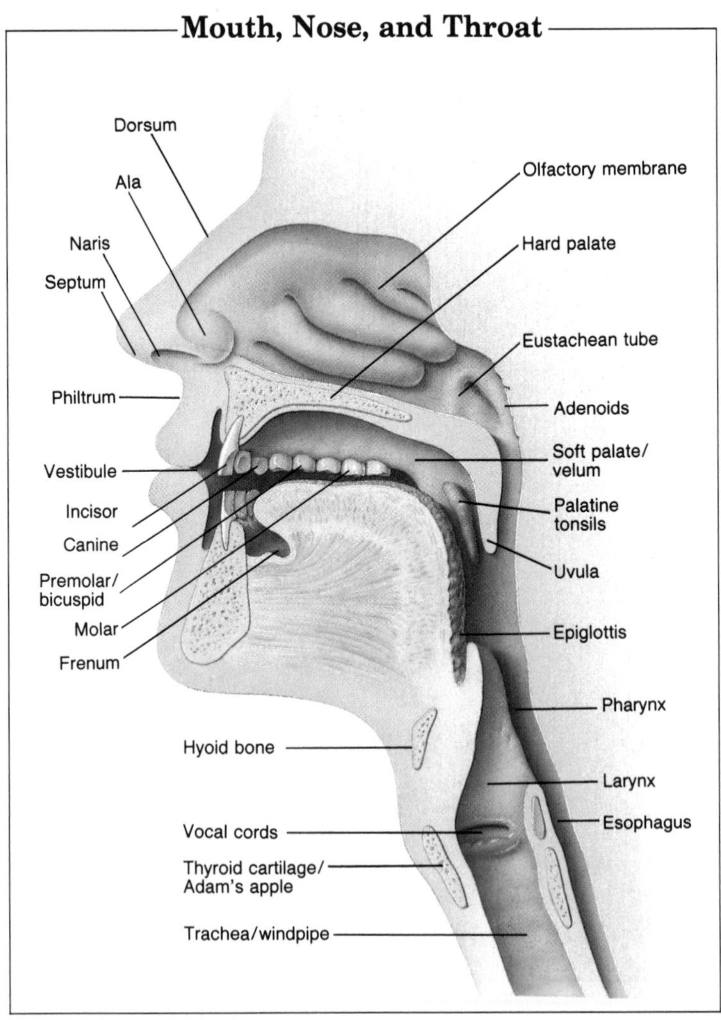

of the water HYDROPLANE

motorcycle escort, as for a VIP's car OUTRIDER
- motorcycle or bicycle with high handlebars CHOPPER
- motorcycle partly propelled by pedals MOPED
- motorcycle-racing arena VELODROME
- seat for a second rider, as on a horse or motorcycle PILLION

motorcyclist carrying official documents or reports DISPATCH RIDER

motto, slogan, or principle BANNER
- motto, slogan, or rallying cry, summing up the principles of a group or project WATCHWORD, MAXIM
- motto or quotation, as at the head of a chapter, suggesting its theme EPIGRAPH

mound covering an ancient burial site BARROW, TUMULUS
- mound of stones serving as a memorial or landmark CAIRN
- mound on which a fort or castle is sited MOTTE
- mound or hillock TUFFET

mountain See also **hill**
- mountain dweller or backwoodsman HILLBILLY
- mountain group within a larger chain MASSIF
- mountain lake TARN
- mountain nymph, in Greek mythology OREAD
- mountain pass or chain in India GHAT
- mountain pass or gap COL
- mountain peak PINNACLE
- mountain range or system of parallel ranges CORDILLERA
- mountain range with a rugged outline SIERRA
- mountain ridge with a knife edge ARÊTE
- mountain ridge projecting sidewise from the main line or range of mountains SPUR
- flat piece of land surrounded by rising slopes, as in the mountains AMPHITHEATER
- flat-topped mountain on the seabed GUYOT
- from or at the other side of the mountains, especially the Alps TRAMONTANE, ULTRAMONTANE, TRANSALPINE
- from or at this side of the mountains, especially the Alps CISMONTANE
- relating to or inhabiting mountains MONTANE
- rocky needle-shaped mountain peak AIGUILLE
- sloping rock surface at the base of a mountain or ridge in an arid region PEDIMENT
- steep or very sharply angled, as the side of a mountain might be PRECIPITOUS
- steep rocky mountain peak CRAG
- steep slope or face of a mountain ridge or plateau ESCARPMENT

mountain (combining form) ORO-, MONT-

mountaineering - descend a steep slope or vertical cliff in mountaineering by sliding down a rope around one's body ABSEIL, RAPPEL
- metal ring for fastening to a spike or running a rope through in mountaineering CARABINER, SNAP RING
- metal spikes fitted to boots, as for mountaineering or walking on ice CRAMPONS
- move sideways or diagonally across a slope, as in skiing or mountaineering TRAVERSE
- rock or ice pillar around which a rope can be tied in mountaineering BOLLARD
- secure a mountaineer at the end of a rope, or secure a rope to a rock or post BELAY
- short rope ladder, with a few solid rungs, as used in mountaineering ÉTRIER
- spike driven into rock to secure a rope in mountaineering PITON
- temporary or overnight camp, as set up by explorers or mountaineers BIVOUAC
- vertical crack in a rock or ice wall, which a mountaineer can fit into CHIMNEY

mounted sentry stationed ahead of an army's outposts VEDETTE

mourn with a wailing lament KEEN

mournful, expressing sadness PLAINTIVE, PLANGENT, WISTFUL
- mournful, sorrowful, sad, in style or substance ELEGIAC

mourning band of black material, worn on the sleeve or hat CRAPE
- mourning clothing, as worn by a widow WEEDS
- mourning fabric, typically of black silk or crepe CYPRESS
- mourning poem or song on someone's death DIRGE, ELEGY, THRENODY, MONODY
- public showing of mourning or repentance SACKCLOTH AND ASHES
- vigil and period of mourning over a dead person before burial WAKE

mouse, rat, squirrel, or related gnawing mammal RODENT
- mouselike, resembling or relating to a rat or mouse MURINE

mouth See illustration
- mouth, as of a shark or lion MAW

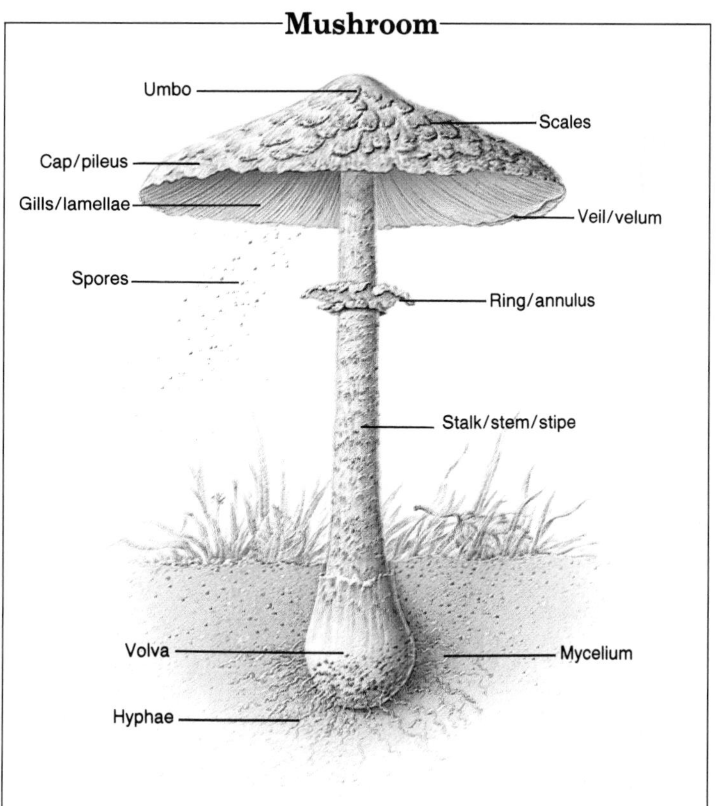

- mouth of a river EMBOUCHURE, ESTUARY
- mouth or other opening in the body ORIFICE
- mouthlike opening, as in a sponge or hookworm STOMA
- adjective for the mouth ORAL
- relating to the mouth or cheeks BUCCAL
- split in the roof of the mouth, often occurring in conjunction with harelip CLEFT PALATE
- technical term for a mouth or other opening OS
- width or gap of the open mouth or beak RICTUS

mouth (combining form) OR-, ORO-, STOMATO-, -STOM-, -STOME, BUCC-

mouthpiece of a wind instrument, especially a brass instrument EMBOUCHURE

move about playfully, jump about FRISK, GAMBOL, FROLIC, ROMP
- move across TRAVERSE
- move along swiftly and easily, as light clouds might SCUD, FLIT
- move away in different directions from a single starting point, separate DIVERGE
- move back, as the tide might RECEDE
- move back to where one started from RETRACE ONE'S STEPS
- move backward, retreat RETIRE
- move backward or get worse RETROGRESS
- move clumsily and heavily LUMBER, GALUMPH, TRUNDLE
- move duties or assets elsewhere HIVE OFF
- move easily and effortlessly, as downhill on a bicycle COAST, FREEWHEEL
- move furtively, sneak SLINK, SIDLE, PROWL
- move hurriedly and out of control, as charging cattle might STAMPEDE
- move in a tired, listless way SHAMBLE, SHUFFLE
- move in a winding or undecided way MEANDER
- move in an easy, carefree manner AMBLE, LOPE, MOSEY, SAUNTER, IDLE
- move lightly and rapidly across a surface in a darting motion, as a fishing fly might SKITTER
- move or get going, rouse oneself, become active BESTIR ONESELF
- move or go hurriedly SCURRY, SCAMPER, SCARPER, SKEDADDLE
- move or go to a specified place REPAIR, RESORT, BETAKE ONESELF
- move or push vigorously forward SURGE
- move or roam about ROVE
- move or roam about aimlessly, frivolously, or irresponsibly GAD ABOUT, GALLIVANT, TRAIPSE
- move rapidly and erratically, as if out of control CAREER, CAREEN
- move reluctantly and little BUDGE, SHIFT
- move round or avoid SKIRT, CIRCUMVENT
- move slowly, lag behind DAWDLE, LOITER
- move to a later time POSTPONE, ADJOURN
- move to another place RELOCATE
- move toward, as if drawn by an irresistible attraction GRAVITATE
- move toward the same point from different directions CONVERGE
- move with an up-and-down motion UNDULATE
- move with bumps and jolts JOUNCE, BOUNCE
- move with exaggerated gestures of displeasure or impatience FLOUNCE, SASHAY
- prevent from moving IMMOBILIZE, PARALYZE

moved easily, readily affected, sensitive SUSCEPTIBLE

movement, as by bacteria, in reflex response to light or a similar stimulus TAXIS
- movement, allegedly by mystical or mental powers, of objects some distance away TELEKINESIS, PSYCHOKINESIS
- movement back and forth ALTERNATION, RECIPROCATION
- diminished power of movement, lack of coordination, caused by brain damage or disease APRAXIA
- movement forward, progress, advance HEADWAY
- movement of the limbs or body to express or reinforce meaning GESTURE
- movement or general direction, as of someone's life TENOR
- movement or transport of goods or people from place to place TRANSIT, CONVEYANCE
- apparent movement of a stationary light, such as a candle flame, when observed in a darkened room AUTOKINETIC PHENOMENON
- force or power resulting from continuing movement MOMENTUM, IMPETUS, ELAN
- instrument for observing, measuring, or adjusting vibration, rotation, or the like by using light flashes to make the moving object appear stationary STROBOSCOPE
- referring to movement MOTIVE, KINETIC

movement (combining form) KIN-, KINET-, KINETO-, -KINESIS, -TROP-, TROPO-, -TROPIC, MOT-, -GRADE, -TACTIC, -DROMOUS

movie See **film**

moving, affecting, or touching, as a memory might be POIGNANT
- moving, arousing sympathy PATHETIC
- moving easily and gracefully LITHE, LIMBER, SUPPLE, LISSOM, AGILE, FLEXIBLE
- moving from place to place, mobile as opposed to stationary AMBULATORY, AMBULANT
- moving or growing inward, toward a center or axis AFFERENT, CENTRIPETAL
- moving or growing outward, away from a center or axis EFFERENT, CENTRIFUGAL
- moving staircase ESCALATOR
- moving under one's own power, as a microorganism might MOTILE, TACTIC

moving (combining form) See **movement** (combining form)

mowing of a second crop of grass in a single season AFTERMATH
- mown grass or hay cut by a scythe or mower SWATH

Mozart - one of the 626 catalog numbers of Mozart compositions KÖCHEL NUMBER

much See also **lots, many, plenty, excessive**
- much in a small space MULTUM IN PARVO

much (combining form) POLY-, MULTI-

mucus - mucuslike discharge from the eyes or nose RHEUM
- mucus secreted in the breathing passages PHLEGM
- mucous matter coughed up from the lungs and windpipe SPUTUM

mud-filled hollow SLOUGH
- muddied through sediment or foreign particles, as river water might be TURBID
- muddy deposit, as on a river bed or the inside of a boiler SLUDGE
- board or boards laid over wet or muddy ground DUCKBOARD
- building material of interlaced sticks plastered with mud or clay WATTLE AND DAUB
- craving for unnatural food, such as mud or chalk, occurring sometimes during pregnancy and in small children PICA
- lie or roll lazily about in mud, a hot bath, or the like WALLOW
- thin, liquid mixture of mud, cement, manure or the like SLURRY
- trapped in mud MIRED

muddle or disorder HAVOC, SHAMBLES, HUGGER-MUGGER
- muddled by many conflicting interests or forces, as political life might be TURBID

mug, tankard, or large cup STOUP,

MUSIC

MUSICAL COMPOSITIONS

arabesque	short, elaborately ornamented piece
aubade	music originally intended for performance in the morning
bagatelle	short, unpretentious composition
barcarole	song with a rhythm resembling that of rowing a gondola
berceuse	lullaby
canon	composition, often choral, where one part is overlapped by other parts in the same or a related key
cantata	work for several solo singers and a choir
capriccio	composition that does not follow any strict form
cavatina	short, simple instrumental piece
chaconne/ passacaglia	piece incorporating variations on a repeated harmonic pattern
concerto	composition for a solo instrument and an orchestra
concerto grosso	composition for several solo instruments and an orchestra
divertimento	light piece for a chamber orchestra, with several short movements
étude	"study," a piece designed as an exercise to develop or embody a particular point of technique
extravaganza	light orchestral work
fantasia	composition in which form takes second place to the composer's fancy
fugue	composition in which several themes are stated separately, then developed in counterpoint
humoresque	playful or humorous composition
idyll	calm, pastoral composition
intermezzo	short piece for performance between the acts of an opera or play
nocturne	composition suggestive of the qualities of night
oratorio	composition, usually on a religious theme, for voices and an orchestra
partita	suite consisting of several instrumental pieces
pastorale	orchestral piece suggesting a rural scene
prelude	piece introducing a larger work; showpiece for piano and orchestra
requiem	composition written as a setting of the Mass for the dead
rhapsody	work with no set form, often based on folk tunes
rondo	composition in which a refrain is repeated between separate sections
scherzo	lively piece, often the third movement of a symphony
serenade	music originally intended for performance in the evening
sonata	composition consisting of three or four independent and contrasting movements
symphonic poem/tone poem	orchestral work interpreting a nonmusical subject such as a folk tale
toccata	free-style composition, usually for organ or harpsichord, with full chords
voluntary	piece, sometimes improvised, played by an organist before or during a church service

MUSIC TERMS

accelerando/ stringendo	gradually quickening
acciaccatura	grace note one step below the principal note
accidental	sign indicating a sharp, flat or natural note outside the key signature of a piece
adagio/lento	slowly
ad libitum/ ad lib	play as desired
affettuoso	tenderly or passionately
agitato	agitatedly
allargando	becoming slower
allegretto	briskly, but more slowly than allegro
allegro	briskly
amoroso	lovingly
andante	at a moderate tempo
andantino	a little faster than andante
animato	animatedly
appassionato	with passion

continued

MUSIC *continued*

appoggiatura	grace note one step above the principal note
arpeggio	notes of a chord played in quick succession
cadence	buildup of chords toward a close
cadenza	unaccompanied, sometimes improvised, passage by a soloist in a concerto
cantabile	in a singing manner
capriccioso	in a free and lively manner
chord	group of three or more notes played together
chromatic scale	scale that consists of all 12 semitones in Western music, as distinct from the diatonic scale
coda	short additional passage at the end of a movement or composition
con brio	vigorously
con sordino	muted
con spirito	with spirit
continuo/ figured bass	bass part with numbered chords
counterpoint	set of two or more melody lines played together and in harmony
crescendo	rising in volume and intensity
decrescendo/ diminuendo	falling in volume and intensity
diatonic scale	scale consisting of five whole tones and two semitones, as distinct from the chromatic scale
double stop	two notes played simultaneously on a stringed instrument
forte	loudly
fundamental	lowest note of a chord
glissando	referring to notes blended together in a rising or falling scale
grace note	embellishing note, with no time value
grave	solemnly
grazioso	gracefully
interval	difference in pitch between two notes
largo	slowly, solemnly
legato	smoothly and evenly
leitmotiv	musical phrase associated with a particular character or situation
ligature	group of notes played as one phrase and indicated by a curved line
maestoso	majestically
major scale	scale with semitones between the third and fourth notes and the seventh and eighth notes
minor scale	scale with semitones between the second and third notes and the fifth and sixth notes
natural	note that is neither flat nor sharp
non troppo	"not too much": term moderating an instruction
obbligato	essential, not to be omitted, not optional
octave	eight notes of a diatonic scale
ostinato	repeated phrase
pentatonic scale	five-note scale
piano	softly
pizzicato	referring to the plucking of notes that are normally bowed
presto	fast
recitative	sung narrative in opera or oratorio, in the rhythm of ordinary speech
reprise	repetition of a phrase, or return to an earlier theme
ritardando	gradual slowing in tempo
rubato	to be played with a varying tempo
segue	continue to the next movement without pause
semitone	smallest standard interval in Western music, or a note separated from another by this interval
sforzando	accented strongly
sostenuto	in a sustained or prolonged manner
spiccato	referring to the playing of notes by bouncing the bow
staccato	referring to notes played crisply and sharply
syncopation	accenting of a beat in a bar that would not normally be accented
tempo	speed at which a piece is played
tonic sol-fa/ solfeggio/ solmization	musical training through singing the *do-re-mi* syllables
tutti	all together
vigoroso	vigorously
vivace	briskly

FLAGON
- mug, typically made of pottery and having a lid, holding about a pint of beer STEIN
- mug in the shape of a man wearing a three-cornered hat TOBY JUG, TOBY
- small mug or cup NOGGIN

Muhammad See also **Muslim** and chart at **Islam**
- Muhammad, or any of his various successors IMAM

mule driver MULETEER
- mulelike hybrid animal, from a female donkey and male horse HINNY
- group or family of mules PACK, BARREN, RAKE, SPAN

mulled wine BISHOP

multi- (combining form) PLURI-, POLY-

multicolored PIED, PIEBALD, MOTLEY, PARTI-COLOR, POLYCHROME, VARIEGATED

multilingual POLYGLOT

multiply by five QUINTUPLE
- multiply by four QUADRUPLE
- multiply plants using graftings and cuttings PROPAGATE
- multiplying by means of buds, shoots, or small bulbs rather than by seeds VIVIPAROUS
- independent of the order of the terms, as an operation such as multiplication is COMMUTATIVE

multitalented VERSATILE

mummy - jar used in ancient Egypt for holding a mummy's entrails CANOPIC JAR

murder See also **kill, killing**
- murder a prominent politician or public figure ASSASSINATE
- killing of a person, as through negligence, that is unlawful though not necessarily murder CULPABLE HOMICIDE, MANSLAUGHTER
- list of people to be murdered HIT LIST
- planned beforehand, deliberate, as a murder may be PREMEDITATED
- plea that mental abnormality at the time of a murder reduces the culprit's responsibility DIMINISHED RESPONSIBILITY

murder (combining form) -CIDE

murderer See **killer**

murmuring, whispering, or rustling sound SUSURRATION

muscle, as at the back of the upper arm, having three points of attachment at one of the ends TRICEPS
- muscle, as on the front of the upper arm, having two points of attachment at one of the ends BICEPS
- muscle, typically regulating an internal organ, that cannot be consciously controlled INVOLUNTARY MUSCLE
- muscle cramp or rigid muscular contraction, as in a fever RIGOR
- muscle on the forearm, helping to turn the palm of the hand downward PRONATOR
- muscle on the forearm, helping to turn the palm of the hand upward SUPINATOR
- muscle sense, awareness of one's own muscles and bodily movements KINESTHESIA
- muscles behind the thigh, or tendons behind the knee HAMSTRINGS
- muscular contraction, involuntary and often violent and painful CONVULSION
- muscular contractions in the intestine or similar tubelike organ that force the contents onward PERISTALSIS
- any of the three buttock muscles GLUTEUS
- circular muscle squeezing or relaxing a body passage SPHINCTER, CONSTRICTOR
- cord of fibers connecting the heel bone to the calf muscles ACHILLES TENDON
- either of two large chest muscles, helping to move the shoulder and upper arm PECTORAL MUSCLE
- exercise through contracting the muscles without changing their length or moving the limbs ISOMETRIC EXERCISE
- fibrous tissue beneath the skin and encasing muscles FASCIA
- flat muscle on the shoulder and back, helping to move the shoulder blade TRAPEZIUS
- health or condition of muscle, as shown by its tension and response to stimuli TONE, TONUS
- long muscle extending from the front of the thigh around to behind the knee, helping bend the knee SARTORIUS
- loss or lack of muscular coordination ATAXIA

Music Symbols

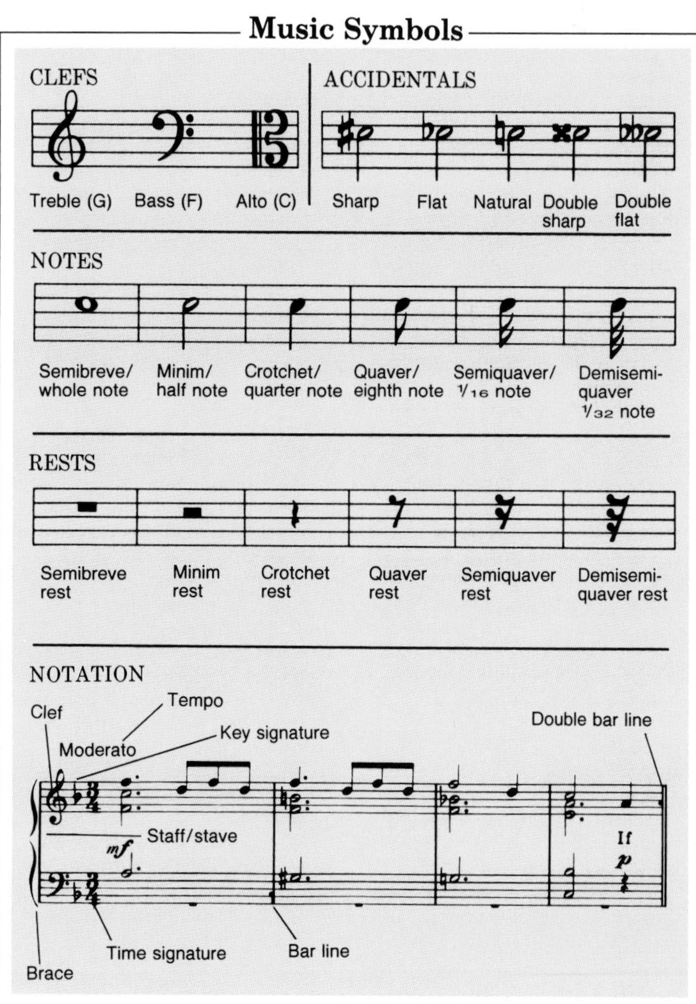

- picture of the body, or a section of the body, without the skin, to show the muscle structure ÉCORCHÉ
- sharpness of outline, as of well-developed muscles DEFINITION
- shortening or tensing of a muscle, either voluntary or involuntary CONTRACTION
- sinew attaching a muscle to a bone or other support TENDON
- thick shoulder muscle, helping to raise the arm DELTOID
- tough band of fibrous tissue connecting moving bones or cartilages, or supporting organs or muscles LIGAMENT
- twitching of muscle fibers FIBRILLATION
- wide swelling section of a muscle VENTER

muscle (combining form) MY-, MYO-, MUSCUL-

Muses - relating to the Muses or artistic inspiration PIERIAN

museum director CURATOR
- museum exhibit, with models of figures set against a background DIORAMA
- museum or place of safekeeping REPOSITORY

mushroom See illustration, page 353, and also **fungus**
- mushroom lover MYCOPHILE
- mushroom-shaped FUNGIFORM
- mushroomlike fungus growing underground, considered a great delicacy TRUFFLE
- cooked or served with a sauce of olive oil, lemon juice, spices, and tomato, as mushrooms might be À LA GRECQUE
- edible mushroom of various types CHAMPIGNON, MOREL, CHANTERELLE
- fungus of the family that includes mushrooms AGARIC
- thin skin or outer covering on the cap of a mushroom PELLICLE

music See chart and illustration, pages 355, 356, and 357, and also **sing, singer**
- music based on an untraditional sequence of notes, typically using a twelve-tone scale SERIAL MUSIC, DODECAPHONY
- music business, popular-music industry TIN PAN ALLEY
- music-loving PHILHARMONIC
- music of a bland kind providing a background in waiting rooms, elevators, and so on MUZAK
- music of a random kind in which the performer is given a great deal of choice by the composer ALEATORY MUSIC
- music played on saloon pianos HONKY-TONK
- music school CONSERVATOIRE, CONSERVATORY
- music stand used by two players in an orchestra, or this pair of players DESK
- music suggesting a story, scene, or idea PROGRAM MUSIC
- music that is purely formal or intellectual, and does not attempt to represent a story, scene, or idea ABSOLUTE MUSIC
- music using short series of notes repeated many times with small variations MINIMALISM
- musical composition, typically numbered in sequence OPUS
- musical dramatic entertainment in England in the 16th and 17th centuries MASQUE
- musical encore or some similar short, pleasant treat LOLLIPOP, BONNE BOUCHE
- musical fanfare or similar dramatic musical passage FLOURISH
- musical medley, based on popular tunes QUODLIBET
- musical training based on rhythmical free-style dance movements to music EURHYTHMICS
- instrument sounding out the beat, used when practicing music METRONOME
- listing of Mozart's 626 musical compositions KÖCHEL LISTING
- play music, composing as one goes IMPROVISE
- range or stock of pieces of music, available to a performer REPERTOIRE
- short line above or below the staff in a piece of printed music, to indicate the position of a high or low note LEDGER LINE
- study of the physical properties of musical sounds HARMONICS
- style of popular musical entertainment in which improvised poetry is recited or chanted to a musical accompaniment RAPPING
- text of the songs and dialogue of an opera or musical LIBRETTO
- words of a song LYRICS

musical instruments See also **percussion, string instruments, wind instruments, electronics**, and chart at **keyboard instruments**
- musical instrument cranked by hand, such as a barrel organ HURDY-GURDY
- distinctive tone of a musical instrument or singing voice, tone color TIMBRE
- range of a musical instrument DIAPASON, REGISTER

musician of masterly technical skill or outstanding flair VIRTUOSO
- musician or performing artist on a specified instrument or in a specified technique EXPONENT
- musician who traveled about in the Middle Ages MINSTREL, TROUBADOUR, JONGLEUR
- musicians playing at public processions or entertainments in former times WAITS
- famous musician MAESTRO
- group of musicians CONSORT
- performance by pop or jazz musicians, as at a club or party GIG

Muslim See also chart at **Islam**
- Muslim at the time of the Crusades SARACEN
- Muslim or Turkish emblem of power THE CRESCENT
- former term for a Muslim MOHAMMEDAN, MAHOMETAN, MUSSULMAN

Mussolini's title as dictator of Italy IL DUCE

mustache of a bushy drooping shape WALRUS MUSTACHE
- mustache with upward-curling ends HANDLEBAR MUSTACHE

mustard, cress, or related plant having a four-petaled cross-shaped flower CRUCIFER
- mustard, spice, vinegar, or other seasoning CONDIMENT

mustard gas or other blistering agent VESICANT

mutant or genetically deviant organism SPORT

mutation of or abrupt variation within a species SALTATION

mute or damper for a musical instrument SORDINO

mutual, given or done in return or exchange RECIPROCAL
- mutually destructive or fatal, as civil war is INTERNECINE

mutual (combining form) INTER-, RECIPROC

my fault MEA CULPA

mysterious, apparently wise but really pompous, as an utterance might be GNOMIC, OBSCURANTIST
- mysterious, awe-inspiring, having a magical aura NUMINOUS
- mysterious, secret, known or understood only by those who have made a special study or been initiated ARCANE, ESOTERIC
- mysterious because uninterpretable, as a facial expression might be INSCRUTABLE, UNFATHOMABLE, DEADPAN, ENIGMATIC
- mysterious or puzzling person or thing, riddle ENIGMA

mystical, as rituals might be OCCULT, ESOTERIC, ORPHIC, CRYPTIC, PERDU, ARCANE, HERMETICAL, SPHINXIAN
- mystical or secret philosophy, specifically one based on the Hebrew scriptures CABALA

mythical creatures See **monster**

N

nag, harass, and dominate one's husband HENPECK
- nag, harass, urge to make haste CHIVY
- nag, make requests persistently IMPORTUNE, HECTOR
- nagging, insistent IMPORTUNATE

nail, claw, hoof, or similar structure UNGUIS
- nail file in the form of a hard, sandpaperlike wooden or cardboard strip EMERY BOARD
- cell tissue from which nails and teeth develop MATRIX
- crescent-shaped mark at the base of a fingernail or toenail LUNULE
- hardened dead skin at the base of a fingernail or toenail CUTICLE
- live sensitive flesh under one's nails QUICK
- painful swelling or abscess around the nail of a finger or toe AGNAIL
- piece of dead but painful skin around a fingernail HANGNAIL
- secure a nail by bending the projecting pointed end over CLINCH
- short, flat-headed nail, as used for fixing metal sheeting to wood CLOUT
- thin headless nail SPRIG
- thin or flattish nail with a small or narrow head BRAD

naive, unsophisticated, simple, innocent ARTLESS, GUILELESS, INGENUOUS
- naive and innocent young woman INGENUE
- naive and overoptimistic person CANDIDE, POLLYANNA
- appearing or pretending to be simple and naive FAUX-NAÏF, DISINGENUOUS

naked, nude AU NATUREL, UNCLAD
- naked person running through a public place, sometimes as a publicity stunt STREAKER

name, give a title, name, or nickname to DESIGNATE, NOMINATE, STYLE, DUB
- name, such as the name of a city or disease, derived from a person's name, or the person or his or her name EPONYM
- name adopted as a disguise, especially a false name assumed for a particular purpose or occasion PSEUDONYM, ALIAS, NOM DE GUERRE, INCOGNITO
- name adopted by an author, as to conceal his or her identity PEN NAME, NOM DE PLUME
- name based on one's mother's name METRONYMIC, MATRONYMIC
- name derived from the first name of one's father or paternal ancestor, typically with an affix such as *-son, Mac-*, or *-ovich* PATRONYMIC
- name explicitly, spell out SPECIFY
- name expressing endearment, often a diminutive form HYPOCORISM
- name in common use, rather than the technical Latin name, of a plant or animal TRIVIAL NAME, VERNACULAR
- name of a category or class RUBRIC
- name of a city or other place used in a foreign language, such as *Florence* for *Firenze* EXONYM
- name of a place or region, or a word derived from it TOPONYM
- name or act of naming DENOMINATION, DESIGNATION
- name or nickname MONIKER
- name or title APPELLATION
- adjective for names ONOMASTIC
- "born," used before the maiden name of a married woman when identifying her NÉE
- having or referring to two names or terms BINOMIAL
- having the same name HOMONYMOUS
- in name only, having the official title but not the real power, as with a figurehead ruler TITULAR, NOMINAL
- line under the title of a magazine or newspaper article giving the writer's name BYLINE
- mark stationery or other belongings with the name, initials, or other form of identification of the owner PERSONALIZE
- nickname or assumed name SOBRIQUET
- nickname or descriptive term forming part of a person's name or title EPITHET, COGNOMEN
- pass or toss something back and forth, such as a person's name in a gossipy conversation BANDY
- preposition such as *von* or *de* accompanying a title or surname, indicating noble rank NOBILIARY PARTICLE
- publicize a product or service by using one's name to recommend it ENDORSE
- referring to a person of unknown or suppressed name, or to a book, contribution, or the like by such a person ANONYMOUS
- referring to the person, fictional hero, or the like, after whom a city, novel, or the like is named EPONYMOUS
- study and history of names ONOMASTICS
- system of names or terms for plants or chemicals NOMENCLATURE
- use of a title or epithet, such as *Her Majesty*, in place of a proper name ANTONOMASIA
- wrong or unsuitable name for someone or something MISNOMER

name (combining form) NOMIN-, -ONYM

nameless, unnamed INNOMINATE

namely - "namely," "that is," term introducing examples I.E., ID EST, VIDELICET, VIZ
- "namely," "to wit," "that is to say," term used to introduce a synonym, explanation, or missing word SCILICET, SC.

nameplate, memorial tablet, or the like, as mounted on a wall or monument PLAQUE
- nameplate or small signboard, as of a doctor or lawyer SHINGLE

nanny or maidservant in India AYAH
- nanny or wet nurse in the East AMAH

nape of the neck NUCHA

Naples - person born or living in Naples NEAPOLITAN

narrow pass or gorge DEFILE
- narrow strip of land joining two larger land areas ISTHMUS
- narrowing toward one end TAPERING
- abnormal narrowing or blocking of a body passage STRICTURE

narrow (combining form) STEN-, STENO-

narrow-minded See also **conservative, old-fashioned**
- narrow-minded, bigoted, intolerant, prejudiced SECTARIAN, BLINKERED
- narrow-minded, limited in perspective, concerned only with

one's immediate surroundings INSULAR, PAROCHIAL, PROVINCIAL
- narrow-minded, self-satisfied, and arrogant person PRIG
- narrow-minded, set in one's ways, incapable of changing with the times HIDEBOUND
- narrow-minded and bigoted white rural American REDNECK
- narrow-minded and embittered, envious, cynical, prejudiced, and hostile JAUNDICED
- narrow-minded and old-fashioned person, unfamiliar with and uninterested in modern urban life BACKWOODSMAN, HILLBILLY
- narrow-minded attitudes LAAGER MENTALITY, BUNKER MENTALITY
- narrow-minded person with old-fashioned ideas TROGLODYTE
- narrow-minded propriety and excessive criticism of the unconventional GRUNDYISM
- narrow-mindedness, inability to take a broad view of things TUNNEL VISION
- person typifying narrow-minded prudishness and conservatism MRS GRUNDY

nasal RHINAL
- nasal or constricted in sound ADENOIDAL
- nasal quality of speech, as in certain accents TWANG

nasal (combining form) NAS-, NASO-, RHIN-, RHINO-

nasty See **bad, spiteful, disgusting**

nation that is not allied with a superpower, a neutral nation NON-ALIGNED NATION
- nations recognizing and accepting the institutions of one another, or the policy of such acceptance COMITY OF NATIONS
- easing of tension, as between nations DÉTENTE
- newly independent, as a nation might be EMERGENT

national anthem of France MARSEILLAISE
- national policy, especially foreign policy, based uncompromisingly on national self-interest rather than on moral considerations REALPOLITIK

nationalism or patriotism of a narrow, militant, fanatical kind CHAUVINISM, JINGOISM, FLAG-WAVING

native, local, restricted to a particular area or group ENDEMIC
- native language or dialect of a country or region VERNACULAR
- native to or originating in a particular place, ABORIGINAL, INDIGENOUS, AUTOCHTHONOUS

Native Americans See chart at **American Indian terms**

Nativity - tableau, as at Christmas, of Jesus' Nativity CRÈCHE, CRIB

natural, inborn, as some skills or talents are NATIVE, INNATE
- natural, simple, and basic, as one's life-style might be ORGANIC
- natural environment or surrounding for an animal or plant HABITAT
- natural in behavior or origin, unrehearsed, unprompted SPONTANEOUS
- natural in manner, frank and honest ARTLESS, UNSTUDIED, GUILELESS
- natural talent, gift, or characteristic ENDOWMENT

natural gas METHANE

nature or wildlife reserve SANCTUARY
- belief in a deity as being present throughout nature, or identical with nature PANTHEISM
- belief that nature is directed or determined by an end or purpose TELEOLOGY
- environmental influences on the development of an organism, as distinguished from genetic influences or nature NURTURE
- imitation or representation of nature or human nature in literature and art MIMESIS
- nature worship, or belief that natural objects have souls ANIMISM
- protection and preservation of the natural environment CONSERVATION
- relate closely to or communicate intimately with someone or something, such as nature COMMUNE
- study or theory of the universe or nature as a whole COSMOGRAPHY

nature (combining form) PHYSI-, PHYSIO-

naughty See also **disobedient**
- naughty, cheeky, or mischievous in an engaging way, roguish, scampish ARCH, INCORRIGIBLE
- naughty, racy, verging on the indelicate or improper, as a joke might be RISQUÉ
- naughty behavior, bad deeds, misconduct MISDEMEANORS, DELINQUENCY

nautical See also **ship, sail**
- nautical mile per hour KNOT

naval See also **military, services, sail**
- naval mechanic ARTIFICER
- naval or military subdivision ECHELON
- naval petty officer in charge of signaling or clerical duties YEOMAN
- naval petty officer responsible for steering or navigating QUARTERMASTER
- small fleet of ships, or small naval task force FLOTILLA, SQUADRON, ESCADRILLE, DETACHMENT

navel UMBILICUS, OMPHALOS

navigation by means of the stars and planets CELESTIAL NAVIGATION, ASTRONAVIGATION
- navigation by visual observation of beacons and landmarks CONTACT FLYING
- navigation technique of estimating one's position by one's speed and direction rather than by radio or observing the stars DEAD RECKONING
- instrument, used in navigation, for measuring the angles of stars and planets to determine the observer's position SEXTANT, ASTROLABE

navy See also **military, services, sail**
- recruit forcibly into the navy PRESS, PRESSGANG, CRIMP, IMPRESS, SHANGHAI

Nazi emblem, consisting of a cross with right-angled ends SWASTIKA
- Nazi Germany's annexation of Austria in 1938 ANSCHLUSS
- Nazi elite troopers SCHUTZSTAFFEL, SS
- Nazi storm troopers, the Brown Shirts STURMABTEILUNG, SA
- chief Nazi ideologist ALFRED ROSENBERG
- Hitler's title as Nazi leader of Germany DER FÜHRER
- person of a northern European gentile racial type, especially Nordic, in Nazi ideology ARYAN
- provincial governor in Nazi Germany GAULEITER
- secret police in Nazi Germany GESTAPO
- territory claimed by a nation, as by Nazi Germany, as being necessary for its well-being LEBENSRAUM

NCO's stripes, worn on the sleeve, indicating rank or length of service CHEVRON

near, touching, bordering, as two plots of land might be ABUTTING, ADJACENT, ADJOINING, CONTIGUOUS
- near, very like, approaching, almost equivalent to VERGING ON
- near enough to be heard WITHIN EARSHOT
- nearby area, local surroundings, neighborhood VICINITY, ENVIRONS, LOCALITY
- nearness in time or position PROPINQUITY, PROXIMITY
- in the near future, about to happen APPROACHING, IMMINENT, IMPENDING
- place things near or next to each other so as to invite comparison JUXTAPOSE
- place things near to each other or

side by side APPOSE
near (combining form) EPI-, PARA-, PERI-, PROS-, PROX-
nearly, practically, in essence but not in appearance VIRTUALLY
- nearly, roughly, more or less APPROXIMATELY, CIRCA
neat in dress or appearance TRIM, DAPPER, SPRUCE, WELL-GROOMED
necessary, inseparable, forming an essential part of the whole INTEGRAL, INTRINSIC, INHERENT
- necessary, required by law or demanded by custom COMPULSORY, STATUTORY, DE RIGUEUR, MANDATORY
- necessary as a duty, inescapable, binding INCUMBENT, OBLIGATORY, IMPERATIVE, IRREMISSIBLE
- necessary minimum of food, shelter, or the like to sustain life SUBSISTENCE
- necessary thing or condition, factor without which something cannot occur SINE QUA NON, PREREQUISITE
- absolutely necessary, vital, essential, impossible to leave out INDISPENSABLE
- be proper or necessary for BEHOVE
- existing or true or false by reason of chance or fact in the real world rather than by logical necessity CONTINGENT
- involve, have as a necessary consequence ENTAIL
neck See illustration at **mouth**
- neck or neck-shaped structure in the body, especially the lower part of the uterus CERVIX
- neck or spine injury caused by sudden jerking of the head, as in a car accident WHIPLASH
- back of the neck SCRUFF, NAPE, NUCHA
- bent abnormally, as the neck might be WRY
- chronic enlargement of the thyroid gland, causing a severely swollen neck, often resulting from iodine deficiency GOITER, STRUMA
- fold of skin hanging from the neck, as of some birds and lizards WATTLE
- frill or ruff of lace or linen formerly worn by women around the neck or shoulders TUCKER
- loose fold of skin at the neck, as in cattle or old people DEWLAP
- natural collar or ring of hair or feathers around the neck of a mammal or bird RUFF, RUFFLE
- referring to the neck or cervix CERVICAL
neckerchief, usually of brightly colored cotton BANDANNA
necklace or collar, typically of twisted metal, worn in ancient times TORQUE
- necklace or jeweled collar in former times CARCANET
- necklace with a medallion, piece of jewelry, or the like hanging freely on it PENDANT
- tight-fitting necklace or band worn around the neck CHOKER
neckline that is low and revealing, or a dress or blouse with such a neckline DÉCOLLETAGE
nectar - food of the gods in classical mythology, corresponding to their drink of nectar AMBROSIA
need - needed thing or necessary quality REQUISITE
- needs that are urgent or pressing EXIGENCIES
- in great danger, distress, or need IN EXTREMITY
- something wished for, needed, or desired DESIDERATUM
needle for pulling ribbon or cord through loops or a hem BODKIN
- needle or jewel in a record-player pickup for tracing the groove of a record STYLUS
- needle or syringe for injections beneath the skin HYPODERMIC
- needle-shaped, pointed ACERATE, ACEROSE, ACULEATE
- needle-shaped natural object or part, such as a crystal, quill, or bristle ACICULA, ACULEUS
- needle-shaped rock mass or mountain peak AIGUILLE
- moving arm that holds the needle of a record player TONE ARM
- small case for needles, cosmetics, or the like ETUI
needlework See also **embroidery, sewing**
- needlework frame in the form of two concentric wooden hoops between which the fabric is locked TAMBOUR
- decorative piece of needlework, often with pictures and mottoes SAMPLER
- make a piece of needlework by looping thread with a hooked needle CROCHET
- thread or loop joining sections of a lace or needlework pattern BRIDE, BAR
negligee, light and loose-fitting dressing gown for a woman PEIGNOIR
negotiate, discuss, or debate PARLEY
- negotiate or perform business TRANSACT
negotiation involving hard bargaining and shrewd compromises HORSE TRADING
- final terms offered in negotiating, to be accepted "or else" ULTIMATUM
neigh gently or quietly WHINNY, NICKER
neighborhood, nearby or surrounding area VICINITY, LOCALITY
- neighborhood with defined boundaries PRECINCTS, ENVIRONS
neon, helium, or other gaseous element formerly considered incapable of chemical reaction INERT GAS, NOBLE GAS, RARE GAS
Neptune's three-pronged spear TRIDENT
nerve See illustrations, pages 362 and 363
- nerve cell NEURON
- nerve ending that receives outside stimuli and converts them into nerve impulses RECEPTOR
- nerve ending that stimulates a muscle to contract or a gland to secrete EFFECTOR
- nerve that produces only coarse sensitivity to pain or heat PROTOPATHIC NERVE
- nerve that produces very fine sensitivity to temperature or pressure EPICRITIC NERVE
- first cranial nerve OLFACTORY NERVE
- second cranial nerve OPTIC NERVE
- third cranial nerve OCULOMOTOR NERVE
- fourth cranial nerve TROCHLEAR NERVE
- fifth cranial nerve TRIGEMINAL NERVE
- sixth cranial nerve ABDUCENS NERVE
- seventh cranial nerve FACIAL NERVE
- eighth cranial nerve STATOACOUSTIC NERVE
- ninth cranial nerve GLOSSOPHARYNGEAL NERVE
- tenth cranial nerve VAGUS NERVE
- eleventh cranial nerve ACCESSORY NERVE
- twelfth cranial nerve HYPOGLOSSAL NERVE
- bundle or cluster of fibers, especially nerve fibers FASCICLE, FASCICULUS, FUNICULUS
- group of nerve-cell bodies usually outside the brain and spinal cord GANGLION
- network of nerves and blood vessels PLEXUS
- referring to nerves directing impulses inward toward the brain or spinal cord AFFERENT
- referring to nerves directing impulses outward from the brain or spinal cord EFFERENT, DEFERENT
- referring to the nerves or nervous system NEURAL
- stalklike structure, as of nerve fibers PEDUNCLE
nerve (combining form) NEUR-, NEURO-
nervous, anxious, tense, in sus-

pense ON TENTERHOOKS
- nervous, or difficult to control SKITTISH
- nervous, on edge, agitated JITTERY, HIGH-STRUNG, FRETFUL
- nervous, very tense or strained, agitated or perturbed FRAUGHT, OVERWROUGHT
- nervous breakdown or nervous exhaustion NEURASTHENIA
- nervous disorder causing uncontrollable, irregular movements of the limbs and face CHOREA
- nervous or emotional disorder, revealed in phobias, obsessions, or the like, that induces anxiety and is mildly disabling NEUROSIS
- nervous twitch or spasm, especially in the face TIC

nervous system See illustration
- nervous system consisting of the brain and spinal cord CENTRAL NERVOUS SYSTEM
- nervous system excluding the brain and spinal cord PERIPHERAL NERVOUS SYSTEM
- division of the nervous system that regulates involuntary processes AUTONOMIC NERVOUS SYSTEM, VEGETATIVE NERVOUS SYSTEM
- subdivision of the nervous system that serves to slow down the heartbeat, dilate the blood vessels, and stimulate secretions PARASYMPATHETIC NERVOUS SYSTEM
- subdivision of the nervous system that serves to speed up the heartbeat, contract the blood vessels, and slow down secretions SYMPATHETIC NERVOUS SYSTEM

nervousness, anxiety, uneasiness HEEBIE-JEEBIES, JITTERS, WILLIES
- nervousness, or a stomach upset resulting from it COLLYWOBBLES
- substance that supposedly produces a surge of excitement, nervousness, or power EPINEPHRINE, ADRENALINE

-ness (combining form) -TUDE

nest, especially for insect or spider eggs NIDUS
- nest building NIDIFICATION
- nest of a bird of prey, built on a cliff or other high place EYRIE, AERIE
- referring to birds born blind and helpless, and requiring lengthy care in the nest NIDICOLOUS
- referring to birds born fairly well-developed, and able to leave the nest fairly soon NIDIFUGOUS

net in which caught fish are kept alive in the water KEEP NET
- net of three layers for catching birds or fish TRAMMEL
- net or network MESH
- netlike in structure, as some bones and the vein patterns of some leaves are CANCELLATE
- netlike, resembling a network or web RETICULAR, RETICULATE, RETIFORM
- catch or tangle in or as if in a net ENMESH
- large, sheetlike fishing net hanging upright in the water SEINE
- small cap or pouch, typically of netting, holding a woman's hair in place at the back SNOOD
- Roman gladiator armed with a net and trident RETIARIUS
- small space, opening, or gap, as between the strands of a net INTERSTICE

nettles - former medical treatment involving lashing with nettles URTICATION

network, context, or environment in which something develops MATRIX
- network, interwoven complex of parts PLEXUS, NEXUS
- network of lines or fine wires, as on a lens, for measuring or locating objects under observation RETICLE, RETICULE, GRATICULE
- network of lines used as a reference grid in photography and measuring stars RESEAU

neutral, specifically not allied with a superpower NONALIGNED
- neutral, applying to both genders EPICENE
- neutral mediator in a dispute GO-BETWEEN, ARBITRATOR, INTERMEDIARY, HONEST BROKER, OMBUDSMAN
- right of a nation at war to use or destroy the property of a neutral nation on condition that full compensation is paid ANGARY

Nerve Cell

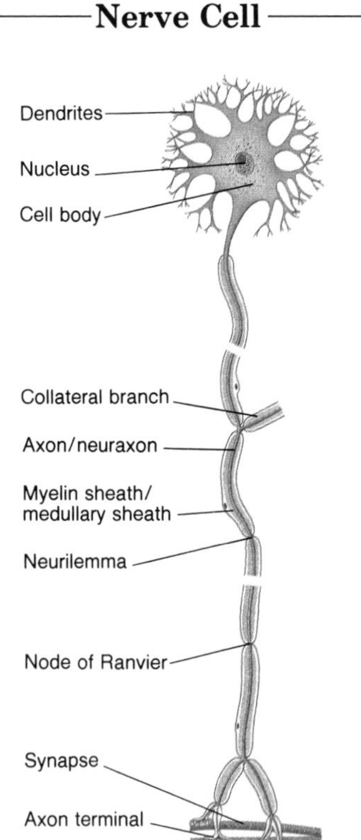

new See also **modern**
- new NOVEL, VERNAL
- new, modern NEOTERIC
- new wine MUST
- newly coined word or expression NEOLOGISM
- newness or something new INNOVATION
- fresh, clean, pure, or perfectly restored, as if brand-new PRISTINE

new (combining form) ANA-, NEO-

New Orleans - carnival in New Orleans celebrating the last day before Lent MARDI GRAS

New Testament event or person supposedly foreshadowed or symbolized by a counterpart in the Old Testament ANTITYPE

New York stock-exchange price index DOW JONES AVERAGE
- New York's banking and financial center, including the Stock Exchange WALL STREET
- names for New York THE BIG APPLE, NEW AMSTERDAM, NEW ORANGE, VANDERHEYDEN'S FERRY, THE GOLDEN DOOR

New Zealand See also chart at **Maori**
- New Zealander of European rather than Maori descent PAKEHA
- coniferous New Zealand tree, cultivated for its wood and resin KAURI
- edible New Zealand shellfish, with a shiny greenish shell like mother-of-pearl, used for ornaments and jewelry PAUA
- extinct large flightless New Zealand bird MOA
- flightless New Zealand bird, also nickname for a New Zealander KIWI
- Maori name for New Zealand AOTEAROA
- rare flightless New Zealand bird NOTORNIS
- small New Zealand tree, valued for its timber NGAIO

newborn child NEONATE

newcomer, inexperienced person, as in the armed forces ROOKIE
- newcomer, novice, beginner NEOPHYTE, TYRO
- newcomer who is typically fumbling and inexperienced TENDERFOOT, GREENHORN, FLEDGLING
- newcomer to wealth or social sta-

tus, Johnny-come-lately UPSTART, PARVENU, NOUVEAU RICHE

news, information INTELLIGENCE, TIDINGS
- news item or story reported at first by only one journalist, newspaper, or the like SCOOP, EXCLUSIVE
- news report or rumor that is false or a deliberate hoax CANARD
- news reporter, typically covering the local news in a specific area, working on a part-time basis STRINGER
- newsworthy and of current interest TOPICAL
- spread gradually, as warmth or news might PERMEATE, DIFFUSE, PERCOLATE
- spread something widely, such as news or knowledge DISSEMINATE, DISPERSE, PROMULGATE

newspaper archives MORGUE
- newspaper of large format, with large wide pages BROADSIDE
- newspaper headline running right across a page BANNER, BANNER HEADLINE, STREAMER
- newspaper of small format, typically having a high proportion of photographs and sensational news reports TABLOID
- newspaper or magazine published in the past, and no longer the current issue BACK NUMBER
- newspapers of a cheap and sensationalizing kind YELLOW PRESS, GUTTER PRESS
- agency selling cartoons, articles, and the like for simultaneous publication in numerous newspapers or magazines SYNDICATE
- column or space in a newspaper for last-minute reports FUDGE, STOP-PRESS
- continuous roll of paper, especially newsprint, for use in a rotary printing press WEB
- number of copies distributed or sold of a newspaper or magazine CIRCULATION
- panel at the top of the front page of a newspaper or magazine, bearing its name, logo, and so on MASTHEAD, FLAG
- report sent over a distance, as by a newspaper correspondent DISPATCH
- small display box, typically for advertisements, in an upper corner of the front page of a newspaper EAR
- small stall, as for selling newspapers KIOSK

newt See illustration, page 364

next to, alongside, side by side ADJACENT, ADJOINING, CONTIGUOUS, JUXTAPOSED, TANGENTIAL, ABUTTING

next to (combining form) EPI-

ng - symbol /ŋ/ used in phonetics to represent the /ng/ sound, as in *long* ENG, AGMA

nice See **friendly, good, fussy**

nickname AGNOMEN
- nickname or assumed name SOBRIQUET
- nickname or descriptive term forming part of a person's name or title EPITHET, COGNOMEN
- nickname or personal name MONIKER
- give a title, name, or nickname to DESIGNATE, NOMINATE, STYLE, DUB

Nietzsche - rational, orderly, and sober, as one side of human nature is, in Nietzsche's terminology APOLLONIAN
- spontaneous, irrational, passionate, and creative, as one side of human nature is, in Nietzsche's terminology DIONYSIAN

night blindness, weak vision in dim light NYCTALOPIA
- either of the two times during the year when day and night are of equal length all over the earth EQUINOX
- official regulation requiring citi-

Nervous System

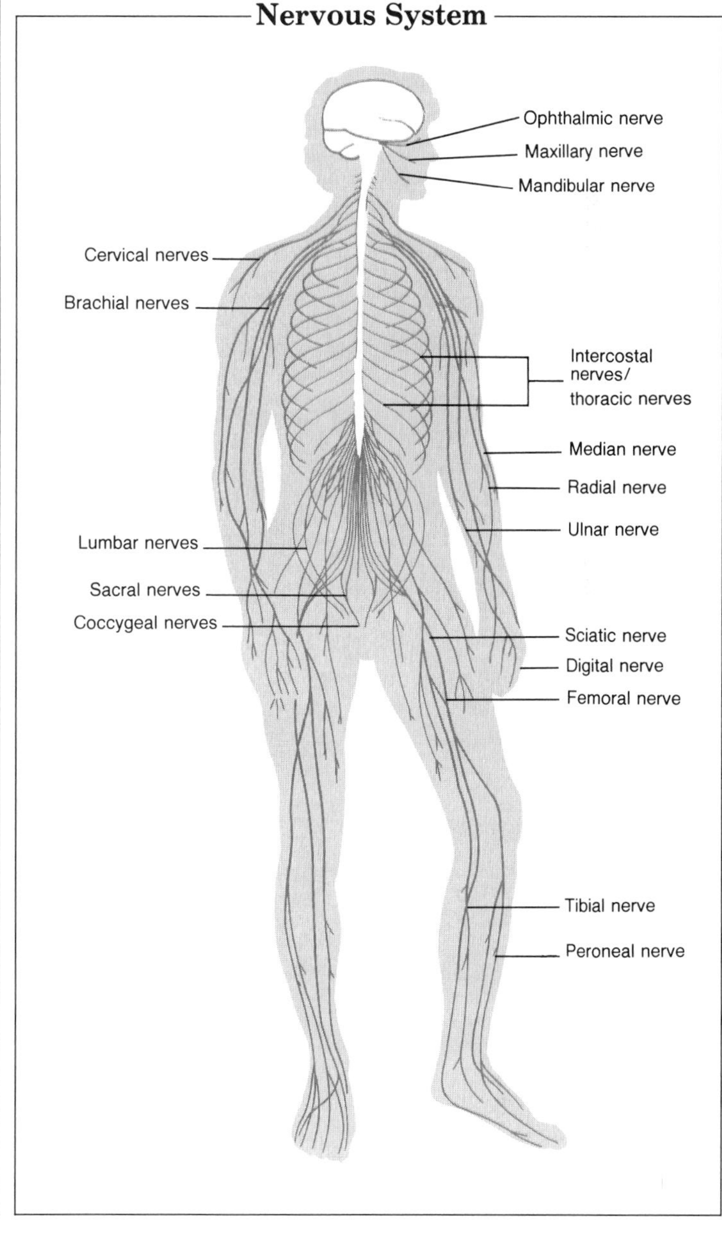

zens to go home or be indoors by a certain hour of night CURFEW
- painting of a night scene or short lyrical composition, especially for the piano, suggestive of or suitable for the night NOCTURNE
- referring to the night NOCTURNAL

night (combining form) NOCT-, NOCTI-, NYCT-, NYCTI-, NYCTO-

nightclub - female singer, as in a nightclub or cabaret CHANTEUSE

nightdress - light, loose-fitting gown, resembling a nightdress, for a woman NEGLIGEE, PEIGNOIR
- nightdress, underwear, and so on for women LINGERIE

nightingale or similar songbird, mentioned in Persian poetry BULBUL
- poetic name for the nightingale PHILOMEL

nightmare or obsessive worry INCUBUS
- nightmarish, disturbingly weird, surreal KAFKAESQUE

Nile houseboat DAHABEAH
- irrigation device, as along the Nile, consisting of a bucket on a pivoted pole SHADOOF

nimble, agile DEXTEROUS, LITHE
- nimble, unpredictable, or changing constantly QUICKSILVER, MERCURIAL

nine (combining form) NONA-

nine-day devotion undertaken by Roman Catholics NOVENA

ninety-degree- (combining form) QUADR-, QUADRI-, QUADRU-

ninety-year-old, or a person aged between 90 and 99 NONAGENARIAN

ninth (combining form) NONA-

nipple or nipple-shaped projection MAMILLA
- nipple or teat PAP
- darkish area, on a breast, surrounding the nipple AREOLA
- small round patches covering the nipples on a striptease artist's breast PASTIES

nitpicking, hairsplitting, needless arguing or drawing of distinctions QUIBBLING, SOPHISTRY, PEDANTRY, SCHOLASTICISM, CASUISTRY
- nitpickingly critical, faultfinding CARPING, CAPTIOUS, CAVILING

nitrogen - conversion of nitrogen in the air into a fertilizer or other compound FIXATION, NITROGEN FIXATION
- relating to or containing nitrogen AZOTIC

Noah - relating to Noah or his time, as the seven pre-Mosaic commandments are NOACHIAN

Nobel prize winner, poet, or other eminent person in the arts or sciences who receives a special honor LAUREATE

nobility See chart, and also **ruler**

noble, held in great honor and esteem VENERATED
- noble, majestic, of great spiritual, intellectual, or moral worth SUBLIME
- noble action or gesture, sometimes empty in effect BEAU GESTE
- noble in character, as an ideal or ambition might be EXALTED, ELEVATED, LOFTY
- noble in quality, unstinted, worthy, as someone's assistance or efforts might be STERLING
- noble in spirit, generous and forgiving MAGNANIMOUS
- noble-looking or high-ranking person MAGNIFICO, GRANDEE
- noble or dignified in appearance DISTINGUÉ, MAJESTIC, STATELY
- noble or gallant man GALAHAD

nobleman See chart, and also **ruler**
- nobleman, or person from an old and distinguished family PATRICIAN
- office, status, or dignity of a judge, king, or nobleman ERMINE
- person who is not a nobleman or noblewoman, ordinary person COMMONER

noise See also **sound**
- noise across a wide range of frequencies, able to block out other sounds WHITE NOISE
- continual, confused noise or racket, such as a babble of voices or series of cries CLAMOR, HUBBUB
- gradual decrease in the volume of a noise or passage of music DECRESCENDO, DIMINUENDO
- gradual increase in the volume of a noise or passage of music CRESCENDO
- harsh creaking or wheezing noise caused by diseased lungs CREPITATION
- harsh whistling or wheezing noise, as caused by congested breathing passages STRIDOR, RHONCHUS
- hold back, cut off, or muffle a scream, noise, or the like STIFLE
- jarring, ugly, unharmonious noise CACOPHONY, DISCORDANCE, DISCORD, DISSONANCE
- light, tinkling noise, as of keys or small bells JANGLE, TINTINNABULATION
- loud, repeated, clanging noise CLANGOR
- loud, resounding, echoing noise REVERBERATION
- make a great noise, cause trouble or an uproar RAISE CAIN
- murmuring noise, rustling, as of light wind through trees SOUGH, SUSURRATION
- murmuring noise of rippling water PURL
- resounding harmoniously and richly as a noise might RESONANT, SONOROUS
- rustling noise, as of silk FROUFROU
- shrill and clear, as a noise or call might be CLARION
- shrill, chirping noise, especially that of crickets STRIDULATION
- slapping noise SKELP
- wailing or lamenting noise KEEN-

Newt

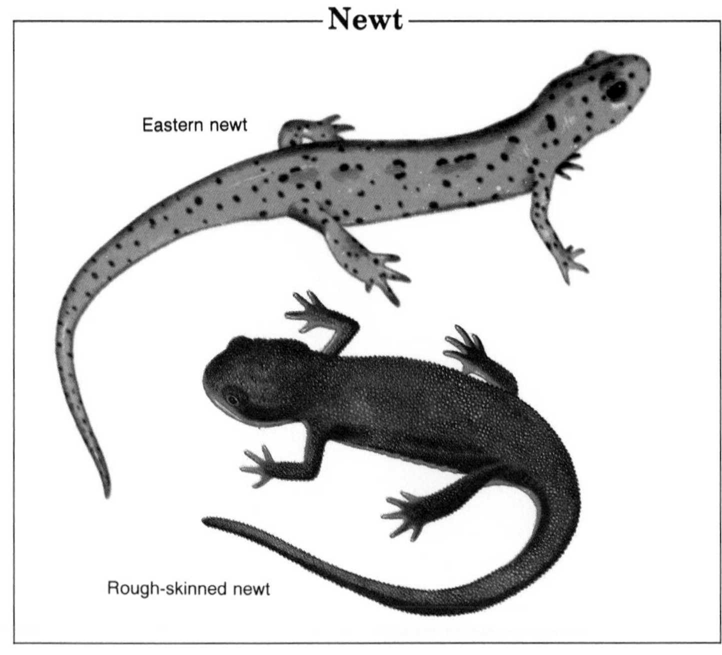

NOBILITY

aetheling/ atheling	Anglo-Saxon nobleman or prince
banneret	knight who led men into battle
boyar/boyard	Russian aristocrat
burgrave	hereditary lord of medieval Germany
chevalier	knight of a French order
daimyo	noble of feudal Japan
dauphin	eldest son of the French king
ealdorman/ alderman	Anglo-Saxon noble, or chief officer of a shire
elector	German prince who took part in the election of the Holy Roman Emperor
eupatrid	noble of ancient Athens
gaekwar	prince of former Indian state of Baroda
graf	German, Austrian, or Swedish count
gräfin	German, Austrian, or Swedish countess
grandee	Spanish or Portuguese nobleman
hidalgo	Spanish nobleman of minor rank
landgrave	medieval German count
marchioness/ marquise	wife of a marquis

ING, ULULATION

noisy and disorderly crowd TUMULT
- noisy and harsh-sounding, grating or blaring JARRING, RAUCOUS, DISCORDANT
- noisy and insistent, as in protest VOCIFEROUS, STRIDENT, CLAMOROUS, BLUSTERING
- noisy and lively in an excited or unruly way RUMBUSTIOUS, BOISTEROUS
- noisy and very enthusiastic, as applause might be TUMULTUOUS
- noisy confusion or upheaval, rowdy stir COMMOTION, FURORE, HULLABALOO, BROUHAHA
- noisy disturbance, uproar, din RUCKUS, RUCTION, RUMPUS
- noisy laughter CACHINNATION
- noisy merrymaking or celebration ROISTERING, REVELRY
- noisy mock serenade to a newlywed couple CHARIVARI
- noisy or showy display, designed to impress or advertise RAZZLE-DAZZLE, RAZZMATAZZ
- noisy place, scene of uproar and disorder BEAR GARDEN, BEDLAM, BABEL
- referring to a very loud or very noisy voice STENTORIAN
- scene of noisy or riotous confusion, utter chaos BEDLAM, PANDEMONIUM, MAYHEM, HAVOC
- screech noisily, especially in argument CATERWAUL

nominal but not real, as a figurehead ruler might be TITULAR

nonbeliever or doubter AGNOSTIC, ATHEIST
- nonbeliever or believer in the wrong religion HEATHEN, PAGAN, INFIDEL, GENTILE, GOY

noncommittal, timid, or cautious behavior PUSSYFOOTING

nondrinker, person who avoids alcohol TEETOTALER, ABSTAINER
- nondrinking, abstaining from alcohol TEMPERATE, ABSTINENT

nonexistence See **nothing**

nonhuman, without human understanding, as a block of wood is INSENSATE, INSENSIBLE

noninterference by governments in commercial activity, free trade LAISSEZ-FAIRE

nonmilitary CIVILIAN

nonprofessional people, those outside a particular profession LAYMEN, LAYWOMEN, LAY PEOPLE

nonreligious in form or content PROFANE, SECULAR

nonsense, foolish speech or writing, rubbish MOONSHINE, TRIPE, BALDERDASH, DRIVEL, POPPYCOCK
- nonsense, stupid or untruthful speech or writing BOSH, BALONEY, BILGE, BUNKUM, FANDANGLE
- nonsense verse, or a nonsense poem or story AMPHIGORY
- confused or nonsensical speech GIBBERISH, GALIMATIAS, JABBERWOCKY
- high-sounding but obscure official language, bureaucratic nonsense or empty jargon GOBBLEDYGOOK, HOCUS-POCUS, MUMBO JUMBO
- insincere, foolish, or empty and long-winded talk, nonsense, waffle CLAPTRAP, HOKUM, FLUMMERY, FLIMFLAM, HUMBUG, MALARKEY, RIGMAROLE, BUNK
- trifling, time-wasting talk or activity, nonsense FIDDLE-FADDLE, FOOTLE, FOLDEROL, TRUMPERY

nonstick - trademark for a nonstick plastic coating material, as used to line frying pans TEFLON

nonviolent opposition, as by fasting and noncooperation, to a law, policy, colonial authority, or the like PASSIVE RESISTANCE
- nonviolent resistance and a refusal to obey laws regarded as unjust, undertaken as a form of political protest, and willingness to bear the legal consequences CIVIL DISOBEDIENCE
- nonviolent resistance, as initiated by Gandhi in India, to press for political reform SATYAGRAHA
- code of nonviolence based on reverence for all living things, as practised in Buddhism and Hinduism AHIMSA

noodles See **pasta**

noon - in the morning, before noon ANTEMERIDIAN
- in the afternoon POSTMERIDIAN

norm or commonest item in a numerical list MODE
- differ or depart from the norm or standard, as of a policy, a route, or one's behavior DEVIATE

normal See also **regular, mediocre**
- normal, standard, traditional CONVENTIONAL, ORTHODOX
- normal, usual, in keeping with custom or current fashion ESTABLISHED, PREVAILING, WONTED
- normal practice or accepted custom, especially when having legal force CONSUETUDE
- abiding strictly by what is normal or accepted CONFORMIST, ACCORDING TO HOYLE

normal (combining form) ORTHO-

Norse bard or minstrel in ancient times SKALD

north - "northern lights", seen flashing in the night sky, especial-

ly near the North Pole AURORA BOREALIS
- Northerner who went to the South after the American Civil War to make a living or to profiteer CARPETBAGGER
- northernmost inhabited land, according to ancient geographers THULE, ULTIMA THULE
- adjective for the north, especially relating to the north wind BOREAL
- of or in the far north, arctic HYPERBOREAN

Norwegian herring, typically canned like sardines SILD
- Norwegian sea inlet that is long, deep, and narrow FJORD

nose See illustration at **mouth**
- nose that is short and slightly turned-up or flattened at the tip SNUB NOSE, PUG NOSE
- nose that turns up slightly at the tip RETROUSSÉ NOSE
- nose with a high, conspicuous, slightly convex bridge ROMAN NOSE
- adjective for the nose NASAL, RHINAL
- blockage of the nose through accumulation of mucus CONGESTION
- bulging and swollen-looking, as a large nose might be BULBOUS
- curved or hooked, resembling an eagle's beak, as a nose might be AQUILINE
- derisive gesture made by thumbing the nose SNOOK
- growth on or under a mucous membrane, as in the nose POLYP
- humorous or slang term for a person's nose, especially a prominent nose PROBOSCIS, SCHNOZZLE
- long, straight nose extending as if in continuation of the line of the forehead GRECIAN NOSE
- relieving congestion, especially in the nose DECONGESTANT

nose (combining form) RHIN-, RHINO-, NAS-, NASO-

nostrils NARES
- air-filled cavity in the skull, leading to a nostril SINUS
- membrane, partition, or division separating tissues or cavities, as between the nostrils SEPTUM

nosy, prying, curious INQUISITIVE

not, *non-*, or similar word or word element indicating the absence or opposite of something positive or real NEGATIVE

not (combining form) NON-, A-, AN-, DIS-, MAL-, UN-

not-guilty verdict ACQUITTAL

notch See also **groove**
- notch or groove, as in a piece of wood CHAMFER, CHASE
- notch or groove, especially around a bullet CANNELURE
- notch or groove made in wood by chopping or sawing KERF
- notch or groove, or a series of them INDENTATION
- notch or groove that houses an inserted part in a joint or hinge MORTISE, GAIN, RABBET
- notch or ridge linking two planks, shafts, or the like SPLINE
- notched or indented like a castle's battlements, as a cliff top might be CASTELLATED
- notched stick formerly used for keeping accounts or records TALLY
- notches or ridges around the edge of a coin MILLING, FLUTING
- notches or teeth in a series, as on a saw or the edge of a leaf SERRATION
- square notches or indentations, as on a molding CRENELLATIONS
- strip or wedge of wood fitting into a notch or groove to make a joint FEATHER, TENON

note, as to a colleague in an organization MEMORANDUM, MINUTE
- note of critical commentary or explanation on a literary text ANNOTATION, GLOSS
- notes or comments written in the margin of a book MARGINALIA
- note or list in detail PARTICULARIZE, ENUMERATE, ITEMIZE, SPECIFY
- note or reference in a text, placed at the end of the text or at the foot of the page FOOTNOTE
- note serving as a reminder MEMORANDUM, AIDE-MÉMOIRE

notebook containing quotations, comments, poems, and the like that strike one as worth recording COMMONPLACE BOOK

nothing, zero ZILCH, NADA, NIL, NIX, RIEN, NICHTS
- nothingness, nonexistence INEXISTENCE, EXISTENCELESSNESS, UNACTUALITY, NONENTITY, NULLITY, NIHILITY, NIHIL, THE NOTHING, DAS NICHTS, LE NÉANT
- person or thing worth nothing NONENTITY, CIPHER

notice, acknowledge, take official note of TAKE COGNIZANCE OF

noticeable, observable, apparent DISCERNIBLE, EVIDENT, MANIFEST, EXPLICIT
- noticeable, possible to feel or distinguish as a difference might be APPRECIABLE, PALPABLE
- noticeable, striking, very marked PROMINENT, CONSPICUOUS, PRONOUNCED
- very noticeable, unmistakable, as an error might be GLARING, PATENT

noun, pronoun, or word or phrase functioning as a noun SUBSTANTIVE
- noun, such as *Jane*, that refers to a particular or unique person or thing PROPER NOUN, PROPER NAME
- noun, such as *leg*, that can refer to any member of a class rather than to a particular or unique person or thing COMMON NOUN
- noun, such as *love*, referring to an idea or quality rather than to a material object ABSTRACT NOUN
- noun, such as *metal*, referring to a material object rather than to an idea or quality CONCRETE NOUN
- noun, such as *milk* (and unlike *pebble*) that cannot normally be used in the plural MASS NOUN, NONCOUNTABLE NOUN
- noun, such as *pebble* (and unlike *milk*) that can easily be used in the plural COUNTABLE NOUN
- case of a noun expressing direction from or cause, as in Latin ABLATIVE
- case of a noun expressing possession, measurement, or source, as in Latin GENITIVE
- case of a noun that is the direct object of a verb or preposition ACCUSATIVE
- case of a noun that is the indirect object of a verb, as in Latin DATIVE
- case of a noun that is the subject of a verb, as in Latin NOMINATIVE
- case of a noun used in addressing a person or thing, as in Latin VOCATIVE
- change of the form of a noun, pronoun, or adjective to indicate gender, number, or case DECLENSION
- referring to a noun NOMINAL
- referring to a noun, such as *baby* or *doctor* that can apply to either a male or a female person or animal EPICENE
- relationship of two nouns or noun phrases set side by side, the one explaining or identifying the other, as in *Socrates, the philosopher, said so* APPOSITION
- use of a name or proper noun, such as *an Einstein*, in place of an idea or common noun ANTONOMASIA
- verb form, ending in *-ing* in English, that can be used as a noun GERUND

nourishing or supporting ALIMENTARY
- nourishing substance, as in food or in the solution absorbed by plant roots NUTRIENT
- process of nourishing or being nourished NUTRITION
- nourishment, food, something that sustains life or promotes growth NURTURE, NUTRIMENT, SUSTENANCE

novel See also **new**
- novel, movie, or the like that continues the story and character development of the previous one

SEQUEL
- novel, movie, or the like that deals with earlier events than those related in the previous one PREQUEL
- novel dealing with the early development and education of a central character BILDUNGSROMAN
- novel depicting real people under fictional names ROMAN À CLEF
- novel in the form of a series of letters EPISTOLARY NOVEL
- novel of a loose, episodic structure dealing with the travels or adventures of a rogue-hero PICARESQUE NOVEL
- novel or series of novels relating the history of a person, family, or community ROMAN-FLEUVE, SAGA NOVEL
- additional section at the end of a novel, piece of music, or the like CODA
- afterword or postscript, such as an additional chapter at the end of a novel outlining the future of the characters EPILOGUE
- introductory chapter at the beginning of a novel PROLOGUE
- passage of conversation in a play, novel, or the like, or the words spoken DIALOGUE
- scene or passage in a novel, movie, or the like that interrupts the main story line to revert to past events FLASHBACK

novice, beginner NEOPHYTE, TYRO
- novice, fumbling or inexperienced newcomer GREENHORN, TENDERFOOT, FLEDGLING
- novice, especially in sports and the armed forces ROOKIE

nuclear bomb's explosive power equivalent to one million tons of TNT MEGATON
- nuclear reaction in which heavy atomic nuclei are split FISSION
- nuclear reaction in which light atomic nuclei combine to form a heavy nucleus FUSION
- nuclear reactor PILE
- nuclear reactor for changing one type of fuel to another CONVERTER REACTOR
- nuclear reactor producing more radioactive nuclear fuel than it consumes BREEDER REACTOR
- nuclear weapons or other arms or defense policy designed to discourage enemy attack DETERRENT
- energy released in a nuclear explosion, expressed in terms of weight of TNT YIELD
- great destruction, as might be caused by nuclear war HOLOCAUST
- heavy water, graphite, or the like in a nuclear reactor's core, used to slow down neutrons and promote fission MODERATOR
- overheating and melting of a nuclear reactor's core MELTDOWN
- person reverting to primitive living in open country to escape the effects of an expected nuclear war SURVIVALIST
- point on the ground at, above, or under the center of a nuclear explosion GROUND ZERO
- radioactive chemical elements used as nuclear fuels and in nuclear weapons URANIUM, PLUTONIUM
- referring to nonnuclear warfare or weapons CONVENTIONAL
- referring to nuclear arms supply greater than required for victory OVERKILL
- round cloud of hot gas and dust generated by a nuclear explosion MUSHROOM, FIREBALL
- treaty restricting the production or deployment of nuclear weapons NONPROLIFERATION TREATY

nuclear accelerator (combining form) -TRON

nucleus (combining form) KARY-, KARYO-, COR-

nudism NATURISM

nuisance or very burdensome task IMPOSITION

numb (combining form) NARCO-

number See chart, and also **mathematics**
- number, numeral CIPHER
- number, such as *third* or *tenth*, indicating position in a sequence ORDINAL NUMBER
- number, such as *three* or *ten*, indicating quantity rather than the position in a sequence CARDINAL NUMBER
- number assigned to a library book to classify and locate it CALL NUMBER
- number needed to make up a whole COMPLEMENT

NUMBERS

LARGE NUMBERS	
million	one thousand thousand, 1 followed by 6 zeros
billion	one thousand million, 1 followed by 9 zeros
trillion	1 followed by 12 zeros
quadrillion	1 followed by 15 zeros
quintillion	1 followed by 18 zeros
sextillion	1 followed by 21 zeros
septillion	1 followed by 24 zeros
octillion	1 followed by 27 zeros
nonillion	1 followed by 30 zeros
decillion	1 followed by 33 zeros
centillion	1 followed by 303 zeros
googol	1 followed by 100 zeros

PREFIXES FOR METRIC UNITS	
exa-	one quintillion
peta-	one quadrillion
tera-	one trillion
giga-	one billion
mega-	one million
kilo-	one thousand
hecto-	one hundred
deca-	ten
deci-	one tenth
centi-	one hundredth
milli-	one thousandth
micro-	one millionth
nano-	one billionth
pico-	one trillionth
femto-	one quadrillionth
atto-	one quintillionth (one million million millionth)

(In other, e.g., British, usage, 1 billion has 12 zeros; 1 trillion, 18 zeros... etc.; 1 decillion, 60 zeros; 1 centillion, 600 zeros ...)

- number or letter printed at the foot of some pages in a book (typically every sixteenth page), specifying the sequence for binding the sections SIGNATURE
- number or letter written or printed slightly above another, as in ab^2 SUPERSCRIPT, SUPERIOR
- number or letter written or printed slightly below another, as in H_2O SUBSCRIPT
- number or quantity by which another is divided DIVISOR
- number or quantity from which another is subtracted MINUEND
- number or quantity into which another is divided DIVIDEND
- number or quantity that divides exactly into another FACTOR
- number or quantity that is added to others in a sum ADDEND
- number or quantity that is subtracted from another in a sum SUBTRAHEND
- number system using base 10, the Arabic or decimal system ALGORISM
- number system using only the digits 0 and 1 BINARY SYSTEM, BINARY NOTATION
- number that occurs most often in a numerical list MODE
- numerical procedure for solving a problem in finite steps ALGORITHM
- adjective for a number or numbers NUMERICAL
- act or system of numbering or counting NUMERATION, RECKONING, TALLYING
- amount obtained as a result of adding numbers together SUM, SUM TOTAL
- any written number between 0 and 9 DIGIT, FIGURE
- based on the number 10, as a fraction, number system, or currency might be DECIMAL
- limited or specified quantity or number, as of imports, members of a group, or the like QUOTA
- real number in the form of a whole number or fraction RATIONAL NUMBER
- referring to a number that divides exactly into a larger number ALIQUOT
- relationship between two numbers or quantities RATIO, PROPORTION
- square layout of numbers in which any row produces the same sum MAGIC SQUARE
- study of the alleged mystical influence or significance of numbers NUMEROLOGY
- very large but indefinite number MYRIAD, MULTITUDE
- whole number or zero INTEGER

numerous See **lots, many, plenty, excessive**

nun of a Roman Catholic teaching order URSULINE
- nun of an austere order, the counterpart of the White Friars CARMELITE
- nun of high rank ABBESS, PRIORESS
- nun or monk VOTARY
- nun or monk holding an office just subordinate to the superior OBEDIENTIARY
- become a nun TAKE THE VEIL
- candidate monk or nun POSTULANT, NOVICE, NEOPHYTE
- dress worn by a nun HABIT
- headdress framing the face, as worn by some nuns WIMPLE
- large white headdress worn by some nuns CORNET
- starched cloth, part of a nun's habit, covering the neck and shoulders GUIMPE
- sum of money paid by a woman when joining certain orders of nuns DOWRY
- woman member of a convent or religious community bound by a rule, but not by vows as a nun is CANONESS

nursemaid, nanny, or maidservant in India AYAH
- nursemaid, nanny, or wet nurse in the East AMAH

nursery for babies or very young children, day-care center CRÈCHE
- nursery school in Europe, preschool in the United States KINDERGARTEN

nut from an evergreen Australian tree, with a tasty round oily kernel MACADAMIA NUT
- nut with a kernel similar to that of the walnut PECAN
- nut with a closed end, capping a bolt LUG
- nutlike seed of an Indian palm, used in a popular chewing mixture in southeastern Asia BETEL NUT
- hazelnut FILBERT
- Mexican nut yielding a valuable liquid wax, as used in shampoos JOJOBA NUT
- North American nut, related to the walnut, with a sweetish kernel HICKORY NUT
- small Asian nut with a tasty greenish kernel PISTACHIO NUT

nutrition, nourishment, development (combining form) TROPH-, TROPHO-, -TROPHIC, -TROPHY

nymph inhabiting a tree, in classical mythology HAMADRYAD
- nymph of rivers or lakes, in classical mythology NAIAD
- nymph of the mountains, in classical mythology OREAD
- nymph of the sea, in classical mythology NEREID
- nymph of the woods or trees, in classical mythology DRYAD
- nymph or virgin in paradise, according to Islamic belief or folklore HOURI

O

oar - blade of an oar or paddle PALM
- looped rope, strap, or the like, as for holding an oar or sliding rope in position BECKET
- peg, pin, or short rod, as for supporting an oar in the side of a boat THOLE
- swiveling support for an oar on the side of a boat OARLOCK
- turn an oar horizontal between strokes in rowing FEATHER

oasis - illusion or image of a nonpresent object, such as an oasis MIRAGE

oath formerly taken by graduating doctors, undertaking to observe professional ethics HIPPOCRATIC OATH
- oath of loyalty by a vassal to his feudal lord HOMAGE, FEALTY
- declaration in writing that is made under oath AFFIDAVIT
- declare under oath, as in a court of law TESTIFY
- formal declaration and undertaking to tell the truth, as in court, in place of an oath AFFIRMATION
- person who makes an affidavit or testifies in writing under oath DEPONENT
- public official authorized to administer oaths, certify documents, and the like NOTARY PUBLIC, NOTARY
- testimony given on oath DEPOSITION
- trial in former times where the accused and 11 neighbors offered to swear to his or her innocence under oath WAGER OF LAW

obedience or cooperation of a token or insincere kind LIP SERVICE
- demand and obtain obedience, vengeance, or the like EXACT
- show obedience RENDER

obedient, easily controlled, governable BIDDABLE, TRACTABLE, CONFORMABLE
- obedient, easily influenced or manipulated, unresistingly submissive PLIABLE, MALLEABLE
- obedient, submissive, or eager to please in a fawning way SERVILE, SYCOPHANTIC, OBSEQUIOUS, UNCTUOUS
- obedient, unquestioningly submissive, even to oppressive or unreasonable demands and rules DOCILE, ACQUIESCENT, MASOCHISTIC
- obedient, willing to listen and follow advice, open to suggestion AMENABLE
- obedient, yielding, submitting to rules or orders easily COMPLIANT
- obedient or submissive in a respectful or humble way OBEISANT, DEFERENTIAL

obey a rule or order, carry out someone's wish or demand, or the like COMPLY WITH
- obey someone's wishes so as to keep the peace HUMOR, INDULGE, ACQUIESCE IN, DEFER TO
- obey the regulations, respect or observe the conventions, or the like ABIDE BY, ADHERE TO
- obey the rules, toe the line CONFORM
- obey too readily, flatter, humble oneself, or the like, so as to curry favor FAWN, TRUCKLE, KOWTOW
- person who obeys and obliges too readily, groveler BOOTLICKER, APPLE-POLISHER, LICKSPITTLE
- person who obeys unquestioningly, such as a self-humbling follower of a patron FLUNKY, LACKY, MINION

obituary NECROLOGY
- obituary speech or composition commemorating a dead person EPITAPH

object believed to have magical powers FETISH, JUJU, RELIC, TALISMAN, LUCKY PIECE
- object grasped by the intellect or intuition rather than as perceived by the senses, thing-in-itself NOUMENON
- object perceived by or apparently real to the senses, rather than known through reasoning or intuition PHENOMENON

objection See also **complain, protest**
- objection, disagreement, refusal to comply or conform DISSENT, DISSIDENCE
- objection, especially to the relevance of an argument raised in court DEMURRER
- objection, hesitation, or misgiving, as based on doubt or conscience QUALM, SCRUPLE
- objection or criticism EXCEPTION
- objection that is trifling and petty CAVIL, QUIBBLE
- confirm as valid or just, uphold something, such as an objection SUSTAIN

objective, unbiased IMPARTIAL, DISINTERESTED
- objective and emotionally detached DISPASSIONATE
- objective or lifelike in its representation, as a painting might be REALISTIC

obligation, debt LIABILITY
- obligation on noble or noble-minded people to be generous and honorable NOBLESSE OBLIGE

oblong or square figure QUADRILATERAL, TETRAGON

obscene or sexually arousing movies, writings, photographs, or the like PORNOGRAPHY
- obscene, coarse sexual language BAWDRY

obscenity - obsessive interest in obscenity, especially in relation to excrement SCATOLOGY

obscure, as with fog or clouds OBNUBILATE
- obscure, confuse, complicate OBFUSCATE
- obscure, known only to experts and connoisseurs ARCANE, RECHERCHÉ, ESOTERIC
- obscure or ambiguous, as though spoken by an oracle DELPHIC

observable by scientific methods or by disinterested outsiders OBJECTIVE
- readily observable, open for all to see, aboveboard OVERT

observant and alert VIGILANT, ARGUS-EYED

observation See also **remark**
- observation or close watch, especially on someone or something suspicious SURVEILLANCE
- observation point that allows a particularly good view COIGN OF VANTAGE, RINGSIDE SEAT, CATBIRD SEAT
- based on or relating to observation or experiment rather than pure theory EMPIRICAL

observation (combining form) -SCOPY

observe or inspect carefully and intensely SCRUTINIZE

observer, as at a card game, offering uninvited advice KIBITZER
- observer or onlooker at an incident, rather than a participant in it

BYSTANDER

obsession See chart at **mania**
- obsession or preoccupation FIXATION, IDÉE FIXE
- obsess or occupy the thoughts of HAUNT
- obsessive interest in obscenity, especially in relation to excrement SCATOLOGY
- obsessive worry or nightmare INCUBUS
- obsessively worried, fussy, sensitive, or the like NEUROTIC

obsolete See **old-fashioned**
- replace something outdated or obsolete SUPERSEDE, PENSION OFF

obstacle See **barrier, obstruction**
- obstacle, minor problem SNAG

obstruct See also **prevent, hinder**
- obstruct, hinder, or delay as a deliberate strategy STONEWALL
- obstruct or ward off a blow, fencing thrust, or the like PARRY
- obstructed or clogged, as by blood or mucus CONGESTED

obstruction, hindrance IMPEDIMENT, ENCUMBRANCE, STUMBLING BLOCK
- obstruction of a blood vessel as by an air bubble or blood clot EMBOLISM
- obstruction of legislation by means of delaying tactics such as lengthy speeches FILIBUSTER
- obstruction or blockage in a body passage or opening, as in the bowels STRICTURE, OCCLUSION, OPPILATION
- obstructive or destructive action of an underhand kind SABOTAGE, SUBVERSION
- causing obstruction, especially in the bowels OBSTRUENT
- deadlock or serious obstruction, as in negotiations or an industrial process LOGJAM
- death of a body organ or tissue because of obstruction of the blood supply, as by a blood clot INFARCTION
- delay in a traffic flow, industrial process, or the like because of an obstruction BOTTLENECK

obtain or achieve COMPASS, ENCOMPASS
- obtain or produce from a source DERIVE

obvious, clear, plain to see EVIDENT, PATENT, MANIFEST
- obvious, dull, or trite remark PLATITUDE, COMMONPLACE, TRUISM
- obvious, highly visible, easily noticed CONSPICUOUS, SALIENT
- obvious, self-explanatory, or self-proving SELF-EVIDENT, AXIOMATIC
- obvious, true by the very nature of its wording or logical form ANALYTIC, TAUTOLOGOUS
- obvious or unmistakable, as a lie or error might be BLATANT, GLARING, GROSS, PALPABLE
- dealing with only the most obvious or apparent features of something SUPERFICIAL, TRIVIAL
- outrageously bad in an obvious way EGREGIOUS
- wrong or evil in an obvious or conspicuous way FLAGRANT

obviously, clearly, plainly PATENTLY

occasional, irregular, periodic INTERMITTENT, SPORADIC

occupation, profession VOCATION
- occupation, trade, or profession to which one is particularly well suited MÉTIER

occupy oneself in a pleasurable activity DISPORT
- occupy or conquer territory, and incorporate it into another state or an empire ANNEX
- occupy or inhabit a place, live in TENANT

occur, happen, take place, come to pass TRANSPIRE
- occur as a result, follow ENSUE, EVENTUATE
- occur at the same time, be or make simultaneous SYNCHRONIZE
- occur or appear as an unexpected but important factor, as fate is said to do INTERVENE, SUPERVENE
- occurring at the same time or place, simultaneous, as two prison sentences might be CONCURRENT
- occurring in fits and starts, intermittent SPASMODIC
- develop into reality, become fact, actually occur MATERIALIZE

occurrence, or the frequency of an occurrence INCIDENCE

ocean See illustration
- ocean, open sea MAIN
- referring to the deep levels or floor of the ocean ABYSSAL
- referring to the deepest levels of the ocean, below about 20,000 feet (6,000 meters) HADAL
- referring to the levels of the ocean below about 300 feet (90 meters), where sunlight no longer penetrates APHOTIC

octopus's sucker ACETABULUM
- armlike flexible projection near the mouth of an octopus, jellyfish, or the like TENTACLE

odd, abnormal, not proper or true to type ABERRANT, DEVIANT
- odd, curious, typical of a closed group with special or secret inter-

Oceans

ests ABSTRUSE, ESOTERIC
- odd, inconsistent, discordant, out of place INCONGRUOUS, ANOMALOUS, ERRATIC
- odd, peculiar, unconventional, in a distorted or ludicrous way BIZARRE, GROTESQUE, OUTLANDISH, OUTRÉ
- odd, seemingly random or individual and not governed by a pattern or reason, as a person, idea, or behavior might be ECCENTRIC, IDIOSYNCRATIC, QUIRKY, WHIMSICAL, SINGULAR, PIXILATED
- odd, without normal or rational explanation INEXPLICABLE, PRETERNATURAL
- odd habit or piece of behavior IDIOSYNCRASY, QUIRK, ECCENTRICITY, MANNERISM
- odd or fanciful action or notion WHIM, CAPRICE, VAGARY, FOIBLE
- oddball, person who does not fit into society MISFIT
- amusingly odd, whimsically comical ZANY, KOOKY, DROLL, QUAINT
- stubbornly holding to eccentric ideas, odd CROTCHETY, CAPRICIOUS, PERVERSE
- weird, inexplicably worrying and odd UNCANNY, EERIE

odds and ends, junk, discarded or miscellaneous objects FLOTSAM, BRIC-A-BRAC
- odds and ends of one's personal property PARAPHERNALIA

Oedipus complex in a girl or young woman, desiring the father and seeing the mother as rival ELECTRA COMPLEX
- negative Oedipus complex, in which the son desires the father and sees the mother as rival, or the daughter desires the mother and sees the father as rival INVERTED OEDIPUS COMPLEX

of one mind, all agreeing UNANIMOUS

of sound mind, sane COMPOS MENTIS

off (combining form) AB-, CATA-

off the cuff, as a speech or statement might be IMPROMPTU, EXTEMPORE, EXTEMPORANEOUS, SPONTANEOUS

offal, especially of a deer, as formerly used for food NUMBLES, UMBLES
- offal of a chicken or other fowl GIBLETS
- offal of animals, especially of pigs, used in cooking FRY, PLUCK, PURTENANCE

offend or hurt, cause a sympathetic or friendly person to become indifferent or hostile ALIENATE, ANTAGONIZE, ESTRANGE
- offend someone by a blow to his or her pride PIQUE
- to be offended, feel resentment, as at a slighting remark TAKE UMBRAGE, TAKE EXCEPTION

offense See **crime**

offensive See also **disgusting**
- offensive, liable to cause ill will or resentment INVIDIOUS
- offensive and unnecessary, as an undeserved insult would be GRATUITOUS
- offensive in a deliberate way, intended or meant to insult or belittle DEROGATORY
- offensive or revolting, as a foul smell is NOISOME
- offensively "gracious," as though dealing with one's subordinate PATRONIZING, CONDESCENDING, PATERNALISTIC

offer or invitation APPROACH, OVERTURE
- offer or propose, present formally PROFFER, TENDER
- amount offered for an item at an auction or the like BID

offering of worship, thanksgiving, an altar gift, or the like OBLATION
- offering to a god, designed to appease PROPITIATION
- based on the fulfillment of a vow, as a religious offering might be VOTIVE

office note or letter MEMORANDUM
- appointed to an office or position though not actually installed yet DESIGNATE
- ceremonial installing of a person in office INVESTITURE, INDUCTION
- holding or occupying of a property, office, or the like TENURE, INCUMBENCY
- promotion or advancement to a higher office or post PREFERMENT
- referring to office work or office workers CLERICAL
- remove from office, power, the throne, or the like DEPOSE

officer See also **military, services**
- officer of a court of justice MARSHAL
- commanding officer of a military post, organization, or the like COMMANDANT
- military officer with a second-lieutenant or higher rank COMMISSIONED OFFICER
- military officer with an intermediate rank, between commissioned and noncommissioned officer WARRANT OFFICER

official See also **diplomat**
- official, orthodox, authoritative CANONICAL
- official, or person discharging official duties FUNCTIONARY
- official, usually a doctor, conducting inquests into deaths that might not stem from natural causes CORONER
- official announcement made to the press and public COMMUNIQUÉ, PROCLAMATION
- official announcement or report COMPTE RENDU
- official approval, formal confirmation or authorization, as of a law RATIFICATION, SANCTION, FIAT, VALIDATION
- official authorized to administer oaths, certify documents, and the like NOTARY PUBLIC, NOTARY
- official authorized to investigate citizens' complaints against government departments or other official bodies OMBUDSMAN
- official badges, emblems, distinguishing symbols, or the like INSIGNIA
- official corruption, private profit derived from a public office JOBBERY, GRAFT
- official document or letter certifying a person's creditworthiness, qualifications, authority, or the like CREDENTIALS
- official in ancient Rome elected by the common people to represent their interests TRIBUNE
- official investigator, especially one who is appointed to root out supposed evil INQUISITOR
- official jargon that is wordy and hard to understand OFFICIALESE, GOBBLEDYGOOK
- official opening ceremony, installation, or beginning INAUGURATION, DEDICATION, COMMENCEMENT, INVESTITURE, INDUCTION
- official regulation on movement, especially one requiring people to be indoors by a certain hour of night CURFEW
- official responsible for maintaining order in a law court, or the like SERGEANT AT ARMS, USHER
- official status, allowing one to be heard at meetings LOCUS STANDI
- official who is unduly zealous or rigid APPARATCHIK
- officially authorized and recognized, as a diplomat should be ACCREDITED
- officially recognized or legally accepted LEGITIMATE
- charge an official such as a president with an offense committed while in office IMPEACH
- communist party official who teaches or enforces party policy COMMISSAR
- court official or sheriff's officer BAILIFF
- government official, or any mean-minded and inflexible official BUREAUCRAT
- senior official in local administration in England during the Middle Ages REEVE

- wrongdoing, especially by a public official MALFEASANCE, MALVERSATION

offset, compensate for, make up for COUNTERVAIL

offspring or descendant, especially male SCION
- bearing more than one offspring at a time MULTIPAROUS
- produce offspring, reproduce PROCREATE
- producing live offspring rather than laying eggs VIVIPAROUS
- producing many offspring PROLIFIC, PHILOPROGENITIVE
- producing offspring by means of eggs that hatch outside the body OVIPAROUS
- producing offspring by means of eggs that hatch within the body, as with some fish and reptiles OVOVIVIPAROUS

offspring (combining form) -PAROUS

often, frequently, over and over again RECURRENTLY, REPEATEDLY
- referring to a person who often or repeatedly engages in a dubious practice, such as smoking or lying HABITUAL, INVETERATE

-ographies (combining form) See chart, pages 374–375

oil See illustration
- oil or other substance used to reduce friction LUBRICANT
- oil from a tropical grass, used in insect repellents and perfume making CITRONELLA OIL
- oil from flax seeds, used as a drying oil in paints, varnishes, and inks LINSEED OIL
- oil from the rind of a small, sour citrus fruit, used in perfume making BERGAMOT OIL
- oil-processing plant REFINERY
- oil-refining unit in which petroleum is converted to fuels with lower boiling points CRACKER
- oil used on the hair, popular in the 19th century MACASSAR OIL
- oily mixture of hydrocarbons from which fuels are prepared PETROLEUM
- pattern of oil when spread thinly on the surface of water OLEOGRAPH
- place or rub oil or ointment on ANOINT
- reduction or decomposition, as by heat-treating oil CRACKING
- referring to natural oils, as used in healthy margarines, having many of the atoms in its molecules linked by double or triple chemical bonds POLYUNSATURATED
- rod for checking the level of oil in a crankcase DIPSTICK
- sesame-seed oil GINGILI
- therapy using fragrant oils AROMATHERAPY

oil (combining form) OLE-, OLEO-, CHRIS-

oil well, mine, or similar asset whose value diminishes over the years WASTING ASSET
- oil well or gas well with an abundant natural flow GUSHER
- begin the drilling of an oil well SPUD
- equipment for a specified purpose, as for drilling or for extracting oil from an oil well RIG
- framework over an oil well for supporting pipes or drilling equipment DERRICK, PLATFORM
- uncontrollable flow from a gas well or oil well, as after an explosion BLOWOUT

oilseed and fodder crop, with a distinctive yellow flower RAPE, COLZA
- residue of oilseed, used as animal fodder EXPELLERS, EXTRACTIONS

oily, fatty, greasy PINGUID, SEBACEOUS
- oily, greasy, or fawningly compliant UNCTUOUS, OLEAGINOUS
- oily substance produced by glands SEBUM, SMEGMA

ointment of olive oil and balsam used in sacramental anointing, as at baptism or confirmation CHRISM
- ointment or bandage applied to produce warmth CALEFACIENT
- ointment or lotion with soothing or healing properties, rubbed into the skin LINIMENT, EMBROCATION, SALVE, UNGUENT
- ointment or oil used for soothing or anointing UNCTION
- fat from sheep's wool, used in cosmetics and ointments LANOLIN
- fragrant ointment in ancient times, or the Indian plant it supposedly derived from SPIKENARD

okra, okra pods, or a soup or stew thickened with okra pods GUMBO

old See also **ancient**
- old, former, previous, as one's divorced spouse is ERSTWHILE, QUONDAM, WHILOM, EX-
- old, shriveled, and wrinkled WIZENED
- old, stale, reworked, as material for a comedy act might be RÉCHAUFFÉ
- old and gray HOARY
- old and respected VENERABLE
- old and unsteady, as through senility DODDERING
- old and weak, in a poor state of repair DECREPIT, DILAPIDATED
- old days, bygone times LANG SYNE
- old quarter of a North African town CASBAH
- old woman of status or wealth DOWAGER
- becoming old, of advanced age SENESCENT
- good because old and mature, as

Oil

THE FORMATION OF AN OIL FIELD

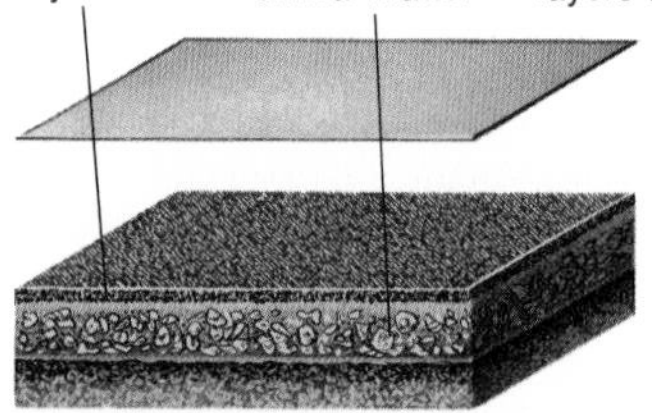

Dead marine organisms collect on the floor of the continental shelf and are broken down by bacteria. They are covered by muddy sediment washed down by the rivers.

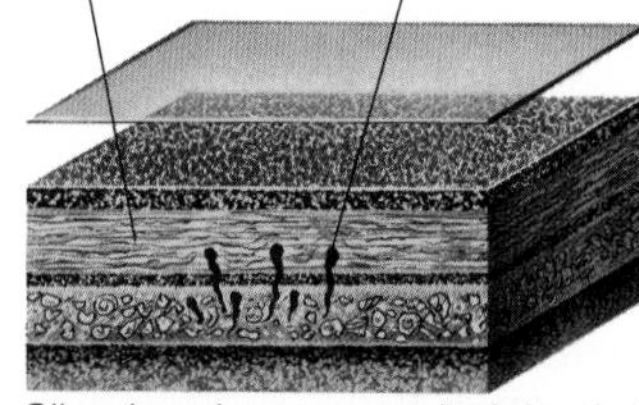

Oil and gas form as a result of chemical changes brought about by high temperatures to which the organic deposits are subjected beneath successive layers of sediment.

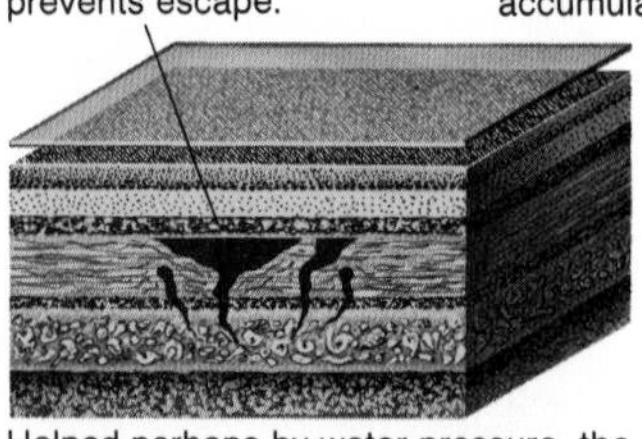

Helped perhaps by water pressure, the oil and gas move up from their bed of shale. Where flat impermeable rock above prevents their escape, they spread out in a thin layer.

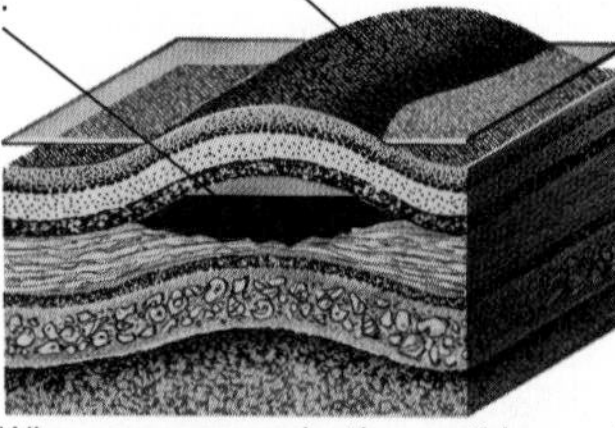

Where pressures in the earth's crust have caused an impermeable layer to rise in a dome shape, the oil and gas rise into it, and are trapped there, forming a potential oil field.

wine might be VINTAGE
- healthy, active, and vigorous, typically in spite of being old SPRY, SPRIGHTLY
- possessed by the same family since olden times, as a house or characteristic might be ANCESTRAL
- so old that its origins are forgotten, as those of a tradition might be IMMEMORIAL
- specialist in or lover of old things, especially books ANTIQUARIAN
- very old, ancient, belonging to bygone times SUPERANNUATED, ARCHAIC, ANTIQUATED
- very old man METHUSALEH
- weak and feeble, resembling a frail old woman ANILE

old (combining form) PALEO-, ARCHEO-, SENESC-

old age, quality of being ancient ANTIQUITY
- feeblemindedness and loss of faculties through old age SENILITY, DOTAGE
- referring to old age, especially showing mental deterioration in old age SENILE
- referring to old age and its medical problems GERIATRIC

old age (combining form) GERONT-, GERONTO-

Old English ANGLO-SAXON
- Old English letter written þ and representing the sounds /th/ and /th/ THORN
- Old English letter written ð and representing the /th/ sound as in *this* EDH, ETH
- Old English letter written ʒ and representing various sounds similar to /y/ or the /kh/ of *loch* or *Bach* YOGH
- Old English letter written æ and representing various sounds including /a/ as in *hat* ASH

old-fashioned, stale FUSTY, MUSTY
- old-fashioned, out of date, dated, having outlasted its usefulness OBSOLETE, SUPERSEDED, ANTIQUATED
- old-fashioned, out of date, not up with the latest trends OUTMODED, PASSÉ, DÉMODÉ
- old-fashioned, shabby, or untidy, as a woman or her clothes might be DOWDY
- old-fashioned and conservative person, seemingly left over from a bygone age ANACHRONISM, RELIC, TROGLODYTE, THROWBACK, ANTEDILUVIAN
- old-fashioned and fussy person FUDDY-DUDDY
- old-fashioned in moral outlook, prudish, square STRAITLACED, VICTORIAN
- completely old-fashioned and incapable of evolving FOSSILIZED, OSSIFIED, STAGNATED
- stubbornly old-fashioned person, one resisting all change DIEHARD, TRADITIONALIST

Old Testament See also **Bible, Scriptures**
- Old Testament figure or event foreshadowing one in the New Testament TYPE
- Old Testament founder or father of the human race or the Hebrew people PATRIARCH
- interpretation of the Old Testament as an allegory or prefiguring, foreshadowing of the New Testament ANAGOGY, ANAGOGE

-ologies (combining form) See chart, pages 374–375

omission of an unstressed vowel or syllable, as in *th' appetite*, commonly in a line of verse ELISION
- omission or loss of sounds or a syllable when pronouncing a word, as when saying *deteriate* for *deteriorate* HAPLOLOGY
- omission or loss of sounds, letters, or syllables at the beginning of a word, as in *'bout* for *about* or *phone* for *telephone* APHAERESIS, APHESIS, FRONT-CLIPPING
- omission or loss of sounds, letters, or syllables at the end of a word as in *walkin'* or *prof*, for *professor* APOCOPE, BACK-CLIPPING
- omission or loss of sounds or letters from the middle of a word, as in *bo's'n* for *boatswain* SYNCOPE
- act of omission or neglect, passing by, disregarding PRETERITION

omnipresent, everywhere UBIQUITOUS

on (combining form) EPI-

on and on, in a boring way INTERMINABLE, REPETITIVE

on behalf of PER PRO, PER PROC.

one, two, three, and so on CARDINAL NUMBERS
- one-legged camera support MONOPOD
- one-wheeled vehicle, as pedaled by acrobats UNICYCLE
- "out of many, one," the U.S. motto E PLURIBUS UNUM

one (combining form) MON-, MONO-, UNI-

one-and-a-half (combining form) SESQUI-

one-sided, without compensation or benefit in return GRATUITOUS
- one-sided conversation, lengthy and uninterrupted speech by one person MONOLOGUE
- one-sided surface made by forming a once-twisted strip into a ring MÖBIUS STRIP
- one-sided surface made by passing the narrow end of a tapered tube through the tube's side then widening it and fusing it to the other open end KLEIN BOTTLE

oneself, in person, or personally IN PROPRIA PERSONA

onion, leek, garlic, or plant related to them ALLIUM
- onionlike bulb, growing in clusters, used for pickling and cooking SHALLOT, SCALLION
- cooked with onions, as potatoes might be LYONNAISE
- having concentric layers such as those of the onion TUNICATE
- smelling or tasting of onions or garlic ALLIACEOUS

onlooker, as at a card game, offering uninvited advice KIBITZER
- onlooker or observer at an incident, rather than a participant in it BYSTANDER

ooze out, emerge slowly, as through pores EXUDE
- oozing, leakage SEEPAGE

open and start using the contents of something, such as a shipment or box BROACH
- open and unobstructed, as ducts or passages in the body should be PATENT
- open country or grassland in South Africa VELD
- open for all to see, observable, aboveboard OVERT
- open formally a building, exhibition, or the like DEDICATE, INAUGURATE
- open stretch of land, sea, or sky EXPANSE
- open to the passage of fluids POROUS, PERMEABLE
- open to view, danger, attack, or the like EXPOSED
- openly acknowledged, candidly admitted, self-confessed AVOWED
- openly expressed, unreserved, outspoken, forthright EXPLICIT
- slightly open, as a door might be AJAR
- wide open, yawning AGAPE

opening See also **hole, gap**
- opening in a wall, wider inside than out, for a door or window EMBRASURE
- opening in fortifications for the passage of troops DÉBOUCHÉ
- opening move or maneuver, as in negotiations, designed to secure an early advantage GAMBIT
- opening part of a sonata, play, or the like that introduces the themes EXPOSITION
- opening quotation, as at the head of a chapter or the start of a book, suggesting its theme EPIGRAPH
- opening words of a speech or letter, such as "Dear friends"

SALUTATION
- abnormal opening or channel, from a hollow organ, abscess, or cavity to the skin's surface or to another hollow organ FISTULA
- small space, opening, or gap, as between the strands of a net INTERSTICE

opening, mouth (combining form) STOM-, -STOME, STOMATO-

opera company's chief female singer PRIMA DONNA, DIVA
- opera or ballet performers' coach REPETITEUR
- opera singer with a strong tenor voice HELDENTENOR
- operatic song for a solo voice ARIA, ARIETTA
- interval entertainment between the acts of an opera or play DIVERTISSEMENT
- interval or interval performance during a play or opera ENTR'ACTE
- text of the songs and dialogue of an opera or operetta LIBRETTO
- translation shown above, as projected above an opera stage SURTITLE

opera glasses supported by a small handle LORGNETTE, LORGNON

-OLOGIES AND -OGRAPHIES

TERM	SUBJECT OF STUDY OR PRACTICE
acarology	mites and ticks
anemology	wind
angiology	blood and lymph vessels
anthropology	humankind
astrology	heavenly magic
bryology	mosses
campanology	bell ringing
cardiology	heart functions and diseases
carpology	fruits and seeds
cetology	aquatic mammals, especially whales
cartography	map making
choreography	dancing, composing ballets
chorography	mapping of regions
chorology	geographical regions; plant and animal distribution
chronology	dates
conchology	seashells
cosmology	the universe
craniology	skulls
criminology	crimes and criminals
cryptology	codes and ciphers
cytology	plant and animal cells
dactylology	fingerprints
demography	population statistics
dendrology	trees
deontology	moral responsibilities
dermatology	human skin
ecology	relationships between living things and their environment
endocrinology	glands
enology	wines
entomology	insects
epidemiology	incidence and risk of disease
epigraphy	ancient inscriptions
epistemology	nature of knowledge
eschatology	death, destiny
ethology	(1) cultures, ethnic groups; (2) animal behavior
etiology	causes, especially of diseases
etymology	word origins
futurology	the future
genealogy	ancestry
gerontology	old age
glotto-chronology	history of language
gynecology	women's disorders
helminthology	worms, especially parasitic worms
hematology	blood
herpetology	reptiles and amphibians
histology	plant and animal tissue
horology	timepieces, measurement of time
hydrology	water
hypnology	sleep
ichthyology	fish
lexicography	dictionaries
lexicology	vocabulary
limnology	freshwater life
lithology	characteristics of rocks
malacology	mollusks
meteorology	weather
metrology	measurement
mycology	fungi
myology	muscles
myrmecology	ants
nomology	lawmaking or scientific laws
nosology	classification of diseases
odontology	teeth
oncology	tumors
oneirology	dreams
ontology	nature of existence

operation See also **surgical**
- operation or experiment on the body of a living animal, especially for research VIVISECTION
- operation or project to control a tricky situation and limit the damage HOLDING OPERATION

opinion, judgment ESTIMATION
- opinion based on incomplete evidence, guess SPECULATION, CONJECTURE, SURMISE
- opinion differing from the orthodox view HERESY, HETERODOXY
- opinion or belief firmly held CONVICTION, DOGMA, PERSUASION
- opinion or belief that is mistaken or misleading DELUSION
- opinion or decision already formed PARTI PRIS
- opinion or idea based on convention rather than real belief IDÉE REÇUE
- opinion or image of someone or something that is conventional, unthinking, and usually oversimplified STEREOTYPE
- opinion poll or similar statistical enquiry SURVEY
- opinion poll taken unofficially or impromptu STRAW POLL
- opinion that is widespread, a general agreement, a majority opinion CONSENSUS
- opinions or prejudices expressing one's outlook SENTIMENTS
- difference of ideas, opinions, or the like DIVERGENCE
- division or classification into two parts, such as conflicting opinions DICHOTOMY
- established, fixed, firmly and immovably settled, as opinions or troops might be ENTRENCHED
- give an opinion RENDER
- growth or increase, as of public feeling or opinion GROUNDSWELL
- passing of opinions on subjects of which one has little knowledge SCIOLISM, ULTRACREPIDARIANISM
- person or group whose reactions serve as a test for new ideas or opinions SOUNDING BOARD
- similarity of ideas, opinions, or the like CONVERGENCE
- test, sample, or probe opinions or intentions SOUND
- unprincipled person who changes his or her policies or opinions to serve personal interests TIMESERVER, TRIMMER, VICAR OF BRAY, TEMPORIZER

opium - medicinal preparation based on opium, widely used in former times LAUDANUM

opponent, enemy, foe ADVERSARY, ANTAGONIST
- opponent, rival, participant in a contest CONTENDER, CORRIVAL
- opponent of mechanization or technical advance LUDDITE
- opponent of or objector to the views, policies, and demands of an authoritarian ruling party DISSIDENT

opportunity - make use of an opportunity, turn to advantage EXPLOIT, UTILIZE, CAPITALIZE ON, CASH IN ON
- place of great wealth or opportunity EL DORADO

oppose, argue against or dispute, contradict or deny GAINSAY, REPUDIATE, OPPUGN, CONTROVERT
- oppose, challenge, stand up to CONFRONT, DEFY
- oppose, offset, or balance with an equal force COUNTERVAIL, COUNTERBALANCE

-OLOGIES AND -OGRAPHIES *continued*

TERM	SUBJECT OF STUDY OR PRACTICE
oology	eggs
ophiology	snakes
ophthalmology	eyes
ornithology	birds
orography	mapping of relief
orology	mountains
osteology	bones
otology	ears
paleography	old manuscripts
paleontology	fossils
palynology	pollen and spores
pathology	diseases
pedology	soils, earth
penology	prisons and treatment of criminals
petrology	rocks
pharmacology	drugs
philology	languages
phrenology	character, by studying skull irregularities
physiology	life processes, functioning of organisms
phytology	plants
polemology	wars
pomology	fruit
potamology	rivers
psephology	elections
pteridology	ferns
radiology	radiation and radiotherapy
reflexology	reflexes; healing through foot massage
rhinology	noses
scatology	excrement; obscene language
seismology	earthquakes
selenology	the moon
semiology	signs and signaling
sinology	China
speleology	caves
stomatology	mouth disorders
teratology	monsters; congenital abnormalities
topography	surface features of a region
topology	shapes and surfaces
toxicology	poisons
tribology	friction and lubrication
trichology	hair
ufology	unidentified flying objects
uranography	mapping of stars and galaxies
vexillology	flags
zymology	fermentation

- oppose or fight vigorously TILT AT
- opposed or hostile to something or someone AVERSE, OPPUGNANT, ANTIPATHETIC
- opposed uncompromisingly, relentlessly hostile IRRECONCILABLE, IMPLACABLE, INEXORABLE
- opposing, conflicting, not in agreement with AT VARIANCE, AT LOGGERHEADS
- opposing or opposite, as winds or criticism might be ADVERSE
- opposing others' wishes or suggestions unreasonably PERVERSE, CONTRARY
- divide into two extreme and opposing positions, groups, opinions, or the like POLARIZE
- linking or shared by opposing parties, as an agreement might be RECIPROCAL
- having opposing senses or implications, as conflicting statements or claims have INCOMPATIBLE, INCONSISTENT, CONTRADICTORY, DILEMMATIC

opposed, opposing (combining form) ANTI-, CONTRA-

opposite, face to face VIS-À-VIS
- opposite, word having a sense directly opposed to that of another word ANTONYM
- opposite or absence of something positive or real NEGATION
- completely contrary, as two opposites might be DIAMETRICAL, POLAR, DILEMMATIC
- completely opposite or contrary to one's nature, experience, or principles ABHORRENT, REPUGNANT, ALIEN
- exact or direct opposite or contrast ANTITHESIS, CONVERSE, INVERSE
- part or number opposite to and completing another COMPLEMENT
- place on the opposite side of the earth, especially Australia and New Zealand ANTIPODES, DOWN UNDER
- use of words to express something markedly different from or opposite to their outward or literal sense IRONY

opposite (combining form) A-, ALLO-, ANTI-, COUNTER-, CONTRA-, UN-, CATA-

opposite direction (combining form) DIA-

opposition, as to government authority or colonial rule, by nonviolent methods such as fasting and noncooperation PASSIVE RESISTANCE
- opposition, disagreement, nonacceptance DISSENT
- opposition, inconsistency, lack of agreement, as between two logically incompatible claims CONTRADICTION, DISPARITY, DISCREPANCY, DISSONANCE, INCONGRUITY
- opposition, refusal to submit to authority CONTUMACY
- opposition or conflict between two rules or laws ANTINOMY, DILEMMA
- opposition or conflict within a group, nation, or the like FACTION
- strong opposition or hostility ANTAGONISM

oppress or ill-treat, especially for racial, religious, or political differences PERSECUTE
- oppressed, unfortunate, or subordinate person UNDERDOG

oppressive or cruel person in authority TYRANT, DESPOT

optical illusion or image of a nonpresent object, such as an oasis MIRAGE
- painting or the like giving an optical illusion or appearance of reality TROMPE L'OEIL

optimist, especially one who is blindly or excessively optimistic POLLYANNA
- optimist in spite of suffering repeated misfortunes MICAWBER
- optimistic and confident, cheerful SANGUINE
- optimistic and confident spirits, as among soldiers MORALE
- optimistic and naive person, especially an innocent young man CANDIDE

optional or contingent, capable of happening or of not happening FACULTATIVE

or else - final terms offered in negotiating, to be accepted "or else" ULTIMATUM

oracle - ambiguous or obscure, as though spoken by an oracle DELPHIC

orange of a bitter variety, used especially for making marmalade SEVILLE ORANGE
- orange or lemon rind used as flavoring ZEST
- orange stuck with cloves, as for scenting linen POMANDER
- oranges, lemons, grapefruit, or related fruit CITRUS FRUIT
- sour, pear-shaped orange with a rind that yields an aromatic oil BERGAMOT
- spongy white tissue between the rind and pulp of oranges or other citrus fruits PITH

oratory, art of effective and persuasive speech RHETORIC

orbit, as of the moon around the earth, in which the same face of the orbiting body is always pointing to the orbited body CAPTURED ROTATION, SYNCHRONOUS ROTATION
- orbit of an artificial satellite timed to keep it apparently fixed over one point on the surface of the earth SYNCHRONOUS ORBIT, GEOSTATIONARY ORBIT
- orbiting in an opposite direction RETROGRADE
- closest or farthest point in the irregular orbit of a celestial body from the body it is orbiting around APSE, APSIS
- elliptical rather than circular, as a planet's orbit might be ECCENTRIC
- point at which a spacecraft in lunar orbit is farthest from the moon APOCYNTHION, APOLUNE, APOSELENE
- point at which a spacecraft in lunar orbit is nearest the moon PERICYNTHION, PERILUNE
- point in its orbit when a planet, comet, or the like is farthest from the sun APHELION
- point in its orbit when a planet, comet, or the like is nearest the sun PERIHELION
- point in its orbit when the moon or a satellite is farthest from the earth APOGEE
- point in its orbit when the moon or a satellite is nearest the earth PERIGEE
- small circle, supposedly followed by a planet, moving in a large orbit around the earth, according to early astronomers EPICYCLE
- star or other celestial body around which a planet or other satellite orbits PRIMARY

orchestra See illustration
- orchestra, as in Java, based on chimes and other such percussion instruments GAMELAN
- orchestra, music society, or a choir PHILHARMONIC
- orchestra or choir leader, as in 18th-century Germany KAPELLMEISTER
- orchestra with only a small number of players, typically performing in a small hall CHAMBER ORCHESTRA
- percussion section of an orchestra BATTERY

orchids of various kinds CALYPSO, CATTLEYA, POGONIA, TWAYBLADE

ordain a bishop CONSECRATE

order See also **column**
- order, arbitrary command, or law as announced by a ruler, autocrat, or authority EDICT, DECREE, PROCLAMATION, UKASE, RESCRIPT, FIAT, DIKTAT, IRADE, PRONUNCIAMENTO
- order, balance between parts SYMMETRY, PROPORTION
- order, command, or instruction MANDATE, DIRECTIVE
- order, distribution, or arrangement DISPOSAL
- order, law, rule, or regulation

STATUTE, ORDINANCE
- order of power or status in a group PECKING ORDER, HIERARCHY
- order or arrange something, as by a decree or guidelines ORDAIN, PRESCRIBE
- order or arrange something in a particular way DISPOSE
- order or cosmic reason in ancient Greek philosophy LOGOS
- order or harmony COSMOS
- order or permission to leave, dismissal NUNC DIMITTIS
- order or rank, as at public ceremonies PRECEDENCE
- order or request, often in writing and official, for needed supplies or equipment REQUISITION
- order or sequence, as of those in line for a title or throne SUCCESSION
- order or urge solemnly, as if under oath ADJURE, ENJOIN, EXHORT
- order something officially, such as a biography or painting COMMISSION
- order warning against a certain action MONITION
- ordered, successive, or serial SEQUENTIAL, CONSECUTIVE
- ordered or requested by AT THE BEHEST OF
- allowing no denial, refusal, or argument, as an order or decree might PEREMPTORY
- arrange something, such as pages, in the correct order COLLATE, COLLOCATE
- cancel or reverse an order or instruction COUNTERMAND
- change or reverse the ordering or relative position of two or more things TRANSPOSE
- court order directed at some lower court, official body, or the like MANDAMUS
- court order requiring a person to appear in court to give evidence SUMMONS, SUBPOENA
- court order requiring an untried prisoner to be brought before a judge, who may order his or her release HABEAS CORPUS
- court order requiring or banning a certain action WRIT, INJUNCTION
- expressing an order IMPERATIVE
- lacking a planned order or arrangement RANDOM, HAPHAZARD, ARBITRARY, ALEATORY
- lay down as an order or condition DICTATE, STIPULATE
- put into order, systematize CODIFY, TABULATE
- rearrangement or reordering PERMUTATION

order (combining form) -TAX-, TAXO-, -TAXY, -TAXIS

orderly, rational, and sober, as one side of human nature is (the opposite of Dionysian), in Nietzsche's terminology APOLLONIAN

ordinary See also **mediocre, dull**
- ordinary, commonplace, day-to-day QUOTIDIAN, WORKADAY
- ordinary, plain, or unstriking INCONSPICUOUS, ANONYMOUS, UNEXCEPTIONAL, PROSAIC
- ordinary, simple, homely, and unpretentious HOMESPUN
- ordinary member of the public, as opposed to a specialist, member of the clergy, or other professional LAY PERSON, LAYMAN, LAYWOMAN
- in ordinary, everyday language COLLOQUIAL, VERNACULAR

ore - separation or refinement of ores or other minerals by skimming off the required particles in bubbles of a liquid FROTH FLOTATION

organ See illustration, page 378, and also **digestion**
- abnormal change to a body part, organ, or tissue LESION
- abnormal opening or channel, from a hollow organ, abscess, or cavity to the skin's surface or to another hollow organ FISTULA
- abnormal rift or gap in a body part or organ DIASTEMA
- adjust organ pipes or a wind instrument to perfect the tone and pitch VOICE
- air valve in the wind chest of an organ PALLET
- body organs, especially those essential for life VITALS
- death of an organ or part of an organ resulting from obstruction of its blood supply INFARCTION
- desklike section of an organ containing the keyboard, pedals, and stops CONSOLE
- displacement of a body part or organ through the wall normally enclosing it HERNIA, RUPTURE
- faulty continuous sounding of an organ pipe even when the key is not being pressed CIPHER
- group of organ pipes producing the same tone color REGISTER, STOP
- health of body organs, as shown by their tension and response to stimuli TONE
- internal body organs ENTRAILS, VISCERA, INNARDS
- internal organs of an animal, especially when regarded as

Orchestra

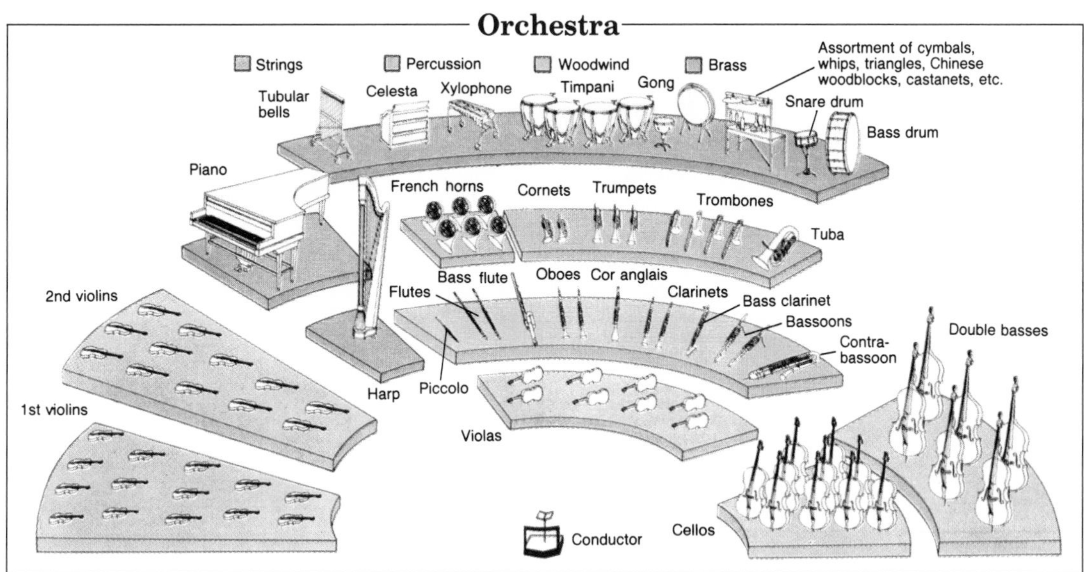

Organ

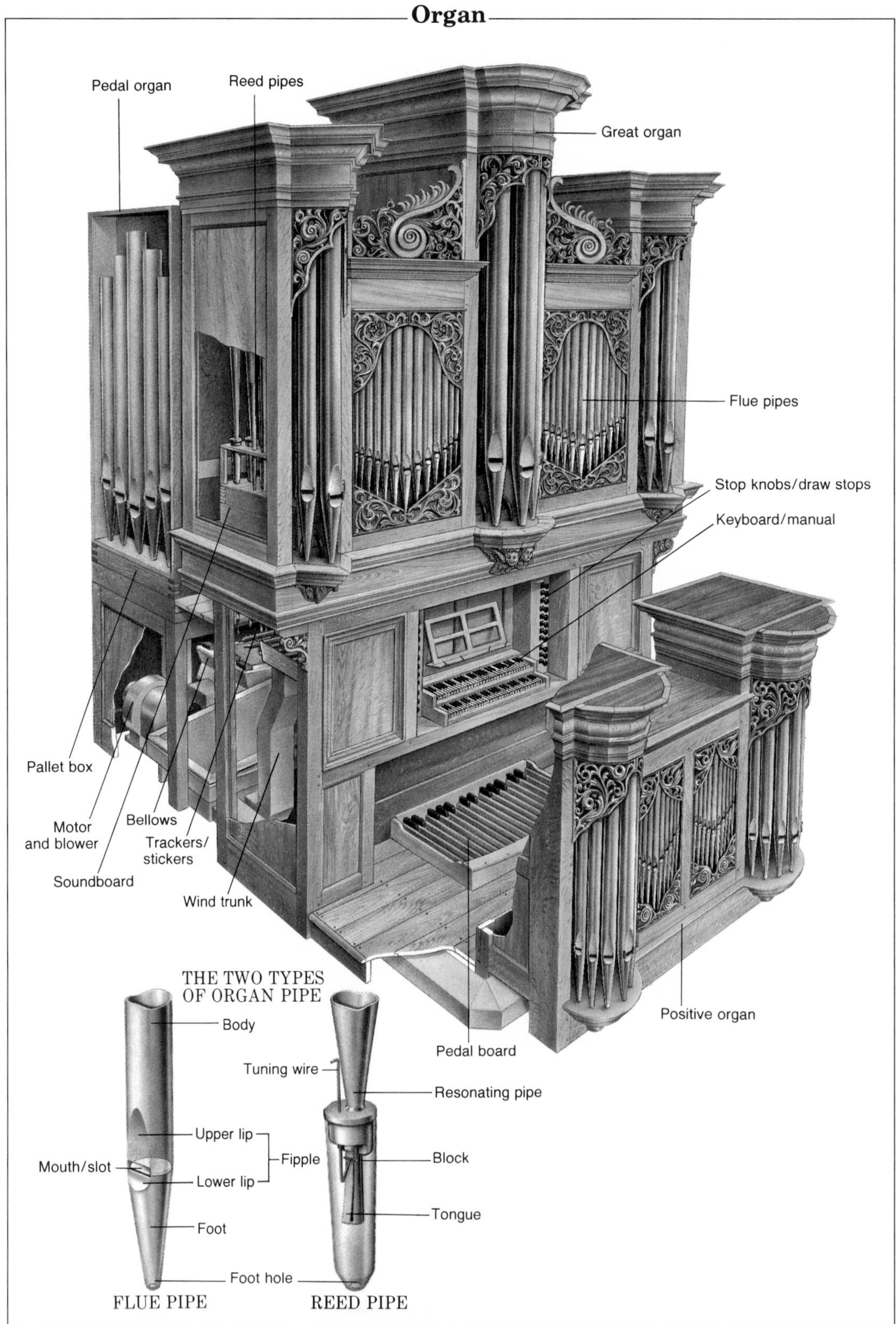
Pedal organ
Reed pipes
Great organ
Flue pipes
Stop knobs/draw stops
Keyboard/manual
Pallet box
Motor and blower
Bellows
Trackers/stickers
Soundboard
Wind trunk
Positive organ
Pedal board
THE TWO TYPES OF ORGAN PIPE
Body
Tuning wire
Resonating pipe
Upper lip
Fipple
Mouth/slot
Lower lip
Block
Tongue
Foot
Foot hole
FLUE PIPE
REED PIPE

edible OFFAL
- leaning or resting against related tissue, as a body organ might be RECUMBENT
- main part of something, such as a body organ CORPUS
- organ stop producing low notes BOURDON, BOMBARDON
- person who provides an organ for transplant DONOR
- person who receives a transplanted organ DONEE, RECIPIENT
- principal organ stop or set of pipes, determining the organ's characteristic tone DIAPASON
- referring to the internal organs VISCERAL, SPLANCHNIC
- set of organ pipes controlled by a single stop RANK
- system of organs and tissues that function as a unit TRACT
- turn a body part or organ inside out EVAGINATE, EVERT
- wall of a body organ such as the heart PARIES

organic matter that decays and fertilizes the soil HUMUS

organism of a basic single-celled type, typically microscopic, such as an amoeba PROTOZOAN
- living together of two organisms in close or dependent association, especially when beneficial to both SYMBIOSIS

organization sponsored but not controlled by the government QUANGO

organize See **arrange**

organizer of stage shows, concerts, or the like IMPRESARIO

organizing of any complicated project, especially one involving transport LOGISTICS
- organizing, supervision, direction, sponsorship AUSPICES, AEGIS

orgy, revelry, unrestrained licentious celebration SATURNALIA
- orgy or drunken, noisy festivity BACCHANAL, BACCHANALIA

orientation (combining form) TROP-, TROPO-, -TROPIC

origin, beginning, or creation, as of an idea or project GENESIS, CONCEPTION
- origin, parentage, descent LINEAGE, EXTRACTION
- origin or descent DERIVATION
- origin and development of a word, or the study of such origins ETYMOLOGY
- origin and historical development of something PEDIGREE
- origin or authorship PATERNITY
- main source or origin, as of an idea FOUNTAINHEAD
- place of origin, as of a work of art PROVENANCE
- point of origin, starting point, beginning in time TERMINUS A QUO
- point of origin or root of an organ or part RADIX
- scientific study of the origin of humankind or the human species ANTHROPOGENESIS
- study of origins or causes, as of a disease or in mythology ETIOLOGY
- study of the origins of personal and place names ONOMASTICS

origin (combining form) -GEN, -GENESIS, -GENY, -GON, GONO-

original, creative, or life-enhancing PROMETHEAN
- original, first, earliest PRIMARY, PRIMAL, ARCHETYPAL, PRIMEVAL
- original and creative, providing a basis for development SEMINAL
- original model or pattern on which other versions or copies are based ARCHETYPE, PROTOTYPE, BLUEPRINT
- original or local, belonging to or relating to a particular place NATIVE, ENDEMIC
- original or special to an individual PATENT
- referring to an original time or condition PRISTINE, PRIMORDIAL
- referring to the original inhabitants of an area ABORIGINAL, AUTOCHTHONOUS, INDIGENOUS

original (combining form) PRIM-, PRIMO-, UR-, INCIP-, INIT-, ARCHE-, PROT-, PROTO-

originality, freshness, or newness NOVELTY

originate See also **begin**
- originate or issue from a source EMANATE
- originating externally, coming from outside EXOGENOUS
- originating in a particular place, native ABORIGINAL, INDIGENOUS, AUTOCHTHONOUS
- originating internally, coming from within ENDOGENOUS

originator of a tradition or trend PROGENITOR, FOUNTAINHEAD, PRECURSOR

ornament See also **decorate**
- ornament, often carved, in the form of a small figure or statuette FIGURINE
- ornament a surface by embedding decorative pieces in it INLAY
- ornament hanging from a wire or thread, with parts that move when pushed or when blown by the wind MOBILE
- ornament of a showy but worthless kind TRINKET, BAUBLE, GEWGAW, GIMCRACK, KNICKKNACK
- ornament of enamelware in differently colored panels within a decorative grid of metal strips CLOISONNÉ
- ornament or sculpture in low relief, such as a cameo ANAGLYPH
- ornamentation or decoration, as of buildings or clothing TRIM
- ornamented, ornate, elaborate CORINTHIAN
- ornamented or styled in an elaborate, uninhibited, or exaggerated way ROCOCO
- ornaments, curios, odd items of furniture, and the like, valued as rare or quaint BRIC-A-BRAC
- small, inexpensive ornament or toy NOVELTY

ornamental loop of drapery, flowers, or the like SWAG, FESTOON
- ornamental ridge running along the top of a roof or wall CRESTING
- ornamental strip of wood, metal, or the like, as for trimming or edging BEADING
- ornamental trim, as lace, on the front of a shirt or blouse JABOT

orthodox, official, authoritative CANONICAL

ostrich, emu, kiwi, or related flightless bird RATITE
- relating to or resembling the ostrich STRUTHIOUS

other - felt or expressed by two people about each other MUTUAL, RECIPROCAL

other (combining form) HETER-, HETERO-, ALT-

otter, badger, ferret, or related mammal MUSTELINE
- otter's den LODGE, HOLT
- rise to the surface to breathe, as beavers and otters do VENT

out-and-out, thoroughgoing, notorious, as a knave is said to be ARRANT

out of (combining form) EC-, EX-, E-

out of control, with uncontrolled force HEADLONG

out of date, no longer in everyday use ANTIQUATED, ARCHAIC, OBSOLETE, OUTMODED, SUPERANNUATED
- replace something that is out of date or out of fashion SUPERSEDE

out of order, not working, in need of repair OUT OF KILTER, MALFUNCTIONING, KAPUT

out of place, inappropriate INOPPORTUNE, INAPPOSITE, MALAPROPOS

out of tune, harsh, or dissonant sound, as of a faulty violin or specially tuned piano WOLF

outbreak of a disease, civil unrest, or the like after a period of inactivity RECRUDESCENCE

outburst, as of anger, hatred, or violence ERUPTION
- outburst, sudden rush, flood SPATE
- outburst or uncontrollable display of rage, laughter, or the like PAROXYSM

outcast from society PARIAH, ISHMAEL, LEPER
outcome or final result, as of a play DENOUEMENT
outdoor bench, typically semicircular and made of stone EXEDRA
- outdoor meal, or entertainment, such as a picnic or garden party FÊTE CHAMPÊTRE
- outdoors, in the open air, as a meal might be ALFRESCO
- outdoorsy, in the style of the British county gentry TWEEDY
outer covering, such as a seed's coat or an animal's skin INTEGUMENT
- outer layer of an organ such as the brain or kidney CORTEX
- outer layer or covering, as of the brain PALLIUM
outer space (combining form) ASTR-
outermost part, the boundary area PERIPHERY
outgoing, friendly, lively person EXTROVERT
- outgoing or sociable, seeking or enjoying the company of others GREGARIOUS
outgrowth or swelling of an organ or other body part APOPHYSIS
outhouse, lavatory PRIVY
outing or short journey, often at a special low fare EXCURSION
outlaw, banish, or exile PROSCRIBE
- person who hunts outlaws or dangerous animals for a reward BOUNTY HUNTER
outlet, as for goods or troops DÉBOUCHÉ
- outlet, exit, means of escape VENT
outline See also **summary**
- outline, shape, form CONFIGURATION, CONTOUR, CONFORMATION, LINEAMENT
- outline, sketch, describe, or draw DELINEATE
- outline of the plot of a novel, play, or the like SCENARIO
- outline or sketch out something, such as a plan ADUMBRATE
- picture formed from shadows or outlines SCIAGRAM
- shadow image or filled-in outline, typically of solid black against a white background, as of a person's profile SILHOUETTE
outmoded See **old-fashioned**
outpouring of emotion in speech or writing EFFUSION
outrage, monstrous behavior or deed ENORMITY
outrageous, unconventional, or provocative person ENFANT TERRIBLE
- outrageously bad EGREGIOUS
- outrageously indelicate or rude SCABROUS
- outrageously or glaringly wrong or evil FLAGRANT
outside and independent of the created universe as God is according to some views TRANSCENDENT
- outside angle of a wall QUOIN, COIGN
- coming from outside, of foreign or external origin EXTRANEOUS, EXOGENOUS, EXTRINSIC
outside (combining form) AB-, ECTO-, EXO-, EXTRA-, SUPER-
outsider, unorthodox thinker or group member MAVERICK
- sense or state of being an outsider, isolated from one's society ALIENATION
outskirts, as of a cathedral close or forest PURLIEUS
- outskirts or suburbs of a town ENVIRONS
outstanding See also **perfect, excellent**
- outstanding, excelling others TRANSCENDENT, SUPERLATIVE, PREEMINENT
- outstanding, striking, conspicuous, as an argument might be SALIENT
- outstanding dish, work of art, performance, or the like within a set or series of related items PIÈCE DE RÉSISTANCE, SHOWPIECE
- outstandingly able or beautiful person PARAGON
outward-moving or -growing CENTRIFUGAL
- outward-tending, especially away from the brain or spinal cord, as some nerves are EFFERENT, DEFERENT
- outward signs, symbolic decorations, or ornamental equipment, as of power TRAPPINGS
- push or jut outward PROTRUDE
- turned outward, as feet might be SPLAYED
oval, almond-shaped AMYGDALOID
ovary - ovaries or testes GONADS
- cavity in the ovary, containing an ovum FOLLICLE
- cell in the ovary that later develops into an ovum OOCYTE
- remove the ovaries from a female animal SPAY
- small fluid-filled sac in the ovary, containing a developing egg cell GRAAFIAN FOLLICLE
ovary (combining form) OOPHOR-
oven or furnace for drying or hardening, as in a pottery KILN
- stove of a large iron make, usually burning coal or wood, with one or more ovens RANGE
over (combining form) EPI-, HYPER-, SUPER-, SUPRA-, SUR-, TRANS-
overabundant See **excessive**
overalls or similar clothing for menial work in a military camp or barracks FATIGUES
- baby's garment or child's playsuit resembling a pair of overalls ROMPERS
- ski trousers resembling a pair of overalls SALOPETTE
overattentive, excessively eager to help or advise OFFICIOUS, SOLICITOUS
overbearing, arrogant, as someone's confident manner might be IMPERIOUS, DOMINEERING, PEREMPTORY, OVERWEENING
overboard - throw overboard JETTISON
overcharging, demanding of an excessive price EXTORTION
overcome a difficulty or obstacle SURMOUNT
- impossible to overcome, as a barrier or obstacle might be INSUPERABLE, INSURMOUNTABLE
overdevelopment of a body part or organ, caused by enlargement of cells HYPERTROPHY
overeating - illness combining bulimia and anorexia nervosa, in which compulsive overeating is followed by bouts of self-induced vomiting BULMOREXIA
overelaborate, flowery, pretentious or fussy in style CHINTZY, CHICHI, PRECIOUS
overflow channel, as around the side of a dam SPILLWAY
- overflow or sudden surge in a stream, as after heavy rains FRESHET, SPATE
- overflowing, abounding, swarming TEEMING
overgrown area, thick with shrubs and undergrowth THICKET, BRAKE
overindulge, surfeit SATIATE, SATE
- overindulgence in sensual or immoral pursuits INTEMPERANCE, DEBAUCHERY, DISSIPATION, DEPRAVITY
overlap INTERSECT
- overlapping circles, used as a diagram to represent mathematical or logical relations VENN DIAGRAM, EULER DIAGRAM
- overlapping in a regular pattern, as fish scales or roof tiles tend to be IMBRICATE
- built with overlapping rather than edge-to-edge planks, as a ship or boat might be CLINKER-BUILT, LAPSTRAKE
overlook, tower above, look down on DOMINATE, COMMAND
overlord SUZERAIN
overmanning, employing more workers than needed, as an employer may be required to do under union rules FEATHERBEDDING
overoptimistic person POLLYANNA, MICAWBER, CANDIDE
overprecise, pedantic, or dogmatic SCHOLASTIC, QUIBBLING

overreacting and seeking confrontation rather than compromise TRIGGER-HAPPY, GUNG HO

overrefined, excessively rich or precious, as a literary style might be DECADENT
- overrefined, affected, overelaborate RECHERCHÉ

overrun and inhabit in large numbers, as vermin might a garden or animal INFEST

oversatisfy, provide or gratify in excess PALL, SATIATE

oversensitive, as to chafing or sunburn IRRITABLE
- oversensitive, easily offended, touchy UMBRAGEOUS

overshadow, reduce from power or importance to obscurity ECLIPSE

oversimplified or given to oversimplifying REDUCTIONIST

oversubtle or devious arguing or reasoning SOPHISTRY, CASUISTRY, QUIBBLING, SCHOLASTICISM

overused, and thereby deprived of its liveliness or force, as a phrase or idea might be CLICHÉD, TRITE, HACKNEYED, SHOPWORN, BANAL
- overused, unoriginal, and predictable remark, phrase, or thought CLICHÉ, PLATITUDE, TRUISM, COMMONPLACE, BROMIDE
- overused moral lesson, sermon, or proverb HOMILY
- overused saying, slogan, or belief SHIBBOLETH

overwhelm or swamp, as with requests or work INUNDATE
- overwhelming influence or activity, that seems to swallow up its participants VORTEX

ovum See **ovary**

own, or take pride or pleasure in owning something, such as an unusual name REJOICE IN

owned and controlled privately PROPRIETARY

owner with exclusive legal rights to something PROPRIETOR

ownership of land DOMAIN
- absolute ownership of inherited land, allowing the owner to dispose of it as he or she wishes FEE SIMPLE
- full and unrestricted ownership, of a house, flat, land, or the like FREEHOLD
- qualified ownership of inherited land, restricting its disposal to a specified heir or heirs FEE TAIL

ox - adjective for oxen BOVINE, TAURINE
- domesticated ox of Asia and Africa, with a hump and a large dewlap ZEBU
- encampment for ox wagons OUTSPAN
- extinct ox, probably the forebear of today's domesticated cattle AUROCHS, URUS
- matching pair of oxen yoked or driven together SPAN

Oxford University's commemoration ceremony ENCAENIA
- autumn, spring, and summer terms at Oxford University MICHAELMAS, HILARY, TRINITY
- dictionary bearing the Oxford imprint OXFORD ENGLISH DICTIONARY, OED
- feast, especially an annual university or college feast, as at Oxford GAUDY
- formal academic wear, especially at Oxford University SUBFUSC
- person born or living in Oxford OXONIAN
- technical term for pronunciation known as Oxford English RECEIVED PRONUNCIATION, RP

oxygen in the form O_3, used in bleaching OZONE
- oxygenate blood VENTILATE, AERATE
- chemical removal of oxygen from a compound or adding of hydrogen to it REDUCTION

oyster, mussel, or similar hinged shellfish MOLLUSK, BIVALVE
- oyster larva SPAT
- large oysterlike shellfish providing mother-of-pearl ABALONE, ORMER
- savory of oysters wrapped in bacon and served on toast ANGELS ON HORSEBACK
- shiny inner surface of the shell of an oyster or related shellfish, used for ornamentation MOTHER-OF-PEARL, NACRE

P

pace, rate, or speed TEMPO

pacify See also **calm**
- pacify, calm down, soothe someone's anger MOLLIFY, PLACATE, APPEASE, PROPITIATE
- pacify, end disputes between CONCILIATE, RECONCILE
- pacify, soothe, make pain or troubles easier to bear ALLAY, ALLEVIATE, PALLIATE

pack down or stamp down tightly tobacco, concrete, or the like by means of light blows TAMP
- pack of hounds CRY

packages - person delivering packages, messages, smuggled drugs, or the like on behalf of another COURIER

packet - small, sealed packet, typically holding one portion of sugar, shampoo, or the like SACHET

packing and insulating material of a synthetic light white solid foam POLYSTYRENE
- packing, as between lengths of piping, machine parts, or the like, serving as a seal GASKET

pad, as of gauze, used to stop bleeding or to reduce pain or inflammation COMPRESS

padding, fabric, and springs used in making a soft covering for furniture UPHOLSTERY
- padding material used in former times BOMBAST
- silky plant fiber used for padding, soundproofing, or the like KAPOK
- wool or cotton waste used for padding furniture or mattresses FLOCK

paddle - blade of an oar or paddle PALM
- blade on a paddle wheel FLOAT

page or insert in a book or magazine that is larger than other pages and is folded to fit GATEFOLD, FOLDOUT
- page or page size equal to a quarter of a large sheet of paper, or a book with such pages QUARTO
- page or page size equal to an eighth of a large sheet of paper, or a book with such pages OCTAVO
- page or page size equal to half a large sheet of paper, or a book with such pages FOLIO
- page width or column width in printing MEASURE
- arrange pages or sheets in the correct order COLLATE
- having the edges of the pages still unslit or untrimmed, as a book might be UNCUT
- headline or title on every page or other page of a book or magazine RUNNING HEAD
- large page printed on one side with news, advertisements, or the like BROADSHEET
- leaf rapidly through files, the pages of a book, or the like RIFFLE
- left-hand page of a book, typically having an even number VERSO
- letter or number printed at the foot of some pages in a book, specifying the sequence for binding the sections, or such a section (typically of 16 or 32 pages) SIGNATURE
- number the pages of PAGINATE
- pair of facing pages in a book, magazine, or newspaper, especially when the text or picture stretches across the fold SPREAD
- right-hand page of a book, typically having an odd number RECTO
- separate multiple copies, continuous stationery, or the like into individual pages or documents DECOLLATE
- set of printed pages, typically 16 or 32, folded from a single sheet, for binding with others to form a book SIGNATURE, GATHER
- white space between facing pages of a book, two postage stamps on a sheet, or the like GUTTER

paid regularly or relating to a regular payment STIPENDIARY

pain, suffering, agony, anguish PURGATORY, TRAVAIL
- pain felt in a part of the body different from its place of origin REFERRED PAIN
- pain reliever that is a common alternative to aspirin ACETAMINOPHEN
- pain-relieving or tranquilizing substance secreted by the brain ENDORPHIN
- pain spasms shooting along the path of a nerve NEURALGIA
- painful, torturing, agonizing EXCRUCIATING
- painful and difficult route or course of action VIA DOLOROSA, CANOSSA
- painful experience, or the distress it causes WORMWOOD
- painful spasms, as on approaching death PANGS, THROES
- acute, sudden, or piercing, as a pain might be LANCINATING, FULGURATING, FULMINANT
- causing or suffering pain, distress, or sorrow DOLOROUS
- enduring pain and grief with unemotional resignation STOICAL
- insensitivity or loss of sensitivity to pain ANESTHESIA, ANALGESIA
- intense, throbbing facial pain in the region of the fifth cranial nerve TRIGEMINAL NEURALGIA, TIC DOLOUREUX
- mildly painful, stinging TINGLING, SMARTING
- minimum level of intensity for registering or tolerating something, such as pain THRESHOLD
- person who enjoys inflicting pain, or is sexually aroused by it SADIST
- person who enjoys undergoing pain, or is sexually aroused by it MASOCHIST
- pull a face or flinch, as from pain WINCE
- relieve pain without getting rid of the cause ALLAY, ALLEVIATE, MITIGATE, PALLIATE
- relieving pain ANALGESIC, LENITIVE, ANODYNE
- sharp and repeated pains in the intestines GRIPES, COLIC

pain (combining form) ALG-, -ALGIA, ALGO-, -DYN-, -DYNIA, DYS-

paint, draw, or engrave using dots or flecks STIPPLE
- paint, mist, or other dispersion of very fine particles in a consistent medium COLLOID
- paint containing a rubbery sap or gum to increase its smoothness and adhesive properties LATEX PAINT
- paint in which the coloring is contained in tiny oil droplets suspended in water EMULSION PAINT
- paint ingredient prepared from chalk WHITING
- paint medium, such as oil, into which the pigments are mixed VEHICLE, BASE
- paint-mixing board of an artist,

or the array of colors on it PALETTE
- paint or draw a picture of LIMN
- paint or similar substance that is applied as a sealer or undercoat PRIMER
- paint that dries to a glossy and hard finish ENAMEL
- paint that dries to a glossy but never quite hard finish POLYURETHANE
- paint thickly, hastily, or crudely DAUB
- paint thinner made of a thin resinous oil TURPENTINE
- becoming liquid when stirred or shaken, as certain paints and some other jellylike substances are THIXOTROPIC
- blue paint coloring made from the crushed particles of a special glass SMALT
- clay or natural earthy substance used as a coloring agent in paints, ink, and the like SIENNA, UMBER, OCHER
- colored powder mixed with oil or water to produce a paint PIGMENT
- drying substance added to paints, inks, some medicines, or the like SICCATIVE
- priming layer of varnish or paint, as in a painting COUCH, SIZING
- producing a dull, unglossy finish, as some paints are MATT
- quick-drying semigloss paint based on a synthetic resin ACRYLIC PAINT
- substance added to paint, glue, or the like, as to thicken or dilute it EXTENDER
- thick paintlike sealer, filler, or glaze, as used for coating paper, cloth, or plastered walls SIZE
- water-based paint, including whitewash DISTEMPER

painting See chart, page 384
- painting in different shades of a single color MONOCHROME, MONOTINT
- painting of a saint or holy person ICON
- painting of a very small yet detailed kind MINIATURE
- painting or sculpture of a person, as on a monument EFFIGY
- painting that is pretentious and sentimentally vulgar KITSCH
- artistic or harmonious arrangement of parts, as in a painting COMPOSITION
- halolike area of light that in medieval paintings surrounds a holy figure MANDORLA, AUREOLE, VESICA, VESICA PISCIS
- plaster-of-paris preparation used as a painting surface GESSO
- represent in words or images, as by painting or describing DEPICT
- representation of a scene, painting, or the like by costumed actors who pose silent and motionless TABLEAU VIVANT
- representing a scene objectively as a painting might be REALISTIC
- shortening of lines in drawing or painting a scene, for apparent depth or distance PERSPECTIVE, FORESHORTENING
- simplified, abstract, stylized, as a painting or design might be CONVENTIONALIZED
- sketch or preliminary drawing, often full-size, for a tapestry, painting, mosaic, or the like CARTOON

pair of similar objects, such as partridges BRACE
- pair of similar things, or one of such a pair DOUBLET
- pair of words differing in only one small respect, helping to identify distinctive sounds or features of the language MINIMAL PAIR
- paired, as compound leaves might be JUGATE
- arrange or occur in pairs GEMINATE

pair (combining form) ZYG-, ZYGO-, JUG-, YOKE-

palace of a sultan SERAGLIO
- adjective for a palace PALATIAL

pale, as through illness, shock, or anger, as someone's complexion might be PALLID, ASHEN, LIVID
- pale and weakened, as through fever or starvation, CADAVEROUS, ETIOLATED
- pale face, or pale-faced person WHEY-FACE
- pale from illness or unhappiness WAN
- pale in complexion, unhealthy-looking, sickly PEAKY, PASTY
- pale yellowish in color or complexion SALLOW
- cause to become white or pale BLANCH, BLEACH

palm See also **hand**
- palm leaf FROND
- palm of the hand, or fleshy base of the thumb THENAR
- any of the seven fleshy pads on the palm of the hand MOUNT
- primitive seed-bearing plant shaped like a palm tree but having fernlike leaves CYCAD
- relating to the palm of the hand or sole of the foot VOLAR

palmistry, alleged reading of a person's life or future by examining the palm of his or her hand CHIROMANCY

pamphlet distributed by hand HANDOUT, HANDBILL
- pamphlet or booklet on some specialist subject MONOGRAPH
- pamphlets, handouts, and other short-lived topical publications EPHEMERA

pan See **cooking**

Pan - rural deity in classical mythology, resembling the god Pan, part man and part goat FAUN, SATYR

pancakes of a savory Russian style, made of buckwheat flour and typically served with caviar or sour cream BLINI
- flat, round pancake, sometimes containing dried fruit BANNOCK
- thin pancake often folded around a filling CREPE

panel - paneling or facing, typically of wood, fixed to the walls of a room WAINSCOTING, DADO
- pair of painted or carved panels hinged together, as for an altarpiece DIPTYCH
- set of three painted or carved panels hinged together, as for an altarpiece TRIPTYCH

panic-stricken headlong rush, as of horses or a crowd of people STAMPEDE

panpipe SYRINX

pantomime featuring the clown Harlequin HARLEQUINADE

pantry or wine cellar BUTTERY

pants See **clothes**

papacy, papal government or authority VATICAN

papal See illustration, page 385, and also **pope**
- papal, relating to the pope considered as the successor of Saint Peter PETRINE
- papal ambassador NUNCIO
- papal delegate or representative LEGATE, EMISSARY
- papal court and administration of the Roman Catholic Church CURIA
- papal document or letter, in antique handwriting BULL
- papal inability to err in doctrinal matters concerning faith and morals INFALLIBILITY
- papal letter of instructions or judgment, in modern handwriting BRIEF
- papal letter or edict on a point of church law or doctrine DECRETAL
- papal letter sent to bishops in all countries ENCYCLICAL
- papal treasurer, cardinal who handles the pope's financial affairs CAMERLENGO
- favoring a policy of centralized and absolute papal authority in the Roman Catholic Church ULTRAMONTANE
- favoring a policy of decentralized authority in the Roman Catholic Church, restricting papal power in the various branches of the church

PAINTING AND RELATED ARTS TERMS

abstract	referring to a style that relies on pure form for its effect, rather than attempting to represent any object
aquarelle	painting made with the use of transparent watercolors
aquatint	etching process producing tonal effects
art brut	"rough" or "raw" works of art that are intended to be "free of artistic culture"
chiaroscuro	arrangement of strongly contrasting light and shade in a painting
collage	picture composed of a variety of materials pasted to a surface
craquelure	network of small cracks in the paint or varnish of an old painting
diptych	altarpiece of two panels
fête champêtre/ fête galante	18th-century French painting of figures in a pleasant, rural setting
figurative	referring to a style, as of painting, that represents humans, animals, or objects, rather than relying purely on abstract forms
fresco	painting on fresh plaster on a wall or ceiling
frieze	decorative horizontal band, as along the top of a wall
frottage	technique of making images by rubbing a soft pencil over paper on a textured surface
genre painting	painting of a scene from everyday life, as in the 17th-century Dutch school
gouache	painting technique using opaque watercolors bound with gum
grisaille	painting in tones of gray, usually striving for an effect of a sculpture or relief
grotesque	decoration combining animal, human, and plant forms
impasto	thick, opaque surface paint in oil painting
mezzotint	engraving process producing tonal effects
minimal art	abstract style using a few simple geometric shapes and primary colors
montage	picture composed of a number of individual pictures
mural	painting on a wall or ceiling
op art/ kinetic art	modern art form using movement or optical illusions to create the impression of movement
pastel	drawing or sketch in delicate colors made by using a chalky crayon
pastoral	painting that portrays rural life, often in an idealized way
paysage	landscape, rural scene
pentimento	reappearance through a painting of traces of an earlier painting from beneath
pietà	representation of the Virgin Mary mourning over the body of Jesus
pointillism	painting technique using closely spaced dots of primary colors
putto	representation of a small boy or angel
secco	painting on dry plaster on a wall or ceiling
sgraffito	design, as on pottery or a wall, scratched through a thin surface layer to reveal the color beneath
still life	representation of inanimate objects, such as vases and fruit
tempera	paint made of color mixed with a substance such as egg white and water
tondo	circular painting, cameo, or medallion
triptych	altarpiece of three panels
trompe l'oeil	technique or style of painting in which a trick effect of three-dimensional reality is produced

CISALPINE, GALLICAN
- seal on a papal bull BULLA

paper See chart, page 386
- paper fragments thrown at festive occasions CONFETTI
- paper frill adorning the end of a drumstick or cutlet PAPILLOTE
- paper impregnated with a purple chemical that turns red in acid solutions and blue in alkaline solutions, used as a pH or acid-base indicator LITMUS PAPER
- paper in a continuous roll, for use in a rotary printing press WEB
- paper made in ancient times from a reedlike plant PAPYRUS
- paper pulp or moistened paper used in molding PAPIER-MÂCHÉ

- paper screen used in a Japanese house SHOJI
- paper trimmer, or frame for the pulp used in handmade paper DECKLE
- paper-trimming device consisting of a long blade hinged to a frame GUILLOTINE
- paper used to protect areas or edges during painting MASKING PAPER
- paperlike transparent wrapping material CELLOPHANE
- cheap paper made from wood pulp or recycled paper, used for newspapers NEWSPRINT
- continuous strip of paper such as that on which stock-exchange re-

Papal Vestments

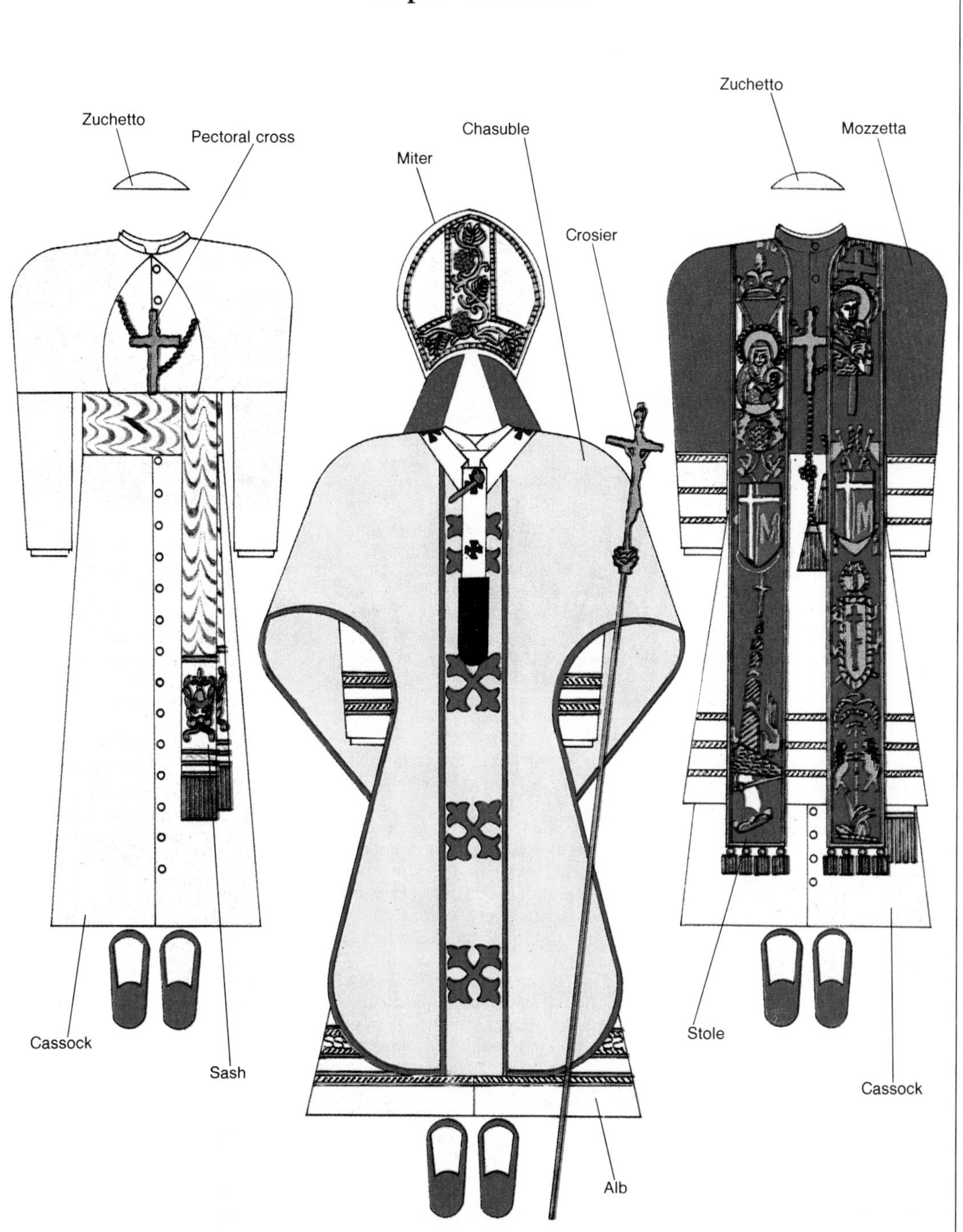

ports used to be printed TICKER TAPE
- crinkled tissue paper used for decorations CREPE PAPER
- drying board, blanket, or roller used in papermaking COUCH
- fine-quality paper resembling thin goatskin VELLUM
- emboss paper with a pattern GOFFER
- file or collection of papers giving information on a particular person or subject DOSSIER
- front side of a sheet of paper, such as a right-hand page in a book, or the side of a letter that is to be read first RECTO
- give a glossy finish to paper, as by pressing it in rollers PLATE
- grainy or crinkled surface, as on leather or paper PEBBLE
- headed writing paper, or the heading on it LETTERHEAD
- identifying mark impressed faintly onto paper, visible when held up to the light WATERMARK
- large sheet of paper printed on one side with news, advertisements, or the like BROADSHEET
- page or page-size equal to a quarter of a large sheet of paper, or a book with such pages QUARTO
- page or page-size equal to an eighth of a large sheet of paper, or a book with such pages OCTAVO
- page or page-size equal to half a large sheet of paper, or a book with such pages FOLIO
- process discarded glass, paper, water, and the like for reuse RECYCLE
- quantity of paper, usually 500 sheets REAM
- quantity of paper, usually 24 or 25 sheets QUIRE
- raised in relief, as words or symbols on specially pressed paper or metal may be EMBOSSED
- reverse side of a sheet of paper, such as a left-hand page in a book, or the side of a letter that is to be read second VERSO
- rough edge of a sheet of paper, especially handmade paper DECKLE EDGE
- smooth, buff-colored paper used for envelopes MANILA PAPER, MANILA
- smooth, heavy paper, as used for drawings CARTRIDGE PAPER
- stiff paper resembling thin goatskin PARCHMENT
- strong, brown wrapping paper made from wood pulp treated with sulfate KRAFT
- strong white paper used especially for writing and typing BOND PAPER
- technique of decorating a surface with paper cutouts DECOUPAGE
- thin, edible paper used in baking RICE PAPER
- thin, tough opaque printing paper BIBLE PAPER, INDIA PAPER
- vegetable matter used in making paper, rayon, and photographic film CELLULOSE
- wood-fiber mixture used in making paper PULP

paper-folding as an art or hobby of Japanese origin ORIGAMI, KIRIGAMI

parachute used to slow down an aircraft or spacecraft, or to drag out the main parachute DROGUE PARACHUTE
- parachuting as a sport SKYDIVING
- cord attaching a parachute pack to the aircraft to open the parachute automatically once the jumper is clear STATIC LINE
- cord pulled by a parachute jumper to open the parachute RIP CORD
- ropes or cords connecting the canopy of a parachute to the jumper's harness SHROUDS
- set of straps attaching a parachute to the jumper's body HARNESS
- silk or nylon hemisphere forming the main part of a parachute CANOPY
- system of ropes or cords on a parachute, hot-air balloon, or the like RIGGING

parade, such as a ceremonial procession of horses or cars CAVALCADE
- parade and carnival held on Shrove Tuesday MARDI GRAS
- parade or costumed procession in a festival PAGEANT
- parade or exhibit in an ostentatious, showy, or vulgar way FLAUNT
- parade or procession of cars or other motor vehicles MOTORCADE
- ceremonial parade or procession, especially a funeral procession CORTEGE
- welcoming parade in which paper strips are thrown down from the buildings lining the streets TICKER-TAPE PARADE

parade (combining form) -CADE

paradise on earth, or idyllic place, especially when purely imaginary SHANGRI-LA, UTOPIA
- paradiselike abode of heroes and virtuous people after death in Arthurian or Celtic mythology AVALON
- paradiselike abode of heroes and virtuous people after death in Greek mythology HESPERIDES, ISLANDS OF THE BLESSED
- paradiselike abode of the blessed after death in Greek mythology ELYSIUM, ELYSIAN FIELDS
- paradiselike hall in Norse mythology, where slain heroic warriors dwell after death VALHALLA
- paradiselike imaginary place of simple and contented country life ARCADIA
- paradiselike place in American Indian folklore HAPPY HUNTING GROUNDS
- nymph or virgin attending the blessed in paradise, according to Islamic belief or folklore HOURI

paradox, contradiction between two equally plausible statements ANTINOMY

paragraph - set in a paragraph from the margin INDENT

parallel, running side by side COLLATERAL

paralysis PALSY, PARESIS
- paralysis from the neck down QUADRIPLEGIA, TETRAPLEGIA
- paralysis from the waist down PARAPLEGIA
- paralysis of a single limb or group of muscles MONOPLEGIA
- paralysis of one side of the body HEMIPLEGIA
- paralysis of the jaw muscles LOCKJAW, TETANUS, TRISMUS
- paralysislike condition together with reduced consciousness, as occurs in schizophrenia and the like CATALEPSY, CATATONIA

paralysis (combining form) -PLEGIA

paralyze IMMOBILIZE
- paralyze or pierce with a spear, one's gaze, or the like TRANSFIX, IMPALE
- paralyze or stupefy, as with fear GORGONIZE, PETRIFY
- device that allows paralyzed pa-

PAPER SIZES

atlas	34 × 26 inches (864 × 660 mm)
crown	20 × 15 inches (508 × 381 mm)
demy	22½ × 17½ inches (572 × 444 mm)
elephant	28 × 23 inches (711 × 584 mm)
foolscap	17 × 13½ inches (431 × 343 mm)
imperial	30 × 22 inches (762 × 559 mm)
medium	23 × 18 inches (584 × 457 mm)
royal	25 × 20 inches (635 × 508 mm)

tients to type, phone, or the like by blowing through a tube POSSUM

parasite, person who takes advantage of another LEECH, SPONGER
- parasitic flatworm such as the fluke TREMATODE
- parasitic worm such as the tapeworm HELMINTH
- intestinal parasite causing dysentery AMOEBA
- inhabit in large numbers, as parasites might their hosts INFEST

parchment of calfskin, lambskin, or kidskin, as used in bookbinding VELLUM
- parchment or manuscript with one or more earlier layers of text erased or still visible PALIMPSEST

pardon See also **excuse, forgive**
- pardon, as of prisoners, granted by a government AMNESTY
- pardon, or declare not guilty ACQUIT
- pardon or release from punishment ABSOLVE, ASSOIL, REMIT
- pardon or overlook an offense readily CONDONE
- corrupt buying and selling of church offices, relics, pardons, and the like SIMONY
- hear the confession of and give a pardon to SHRIVE

pardonable, easily excused or forgiven VENIAL

parent or forbear PROGENITOR
- father, be the parent of BEGET, SIRE
- murder of one's parent PARRICIDE
- in place of or with the responsibilities of parents, as a school principal might be IN LOCO PARENTIS
- influenced by or derived from one's parents HEREDITARY

Paris stock exchange LA BOURSE
- Parisian borough ARRONDISSEMENT

parish meeting of the administrative committee or congregants VESTRY
- relating to a parish PAROCHIAL

parliament See chart, and also **member of parliament, government**
- parliament, congress, or similar lawmaking body or assembly LEGISLATURE
- chairperson controlling the debate in a parliament, a similar legislative body, or the like SPEAKER
- close at the end of a session, as the court, parliament, and congress do ADJOURN
- discontinue a parliament or a similar body, without actually dissolving it PROROGUE
- end and dismiss a meeting, parliament, or the like DISSOLVE
- ending of a debate, as in a parliament or congress, and the immediate voting on the motion CLOSURE, CLOTURE
- having only one chamber or house, as many parliaments are UNICAMERAL
- having two chambers or houses, as many parliaments or legislative bodies are BICAMERAL
- meeting or series of meetings of a parliament, congress, or court, or the period during which meetings are held SESSION
- method of limiting a debate in parliament by the imposition of time limits beforehand GUILLOTINE
- obstruct parliamentary or congressional proceedings deliberately, as by rambling debate STONEWALL, FILIBUSTER
- official doorkeeper in a court of law, parliament, congress, or the like USHER
- official who maintains order in a court of law, parliament, or the like SERGEANT-AT-ARMS
- presentation of a bill to parliament at the various stages of its passage READING
- question a minister, in some European parliaments, on a point of policy INTERPELLATE
- representative assembly or lower chamber of the Irish parliament DAIL
- speech read at the opening of parliament in Commonwealth countries, by the Queen, governor, or the like SPEECH FROM THE THRONE, GRACIOUS SPEECH
- seating in parliament for government or opposition members who are not ministers or shadow ministers BACKBENCHES
- seating in parliament for neutral or independent members committed neither to the government nor to the opposition CROSSBENCHES
- temporary ending of business, as between court sessions or during the parliamentary or congressional holiday RECESS
- transcript or report of British parliamentary debates HANSARD
- unrepresentative parliament that occurs after most of its members have left, died, or been driven out RUMP

PARLIAMENTS

Alderney	**States of Alderney**
Austria	**Bundesversammlung**
Bulgaria	**Narodna Subranie**
Denmark	**Folketing**
Ethiopia	**Shergo**
Finland	**Eduskunta**
France	**Assemblée Nationale**
Germany	**Deutscher Bundestag**
Greenland	**Landstraad**
Guernsey	**States of Deliberation**
Iceland	**Althing**
India	**Rajya Sabha and Lok Sabha**
Iran	**Majlis**
Ireland	**Oireachtas**
Isle of Man	**Court of Tynwald**
Israel	**Knesset**
Japan	**Diet**
Jersey	**States of Jersey**
Mongolia	**Khural**
Nepal	**National Panchayat**
Netherlands	**Staten-Generaal**
Norway	**Storting**
Sark	**Court of Chief Pleas**
Spain	**Cortes**
Sweden	**Riksdag**
Switzerland	**Bundesversammlung**

parody, imitation or representation that is crudely distorted TRAVESTY, CARICATURE
- parody of the style of a literary, musical, or other artistic work PASTICHE
- mocking parody or satire SPOOF, LAMPOON, BURLESQUE

parrot - adjective for a parrot PSITTACINE
- virus disease in parrots, producing a pneumonialike fever in humans PSITTACOSIS

part, subdivision, offshoot, or branch RAMIFICATION
- part attached as an accessory, as to a machine FITMENT
- part into which an area, building,

train, or the like is divided COMPARTMENT
- part of a book, TV drama, or the like EPISODE, INSTALLMENT
- part of a group within a conference, military force, or the like CONTINGENT, DETACHMENT
- part of a whole, element, or section CONSTITUENT, COMPONENT, INGREDIENT
- part or division, especially that bounded by a chord of a circle SEGMENT
- part or division, especially that bounded by two radii of a circle SECTOR
- part or portion, especially a half MOIETY
- part or side of an issue, argument, or the like FACET, FACTOR
- part viewed as a fraction of a whole PROPORTION, PERCENTAGE
- break down into small or basic parts, analyze DECOMPOSE, DISINTEGRATE, DECONSTRUCT
- combining of parts or elements to form a whole SYNTHESIS
- corresponding or complementary part COUNTERPART
- distinct part or stage in the course of an extended process PHASE
- having a uniform structure or similar parts, aspects, or elements throughout, consistent HOMOGENEOUS
- having dissimilar parts, aspects, or elements HETEROGENEOUS
- having many and varied aspects or parts MULTIFARIOUS
- having or divided into two parts BIPARTITE
- made up of several parts COMPOUND, COMPOSITE
- referring to equal parts, especially when they jointly make up the whole ALIQUOT
- small part, fraction MODICUM
- small part or shred of a conversation, book, or the like SNIPPET

part (combining form) -MERE, -MER-, MERO-, -OME, -TOME, HYPO-

part and parcel, inseparable, vital, forming an essential part of the whole INTEGRAL, INTRINSIC, INHERENT

parts of speech GRAMMATICAL WORD CLASS, MAJOR FORM CLASS

part-song - unaccompanied secular song or part-song, developed in Renaissance Italy MADRIGAL

participle incorrectly or inadequately connected to the word it modifies MISRELATED PARTICIPLE, DANGLING PARTICIPLE, HANGING PARTICIPLE

particle, pellet, small grain GRANULE
- suspension of particles, as in smog or a colloid DISPERSION

particular, definite, individual SPECIFIC

parting shot, clinching argument, or hostile remark made when leaving PARTHIAN SHOT

partition dividing up a ship, aircraft, or spacecraft BULKHEAD

partly (combining form) QUASI-, SEMI-, SECT-

partner, comrade, companion COMPEER, YOKEFELLOW, MATE, BUDDY
- partner, especially the spouse of a monarch CONSORT
- partner, helper, especially a spouse HELPMEET, HELPMATE
- partner, helper, or fellow worker ASSOCIATE, COLLABORATOR, COLLEAGUE, CONFRERE, CONSOCIATE
- partner, member of a group of fellow students, sportsmen, workers, or the like STABLEMATE
- partner in a friendly contest, rival SPARRING PARTNER
- partner or follower, often one who is willing to do the "dirty business" COHORT, HENCHMAN, SIDEKICK, CRONY
- partner or helper, sometimes in a dubious or criminal enterprise ACCESSORY, ACCOMPLICE, CONFEDERATE
- temporary partner, associate, or companion BEDFELLOW

partner (combining form) CO-

partnership - collaborating, in partnership with, especially in some dubious enterprise IN CAHOOTS, COLLUDING

partridges - pair of similar objects, such as partridges BRACE
- small flock or family of partridges COVEY

party See also **celebration, political**
- party, banquet, or outing JUNKET
- party attended by men only, typically one held just before the groom's wedding BACHELOR PARTY, STAG PARTY
- party or excursion for women only HEN PARTY
- party or festivity that is drunken and noisy, or a reveler at such an event BACCHANAL
- party or gathering for a special occasion, as after a wedding or to welcome visitors RECEPTION
- party or gathering for discussion of the arts SALON, CONVERSAZIONE
- party where gifts are given to a bride before marriage or a mother-to-be SHOWER
- party with dancing at teatime in the afternoon THÉ DANSANT
- formal evening party, often with musical or literary entertainments SOIREE
- formal royal reception or party LEVEE
- move about from person to person, as at a party CIRCULATE, WORK THE ROOM
- outdoor party or picnic of various kinds BURGOO, CLAMBAKE, COOKOUT, FÊTE CHAMPÊTRE
- personally involved or affected, as parties in a dispute would be INTERESTED
- traditional Irish or Scottish party with dances, music, and the like CEILIDH

pass, ooze, or seep slowly through or as if through a filtering substance PERCOLATE
- pass allowing entry to a specific area LAISSEZ-PASSER
- pass between two mountain peaks COL
- pass beyond or rise above the limits of TRANSCEND
- pass on property, especially land or buildings, by a will DEVISE
- pass on something from one person or point to another RELAY
- passing of the soul into another body after death TRANSMIGRATION, METEMPSYCHOSIS
- passing on of rights or duties, as to a substitute or successor DEVOLUTION
- passing through or across TRANSIT
- passing through, staying only temporarily, as a farmworker or bird might be TRANSIENT, MIGRATORY
- gain possession of the ball by cutting off a pass INTERCEPT

passage copied from a text, speech, or the like, as for separate publication EXTRACT, EXCERPT
- passage of writing that is more striking, elaborate, or extravagant than the surrounding text PURPLE PATCH, PURPLE PASSAGE
- passage or extract from a text GOBBET, SNIPPET

passageway, roofed but often without walls, between two buildings BREEZEWAY
- passageway, typically lined with shops, as through a building ARCADE
- passageway to a bank of seats in a stadium or amphitheater, as in the Colosseum in Rome VOMITORY
- network of hedged or walled passageways in a puzzling pattern MAZE, LABYRINTH
- public passageway or right of passage from one point to another THOROUGHFARE

passenger list MANIFEST

passion, typically short-lived, especially for another person INFATUATION
- passion or burning enthusiasm

ARDOR, RAPTURE, FERVOR
- not returned or reciprocated, as a person's love or passion for another might be UNREQUITED
passionate, fiery, intense, or emphatic VEHEMENT
- passionate, rabble-rousing orator FIREBRAND, DEMAGOGUE, INCENDIARY
- passionate, stormy, chaotic, as a love affair might be TEMPESTUOUS, TURBULENT, TUMULTUOUS
- passionate and energetic in a creative way DIOANYSIAN, DIONYSIAC
- passionate and volatile, easily angered INFLAMMABLE
- passionate choral hymn and dance in ancient Greece, in honor of Dionysus DITHYRAMB
- passionate speech of denunciation TIRADE, DIATRIBE
- passionately angry, infuriated INCENSED
- passionately enthusiastic and zealous in promoting a cause EVANGELISTIC
- passionately enthusiastic or devoted AVID, ARDENT, FERVENT, PERFERVID, IMPASSIONED
- passionately enthusiastic or devoted, to an extreme or excessive and irrational degree FANATICAL, RABID
- passionately enthusiastic or highly delighted ECSTATIC, RHAPSODIC
- passionately in love, though usually only temporarily INFATUATED, BESOTTED
passive, slack, weak-willed SUPINE
- passive resistance, as initiated by Gandhi in India, to press for political reform SATYAGRAHA
Passover PESACH
- Passover feast SEDER
- adjective for Easter or the Passover PASCHAL
- book read at the Passover feast, relating the story of the Exodus HAGGADAH
- flat, crisp bread, eaten by Jews during Passover MATZO
- made of dough without yeast or other fermentation agent, as Passover bread is UNLEAVENED
passport allowing entry to a specific area LAISSEZ-PASSER
password COUNTERSIGN, PAROLE
- password, catchphrase, slogan, or the like that distinguishes a group from others SHIBBOLETH
- password used for identification or recognition among members of a group WATCHWORD
past, early life, or background of a person ANTECEDENTS
- applying to the past, or taking effect as from a date in the past, as a law might RETROACTIVE, RETROSPECTIVE
- calculation of the dates of past events, or ordering of events according to their dates, or a list of such events CHRONOLOGY
- looking back on the past, with hindsight IN RETROSPECT
- scene or passage in a novel, movie, or the like that interrupts the main story line to revert to past events FLASHBACK
- something handed down from the past LEGACY, HERITAGE
past perfect tense of a verb, as in *had climbed* PLUPERFECT
pasta See illustration, page 390
- pasta in the form of long narrow ribbons FETTUCINE
- pasta in the form of long, thin, flat strands LINGUINE
- pasta in the form of short ribbed noodles, hollow and often slightly curved RIGATONI
- containing or relating to pasta FARINACEOUS
- firm and chewy though lightly cooked, as pasta might be AL DENTE
paste, semisolid mixture MAGMA
- art form or work in which many pieces of fabric, cloth, or the like are pasted on a surface COLLAGE
- patchwork, embroidery, or similar decoration consisting of different materials pasted or sewn together APPLIQUÉ
pastille of a medicinal substance, for chewing or sucking TROCHE, LOZENGE
pastry See also **cake** and chart at **dessert**
- pastry case, filled with a savory mixture and served hot as an hors d'oeuvre or snack BOUCHÉE
- pastry made with eggs, of a very light consistency, as used for éclairs CHOUX PASTRY
- pastry or pastries PATISSERIE
- pastry shell filled with a savory mixture of fish, mushrooms, or the like in thick sauce VOL-AU-VENT
- pastry strip sealing the edge of a pie crust FLUTING
- crescent or other small ornamental piece of puff pastry used as a garnish in cooking FLEURON
- fat, such as butter or lard, as used to make crumbly biscuits or flaky pastry SHORTENING
- light pastry in paper-thin layers, as in some Greek sweet and savory dishes PHYLLO
- pinch the edges of pastry for a fluted appearance CRIMP
patch of color on an animal's coat FLASH
- brown or gray with darker streaks or patches, as a dog, cat, or cow might be BRINDLED
- marked with black and white patches, as some horses are PIEBALD, PINTO
- marked with patches of different colors PIED
- marked with white, gray, brown, or reddish patches, as some horses are SKEWBALD
patchwork, embroidery, or similar decoration consisting of different materials pasted or sewn together APPLIQUÉ
patent medicine, especially one boasting of secret ingredients NOSTRUM, PANACEA, SNAKE OIL
path along a canal or river, as still sometimes used by horses pulling boats TOWPATH
- path or promenade made of wooden planks, as beside a beach BOARDWALK
- path or road from one point to another THOROUGHFARE
- path or strip, such as that left behind by a scythe or mower SWATH
- pathway used for horse riding BRIDLEPATH
- curved flight path of a missile, ball, or the like TRAJECTORY
- narrow pathway or platform, as along the side of a bridge CATWALK
pathfinder TRAILBLAZER
patient, calm, and uncomplaining in the face of provocation LONG-SUFFERING, FORBEARING
- patient receiving blood, tissue, a transplanted organ, or the like from a donor RECIPIENT, DONEE
- patient's full case history or medical records ANAMNESIS
- relating to the direct treatment of patients, as in the practical section of medical training CLINICAL
- restraining garment with long sleeves for binding the arms of a violent patient or prisoner STRAITJACKET
patriot of an extreme or uncritical kind CHAUVINIST, JINGO, JINGOIST, FLAG-WAVER
- patriotism of a narrow, militant, fanatical kind CHAUVINISM, JINGOISM
patron or sponsor of artists, writers, and the like MAECENAS
- person whose welfare is protected or career advanced by an influential patron (masculine and feminine, respectively) PROTÉGÉ, PROTÉGÉE
patronizing system of government or authority, typically generous and concerned but restricting individual responsibility PATERNALISM
patter, long-winded or slick sales talk or attempt at persuasion SPIEL
pattern See also **design**

- pattern, mold, plate, or similar guide, as in woodwork, for making or reproducing something accurately TEMPLATE
- pattern, routine, or way of operating REGIMEN
- pattern, structure, or framework, as of an argument SCHEMA
- pattern of colored lines forming squares against a plain background TATTERSALL
- pattern of complicated curved shapes, as on colorful woolen shawls PAISLEY
- pattern of draped or curved strings of leaves, ribbons, or the like FESTOON
- pattern of elements forming an identifiable problem, undesirable condition, behavior disorder, or the like SYNDROME
- pattern of five things of which four outline a square and the fifth is in the center QUINCUNX
- pattern of four leaves or petals, as in heraldry or tracery QUATREFOIL
- pattern of inlaid work, as used in decorating furniture MARQUETRY
- pattern of multicolored diamond-shaped areas, as used in knitting ARGYLE
- pattern of overlapping edges, as of roof tiles or fish scales IMBRICATION
- pattern of slanted parallel lines in alternating rows HERRINGBONE
- pattern of superimposed letters, as for making an emblem MONOGRAM, CIPHER
- pattern or arrangement of parts CONFIGURATION, CONFORMATION
- pattern or cycle of one's mental, physical, or emotional condition BIORHYTHM
- pattern or design of three curved or bent branches radiating from a center TRISKELION
- pattern or design on metal, raised in relief by hammering REPOUSSÉ
- pattern or direction of the fibers in wood, meat, muscle or the like GRAIN
- pattern or distinctive quality of a piece of music, historical period, or the like TEXTURE, ETHOS
- pattern or method of procedure, as in a criminal's actions MODUS OPERANDI, MO
- pattern or model on which other versions or copies are based BLUEPRINT, ARCHETYPE, PROTOTYPE
- pattern or symbol, as on a flag or in embroidery DEVICE
- pattern produced by superimposing one design on another MOIRÉ PATTERN
- patterned fabric produced by shielding various areas with wax before dyeing the fabric BATIK
- patterning or artistic arrangement of the elements in a poem, painting, building plan, or the like ORDONNANCE
- complex pattern of interlaced leaves, flowers, or geometrical shapes ARABESQUE
- example or model serving as a standard or pattern for others PARADIGM, TOUCHSTONE
- leaf pattern in architecture, as engraved on Corinthian columns ACANTHUS
- make a design or pattern by embedding decorative pieces in a surface INLAY
- ornamental pattern of interlaced lines or repeated geometrical shapes within a band, as on wall decorations or moldings FRET, MEANDER
- repeated shape or theme in a pattern, composition, or the like MOTIF
- traditional Chinese blue-on-white design, as on a patterned china plate WILLOW PATTERN

pause, interval, temporary stop, as between acts of a play INTERMISSION
- pause, rest, or postponement,

Pasta

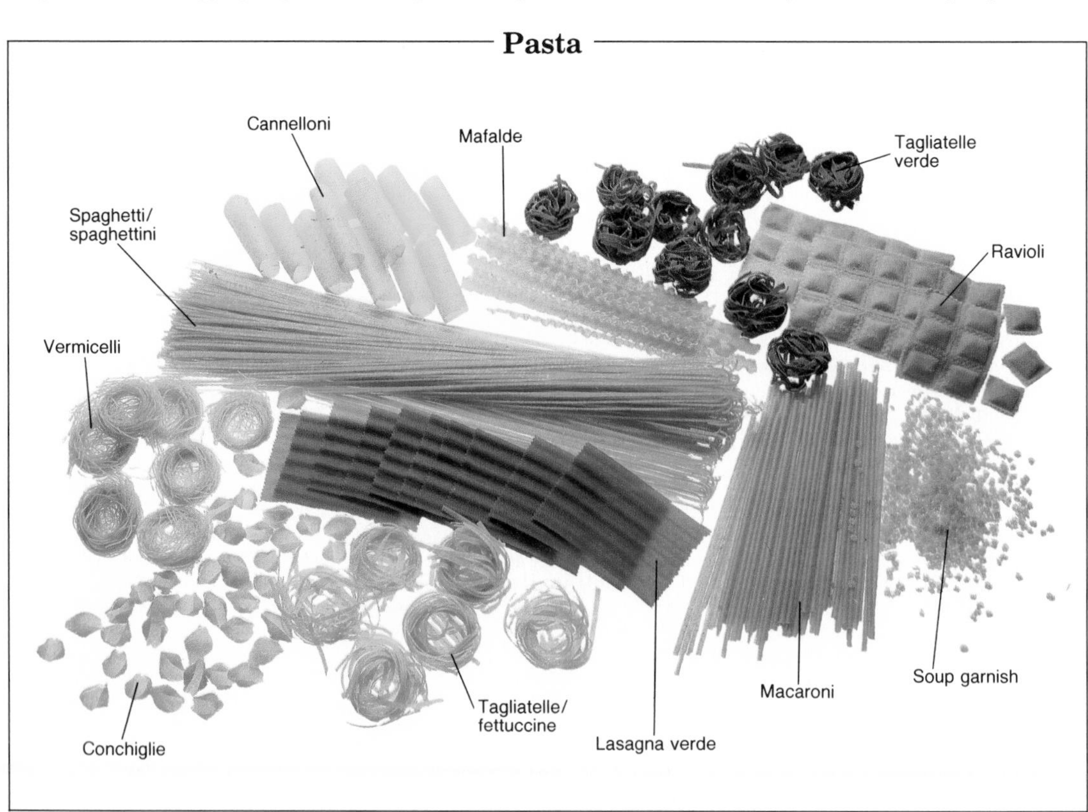

typically in the middle of something unpleasant RESPITE
- pause in a line of verse, especially at a natural sense division CAESURA
- pause or discontinuity, specifically between two successive reigns or governments INTERREGNUM
- pause or break in proceedings or continuity HIATUS
- pause or interval in the sessions of a committee, court, or the like RECESS, ADJOURNMENT

paved outdoor area adjoining a house PATIO

pavement - canvas canopy over the pavement, marking the entrance to a theater, club, or the like MARQUEE
- glass tile or disc set in a pavement, deck, or the like to admit light BULL'S-EYE

paving brick CLINKER
- paving stone FLAGSTONE

pawn - in pawn IN HOCK
- pawned item PLEDGE
- recover or regain something, such as pawned goods, by payment REDEEM

pay, meet the costs or expenses DEFRAY
- pay back REIMBURSE
- pay off a debt or mortgage by installments AMORTIZE
- pay or give what is due RENDER
- pay out, as from a fund DISBURSE
- difference in rates of pay for different types of work DIFFERENTIAL
- money paid by an employer as a compensation to an employee who has lost his or her job SEVERANCE PAY, REDUNDANCY PAY

payment, as made initially to a lawyer or regularly to an occasional consultant RETAINER
- payment, as of dividends or a pension, made once a year ANNUITY
- payment, gift, or other expression of respect, submission, or the like TRIBUTE
- payment, such as an allowance or salary, that is received regularly STIPEND
- payment, usually small, for a service that is technically free HONORARIUM
- payment made in an illegal or underhand way to secure a favor BRIBE
- payment made periodically by a divorced person to an ex-spouse ALIMONY, MAINTENANCE
- payment made to a salesman or agent for successfully completed services COMMISSION
- payment made to workers to encourage increased production INCENTIVE, BONUS
- payment or gift in return for a service or favor CONSIDERATION, RECOMPENSE, REMUNERATION
- payment or maintenance settlement made to a lover after separation PALIMONY
- payment or order for an advance purchase, as of concert tickets or issues of a magazine over a specified period of time SUBSCRIPTION
- payment or profit from one's job or office EMOLUMENT
- payment or reward GUERDON
- based on personal decision rather than on regulations, as powers or payments might be DISCRETIONARY
- force payment, tribute, or the like EXACT, EXTORT, BLACKMAIL
- given as a favor rather than out of legal obligation, as a payment might be EX GRATIA
- make amends for a loss or injury, as by a payment COMPENSATE
- reduce or revise a debt, payment, or the like COMMUTE
- return of part of the payment made REBATE
- something, especially money, that is offered as payment TENDER
- system of making wage payments in goods or vouchers rather than cash TRUCK SYSTEM
- without constraint and without payment VOLUNTARY

pea, bean, or related pod-bearing plant LEGUME
- pealike pickled bud with a pungent flavor used as a condiment CAPER
- small tender green pea PETIT POIS

peace agreement PACT, TREATY
- "peace," "truce," used as an immunity or exemption call, as in children's games FEN, VENTS, FAINS, FAIN IT, FAINS I, FAINITES, PAX
- peace agreement and informal decision to cooperate, as between two countries ENTENTE CORDIALE
- peace established temporarily, agreed suspension of hostilities TRUCE, ARMISTICE
- peace of mind, emotional tranquillity EQUANIMITY, ATARAXIA
- peace or harmony CONCORD
- "peace to," "with deference to," used to acknowledge someone when disagreeing with his or her opinion PACE
- peaceful relations, friendship, especially between countries AMITY
- policy of agreeing to the demands of a potential enemy for the sake of maintaining peace APPEASEMENT
- politician or adviser favoring aggression rather than peace HAWK
- politician or adviser favoring peaceful solutions DOVE
- promoting peace, reducing conflict IRENIC, PACIFIC, PLACATORY, CONCILIATORY
- resumption of or the approach toward peaceful relations, as between two countries or nations RAPPROCHEMENT, DETENTE

peace pipe CALUMET

peaceful See **calm**

peach or related fruit whose stone or pip tends to cling to the flesh CLINGSTONE
- peach or related fruit whose stone or pip tends to separate easily from the flesh FREESTONE

peacock - eyelike marking, as on a peacock's tail OCELLUS
- flock of peacocks or peafowl MUSTER, PRIDE, OSTENTATION
- relating to or resembling a peacock or peacock's tail PAVONINE

peak, high point, final development or achievement PINNACLE, ZENITH, MERIDIAN, SUMMIT, CLIMAX

peanuts - poison produced by fungus on peanuts and corn AFLATOXIN

pear-shaped PYRIFORM
- alcoholic drink made from fermented pear juice PERRY

pearl produced through artificial stimulation of an oyster by the insertion into it of a small bead CULTURED PEARL
- pearl that is smooth, round, and very large PARAGON
- pearl that is very small and often imperfect SEED PEARL
- pearl's quality of luster, or a high-quality pearl ORIENT
- adjective for a pearl MARGARIC
- irregularly shaped, as a pearl might be BAROQUE

pearly, consisting of or resembling mother-of-pearl NACREOUS
- pearly, shiny inner surface of some mollusk shells, used for ornamentation MOTHER-OF-PEARL, NACRE

peasant in a slavelike condition, bound to a feudal lord or estate SERF
- peasant in feudal times who had the status of a freeman but owed services or rent to his lord in return for land VILLEIN
- peasant in feudal times who occupied a cottage and smallholding in return for labor COTTER
- peasant in Russia in czarist times MUZHIK
- peasant or unskilled worker, especially in Latin America PEON
- peasants or farm laborers in Arab countries FELLAHIN
- Anglo-Saxon peasant or other person of the lower classes ESNE

peat bog TURBARY
- peat moss SPHAGNUM
peculiar See **odd**
peculiar (combining form) IDIO-
peculiarity of behavior, or odd notion or action QUIRK, MANNERISM, FOIBLE, WHIM, ECCENTRICITY, IDIOSYNCRASY, VAGARY, CAPRICE
pedal on a piano for prolonging a note, the loud pedal SUSTAINING PEDAL, REVERBERATION PEDAL
- pedal or foot-operated lever for driving a sewing machine, potter's wheel, or the like TREADLE
pedantic, dogmatic, excessively precise or subtle SCHOLASTIC, NITPICKING, CASUISTIC
peddler, trader, or supplier in former times CHAPMAN
pedestrian crossing at which pedestrians have priority over vehicles at all times ZEBRA CROSSING
- area for pedestrians, such as a concourse or wide passageway, lined with shops MALL, ARCADE
pedigrees - study of pedigrees, coats of arms, precedence, and the like HERALDRY
peephole in a door for identifying visitors JUDAS, JUDAS HOLE
peeping Tom VOYEUR
peg, pin, or short rod fitting into holes to fasten adjoining pieces of wood or stone DOWEL
- peg or pin, especially one used as a oarlock in the side of a boat THOLE
- peglike crosspiece inserted to fasten a loop or strap, or secure a knot TOGGLE
pen pen made of the hollow main shaft of a feather QUILL
- pen or pound for animals, such as stray sheep PINFOLD
- pen with a felt tip, used to pick out printed words by broad colored strokes HIGHLIGHTER
- pen with a hollow needle instead of a nib for the release of the ink STYLOGRAPH
- downward stroke of the pen in handwriting MINIM
pen name NOM DE PLUME, NOM DE GUERRE, PSEUDONYM
penalty, especially a fine, imposed at the court's discretion AMERCEMENT
- penalty imposed or threatened, as a means of enforcing a law, standard, or decree SANCTION
- reduce to a lighter sentence, penalty, or the like COMMUTE
- suspend or refrain from enforcing a rule, penalty, or the like WAIVE
pencil-like stick containing a chemical for stopping the bleeding from small cuts, as after shaving STYPTIC PENCIL
- pencil whose writing cannot be erased INDELIBLE PENCIL
- dark gray allotropic form of carbon used in lead pencils and as a lubricant GRAPHITE, PLUMBAGO
pendulum - long, heavy, free-swinging pendulum that demonstrates the rotation of the earth FOUCAULT PENDULUM
penetrate or spread through DIFFUSE, PERMEATE, METASTASIZE
- impossible to penetrate, resisting penetration by liquids or gases IMPERMEABLE, IMPERVIOUS
penetrating, cutting, to the point, as a remark might be INCISIVE, TRENCHANT, MORDANT, CAUSTIC
penicillin or related medicine used in treating or preventing bacterial infections ANTIBIOTIC
penis, or a sculpture or other symbolic representation of it PHALLUS
- penis symbol or phallic image of the Hindu god Shiva LINGAM
- canal in the penis for the passage of urine and semen URETHRA
- gland between the bladder and penis, secreting seminal fluid PROSTATE
- image or representation of the penis, as in sculpture PRIAPUS
- loose fold of skin covering the tip of the penis FORESKIN, PREPUCE
- referring to a statue, painting, or the like of a man or fertility god with a prominent penis ITHYPHALLIC
- tip or head section of the penis GLANS
penmanship, fine handwriting CALLIGRAPHY, CHIROGRAPHY
pension, dividends, or the like paid once a year ANNUITY
- pension rights or other benefit enjoyed by an employee, in addition to his or her wages or salary FRINGE BENEFIT
- pensioned off, retired, or discharged because of old age or illness SUPERANNUATED
- rising in keeping with the cost of living, as a salary or pension might INDEX-LINKED
people, the masses POPULACE, PLEBS
- people in the mass, the mob, rabble CANAILLE, HOI POLLOI, RAGTAG, RIFFRAFF
- people of a nation, regarded as a political group DEMOS
- common people, the lower classes or working people PLEBEIANS, PLEBS, PROLETARIAT
- common people or inhabitants of a place POPULACE, COMMONALTY
- relating to the common people, unsophisticated DEMOTIC, PLEBEIAN
people (combining form) DEM-, DEMO-, ETHN-, ETHNO-
pepper-like condiment with a fierce burning taste, red pepper CAYENNE PEPPER
- pepper shaker, salt cellar, mustard pot, or the like, or a set of such containers CRUET
- sweet pepper, red or green pepper or similar vegetable PIMIENTO, CAPSICUM
peppermint flavoring MENTHOL
per day, daily PER DIEM
per month, monthly PER MENSEM
per person PER CAPITA
per thousand PER MILL
per year, annually PER ANNUM
perception, allegedly by means of a sixth sense, supernatural powers, intuition, or the like EXTRASENSORY PERCEPTION, ESP, CRYPTESTHESIA, TELESTHESIA
- below a person's threshold of consciousness or perception SUBLIMINAL
- fine feeling, keen power of perception, sensitive openness to emotional influences SENSIBILITY
- object grasped by the intellect or intuition rather than known through sense perception THING-IN-ITSELF, NOUMENON
- object known through sense perception, rather than known through reasoning or intuition PHENOMENON
percussion See chart
- percussion section of an orchestra BATTERY
- percussionist in an orchestra, especially one who plays the kettledrums TYMPANIST
perfect See also **excellent**
- perfect, free of error or failing IMMACULATE, IMPECCABLE, FLAWLESS, UNBLEMISHED
- perfect, impossible to fault or blame, beyond criticism IRREPROACHABLE, UNIMPEACHABLE
- perfect, inevitably correct, and incapable of making a mistake INFALLIBLE
- perfect example or specimen, serving as a model for others EXEMPLAR, PARAGON
- perfect example or typical representative of a specified vice or virtue PERSONIFICATION, EMBODIMENT, INCARNATION
- perfect example, representative, or embodiment of an idea or ideal EPITOME, ARCHETYPE, AVATAR
- perfect place, paradise on earth, especially when imaginary SHANGRI-LA, UTOPIA, ARCADIA
- perfect society, looked forward to in the future MILLENNIUM
- perfect state or extreme point

NE PLUS ULTRA

perforation between rows of stamps for easy separation ROULETTE

perform or celebrate with formal or religious rites SOLEMNIZE
- perform a hoax, commit a crime, or the like PERPETRATE
- perform official duties on a formal occasion OFFICIATE
- perform or devise a poem, play, melody, or the like, composing as one goes IMPROVISE
- perform business TRANSACT
- perform or speak without preparation EXTEMPORIZE

performance, as by a musician, that is additional to the scheduled program, in response to audience applause ENCORE
- performance by a solo musician RECITAL
- performance of a dramatic role or musical composition RENDERING, RENDITION
- performance of a play or show, or screening of a film in the afternoon MATINEE
- brilliant technically, or showy, as a musical performance might be BRAVURA

performer of considerable experience, veteran performer TROUPER
- performer of miracles, magician THAUMATURGIST
- performer on a specified instrument or in a specified technique EXPONENT
- range of jokes, pieces of music, or the like, available to a performer REPERTOIRE, REPERTORY

perfume box with a perforated lid POUNCET-BOX
- perfume fixative based on a waxy cholesterol substance that is secreted by whales AMBERGRIS
- perfume fixative derived from glands under a beaver's tail CASTOR
- perfume made from sandalwood CHYPRE
- perfume made from the oil derived from the leaves of an Asian tree PATCHOULI
- perfume or fragrant oil extracted from petals ATTAR
- perfumed mixture, as of dried petals, in a small packet or box, as for scenting linen POMANDER
- perfumed oil or cream for the hair POMATUM, MACASSAR OIL, MOUSSE, POMADE
- perfumed smoke, or the substance producing it INCENSE
- perfumed stick, burned as incense JOSS STICK
- perfumed toilet water EAU DE COLOGNE
- fragrant glandular secretion from various mammals, used in making perfume CIVET, MUSK
- gum or resin used in making perfume MYRRH
- jar of dried petals or spices, used to perfume the air POTPOURRI
- oil extracted from a tropical grass, used in insect repellents and making perfume CITRONELLA
- oil extracted from the rind of a citrus fruit, and used in making perfume BERGAMOT
- rootstock of a type of iris, used in

PERCUSSION INSTRUMENTS

bones	pair of small bones, making a clicking sound
bongo drums	pair of small Cuban hand drums
castanets	concave wooden discs or shells, clicked together in the hand
chimes	set of hanging metal tubes, struck with a small hammer
claves	wooden sticks beaten together rhythmically
conga	tall Cuban hand drum
cymbal	metal plate struck with a drumstick or clashed against another cymbal
glockenspiel	set of tuned metal bars struck with a small hammer, sounding like bells
kettledrum/ timbal	large bowl-shaped drum that can be tuned; used in orchestras and mounted military bands
lithophone	xylophonelike instrument, with tuned stones instead of bars
maraca	seed-filled gourd that rattles when shaken
marimba	large, deep-pitched xylophonelike instrument, usually played with soft-headed hammers
nakers	pair of small, shallow drums, played in medieval times
pedal drum	kettledrum, mechanically tuned by pedals
snare drum/ side drum	small, shallow, cylindrical drum with a skin at either end, making a rattling tone
tabla	pair of small Indian hand drums
tabor	small drum beaten by hand rather than with sticks
tambourin	long, narrow Provençal drum
tambourine	small drum, with jingles or bells set in the frame, that is rattled or struck
tenor drum	drum similar to a side drum, but deeper pitched
timpani	set of two or three kettledrums
tom-tom	oriental drum, often used in pairs
vibraphone	set of tuned metal bars, arranged like a keyboard, with motor-driven resonators below
washboard	board with a ridged metal or wooden surface, used to make a rattling sound
wood block/ Chinese temple block	resonant, hollow block of wood, struck with wooden sticks
xylophone	set of tuned wooden bars, arranged as a keyboard and struck with small, hard hammers

making perfume ORRIS
- small bottle for perfume PHIAL, VIAL
- small packet or bag containing perfumed powder, to scent clothes and linen SACHET
- spray device, as for perfume ATOMIZER
- substance added to a perfume to reduce evaporation FIXATIVE

period during which a human or animal fetus is carried in the womb GESTATION PERIOD
- period of greatest strength or success HEYDAY, PRIME
- period of history, era EPOCH
- period of time for which something continues or lasts DURATION
- woman's period, monthly discharge of blood from the uterus MENSTRUATION, MENSES

periodic, stopping and starting at intervals INTERMITTENT

perjury - induce someone to commit a wrongful act, especially perjury SUBORN

perk or other customary benefit attached to a position APPANAGE, PERQUISITE, FRINGE BENEFIT

permafrost region between the Arctic's perpetual snow and the tree line TUNDRA

permanent See also **constant**
- permanent, everlasting ETERNAL, SEMPITERNAL, IN PERPETUITY
- permanent, indestructible, or immortal IMPERISHABLE, INDISSOLUBLE, ABIDING, ENDURING
- permanent, lasting indefinitely or forever PERPETUAL, PERENNIAL, PERDURABLE
- permanent, unchangeable, irreversible IRREVOCABLE
- permanent, unchanging IMMUTABLE
- permanent, unerasable INDELIBLE
- permanent and definite, not merely acting or temporary SUBSTANTIVE
- permanent and unbreakable, as a union or contract might be INDISSOLUBLE
- permanent or secure employment status, as enjoyed by some university teachers TENURE
- permanently attached or fixed ENTRENCHED, INGRAINED
- permanently beautiful, everlasting AMARANTHINE
- permanently fitted item of furnishings or the like FIXTURE
- permanently frozen ground, as in the Arctic PERMAFROST
- make permanent or everlasting PERPETUATE

permission, official authorization FIAT
- permission for an aircraft or ship to proceed, as after a traffic delay, or the like CLEARANCE
- permission for the publication of a book, as granted by a bishop or censor IMPRIMATUR
- permission or order to leave, dismissal NUNC DIMITTIS
- permission or toleration implied by the absence of an explicit prohibition SUFFERANCE
- permission to leave CONGÉ

permit, authorize, or approve COUNTENANCE, EMPOWER, WARRANT, SANCTION, RATIFY
- permit allowing entry to a specific area LAISSEZ-PASSER
- permit for the temporary import of a car, or for a motorist to cross certain frontiers CARNET
- permit or accept as rightful, justify LEGITIMATE

permitting, making possible but not obligatory FACULTATIVE
- permitting or admitting of something, such as an interpretation SUSCEPTIBLE

perpendicular, exactly vertical PLUMB

perpendicular (combining form) ORTHO-

perpetual See **constant, permanent**

persecution complex PARANOIA
- persecution of suspected communist sympathizers in the United States in the 1950's McCARTHYISM

persevering, dogged INDEFATIGABLE, UNREMITTING, TENACIOUS, PERTINACIOUS, PERSISTENT

Persian lamb or the fur prepared from it KARAKUL
- Persian title of respect, placed before the surname of a distinguished man MIRZA
- provincial governor in ancient Persia SATRAP
- title of the king of Persia in ancient times SOPHY

personal, and hence often unfounded or biased SUBJECTIVE
- personal, deeply private, secret INTIMATE
- personal belongings PARAPHERNALIA, EFFECTS, CHATTELS
- personal charm and magnetic power of inspiration CHARISMA
- personally, without an intermediary IN PROPRIA PERSONA
- personally involved or affected, as parties in a dispute would be INTERESTED
- report or summary of one's education, career, and other personal details, as for job applications CURRICULUM VITAE, , VITA, RÉSUMÉ

personality, character HUMOR, DISPOSITION, TEMPERAMENT
- personality assets or requirements in one's profession or pursuits STOCK IN TRADE
- personality test based on the subject's interpretations of various abstract inkblot designs RORSCHACH TEST, INKBLOT TEST
- aspect or feature, as of someone's personality FACET, TRAIT
- changeable, as someone's personality might be MERCURIAL, VOLATILE
- harmonious organization of the psychological and intellectual characteristics into a unitary and effective personality INTEGRATION
- sense of a loss of personality, personal identity, and self-esteem, as often found in modern society ALIENATION
- sense of rootlessness, confusion, and loss of personality or personal identity, in the absence of a supportive community ANOMIE

personnel - guns, ammunition, and other equipment of an army, as distinct from personnel MATÉRIEL

perspective in a drawing or painting, through shortening of lines FORESHORTENING

perspiration See **sweat**

persuadable, easily led DUCTILE, MALLEABLE, IMPRESSIONABLE
- persuadable, obliging, cooperative FLEXIBLE, TRACTABLE

persuade by craftiness, trickery, and deceit FINAGLE, WANGLE
- persuade or force someone into doing something, as by threats COERCE, DRAGOON
- persuade or pressure someone into doing something INDUCE, PREVAIL UPON
- persuade someone to go along with one by promises or gifts ENTICE
- persuade with flattery CAJOLE, WHEEDLE, INVEIGLE, COAX, SMOOTH-TALK, SOFT-SOAP
- persuade with private hints or intrigue EARWIG
- incite or persuade someone to act wrongly SUBORN, SEDUCE
- try to persuade or influence legislators or other officials in favor of special interests LOBBY
- try to persuade people to support someone or buy from someone specified TOUT, CANVASS

persuasion - long-winded or slick sales talk or attempt at persuasion SPIEL, PATTER

persuasive, forceful, telling, as an argument might be COGENT, TRENCHANT, INCISIVE, COMPELLING, POINTED
- persuasive or believable, as an excuse or politician might be PLAUSIBLE

- possible and defendable, but not really persuasive, as an argument might be TENABLE

perversions See **sex**

pervert, corrupt, or undermine SUBVERT

pessimism - sentimental or romantic pessimism about life in general WELTSCHMERZ

pessimist, warning others of disaster JEREMIAH, CASSANDRA

- pessimistic, doubting, disbelieving SKEPTICAL, CYNICAL
- pessimistic, predicting disaster APOCALYPTIC

pestle - bowl in which something is ground with a pestle MORTAR

pests See illustration

pet animal, especially a lamb COSSET

- pet name HYPOCORISM, DIMINUTIVE
- sawdust or similar material, in a tray, for pets to excrete on indoors LITTER, CAT LITTER

petals or leaves in a radiating pattern WHORL

- relating to or having petals and sepals CHLAMYDEOUS
- short-lived, dying or falling quickly, as petals might be FUGACIOUS

petition on which the signatures are arranged in a circle ROUND-ROBIN

petrified wood or similar substance hardened by calcium salts CALCIFICATION

petroleum - reduction or decomposition by heat, as of petroleum CRACKING

- separation of petroleum and other chemical mixtures into their components, as on the basis of different boiling points FRACTIONATION

petting, kissing and cuddling NECKING, CANOODLING

petty but nagging, as minor doubts or anxiety might be NIGGLING

- petty criticism or faultfinding NIT-PICKING, CARPING, CAVILING

phantom limb or phantom breast PSEUDOESTHESIA

phantom pregnancy, false pregnancy PSEUDOCYESIS

pharmacist - former term for a pharmacist APOTHECARY

philosopher, scholar, or thinker, especially a devious or oversubtle one SOPHIST

- philosopher, wise teacher, or the like, deeply respected for his experience and judgment SAGE

philosophy See chart, page 396

- philosophical, abstract, speculative METAPHYSICAL
- philosophical discussion and logical disputing DIALECTIC
- philosophical or theological argument, as by students QUODLIBET
- philosophical principle, devised by Descartes, that the very fact of one's thinking or consciousness is a proof of one's existence COGITO, ERGO SUM
- philosophical standpoint from which one views and interprets the world WELTANSCHAUUNG
- philosophical study and theory of the nature and grounds of knowledge EPISTEMOLOGY
- philosophical work, as by Plato, in the form of a conversation DIALOGUE
- actuality or realization of a thing, rather than just potentiality, according to Aristotle's philosophy ENTELECHY
- combine or try to reconcile different philosophical, religious, or other beliefs SYNCRETIZE
- mind of a newborn baby considered, as in Locke's philosophy, a clean slate until receiving sense impressions TABULA RASA
- principle of philosophical and scientific investigation that the simpler a theory is and the fewer unproved assumptions it makes the better OCCAM'S RAZOR
- relating to philosophical thought or pure intellect NOETIC
- relating to the concepts of duty and obligation, in philosophy and logic DEONTIC
- secret or mystical philosophy, specifically occult philosophy based on the Hebrew scriptures CABALA
- thing as it appears, according to Kantian philosophy, as experi-

Pests

PEST	HABITAT	PEST	HABITAT
Flour beetle and flour moth larvae (wormlike) 	Flour, grain, bird seed, pet food	Carpenter ant 	Nests in moist or decaying wood.
Housefly 	Food, garbage, and decaying organic matter, such as manure or cut grass	Household ant 	Attracted from outdoor colonies by sweet or greasy food
Mosquito 	Stagnant water	Bedbug 	Mattresses, box springs, floor and wall cracks, furniture, wallpaper
Silverfish 	Cool, damp areas, such as basements	Book louse 	Warm, humid areas
Spider 	Spins webs in corners and crevices.	Carpet beetle 	Carpets, feathers, furs, hair, silk, upholstery, wool
Wasp, hornet 	Attics, porch ceilings, roof overhangs, roof trees, holes in ground	Cockroach 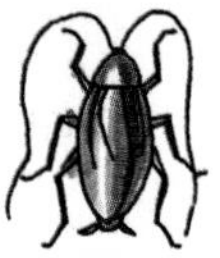	Moist, warm, dark areas

enced by the senses rather than as understood by reason or intuition PHENOMENON
- thing-in-itself, according to Kantian philosophy, as understood by reason or intuition rather than as it appears to the senses NOUMENON
- universally applicable moral law derived from pure reason, according to Kantian philosophy CATEGORICAL IMPERATIVE

phobias See chart, page 398

phone See **telephone**

phonetics See **pronunciation, sound, speech, voice**

photocopying process using light and a resinous powder XEROGRAPHY, XEROX

photographer or freelance journalist who badgers celebrities and the like PAPARAZZO

photography See also **camera, lens, film**
- photograph, engraving, or the like with blurry edges VIGNETTE
- photograph in a brownish tint, especially from earlier times SEPIA
- photograph of a person's face, as of a criminal MUG SHOT
- photograph or photographic process of an early type, based on a silver-coated metal plate DAGUERROTYPE
- photographs, as in magazine advertisements, of handsome or muscular men scantily clothed BEEFCAKE
- photographs, as in magazine advertisements, of sexually attractive women scantily clothed CHEESECAKE
- photographs, particularly aerial photographs, set side by side to form a large composite picture MOSAIC
- photographic film or plate EXPOSURE
- photographic print of the same size as the negative, for preliminary viewing CONTACT PRINT
- photographic print on rough, dull paper TEXTURED PRINT, MAT
- photographic print on smooth, shiny paper GLOSSY
- photographic slide, lit from behind, TRANSPARENCY
- device used in photography for softening the lighting and the shadows, such as a screen of fabric placed in front of a spotlight DIFFUSER
- difference in brightness, as of separate areas of a photograph or television picture CONTRAST
- having poor definition and a speckled appearance, as some photographs are when an inappropri-

PHILOSOPHIES

antinomianism	rejection of conventional morality; doctrine rejecting moral law on the ground that salvation derives from grace or faith alone
behaviorism	doctrine that behavior, rather than mind or consciousness, is all that can really be known or studied about human nature
determinism	doctrine that every event happens according to physical laws, is causally determined, and is independent of human will
empiricism	doctrine that knowledge can be gained only through sense perception and experience
epicureanism	classical Greek doctrine that good was pleasure and evil was pain
epistemology	study of the nature and origin of knowledge
estheticism	doctrine that beauty is the basic principle or chief good in life and underlies morality
ethics	philosophy of morals and moral choices
existentialism	doctrine that human beings have complete free will but no given essence, and have to define themselves with absolute responsibility by their choices in a world that is without independent moral values
Fabianism	political doctrine favoring gradual, nonconfrontational social progress and change
fatalism	doctrine that everything is predestined, as by fate, and that human will and action are powerless to affect events
hedonism	doctrine that pleasure is the basic principle or chief good in life, and underlies morality or determines one's actions
historicism	doctrine that history is governed by inevitable processes; doctrine that a past age should be judged on its own terms rather than by modern values
humanism	doctrine that the basic principle of morality is human culture and the well-being of humanity
idealism	doctrine that the true reality lies beyond the observable world; doctrine that consciousness or reason is the true reality, or the only thing really knowable
instrumentalism	doctrine that the value of ideas lies not in their correctness but in their practical success
jurisprudence	philosophy of law
logical positivism	doctrine that the only meaningful statements are either self-evident or scientifically confirmable, and that statements about unobservable things, such as God or mental states, are therefore meaningless
materialism	doctrine that physical matter is the basic reality and that thoughts and emotions are simply results of it, and that religious and supernatural beliefs are baseless; doctrine that history and social and economic changes have mechanical material causes
metaphysics	study of underlying principles and ultimate reality
nihilism	doctrine that denies the existence of everything; political theory or movement based on the rejection of all authority or any curtailment of individual freedom

PHILOSOPHIES *continued*	
nominalism	doctrine that only actual individual objects really exist, and that essences, universals, or abstract concepts exist only as names
ontology	study of the nature of absolute being as different from the nature of becoming
perspectivism	doctrine that there can be no absolute knowledge of truth because no observer can judge from an absolute position—rival conceptual systems produce different views; doctrine that several points of view are needed to understand reality
phenomenalism	doctrine that the only thing knowable for certain is our set of sense perceptions or sensations
phenomenology	study of awareness and of perceived objects rather than of objective reality
positivism	doctrine that knowledge consists of or is derived from actual facts, and that mere feelings and religious or supernatural beliefs are not true knowledge
pragmatism	practical approach to political or personal dealings, rejecting ideological and historical considerations
prescriptivism	doctrine that statements about good and evil cannot be either true or untrue, but simply reflect and prescribe moral attitudes
rationalism	doctrine that knowledge can be gained only through reason; doctrine that rejects religion on the grounds that it is contrary to reason
realism	doctrine, in modern philosophy, that objects exist independently of being observed (the opposite of idealism); doctrine, in medieval philosophy, that universals, general concepts, exist independently of being thought (the opposite of nominalism)
reductionism	analysis of a subject or problem into its components, even if it means oversimplifying it
relativism	doctrine that truth is not absolute but varies from individual to individual, culture to culture, and age to age
scholasticism	medieval Christian philosophy and theology associated with the Church Fathers, sometimes influenced by Aristotle
solipsism	belief that the self—consciousness—is the only thing in existence or, at any rate, the only thing knowable for certain
stoicism	classical Greek doctrine that the only worthwhile human aim is virtue, and that this involves submitting to nature and suppressing one's emotions
structuralism	theory or movement in many academic fields based on the view that the subject has various underlying structures, contrasts, and assumptions; study of the structure rather than the history of a language
transcendentalism	doctrine that the ultimate reality is in a realm beyond everyday experience; doctrine that knowledge is obtained by intuition or by reflecting on the reasoning process itself
utilitarianism	doctrine that the greatest good is what produces most happiness for the greatest number of people

ate film is used GRAINY
- improve a photographic negative or print by adjusting details or removing flaws RETOUCH
- laser-produced photograph or pattern creating a powerful three-dimensional effect HOLOGRAM
- light-sensitive coating, on photographic film or paper EMULSION
- prepare photographs for display, as by pasting them onto cardboard MOUNT
- screen or network of fine lines, used in astronomical and color photography RESEAU
- sharpness or clarity of outline, as of a photograph or television image DEFINITION, ACUTANCE
- title or short account of a photograph, illustration, cartoon, or the like CAPTION

phrase in popular use, especially one associated with a particular entertainer CATCHPHRASE
- phrase or clause, group of words forming part of a sentence or a sentence CONSTRUCTION
- phrase or expression that has been shortened, such as *morning* for *good morning* BRACHYLOGY
- phrase or expression that is roundabout or long-winded CIRCUMLOCUTION
- phrase or remark, with independent syntax, within a sentence PARENTHESIS
- phrase or word, recorded only once in a given text or language HAPAX, HAPAX LEGOMENON
- phrase or word used for the first time COINAGE, NEOLOGISM
- phrase or word whose letters are rearranged from or into those of another phrase or word ANAGRAM, TRANSPOSITION

physical, bodily, having a real or material rather than spiritual nature CORPOREAL, TANGIBLE
- physical, fleshly, relating to bodily desires and appetites SENSUAL, CARNAL
- physical, material, or actual rather than conceptual or imaginary OBJECTIVE
- physical exercises done rhythmically to improve or maintain one's fitness and muscle tone CALLISTHENICS
- physical exercise done to improve or maintain one's overall cardiovascular health AEROBICS
- physical exercises done to increase one's muscle tone through muscular contraction against resistance ISOMETRICS

physics See chart, page 399

piano See illustration, page 400

PHOBIAS

IRRATIONAL OR EXCESSIVE FEAR OF:	
airplanes or flying	**aerophobia/ pterophobia**
animals	**zoophobia**
bees	**apiophobia/ melissophobia**
birds	**ornithophobia**
blood	**hemophobia/ hematophobia**
bridges, or crossing bridges	**gephyrophobia**
burial alive	**taphephobia**
cats	**ailurophobia/ gatophobia**
children	**pedophobia**
choking	**pnigophobia**
cold	**psychrophobia/ cheimophobia/ cyrophobia**
confined spaces	**claustrophobia/ clithrophobia**
crowds	**ochlophobia/ demophobia**
dark	**scotophobia/ nyctophobia/ achluophobia/ lygophobia**
death or corpses	**necrophobia/ thanatophobia**
depths, deep places	**bathophobia**
deserts, dry places	**xerophobia**
dirt	**rhypophobia/ rupophobia/ mysophobia**
dogs	**cynophobia**
drinking, drunkenness	**dipsophobia**
fear, being alarmed	**phobophobia**
fire	**pyrophobia**
fish	**ichthyophobia**
foreigners	**xenophobia**
fur	**doraphobia**
germs	**microbiophobia**
ghosts	**phasmophobia**
heat	**thermophobia**
heights	**acrophobia/ hypsophobia/ cremnophobia**
horses	**hippophobia**

IRRATIONAL OR EXCESSIVE FEAR OF:	
illness	**nosophobia/ pathophobia**
injury	**traumatophobia**
insects	**entomophobia**
lightning	**astrapophobia/ keraunophobia**
loneliness	**eremiophobia/ autophobia/ monophobia**
madness	**maniaphobia/ lyssophobia**
men and boys	**androphobia**
mice	**musophobia**
name or a particular word	**onomatophobia**
night	**nyctophobia**
noise	**phonophobia**
old age	**gerascophobia**
open spaces, or going out in public	**agoraphobia/ kenophobia**
pain	**algophobia/ odynophobia**
particular place	**topophobia**
poisoning	**toxicophobia/ iophobia**
pregnancy	**maieusiophobia**
sea	**thalassophobia**
sharks	**galeophobia**
sleep	**hypnophobia**
snakes	**ophidiophobia**
speaking, public speaking	**lalophobia/ glossophobia**
speed	**tacophobia**
spiders	**arachnaphobia**
streets, or crossing streets	**dromophobia**
surgery	**tomophobia**
thirteen	**triskaidekaphobia**
thunder	**keraunophobia/ brontophobia/ tonitrophobia**
trains	**siderodromophobia**
travel	**hodophobia**
water or wetness	**hydrophobia/ aquaphobia/ hygrophobia**
women or girls	**gynophobia**
worms	**helminthophobia/ scoileciphobia**

- piano accompanist assisting at opera rehearsals REPETITEUR
- piano having two sets of strings crossing each other OVERSTRUNG PIANO
- piano of the largest size CONCERT GRAND
- piano operated mechanically, sounding the notes indicated on a perforated paper roll PLAYER PIANO, PIANOLA
- piano or similar early keyboard instrument CLAVIER
- piano or similar stringed instrument KEYBOARD INSTRUMENT
- any key on a piano or similar instrument DIGITAL

pick See also **choose**
- pick out or select the best or worst specimens CULL
- picklike hoe for farming or gardening MATTOCK

pickle, soak in brine or vinegar in order to pickle SOUSE
- pickle or soak meat or fish in a sauce before cooking MARINATE
- pickled bud with a pungent flavor, used as a condiment CAPER
- pickling sauce in which meat or fish is left to soak before cooking MARINADE
- salty water, as used for pickling BRINE
- small cucumber usually used for pickling GHERKIN

pickpocket - former term for a pickpocket CUTPURSE

picnic, garden party, or other outdoor meal or entertainment FÊTE CHAMPÊTRE, ALFRESCO

picture See also **painting**
- picture, as of a battle scene, around the inside wall of a circular room CYCLORAMA
- picture, graphic description or

PHYSICS TERMS

absolute zero	lowest temperature that theoretically can be reached: 0°Kelvin, −273.15°C, or −459.67°F
Archimedes' principle	principle that a body's apparent loss of weight when it is immersed in a fluid is equal to the weight of the fluid it displaces
Avogadro's law	law stating that equal volumes of all gases under the same temperature and pressure conditions contain the same number of molecules
Boyle's law	law stating that at constant temperature the volume of a gas varies inversely with its pressure
Brownian motion	random motion of microscopic particles suspended in a liquid or gas
Charles's law	law stating that at constant pressure the volume of a gas varies directly with its absolute temperature
conservation of energy	law stating that in a closed system the total energy remains constant
Doppler effect	apparent change in the frequency of a wave when the observer and the source are moving relative to each other, as in the changing pitch of a train's whistle as it approaches
dynamics	branch of mechanics concerned with the forces that produce or alter the motions of bodies
half-life	time taken for half the nuclei in a sample of radioactive material to decay
Hooke's law	law stating that the strain produced in a solid body is proportional to the stress applied to it
hydraulics/ fluid mechanics	branch of mechanics concerned with the flow of liquids
inertia	tendency of a body to remain at rest or in a state of uniform motion unless disturbed by an external force
kinetics	branch of mechanics concerned with all aspects of motion
mechanics	branch of physics concerned with the action of forces on matter
Planck's constant	universal constant relating the frequency of a radiation to its energy
quantum jump/ quantum leap	transition of an atomic or molecular system from one distinct energy level to another without traveling through the intervening space
quantum theory	theory that light and other forms of energy are emitted not as a wave motion but in small "packets," or quanta
scalar	quantity, such as time or mass, that has magnitude but no direction
statics	branch of mechanics concerned with the action of forces on bodies at rest
surface tension	property of liquids in which the surface acts like a stretched elastic skin
thermodynamics	branch of physics concerned with the relationship of heat to other forms of energy
torque/ moment of force	turning effect of a force on a body free to rotate about an axis
vector	quantity, such as velocity, that has direction as well as magnitude

Piano

UPRIGHT PIANO

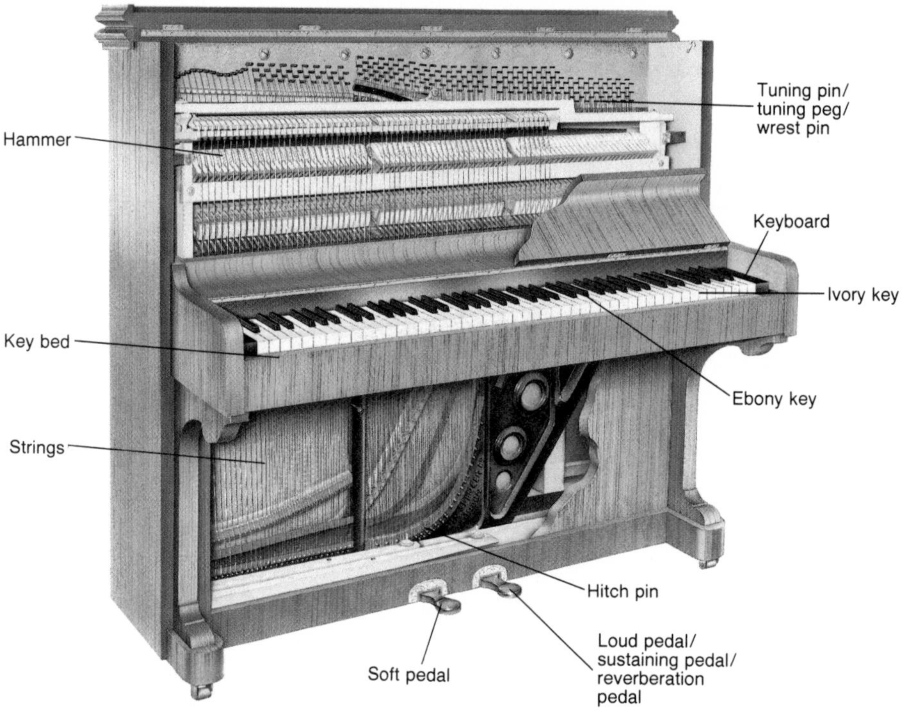

Tuning pin/
tuning peg/
wrest pin
Hammer
Keyboard
Ivory key
Key bed
Ebony key
Strings
Hitch pin
Loud pedal/
sustaining pedal/
reverberation
pedal
Soft pedal

STRIKING MECHANISM

Damper/sordino/muter
Hammer
Damper rest/
damper rail
Hammer rest/
hammer rail
String
Butt
Damper lifter
Check
Escapement/
hammer lever
Regulating button
Action lever
Pivot point
Key
Pilot

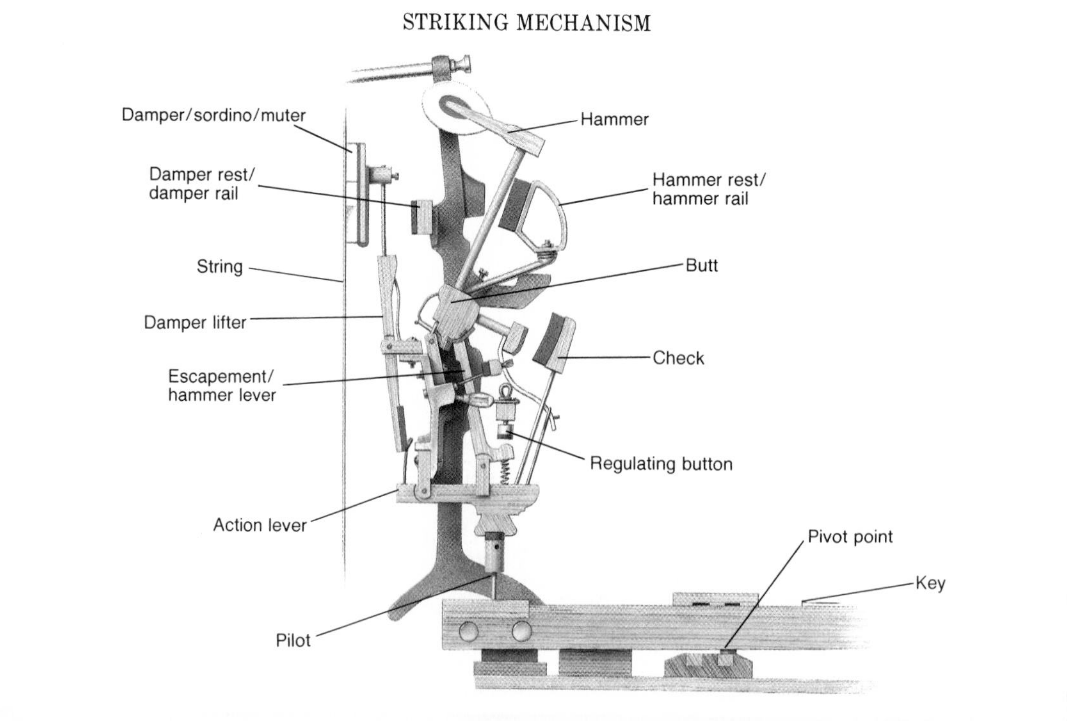

representation TABLEAU
- picture, typically an engraved or photographic portrait, with blurry edges VIGNETTE
- picture at the front of a book, often opposite the title page FRONTISPIECE
- picture frame with crossing and projecting edges OXFORD FRAME
- picture-framing method in which the glass and backing are taped together, or the tape used for this purpose PASSE-PARTOUT
- picture made up of many other pictures overlapping or stuck side by side MONTAGE, COLLAGE
- picture of a memorial plaque made by rubbing graphite or wax on paper pressed against it BRASS RUBBING
- picture or design made up of many small pieces of stone, tile, or glass MOSAIC, TESSELLATION
- picture or scene, as viewed through a slit, that is formed on a series of translucent cloth sheets DIORAMA
- picture representing a word or idea, as in ancient writing systems PICTOGRAPH, HIEROGLYPH
- picture writing, as used in ancient Egypt HIEROGLYPHICS
- card or disc that is spun or twirled to produce a merged image of the partial words or pictures on either side THAUMATROPE
- pair of nearly identical pictures that give a three-dimensional effect when viewed through special lenses STEREOGRAPH
- prepare pictures for display, as by pasting them onto cardboard MOUNT
- puzzle in the form of pictures or symbols representing syllables or words REBUS
- relating to pictures PICTORIAL
- represent in words or images, as by painting or describing DEPICT, LIMN
- title or short account of a photograph, illustration, or other picture CAPTION

picturesque in a simple way IDYLLIC, ARCADIAN

pier or mole to protect a harbor or shore JETTY, GROIN

pierce or paralyze with a weapon, one's gaze, or the like TRANSFIX, IMPALE
- pierce with many holes RIDDLE

pig See also **bacon, pork**
- pig offal used in cooking FRY, HASLET, PLUCK, PURTENANCE
- pig or other male animal castrated after maturity STAG
- pig that has been castrated when young BARROW
- pig's feet, used as food TROTTERS, PETTITOES
- pig's jaw or cheek, used as food CHAP
- piglet newly weaned SHOAT
- piglet or puppy that is the smallest of the litter RUNT
- adjective for a pig PORCINE
- female piglet, or young sow that has not yet produced a litter GILT
- fodder or pasturage for pigs, as in a forest PANNAGE
- food for pigs consisting of acorns and beech nuts MAST
- food for pigs consisting of kitchen scraps and liquid SWILL, SLOPS, WASH
- group of piglets produced at a single birth LITTER, FARROW
- small intestines of pigs, prepared as food CHITLINS, CHITTERLINGS
- viral disease of pigs, causing fever and blistering on feet and snout SWINE VESICULAR DISEASE

pigeon loft or a dovecote COLUMBARIUM
- adjective for a pigeon COLUMBINE
- baby pigeon SQUAB
- captive or dummy pigeon used to decoy others STOOL PIGEON
- domestic pigeon that can perform backward somersaults while flying TUMBLER, ROLLER
- domestic pigeon with a large crop that can be puffed out POUTER
- domestic pigeon with a rounded tail than can be spread out like a fan FANTAIL
- person who has a specified hobby, especially breeding pigeons, roses, or the like FANCIER

pigeonhole, divide into different classes, categories, sections, or the like COMPARTMENTALIZE

pigment See also **color, paint**
- pigment consisting of a natural clay or brown earthy substance UMBER, SIENNA, OCHER
- bright blue pigment made from the crushed particles of a special glass SMALT
- bright red pigment or dye obtained from a tropical cactus insect COCHINEAL, CARMINE
- gray-green pigment used in paints, derived from a greenish sandstone TERRE VERTE
- yellow-brown pigment made from wood soot BISTER

pigtail or plait BRAID, QUEUE

pike - young pike PICKEREL

pile, heap, or mound CUMULUS
- pile or bank of snow or sand, accumulated by wind or water DRIFT

piles, swollen anal tissue HEMORRHOIDS

pilgrim, especially one in former times who carried a palm branch as an indication of having visited the Holy Land PALMER
- pilgrim to Mecca HAJJI
- pilgrimage to Mecca by Muslims HAJJ

pill or medicinal tablet of large size BOLUS
- package of pills in which each pill is contained in a separate plastic bubble on a card BLISTER PACK

pillar See also **column**
- pillar, typically rectangular, set into a wall and projecting slightly from it PILASTER
- pillar, typically rectangular, supporting an arch or vault PIER
- pillar carved and painted with kinship symbols, as by certain North American Indians TOTEM POLE
- pillar in classical architecture in the form of a statue of a man TELAMON, ATLAS
- pillar in classical architecture in the form of a statue of a woman CARYATID
- pillar of stone, four-sided and tapering up to a pyramidal top, of a kind used as a monument in ancient Egypt OBELISK
- pillar or other construction supporting the edge of an arch or end of a bridge ABUTMENT
- pillar or slab of stone, with an engraved surface, as used in ancient times as a monument, gravestone, or the like STELE
- pillar with a stone bust on top, used as a boundary marker or architectural ornament in ancient Rome TERM, TERMINUS
- pillarlike stone, large and flat, usually part of a prehistoric monument MEGALITH, MONOLITH, DOLMEN, MENHIR
- early Christian hermit who lived on top of a pillar STYLITE
- prehistoric monument or chamber formed by stone pillars with a crossbeam DOLMEN, TRILITHON
- ring of stone pillars forming part of a prehistoric monument HENGE, CROMLECH
- row of pillars, columns, or trees that are positioned at regular intervals COLONNADE

pillar (combining form) STYL-, STYLO-, -STYLAR

pillow or long cushion that is often hard, stiff, and narrow BOLSTER
- silky plant fiber used for stuffing pillows KAPOK
- strong cloth used to cover a mattress or pillow TICKING

pilot of a balloon or lighter-than-air

aircraft AERONAUT
- pilot of an aircraft, especially in the early days of flying AVIATOR, AVIATRIX
- seat in a military aircraft that is designed to hurl the pilot or a crew member clear in an emergency EJECTION SEAT, EJECTOR SEAT
- suicide pilot in the Japanese armed forces during World War II, "divine wind" KAMIKAZE

pimp, or go-between in a sexual relationship PANDER, PANDERER, PROCURER

pimple - pimplelike protuberance, as on the tongue or at the root of a hair PAPILLA
- pimple on the eyelid, caused by the inflammation of an oil gland STY
- pimplelike pus-filled skin inflammation PUSTULE, PAPULE, TETTER
- break out, appear on the skin, as a pimple or other blemish does ERUPT
- dark oily plug blocking a pore of the skin and forming a pimple, especially on the face BLACKHEAD, COMEDO
- goose pimples, gooseflesh, bristling of the body hair, as from fear or cold HORRIPILATION, PILOERECTION
- hard, lightish, pimplelike mass under the skin, caused by the blockage of the outlet of an oil gland MILIUM
- inflamed area surrounding a pimple AREOLA
- large, oily pimple or cyst, especially on the scalp WEN
- slang term for a pimple, especially in acne ZIT

pin, bolt, revolving axle, or the like, as in a lock or between two door handles SPINDLE
- pin, peg, or short rod fitting into holes to fasten adjoining pieces of wood or stone DOWEL
- pin at the end of an axle, to hold the wheel in place LINCHPIN
- pin for fastening two parts or objects together, either by spreading its split end or by bolting its threaded end COTTER PIN
- pin or fastener with two flexible arms as for securing a wheel to an axle SPLIT PIN
- pin or pierce with a stake or sharp object IMPALE, TRANSFIX

pinch into tight curls, folds, or the like CRIMP

pine, fir, or other cone-bearing tree CONIFER

pineal gland EPIPHYSIS

pink, carnation, or related flower DIANTHUS

pinkish, "flesh"-colored INCARNADINE

pinniped See illustration

pioneer or leader in any field of endeavor TRAILBLAZER

pious hypocrite TARTUFFE
- pious in a hypocritical or self-satisfied way, pretending to be holy, smug SANCTIMONIOUS, CANTING, HOLIER-THAN-THOU
- piously and narrow-mindedly convinced of the value of one's own virtues SELF-RIGHTEOUS

pip or seed of a grape berry, or the like ACINUS
- peach or related fruit whose stone or pip tends to cling to the flesh CLINGSTONE
- peach or related fruit whose stone or pip tends to separate easily from the flesh FREESTONE

pipe, tube, or canal for the passage of fluids, as in a building, a plant, or the human body DUCT
- pipe carrying sewage from a toilet SOIL PIPE
- pipe connecting smaller pipes HEADER
- pipe fitting, typically a U- or S-shaped bend, for holding water as a barrier against the return flow of gases TRAP
- pipe or channel, as for rainwater or an electric cable CULVERT, CONDUIT
- pipe or duct for hot air, smoke, or the like, as in a boiler or chimney FLUE
- pipe rising vertically within a building RISER
- pipe running up a building, for pumping water from street level in the event of a fire DRY RISER
- pipe smoked in the East, in which the smoke is bubbled through water to cool it HOOKAH, HUBBLE-BUBBLE, CALEAN, WATER PIPE, NARGHILE

Pinniped

- pipe with many holes and connections MANIFOLD
- access opening in the side of a pipe for inspection or cleaning FERRULE
- ceremonial pipe with a long stem, used by Native Americans, "peace pipe" CALUMET
- clay pipe with a long stem CHURCHWARDEN
- fiber of hemp or jute, often treated with tar, used for sealing pipe joints and caulking the seams in wooden ships OAKUM
- rubber suction cup on a handle, used for clearing blocked drains and pipes PLUNGER, PLUMBER'S HELPER
- short tobacco pipe made of clay DUDEEN
- small tool for packing tobacco down into the bowl of a pipe TAMPER
- threaded adaptor or linking pipe for two pipes of different diameters BUSHING
- tobacco pipe made of wood, especially from a woody root BRIAR
- tobacco pipe with a bowl made from a light whitish earthy mineral MEERSCHAUM
- tobacco pipe with a short stem CUTTY
- Turkish pipe with a clay or meerschaum bowl and very long stem CHIBOUK
- upright outdoor water pipe with a tap STANDPIPE

piping or roll of ribbon as used for trimming ROULEAU

pirate, especially along the Barbary Coast of North Africa in former times CORSAIR
- pirate, especially one frequenting the Caribbean in the 17th and 18th centuries BUCCANEER
- pirate, plunderer, military adventurer, or the like in former times FREEBOOTER, FILIBUSTER
- pirate flag JOLLY ROGER, SKULL-AND-CROSSBONES
- pirate or pirate ship ROVER, PICAROON
- pirate's sword, of a short and curved design CUTLASS

pistil or all the pistils of a flower GYNOECIUM

pit or small crater used by soldiers as protection against enemy fire FOXHOLE

pitch - pitchlike bitumen mixture, as used in roofing and roadmaking ASPHALT
- pitchlike, especially in being glossy and blackish PICEOUS
- adjust the pitch of a musical instrument, string, note, or the like TEMPER
- fibers, often treated with pitch, used for sealing the seams in wooden ships OAKUM
- waterproof the hull or seal the seams of a wooden ship, as with tar or pitch PAY, CAULK

pith of a stem or marrow of a bone MEDULLA

pituitary gland HYPOPHYSIS

pity, sympathize with, feel sorry for COMMISERATE
- pity, sympathy, mercy COMPASSION
- arousing pity or sympathy, pitiful, piteous PATHETIC

pivot SWIVEL
- pivot pin, as on a rudder, gun carriage, or towing vehicle PINTLE
- pin on either side of a cannon, container, or the like enabling it to be pivoted on a supporting frame TRUNNION

place See also **position**
- place, setting, or surroundings MILIEU
- place ceremonially in office INSTATE, INSTALL
- place frequently visited HAUNT, PURLIEU
- place in order, arrange, set up ARRAY
- place in society or a profession, prestige STATUS
- place in the care of another, entrust CONSIGN
- place inside something else, such as a new word into a sentence EMBED, INSERT
- place of security or refuge STRONGHOLD
- place or area where some particular event occurred, or where a play or novel is set LOCALE, SETTING, LOCUS
- place or arrange correctly in relation to other things COORDINATE
- place or hide securely ENSCONCE
- place or state of perfect happiness ELYSIUM, ELYSIAN FIELDS
- place or way of life considered empty of spiritual values, cultural interest, or the like WASTELAND
- place over or on top of something else, as one film sequence over another SUPERIMPOSE
- place selected or designated for a trial, sports match, or the like VENUE
- place side by side, as for contrast JUXTAPOSE
- place that is perfect and idyllic, especially when purely imaginary SHANGRI-LA, UTOPIA
- place that is very unpleasant, especially when purely imaginary DYSTOPIA, CACOTOPIA
- place where things are stored for safekeeping REPOSITORY
- approximate place or location WHEREABOUTS
- assign to a place, position LODGE, SITUATE, STATION
- distinctive feeling of a place GENIUS LOCI
- find or specify the place of something, as on a map LOCATE, PINPOINT
- listing or dictionary of places GAZETTEER
- neighborhood, district, places nearby LOCALITY, VICINITY

place (combining form) TOP-, TOPO-, -ORY, -ARIUM, -ORIUM

place error, geographical mistake, positioning something in the wrong region (analogous to anachronism) ANACHORISM

place name, or a word derived from it TOPONYM

plague fever spread by rats' fleas, black death BUBONIC PLAGUE
- plague or other epidemic and deadly disease PESTILENCE
- hospital for treating the plague, leprosy, or other contagious diseases in former times LAZARETTO

plain, as in Russia, that is flat, treeless, and grass-covered STEPPE
- plain, clear, unambiguous, not open to doubt UNEQUIVOCAL
- plain, cooked in a simple way AU NATUREL
- plain, stretch of open, treeless country CHAMPAIGN
- plain to see, obvious EVIDENT, MANIFEST, CONSPICUOUS, SALIENT
- plainly and simply, without mincing words TOUT COURT

plainsong GREGORIAN CHANT
- plainsong opening, sung as a solo INTONATION
- music of a single melodic line, as in plainsong MONOPHONY

plait or pigtail QUEUE
- plaited braid, or its metal tag, as on the shoulder of a military uniform AIGUILLETTE

plan See also **plot**
- plan, outline, or arrangement, as for a radio program FORMAT
- plan, proposal, intended or suggested scheme PROJECT, PROPOSITION
- plan, sketch, or rough drawing of something DRAFT
- plan or arrangement, ordering DISPOSITION
- plan or intend MEDITATE, PURPOSE, CONTEMPLATE, DESTINE, ENVISAGE
- plan or invent, scheme DEVISE, CONTRIVE, CONCOCT, CAST ABOUT, DESIGN
- plan or method based on a long-range or overall view of things STRATEGY
- plan or model, original and detailed, that forms the basis for subsequent versions PROTOTYPE, BLUEPRINT
- plan or record of a trip ITINERARY

- planned, intended PROJECTED
- planned beforehand, deliberate, as a murder might be PREMEDITATED
- planned or performed together, combined, as an effort might be CONCERTED, COORDINATED
- planning, preparation FORETHOUGHT
- planning of any complicated project, especially one involving transport LOGISTICS
- planning technique for a complex project, based on comparing various combinations of stages CRITICAL-PATH ANALYSIS
- plans or methods designed to achieve short-term, local, or immediate objectives TACTICS
- carry out a plan IMPLEMENT, EXECUTE
- course of action for carrying out a plan, process, or the like PROCEDURE
- delay or difficulty in one's plans HITCH
- draft or specify a plan, ideas, or the like FORMULATE
- precise description, list of details, plan, or proposal SPECIFICATION, SPECS
- providing for some possible though unlikely future occurrence or emergency, as a fund or plan might be CONTINGENCY
- provisional, incompletely developed, or experimental, as a plan might be TENTATIVE, STOPGAP, MAKESHIFT
- sketch out or give a rough outline of something, such as a plan ADUMBRATE
- success or realization of plans or wishes FRUITION

planet See illustration
- planet, star, or comet CELESTIAL BODY
- planet of very small size, especially in an orbiting belt between Mars and Jupiter PLANETOID, MINOR PLANET, ASTEROID
- planet that is closer to the sun than earth is INFERIOR PLANET
- planet that is farther from the sun than earth is SUPERIOR PLANET
- chart of the relative positions of planets and signs of the zodiac at a given time HOROSCOPE
- elliptical rather than circular, as a planet's orbit might be ECCENTRIC
- imaginary band around the celestial sphere, as used by astronomers and astrologers, representing the path of the sun, moon, and planets ZODIAC
- point in its orbit when a planet, comet, or the like is farthest from the sun APHELION
- point in its orbit when a planet, comet, or the like is nearest the sun PERIHELION

plank or ramp, as on a building site, used for crossing a muddy area GANGPLANK, DUCKBOARDS
- plank used for strengthening the side of a trench, ship, or the like WALE
- path or promenade made of wooden planks, as beside a beach BOARDWALK
- referring to a ship or boat built with overlapping planks CLINKER-BUILT, LAPSTRAKE
- referring to a ship or boat built with the planks lying edge to edge on the hull, rather than overlapping CARVEL-BUILT
- strip of planking or metal plating stretching the entire length of a ship's hull STRAKE

plant See also **flower**
- plant, such as moss, growing on another plant without being parasitic on it EPIPHYTE
- plant cultivation, especially of flowers HORTICULTURE
- plant cultivation without soil, using nutrients dissolved in water HYDROPONICS, AQUICULTURE
- plant cutting, as for grafting SLIP, SCION
- plant disease affecting cereals, caused by various fungi SMUT, ERGOT
- plant disease causing the withering and death of leaves and other parts without rotting BLIGHT
- plant eating, feeding solely on plants as many animals are HERBIVOROUS, PHYTOPHAGOUS
- plant life of an area VEGETATION, FLORA

Planets

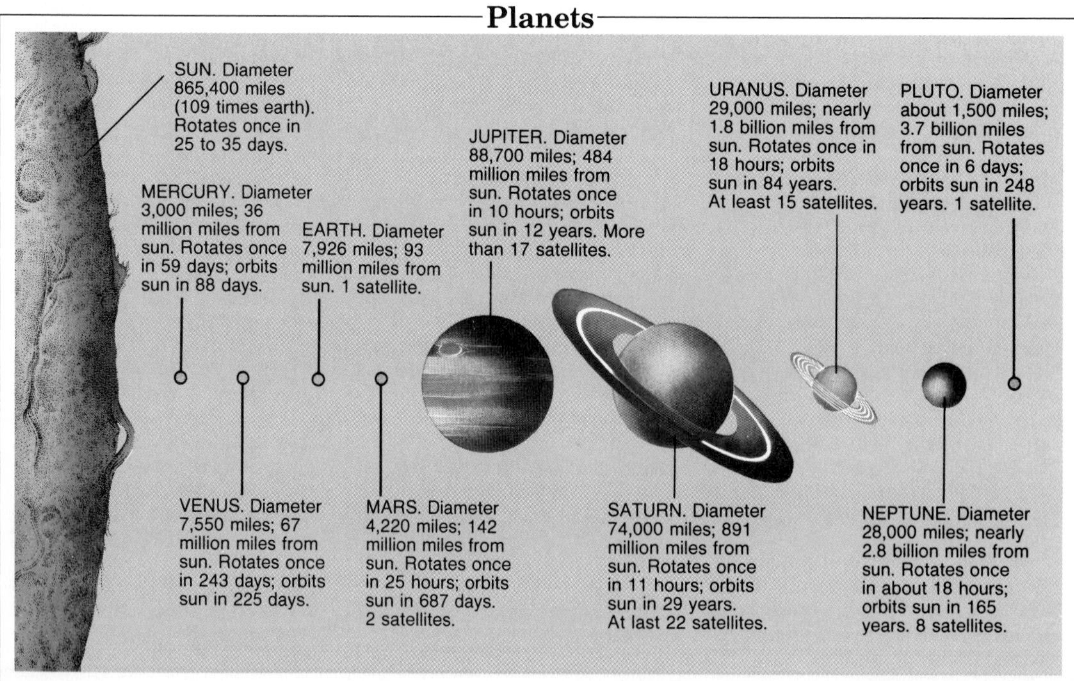

- plant living for one year or a single season ANNUAL
- plant living for three or more years, typically with new growth or flowering each year PERENNIAL
- plant living for two years BIENNIAL
- plant of a cultivated rather than natural variety CULTIVAR
- plant of the common group including most trees and shrubs, characterized by two embryonic seed leaves DICOTYLEDON, DICOT
- plant of the group including grasses, orchids, and lilies, characterized by a single embryonic seed leaf MONOCOTYLEDON
- plant or animal established in a region although not indigenous to it DENIZEN
- plant or crop growing from seed that was not deliberately sown VOLUNTEER
- plant or flower bred from two different varieties or species HYBRID
- plant or grow crops in a fixed sequence ROTATE
- plant part resembling a leaf, just beneath a flower or cluster of flowers BRACT
- plant pot of a large, decorated type JARDINIERE
- plant that keeps its color when dried IMMORTELLE, EVERLASTING
- plant tissue conducting nutrients, made up of sieve tubes PHLOEM, BAST
- plant tissue conducting water and providing support, woody tissue XYLEM
- plant used in making medicines OFFICINAL, SIMPLE
- plantlike, relating to plants or plant growth VEGETAL
- plantlike animal, such as a sea anemone ZOOPHYTE
- plantlike organisms that formerly were, falsely, classified as plants FUNGI, ALGAE
- bell-shaped cover of plastic or glass, placed over young plants for protection CLOCHE
- box or small case used by botanists for carrying plant specimens collected on their expeditions VASCULUM
- branch, leaf, or other secondary or projecting part of a plant APPENDAGE
- building in which plants are cultivated under controlled conditions PHYTOTRON
- cultivate wild plants or adapt foreign plants to a new environment DOMESTICATE
- enclosure for keeping or breeding animals or plants indoors VIVARIUM
- fleshy part of plants, often edible HERBAGE
- go limp, droop, as a plant might WILT
- green pigment in plants that traps energy from sunlight for photosynthesis CHLOROPHYLL
- primitive seed-bearing plant shaped like a palm tree but having fernlike leaves CYCAD
- protective layer covering the epidermis of a plant CUTICLE
- radiating pattern of leaves or petals around the stem of a plant WHORL
- referring to a plant that is local or native to the region INDIGENOUS
- referring to a plant that is not local or native to the region EXOTIC
- referring to a plant's growth or movement in a particular direction through internal rather than external factors NASTIC
- repeated branching or forking of a plant into two equal parts DICHOTOMY
- reproduce, breed, or cause plants or animals to reproduce themselves PROPAGATE
- study of plants BOTANY, PHYTOLOGY
- tendency of a plant to grow in a particular direction TROPISM
- tropical American plant with fleshy leaves, of a family including the pineapple BROMELIAD
- tropical American plant with fleshy leaves, some species yielding fiber such as sisal and alcoholic drinks such as tequila AGAVE
- use of light energy by a plant, absorbed by chlorophyll, for forming organic compounds from carbon dioxide and water PHOTOSYNTHESIS

plant (combining form) ANTHO-, -PHYT-, PHYTO-, -PHYTE

plaster a wall or surface RENDER
- plaster of a coarse, gravely kind, applied to outside walls ROUGHCAST
- plaster of a smooth kind used for frescoes or moldings STUCCO
- plaster-of-paris preparation, used as a painting surface or for bas-relief sculpture GESSO
- plaster used as a finishing coating on walls GROUT
- decoratively patterned plasterwork on walls PARGETING
- rough finish for outside walls, produced by small pebbles embedded in the plaster PEBBLE DASH, ROCK DASH
- roughen or scratch plaster KEY
- smooth or level plaster FLOAT
- tray with a handle underneath, as for carrying plaster HAWK
- wall painting made on dry plaster SECCO
- wall painting made on damp plaster FRESCO
- white mineral used in fertilizers and plaster of paris GYPSUM
- wooden or metal strip used as a thickness guide or leveler, as when plastering SCREED

plastic of a light, foamy consistency, as used for packaging material EXPANDED PLASTIC, POLYSTYRENE
- chemical compound with large molecules containing repeated units, forming the basis of plastics POLYMER
- clear plastic specially treated to reduce glare, as used in sunglasses POLAROID
- clear resilient plastic used as a substitute for glass PERSPEX
- floor covering of a plasticlike material, produced either in sheets or in tiles LINOLEUM
- glossy plastic sheeting, as used for table tops FORMICA
- heavy plastic of a hard resistant kind, as formerly used for the casings of radio sets BAKELITE
- lightweight resilient plastic of various kinds ACRYLIC
- produce wire or plastics, or the like by pressing through a nozzle or die EXTRUDE
- tough, flexible, shiny plastic of various kinds VINYL

plastic surgery ANAPLASTY
- plastic surgery, such as a facelift, designed to improve one's physical appearance COSMETIC SURGERY

plate, protective shell, or similar hard covering, as on some animals or ships CUIRASS
- plate, scale, or similar thin layer of plant or animal tissue LAMELLA, LAMINA
- plate, typically of silver or gold, used for holding the bread at Communion PATEN
- plate of a large shallow design CHARGER, PLATTER
- plate or shield, as worn by fencers, or forming the underside of a tortoise PLASTRON
- plate or tray of wood, used for carving or serving food TRENCHER
- plate set on a hot plate or warmer, used to cook food or keep it warm CHAFING DISH
- plated or scaled, as an armadillo or lobster is MAILED
- covered in scales or bony plates, as some insects and seeds are SCUTATE, SCUTELLATE
- having a traditional blue-on-white Chinese design, as a china plate might be WILLOW-PATTERN

plateau of uplands or a well-defined block of mountains MASSIF

platform, as for a lecturer or conductor DAIS, PODIUM, ROSTRUM
- platform, or the stairway leading to it, outside the entrance of a large building PERRON
- platform or raised wooden framework, as for hanging or beheading criminals SCAFFOLD
- platform supporting cargo or stored goods, typically moved by a forklift truck PALLET, SKID
- platform which election candidates formerly used to make speeches HUSTINGS
- raised platform in a public place TRIBUNE

Plato - philosophical work, as by Plato, in the form of a conversation DIALOGUE

platypus or related egg-laying mammal MONOTREME

play See also **theater** and chart at **drama**
- play about with, treat disrespectfully TRIFLE WITH
- play at some pursuit, take a casual interest in something DABBLE
- play down, minimize the importance of, detract from SOFT-PEDAL
- play for time, evade or postpone commitments TEMPORIZE
- play on words, especially a pun PARANOMASIA
- play or scene in a play in which only two actors have speaking parts DUOLOGUE
- play or write a musical composition in a different key TRANSPOSE
- play's scenery and props MISE-EN-SCÈNE
- playing or expected to play similar roles continually TYPECAST
- climax, solution, or unraveling of a play DENOUEMENT, CATASTROPHE
- closing poem or speech following the end of the action of a play EPILOGUE
- early or afternoon performance of a play MATINEE
- first public presentation of a movie, play, or the like PREMIERE
- interval entertainment between the acts of an opera or play DIVERTISSEMENT, INTERLUDE, ENTR'ACTE
- "into the middle of things," straight into the narrative or plot, as a book or play might begin IN MEDIAS RES
- list of characters in a play DRAMATIS PERSONAE
- outline of the plot of a play, novel, or the like SCENARIO
- passage of conversation in a play, novel, or the like, or the characters' spoken words in such a passage DIALOGUE
- relating to play or games LUDIC
- scene in a play in which the actors freeze in position TABLEAU
- speech addressed only to oneself, such as a character in a play might utter SOLILOQUY
- supporting actors in a play ENSEMBLE
- test for a part in a play, concert, or the like, by giving a sample performance AUDITION
- theatrical company performing a variety of plays during a season REPERTORY COMPANY
- writer of plays, dramatist DRAMATURGE

playboy, lecherous man, or compulsive womanizer RAKE, ROUÉ, PROFLIGATE, SKIRTCHASER, LIBERTINE, DEBAUCHEE
- playboy, sexually promiscuous man, seducer LADYKILLER, DON JUAN, LOTHARIO

playful, abounding in high spirits FROLICSOME, SPORTIVE
- playful and joking conversation BADINAGE, BANTER, REPARTEE
- move about in a playful way, jump and skip about FRISK, GAMBOL, FROLIC, ROMP, SPORT, ROLLICK, CAPER, CAVORT

playing card See **card, card** games

playwright, dramatist DRAMATURGE

plead or beg on behalf of another INTERCEDE

pleasant See **good, friendly**
- pleasant, agreeable, or satisfying GRATIFYING
- pleasant-sounding, pleasing to the ear EUPHONIOUS
- pleasantness AMENITY
- having an appropriate and pleasant style, as a writer might FELICITOUS

pleasant (combining form) EU-

please or satisfy GRATIFY
- pleased or self-satisfied, to the point of feeling that nothing more needs to be done COMPLACENT
- pleasing, or trying to please or gain favor, as by excessive flattery, humility, or obligingness TOADYING, SYCOPHANTIC, SERVILE, OBSEQUIOUS, UNCTUOUS, FAWNING
- hugely pleased or overwhelmed with delight TRANSPORTED, ECSTATIC, ENRAPTURED

pleasure, delight, or enjoyment DELECTATION, GRATIFICATION
- pleasure in or satisfaction at the misfortunes of someone else GLOATING, SCHADENFREUDE
- pleasure-loving, devoted to food and drink and other sensual pleasures HEDONISTIC, EPICUREAN
- pleasure-loving person, devoted to luxurious and sensual living SYBARITE, VOLUPTUARY
- pleasurable and intense emotions RAPTURES, TRANSPORT, ECSTASY
- experienced or enjoyed through the actions or achievements of someone else, as pleasure might be VICARIOUS
- occupy oneself in a pleasurable activity DISPORT
- regard with cruel satisfaction or smug pleasure GLOAT
- relating to or gratifying the pleasures of the senses or the bodily appetites SENSUAL

pleasure (combining form) -PHILIA, -MANIA

pleat, flute, or crimp material, as with a heated iron GOFFER
- pleated or gathered strip of lace or fabric, used as a trimming RUCHE, RUFFLE
- pleated or gathered strip of material sewn to the lower edge of a garment or curtain FLOUNCE

pledge or mortgage something as security HYPOTHECATE
- fulfill a promise, pledge, or the like REDEEM

plenty See also **lots, many, excessive**
- plenty, abundance or fullness AMPLITUDE, PLENITUDE
- plentiful, endless or countless BOTTOMLESS, INEXHAUSTIBLE, INFINITE, UNTOLD
- plentiful, generous, numerous, in good supply ABOUNDING, ABUNDANT, BOUNTEOUS, BOUNTIFUL, OPULENT, PRODIGAL
- plentiful harvest or supply FOISON
- plentiful or generous, as a helping of food might be LAVISH, AMPLE, COPIOUS
- plentiful or luxurious only in appearance or by report, as an illusory feast BARMECIDAL
- plentiful supply, as of wealth or choices, overabundance EMBARRAS DE RICHESSES, EMBARRASSMENT OF RICHES
- extremely plentiful, excessively abundant or productive, swarming THRONGING, TEEMING, PULLULATING
- full, well-stocked, having a plentiful supply BRIMMING, POPULOUS, FLUSH, REPLETE
- given generously or plentifully UNSTINTED
- horn of plenty, overflowing store, abundance CORNUCOPIA
- in plenty, in abundance GALORE
- produced or producing plentifully, fertile, fruitful, as an imagination or vegetation might be FECUND, EXUBERANT, LUXURIANT, PROFUSE, PROLIFIC
- too plentiful, oversupplied RIFE,

AWASH

pliable, flexible, easily molded DUCTILE, MALLEABLE, PLASTIC

plot See also **plan**

- plot, conspire, cooperate in a secret or underhand way COLLABORATE, COLLUDE, COLLOGUE, CONNIVE, INTRIGUE
- plot, intrigue, conspiracy MACHINATIONS, COMPLOT
- plot or group of plotters CONSPIRACY, CABAL, CONFEDERACY
- plot or secret agreement for sinister or illegal purposes COLLUSION, CONNIVANCE
- plot or use of false evidence to incriminate an innocent party FRAME-UP
- criminal plot to cheat, harm, or injure a victim COVIN
- outline of the plot of a novel, play, or the like SCENARIO
- resolution or clarification, as of the plot of a play or a story DENOUEMENT
- sinful, wicked, infamous, as an evil plot or notorious murderer is NEFARIOUS
- straight into the plot, as a book or play might begin IN MEDIAS RES

plow - plowlike implement used to level or break up soil HARROW

- plow of an ancient design ARD
- plowable, and suitable for cultivating crops, as land might be ARABLE
- plowing at right angles to the slope of the land, in order to reduce erosion CONTOUR PLOWING
- blade or cutting wheel at the front of a plow, cutting a preliminary furrow COULTER
- ridge between plowed furrows LIST

plucking device for the strings of a harpsichord or related instrument QUILL

- played by plucking rather than bowing the strings, as a passage for the violin might be PIZZICATO
- small thin disc or plate, as of plastic, used for plucking the strings of a guitar, lute, or related instrument PLECTRUM, PICK

plug connecting one or more other plugs to an electrical socket ADAPTER

- plug or bung in the vent of a cask SPIGOT, SPILE
- plug or cover for the muzzle of a gun when not in use TAMPION
- plug such as a cork or bung STOPPLE

plum of a small, blue-black variety DAMSON

plum brandy from Eastern Europe SLIVOVITZ

plume on a helmet or hat PANACHE

plump or full-bosomed, and healthy and energetic, as some women are BUXOM

plunder, rob violently PILLAGE

- plunder and destruction DEPREDATION, RAPINE, SPOLIATION
- plundered or stolen goods LOOT, BOOTY, SPOILS
- plundering and destructive, as an advancing army might be RAPACIOUS
- raider in search of plunder MARAUDER, LOOTER, PILLAGER

plus (combining form) CON-, -CUM-

plywood or similarly layered sheet of material LAMINATE

- any of the thin layers bonded together to form plywood VENEER

pneumonia - crackling sound in the chest, as of pneumonia sufferers CREPITUS

pocket, as on a waistcoat, designed for a pocket watch FOB

- slit in a dress, skirt, or the like, as for fitting a fastening or for access to a pocket PLACKET

pod or seed of the pea, bean, or related plant LEGUME

- split or burst open along a seam, as a pod or fruit might, to release seeds or pollen DEHISCE

poem See also **poetry**

- poem about rural life BUCOLIC, GEORGIC, ECLOGUE, IDYLL
- poem in which some letters, usually the first, of the lines spell out a name or message ACROSTIC
- poem of a formal, dignified, and stylistically complex kind ODE
- poem of a simple, musical, and often emotional kind, rather than dramatic or narrative LYRIC
- poem of grief, lament, usually over lost love COMPLAINT
- poem of lament for someone's death ELEGY, THRENODY, MONODY
- poem of recantation PALINODE
- poem or other material spoken from memory in front of an audience RECITATION
- poem or song in celebration of a marriage EPITHALAMIUM
- poem to be sung or recited before a wedding PROTHALAMION
- poem to be sung or recited at dawn AUBADE
- Japanese three-line, 17-syllable poem HAIKU
- long poem with a heroic narrative EPIC
- loosely structured verse with intentionally or unintentionally comic effect DOGGEREL
- narrative poem of simple rhyming stanzas and a repeated refrain BALLAD
- rhymed poem of 14 lines SONNET
- short poem with a heroic narrative LAY
- verse or stanza of a poem STAVE

poet, bard, or minstrel in ancient Scandinavia SKALD

- poet, bard, or minstrel in Anglo-Saxon England SCOP
- poet, especially an ancient Celtic singing poet, an honored national poet, or a prizewinning Eisteddfod poet BARD
- poet, Nobel prize winner, or other eminent person in the arts or sciences who receives a special honor LAUREATE
- poet and musician in medieval France TROUBADOUR, TROUVÈRE, JONGLEUR
- poet of poor quality RHYMESTER, POETASTER, VERSIFIER
- poets of the 17th century, such as Donne and Herbert, using far-fetched metaphors METAPHYSICALS
- poetic inspiration or other creative impulse AFFLATUS

poetry See chart, page 408, and also **poem, figure of speech**

- book or collection of poetry ANTHOLOGY, CHRESTOMATHY
- complex metaphor used in Old English and Old Norse poetry KENNING
- pair of consecutive and rhyming lines in poetry COUPLET
- referring to artistic inspiration, especially poetry PIERIAN
- referring to lines of poetry that continue as a single flowing sentence without pause to the next ENJAMBED
- referring to lines of poetry that end with a distinct pause END-STOPPED
- referring to poetry or drama that is refined and classically elegant in style AUGUSTAN
- referring to the world of poetry PARNASSIAN
- rhymed verse forms common in English poetry OTTAVA RIMA, SPENSERIAN STANZA
- rhythm or metrical lines in poetry NUMBERS
- rhythmical or metrical stress in a line of poetry ICTUS
- study of the forms and meters of poetry PROSODY
- style of popular musical entertainment, in which improvised poetry is recited or chanted to a musical accompaniment RAPPING, RAP MUSIC
- vivid comparisons, metaphors, and the like, that are used in poetry to evoke pictures in the mind IMAGERY

POETRY TERMS

anapest	metrical foot consisting of two short or unstressed syllables followed by one long or stressed syllable
blank verse	verse form, as in Shakespeare's plays, of unrhymed 10-syllable lines
caesura	pause or break within a line of verse
canto	section or "chapter" of a long poem
clerihew	comic four-line verse, typically about a person named in one of the lines
concrete poetry	poetry in which the shape of the words on the page conveys added meaning
dactyl	metrical foot consisting of one long or stressed syllable followed by two short or unstressed syllables
eclogue	short pastoral poem, often in the form of a dialogue
elegy	poem lamenting a dead person; broadly, any wistful poem
envoi	short, final stanza of certain poems, especially French poems
feminine rhyme	rhyme of two or more syllables of which the first is stressed, such as *measure* and *treasure*
foot	unit of meter in poetry, corresponding to a bar in music
free verse/vers libre	verse without conventional meter or rhyme
georgic/bucolic	poem about rural, pastoral, or farming life
haiku	Japanese three-line poem of 17 syllables
heroic couplet	verse form of two rhyming 10-syllable lines
hexameter	line of six metrical feet
iambic/ iambus/iamb	metrical foot consisting of one short or unstressed syllable followed by one long or stressed syllable
idyll	short lyrical poem about everyday life in rural surroundings
internal rhyme	rhyme occurring within a line of verse rather than at the ends of two or more lines
limerick	light witty poem or nonsense verse of a fixed five-line form
macaronic verse	humorous verse written in a jumble of languages
ode	long, usually rhymed, heroic poem
pentameter	line of five metrical feet
quatrain	stanza consisting of four lines rhyming alternately
rondeau/rondel	lyrical poem of French origin using only two rhymes throughout
roundelay	poem or song with a regularly repeated refrain
scansion	rhythmic or metrical pattern of a verse
spondee	metrical foot, as in Latin poetry, consisting of two long syllables
sprung rhythm	heavily accented verse rhythm with an irregular number of unstressed syllables in each foot
stanza	complete verse or "paragraph" of a poem
stich	line of verse
strophe	verse, especially the first of two differently structured verses making up a poem
tanka	Japanese five-line poem of 31 syllables
tetrameter	line of verse consisting of four feet
trochee	metrical foot consisting of one long or stressed syllable followed by one short or unstressed one
villanelle	poem of a complex 19-line form of French origin, using much repeated rhyme

point at which lines intersect or diverge NODE
- point at which three or more lines in geometry intersect CONCURRENCE
- point of crisis beyond which a tense situation will erupt into war or violence FLASHPOINT
- point of greatest intensity, as of a series of events, or in a story, play, or the like CLIMAX
- point of no return, limit beyond which one becomes fully committed to a course of action RUBICON
- point of origin, starting point TERMINUS A QUO
- point of view, attitude PERSPECTIVE, STANDPOINT
- point on the body where an artery can be pressed shut to stop the bleeding of a wound farther on PRESSURE POINT

- point or detail based on a strict ruling or literal interpretation of a law TECHNICALITY
- point that is open to debate or no longer important MOOT POINT
- pointing or jutting outward, projecting, as an angle or the like might SALIENT
- acknowledgment of a telling point, argument, or accusation made against one TOUCHÉ
- approach the same point from different directions CONVERGE
- move away from the same point in different directions DIVERGE

point (combining form) ACRO-, -STYL-, STYLO-, -STYLAR

pointed, cutting, or piercing, as a witty retort might be POIGNANT
- pointed, needle-shaped ACERATE, ACEROSE, ACULEATE
- pointed, tapering, narrowing to a point, as a leaf might ACUMINATE
- pointed end or figure CUSP
- pointed writing instrument, as used on wax tablets in ancient times STYLUS

poison, germ, or any other harmful substance that prompts the body's immune system to produce antibodies ANTIGEN
- poison extracted from an Indian tree, much favored by early mystery writers STRYCHNINE
- poison produced by a fungus on peanuts and maize AFLATOXIN
- poisoning by a cereal fungus, capable of producing itching, gangrene, or convulsions ERGOTISM, SAINT ANTHONY'S FIRE
- poisonous chemical element, used in insecticides, weed killers, and the like ARSENIC
- poisonous compound, smelling of almonds, as used for fumigation CYANIDE
- poisonous flowering plant, or the poison derived from it, which Socrates drank when condemned to death HEMLOCK
- poisonous fluid secreted in a snakebite, scorpion sting, or the like VENOM
- poisonous plant of various kinds, of the buttercup and lily families, or the poison extracted from its underground stem HELLEBORE
- poisonous substance, especially of organic origin TOXIN
- poisonous substance extracted from deadly nightshade, used in various medical treatments ATROPINE, BELLADONNA
- affecting the entire body, as a disease or poison might SYSTEMIC
- antidote to poison obtained from the blood or tissue of immunized animals SERUM
- arrow poison used by South American Indians, obtained from the resin of tropical trees CURARE
- chemical compound used to prevent blood clotting and as a rat poison WARFARIN
- deadly poison BANE
- effective, powerful, or still active, as a drug or poison might be POTENT
- extremely harmful or rapid in effect, as a disease or poison might be VIRULENT
- food poisoning PTOMAINE POISONING
- food poisoning, often fatal, caused by a bacterial toxin found in badly canned, preserved, or smoked food BOTULISM
- food poisoning caused by rod-shaped bacteria of a kind often found in inadequately cooked meat SALMONELLA POISONING, SALMONELLOSIS
- glass box with protective gloves sealed into the side for handling radioactive or poisonous substances GLOVE BOX
- immunity to poison through habituation to it by taking small doses MITHRIDATISM
- Indian tree with poisonous seeds, the source of strychnine and other poisons NUX VOMICA
- Japanese fish with some poisonous parts that have to be removed before it is eaten FUGU
- medicine, serum, or antibody that counteracts the effects of a poison ANTIDOTE, ANTITOXIN, ANTIVENIN
- small container for medicine, poison, or other liquid, typically a stoppered glass bottle VIAL, PHIAL
- study of poisons and the treatment of poisoning TOXICOLOGY
- supposed antidote against all poisons MITHRIDATE
- tropical American plant with poisonous seeds used in insecticides SABADILLA
- weed killer or other poison for destroying plants HERBICIDE

poison (combining form) TOX-, TOXO-, TOXICO-

poisonous TOXIC, VENOMOUS
- poisonous gas remaining in a mine, especially a coal mine, after an explosion or fire AFTERDAMP

poker or other heat-resistant implement used in fire SALAMANDER

poker hand containing five consecutive cards, but not all of the same suit STRAIGHT
- poker hand containing three cards all with the same value, and two cards both with the same value FULL HOUSE
- poker hand in which all five cards are in a single suit FLUSH
- poker hand of five consecutive cards in a single suit STRAIGHT FLUSH
- poker hand of the top five cards of a single suit ROYAL FLUSH
- bet made by a poker player before looking at his or her cards BLIND
- demand by a poker player to see an opponent's hand, made by matching but not increasing his or her bet CALL
- drop out of the betting during a hand of poker FOLD
- form of poker in which some cards are dealt face upward STUD
- increase the bet in a poker game RAISE
- showing of the cards at the end of a poker game SHOWDOWN
- stake put into the pool by a poker player receiving his or her cards ANTE

polar weather condition producing very low visibility WHITEOUT

pole for marking positions in surveying RANGING POLE
- pole or pillar carved and painted with kinship symbols, as by certain Native Americans TOTEM POLE
- pole used as a mast or boom SPAR
- pole with a bucket on the end for drawing water from a well SWEEP, SWIPE
- pole with a spring at the base, on which one can bounce along POGO STICK
- variation, in 14-month cycles, of the position of the geographical poles CHANDLER WOBBLE

police force of a town or district CONSTABULARY
- police hunt of a widespread and coordinated kind DRAGNET
- police informer STOOL PIGEON
- police kit or method for creating a picture of a wanted criminal IDENTIKIT, PHOTOFIT
- police line, series of ships, or the like, surrounding or guarding an area CORDON
- police officer of fairly senior rank SUPERINTENDENT
- police or military trainee CADET
- police van for transporting offenders BLACK MARIA, PADDY WAGON
- civilian who takes on, without legal right, judicial or police powers for himself or herself VIGILANTE
- detention, being held under arrest or under guard, as by the police CUSTODY
- district of a city under a particular administrative or police authority PRECINCT

- senior police officer of a metropolitan district COMMANDER
- tricking or luring of someone, as by the police, into danger or self-incrimination ENTRAPMENT

police-state system aiming at total control TOTALITARIANISM

policeman in Canada MOUNTY
- policeman in France FLIC, GENDARME
- policeman in Ireland GARDA
- policeman under military command in Italy CARABINIERE
- policeman in London in the 18th and early 19th centuries BOW STREET RUNNER
- policeman's short club or truncheon NIGHTSTICK, BILLY CLUB
- slang or informal terms for a police officer or detective COP, COPPER, FLATFOOT, PIG, THE HEAT, THE FUZZ, SHAMUS, PEELER, BOBBY, JOHN LAW

policy, plan, or method based on a long-range or overall view of things STRATEGY
- policy of burning or destroying all crops, food, and anything else likely to be of use to an advancing enemy SCORCHED-EARTH POLICY
- declaration of policies, as by a political party MANIFESTO
- reversal or about-turn of attitude or policy VOLTE-FACE

polio INFANTILE PARALYSIS, POLIOMYELITIS
- polio vaccine, formerly injected, based on a weakened or killed virus SALK VACCINE
- polio vaccine, taken orally, based on a live but weakened virus SABIN VACCINE

polish and brighten BURNISH, FURBISH
- polish or gloss LUSTER
- polish or smoothness, as of speech or manners FINISH
- polish with wax SIMONIZE
- polished surface layer or finishing, as of fine wood VENEER

polite, proper, avoiding disrespect and impropriety DEFERENTIAL, DECOROUS
- polite, refined, polished in social behavior GENTEEL
- polite, socially gracious, and charming, often in a superficial way SUAVE, URBANE
- polite, well-mannered CIVIL, COURTEOUS
- polite or extremely formal CEREMONIOUS, PUNCTILIOUS
- polite remarks, small talk PLEASANTRIES
- polite social gestures, courtesies CIVILITIES
- accepted or expected forms or standards of polite social behavior CONVENTIONS, ETIQUETTE, PROTOCOL, CONVENANCES
- referring to polite remarks, as about the weather, made for the sake of social contact rather than true communication PHATIC

political activity, especially foreign policy, based uncompromisingly on national self-interest rather than on moral considerations REALPOLITIK
- political agitation and propaganda, especially that by left-wing radicals AGITPROP
- political agitator provoking civil discontent or strife INCENDIARY
- political and social system that prevailed in former times but has now been replaced ANCIEN RÉGIME
- political campaigning, especially for elections HUSTINGS
- political cooperation between different parties or groups in power COHABITATION
- political cunning or opportunism MACHIAVELLIANISM
- political deals among legislators, such as the swapping of votes and other mutual favors LOGROLLING
- political elimination of opponents or dissidents PURGE
- political extremist in favor of basic and far-reaching social and economic changes RADICAL
- political extremist or revolutionary SANSCULOTTE, MAXIMALIST, JACOBIN
- political extremist advocating the destruction of all existing social and political institutions NIHILIST, ANARCHIST
- political grouping or agreement ALIGNMENT
- political leader or agitator rallying support by crude emotional speeches DEMAGOGUE
- political manipulation of the boundaries of an electoral constituency for party advantage GERRYMANDER
- political opponent of a government, especially in a one-party state DISSIDENT
- political or military grouping that forms the core of a potentially larger unit CADRE
- political or other group, typically causing dissension, within a larger group FACTION
- political or religious document or pamphlet containing a forceful declaration or rallying call TRACT
- political party's declaration of its policies, as before an election PLATFORM, MANIFESTO
- political party's subgroup or policy meeting CAUCUS
- political policies and actions based on the wishes of the majority CONSENSUS POLITICS
- political principles of a country, concerning basic rights and duties, either unwritten or embodied in statutes CONSTITUTION
- political protest in the form of nonviolent resistance and a refusal to obey laws regarded as unjust CIVIL DISOBEDIENCE
- political protester or energetic campaigner ACTIVIST, MILITANT
- political reformer or rebel within a particular group or party YOUNG TURK
- political reformer or theorist who is hopelessly idealistic and impractical VISIONARY, UTOPIAN
- political style or presentation aimed at appealing to ordinary people POPULISM
- political union, league, or association of states with a fairly strong central government FEDERATION
- politically committed, active in promoting a moral or political cause ENGAGÉ
- alliance, typically temporary, of political parties or other groups COALITION
- catchphrase, motto, jingle, or the like used repeatedly, as in political campaigns SLOGAN
- change a person's beliefs or political attitudes by indoctrination or intensive conditioning BRAINWASH
- extreme or uncompromising, as one's political stance might be INTRANSIGENT
- overthrow or attempt to destroy something, especially a government or political system, by means of concerted secret undermining SUBVERT
- place, platform, or occasion for public speeches, especially on political issues STUMP
- relating to a politically corrupt organization in city or state government TAMMANY
- secret agent who joins a political or criminal group and tries to entrap it into punishable or discreditable activities AGENT PROVOCATEUR
- sympathizer with the aims and ideals of a political or other group, without being a member of it FELLOW TRAVELER, CAMP FOLLOWER

politician who is neutral or independent MUGWUMP
- politician responsible for ensuring that fellow party members attend and vote correctly in a lawmaking body WHIP
- government-funded project benefiting a particular politician's constituency PORK BARREL

poll that is taken in a cross section

of society, especially to forecast election results GALLUP POLL
- rough-and-ready unofficial opinion poll, especially on an election or political issue STRAW POLL

pollen - pollinated by insects, as many flowering plants are ENTOMOPHILOUS
- pollinated by wind-blown pollen, as grass flowers are ANEMOPHILOUS
- pollination between two flowers on a single plant ENDOGAMY
- pollination from one plant to another plant, cross-fertilization XENOGAMY
- drug used in the treatment of allergic reactions, as to pollen or bee stings ANTIHISTAMINE
- self-pollination by a flower, self-fertilization AUTOGAMY

polo stick MALLET
- any of the sessions of play, each lasting about seven minutes, in a polo match CHUKKER

Polynesian skirt formed by a wraparound rectangular cloth LAVALAVA, PAREU

pomegranate or red-currant syrup, used as a cordial or flavoring GRENADINE

pomp and ceremony, grand spectacle PAGEANTRY

pompous See also **highfalutin, pride, proud**
- pompous, putting on airs, behaving in an artificial way to impress others AFFECTED, PORTENTOUS, PRETENTIOUS
- pompous, self-important, swaggering STRUTTING, BUMPTIOUS, PUSHY, CONSEQUENTIAL, VAINGLORIOUS
- pompous, snobbish, stuck-up ALOOF, HOITY-TOITY, LA-DI-DA, LOFTY, SNIFFY, SNOOTY, SNOTTY, UPPISH
- pompous, standing on ceremony, and bossy OFFICIOUS
- pompous and arrogant, assuming an air of superiority CONDESCENDING, DISDAINFUL, PATRONIZING, SUPERCILIOUS
- pompous and reactionary man, especially an officer or bureaucrat COLONEL BLIMP
- pompous or affected in style, stiff and unnatural MANNERED, STILTED, STARCHY
- pompously moralizing, especially by means of proverbs and platitudes SENTENTIOUS, PONTIFICAL, PREACHY
- pompously moralistic, precise, or narrow-minded CANTING, HOLIER-THAN-THOU, PUNCTILIOUS, PIOUS, PRIGGISH, SERMONIZING, SANCTIMONIOUS
- pompously self-assured and inflexible, arrogant OPINIONATED, COCKSURE
- pompously self-satisfied COMPLACENT, SMUG
- angry or peevish in a pompous way, as from an affront to one's supposed dignity HUFFISH

pond or small lake MERE

pool - still, filled with motionless water, as a pool or pond might be STAGNANT
- fabric, usually green and woolen, used on top of pool or billiards tables BAIZE
- shot in pool in which the red ball struck by the cue ball goes on to strike another red ball PLANT
- shot made with a near-upright cue in pool or billiards, designed to curve the cue ball around an obstructing ball to hit another MASSÉ
- support or rest on legs for a cue during a difficult or inaccessible pool or billiards shot SPIDER

poor, down and out, poverty-stricken, having few or no possessions DESTITUTE, PENURIOUS, INDIGENT
- poor, down at heel, deprived of one's former wealth or comforts DISTRESSED, IMPOVERISHED, IN STRAITENED CIRCUMSTANCES, IN REDUCED CIRCUMSTANCES
- poor, penniless, needy IMPECUNIOUS, NECESSITOUS, PINCHED
- poor, underprivileged, lacking most of the advantages in life DEPRIVED, DISADVANTAGED
- poor but refined SHABBY GENTEEL
- poor person, sometimes living on public charity PAUPER

pop music of a black American style, often with blues or gospel rhythms MOTOWN

pope See also **papal**
- pope PONTIFF, VICAR OF CHRIST, VICEGERENT
- pope's ambassador NUNCIO
- pope's authority, office, or term of office PAPACY
- pope's beehive-shaped three-tiered crown or hat TIARA
- pope's meeting with the cardinals CONSISTORY
- pope's unfailing correctness in doctrinal matters of faith and of morals INFALLIBILITY
- adjective for the pope PAPAL
- authorized by the pope, as a doctrine might be EX CATHEDRA
- cardinal who handles the pope's financial affairs, papal treasurer CAMERLENGO
- delegate or representative of the pope EMISSARY, LEGATE
- favoring a policy of centralized authority in the Roman Catholic Church, investing the pope with absolute power ULTRAMONTANE
- favoring a policy of decentralized authority in the Roman Catholic Church, restricting the pope's power in the various branches of the church CISALPINE, GALLICAN
- formal agreement, especially between the pope and a country's government, over religious affairs CONCORDAT
- formal meeting with a monarch, the pope, or the like AUDIENCE
- letter from the pope to bishops in all countries ENCYCLICAL
- letter of instructions or judgment, in modern handwriting, issued by the pope BRIEF
- letter or document, in antique handwriting, issued by the pope BULL
- letter or edict issued by the pope on a point of church law or doctrine DECRETAL
- meeting of cardinals to elect the pope CONCLAVE
- relating to Saint Peter or to the pope considered as his successor PETRINE

popular, commonly used, as the ordinary form of a language is DEMOTIC, VERNACULAR
- popular, fashionable EN VOGUE, IN VOGUE
- popular feeling, public opinion VOX POPULI

popularity or fashion VOGUE

population growth that is optimal and therefore accelerating EXPONENTIAL GROWTH
- increase dramatically, as an animal population might in favorable conditions IRRUPT
- referring to the population of an area that seems always to have been there INDIGENOUS, ABORIGINAL, AUTOCHTHONOUS
- sample taken at random, as of the general population, regarded as typical of the whole CROSS SECTION
- science of population statistics, such as distribution and birth rate DEMOGRAPHY

population (combining form) DEM-, DEMO-

porcelain See chart at **pottery**

porch, especially at the entrance to a temple PROPYLAEUM
- porch or entrance stairway at a house door STOOP
- porch or corridor used by athletes for exercise in ancient Greece XYST
- porch with a roof and columns, sometimes surrounding a building PORTICO

porcupine - spines covering the body of a porcupine QUILLS

pork See illustration, page 412, and also **bacon**
- forbidden as food in Islam, as pork is HARAM

- forbidden as food in Judaism, nonkosher, as pork is TREF
- salted and cured side of pork FLITCH

pornography, sexually explicit art or writing EROTICA
- pornography of a mild kind SOFT-CORE PORNOGRAPHY
- pornography of a very explicit or deviant kind HARD-CORE PORNOGRAPHY
- pornographic film STAG FILM, BLUE MOVIE, PORNO
- pornographic film in which an actor is killed in reality before the camera SNUFF MOVIE
- detailed in describing or representing sexual acts, as some pornographic films are EXPLICIT
- euphemism for "pornographic" ADULT

porpoise, dolphin, whale, or similar aquatic mammal CETACEAN

porridge - porridgelike dish of boiled sweetened wheat FRUMENTY
- thick corn porridge SAMP, POLENTA, PUTU, HOMINY GRITS, GRITS
- thick oatmeal porridge, as served to sailors in former times BURGOO, LOBLOLLY
- thin, watery porridge GRUEL, SKILLY

port side of a ship LARBOARD
- crust forming in bottles of old wine, especially port, or a wine containing this crust BEESWING

porthole, hinged hatchway, or the like on a ship SCUTTLE

portion or share specially set aside ALLOCATION, ALLOTMENT

portmanteau word TELESCOPED WORD, BLEND

portrait, typically an engraving or photograph, in which the edges have been blurred VIGNETTE
- portrait in profile in the form of a shadow image or filled-in outline SILHOUETTE
- portrait of a person, such as a cartoon or written parody, exaggerating his or her features and qualities for comic or satirical effect CARICATURE
- portrait sculpture of a person, as on a monument EFFIGY
- referring to a statue or portrait in which the subject is depicted on horseback EQUESTRIAN

portray or describe LIMN

Portuguese and Spanish IBERIAN
- melancholy Portuguese folk song FADO

Portuguese (combining form) LUSO-

Poseidon's three-pronged spear TRIDENT

position See also **place**
- position, job, or activity particularly suited to a person NICHE
- position accurately, find or specify the position of something, as on a map LOCATE, PINPOINT
- position accurately in relation to something else, especially by placing in a straight line ALIGN
- position in relation to one's surroundings BEARINGS, ORIENTATION
- position or locate in a specified direction, as when facing a church east ORIENT, ORIENTATE
- position or outlook of a house, as in a specified direction EXPOSURE, ASPECT
- position or ranking on a scale RATING
- position side by side JUXTAPOSE
- change in the apparent position of an object when the observer changes position PARALLAX ERROR
- change or reverse the ordering or relative position of two or more things TRANSPOSE
- defensible or maintainable, as a military or philosophical position might be TENABLE
- force out from a fixed position, hiding place, dwelling, or the like DISLODGE
- have the most prominent position, as in a room or landscape DOMINATE
- important or high in status, position, or the like EXALTED
- occupying the same space or position, or identical in size and shape COINCIDENT
- two or more numbers, readings, or measurements that define a position, as on a map or graph COORDINATES

position (combining form) -WISE

positioned (combining form) -TACTIC

possess, or take pride or pleasure in possessing something, such as an unusual name REJOICE IN

possessed - allegedly drive out demons or evil spirits, or free a possessed person from them, as by religious rites EXORCISE
- person allegedly possessed by an evil spirit DEMONIAC, ENERGUMEN

possession, gift, or project that is expensive or inefficient, requiring more trouble than it is worth WHITE ELEPHANT
- possession desired or valued as an indicator of wealth or social prestige STATUS SYMBOL
- interest in possessions rather than spiritual or moral values MATERIALISM
- valued household possessions LARES AND PENATES

possible, practicable, or imaginable CONCEIVABLE, FEASIBLE
- possible, uncertain CONTINGENT
- possible, workable, practicable, realistic VIABLE
- possible but not yet actual POTENTIAL, LATENT

Pork Cuts

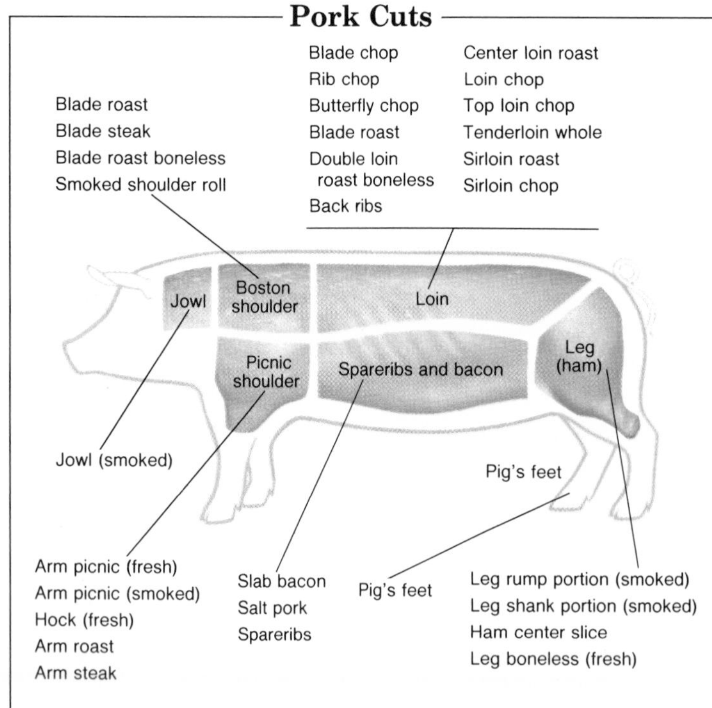

- possible occurrence or event CONTINGENCY, EVENTUALITY
- possible or projected course of action or chain of events SCENARIO
- possibly true, apparently valid, as an excuse might be PLAUSIBLE
- enabling, making possible but not obligatory FACULTATIVE

post See also **letter**
- post, stake, pile as for foundations SPILE
- post for tethering a horse HITCHING POST
- post, mail, officially recorded and insured REGISTERED MAIL
- post or pointed stake driven into the ground, as for defense PICKET
- post or target to be tilted at as by horsemen QUINTAIN
- postal code ZIP CODE, ZONE-IMPROVEMENT PLAN
- centralized European system for banks and post offices to transfer money GIRO
- department of a post office, holding letters for collection by the addressee GENERAL DELIVERY, POSTE RESTANTE
- fortress or defensive barrier made of upright posts or stakes STOCKADE, PALISADE
- mark or stamp a letter or package to indicate payment of postage FRANK

postcard collector DELTIOLOGIST

postmortem, medical examination or dissection of a dead body to establish the cause of death AUTOPSY
- postmortem investigation, as into the cause of a death or failure INQUEST
- medical specialist who conducts a postmortem examination to establish the cause of death PATHOLOGIST
- public officer presiding at postmortem investigations CORONER

postpone, delay doing something until later, waste time PROCRASTINATE
- postpone, put aside temporarily, put off WAIVE, DEFER, REMIT, PUT ON THE BACK BURNER
- postpone, suspend, put aside for later consideration PIGEONHOLE, SHELVE, MOTHBALL, TABLE, HOLD IN ABEYANCE
- postpone acceptance of an offer that will remain open TAKE A RAIN CHECK
- postpone decisions or draw out discussions as a way of gaining time TEMPORIZE
- postpone discussions, break off a court hearing or meeting temporarily ADJOURN
- postpone or avoid giving direct answers, beat about the bush EQUIVOCATE, PREVARICATE
- postpone or discontinue temporarily the sessions of a lawmaking body PROROGUE
- postponement or delay, as of payments MORATORIUM
- temporary postponement, especially of something unpleasant REPRIEVE, RESPITE

postulate, put forward a proposition or idea for the sake of argument POSIT, PREMISE

posture, way of walking or standing POISE, BEARING, CARRIAGE, GAIT
- woman's fashionable forward-tilting posture in the late 19th century, often enhanced by a bustle GRECIAN BEND

posy, small bunch or bouquet of flowers NOSEGAY

pot See also **cooking**
- pot for cooking, covered and often of earthenware CASSEROLE, MARMITE
- pot or large kettle with a hooped handle for hanging over an open fire CALDRON
- pot or small pan of earthenware PIPKIN
- large, decorated pot or stand for plants JARDINIERE

pot marigold CALENDULA

pot plant - tree or shrub of dwarf size, produced by rigorous pruning, and displayed as a pot plant BONSAI

potato SPUD, MURPHY
- potato beetle COLORADO POTATO BEETLE
- potato flour or the starch from it FARINA
- potato or similar swollen underground bud-bearing stem or root TUBER
- potato pancake of traditional Jewish style LATKE
- baked cakes of mashed potatoes bound with egg DUCHESSE POTATOES
- cooked with onions, as potatoes might be LYONNAISE
- fried potatoes of traditional Swiss style RÖSTI
- Scottish dish of steamed potatoes STOVIES
- shredded or sliced into narrow strips, as potatoes might be JULIENNE
- sliced thin and baked in a sauce, as potatoes might be SCALLOPED
- thick, creamy leek and potato soup, typically served cold VICHYSSOISE

potency, sexual functioning or prowess in an adult male VIRILITY

potential, present but not visible, as a tendency might be LATENT
- potential, unfulfilled MANQUÉ

pottery See chart, page 414
- pottery or vessels made of baked clay EARTHENWARE
- potter's wheel THROW
- potter's wooden spatula used for mixing or molding clay PALLET
- fragment of pottery, as found in archeological excavations SHARD, POTSHERD, SHERD, CROCK
- fragment of pottery used in ancient Greece when voting for the banishment of an unpopular citizen OSTRACON
- oven or furnace for drying and hardening pottery KILN
- soluble fusible white mineral used in making glass and pottery BORAX

pouch-bearing mammal, such as a kangaroo MARSUPIAL
- pouch for sheltering the young, as in the kangaroo MARSUPIUM
- pouch in the body, especially that between the small and large intestines CECUM
- pouch of furry leather worn in front of the kilt in traditional Highland dress SPORRAN
- pouch or baglike part, often filled with fluid, in a plant or animal SAC
- pouch or sac formed in the weakened wall of a hollow body part, especially the intestines DIVERTICULUM
- pouchlike sac or cavity in the body, either normal or abnormal CYST

poultry See **chicken**

pound or pen for animals, such as stray sheep PINFOLD

pound - system of weights including the ounce, pound, and ton AVOIRDUPOIS

pounding, crushing, or grinding implement, as in a mill PESTLE

pour a liquid from one container to another, as when separating wine from its sediment DECANT
- pour or transfer a liquid from one container or vessel to another TRANSFUSE
- pour out, emerge, or issue, as a river might DISCHARGE, DISGORGE, DEBOUCH
- pouring of a liquid, as a religious ritual LIBATION
- pouring of water, especially on the head at baptisms AFFUSION
- pouring out, or something that is poured out EFFUSION

pout, sulky expression MOUE

poverty See also **lack**
- poverty, financial embarrassment or seriously reduced circumstances DIRE STRAITS, IMPOVERISHMENT
- poverty, lack of basic comforts or essentials of life PRIVATION
- poverty, complete lack of money,

pennilessness IMPECUNIOUSNESS
- poverty, state of want or neediness INDIGENCE
- extreme poverty, lack of all comforts and even necessities, beggary PENURY, DESTITUTION
- miserable, pitiable, grindingly wretched, as poverty might be ABJECT

POW camp - German POW camp for noncommissioned officers and privates during World War II STALAG
- German POW camp for commissioned officers during World War II OFLAG

powder - mineral used in cosmetic powder, pills, tablets, and so on TALC, TALCUM
- crush to a powder, as with a mortar and pestle BRAY
- grind, crush, pound, or reduce to powder PULVERIZE, COMMINUTE, TRITURATE
- small flat case containing face powder, a mirror, and a powder puff, as carried in a woman's handbag COMPACT

powdery coating, as on plums or new coins BLOOM
- powdery or mealy in texture FARINACEOUS

power See also **authority, force, government**
- power, authority, or influence of one state over another HEGEMONY, SUZERAINTY
- power, governing control, authority DOMINION, SOVEREIGNTY
- power, influence SWAY, CLOUT
- power, inherent ability, or skill FACULTY, APTITUDE
- power, strength, or vitality THEWS, SINEW
- power, superiority, clear advantage ASCENDANCY, DOMINANCE, PREDOMINANCE, PREEMINENCE, SUPREMACY
- power and control, or the legal and territorial extent of power JURISDICTION
- power center, hub of influence, activity, or interest GANGLION
- power failure OUTAGE
- power-mad person, typically with delusions of grandeur MEGALOMANIAC
- power of a microscope, photographic emulsion, or the like to separate and reveal fine details RESOLUTION

POTTERY AND CHINA TERMS

argil	clay used by potters
basalt ware	black, unglazed pottery
biscuit/ bisque	unglazed pottery
blunger	vessel in which pottery ingredients are mixed
bone china	semitranslucent porcelain made of clay mixed with bone ash
cameo ware	pottery with raised white designs on a contrasting background
celadon ware	pottery with a pale gray-green glaze
clair de lune	pale gray-blue glaze applied to certain porcelain
crackleware	pottery or porcelain with a network of fine cracks in the glaze
delftware	blue and white pottery originally made in Delft, Holland
faience	fine pottery with a colorful glaze, named after Faenza, Italy, one of its sources
glost/glaze	lead glaze used for pottery
ironstone	hard, white pottery
jasperware	colored stoneware with raised designs in white, invented by Josiah Wedgwood
lambrequin	scalloped edging decorating the top of an item of porcelain
majolica	brightly decorated pottery in 16th-century Italian style
muffle	kiln in which pottery is fired without direct exposure to the flames
Nankeen	Chinese-style porcelain with a blue and white pattern, originally imported into Europe from Nanking
pallet	spatula or paddlelike implement used for mixing or shaping clay
sagger	casing of fire clay in which delicate ceramic ware is fired
slip	thin clay used by a potter for coating or decorating
stoneware	heavy pottery fired at a high temperature, and often glazed with salt
terra-cotta	unglazed pottery made of clay and fine sand
throw	shape clay on a potter's wheel
underglaze	pigment or decoration applied to pottery before it is glazed

FAMOUS MAKES OF CHINA AND PORCELAIN

Adams	**Coalport**	**Dresden**	**Minto**	**Royal Crown Derby**	**Sèvres**
Belleek	**Copeland**	**Goss**	**Rockingham**	**Royal Doulton**	**Spode**
Bow	**Crown Staffordshire**	**Limoges**	**Rosenthal**	**Royal Worcester**	**Sunderland**
Bristol	**Davenport**	**Longton Hall**	**Royal Copenhagen**		**Swansea**
Chelsea		**Meissen**			**Wedgwood**

- power of choosing, will VOLITION
- power of jurisdiction that a country has beyond its borders, as over its citizens living abroad EXTRATERRITORIALITY
- power or ability that is as yet unrealized POTENTIAL
- power or capacity to produce results EFFICACY
- power or force, especially as a result of continuing movement MOMENTUM, IMPETUS, INERTIA
- power or influence, moral authority or prestige MANA
- power or rule of an absolute kind AUTARCHY, AUTOCRACY
- power to make use of something or someone DISPOSAL
- area in someone's power, or sphere of someone's influence FIEFDOM, DOMAIN, REALM, PARISH, BAILIWICK
- assign work, duties, or powers to one's agent or subordinate DELEGATE, DEPUTE
- based on personal decision rather than on regulations, as powers or payments might be DISCRETIONARY
- be superior to in power, importance, influence, or quantity PREDOMINATE
- body-produced substance that can provide a surge of excitement or power EPINEPHRINE, ADRENALINE
- complete, full, unlimited, as a dictator's powers would be, absolute PLENARY, PLENIPOTENTIARY
- give up or relinquish power or responsibility formally ABDICATE, RENOUNCE
- increase in power, reputation, or the like AGGRANDIZEMENT
- level of power or responsibility in a hierarchical organization ECHELON
- order of power or status in a group PECKING ORDER, HIERARCHY
- outward signs, symbolic decorations, or ornamental equipment, as of power TRAPPINGS
- referring to power derived from heat in the interior of the earth GEOTHERMAL
- remove from office, power, the throne, or the like, overthrow DEPOSE
- seize by force and hold illegally the power, rights, throne, or the like of another USURP
- seize or wrench something forcibly or unlawfully, such as power WREST
- transfer of power from central government to regional or local authorities DEVOLUTION
- unlimited power to act as one wishes, or a document conferring it CARTE BLANCHE

power (combining form) DYNAM-, DYNAMO-

powerful See also **large, strong**
- powerful, mighty, strong PUISSANT
- powerful, rich, or important man NABOB, MOGUL, POTENTATE
- powerful and convincing, as someone's reasoning might be COGENT, COMPELLING, TRENCHANT, INCISIVE
- powerful and influential person, typically a rich industrialist MAGNATE
- powerful controlling and constricting force, such as one that is imposed by tradition or custom TYRANNY
- powerful in a wide-ranging and effective way, as a remedy or the like might be SOVEREIGN, EFFICACIOUS, POTENT
- powerful in an irresponsibly bullying or overbearing way IMPERIOUS, DOMINEERING, DICTATORIAL
- powerful in effect, or forceful, arresting, as an advertisement might be PUNCHY
- powerful in or having control over an enterprise IN THE DRIVER'S SEAT
- powerful official or authority OVERLORD
- powerful to a great or excessive degree OMNIPOTENT, OVERWHELMING
- conclusive, with powerful influence, as a textbook might be AUTHORITATIVE, DEFINITIVE
- huge and powerful TITANIC

powerless, inoperative, or invalid, as a disregarded law or regulation is NUGATORY, DEAD-LETTER

practicable, capable of working, realistic VIABLE, FEASIBLE

practical, dealing with, ruled by, or relating to facts and actual circumstances rather than theories or ideals PRAGMATIC, REALISTIC
- practical and purely functional, wholly mechanical or materialistic BANAUSIC
- practical rather than decorative UTILITARIAN, FUNCTIONAL
- practical shrewdness, common sense GUMPTION
- based on practical experience rather than theory or proof, as a medical treatment might be EMPIRICAL

practically, nearly, in essence but not in appearance VIRTUALLY

practice or practical side of a profession or field of study as distinct from the theory PRAXIS
- practice or engage in one's trade PLY
- practice or rehearsal DUMMY RUN, DRY RUN
- disuse, state of being out of use or practice DESUETUDE

praise, acknowledgment of qualities HOMAGE, TRIBUTE
- praise, adore, worship REVERE, VENERATE
- praise, applause, compliment ACCLAIM, ACCOLADE, BOUQUET
- praise, compliment, or express approval of COMMEND
- praise, enthusiastic approval PLAUDITS, APPROBATION
- praise, or a speech of praise or a tribute that is written EULOGY, ENCOMIUM, PANEGYRIC
- praise highly, glorify, honor EXALT, EXTOL, LAUD
- praise of an excessive kind, idolization HAGIOGRAPHY, ADULATION
- praise or prestige as a result of achievements or success KUDOS
- praise or recommend, as in an advertisement ENDORSE
- praise or recommend highly or with suspect enthusiasm TOUT, PUFF
- praise or talk in an extremely enthusiastic way RHAPSODIZE
- praise publicly and in a conspicuous way, celebrate EMBLAZON, EULOGIZE, PROCLAIM
- cry of praise to God HOSANNA
- hymn, verse, or formula praising God in the liturgy DOXOLOGY
- lavish in an excessive and distasteful way, as praise might be FULSOME
- song or expression of joy and praise PAEAN

praiseworthy LAUDABLE, COMMENDABLE

pranks or high-spirited adventures CAPERS, TOMFOOLERY, HIGH JINKS, HORSEPLAY, SKYLARKING, ESCAPADES, ANTICS, SCRAPES

pray - desk at which a person may kneel to pray PRIE-DIEU
- "praying" insect MANTIS

prayer See chart, page 416, and also **hymn**
- prayer beads ROSARY
- prayer book, especially for the Roman Catholic Mass MISSAL
- prayers or other, usually private, acts of religious observance DEVOTIONS
- endowment for the saying of prayers or Mass, usually for the soul of the benefactor CHANTRY
- expressing or based on a vow or wish, as a prayer might be VOTIVE
- former term for a prayer ORISON
- person in former times who prayed, often for pay, for another's soul or welfare BEADSMAN
- psalm, anthem, or the like sung as an invitation to prayer during a church service INVITATORY
- psalm, prayer, or hymn sung at

the beginning of a church service INTROIT

preacher or evangelizer full of enthusiasm HOT-GOSPELER
- belonging to the congregation or general public as opposed to the clergy, as a preacher might be LAY
- traveling from place to place, as some judges or preachers are ITINERANT

preachy, pompously moralizing, as by means of clichéd advice SENTENTIOUS, PONTIFICAL
- preachy or priggish explanations or criticisms MORALIZING, CANT, SERMONIZING

precautions - taking appropriate precautions CIRCUMSPECT

precious or high-quality, as a ruby or amethyst might be ORIENTAL
- extremely precious, beyond price INVALUABLE

precious stones See chart, and also **gemstone**

precise description, list of details, plan, or proposal SPECIFICATION, SPECS
- precise details, sometimes needlessly fussy MINUTIAE, TRIVIA
- precise or careful to a fault, extremely painstaking METICULOUS, FASTIDIOUS, SCRUPULOUS, PUNCTILIOUS
- precise to a fault, oversubtle, pedantic, or dogmatic SCHOLASTIC, ACADEMIC, SOPHISTICAL
- demanding person, insisting on precise accuracy, obedience, and the like STICKLER, PURIST, PERFECTIONIST
- quoting precisely, using the identical words, word for word VERBATIM

precision, delicacy, subtlety, as in negotiations NICETY

preconceived opinion, prejudice PARTI PRIS

predict See **forecast, foretell, prophetic, fortune-telling**

predictable or automatic, as a reaction or response may be PAVLOVIAN, KNEE-JERK

pregnancy in which the fertilized egg develops outside the uterus, typically in a fallopian tube ECTOPIC PREGNANCY, TUBAL PREGNANCY
- pregnancy occurring in a female who is already pregnant SUPERFETATION
- pregnancy test by prodding the uterus to feel a rebound from the fetus BALLOTTEMENT
- clawed toad used in pregnancy testing XENOPUS, PLATANNA
- craving for unnatural food, such as mud or chalk, occurring sometimes during pregnancy PICA
- custom in some cultures in which the husband, too, takes to his bed during the later stages of his

PRAYERS

Agnus Dei	"Lamb of God," prayer in three parts spoken or sung in the Mass	**Kaddish**	daily prayer in praise of God in Jewish services; also recited by those mourning the death of a close relative
Aleinu	prayer near the end of a Jewish service	**Kol Nidre**	prayer on the eve of Yom Kippur, the Jewish Day of Atonement
Amidah	main prayer at a Jewish service	**Kyrie Eleison**	"Lord have mercy," prayer, often sung, in Christian worship
Angelus	prayer said morning, noon, and night by Roman Catholics to commemorate the Annunciation	**litany**	prayer in which the congregation's responses alternate with the leader's invocations
Ave Maria	"Hail Mary," prayer honoring the Virgin Mary, in Roman Catholic worship	**matins**	first of the seven canonical hours
canonical hours	prayers or services set for specific times of day in the Roman Catholic Church	**Miserere**	prayer for mercy in Christian worship
collect	brief prayer spoken before the epistle at Mass or Holy Communion	**none**	fifth of the seven canonical hours
compline	last of the seven canonical hours	**Pater Noster**	"Our Father," the Lord's Prayer
Confiteor	prayer including a standardized confession of sins, in Roman Catholic worship	**prime**	second of the seven canonical hours
epiclesis	prayer in the Mass calling on the Holy Spirit to transform the bread and wine into the body and blood of Christ	**Requiescat**	prayer for the souls of the dead
Fatiha	standard prayer and declaration of faith in Islamic worship	**rogation**	prayer said during the Rogation Days, preceding Ascension Day
Gloria	prayer of praise in Christian worship	**sext**	fourth of the seven canonical hours
intercession	prayer to God on behalf of another	**Shema**	"Hear, O Israel," the confession of the Jewish faith
invocation	prayer asking for God's help	**terce**	third of the seven canonical hours
		vespers	sixth of the seven canonical hours

wife's pregnancy COUVADE
- developing embryo during the later stages of pregnancy FETUS
- illusory pregnancy, often including such signs as a swollen abdomen, typically resulting from an emotional disorder PHANTOM PREGNANCY, PSEUDOCYESIS, FALSE PREGNANCY
- occurring during or relating to pregnancy PRENATAL, ANTENATAL
- premature expulsion of a fetus in midpregnancy MISCARRIAGE, SPONTANEOUS ABORTION
- referring to the care of women during pregnancy and after childbirth OBSTETRIC
- toxic condition, involving convulsions and sometimes coma, during the last three months of pregnancy ECLAMPSIA

pregnant, with child GRAVID, ENCEINTE, EXPECTANT
- be pregnant, carry unborn young GESTATE
- fertilize, make pregnant FECUNDATE, IMPREGNATE, INSEMINATE
- not pregnant, as a mare might be FALLOW
- not pregnant or not calving in a particular year, as a cow might be FARROW
- withdrawal by syringe of some of the fluid in a pregnant woman's womb, to monitor the health of the fetus AMNIOCENTESIS

prehistoric See **archeology**

prehistoric (combining form) EO-, PALEO-

prehistoric animals See **dinosaur, extinct**

prehistoric humans known from skeleton remains in Europe, an early form of modern humans CRO-MAGNON
- prehistoric-human hoax, a well-known forgery that used modern bones PILTDOWN MAN
- prehistoric human of Europe, Asia, and North Africa, an early user of tools and early species of Homo sapiens NEANDERTHAL MAN
- prehistoric humanlike creature, of several species PROTOHUMAN
- prehistoric humanlike creature of eastern and southern Africa AUSTRALOPITHECINE, PARANTHROPUS, ZINJANTHROPUS
- apelike prehistoric human, such as Peking Man or Java Man HOMO ERECTUS, SINANTHROPUS, PITHECANTHROPUS

prejudice, preformed judgment or preference PREDISPOSITION, PRECONCEPTION, PREDILECTION, PARTI PRIS, PARTIALITY
- prejudice against or hatred of foreigners XENOPHOBIA
- prejudice against or hatred of men MISANDRY
- prejudice against or hatred of people MISANTHROPY
- prejudice against or hatred of women MISOGYNY
- prejudiced, mindlessly devoted or loyal PARTISAN
- prejudiced and intolerant person BIGOT
- prejudiced attitudes or actions, as on the basis of race or sex DISCRIMINATION
- prejudiced by one's fixed beliefs or ideology, not open-minded DOGMATIC, DOCTRINAIRE
- prejudiced favoring of one's own group or country JINGOISM, CHAUVINISM, FLAG WAVING
- prejudiced or biased against something, pessimistic or cynical JAUNDICED
- prejudiced or narrow-minded, blinkered MYOPIC, PAROCHIAL

preliminary See also **introduction**
- preliminary, introductory, or preparing for something to come PREPARATORY, PREFATORY, PRECURSORY
- preliminary draft for a treaty or other document PROTOCOL
- preliminary event, entertainment, or the like, as before the main sports match or play CURTAIN RAISER
- preliminary inspection of a region, as to assess the terrain or study enemy positions RECONNAISSANCE, RECONNOITER
- preliminary statement or explanation, as in a formal document PREAMBLE

preliminary (combining form) FORE-

premature, ill-prepared HALF-COCKED
- give premature birth to a calf SLINK, SLIP
- temperature-controlled hospital container, as for premature babies INCUBATOR

premise - pattern of logical reasoning in which two premises generate a conclusion SYLLOGISM
- put forward as a premise or axiom, as in a geometry theorem POSTULATE, POSIT, HYPOTHESIZE

preoccupation or obsession FIXATION, IDÉE FIXE

prepare See also **make**
- prepare for something difficult, dangerous, or undesirable MAKE PROVISIONS, GIRD UP ONE'S LOINS, PRIME ONESELF, BATTEN DOWN THE HATCHES
- prepare something, as in cooking, by mixing various elements CONCOCT

prepared, ready POISED, BRACED

prescription - "equal quantities of," referring to the ingredients in a prescription ANA
- referring or relating to a medical drug available only on prescription ETHICAL, MAGISTRAL
- referring or relating to a medical drug available without prescription OVER-THE-COUNTER, OFFICINAL

present See also **gift**
- present, current, happening or existing at the present time, now CONTEMPORARY
- present but not visible, as a tendency might be LATENT
- present or bestow a degree or honor CONFER

PRECIOUS AND SEMIPRECIOUS STONES

COLORLESS

diamond
topaz
white sapphire
zircon

YELLOW AND ORANGE

amber
chrysoberyl
citrine
fire opal/girasol
topaz

BROWN

agate
andradite
cairngorm/smoky quartz
cat's-eye
jade
jadeite
jasper
sardonyx
tiger-eye

RED AND PINK

almandine
beryl
carbuncle
carnelian/cornelian
garnet
morganite
red zircon/hyacinth/jacinth
rose quartz
rubasse/Mont Blanc ruby
rubellite
ruby
rutile
spinel

PURPLE AND VIOLET

almandine
amethyst
garnet
spinel

BLUE

lapis lazuli
lazurite
sapphire
turquoise
water sapphire
sodalite

GREEN

alexandrite
amazonstone/amazonite
aquamarine
beryl
chrysoberyl
chrysoprase
emerald
heliotrope/bloodstone
jade
jadeite
malachite
nephrite
olivine
peridot
tourmaline
verditer

WHITISH

moonstone
onyx
opal

BLACK

jet
melanite
rutile

- present or bestow a degree or honor CONFER
- present or offer formally TENDER
- present or submit something, such as a bill RENDER
- for the present, for the time being FOR THE NONCE

present tense of verbs used when narrating events of the past HISTORICAL PRESENT

preservative, as of specimens for dissecting FORMALDEHYDE
- preservative or protective substance FIXATIVE
- potassium nitrate, used as a preservative of meat SALTPETER

preserve See also **keep, protect**
- preserve a corpse from decay by means of chemical treatment EMBALM
- preserve food, especially meat, in brine or with salt CORN
- preserve food by drying DESICCATE
- preserve meat, fish, tobacco, rubber, or the like CURE

presidency or government of France ELYSÉE
- presidency or presidential power in the United States OVAL OFFICE, WHITE HOUSE

president of the United States during his remaining time in office after his successor has been elected LAME-DUCK PRESIDENT
- president or other official currently in office INCUMBENT
- charge a president or other public official with an offense committed while in office IMPEACH
- install someone, such as a president, formally in office INDUCT, INAUGURATE, INVEST, SWEAR

press of a cheap and sensationalizing kind YELLOW PRESS
- press through which paper or cloth is rolled for a smooth or glossy finish CALENDER

pressure cooker, or similar sealed vessel for sterilizing surgical instruments AUTOCLAVE
- pressure gauge MANOMETER, SPHYGMOMANOMETER
- enclosed space inside which the air or gas pressure is greater than that outside PLENUM
- feeling of tightness or pressure, as in the chest CONSTRICTION
- instrument for measuring the atmospheric pressure, used in calculating altitude and making weather forecasts BAROMETER
- line on a weather map linking places with the same atmospheric pressure ISOBAR
- operated by or involving fluid pressure HYDRAULIC
- painful condition, as in deep-sea divers, after sudden change of pressure THE BENDS, CAISSON DISEASE, DECOMPRESSION SICKNESS, AEROEMBOLISM
- rotating cylinder on which a pen records changes in pressure, heartbeat, or the like KYMOGRAPH
- tube with a narrow throat, as in a pipe or carburetor, for measuring fluid pressure or for providing suction VENTURI
- unit of atmospheric pressure MILLIBAR

pressure (combining form) BARO-, PIEZO-

pressure point - artery that can be constricted at the pressure point against the collarbone SUBCLAVIAN ARTERY
- artery that can be constricted at the pressure point at the base of the neck COMMON CAROTID ARTERY
- artery that can be constricted at the pressure point below the jaw FACIAL ARTERY
- artery that can be constricted at the pressure point in front of the ear TEMPORAL ARTERY
- artery that can be constricted at the pressure point in the groin FEMORAL ARTERY
- artery that can be constricted at the pressure point in the inner side of the upper arm BRACHIAL ARTERY

prestige or glory resulting from some achievement KUDOS
- prestige or social distinction CACHET

pretend, fake, or falsely display something, such as relief FEIGN, SIMULATE, AFFECT, ASSUME, COUNTERFEIT, SHAM
- pretend, mislead, hide one's true thoughts or feelings DISSEMBLE, DISSIMULATE
- pretend to be dead, asleep, or ignorant PLAY POSSUM
- pretend to be ill, as to get off work MALINGER, SKIVE
- pretend to be someone else IMPERSONATE, MASQUERADE, MIMIC
- pretended, feigned, false, as an emotion might be SIMULATED, SHAM, BOGUS
- pretended, merely apparent or outward, as a given reason might be PROFESSED, SPECIOUS, OSTENSIBLE
- pretended reason, apparent purpose or justification PRETEXT
- pretending or appearing to be unsophisticated and naive FAUX-NAÏF
- pretending to be ignorant, insincere DISINGENUOUS

pretending (combining form) PSEUD-, PSEUDO-

pretense, caricature, or a crudely distorted imitation TRAVESTY, PARODY
- pretense, false appearance GUISE
- pretense, hypocrisy HUMBUG
- pretense, trickery DECEIT, GUILE, FINESSE
- pretense intended to mislead, especially a misleading movement or feigned attack FEINT
- scheme or trick relying on pretense and deceit ARTIFICE, DODGE, RUSE, STRATEGEM, SUBTERFUGE, WILE

pretentious See also **pompous**
- pretentious, flowery, affected, fussy, or overelaborate in style, pretty-pretty CHINTZY, PRECIOUS, CHI-CHI
- pretentious and typically sentimental art KITSCH
- pretentious newcomer in a social circle, upstart PARVENU, ARRIVISTE, NOUVEAU RICHE
- pretentious things, such as over-ornate clothes FRIPPERY
- socially pretentious, affecting posh manners GENTEEL

pretty See also **attractive, beautiful**
- pretty girl or woman BELLE

prevent See also **hinder, limit, prohibit**
- prevent, hold back, or hide laughter, a yawn, or the like STIFLE, SUPPRESS
- prevent, nip in the bud, take advance action against ANTICIPATE, FORESTALL, OBVIATE, PRECLUDE, PREEMPT
- prevent, ward off, or deflect a blow, problems, or the like AVERT, FORFEND, PARRY, STAVE OFF
- prevent acceptance of a proposal by exercising one's absolute right to decide VETO
- prevent from continuing, cut short, or end prematurely ABORT, ARREST
- prevent from happening or moving, put obstacles in front of, restrain, check BAULK, BILK, CURB, FRUSTRATE, PUT THE KIBOSH ON, SPIKE, THWART
- prevent from joining a social group, exclude BLACKBALL, DEBAR, OSTRACIZE
- prevent from moving IMMOBILIZE, PARALYZE
- prevent or discourage someone from doing something, as by threatening DETER
- prevent or restrain oneself from doing something, refrain or desist from FORBEAR
- prevent the free or unregulated publication of a book, newspaper, or the like, as by inspecting and making cuts CENSOR, BOWDLERIZE
- preventing or protecting against something, especially against disease PROPHYLACTIC

- preventing or trying to prevent, anticipating PREVENIENT

previous, earlier, being before in time, rank, order, or the like PRECEDING
- feeling of having undergone previously an experience that one is only having for the first time DÉJÀ VU
- "in the previous month," formerly used in business correspondence ULTIMO, ULT.

previous (combining from) EX-, SUPRA-

prey, hunted game QUARRY
- animal that kills and eats prey PREDATOR
- seizing and eating prey, as birds of prey are PREDACIOUS, PREDATORY, RAPACIOUS, RAPTORIAL, RAVENING

price index issued each month, used as a guide to inflation RETAIL PRICE INDEX
- price list TARIFF
- price that is the minimum the owner will accept at an auction RESERVE PRICE
- excessive, unreasonable, as prices or demands might be EXORBITANT, EXTORTIONATE
- maintain or increase the price of a commodity or service, as by government subsidies, levies, or the like VALORIZE

prick or stab lightly, as with a sword PINK

prickly bush or shrub, especially a wild rose BRIAR
- prickly husk or seedpod BURR
- prickly shrub or plant such as the blackberry or dog rose BRAMBLE

prickly (combining form) ECHINO-

prickly pear OPUNTIA

pride See also **proud, boast, pompous**
- pride in attitude, arrogance, habit of putting on airs HAUTEUR, GRANDEUR, CONCEIT
- pride in oneself, sense of one's own worth and dignity SELF-ESTEEM, AMOUR PROPRE
- pride or arrogance, which often leads to downfall HUBRIS
- pride or plume oneself on something, congratulate oneself PIQUE, PREEN
- downfall or undoing, typically just retribution, as following pride or overconfidence NEMESIS
- excessive, out of proportion, as ambitions or pride might be OVERWEENING
- excessive pride in one's appearance or abilities, boastfulness and vanity VAINGLORY
- humble, reduce the pride or confidence of DEFLATE
- please, satisfy, or indulge something, such as one's pride GRATIFY

priest See also **clergyman** and illustration at **clerical clothing**
- priest, clergyman, clergywoman ECCLESIASTIC
- priest in ancient Rome, serving a specific deity FLAMEN
- priest of highest status in ancient Rome PONTIFEX MAXIMUS
- priest of senior status in ancient Rome PONTIFEX
- priest officiating at the Eucharist or other religious ceremony or rite CELEBRANT
- priest or elder in various churches PRESBYTER
- priest's acceptance into the ministry, or the ceremony of admission ORDINATION
- priest's assistant when at the altar ACOLYTE
- priest's official clothing CANONICALS, VESTMENTS
- priestlike, relating to priests HIERATIC, SACERDOTAL
- abstaining from sexual intercourse, as priests are, and others who have taken a vow of chastity

Primates

Gorilla

Chimpanzee

Langur monkey

CELIBATE
- authorize to be a priest, invest with holy orders ORDAIN
- Buddhist priest or monk in Tibet or Mongolia LAMA
- calling or strong urging or inclination, as to the priesthood VOCATION
- confession heard or absolution granted by a priest SHRIFT
- deprive a priest of his or her clerical rights and functions UNFROCK, DEFROCK
- residence of a Roman Catholic parish priest PRESBYTERY
- right to nominate a priest to a vacant benefice or to a position ADVOWSON

priestess in ancient Rome tending the sacred fire in the temple of the goddess Vesta VESTAL VIRGIN
- priestess or nun VOTARESS

prim, affectedly delicate or refined MINCING, NIMINY-PIMINY, FINICKY

primates See illustration, page 419

primitive See also **prehistoric humans**
- primitive, original PRIMAL, PRIMEVAL
- person who takes to the hills, living a primitive life, to escape the effects of an expected nuclear war SURVIVALIST
- relating to a primitive time or condition PRISTINE, PRIMORDIAL
- reversion to a more primitive state ATAVISM

primitive (combining form) UR-

prince or high nobleman in Anglo-Saxon times ATHELING

princess of a Spanish or Portuguese royal family other than the heir apparent INFANTA

principal See also **main**
- principal, foremost, leading, supreme PARAMOUNT, PREDOMINANT, PREEMINENT, PREPONDERANT
- principal or capital sum of money, value of an estate, or the like, as distinct from the interest or income CORPUS

principle, body of beliefs, or the like CREDO, CREED, DOGMA, DOCTRINE, TENET
- principle, guiding doctrine, or the like, adhered to unwaveringly GOSPEL
- principle, standard, or basis or measure for judgment CRITERION, CANON
- principle or ideal expressed by a word or maxim, as on a coat of arms MOTTO
- principle or mock-scientific law to the effect that if anything can go wrong it will MURPHY'S LAW
- principle or mock-scientific law to

PRINTING TERMS

boldface	heavy thick-lined type presenting an emphatic black appearance
caret	arrowhead mark indicating to the typesetter where material is to be inserted
cast-off	calculation of the amount of space that a manuscript will take when set in type
chase	metal frame that holds type for printing or platemaking
composing stick	small, hand-held adjustable tray in which type is set before fitting in the galley
feathering/ carding	adjustment of the spacing between lines to fill the column exactly
flong	papier-mâché sheet used for making stereotype molds; mold made of this
font	set of type characters of a particular design
form	type assembled in a chase and ready for printing
galley	metal tray in which set type is held before pagination; printer's proof from such type
guide word/ catchword	word printed at the top of a page or column, as in a dictionary, to indicate the alphabetically first and last of its entries
gutter	white space running down between the facing pages of a book
imposition	arrangement of pages of type in a form to read consecutively when the printed sheet is folded
impression	printed sheet produced by a letterpress machine; copies of a book printed at one time from a single set of type
indent	set in from the margin, as for the first line of a paragraph
intaglio/ gravure	technique of printing from a plate in which the images are incised rather than raised
justification	equal spacing of words to produce a line to the full width of a given column
kern	part of a piece of type that projects beyond the body or shank
kerning	letting the kern of adjacent letters overlap for tighter setting
leaders	dots or dashes along a line linking separated words, as in a table of contents
leading	spacing (the amount of lead) between lines
letterpress	technique of printing from raised inked surfaces
Linotype	machine for setting an entire line of type on a single slug or metal bar
lithography	technique of printing from a plate treated so that some areas accept ink while others repel it
logotype	single piece of type bearing two or more characters
lowercase	referring to small letters, the type for which was originally held in the lower frame of a case of type
mackle	blur or double impression on a printed sheet
matrix	metal plate for casting typefaces

PRINTING TERMS *continued*	
offset	printing process in which ink is transferred from the plate to an offset cylinder and then to the paper
proof	trial sheet of print on which corrections are written
quoin	wedge used to lock type in a chase
range	lie flush at the margin
registration	exact alignment of print on a page
running head	title printed at the top of every page or every alternate page
signature/ gathering/ section	groups of printed pages, usually 16 or 32, folded from a large single sheet and bound with others to make up a book
stereotype/ cliché	printing plate cast from a papier-mâché mold
stet	instruction to a typesetter to ignore a correction
uppercase	referring to capital letters, the type for which was originally held in the upper frame of a case of type
widow	word or very short line, especially when ending a paragraph or standing by itself at the top of a column or page

the effect that people tend to get promoted until they reach a position in which they are incompetent PETER PRINCIPLE
- principle or mock-scientific law to the effect that work expands to fill the time available for its completion PARKINSON'S LAW
- principle or rule of conduct, command or maxim PRECEPT
- principle or rule widely accepted AXIOM
- principle underlying something, foundation SUBSTRATUM
- principles allowing different behavior in one person or group from that expected of another DOUBLE STANDARD
- principles and techniques of a discipline, art, or science METHODOLOGY

principles (combining from) -NOMY

print made from a specially carved or etched block or printing plate ENGRAVING

printing See chart, and also **typesetting, paper**, and illustrations at **script** and **typeface**
- printing error or typing error TYPOGRAPHICAL ERROR, TYPO
- printing plate or mold MATRIX
- printing symbol, *, as for referring to a footnote ASTERISK
- printing symbol, †, as for referring to a footnote DAGGER, OBELISK, OBELUS
- printing symbol, ‡, as for referring to a footnote DIESIS, DOUBLE DAGGER
- printing type of a sloping style, as used for emphasis ITALIC
- printing worker who sets type, typesetter COMPOSITOR
- printed character of two or more letters joined together, such as *fi* LIGATURE
- printed pamphlets, handouts, and other short-lived topical publications EPHEMERA
- printer for a word processor, printing each character in the form of a set of tiny dots DOT-MATRIX PRINTER
- check a printer's copy for mistakes against the original manuscript or typescript PROOFREAD
- short ornamental line finishing off a stroke of a printed letter SERIF
- small wheellike device supporting the printing characters on a modern typewriter or word-processor printer DAISY WHEEL

priority given according to position or rank PRECEDENCE

prison PENITENTIARY
- prison for persons awaiting trial JAIL, CUSTODY, DETENTION
- prison guard who keeps the keys to an old-style jail TURNKEY
- prison or fortress BASTILLE
- prison sentence whose length is not specified when imposed INDETERMINATE SENTENCE
- prison where short-term sentences are served by manual labor WORKHOUSE
- prisonlike institution for young offenders REFORMATORY
- center to help people readjust to society after release from prison or a mental hospital REHABILITATION CENTER, HALFWAY HOUSE
- confinement in isolation within a prison, usually as a punishment SOLITARY CONFINEMENT
- dark cell or prison, usually underground DUNGEON, OUBLIETTE
- early release from a prison, on condition of good behavior PAROLE
- enclosed area inside a prison or prison camp COMPOUND
- German prison camp for captured noncommissioned officers and privates during World War II STALAG
- German prison camp for captured commissioned officers during World War II OFLAG
- labor camp or prison, especially for political prisoners in the U.S.S.R. GULAG
- legal writ for release from prison or other rights for a prisoner HABEAS CORPUS
- local prison for holding offenders awaiting a court hearing LOCKUP, JAIL
- military prison enclosure STOCKADE
- official sending of a person to prison or a mental hospital COMMITTAL
- person confined in an institution, such as a prison or a mental hospital INMATE
- reduction of the duration of a prison sentence, as for good behavior REMISSION
- remain neglected and disheartened, as in prison LANGUISH
- release from jail or prison against payment of a security BAIL
- running simultaneously, as two prison terms might be CONCURRENT
- send to prison CONSIGN
- ship used as a prison HULK
- short-term prison for young offenders DETENTION CENTER
- slang term for a prison sentence STRETCH
- slang term for a prison or jail SLAMMER, CLINK, COOLER, BIG HOUSE, CALABOOSE, BRIG, CAN, BOOBYHATCH, POKEY
- study of the punishment and treatment of criminals, especially prison management PENOLOGY
- unable to communicate with others, as when detained in prison INCOMMUNICADO

prisoner serving as an informer to the authorities STOOL PIGEON
- prisoner with special privileges,

as for good behavior TRUSTY
- guardianship, as of an orphan or prisoner CUSTODY
- restraining garment with long sleeves for binding the arms of a violent patient or prisoner STRAIT-JACKET
- separation or isolation of an individual or small group from the group as a whole, as of prisoners SEGREGATION
- tendency of former prisoners to revert to crime RECIDIVISM

privacy - person who values his or her privacy and lives in solitude RECLUSE, HERMIT

private See also **secret**
- private, deeply personal, secret INTIMATE
- private, hidden, tucked away or sheltered alone SOLITARY, SEQUESTERED, SECLUDED
- private conversation between two people TÊTE-À-TÊTE
- privately, in confidence SUB ROSA
- privately owned and controlled PROPRIETARY
- in private, especially relating to a court hearing from which the public is excluded IN CAMERA
- knowing something secret or private PRIVY TO
- person to whom one tells one's secrets or with whom one discusses private matters (masculine and feminine, respectively) CONFIDANT, CONFIDANTE

private enterprise, noninterference by governments in commercial activity LAISSEZ-FAIRE

privilege or right, as conferred by rank, the law, or the like PREROGATIVE

prize, award, or some other honor ACCOLADE
- prize for a particular deed PREMIUM
- prize given in a mocking spirit to the contestant who comes last BOOBY PRIZE, WOODEN SPOON
- prize given to a worthy loser CONSOLATION PRIZE
- prize or high distinction CORDON BLEU, THREE STARS
- prizes awarded annually for journalism, literature, and music PULITZER PRIZES
- second prize, or a person who nearly wins an academic prize or other award PROXIME ACCESSIT
- prize winner, poet, or other eminent person in the arts or sciences who receives a special honor LAUREATE

probability - having an even probability, not planned to favor any particular outcome ACCIDENTAL, RANDOM, ALEATORY
- mathematical analysis of data using sampling techniques and probability theory STATISTICS

probable, believable, likely or possible FEASIBLE
- probable, in the offing, likely to become someone or something specified PROSPECTIVE
- probable, seemingly true, as an excuse might be PLAUSIBLE, COLORABLE

probably, clearly, or obviously EVIDENTLY

problem, behavior pattern, or the like consisting of several associated elements SYNDROME
- problem, condition of difficulty or distress PLIGHT, PREDICAMENT, DILEMMA
- problem, confused or entangled situation IMBROGLIO, MARE'S NEST
- problem, minor obstacle SNAG, HITCH
- problem-solving by means of an imaginative and free-ranging rather than strictly logical mode of thinking LATERAL THINKING
- problem that can be resolved only by bold or drastic action GORDIAN KNOT
- problem that is hard, difficult to solve, puzzle POSER, CONUNDRUM, ENIGMA
- problem that is unresolvable and blocks progress IMPASSE, DEADLOCK, STALEMATE
- problem that is very complicated, with each apparent solution leading only to further difficulties LABYRINTH
- problem that is very demanding and difficult to escape from MORASS, QUAGMIRE
- problem that seems to have no satisfactory solution DILEMMA, QUANDARY
- difficult to solve or deal with, as a knotty problem would be SCABROUS
- having many aspects, as a difficult problem might be HYDRA-HEADED
- having very serious problems IN EXTREMIS
- identification of a disease, injury, or problem DIAGNOSIS
- referring to a problem that cannot be solved INSOLUBLE
- relating to problem-solving techniques based on trial and error HEURISTIC
- supposed source of problems, errors, or mischief GREMLIN

procedure that is pointlessly long and complicated RIGMAROLE
- procedure or program, as of daily exercise REGIMEN
- characteristic procedure, way of operating MODUS OPERANDI, MO

processes or functions maintaining life METABOLISM

procession, especially a funeral procession CORTEGE
- procession, such as a ceremonial parade of horses CAVALCADE
- procession of the choir and clergy out of the chancel at the end of a church service RECESSION
- procession or costumed parade in a festival PAGEANT
- procession or parade of cars or other motor vehicles MOTORCADE
- placard or message carried in a demonstration or procession BANNER, SIGN
- precedence, or right of priority in a procession PAS

procession (combining form) -CADE

produce, give rise to ELICIT, EVOKE
- produce or obtain from a source DERIVE

producer or sponsor of stage shows, concerts, or the like IMPRESARIO

producing or about to produce a discovery, inspired idea, or the like PARTURIENT

producing, production (combining form) -GEN-, -GENIC, -GENOUS, -GON-, GONO-, FER-, -FACIENT, -FIC, -POIETIC, -POIESIS

product that is the most successful of a business's output FLAGSHIP
- anything commercially useful, such as a farm product, or any tradable goods or services COMMODITY
- crop or product that is the major one of its kind in a region STAPLE

profession, occupation to which one is suited VOCATION, CALLING, MÉTIER
- members collectively of the medical, legal, or other learned profession FACULTY
- person who works in a profession or teaches, by contrast to a theoretician PRACTITIONER
- requirements in one's profession or pursuits STOCK IN TRADE

professional misconduct, offense or offenses committed by a public official MALVERSATION

professor - retired but retaining an honorary title, as a professor might be EMERITUS

profile portrait in the form of a shadow image or filled-in outline SILHOUETTE

profit or payment from one's job or office EMOLUMENT
- profits of a business, charity campaign, or the like PROCEEDS
- anything that can be turned to

one's profit or advantage GRIST
- referring to the final profit, weight, price, or the like after all deductions have been made NET, BOTTOM LINE
- referring to the profit, weight, price, or the like before deductions have been made GROSS
- share of profits or a bankrupt's assets DIVIDEND

profitable, fruitful, producing a great deal of money LUCRATIVE, REMUNERATIVE
- profitable job requiring little work, or similar easy source of income GRAVY TRAIN, MILCH COW, SINECURE

program See also **radio, television**
- program at the end of a day's broadcasting in England, typically a short religious program EPILOGUE
- program of events, schedule of activities CURRICULUM, ROSTER
- program or procedure, as of daily exercise REGIMEN
- program that has been prerecorded for broadcasting TRANSCRIPTION
- program that is broadcast simultaneously on radio and television SIMULCAST
- announcements or linking items designed to avoid breaks between broadcast programs CONTINUITY
- broadcast live a program via a transmitter RELAY

progress, movement forward HEADWAY
- progress or general direction, as of someone's life TENOR
- progress to a more important role GRADUATE

progression (combining form) -GRADE

progressive or rebellious activist within a political group or party YOUNG TURK

prohibit See also **hinder, limit, prevent**
- prohibit, forbid, ban DEBAR, OUTLAW, PROSCRIBE, VETO
- prohibit or cut off from membership of a church EXCOMMUNICATE
- prohibit or forbid by force of law ENJOIN, INTERDICT, RESTRAIN
- prohibited, forbidden VERBOTEN
- prohibited because blasphemous, cursed, or holy TABOO
- prohibited goods, obtainable only by smuggling CONTRABAND
- court order prohibiting or enforcing an action INJUNCTION, WRIT

prohibition, as of foreign ships or of arms trading EMBARGO
- make, sell, or transport goods illegally, especially alcohol during the Prohibition era in the United States BOOTLEG

project, gift, or possession requiring more trouble than it is worth WHITE ELEPHANT
- project or enterprise, often risky VENTURE, UNDERTAKING
- projected or possible course of action or chain of events SCENARIO
- dark chamber in which the image of an outside view is projected onto a surface by a lens set above or opposite CAMERA OBSCURA
- organizing of any complicated project, especially one involving transport LOGISTICS

projecting, jutting out PROTRUDING, EXTRUDING
- projecting, rounded part, as on the ear or a leaf LOBE
- projecting end of a piece of wood fitting into a corresponding mortise in another piece to form a joint TENON
- projecting from the surrounding wall or surface PROUD
- projecting or swelling part, bulge PROTUBERANCE
- projecting pin on either side of a cannon, container, or the like enabling it to be pivoted on a supporting frame TRUNNION
- projecting rim or edge, as on a wheel or beam, for strengthening, attaching, or the like FLANGE
- pointing or jutting outward, projecting, as an angle might be SALIENT

projector for showing images, as written or drawn on transparent material such as film, or on opaque material, onto a screen EPIDIASCOPE
- projector or camera for cinematic films CINEMATOGRAPH
- projector or other apparatus giving brief exposures of visual images, as for experiments in memory or perception TACHISTOSCOPE

prolong, extend, cause to continue PERPETUATE, PROTRACT

promise, token, or guarantee EARNEST, PLEDGE, UNDERTAKING
- promise of support and vow of faith by members of a church COVENANT
- promise or obligation, recorded in court BOND, RECOGNIZANCE
- promise solemnly to be faithful, especially when getting married PLIGHT ONE'S TROTH
- fail to honor one's debts, promises, or the like WELSH
- fulfill a promise REDEEM
- go back on one's promise or commitment RENEGE, WELSH
- obtain a promise, commitment, or the like by persuasion EXTRACT
- written promise to pay a specified sum IOU, PROMISSORY NOTE

promised land, utopia ZION

promising, developing, up-and-coming BUDDING
- promising, favorable, boding well AUSPICIOUS, PROPITIOUS

promote, move to a new and grander role TRANSLATE, PREFER
- promoting or favorable to a given result CONDUCIVE

promoter or financial supporter of a project, sportsman, cultural activity, or the like SPONSOR, PATRON, ANGEL

promoter (combining form) -MONGER

promotion of a military officer to a higher rank, without the corresponding rise in pay or authority BREVET
- promotion or advancement to a higher office or post PREFERMENT
- lowering of rank or status, as opposed to promotion DEMOTION, RELEGATION

prong of a fork or fork-shaped tool TINE

pronoun, in English ending in *-self*, that refers back to the subject of the verb, such as *herself* in *she hurt herself* REFLEXIVE PRONOUN
- adjective for a pronoun PRONOMINAL
- use of pronouns or similar reference to something previously mentioned ANAPHORA
- word, phrase, or clause to which a pronoun refers ANTECEDENT

pronounce, especially in a clear way ARTICULATE, ENUNCIATE
- name, sentence, or the like that is difficult to pronounce or to say quickly TONGUE TWISTER

pronouncement - from the source of authority, as an official pronouncement might be EX CATHEDRA

pronunciation See also **sound, voice, speech**
- pronunciation of a final consonant that is normally silent, especially in French, when the next word begins with a vowel LIAISON
- pronunciation of American English that comes close to being a "formal" norm AMERICAN TELEVISION-ANNOUNCER ENGLISH, ATVAE
- pronunciation of the sound /r/ as /l/, as by many Chinese people speaking English LALLATION
- pronunciation of words, or the study of it ORTHOEPY
- pronunciation or spelling differing slightly from another form of the same word VARIANT
- pronunciation that is incorrect CACOEPY
- pronunciation widely used by the upper-middle classes in England

and often considered standard BBC ENGLISH, RECEIVED PRONUNCIATION, RP
- conforming to pronunciation, as Spanish spelling is approximating PHONETIC
- error in pronunciation or grammar produced by the avoidance of another, often imaginary error HYPERCORRECTION
- excessive or inconsistent use of the /r/ sound in pronunciation RHOTACISM
- insertion of an extra sound into a word to make its pronunciation easier, as when *umbrella* is pronounced as though it were spelled *umbarella* EPENTHESIS
- manner or clarity of one's pronunciation DICTION, ELOCUTION, ENUNCIATION, ARTICULATION
- mispronunciation, as when pronouncing *forte* as /for'tay/ (a two-syllable Italian music term meaning "loud") instead of *forte* /fort/ (a one-syllable French term meaning "strength," "strong point") MALAPROPISMS
- omitting or slurring of a vowel or syllable in pronunciation, as to make a verse scan ELISION
- study of pronunciation and speech sounds PHONETICS, PHONEMICS, PHONOLOGY
- tendency to change a speech sound for the sake of easier pronunciation EUPHONY
- throaty and harsh, as a person's pronunciation might be GUTTURAL

proof See also **prove**
- proof, evidence, or arguments used in justifying a claim or action VINDICATION
- proof or disproof of a proposition by showing that the logical consequences of it or its opposite are absurd or ridiculous REDUCTIO AD ABSURDUM
- proof or firm evidence or witness TESTAMENT
- proof or process of deduction in mathematics or logic DERIVATION
- additional proposition following from the proof of another proposition COROLLARY
- be evidence or proof of, be a witness for ATTEST, TESTIFY
- establish or confirm by evidence or proof VERIFY, SUBSTANTIATE, CORROBORATE
- referring to the method of step-by-step logical proof AXIOMATIC-DEDUCTIVE
- responsibility in law to provide proof for one's charge or claim BURDEN OF PROOF
- substantial, as concrete proof is TANGIBLE, SUBSTANTIVE
- supposed or presumed, but without proof, and often doubtful ALLEGED, HYPOTHETICAL
- theory that awaits proof HYPOTHESIS, WORKING HYPOTHESIS
- unquestionable, impossible to dispute or contradict, as a watertight proof is INCONTROVERTIBLE
- "which was to be proved," formula indicating that full proof has been achieved, as in a geometry theorem QUOD ERAT DEMONSTRANDUM, QED

proofreader's marks See illustration
- proofreading mark in the shape of an inverted V, placed in the text to indicate where new material is to be inserted CARET
- word written by a proofreader to reinstate a deleted piece of text or overrule a correction STET

propaganda or presentation of awkward facts, policies, or the like in a selectively favorable way WINDOW DRESSING
- propaganda and agitation, especially by left-wing radicals AGITPROP
- propaganda pamphlet or book containing a forceful declaration or rallying call TRACT
- influence someone into accepting an ideology, belief, or point of view uncritically, as by propaganda INDOCTRINATE, BRAINWASH

propeller blade VANE
- powerful rush of air or water forced backward by a propeller SLIPSTREAM, RACE

proper, in keeping with good manners and social conventions SEEMLY, DECOROUS, COMME IL FAUT
- proper, legal, officially approved, conforming with the requirements CANONICAL
- proper or formal behavior, good manners, observing of the formalities ETIQUETTE, PROTOCOL
- be proper or necessary for BEHOOVE, BEFIT

property See also **land, estate**
- property, as of a bankrupt, used to pay debts ASSETS
- property abandoned by its owner DERELICT
- property in one's personal possession CHATTELS, CHOSES
- property owned or the ownership of it DOMAIN
- property-owning or landed gentry class, or government by it SQUIREARCHY
- property pledged as security for a loan COLLATERAL
- property returning to a lessor or grantor after the agreed term, or the right to this property REVERSION
- property right retained by the lessor or seller RESERVATION
- property to be left in a will by a husband to his widow JOINTURE
- divide land or property into several small units COMMINUTE
- full ownership of land or property FREEHOLD
- government's right to take over private land or property for public use, compensation usually being paid EMINENT DOMAIN
- holding or occupying of a property, office, or the like TENURE
- intrude slowly on the property or rights of someone else, trespass ENCROACH
- large landed property or estate DEMESNE
- legal document certifying a contract or transfer of property DEED
- legal right to the use of benefits from someone else's property USUFRUCT
- legally attested right to a property TITLE
- limit the inheritance of property to a particular line of heirs ENTAIL
- mortgage or other charge or claim on a property ENCUMBRANCE
- repossess mortgaged property when the scheduled payments are not met FORECLOSE
- return of land or property to a feudal lord in the absence of legal heirs, in former times ESCHEAT
- right of use over another person's land or property for specific purposes SERVITUDE
- seize or confiscate property temporarily, especially a debtor's goods SEQUESTRATE
- seize property, as to force payment of a debt DISTRAIN, DISTRESS, LEVY
- share of the proceeds paid to a landowner for the use or development of his or her property ROYALTY
- strip or deprive of something, such as clothes, rights, or property DIVEST
- take away a person's private property or land, especially for public ownership EXPROPRIATE
- take or use fraudulently for oneself money or property entrusted to one EMBEZZLE, PECULATE, DEFALCATE
- transferrable to another owner, as some inherited property is ALIENABLE
- value of property once all debts are taken into account EQUITY

prophecy See also **fortune-telling**
- prophecy, shrine, or priest of a

prophetic god, as in ancient Greece ORACLE
- prophecy, vision, or revelation of a great disaster APOCALYPSE

prophecy (combining form) - MANCY

prophesy See **foretell, fortune-telling**
- prophesy or predict on the basis of signs and omens AUGUR, VATICINATE

prophet, astrologer, or sorcerer CHALDEAN
- prophet, visionary, or clairvoyant SEER
- prophet of doom whose warnings are ignored CASSANDRA
- prophet who warns of disaster JEREMIAH
- prophetess or sorceress SIBYL

prophetic, able to tell the future MANTIC, ORACULAR, CLAIRVOYANT
- prophetic, relating to a prophet VATIC, FATIDIC, PYTHONIC
- prophetic sign OMEN, PORTENT, PRESAGE, HARBINGER

proportion or correct relationship between things, especially their relative importance PERSPECTIVE

proportionate, corresponding in amount or degree, as one's salary might be with one's qualifications COMMENSURATE
- proportionate or balanced arrangement of parts, harmony SYMMETRY

proposal, precise description, list of details, or plan SPECIFICATION, SPECS

propose or name as a candidate NOMINATE
- propose or put forward for consideration PROPOUND

proposition in logic, forming either of the first two parts of a syllogism, from which the conclusion can be deduced PREMISE
- proposition in logic containing two simple statements joined by the word *or* DISJUNCTION
- logically inconsistent or conflicting, as two opposed propositions might be INCOMPATIBLE, DILEMMATIC
- minor proposition taken as valid and used to prove a more important proposition LEMMA
- referring to a proposition whose truth value depends entirely on the meanings of its terms rather than on real-life facts ANALYTIC
- referring to a proposition whose truth value depends on real-life facts rather than on the meanings of its terms SYNTHETIC

Proofreader's Marks

Proof with errors marked

1. sc/	2. not/	It does appear that the earlieest priters	3.	4. n/
5. #/	6. ital/	hadany consistent method of correkting errors,	7. c/	8. :/
9. cap/	10. rom/	they were not proofreaders in *our* sense. They	11. ;/	12. lc/
13. little/	14. tr/	cared much about spellign or "printers errors.	15. ’/	16. ”/
17. ¶/	18.	Impor tant that was the proof corresponded to	19. tr/	20. stet/
21. [/	22. —/	[the copy and the sense had to be right. English	23. bf/	24. !/
23. bf/	25. ,/	orthography, after all was fluctuating.	26. still in flux/?	

1 set in small capitals

2 insert "not"

3 delete "e" and close up

4 insert "n"

5 insert space

6 set in italics

7 set "c" for "k"

8 set colon for comma

9 set capital "T"

10 set in roman

11 set semicolon for period

12 set lowercase "t"

13 set "little" for "much"

14 transpose letters

15 insert apostrophe

16 insert closing quotation mark

17 indent as paragraph

18 close up

19 transpose words

20 "let it stand"

21 move to left

22 insert em-dash (dash the length of the letter "m")

23 set in boldface

24 set exclamation mark for period

25 insert comma

26 question to author

Proof after corrections have been made

IT DOES not appear that the earliest printers had any *consistent method* of correcting errors: They were not proofreaders in our sense; they cared little about spelling or "printer's errors."

Important was that the proof corresponded to the copy—and the **sense** had to be right! English **orthography**, after all, was still in flux.

props and scenery in a play MISE-EN-SCÈNE

prostitute, typically with wealthy clients, or the mistress of a high-ranking man COURTESAN, DEMIREP, DEMIMONDAINE, COCOTTE, HETAERA
- prostitute, whore, promiscuous woman CYPRIAN, DOXY, FILLE DE JOIE, HOOKER, STREETWALKER, WORKING GIRL, FLOOZY, CHIPPY, HARLOT, MOLL, STRUMPET, TROLLOP
- prostitute now reformed MAGDALEN
- prostitute or other civilian who follows an army unit to provide unofficial services CAMP FOLLOWER
- prostitute who makes appointments by telephone CALL GIRL
- prostitute's child by a client TRICK BABY
- prostitute's client JOHN, TRICK
- prostitute's session with a client TRICK
- approach someone with an offer of sex, as a prostitute might SOLICIT, ACCOST, HUSTLE, IMPORTUNE
- engage someone to act as a prostitute PROCURE, TURN OUT
- male prostitute or boy kept for sexual purposes CATAMITE, GANYMEDE, RENT BOY
- man who finds clients for a prostitute or brothel PIMP, PANDER, PROCURER, WHOREMONGER, SWEETMAN, MAQUEREAU, FLESH-PEDDLER
- woman kidnapped into prostitution WHITE SLAVE

protect or make immune to attack SECURE
- protect, shield, cushion BUFFER, BUTTRESS
- protect against disease by introducing resistance-building materials into the body IMMUNIZE, INOCULATE, VACCINATE
- protect and rear a child FOSTER, NURTURE
- protect or exempt from loss or legal responsibility INDEMNIFY
- protect or preserve nature, food, or the like from decay CONSERVE
- protect or shelter HARBOR, SAFEGUARD
- protect or shield someone from what is considered unsuitable INSULATE
- protected, supported, sponsored, or supervised by UNDER THE AEGIS OF, UNDER THE AUSPICES OF
- protected by a trademark, as a medicine might be PROPRIETARY, PATENT
- overprotect or indulge, spoil by pampering COCOON, MOLLYCODDLE
- person whose welfare is protected or career advanced by an influential patron (masculine and feminine, respectively) PROTÉGÉ, PROTÉGÉE

protection See also **defense, fortification**
- protection, as against inflation HEDGE
- protection, sponsorship, supervision, especially of a young person PATRONAGE, TUTELAGE
- protection and preservation, as of a house UPKEEP, MAINTENANCE
- protection and preservation of the environment CONSERVATION
- protection money, as paid by a vassal nation to a dominant nation TRIBUTE
- protection or defense, specifically the walls of a fortification RAMPART, BULWARK
- protection or guardianship, as granted by a court CUSTODY
- protection or shelter, as from persecution, or a place offering such safety ASYLUM, REFUGE, SANCTUARY, HAVEN
- child, senile person, or the like under the legal protection of a guardian or court of law WARD
- demand protection money EXTORT

protective, as a deity is supposed to be toward his or her shrine TUTELARY
- protective, jealously defensive TERRITORIAL
- protective, on one's guard, watchful VIGILANT
- protective against or preventing something, especially against disease PROPHYLACTIC
- protective charm AMULET, TALISMAN, LUCKY PIECE
- protective charm or practice, guarantee, safeguard PALLADIUM
- protective coloring of an animal, by which it resembles an unrelated animal that is unpalatable or poisonous to its predators BATESIAN MIMICRY
- protective or preservative substance FIXATIVE
- protective shell or the outer covering of an animal or plant ARMATURE, INTEGUMENT

protector, in the form of a person, institution, or place, of a cause, attitude, or principle BASTION, OUTPOST, BULWARK, STRONGHOLD
- protector or supporter PATRON, BENEFACTOR, SPONSOR, ANGEL
- outstanding protector or defender of a cause, champion PALADIN
- escort, usually a mature woman, serving as protector of a young woman's reputation CHAPERON, DUENNA

protein in milk, forming the basis of cheese CASEIN
- protein of various kinds in blood, milk, and the like GLOBULIN
- protein produced by living cells and serving as a biochemical catalyst ENZYME
- protein substance made from soya beans, processed to resemble meat TEXTURED VEGETABLE PROTEIN, TVP, SPUN PROTEIN
- acid forming a basic part of proteins AMINO ACID
- common protein found in blood plasma and egg white ALBUMIN
- egg white, consisting mostly of protein ALBUMEN

protest See also **complain, criticize, objection**
- protest or object earnestly REMONSTRATE, EXPOSTULATE
- protest, complaint, or statement, as in diplomatic matters or to the public authorities DEMARCHE
- protest, raise objections, take exception DEMUR
- protest against, disapprove of, condemn, or discourage DEPRECATE, DEPLORE, REPREHEND, REPROBATE
- protest against bitterly, rail against INVEIGH, LAMBAST
- protest demonstration MANIFESTATION
- protest in the form of nonviolent resistance and a refusal to obey laws regarded as unjust CIVIL DISOBEDIENCE
- protest or complaint, or the injustice giving rise to it GRIEVANCE
- protest or demonstrate outside a place of work, typically during a strike, as to discourage other workers or customers from entering PICKET
- protest speech that is typically loud, emotional, and rhetorical TIRADE, HARANGUE, PHILIPPIC, DECLAMATION
- protester or devoted and energetic campaigner in pursuing a political aim ACTIVIST, MILITANT
- protesting noisily VOCIFEROUS
- protesting disagreement, refusal to comply or conform DISSENT, DISSIDENCE
- protests or appeals, as to an authority REPRESENTATIONS
- launch or hand in a protest REGISTER, LODGE
- noisy and insistent, as a protest might be VOCIFEROUS
- noisy and insistent public protest CLAMOR, OUTCRY
- refuse to buy, deal with, or the like, as a form of protest or coercion BOYCOTT

Protestant, especially Calvinist or Zwinglian rather than Lutheran REFORMED

- Protestant, especially fundamentalist or Low-Church EVANGELICAL
- Protestant from France in the 16th and 17th centuries HUGUENOT
- Protestant in Northern Ireland ORANGEMAN
- Protestant in the early Scottish Presbyterian church COVENANTER
- Protestant or person who refuses to comply with an established church NONCONFORMIST, DISSENTER
- Christian reform movement in 16th-century Europe that gave rise to Protestantism REFORMATION

proud See also **pride, pompous, boast**
- proud, self-centered, full of oneself EGOCENTRIC
- proud, stately, dignified MAJESTIC, OLYMPIAN
- proud and boastful of one's appearance or abilities, stuck up VAIN, BLOATED, BLUSTERING, INFLATED, SWANKY
- proud and rude INSOLENT
- proud in a scornful way, pompous PRESUMPTUOUS, ARROGANT, ASSUMING, CONCEITED, GRANDIOSE, HAUGHTY, IMPERIOUS, LOFTY, LORDLY, OVERBEARING, OVERWEENING
- proudly distant, reserved, and unfriendly ALOOF, SNIFFY, SNOOTY
- excessively proud in one's appearance, totally taken up in self-admiration NARCISSISTIC

prove See also **proof**
- prove, confirm as genuine or correct VERIFY, AUTHENTICATE, VALIDATE
- prove, establish or confirm by convincing evidence, bear out CORROBORATE, SUBSTANTIATE
- prove false, disprove, contradict BELIE, CONFUTE, GIVE THE LIE TO, REBUT, REFUTE
- prove or justify, in the face of adverse criticism or evidence VINDICATE
- proving something directly by means of logical argument DEICTIC
- proving something indirectly by means of logical argument ELENCTIC, ELENCHTIC
- bear witness to or provide evidence for in an attempt to prove or justify VOUCH FOR, TESTIFY TO
- show plainly or prove, demonstrate clearly with convincing examples EVIDENCE, MANIFEST, ATTEST TO
- support or give good reasons for, but without actually proving AFFIRM, SUSTAIN

proven beyond doubt, indisputably certain APODICTIC, INCONTROVERTIBLE, IRREFUTABLE

Provençal courtly poet-musician in the Middle Ages TROUBADOUR
- region of southern France where Provençal is spoken LANGUEDOC

proverb or clichéd moral speech or lesson HOMILY
- proverb or motto MAXIM, ADAGE, APOTHEGM, GNOME, SAW, APHORISM, PRECEPT
- pompously moralizing, especially by means of proverbs and platitudes SENTENTIOUS

provide for, make allowance for something LEGISLATE FOR
- provide or supply FURNISH, PURVEY

provisional, incompletely developed, or experimental TENTATIVE
- provisional, temporary INTERIM

provisions or allowance for a journey VIATICUM
- supplier of provisions and food to an army, a ship, or the like VICTUALLER, SUTLER

provoke or arouse discontent, friction, or the like, agitate FOMENT
- provoke something, often something wrong, or provoke someone into doing it INSTIGATE
- provoked or aroused very easily HAIR-TRIGGER
- provoking anger or violence, as a speech might be INCENDIARY, INFLAMMATORY

prow, of a ship NOSE, STEM, FRONT, FOREPART, FORE, BOW, ROSTRUM

prudent, careful or reserved in one's behavior, wary CIRCUMSPECT, JUDICIOUS, GUARDED
- prudent, tactful, cautious in one's social dealings DISCREET, DIPLOMATIC, POLITIC
- prudent in the circumstances, advisable EXPEDIENT

pruning shears SECATEURS

prying into other people's business, nosy INQUISITIVE

psalm See also **prayer, hymn**
- psalm or hymn sung with responses, or in alternating parts ANTIPHON
- psalms, or a book of psalms, or music for the psalms PSALTER

pseudonym, pen name NOM DE PLUME, NOM DE GUERRE

psychiatrist specializing in legal aspects of mental illness ALIENIST

psychiatry See chart, pages 428–429

psychic or supernatural, beyond normal experience or scientific laws PARANORMAL
- study of telepathy and other alleged psychic phenomena PARAPSYCHOLOGY

psychology See chart, pages 428–429, and also **Freudian, Jung**
- psychologically disordered person, typically aggressive, moody, and lacking in conscience PSYCHOPATH, SOCIOPATH
- psychologically unhealthy or obsessed MORBID
- referring to physical diseases or disorders caused or aggravated by psychological factors such as stress PSYCHOSOMATIC

psychotic condition that involves personality disturbances and a weakened grip on reality SCHIZOPHRENIA

public announcement by a government or official body COMMUNIQUÉ, PROCLAMATION
- public announcement or brief official report, as of the latest news of a battle BULLETIN
- public appearance or presentation, as on television EXPOSURE
- public attention LIMELIGHT
- public baths, especially in ancient Greece and Rome THERMAE
- public building, as for lectures and concerts LYCEUM
- public funds set aside or assigned by vote for a particular purpose APPROPRIATION
- public image or self-projection adopted by a person PERSONA
- public meeting and discussion FORUM
- public meeting or local court in Anglo-Saxon England GEMOT
- public prosecutor and coroner in Scotland PROCURATOR FISCAL
- public-record office or archive CHANCERY
- public ridicule or abuse PILLORY
- public right of way THOROUGHFARE
- public service such as water, electricity, or transport UTILITY
- public speaking, or the art or style of a public speaker ORATORY, RHETORIC, ELOCUTION
- public square or open space, especially in a Spanish-speaking town PLAZA
- public square or open space, especially in an Italian town PIAZZA
- public square or open space in ancient Greece AGORA
- public square or open space in ancient Rome FORUM
- belonging to the congregation or general public as opposed to the clergy, as a preacher might be LAY, SECULAR
- make public or reveal some private or confidential information DIVULGE

public opinion as a court of appeal or judgment TRIBUNAL
- public opinion or popular feeling VOX POPULI
- survey public opinion on certain topics, as by questionnaires POLL, CANVASS

publication - stop the publication or circulation of SUPPRESS
publicity, or a liking for or power to attract publicity RÉCLAME, SHOWMANSHIP
- publicity or advertising campaign, or publicity in general PROMOTION
- attracting little attention or publicity LOW-PROFILE, UNOBTRUSIVE, UNOSTENTATIOUS, INCONSPICUOUS
publicize, announce or proclaim publicly or widely BLAZON ABROAD, BRUIT ABOUT
- publicize a product by using one's name to recommend it ENDORSE
publish a law and thereby bring it into operation PROMULGATE
- published after the writer's death POSTHUMOUS
- publisher's list of books still available even though published in the distant past BACKLIST
pudding See chart at **dessert**
- beadlike granules of cassava-root starch, used in milk puddings, and as a thickener in soup and the like TAPIOCA
puff-pastry case that is filled with a savory mixture and served hot as an hors d'oeuvre or snack BOUCHÉE, VOL-AU-VENT
- puff-pastry cream and jam slice MILLE FEUILLE, NAPOLEON
puffed or made light by beating or cooking SOUFFLÉ
- puffed out, as a sleeve or hairstyle might be BOUFFANT
puffy, swollen, bloated TURGID, TUMESCENT
- puffy or swollen condition, or the process leading to it TUMEFACTION
pull a heavy object on wheels or rollers TRUNDLE
- pull limb from limb DISMEMBER
- pull or drag behind ENTRAIN
- pull or wrench from someone's grasp or control WREST
- pull out something, such as a tooth, by force EXTRACT
- pulling power, as of a locomotive TRACTION, DRAFT
pulley or system of pulleys set in a casing BLOCK
- pulley wheel with a grooved rim SHEAVE
- lower section of a pulley BREECH
- system of ropes and pulleys for hoisting, or the like TACKLE
pulp left over after fruit, especially grapes, has been pressed MARC
- pulp remaining after apples or other fruits have been crushed to extract the juice POMACE
pulpit, used in pairs, in the early Christian church AMBO
- pulpit in a mosque MINBAR
- pulpit cloth or altar covering ANTEPENDIUM
- pulpit or reading desk in a synagogue ALMEMAR, BEMA
- rooflike covering over an altar, pulpit, or the like CANOPY, BALDACHIN
pulse - technique for regulating one's own pulse rate, blood pressure, or other apparently involuntary bodily functions BIOFEEDBACK
pulse (combining form) SPHYGM-, SPHYGMO-
pulsing, rippling, swaying, or other wavelike movement UNDULATION
pulverize, reduce to a powder by crushing or grinding TRITURATE
pump based on suction, as used in surgery for removing fluids from a body cavity ASPIRATOR
- small hand pump whose lower end is placed in a bucket of water, as used in fighting fires STIRRUP

PSYCHOLOGY AND PSYCHIATRY TERMS

abulia/aboulia	chronic inability to decide or act independently
alienation	state of estrangement from the social world
amentia	lower-than-normal mental development
amnesia	loss of memory, as through hysteria or brain damage
behaviorism	school of psychology emphasizing the study of behavior or of stimulus and response, rather than of mental processes
Binet-Simon scale	scale in IQ tests of children
classical conditioning/ Pavlovian conditioning	learning process of associating two stimuli and eventually securing a response from each of them that was originally elicited only by one of them
compensation	exaggerated action or behavior intended to make up for real or supposed defects or losses
complex	set of unconscious ideas or urges that continue to influence a person's behavior
conditioned response/ conditioned reflex	reaction to a specially contrived stimulus that replaces the original stimulus
configurationism/ Gestalt psychology	school emphasizing the indivisibility of various behavior patterns and psychological experiences
displacement	unconscious redirecting of feelings or urges to a more acceptable person or thing
ego	conscious part of the personality that deals with external reality
Electra complex	Oedipus complex in a girl or young woman
fixation	persistent attachment to a person or thing continuing from childhood
fugue	dreamlike state in which a person loses his or her memory and often wanders from home
id	unconscious and deepest part of the personality, the basis for instinctive and biological drives
imago	idealized impression of oneself, a parent, or another person, based on an image formed in childhood

PUMP
- type of vacuum pump in which steam is condensed in, and water admitted to, two chambers alternately PULSOMETER
- water pump using the momentum of running water to direct some of the water upward through a pipe HYDRAULIC RAM

pumpkin - lantern made from a pumpkin JACK-O'-LANTERN

pun that creates ambiguity through similar-sounding words PARANOMASIA

punctuation See illustration, page 430
- joining phrases or clauses with conjunctions rather than punctuation HYPOTAXIS
- joining phrases or clauses with punctuation rather than conjunctions PARATAXIS

- sign or mark added to a letter to indicate a special pronunciation DIACRITIC

punish See also **criticize**
- punish, as by flogging with a whip SCOURGE
- punish, usually at the court's discretion, as by a fine AMERCE
- punish by demoting, sending away, consigning to an inferior locality, or the like RELEGATE
- punish by subjecting to a penalty PENALIZE
- punish or criticize severely CHASTIZE, CASTIGATE
- punish or discipline in order to improve CHASTEN
- punish unfairly, bully, or discriminate against VICTIMIZE

punishment, as formerly in the army or navy, in which two lines of men beat an offender running between them GAUNTLET
- punishment fitted to the crime, or the system or principle of such retaliatory punishment TALION, LEX TALIONIS
- punishment for sailors, consisting of being dragged under the ship KEELHAULING
- punishment by being made to stay in class after the end of the school day DETENTION
- punishment in which the victim is hoisted on a rope attached to his or her arms tied behind his back, and then dropped to the length of the rope STRAPPADO
- punishment or adverse result that is well-deserved COMEUPPANCE, JUST DESERTS
- punishment or affliction, especially when regarded as imposed by a deity VISITATION
- punishment or other steps taken to correct someone's behavior and restore discipline DISCIPLINARY ACTION
- punishment or revenge for mistreatment or wrongdoing RETRIBUTION
- cancel or reduce a punishment REMIT
- cancellation or postponement of a punishment, such as the death penalty REPRIEVE, RESPITE
- deserved and appropriate, as a punishment might be CONDIGN, COMMENSURATE
- designed to inflict punishment PUNITIVE
- exemption or immunity from punishment IMPUNITY
- large wheel, as for driving a mill, turned by people walking on steps at the ends of its spokes, formerly used as a punishment TREADMILL

PSYCHOLOGY AND PSYCHIATRY TERMS *continued*

inhibition	restraint of an instinctive impulse
libido	psychic energy derived from deep biological urges, underlying the sex drive
Oedipus complex	set of unconscious emotions affecting a young child, including sexual desire for the parent of the opposite sex
operant conditioning/ instrumental learning	simple learning process or training in which a particular action or response to a given stimulus is reinforced by means of reward
paranoia	mental disorder involving delusions, as of persecution or grandeur
person/persona	social mask or front adopted by a individual in keeping with his or her outward role in life
projection	attribution of one's own feelings or urges to others
psychosomatic	referring to the link between the physical and the psychological, as in stress-related illness
Rorschach test	personality test in which the subject offers interpretations of a variety of abstract inkblots
schizophrenia	psychotic condition involving personality disturbances and a weakened grip on reality
Stanford-Binet scale	scale in IQ tests of children
sublimation	conversion of instincts or impulses into other usually most socially acceptable urges and activities
subliminal	below the threshold of conscious awareness
superego	partially unconscious part of the personality, based on parental and social standards of morality, and underlying the conscience
Terman scale	scale in IQ tests of children
transactional analysis/TA	psychotherapy analyzing one's social exchanges and relating them to roles, games, and hidden aspects of the personality
transference	unconscious shifting of emotions, thoughts, and wishes regarding one person or object to another

- relating to punishment or legal penalties PENAL
- right or possession that one has to surrender by way of punishment FORFEIT
- send abroad to a penal colony, formerly a punishment for convicts TRANSPORT
- serving as a warning or example to others, as a harsh punishment might be EXEMPLARY
- stool to which wrongdoers or suspects were formerly tied as a punishment, as for ducking or public mockery CUCKING STOOL
- study of the punishment and treatment of criminals, especially prison management PENOLOGY
- take away someone's private property by way of punishment CONFISCATE
- very harsh, as laws or punishments might be DRACONIAN
- wooden frame with holes for locking the feet, hands, or head of an offender and exposing him or her to public abuse as a punishment STOCKS, PILLORY

puny person RUNT

pupa of a moth or butterfly, often encased in a cocoon CHRYSALIS

pupil or disciple of a guru CHELA
- pupil who is top of the class, in Europe DUX
- relation between pupil and tutor TUTELAGE

puppet leader set up by an occupying foreign power QUISLING
- puppets moved by strings or wires MARIONETTES, FANTOCCINI
- puppet theater of a traditional Japanese school BUNRAKU

puppy WHELP
- puppy or piglet that is the smallest of the litter RUNT
- group of puppies produced at a single birth LITTER

pure, as in sexual morality CHASTE
- pure, flawless, as perfect behavior is IRREPROACHABLE, UNIMPEACHABLE, IMPECCABLE
- pure, out-and-out, utter, as a downright scoundrel or scandal is UNMITIGATED, VERITABLE
- pure, uncorrupted IMMACULATE, UNBLEMISHED, PRISTINE
- pure, unmixed, or undiluted UNALLOYED, UNADULTERATED
- pure and noble man GALAHAD

purely and simply, without mincing words TOUT COURT

purify, cleanse of germs, pollutants, or impurities, disinfect SANITIZE, DECONTAMINATE
- purify, make holy, cleanse of sin SANCTIFY, CONSECRATE, HALLOW
- "purify" a text by changing or removing objectionable passages EXPURGATE, BOWDLERIZE
- purify or cleanse something, such as the body DEPURATE
- purify or refine DISTILL
- purify or separate a substance or mixture, such as crushed ore, by washing and then filtering, straining, or the like ELUTRIATE
- purifying or straining by filtering FILTRATION
- purifying power, agent, or device ALEMBIC
- purification of the emotions through pity and fear, as when watching a tragedy on stage CATHARSIS

Punctuation

( )	Brackets, parentheses
< >	Angle brackets
[ ]	Square brackets
{	Brace
•	Bullet
†	Dagger/obelisk
‡	Double dagger/diesis
*	Asterisk/star
/	Solidus/oblique/ slash/virgule
§	Section
~	Swung dash
. . .	Ellipsis/suspension points
¶	Paragraph

ACCENTS AND DIACRITICS

´	é	Acute
°	Å	Bolle
ˇ	ŭ	Breve
¸	ç	Cedilla
ˆ	ê	Circumflex
¨	ö	Diaeresis/umlaut
`	è	Grave
ˇ	Č	Haček
¯	ō	Macron
/	ø	Streg
˜	ñ	Tilde

- purification plant, as for crude oil, sugar, or ore REFINERY

puritanical See **strict, old-fashioned**
- puritanical belief in the virtues of hard work WORK ETHIC
- puritanically disapproving, self-righteous and usually hypocritical PHARISAICAL

purpose, destination, goal, finishing point TERMINUS AD QUEM
- purpose, intention, or motive ANIMUS, IMPULSION
- purpose or design in nature, or the study of or belief in it TELEOLOGY
- purpose or intention that is concealed, especially so as to deceive ULTERIOR MOTIVE, HIDDEN AGENDA, ARRIÈRE-PENSÉE
- pretended or apparent purpose PRETEXT

purposeful, directed or tending toward a specific goal TELIC

purse - cord or ribbon running inside a hem, as to tighten a sleeve or close a purse DRAWSTRING

pursue in an irritating and persistent way HARASS, HOUND

pus-filled channel, as from a boil SINUS
- pus-filled skin inflammation resembling a blister PUSTULE
- puslike liquid from an ulcer or wound ICHOR
- discharge pus, as a wound might SUPPURATE, MATURATE, FESTER
- relating to or containing pus PURULENT

pus (combining form) PY-, PYO-

push, squeeze, or force out EXTRUDE
- push in or enter uninvited or inappropriately INTRUDE
- push oneself or one's opinions on others OBTRUDE
- push or elbow one's way in a crowd JOSTLE
- push or prod lightly or surreptitiously NUDGE
- set in motion by a push PROPEL

pushy, assertive, or insistent in manner STRIDENT, SELF-AGGRANDIZING
- pushy, self-important, meddlesome, and pompous OFFICIOUS, INTRUSIVE
- pushy or aggressive BRASH, BUMPTIOUS, ASSERTIVE, OBTRUSIVE

put aside for a specific use APPROPRIATE
- put forward a proposition or idea for the sake of argument POSTULATE, POSIT
- put into words VERBALIZE
- put on an act, show off, try to impress POSE, POSTURE, GRANDSTAND
- put on one's hat or clothes DON

put off doing something until later

PROCRASTINATE, DEFER

put out a fire or flame EXTINGUISH, DOUSE, QUENCH

putty - rubbery puttylike filler or sealer MASTIC

- thin mortar used like putty, as for filling cracks between tiles GROUTING

puzzle, confront with an insoluble problem STUMP, STYMIE, BAFFLE, CONFOUND, FLUMMOX, NONPLUS

- puzzle, confuse, mystify BEMUSE, BEFUDDLE, BEWILDER, PERPLEX, BAMBOOZLE, OBFUSCATE, STUPEFY
- puzzle, extremely difficult decision, problem with no satisfactory solution DILEMMA, QUANDARY
- puzzle, troublesome problem or embarrassing situation PREDICAMENT, PLIGHT
- puzzle in the form of pictures or symbols representing syllables or words REBUS
- puzzle of Chinese origin consisting of a set of simple shapes for reassembling into different figures TANGRAM
- puzzle or poem in which some letters, usually the first, of the lines spell out a name or message ACROSTIC
- puzzle that is difficult to solve POSER, CONUNDRUM, ENIGMA

puzzling, mysterious, as a brief and ambiguous comment might be CRYPTIC, ORACULAR

- puzzling because uninterpretable, as a facial expression might be INSCRUTABLE, UNFATHOMABLE, DEADPAN, ENIGMATIC
- puzzling network of hedged or walled pathways MAZE, LABYRINTH
- puzzling or mysterious person or thing, riddle ENIGMA, SPHINX

pyramid-shaped temple tower, as in ancient Babylon ZIGGURAT

- pyramid of progressively larger numbers PASCAL'S TRIANGLE
- base part or midsection of a cone, pyramid, or other solid object FRUSTUM

quack doctor or other fraudulent self-proclaimed expert CHARLATAN
- quack remedy, especially one claiming to have secret ingredients NOSTRUM
- seller of quack medicines MOUNTEBANK, SNAKE-OIL SALESMAN

quadrangle surrounded by covered corridors GARTH
- covered and colonnaded walk around a quadrangle CLOISTERS

quail flock or family BEVY

quaint, folksy ETHNIC
- quaint and attractive, visually appealing PICTURESQUE
- quaint idea, eccentric gesture, odd piece of behavior, or the like WHIMSY

qualifications - letter or certificate of a person's qualifications or rights CREDENTIALS

qualified, authorized, or valid, as a representative or deputy might be LEGITIMATE
- qualified, worthy, appropriate, as for a task or post ELIGIBLE

qualifying phrase or remark within a sentence PARENTHESIS

quality, degree of excellence or worthiness CALIBER
- quality, feature, characteristic ATTRIBUTE, TRAIT
- distinctive and characteristic air or quality ACCENT, AURA, ETHOS
- indication of quality HALLMARK, CACHET

quantity See **plenty**
- quantity, size, extent MAGNITUDE, AMPLITUDE, PROPORTIONS

quarantine building or ship in former times LAZARETTO

quarrel, dispute, or difference of opinion DISSENSION, VARIANCE
- quarrel, heated argument or disagreement CONTRETEMPS, ALTERCATION, ARGY-BARGY
- quarrel, wrangle, squabble over something petty BICKER
- quarrel or feud persisting over a long period of time VENDETTA
- quarrel or noisy disturbance, uproar, commotion RUCTION
- quarrel with a statement, call into question, dispute or contradict OPPUGN, GAINSAY, REPUDIATE, CONTROVERT
- quarreling, disputing, conflicting, at odds AT LOGGERHEADS, AT VARIANCE
- quarrelsome, argumentative DISPUTATIOUS, CONTENTIOUS
- causing quarrels or disputes DIVISIVE
- come forward to try to settle a quarrel or dispute INTERCEDE
- go-between or judge in a quarrel or dispute ARBITRATOR, HONEST BROKER, MEDIATOR, MODERATOR, INTERMEDIARY, ADJUDICATOR, OMBUDSMAN
- involved in a quarrel, dispute, scandal, or the like EMBROILED
- resolve or attempt to end a quarrel or dispute between others CONCILIATE
- settle a quarrel, dispute, or differences RECONCILE, COMPOSE, DETERMINE

quarter circle, or quarter of a disc QUADRANT
- quarter at the outer parts of a city, especially a French-speaking city FAUBOURG

quay - pier or mole to protect a quay or shore JETTY, GROIN

queasy, seasick, or dizzy WOOZY

queen's husband or king's wife CONSORT
- attain or ascend the throne, as when a princess becomes queen ACCEDE
- attendants or companions of a queen or king RETINUE
- "defender of the faith," one of the titles of the British queen or king FIDEI DEFENSOR
- give up or relinquish the throne formally, as a queen or king might ABDICATE
- referring to a queen or king, royal REGAL
- ruling by hereditary right, as a queen might be LEGITIMATE
- staff carried by a queen or king as a sign of royal authority or power SCEPTER
- title of a queen, as used in legal documents REGINA

quench one's thirst SLAKE

question a witness who is called to the witness box by the opposing side in a court case CROSS-EXAMINE, CROSS-QUESTION
- question-and-answer examinations or instruction book, particularly one on the basic principles of Christianity CATECHISM
- question-and-answer method of instruction, aimed at drawing out the student's supposedly inborn knowledge SOCRATIC METHOD
- question closely, intensely, or systematically, sometimes using threats INTERROGATE
- question or examine in a probing way, interrogate CATECHIZE
- question such as *isn't it?* added at the end of a remark TAG QUESTION
- question that is fairly difficult to answer POSER, CONUNDRUM
- question that is put for effect or to make a point rather than to secure an answer RHETORICAL QUESTION
- questioning of or report by a spy, astronaut, diplomat, or the like on his or her return from a mission DEBRIEFING
- always asking questions, in the way a child might be INQUISITIVE
- evade or counter a hostile or embarrassing question PARRY
- relating to Socrates' method of eliciting someone's submerged knowledge by means of a series of questions MAIEUTIC
- sustained delivery of punches, questions, words, or the like BARRAGE

question mark combined with an exclamation mark into a single punctuation mark INTERROBANG

questionable, still uncertain or unresolved, as a point under debate would be MOOT
- questionable, widely disputed or earnestly debated CONTROVERSIAL

quibbling, hairsplitting, and oversubtle in argument SOPHISTIC, CASUISTIC

quick, prompt, done speedily and efficiently EXPEDITIOUS
- quick, rapid, swift FLEET
- quick and informal, as an execution might be SUMMARY
- quick cooperation, prompt and eager willingness ALACRITY
- quick glance COUP D'OEIL
- quick movement or action, speed or briskness CELERITY, DISPATCH
- quick or brief, and typically half-hearted, as a routine inspection would be CURSORY, PERFUNCTORY
- quick or brief to the point of rude-

ness, abrupt, or gruff, as a reply might be CURT
- quick to respond, rashly over-reacting TRIGGER-HAPPY
- quicker than normal, speeded up ACCELERATED
- quickly, at a very rapid pace HOT-FOOT, LICKETY-SPLIT, LICKETY-CUT, LICKETY-BRINDLE
- dangerously or recklessly quickly, hurtling, hell-for-leather PELL-MELL, HEADLONG, HELTER-SKELTER
- excessively quick, rash, impulsive, as a decision might be PRECIPITATE
- lively, full of vitality, quick and agile SPRIGHTLY
- moving about quickly, nimble, nippy VOLANT, VOLITANT

quick-tempered, easily angered, very touchy, snappish IRASCIBLE, INFLAMMABLE, VOLATILE

quickly or suddenly PRESTO, SUBITO, TOUT DE SUITE

quiet, avoiding drawing attention to oneself SUBDUED, LOW-KEY, LOW-PROFILE, INCONSCPICUOUS
- quiet, silent, not speaking, as though stunned into silence MUTE, DUMBSTRUCK
- quiet and calm, tranquil SERENE, REPOSEFUL
- quiet and inactive, still QUIESCENT, PASSIVE
- quiet and reserved, not saying as much as one could UNCOMMUNICATIVE, RETICENT, TACITURN
- quiet and thoughtful PENSIVE, REFLECTIVE, MEDITATIVE, CONTEMPLATIVE, INTROSPECTIVE
- quiet place or situation BACKWATER
- quietly spoken utterance or the subdued sound of it UNDERTONE

quill, hollow, stemlike shaft of a feather CALAMUS
- quill, crystal, bristle, or similar needle-shaped natural object or part ACICULA, ACULEUS

quilt stuffed with down, feathers, or synthetic insulating material, used in place of a sheet and blankets DUVET, CONTINENTAL QUILT
- quilting with a stitched design TRAPUNTO

quinine or related drug, or the bark or tree from which it is derived CINCHONA

quivering, shaking, or trembling movement TREMOR

quota ALLOTMENT, ALLOCATION

quotation considered a standard or definitive example LOCUS CLASSICUS
- quotation or reference used as an authority, as for a dictionary or legal argument CITATION
- quotation or statement printed at the start of a book or chapter to indicate its theme MOTTO, EPIGRAPH

quote as an example, authority, or proof CITE
- "so," "thus," term used in a printed text to indicate the deliberate reproduction of a mistaken or the quoting of a surprising term or fact SIC

R

r - /r/ sound inserted inappropriately into a word or phrase, as when *drawing* is pronounced as though it were spelled *draw-ring* INTRUSIVE *R*
- excessive or inconsistent use of the /r/ sound in pronunciation RHOTACISM
- pronunciation of the /r/ sound as an /l/ sound, as by many Chinese people speaking English LALLATION
- relating to varieties of English in which the /r/ sound is retained before a consonant or pause RHOTIC
- trilling or braying pronunciation of *r*, as in Scotland or Northumbria BURR, ROLL

rabbit colony or breeding area WARREN
- rabbit of a grayish, thick-coated breed CHINCHILLA
- rabbit of a white, long-haired breed ANGORA RABBIT
- rabbit or similar animal CONEY
- infectious viral disease of rabbits, producing skin tumors and usually fatal MYXOMATOSIS

rabble-rousing, inciting, as a political speech might be INFLAMMATORY
- rabble-rousing political leader or agitator, rallying support by crude emotional speeches and the like DEMAGOGUE
- rabble-rouser, person causing anger or violent quarrels INCENDIARY, FIREBRAND

rabies HYDROPHOBIA
- rabies, malaria, or any other disease transmitted by insects or other animals ZOONOSIS

race See also **horse racing**
- race or contest in which the advantages are adjusted to give all the competitors an equal chance of winning HANDICAP
- race or contest forming the basis of a lottery SWEEPSTAKE
- race or series of races for boats REGATTA
- checkpoint in a race, such as a car rally, where progress is confirmed and assessed CONTROL

race, racial (combining form) ETHN-, ETHNO-

racecourse HIPPODROME
- racecourse enclosure for preparing the horses PADDOCK

racehorse See **horse**

racial separation within a society SEGREGATION
- abolish racial separation, as in a school DESEGREGATE
- open a neighborhood, a school, or the like to all races INTEGRATE
- prejudiced attitudes or actions, as on the basis of racial, sexual, or age difference DISCRIMINATION

racing See **horse racing**

racing car - air deflector, as on an aircraft's wing or a racing car, to increase drag and reduce the tendency to lift SPOILER
- assembly area for racing cars, next to the track PADDOCK
- team of racing cars ÉCURIE

radar antenna's domelike covering, as in some aircraft RADOME
- radarlike establishing of the position of an object, as in bats or dolphins, by high-frequency sound waves ECHOLOCATION
- radarlike sonar device or system, as used for detecting enemy submarines ASDIC, ECHO SOUNDER
- radarlike system or apparatus for detecting or locating objects underwater by means of sound waves SONAR
- airborne radar system for detecting enemy bombers AWACS
- electronic valve helping to generate high-power microwaves, as in radar systems MAGNETRON
- metal foil released in strips into the air to thwart an enemy's radar system CHAFF, WINDOW

radiant, shining brilliantly RESPLENDENT, EFFULGENT, SCINTILLATING, CORUSCATING

radiation having wavelengths between those of visible light and radio waves INFRARED
- radiation having wavelengths between those of visible light and X-rays ULTRAVIOLET
- allowing the passage of specified radiation, such as X-rays or visible light TRANSPARENT
- apparatus for radiation treatment, directing gamma rays from cobalt-60 COBALT BOMB
- preventing the passage of specified radiation, such as X-rays or visible light OPAQUE
- send out or give off something, such as gas or radiation EMIT

radiation (combining form) ACTINO-, RADIO-

radical, extremist, or revolutionary in politics SANSCULOTTE, JACOBIN, MAXIMALIST
- radical or reforming activist within a political group or party YOUNG TURK
- radical political revolutionary advocating the destruction of all social and political institutions before building new ones NIHILIST, ANARCHIST

radio See illustration
- radio-frequency band assigned for private radio communication between members of the public, such as motorists CITIZENS BAND, CB
- radio of an early kind, using a semiconducting crystal to receive signals, and requiring earphones CRYSTAL SET
- radio or television announcements or linking of items designed to avoid breaks between programs CONTINUITY
- radio or television network GRID
- radio or television program that has been prerecorded TRANSCRIPTION
- broadcast live a concert, speech, or the like, as over the radio RELAY
- broadcast of a program simultaneously on radio and television SIMULCAST
- capable of transmitting or receiving two signals at once over a radio channel DIPLEX
- degree of accurate reproduction, as by a radio or amplifier, of an input signal FIDELITY
- device in or part of a radio, television, telephone, or the like that receives and converts incoming signals RECEIVER
- estimates of the audience figures, and hence popularity, of radio or television programs RATINGS
- fine wire used for electrical contact in a crystal radio set CAT'S WHISKER, CAT WHISKER
- referring to radio in which members of the general public rather than professionals make the programs PUBLIC-ACCESS, ACCESS

- small, portable radio receiver that sounds a coded alert signal BLEEPER, BEEPER
- unwanted electric signals that produce random noise in a radio STATIC

radioactive, especially when decomposing rapidly UNSTABLE
- radioactive particles in the atmosphere, caused by a nuclear explosion or leakage FALLOUT
- radioactive substance, dye, or the like, whose course can be monitored through a system, as used in medical diagnosis TRACER
- chemical elements with radioactive isotopes of various uses CESIUM, COBALT, PLUTONIUM, RADIUM, STRONTIUM, THORIUM, URANIUM
- dangerous as a result of exposure to radioactivity CONTAMINATED
- gas produced in the process of radioactive decay EMANATION
- glass box with protective gloves sealed into the side in which radioactive substances can be handled GLOVE BOX
- instrument for detecting radioactivity GEIGER COUNTER

radiotherapy apparatus, directing gamma rays from cobalt-60 COBALT BOMB

raft of a light, buoyant kind BALSA
- raft of logs or floats tied together CATAMARAN

rage - attack or fit, as of rage ACCESS
- fit of rage or hysterics CONNIPTIONS
- outburst or uncontrollable display of rage, laughter, or the like PAROXYSM
- pale or ashen-faced, as through rage LIVID

ragtime music as played on saloon pianos HONKY-TONK

raid See also **attack**
- brief military excursion or attack SORTIE, SALLY, FORAY
- raid an enemy, village, or the like SACK, PILLAGE, MARAUD, FREEBOOT, PLUNDER, HARRY
- raid or invasion INCURSION
- raiding and looting a village, community, or the like PREDATION

rail and its supporting posts, as along the edge of a staircase BALUSTRADE
- rail around the stern of a ship TAFFRAIL
- railing or wall on the edge of a balcony or roof PARAPET
- handrail along the edge of a staircase BANISTER

railroad carriage of a comfortable and spacious design PULLMAN
- railroad car behind a steam locomotive, carrying fuel and water TENDER
- railroad car that unloads through its floor HOPPER
- railroad carriage's enclosed entrance area VESTIBULE
- railroad carriages, freight cars, and locomotives ROLLING STOCK
- railroad freight car of a low and open design GONDOLA
- railroad or road bridge, typically supported by a series of arches, as over a valley VIADUCT
- railroad sleeping car, especially on a European continental train WAGON-LIT
- railroad system, often elevated, in which a single rail supports the trains MONORAIL

Radio Waves

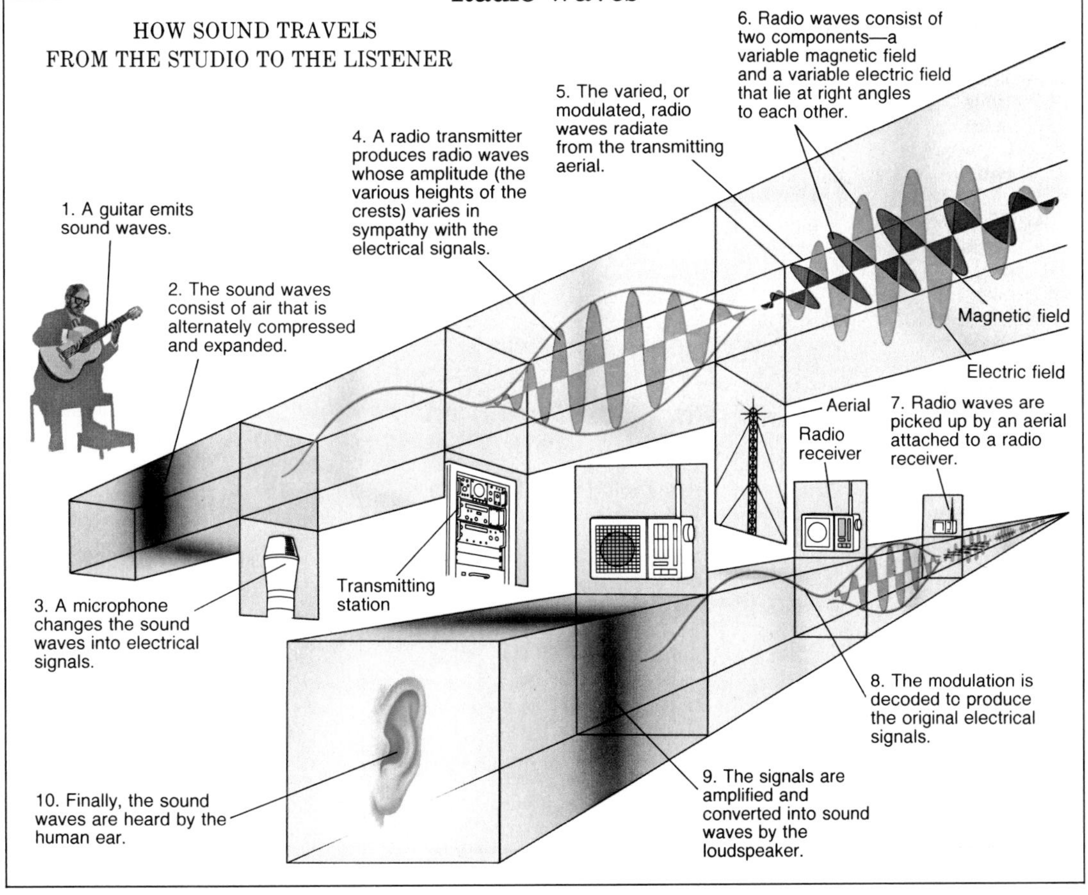

HOW SOUND TRAVELS
FROM THE STUDIO TO THE LISTENER

1. A guitar emits sound waves.

2. The sound waves consist of air that is alternately compressed and expanded.

3. A microphone changes the sound waves into electrical signals.

4. A radio transmitter produces radio waves whose amplitude (the various heights of the crests) varies in sympathy with the electrical signals.

Transmitting station

5. The varied, or modulated, radio waves radiate from the transmitting aerial.

6. Radio waves consist of two components—a variable magnetic field and a variable electric field that lie at right angles to each other.

Magnetic field

Electric field

Aerial

Radio receiver

7. Radio waves are picked up by an aerial attached to a radio receiver.

8. The modulation is decoded to produce the original electrical signals.

9. The signals are amplified and converted into sound waves by the loudspeaker.

10. Finally, the sound waves are heard by the human ear.

Rainbow

Look for rainbows on days when rainy spells alternate with sunshine. You might even see a double bow, like this one. In a single bow, the red is always on top; the second, fainter bow reverses the order of the colors.

- railway yard in which carriages, engines, and so on are joined up MARSHALING YARD
- bed or folding bunk in a railroad carriage COUCHETTE
- bumper or grid in front of a railroad locomotive to clear the track FENDER, COWCATCHER
- device for linking any two railroad carriages or cars COUPLING, DRAWBAR
- frame on the roof of a railroad train, streetcar, or bus collecting electric current from an overhead wire PANTOGRAPH
- gravel, rock chips, or the like used as foundation for a road or railroad track BALLAST
- heavy beam supporting railroad rails TIE, SLEEPER
- open, elevated railway in an amusement park providing visitors with a fast exciting ride ROLLER COASTER
- overhead cable of an electric rail, streetcar, or bus system CATENARY
- shock-absorbing or cushionlike device, such as the steel springs or pads at the ends of railroad carriages BUFFER
- sloping section or incline, as of a road or railroad track GRADIENT

rain gage UDOMETER, PLUVIOMETER
- rainy, or referring to rain or rainy regions HYETAL
- rainy season in south and southeast Asia MONSOON
- formation or fall of rain, snow, dew, or the like PRECIPITATION
- great downpour of rain CATARACT, DELUGE
- pouring or flooding copiously, as heavy rain is TORRENTIAL
- spray dry-ice crystals or sprinkle chemicals onto a cloud to cause condensation and so produce rain SEED

rain (combining form) PLUVI-, PLUVIO-, HYET-, HYETO-

rainbow See illustration
- colors of the rainbow RED, ORANGE, YELLOW, GREEN, BLUE, INDIGO, VIOLET
- having all the colors of the rainbow, multicolored PRISMATIC
- range or image of the colors of the rainbow SPECTRUM
- shimmering with a rainbowlike effect, as a soap bubble or opal is IRIDESCENT

raise an anchor, as in preparation for sailing WEIGH, TRIP
- raise from obscurity, unearth DREDGE UP
- raise from the dead, revive RESUSCITATE
- raise in rank, status, or the like EXALT, ELEVATE, PROMOTE, PREFER
- raise or hoist, especially by machine WINCH
- raise or lift up UPREAR
- raise or lift up jerkily HOICK
- raised in relief, as words or symbols on specially pressed paper or metal may be EMBOSSED
- raised platform in a public place TRIBUNE, DAIS, PODIUM, ROSTRUM
- raising agent or fermentation agent added to dough, such as yeast in bread making LEAVEN
- woven with a raised pattern, as brocade and some other fabrics are BROCHÉ

raja - wife of a raja, or a woman with the rank of raja RANI

rake, immoral and debauched man, especially an aging one ROUÉ
- rakelike farm implement used to level or break up soil HARROW

rakish, unconventional RAFFISH, DISREPUTABLE

ram that has been gelded before maturity WETHER
- ram that leads a flock of sheep BELLWETHER

rambling, as a speech or argument might be DIGRESSIVE, DISCURSIVE
- rambling or disorderly, as a conversation might be DESULTORY, EXCURSIVE

ranch or ranch house of Spanish style HACIENDA

random, depending on mere chance ALEATORY, HAPHAZARD
- random, done or applied without making any sensitive distinctions INDISCRIMINATE, ARBITRARY
- random, especially in statistics STOCHASTIC
- random, rambling, or casual DESULTORY
- random, willful, unprovoked, as vandalism or mindless destruction is WANTON, GRATUITOUS
- random or based on personal decision rather than on regulations DISCRETIONARY
- acquired or added at random, not inherent ADVENTITIOUS
- acting randomly or according to whim CAPRICIOUS, FICKLE, IMPULSIVE
- happening at random, usually to one's benefit FORTUITOUS
- occurring irregularly or at random SPORADIC, INTERMITTENT
- tendency to make lucky discoveries at random or by accident SERENDIPITY

range, distribution, or spread, as of colors or radiation SPECTRUM
- range, extent, or scope, as of a law or one's outlook PURVIEW
- range of a musical instrument or

a singer's voice COMPASS, REGISTER, DIAPASON
- range of one's understanding, perception, or knowledge COGNIZANCE
- range or extent of something, from the beginning to the end GAMUT
- range or field of activity, sphere of operation or expertise PRESERVE, DOMAIN, BAILIWICK, PROVINCE
- range or scope of possible activity, reach, extent AMBIT, ORBIT, RADIUS
- range or stock of jokes, pieces of music, operatic roles, or the like available to a performer REPERTOIRE
- acting or speaking beyond the range of one's ability or expertise ULTRACREPIDARIAN

rank - deprivation of rank, status, office, or the like DEGRADATION, CASHIERING
- organization according to rank or importance HIERARCHY
- priority given according to position or rank PRECEDENCE

ranks See also **services**
- crowded, pressed together, tightly packed, as ranks of troops might be SERRIED

ransom - captive for whose safety a ransom is demanded HOSTAGE

rape RAVISH, VIOLATE
- criminal offense, considered a form of rape, of having sexual intercourse with a girl who is below the age of consent even if it took place on her initiative STATUTORY RAPE

rapid See **quick**

rapid (combining form) TACH-, TACHY-, TACHEO-

rare, obscure, known only to experts and connoisseurs RECHERCHÉ, ABSTRUSE, ARCANE
- referring to meat served medium-cooked or slightly rare À POINT
- referring to meat served underdone or fairly rare SAIGNANT
- referring to meat served very rare AU BLEU

rash See also **reckless**
- rash, frantic, disorderly, confused HEADLONG, HARUM-SCARUM, HELTER-SKELTER, PELL-MELL
- rash, giddy, wild, unreasonable MADCAP
- rash, out of one's personal control, as passion might be UNBRIDLED
- rash, overhasty, reckless, devil-may-care IMPETUOUS, IMPULSIVE, PRECIPITATE
- rash, scar, birthmark, or spot on the skin STIGMA
- rash in overreacting TRIGGER-HAPPY, GUNG HO
- rash or careless, heedless, ill-advised, unthinking IMPROVIDENT, IMPRUDENT, INJUDICIOUS
- rash or ulcerous skin disease LUPUS
- red skin rash, as that which occurs in measles ROSEOLA

raspberry brandy FRAMBOISE

rat, mouse, squirrel, or related gnawing mammal RODENT
- ratlike, resembling or relating to a rat or mouse MURINE
- rats, cockroaches, lice, or similar small animals that are harmful or annoying to humans VERMIN

ratchet - locking hinge or small lever engaging the teeth of a ratchet PAWL, PALLET, DETENT

rate, pace, or speed TEMPO
- rate at which body processes function METABOLISM
- rate of change, action, or the like VELOCITY
- rate or frequency of occurrence INCIDENCE
- currency equivalent, at the official rate of exchange PARITY

ratio, rate, or proportion QUOTIENT
- first term in a ratio ANTECEDENT
- second term in a ratio CONSEQUENT

rational and deliberate rather than emotional and spontaneous, as one side of human nature is, in Nietzsche's terminology APOLLONIAN

rattle or creak as diseased lungs or broken bones might CREPITATE

rattlesnake - tip of a rattlesnake's tail BUTTON

raven - adjective for a raven CORVID
- flock or family of ravens UNKINDNESS

ravine or gorge, as gouged out by a river or flood water ARROYO, CANYON, GULLY, COULÉE, WADI, GULCH, KLOOF
- narrow ravine or gorge, usually with a stream flowing through it FLUME

raw material STAPLE

ray - relating to rays, beams, or radii from a common source or point RADIAL

ray (combining form) RAD-, ACTINO-

raze, tear down, flatten, knock down, dismantle, wreck DEMOLISH, DESTROY, RUIN, OBLITERATE, REMOVE

razor - principle urging the simplest and most sparing use of terms and assumptions to argue or explain something OCCAM'S RAZOR
- leather or canvas strip for sharpening a straight razor STROP

reach or retrieve something, such as computer data ACCESS

reacting too quickly and seeking confrontation rather than compromise TRIGGER-HAPPY, GUNG HO

reaction of a violent kind HORNET'S NEST
- reaction of an adverse or hostile kind, as to an apparent social threat BACKLASH
- reaction that is unthinking and automatic KNEE-JERK REACTION
- reactions, speed of response REFLEXES
- person or group whose reactions serve as a test for new ideas or opinions SOUNDING BOARD
- referring to a reflex reaction or conditioned response to a stimulus PAVLOVIAN

read, especially with care and in detail PERUSE, PORE OVER
- read, interpret, or clarify a code, obscure text, mystery, or the like DECIPHER
- read or recite expressively a poem, speech from a play, or the like DECLAIM
- able to read and write LITERATE
- unable to read and write ILLITERATE

readable, as handwriting ought to be LEGIBLE

reader of a manuscript of an academic article who advises the editor or publisher on its suitability for publication REFEREE
- reader of lessons from the Bible in a church service LECTOR
- eager, insatiable, taking in everything available, as some readers are AVID, VORACIOUS, OMNIVOROUS

reading disability caused by brain damage or disease, "word blindness" ALEXIA
- reading disability caused by learning difficulties or a brain disorder DYSLEXIA
- reading of a text to a musical accompaniment DECLAMATION
- reading of printed text by a machine for conversion to computer data OPTICAL CHARACTER RECOGNITION, OCR
- reading room, library, or similar institution ATHENAEUM
- reading stand for supporting a book or notes, as in a church or lecture hall LECTERN

ready, prepared POISED, BRACED
- ready, waiting to be called in or activated PRIMED, ON STANDBY, IN THE WINGS

ready-reference manual or guidebook VADE MECUM

real, actual, assumed to be existing in the real world independently of the mind OBJECTIVE
- real, genuine, not imaginary or merely apparent SUBSTANTIVE, SUBSTANTIAL
- real, genuine, true, reliable, actual AUTHENTIC, VERITABLE, BONA FIDE
- real, physical, material CORPOREAL,

TANGIBLE, PALPABLE
realistic, capable of working, practicable VIABLE
- realistic and lifelike in art or literature NATURALISTIC, REPRESENTATIONAL
- realistic painting that deceives the eye by its striking three-dimensional effect TROMPE L'OEIL

reality - lacking a body or lacking in reality INCORPOREAL, DISEMBODIED
- quality of appearing to be reality or the truth VERISIMILITUDE
- regard a concept as having concrete reality HYPOSTATIZE, REIFY

really, actually, in fact DE FACTO

rear end of a horse or other domestic animal CROUP, HAUNCHES, RUMP, CRUPPER
- referring to the rear or tail end of the body of an animal POSTERIOR, CAUDAL
- to the rear of a ship ASTERN

rearing up on the hind legs, as a heraldic animal might be RAMPANT

rearrangement or reordering PERMUTATION

reason for an action MOTIVE
- reason for being, point of or justification for existence RAISON D'ÊTRE
- reason or cosmic order in ancient Greek philosophy LOGOS
- reason or mind, especially as the governing principle in the universe NOUS
- adjective for reason RATIONAL
- against reason, illogical IRRATIONAL
- for an even stronger reason, all the more so A FORTIORI
- pretended, merely apparent or outward, as a given reason might be OSTENSIBLE, PURPORTED, COLORABLE, SPECIOUS
- pretended or apparent reason PRETEXT
- produce or cite an example, argument, or reason as evidence or proof ADDUCE

reasonable or valid, as a grievance or conclusion might be LEGITIMATE

reasoning See also **logic, fallacy**
- reasoning by inferring general truths from particular instances, as distinct from strict logical deduction INDUCTION, REASONING A POSTERIORI
- reasoning from the general to the particular, deduction SYNTHESIS, AXIOMATIC-DEDUCTIVE REASONING
- reasoning in a logical and systematic way RATIOCINATION
- reasoning or argument that is plausible but oversubtle, faulty, or deliberately deceptive CHOPLOGIC, CASUISTRY, SOPHISTRY
- reasoning that is faulty or illogical and that invalidates the conclusion FALLACY
- reasoning that is faulty or invalid, though not deliberately so PARALOGISM
- based on abstract, transcendent reasoning METAPHYSICAL
- conclusion based on strict logical reasoning DEDUCTION
- logical reasoning through disputation DIALECTIC
- pattern of logical reasoning in which two premises generate a conclusion SYLLOGISM
- powerful and convincing, as someone's reasoning might be COGENT, COMPELLING, INCISIVE, TRENCHANT
- referring to reasoning from the general to the particular, from principles or causes to facts or effects DEDUCTIVE, A PRIORI
- relating to reasoning from the particular to the general, from facts or effects to principles and causes EMPIRICAL, INDUCTIVE, A POSTERIORI

Rebus

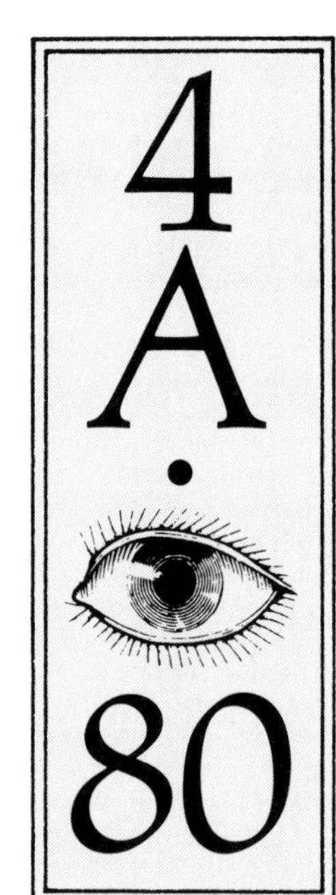

An ingenious beggar's rebus sign, which made many passersby curious enough to pay to discover its meaning: "For a period, I ate next to nothing."

- using the premise and conclusion to prove each other, as faulty reasoning might be CIRCULAR
- work out or prove by reasoning, deduce, infer DERIVE

rebel against accepted rules, practices, and religious beliefs DISSENTER, NONCONFORMIST, RECUSANT
- rebel against an official church, person holding forbidden religious views HERETIC
- rebel or reformer within a political group or party YOUNG TURK
- military action taken by the authorities against rebels or terrorist groups COUNTERINSURGENCY

rebellion, revolt, uprising INSURGENCE, INSURRECTION
- rebellion by soldiers or sailors against their officers MUTINY
- rebellion leading to the sudden overthrow of a government COUP, COUP D'ÉTÂT, PUTSCH
- put down, crush, or suppress something, such as a rebellion REPRESS, QUELL
- stir up trouble, rebellion, or the like FOMENT, INSTIGATE
- suppression of a rebellion or terrorism in a region PACIFICATION

rebellious MUTINOUS, DISAFFECTED
- rebellious, discontented person MALCONTENT
- rebellious, disobeying orders, behaving badly RESTIVE, UNRULY, INSUBORDINATE, DEFIANT
- rebellious, uncooperative, obstinate, difficult to manage RECALCITRANT, REFRACTORY, CONTUMACIOUS
- rebellious person who stirs up unrest or discontent FIREBRAND, INCENDIARY, AGITATOR, SUBVERSIVE
- rebellious speech or action, incitement to undermine authority SEDITION

rebirth in another body or form REINCARNATION
- rebirth or revival, as of a cultural heritage RENASCENCE, RENAISSANCE

reborn - person, project, or the like that seems to be reborn after destruction or downfall PHOENIX

rebus See illustration

recantation in the form of a poem or official declaration PALINODE

receiver - person who receives or takes delivery of something RECIPIENT, ADDRESSEE
- receiver and seller of stolen goods FENCE
- person who receives charity, a favor, money from a will, or the like BENEFICIARY

recent (combining form) NEO-

recently LATTERLY

reception, as for a VIP LEVEE

recess in a wall, as for a statue NICHE

recite expressively a poem, speech from a play, or the like DECLAIM
- recite or chant in a half-musical tone INTONE, CANTILLATE

reckless See also **rash**
- reckless, heedless, negligent, slack REMISS
- reckless, thoughtless, without due reflection beforehand UNADVISED, UNCONSIDERED
- reckless disregard of danger TEMERITY
- reckless or rash, without regard for possible dangers or consequences IMPETUOUS, IMPULSIVE, PRECIPITATE
- reckless person TEARAWAY, MADCAP
- recklessly bold and brave, or lacking restraint AUDACIOUS

reckon, count TALLY

recluse or hermit, person who has gone into seclusion for religious reasons ANCHORITE, ANCHORESS, EREMITE
- reclusive person TROGLODYTE

recognition (combining form) -GNOSIS

recognized officially, authorized, having acceptable credentials ACCREDITED
- generally recognized, accepted RECEIVED, ACKNOWLEDGED

recommend, approve, give one's backing to SANCTION, ENDORSE
- recommend highly or with suspect enthusiasm TOUT, PUFF
- recommend or argue in favor of a proposal, course of action, or the like ADVOCATE

reconcile, or attempt to reconcile, disputing people or groups MEDIATE, MODERATE, CONCILIATE, ARBITRATE, INTERCEDE

record, list, or check off item by item TALLY
- record an interview, program, or the like for broadcasting at a later time TRANSCRIBE
- record of ancestral line or purity of breeding PEDIGREE
- record of negotiations used as a first draft for a treaty or similar document PROTOCOL
- record or report in detail, and support with evidence DOCUMENT
- recording using separate electronic signals rather than a continuous fluctuating signal DIGITAL RECORDING
- records of an institution, group of people, or the like ARCHIVES, DOSSIERS
- records of events over the years ANNALS, CHRONICLES
- records or files held on a particular person or subject DOSSIER
- records or published transcripts of a conference, learned society's meetings, or the like ACTS, PROCEEDINGS, TRANSACTIONS, ANNALS
- records stored in a computer ELECTRONIC DATA, ELECTRONIC FILES
- hard, plasticlike resin from which old 78-RPM records were made SHELLAC
- official record of events at a meeting MINUTES
- person in charge of official registers and records REGISTRAR
- personal record of one's education and career details, as shown to prospective employers CURRICULUM VITAE, CV, VITA, RÉSUMÉ
- place where records or ledgers are stored REGISTRY
- small laser-read metal disc for reproducing music or other recorded sound on a special player COMPACT DISC

record (combining form) -GRAM

record player See also **stereo**
- record player PHONOGRAPH, GRAMOPHONE
- moving arm of a record player, holding the cartridge and needle TONE ARM, PICKUP ARM, PICKUP
- needle or jewel in a record-player pickup for tracing the groove of a record STYLUS
- rapid distortion or variation of pitch, as produced by a faulty record player or tape recorder FLUTTER
- slow distortion or variation of pitch, as produced by a faulty record player or tape recorder WOW
- small shaft or protuberance, on the turntable of a record player, passing through the center hole of a record CAPSTAN

recorder - lip or plug producing the vibration in an organ pipe, the mouthpiece of a recorder, or the like FIPPLE

recording (combining form) -GRAPH

recover from a loss or setback, and regain a favorable position RECOUP
- recover or regain something, such as pawned goods, by payment REDEEM
- recover or regain something that was lost, left behind, or confiscated RECLAIM, RETRIEVE
- recover or save property or damaged materials, as from a fire or a sinking ship SALVAGE
- recover strongly, improve rapidly, as one's health or spirits might RALLY
- recovering from illness or injury, trying to return to health CONVALESCENT, RECUPERATING, VALETUDINARIAN
- recovery of one's status, good name, or the like REHABILITATION
- ability to recover quickly from illness or other setbacks RESILIENCE, BUOYANCY
- help to recover, restore to life REVIVE, RESUSCITATE
- legal action to recover personal property REPLEVIN, REPLEVY
- medical drug, tonic, or the like that helps in the recovery of health or strength RESTORATIVE

recruit forcibly into military service PRESS, PRESS-GANG, IMPRESS, SHANGHAI
- recruiting of managers or officials from other firms HEADHUNTING

rectangular but not square OBLONG
- rectangular slot into which the matching tenon is fitted when joining two pieces of wood, stone, or metal MORTISE

rectory or similar office having fixed capital assets, or the revenue derived from these BENEFICE

rectum See also **anus**
- injection of liquid into the rectum as for medication or purging the bowels ENEMA
- medication in solid form designed to be inserted into a body cavity, especially the rectum SUPPOSITORY

rectum (combining form) PROCT-, PROCTO-

recurring phrase, design, or thematic element in music, art, or literature MOTIF, MOTTO
- recurring regularly CYCLICAL, RECURRENT

red See also **colors**
- red-currant or pomegranate syrup, used as a cordial or flavoring GRENADINE
- red-faced and often swollen and coarse-looking BLOWSY
- red-handed, in the very act of committing an offense IN FLAGRANTE DELICTO
- red-hot or white-hot, glowing with heat INCANDESCENT
- red lead, as used formerly in paint MINIUM, CINNABAR
- red pepper, sweet pepper PIMIENTO, CAPSICUM
- red pepper as a condiment CAYENNE PEPPER

red (combining form) ERYTHR-, ERYTHRO-, RHOD-, RHODO-, RUB-

reddening or blushing ERUBESCENCE

reddish in appearance or complexion, rosy, ruddy, flushed FLORID, RUBICUND

reduce See **lessen**

reduction, or the amount lost or wasted in a reduction DECREMENT

redundancy, needless repetition of a single idea in separate sets of words TAUTOLOGY
- redundancy, use of more words than necessary in expressing the

same idea PLEONASM
- reduction in the work force as through retirement or resignation rather than through redundancies NATURAL WASTAGE, ATTRITION

redundant See **excessive, long-winded**
- redundant, purposeless, having no real use OTIOSE
- make something redundant, make unnecessary by anticipating OBVIATE, PREEMPT

reed - reedlike, relating to or resembling a reed ARUNDINACEOUS
- reedlike marsh plant related to the grass family SEDGE
- reedlike plant, or the paper once made from its pith PAPYRUS
- metal band securing the reed to the mouthpiece of a clarinet or saxophone LIGATURE

reef of coral, parallel to the coastline and forming a deep, wide lagoon BARRIER REEF
- reef or small rocky island, as in a river or off the coast SKERRY
- ring of islands around a lagoon, formed of coral reefs ATOLL
- seawater separated from the sea, as by coral reefs LAGOON

reel or spool around which yarn is wound in weaving SPINDLE, BOBBIN, QUILL
- reel used for spinning silk from cocoons, or the place where such spinning is done FILATURE

refectory in a medieval monastery FRATER

refer a case or decision to a lower court, committee, or the like REMIT
- refer to indirectly ALLUDE
- refer to something, call attention or remark ADVERT

reference See also **footnote**
- reference, letter of commendation TESTIMONIAL
- reference book presenting a specialized vocabulary or selected information THESAURUS, LEXICON
- reference line, as on a graph or technical drawing AXIS
- reference manual or handy guidebook VADE MECUM
- reference or note in a text, placed at the end of the text or at the foot of the page FOOTNOTE
- reference or quotation used as an authority, as for a dictionary or legal argument CITATION
- reference point, starting point, or standard, as in surveying or sociology DATUM LINE
- list of references used in researching or compiling a book or report BIBLIOGRAPHY
- person writing a reference for a job applicant, scholarship candidate, or the like REFEREE
- "and the following," used in references and footnotes to refer to the lines, pages, or the like following the one just listed FF
- "in the place cited," used in references and footnotes to refer to the work or page previously cited LOC CIT, LOCO CITATO
- "in the same place," used in references and footnotes to refer to the chapter, page, or the like cited immediately before IB, IBID, IBIDEM
- "in the text above," used in references and footnotes to refer to a previous passage in the text SUPRA
- "in the text below," used in references and footnotes to refer to a later passage in the text INFRA
- "in the work cited," used in references and footnotes to refer to the book, article, or other work previously cited OP CIT, OPERE CITATO
- "see" or "which see," used in references and footnotes to direct the reader's attention to a specified page, work, or the like VIDE, QV, QUOD VIDE
- "the same," used in references and footnotes to indicate a reference already mentioned IDEM
- "throughout", "here and there," used in references and footnotes to indicate the frequent occurrence of an item in a text PASSIM

referring to or relating to, concerning PERTAINING TO, ANENT, APROPOS OF

referring to (combining form) -WISE

refined, elegant, exquisite, especially in a pretentious way RECHERCHÉ
- refined, often in an affected way GENTEEL
- refined, sensitive, capable of or based on fine distinctions SUBTLE
- refined, very delicate ETHEREAL
- refined and very well-bred man PATRICIAN
- refined or dainty in an affected way MINCING, NIMINY-PIMINY
- refined or elegant feature NICETY

reflector or mirror in some optical instruments SPECULUM

reflex, knee-jerk, sleepwalking, or similar involuntary, unthinking action AUTOMATISM
- reflex movement, as by bacteria, in response to light or a similar stimulus TAXIS
- referring to a reflex reaction or conditioned response to a stimulus PAVLOVIAN
- small rubber-headed hammer used for testing reflexes and tapping the chest for purposes of diagnosis PLEXOR

reformer or rebel within a political group or party YOUNG TURK
- reformer or social theorist who is hopelessly idealistic and impractical VISIONARY, UTOPIAN

reforms - superficial, just for show, shallow rather than really effective, as reforms might be COSMETIC, TOKEN, PRO FORMA

refrigeration (combining form) CRYO-

refrigerator - chemical commonly used as refrigerant in refrigerators and air conditioners FREON
- switching or controlling device for regulating temperature, as in a refrigerator or central-heating system THERMOSTAT

refuge, haven, or relief OASIS
- immunity from arrest or punishment, as by taking refuge in a church or embassy SANCTUARY

refugee or emigrant, specifically one who has fled his or her homeland for political reasons (masculine and feminine, respectively) ÉMIGRÉ, ÉMIGRÉE

refund of part of a sum paid, as of one's taxes REBATE

refusal, denial, or contradiction NEGATION
- refusal or blunt rejection, as of an offer REBUFF, SNUB, REPULSE

refuse or neglect to carry out the wishes of DISOBLIGE
- refuse or reject a proposal by exercising one's absolute right to decide VETO
- refuse or reject an offer, approach, or the like REPEL, REPULSE
- refuse to acknowledge a debt, authority, claim, or the like REPUDIATE
- refuse to buy, deal with, or the like, as a form of protest or economic pressure BOYCOTT
- refuse to continue, be reluctant, avoid JIB, BALK, SHRINK
- refuse to do or accept something DECLINE
- refuse to obey, approve, or conform to DISSENT, DEFY, OUTFACE
- refuse to recognize or acknowledge, turn one's back on DISOWN
- refuse to speak to or deal with, exclude, shun OSTRACIZE
- refuse with scorn DISDAIN, SPURN

regain a favorable position, as by recovering from a loss RECOUP
- regain one's health, wealth, social standing, or the like RECUPERATE

regard as having a particular quality, consider to be ADJUDGE, DEEM, PRONOUNCE
- regards, greetings, good wishes COMPLIMENTS, SALUTATIONS
- high regard, respect DEFERENCE, REVERENCE

regarding, in relation to, compared with VIS-À-VIS

- regarding, relating to, concerning PERTAINING TO, ANENT, APROPOS OF

regardless of, without reference to, without consideration of IRRESPECTIVE OF

region See also **area**
- region into which a county might be divided in former times HUNDRED, WAPENTAKE, RIDING
- region into which French cities and départements are divided ARRONDISSEMENT
- electoral region or police district of city PRECINCT
- English county, or regional division of an Australian state SHIRE
- geographical features of a region, or their display on a map TOPOGRAPHY

region (combining form) TOP-, TOPO-

register of workers, soldiers, or the like, or the list of duties to be performed by them ROSTER

registration plates that include the initials of the vehicle's owner VANITY PLATES

regret, feel sorry about RUE
- regretting one's sins or offenses REPENTANT, PENITENT, CONTRITE

regular, typical, predictable STATUTORY
- regular, unbroken, and typically unpleasant, as boredom might be UNRELIEVED
- regular, uniform, solid, and impersonal MONOLITHIC
- regular, with little variation, as a climate or personality might be EQUABLE
- regular throughout, predictable, forming a coherent whole CONSISTENT, INTEGRATED, OF A PIECE, UNIFORM
- flowing regularly and rhythmically, as good prose does SEAMLESS, MEASURED
- occurring at regular intervals CYCLICAL, RECURRENT
- system or institution, such as a college, with a regular and reliable output of dull standardized products, graduates, or the like PRODUCTION LINE, SAUSAGE MACHINE, RUBBER STAMP

regulator (combining form) -STAT

rehearsal or practice DUMMY RUN
- rehearsal or trial run, as of a military attack DRY RUN

reheated before serving, as leftover food might be RÉCHAUFFÉ

reign - reigning or ruling REGNANT
- period of time between two successive reigns, governments, or the like INTERREGNUM
- referring to a particular year of the reign of a named king or queen REGNAL

reincarnation - reverence for all life, as in some Indian religions, often with a belief in nonviolence and reincarnation AHIMSA

reindeer in North America CARIBOU
- Santa's reindeer DASHER, DANCER, PRANCER, VIXEN, COMET, CUPID, DONNER, BLITZEN, RUDOLPH

reinforced concrete FERROCONCRETE

reinforcing triangular metal plate for a corner joist GUSSET

reins See illustration at **harness**

reject a proposal by exercising one's absolute powers of refusal VETO
- reject a sweetheart in a cruel way JILT
- reject as being of no further use DISCARD, JETTISON
- reject or abandon a cause, commitment, or the like, turn one's back on, desert DISAVOW, FORSAKE, DISOWN
- reject or cold-shoulder, treat dismissively SLIGHT
- reject or deny a claim or accusation REPUDIATE
- reject or disregard something as irrelevant or unreliable DISCOUNT
- reject or give up solemnly or resolutely ABJURE, FORSWEAR, RENOUNCE
- reject or shun someone utterly from all social dealings in one's community BOYCOTT, OSTRACIZE
- reject the authority of a person or group, refuse to obey or conform DISSENT, DEFY, OUTFACE
- reject with scorn DISDAIN, SPURN

rejection of all moral and social values NIHILISM, ANARCHISM
- rejection or blunt refusal of an offer REBUFF, SNUB, REPULSE

relate to, be connected with, or belong to as a rightful part or function APPERTAIN
- relate to closely or communicate intimately with someone or something, such as nature COMMUNE

related, especially through the father's line AGNATE
- related, especially through the mother's line COGNATE
- related but separated by a specified number of generations, as distant cousins might be REMOVED
- related but subordinate ADJUNCT
- related by blood CONSANGUINEOUS
- related in form, development, or function, as a human arm and a bird's wing are HOMOLOGOUS
- related or resembling AKIN, KINDRED

relating to or referring to PERTAINING, ANENT, APROPOS
- relating to a number divided into one RECIPROCAL

relations - resumption of friendly relations, as between two countries RAPPROCHEMENT, DÉTENTE

relationship, especially a sexual relationship LIAISON
- relationship, or quality of relationship, as between business associates FOOTING, STANDING
- relationship between two numbers or quantities RATIO, PROPORTION
- relationship by adoption or marriage, as distinct from a blood relationship AFFINITY
- relationship by blood CONSANGUINITY
- relationship of close and beneficial association, with dependency but without parasitism, as between two different organisms SYMBIOSIS
- relationship of close and beneficial association, without dependency or parasitism, as between two different organisms COMMENSALISM, MUTUALISM
- relationship of correspondence, equivalence, or identity between systems or parts of a system SYMMETRY
- relationship of correspondence between two things CORRELATION
- relationship of equivalent giving and taking on both sides RECIPROCITY, MUTUALITY
- relationship of mutual trust and participating in another's thoughts and feelings RAPPORT, COMMUNION
- relationship or similarity KINSHIP
- capable of living or working together harmoniously, as the partners in a relationship should be COMPATIBLE, ON THE SAME WAVELENGTH
- correct relationship between things, especially their relative importance PERSPECTIVE
- formation of a close relationship, usually between mother and child BONDING
- having the same relationship to each other MUTUAL, RECIPROCAL
- referring to love or a close relationship between two unrelated people that is free of sexual desire PLATONIC
- set of social or psychological factors underlying a relationship DYNAMIC
- value or thing having a close relationship with another, or corresponding to it closely and dependent on it FUNCTION

relative, blood relation KINSMAN, SIB
- relative importance of things, or the ability to see them objectively PERSPECTIVE
- relative or relatives closest to a person NEXT OF KIN
- favoritism, such as political appointments, shown to relatives or

friends by those in positions of power NEPOTISM
- murder of one's parent PARRICIDE

relative density SPECIFIC GRAVITY
- apparatus to measure the relative density of liquids, as used in beer- and winemaking HYDROMETER
- scale in measuring the relative density of liquids BAUMÉ SCALE

relax See also **calm**
- relax, ease up, cease being tense THAW, UNBEND, UNCLENCH
- relax in a listless or apathetic way LANGUISH, LOLL
- relaxation of or release from a rule, law, obligation, or the like DISPENSATION
- relaxation technique popular in Western countries, based on Hindu traditions of meditation TRANSCENDENTAL MEDITATION, TM
- relaxed and friendly MELLOW, GENIAL, COOL
- relaxing, calming, soothing, as a medical drug might be SEDATIVE, ANODYNE
- relaxing of tension, as between nations DÉTENTE, RAPPROCHEMENT
- relaxing or sleep-inducing drug NARCOTIC, OPIATE, SOPORIFIC

relay race - last runner or swimmer in a relay race ANCHORMAN, ANCHORWOMAN
- short stick that is passed from one runner to the next in a relay race BATON

release See also **free**
- release, as from duty, debt, or life QUIETUS
- release a dog, hawk, or the like from its leash or other restraint SLIP
- release of a prisoner before the end of his or her sentence, on condition of good behavior PAROLE
- release or discharge from obligation, debt, or penalty QUITTANCE
- release or discharge smoke, steam, or the like VENT
- writ to release a person from unlawful imprisonment, or the right to demand such a writ HABEAS CORPUS

relentless, deaf to all pleas REMORSELESS, INEXORABLE

relevant, applicable, or to the point APPOSITE, APROPOS, APPROPRIATE, AD REM, GERMANE, PERTINENT, APT
- relevant, crucially important MATERIAL
- relevant or well-suited to the occasion OPPORTUNE, SEASONABLE, TIMELY
- relevance, applicability to the matter at hand BEARING
- be suitable, appropriate, or relevant PERTAIN

reliable, expert, and conclusive, as a textbook might be DEFINITIVE
- reliable, honest, as a lawyer or shopkeeper might be REPUTABLE
- reliable, official, based on expert sources AUTHORITATIVE
- reliable, trusty, loyal, and resolute STALWART, STAUNCH, STEADFAST
- reliable all the time and in every case, unfailing, as a remedy might be INFALLIBLE, FOOLPROOF, FAIL-SAFE, DEPENDABLE
- reliable colleague or adviser TROUPER
- reliable or believable CREDIBLE

relief in sculpture in which the forms project only very slightly from the background BAS-RELIEF, BASSO-RELIEVO, LOW RELIEF
- relief or assistance in time of distress SUCCOR

relieve of or free from a problem DISEMBARRASS, DISENCUMBER
- relieve oneself by disclosing the thoughts or feelings that are troubling one UNBOSOM, CONFESS
- relieve or stand in for somebody at work, by taking a turn SPELL

religion See chart, pages 444–445, and also **church, Communion, clergyman, prayer, Roman Catholic,** and charts at **Buddhism, Hinduism, Islam,** and **Judaism**
- religion based on belief in a single god MONOTHEISM
- religion based on belief in several gods POLYTHEISM
- religion based on belief in two gods or forces, one good and one bad DUALISM, MANICHAEISM
- religion based on the belief that all things have a spirit ANIMISM
- religious act or rite, such as baptism, representing or helping to achieve grace SACRAMENT
- religious annointing UNCTION
- religious belief of a strict or passionate kind FUNDAMENTALISM
- religious beliefs PERSUASION
- religious custom, ceremony, or ritual marking a change of status in a person's life RITE OF PASSAGE
- religious devotion PIETY
- religious doctrine or belief differing from the orthodox view HERESY, HETERODOXY
- religious festival, as on a saint's day, especially in a Spanish-speaking country FIESTA
- religious gift or offering OBLATION
- religious hermit, living in discomfort and solitude for prayer and meditation RECLUSE, ANCHORITE, ANCHORESS, EREMITE, STYLITE
- religious hypocrite TARTUFFE
- religious in a deeply sincere or observant way DEVOUT, PIOUS
- religious in an affected or excessive way PHARISAICAL, RELIGIOSE, HOLIER-THAN-THOU, SANCTIMONIOUS
- religious meditation as a means of experiencing communion with the divine MYSTICISM
- religious meeting, especially when illegal and held in secret CONVENTICLE
- religious or formal celebration of a rite, performance of a ceremony, or the like SOLEMNIZATION, CONSECRATION
- religious or philosophical system holding that knowledge of God comes through mystical intuition THEOSOPHY
- religious or political document or pamphlet containing a forceful declaration or rallying call TRACT
- religious person living a monastic life but without having taken formal vows OBLATE
- religious principle, body of beliefs, or the like DOGMA, DOCTRINE, CREED, CATECHISM, GOSPEL, TENETS
- religious rite of removing the foreskin CIRCUMCISION
- religious ritual considered foolish and obscure MUMBO JUMBO
- religious ritual involving the pouring of a liquid LIBATION
- religious sacrament including confession, absolution, and penalties PENANCE
- religious separation or exclusivity SECTARIANISM, DENOMINATIONALISM
- religious song, poem, or hymn CANTICLE
- religious system or code DISPENSATION
- religious system or group, especially as seen by the dominant religion or society CULT
- religious view that God created the universe and natural laws but no longer directs them DEISM
- religious view that God is both the creator and director of the universe THEISM
- religious view that God includes the worlds but is more than it PANENTHEISM
- religious view that God is present throughout nature and is identical with it PANTHEISM
- calling or strong urging or inclination, as to a religious life VOCATION
- combine or try to reconcile different philosophical, religious, or other beliefs SYNCRETIZE
- conversion from or abandoning of one's religion or loyalty APOSTASY
- cut off from membership of a church or religion EXCOMMUNICATE

- declare a belief in something, especially in a religion PROFESS
- disclosure or realization of God's will or some religious truth REVELATION
- lacking religious beliefs, or lacking the beliefs regarded as the correct ones INFIDEL
- lacking religious beliefs, or not belonging to a monotheistic religion that is considered the right one PAGAN, HEATHEN
- liberal, especially in matters of religion LATITUDINARIAN
- living a strict, self-denying life, with minimum comforts and pleasures, often for religious reasons ASCETIC, AUSTERE
- movement or doctrine favoring greater unity among the various churches or religions ECUMENISM, ECUMENICALISM
- officiating priest or lay participant in a religious ceremony or rite CELEBRANT
- person enthusiastically following a specified religion, cause, or god VOTARY, DEVOTEE
- person on probation in a religious order, before taking vows NOVICE
- place or rub oil or ointment on, as part of a religious ceremony ANOINT
- recent convert to a religion NEOPHYTE, PROSELYTE
- recognition of others' rights to dissenting beliefs, especially in matters of religion TOLERATION
- rejection of religion as lacking a human and logical basis RATIONALISM
- rejection of religion on the ground that the existence of gods remains unknowable or at least unprovable AGNOSTICISM
- rejection of religion on the ground that there are no gods ATHEISM
- reserve or ceremonially set aside for sacred or religious use CONSECRATE, SANCTIFY, DEDICATE
- spoiling or destruction of the sacred quality of a religious building, graveyard, or the like DESECRATION, PROFANATION, VIOLATION, SACRILEGE, DEFILEMENT
- strict and stiffly correct observer of the rules, a religion, or the like PRECISIAN
- study of religion THEOLOGY
- referring to worldly rather than spiritual or religious matters SECULAR, TEMPORAL, PROFANE

reluctant, unwilling, forced, involuntary GRUDGING
- be reluctant, refuse to continue JIB, BALK, DIG ONE'S HEELS IN

remain, continue, or survive, as pain might PERSIST
- remain in or at a place temporarily TARRY, SOJOURN
- remain or hang about aimlessly, or dawdle idly LINGER, LOITER
- remain unmoved or unchanged, especially in the face of outside pressures ABIDE, ENDURE
- remaining only temporarily, passing through, as a laborer or bird might be TRANSIENT, ITINERANT, MIGRANT

remains, leftovers, scraps, remainders ODDMENTS, REMNANTS
- remains, traces left by something that has mostly disappeared VESTIGES
- remains from a past age RELICS
- remains of something destroyed WRACK
- remaining quantity or substance at the end of a chemical process, settling of debts, or the like RESIDUE
- amount that remains after part is deducted, as from a bank account BALANCE
- inferior remains, part left over once the best has been removed RUMP
- solid remains or residue of oilseed after processing, used as animal fodder EXPELLERS, EXTRACTIONS
- solid remains settling at the bottom of a liquid DREGS, SEDIMENT
- solid remains settling at the bottom of a liquid, especially coffee GROUNDS
- solid remains settling at the bottom of a liquid, especially wine LEES
- solid remains settling or filtered out when refining oil, distilling liquids, or the like FOOTS

remark, clinching argument, or hostile gesture made when leaving or pretending to leave PARTHIAN SHOT
- remark made in passing, incidental comment OBITER DICTUM
- remark or carefully considered observation, usually very critical ANIMADVERSION
- remark or phrase, with independent syntax, within a sentence PARENTHESIS
- remark or statement having no apparent relevance to what came before it NON SEQUITUR
- remark spoken in an undertone, as by a character in a play, for the audience and pretending to be inaudible to other actors ASIDE, STAGE WHISPER
- clear, crisp, and forceful, as a remark or argument might be TRENCHANT, COGENT
- cutting, penetrating, to the point, as a remark might be INCISIVE, MORDANT
- hurtfully direct, cutting, as a remark might be BARBED
- inappropriate or ill-chosen, as a remark, style, or expression might be INFELICITOUS
- insulting in a deliberate way, intended to offend or belittle, as a slighting remark is DEROGATORY
- perceptive remark, insightful observation APERÇU
- throw in a remark by way of interruption INTERJECT, INTERPOSE

remarkable, exceptional, extraordinary SURPASSING, SINGULAR
- remarkable or wonderful PRODIGIOUS

remedial, curative THERAPEUTIC

remedy for all ailments or problems PANACEA, CATHOLICON
- remedy intended for a particular disease or disorder SPECIFIC
- remedy or scheme, as for social problems, that is considered facile or simplistic NOSTRUM
- effective all the time and in every case, as a remedy might be INFALLIBLE, FOOLPROOF, FAIL-SAFE
- having wide-ranging and effective power, as a remedy might be SOVEREIGN
- powerful or successful, as a remedy might be EFFICACIOUS

remember, bring to mind again RECALL, RECOLLECT, RETRIEVE
- remember and honor a person or event by means of a ceremony COMMEMORATE
- remember and recount past events, especially with nostalgia REMINISCE
- remember by conscious effort, commit to memory, learn by rote MEMORIZE, CON
- remember consciously, go back over in one's mind RETRACE
- remember or keep in mind, especially after a long time RETAIN
- be remembered, come back to mind, as a dream might RECUR
- things or events that deserve to be remembered MEMORABILIA

remembering, recall, recollection ANAMNESIS
- remembering by repetition rather than through understanding ROTE
- formula, rhyme, or the like used as an aid to remembering MNEMONIC, MNEMONIC DEVICE

reminder, usually in the form of a note MEMORANDUM, AIDE-MÉMOIRE
- reminder of eventually inescapable death, such as a skull MEMENTO MORI

- object that reminds one of a person or place SOUVENIR, KEEPSAKE, MEMENTO
- serving as a reminder of, prompting memories, suggestive REMINISCENT, EVOCATIVE, REDOLENT

remorse for one's sins CONTRITION, REPENTANCE, PENITENCE

remote, separated, lonely, as a place or life might be SECLUDED, CLOISTERED, SEQUESTERED, SOLITARY
- remote and difficult to reach INACCESSIBLE
- remote country areas, the sticks, the bush BOONDOCKS, BOONIES, OUTBACK, HINTERLAND, BACKVELD, BACKBLOCKS, BUNDU
- remote from the center, far

RELIGION

RELIGIONS AND BELIEFS	
Babism	Persia: religion founded in the 19th century by Ali Muhammad, known as "the Bab," the "Gateway," who tried to combine the best of all religions
Bahaism	Persia: religion developed from Babism by the 19th-century religious leader Bahaullah
Buddhism	India, China, southeast Asia: philosophical-religious system founded in the 6th century BC in India by Gautama Siddhartha, "the Buddha"
Confucianism	formerly China: religious and moral system based on the teachings of Confucius, the 6th-century- BC philosopher
Druses	Lebanon: followers of a religion based on Islam, founded in the 11th century by Al-Hakim Bi-Amr Allah
Hinduism	India: traditional religion of the greater part of the Indian subcontinent
Islam	Middle East and worldwide: religion founded by the 7th-century prophet Muhammad
Jainism	northern India: religion developed from Hinduism by "Jinas" or "conquerors," such as Mahavira, a 6th-century-BC sage
Judaism	Israel and worldwide: the religion of the Jewish people
Manichaeism	Persia: religion based on the teachings of the 3rd-century teacher Manes, similar to Mazdaism
Mazdaism/ Zoroastrianism	Persia: religion based on the teachings of the 6th-century-BC prophet Zoroaster (Zarathushtra), who regarded the world as a battleground between good and evil
Mithraism	Persia: ancient worship of Mithras, god of light
Parseeism	western India: surviving form of Zoroastrianism
Rastafarianism	Jamaica: militant religion including the veneration of Ras Tafari, or Haile Selassie, the former emperor of Ethiopia, as God
Shamanism	northern Siberia and North America: belief that spirits control life and can be influenced by priests
Shintoism	Japan: traditional religion, involving the worship of numerous gods
Sikhism	Punjab: religion developed from Hinduism in the 16th century by Guru Nanak, incorporating elements of Islam
Sufism	Iran: a mystical form of Islam
Taoism	China: religious and philosophical system based on the teachings of the 6th-century- BC philosopher Lao-tzu
Wahhabism	Saudi Arabia: beliefs of a rigid Islamic sect, strict observers of the Koran
Zen Buddhism	Japan, and formerly China: a mystical form of Buddhism, seeking enlightenment through meditation
CHRISTIAN GROUPS	
Albigensians	ascetic Catharian religion in 12th- and 13th-century France, believing that the material world was purely evil
Amish	U.S. Anabaptist religion that broke away from the Mennonites in the 17th century
Anabaptists	radical Protestant movement that developed in the 1520's, believing in pacifism and adult baptism
antinomians	believers in the doctrine that salvation depends on faith alone
Calvinists	followers of the 16th-century Protestant theologian John Calvin, believing in the strict authority of the Bible, and in salvation through God's grace alone

away, fairly distant OUTLYING
- remote region, goal, or ideal ULTIMA THULE

removal or seclusion from public view, as of some women, or as when in disgrace PURDAH

removal (combining form) EX-, -ECTOMY

remove, separate, or isolate from the main group SEGREGATE
- remove a limb, as by surgery AMPUTATE
- remove an organ or other body party by surgery EXCISE
- remove all trace of ERADICATE, OBLITERATE
- remove and set aside a passage from a text for special consider-

RELIGION *continued*

charismatics	followers of a movement seeking to reassert the influence of the Holy Spirit, and marked by such practices as spiritual healing and speaking in tongues
Christadelphians	religion founded in the United States in the late 1840's, rejecting the Holy Trinity and believing in the complete obliteration of the wicked
Christian Scientists	members of the Church of Christ, Scientist, founded in 1879, emphasizing spiritual healing
Copts	members of the Coptic Church centered in Egypt, professing monophysitism
Dunkers	German-American Baptist sect opposed to military service and the taking of oaths
Gnostics	early Christian sect believing that salvation was attainable only by the few with a special knowledge of God
Huguenots	French Protestants of the 16th and 17th centuries
Hussites	followers of the 14th-15th-century Bohemian reformer John Huss
Illuminati	16th-century Spanish religion claiming special religious enlightenment
Jehovah's Witnesses	religion founded in 1879, active in missionary work, whose dedication to the Bible can entail opposition to established religion and government authority
Lollards	followers of the 14th-century English reformer John Wycliffe
Maronites	members of an ancient Uniate church from Syria, now mainly in Lebanon
Melchites	members of the Greek Catholic Church in the Middle East
Mennonites	pacifist Protestant religion arising from the Anabaptist movement
Monophysites	believers in the doctrine that Christ had only one nature, being purely divine rather than both human and divine
Moravians	members of the Protestant Moravian Church founded by Hussites in 1722
Mormons	members of the Church of Jesus Christ of Latter-Day Saints, founded in the United States in the 1830's, whose Book of Mormon supplements the Bible as official scripture
Mozarabs	Spaniards who continued to practice modified Christianity under Muslim rule
Plymouth Brethren	puritanical religion founded in 1830 in Plymouth, England, holding the Bible to be the sole source of truth
Seventh-Day Adventists	religion observing the Sabbath on Saturday and believing that Christ's Second Coming and the end of the world are about to happen
Shakers	radical Quaker sect founded in 1747, believing in common ownership of property, named from their former custom of dancing and shaking movements during ceremonies
Swedenborgians	followers of the 18th-century Swedish theologian Emanuel Swedenborg, or members of the New Jerusalem Church, believing in direct mystical communication between the world and the spiritual realm
Tractarians	followers of the 19th-century Oxford Movement, who sought closer ties between the Anglican and Roman Catholic churches
Uniates	members of the Eastern Orthodox churches that acknowledge the pope but keep their own liturgy
Zwinglians	followers of the 16th-century Swiss Protestant reformer Ulrich Zwingli, holding that Christ's presence in the Communion is symbolic rather than actual

ation ABSTRACT, EXTRACT
- remove bad or weak parts or members, weed out CULL
- remove entirely, pull up by the roots DERACINATE, EXTIRPATE, UPROOT
- remove from office, especially by force, overthrow, unseat DEPOSE, DISPLACE, SUPPLANT, OUST
- remove or cut the end from, abbreviate PRUNE, TRUNCATE, CURTAIL
- remove or delete offending parts from a text EXCISE, EXPUNGE, EXPURGATE
- remove or rescue from difficulties EXTRICATE
- remove something from, relieve or deprive of something, such as powers, duties, or problems DISBURDEN, DIVEST, DISEMBARRASS, DISENCUMBER
- remove soluble parts from a substance such as soil, as by flushing with water LEACH
- removed, remote, lonely, solitary, as a place or life might be SECLUDED, CLOISTERED, SEQUESTERED

remove (combining form) DE-, DIS-, UN-
rendezvous, especially of lovers or with one's destiny TRYST
renew See also **repair**
- renew, reestablish, repair RESTORE
- renew, start again RESUME
- renew or reform spiritually, morally, or culturally REGENERATE, REVITALIZE, REVIVIFY
- renew or revive, return to consciousness or life RESUSCITATE
- renew the social standing of, restore to power or favor REHABILITATE, REINSTATE
- renew the supply of, refill REPLENISH
- renew the vigor of, restore the youth of REJUVENATE

renewal or revival of culture RENASCENCE, RENAISSANCE
renewed bout of ill health after an apparent recovery RELAPSE
- renewed outbreak of disease, civil unrest, or the like after a period of inactivity RECRUDESCENCE

rent-free, referring to property owned by the sovereign and let free of charge to a favored tenant GRACE-AND-FAVOR
- rent, tax, or the like that remains unpaid ARREARS
- rent of a very small, purely nominal amount PEPPERCORN RENT
- rent that is outrageously high RACK RENT
- person whose income is derived chiefly from rents or investments RENTIER

reordering or rearrangement PERMUTATION, COMBINATORY ORDERING
repair See also **renew**
- repair, improve, make better or easier AMEND, AMELIORATE
- repair, patch up, restore to an acceptable or original state REVAMP, RECONDITION
- repair, rebuild, or restore from fragments or original plans RECONSTRUCT, RECONSTITUTE
- repair and restore something, such as a house FURBISH, REFURBISH, RENOVATE
- repair in a desultory or inexpert fashion TINKER
- repair or remedy an injustice or inequality REDRESS
- dismantle, examine, and repair DEBUG, OVERHAUL
- impossible to repair or make good, as devastating damage might be IRREPARABLE

repay REIMBURSE
- repay an injury like for like RETALIATE
- repay for loss or injury COMPENSATE, INDEMNIFY, RECOMPENSE
- repay or reward someone REQUITE

repayment RECOMPENSE, REQUITAL, QUITTANCE
- repayment, compensation, making good RESTITUTION, REPARATIONS, INDEMNIFICATION, AMENDS, REDRESS, ATONEMENT

repeat, say again ITERATE, REITERATE, REAFFIRM, INGEMINATE
- repeat in concise form, sum up RECAP, RECAPITULATE, PUT IN NUCE
- repeat or make a copy of REPRODUCE, DUPLICATE
- repeat or reproduce facts in an unthinking way REGURGITATE
- repeat or rework old material without any significant alteration REHASH

repeated phrase, design, or thematic element in music, art, or literature MOTIF, LEITMOTIV, MOTTO
- repeated verse, tune, theme, or the like REFRAIN, CHORUS, BURDEN

repentance for sin based on fear rather than on love of God ATTRITION
- repentance for sin based on love of God rather than fear CONTRITION
- repentant, humbly or sorrowfully regretting one's sins or offenses PENITENT, CONTRITE
- act of self-punishment or devotion to demonstrate sorrow or repentance for sin PENANCE
- forgiveness or release from punishment, as after sincere repentance ABSOLUTION
- making good, atonement, reparations or compensation, as after repentance RESTITUTION, REDRESS, AMENDS, EXPIATION, REDEMPTION
- public show of mourning or repentance SACKCLOTH AND ASHES

repetition, at the start of a phrase, of the word or words ending the previous phrase ANADIPLOSIS
- repetition, especially of a phrase or theme in music REPRISE
- repetition, unthinking routine ROTE
- repetition of a single idea in separate sets of words TAUTOLOGY
- repetition of a word or phrase at the start of successive clauses, lines of verse, or the like ANAPHORA
- repetition of conjunctions for stylistic effect, as in *blood and sweat and tears* POLYSYNDETON
- repetition or excess of information, either deliberately, as in telegrams or computer programs, or carelessly, as in tautology REDUNDANCY, PLEONASM
- repetition or uncontrollable recurrence of an idea, spoken word, or the like PERSEVERATION

replace a lost or damaged body part by the formation of new tissue REGENERATE
- replace another in a position or office, especially by force or intrigue SUPPLANT, OUST, DISPLACE, DEPOSE
- replace another in a position or office, especially on the death or retirement of the incumbent SUCCEED
- replace something outdated or obsolete SUPERSEDE
- replace temporarily, stand in for DEPUTIZE

replacement, stand-in SUBSTITUTE
- replacement doctor, priest, or the like, a temporary stand-in LOCUM, LOCUM TENENS
- person serving as a replacement for another, such as a teacher who fulfills the emotional role of a parent SURROGATE

reply, quick retaliatory action or retort RIPOSTE, REJOINDER
- deliberately vague, ambiguous, or noncommittal, as a reply might be EVASIVE, EQUIVOCAL
- sharp and witty reply in a conversation, piece of clever backchat RETORT, REPARTEE
- witty reply or retort that occurs to one only when it is too late ESPRIT D'ESCALIER, TREPPENWITZ

report or record in detail, and support with evidence DOCUMENT
- report or rumor that is false or a deliberate hoax CANARD
- report sent over a distance, as by a newspaper correspondent or military field officer DISPATCH
- government report in Great Britain containing proposals for legislation, issued to interested parties

for comments and discussion GREEN PAPER
- government report or policy statement before discussion by a lawgiving body WHITE PAPER
- government report or publication providing information on a special topic BLUE BOOK
- revealing of a scandal or crime, or the book, broadcast, or the like in which it is reported EXPOSÉ
- spread a rumor or report BRUIT

reporter, typically covering the local news in a specific area, working on a part-time basis STRINGER
- reporter doing routine or mediocre work HACK
- reporter or free-lance photographer who badgers celebrities PAPARAZZO

repossess mortgaged property when the scheduled payments are not met FORECLOSE

represent graphically in pictures or words, describe, portray DEPICT, DELINEATE, REALIZE, RENDER, LIMN
- represent perfectly, be a typical example of TYPIFY, EMBODY, PERSONIFY, INCARNATE, EPITOMIZE
- representing a scene objectively, lifelike, as a painting might be REALISTIC

representational, not abstract, as a painting might be FIGURATIVE

representative See also **diplomat**
- representative, agent, or deputy, performing duties for someone else PROXY, MINISTER, COMMISSARY, ASSIGNEE
- representative, agent, or messenger sent on a mission, typically by a government or head of state EMISSARY, LEGATE, ENVOY
- representative, agent, or middleman in business dealings BROKER, FACTOR
- representative, as of a university, in business matters SYNDIC
- representative, especially at a conference DELEGATE
- representative, stand-in, or replacement DEPUTY, SUBSTITUTE
- representative or agent in former times, as for collecting tithes or conducting a case in court PROCTOR
- representative or agent legally entitled to control or administer the property or funds of someone else TRUSTEE
- representative or agent legally entitled to control or administer the will of a dead person or the funds that have been bequeathed EXECUTOR, EXECUTRIX
- representative or agent secretly standing in for someone else FRONT, FRONT PERSON, DUMMY
- representative or agent who runs a landowner's estate STEWARD, BAILIFF
- representative or assistant performing a wide range of duties FACTOTUM
- representative or means mediating between people or things, gobetween INTERMEDIARY
- representative or perfect example or embodiment of an idea or ideal EXEMPLAR, ARCHETYPE, AVATAR, PERSONIFICATION, EPITOME, INCARNATION
- representative or substitute for another, such as someone fulfilling the emotional role of a parent SURROGATE
- representative trained to replace someone when necessary, as in the theater UNDERSTUDY
- representative who speaks for someone else, spokesperson MOUTHPIECE
- appoint as one's agent, substitute, or representative DEPUTE
- deputy administrative officer or representative assisting a king, magistrate, or the like VICEGERENT
- performed or experienced through a representative or substitute VICARIOUS
- person or group acting as representative, especially on a mission DEPUTATION, DELEGATION
- put into the hands of a representative or those of a subordinate DELEGATE

reprint of an article on its own, after it has appeared in a journal or book OFFPRINT

reproduce, or cause plants or animals to reproduce PROPAGATE
- reproduce or spread rapidly PROLIFERATE

reproducing by means of splitting, as some one-celled plants and animals are FISSIPAROUS
- reproducing or developing without sexual union and fertilization, asexual AGAMIC, AGAMOGENETIC, PARTHENOGENETIC
- reproducing young by means of eggs that hatch outside the body OVIPAROUS
- reproducing young by means of eggs that hatch within the body, as with some fish and reptiles OVOVIVIPAROUS
- reproducing young in the form of live offspring developed within the body VIVIPAROUS

reproduction, producing of offspring PROCREATION
- reproduction that is asexual, in which there is no direct fertilization of an egg by a sperm APOMIXIS, APOGAMY, PARTHENOGENESIS
- reproduction that is sexual, involving fertilization of the egg by the sperm AMPHIMIXIS
- barren, incapable of further reproduction, as a plant or animal might be EFFETE

reproduction (combining form) -GON, GONO-, -GEN-, -GENESIS

reproductive gland in female mammals OVARY
- reproductive gland in male mammals TESTIS
- reproductive gland in mammals GONAD
- exterior parts of reproductive organs GENITALIA, GENITALS

reptile (combining form) HERPET-, HERPETO-

repulsive, dreadful, grim, as the sight of bloodshed is GRISLY, GRUESOME
- repulsive, hideous, horrible, or hateful LOATHSOME, ABOMINABLE, HORRENDOUS, UNSPEAKABLE
- repulsive, offending one's tastes or senses, causing aversion REPELLENT, REPUGNANT
- repulsive, offensive, disgusting, sickening NAUSEATING

reputation, especially good reputation REPUTE, REGARD, RENOWN
- reputation, status or renown as through success or wealth PRESTIGE, CACHET, KUDOS
- reputation, status, rank, or level of achievement STATURE, STANDING, STOCK
- reputation for evil or wickedness, or an act contributing to such a reputation INFAMY
- damage or spoil someone's reputation, name, or the like SULLY, DEFILE, TARNISH, PROFANE, DISCREDIT
- disgrace, dishonor, bad reputation DISREPUTE, NOTORIETY
- restore someone to his or her former status or reputation, as after a counterrevolution REHABILITATE

reputed or commonly considered, as a child's supposed father might be PUTATIVE

request See **ask**

requested or commanded by AT THE BEHEST OF

require, demand or lay down as a condition in an agreement or contract STIPULATE
- required as a duty INCUMBENT
- required by law or enforced by custom COMPULSORY, OBLIGATORY, MANDATORY

requirements that are listed precisely SPECIFICATIONS, SPECS

rescue from sin, ignorance, danger, or the like SALVATION, DELIVERANCE
- rescue or save, as from loss, damage, or cancellation SALVAGE

- rescue or save from danger or trouble RETRIEVE
- rescue or save from sin and punishment REDEEM
- rescue or save someone from evil ways by reforming him or her RECLAIM

research into and analysis of the efficiency of a work force, machine system, or the like, as an aid to policy making OPERATIONAL RESEARCH
- research report or treatise, especially for an academic degree THESIS, DISSERTATION

resemble or imitate, often for camouflage MIMIC, SIMULATE
- resembling but not really being QUASI-, BOGUS, ERSATZ

resembling (combining form) QUASI-, PARA-, -INE, -OSE, -OID

resentment, feeling of anger and ill will GRUDGE
- resentment, offense, feeling of anger at some supposed insult UMBRAGE
- resentment or temper, as from a blow to one's pride PIQUE
- offensive, liable to cause ill will or resentment INVIDIOUS

reserve or book, claim or arrange in advance, or order specifically BESPEAK
- reserve stratagem or device whereby one may snatch victory from defeat TRUMP CARD
- reserve supply or store accumulated for future use STOCKPILE
- nature or wildlife reserve SANCTUARY

reserved See **shy**
- reserved, silent, uncommunicative TACITURN, RETICENT

resident or inhabitant of a place or region DENIZEN

resin-flavored Greek wine RETSINA
- resin of various pine trees, used on the bows of stringed instruments ROSIN, COLOPHONY
- resin or gum from various acacia trees, used in ink, glues, and the like GUM ARABIC, GUM ACACIA
- resin or gum used in making perfume MYRRH, BDELLIUM
- resin or gum, as used in varnish MASTIC, GUAIACUM
- resin used in incense FRANKINCENSE, OLIBANUM
- artificial resin used in synthetic rubber, paints, plastics, and the like ACRYLIC RESIN
- artificial resin used in tough adhesives EPOXY
- fragrant, oily resins from various trees, used in lotions, perfumes, and the like BALM, BALSAM, TOLU
- gum resin used as the source of a yellow pigment for paints GAMBOGE
- gum resin with onionlike smell, used in Eastern cooking and formerly in medicines ASAFETIDA, ASFETIDA
- purified resin from various insects, as used in making old phonograph records SHELLAC
- turpentine resin from pine trees GALIPOT, BORDEAUX TURPENTINE

resistance, as to government authority or colonial rule, by nonviolent methods such as fasting and noncooperation PASSIVE RESISTANCE
- resistance, capacity of enduring or withstanding something burdensome or unpleasant TOLERANCE
- deliberate damaging or destruction of property, as by underground resistance groups or dissatisfied workers SABOTAGE
- unit of electrical resistance OHM

resistant to damage, harm, or injury INVULNERABLE, IMMUNE, UNASSAILABLE

resolve or solve a mystery, puzzle, or problem UNRAVEL, DECIPHER

resort area with mineral springs SPA

resources, especially money, required for a particular purpose WHEREWITHAL
- use or spend resources thriftily HUSBAND

respect, courteous or submissive regard DEFERENCE
- respect, great devotion, awe, as shown to God REVERENCE, VENERATION
- respect, honor, or duty, as granted to someone or to a belief or cause HOMAGE
- respect or admire greatly, honor ESTEEM
- gift, payment, or other expression of respect, submission, or the like TRIBUTE

respectable, often in an affected way GENTEEL

respected, especially because of old age VENERABLE
- respected or feared as awesome or very impressive FORMIDABLE, REDOUBTABLE
- made respected or honored, as by time CONSECRATED, VENERATED

respectful - courteously respectful and compliant DEFERENTIAL, SUBSERVIENT
- excessively respectful and humble, slavish OBSEQUIOUS, SERVILE, FAWNING, UNCTUOUS, SYCOPHANTIC
- submissively respectful and admiring OBEISANT, REVERENTIAL

respects, greetings, compliments DEVOIRS

response See also **reaction**
- response sung during a church service ANTIPHON
- response to a stimulus that does not directly cause it but has come to be associated with it, as through training CONDITIONED RESPONSE
- response to or information resulting from an inquiry, experiment, program, or the like FEEDBACK
- referring to a reflex reaction or conditioned response to a stimulus PAVLOVIAN

responsibility or burden ONUS
- deny or reject responsibility DISCLAIM
- factor that shares in the responsibility for something CONTRIBUTORY FACTOR
- give up or relinquish responsibility ABDICATE, DEROGATE, RENOUNCE
- plea that mental abnormality at the time of a crime, especially a murder, reduces the culprit's responsibility DIMINISHED RESPONSIBILITY
- relating to or shared by a united body, as responsibility might be COLLECTIVE, CORPORATE

responsible, legally required LIABLE
- responsible and punishable for wrongdoing, blameworthy CULPABLE
- person guilty of a crime or responsible for a mistake or accident CULPRIT

responsive to stimuli, conscious, aware SENTIENT

rest See also **remains, pause, stop**
- rest, pause, or postponement, typically in the middle of something unpleasant RESPITE
- rest, state of inactivity or relaxation REPOSE
- resting, alive but in a suspended or inactive stage of biological development DORMANT, LATENT
- allow a brief rest to SPELL
- relating to bodies at rest or to forces in equilibrium STATIC
- tendency of a physical body to remain at rest or in unchanged motion unless acted on by external forces INERTIA

restaurant See also chart at **menu**
- restaurant, typically sharing premises with a bar BRASSERIE
- restaurant, typically small, cosy, and modest BISTRO
- restaurant counter, or a restaurant having such a counter BUFFET
- restaurant dispensing food by means of vending machines AUTOMAT
- restaurant or inn in former times CHOPHOUSE, PORTERHOUSE
- restaurant or shop specializing in roast meat ROTISSERIE, CARVERY
- beer hall or German restaurant,

originally in the cellar of a town hall RATHSKELLER
- cheap, unhygienic, and unappetizing restaurant GREASY SPOON
- deep tray containing hot water, in which deep dishes of food are kept warm, as in a self-service restaurant BAIN-MARIE
- Greek or Greek-style restaurant TAVERNA
- Italian or Italian-style restaurant TRATTORIA
- table setting in a restaurant, or the cover charge for it COUVERT

restless, agitated TURBULENT
- restless or impatient, as to go traveling FOOTLOOSE
- restlessness or feeling of unease FANTODS, FIDGETS

restore oneself to favor REDEEM
- restore or patch up, return to an acceptable or original state RECONDITION, REVAMP
- restore or reform spiritually, morally, or culturally REGENERATE, REVITALIZE, REVIVIFY
- restore or repair something, such as a house FURBISH, REFURBISH, RENOVATE
- restore or return to life, revive RESUSCITATE, RESURRECT
- restore something to its natural state, such as dried food or concentrated lemon juice, as by adding water RECONSTITUTE
- restore the social status of, return to power or favor REHABILITATE, REINSTATE
- restore to youth or vigor REJUVENATE
- restoring of property to its rightful owner RESTITUTION

restrain or check a smile, groan, or the like SUPPRESS, STIFLE
- restrain someone by binding his or her arms PINION
- restraining garment with long sleeves for binding the arms of a violent patient or prisoner STRAITJACKET

restrained, sparing, or disciplined, especially in eating and drinking ABSTEMIOUS, TEMPERATE

restraint, restriction, confining influence SHACKLES, FETTERS
- restraint or moderation, especially in drinking alcohol TEMPERANCE

restrict See also **limit, hinder, prevent, prohibit**
- restrict an animal's movements by tying a rope around its head and one of its legs HAMSHACKLE
- restrict an animal's movements by tying it to a tree, post, or the like TETHER
- restrict an animal's movements by tying its legs together HOBBLE
- restrict someone's movements by holding or tying him or her around the arms PINION
- restrict the freedom or movement of, as by strict rules or physical restraint STRAITJACKET
- restrict the freedom of expression of GAG

restricted by rules or prejudices HIDEBOUND, INFLEXIBLE
- restricted or specified number or quantity, as of imports, employees, immigrants, and the like QUOTA
- restricted to a relatively small group EXCLUSIVE, SELECT, ESOTERIC, RAREFIED, ARCANE

restriction, restraint, confining influence FETTERS, SHACKLES
- restriction or condition, as in an agreement or document PROVISO
- restriction or regulation requiring people to go home or be indoors by a certain hour of night CURFEW

result considered definite or inevitable FOREGONE CONCLUSION
- result from or follow from immediately ENSUE, SUPERVENE
- result or final outcome, as of a play DENOUEMENT
- result or occur eventually or ultimately EVENTUATE
- resulting, following as an effect or conclusion CONSEQUENTIAL
- resulting state or period, as after a disaster or misfortune AFTERMATH, BACKWASH
- results, often disastrous, of one's actions HANDIWORK
- results, often indirect and harmful, of an action, decision, or event REPERCUSSIONS, REVERBERATIONS, FALLOUT
- results, unavoidable but usually undesirable, of an action or decision RAMIFICATIONS
- adverse reaction resulting from a perceived threat BACKLASH
- final result, outcome UPSHOT
- have a favorable or unfavorable result or effect REDOUND
- incidental result or secondary effect, usually desirable BY-PRODUCT, SPIN-OFF
- incidental result or secondary effect, usually undesirable FALLOUT, SIDE EFFECT
- information or response resulting from an experiment, inquiry, or the like FEEDBACK
- logical result or effect of an action or condition CONSEQUENCE, COROLLARY, SEQUEL

retail - sale of goods in bulk, as to a store, as distinct from retail WHOLESALE

retain See also **keep**
- word written to instruct a typesetter or printer to retain deleted or changed text STET

retaining wall REVETMENT

retired but retaining an honorary title, as a professor might be EMERITUS
- retired into seclusion, isolated SEQUESTERED, IMMURED, CLOISTERED
- retired or discharged because of old age or illness SUPERANNUATED

retort or quick retaliatory action RIPOSTE

return an accused person to prison, another court, or the like REMAND
- return feelings, invitations, or the like RECIPROCATE, REQUITE
- return of like for like, equal exchange QUID PRO QUO
- return like for like, especially evil for evil, repay in kind RETALIATE
- return of disease, rebellion, or the like after a period of improvement RECRUDESCENCE
- return of part of the payment made REBATE
- return someone or something to the country of origin REPATRIATE
- return someone to his or her former power, favor, or fitness for society REHABILITATE, REINSTATE
- return something to a correct, proper, or balanced state RECTIFY, REDRESS
- return to an earlier, more primitive state or pattern of behavior, throwback ATAVISM
- return to an earlier and less favorable condition RELAPSE, REVERT, REGRESS, BACKSLIDE
- return to harm the originator, as a hurtful policy might BOOMERANG, REBOUND, RECOIL, REDOUND
- return to life or active use after apparent death RESURRECTION, RESUSCITATION, ANABIOSIS
- returning, strengthening, reemerging RESURGENT
- returning of property to its rightful owner RESTITUTION
- person who returns, sometimes allegedly as a ghost, after an absence REVENANT
- person who returns or relapses into a former habit, especially crime RECIDIVIST

reveal, bring to light, uncover UNEARTH, EXHUME, DISINTER
- reveal, expose, or betray UNMASK
- reveal, introduce, or make public formally or officially, as in announcing plans or dedicating a monument UNVEIL
- reveal, show, make public, be evidence of MANIFEST
- reveal a scandal or the like DISINTER

- reveal or confide one's thoughts or feelings UNBOSOM, CONFESS
- reveal something, such as a secret DISCLOSE, DIVULGE

revelation, vision, or prophecy of a great disaster APOCALYPSE
- revelation or appearance of a god, angel, or the like EPIPHANY, MANIFESTATION, THEOPHANY
- revelation or public exposure of a scandal, corruption, or the like EXPOSÉ

revenge VENGEANCE
- revenge attack, striking back RETALIATION
- revenge by one state or nation upon the citizens of another RETORTION
- revenge or just retribution, or an agent of it NEMESIS
- revenge or punishment in return for mistreatment or wrongdoing RETRIBUTION, REPRISALS
- blood feud, maintained by a cycle of revenge VENDETTA
- clear of an accusation or dishonor, as by legal action or revenge VINDICATE
- fitting repayment, restoring of the balance, or the like, as through revenge REDRESS, REQUITAL
- foreign policy based on revenge or on the regaining of lost territory REVANCHISM
- principle of revenge or retaliation, law of "an eye for an eye" LEX TALIONIS
- referring to or motivated by revenge VINDICTIVE

reversal of direction, policy, attitude, or results TURNAROUND, ABOUT-TURN, VOLTE-FACE, U-TURN
- reversal or sudden change in fortunes or the course of events, especially in a play or other literary work PERIPETEIA

reversal (combining form) CATA-

reverse, backward, or unprogressive RETROGRADE, REGRESSIVE, RECESSIVE, RETROGRESSIVE
- reverse in position, order, or the like INVERT
- reverse or change the ordering or relative position of two or more things TRANSPOSE
- reverse side of a leaf of printed paper, or of a coin or medal, "tails" VERSO
- in a reverse direction, opposite to the movement of the sun, or anticlockwise WIDDERSHINS, WITHERSHINS

review or analysis of a recent event, game, failure, or the like POSTMORTEM
- review or criticism of a book, movie, play, or the like CRITIQUE, NOTICE
- review or description for promotional purposes, as on the dust jacket of a book BLURB
- review or short criticism, especially of a book COMPTE RENDU

revise a text, plan, or the like REVAMP

revision or critical edition of a text, incorporating the most plausible variant readings RECENSION

revival, return to life after apparent death RESUSCITATION, ANABIOSIS, RESURRECTION
- revival of a disease, civil unrest, or the like after a period of inactivity RECRUDESCENCE
- revival or rebirth, as of a culture RENASCENCE, RENAISSANCE

revive, especially spiritually or morally REGENERATE
- revive, refresh, give new life or vigor to QUICKEN, REANIMATE, REVITALIZE, REVIVIFY
- revive, restore or return to life RESUSCITATE, RESURRECT

revolt See **rebel, rebellion**

revolution, as of the moon's around the earth, in which the same face of the satellite is always pointing to the primary CAPTURED ROTATION, SYNCHRONOUS ROTATION
- revolution in the form of a sudden seizing of power COUP D'ÉTAT, PUTSCH

revolutionary See also **rebellious**
- revolutionary, radical, or extremist in politics SANSCULOTTE, JACOBIN
- revolutionary believing in or urging the seizure by workers of economic and government control, as through strikes and sabotage SYNDICALIST
- revolutionary of an extreme, uncompromising kind MAXIMALIST
- revolutionary of an extremist tendency, advocating the destruction of all existing social and political institutions before rebuilding them NIHILIST, ANARCHIST
- revolutionary or reforming activist within a political group or party YOUNG TURK

revolve around a point or axis GYRATE

revolver - foolhardy risk or betting game in which a person pulls the trigger of a revolver loaded with one bullet and aimed at the head RUSSIAN ROULETTE

revolving, whirling VERTIGINOUS
- revolving circular tray holding food on a dining table DUMBWAITER, LAZY SUSAN
- revolving door or gate that lets people or animals through one by one TURNSTILE
- revolving or rolling movement VOLUTION
- revolving part in a motor, generator, or other machine ROTOR

reward in psychology, or the strengthening of a learned response as by means of rewards REINFORCEMENT
- reward or payment, as for services rendered RECOMPENSE, GUERDON
- reward or payment offered by the authorities in return for helpful service, such as arresting outlaws BOUNTY
- reward or repay someone REQUITE, REIMBURSE

reword a passage to clarify its meaning PARAPHRASE
- rewording or summary of a text ABSTRACT, PRÉCIS

rhetorical See also **highfalutin, figure of speech**
- rhetorical figure of speech, such as metaphor TROPE

Rhine siren in German mythology whose singing lured sailors to destruction LORELEI
- adjective for the river Rhine RHENISH

rhinoceros See illustration
- herd or family of rhinoceroses CRASH

rhyme of a rough or approximate kind, as where the stressed vowels are the same but the final consonants differ ASSONANCE
- rhyme of a single stressed syllable MASCULINE RHYME
- rhyme of two or more syllables, of which the first is stressed FEMININE RHYME
- rhyme or tune of a simple, catchy kind, as used in advertisements JINGLE
- false rhyme between words similar in spelling rather than sound, such as *blood* and *mood* EYE RHYME, SIGHT RHYME
- initial rhyme, similarity of sounds at the beginning of words ALLITERATION
- word game in which one player or team produces a word or line rhyming with a cue from the other CRAMBO

rhythm in music TEMPO
- rhythm of biological processes in response to environmental changes or internal control mechanisms BIORHYTHM
- rhythm of biological processes that have a regular 24-hour cycle CIRCADIAN RHYTHM
- analysis of the metrical or rhythm patterns of verse SCANSION
- regular in rhythm MEASURED
- study of rhythm and meter in poetry or speech PROSODY

rhythmic flow, as of poetry or tune-

ful speech CADENCE
- rhythmic irregularity in music, as caused by stressing a weak beat SYNCOPATION
- rhythmic swinging movement OSCILLATION
- rhythmic variation within a phrase or bar of music without changing its length RUBATO
- rhythmical, springy flow or swing, as in a person's voice or walk LILT
- rhythmical free-style dance to music, or a form of musical training using such movement EURHYTHMICS
- rhythmical stress in verse ICTUS

rib, ridge, or large vein, as on a leaf or insect's wing COSTA
- rib or ridge on corduroy or a similar fabric, or the texture of such a fabric WALE
- relating to or located in the space between ribs INTERCOSTAL

ribbon, feather, or rosette worn on the hat, especially by soldiers COCKADE
- ribbon worn on the chest as an honor or sign of rank CORDON
- decorative chain or garland of flowers, ribbons, or the like suspended in a loop FESTOON
- rose-shaped design or structure, such as a pleated ribbon badge ROSETTE
- strip of ribbon, lace, or metal worn in the hair or around the neck FILLET

rice, or rice field PADDY, PADI
- rice of a long-grained variety used for savory dishes PATNA RICE
- dish of eastern origin, consisting of rice cooked in a spicy stock, often with meat or fish added PILAU, PILAF
- Indian dish of spiced rice with meat or fish BIRYANI
- Italian dish of rice cooked in stock, mixed with cheese, vegetables, seafood, or the like RISOTTO
- Spanish dish of rice cooked in stock, mixed with shellfish, chicken, and vegetables PAELLA
- yellow spice, made from crocuses, used to flavor and color rice SAFFRON

rich See also **money, plenty**
- rich, comfortably off, well-to-do AFFLUENT, PROSPEROUS, SUBSTANTIAL, WELL-HEELED
- rich, loaded, especially temporarily FLUSH
- rich, plentiful, or luxurious OPULENT, SUMPTUOUS
- rich, powerful, and important man NABOB, MOGUL, TYCOON, MAGNATE
- rich class of people exercising power in a society PLUTOCRACY
- extremely rich person CROESUS, MIDAS, DIVES
- person who has recently become rich, especially when living in a showy but unrefined style NOUVEAU RICHE, PARVENU

riches, wealth, or money, especially if acquired in a dubious way PELF, LUCRE
- riches regarded as a corrupting influence MAMMON
- mine or other source of great riches GOLCONDA
- place of great riches or opportunity EL DORADO
- source of great riches or good luck BONANZA

rickets RACHITIS
- preventing or curing rickets, as a drug might be ANTIRACHITIC

riddle, mysterious or puzzling person or thing ENIGMA
- riddle, typically based on a pun CONUNDRUM
- riddle in the form of pictures or symbols representing syllables or words REBUS
- riddle or brainteaser in Zen Buddhism, designed to free the mind from the constraints of logic KOAN

rider of the left front horse of a coach POSTILION
- rising and falling of the rider in the saddle in time with a horse's trot POST

ridge, as on corduroy or around a basket or ship's rail WALE
- ridge of land jutting into the sea PROMONTORY, NESS, NAZE
- ridge of sand or shingle extending from the shore into the sea or across an estuary SPIT
- ridge or arch in the earth's folded rocks ANTICLINE
- ridge or bank bordering a river or irrigated field LEVEE
- ridge or crest of land CHINE
- ridge or groove linking two planks, shafts, or the like SPLINE
- ridge or hill of streamlined shape formed of glacial deposits DRUMLIN

Rhinoceros

- ridge or low hill KNOLL, HUMMOCK
- ridge or low mound of sand or gravel left by melting glacial ice ESKER, OS, KAME
- ridge or upland formed by an upthrust between two parallel, or two sets of parallel, geological faults HORST
- ridge with steep eroded sides HOGBACK, HOG'S BACK
- ridged, grooved, or striped STRIATE, STRIGOSE
- ridges or grooves around the edge of a coin MILLING, FLUTING
- ridges or teeth in a series, as on a saw or the edge of a leaf SERRATION

ridicule See also **mock**
- ridicule, crude parody LAMPOON, BURLESQUE, SPOOF, SQUIB, SKIT, TRAVESTY, FARCE
- ridicule and expose the falseness or pretentiousness of DEBUNK, DEFLATE
- ridicule or abuse in public, mock or jeer at PILLORY
- ridicule or mock by imitating MIMIC, APE, PASTICHE, SATIRIZE, PARODY, CARICATURE
- light ridicule, poking fun in a playful manner BADINAGE, BANTER, CHAFF, PERSIFLAGE, RAILLERY
- object of ridicule or scorn LAUGHINGSTOCK, BUTT

ridiculous See also **nonsense**
- ridiculous, laughable, or absurd LUDICROUS, FARCICAL, PREPOSTEROUS, RISIBLE
- ridiculous, senseless, empty and silly, as a remark might be ASININE, FATUOUS, INANE
- ridiculous, strange, incomprehensible BIZARRE, OUTLANDISH, OUTRÉ
- ridiculously impractical or visionary LAPUTAN
- ridiculously small or inadequate, as a pay offer might be DERISORY

riding breeches JODHPURS

riding school MANÈGE

rifle See also **gun**
- carry a rifle diagonally across the body PORT
- rod for cleaning a rifle or inserting the charge into a muzzle-loading firearm RAMROD
- sighting lines, at right angles to each other, in a riflesight, theodolite, or the like CROSS WIRES, CROSS HAIRS

rift valley, trough formed between two roughly parallel geological faults GRABEN

rigging See **sail**

right See also **correct**
- right, granted temporarily, to buy or sell property, shares, or the like exclusively OPTION
- right, power, or authorization FACULTY
- right and proper, acceptable or satisfactory KOSHER
- right and proper, genuine PUKKA
- right-hand page of a book RECTO
- right-handed, on the right, or relating to the right side DEXTRAL
- right in law DROIT
- right in law, as to a property or claim TITLE
- right of an untried prisoner to appear before a judge or to be released HABEAS CORPUS
- right of the eldest son to inherit the entire estate PRIMOGENITURE
- right of the government to take over private land or property for public use, compensation usually being paid EMINENT DOMAIN
- right of the youngest son to inherit the estate ULTIMOGENITURE
- right of use over another person's land or property for specific purposes SERVITUDE, EASEMENT
- right or claim considered absolute or God-given DIVINE RIGHT
- right or possession, claimed as one's exclusive own PERQUISITE
- right or privilege, as conferred by rank, the law, or the like PREROGATIVE
- right or status, as of appearing in court, speaking at a meeting, and the like LOCUS STANDI
- right side of a ship STARBOARD
- right to freedom of speech, assembly, and the like CIVIL LIBERTY
- right to market a particular product in a given area CONCESSION
- right to the first offer of something, especially the chance of buying something such as a house FIRST REFUSAL
- right to the help, company, or affection of one's husband or wife CONSORTIUM
- right to the use of benefits from someone else's property USUFRUCT
- right to vote FRANCHISE, SUFFRAGE
- rights of a citizen within society CIVIL RIGHTS
- rights retained by the lessor or seller of a property RESERVATION
- at right angles PERPENDICULAR
- both right-handed and left-handed, able to use both hands equally expertly AMBIDEXTROUS
- champion of rights, especially for the oppressed TRIBUNE
- defend or enforce one's rights ASSERT
- give up a claim or right voluntarily WAIVE, RELINQUISH
- intrude slowly on the property or rights of someone else, trespass ENCROACH
- political principles, of a country, concerning basic rights and duties, either unwritten or embodied in statutes CONSTITUTION
- referring to rights, duties, and similar ethical concepts DEONTIC
- referring to rights that cannot be withdrawn or transferred INALIENABLE
- strip or deprive of something, such as clothes, rights, or property DIVEST

right (combining form) DEXT-, DEXTRO-, ORTHO-, RECT-

right of way THOROUGHFARE
- right of way or similar legal right over another person's land EASEMENT

rightful, in accordance with the law LEGITIMATE

rigidity and temporary insensitivity in reaction to shock RIGOR

rim or projecting edge, as on a wheel or beam, for strengthening, attaching, or the like FLANGE

rind, bark, husk, or similar outer layer CORTEX

ring, usually of gold, worn in a pierced ear to prevent the hole from sealing up SLEEPER
- ring engraved with initials or a design, originally for use as a seal SIGNET RING
- ring made of two interlocking rings GIMMAL
- ring of faint light, as around the moon when viewed through a haze CORONA
- ring of light around the sun or moon, as when viewed through mist AUREOLE
- ring of light or halo, especially in art GLORIA, GLORIOLE, GLORY, NIMBUS
- ring of metal, such as a key ring, consisting of a tight double coil of wire SPLIT RING
- ring of muscle constricting or relaxing a body passage, as at the mouth or the anus SPHINCTER
- ring of stone at the top of a column, directly beneath the capital ANNULET
- ring of stone or wooden pillars, from prehistoric cultures HENGE
- ring of three braided loops of different kinds of gold RUSSIAN WEDDING RING
- ring or eyelet, as of rope or rubber, for securing a sail, protecting a wire from chafing, or the like GROMMET
- ring or other ornament worn in the lip LABRET
- ring shape, shape of a ring doughnut TORUS
- ring-shaped ANNULAR, TOROID, CIRCULAR

- ring-shaped figure, space, marking, part, or object ANNULUS
- ring-shaped or coiled, as the frond of a young fern might be CIRCINATE
- ring with an oval-shaped gemstone or oval cluster of stones MARQUISE
- circular rim securing the gemstone in a ring or other piece of jewelry COLLET
- large ring, open at the top, through which a cable or rope is run on shipboard CHOCK
- made of or marked with rings, as an annelid worm might be ANNULATE
- medallion, on a brooch, ring, or the like, with a head in profile in raised relief CAMEO
- study of seals and signet rings SPHRAGISTICS

ring (combining form) GYRO-, CIRC-

ringing, loud or repeated metallic noise CLANGOR
- ringing of bells or chimes using all possible variations CHANGE RINGING

ringworm, athlete's foot, or similar fungal skin disease TINEA, DERMATOPHYTOSIS

rinsing - kitchen utensil for rinsing or draining, consisting of a perforated bowl COLANDER

Rio de Janeiro - person born or living in Rio de Janeiro CARIOCA

riot with much noise and disorder TUMULT, MELEE
- break up a riot or drive off the rioters DISPERSE
- encourage or provoke unrest, a riot, or the like FOMENT
- suppress something forcibly, such as a riot QUELL

riotous and uninhibited, as a drunken party might be BACCHANALIAN, BACCHANT, BACCHANTIC, BACCHIC

ripe and sweet, as a fruit might be MELLOW

rippling, swaying, pulsing, or other wavelike movement UNDULATION

rise See also **increase**
- rise, climb ASCEND
- rise above or extend beyond the limits of TRANSCEND
- rise above, overcome SURMOUNT
- rise and fall with a strong regular rhythm, as waves do in the open sea SURGE, HEAVE, SWELL
- rise and float in the air, apparently in defiance of gravity LEVITATE
- rise or increase INCREMENT
- rise or increase that is very rapid UPSURGE
- rise steeply or suddenly, as prices might SKYROCKET, SOAR, SPIRAL
- rise up on its hind legs, as a horse might REAR UP
- rising and falling movement, as of waves UNDULATION
- rising again RESURGENT
- very fast, impressive, as a rise to fame might be METEORIC

risk, endanger IMPERIL, JEOPARDIZE
- risk, gamble, expose to danger HAZARD, VENTURE, BRAVE
- risk, threat, danger MENACE
- risk assessor, as for an insurance company UNDERWRITER
- risk everything on a single bet or chance GO NAP
- risk or danger associated with one's job or a specified activity OCCUPATIONAL HAZARD
- risk taking of a foolhardy kind, reckless and open disregard of danger TEMERITY
- risk to an insurance company based on a policyholder's possible dishonesty or carelessness MORAL HAZARD
- risky, insecure, or unstable PRECARIOUS, SHAKY
- risky buying and selling of a commodity in the hope of a large profit SPECULATION

ritual, custom, or ceremony marking a change of status in a person's life RITE OF PASSAGE
- ritual ban or restriction of something considered either too holy or too unholy TABOO
- ritual chanting of magic sounds or spells INCANTATION
- ritual or ceremony of admission, as to group membership INITIATION
- ritual or religious ceremony that is considered foolish and obscure MUMBO JUMBO
- ritual pouring of a liquid LIBATION
- ritual revel or celebration, typically marked by sexual acts and heavy drinking, in ancient Greek cults ORGY, BACCHANAL
- ritual washing ABLUTION
- designed to prevent or turn away evil, as a ritual ceremony might be APOTROPAIC
- mystical and obscure, as rituals might be OCCULT, ESOTERIC, ORPHIC

river See illustration, page 454
- river embankment, or landing place or pier LEVEE
- river of ice and snow moving slowly down a valley GLACIER
- river or stream flowing into a larger one TRIBUTARY
- river or stream flowing out of a lake EFFLUENT
- adjective for a river POTAMIC, FLUVIAL
- adjective for a river bank RIPARIAN
- area, typically triangular, at the branching mouth of a river DELTA
- branch of a river, especially in a delta, that flows away from it without returning DISTRIBUTARY
- dam in a river or canal to raise the water or regulate its flow WEIR
- flight of steps beside a river in India GHAT
- flow out of a valley to emerge into a more open area, as a river might DEBOUCH
- flow out or discharge at the mouth of a river DISEMBOGUE
- flowing together or meeting point of two or more rivers CONFLUENCE
- flowing with a violently agitated movement, as a river or stream might be TURBULENT
- follow a winding course, as some rivers do MEANDER
- formation of land, especially by deposition in a river ALLUVION
- gorge of a river, typically dry except after heavy rain WADI
- gorge with high walls, cut by a river CANYON, RAVINE, GULCH
- migrating down a river to the sea to breed, as some fishes are CATADROMOUS
- migrating up a river to breed, as salmon are ANADROMOUS
- mouth of a river, outlet for a channel, or the like DEBOUCHURE, EMBOUCHURE
- mouth or wide lower reaches of a river where it approaches or meets the sea ESTUARY
- muddy or cloudy, as a river might be TURBID
- name used formerly for a branch of a river that flows away but rejoins the main stream later ANABRANCH
- path along a canal or river, as used by horses pulling boats TOWPATH, BRIDLE PATH
- referring to a river whose direction is directly related to the original main slope of the land CONSEQUENT
- referring to a river that is a tributary of a consequent river SUBSEQUENT
- referring to a tributary river flowing in a direction opposite to a consequent river OBSEQUENT
- rippling or swirling movement in a river EDDY, PURL
- search the bed of a river, lake, or canal by trailing a hook or net along it DRAG, DREDGE
- section of a river where the flow is very strong and rough RAPIDS
- sediment of fine sand deposited in or by a river SILT
- small island, especially in a river AIT, EYOT
- small river or brook RIVULET

- small river or stream, as referred to in various regions BECK, BOURN, BURN, RILL, CREEK, RUNLET, RUNNEL
- small, swift-flowing mountain river or stream GILL
- source of a river HEADWATERS
- source of a river in the form of a spring FOUNTAINHEAD
- uninterrupted stretch of water on a river or canal REACH
- U-shaped bend in a river OXBOW
- usually dry river bed in an arid area of the Americas ARROYO
- valley or pass that no longer holds a river WIND GAP
- wave moving upstream on a river, as caused by tidal currents BORE, EAGRE

road, as across marshy ground, made of logs laid sideways CORDUROY ROAD
- road along the coast, often built into the side of a cliff CORNICHE
- road ascending a steep slope in a winding course SWITCHBACK
- road junction with an overpass and four curving and four straight access roads CLOVERLEAF
- road on which cars may not stop except in an emergency FREEWAY, THRUWAY, INTERSTATE
- road or passage from one point to another THOROUGHFARE
- road or railroad bridge, typically supported by a series of arches, as over a valley VIADUCT
- road or route deviating from the standard or direct one DETOUR
- road or similar area lined with shops and closed to motor vehicles MALL, PEDESTRIAN AREA
- road or track used for carrying boats or supplies between waterways PORTAGE
- road passing above another road OVERPASS, FLYOVER
- road surface consisting of small stones, commonly bound with tar MACADAM, TARMAC
- road that leads through traffic around congested areas BYPASS, RELIEF ROAD, BELTWAY
- road with a central barrier or strip of land dividing traffic moving in opposite directions DIVIDED HIGHWAY
- road with no exit, dead-end road CUL-DE-SAC, IMPASSE
- roadway or bridge, hinged near a weighted end so as to be raised or lowered BASCULE, DRAWBRIDGE
- arched or upwardly curved surface of a road CAMBER
- black, often syrupy, naturally occurring hydrocarbon mixture used in roadmaking and roofing BITUMEN, ASPHALT
- break up and loosen the surface of a road, topsoil, a field, or the like SCARIFY
- broad city road or avenue, especially in Paris BOULEVARD
- broad road or square, especially in a city CONCOURSE
- central or highest part of a cambered road CROWN
- circular one-way road around a central island at a road junction ROUNDABOUT, ROTARY
- grassy border of a road VERGE
- gravel, rock chips, or the like used as foundation for a road or railroad track BALLAST
- hump built across a road to limit the speed of vehicles SLEEPING POLICEMAN
- junction between a turnpike and another road INTERCHANGE
- junction where two or more roads meet CROSSROADS, INTERSECTION
- major road linking towns or cities ARTERY, TRUNK ROAD
- minor or side road BYROAD
- narrow one-way road connecting a turnpike with another road ACCESS ROAD
- raised roadway, as across water or marshland CAUSEWAY
- reflector set in a road at intervals to indicate traffic lanes at night CAT'S-EYE
- relating to traveling or roads

River

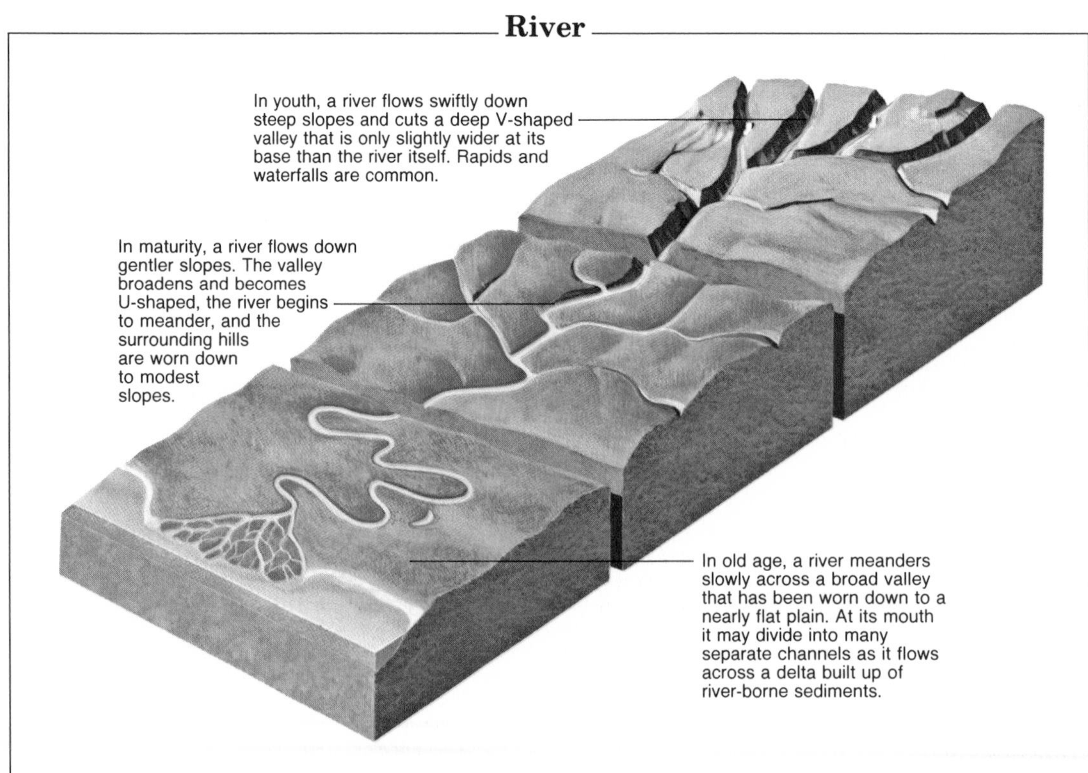

VIATIC
- secondary road linking smaller communities with a trunk road or turnpike FEEDER
- sloping section or incline, as of a road or railroad track GRADIENT
- small street behind a residential road, formerly containing stables, now usually converted to small houses MEWS, BACK STREET, ALLEY
- subsidiary road, leading to a sandbank, built at a corner on a steep slope, to avert accidents if drivers lose control ESCAPE ROAD
- thin coating of ice, as on a road GLAZE ICE, BLACK ICE
- turnpike or fast road for motor vehicles only, in various countries AUTOBAHN, AUTOROUTE, AUTOSTRADA, EXPRESSWAY, FREEWAY, PARKWAY
- very sharp bend in a road, as on a mountainside HAIRPIN
- winding or twisting, as a mountain road might be TORTUOUS

roast - moisten roasting meat with melted fat or sauce BASTE

roasting appliance fitted with a rotating spit ROTISSERIE
- roasting spit or skewer BROACH, BROCHETTE

rob See also **steal**
- rob by force, as in wartime PLUNDER, PILLAGE, LOOT, RAVAGE, DESPOIL, RANSACK, MARAUD
- rob or deprive of DISPOSSESS, RELIEVE

robber in an armed band in the hills in India or Myanmar DACOIT
- rob by plunder PILLAGE
- robber or bandit BRIGAND
- robber who formerly held up coaches or travelers HIGHWAYMAN

robbery and destruction PILLAGE, DEPREDATION, PLUNDER, SPOLIATION
- robbery of public, private, or company funds entrusted to one EMBEZZLEMENT, MALVERSATION, PECULATION
- robbery or large theft HEIST
- robbery or misappropriation of property left in one's care CONVERSION
- involved in a robbery or other crime IMPLICATED
- proceeds of a robbery LOOT, HAUL, BOOTY

robot or robotlike person behaving mechanically as if not under his or her own control AUTOMATON, ZOMBIE
- having certain robotlike or electronically enhanced functions, as some science-fiction characters and creatures are BIONIC
- person with certain robotlike or other artificial body parts or body implants CYBORG

robust, lusty, or coarsely humorous RABELAISIAN

rock See chart, page 456, and also **geology, gemstone,** and chart at **precious stones**
- rock, stones, or soil covering a mineral vein or archeological stratum OVERBURDEN
- rock base lying under topsoil, loose sand or the like BEDROCK
- rock cavity lined with crystals pointing inward GEODE
- rock containing metal or mineral deposits LODE
- rock-forming mineral of a common kind, consisting of any of various types of aluminum silicate FELDSPAR
- rock fragment CLAST
- rock fragment of medium size COBBLE
- rock fragments, rubble DEBRIS
- rock fragments or rubble at the foot of a hill or cliff SCREE, TALUS
- rock-hurling weapon of various kinds in ancient warfare CATAPULT, BALLISTA, ONAGER, MANGONEL, TREBUCHET, TREBUCKET
- rock layer STRATUM
- rock mass or mountain peak that is steep and pointed AIGUILLE
- rock or pile of stones on a hilltop TOR
- rock painting, carving, or inscription from ancient or prehistoric times PETROGLYPH
- rock projecting beyond a cliff face OVERHANG
- rock shaped in a large, usually upright, block MONOLITH
- rocky cliff or peak CRAG
- rocky plateau with distinct borders, or a distinct mountain group in a chain MASSIF
- rocky ridge of land jutting into the sea PROMONTORY
- basin or layer of porous rock, between layers of hard rock, in which water is trapped ARTESIAN BASIN
- crack in the earth's crust and resulting shift and discontinuity of the rocks on either side FAULT
- cross section of the earth's crust showing rock and soil layers PROFILE
- crust of porous rock formed from mineral deposits around a geyser or hot spring SINTER
- delicate curving decoration of rock fragments or shells, used in rococo design ROCAILLE
- having small bubbles or cavities, as some rocks are POROUS, CELLULAR
- intensely folded rock formation displaced from its site of origin by the forces causing the folding NAPPE
- lacking a crystalline structure, as a rock or chemical might be AMORPHOUS
- narrow layer of rock LAMINA
- oval cavity, originally a bubble, in lava rock, often filled with quartz or mineral crystals AMYGDULE
- pillar or cone of rocky lime deposit hanging from the roof of a cave STALACTITE
- pillar or cone of rocky lime deposit rising from the floor of a cave STALAGMITE
- rubbing down or wearing away of rock through friction, as by wind-blown sand ATTRITION
- small lump of a mineral or rock, typically found in a different kind of rock NODULE
- wear or rub away, as rock might ABRADE, CORRADE
- splitting or flaking easily, as some rocks are SPATHIC

rock (combining form) -LITE, -LITH-, LITHO-, PETRO-

rocket See also **missile**
- rocket, shell, missile, bullet, or other object fired or hurled PROJECTILE
- rocket engine used to slow down or reverse a missile, spacecraft, or the like BRAKING ROCKET, RETROROCKET, RETRO
- rocket fuel, explosive charge, or similar agent generating thrust PROPELLANT
- rocket propelled by successive firings MULTISTAGE ROCKET, STEP ROCKET
- rocket that supplements the main power system of a jet or spacecraft, often as the first stage of a multistage rocket BOOSTER
- curved flight path of a rocket, ball, or the like TRAJECTORY
- spin or wobble in flight, as a rocket or aircraft might YAW
- supporting tower or scaffolding for a rocket on the launching pad GANTRY

rococo - decoration of or resembling rock fragments or shells, used in rococo design ROCAILLE

rod, forked stick, or the like that supposedly quivers or dips when held above ground containing water or minerals DIVINING ROD, DOWSING ROD
- rod for cleaning a rifle or inserting the charge into a muzzle-loading firearm RAMROD
- rod for marking positions in surveying RANGING POLE
- rod or pin holding a spool or bobbin, as in a spinning machine SPINDLE
- rod or staff carried as an emblem

ROCKS AND MINERALS

ROCKS AND ROCK TERMS

agglomerate	rock composed of volcanic fragments
aggregate	rock of mixed minerals or separable fragments
basalt	dark, fine-grained, hard extrusive rock
breccia	rock composed of angular fragments
calcite/ calcspar	white calcium mineral that is the main constituent of limestone, chalk, and marble
conglomerate/ pudding stone	rock composed of rounded rock fragments cemented together
detritus	mineral particles derived from rocks by weathering and erosion
dolomite	type of limestone found in the Dolomites, in north Italy
erratic	large fragment of rock that is different from surrounding rock types
extrusive rock	fine-grained igneous rock that has cooled and solidified on the earth's surface or on the seabed
gabbro	coarse-grained igneous rock containing the same minerals as basalt
gneiss	metamorphic rock with alternating bands of light and dark material
igneous rock	rock that has solidified from molten rock
intrusive rock	coarse-grained igneous rock that has solidified in cracks or cavities in existing rocks
lodestone	highly magnetic rock
metamorphic rock	rock that has been altered in chemical composition or texture by high temperatures or pressures, or both
obsidian	hard, black volcanic glass used to make cutting tools in prehistoric times
oolite/oolitic limestone	limestone composed mainly of tiny rounded particles
outcrop	section of a rock formation exposed at the earth's surface or covered only by a thin layer of soil or the like
plutonic rock	intrusive rock formed at great depth
pumice stone	rock with many small cavities formed from lava
sarsen stone/ druid stone	sandstone block found on the chalk of southern England, and probably a remnant of an eroded sandstone layer
schist	metamorphic rock with minerals arranged in wavy bands, which split easily
sedimentary rock	rock formed from particles of preexisting rock, or other material, deposited by water, wind, or ice
shale	sedimentary rock formed from clay, mud, or silt, with narrow layers
tufa	calcium carbonate deposited around a spring
vesicle	small cavity in a rock formed by a bubble of gas in the rock in its molten state

MINERALS AND THEIR USES AND PRODUCTS

alabaster	sculpture, ornaments
albite	glass, ceramics
anhydrite	cement, fertilizers
azurite	copper
bauxite	aluminum
blue john	jewelry and ornaments
calcite/ calcspar/ Iceland spar	cement, plaster, paint, glass, fertilizer, optical instruments
cassiterite	tin
cinnabar	mercury
corundum	abrasives, gemstones
dolomite	cement, building stone
fluorite	glass, enamel, jewelry
galena	lead
graphite/ plumbago	lead pencils
gypsum	plaster of paris, cement, blackboard chalk
halite/ rock salt	common salt, chlorine, pottery glazes, glass
hematite	iron
jet	jewelry
kaolinite	porcelain, coating, and filler in making paper
malachite	copper, ornaments
microlite	glass, ceramics
muscovite mica/ isinglass	insulators, lubricants, paints
orthoclase	glass, ceramics
pyrite/ fool's gold/iron pyrite	sulfur, iron
quartz	abrasives, cement, glass, gemstones
rutile	titanium
serpentine	ornaments. A variety is known as asbestos.
sphalerite	zinc
talc	talcum powder, electrical insulators

of authority or office VERGE
- rod-shaped BACILLARY, BACILLIFORM, PENICILLARY, VIRGATE, VIRGULATE
- bundle of rods with an ax, carried as a symbol of the magistrates' authority in ancient Rome FASCES

rodents See illustration

roe of a lobster or crab, pink when cooked CORAL
- roe of the male fish, soft roe MILT
- salted female roe of fish such as sturgeon, eaten as a delicacy CAVIAR

rogue, adventurer PICARO, PICAROON

role or public face that a person adopts in social situations, "mask" PERSONA
- role or status of a plant or animal within its ecological community NICHE
- brief role or small part played by a famous actor or actress CAMEO ROLE
- playing or expected to play similar roles continually TYPECAST

roll, lie, or toss about in WELTER, WALLOW
- roll heavily or noisily along TRUNDLE
- roll of cloth BOLT
- roll of coins wrapped in paper ROULEAU
- roll of paper, especially newsprint, for use in a rotary printing press WEB
- roll of parchment or paper used for written documents SCROLL
- roll or breadstick made into a long sandwich HERO, SUBMARINE, GRINDER
- roll up a flag, umbrella, or the like FURL
- rolled up or coiled CONVOLUTE, CONVOLUTED
- rolling or revolving movement VOLUTION

roller of a typewriter PLATEN
- device for squeezing water from wet laundry by pressing it between rollers WRINGER, MANGLE

Roman See chart, page 458
- Roman and Greek culture as a subject of study HUMANITIES
- Roman army unit, originally of 100 troops CENTURY
- Roman body armor LORICA
- Roman building, divided by columns into a long nave and side aisles, used for public assembly and administration BASILICA

Roman Catholic See chart, page 459
- Roman Catholic in 16th- to 18th-century England who defied the law requiring attendance at Church of England services RECUSANT

romance in verse or prose, especially as written in the Middle Ages GEST

romantic-idealistic, but impractical or absentminded QUIXOTIC
- writer or artist favoring a real-life representation of everyday subject matter rather than a romantic approach REALIST

romanticism - style and artistic principles marked by simple and regular form and by restraint in emotions and in association of ideas, in contrast to romanticism CLASSICISM

Rome - arch of spears through which the defeated enemies of ancient Rome had to walk as a gesture of submission YOKE
- chief of the seven hills of Rome PALATINE
- relating to the civilization of ancient Greece and Rome CLASSICAL
- underground galleries and tunnels with niches or ledges for graves, especially those in Rome CATACOMBS

roof See illustration, page 460
- roof, or structure on a roof, in the shape of a dome CUPOLA
- roof at the entrance of a building, providing sheltered access PORTE COCHERE
- roof of the mouth PALATE
- roofing slate with one side left rough RAG
- roof with a ridge, and a gable at each end SADDLE ROOF, SADDLEBACK
- roof with double-sloping sides, the lower slope being steeper in each case CURB ROOF
- roof with two sloping sides of equal angle and size SPAN ROOF
- arched roof or ceiling, typically of stone or masonry VAULT
- apartment on the roof or top floor of a large building PENTHOUSE
- beam in the frame of a vaulted roof LAMELLA
- black, sticky, hydrocarbon mixture used in roadmaking and roofing BITUMEN, ASPHALT
- circular or crescent-shaped opening in a roof LUNETTE
- covering of overlapping boards, as for a roof or wall WEATHERBOARDING, CLAPBOARDS, SIDING
- gutter in the eaves of a roof CULLIS
- horizontal beam forming the ridge of a roof, to which the rafters are attached RIDGEPOLE
- horizontal bracket on the top of a wall, for supporting a roof HAMMER BEAM
- horizontal beams supporting the rafters of a roof PURLINS
- metal strips or similar strong weatherproof material covering the joints and angles of a roof FLASHING
- ornamental ridge running along the top of a roof or wall CRESTING
- pair of sloping wooden beams, often curved, helping to support a roof CRUCKS
- room just under a pitched roof

Rodents

GARRET, ATTIC
- slanting upper part of a roof or wall COPING
- sloping beam forming part of the framework of a roof RAFTER
- sloping roof PITCHED ROOF
- small turret or spire, as on the roof of a Gothic building PINNACLE
- supporting framework of struts, or the like, as for a roof TRUSS
- triangular upper wall at the edge of a pitched roof GABLE
- upright pole or post, as for supporting a roof STANCHION
- wall or railing on the edge of a balcony or roof PARAPET

rook - adjective for a rook or related bird CORVID
- flock or family of rooks PARLIAMENT, CLAMOR, BUILDING

room for maneuver, margin for error, freedom within limits LEEWAY, LATITUDE, PLAY
- room for play or parties RUMPUS ROOM
- room in a church for storing sacred vessels and vestments SACRISTY, VESTRY
- room or attic just under a pitched roof GARRET
- room or building where records are stored ARCHIVES
- room or cell in a dungeon, entered

ROMAN TERMS

aedile	official responsible for public works
agnomen	additional, usually fourth, name as bestowed on military heroes
atrium	open courtyard within a house or villa
augur/ auspex	religious official who interpreted omens, soothsayer
basilica	large public hall or court
calends	first day of the month
censor	either of two officials who were responsible for the public census, and public morals and behavior
centurion	officer commanding a small military unit
cognomen	third name of a citizen
cohort	subdivision of a legion, numbering 300 to 600 men
consul	either of two chief officials of the republic, elected for one year
curia	senate house
decimate	kill every tenth man in a cowardly or mutinous military unit
denarius	silver coin issued by magistrates
fasces	bundle of rods tied around the handle of an ax, carried before magistrates as a symbol of authority
forum	marketplace, public square, and place for political assembly
haruspex	priest who foretold the future by examining animal entrails
ides	13th or 15th day of the month
lares and penates	household gods
legion	basic military unit, numbering 3,000 to 6,000 men
lemures	unfriendly spirits of the dead
lictor	official who carried the fasces
lupercalia	fertility festival of the god Lupercus, celebrated in February
manes	friendly spirits of the dead; deified souls of ancestors
maniple	subdivision of a cohort, 60 to 120 men
nomen	second or family name of a citizen
nones	ninth day before the ides of a month
patrician	noble
plebeians/ plebs	ordinary citizens, the masses, the common people
pontifex	priest of high status
praenomen	first or personal name of a citizen
praetor	leading magistrate of the republic
praetorian guard	elite troops of the emperors
proletarian	citizen of the lowest class
quaestor	financial and administrative official
retiarius	gladiator armed with a net and trident rather than a sword
saturnalia	bawdy festival of the god Saturn, celebrated in December
sesterce	quarter of a denarius
SPQR	"the Senate and the People of Rome" (senatus populusque Romanus)
testudo	"turtle," siege device formed by interlocking shields held above legionaries' heads to protect them against missiles
thermae	public baths
tribune	official elected by the plebeians to champion their rights against the patricians
triclinium	couch around three sides of a table, on which Romans reclined at meals; a dining room
triumvir	any of three joint rulers

only through a trapdoor in the ceiling OUBLIETTE
- room or shed built onto the side of a house LEAN-TO
- room or vault housing the bones or bodies of dead people CHARNEL HOUSE
- room or wardrobe for storing clothes GARDEROBE
- room such as a private study where one can remain undisturbed, den SANCTUM

ROMAN CATHOLIC TERMS

aggiornamento	modernization of the ideas and administration of the church
beatification	official recognition and proclaiming of a dead person to be blessed, usually preliminary to canonization
breviary	book of daily prayers for the canonical hours; or these prayers
bull	edict issued by the pope, often sealed with a bulla, or lead seal
canonization	official recognition and proclaiming of a dead person to be a saint
Codex Juris Canonici	code of law governing the church since 1918
conclave	meeting of cardinals to elect a new pope
consistory	meeting of the pope and cardinals to announce papal acts officially
curia	papal court and its officials
decretal	papal decree deciding a point of canon law
de fide	referring to a doctrine that is an article of faith
devil's advocate/ promoter of the faith/promotor fidei	official appointed to argue against a proposed beatification or canonization
Dom	title given to monks of certain orders, especially Benedictines
encyclical	letter sent by the pope to bishops in all countries
extreme unction/ Sacrament of the Sick	ceremony in which a priest anoints and prays for a very ill or dying person
host/eucharistic host	wafer consecrated and consumed during Mass
Index Librorum Prohibitorum/ Index	official list of books banned by the Church
indulgence	reduction in or cancellation of the punishment, especially in purgatory, for a sin, after it has been forgiven
infallibility	principle of the pope's unfailingly correct judgment in matters of faith and morals, accepted by the First Vatican Council, in 1870
limbo	eternal home of the souls of unbaptized infants, and of the just who died before the birth of Christ
metropolitan	archbishop with authority over other bishops
Monsignor	title or form of address for certain church officials
mortal sin	willfully committed serious sin, seen as involving spiritual death and loss of divine grace
nihil obstat	censor's approval of a book, certifying that it is doctrinally acceptable
novena	nine-day period of prayer
ordo	calendar with details for services for each day of the year
Propaganda Fide/ Propaganda	Vatican department in charge of training, placing, and supervising missionaries
purgatory	condition or temporary home in which the souls of the dead suffer remorse for their venial sins, and are purified for heaven
requiem	Mass for a dead person
Rota	supreme ecclesiastical court
sodality	society or association of lay members of the church for devotional or charitable purposes
transubstantiation	doctrine that the bread and wine used during Mass actually turn into the body and blood of Christ
Tridentine Mass	Mass in the form used from 1570 until recent times
Venerable	title given to a dead person who is at the first level of sainthood
venial sin	sin that is not fully evil, and does not deprive the soul of God's grace
Vulgate	4th-century Latin translation of the Bible by Saint Jerome

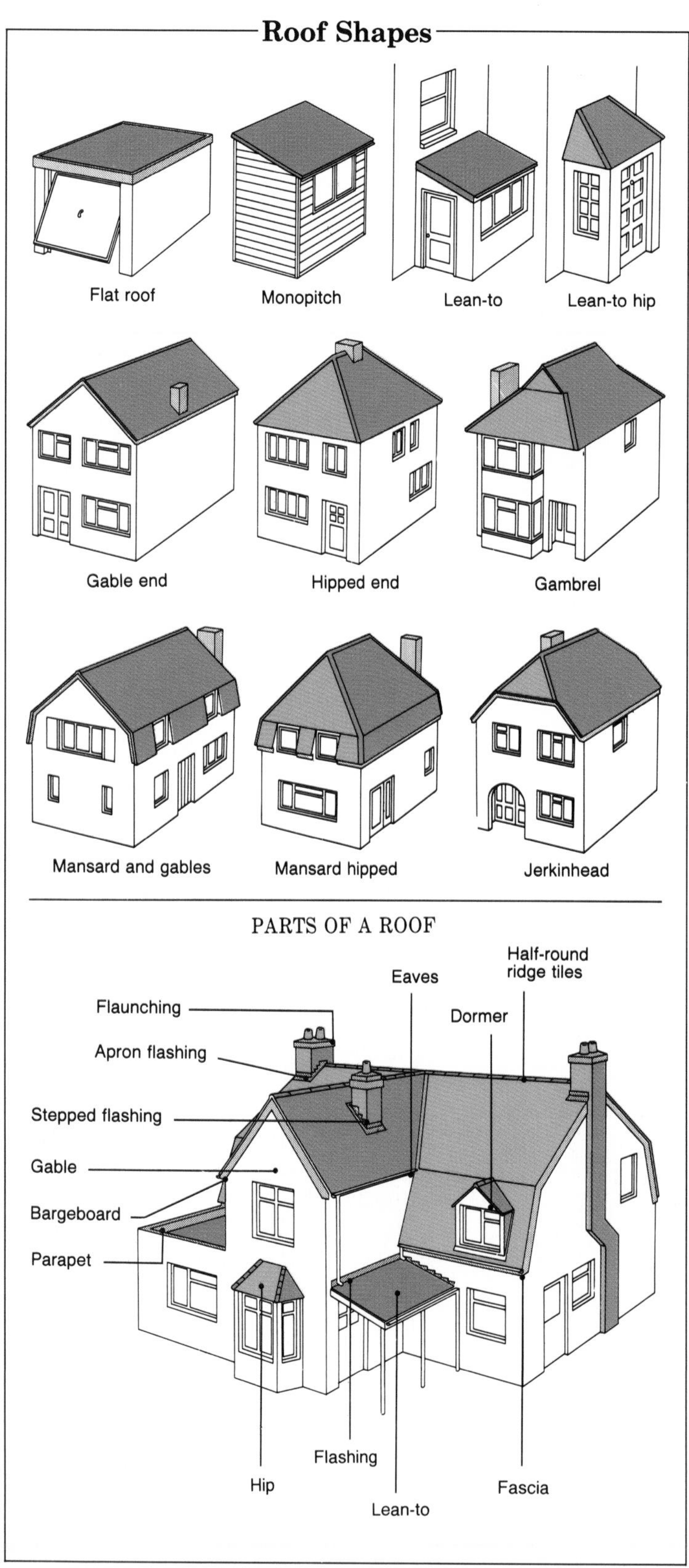

- "room to live," space to expand, especially as used in Nazi philosophy to justify invasions and genocide LEBENSRAUM
- room with boiler, washing equipment, and the like, often used for storage UTILITY ROOM
- alcove in a larger room for informal meals DINETTE
- circular, often domed, building or room ROTUNDA
- connect, as two rooms might, through a shared door, passage, or the like COMMUNICATE
- darkened room into which an image from the outside is projected through an opening or lens CAMERA OBSCURA
- dining room or hall in a college or monastery REFECTORY
- dining room with low tables and couches, especially in ancient Rome TRICLINIUM
- entrance and reception room of a hotel, theater, or the like LOBBY, FOYER
- forming a set, especially of rooms EN SUITE
- furnished accommodation consisting of a single room for both sleeping and living in STUDIO APARTMENT, EFFICIENCY APARTMENT, EFFICIENCY
- glassed-in room or porch for sunning oneself, as in a sanatorium SOLARIUM
- hot-air room for sweat baths, especially in ancient Rome SUDATORIUM
- large drawing room or hall for receiving guests SALON
- meeting room or hall of a guild or corporation in former times GUILDHALL
- open, central room or court of a house, especially in ancient Rome ATRIUM
- private cabin or room on a passenger ship STATEROOM
- reading room, library, or the like ATHENAEUM
- separate room or section, especially of a railroad carriage COMPARTMENT
- sleeping room with many beds, in a school or the like DORMITORY
- small dining room, usually on an upper floor CENACLE
- small room, cupboard, or cabin on a ship CUDDY
- small room off a kitchen, for dishwashing, storing pots and pans, and the like SCULLERY
- small room partitioned off, as for sleeping, changing, or washing CUBICLE
- small room serving as an en-

trance to a reception room ANTECHAMBER, ANTEROOM, VESTIBULE
- small separate room or table section in a library, used for private study CARREL
- smoking room or coffee house with couches, in former times DIVAN
- snug or cramped room, cupboard, or compartment CUBBYHOLE
- woman's private sitting room, dressing room, or bedroom BOUDOIR, BOWER

room and board, as in a small European hotel PENSION

roomy, large, bulky, or baggy VOLUMINOUS
- roomy, spacious CAPACIOUS, COMMODIOUS

rooster's comb or similar outgrowth, normal or abnormal, on an animal, a seed, the skin, or the like CARUNCLE
- name for a rooster, as in fables CHANTICLEER

root See illustration
- root, especially of ginger RACE
- root on some bulbs, serving to draw the bulb downward in the soil CONTRACTILE ROOT
- root or underground stem that is swollen and bears buds, as of the potato or dahlia TUBER
- root that grows from and supports the stem or trunk of a plant, as in corn or the mangrove tree BUTTRESS ROOT, PROP ROOT
- root valued in the East for its assumed medicinal properties GINSENG
- rootlike stem growing under the ground, as in the iris or grasses RHIZOME
- rootstock of a type of iris, used in making perfume ORRIS
- adjective for a root RADICAL
- determine the root of a number EXTRACT
- located or active in the air, as some plants' roots are AERIAL
- main root of certain plants, growing straight downward and giving off small lateral roots TAPROOT
- mathematical extraction of the root of a number or quantity EVOLUTION
- part of a plant embryo that develops into the main root RADICLE
- plant with a forked root, formerly used as a narcotic drug and thought to shriek when pulled from the ground MANDRAKE
- tropical plant whose starchy root is eaten as a vegetable, and used as the basis of tapioca CASSAVA, MANIOC
- uproot, pull up by or as if by the roots DERACINATE

root (combining form) RADIC-, -RAC-, RHIZ-, RHIZO-

rooted, fixed, immobile, as barnacles are SESSILE
- rooted firmly and too deeply to be removed, as incorrigible vices are INERADICABLE, INGRAINED

rootless, separated from one's homeland, social origins, familiar culture, or natural environment DERACINATED, DÉRACINÉ, ALIENATED

rope, chain, or the like, as used for steadying a load or mooring an aerial or tent GUY, STAY
- rope, used on ships, of two twisted strands MARLINE
- rope at the front of a boat for tying it up PAINTER
- rope between the top of a boom

Roots

Roots—the underground (and sometimes aboveground) parts of plants—have two purposes: They serve as anchors, and they absorb nourishing substances.

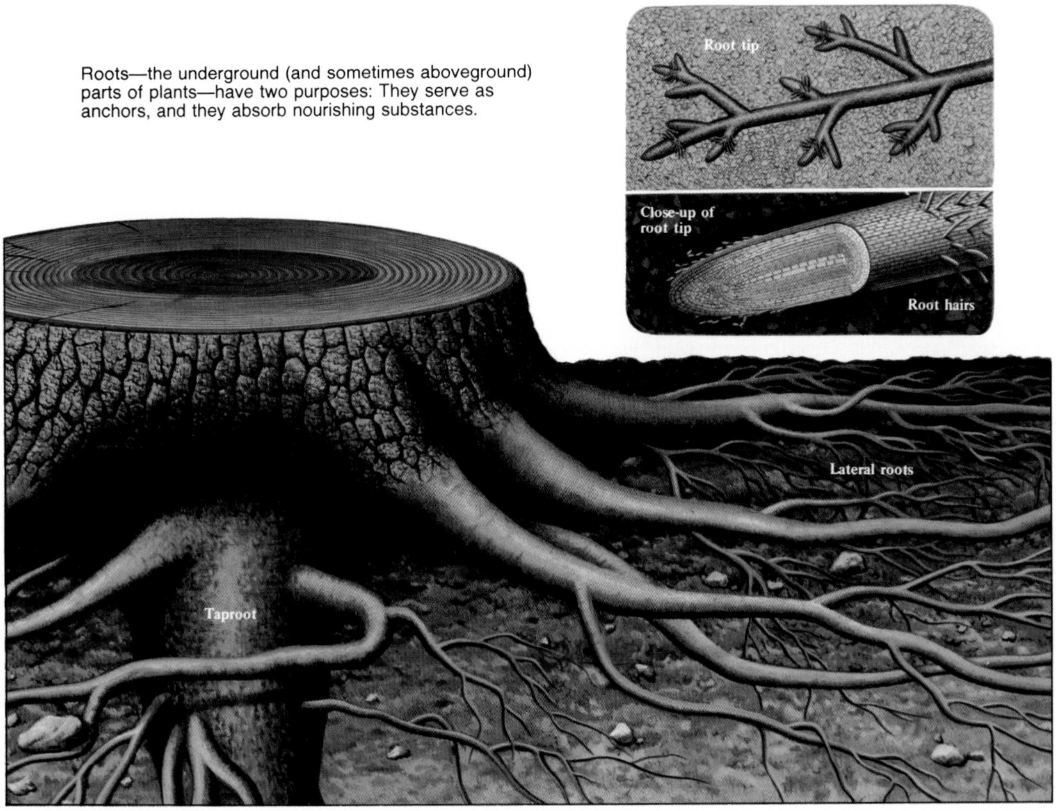

Root tip
Close-up of root tip
Root hairs
Lateral roots
Taproot

or gaff and the deck VANG
- rope for raising or lowering a sail or flag HALYARD
- rope for restricting an animal to a small range of movement or grazing area TETHER
- rope for securing a horse or cow, or for a noose in hanging HALTER
- rope for tying together the legs of a horse or cow HOBBLE
- rope handrail on a ship's ladder or gangplank MANROPE
- rope ladder with rigid rungs JACOB'S LADDER
- rope ladder with two or three rungs of metal or wood, used in mountaineering ÉTRIER
- rope or cable for tying up or towing a ship HAWSER, TOWLINE, WARP
- rope or chain attached to and controlling the lower corner or corners of a sail SHEET
- rope or cord used for tying or binding LASHING
- rope passed over a beam, as on a mast, and used for hoisting GANTLINE
- rope sling for sliding or lifting tree trunks, barrels, or the like PARBUCKLE
- rope trailing from a balloon or airship, used for mooring or braking DRAGROPE
- rope with attached weights, used in South America for catching cattle or game by snaring the legs BOLA
- ropes, cables, and the like supporting or controlling the masts, spars, and sails of a sailing ship RIGGING
- ropes across the sail of a ship, forming a rope ladder RATLINE
- ropes in a ship's rigging CORDAGE
- ropes or cables supporting the mast on a ship or boat SHROUDS
- bind a rope end with twine to stop it fraying WHIP
- coconut-husk fiber, as used for ropes and matting COIR
- descend, as from a cliff top or helicopter, by means of a supporting rope around one's body ABSEIL
- fasten a rope, as on a ship or in mountaineering BELAY
- fiber used in making ropes, or the plant that yields the fiber SISAL, JUTE
- iron device with hooks, attached to a rope, thrown onto a wall, nearby ship, or the like to grip it and create a connection GRAPNEL, GRAPPLING
- join two strips of film, rope, or the like at the ends SPLICE
- lifting machine, typically using ropes for hoisting WINDLASS
- loop in a rope for hitching to a hook, as on shipboard CAT'S-PAW
- loop in a rope, or slack middle part of a rope BIGHT
- loop or coil, as of rope HANK
- peg or crosspiece, attached to a rope, chain, or the like, used for fastening or to prevent slipping TOGGLE
- relating to rope, string, or cable FUNICULAR
- restrict the movement of a horse or farm animal by means of a rope, hobble or tether HAMSHACKLE
- short rope or nautical cord, as for fastening sails LANYARD
- strand twisted with others to make wool, rope, or the like PLY
- thread a rope through a ring, pulley, or the like REEVE
- T-shaped bar or post for securing ropes, as on a ship's deck CLEAT
- willow twig used as a rope WITHE, WITHY

rose of Asian origin with fragrant red or pink petals, used in making perfume DAMASK ROSE
- rose of Sharon ALTHAEA
- rose-shaped design or structure, such as a pleated ribbon badge ROSETTE
- rose that blooms twice or more during a season REMONTANT ROSE
- climbing or sprawling rose bearing clusters of small flowers RAMBLER
- cultivated hybrid rose bearing abundant clusters of flowers FLORIBUNDA
- having prickles or thorns, as a rose is ACULEATE
- perfume or fragrant oil extracted from petals, especially rose petals ATTAR
- wild rose with pinkish petals and fragrant leaves SWEETBRIER, EGLANTINE

rose (combining form) RHOD-, RHODO-

rosy, reddish, ruddy RUBICUND

rot, become gangrenous or ulcerous FESTER, SUPPURATE, MATURATE, PUSTULATE
- rot or decay DECOMPOSE, PUTREFY, PERISH

rotating blade, as on a propeller, windmill, or turbine VANE
- rotating fireworks or jets of water GIRANDOLE
- rotating flow or rush, such as a whirlwind or whirlpool VORTEX

rotation - force, or moment of a force, tending to produce rotation TORQUE
- straight line around which an object rotates, as in geometry AXIS

rotation(combining form) GYRO-

rotten, decayed, as bad teeth or bones become CARIOUS
- rotten, full of pus, as a wound might be MATURATING, PURULENT, PUSTULATING, SUPPURATING
- rotten, spoiled by decay PERISHED
- rotten, ulcerous, dying, as a body part might be FESTERING, GANGRENOUS
- rotten and foul-smelling DECOMPOSED, FECULENT, FETID, PUTRID, PUTRIFIED, RANK, HIGH, OFF
- rotten, off, bitter-tasting or -smelling, as bacon fat might be RANCID

rotting and death of a limb, body tissue, or the like, typically through a failure of blood supply GANGRENE, NECROSIS, MORTIFICATION
- rotting flesh of a dead animal CARRION
- rotting of teeth or bones CARIES
- rotting or decaying smell, as from a swamp or rubbish heap EFFLUVIUM
- hyena, vulture, insect, or the like that feeds on dead animals, rotting meat, or other decaying organic matter SCAVENGER

rotting matter (combining form) SAPR-, SAPRO-

rouge - apply rouge to the face coarsely RADDLE

rough, gruff, abrupt, discourteously blunt BRUSQUE, CURT, ABRASIVE, CRUSTY
- rough, harsh, or throaty, as some speech sounds seem GUTTURAL, RASPING
- rough, unrestrained, and noisy, usually in a playful manner BOISTEROUS
- rough and harsh, as sandpaper is or as someone's manner might be ABRASIVE
- rough drawing, plan, or sketch of something DRAFT
- rough edge or bump, as on processed metal, or a burl on a tree trunk BURR
- rough or disturbed, as water might be CHOPPY, TURBULENT
- rough or grainy surface, as of leather or the like TEXTURE
- rough or jagged projection SNAG
- rough to the touch, horny or scaly, as hard dry skin might be SCABROUS
- roughened with a metal brush, as the plaster on a wall might be KEYED

rough-and-ready temporary device or substitute MAKESHIFT, STOPGAP

roughness or harshness, as of climate, mood, voice, or surface ASPERITY

roulette - bet in roulette made on any one single number EN PLEIN, PLEIN, STRAIGHT UP

- bet in roulette made on four numbers forming a square CARRÉ
- bet in roulette made on numbers 1 to 18 MANQUE, LOW
- bet in roulette made on numbers 19 to 36 PASSE, HIGH
- bet in roulette made on numbers 1 to 12 PREMIÈRE DOUZAINE, FIRST DOZEN
- bet in roulette made on numbers 13 to 24 DEUXIÈME DOUZAINE, SECOND DOZEN
- bet in roulette made on numbers 25 to 36 TROISIÈME DOUZAINE, THIRD DOZEN
- bet in roulette made on six numbers forming two rows TRAVERSAL PLEIN
- bet in roulette made on the 12 numbers of the column beginning with 1 PREMIÈRE COLONNE, FIRST COLUMN
- bet in roulette made on the 12 numbers of the column beginning with 2 DEUXIÈME COLONNE, SECOND COLUMN
- bet in roulette made on the 12 numbers of the column beginning with 3 TROISIÈME COLONNE, THIRD COLUMN
- bet in roulette made on three numbers forming a row TRAVERSAL
- bet in roulette made on two numbers side by side À CHEVAL, CHEVAL
- bet in roulette that the winning number will be an even number PAIR
- bet in roulette that the winning number will be an odd number IMPAIR
- bet in roulette that the winning number will be black NOIR
- bet in roulette that the winning number will be red ROUGE
- call by the croupier to end the placing of bets for any one spin of the wheel RIEN NE VA PLUS
- call by the croupier to roulette players or other gamblers to place their bets FAITES VOS JEUX
- doubling-up system in gambling, especially in roulette MARTINGALE
- lay a bet against the bank in roulette, faro, or other gambling games PUNT

round object, ball SPHERE, ORB, GLOBE

round (combining form) CYCL-, CYCLO-, GLOB-, SPHER-

roundabout, long and indirect, as a trip argument might be CIRCUITOUS

rounded, bulging CONVEX, PROTUBERANT, GIBBOUS
- rounded, spherical GLOBULAR
- rounded line or shape, as of a whirlpool SPIRAL, HELIX, VOLUTE, WHORL

rouse to action, as by nagging or irritating GOAD, INCITE

route of principal importance in a transport system TRUNK LINE
- route or road deviating from the standard or direct one DETOUR
- route or road that bears the main flow of traffic, messages, or the like ARTERY
- route planned for a trip ITINERARY
- sail regularly over a particular route PLY

routine, mechanical repetition ROTE
- routine, mechanical, superficial, as a glance or smile might be PERFUNCTORY
- routine, pattern, or way of operating REGIMEN, MODUS OPERANDI, MO
- routine and boring STULTIFYING
- routine or monotonous task TREADMILL

row of columns or trees positioned at regular intervals COLONNADE
- row or level, as of theater seating, in a rising series TIER

row, line (combining form) STYCH-, STYCHOUS

row cart, hand-activated toy vehicle IRISH MAIL, HOLLÄNDER

rowing - catch up and touch the boat ahead, in university rowing races BUMP
- covered section at the front or back of a racing boat in rowing CANVAS
- mishandle the oar in rowing, as by striking the water with the blade when recovering from a stroke CATCH A CRAB
- oar or small racing boat used in rowing SCULL
- oarsman nearest the cox at the stern of a racing crew, setting the tempo STROKE
- person who steers the boat or directs the crew in rowing races COXSWAIN, COX
- turn the blade of the oar upright when rowing PEAK
- turn the blade of the oar horizontal between strokes in rowing FEATHER

rowing boat - bracket supporting a oarlock, projecting from the side of a racing or rowing boat OUTRIGGER, RIGGER
- light rowing boat, used in races, for a single oarsman WHERRY
- peg or pin, especially one used as an oarlock in the side of a rowing boat THOLE
- seat extending across a rowing boat, typically for the oarsman THWART
- spaces at the front and back of a rowing boat SHEETS

royal, dignified, or gracious REGAL
- royal attendant, formerly responsible for the horses of the royal household EQUERRY
- royal authority or power, or the symbol or insignia of it SCEPTER, DIADEM
- royal power, rank, or authority SOVEREIGNTY
- royal reception formerly held by a sovereign just after getting out of bed LEVEE
- royal seal on documents GREAT SEAL, PRIVY SEAL
- funds voted each year by parliament to maintain members of the royal family CIVIL LIST
- marriage between a royal or noble person and a partner of lower rank, with strict limitations on inheritance rights MORGANATIC MARRIAGE
- money voted by parliament for the running of the royal household PRIVY PURSE
- regularly and officially employed by the royal family IN ORDINARY

royalty - symbol of royalty in the form of a cross attached to a globe ORB
- symbol of royalty, or royal authority or power SCEPTER, DIADEM
- symbols or trappings, especially of royalty REGALIA

rub down a horse, groom CURRY
- rub or wear away, as by rust or acid CORRODE
- rub out, wipe out, erase EFFACE
- rub to produce a smooth and polished finish BURNISH, LEVIGATE
- rubbing against another person's body, as in a crowded bus, for sexual satisfaction FROTTAGE
- rubbing between two surfaces in contact, reducing or preventing slipping FRICTION
- rubbing or wearing away, as of rock during erosion ABRASION, CORRASION, ATTRITION
- lotion for rubbing onto the skin EMBROCATION, LINIMENT
- study of friction, rubbing, and lubrication TRIBOLOGY
- taking of a rubbing, as from a rough wooden surface, in art FROTTAGE
- wear away by, or as if by, rubbing ABRADE, CORRADE
- wear away or become tattered or irritated by rubbing CHAFE, FRAY, FRAZZLE

rubber for removing pencil marks or writing ERASER
- rubber or leather blade, fixed to a handle, for wiping liquid, as in cleaning windows SQUEEGEE
- rubber shoes worn over other shoes to keep them dry GALOSHES
- rubber suction cup fitted with a

handle, used for clearing blocked drains and pipes PLUNGER, PLUMBER'S HELPER
- rubbery latex substance used in electrical insulation and waterproofing GUTTA-PERCHA
- milky sap of certain plants, used in the manufacture of rubber LATEX
- raw or natural rubber INDIA RUBBER, CAOUTCHOUC
- resilient chemical polymer used as a rubber additive, in paints and varnishes, in electrical insulators, and in cosmetic surgery SILICONE
- treat rubber with sulfur, heat, and pressure to improve its strength VULCANIZE
- whitish or yellowish crinkly, raw rubber, as used on the soles of shoes CREPE RUBBER

rubbing, friction (combining form) TRIBO-, FROTT-

rubbish See also **nonsense**
- rubbish consisting of fragments of broken rocks or masonry BRASH, DEBRIS, RUBBLE
- rubbish heap or dunghill MIDDEN
- rubbish or scum produced in cooking, a chemical process, or the like OFFSCOURING
- furnace used for burning rubbish INCINERATOR
- search through rubbish or refuse for food or useful objects SCAVENGE
- waste products or slag from smelting, or stupid and worthless rubbish generally DROSS, RECREMENT

rubble, scattered remains, or the like of something broken DEBRIS, BRASH

rudder - crossbar on a rudder, to which the steering ropes or cables are attached YOKE
- socket, as for the rudder of a boat or the pin of a hinge GUDGEON
- upright pivot pin, as on a rudder or towing vehicle PINTLE

rude, abrupt, gruff, discourteously blunt BRUSQUE, CURT, TERSE, UNCEREMONIOUS, CRUSTY
- rude, abusive, or blasphemous language PROFANITY
- rude, impolite, or discourteous UNCIVIL, UNMANNERLY, ILL-BRED, ILL-MANNERED
- rude, in bad taste, improper, as indelicate behavior would be INDECOROUS, UNBECOMING, UNSEEMLY
- rude, obsessed with or dealing explicitly with excrement SCATOLOGICAL
- rude, obsessed with sexual matters PRURIENT
- rude, saucy and lively, broadly and lustily humorous BAWDY, RABELAISIAN, RACY, RAUNCHY, SALTY, RIBALD
- rude, uncultured, unpolished, or coarse AGRESTIC, CHURLISH, UNCOUTH
- rude in a cheeky, disrespectful way IRREVERENT
- rude in a coarse, unrefined way EARTHY
- rude in a contemptuous, insulting way CONTUMELIOUS, INSOLENT
- rude in a perverted or sick way DEPRAVED
- rude or indecent, especially through being sexually suggestive, as a poem or play might be SALACIOUS, LEWD, LUBRICIOUS, LASCIVIOUS
- rude or profane exclamation or oath EXPLETIVE
- rude sexual language BAWDRY
- dealing with rude and explicitly sexual material, as an X-rated movie would be PORNOGRAPHIC
- extremely rude, offensively coarse, outrageously vulgar UNPRINTABLE, SCURRILOUS, SCABROUS, OBSCENE, FESCENNINE
- fairly rude, rather dirty or vulgar SMUTTY, UNSAVORY
- mildly rude, slightly improper, off-color, as a joke might be RISQUÉ
- mildly rude, hinting at sexual matters, as a saucy remark might be SUGGESTIVE

rudeness or insult CONTUMELY

rug See also **carpet**
- rug of Asian origin, typically with a black-and-white pattern on a reddish background BOKHARA RUG
- Persian rug with an ornate border KIRMAN
- tapestry-woven rug of Asian origin KILIM

rugby - kick in rugby that sends the ball bouncing along the ground GRUBBER
- loose informal scrum in rugby MAUL, RUCK
- player of position in rugby providing the link between the scrum half and the other backs FLY HALF, STAND-OFF HALF, OUTSIDE HALF
- pretended pass in rugby to deceive an opponent DUMMY
- swerve suddenly when running in rugby, to evade an opponent JINK

ruin See also **destroy, destruction, damage**
- ruin, as caused by war HAVOC, DEVASTATION, DESPOLIATION, DESOLATION
- ruin, damage extensively, spoil or destroy, as grief or fire might RAVAGE, DEVASTATE, DESOLATE
- ruin, decay, extremely run-down condition, as in a slum area BLIGHT
- ruin, destroy, or damage something, such as a plan or ship SCUTTLE
- ruin, destruction, or doom, often self-inflicted UNDOING, DOWNFALL
- ruin, loss of everything, utter impoverishment DESTITUTION
- ruin, wreck, cause the downfall or loss of reputation of WRACK
- ruin or destroy personal or public property wantonly VANDALIZE
- ruin or spoil, make imperfect VITIATE
- ruined, beyond saving or repair IRREPARABLE, IRREMEDIABLE
- ruined or completely destroyed FORDONE
- ruined or deserted, as a dilapidated old house or the like might be DERELICT
- sudden and violent change, upheaval, or ruin CATACLYSM

ruins - archeological diggings, or the hollow formed or the ruins revealed by them EXCAVATION

rule See also **authority, power, government, order**
- rule, authority, or influence of one state over another HEGEMONY, SUZERAINTY
- rule, control, or authority DOMINION, SOVEREIGNTY, SUPREMACY
- rule, doctrine, or a principle widely accepted AXIOM, TENET, PRECEPT, CREED
- rule, law, or code of laws CANON
- rule, order, regulation, or an authoritative ruling or pronouncement DECREE, DICTUM, ORDINANCE, PRESCRIPT
- rule, test, or standard on which a judgment or decision is based CRITERION, NORM, YARDSTICK, TOUCHSTONE
- rule of behavior, as expressed in a brief saying MAXIM
- rule or custom, as for the conducting of a church ceremony RUBRIC
- rule or law no longer enforced though still officially valid DEAD LETTER
- rules, customs, or code of proper behavior within a given group or society ETIQUETTE, MORES
- rules formally and permanently guiding the internal affairs of a club, university, or the like STATUTES, ARTICLES, BYLAWS
- rules governing grammatical correctness, formulas in logic, computer programming, and the like SYNTAX
- rules of behavior and etiquette, especially among diplomats and rulers PROTOCOL
- rules of fair play in boxing MARQUIS OF QUEENSBERRY RULES
- breaking of a law or rule VIOLATION, BREACH, TRANSGRESSION, INFRINGEMENT, INFRACTION
- breaking or ignoring a rule PECCANT

RUSSIAN TERMS

apparat	communist party machine or administrative system; bureaucracy
apparatchik	bureaucrat
artel	workers' cooperative
babushka	grandmother; old woman; headscarf
balalaika	three-stringed guitarlike instrument
blini	buckwheat pancakes
Bolshevik	member of the communist party; formerly, supporter of Lenin
borscht/borsch	beet or cabbage soup
boyar	aristocrat in former times
commissar	communist party official supervising party loyalty and education
Cossack	member of a southern Russian people, formerly famous as cavalrymen
czarevitch	son of the czar
czarina	empress; wife of the czar
dacha	country house
droshky	open horse-drawn carriage
Duma	pre-Revolutionary parliament
glasnost	policy of "openness" in government
gospodin	polite form of address to foreign men
guberniya	administrative division or region
gulag	forced-labor camp
Izvestia	"News," used as the title of a newspaper
kibitka	covered cart or sled
kolkhoz	collective farm
Komsomol	communist youth organization
kopeck/kopek	smallest unit of currency
kremlin	citadel
Kremlin	chief government building in Moscow; Soviet government
kulak	formerly, a prosperous peasant or usurer
kvass	beerlike drink
matrioshka	traditional set of hollow wooden dolls, encased one inside another
Menshevik	moderate socialist, at the time of the Russian Revolution
mir	"peace"; the world; pre-Revolutionary peasant community
muzhik/moujik	pre-Revolutionary peasant
oblast	local administrative division
perestroika	policy of "restructuring" the Soviet system
piroshki/pirogi	small pies or pastry turnovers
pogrom	massacre or persecution
Politburo	communist party's ruling committee
Pravda	"Truth," used as the title of a newspaper
Presidium	highest policy-making committee of the supreme soviet, the legislature
refusenik	Soviet citizen refused permission to emigrate
ruble/rouble	monetary unit, equal to 100 kopecks
samizdat	underground publishing unit or press
samovar	tea urn
soviet	national, regional, or local council
sovkhoz	state farm
sputnik	satellite, orbiting spaceship
Stakhanovite	outstanding industrial worker
steppe	wide, grassy plain of southern U.S.S.R.
taiga	subarctic pine forest of Siberia
tovarich	comrade, used as a polite form of address
troika	three-horse carriage or sledge
ukase	command or edict, as issued by the czars
verst	measure of distance, about two-thirds of a mile
volost	pre-Revolutionary local council in a rural area
zemstvo	pre-Revolutionary district council

- exemption or release from a rule, law, obligation, or the like DISPENSATION
- making or relating to rules or laws PRESCRIPTIVE, NORMATIVE
- mathematical statement of a rule, proof, principle, or the like FORMULA, THEOREM
- obey a rule or order, carry out someone's wish or demand, or the like COMPLY WITH
- obeying the rules needlessly closely HIDEBOUND, FASTIDIOUS
- put forward as a rule or guide PRESCRIBE
- referring to extremely harsh laws, rules, or penalties DRACONIAN
- referring to or enforcing strict rules, demanding standards, or the like STRINGENT
- rough rules or principles on which to base actions or judgments GUIDELINES
- strict and stiffly correct observer of the rules, a religion, or the like PRECISIAN
- strict or rigorous, as a rigid rule is IRONCLAD
- suspend a rule, penalty, or the like, or refrain from enforcing it WAIVE
- unbreakable, as a sacred rule should be INVIOLABLE

rule (combining form) -ARCHY, -CRACY, -OCRACY

ruler See also **leader**
- ruler, hereditary lord DYNAST
- ruler, stick, or the like for beating children, especially on the hand FERULE, FERULA
- ruler during the absence, illness, or minority of the monarch PROTECTOR, REGENT
- ruler who is harsh, absolute, and arbitrary TYRANT, DESPOT, DICTATOR
- ruler's staff carried as a sign of royal authority or power SCEPTER
- remove a ruler or other high officeholder from his or her position of power DEPOSE
- subordinate ruler or dictator SATRAP

ruler (combining form) -ARCH

ruling, governing, in authority DOMINANT
- ruling by hereditary right, as a monarch might be LEGITIMATE
- ruling group of officers after a military takeover JUNTA
- ruling in a fatherly way, typically generous and concerned but restricting individual freedom and responsibility PATERNALISTIC
- ruling itself, relatively independent of outside control, government, or domination AUTONOMOUS
- ruling or reigning REGNANT

rumbling in the abdomen, caused by intestinal fluids and gas BORBORYGMUS

rumor, idle talk, gossip SCUTTLEBUTT, PRATTLE, TITTLE-TATTLE
- rumor or news report that is false or a deliberate hoax CANARD
- rumor or unconfirmed report HEARSAY
- crush or put an end to something, such as a rumor, plan, or rebellion SCOTCH
- informal or secret means of passing on rumors or information GRAPEVINE, BUSH TELEGRAPH
- long-lasting, continuing despite discouragement, as a rumor might be PERSISTENT
- spread a rumor or report widely BRUIT, DISSEMINATE, CIRCULATE

run or walk awkwardly LOLLOP
- running naked through a public place as a stunt STREAKING
- adapted for running, as some birds or bones are CURSORIAL

run away, depart hastily, flee SCRAM, SPLIT, SKEDADDLE, VAMOOSE
- run away secretly, as after committing a theft ABSCOND, DECAMP, ABSQUATULATE, HIGHTAIL
- run away secretly with a lover, especially to marry ELOPE

run-down, abnormally weak and tired DEBILITATED, ENERVATED
- run-down, worn out, or untidy, as through debauchery RADDLED

runaway, fleeing or escaped criminal FUGITIVE

rung of a ladder SPOKE, STAVE

runic alphabet FUTHARK
- runic letter æ, representing the sound /a/ as in *cat*, as used in Old English ASH
- runic letter ð, representing the sounds /th/ and /th/, as used in Old and Middle English ETH, EDH
- runic letter þ, representing the sounds /th/ and /th/, as used in Old and Middle English THORN

runner, creeping stem or branch, as of the strawberry STOLON
- runner or long whiplike shoot of a primitive plant FLAGELLUM

running (combining form) -DROMOUS

running down of the energy in the universe or any closed system ENTROPY

runway - land or run past the end of the runway, as an aircraft might OVERSHOOT
- land short of the runway, as an aircraft might UNDERSHOOT

rupture, displacement of a body organ through the wall that normally contains it HERNIA

rural scene or event of simple charm IDYLL
- idealistically rural, peaceful, and simple ARCADIAN, PASTORAL
- old-fashioned, rural, and unspoiled RUSTIC

rush, sudden flood, outburst SPATE
- rush about wildly, as a frenzied animal might RAMPAGE
- rush in violently IRRUPT
- panic-stricken headlong rush, as of horses or a crowd of people STAMPEDE

Russian See chart, page 465, and also chart at **menu**
- Russian alphabet CYRILLIC
- traditional liturgical language of the Russian Orthodox Church OLD CHURCH SLAVONIC
- Russian-style picture of a saint or holy person ICON

rusting, eating away, or dissolving of metals CORROSION

rustling, whispering, or murmuring sound, as of wind or surf SOUGH, SUSURRATION

rustproof iron or steel by coating it with zinc GALVANIZE

rye bread - aromatic seeds, as sometimes used in rye bread CARAWAY

S

s - /s/, /z/, or related hissing sound SIBILANT
S-shaped SIGMOID
- S-shaped curve in architecture OGEE

Sabbath - person who observes the Sabbath strictly SABBATARIAN
sacking, or the plant or its fiber used in making sacks JUTE
- sacking made of jute HESSIAN, BURLAP

sacred, very holy HALLOWED, SACROSANCT, INVIOLABLE, VENERATED
- sacred and not to be mentioned or described INEFFABLE, TABOO
- sacred object or notion reputedly protecting a city or state PALLADIUM
- sacred place, or a place treated as sacred HOLY OF HOLIES, SANCTUM SANCTORUM
- sacred place, or the holiest part of a church SANCTUARY, SACRARIUM
- sacred place associated with a saint or revered person SHRINE
- anything seen as sacred, or the quality of being sacred SANCTITY
- make or declare something sacred CONSECRATE, SANCTIFY
- relating to everyday earthly matters rather than to anything sacred SECULAR, PROFANE
- shrine or container for sacred relics RELIQUARY
- spoiling of the sacred quality of a place of worship, as by blasphemy or vandalism DESECRATION, PROFANATION, VIOLATION, SACRILEGE
- treat as sacred, cherish ENSHRINE

sacred (combining form) HIER-, HIERO-
sacred books See **Scriptures**
sacrifice or slaughter on a large scale HECATOMB
- sacrificial offering burned in flames HOLOCAUST
- atoning or expiatory, as a sacrifice might be PIACULAR
- kill as a sacrifice IMMOLATE
- pouring of a liquid as a religious sacrifice LIBATION

sad See also **unhappy**
- sad, depressing, or dreary, CHEERLESS, BLEAK, MELANCHOLY, DISMAL
- sad, gloomy, or threatening, as a look might be BALEFUL
- sad, gloomy, quietly mournful DOLEFUL, LUGUBRIOUS
- sad, mournful, expressing sorrow, as some poems are ELEGIAC
- sad, sorrowful, mourning TRISTFUL, DOLOROUS
- sad and subdued, melancholy or gloomy, as a mournful atmosphere is FUNEREAL, SOMBER
- sad and tearful, as through grief or depression LACHRYMOSE
- sad or discouraged, depressed DEJECTED, DESPONDENT, DOWNCAST, DISCONSOLATE, DISPIRITED, CRESTFALLEN, CHAPFALLEN, CHOPFALLEN
- sad or ill-humored, quietly gloomy or resentful DYSPEPTIC, GLUM, MOROSE, SULLEN, DOUR
- sad or mournful, expressing sorrow or yearning, as a song might be PLAINTIVE, PLANGENT, WISTFUL
- sad or mournful in appearance, sorrowful WOEBEGONE
- sad or suffering through frustrated love LOVELORN
- sad yearning pessimism about life, typically sentimental or romantic WELTSCHMERZ
- extremely sad, heartbroken, INCONSOLABLE, PROSTRATE
- extremely sad, as a tragic play might be HEARTRENDING
- extremely sad as a result of loss, as on the death of a loved one BEREFT, DESOLATE, FORLORN
- sorry for one's misdeeds, sad at what one has done CONTRITE, RUEFUL, REMORSEFUL
- tending to be sad or melancholy ATRABILIOUS, ATRABILIAR
- thoughtful in a sad, quiet way, brooding PENSIVE

saddle See illustration, page 468
- saddle, as for a mule, to which loads can be fastened PACKSADDLE
- saddle or canopied seat on an elephant's back HOWDAH
- saddle or seat for a second rider, as on a motorcycle PILLION
- leather gaiters attached to a saddle GAMBADOES
- ornamental covering, especially for a horse's saddle or harness CAPARISON
- soft, flexible saddle made without a frame PAD

sadism or masochism, any sexual pleasure derived from pain ALGOLAGNIA
safe, reliable, almost risk-free, as secure investments are BLUE-CHIP
- safe and sound, unhurt despite the dangers UNSCATHED
- safe place or retreat HAVEN, REFUGE, SANCTUARY
- place of safekeeping REPOSITORY
- utterly safe or secure, impossible to overcome UNASSAILABLE, INVULNERABLE, IMPREGNABLE

safecracker, burglar skilled in opening safes PETEMAN
safeguard, insurance measure against harm SAFETY NET, BACKSTOP, BACKUP
- safeguard or guarantee of society PALLADIUM

safekeeping - person entrusted with something for safekeeping DEPOSITORY, TRUSTEE
safety or shelter, as from persecution, or a place offering such protection ASYLUM, REFUGE, SANCTUARY
- safety precaution, person or thing that double-checks for safety SAFEGUARD, LONGSTOP, SAFETY NET, FAIL-SAFE FEATURE
- safety switch or lever, as on a train, that causes mechanical shutdown if released either intentionally or when the operator faints or dies DEADMAN BRAKE

Sahara - region of northwestern Africa, between the Sahara and the Mediterranean MAGHREB
- semidesert region just south of the Sahara SAHEL

sail See chart and illustration, pages 470 and 472, and also **ship**
- sail, travel on water NAVIGATE
- sail on the lowest yard on a square-rigged ship COURSE
- sail successfully, as around a tight bend NEGOTIATE
- sail or fly completely around something CIRCUMNAVIGATE
- sail regularly on a route PLY
- sails, ropes, and other equipment of a sailing ship GEAR
- adjust sails to catch the wind better TRIM
- baggy middle section of a fishing net or square sail BUNT
- bulging section of a sail BAG
- corner of a sail CLEW, HEAD, TACK
- crossbeam attached to a mast and supporting a sail YARD
- fasten a sail securely LASH, FRAP

Saddle

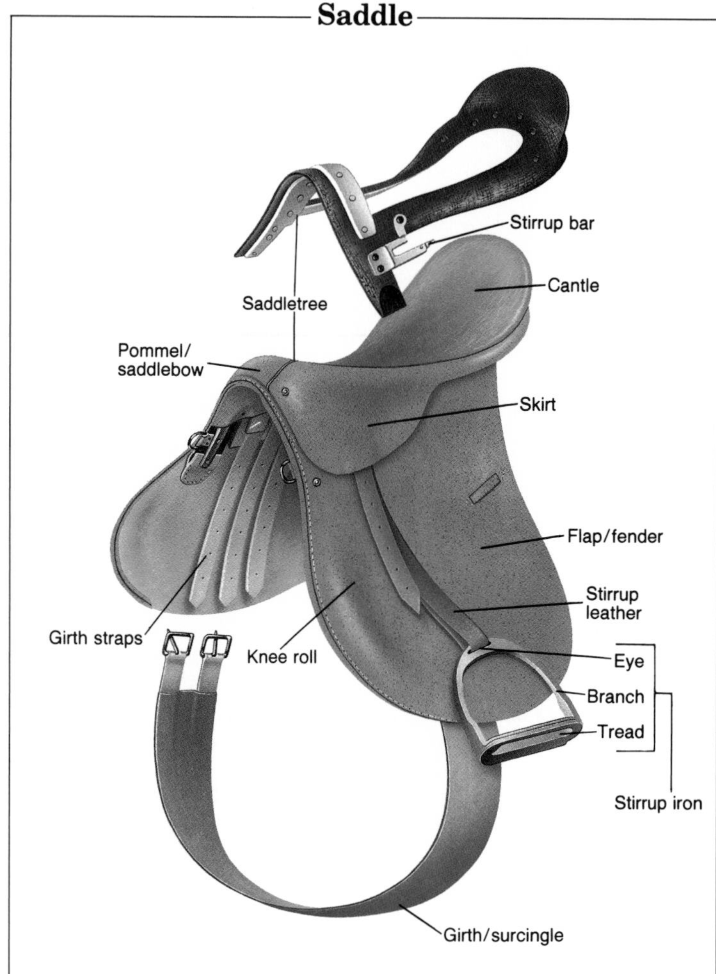

- gather in and fasten a sail FURL
- let the wind out of a sail SPILL
- lower a boat's mast, sail, or flag STRIKE
- number, shape, and pattern of masts and sails on a vessel RIG
- rope for raising or lowering a sail or flag HALYARD
- rope or chain attached to and controlling the lower corner or corners of a sail SHEET
- rope or strap attaching a furled sail to a crossbeam GASKET
- ropes across a ship's sail, forming a rope ladder RATLINE, RATTLING
- ropes, cables, or the like supporting or controlling the masts and sails of a sailing ship RIGGING
- small ring of rope or metal on the edge of a sail CRINGLE

sailor See also **services**
- sailor, soldier, or army servant from the East Indies LASCAR
- sailor or seaman MARINER
- sailors' chapel BETHEL
- sailors' rebellion MUTINY
- sailors' work song SHANTY
- bed of canvas or string, suspended at both ends, as formerly used by sailors HAMMOCK
- carved or engraved articles of ivory, whalebone, or the like, typically made by sailors SCRIMSHAW
- crackers or bread eaten by sailors HARDTACK, SHIP BISCUIT
- informal term for a sailor GOB, TAR, MATELOT
- person considered by sailors to be inexperienced LANDLUBBER
- punishment for sailors in former times, involving being dragged under the ship KEELHAULING
- trick or force men into serving as sailors or soldiers PRESS, IMPRESS, COMMANDEER, PRESS-GANG, SHANGHAI

saint considered the special protector of a person, group, city, or the like PATRON SAINT
- biography of a saint or saints HAGIOGRAPHY
- declare a person to be a saint CANONIZE
- honor a deceased person as blessed, as a first step toward declaring him or her a saint BEATIFY
- list or calendar of the saints that are recognized by the Roman Catholic Church CANON
- picture of a saint or holy person ICON
- relating to Saint Peter PETRINE
- revered object, associated with a saint or martyr RELIC
- ring of light around a saint's head in a painting HALO, MANDORLA, AUREOLE
- Roman Catholic official arguing the case against sainting a deceased person DEVIL'S ADVOCATE, PROMOTER OF THE FAITH, PROMOTOR FIDEI
- Roman Catholic official arguing the case for sainting a deceased person POSTULATOR
- title given to a deceased Roman Catholic at the first level of sainthood VENERABLE

saint (combining form) HAGI-, HAGIO-

saintliness, holiness SANCTITY

saintly, joyful BEATIFIC

salad See **vegetable** and chart at **menu**

salad - oil-and-vinegar salad dressing FRENCH DRESSING, VINAIGRETTE
- small toasted or fried square of bread served in soups and salads CROUTON

salary, allowance, or similar regular payment STIPEND
- salary, wages, or profit from one's job or office EMOLUMENT
- deduct a part from someone's salary or wages DOCK, GARNISHEE
- rising in keeping with the cost of living, as a salary or pension might be INDEX-LINKED

sale item offered very cheaply as an inducement LOSS LEADER
- collection of varied items for sale as a single lot JOB LOT
- slick sales talk, patter SPIEL

salesperson using dishonest or aggressive selling techniques HUCKSTER

saliva, spittle SPUTUM
- dribble saliva from the mouth SLOBBER, DROOL, SLAVER

salmon after spawning, usually in an exhausted condition KELT
- salmon in the freshwater phase of its life PARR
- salmon of about two years old, when it turns silvery and begins to migrate to the sea SMOLT
- salmon of between two and three years old MORT
- female salmon that has recently

spawned BLACKFISH
- male salmon that has recently spawned REDFISH
- migrating from the sea to breed, as salmon are ANADROMOUS
- smoked salmon LOX
- young salmon or trout ALEVIN
- young salmon returning from the sea to inland waters for the first time to spawn GRILSE

salt, pepper, mustard, or other sauce or seasoning CONDIMENT
- salt deposit frequented by animals to lick minerals LICK
- saltcellar, pepper shaker, mustard pot, or the like, or a set of such containers CRUET
- saltlike flavor-enhancer MONOSODIUM GLUTAMATE, MSG
- remove salt, as from sea water DESALINATE
- turn into, treat with, or mix with salt or a salt SALIFY
- with a grain (or pinch) of salt CUM GRANO SALIS

salt (combining form) SALI-, HAL-, HALO-

salts - chemical salts used in making paper and glass, and as a laxative GLAUBER'S SALT
- medicinal salts used as a vigorous laxative, and for reducing inflammation EPSOM SALTS

salty, as water might be BRACKISH, BRINY
- salty, relating to salt, or mineral salts SALINE
- salty or spicy to the taste, rather than sweet SAVORY
- salty water, as used for pickling BRINE

salvation from sin through Christ's death on the Cross REDEMPTION, DELIVERANCE
- chosen by God's will for salvation ELECT

Salvation Army meeting hall CITADEL

same in age, duration, or period CONTEMPORARY, COETANEOUS, COEVAL
- same in size or duration COMMENSURATE
- same in status, type, or the like COORDINATE
- same or coinciding in meaning, range, proportions, or the like COTERMINOUS, COEXTENSIVE
- sameness or equivalence, as of amount PARITY
- amounting to, the same as, equivalent to TANTAMOUNT TO
- be the same as or equivalent to CONSTITUTE
- coinciding in shape, having exactly the same proportions, as two identical geometrical figures are CONGRUENT
- having the same meaning SYNONYMOUS
- having the same shape or form about a given axis, point, line, or plane SYMMETRICAL
- having the same structure, force, or the like, such that an exchange of positions or roles is possible INTERCHANGEABLE
- make equal or treat as the same EQUATE
- person or thing exactly the same as another, perfect copy DUPLICATE, CLONE

same (combining form) AUT-, AUTO-, HOM-, HOMO-, IS-, ISO-, SYN-, SYM-, TAUT-, TAUTO-

sample piece of fabric SWATCH
- sample taken at random, as of the general population, regarded as typical of the whole CROSS SECTION

Samson - Jew in biblical times, such as Samson, committed by sacred vows to a life of purity and austerity NAZIRITE

sanctuary or sacred part of a church SACRARIUM

sand or other sediment deposited in a tidal estuary WARP
- chemical compound that is a major constituent of sand and is used in the manufacture of glass SILICA, SILICON DIOXIDE, QUARTZ
- fine light sand or clay particles deposited by the wind LOESS
- growing or living in sand ARENACEOUS, ARENICOLOUS
- rock particles finer than sand but coarser than clay, deposited by rivers and streams SILT
- strip of sand or shingle extending from a shore SPIT

sandbags, stones, concrete, or other covering supporting a wall or embankment REVETMENT

sandbank, mudbank, or the like, often dangerous to shipping, sometimes exposed at low tide SHOAL

sandpaper - abrasive mineral or mixture, as on sandpaper, for grinding and polishing CORUNDUM, EMERY

sandwich made of a long roll or breadstick HERO, SUBMARINE
- snack or appetizer in the form of a small open sandwich CANAPÉ

sandy in composition, texture, or appearance ARENACEOUS

sane, coherent, conscious and reasonable LUCID, RATIONAL
- sane, of sound mind COMPOS MENTIS

Sanskrit - syllabic script used for Sanskrit and Hindi DEVANAGARI

sap - milky sap of certain plants, used in making rubber LATEX

sarcasm - belittling, causing embarrassment, as sarcasm or a disapproving look might WITHERING
- sarcastic, biting CAUSTIC, MORDANT
- sarcastic in a sneering or insulting way, as a cruel remark might be SNIDE
- humorous or mildly sarcastic use of words to express something markedly different from or opposite to their literal sense IRONY
- joking in a sarcastic or inappropriate way FACETIOUS
- mocking or scornful in a cynical or sarcastic way SARDONIC

sardines - Norwegian herring, typically canned like sardines SILD

sash, wide and often pleated, worn around the waist with a dinner jacket CUMMERBUND
- sash or belt crossing the chest from the shoulder, used for carrying a sword or bugle BALDRIC

Satan LUCIFER

satellite See also **spacecraft**
- satellite orbiting in a fixed position relative to a point on the equator GEOSTATIONARY SATELLITE, GEOSYNCHRONOUS SATELLITE

satire, takeoff SKIT, SPOOF
- satirical portrait CARICATURE
- satirical literary work, usually treating a subject in an inappropriate style BURLESQUE
- satirical literary work treating a lowly or comic subject in a heroic or high literary style MOCK-HEROIC
- satirical mimicry, as of a writer's or composer's work PARODY, PASTICHE
- satirical work in the form of a grotesque imitation of an original work TRAVESTY
- satirize or mock by imitating MIMIC, APE
- mocking satire of another work LAMPOON, PASQUINADE, SQUIB

satisfaction - experienced or enjoyed through the actions or achievements of someone else, as satisfaction might be VICARIOUS

satisfactory See **mediocre**

satisfied or self-satisfied to the point of feeling that nothing more needs to be done COMPLACENT
- satisfied with or complacent about one's past achievements RESTING ON ONE'S LAURELS

satisfy a whim or craving INDULGE, GRATIFY
- satisfy one's lust, appetites, or the like to the full SATE, SATIATE
- satisfy one's thirst QUENCH, SLAKE
- satisfy someone's whims or wishes, especially unworthy wishes PANDER TO

Saturday - one who observes Saturday as the Sabbath SABBATARIAN

sauces See chart, page 473
- sauce in which meat or fish is

soaked before cooking MARINADE
saucepan, typically with legs and a long handle, for cooking on a hearth SKILLET
sausage, ham, and other cold cooked meats CHARCUTERIE
- sausage made with pig's blood, blood sausage BLACK PUDDING, BLUTWURST
- sausage-shaped, as a plant part might be ALLANTOID
- British informal term for sausages BANGERS
- German sausages of various kinds BRATWURST, KNACKWURST, BLUTWURST
- highly seasoned smoked pork sausage CHORIZO, SAVELOY
- large, mild sausage sliced and eaten cold in salads or sandwiches BOLOGNA, MORTADELLA, POLONY
- mild smoked sausage FRANKFURTER, WIENER, WIENERWURST
- smoked Polish sausage KIELBASA
- spicy sausage of various kinds, as used in sandwiches CERVELAT, SALAMI
- very spicy Italian sausage, eaten cold PEPPERONI
savage, untamed, wild FERAL
save, keep in existence SUSTAIN
- save, use economically, budget HUSBAND
- save from loss, damage, or cancellation SALVAGE
- save or protect from harm, loss, or decay CONSERVE
- save or rescue from danger or trouble RETRIEVE
- save or rescue from sin and punishment REDEEM
- save someone from evil ways by reforming him or her RECLAIM
- saving or rescue from sin, ignorance, danger, or the like SALVATION, DELIVERANCE, REDEMPTION
- gather, store, and save, accumulate a reserve AMASS, GARNER, STOCKPILE
saving grace REDEEMING CHARACTERISTIC, MITIGATING FACTOR
saw - groove or notch made in wood by an ax or saw KERF
- having small notches or teeth, as the edge of a saw is SERRATED
say See also **speak, speech, state, conversation**
- say, put into words, give voice to VOCALIZE, ARTICULATE, PRONOUNCE, UTTER, VERBALIZE
- say something deliberately or formally DELIVER ONESELF OF
- say something impulsively and suddenly BLURT OUT
- say something that one should not, give away secret or private information DIVULGE, DISCLOSE
- say emphatically ASSEVERATE
saying expressing a deep truth or principle in a concise and elegant or witty way APHORISM
- saying or proverb expressing a general truth ADAGE, AXIOM, APOTHEGM, APOPHTHEGM, DICTUM
- insight or sharp observation, or a saying expressing it APERÇU
- overused, unoriginal, or obvious saying CLICHÉ, COMMONPLACE, TRUISM, PLATITUDE, BROMIDE
- proverb or similar short saying, typically overused or outdated SAW, BYWORD
- rule of conduct, or a saying summing it up PRECEPT
- short saying that sums up a guiding principle MAXIM, MOTTO, SLOGAN
- short witty saying, often with a paradoxical twist EPIGRAM, MOT, GNOME
scab or layer of dead skin, as caused by a burn ESCHAR
scale, flake of skin, or similar structure SQUAMA
- scale, plate, or similar thin layer of plant or animal tissue LAMELLA, LAMINA
- scale for comparison, as for the cost of living INDEX
- scale indicating one's weight by a pointer shifted along a marked bar PLATFORM SCALE
- scale of colors, based on equal changes of hue MUNSELL SCALE
- scale of hardness of metals, based on resistance to indentation from the pressure of a standard steel ball BRINELL SCALE
- scale of hardness of minerals, based on resistance to scratching MOHS SCALE
- scale of magnitude of earthquakes RICHTER SCALE
- scale of mental ability or IQ in children BINET-SIMON SCALE, STANFORD-BINET SCALE, S-B, WECHSLER SCALE, WISC, TERMAN-MCNEMAR SCALE

Sailing Boats and Sailing Ships

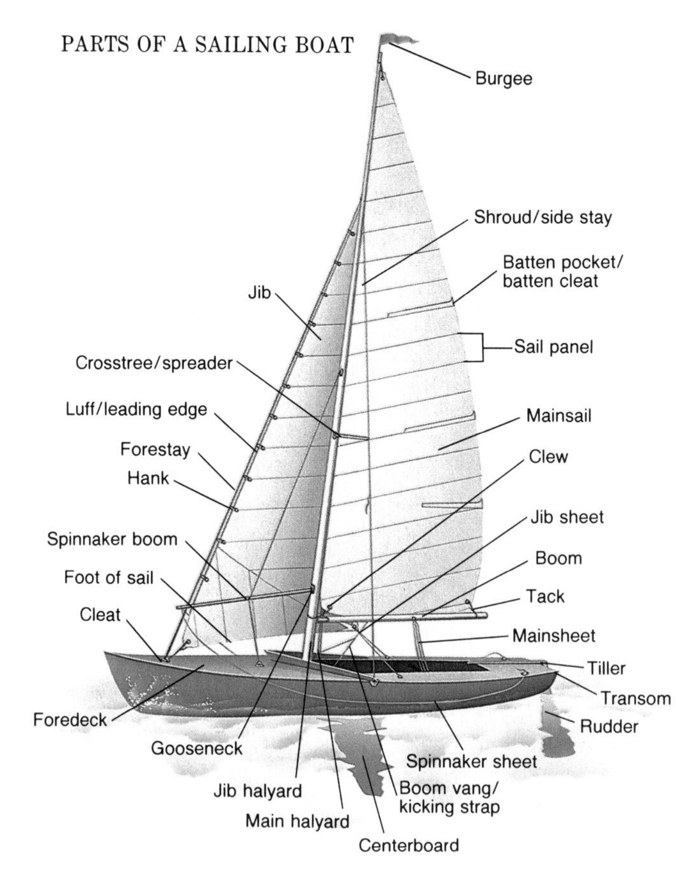

- scale of relative density of liquids BAUMÉ SCALE, TWADDELL SCALE
- scale of wind velocities BEAUFORT SCALE
- scale or balance consisting of a pivoted bar STEELYARD
- scale or series of steps, stages, or degrees, a gradual progression GRADATION
- scale systems in music, such as major and minor MODES
- scaly dry skin, as in dandruff SCURF
- scaly or rough to the touch, as hard dry skin might be SCABROUS
- covered in scales or bony plates MAILED, SCUTATE, SCUTELLATE
- drawing made to scale PROTRACTION
- drawing made to scale of an outside face of a building or structure ELEVATION
- finely marked scale supplementing the main scale of a measuring instrument VERNIER
- mark, adjust, or check the scale of a measuring instrument CALIBRATE
- position or ranking, as on a scale RATING
- relating to a musical scale consisting of all twelve semitones of an octave CHROMATIC, DODECAPHONIC, TWELVE-TONE
- relating to the basic Western major or minor musical scale, without modifications DIATONIC
- system or practice of using the *do-re-mi* syllables to correspond to notes of the scale SOLMIZATION, TONIC SOL-FA, SOLFEGGIO, SOLFÈGE

scale (combining form) LEPID-, LEPIDO-

scalpel - long, narrow scalpel for delicate surgery BISTOURY
- surgical cut, as made by a scalpel INCISION

scandal or controversy arousing public interest CAUSE CÉLÈBRE
- revealing of a scandal or crime, or the book, broadcast, or the like in which it is reported EXPOSÉ

Scandinavian NORSE
- Scandinavian in ethnic grouping or appearance NORDIC
- Scandinavian-style buffet meal SMORGASBORD

scar formed by the stitching up of a wound SUTURE
- scar or mark from branding, as formerly on the skin of a slave or criminal STIGMA
- scar resulting from a flesh wound CICATRIX, CICATRICE
- hard pink scar tissue KELOID

scarcity See **lack**

scared See also **frighten, cowardly, fear**
- scared, timid, fearful TIMOROUS, TREMULOUS
- scared in a base or cowardly way CRAVEN, LILY-LIVERED
- scared into silence or inaction, as by threats INTIMIDATED, UNNERVED
- scared or suspicious to an unreasonable degree PARANOID

FULL-RIGGED SAILING SHIP

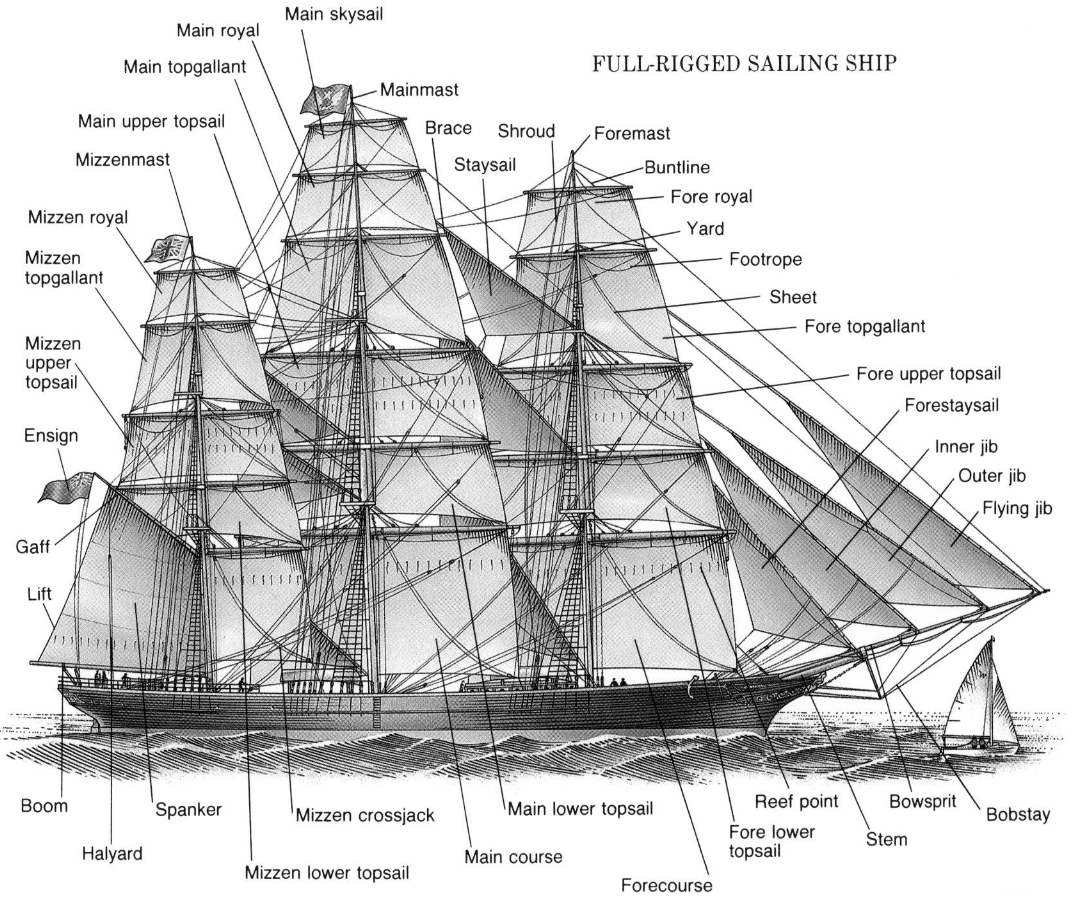

SAILING TERMS

belaying pin	pin fitted to a rail to secure a rope without knotting
broaching	turning dangerously sideways to the wind and waves
careening	turning a boat on its side for cleaning and repairs
carvel-built	built with planks meeting flush at the seams
clinker-built	built with overlapping planks
close-hauled	sailing as nearly as possible into the wind
crabbing	sailing slightly sideways to offset the drift caused by a current
davits	cranes on deck for hoisting or lowering smaller boats
dogwatch	two-hour spell of duty, from 4 to 6 or from 6 to 8 PM
fiddle	rail around a table to prevent objects from sliding off
fore-and-aft	referring to a sail that lies along a vessel, not across it
forecastle/ fo'c'sle	cabin farthest to the front of a vessel
Genoa jib	large triangular sail, as used on racing yachts
gunwale	upper section or top plank of the side of a vessel
heaving to	bringing a ship to a standstill by heading into the wind and trimming the sails
heeling	leaning or tilting when sailing into the wind
jibing	causing a fore-and-aft sail to swing to the other side of the vessel when sailing before the wind
kite	small sail, set high on a mast, used in a light wind
lateen	triangular sail slung from a long diagonal spar attached to the top of a mast
luffing	turning into the wind, making the sails flap
lugsail	four-sided sail, widest at the bottom, on a diagonal yard
Marconi rig/ Bermuda rig	rig with a triangular mainsail, as used on cruising and racing vessels
painter	rope attached to the bow of a small boat
reaching	sailing with the wind blowing from the side
reefed sail	a sail partly lowered and secured
running	sailing with the wind blowing from directly behind
spar	any pole used to support rigging or sails
spinnaker	billowing sail, usually triangular, as used on racing yachts
tacking	sailing into the wind on a zigzag course
thwart	seat across a small boat, as for the oarsman
trimming	adjusting the tightness of sails according to wind conditions
warp	mooring line; to move a small boat by pulling at this line
yawing	deviating briefly from a straight course

- extremely scared, paralyzed with fear PETRIFIED
- extremely scared, to the point of loss of self-control PANIC-STRICKEN
- nervous, scared, ill at ease JITTERY, FRETFUL, APPREHENSIVE

scarlet fever SCARLATINA

scatter, break up, as troops of a defeated army might DISBAND, DISPERSE
- scatter in a squandering or irresponsible way DISSIPATE
- scatter or drive off rioters or enemy troops ROUT, DISPEL
- scatter or spread something widely, such as news DISSEMINATE
- scatter randomly or untidily STREW
- scatter throughout a speech, text, or the like, interlace INTERLARD, INTERSPERSE
- scattered, isolated, occasional, intermittent SPORADIC
- scattered or spread out in an untidy, irregular way STRAGGLY
- scattered widely, widespread, widely distributed BROADCAST, DIFFUSE, DISPERSED
- scattering of a nation's people, especially of the Jews DIASPORA
- scattering of people or things DISPERSION

scene in a play in which the actors freeze briefly in position TABLEAU
- scene of a crime VENUE
- scene or setting, as in museums, with models of figures exhibited against a background DIORAMA
- scene or view, especially through a frame such as an avenue of trees VISTA, PROSPECT
- representation of a historical scene, painting, or the like by costumed actors posing silent and motionless TABLEAU VIVANT

scene (combining form) -SCAPE

scenery See also **theater**
- scenery and props in a play MISE-EN-SCÈNE

scent See also **perfume**
- scented mixture, as of dried petals, in a sachet or box, as for scenting linen POMANDER
- scented oil or cream for the hair POMADE, POMATUM, MACASSAR OIL
- scented toilet water EAU DE COLOGNE, EAU DE TOILETTE
- jar of dried petals or spices, used to scent the air POTPOURRI
- small packet or bag containing perfumed powder, for scenting clothes and linen SACHET

scheming, crafty CALCULATING, CONNIVING

scholar of or expert in Sanskrit or Hinduism PUNDIT, PANDIT
- scholar or religious leader in Is-

lam IMAM, AYATOLLAH
- scholar who shows off his or her knowledge PEDANT
- servant of a scholar or magician in medieval times FAMULUS

scholarly comments, footnotes, variant readings, and the like in an edition of a text APPARATUS CRITICUS, CRITICAL APPARATUS
- scholarly edition of a writer's works, together with notes by various commentators VARIORUM
- scholarly knowledge, deep learning ERUDITION

school, university, or college that one used to attend as a student ALMA MATER
- school classes specially designed for pupils with learning difficulties REMEDIAL CLASSES
- school elementary textbook PRIMER
- school for very young children KINDERGARTEN
- school of music CONSERVATORY, CONSERVATOIRE
- school pupil who is top of the class in England DUX
- school pupil who stays away from school without permission TRUANT
- school to which juvenile offenders are sent REFORMATORY
- school training corps in military techniques and discipline CADET CORPS
- abolish racial separation, as in a school DESEGREGATE
- academic secondary school in France LYCÉE
- academic secondary school in Germany GYMNASIUM
- area that is served by a particular school, hospital, or the like CATCHMENT AREA
- British private school PUBLIC SCHOOL
- divided along racial lines or restricted to certain racial groups, as some schools or buses are SEGREGATED
- head of school PRINCIPAL, HEADMASTER
- occurring outside the normal course of studies or timetable, as in a school or university EXTRACURRICULAR, EXTRAMURAL
- principal of a school or university RECTOR
- private day or boarding school PREPARATORY SCHOOL, PREP SCHOOL
- traditional Jewish school emphasizing religious studies YESHIVA

science See also charts at **chemistry** and **physics**
- science as used in establishing facts for evidence in legal cases FORENSIC SCIENCE
- medieval precursor of science seeking a cure-all medicine and a means of turning base metal into gold ALCHEMY

science (combining form) -GRAPHY, -LOGY, -NOMY, -SOPHY

science-fiction magazine or other magazine for those with a particular hobby or interest FANZINE
- having certain robotlike or electronically enhanced body functions, as some characters and creatures of science fiction BIONIC

scientific and rigorously objective, accurate and thorough in detail CLINICAL
- referring to scientific observation or experiment rather than theory EMPIRICAL

scientific instruments See chart, page 474, and also **electricity, laboratory, measuring instrument, medical**

scimitar-shaped, curved, as some leaves are ACINACIFORM

scissors with toothed blades for cutting a zigzag edge on cloth to prevent fraying PINKING SHEARS

scold See also **criticize**
- scold, dress down, take to task CHIDE, REPROVE
- scold, punish, or criticize severely CASTIGATE, CHASTIZE, KEELHAUL
- scold or blame for a failing or

SAUCES

aioli	garlic mayonnaise
béarnaise	sauce of egg yolk, butter, lemon juice or vinegar, and herbs
béchamel	white sauce made with milk, butter, and flour, flavored with herbs
chasseur	brown sauce with white wine, shallots, mushrooms, and tomatoes, for hot meat
espagnole	brown sauce, as made with stock, bacon, and vegetables
hollandaise	sauce of butter, egg yolk, and lemon juice or vinegar, for fish or vegetable dishes
matelote	wine sauce for fish
mornay	béchamel sauce with added cheese
pesto	Italian sauce of olive oil, basil, pine nuts, and garlic
pistou	Provençal sauce of crushed basil leaves, tomatoes, Parmesan cheese, garlic, and olive oil
ravigote	oil and vinegar sauce with herbs, for boiled meat or fish
remoulade	mayonnaise with herbs and chopped capers and gherkins, for cold shellfish and egg dishes
sambal	vinegary chutney used as a relish for curries, or in Malay cooking
satay	spicy peanut and coconut sauce, served with Indonesian dishes
soubise	white sauce with puréed onions
suprême	white sauce made with veal or chicken stock, with added cream and egg yolk, for eggs, poultry, and vegetables
Tabasco	pungent pepper sauce
tartare	mayonnaise with chopped gherkins, chives, and cream, for hot fish
velouté	white sauce made with veal, chicken, or fish stock, with added cream and egg yolk
vinaigrette	oil, vinegar, and seasoning sauce, as served with salads and the like

misdeed REPROACH
- scold or criticize sharply REBUKE, REPRIMAND, OBJURGATE
- scold or warn gently but firmly ADMONISH
- scold sternly or severely BERATE, UPBRAID
- scolding by a wife of her husband in private, or similar private reproach CURTAIN LECTURE
- bridle with an iron bit formerly used to silence scolding women BRANKS

scope, extent, or range, as of a law or one's outlook PURVIEW, COMPASS
- scope for freedom of thought or action LATITUDE, LEEWAY
- scope of one's understanding, perception, or knowledge COGNIZANCE
- scope or field of activity, sphere of expertise PRESERVE, DOMAIN, BAILIWICK, PROVINCE
- scope or range of possible activity, reach, extent AMBIT, ORBIT, RADIUS
- acting or speaking beyond the scope of one's ability or expertise ULTRACREPIDARIAN

scorn See also **mock, ridicule**
- scorn or despise DISDAIN
- object or target of scorn LAUGHINGSTOCK, BUTT, BYWORD

scornful, contemptuous, and reproachful, as a remark might be OPPROBRIOUS
- scornful in a condescending or haughty way SUPERCILIOUS, DISDAINFUL
- scornful in a dismissive, belittling, or mocking way DISPARAGING, DERISIVE
- scornful in a mocking or cynical way SARDONIC
- scornful in an arrogant and overbearing way OVERWEENING

scorpion - pincerlike claw of a scorpion CHELA

Scottish, relating to Scotland CALEDONIAN
- Scottish Highlander GAEL

scouring or cleansing, as a cleaning powder might be ABSTERGENT
- scouring substance, such as pumice or emery, for smoothing or cleaning ABRASIVE

scout or advance patroler OUTRIDER
- scout or sentry on horseback stationed ahead of an army's outposts VEDETTE
- scout out or survey a stretch of land, an enemy position, or the like RECONNOITER, RECCE

scowl, frown, stare angrily GLOWER

scrape, grate, or file RASP
- scraping instrument used by ancient Greeks and Romans for cleaning the skin STRIGIL
- scraping or scouring substance, such as emery, used for cleaning or smoothing ABRASIVE

scraps or fragments, as of fabric ODDMENTS, REMNANTS

scratch about or feel around for with the hands, grope GRABBLE
- scratch or cut the skin slightly, as for vaccination SCARIFY
- scratch or graze something, such as a shoe SCUFF
- scratch or wear away, rub off, as by chafing ABRADE
- scratch the flesh deeply and jag-

SCIENTIFIC INSTRUMENTS

barostat	maintains constant pressure
chronograph	records short time intervals
dephlegmator	condenses the constituents having high boiling points of a mixed vapor
electromyograph	records electrical activity in a muscle
hodoscope	traces the paths of high-energy particles
hydrophone	detects and monitors sounds underwater
hydroscope	views objects deep underwater
hydrostat	detects the presence or absence of water
hygrograph	records variations in the humidity of the atmosphere
hygrostat/ humidistat	controls the relative humidity of the air
image converter/image tube	converts X-rays or other radiation into a visual image
microtome	cuts very thin slices for examination by microscope
nephograph	photographs cloud patterns
optical character reader	converts printed characters into digital form, as for computers
oscillograph	records electric currents as a graph
pantograph	copies pictures and diagrams to scale
radarscope	displays radar signals
radiosonde	transmits meteorological data from a balloon at high altitudes
spectroscope	observes optical spectra
stauroscope	helps in the study of the crystal structure of minerals
stroboscope	helps in the adjustment of moving machine parts by making them appear stationary while operating
tachistoscope	tests perception and memory by displaying visual images very rapidly
tachograph	records speeds and times of use of vehicles
telethermoscope/ telethermometer	indicates the temperatures of remote locations
thermostat	maintains a constant temperature
transponder	transmits information in response to a radio signal
zymoscope	monitors fermentation by recording the amount of carbon dioxide produced

gedly, tear roughly LACERATE

scream or howl in a loud, lamenting way, wail ULULATE
- scream shrilly, shriek like a cat in heat CATERWAUL
- hold back, cut off, or muffle a scream, noise, or the like STIFLE

screech or cry, as of a cat in heat CATERWAUL

screen of rice paper used as a sliding door or partition in a Japanese house SHOJI
- screen used to conceal women, especially in India PURDAH

screenplay or shooting script for a movie SCENARIO

screw - screwlike device within a tube, used in ancient times for raising water ARCHIMEDES' SCREW
- screw that is sunk so deep that its head lies flush with or below the surface COUNTERSUNK SCREW
- screw with a cross-shaped groove in the head PHILLIPS SCREW, CROSS-HEAD SCREW
- screw with holes through the head, turned by a bar inserted through one of the holes CAPSTAN SCREW
- cut or finish the thread of a screw CHASE
- tool for cutting internal screw threads on nuts, pipes, sockets, and the like TAP
- width of the thread of a screw, or distance advanced by a screw in one full turn PITCH

screwdriver - sloping surface leading to the tip or cutting edge of a chisel, screwdriver, or other tool BEZEL
- tool serving as a screwdriver, consisting of a small bent metal bar whose tip fits into the six-sided recess in the head of special screws or bolts ALLEN KEY

scribbled messages or drawings, often witty or obscene, in public places, typically on walls GRAFFITI

scribe or copyist in former times SCRIVENER

Scriptures See also **Bible, Old Testament, Koran**
- Scriptures of Islam, containing Allah's revelations to Muhammad KORAN, QUR'AN, ALCORAN
- Scriptures of the Sikh religion GRANTH
- Scriptures of the Zoroastrian religion ZEND-AVESTA, AVESTA
- body of ancient rabbinical writings or Scriptures, forming the basis of religious authority in orthodox Judaism TALMUD
- epic poems in Sanskrit, forming Hindu Scriptures RAMAYANA, MAHABHARATA
- Hindu and Buddhist mystical Scriptures, written in Sanskrit TANTRAS
- Hindu Scriptures and holy verses from ancient times, gathered in four collections VEDAS
- Hindu Scriptures that comment and build upon the four Vedas UPANISHADS
- first five books of the Old Testament, or the scroll used in a synagogue on which these Scriptures are written TORAH

scroll-like or spiral shell, architectural ornament, or the like VOLUTE
- scroll-shaped TURBINAL
- scroll-shaped ornamental tablet of stone, plaster, or the like, sometimes carrying an inscription CARTOUCHE

scrubbing - spongelike, fibrous interior of the dishcloth gourd, used for scrubbing the skin LOOFAH

sculpture See chart, page 477

scurvy - relating to scurvy, scurvy-like, or suffering from scurvy SCORBUTIC
- preventing or curing scurvy, as a medical drug might be ANTISCORBUTIC

scythe - Death viewed as Father Time with his scythe GRIM REAPER
- path or strip, such as that left behind by a scythe or mower SWATH

sea See also **ship**
- sea, open ocean MAIN
- sea foam or froth SPUME
- sea inlet at the mouth of a river ESTUARY, FIRTH
- sea inlet that is long and narrow FJORD
- sea inlet that is long and wide SOUND
- "sea" on the moon MARE
- sea-wall or jetty jutting into the water to control erosion, direct a current, or the like BREAKWATER, GROIN, MOLE, BULWARK
- seawater BRINE
- seawater separated from the sea, as by coral reefs LAGOON
- adjective for the sea MARINE, NAUTICAL, MARITIME, PELAGIC, THALASSIC
- backward pull in the sea caused by receding waves after breaking on the shore UNDERTOW
- cargo or wreckage floating on the sea after a ship has sunk FLOTSAM, JETSAM
- cargo thrown overboard at sea and washed ashore JETSAM
- floating or drifting mass of tiny animal or plant organisms at or near the surface of the sea or a lake PLANKTON
- fresh, invigorating sea air OZONE
- humorously informal term for the sea THE BRINY, BRINY DEEP
- large expanse of sea partially enclosed by land GULF
- narrow strip of land allowing an inland country access to the sea CORRIDOR
- narrow strip of land extending into the sea from the mainland PENINSULA
- narrow waterway linking two seas or other large bodies of water STRAIT
- person inexperienced at sailing or unsuited to life at sea LANDLUBBER
- remove salt, as from seawater DESALINATE
- ridge of land, usually with cliffs, jutting into the sea PROMONTORY
- rise and fall with a strong regular rhythm, as waves do in the open sea SURGE, HEAVE, SWELL
- without access to the sea, as some countries are LANDLOCKED

sea (combining form) HAL-, HALO-, MAR-, THALLAS-, PELLAG- NAUT-

sea anemone coral, or related creature, typically tubelike and with tentacles POLYP
- sea anemone, sponge, or similar plantlike animal ZOOPHYTE, ANTHOZOAN
- armlike flexible projection near the mouth of a squid, sea anemone, or the like TENTACLE

sea horse in mythology, having a horse's front legs and a fish's tail HIPPOCAMPUS

seafood See **fish**

seal a boat, pipe, or the like by packing the seams or cracks with a filler CAULK
- seal between lengths of piping, machine parts, or the like, to prevent the escape of gas or liquid GASKET
- seal on a document in former times CACHET
- seal on a papal bull BULLA
- seal the seams of a wooden ship, as with tar or pitch PAY
- seal or enclose an area, as with a line of troops CORDON OFF
- seal or sealed impression as used on official documents SIGNET
- sealed, airtight HERMETIC
- sealing material of cement and clay LUTE, LUTING
- seallike mammal with small paddlelike forelimbs MANATEE
- adjective for a seal or related animal PHOCINE
- document under a sovereign's seal in former times, typically authorizing imprisonment without trial LETTRE DE CACHET
- group or school of seals POD
- royal seal on documents GREAT

SEAL, PRIVY SEAL
- strip a whale, seal, or the like of its skin or blubber FLENSE
- study of seals and signet rings SPHRAGISTICS, SIGILLOGRAPHY

seam or joint line, as on a seedpod or between the bones of the skull SUTURE

seaplane or its broad float HYDROPLANE
- float supporting a seaplane PONTOON

search a person as for concealed weapons or the like FRISK
- search for food or provisions, as by scouring the country FORAGE
- search for something, such as an explanation, without much hope CAST ABOUT FOR
- search for something in an unmethodical way RUMMAGE, FOSSICK
- search intensely and thoroughly, inquire deeply DELVE, PROBE
- search the bed of a river, lake, or canal by trailing a grappling hook or net along it DRAG
- search through and examine closely to separate the good from the bad, sift WINNOW
- search through rubbish for food or useful objects SCAVENGE
- search for senior employees from other firms HEAD-HUNTING
- close examination or search, as by careful reading PERUSAL, SCRUTINY
- expedition made in search of something FORAY
- judicial writ, as for authorizing a search or arrest WARRANT
- make a preliminary search or survey of an area RECONNOITER
- object of a long search GRAIL
- solve a problem, penetrate a mystery, or the like, by painstaking searching or research FATHOM

seasick, queasy, or dizzy WOOZY
- seasickness MAL DE MER
- seasickness or similar queasy feeling preceding vomiting NAUSEA

season or time of year when hunting, fishing, shooting of game, or the like is permitted OPEN SEASON
- season or time of year when hunting, fishing, or the like is prohibited CLOSED SEASON

seasonings See **herbs**

seat extending across a small boat, typically for an oarsman THWART
- seat in a military aircraft designed to hurl the pilot or crew member clear in an emergency EJECTION SEAT, EJECTOR SEAT
- seat or saddle for a second rider, as on a horse or motorcycle PILLION
- seat that folds down, as in a taxi or aircraft JUMP SEAT
- seats facing each other by or beside a large fireplace INGLENOOK
- open-air rows of seats, especially in a sports stadium BLEACHERS
- row of seats in a rising series TIER

seaweed ash used as a source of iodine and potash KELP, VAREC

second self, another side of oneself ALTER EGO

second (combining form) DEUT-, DEUTO-, DEUTERO-

second-last, last but one PENULTIMATE

second-year student SOPHOMORE

secondary, accompanying or associated rather than central AFFILIATED, APPENDANT, ATTENDANT, ACCESSORY, APPURTENANT, CONCOMITANT
- secondary, having a helping or enabling rather than central function AUXILIARY, ANCILLARY
- secondary, less important SUBORDINATE, COLLATERAL, INCIDENTAL
- secondary or lower in rank or status SUBSIDIARY, SUBSERVIENT, SUBALTERN
- secondary remark or action AFTERTHOUGHT, FOOTNOTE, POSTSCRIPT

secondary (combining form) BY-, SUB-

secondhand or indirect, as pleasure is when gained through someone else's achievements or actions VICARIOUS

secret, as official information or documents might be CLASSIFIED
- secret, hidden SUBTERRANEAN, COVERT
- secret, hidden, or secluded places RECESSES, FASTNESSES
- secret, mysterious, known or understood only by those who have made a special study or been initiated ARCANE, ESOTERIC, OCCULT, CRYPTIC
- secret, private, very personal INTIMATE
- secret agent who joins a political or criminal group and tries to incite it into punishable or discrediting activities AGENT PROVOCATEUR
- secret agreement for sinister or illegal purposes COLLUSION, CONNIVANCE
- secret and hidden, and often probably illegal CLANDESTINE, FURTIVE, BACKSTAIR
- secret and stealthy, as political maneuvering might be SURREPTITIOUS
- secret entry into or establishment in an organization, region, or the like, as by spies or enemy troops INFILTRATION
- secret group or committee as of plotters CABAL, JUNTO
- secret information, especially about an enemy, as obtained by spies INTELLIGENCE
- secret meeting or appointment, especially between lovers ASSIGNATION
- secret or in private, especially relating to a court hearing from which the public has been excluded IN CAMERA
- secret or mystical philosophy, specifically one based on the Hebrew Scriptures CABALA
- secret store of money, drugs, or the like STASH, CACHE
- secret thought or intention that is deliberately held back ARRIÈRE-PENSÉE
- secret weapon to pull out when all else has failed TRUMP CARD
- secret writing system or code in which letters are substituted according to a key CIPHER
- secretive, done or carried out in a stealthy or underhand manner SURREPTITIOUS, FURTIVE
- secretly, in confidence SUB ROSA
- secretly, in disguise or under an assumed name, to avoid being recognized INCOGNITO
- secretly or stealthily harmful, treacherous INSIDIOUS
- announcement of some new information or secret fact REVELATION, DISCLOSURE
- bring a secret or obscure information to light DISINTER
- done or acting in secret UNDERCOVER
- done or told in secret, private CONFIDENTIAL
- knowing something secret or private PRIVY
- person to whom one tells one's secrets or private worries (masculine and feminine, respectively) CONFIDANT, CONFIDANTE
- place for depositing secret letters, stolen goods, or the like for collection DROP
- reveal some private or secret information DISCLOSE, DIVULGE
- security classification for documents that is less tight than a secret status RESTRICTED
- uncommunicative, keeping or appearing to be keeping secrets TACITURN, CLOSE

secret (combining form) CRYPT-, CRYPTO-

secret service, secret police, or intelligence agency of the U.S.S.R., in its various forms prior to the KGB CHEKA, GPU, OGPU, NKVD, MVD
- secret service and private police force under the Duvalier dictatorship in Haiti TONTONS MACOUTE
- secret service and foreign intelli-

gence agency of the United States CENTRAL INTELLIGENCE AGENCY, CIA
- secret service department of the KGB, used to eliminate spies overseas SMERSH
- secret service of France SERVICE DE DOCUMENTATION EXTÉRIEURE ET CONTRE-ESPIONAGE, SDECE
- secret service of Israel MOSSAD
- secret service or security police in Nazi Germany GESTAPO, GEHEIME STAATSPOLIZEI, ABWEHR, SICHERHEITSDIENST, SD
- military secret service in the U.S.S.R., covering international intelligence GRU

secret society of French settlers in Algeria opposed to Algerian independence OAS, ORGANISATION DE L' ARMÉE SECRÈTE
- secret society in China at the turn of the century that sought to drive out foreigners BOXERS, HARMONIOUS FISTS
- secret society of prominent Afrikaners in South Africa, promoting Afrikaner interests BROEDERBOND
- secret society of racist white supremacists terrorizing African-Americans, Jews, and Catholics KU KLUX KLAN
- body of people joined in a religious order, guild, secret society, or the like FRATERNITY
- Chinese secret society, often engaged in criminal activities TONG
- criminal secret society of Sicilian origin COSA NOSTRA, MAFIA
- fanatical Muslim secret society that preyed upon Christian Crusaders ASSASSINS
- French secret society that organized underground resistance to the Germans in World War II MAQUIS
- international charitable and quasi-religious secret society FREEMASONS, MASONS
- international Chinese secret society, often engaged in drug trafficking TRIAD
- Kenyan secret society of Kikuyu tribespeople that used terrorism in the 1950's to end white colonial rule MAU MAU
- liberal and republican German secret society of the 18th century ILLUMINATI, ILLUMINATEN
- member of a Japanese secret society similar to the Mafia YAKUZA
- members of a 17th-18th century religious secret society, claiming to have mystical knowledge, or of a modern society descended from it ROSICRUCIANS
- Neapolitan secret society, similar to the Mafia CAMORRA
- Sicilian criminal secret society active in the United States in the early 20th century BLACK HAND

secretary or official clerk SCRIBE
- secretary or scribe who takes dictation or makes neat copies of doc-

SCULPTURE TERMS

alabaster	marblelike stone, usually white
anaglyph	carving or ornament in bas-relief
armature	frame used to support clay, wax, or plaster in modeling
atlas/telamon	male statue used as a column, as in an ancient Greek temple
banker	sculptor's workbench
bas-relief/ basso-relievo/low relief	sculpture in which the figures project only slightly from the background
calvary	representation of the Crucifixion
cameo	small bas-relief carving in stone, glass, or shell, the design in relief in a color different from the background
caryatid	female statue used as a column, as in an ancient Greek temple
chryselephantine	made or decorated with gold and ivory, as ancient Greek statues were
cire perdue/ lost-wax process	technique in bronze casting in which the wax layer between core and mold is melted away and replaced by bronze
corbeil	sculpture of a basket of fruit or flowers, used as an architectural ornament
diaglyph	carving or ornament in intaglio
gesso	mixture of plaster of paris or gypsum and glue, used as a base for bas-relief or to prepare a painting surface
intaglio	carving in which the design is cut into the surface, the opposite of relief
kore	ancient Greek female statue, usually draped
kouros	ancient Greek male statue, usually nude
mantle	clay mold around a wax model
maquette/ bozzetto	preliminary model for a sculpture
mobile	abstract construction with parts that move when pushed or blown
pietà	representation of Mary holding the body of Jesus
putto/amorino	figure of a small child or cherub
relief/relievo	sculpture in which the figures half project from a flat background
restrike	impression taken from a sculptor's mold at some time after the original edition
spall	chip broken from a stone carving
stabile	construction resembling a mobile in appearance, but at least partly stationary

uments AMANUENSIS
- secretary to a king or nobleman in former times CHANCELLOR

section See **part**
- section, as of a text or recital, that is more striking or elaborate than the rest PURPLE PATCH, PURPLE PASSAGE
- section of a document, contract, law, or the like CLAUSE

secular, lay, or civil rather than spiritual or religious TEMPORAL

secure See **safe, tight, join**

security classification for documents that is less tight than a secret status RESTRICTED
- security in the form of a deposit or pledge GAGE
- security or guarantor against loss or damage SURETY
- security pledged for a loan COLLATERAL
- pledge or mortgage something as security HYPOTHECATE
- something giving security or emotional stability MOORING

sediment of fine sand deposited in or by a river SILT
- sediment of wine, cider, or the like DREGS, LEES

seduce or corrupt someone, especially someone young and innocent DEBAUCH
- man who pursues and seduces women regularly, playboy DON JUAN, ladykiller, LOTHARIO, RAKE

see See also **look**
- see, catch sight of, especially when on the lookout DETECT, DISCERN, DESCRY
- "see above," term directing a reader to consult an earlier passage VIDE SUPRA
- "see below," term directing a reader to consult a later passage VIDE INFRA
- see clearly, make out, notice distinctly DISTINGUISH
- see in the mind's eye, imagine, fancy VISUALIZE, ENVISION
- see or glimpse something elusive or far away, catch sight of ESPY
- see or hear, observe clearly PERCEIVE, REMARK, WITNESS
- see the point of, understand, grasp APPREHEND, PENETRATE

seed See illustration, page 480, and also **flower**
- seed coat, animal skin, or similar natural covering INTEGUMENT
- seed-eating, feeding on seeds or grain GRANIVOROUS
- seed-eating, feeding on seeds or grass GRAMINIVOROUS
- seed leaf, a simple food-storing leaf in some sprouting seeds COTYLEDON
- seed or pip of a grape or berry ACINUS
- seed or pod of the pea, bean, or related plant LEGUME
- seed pod of cotton, flax, or similar plants BOLL
- seed used as an aromatic flavoring in cooking and baking, as in rye bread CARAWAY
- seeds of a leguminous plant such as lentils PULSES
- begin to grow, as seeds do GERMINATE
- casing of a seed or seeds of a fruit, developed from the plant's ovary PERICARP
- cut or soften the coat of a hard seed to speed up germination SCARIFY
- embryonic seed of a plant, before fertilization OVULE
- furrow or implement for planting seeds DRILL
- having two winglike projections, as some seeds are DIPTEROUS
- lightweight fragments of mica-derived material used in seedbeds and for insulation VERMICULITE
- part of a seedling plant between the cotyledons and the radical HYPOCOTYL
- part of the seed that develops into the main root RADICLE
- part of the seed that develops into the shoot or stem PLUMULE
- referring to seeds SEMINAL
- referring to seeds that germinate while still attached to the parent plant VIVIPAROUS
- reproductive cell or organ, the counterpart of a seed, in non-flowering plants such as mosses and ferns and in fungi SPORE
- scar on the coat of a bean or other seed, marking the point where it was joined to the stalk HILUM, UMBILICUS
- seam or joint line, as on a seedpod or between the bones of the skull SUTURE
- seam or raised ridge on the coat of some seeds RAPHE
- small, flattish seed used for flavoring food, often sprinkled on bread rolls SESAME, BENNE
- sow seed over a wide area, typically by hand BROADCAST
- split or burst open along a seam, as a pod or fruit might, to release seeds or pollen DEHISCE
- stalk connecting a seed to the wall of the ovary FUNICULUS
- swelling or fleshy outgrowth on the coat of a seed CARUNCLE
- thick hard outer coat of a seed TESTA
- thin delicate inner coat of a seed TEGMEN
- thin membrane covering a seed or other plant part TUNIC
- tiny opening in a plant ovule through which the pollen tube can enter to produce a fertilized seed MICROPYLE
- tissue surrounding and feeding the embryo in the seed of a flowering plant ENDOSPERM
- tray of soil in which seeds or cuttings are grown, or such seeds or cuttings PROPAGATOR
- tuft of hairs on the seed coat of some seeds COMA

seed (combining form) -SPERM-, -GON-, GONO-, GRANI-

seeing or knowing things by allegedly superhuman or telepathic means CLAIRVOYANCE
- seeing or showing everything PANOPTIC

seek See **search**

seem - *seem, be, feel*, or similar verb that identifies the predicate of a verb with the subject COPULA

seeming, apparent, but usually just pretended, as someone's alleged purpose might be PURPORTED, PROFESSED
- seeming, apparent, outward, as a given reason might be OSTENSIBLE
- seeming change in the position of an object when the observer changes position PARALLAX
- seemingly, apparently, supposedly REPUTEDLY
- seemingly attractive, genuine, or sound, but not really so SPECIOUS
- seemingly but not really, in name only NOMINALLY

seemingly (combining form) QUASI-

seesaw, balance precariously TEETER
- seesawlike bridge or roadway, hinged near a weighted end so as to be raised or lowered BASCULE
- arm of a seesaw, or other extension from a fulcrum CANTILEVER

seize territory and incorporate it into another country ANNEX
- seize, interrupt, or stop something, such as a message, in its course INTERCEPT
- seize and kill without trial an alleged offender, as an impassioned mob might LYNCH
- seize at customs IMPOUND, EMBARGO
- seize by force and hold illegally the power, rights, throne, or the like of another USURP
- seize or take possession, especially under wartime regulations COMMANDEER
- seize or take temporary possession of someone's property, as to force payment of a debt DISTRAIN, DISTRESS, SEQUESTRATE

- seize someone's property as an official penalty APPROPRIATE, CONFISCATE, LEVY
- seizing property by force PILLAGE, RAPINE
- seizure of a neutral ship in wartime SPOLIATION

seizure, fit (combining form) -LEPSY

select See **choose**

selection of literary passages, as used for studying a foreign language CHRESTOMATHY
- selections from a literary work or works ANALECTS

self - another side to oneself, a second self ALTER EGO
- self-assured, poised, not embarrassed UNABASHED
- self-confessed, openly acknowledged by oneself, candidly admitted AVOWED, PROFESSED
- self-confidence, assured manner COMPOSURE, POISE, APLOMB
- self-confident and self-assertive, pushy BUMPTIOUS
- self-contradictory or apparently absurd statement that is not necessarily untrue PARADOX
- self-control, ability to keep one's temper COUNTENANCE, COMPOSURE
- self-control or restraint, such as urinary or sexual restraint CONTINENCE
- self-defense techniques, such as kung fu and karate MARTIAL ARTS
- self-denial, especially restraint in eating and drinking ABSTINENCE, ABSTEMIOUSNESS, TEMPERANCE
- self-denying, living a strict life, with minimum comforts and pleasures, often for religious reasons ASCETIC
- self-evident, obvious AXIOMATIC
- self-evident or self-confirming, as a proposition in logic might be ANALYTIC, A PRIORI
- self-examination, reflection on one's feelings or motives HEART-SEARCHING, INTROSPECTION
- self-generated, apparently uncaused SPONTANEOUS
- self-government, independence SOVEREIGNTY, AUTONOMY
- self-importance in a minor official OFFICIOUSNESS, BUMBLEDOM
- self-indulgence in immoral or sensual pursuits DISSIPATION, DISSOLUTION, INTEMPERANCE, DEBAUCHERY, DEPRAVITY
- self-indulgent or luxuriously sensual living FLESHPOTS
- self-indulgent, decadent, self-absorbed EFFETE
- self-interest, advantageous rather than fair behavior EXPEDIENCY
- self-love or excessive admiration of oneself NARCISSISM, EGOTISM
- self-opinionated and reactionary man, especially an officer or bureaucrat COLONEL BLIMP
- self-persuasion, either conscious or unconscious AUTOSUGGESTION
- self-reflecting, turned back upon the source, as thoughts might be REFLEXIVE
- self-reliance as a government policy, or a self-sufficient territory or country AUTARKY
- self-respect, appropriate pride in oneself, sense of one's own worth and dignity AMOUR PROPRE
- self-righteous, holier-than-thou MORALISTIC, SANCTIMONIOUS
- self-righteous or puritanically disapproving, usually in a hypocritical way PHARISAICAL
- self-sacrifice or self-denial ABNEGATION
- self-taught person AUTODIDACT
- self-satisfied, narrow-minded, and arrogant person PRIG
- self-satisfied or smug, to the point of feeling that nothing more needs to be done COMPLACENT
- self-seeking, largely or purely self-interested EGOISTIC
- self-service meal in which the dishes are all placed on a counter or table BUFFET, SMORGASBORD
- having great self-discipline, fortitude, and endurance SPARTAN
- indulge oneself luxuriously, as in sensual pleasures or self-pity REVEL, WALLOW
- relating to or arising from the individual self or mind rather than external reality SUBJECTIVE
- theory that the self is the only knowable and thus the only existing reality SOLIPSISM
- universal life-enhancing drive or instinct for self-preservation, in Freudian theory EROS
- universal death wish or instinct for self-destruction, in Freudian theory THANATOS

self (combining form) AUT-, AUTO-

self-important See **pompous**

selfish, self-centered EGOCENTRIC
- selfish, self-seeking, intent only on increasing one's own power or status SELF-AGGRANDIZING
- selfishly advantageous rather than fair or moral EXPEDIENT

selfless, concerned for others' welfare ALTRUISTIC

sell assets for cash, as to pay off debts LIQUIDATE
- sell goods in the street or while traveling from place to place VEND, PEDDLE, HAWK
- sell in a forceful way HUSTLE
- sell or give away DISPOSE OF
- sell or transfer the ownership of documents, shares, or the like NEGOTIATE
- selling and buying, especially of disreputable goods such as drugs TRAFFICKING
- selling of goods in a foreign country cheaply, often at below cost price DUMPING
- selling system in which the goods are sold in turn to several agents or distributors before going on retail sale PYRAMID SELLING
- selling through advertising, exhibitions, and other techniques MERCHANDISING
- do business, buy, sell TRANSACT

seller of cloth and sewing materials, in England DRAPER
- seller of goods in the street or door-to-door HAWKER, PEDDLER, HUCKSTER
- seller of provisions who accompanied an army in former times SUTLER
- seller of quack remedies, as in the Wild West MOUNTEBANK
- seller or manufacturer of candles CHANDLER
- seller or manufacturer of socks and knitted underwear HOSIER
- seller or provider of food, such as a wholesale grocer PURVEYOR, PROVISIONER

seller (combining form) -MONGER

semaphore See illustration, page 482

semen - glandular tissue at the base of the bladder in men, secreting the fluid for semen PROSTATE
- impregnate with semen INSEMINATE
- person or animal that provides semen for artificial insemination DONOR
- sudden discharge of semen EJACULATION

semiprecious stones See chart at **precious stones**

send away or withdraw troops or inhabitants from a place of danger EVACUATE
- send money, as through the post REMIT
- send out or give off something, such as radiation EMIT, EMANATE
- send to a particular destination DISPATCH
- hand over goods to someone to send or deliver CONSIGN

senile person DOTARD
- senility DOTAGE
- presenile mental deterioration ALZHEIMER'S DISEASE

senior or eldest member of a group, society, diplomatic circle, or the like (masculine and feminine, respectively) DOYEN, DOYENNE

sensational, macabre, or gruesome, often in a deliberately artificial way GRAND GUIGNOL
- sensationalizing journals and newspapers YELLOW PRESS

sense See **meaning**

senseless and irresponsible, as a wild spree might be INSENSATE

senses, such as sight, smell, and touch MODALITIES
- sensing cell, nerve, organ, or the like RECEPTOR
- sensing or perceiving allegedly by means of a sixth sense TELESTHESIA
- detectable by any of the senses PERCEPTIBLE
- doctrine that all true knowledge derives from experience, especially from sense perceptions EMPIRICISM
- object or experience perceived by or apparently real to the senses, rather than known through reasoning or intuition PHENOMENON
- object or experience that is known through reasoning or intuition rather than perceived by the senses, thing in itself NOUMENON

sensitive, delicate, capable of or based on fine distinctions SUBTLE
- sensitive emotionally, easily affected SUSCEPTIBLE, VULNERABLE, THIN-SKINNED
- sensitive part, as of one's nails or emotions QUICK
- sensitive to emotion or suffering, able to feel PASSIBLE

sensory organs or feelers near the mouth, as in some insects and shellfish PALPS, PALPI
- sensory organs or feelers on the head of an insect, shellfish, or the like ANTENNAE
- sensory organs or feelers on the head of the catfish and some other fishes BARBELS

sensual, luxurious, and self-indulgent living FLESHPOTS
- sensual overindulgence, especially in immoral pursuits DISSIPATION, INTEMPERANCE, DISSOLUTION, DEBAUCHERY, DEPRAVITY
- sensualist, person devoted to luxurious living and the sensual pleasures VOLUPTUARY, SYBARITE, HEDONIST

sentence, name, or the like that is difficult to pronounce or to say quickly TONGUE TWISTER
- sentence, word, or phrase reading exactly the same forward or backward, such as *poor Dan in a droop* PALINDROME
- sentence containing every letter of the alphabet, such as *The quick brown fox jumps over the lazy dog* PANGRAM
- sentence formation in which subordinating clauses are joined by conjunctions HYPOTAXIS
- sentence formation through joining phrases or clauses with punctuation rather than conjunctions PARATAXIS
- sentence in which the completion of the main clause comes right at the end PERIODIC SENTENCE
- sentence in which there is a sudden change to a second, inconsistent grammatical pattern ANACOLUTHON
- sentence or utterance that is very short or curt, specifically one of a single syllable MONOSYLLABLE
- sentence stating the main idea in a paragraph, often placed at the beginning TOPIC SENTENCE
- sentence with several carefully arranged clauses PERIOD
- break down a sentence into its component parts of speech and give a grammatical explanation of these PARSE
- breaking off speech or writing in midsentence, for dramatic effect APOSIOPESIS
- phrase or clause, group of words forming part of a sentence CONSTRUCTION
- prison sentence or detention order, imposed by a court CUSTODIAL SENTENCE
- prison sentence that is served only in the event of a subsequent sentence SUSPENDED SENTENCE
- prison sentence whose length is not specified at the time it is imposed INDETERMINATE SENTENCE
- reduction of the length of a prison sentence, as for good behavior REMISSION
- reduce to a lighter prison sentence, penalty, or the like COMMUTE
- referring to a subordinate clause within a sentence EMBEDDED
- release of a prisoner before the full completion of his or her sentence, on condition of good behavior PAROLE
- running simultaneously, as two prison sentences might be CONCURRENT
- suspending of an offender's prison sentence subject to good behavior and submission to supervision PROBATION

sentimental about things of the past NOSTALGIC
- sentimental and clichéd material, as in a film or play HOKUM

Seeds

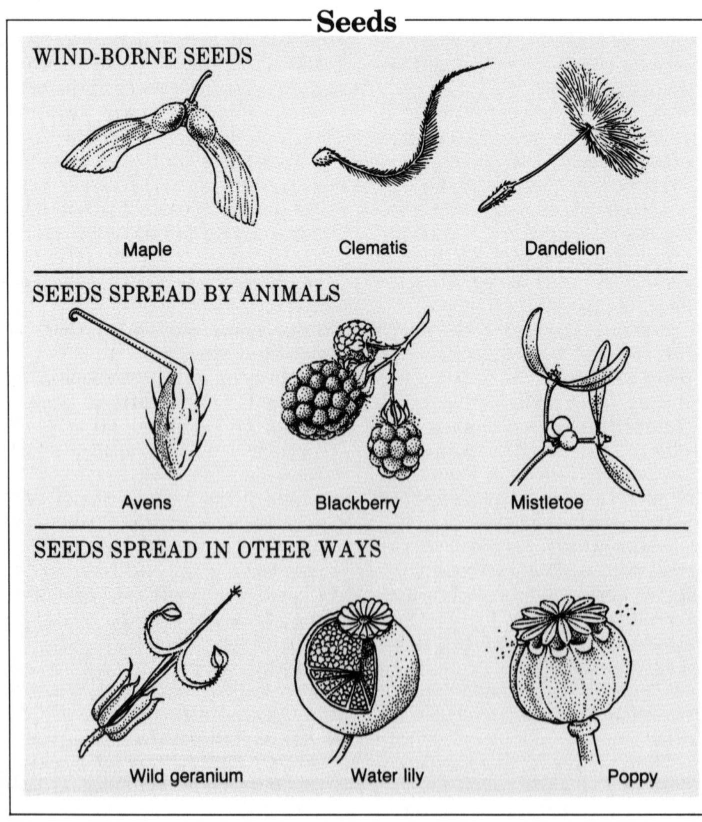

- sentimental and pretentious art KITSCH
- sentimental in a cheap or vulgar way, mushy MAUDLIN, MAWKISH
- sentimental in a weak, affected way, as manners or poetry might be NAMBY-PAMBY, INSIPID
- sentimentality, as in art and music SCHMALTZ
- sentimentally affecting or touching POIGNANT
- sentimentally or excessively sweet, polite, or friendly SACCHARINE, CLOYING

sentry, guard SENTINEL
- sentry on horseback stationed ahead of an army or formation on the move VEDETTE

separate See also **divide**
- separate, disconnect, remove without breaking DETACH, DISJOIN, DISLODGE
- separate, distinct, or individual DIVERSE
- separate, remove, or distance, as when distancing oneself from a decision DISSOCIATE
- separate, remove, or take out as for special attention or treatment PRESCIND
- separate, unconnected, individual, distinct DISCRETE
- separate and move in different directions from a point DIVERGE, DIVARICATE
- separate from the surrounding environment INSULATE, ISOLATE, CORDON OFF
- separate grain or seed from the stems and husks by means of beating THRESH, FLAIL
- separate grain or seed from the stems and husks by means of wind WINNOW
- separate into sections, divide up PARTITION, DISMEMBER, FRAGMENT, SEGMENT
- separate into small or basic parts DECOMPOSE, DISINTEGRATE
- separate multiple copies, continuous stationery, or the like into individual documents DECOLLATE
- separate or divide into branches, fork BIFURCATE, RAMIFY
- separate or divide into different classes, categories, or the like PIGEONHOLE, COMPARTMENTALIZE
- separate or extract an essence, idea, or the like DISTILL
- separate or isolate someone, especially to prevent spread of a disease QUARANTINE
- separate or remove from others or from an entire group SEGREGATE
- separate or scatter, as troops might after a defeat DISBAND
- separated, divided, split CLEFT, CLOVEN, ASUNDER
- separated, remote, lonely, solitary, as a place or life might be SECLUDED, SEQUESTERED, CLOISTERED
- separated or unfriendly through having been offended or antagonized ESTRANGED, ALIENATED
- come between, as to separate people fighting INTERPOSE, INTERVENE

separate (combining form) DIA-, -SECT

separately or severally, in the order stated RESPECTIVELY

separation into constituent parts or elements RESOLUTION
- separation of a chemical mixture into its components, as on the basis of different boiling points FRACTIONATION
- separation or classification into two parts, such as conflicting opinions DICHOTOMY

separation (combining form) AP-, APO-, DIS-

sequence of those in line for a title or throne SUCCESSION
- sequence or order of priority, based on rank, as at public ceremonies PRECEDENCE
- arrange something, such as pages, in the correct sequence COLLATE, COLLOCATE
- change or reverse the sequence or relative positioning of two or more things TRANSPOSE
- lacking an orderly arrangement or sequence HAPHAZARD, RANDOM, ARBITRARY, ALEATORY, ALEATORIC
- ordered, in sequence, successive, serial SEQUENTIAL, CONSECUTIVE
- put into sequence, systematize CODIFY, TABULATE
- rearrangement, shuffling, change of sequence PERMUTATION

serf See also **peasant**
- serf in ancient Sparta HELOT
- serf in Russia in czarist times MUZHIK

serial, successive, ordered SEQUENTIAL, CONSECUTIVE
- installment of a serial EPISODE

series, as of electrical components CASCADE
- series, full range or extent, from the beginning to the end, as of musical notes GAMUT
- series, unbroken chain of events, officeholders, or the like SUCCESSION, PROGRESSION, SEQUENCE
- series graded according to rank or importance HIERARCHY
- series of changes without any obvious divisions CONTINUUM, SPECTRUM, CLINE
- series of events in which each causes or influences the one following CHAIN REACTION, CAUSALITY
- series of linked events, ideas, terms, or the like CONCATENATION, CATENATION
- series of steps, stages, degrees, or the like, a gradual progression GRADATION
- series of things occurring or used together and forming a unit SUITE
- series of tunes played as a single piece of music MEDLEY
- one after another in sequence, item by item in series SERIATIM

serious, deep, and sincere, as desires might be FERVENT, HEARTFELT
- serious, critically important MOMENTOUS, CONSEQUENTIAL
- serious, determined, meaning business RESOLUTE, INTENT
- serious, dignified, earnest, sober in manner STAID, SEDATE
- serious, grim, grave, unsmiling, solemn SOMBER, POKER-FACED
- serious, intense, very dangerous, as a hardship or shortage might be DRASTIC, ACUTE, GRIEVOUS
- serious and dutiful hard work DILIGENCE, ASSIDUITY, CONSCIENTIOUSNESS, APPLICATION
- serious or solemn manner, bearing, or quality GRAVITAS, GRAVITY
- intensify, make something more serious, as an error or anxiety COMPOUND, AGGRAVATE
- keeping a straight face or being apparently serious, as when telling a joke DEADPAN
- lightness or frivolity of manner, especially when seriousness would be more appropriate LEVITY
- make something more serious or severe, such as a pain or difficulty EXACERBATE, AGGRAVATE
- represent a crime, fault, or the like as less serious or blameworthy, as by making certain excuses EXTENUATE, MITIGATE
- thoughtful, serious, or reflective PENSIVE, INTROSPECTIVE

servant, assistant, or private secretary of a scholar, magician, or the like in former times FAMULUS
- servant, attendant, or disciple ACOLYTE, VARLET
- servant, attendant, or minor official in a royal or noble household in former times YEOMAN
- servant, employee, or assistant with varied duties FACTOTUM
- servant, usually a foreign young woman, employed to help with children and domestic chores AU PAIR
- servant or assistant with numerous duties and responsibilities MAN FRIDAY, GIRL FRIDAY, FACTOTUM
- servant employed to breast-feed her employer's baby WET NURSE

- servant of long-standing service with a particular family or household RETAINER
- servant or stableman in former times who took care of horses, as at a coaching inn OSTLER
- servant who cares for or supervises the horses GROOM
- servant who supervised the serving of meals in medieval times SEWER
- servant whose work is within a house rather than in the gardens, stables, or the like DOMESTIC
- adjective for a servant MENIAL, ANCILLARY
- boy or young man employed at a hotel, club, or the like as a messenger or general junior servant PAGE, BELLHOP
- boy servant at an inn in former times POTBOY
- boy servant in former times who cleaned shoes BOOTBLACK, BOOTS
- castrated male servant in a harem EUNUCH

Semaphore

Semaphore alphabet: Signals can be sent by arm movements, with or without flags, as well as by machine. The receiver may be in front of or behind the signaler; therefore, the direction sign—with left arm horizontal—is given first to show which way the signs are to be read.

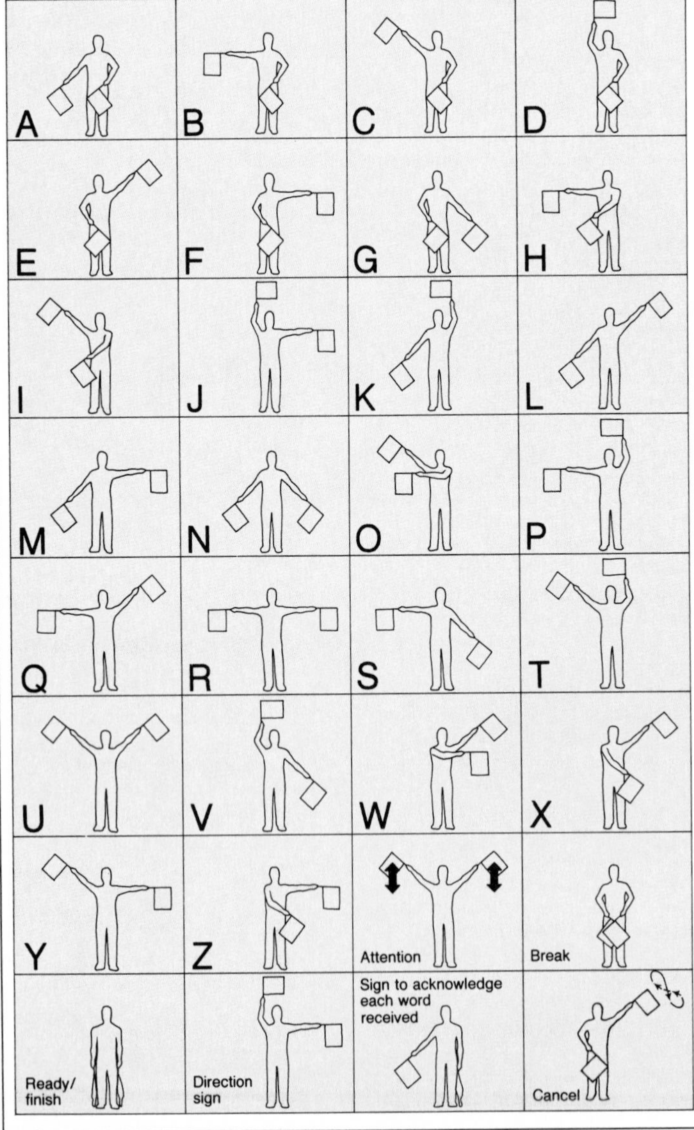

- devil or spirit acting as servant to a witch or magician FAMILIAR
- female attendant or servant in former times HANDMAID
- female servant in the East, especially a nursemaid AMAH
- female servant who cleans, makes beds, and the like in a hotel or similar establishment CHAMBERMAID, FEMME DE CHAMBRE
- group of servants or employees in attendance upon a person or household RETINUE, TRAIN, SUITE
- high-ranking servant or steward in a royal or noble household in former times CHAMBERLAIN, SENESCHAL
- highest-ranking male servant in a household BUTLER, MAJORDOMO
- Indian nursemaid or female domestic servant AYAH
- Indian or Chinese laborer or outdoor servant, especially in former times COOLIE
- junior employee or low-ranking servant in a large organization MINION, VASSAL
- knight's attendant or personal servant in former times SQUIRE, ESQUIRE, VARLET
- lady's maid, personal servant of a woman ABIGAIL, FEMME DE CHAMBRE, TIREWOMAN
- liveried servant in former times who ran messages and accompanied his employer on outings FOOTMAN, CHASSEUR
- male servant such as a footman, especially one dressed in a uniform FLUNKY, LACKEY
- man's personal servant VALET, VALET DE CHAMBRE
- person who fetches and carries, runs errands, and is generally treated as a servant GOFER
- personal servant or employee performing various secretarial tasks AMANUENSIS
- trusted female servant who acts as governess or chaperon to the daughters of the family, especially as formerly in Spanish-speaking countries DUENNA

service or assistance MINISTRATIONS
- services or features of a place that are convenient and helpful FACILITIES, AMENITIES

services See **military**
- units in the armed services GROUP, COMMAND, CORPS, DIVISION, WING, FLIGHT, BRIGADE, REGIMENT, BATTALION, COMPANY, BATTERY, TROOP, PLATOON, SQUAD

serving as host, priest, or other official for the occasion OFFICIATING
- serving only as a means to an end, purely instrumental SUBSERVIENT, EXPEDIENT

- serving stand or cart next to a dining table DUMBWAITER

sesame seed or oil BENNE
- sesame-seed oil GINGILI
- sesame-seed paste TAHIN, TAHEEN
- sweetmeat made of honey and crushed sesame seeds HALVAH

session - fully attended or open to all, as a session of a conference might be PLENARY

set, as of matching clothes or furniture ENSEMBLE
- set in motion, start ACTUATE
- set in one's ways, refusing to change mind or course IMPLACABLE, INTRACTABLE, INEXORABLE
- set in one's ways, unyielding or blinkered RIGID, INFLEXIBLE, OSSIFIED, FOSSILIZED, MONOLITHIC
- set up or establish a court, institution, or the like CONSTITUTE
- setting forth of information, intentions, or the like EXPOSITION
- associating the members of one set with those of another MAPPING
- person who sets type, in preparation for printing COMPOSITOR, KEYBOARDER
- forming a set, especially of rooms EN SUITE

set fire to IGNITE, KINDLE

setting for a jewel, or a jeweled brooch or clasp OUCH
- setting of a play or novel LOCALE
- setting or surroundings MILIEU, AMBIENCE

settle a debt or claim LIQUIDATE
- settle an argument or differences COMPOSE, RECONCILE, DETERMINE
- settle or attempt to settle a dispute between other people or groups MEDIATE, ARBITRATE, CONCILIATE, MODERATE
- settle or sink, as the sediment in a liquid does SUBSIDE
- settling of a bill or account RECKONING

settled or established firmly or securely in a position ENSCONCED, ENTRENCHED

seven - relating to or based on the number seven, or having seven parts SEPTENARY
- seven deadly sins CARDINAL SINS
- seven dwarfs DOPEY, SLEEPY, GRUMPY, DOC, HAPPY, SNEEZY, BASHFUL
- lasting for seven years, or occurring once every seven years SEPTENNIAL
- meeting or occurring every seven days, as a weekly committee would HEBDOMADAL, HEBDOMATARY

seven (combining form) SEPT-, SEPTI-, HEBDO-, HEPT-, HEPTA-

seventy-year-old, or aged between 70 and 79 SEPTUAGENARIAN

several See also **many**
- several, various MISCELLANEOUS, SUNDRY, DIVERS, MYRIAD

several (combining form) PLURI-, MULTI-, POLY-

severe, demanding, strict, as a law might be EXACTING, IRONCLAD
- severe, strict, moralistic, and self-denying, especially from religious considerations ASCETIC, PURITANICAL, BLUENOSED, STRAITLACED
- severe, strict, rigid, demanding RIGOROUS
- severe, strict, stern, and serious in life-style and morality AUSTERE
- severe, tough, very disciplined, as an upbringing might be SPARTAN
- severe, very harsh, as a law or punishment might be DRACONIAN
- severe, very harsh, as scornful criticism might be SCATHING
- severe and stiff in discipline, allowing little individualism PRUSSIAN, TEUTONIC
- severe disciplinarian or strict authoritarian MARTINET, RAMROD
- reduce the severity of a crime, pain, or the like MITIGATE, PALLIATE, EXTENUATE, ALLEVIATE

sewing See chart, pages 486–487, and also **embroidery**
- sewing or stitching together of edges of a wound SUTURE
- foot-operated lever for driving a sewing machine, potter's wheel, or the like TREADLE
- tapered tuck made when sewing an item of clothing DART

sewage, chemical waste, or other waste liquid EFFLUENT
- sewage enriched by air and added to untreated sewage to encourage bacterial action and speed up purification ACTIVATED SLUDGE
- sewage tank in which solid waste is decomposed by bacteria SEPTIC TANK
- pit or hole for sewage or waste from household drains CESSPOOL
- solid deposit produced during the early stages of sewage treatment SLUDGE

sewer CLOACA
- sewer or drain, as under a road CULVERT, CONDUIT

sex attractant, warning chemical, or other substance secreted by certain animals and affecting others of the same species PHEROMONE
- sex between closely related people INCEST
- sex classification GENDER
- sex gland, specifically an ovary or testis GONAD
- sex party, or gathering involving unrestrained promiscuity ORGY
- sexual activity, typically in short casual relationships, with new partners PROMISCUITY
- sexual arousal by or obsession with inanimate objects, such as shoes, or exclusive obsession with parts of the body other than the sexual organs FETISHISM
- sexual capability in the male POTENCY, VIRILITY
- sexual drive LIBIDO, EROS
- sexual excitement in female mammals HEAT, ESTRUS
- sexual excitement or frenzy in male camels, elephants, and other large mammals MUSTH, MUST
- sexual harassment, abuse, or assault MOLESTATION
- sexual intercourse, copulation, as referred to in formal contexts or in former times COITUS, COITION, CARNAL KNOWLEDGE, UNION, CONGRESS, CONJUNCTION, CONJUGATION, CONVERSATION, CONSUMMATION, COMMERCE
- sexual intercourse, especially when adulterous or considered immoral FORNICATION
- sexual intercourse between a man and a boy or youth PEDERASTY
- sexual intercourse cut short before ejaculation, as a supposed means of contraception COITUS INTERRUPTUS
- sexual interest in or attraction toward children PEDOPHILIA
- sexual intimacy between women, of a kind mimicking sexual intercourse between men and women TRIBADISM
- sexual language of an obscene kind BAWDRY
- sexual or emotional attachment, typically immature and neurotic, to a person or thing FIXATION
- sexual organs GENITALS, GENITALIA, PRIVATE PARTS, PRIVATES, REPRODUCTIVE ORGANS
- sexual perversions of various kinds ALGOLAGNIA, BESTIALITY, BONDAGE AND DISCIPLINE, COPROPHILIA, EXHIBITIONISM, FETISHISM, FROTTAGE, MASOCHISM, NECROPHILIA, PEDOPHILIA, SADISM, SCOPOPHILIA, VOYEURISM, ZOOPHILIA
- sexual relationship, an affair LIAISON
- sexual relationship of three people living together MÉNAGE À TROIS
- sexual reproduction involving fertilization of the egg by the sperm AMPHIMIXIS
- sexual restraint, abstinence, or self-control CONTINENCE
- sexual unfaithfulness, especially adultery INFIDELITY
- sexually abnormal behavior PARAPHILIA, DEVIANCE, PERVERSION
- sexually active woman who technically remains a virgin DEMIVIERGE

- sexually appealing VOLUPTUOUS
- sexually arousing or arousable, as a part of the body might be EROGENOUS
- sexually arousing or tantalizing TITILLATING, PROVOCATIVE
- sexually arousing writings, movies, photographs, or the like PORNOGRAPHY, EROTICA
- sexually attracted to other women, as homosexual women are LESBIAN, SAPPHIC
- sexually attracted to persons of one's own sex HOMOSEXUAL, GAY
- sexually attracted to persons of the opposite sex HETEROSEXUAL
- sexually attractive, as a young marriageable woman is said to be NUBILE
- sexually inactive period in female mammals METESTRUS, ANESTRUS
- sexually promiscuous man, stud, playboy RAKE, LADYKILLER, DON JUAN, PHILANDERER, LOTHARIO, LIBERTINE
- sexually promiscuous or immoral WANTON
- sexually promiscuous woman living on the fringes of respectable society, especially in the 19th century DEMIMONDAINE
- sexually uninhibited person, especially one who enjoys swapping partners SWINGER
- abnormally strong sexual desire in a man SATYRIASIS, DON JUAN SYNDROME
- abnormally strong sexual desire in a woman NYMPHOMANIA
- abstaining from or uninterested in sexual intercourse CELIBATE, MONASTIC, ASCETIC, ASEXUAL
- abstaining from unlawful or all sexual activity CHASTE, CONTINENT
- annual state of heat or sexual excitement, as in male deer RUT
- approach someone with an offer of sex, as a prostitute might SOLICIT, ACCOST, PROPOSITION
- broad-minded or tolerant, especially in matters of sexual conduct PERMISSIVE
- characteristic of or resembling both male and female sexes HERMAPHRODITIC, EPICENE, ANDROGYNOUS, MONOECIOUS
- channel or transform a sexual or other instinctual impulse into a socially or more acceptable activity SUBLIMATE
- detailed in describing or representing sexual acts EXPLICIT
- developing or reproducing without sexual union and fertilization, asexual AGAMIC, AGAMOGENETIC, PARTHENOGENETIC
- devil or spirit adopting female form to have sexual intercourse with a sleeping man SUCCUBUS
- devil or spirit adopting male form to have sexual intercourse with a sleeping woman INCUBUS
- early phase of adolescence in which adult sexual characteristics begin to develop PUBERTY
- external sexual organs, especially the female's PUDENDA
- feudal lord's alleged right (legendary, having existed only in literature) to sexual intercourse with the bride of a vassal on her wedding night DROIT DU SEIGNEUR, VIRGINAL TRIBUTE, IUS PRIMAE NOCTIS, RIGHT OF THE FIRST NIGHT
- go-between in a sexual relationship PIMP, PANDER, PANDERER, PROCURER
- having an obsessive interest in sexual matters PRURIENT
- in the very act of having sexual intercourse, especially when illicit IN FLAGRANTE DELICTO
- legal right to sexual intercourse with one's spouse CONJUGAL RIGHTS
- living together and having a sexual relationship but without being formally married POSSLQ, COHABITATION, COMMON-LAW MARRIAGE
- lustful or lewd, given to or arousing sexual desires LASCIVIOUS, LECHEROUS, DEBAUCHED, LIBERTINE, LIBIDINOUS, SALACIOUS, CONCUPISCENT, LUBRICIOUS
- man deriving sexual pleasure from secretly watching courting couples, women undressing, or the like VOYEUR, PEEPING TOM
- person who feels an urge to belong to the opposite sex, specifically one who has undergone a sex-change operation TRANSSEXUAL
- practice of habitually dressing in clothing intended for people of the opposite sex TRANSVESTISM, EONISM, CROSS-DRESSING
- referring to love or a close relationship between two unrelated people that is free of sexual desire PLATONIC
- referring to or suitable for people of either sex UNISEX, EPICENE
- referring to or transmitted by sexual intercourse VENEREAL
- referring to sexual and other physical desires and appetites, sexually suggestive SENSUAL, CARNAL
- referring to sexual love or desire EROTIC, AMATORY
- referring to the region around the sexual organs PUBIC
- stimulating or increasing sexual desire, as certain drugs or foods allegedly do APHRODISIAC
- unable to achieve full sexual satisfaction FRIGID
- unable to have sexual intercourse IMPOTENT
- unconscious or unacknowledged, as secret fears or sexual feelings might be REPRESSED
- whip, flog, or scourge, as for religious discipline or sexual gratification FLAGELLATE
- woman deriving sexual pleasure from secretly watching courting couples, men undressing, or the like VOYEUSE

sexless, neither male nor female NEUTER, EPICENE, UNISEX

sexton of a synagogue BEADLE, SHAMMES

sexual (combining form) -GON-, GONO-

sexual desire (combining form) EROT-, EROTO-

sexual union (combining form) -GAM-

sexy, as a shapely and sensual woman would be CURVACEOUS, VOLUPTUOUS

shackles, restraint, restriction, chains FETTERS

shade a drawing or map with intersecting sets of parallel lines CROSSHATCH
- shade of meaning, subtle distinction NUANCE
- shading of fine lines in a drawing or map HATCHING
- shady, or covered by trees or shrubs BOSKY
- shady, providing shade UMBRAGEOUS
- shady garden shelter, nook, or retreat, often made of trellising BOWER, ARBOR

shadow image or filled-in outline, typically of solid black against a white background, as of a person's profile SILHOUETTE
- shadow picture SCIOGRAM
- shadow play, using small paper figures GALANTY SHOW
- darkest part of a shadow UMBRA
- object, such as the arm of a sundial, that casts a shadow to indicate the time GNOMON
- partial shadow, as during an eclipse, lying between the areas of full shadow and full illumination PENUMBRA

shadow boxing, fighting imaginary enemies SCIAMACHY

shaft that rotates, as in a machine tool ARBOR, SPINDLE, MANDREL

shake, quiver, tremble, or vibrate PALPITATE, QUAVER, PULSATE
- shake, quiver, or tremble, as with rage or from shock QUAKE
- shake or flap rapidly and irregularly FLUTTER
- shake or move in a smooth, wavy rhythm, ripple UNDULATE

- shake or swing regularly back and forth OSCILLATE, VACILLATE, FLUCTUATE
- shake or twitch VELLICATE
- shake or waggle the body rapidly, as if dancing vigorously SHIMMY
- shake or vibrate abnormally, as when changing gear JUDDER
- shake or wave something energetically, such as a weapon or flag BRANDISH, FLOURISH
- shake something vigorously AGITATE, CONVULSE
- shaking, quivering, trembling, or vibrating TREMULOUS
- shaking, quivering, or trembling movement, as from illness or fear TREMOR, TREPIDATION
- shaking a patient vigorously to listen for abnormal pockets of body fluid SUCCUSSION

Shakespeare - excessive enthusiasm for Shakespeare's works BARDOLATRY
- index of all the words in a text, such as the works of Shakespeare, listing every occurrence of each word CONCORDANCE

shaky, badly built or maintained, as a house might be RICKETY, RAMSHACKLE, DILAPIDATED, DECREPIT
- walk in a shaky, unsteady way TEETER, TOTTER

shallow, lacking in depth, interest, or originality SUPERFICIAL, FACILE
- shallow, merely for show, decorative rather than effective, as reforms might be COSMETIC, TOKEN
- shallow stretch of water SHOAL
- shallow stretch of water where the depth can be measured by a weighted line SOUNDING
- effortless or fluent, as in speaking or writing, but typically shallow and insincere GLIB

sham compliance with a law or custom by means of a small gesture TOKENISM

shame, modesty, or prudishness PUDENCY
- shame, dishonor, or disgrace HUMILIATION, DEGRADATION, IGNOMINY, INFAMY
- mark or sign of shame or disgrace STIGMA

shampoo - reddish dye often added to shampoo HENNA
- waxy plant extract used in shampoos, polishes, or the like JOJOBA

shape See chart, page 488, and also **geometry**
- shape, form, outline CONFIGURATION, CONFORMATION
- shape of a person or thing when set against a lighter background SILHOUETTE
- shape or outline, as of a stretch of land CONTOUR
- shape or view of something from the side PROFILE
- shaped wrongly or abnormally MALFORMED, DEFORMED
- ability to revert to an earlier shape or condition RESILIENCE
- change of a spectacular kind in shape, appearance, or attitude METAMORPHOSIS, TRANSFIGURATION, TRANSMOGRIFICATION
- distinctive shape or outline of something, especially of the face LINEAMENTS
- general shape or plan, as of a complicated project FORMAT
- shadow image or shape of something, filled-in outline SILHOUETTE
- twisted out of its natural shape DISTORTED

shape (combining form) -MORPH-, MORPHO-, -MORPHIC, -FORM

shapeless, lacking a distinct form AMORPHOUS, APLASTIC

share, as of work, given to or required by a participant QUOTA
- share of the proceeds paid to a writer, composer, or the like from sales or performances of his or her work ROYALTY
- share or portion specially set aside ALLOCATION, ALLOTMENT
- shared, common, joint MUTUAL
- shared, common, relating to all members of a group COMMUNAL
- sharer, equal heir PARCENER, COPARCENER
- sharing in or being an accomplice to a criminal act, cruel deed, or the like COMPLICITY

shares shares and other assets and investments, in a detailed list PORTFOLIO
- shares bearing the name of the owner or original purchaser NOMINAL SHARES
- share-buying for quick resale at a higher price ARBITRAGE
- share certificate or other document of entitlement SCRIP
- share considered safe and profitable through having a long record of reliability BLUE CHIP
- share dealing, stockbroking, or financial speculation AGIOTAGE, STOCKJOBBING
- agree to buy or guarantee the purchase of a share issue UNDERWRITE
- application to purchase newly issued shares SUBSCRIPTION
- convert shares into cash, paper money into bullion, or the like REDEEM
- daily average of various share prices on the London Stock Exchange FT INDEX
- daily average of various share prices on the New York Stock Exchange DOW-JONES INDEX
- face value, value printed on the face of a share certificate or bond, as used for assessing dividends PAR VALUE
- finance and investment company buying a variety of shares, and selling units from the combined portfolio to the public MUTUAL FUND
- formal statement or brochure giving details of a forthcoming share issue PROSPECTUS
- issue of new shares free to current shareholders SCRIP ISSUE, BONUS ISSUE
- launching or financing of a business venture by means of a share issue FLOTATION
- offer shares, bonds, or the like for sale FLOAT
- ordinary shares EQUITIES, COMMON STOCK
- referring to stocks and shares not quoted on the stock exchange UNLISTED
- speculator who anticipates falling prices, and sells shares hoping to buy them back later at a lower price BEAR
- speculator who anticipates rising prices, and buys shares hoping to sell them later at a profit BULL
- total value of a business's shares CAPITALIZATION

shark, ray, or similar fish whose skeleton is of cartilage rather than hard bone CARTILAGINOUS FISH
- shark with a flattened head, with the eyes at the ends of the bulging sides HAMMERHEAD
- large shark that often floats near the surface of the water BASKING SHARK, SAILFISH
- relating to sharks or rays SELACHIAN
- small shark with a pointed nose and a crescent-shaped tail PORBEAGLE, MACKEREL SHARK

sharp or cutting, as wit might be SARCASTIC, CAUSTIC, ACERBIC, MORDANT
- sharp, harsh, or irritating, as a smell or taste might be ACRID, PUNGENT
- sharp fragment, splinter SLIVER
- sharp or penetrating, as a comment might be TRENCHANT, INCISIVE
- sharp-sighted LYNX-EYED
- sharp smell or taste TANG
- sharply tipped, narrowing to a point, as a leaf might be ACUMINATE, APICULATE

sharp (combining form) OXY-, BELONE-, AICHMO-

sharpen a blade or the like, as on a grindstone HONE, WHET

- sharpen a straight razor on a leather or canvas strip STROP
- sharpening wheel, abrasive wheel CARBORUNDUM WHEEL
- stone for sharpening knives and other cutting tools WHETSTONE, GRINDSTONE

sharpness or clarity of outline, as of a photograph or television image DEFINITION, ACUTANCE, RESOLUTION
- sharpness or keenness of the senses or the mind ACUITY

shaven head, or top part of the head, especially of a monk or priest TONSURE

shaving - stick of chemical for stopping bleeding from small cuts, as after shaving STYPTIC PENCIL

sheath - clear thick liquid secreted by membranes in joints, tendon sheaths, and the like SYNOVIA
- forming a sheath or enclosed in a sheath VAGINATE
- metal tip or trimming for a sheath or scabbard CHAPE

shed, typically with a sloping roof, against the side of a building PENTHOUSE, LEAN-TO
- shed feathers or fur MOLT
- shedding of a body part, such as a lizard's tail, as a means of protection when attacked AUTOTOMY
- shedding of the outer layer, shell, or skin, as in insects and snakes SLOUGHING, ECDYSIS
- shedding all their leaves at a particular time each year, as some trees are DECIDUOUS
- performer who sheds her or his clothes, stripteaser ECDYSIAST

sheen on a surface produced by age or handling PATINA
- sheen or wavy finish, as given to silk WATER

sheep, horse, or the like regarded as the mother of another DAM
- sheep of a breed originally from Spain, producing a soft fine wool MERINO
- sheep of a central Asian breed whose young have a curled glossy coat yielding Persian lamb fur KARAKUL, BROADTAIL
- sheep of a wild variety in North Africa BARBARY SHEEP, AOUDAD
- sheep of a wild variety in Sardinia and Corsica MOUFLON
- adjective for a sheep OVINE
- gelded male sheep WETHER
- male sheep that leads the flock BELLWETHER
- person who herds and drives cattle or sheep DROVER
- young sheep, lamb YEANLING

sheet, as of folded paper or wooden boarding PLY
- sheet for wrapping a corpse SHROUD, WINDING-SHEET
- sheet of natural or artificial tissue through which fluids can pass slowly MEMBRANE
- split or beat into thin sheets, or join several parallel sheets together LAMINATE

shelf, as above a fireplace MANTELPIECE, MANTEL

shell See illustration, page 491, and also **bomb**
- shell, bullet, missile, rocket, or other object fired or hurled PROJECTILE
- shell, protective plate, or similar hard covering, as on some animals or ships CUIRASS
- shell beads formerly used as currency by North American Indians WAMPUM, PEAG
- shell fragments produced by an explosion SHRAPNEL
- shell-like protective horny covering on some insects, crustaceans, and the like CUTICLE
- shell of a tortoise, crab, lobster, or the like CARAPACE
- shell of various sea mollusks, used as money in some cultures COWRIE
- shell or hard coating, as of some insects TEST
- shell or protective outer covering of an animal or plant ARMATURE
- shell-producing or -containing CONCHIFEROUS
- coil or single turn, as of a spiral shell VOLUTE, WHORL, VOLUTION
- delicate curving decoration of rock fragments or shells, used in rococo design ROCAILLE
- diameter of the inside of a tube, the bore of a gun, or a bullet or shell CALIBER
- fossil shell of a common, flat, coiled type, from various extinct squidlike creatures AMMONITE
- hornlike substance occurring in some fungi and in the shell of a lobster, crab, or the like CHITIN
- knoblike protruberance, as in the center of a shield or at the top of a clam's shell UMBO
- opening or hollow at the base of a mollusk's shell UMBILICUS
- shiny inner surface of some mollusk shells, used for ornamentation MOTHER-OF-PEARL, NACRE
- scallop, oyster, or similar mollusk having a pair of hinged shells

SEWING AND DRESSMAKING TERMS

appliqué	decorative finish made by stitching shapes of one material onto a different material
basting/ tacking	temporary stitching to hold pieces of fabric together
bias	line diagonal to the selvage of a fabric
bias binding	strip of fabric, cut on the bias, used for binding edges
blackwork	black embroidery on white material
blocking board	board used to stretch and straighten pieces of embroidery
bobbin	small spool holding the lower thread supply of a sewing machine
bodkin	tool shaped like a long, blunt needle, used to thread elastic or ribbons through a casing
broderie anglaise	embroidery of perforated shapes on fine white linen, cotton, or the like
couching	stitching with two threads, the couching thread being used to stitch a laid thread to the fabric
crewel needle	standard, long-eyed embroidery needle
curve square	instrument for measuring curves, seam allowances, and buttonholes
gusset	piece of fabric, usually triangular, inserted to enlarge or strengthen a garment
hardanger	openwork embroidery on even-weave fabric, of Norwegian origin

BIVALVE
- snail, whelk, or similar mollusk having a single shell UNIVALVE
- spiraling and cone-shaped, as some shells are TURBINATE
- top section of a coiled shell, including the apex SPIRE

shell (combining form) CONCH-, CONCHO-

shellfish See illustration, page 490, and also **fish**
- shellfish such as a lobster or prawn CRUSTACEAN
- shellfish such as a shrimp or lobster, or any insect, spider, or the like, having a horny, segmented covering and jointed limbs ARTHROPOD
- shellfish, such as a whelk or limpet, having a single shell and a footlike muscle used for crawling about UNIVALVE, GASTROPOD
- shellfish, such as an oyster or mussel, having a pair of hinged shells BIVALVE
- shellfish such as an oyster or whelk MOLLUSK
- shellfish of the kind clinging to ships' hulls BARNACLE
- shellfish resembling a small lobster CRAYFISH, LANGOUSTE
- shellfish with a ridged, fan-shaped shell SCALLOP
- shellfish with a spiraled shell, related to the squid NAUTILUS
- large edible shellfish with a large ear-shaped shell yielding mother-of-pearl ABALONE, ORMER
- New Zealand shellfish with a shimmering greenish shell resembling mother-of-pearl PAUA
- small shrimplike shellfish forming the principal food of some whales KRILL
- squidlike shellfish whose calcified internal shell is sometimes placed in bird cages to supplement the bird's diet CUTTLEFISH

shelter of arched corrugated iron sheets NISSEN HUT
- shelter or cover providing protection against the wind LEE
- shelter or inn for the needy or travelers HOSPICE
- shelter or protect HARBOR
- shelter or protection, as from persecution, or a place offering such safety ASYLUM, HAVEN, REFUGE, SANCTUARY
- sheltered, private, or hidden SECLUDED, SEQUESTERED, CLOISTERED
- sheltered place, especially a small bay COVE

shepherds - relating to shepherds BUCOLIC, PASTORAL

sheriff or similar peace officer MARSHAL
- sheriff's office, term of office, or authority, in England SHRIEVALTY
- sheriff's officer in medieval times who arrested debtors CATCHPOLE
- sheriff's officer who serves writs and carries out a court's orders, in England BAILIFF
- group of people assembled by a sheriff, as to pursue a fugitive POSSE

sherry, port, or other strengthened wine FORTIFIED WINE
- sherry of a pale dry variety from Spain MANZANILLA
- large glass for sherry or beer SCHOONER

shield, as in heraldry, bearing a coat of arms ESCUTCHEON
- shield large enough to protect the whole body, used in medieval times PAVIS
- shield-shaped SCUTATE, SCUTELLATE, PELTATE, CLYPEATE
- shieldlike plate covering a keyhole, surrounding a door handle, protecting a light switch, or the like ESCUTCHEON
- ornamental knob in the center of a shield BOSS, UMBO
- overhead cover, of an overlapping roof of shields, protecting an ancient Roman military unit TESTUDO, TORTOISE
- small, round shield worn or carried on the arm in former times BUCKLER, TARGET, TARGE

shift of duty on guard or on shipboard WATCH
- shift or session of duty, as at the helm of a ship TRICK

shimmering, changing in brightness, twinkling, as a cat's-eye or similar gemstone is CHATOYANT
- shimmering with a rainbowlike effect, as a soap bubble or opal is IRIDESCENT, OPALESCENT

shinbone TIBIA

shine, smooth polished finish LUSTER, GLOSS, BURNISH, SHEEN
- shining brightly RELUCENT
- shining brilliantly, radiantly illuminated, dazzling RESPLENDENT, EFFULGENT, REFULGENT
- shining or flickering gently, shimmering or glistening LAMBENT
- shining or glittering brilliantly, sparkling, as a person's wit or a gemstone might be SCINTILLATING, CORUSCATING
- shining or glowing intensely, bril-

SEWING AND DRESSMAKING TERMS *Continued*

interfacing	crisp, fibrous backing material giving shape and body
interlining	insulating lining sewn between the outer garment or curtain and the lining
lettuce edge	decorative finish giving a frilly effect to knitted fabrics
mercerized	referring to a cotton or linen fabric or thread that has been preshrunk and treated for greater luster and strength
mitering	diagonal joining of two edges at a corner
nap	raised fabric surface, as in velvet and corduroy
piping	rounded strip of cloth, sometimes covering a cord, used for trimming furniture covers or garments
placket	slit in a garment, such as a cuff or zipper opening, to make it easier to put on and take off
quilting	embroidery dividing padded material into decorative shapes
rickrack braid	wavy braid used for decorative trimming
selvage	ribbonlike, nonfraying edge running lengthwise along each side of a woven fabric
shirring	decorative, multiple gathering of a fabric, often with elastic thread, to control fullness, especially at the waist and cuffs
smocking	decorative stitching of evenly gathered material to give a regular, patterned effect
tambour/ taboret	round embroidery frame
trapunto	quilting made by filling stitched areas with padding

liantly bright INCANDESCENT

shiny, flaky mineral MICA

- shiny, glossy LUSTROUS
- shiny disc or button, used to ornament clothing, handbags, or the like SEQUIN
- shiny in a shimmery way IRIDESCENT, OPALESCENT
- shiny surface layer or finishing,

SHAPES

IN THE SHAPE OF	DESCRIPTION
almond	**amygdaloid**
arrowhead	**sagittate**
bell	**campanulate**
berry	**bacciform**
boat	**navicular/ scaphoid**
bow, arch	**fornicate/ arcuate**
bristle	**setiform/ acicular/ styliform**
brush	**penicilliform**
bunch of grapes	**botryoidal/ aciniform**
club	**clavate/ claviform**
coil	**circinate**
coin	**nummular**
comb	**pectinate**
cone	**fastigiate**
crescent	**bicorn/ lunular**
cross, X	**decussate/ cruciform/ cruciate**
cup	**cotyloid/ cupulate/ acetabular**
diamond	**rhomboidal**
dish, pan	**patelliform**
doughnut, ring	**toroid**
droplet	**guttate/ stilliform/ globular**
eagle's beak	**aquiline**
ear	**auriculate**
eel	**anguilliform**
egg	**oval/ovoid**
fan	**flabellate**
feather	**pinnate**
fingers	**digitate/ dactyloid**
fish	**pisciform**
foot	**pediform**
fork	**furcate/ bifurcate**
funnel	**infundib- ular**
hand	**palmate/ chiroform**
head	**capitate**
heart	**cordate**
helmet	**galeate**
hood, cowl	**cucullate**
hook	**uncinate/ unciform**
horn	**cornual**
keel	**carinate**
kidney	**reniform**
knife blade	**cultrate**
ladder	**scalariform**
lance	**lanceolate**
lens, lentil seed	**lenticular**
lyre	**lyrate**
needle	**acerose/ beloneform**
pear	**pyriform**
pine cone	**strobila- ceous**
pouch, sac	**bursiform/ saccate**
ribbon, belt	**cestoid**
ring	**annular/ toroid**
rod	**bacillary/ bacilliform/ virgate/ virgulate**
S (the letter)	**sigmoid**
sausage	**allantoid**
saw, teeth of a saw	**runcinate/ serrate**
scimitar	**acinaciform**
shield	**scutate/ scutellate/ peltate/ clypeate**
sickle	**falcate**
slipper	**calceolate**
snail's shell	**cochleate**
snake	**anguiform/ colubriform/ colubroid/ ophidiform**
spearhead	**hastate**
spiral	**helical/ turbinal/ volute**
spokes of a wheel	**rotate**
star	**stellate/ astroid**
strap	**ligulate**
string of beads	**moniliform**
sword	**ensiform/ gladiate/ xiphoid**
tongue	**lingulate**
tooth	**dentiform**
tree	**dendriform/ dendroid**
triangle	**deltoid**
urn	**urceolate**
violin	**pandurate**
wand, rod	**virgate**
wedge	**cuneal/ sphenic**
wheel	**rotary/ rotate/ trochal**
whip	**flagellate**
wing, wings	**alary/ aliform**
worm	**vermicular/ vermiform/ lumbricoid**

as of fine wood or plastic VENEER

ship See illustration and chart, pages 493 and 494, and also **boat, sail**
- ship abandoned at sea DERELICT
- ship escorting another CONSORT
- ship of a heavy and awkward design HULK
- ship's bearing calculated from a fixed reference, such as due north on the horizon, typically measured clockwise in degrees AZIMUTH
- ship's boat or lifeboat, typically a small rowing boat YAWL, JOLLY BOAT
- ship's cabin, especially a large, comfortable private cabin STATEROOM
- ship's officer in charge of equipment, maintenance, and deck crew BOATSWAIN, BO'S'N
- ship's officer in charge of finances and passenger welfare PURSER
- ship's officer supervising the food and provisions STEWARD
- ship's officers' living quarters WARDROOM
- ship's rigging TACKLE
- ship's steering equipment, tiller, or wheel HELM
- ship's supplier or other dealer in a specified trade or commodity CHANDLER
- ships traveling in a group, especially when protected by an escort of warships CONVOY
- armored pilot house on a ship, or the superstructure of a submarine CONNING TOWER
- cargo or wreckage found floating after a ship has sunk FLOTSAM, JETSAM
- cargo thrown overboard from a ship or washed ashore JETSAM
- cargo thrown from a ship but marked by buoys for later recovery LAGAN
- carved bust or full figure in the prow of some sailing ships FIGUREHEAD
- complete staff of officers and crew of a ship COMPLEMENT, COMPANY
- curved wooden rib forming part of a ship's frame FUTTOCK
- deep, wide, and safe enough for ships or boats to sail on or through NAVIGABLE
- depth below the water line of the keel of a loaded ship DRAFT
- dock worker who boards ships to load and unload them STEVEDORE
- document recording details of goods for shipment, especially in foreign trade BILL OF LADING, WAYBILL, MANIFEST
- equip and check a ship for active service COMMISSION
- fiber of hemp or jute, often treated with tar, used for sealing pipe joints and caulking the seams in wooden ships OAKUM
- fleet of small ships, or small fleet of ships FLOTILLA
- force a person, by trickery or threats, into service on a ship SHANGHAI, PRESS, IMPRESS, PRESS-GANG, CRIMP
- raised frame of windows on a ship's upper deck, affording light below COMPANION
- heavy material, such as sandbags, helping to stabilize a ship or balloon BALLAST
- inside of the lowest part of a ship's hull, or the water collecting there BILGE
- kitchen on the deck of a ship CABOOSE
- ladder, usually of rope but with rigid rungs, used on a ship JACOB'S LADDER
- ladder or portable staircase that can be hung over the side of a ship for access ACCOMMODATION LADDER
- large section of a passenger ship for those paying the cheapest fares STEERAGE
- large spike on the prow of an ancient warship for puncturing an enemy ship's hull ROSTRUM, RAM, BEAK
- line of plates or planking running the length of a ship's hull STRAKE
- line or set of lines marked on the side of a cargo ship, showing its legal load level in various conditions PLIMSOLL MARK
- lookout platform near the top of a mast of a sailing ship CROW'S NEST
- main body or shell of a ship HULL
- modernize and reequip a ship REFIT
- person who hides on board a departing ship, train, or the like for a free journey STOWAWAY
- pier, docking platform, or the like at which ships can moor for loading or unloading WHARF
- plate or place on the stern of a ship or boat bearing the vessel's name ESCUTCHEON
- platform above the main deck on a ship, housing the controls BRIDGE
- porthole, hinged hatchway, or the like on a ship SCUTTLE
- prohibition, as of foreign ships or of arms trading EMBARGO
- protective plate, shell, or similar hard covering, as on some animals or ships CUIRASS
- rail around the stern of a boat or ship TAFFRAIL
- ramp sloping into the water, supporting a ship being built or repaired SLIPWAY
- relating to ships or seafaring NAUTICAL, MARITIME
- rescue of a ship, cargo, or crew SALVAGE
- rope or cable used in mooring or towing a ship HAWSER
- ropes or cables supporting the mast on a ship or boat SHROUDS
- rotating drum on the deck of a ship around which ropes or cables are wound CAPSTAN
- run before a gale, as a ship might even when carrying little sail SCUD
- seaworthy or strongly built, as a wooden ship might be SNUG
- section of a ship's structure situated above the main deck SUPERSTRUCTURE
- seizure of a neutral ship in wartime SPOLIATION
- senior captain of a shipping line, merchant fleet, or naval squadron COMMODORE
- shellfish with hard shells that often cling to and foul the bottoms of ships BARNACLES
- shelter against rain or spray on a yacht or ship's bridge DODGER
- shift or session of duty, as at the helm of a ship TRICK
- shift or session of duty as on guard or on shipboard WATCH, SPELL
- side of a ship to the left when facing the bow or front LARBOARD, PORT
- side of a ship to the right when facing the bow or front STARBOARD
- small squadron of ships ESCADRILLE, FLOTILLA
- stairway from a ship's upper deck to the cabins or deck below COMPANIONWAY
- supplier of provisions or equipment, as for a ship CHANDLER
- track of visible foam or waves in water, as left by a ship WAKE
- T-shaped bar or post for securing ropes, as on a ship's deck CLEAT
- vertical exhaust pipe or "chimney" on a steamship STACK
- waterproof the hull or seal the seams of a wooden ship, as with tar or pitch PAY, CAULK
- window, usually circular, in the side of a ship PORTHOLE
- wooden strip or plank forming part of a barrel, ship's hull, or the like STAVE
- wreckage from a shipwrecked ship WRACK

shipping and sailing within a country's territorial waters CABOTAGE
- adjective for shipping MARITIME, MARINE

shiver or thrill of fear or excitement FRISSON
- shivering attack and chills, as in malaria AGUE, RIGOR

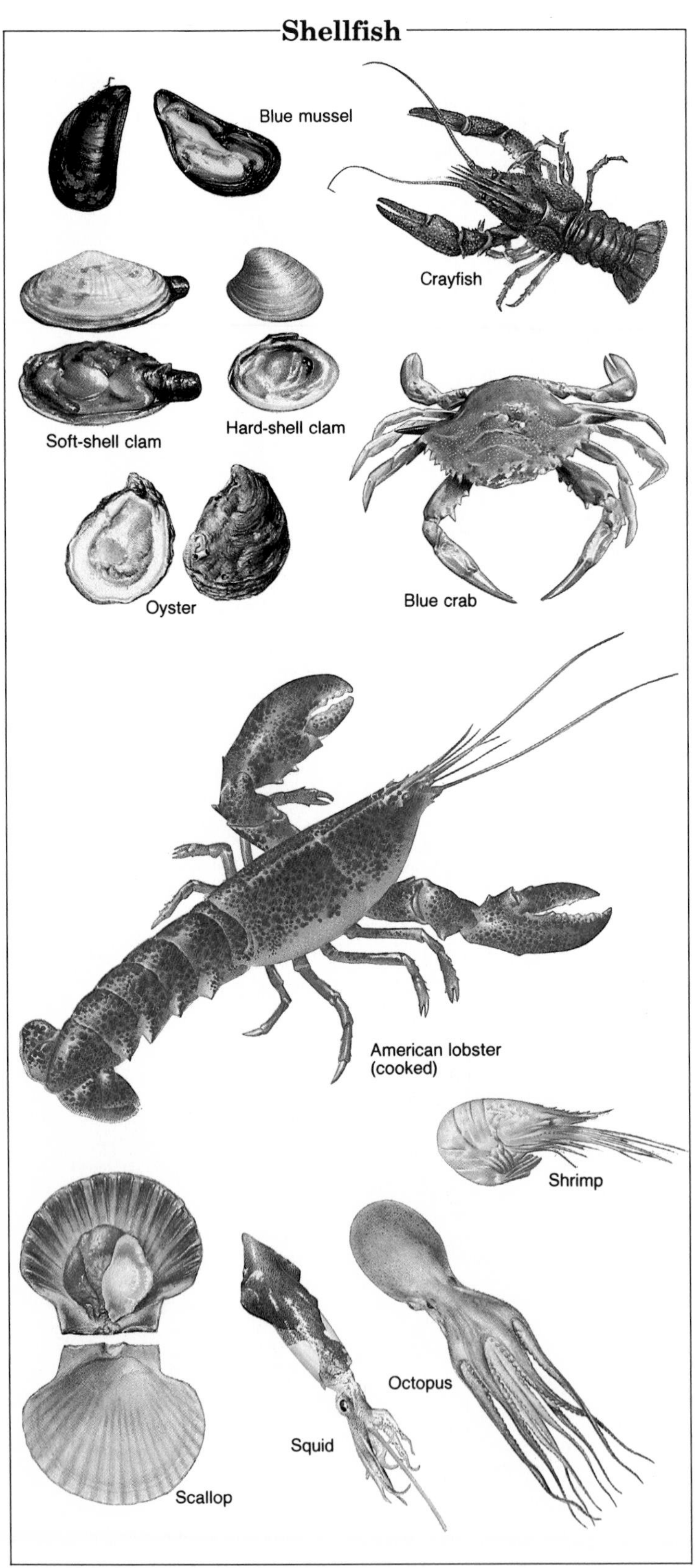

shock See also **surprise**
- shock having long-lasting psychological effects TRAUMA
- shock or violent jarring, especially to the brain, typically producing temporary loss of bearings and alertness CONCUSSION
- shocked or amazed STUPEFIED
- shocked or amazed by something horrible AGHAST, APPALLED
- temporary rigidity and insensitivity in reaction to shock RIGOR
- therapy for treating psychiatric patients, involving an electric shock to the brain ELECTROSHOCK THERAPY, EST, ELECTROCONVULSIVE TREATMENT, ECT

shock-absorbing system in motor vehicles, based on pistons in fluid-filled cylinders rather than with springs HYDRAULIC SUSPENSION

shocking, sensational, or gruesome, often in a deliberately artificial way GRAND GUIGNOL
- shocking or startling, outrageously unconventional ÉPATANT
- shockingly or glaringly wrong or evil FLAGRANT
- shockingly unjust or unreasonable UNCONSCIONABLE

shoddy and cheap GIMCRACK, BRUMMAGEM, TAWDRY

shoe See illustration and chart, pages 495 and 496
- covering of cloth or leather protecting the upper shoe and ankle SPAT
- large, heavy, and ugly shoes or boots CLODHOPPERS
- layers forming the heel of a shoe LIFTS
- small protective metal plate attached to the sole or heel of a shoe TAP
- spiked plate on the sole of a shoe to prevent slipping on ice CLAMPER
- spikes fastened to a shoe or boot, as for mountaineering or walking across ice CRAMPONS
- strip of iron, rubber, or leather attached to the sole of a shoe to reduce wear or prevent slipping CLEAT

shoe (combining form) CALC-

shoelace - metal or plastic tip on a shoelace, to prevent fraying and make threading easier AGLET, TAG

shoot from the roots or lower stem of a plant SUCKER
- shoot or long thin runner of a plant FLAGELLUM
- shoot or twig cut for planting or grafting SLIP, SCION
- shootlike twining part, as on a grapevine, serving to attach a climbing plant to its support, trellis, or the like TENDRIL

Shells

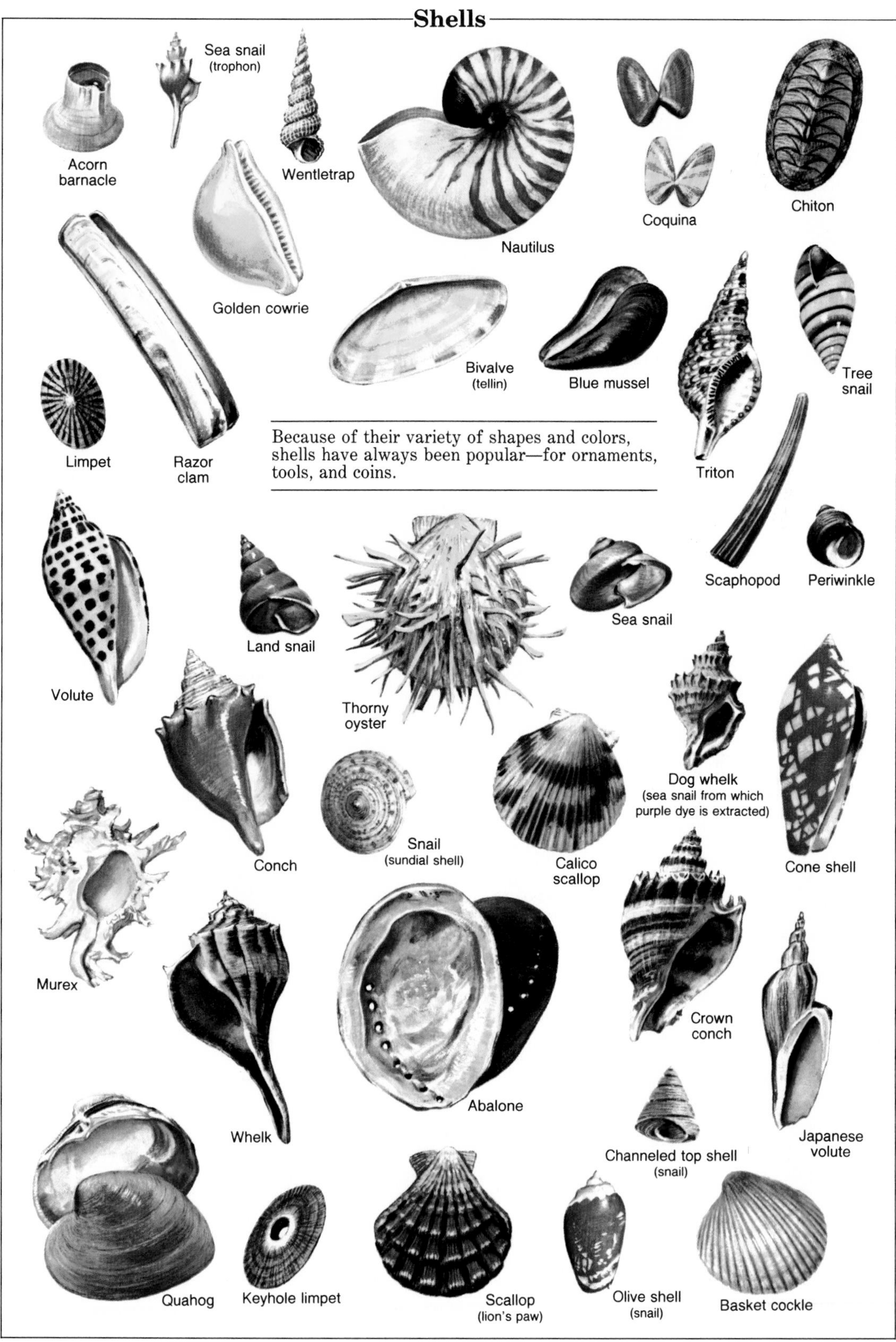

Because of their variety of shapes and colors, shells have always been popular—for ornaments, tools, and coins.

- shoots, as of willow, used in basketwork WICKER

shooting - clay disc hurled into the air for use as a shooting target CLAY PIGEON
- hidden marksman shooting at exposed individuals SNIPER
- time of year when hunting or shooting is permitted OPEN SEASON
- time of year when hunting or shooting is prohibited CLOSED SEASON

shop See **store**

shop window - life-size model used for displaying clothes in shop windows MANNEQUIN

shoplifting - loss of goods from a shop or supermarket, as through shoplifting SHRINKAGE

shore or beach STRAND
- adjective for a shore LITTORAL

short See also **brief, concise, summary**
- short and abrupt CURT
- short and heavily built PYKNIC, ENDOMORPHIC
- short and mysterious, pithy, as an utterance might be GNOMIC
- short literary work, scene, or the like VIGNETTE, CAMEO

short (combining form) BRACHY-

short-lived, lasting only a short time EPHEMERAL, TRANSITORY, VOLATILE
- short-lived, passing quickly, brief FLEETING, FUGITIVE, FUGACIOUS, TRANSIENT
- short-lived, vanishing rapidly EVANESCENT, MOMENTARY

shortage See **lack**

shorten, abbreviate TRUNCATE, CURTAIL
- shorten, cut, or summarize a text ABRIDGE, CONDENSE
- shortened version of a text, summary ABSTRACT, SYNOPSIS, DIGEST, ABRIDGMENT, EPITOME, PRÉCIS

shortsightedness, defective distance vision MYOPIA

shoulder belt fitted with cartridge pockets, worn across the chest BANDOLIER
- shoulder blade SCAPULA
- shoulder socket GLENOID CAVITY
- braid, fringed strap, or the like worn on the shoulder, as on a military uniform EPAULET
- garment worn by monks, consisting of a long band of cloth hanging at the front and back from the shoulders SCAPULAR

show, demonstrate plainly MANIFEST
- show, display, activity, or the like that is elaborate, fanciful, or spectacular EXTRAVAGANZA
- show, prove, or suggest strongly EVIDENCE
- show a feeling clearly, such as surprise REGISTER, EVINCE
- afternoon performance of a play, movie, or other show MATINEE
- first or opening performance of a play, film, or other show PREMIERE
- producer or organizer of stage shows, concerts, or the like IMPRESARIO

show off, parade or exhibit ostentatiously FLAUNT
- show off, put on an act, parade, try to impress POSE, POSTURE, GRANDSTAND, ATTITUDINIZE
- showing off, drawing attention to oneself, as by rowdy behavior EXHIBITIONISM
- person who puts on an act, shows off, or assumes a role in an attempt to impress others POSEUR

showing or demonstrating directly OSTENSIVE, DEICTIC
- showing or demonstrating indirectly ELENCTIC, ELENCHTIC
- showing or seeing everything PANOPTIC

showmanship, liking for or power to attract publicity RÉCLAME

showpiece, outstanding item in a group PIÈCE DE RÉSISTANCE

showy, artificially spectacular, garishly brilliant TECHNICOLOR
- showy, demonstrative, gushing EFFUSIVE
- showy, drawing attention to oneself OSTENTATIOUS, OBTRUSIVE
- showy, elaborately decorated or unrestrained FLAMBOYANT, FLORID, ROCOCO
- showy, flashy, ornate or brightly colored in a tasteless way GAUDY, GARISH, TAWDRY, TINSEL
- showy, swanky, swish, luxurious RITZY, GLITZY
- showy, trifling ornament TRINKET, FALLAL
- showy and brightly colored EMBLAZONED
- showy but brilliant, as a musical performance might be BRAVURA
- showy but worthless TRUMPERY
- showy clothing or decoration FROUFROU, FRIPPERY, FURBELOWS
- showy display or public ceremony FANFARE
- showy in a vulgar way RAFFISH
- showy or colorful display or symbol BLAZON
- showy or dramatic gesture, movement, or action FLOURISH
- showy or noisy display, designed to impress or advertise RAZZLE-DAZZLE, RAZZMATAZZ

shredded or finely sliced, as vegetables are in some dishes JULIENNE

shriek - "shrieking root," plant with a forked root, formerly used for sorcery and a narcotic drug, and thought to shriek when pulled from the ground MANDRAKE, MANDRAGORA

shrill grating chirp of a cricket or grasshopper STRIDULATION
- shrill or high-pitched TREBLE

shrimp, crab, lobster, or related animal having a segmented body, jointed limbs, and horny shell CRUSTACEAN
- shrimplike, small marine organisms, forming the main food of some whales KRILL

shrine or container for sacred relics RELIQUARY
- canopied niche or recess used as a shrine TABERNACLE

shriveled and wrinkled, as an old person's face might be WIZENED

shroud - wax-coated cloth formerly used as a shroud CERECLOTH, CEREMENT

Shrove Tuesday or its carnival celebrations MARDI GRAS

shrunk - referring to a kind of preshrunk fabric used for clothing SANFORIZED

shun - shunned person or social outcast ISHMAEL, PARIAH, LEPER
- shun, ostracize SEND TO COVENTRY
- shunning, exclusion from society OSTRACISM, PURDAH

shut away from the world, confine or hide SECLUDE, CLOISTER, SEQUESTER, IMMURE
- shut oneself away, as for a private discussion CLOSET

shut out See **exclude**

shutter or blind with adjustable horizontal slats JALOUSIE
- shutter or screen protecting a window from the sun in hot countries BRISE-SOLEIL

shy, avoiding public exposure, not drawing attention to oneself RETIRING, RESERVED, UNDEMONSTRATIVE
- shy, hesitant, or uncertain, as a smile might be TENTATIVE
- shy, inward-looking, socially withdrawn INTROVERTED
- shy, self-conscious, and easily embarrassed BASHFUL
- shy, timid, lacking in confidence or self-assertiveness DIFFIDENT
- shy, unassertive, or unattractive person who is left out of social activities, as at a dance WALLFLOWER
- shy, uncommunicative, saying less than one could RETICENT, TACITURN, UNFORTHCOMING
- shy away, draw back RECOIL, FLINCH, QUAIL, BLENCH
- shy or embarrassed to the point of being speechless TONGUE-TIED
- shy or modest, often in a way suggesting flirtatiousness COY, DE-

Ships

Egyptian seagoing ship
c. 2500 BC
Greek trireme—c. 500 BC
Roman merchant ship
c. 100 AD
Viking ship—c. 900 AD
Merchantman
14th century
Caravel
15th century
Pinnace
17th century
Galleon—16th century
HMS
"Victory"
1765
East Indiaman
18th century
Venetian galleass—17th century
Although ship design has changed greatly, basic features remain the same.
"Clermont"
1862
"Monitor"
1862
"Constitution"
1797
Whaler—19th century
Chinese junk
19th century
Clipper ship—c. 1850
"Great Eastern"—1858
Mississippi steamboat—c. 1870
Cargo ship and tug—c. 1910
"Queen Mary"—1934
USS "Long Beach"
(atomic-powered missile
cruiser)—1961
Supertanker—1969
USS "Enterprise"
1961
Atomic-powered hydrofoil
of the future

MURE, SKITTISH
- shy or socially awkward and ill at ease GAUCHE, FAROUCHE
- shy or timid, very nervous TREMULOUS, TIMOROUS
- shy or wary, as of meeting people CHARY, CAUTIOUS
- shy person, very reluctant to come forward SHRINKING VIOLET
- shyly or sheepishly guilt-stricken SHAMEFACED, RUEFUL
- distant or standoffish out of a sense of superiority rather than shyness ALOOF
- embarrassed and too shy to speak out CONSTRAINED
- excessively modest, as through shyness, about one's own qualities, running oneself down SELF-EFFACING, SELF-ABNEGATING

sick See also **ill, illness, disease**
- sick, vomiting or feeling as if about to vomit NAUSEOUS, BILIOUS, QUEASY

sickeningly often, regularly or repeatedly to a tiresome extent AD NAUSEAM

sickle-shaped, as some leaves are FALCATE

sickly and chronically weak person INVALID, VALETUDINARIAN
- sickly in appearance, pale PEAKY
- sickly yellowish in color or complexion SALLOW

side of a ship above the water, or the guns along the side BROADSIDE
- side view, especially of a human head PROFILE
- side with a contestant, opinion, political party, or the like ALIGN
- having sides of equal length, as a triangle might be EQUILATERAL
- place or be placed on both sides of a divide STRADDLE
- referring to the side or flank LATERAL

side by side, often for the sake of contrast JUXTAPOSED
- side by side, running parallel COLLATERAL

side effects - signs, such as allergies or dangerous side effects, that argue for the discontinuation of a medicine or treatment CONTRAINDICATIONS

-sided (combining form) -GON, -GONAL

sideways, glancingly, obliquely, the way one might look at a person ASKANCE
- sideways on BROADSIDE

siege - catapultlike launcher of rocks or other missiles, as used in ancient siege warfare ONAGER, BRICOLE, BALLISTA
- lay siege to, besiege, surround with soldiers BELEAGUER
- lifting of a siege RELIEF
- raid against the enemy by those under siege SORTIE
- tall wheeled wooden frame used to scale fortress walls during a siege in ancient times TURRET

sieve or mash boiled food to produce a pulpy consistency PUREE
- coarse sieve, as for sifting grain or gravel RIDDLE

sift grain, gravel, or the like RIDDLE
- sift or filter PERCOLATE

sigh or breathe SUSPIRE
- sighing or rustling sound, as of wind or surf SOUGH, SUSURRATION

sight See also **eyesight**
- sudden or unusual sight APPARITION

sighting lines, at right angles to each other, in the sight of a rifle, theodolite, or the like CROSS WIRES, CROSS HAIRS

sign See also **symbol**
- sign, indication, token INDEX
- sign, symbol, or letter standing for an entire word, such as # for *number* LOGOGRAM, LOGOGRAPH
- sign a document that already bears a signature, to ratify or authenticate it COUNTERSIGN
- sign of illness, deterioration, or the like SYMPTOM
- sign one's name at the foot of a document as a witness or contracting party SUBSCRIBE
- sign or character representing an entire idea, as in Chinese writing IDEOGRAM
- sign or design made up of initial letters MONOGRAM
- sign or emblem of a company or corporation LOGO, LOGOTYPE
- sign or endorse a document or the like UNDERWRITE
- sign or evidence that one possesses a specified quality PATENT
- sign or indication of the reality or existence of something, such as envy MANIFESTATION
- sign or mark of shame or disgrace STIGMA
- sign or nameplate, as of a doctor or lawyer SHINGLE
- sign or pictorial character used in ancient Egyptian writing HIEROGLYPH
- sign or signal of the approach of something HARBINGER, HERALD
- sign or symbol, or its intended meaning or reference DENOTATION
- sign or warning of a coming event OMEN, AUGURY, AUSPICE, PORTENT, PRODIGY, PRESAGE
- signs, such as allergies or dangerous side effects, that argue for the discontinuation of a medicine or treatment CONTRAINDICATIONS
- make signs or signals by gesturing vigorously GESTICULATE
- person, party, government, or the like that has signed and is bound to a convention or treaty SIGNATORY
- promising, favorable, as a sign or outlook might be AUSPICIOUS
- publisher's or printer's sign or emblem on a book COLOPHON
- science or study of signs and symbols SEMIOTICS

sign language with the hands, as used by deaf-mute people DACTYLOLOGY

sign of the zodiac See charts at **astrology, zodiac**

signal flare fired from a special pistol, especially at sea VERY LIGHT
- signal or call to action TOCSIN
- signal or signaling device based on flashes of sunlight from a mirror HELIOGRAPH
- signaling system or apparatus, as on a railroad line, using lights, flags, or pivoted arms SEMAPHORE

SHIPS

POWERED BY OARS

bireme
bucentaur
galley
galliot
longship
quinquereme
trireme

POWERED BY SAIL

argosy
bark
barkentine
bilander
brig
brigantine
caravel
carrack
clipper
cutter
dandy
dromond
galleass
galleon
Indiaman
ketch
knockabout
schooner
sloop
square-rigger
tartan
windjammer
xebec
yawl

POWERED BY ENGINE

collier
container ship
freighter
liner
motorized fishing vessel/ MFV
packet
paddle steamer
stern-wheeler
tanker
trawler
tug
whaleback

WARSHIPS

aircraft carrier
battle cruiser
battleship
corvette
cruiser
destroyer
dreadnought
escort carrier/ baby carrier
frigate
man-of-war
minelayer
minesweeper
monitor
Q-ship
submarine

signature written on behalf of another person ALLOGRAPH
- signature of the writer's own name AUTOGRAPH
- petition or protest on which the signatures are arranged in a circle ROUND ROBIN
- place one's signature on a document, the back of a check, or the like, as to indicate agreement, receipt, or transfer ENDORSE
- showy decoration or squiggle under a signature FLOURISH, PARAPH, CURLICUE

signet rings - study of seals and signet rings SPHRAGISTICS

Sikh scriptures GRANTH
- short sword traditionally carried by Sikh men as a symbol of loyalty KIRPAN

silence - bridle with an iron bit, formerly used to silence scolding women BRANKS
- monk of a Cistercian order noted for its austerity and vow of silence TRAPPIST

silencer or other sound-reducing device BAFFLE, MUFFLER

silent, not speaking, as though stunned into silence MUTE, DUMBSTRUCK, MUMCHANCE
- silent, reserved, not saying as much as one could RETICENT, UNCOMMUNICATIVE, TACITURN
- silent and inactive, still QUIESCENT, PASSIVE
- silent and thoughtful PENSIVE, REFLECTIVE, MEDITATIVE, CONTEMPLATIVE, INTROSPECTIVE

silk or gauze fabric of very fine texture GOSSAMER
- silk production by rearing silkworms SERICULTURE
- silk-screen print SERIGRAPH
- allowing some light through, as silk or a similar fine fabric is DIAPHANOUS
- spinning of silk from cocoons, or the reel used for it, or the place where such spinning is done FILATURE
- swishing or rustling sound, as of silk FROUFROU

silky fiber used in pillows, for soundproofing, or the like KAPOK
- silky mass of fibers, as from cotton, or silkworm cocoons FLOSS
- silky protective capsule spun by worms, larvae, or the like, to house the developing pupa COCOON

silly See also **stupid, fool**
- silly, asslike, as a remark might be ASININE
- silly, gooselike ANSERINE
- silly, inappropriately joky or lightweight, as a response to a serious inquiry might be FACETIOUS, FLIPPANT, FRIVOLOUS, TRIVIALIZING
- silly, ridiculous, laughable, as an absurd suggestion would be RISIBLE, LUDICROUS
- silly, senseless, empty of thought or purpose, as a speech might be VACUOUS
- silly, talkative, flighty person FLIBBERTIGIBBET
- silly, thoughtless, showing poor judgment INJUDICIOUS
- silly, trifling, foolish, as an objection might be FOOTLING
- silly, unrealistic, whimsical, as a scheme might be FANCIFUL
- silly, vain, pretentious person COXCOMB
- silly in a childish way PUERILE
- extremely silly, utterly foolish or thoughtless, as a comment might be INANE

silver as referred to in alchemy LUNA
- silver or gold thread used in embroidery PURL
- silver or silvery ornament or object decorated by the insertion of colored enamel into cut grooves CHAMPLEVÉ
- silver that is 92.5 percent pure STERLING, STERLING SILVER
- silver tray or platter for serving food, presenting visiting cards, or the like SALVER
- silvery ARGENTINE
- silvery decoration of thin strips, as on a Christmas tree TINSEL
- mark stamped on gold or silver objects, indicating the purity of the metal HALLMARK, PLATEMARK
- work of twisted wire, especially of gold or silver FILIGREE

silver (combining form) ARGENT-

similar, corresponding, consistent, or harmonious CONGRUOUS
- similar or corresponding, especially in shape, as two triangles might be CONGRUENT
- similar or corresponding, especially in sound CONSONANT
- similar or equivalent in certain respects, close enough to be compared COMPARABLE, ANALOGOUS, AKIN, COGNATE
- similar or related KINDRED
- similar or uniform in kind or structure HOMOGENEOUS
- person or thing very similar in appearance to another RINGER, DOPPELGÄNGER
- very similar, impossible to tell apart IDENTICAL, INDISTINGUISHABLE

similar (combining form) HOMEO-, HOMO-, IS-, ISO-, PARA-, SYN-, SYM-, -OSE

similarity, as of people's interests COMMUNITY
- similarity between things, such as languages, based on a relationship or causal connection AFFINITY
- similarity of a rough or approximate kind ASSONANCE
- similarity of shape or form about a given axis, point, line, or plane SYMMETRY
- similarity, correspondence, or agreement between otherwise differing elements ANALOGY
- similarity or relationship KINSHIP
- figure of speech pointing directly to a similarity between two things, as in *a wind like a whetted knife* SIMILE
- figure of speech pointing indirectly to a similarity between two things, as in *a razor-sharp wind* METAPHOR
- person or thing having a similar or related form, function, job, or the like COUNTERPART

simple, austere, frugal SPARTAN
- simple, charming, or picturesque event or scene IDYLL
- simple, cooked in a plain way

Shoe

AU NATUREL
- simple, plain, without decoration or fussy additions UNADORNED, UNEMBELLISHED
- simple, relating to basic knowledge, elementary RUDIMENTARY
- simple, unadorned, austere, as furniture might be CLINICAL
- simple, unsophisticated, innocent, as through inexperience NAIVE, INGENUOUS
- simple, unsophisticated, or unpretentious HOMESPUN
- simple and forthright, unscheming, frank ARTLESS, GUILELESS, UNCONTRIVED
- simple and modest in manner, life-style, or the like UNASSUMING, UNPRETENTIOUS, UNOSTENTATIOUS
- simple and unsophisticated in a charming way RUSTIC
- simple habits and living conditions, as wartime policy might impose AUSTERITY
- simple to follow or grasp, understandable COMPREHENSIBLE, INTELLIGIBLE, ACCESSIBLE
- simple to understand, very clearly expressed LUCID, PERSPICUOUS, TRANSPARENT

simplified, abstract, stylized, as a painting or design might be CONVENTIONALIZED
- simplified and often prejudiced image or opinion of someone or something STEREOTYPE

simplify by drawing conclusions, on the basis of evidence that is not or cannot be exhaustive GENERALIZE
- simplify or clarify a passage by rewording it PARAPHRASE
- simplifying of complex information, plans, or the like, especially in an unsophisticated and misleading way REDUCTIONISM

simply, without mincing words TOUT COURT

simultaneous, happening or existing at the same time CONTEMPORARY, CONTEMPORANEOUS, CONCURRENT, COINCIDENT
- simultaneous occurrence, coinciding CONJUNCTION
- simultaneously IN UNISON
- happen at the same time, be simultaneous SYNCHRONIZE

simultaneous (combining form) SYN-, SYM-

sin or crime TRESPASS, TRANSGRESSION
- sin or fault considered petty or trifling PECCADILLO
- sin so grave that it leads to the forfeiting of God's grace, in Roman Catholicism MORTAL SIN
- sin that is relatively minor and excusable, and does not cut the soul off from God's grace, in Roman Catholicism VENIAL SIN
- act of self-punishment or devotion to demonstrate sorrow or repentance for sin PENANCE
- canceling of or release from punishment for a sin, after pardoning, in Roman Catholicism INDULGENCE
- liable to sin, open to temptation PECCABLE
- pardon or forgive for a sin ABSOLVE, REMIT
- remorse for one's sins CONTRITION, REPENTANCE, PENITENCE
- rescue or save from sin REDEEM
- seven deadly sins CARDINAL SINS

sincere, deeply or truly felt HEARTFELT

SHOES AND BOOTS

balmoral	heavy walking boot
brogan	ankle-high work shoe
brogue	stout walking shoe with decorative punch marks
buckskin	shoe made from deerskin or sheepskin
chukka/ chukka boot	suede ankle boot, usually with two eyelets
clog	shoe with a heavy, usually wooden, sole
cothurnus/ cothurn/ buskin	thick-soled, calf-length or knee-length boot, as worn by ancient Greek actors
espadrille	rope-soled shoe with canvas top
galosh	waterproof overshoe
geta	Japanese wooden-soled sandal
gillie/ghillie	shoe with decorative laces
gumshoe	rubber shoe or overshoe; sneaker
Hessian boot	high, tasseled man's boot
larrigan	moccasin with knee-length leggings
Loafer	casual shoe resembling a moccasin, with broad, flat heel
moccasin	soft, heelless, slip-on leather shoe with a stitched top
mukluk	Eskimo boot of soft reindeer skin or sealskin
mule	loose, backless, strapless slipper
oxford	stout shoe with a low heel
pantofle	bedroom slipper
patten	wooden overshoe or clog on a raised wooden sole or metal platform
plimsoll	light rubber-soled shoe with a canvas top, usually laced
pump/court shoe	light, flat or low-heeled, shoe, without fastenings, often worn for dancing
sabot	clog made from a single piece of wood
sneaker/ tennis shoe/ gym shoe	soft-soled, usually rubber-soled, shoe with canvas or soft leather top
stiletto heel	woman's shoe with a narrow, tapering high heel
veldschoen/ velskoen	South African rawhide shoe or boot
wader	waterproof combination of boots and trousers, usually up to the armpits, as worn by anglers
Wellington	unlaced rubber boot for wet conditions; high leather riding boot

- sincere, genuine, wholehearted, without pretending UNFEIGNED, FOURSQUARE
- sincere and modest, not making any false claims for oneself UNAFFECTED, UNPRETENTIOUS
- sincere or devoted in one's affections, religious duties, or the like DEVOUT

sinew attaching a muscle to a bone or other support TENDON
- sinews, muscles THEWS

sinful See **evil, immoral**

sing a love song to one's sweetheart SERENADE
- sing a part-song, such as a carol or round TROLL
- sing in a voice wavering between normal and falsetto, as among folksingers in the Alps YODEL
- sing or recite in a half-musical tone, chant INTONE, CANTILLATE
- sing with trills, as a thrush does WARBLE
- singing or chanting that involves responses or alternating parts ANTIPHONY
- singing training through the use of the *do-re-mi* syllables TONIC SOL-FA, SOLFEGGIO, SOLMIZATION
- singing voice, typically male, when forced into an unnatural register much higher than the normal range FALSETTO
- director of singing in a church PRECENTOR
- highest singing part in a choral song, or a decorative air sung above a melody DESCANT
- operatic singing of a pure, rich, unstrained, even-toned style BEL CANTO
- referring to male voices singing unaccompanied in four-part harmony BARBERSHOP
- referring to singing or compositions based on the harmonizing of two or more different melodic lines POLYPHONIC
- referring to singing performed without instrumental accompaniment A CAPPELLA

singer, as in a band or pop group VOCALIST
- singer, especially a soprano, who specializes in ornamental trills and runs COLORATURA
- singer in the role of a young woman, especially a flirtatious lady's maid, in a comic opera SOUBRETTE
- singer or poet in 15th- to 16th-century German guilds MEISTERSINGER
- singer-poet and storyteller in medieval times MINSTREL, JONGLEUR, TROUBADOUR
- singer's range of notes from high to low COMPASS, REGISTER
- boy singer performing the highest voice part TREBLE
- choir leader, lead singer, or soloist, as in a church or synagogue CANTOR, PRECENTOR
- female singer, as in a nightclub or cabaret CHANTEUSE
- female singer or boy singer with the highest natural range SOPRANO
- female singer with a medium-high natural range MEZZO-SOPRANO
- female singer with a relatively low natural range CONTRALTO, ALTO
- group of singers typically performing choral music GLEE CLUB
- leading female opera singer PRIMA DONNA, DIVA
- male singer, usually a bass, performing comic-opera roles BUFFO
- male singer castrated in boyhood, until the 19th century, to keep his high-pitched voice CASTRATO
- male singer with a strong high voice, especially suited to Wagnerian opera HELDENTENOR
- male singer with an extremely high natural range COUNTERTENOR, ALTO
- male singer with a high natural range TENOR
- male singer with a medium-low natural range BARITONE
- male singer with the lowest normal range BASS
- male singer with an extremely low natural range BASSO PROFUNDO
- melodic rather than dramatic, as a singer might be LYRIC

single, sole SOLITARY
- single, undivided UNITARY
- single-celled organism MONAD
- single out, mention individually PARTICULARIZE, SPECIFY

single (combining form) UNI-, MONO-

singly, individually, in the order stated RESPECTIVELY

sinister - person exerting or trying to exert a sinister influence over another's will SVENGALI

sink, as a ship might FOUNDER
- sink one's ship, accidentally or deliberately SCUTTLE
- sink or settle SUBSIDE

sinning, guilty PECCANT

sister or brother SIBLING
- custom in some societies by which a man marries two or more sisters successively SORORATE
- murder of one's sister SORORICIDE

sisterhood, state of being sisters or sisterly SORORITY

sitting a great deal, or requiring much sitting, as a job might be SEDENTARY
- upright, cross-legged sitting position, as in yoga and meditation, with the hands resting on the knees LOTUS POSITION

situation requiring a choice between two equal and typically undesirable alternatives DILEMMA, DOUBLE BIND
- situation requiring a choice between two equally desirable alternatives BURIDAN'S ASS
- situation that is difficult, embarrassing, or unpleasant PREDICAMENT

six children or young born at one birth SEXTUPLETS
- six-pointed star, such as the Star of David HEXAGRAM
- group of six people or things, especially musicians SEXTET
- lasting for six years, or occurring once every six years SEXENNIAL
- referring to or based on the number six, or having six parts SENARY

six (combining form) HEX-, HEXA-, SEX-

sixteenth century in Italian art and architecture CINQUECENTO

sixth sense - alleged perception by means of a sixth sense, supernatural powers, intuition, or the like EXTRASENSORY PERCEPTION, ESP, CRYPTESTHESIA, TELESTHESIA

sixty-year-old, or a person aged between 60 and 69 SEXAGENARIAN
- referring to or based on the number 60 SEXAGESIMAL

size or extent DIMENSIONS, PROPORTIONS, MAGNITUDE, AMPLITUDE

skating - blade of a skate or sled RUNNER
- notched section on the front of the blade of a skate, used for braking TOE RAKE, TOE PICKS

skeleton key or master key PASSKEY, PASSE-PARTOUT

sketch, outline, draw or describe DELINEATE, LIMN
- sketch, plan, or rough drawing of something DRAFT
- sketch or brief incident or scene in a book, movie, or play VIGNETTE, CAMEO
- sketch or preliminary drawing, often full-size, for a tapestry, painting, or the like CARTOON
- sketch out or give a rough outline of something, such as a plan ADUMBRATE

ski See chart, page 500
- ski-lift cable car typically for one or two skiers GONDOLA
- ski lift for a single skier, who is dragged uphill by a plastic disc on the end of a bar placed between the legs POMA LIFT
- skilike blade on the hull of a boat that raises it when speeding HYDROFOIL
- device on a ski for securing the

boot firmly but releasing it when strain arises, as during an accident RELEASE BINDING, SAFETY BINDING
- disc near the tip of a ski pole to stop it from sinking into the snow BASKET

skill, power, or ability FACULTY, APTITUDE
- skill at conjuring or card tricks, involving deceptive hand movements LEGERDEMAIN, SLEIGHT OF HAND
- skill displaying outstanding technical ability, especially in playing a musical instrument VIRTUOSITY
- skill of a delicate or subtle kind, as in painting style, negotiations, or tennis strokes FINESSE
- skill of an effortless kind FACILITY
- skill or sensitivity, as in one's dealings with other people, social know-how TACT, SAVOIR FAIRE
- inventive skill or cleverness INGENUITY, ARTIFICE
- outstanding skill PROWESS
- strong point, major skill, speciality FORTE, MÉTIER

skillful, very able in a confident way PROFICIENT, ACCOMPLISHED
- skillful at, expert in AU FAIT, ADEPT
- skillful craftsperson or manual worker ARTISAN, ARTIFICER
- skillful or clever, especially with one's hands DEXTEROUS, DEFT, ADROIT, HABILE
- skillful or knowledgeable VERSED
- skillful or talented in a wide variety of ways VERSATILE
- reasonably skillful COMPETENT

skim, glide, or skip lightly SKITTER
- skim or glide in the wind, as clouds do SCUD

skin See illustration, page 501
- skin, membrane, seed coat, or similar natural outer covering INTEGUMENT
- skin, strip the skin of, as by whipping FLAY
- skin blemish, scar, birthmark, or rash STIGMA
- skin blemish or growth, such as a mole or strawberry mark, present from birth NEVUS
- skin blemish or spot MACULA
- skin cancer of a slow-growing type CANCROID
- skin condition marked by a horny patch or growth, such as a wart KERATOSIS
- skin condition or allergy involving itching and bumps HIVES, NETTLE RASH, URTICARIA, UREDO
- skin grafting in plastic surgery DERMATOPLASTY
- skin inflammation in the form of a pus-filled blister or pimple PUSTULE
- skin irritation caused by the wind WINDBURN
- skin lotion for relieving pain or stiffness LINIMENT, EMBROCATION, UNGUENT
- skin lotion for soothing and softening EMOLLIENT
- skin of a sheep or goat, treated for writing or painting on PARCHMENT
- skin of an animal, hide PELT, FELL
- skin pigment MELANIN
- skin rash, as in measles ROSEOLA
- skinlike sheet of natural or artificial tissue through which fluids can pass slowly MEMBRANE
- skinlike sheet of tissue covering or lining all body parts EPITHELIUM
- break out, appear on the skin, as a pimple or other blemish does ERUPT
- brownish patches on the skin, as occurring during pregnancy CHLOASMA
- cold and clammy, as the skin of malaria patients is ALGID
- curved blunt blade used by ancient Greeks and Romans for scraping the skin STRIGIL
- fibrous tissue beneath the skin and encasing muscles FASCIA
- fold of skin hanging from the throat, as of some birds and lizards WATTLE
- fold or flap of skin, such as that under the tongue FRENUM
- itching sensation, as though ants were crawling all over one's skin FORMICATION
- large freckle or discoloration developing on the skin of elderly people LIVER SPOT, LENTIGO
- located or made just beneath the skin, as fat or an injection might be SUBCUTANEOUS
- medical name for the skin DERMIS, CUTIS
- medical technique of attaching a glass cup to the skin by a partial vacuum, in order to draw blood to the surface, seldom used today CUPPING
- oil secreted by small glands in the skin SEBUM, SMEGMA
- outgrowth on an animal, seed, the skin, or the like, such as a rooster's comb CARUNCLE
- painful piece of skin pulled away but partially attached beside a fingernail HANGNAIL
- referring to the region just beneath the skin HYPODERMIC
- referring to the skin CUTANEOUS, DERMAL
- rough to the touch, horny or scaly, as hard dry skin might be SCABROUS, SQUAMOUS
- rub or tear away the skin of EXCORIATE
- scab or layer of dead skin, as caused by a burn ESCHAR
- scaly dry skin, as in dandruff SCURF, FURFURES
- shedding of the outer layer, shell, or skin, as in insects and snakes SLOUGHING, ECDYSIS
- slit or scratch the skin slightly, as for vaccination SCARIFY
- strip of hardened skin at the base of a fingernail or toenail CUTICLE
- temporary roughness of the skin because of cold, fear, or excitation, gooseflesh, goose pimples PILOERECTION, HORRIPILATION
- thickened or horny patch of skin, caused by pressure or friction, as on the hand or foot CALLUS, CALLOSITY
- tiny hole in the skin for perspiration to pass through PORE

skin (combining form) -DERM-, DERMO-, DERMATO-

skin diseases See **disease**

skip, glide, or skim lightly SKITTER
- skip or jump about playfully FROLIC, CAVORT, FRISK, GAMBOL, SPORT, ROLLICK, CAPER, ROMP

skirt See also **clothes**
- skirt of an old style, very tight below the knees HOBBLE SKIRT
- skirt that is bell-shaped, being draped over a structure of hoops HOOPSKIRT
- skirt worn as folk costume by Greek men, as on ceremonial occasions FUSTANELLA
- ballerina's very short skirt TUTU
- frame or pad formerly worn under a woman's skirt to expand it at the rear BUSTLE
- hoop or series of hoops formerly worn under a skirt to support it, or the skirt itself FARTHINGALE
- support, as of wire, spreading a skirt at the hips PANNIER

skull See also **bone, head**
- skull CRANIUM
- skull or a picture of it, representing mortality or death DEATH'S-HEAD
- cut a hole in or remove a disc of bone from the skull, using a special instrument TREPAN, TREPHINE
- farthermost point at the back of the skull INION
- former pseudoscience studying the shape and irregularities of a person's skull as a supposed indication of his or her character and mental powers PHRENOLOGY
- front upper part of the skull, the forehead area SINCIPUT
- opening at the base of the skull, through which the spinal cord passes FORAMEN MAGNUM
- referring to the head or skull CE-

PHALIC
- reminder of inescapable death, such as a skull MEMENTO MORI
- seam or joint line, as on a seedpod or between the bones of the skull SUTURE
- spongy bone between the hard inner and outer bone layers of the skull DIPLOE
- top of the head, highest point of the skull VERTEX
- top part of the skull, skullcap CALVARIA

skull (combining form) -CEPHAL-, CEPHALO-

skull and crossbones, pirate flag JOLLY ROGER

skullcap worn by religious male Jews YARMULKE, KIPA, KAPPEL
- skullcap worn by some Roman Catholic clergymen CALOTTE, ZUCCHETTO

sky, arching vault of the heavens WELKIN, FIRMAMENT
- look menacing and dark, as the sky or weather might LOWER
- referring to the sky or heavens SUPERNAL, CELESTIAL, EMPYREAL

sky (combining form) URAN-, URANO-

sky blue AZURE, CERULEAN

slander, insult in a false or unfairly demeaning way DEFAME, MALIGN, VILIFY, CALUMNIATE, SMEAR
- slander, knowingly false statement that injures someone's reputation CALUMNY, DEFAMATION
- slander, malicious injury or damage to someone's reputation CHARACTER ASSASSINATION
- slander or betray TRADUCE
- circulate slander openly UTTER
- defamation that is in writing or similarly on record, not spoken as slander is LIBEL

slang or jargon of a group ARGOT, CANT, PATOIS
- informal, slightly slangy word or phrase COLLOQUIALISM

slant See **slope**

slant (combining form) -CLIN-, CLINO-

slanting (combining form) PLAGI-, PLAGIO-

slash, punctuation mark as in *and/or* SOLIDUS, VIRGULE, OBLIQUE, SHILLING MARK, SLANT

slat or strip of wood or metal used in sheets as a backing for plaster, slates, tiles, or the like LATH
- slatted shutter or blind that can be adjusted to regulate the air or light admitted JALOUSIE
- slatted window or door, or any of the slats LOUVER

slaughter or massacre, especially in war CARNAGE
- slaughter or sacrifice on a large scale HECATOMB
- without making any distinctions, as among the victims of wholesale slaughter INDISCRIMINATE

slaughterhouse ABATTOIR, SHAMBLES

slave in Muslim countries MAMELUKE
- slavelike, relating to a slave SERVILE
- slavelike laborer, bound to a lord or estate SERF, BOND SERVANT, HELOT
- slave or concubine forming part of a harem ODALISQUE
- slave owned by a specific person CHATTEL
- slave who escaped or was freed during the American Civil War CONTRABAND
- supervisor of a gang of slaves OVERSEER, TASKMASTER, SLAVE DRIVER
- temporary barracks for slaves or convicts in former times BARRACOON

slavery or enslavement BONDAGE, SERVITUDE, THRALL
- ending of slavery and the slave trade ABOLITION
- free from slavery EMANCIPATE, MANUMIT, ENFRANCHISE

sled with an upturned front, used for transport or sliding downhill TOBOGGAN
- blade of metal or wood on a skate or sled RUNNER
- command to sled dogs to speed up MUSH

sleep-inducing NARCOTIC, SOPORIFIC, HYPNOTIC, HYPNAGOGIC, SOMNIFEROUS, SOPORIFEROUS, SOMNOLENT
- "sleep learning" HYPNOPEDIA
- sleep of the commonest kind, involving deep relaxation and no dreaming ORTHODOX SLEEP, NREM, SLOW-WAVE SLEEP, SYNCHRONIZED SLEEP
- sleep of the kind involving dreaming and eye movements, occurring in phases during the sleep cycle PARADOXICAL SLEEP, REM, RAPID-EYE-MOVEMENT SLEEP, DESYNCHRONIZED SLEEP, ACTIVATED SLEEP
- sleep or remain in a dormant state throughout the winter, as some animals do HIBERNATE
- sleep or remain in a dormant state throughout the summer, as some animals do ESTIVATE
- sleep or rest taken in the afternoon, especially in hot southern countries SIESTA
- sleep personified, or the god of sleep MORPHEUS
- calm someone to sleep LULL
- movement of the eyeballs behind closed lids during the dreaming phase of sleep REM, RAPID EYE MOVEMENT

sleep (combining form) HYPN-, HYPNO-, SOMN-, SOMNO-, MORPH-

sleeping, inactive DORMANT
- sleeping car, especially on a European train WAGON-LIT
- sleeping quarters, as in a boarding school DORMITORY

sleeping pill or potion HYPNOTIC, SOPORIFIC, NARCOTIC, SEDATIVE, OPIATE
- sleeping pill or tranquilizer of a common synthetic type DIAZEPAM, CHLORDIAZEPOXIDE, VALIUM

sleeping sickness ENCEPHALITIS LETHARGICA, HYPERSOMNIA, ECONOMO'S DISEASE, HYPERSOMNIC ENCEPHALITIS, TRYPANOSOMIASIS
- bloodsucking fly in Africa that causes sleeping sickness TSETSE FLY

sleeplessness INSOMNIA

sleepwalking SOMNAMBULISM, NOCTAMBULISM
- sleepwalking, knee jerk, or similar involuntary, unthinking action AUTOMATISM

sleepy DROWSY
- sleepy feeling, sluggishness TORPOR, SOMNOLENCE
- sleepy or yawning OSCITANT
- sleepy semiconsciousness induced by anesthetics TWILIGHT SLEEP

sleepy (combining form) NARCO-

sleeve extending all the way to the collar RAGLAN SLEEVE
- sleeve that is wide at the armhole and tapers to a narrow wrist DOLMAN SLEEVE
- full at one end and tapering at the other, as a sleeve or sail might be LEG-OF-MUTTON
- puffed out, as a sleeve or hairstyle might be BOUFFANT

sleight of hand, as of a magician in performing tricks PRESTIDIGITATION, LEGERDEMAIN

slide, slip, or skid, as on a wet road SLITHER, SLEW, VEER
- slide or sloping channel or duct down which water, coal, parcels, or the like can be conveyed CHUTE
- slide, X-ray photograph, or the like TRANSPARENCY
- projector for slides, diagrams on transparent plates, or the like DIASCOPE
- spiral slide at an amusement park HELTER-SKELTER

slide rule - sliding transparent indicator on a slide rule CURSOR

sling for sliding or lifting tree trunks, barrels, or the like PARBUCKLE
- giant sling or catapult, as for hurling rocks, used in medieval warfare TREBUCHET, TREBUCKET

slip of the tongue, verbal blunder LAPSUS LINGUAE
- slip of the tongue or similar lapse that discloses someone's real feelings or unconscious thoughts FREUDIAN SLIP, PARAPRAXIS

slipper-shaped, as some orchids are

CALCEOLATE

slippery, difficult to catch or pin down ELUSIVE
- slippery and smooth LUBRICIOUS

slope, slant, be at an angle BEVEL, SPLAY
- slope, slant, tilt INCLINATION, DEVIATION, CANT
- slope backward, as someone's forehead might RECEDE
- slope of a roof PITCH
- slope or angle, as of a mast, theater stage, aircraft's wings, or cutting edge of a tool RAKE
- slope or gentle incline GLACIS
- sloping or slanting, at an angle INCLINED, OBLIQUE
- sloping section or incline, as of a road or railroad track GRADIENT
- sloping typeface, as used for emphasis ITALIC
- diagonal or crosswise route across a slope, as in skiing TRAVERSE
- downward slope or tendency DECLENSION, DECLINATION, DECLINE, DECLIVITY
- flat shelf cut, usually as part of a series, into the side of a slope, for cultivation, preventing erosion, or the like TERRACE
- less steep, sloping rock surface at the base of a mountain in dry areas PEDIMENT
- long, steep slope, as from a plateau or in front of a castle ESCARPMENT
- upward slope ACCLIVITY

slope (combining form) -CLIN-, CLINO-

sloping (combining form) PLAGI-, PLAGIO-

slot, groove, or notch CHASE
- slot into which a matching tenon is fitted when joining two pieces of wood, stone, or metal MORTISE

sloth - two-toed sloth UNAU

slow, causing delays DILATORY
- slow, unhurried, at a comfortable pace LEISURELY
- slow absorption or acquisition, as of knowledge OSMOSIS
- slow and unhurried, thinking out each move DELIBERATE
- slow down DECELERATE, RETARD
- slow down or reduce in intensity or volume, peter out, dwindle SUBSIDE, RECEDE, TAPER OFF
- slow-motion meditative Chinese body movements T'AI CHI, T'AI CHI CHUAN
- slow-moving, sluggish TARDY
- slow or sluggish, as though constipated COSTIVE
- slow person, lagging behind LAGGARD, DAWDLER, SLOWPOKE
- slow through lacking energy or interest LANGUID, LACKADAISICAL
- slow to finish, long and drawn out PROLONGED, INTERMINABLE, PROTRACTED
- delay, be late or slow in doing something TARRY, PROCRASTINATE
- emerge or discharge slowly, as through pores EXUDE

slow (combining form) BRADY-

slowing or stoppage of blood flow, digestion, or the like STASIS

slowing (combining form) -STASIS, -STAT

sluggish, inactive TORPID, LETHARGIC

slum clearance URBAN RENEWAL, GENTRIFICATION
- slum area or old area of a city, inhabited by a poor minority group GHETTO
- large building, often in a slum area, divided into rooms or flats for rent TENEMENT
- building, often in a slum area, divided into rooms just large enough for one person SRO, SINGLE-ROOM OCCUPANCY

slur or slight of an oblique or veiled kind INNUENDO, ASPERSION, INSIN-

SKIING TERMS

Alpine	referring to downhill and slalom racing
biathlon	winter-sports contest involving cross-country skiing and target shooting
christiania/ christy	medium-fast turn with the skis kept parallel
fall line	most direct line of descent
geländesprung	jump launched from a crouching position during a downhill run
herringboning	climbing uphill by turning skis outward to form a V
hotdogging	spectacular freestyle skiing
kick-turn	pivot while stationary by raising and reversing the skis one by one
langlauf	cross-country skiing
mogul/bosse	mound or hillock of compacted snow
Nordic	referring to cross-country racing and related events
off-piste	referring to skiing on unmarked slopes
piste	marked ski run
schuss	fast, straight downhill run
skibob	bicyclelike vehicle that has short skis in place of wheels
skijoring	skiing behind a towing horse or vehicle
slalom	zigzag downhill race between poles or posts
snowplowing	slowing by turning the tips of the skis inward to form a V
stem turn	turn made by pushing the heel of one or both skis outward
swing	high-speed turn with the skis kept parallel
telemark	turn across the fall line made by pushing one ski well forward and around; possible only with bindings that leave the heel free, as in cross-country skiing
traversing	skiing diagonally or almost horizontally across the slope
vorlage	position in which the skier or ski jumper leans forward from the ankles
wedeln	series of short zigzag turns down the fall line

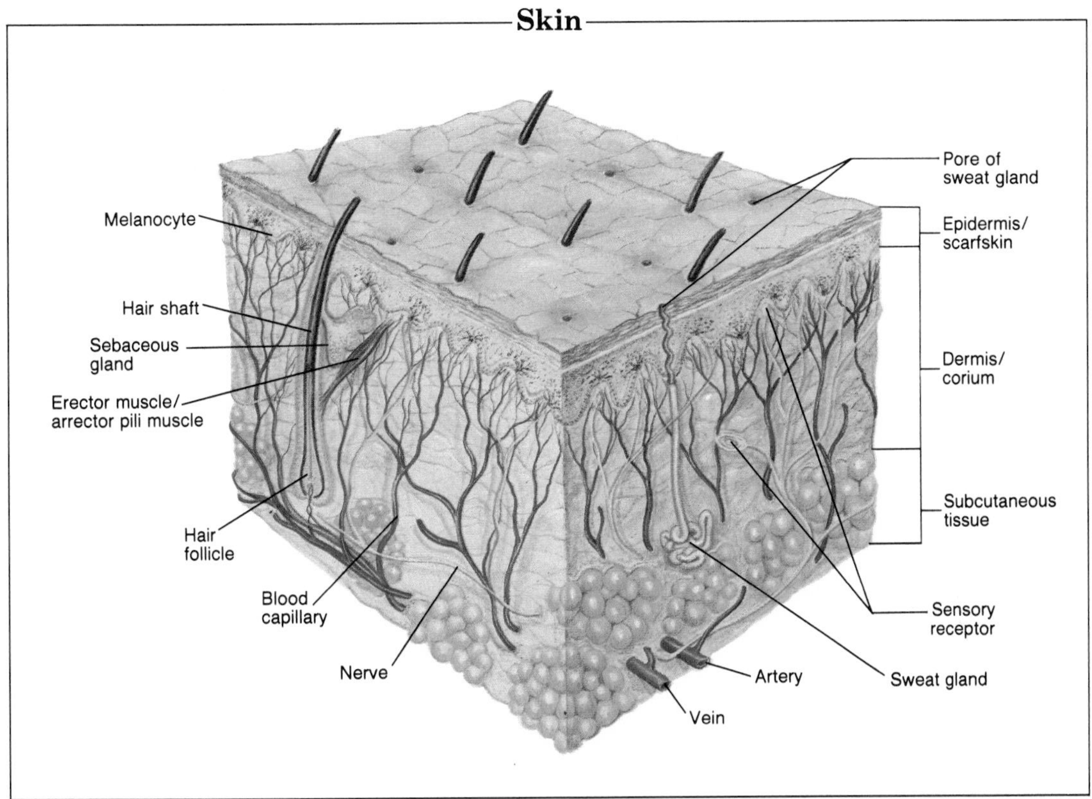

UATION

sly, cunning, crafty, full of tricks ARTFUL, INGENIOUS, WILY
- sly, shifty, calculating, or sneaky DEVIOUS, GUILEFUL
- sly, shrewd ASTUTE
- sly or knowing look LEER
- sly or secret, as a rendezvous might be CLANDESTINE
- sly or stealthy in a secretive or underhand way FURTIVE, SURREPTITIOUS
- slyly feigning ignorance or innocence, insincere DISINGENUOUS
- slyly imply, hint, or introduce something INSINUATE

small, charming, and delicate trinket or other object BIJOU
- small, puny person RUNT, MINNOW, PIPSQUEAK
- small, ungenerous, skimpy, as an allowance might be BEGGARLY, MEAGER, PALTRY
- small allowance, salary, or the like PITTANCE
- small amount, especially a slight knowledge of a language SMATTERING
- small amount, modest quantity SEMBLANCE, MODICUM
- small and trim, dainty, compact, as a woman might be PETITE
- small but self-important man COCKALORUM
- small or ridiculously inadequate, as a pay offer might be DERISORY
- smallest possible, as in amount or degree MINIMAL
- extremely small, microscopic, insignificant INFINITESIMAL
- so small as to pass unnoticed IMPERCEPTIBLE
- very small, barely noticeable, as a slight difference or increase might be MARGINAL, NEGLIGIBLE
- very small amount, merest hint or trace SOUPÇON, TINCTURE, VESTIGE
- very small amount, tiny bit SLIVER, IOTA, SCINTILLA, SMIDGEN
- very small in size or stature MINIATURE, DIMINUTIVE, MIDGET, LILLIPUTIAN, MINUSCULE

small (combining form) -CLE, -CULE, -KIN, -ULE, -Y, -EY, -IE, MINI-, MICRO-, NANO-, PICO-

small letters, as distinct from capital letters LOWERCASE, MINUSCULE LETTERS

small talk, polite remarks PLEASANTRIES, PATHIC TALK

smallness See **lack**

smallpox VARIOLA

smart, well-groomed, elegant SOIGNÉ
- smart in a cheeky way, jaunty, as the angle of a hat might be RAKISH
- smartly dressed, neat and trim, spruce DAPPER

smarten up in appearance as by adornment or refurbishment TITIVATE, SPRUCE UP

smear or spread roughly a substance such as mud, plaster, or grease DAUB

smear test in gynecology PAP TEST

smell, or smelly gas or vapor, as from a swamp or rubbish heap EFFLUVIUM
- smell of a wine, brandy, or liqueur BOUQUET
- bad smell, stink, stench, as of rotting organic material FETOR, MEPHITIS
- carry lightly, as the wind carries the smell of flowers WAFT
- loss of the sense of smell ANOSMIA
- pleasant smell, as of food AROMA, SAVOR
- pleasant smell, as of perfume or flowers FRAGRANCE, INCENSE
- referring to the sense of smell OLFACTORY, OSMATIC
- sharp or harsh, as a smell or taste might be ACRID, PUNGENT
- spray, liquid, or other substance used to suppress or mask smells such as those of sweat or cooking DEODORANT

smelling, especially pleasant-smelling FRAGRANT, REDOLENT, ARO-

MATIC
- smelling, especially unpleasant-smelling ODOROUS, ODORIFEROUS
- smelling moldy or stale FUSTY, MUSTY, FROWSY
- smelling of decay, foul-smelling MEPHITIC
- smelling off, stale, decomposing, as old butter or bacon fat might be RANCID, RANK
- smelling or tasting bad or rotten RANK, GAMY
- smelly, stinking FETID, MALODOROUS, REEKING, NOISOME
- smelly as a goat HIRCINE

smelling salts containing ammonium carbonate SAL VOLATILE
- bottle for smelling salts VINAIGRETTE

smelting - solid waste material from a furnace after smelting or refining SLAG, SINTER, CINDER, SCORIA

smile in an irritatingly shy or affected way SIMPER
- smile in an irritatingly smug or knowing way SMIRK
- smiling expression on the face of early Greek statues ARCHAIC SMILE
- apologetic or regretful, in a slightly cynical way, as a wry smile might be RUEFUL
- joyful in a serene or saintly way, as a smile might be BEATIFIC
- puzzling or mysterious, as a smile might be ENIGMATIC
- shy, hesitant, or uncertain, as a smile might be TENTATIVE
- unnatural gaping expression or smile RICTUS

smoke, vapor, or gas that is blown or breathed out EXHALATION
- dark and oppressive covering, as of smoke PALL, SHROUD
- fill a room or building with poisonous smoke to disinfect it or rid it of vermin FUMIGATE
- referring to smoke FUMATORY
- wood used for smoking food HICKORY

smoked salmon LOX

smoking - inhaling by nonsmokers of other people's tobacco smoke, now confirmed as a health hazard PASSIVE SMOKING

smoky or sooty FULIGINOUS

smooth, socially gracious and charming, often in a superficial way SUAVE, URBANE
- smooth and bald GLABROUS
- smooth and charming but often deceiving talk BLARNEY
- smooth and polished, as leather might be GLACÉ
- smooth and shiny, having a satiny finish SLEEK
- smooth and sweet, as a voice might be MELLIFLUOUS
- smooth surface on a bone or tooth FACET
- smoothly charming in an insincere, overearnest way UNCTUOUS, INGRATIATING
- smoothly or easily done FACILE
- make plaster or a similar surface smooth or level FLOAT
- speaking or writing in a smooth and effortless but sometimes shallow way FLUENT, GLIB

smuggling, or smuggled goods CONTRABAND
- smuggled or illicitly manufactured goods, especially alcohol during the U.S. Prohibition era BOOTLEG
- official who prevented smuggling in former times EXCISEMAN

snack or appetizer of a small open sandwich or spread biscuit CANAPÉ

snail or related land creature HELIX
- snail or related shell-covered land or sea creature MOLLUSK
- edible snail, especially when cooked ESCARGOT
- shaped like a snail shell, twisted spirally COCHLEATE

snake See illustration, page 505
- snake, such as the anaconda, python, or boa, that coils around and crushes its prey CONSTRICTOR
- snake's long, pointed tooth FANG
- snakelike monster with multiplying heads, killed by Hercules HYDRA
- adjective for a snake ANGUINE, COLUBRINE, OPHIDIAN
- curving gracefully, as a winding road or the movements of a snake might be SINUOUS
- poisonous snake, probably a small cobra, that killed Cleopatra ASP
- shedding of the outer layer, shell, or skin, as in insects and snakes SLOUGHING, ECDYSIS
- staff with wings and two twining snakes, serving as a symbol of the medical profession CADUCEUS
- weasellike mammal noted for its skill in killing snakes MONGOOSE

snakebite antidote obtained from the blood or tissue of immunized animals SERUM
- poisonous fluid secreted in a snakebite, scorpion sting, or the like VENOM

snare See **trap**

sneeze, or the act or noise of sneezing STERNUTATION
- equivalent of "bless you," of German origin, said to someone who has sneezed GESUNDHEIT

snobbish, haughty, or pretentious HOITY-TOITY
- snobbishness, exclusiveness, and standoffishness ELITISM

snoring heavily, or referring to a heavy snoring noise STERTOROUS

snow - referring to snow NIVEOUS, NIVAL
- snow pellets, soft hail GRAUPEL
- ledge of snow overhanging a cliff or mountain top CORNICE
- mass of porous ice formed from snow but not yet turned into glacier ice FIRN, NÉVÉ

snowshoe consisting of a stringed loop RACKET

snowstorm that is heavy and cold, with high winds BLIZZARD

so - "so," "thus," term used in a text to indicate the deliberate reproduction of a mistaken or surprising wording or fact being quoted SIC
- so-called, self-styled SOI-DISANT
- so much the better TANT MIEUX
- so much the worse TANT PIS

soak, cover completely in a liquid IMMERSE, SUBMERGE
- soak, wet, or fill with a substance IMPREGNATE, SATURATE, INFUSE, IMBUE
- soak or pickle meat or fish in a sauce before cooking MARINATE
- soak or steep herbs, tea, or the like without boiling INFUSE
- soften, separate, or disintegrate by means of soaking MACERATE

soap - soaplike or soapy SAPONACEOUS

soccer - player in soccer who defends from a position near his or her own goal SWEEPER
- player in soccer who is usually positioned in the opponent's half to exploit scoring opportunities STRIKER
- pretended pass or swerve, as in soccer or rugby, to deceive an opposing player DUMMY

sociable See also **friendly**
- sociable, enjoying the company of others GREGARIOUS
- sociable, friendly, lively person EXTROVERT
- sociable, jolly, or festive, as a party atmosphere or companion might be JOVIAL, CONVIVIAL

social distinction or prestige CACHET
- social blunder GAFFE, FAUX PAS
- social climber, upstart, johnny-come-lately ARRIVISTE, PARVENU, NOUVEAU RICHE
- social disturbance or agitation of a violent kind UPHEAVAL, CONVULSION
- social group of the same age and status as oneself PEER GROUP
- social group or clique, such as a literary discussion group CENACLE
- social mixing or friendly relations, as with the people of an enemy country FRATERNIZATION
- social outcast ISHMAEL, PARIAH,

LEPER
- social reformer or theorist who is hopelessly idealistic and impractical VISIONARY, UTOPIAN
- social role or self-projection adopted by a person when in the company of others, his or her "front" PERSONA
- social self-assurance and adeptness, tact SAVOIR FAIRE
- social success, acclaim, or distinction ÉCLAT
- social system in medieval Europe, in which vassals exchanged homage and service for land and protection from a lord FEUDALISM, FEUDAL SYSTEM
- social worker responsible to a court for supervising offenders with suspended sentences PROBATION OFFICER
- possession desired or valued as an indicator of wealth or social prestige STATUS SYMBOL
- raising one's social status UPWARDLY MOBILE
- rejection of all moral and social values NIHILISM
- treat someone as a social idol or celebrity LIONIZE

socialism of a nonrevolutionary, democratic, gradually developing kind FABIANISM

socialize or associate in a familiar way HOBNOB, CONSORT
- socialize or flirt, especially while wandering about GAD ABOUT, GALLIVANT

socially acceptable and polite remarks, small talk PLEASANTRIES, CIVILITIES, PATHIC TALK
- socially awkward or ill-at-ease teenager or young man or woman HOBBLEDEHOY
- socially correct and acceptable, proper COMME IL FAUT
- socially exclusive and cultivated person, intellectual snob BRAHMIN
- socially gracious and charming, often in a superficial way SUAVE
- socially humbled, reduced in social status or class DÉCLASSÉ
- socially skillful, tactful, or sensitive DIPLOMATIC

society or association, specifically a charitable society of lay Roman Catholics SODALITY
- society's basic structures and institutions, such as transport and education INFRASTRUCTURE
- divided according to castes or classes, as a nation or society might be STRATIFIED
- influential conservative group of people, subtly directing political trends, artistic activity, or the like within society THE ESTABLISHMENT
- level, such as a class or caste, within a society or series STRATUM
- local branch of a society or club CHAPTER, LODGE, CELL
- referring to a society in which several racial, religious, or cultural groups coexist PLURALISTIC
- sense or state of being an outsider, isolated from one's society ALIENATION
- young upper-class lady undergoing a formal presentation to society, as at a ball DEBUTANTE

Socrates - poison drunk by Socrates in accordance with his death sentence HEMLOCK
- process of reaching the truth, as in Socrates or Hegel, by examining contradictions DIALECTIC
- relating to Socrates' method of eliciting someone's submerged knowledge by means of a series of questions MAIEUTIC

soda water, sparkling water CARBONATED WATER, CLUB SODA, SELTZER WATER
- emitting small bubbles of gas, as soda water is EFFERVESCENT

sofa See **furniture**

soft and crumbly, as soil might be FRIABLE
- soft and flexible enough to be bent or shaped, as some metals are PLIABLE, DUCTILE, MALLEABLE
- soft and limp, drooping, flabby, lacking firmness FLACCID
- soft or mashed food, as for a baby or sick person PAP
- soft sighing sound, as of the wind SOUGH, SUSURRATION

soft (combining form) MALACO-

soft coal BITUMINOUS COAL

soft hail, snow pellets GRAUPEL

soft roe MILT

soften, ease, make gentler, or pacify MOLLIFY
- soften, separate, or disintegrate by means of soaking MACERATE
- soften or reduce the intensity of something, such as anger MITIGATE, MODERATE, TEMPER
- soften the sound of a trumpet or other instrument MUTE, MUFFLE

softly and privately, in a subdued voice, under one's breath SOTTO VOCE
- softly spoken utterance or the subdued sound of it UNDERTONE

soil consisting of a fertile mix of clay, sand, and silt LOAM
- soil formed from crumbled limestone MALM
- soil of very fine rock particles SILT
- soil or other sediment deposited by a river or flood ALLUVIUM
- break up and loosen the surface of topsoil, a field, a road, or the like SCARIFY
- crumbly, as soil might be FRIABLE
- crumbly clay soil MARL
- dark, fertile soil, rich in humus CHERNOZEM
- harrow used for crushing clods or leveling the soil DRAG
- layer of humus in soil MULL
- loose, crumbly soil, rich in organic matter MOLD
- referring to rich, fertile, workable soil UNCTUOUS, PINGUID
- remove soluble parts from a substance such as soil, as by flushing with water LEACH
- scientific study of soil PEDOLOGY
- any soluble mineral salt found in natural water and arid soils ALKALI
- sudden shifting of soil from one property to another, as through flooding AVULSION
- wearing away or washing away, as of the soil cover EROSION

soil (combining form) AGR-, AGRI-, AGRO-, PED-, PEDO-

solar system - model of the solar system, used in studying astronomy ORRERY

solder - join or fuse two metal surfaces with a nonferrous solder BRAZE

soldier See chart, page 507, and also **services, military, troops**
- soldier assisting a duty officer ORDERLY
- soldier in a small irregular military unit carrying out sabotage and harassment operations GUERRILLA, PARTISAN
- soldier or soldiers assigned to a particular duty DETAIL
- soldier serving in a foreign army or organization for payment MERCENARY
- soldier who is enrolled compulsorily for military service CONSCRIPT, RECRUIT
- soldier who signs up for military service of his or her own free will VOLUNTEER
- soldiers' lodgings in a civilian building BILLET
- soldiers' quarters, building or group of buildings for housing soldiers BARRACKS
- soldiers' quarters, especially in a garrison town, in former times CASERN
- acquire new soldiers, members, or the like RECRUIT, ENLIST, ENROLL
- acquire new soldiers for service by force of law CONSCRIPT, LEVY, DRAFT
- adjective for a soldier MILITARY, MARTIAL
- band of soldiers, strikers, protesters, or the like COHORT

- dismiss a soldier from a military unit, impose a dishonorable discharge on CASHIER, DRUM OUT
- persecution by soldiers, military subjection or bullying DRAGOONING
- person who is not a soldier or other military employee CIVILIAN
- person who, on moral grounds, refuses to serve as a soldier CONSCIENTIOUS OBJECTOR
- pit or crater serving as protection for soldiers against enemy fire FOXHOLE
- release or discharge soldiers from military service DEMOBILIZE, DEMOB, DISBAND
- trick or force men into serving as sailors or soldiers PRESS, IMPRESS, COMMANDEER, PRESS-GANG, SHANGHAI
- unit of part-time or civilian soldiers MILITIA

sole - relating to the sole of the foot PLANTAR, THENAR, VOLAR

solid ground, dry land TERRA FIRMA

solid (combining form) STERE-, STEREO-

solidify CONSOLIDATE
- solidify into a soft mass, as liquids might COAGULATE, CLOT, CURDLE, CONGEAL
- solid mass, such as a kidney stone CALCULUS, CONCRETION

solitaire card game PATIENCE

solitary person who has withdrawn from society, as for religious reasons HERMIT, RECLUSE

solo song, as in an opera or oratorio ARIA, ARIETTA

solution or final result, as of a play DENOUEMENT
- solution or molten material that conducts electricity ELECTROLYTE
- solution or scheme, as for social problems, that is considered facile or simplistic NOSTRUM
- containing as much dissolved substance as possible, as a solution might SATURATED
- gradual evening out of differently concentrated solutions by the transfer of molecules through the separating membrane OSMOSIS
- Hitler's "final solution" THE HOLOCAUST
- separation of different types of molecule in a solution by means of a membrane DIALYSIS
- solid substance separated out from a solution PRECIPITATE

solve or interpret something puzzling or obscure DECIPHER
- solve or penetrate to the meaning of a mystery or puzzle FATHOM, UNRAVEL
- capable of being solved, resolved, or dissolved SOLUBLE
- impossible to solve, resolve, or dissolve INSOLUBLE
- triumphant exclamation on finding, solving, or discovering something EUREKA

solvent supposedly capable of dissolving anything, as sought by the alchemists ALKAHEST

sometimes, now and then, occasionally, from time to time INTERMITTENTLY, PERIODICALLY

son - adjective for a son or daughter FILIAL
- "son of" MC-, MAC-, O'-, -SON, -SOHN, -SEN, -OVICH, BEN

song, hymn, or religious poem CANTICLE
- song about unrequited or passionate love TORCH SONG
- song business or popular-music industry TIN PAN ALLEY
- song for a solo voice, as in an opera or oratorio ARIA, ARIETTA
- song of a simple kind DITTY
- song of lamentation, mourning song THRENODY
- song of a Venetian gondolier BARCAROLE
- song of West Indian origin with a syncopated rhythm and lyrics, typically improvised on a humorous or topical theme CALYPSO
- song or expression of joy and praise PAEAN
- song or round for three or more voices, popular in the 17th and 18th centuries CATCH
- song sung by sailors, typically in rhythm with their work SHANTY
- song to celebrate a wedding PROTHALAMION, EPITHALAMIUM
- chorus or bass accompaniment of a song BURDEN
- chorus or repeated section of a song REFRAIN
- cradle song, lullaby BERCEUSE
- formal song or poem honoring and praising someone PANEGYRIC
- German song or art song LIED
- range or stock of jokes, songs, operatic roles, plays, or the like REPERTOIRE
- sung without instrumental accompaniment, as some choral songs are A CAPPELLA
- text of the songs and dialogue of an opera, musical, or other musical work LIBRETTO
- unaccompanied secular song or part-song, developed in Renaissance Italy MADRIGAL
- words of a song LYRICS

songwriter LYRICIST

sonnet with a strict rhyming pattern, unlike the loose English or Shakespearean sonnet ITALIAN SONNET, PETRARCHAN SONNET
- sonnet's first eight lines OCTET
- sonnet's last six lines SESTET

soon to happen IMMINENT, IMPENDING, LOOMING, PROXIMATE
- soon, tomorrow MAÑANA

soot particle SMUT
- referring to soot FULIGINOUS

soothe See **calm**

soothing, comforting, relaxing ANODYNE, LENITIVE
- soothing, relaxing, or sleep-inducing substance SEDATIVE, NARCOTIC, OPIATE, SOPORIFIC
- soothing and softening, as a skin lotion should be EMOLLIENT
- soothing ointment or lotion LINIMENT, EMBROCATION, UNGUENT
- soothing or healing substance, person, or influence SALVE
- soothing potion or drug, or technique for forgetting one's pains and sorrows NEPENTHE
- something, such as an idle promise or excuse, used to soothe or humor someone PLACEBO

soothsayer See also **prophet**
- soothsayer in ancient Rome HARUSPEX, AUGUR

sophisticated, elegant, or fashionable SOIGNÉ
- sophisticated, very cultured or learned HIGHBROW, CULTIVATED
- sophisticated and broad-minded, as through being familiar with a variety of cultures COSMOPOLITAN
- sophisticated and charming in company, socially refined SUAVE, URBANE, DEBONAIR
- sophisticated or clever beyond his or her years, as an advanced child would be PRECOCIOUS
- stylish or fashionable in a pretentious way, oversophisticated or overelaborate CHICHI

soprano specializing in ornamental trills and runs COLORATURA

sorcery See **magic, black magic,** prophet

sore, blister, or blotch on the skin BLAIN
- sore, broken or scraped skin ABRASION, EXCORIATION
- sore, raised patch or stripe on the skin, as caused by a blow or an insect bite WEAL, WELT
- sore, wound, or injury LESION, TRAUMA
- sore in the form of a hard, infected, pus-filled swelling, boil FURUNCLE
- sore in the form of a hard, pale mass under the skin, caused by a blocked oil gland MILIUM
- sore in the form of a pocket of pus in inflamed tissue ABSCESS
- sore or cyst in the eyelid, caused by a blocked oil gland CHALAZION
- sore or cyst under the tongue, caused by a blocked salivary gland

or duct RANULA
- sore or itchy inflammation on the hands, feet, or ears, caused by exposure to the cold and damp CHILBLAIN
- sore or pus-filled inflammation near a fingernail or toenail FELON, WHITLOW
- sore or scab formed by a burn, chafing, or the like ESCHAR
- sore or ulcer in the mouth or on the lips CANKER

Snakes

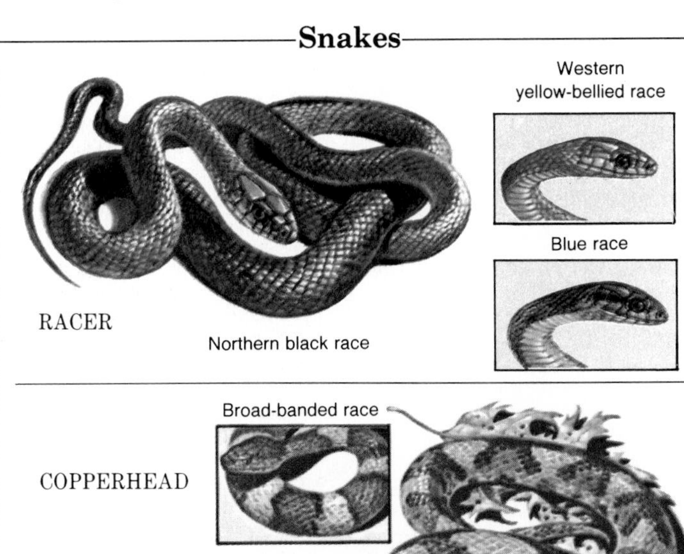

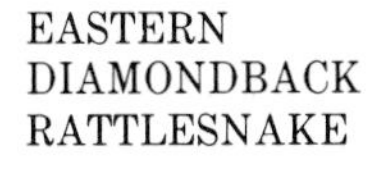

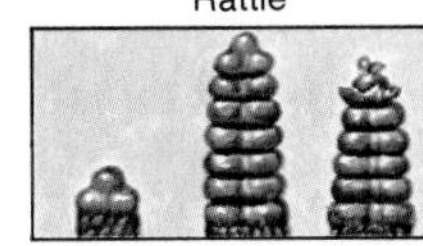

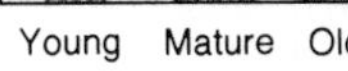

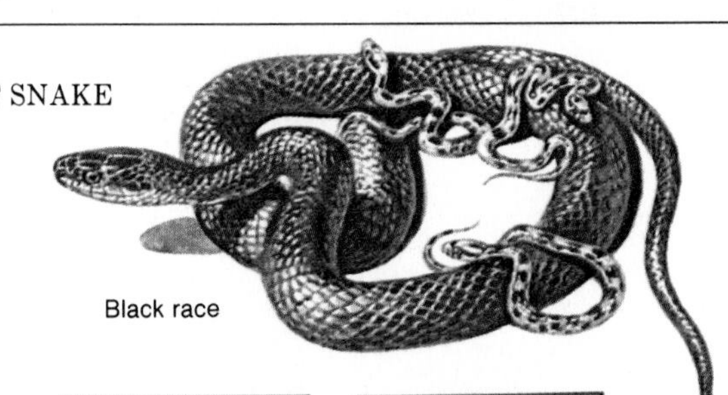

- sore resembling a large boil, caused by bacterial infection CARBUNCLE
- sore swelling of the first joint of the big toe BUNION
- sore swelling under the hide of cattle or horses WARBLE
- bedsore, pressure sore DECUBITUS ULCER
- hard reddish sore that is an early indication of syphilis CHANCRE
- oily sore or cyst, especially on the scalp WEN
- small, pus-producing sore or ulcer FESTER, GATHERING
- small sore on the skin or a mucous membrane, caused by a tiny hemorrhage PETECHIA
- swollen pimple, blister, or sore, typically filled with pus PUSTULE, PAPULE, WHELK, BLEB, BULLA
- wartlike sore in the rectal or genital area CONDYLOMA

sore throat caused by a common bacterial infection STREP THROAT

sorrowful See **sad**

sorry for one's sins, or regretting one's misdeeds REPENTANT, PENITENT, REMORSEFUL, CONTRITE
- be sorry about, lament REGRET, DEPLORE, RUE
- feel sorry for or sympathize with someone COMMISERATE

S.O.S., distress call MAYDAY

soul, in Hindu philosophy ATMAN
- soul, vital spirit PNEUMA
- soul or spirit, as distinct from the body PSYCHE
- soul or true inner self in Jungian psychology ANIMA, ANIMUS
- soul's migration, after a person's death, into another body or cycle of existence TRANSMIGRATION, REINCARNATION, METEMPSYCHOSIS, PALINGENESIS
- abode, in Christian theology, of just souls barred from heaven, as through not having been baptized LIMBO
- condition or place in which souls are purified of their sins before admission to heaven PURGATORY
- damnation, loss of the soul PERDITION
- religious belief that each thing, both living and nonliving, has its own individual soul ANIMISM

sound See also **noise, pronunciation, speech, voice**
- sound, effective, or acceptable, as an argument, title, or passport might be VALID
- sound, especially in speech, that is pleasant to listen to EUPHONY
- sound or sound reproduction, as of a television or stereo set AUDIO
- sound quality produced by over-

tones rather than volume and pitch TIMBRE
- sound-regulating device, as in a microphone or loudspeaker BAFFLE
- sound reproduction that creates the effect in the listener of being bombarded with sound from all sides SURROUND-SOUND
- sound system of a particular language PHONOLOGY
- sound that is ugly and jarring CACOPHONY, DISCORDANCE, DISSONANCE
- sounding harsh or hoarse RAUCOUS
- sounding of a final consonant that is normally silent, especially in French, when the next word begins with a vowel LIAISON
- sounding of the /r/ after vowels, as in *card* or *teacher,* in keeping with the spelling, by people who are "R speakers" as opposed to "R droppers" RHOTACISM
- sounding pleasant, pleasing to the ear EUPHONIOUS
- sounding pleasantly melodious DULCET
- sounding rich, deep, or impressively loud SONOROUS, RESONANT
- soundproof, heatproof, or prevent the transfer of electricity INSULATE
- sounds of prolonged vibration or echoing REVERBERATIONS
- alter or insert the soundtrack of a movie or tape DUB
- apparent change in pitch of sound, as of a siren, as the source approaches or moves away from the listener DOPPLER EFFECT
- change in the sound of a consonant because of the influence of another consonant, as in pronouncing *incline* as though it were *ingcline* ASSIMILATION
- change in the vowel sound of a verb, as in *sing, song, sung* ABLAUT, GRADATION
- change in the vowel sound of a word, especially of a verb, originally because of the influence of a nearby vowel UMLAUT, MUTATION
- deaden a sound MUFFLE, MUTE
- fall in the sound level or pitch of the voice, as at the end of a sentence CADENCE
- glorious or harmonious burst of musical sound DIAPASON
- gradual decrease in the volume of sound, as in a passage of music DIMINUENDO, DECRESCENDO
- gradual increase in the volume of sound, as in a passage of music CRESCENDO
- hissing sound, as of /s/ or /z/ SIBILANT
- increase in volume or length of a sound, as by an echo or vibration RESONANCE
- insertion of an extra sound into a word to make its pronunciation easier, as when *umbrella* is pronounced as though it were spelled *umbarella* EPENTHESIS
- letter, symbol, or group of characters that can represent more than one sound, such as the English *g* in *gin* and *gain* POLYPHONE
- loss or cutting off of a letter, syllable, or sound at the beginning of a word, as with *squire* from *esquire* APHAERESIS, APHESIS, FRONT-CLIPPING
- loss or cutting off of a letter, syllable, or sound from the end of a word, as with *prof* from *professor* APOCOPE, END-CLIPPING
- loss or cutting off of a letter, syllable, or sound from the middle of a word, as with *fo'c's'le* from *forecastle* SYNCOPATION, SYNCOPE
- loss or cutting off of a syllable or sound from the middle of a word, as when *deteriorate* is pronounced as though it were spelled *deteriate* HAPLOLOGY
- omitting or slurring of a vowel sound or syllable, as to make a line of verse scan ELISION
- pronunciation of the sound /r/ as /l/, as by many Chinese people speaking English LALLATION
- quality of sound reproduction in a hall, auditorium, stadium, or the like ACOUSTICS
- recording or transmitting sound by means of only one channel MONOPHONIC, MONAURAL, MONO
- recording or transmitting sound by means of two separate channels STEREOPHONIC, BINAURAL, STEREO
- referring to sound or hearing ACOUSTIC, AURAL
- referring to sound, sound waves, audible sound, or the speed of sound SONIC
- referring to speech sounds PHONETIC
- referring to speed greater than the speed of sound SUPERSONIC
- repeated occurrence of a consonant sound, especially at the start of words ALLITERATION
- repeated occurrence of sounds, especially vowels, as in poetry ASSONANCE
- sensation of color evoked by a sound, or similar sensation of a sense different from the one stimulated SYNESTHESIA
- speech sound identified as significant in a given language through serving to distinguish one word from another PHONEME
- speech sound of a breathy kind, such as the /h/ sound in English ASPIRATE
- speech sound of a throaty kind, such as the Parisian /r/ sound UVULAR
- speech sound of an unstressed midcentral vowel, as at the end of *teacher* or the beginning of *about,* or the symbol /ə/, which represents it SCHWA
- speech sound produced in the throat GUTTURAL
- speech sound such as the /ī/ sound in *side,* in which a vowel changes in quality during the syllable DIPHTHONG
- speech sound such as /ch/ or /j/, produced by the sudden release of the breath AFFRICATE
- speech sound such as /d/ or /t/, formed with the tip of the tongue just behind the upper teeth ALVEOLAR
- speech sound such as /f/ or /z/, formed by partially blocking the flow of breath FRICATIVE, SPIRANT
- speech sound such as /j/ or /k/, formed with the back of the tongue near or against the soft palate VELAR
- speech sound such as /m/ or /p/, involving the use of the lips LABIAL
- speech sound such as the /p/ in *top,* involving the brief blocking of the breath PLOSIVE
- study of pronunciation and speech sounds PHONETICS, PHONEMICS, PHONOLOGY
- switching, usually unintended, of the initial sounds of two or more words, as when *crushing blow* comes out as *blushing crow* SPOONERISM
- system or apparatus for detecting or locating objects underwater by means of sound waves SONAR, ECHOLOCATION
- unit for measuring the loudness of a sound DECIBEL
- word in which the sound echoes the meaning ONOMATOPOEIA

sound (combining form) PHON-, PHONO-, -PHONE, -PHONY, AUDI-, AUDIO-

soup See chart, page 510
- souplike mixture of organic chemicals in early times from which life may have developed PRIMORDIAL SOUP
- broad deep bowl, as used for serving soup TUREEN
- small toasted or fried square of bread, served in soups or salads CROUTON

sour, tart, bitter to the taste ACERBIC, ACETOUS, ACIDULOUS

source See also **origin**
- source in the form of a spring

FOUNTAINHEAD
- source of a river HEADWATERS
- source of easy money or help MILCH COW, GRAVY TRAIN
- source of supply, as of raw materials LODE
- selecting or selected from several different sources ECLECTIC

south, southerly MERIDIONAL, AUSTRAL, MIDI
- southern lights, seen flashing in the night sky, especially near the South Pole AURORA AUSTRALIS
- southern U.S. states DIXIE
- alliance of the southern states during the American Civil War CONFEDERACY

south (combining form) AUSTR-, AUSTRO-, NOT-, NOTO-

South America - blanketlike cloak with a hole in the center for the head, originally from South America PONCHO
- cowboy on the South American grassland plains GAUCHO
- grassland plains of South America PAMPAS
- mammals from South America that are closely related to the llama ALPACA, GUANACO, VICUÑA
- tealike drink popular in South America MATÉ, YERBA MATÉ, PARAGUAY TEA

souvenir, especially a gift that serves as a reminder KEEPSAKE, MEMENTO

sovereign See **king**

Soviet See **Russian**

space allowing access or free play, as the headroom for a vehicle under an overhead bridge or the gap between two parts of a machine CLEARANCE
- space of four dimensions in mathematics HYPERSPACE
- space or heavens beyond the earth's atmosphere, according to Greek myth ETHER
- space or missing part, as in a bone or manuscript LACUNA
- creature from another world or from outer space ALIEN, EXTRATERRESTRIAN, EXTRATERRESTRIAL
- depth appearance of various objects in different spatial relationships PERSPECTIVE
- relating to outer space COSMIC, SPA-

SOLDIERS

askari	East African colonial soldier
bashi-bazouk	irregular 19th-century Turkish cavalryman
berserker	Norse warrior fighting in a drugged frenzy
carabineer	soldier armed with a carbine, or short rifle
centurion	Roman officer in command of a century, which originally consisted of 100 men
chasseur	light cavalryman or infantryman in the French army
Chetnik	Serbian nationalist guerrilla, especially in World War II
Chindit	member of the Allied commando force in Burma during World War II
condottiere	mercenary in Europe between the 14th and the 16th century
doughboy	U.S. infantryman of World War I
fusilier	soldier armed with a fusil, or light musket
ghazi	highly honored Muslim warrior
Gurkha	Nepalese soldier serving in the British or Indian army
halberdier	medieval soldier armed with a halberd, or axlike weapon on a long shaft
Hessian	German mercenary in the British army during the American War of Independence and Napoleonic Wars
hoplite	heavily armed foot soldier in ancient Greece
hussar	Hungarian light cavalryman of the 15th century; light cavalry soldier
Ironsides	Puritan cavalryman in Cromwell's army in the English Civil War
janissary	Turkish soldier of an elite guard, between the 14th and the 19th century
kern	medieval Irish or Scottish foot soldier
landsknecht	German 15th-17th century mercenary
lascar	soldier, sailor, or army servant from the East Indies
legionnaire/ legionary	member of a legion, as in ancient Rome or in the French Foreign Legion
minuteman	American militiaman during the War of Independence
Myrmidon	Greek warrior at the siege of Troy
peltast	lightly armed foot soldier of ancient Greece
poilu	French infantryman, especially one in the front line during World War I and II
rapparee	Irish freebooting soldier of the 17th century
sepoy	Indian soldier formerly serving under British command
sowar	mounted soldier (or policeman) in India
spahi	Turkish cavalryman; Algerian cavalryman in the French army
vexillary	ancient Roman veteran; standard-bearer
Zouave	Algerian infantryman in the French army

CIAL, EXTRATERRESTRIAL
- small space or gap, as between the strands of a net INTERSTICE
- unsuccessful or prematurely ended, as a space flight might be ABORTIVE

spacecraft that was the first to orbit the earth, launched by the U.S.S.R. SPUTNIK 1
- spacecraft's heat shield ABLATOR
- activity, such as spacewalking, by an astronaut outside the spacecraft while away from earth EVA, EXTRAVEHICULAR ACTIVITY
- load of equipment or cargo on a spacecraft PAYLOAD
- minimum speed needed by a spacecraft to overcome the gravitational field ESCAPE VELOCITY
- pilot or crew member of a spacecraft ASTRONAUT, COSMONAUT
- point at which a spacecraft in lunar orbit is farthest from the moon APOCYNTHION, APOLUNE, APOSELENE
- point at which a spacecraft in lunar orbit is nearest to the moon PERICYNTHION, PERILUNE, PERISELENE
- point in its orbit when the moon or a spacecraft is farthest from the earth APOGEE
- point in its orbit when the moon or a spacecraft is nearest to the earth PERIGEE
- rocket supplementing the main power system of a jet or spacecraft BOOSTER
- self-contained unit, usually separable, of a spacecraft MODULE, LANDER
- supply tube to a spacecraft before launching UMBILICAL CORD
- supporting tower or scaffolding for a spacecraft on the launching pad GANTRY

spacious, large, bulky, or baggy VOLUMINOUS
- spacious or roomy, as an office might be COMMODIOUS, CAPACIOUS

spaghetti See also **pasta**
- firm and chewy through being lightly cooked, as spaghetti might be AL DENTE

Spain - adjective for Spain and Spanish America HISPANIC

Spanish See chart, page 512, and also charts at **menu, bullfighting**
- Spanish and Portuguese IBERIAN
- Spanish dancer's small wooden shells clicked in the hand in time to the music CASTANETS
- Spanish dialect spoken by Sephardic Jews, as formerly in the Balkans LADINO, JUDEZMO, JUDEO-SPANISH
- Spanish dialect that is now the standard and official form of Spanish in Spain CASTILIAN
- Spanish fascist organization that became the ruling party in Spain under General Franco FALANGE
- Spanish invader of Mexico and Peru in the 16th century CONQUISTADOR
- Spanish-speaking neighborhood or community, as in a U.S. city BARRIO
- elderly woman employed by Spanish or Portuguese families as governess and chaperon for the daughters DUENNA
- group of confidential advisers, as formerly to the Spanish kings CAMARILLA
- powerful politician in a Spanish-speaking country CACIQUE

Spanish (combining form) HISPANO-

Spanish fly, an alleged aphrodisiac CANTHARIDES, LYTTA VESICATORIA

sparing, restrained, in eating and drinking ABSTEMIOUS, TEMPERATE

spark, excite, or inspire KINDLE, INFLAME
- spark or flash SCINTILLATION
- sparking system in an engine IGNITION
- device in an internal-combustion engine for supplying current in the correct sequence to the spark plugs DISTRIBUTOR

sparkle, flash, or shine SCINTILLATE, CORUSCATE, SPANGLE, FULGURATE
- sparkle gently, gleam GLISTEN, SHIMMER
- sparkle or sheen LUSTER
- sparkle or shine producing a variety of colors IRIDESCENCE
- sparkling, as with sequins CLINQUANT
- sparkling, decorated with sequins, powdered glass, or artificial jewels to produce a diamondlike effect DIAMANTÉ
- sparkling decoration of thin threads or strips, as on a Christmas tree TINSEL
- sparkling fabric containing silver or golden threads LAMÉ

sparrow - referring to sparrows, finches, and related birds FRINGILLID

spasm, fit PAROXYSM, CONVULSION
- spasm or twitch, especially in the face TIC
- spasms of facial pain caused by the trigeminal nerve TIC DOLOUREUX
- impaired control of the muscles and limbs, sometimes including spasms or convulsions, resulting from brain damage before or during birth CEREBRAL PALSY, CP

speak See also **spoken, speech, say, state, conversation, talkative**
- speak about business matters or private concerns, discuss, exchange views CONFER, CONSULT
- speak about familiar things in a relaxed way, chat or gossip CHEW THE FAT, CONFABULATE, SCHMOOZE
- speak about openly, bring into public discussion VENTILATE
- speak aimlessly and at tedious length MAUNDER, PRATE
- speak cautiously and in a noncommittal way HEDGE
- speak evasively, hedge EQUIVOCATE, PREVARICATE, QUIBBLE
- speak in a long-winded, lengthy, pompous, and rhetorical way PERORATE, DECLAIM, SPEECHIFY
- speak in a lazy, drawn-out way DRAWL
- speak in a monotonous or boring way DRONE
- speak in a preachy or moralizing way SERMONIZE
- speak in an extremely enthusiastic way, as in praising something overeagerly RHAPSODIZE
- speak in an incoherent or stammering way, as when very angry SPLUTTER, STUTTER
- speak in an overconfident and opinionated way PONTIFICATE, DOGMATIZE
- speak incoherently or nonsensically, as after a shock GIBBER
- speak long and often irrelevantly in a debate as a delaying tactic to obstruct legislation FILIBUSTER
- speak loudly in a boastful or threatening way BLUSTER
- speak or perform without preparation EXTEMPORIZE
- speak or write about formally DISCOURSE
- speak or write lengthy details on a subject ELABORATE, EXPATIATE, ENLARGE, DILATE, EXPOUND
- speak out, as in open protest CLAMOR, YAMMER
- speak rapidly and casually or aimlessly, chatter JABBER, BLABBER, GABBLE, TATTLE, PALAVER, CLACK, BABBLE, PRATTLE, NATTER
- speak to a gathering, in a passionate, ranting, or argumentative way HARANGUE
- speak with an irritatingly shy or affected smile SIMPER
- speaking clearly and effectively, expressive ARTICULATE
- speaking disability or writing disability caused by brain damage or disease APHASIA
- speaking in a hesitant or devious way MEALYMOUTHED
- speaking or chanting rhymed verses to a musical beat RAPPING
- speaking or writing effortlessly FLUENT

- speaking or writing in an effortless but shallow manner GLIB
- speaking style or delivery, especially in public ELOCUTION
- chronic compulsion to speak or shout obscenities, accompanied by rapid muscle movements TOURETTE'S DISORDER, GILLES DE LA TOURETTE'S SYNDROME
- excessive or uncontrollable speaking, sometimes caused by mental illness LOGORRHEA
- person speaking to another COLLOCUTOR, INTERLOCUTOR

speaker who is impressive and persuasive or else excessively high-flown RHETORICIAN
- speakers' platform, as in a lecture hall DAIS, ROSTRUM
- jeer at a speaker with repeated critical comments HECKLE

speaker (combining form) -PHONE

spear, as used formerly by warriors in southern Africa ASSEGAI
- spear used in sporting competitions or formerly as a weapon JAVELIN
- spear with three prongs, as used by gladiators or carried by Neptune TRIDENT
- spear with three or more prongs, used in salmon fishing LEISTER
- arch of spears through which the defeated enemies of ancient Rome had to walk as a gesture of submission YOKE
- shaped like a spearhead or arrow, as some leaves are HASTATE

specialist adviser CONSULTANT
- person with wide-ranging knowledge or interests, as distinct from a specialist GENERALIST

specialist (combining form) -ICIAN

specialized or technical vocabulary TERMINOLOGY, NOMENCLATURE

species name following the genus name in biological classification TRIVIAL NAME, SPECIFIC EPITHET
- species designating humans HOMO SAPIENS
- continuous variation in form among members of a widespread species or population CLINE
- development by slow or natural means, as of species, art, or social systems EVOLUTION
- development of a species into several different species adapted to different environments ADAPTIVE RADIATION
- evolution or development of a species, genus, or the like PHYLOGENY
- mutation of or abrupt variation within a species SALTATION
- protective or cooperative instinct or behavior among animals, serving to benefit the species as a whole ALTRUISM
- still in existence, not extinct, as surviving species are EXTANT
- system of classifying and naming animals or plants using two Latin names, indicating the genus and then the species BINOMIAL NOMENCLATURE

specific gravity RELATIVE DENSITY
- apparatus to measure the specific gravity of liquids, as used in making beer and wine HYDROMETER
- scale in measuring the specific gravity of liquids BAUMÉ SCALE

specify, require, or lay down as a condition in an agreement or contract STIPULATE

speckled or dotted, as with paint or natural colors STIPPLED

spectacles See **glasses**

spectacular, elaborate, or fanciful entertainment, display, or the like EXTRAVAGANZA

spectrum or other unbroken series of changes without any obvious divisions CONTINUUM

speech See also **conversation, speak, sound, voice, pronunciation, style**
- speech, as to a party conference, stating important plans or principles KEYNOTE SPEECH
- speech, story, sales talk, or the like that is glib or long-winded SPIEL, PATTER
- speech, way of talking, specific or personal language or style PARLANCE, IDIOM
- speech addressed only to oneself, such as a character in a play might utter SOLILOQUY
- speech colored by a nasal quality, often suggesting a regional accent TWANG
- speech defect, such as a stammer IMPEDIMENT
- speech made by a recently installed professor, president, or the like INAUGURAL SPEECH
- speech of an elegant rhetorical style PERIODS
- speech of denunciation that is long and passionate TIRADE, DIATRIBE, HARANGUE, PHILIPPIC
- speech of farewell VALEDICTION, VALEDICTORY
- speech of lamentation that is long and passionate JEREMIAD
- speech of praise or a written tribute, as for someone recently dead EULOGY
- speech of praise that is long, elaborate, and formal ENCOMIUM, PANEGYRIC
- speech of some length, dominating a conversation or addressed only to oneself MONOLOGUE
- speech of the people, informal everyday language VERNACULAR, VULGATE, DEMOTIC, COLLOQUIALISM
- speech of urgent appeal or encouragement EXHORTATION
- speech or formal address, as at a ceremony or funeral ORATION
- speech or formal address or explanation, lecture DISQUISITION
- speech or language exclusive to a profession or other group CANT, JARGON, ARGOT
- speech or language pattern of a particular regional or social group DIALECT, PATOIS
- speech or language pattern of an individual person IDIOLECT
- speech or other sound that is pleasant to listen to EUPHONY
- speech or other sound that is unpleasant to listen to CACOPHONY, DISSONANCE
- speech or writing, especially of a formal kind DISCOURSE
- speech or writing of a light, teasing style PERSIFLAGE, BANTER, BADINAGE, JEST, RAILLERY
- speech or writing that is graceful, moving, or effective ELOQUENCE
- speech or writing that is high-flown, showy, and also pompous BOMBAST, FUSTIAN, FLATULENCE, GRANDILOQUENCE, EUPHUISM
- speech or writing that is hypocritically moralizing CANT
- speech or writing that is impressively high-flown but may be empty of real meaning RHETORIC
- speech or writing that is long-winded, roundabout, or evasive CIRCUMLOCUTION, PROLIXITY, PERIPHRASIS, EQUIVOCATION
- speech that is charming and smooth but often deceiving BLARNEY
- speech that is deliberately emotional or rhetorical ORATORY, DECLAMATION
- speech that is ecstatic and unintelligible, as some religious speech is, "gift of tongues" GLOSSOLALIA
- speech that is long and tedious LITANY, HOMILY
- speech with another or others, conversation, especially of a formal or literary kind COLLOQUY
- speeches or discussions, especially between enemies over terms of a truce PARLEY
- ability to use and understand speech ORACY
- administrative or governmental speech or writing that is pretentiously wordy and difficult to understand GOBBLEDYGOOK, BUREAUCRATESE, OFFICIALESE, WASHINGTONESE

- capable of logical thought, comprehensible speech, and so on COHERENT
- capable of speech ARTICULATE
- concluding part of a long speech, often recapitulating its main themes PERORATION
- conversational or informal in style, characteristic of casual everyday speech COLLOQUIAL
- decorate speech and writing with quotations, anecdotes, or the like LARD
- degree of clarity of one's speech DICTION, ELOCUTION, ENUNCIATION, ARTICULATION
- deliver a speech without having prepared it IMPROVISE, AD-LIB, EXTEMPORIZE
- digression in a speech for rhetorical effect, especially to address an imaginary or absent person APOSTROPHE
- distinctive type, style, or level of speech and language, varying according to profession, social environment, or the like REGISTER
- harsh or curt in speech or manner BRUSQUE, ABRASIVE
- harsh or cutting in speech or manner ACERBIC, CAUSTIC, ACIDULOUS, ACRID
- heavily accented speech, especially Irish BROGUE
- hesitant or jerky, as uncertain speech is HALTING
- impressive, grand, or highfalutin in style or speech SONOROUS
- "ladies and gentlemen," or similar conventional opening words of a speech SALUTATION
- line on a language map linking places using the same distinctive form of speech ISOGLOSS
- loss of one's powers of speech, as by injury or disease APHONIA
- observation, as in a conversation or speech, that departs briefly from the main subject DIGRESSION, ASIDE, PARENTHESIS
- obstruction of legislation by means of delaying tactics such as lengthy speeches FILIBUSTER
- outpouring of emotion in speech or writing EFFUSION
- place, platform, or occasion for public speeches, especially on political issues STUMP
- political leader or agitator rallying support by crude, emotional speeches DEMAGOGUE, RABBLE-ROUSER
- produce speech sounds VOCALIZE
- quick counter or reply in speech or action REPARTEE, RIPOSTE, RETORT
- rabble-rousing, inciting, as a political speech might be INFLAMMATORY
- referring to speech ORAL
- referring to speech sounds PHONETIC
- referring to speech that is disorganized or unconnected INCOHERENT
- scattered throughout a speech, text, or the like INTERSPERSED, INTERLARDED
- showing effortless ease in speech or writing, flowing and graceful FLUENT
- study or science of speech sounds PHONETICS, PHONOLOGY, PHONEMICS
- style of speech or writing, way of putting things PHRASEOLOGY, DICTION
- unrehearsed, off-the-cuff, as a spontaneous, unprepared speech EXTEMPORANEOUS, IMPROMPTU
- wandering or digression from the main topic or course, as in a speech EXCURSION, EXCURSUS

speech (combining form) LOG-, -LOGUE, LOGO-, PHON-, PHONO-, -PHONE, -PHONY

speech disorder (combining form) -PHASIA

speech therapy LOGOPEDICS

speed See also **quick**
- speed, eager promptness ALACRITY
- speed, especially in a given direction VELOCITY
- speed, force, or other quantity having both magnitude and direction VECTOR
- speed, haste or promptness DISPATCH, EXPEDITION
- speed, swiftness CELERITY
- speed at which a piece of music is or should be played TEMPO
- speed needed by a spacecraft to overcome the earth's gravitational field ESCAPE VELOCITY
- speed of one nautical mile per hour KNOT
- speed up the progress of something, such as a business matter EXPEDITE
- maximum possible speed of a missile, falling object, aircraft, or the like, as determined by such factors as air resistance TERMINAL VELOCITY
- relating to speed greater than the speed of sound SUPERSONIC

speed (combining form) TACH-, TACHO-

speedboat that skims the surface of the water HYDROPLANE

spell cast through ritual chanting INCANTATION

spelling, or the study of spelling ORTHOGRAPHY
- spelling change produced by the transposing of letters within a word METATHESIS
- spelling or pronunciation differing slightly from another form of the same word VARIANT
- spelling or writing in the letters of another alphabet TRANSLITERATION
- spelling words in keeping with their pronunciation, which a lan-

SOUPS

bisque	thick French soup, usually made with shellfish
borscht/ borsch	Russian beet soup
chowder	thick soup or stew made with shellfish or fish
cock-a-leekie	Scottish soup of chicken and leek
consommé	clear, stock-based soup
gazpacho	spicy Spanish vegetable soup, usually served chilled
gumbo	African, Caribbean, and U.S. soup or stew thickened with okra
madrilene	French tomato-flavored consommé, served chilled or hot
minestrone	Italian vegetable soup with bacon and rice or pasta
mulligatawny	curry-flavored soup of Anglo-Indian origin
potage	thick soup
pot-au-feu	thick French soup of vegetables and meat, sometimes with pasta or rice
vichyssoise	thick soup of potato and leek or onion, usually served chilled

guage such as Spanish almost is PHONETIC
- change in the form or spelling of a word through a mistaken association with some other word POPULAR ETYMOLOGY, FOLK ETYMOLOGY

spend, lay out EXPEND, DISBURSE
- spend extravagantly or use up wastefully SQUANDER, DISSIPATE
- spend or give something generously, such as affection or money LAVISH

spending in a showy and extravagant way, especially to impress others CONSPICUOUS CONSUMPTION

spendthrift PRODIGAL, PROFLIGATE, WASTREL

sperm cell, male reproductive cell SPERMATOZOON
- sperm cell, ovum, or other cell that can combine to form a fertilized cell GAMETE
- sperm or testis of fish MILT

sphere imagined as surrounding the earth at a great distance, and housing the stars and planets on its surface CELESTIAL SPHERE
- sphere of operation or expertise, field of activity PROVINCE, PRESERVE, DOMAIN, BAILIWICK
- sphere or range of possible activity, scope, reach AMBIT, ORBIT, COMPASS
- elongated sphere SPHEROID
- model of the universe, with solid rings within a sphere to represent planetary paths ORRERY, ARMILLARY SPHERE

spice See also **herbs**
- spice, mustard, vinegar, or other seasoning CONDIMENT
- spice and heat wine or ale MULL
- spice mill QUERN

spicy or pleasantly sharp to the taste PIQUANT
- spicy or salty to the taste, rather than sweet SAVORY
- spicy sauce RELISH, CHUTNEY
- spicy sauce in which meat or fish is left to soak before cooking MARINADE

spider See illustration, page 514, and also **insect**
- spider, insect, crustacean, centipede, or related creature having jointed limbs, a horny shell, and a segmented body ARTHROPOD
- spider, tick, or related creature ARACHNID
- spider's nest NIDUS
- large hairy spider with a painful bite TARANTULA
- organ on a spider, caterpillar, or the like for producing silky threads for a web or cocoon SPINNERET

spike or peg, usually with an eye or ring for a rope, driven into a rock or ice surface for support in mountaineering PITON
- spiked heel, high and tapering, on a woman's shoe STILETTO
- spiked iron ball, formerly used to slow down enemy troops, as by laming horses CALTROP, CROWFOOT
- spiked plate on the sole of a shoe to prevent slipping on ice, as used in mountaineering CRAMPON, CLAMPER
- heavy war club with a spiked metal head, used to crush armor MACE

spike (combining form) ACANTH-, ACANTHO-, ECHINO-

spin See also **turn, twist**
- spin around a point or axis GYRATE, REVOLVE
- spin on tiptoe or on the ball of a foot, as in ballet PIROUETTE
- spin or turn on an axis ROTATE
- spin or wobble in flight, as a missile or aircraft might YAW
- spin round and round, whirl, twirl REEL, TRUNDLE
- spinning flywheel maintaining a stable angle or direction in a frame of pivoted supports GYROSCOPE
- rod, hinge, or axis around which something fixed spins PIVOT

spin (combining form) GYRO-

spinal cord (combining form) MYEL-, MYELO-

spine See also **nerve**
- spine, or the second vertebra from the top of the spine AXIS
- spine manipulation as a form of therapy OSTEOPATHY, CHIROPRACTIC
- abnormal curving or bending, as of the spine CURVATURE
- abnormal frontal and backward curvature of the spine LORDOSIS, KYPHOSIS, SWAYBACK, SADDLEBACK
- abnormal sideways curvature of the spine SCOLIOSIS
- having a backbone or spinal column VERTEBRATE
- having no backbone or spinal column INVERTEBRATE
- insertion of a syringe needle into the lower spine to inject drugs or withdraw spinal fluid LUMBAR PUNCTURE
- referring to the same "side" of the body as the spinal cord DORSAL, NEURAL
- small bone at the base of the spine COCCYX
- surgeon specializing in spinal and joint disorders ORTHOPEDIC SURGEON
- triangular bone near the base of the spine, consisting of five fused vertebrae SACRUM
- top vertebra of the spine, supporting the skull ATLAS

spines covering a porcupine or hedgehog QUILLS

spinning machine of an early design SPINNING JENNY, MULE, THROSTLE
- spinning or twisting of silk, cotton, or the like into threads FILATURE
- cleft stick for holding raw flax or wool before spinning DISTAFF
- spool or reel, for the yarn in spinning or for the wire in an electromagnetic buzzer BOBBIN
- stick or pin on which thread is twisted in spinning SPINDLE

spiny (combining form) ECHINO-

spiny anteater ECHIDNA

spiny lobster LANGOUSTE

spiral device within a tube, as used in ancient times for raising water ARCHIMEDES' SCREW
- spiral around a point or axis, revolve GYRATE
- spiral structure or shape HELIX, VOLUTE, WHORL
- spiraling and cone-shaped, as some shells are TURBINATE
- spiraling flow or rush, such as a whirlwind or whirlpool VORTEX
- spiraling shootlike part, as on a grapevine, serving to attach a plant to its support TENDRIL
- shaped like a spiral or snail shell COCHLEATE

spiral (combining form) GYRO-, HELIC-, HELICO-

spire or turret, as on the roof of a Gothic building PINNACLE

spirit, soul PNEUMA, ATMAN
- spirit, wit, liveliness ESPRIT
- spirit in Scottish legend, in the form of a horse that drowns its rider KELPIE
- "spirit matter" or specter allegedly conjured up by a medium during a spiritualism session ECTOPLASM
- spirit of enterprise or adventure, initiative or pluck GUMPTION
- spirit of optimism and confidence, as among soldiers MORALE
- spirit or atmosphere, or its guardian deity of a place GENIUS LOCI
- spirit or divine force supposedly guarding a place, inhabiting a natural object, or guiding a person NUMEN
- spirit or divinity of forests and trees in classical mythology, wood nymph DRYAD, HAMADRYAD
- spirit or divinity of the fields and woodlands in classical mythology, with a human head and goat's legs, noted for its lechery FAUN, SATYR
- spirit or divinity of the mountains in classical mythology, a mountain nymph OREAD
- spirit or elflike creature, such as

a water nymph SPRITE
- spirit or ghost that is noisy or mischievous POLTERGEIST
- spirit or imaginary creature living in the air SYLPH
- spirit or mood of the times ZEITGEIST
- spirit or soul, as distinct from the body PSYCHE
- spirit taking human form, in Muslim legend GENIE, JINNI
- spirit that allegedly acts through a spiritualist medium, especially at a seance CONTROL
- appear or become visible, as a spirit might MANIFEST
- arrival or visit of a ghost, spirit, angel, or the like VISITATION
- beautiful fairylike creature or spirit, especially in Persian folklore PERI
- benevolent spirit or demon EUDEMON
- calling up spirits of the dead, as in black magic NECROMANCY
- drive out an evil spirit, or free a possessed person from evil spirits, as by religious rites EXORCISE
- emergence or appearance of a spirit, as allegedly at a seance, in visible bodily form MATERIALIZATION, PRECIPITATION
- evil spirit in the shape of a man that has sex with sleeping women INCUBUS
- evil spirit in the shape of a woman that has sex with sleeping men SUCCUBUS
- female spirit in Irish folklore, whose wailing foretells a death in the household BANSHEE
- guiding spirit, guardian genius DAEMON
- malicious spirit in Jewish folklore, usually the soul of a dead sinner, that enters a person's body DYBBUK
- malicious spirit in German mythology, who carries children away to death ERLKING
- migration of a spirit, after a person's death, into another body or a new cycle of existence TRANSMIGRATION, METEMPSYCHOSIS, PALINGENESIS, REINCARNATION
- mischievous or wicked spirit or elf PUCK, BOGEY, HOBGOBLIN, BUGABOO, BUGBEAR
- person allegedly able to communicate with the spirits of dead people MEDIUM
- person supposedly possessed by an evil spirit DEMONIAC, ENERGUMEN
- summon up a spirit by means of spells or incantations CONJURE, INVOKE
- water spirit in Germanic folklore, usually hostile to humans NIX
- water spirit or nymph UNDINE

spirit (combining form) PNEUMAT-, PNEUMATO-

spirits See **alcohol, drinks**

spiritual divine, heavenly CELESTIAL
- spiritual, referring to the spirit or vital spark PNEUMATIC
- spiritual, unearthly, impalpable ETHEREAL
- spiritual, without material substance INCORPOREAL, INTANGIBLE, INSUBSTANTIAL, IMMATERIAL
- spiritual contemplation or meditation as a means of experiencing communion with the divine MYSTICISM
- spiritual damnation, loss of the soul PERDITION
- spiritual leader or teacher in Hinduism GURU, MAHARISHI
- spiritual lethargy, despairing indifference ACCIDIE, ACEDIA
- spiritually uplifting NUMINOUS
- civil, lay, or secular rather than spiritual or religious TEMPORAL, HUMANISTIC
- symbol, relationship, or the like considered to have sacred or spiritual significance SACRAMENT

spiritualist meeting in which people try to communicate with the dead SEANCE
- spiritualist religious and medical practices, as among Native Americans, in which the priest's spirit leaves his body during drumming or dancing SHAMANISM
- spiritualist's trick or the act of allegedly conjuring up or transporting a physical object APPORT
- alleged ability of spiritualists or clairvoyants to speak a foreign language they do not know XENOGLOSSIA
- board displaying the alphabet used in spiritualism sessions to register messages OUIJA BOARD
- ghostlike substance allegedly emerging from a spiritualist medium during a seance ECTOPLASM
- mobile board with a pencil, used in spiritualism sessions to write or spell out messages from the spirit world PLANCHETTE

spit, saliva SPUTUM
- spit for roasting meat BROACH
- spit or small skewer for grilling or roasting, or the food cooked on it BROCHETTE
- spit or spit out EXPECTORATE
- helping the flow of spit, easing the production and expulsion of phlegm or sputum EXPECTORANT
- produce or secrete spit or saliva SALIVATE
- thick mucus or spit PHLEGM

spiteful, bitter, vengeful VINDICTIVE
- spiteful, bitterly hostile, hate-filled VIRULENT, MALIGNANT
- spiteful, ill-willed, intending to hurt MALEVOLENT, MALICIOUS
- spiteful, vicious, hurtful, as a comment might be VENOMOUS, VIPEROUS

spittoon CUSPIDOR

splendid in appearance, magnificent, dazzling RESPLENDENT

splendor of achievement, appearance, or the like LUSTER

splinter, chip, or break stone, especially with a hammer SPALL
- splinter, a thin and sharp fragment SLIVER

split, separated, divided CLEFT
- split or burst open along a seam, as a pod or fruit might, to release

SPANISH TERMS

alcalde	mayor or chief magistrate
alcazar	palace or fortress, as built by the Moors
bodega	wineshop or wine store
caballero	gentleman
cantina	bar or wineshop
caudillo	military leader, dictator
Cortes	parliament in Spain
fiesta	holiday, religious festival, or saint's day
grande/ grandee	man of elevated rank
Guardia Civil	national police force in Spain
hacienda	ranch or ranch house
hidalgo	minor nobleman
hostería	restaurant
infanta	princess
mañana	tomorrow, shortly
parador	state-supervised country hotel
plaza	public square
posada	inn
siesta	afternoon nap or rest

seeds or pollen DEHISCE
- split or cut, as by chopping with an ax CLEAVE
split (combining form) FISSI-, SCHIZ-, SCHIZO-
splitting, cutting SCISSION
- splitting, especially of heavy atomic nuclei in a nuclear reaction FISSION
- splitting into opposing factions, as within a church SCHISM
- splitting or flaking easily, as some minerals are SPATHIC
- splitting up of a word by an expression put between its parts, as in *what place soever* for *whatsoever place* TMESIS
spoil, corrupt, lower in moral or intellectual character BASTARDIZE, DEGRADE
- spoil, make crude or savage BARBARIZE
- spoil by drying up, shrinking, or fading SHRIVEL, WITHER, WIZEN
- spoil by making impure or dirty DEFILE, FOUL, POLLUTE, SOIL, SULLY
- spoil one's chances or plans QUEER ONE'S PITCH
- spoil oneself or someone else by yielding to wishes INDULGE, PAMPER, GRATIFY, PANDER TO
- spoil or corrupt morally DEPRAVE, PERVERT
- spoil or degrade oneself for money or an unworthy cause PROSTITUTE
- spoil or frustrate something, especially someone's hopes or opportunities BLIGHT
- spoil or make dangerous, impure, or poisonous CONTAMINATE
- spoil or reduce the importance, quality, or value of DEVALUE, IMPAIR, VITIATE
- spoil or reduce the purity of something valuable by adding inferior material ADULTERATE, ALLOY, DEBASE
- spoil or ruin, by harassment BEDEVIL
- spoil or stain something, such as a person's reputation BLEMISH, BESMIRCH, TAINT, TARNISH
- spoil someone, especially a child, through excessive affection and compliance CODDLE, MOLLYCODDLE, COSSET
- spoil the appearance of, damage, harm, injure DISFIGURE, DEFACE, MAR, MUTILATE
- spoils of victory, including captured weapons TROPHY
spoiled, excessively demanding, whimsical, self-pitying, or the like SELF-INDULGENT
- spoiled, overprotected, as a child might be CODDLED, COSSETED, INDULGED, MOLLYCODDLED, PAMPERED, SPOON-FED
- spoiled by overfamiliarity or overindulgence, hence bored and unenthusiastic BLASÉ, JADED
spoils, booty, loot, as from a plundering expedition PILLAGE
spoken See also **speak**
- spoken, by word of mouth ORAL, VIVA VOCE, VERBAL
- spoken clearly and distinctly ARTICULATE
- conversational, informal, characteristic of casual spoken language COLLOQUIAL
- passage of conversation in a play, novel, or the like, or the characters' spoken words DIALOGUE
sponge, sea anemone, or similar plantlike organism ZOOPHYTE
- spongelike, fibrous interior of the dishcloth gourd, used for scrubbing the skin LOOFAH
- opening in a sponge, for the passage of water OSCULUM, OSTIUM, STOMA
sponsor or benefactor PATRON
- sponsor or patron of artists MAECENAS, ANGEL
spontaneous, automatic, involuntary or unthinking, as a reaction might be REFLEX, KNEE-JERK
- spontaneous, off the cuff, without preparation, as a speech might be IMPROMPTU, EXTEMPORE, AD-LIB, IMPROVISED
- spontaneous, without forethought, spur-of-the-moment UNPREMEDITATED
- spontaneous and emotional rather than rational and deliberate, in Nietzsche's terminology DIONYSIAN
- devised spontaneously as a temporary measure MAKESHIFT, STOPGAP
- knowing or acting spontaneously, insightful INTUITIVE
- offered or given freely or spontaneously, without being asked GRATUITOUS, UNPROMPTED
- rational and deliberate rather than spontaneous and emotional, in Nietzsche's terminology APOLLONIAN
spool or reel, as for yarn in spinning or wire for an electromagnetic buzzer BOBBIN
spoon - spoonlike piece of cutlery with prongs and a sharp edge, combining the features of knife, fork, and spoon RUNCIBLE SPOON
sports See chart, page 516
- sports arena, hall, or the like, with seating all the way around AMPHITHEATER
- sports arena, stadium, or large entertainment hall COLISEUM
- sports car or similar sleek high-speed car GRAN TURISMO, GT
- sports car with two doors COUPE, COUPÉ
- sports or games festival in ancient Greece AGON
- sports stadium's open-air grandstand BLEACHERS
- sportsman at a college or university JOCK
- artificial male sex hormone increasing muscle and bone growth, sometimes illegally used in sports ANABOLIC STEROID
- fail to appear in a sports match, thereby forfeiting it DEFAULT
- fan or enthusiastic follower of a specified sport or pastime DEVOTEE, AFICIONADO
- grasslike nylon or vinyl surfacing material, as used on sports grounds ASTROTURF
- promoter or financial supporter of a project, sportsperson, cultural activity, or the like SPONSOR
spouse See **husband, wife**
spray device, as for perfume or deodorant ATOMIZER
- convert a liquid to a fine spray, as by an atomizer NEBULIZE
spread, distribution, or range, as of colors or radiation SPECTRUM, GAMUT
- spread a rumor or report BRUIT
- spread across or through, as an idea or a color might SUFFUSE, INFUSE, INTERFUSE, IMBUE
- spread by physical contact, as a disease might be CONTAGIOUS
- spread from one person to another, as some diseases are COMMUNICABLE, TRANSMISSIBLE, INFECTIOUS
- spread gradually, as warmth or news might PERMEATE, PERVADE, DIFFUSE, PERCOLATE
- spread information, doctrines, rumors, or the like widely CIRCULATE, PROMULGATE, PROPAGATE, DISSEMINATE
- spread or increase rapidly PROLIFERATE
- spread or pass on rumors, words, or the like frivolously or indiscriminately BANDY ABOUT
- spread or smear roughly a substance such as mud, plaster, or grease DAUB
- spread or throw here and there, sprinkle, scatter STREW
- spread or try to circulate ideas or opinions PEDDLE
- spread out, unroll, or unfold something, such as a flag UNFURL
- spread out and irregular in design, as a large house might be SPRAWLING, RAMBLING
- spread out in an untidy or irregular way STRAGGLY
- spread out like rays from a common source or point RADIATE
- spread out or apart, as limbs

might be SPLAYED
- spread through or introduce gradually, implant, teach INSTILL
- spread widely, scattered, widespread DIFFUSE, DISPERSED
- ordered and impressive spread, selection, or arrangement, as of clothes, facts, or troops ARRAY

spreading freely, unchecked, as vegetation might be RAMPANT
- spreading from one person to another easily, as laughter or enthusiasm might be INFECTIOUS, CONTAGIOUS
- spreading implement having a wide-tipped and flexible blade, as for icing SPATULA
- spreading of a cancer, bacteria, or the like from the original site to other parts of the body METASTASIS
- spreading of information, often dubious, to further a cause, or the information itself PROPAGANDA
- spreading or gradual widening, as of a trouser leg FLARE
- spreading rapidly throughout an area, as an infectious disease might be EPIDEMIC

spring, as on a truck's back axle, consisting of a set of layered metal strips LEAF SPRING
- spring, daybreak, or similar early part or beginning of something PRIME
- spring from a source, originate DERIVE
- spring of mineral water SPA
- spring that forms the source of a river FOUNTAINHEAD
- spring throwing up a column of hot water and steam GEYSER
- springs, padding, and fabric, as used in making a soft covering for furniture UPHOLSTERY
- springs, shock absorbers, or the like to help a vehicle run more smoothly SUSPENSION
- adjective for the spring VERNAL
- crust of porous mineral deposit formed around a geyser or hot spring SINTER
- hot spring THERMAL SPRING

sprout or germinate PULLULATE

sprout (combining form) -BLAST-

spur See also **stimulate**
- spur into action, startle GALVANIZE
- spur or jutting part, as on a chicken's leg or a flower's corolla CALCAR
- spur to action INCENTIVE, GOAD, INCITEMENT, STIMULUS
- ironsmith who made spurs and bits for horses LORIMER
- small toothed wheel on the end of a cowboy's spur ROWEL

spy, intelligence officer, or secret agent who joins a political or criminal group and tries to incite it into punishable or discrediting activities AGENT PROVOCATEUR
- spy planted for future use rather than current activity SLEEPER
- spy who is given a mission only after he or she is established in a foreign organization MOLE
- spying, intelligence gathering ESPIONAGE
- informer, decoy, or police spy STOOL PIGEON, STOOLIE
- report by or questioning of a spy, astronaut, diplomat, or the like on his or her return from a mission DEBRIEFING
- secret entry into or establishment in an organization, region, or the like, as by spies or enemy troops, for the purpose of subversion INFILTRATION
- woman spy MATA HARI

square or oblong figure RECTANGLE, QUADRILATERAL, TETRAGON
- large public square, wide street, or open space where crowds can gather CONCOURSE
- large public square or open space, especially in a Spanish-speaking town PLAZA
- large public square or open space, especially in an Italian town PIAZZA
- layout of numbers in the form of a square, in which any of the rows produces the same sum MAGIC SQUARE

square (combining form) QUADR-, QUADRI-, QUADRU-

square root or other root of a quantity as indicated by the sign $\sqrt{}$ RADICAL

squeaky, unnaturally high-pitched, as a teenage boy's voice might be FALSETTO

squeeze, push, or force out EXTRUDE
- rubber blade or roller used in printing or photography, as for squeezing water from wet prints SQUEEGEE

squid, cuttlefish, or related 10-tentacled creature DECAPOD
- squid, octopus, nautilus, or related mollusk CEPHALOPOD
- long horny internal shell of a squid PEN

squint caused by a malfunction of the eye muscles STRABISMUS
- slight squint of the eye CAST

squire for a knight, armor-bearer ARMIGER

squirrel - squirrellike, or relating to squirrels SCIURINE, SCIURID
- squirrellike rodent living in burrows MARMOT
- squirrel's nest DREY

stab lightly or prick, as with a sword PINK

stability, state of balance of forces EQUILIBRIUM
- road vehicle's degree of stability, as at high speeds or on wet roads ROADHOLDING
- something giving security or emotional stability MOORINGS

stabilization (combining form) -STASIS

Spiders

Wolf spider (female with young on back)

Comb-footed spider (black widow)

Tarantula

stabilizing material or device, such as an electrical resistor, or sandbags in a ship's hold BALLAST
stable condition or period, as of economic activity PLATEAU
- stable for boarding horses or letting out horses and carriages LIVERY STABLE
stableman at an inn OSTLER
staff See also **stick**
- staff, typically decorated with leaves and tipped with a pine cone, carried by Dionysius or Bacchus THYRSUS
- staff carried by a bishop or abbot, having a crook or cross at the top CROSIER
- staff of office carried as a symbol of authority VERGE, SCEPTER, MACE
- staff or wand decorated with wings and two twining snakes, serving as a symbol of the medical profession CADUCEUS
- long wooden staff, often with a metal point or blade, used as a weapon in former times QUARTERSTAFF, PIKESTAFF, PARTISAN, HALBERD
stage See also **theater** and chart at **drama**
- stage, step, or degree in a gradual progression GRADATION
- stage direction indicating a speech or the start of a speech by a character LOQUITUR
- stage direction indicating the exit of all the characters EXEUNT OMNES
- stage or platform, as for a public speaker or music conductor ROSTRUM, PODIUM, DAIS
- stage setting in a play MISE-EN-SCÈNE
- passing down from stage to stage DEVOLUTION
stain DISCOLORATION
- stained blood-red INCARNADINE
- stained or discolored, as old books might be FOXED
stairs See illustration, page 518
- stair in a straight rather than winding staircase FLIER
- stair in a winding rather than straight staircase WINDER
- stair post, table leg or the like, typically turned and decorated SPINDLE
- baseboard along the side of a staircase STRINGBOARD, STRINGER, STRING, SKIRTBOARD
- central pillar, typically of stone, about which a spiral staircase winds NEWEL
- underside of an arch, staircase, or other overhang SOFFIT
stale, reworked, as material for a comedy act might be RÉCHAUFFÉ
- stale, unoriginal, or predictable remark, phrase, or thought CLICHÉ, PLATITUDE, COMMONPLACE, BROMIDE
- stale, unoriginal and overused, theadbare and uninspiring, as a boring remark might be HACKNEYED, TRITE, BANAL, SHOPWORN
- stale and usually oversimplified image or opinion of someone or something STEREOTYPE
- stale joke, old story, or the like CHESTNUT
- stale-smelling MUSTY, FUSTY, FROWSY
stalemate or unresolvable difficulty blocking progress IMPASSE, DEADLOCK
stamens of a flower ANDROECIUM
stamp collector PHILATELIST
- stamps in a rectangular sheet, as a page of a stamp book PANE
- cancel a stamp by means of a postmark FRANK
- cancellation mark on a postage stamp KILLER
- design stamped on an envelope to commemorate a postal event CACHET
- issued in honor of the memory of a person or event, as stamps or coins might be COMMEMORATIVE
- picture in a postage stamp, as distinct from the frame and lettering VIGNETTE
- referring to a pair of postage stamps in which one is upside down in relation to the other TÊTE-BÊCHE
- series of holes, or of ridges and indentations, around postage stamps PERFORATION
- series of tiny slits between rows of stamps for easy separation ROULETTE
- white space between two postage stamps on a sheet, facing pages of a book, or the like GUTTER
stamped mark on gold or silver objects indicating the purity of the metal HALLMARK, PLATEMARK
stand, usually with three short legs, as used to support hot dishes on the table TRIVET
- stand for supporting a book or notes, as in a church or lecture hall LECTERN
- stand or sit astride BESTRIDE, STRADDLE
- stand or support having just one leg, as for a camera MONOPOD
- stand or support having three legs, as for a camera TRIPOD
stand-in See **agent, substitute**
stand in for or relieve somebody at work, by taking a turn SPELL
- stand in for temporarily, replace, serve as a substitute DEPUTIZE, UNDERSTUDY
standard, guiding principle POLESTAR, LODESTAR
- standard, principle, or basis or measure for judgment CRITERION, CANON
- standard, reference point, or starting point, as in surveying or sociology DATUM LINE
- standard, unoriginal, or oversimplified image of someone or something STEREOTYPE
- standard-bearer, flag bearer VEXILLARY
- standard example or measurement used as a reference for comparisons BENCHMARK, TOUCHSTONE, YARDSTICK, LITMUS PAPER
- standard of acceptability, model of behavior, or the like NORM
- standard of comparison as used in a statistical analysis, scientific experiment, or the like CONTROL
- standard of living that is adequate but modest SUFFICIENCY
- standard of living that is the minimum for reasonable survival SUBSISTENCE LEVEL
- standard that is arbitrary but is rigidly enforced PROCRUSTEAN BED
- differ or depart from the norm or standard, as of a policy, a route, or one's behavior DEVIATE
- meet the required standards PASS MUSTER
standard (combining form) ORTHO-, NORM-
standpoint, point of view PERSPECTIVE
stanza of a poem, verse STAVE, STROPHE
star See also charts at **astronomy, astrology, zodiac**
- star, especially the North Star, used as a guide by sailors and astronomers LODESTAR, CYNOSURE
- star, planet, or comet CELESTIAL BODY
- star cluster ASTERISM
- star of a large, cool, and old type RED GIANT
- star of a small, cool type RED DWARF
- star of a small, hot, dense type WHITE DWARF
- Star of David MAGEN DAVID
- star-shaped ASTEROID, ACTINOID
- star-shaped printing symbol, *, as for referring to a footnote ASTERISK
- star system, any of the millions of groups of stars held together by gravity GALAXY
- star system, any of the major groupings of stars as viewed from the earth CONSTELLATION
- star that, from a given viewing point, never dips below the horizon CIRCUMPOLAR STAR
- star that is the brightest or largest in its constellation ALPHA

- star with five points, formed by five straight lines, and sometimes credited with magic powers PENTACLE, PENTANGLE, PENTAGRAM
- adjective for a star or stars STELLAR, ASTRAL, SIDEREAL
- brightness of a star MAGNITUDE
- building housing telescopes for observing the stars OBSERVATORY
- fainter of the two units of a double star COMPANION
- instrument for measuring the angles of stars and planets to determine the observer's position on earth SEXTANT, ASTROLABE
- network of lines used as a reference grid, as in photography and in measuring stars RESEAU
- pair of stars circling each other BINARY STAR
- projector of images of the stars and planets, or the domed room or building in which it operates PLANETARIUM
- scientific study of the stars and planets, and outer space generally ASTRONOMY
- superstitious interpretation of the stars and planets as affecting human life and destiny ASTROLOGY

star (combining form) ASTR-, ASTRO-, STELL-

starch, sugar, or a related compound CARBOHYDRATE
- starch from potato flour FARINA
- starch from the root of a tropical plant, as used for making tapioca CASSAVA, MANIOC
- starch used in cooking, or the tropical American plant from which it is extracted ARROWROOT
- starchy, heavy and filling, as thick porridge or similar food is STODGY
- starchy or floury FARINACEOUS

starch (combining form) AMYL-, AMYLO-

stare at, especially in a lustful way LEER, OGLE
- stare down, outstare OUTFACE
- stare or look angrily or frowningly GLOWER, SCOWL

starling - flock or family of starlings MURMURATION

start See also **begin, beginning**
- start a car by means of cables connected to another car's battery JUMP-START

starvation - exhaustion, often fatal, as caused by starvation INANITION

starve - starved and extremely thin EMACIATED, MACERATED, CADAVEROUS, ANOREXIC
- starving, or extremely hungry RAVENOUS, FAMISHED
- condition of extreme thinness and weakness, as among starving people MALNUTRITION

state See also **government, speak**
- state, put into words, or say ARTICULATE, PRONOUNCE, UTTER, VERBALIZE
- state economically or politically dependent on a more powerful country CLIENT STATE
- state emphatically ASSEVERATE
- state explicitly or in detail, spell out SPECIFY
- state formally ENUNCIATE
- state in detail, set forth or explain fully EXPOUND, PROPOUND
- state openly, or under oath TESTIFY
- state or announce publicly and officially PROCLAIM
- state or claim, typically without proving ALLEGE
- state or declare, claim MAINTAIN, ASSERT, CONTEND, SUBMIT
- state or declare, confidently or forcefully AFFIRM, AVER, AVOUCH, AVOW, WARRANT, PROFESS
- state or declare as belonging to or characteristic of someone or something PREDICATE
- state or declare to be true, back up, confirm ATTEST, CORROBORATE
- state or declare to be true or existing, assume or put forward, as for the sake of argument POSTULATE, PREMISE, POSIT
- state or zone, usually small and neutral, lying between two enemy forces or rival powers BUFFER STATE, BUFFER ZONE, CORRIDOR
- state that exercises control or dominion over a dependent state, especially over its foreign affairs SUZERAIN
- state's authority or power of jurisdiction beyond its borders, as over its citizens living abroad EXTRATERRITORIALITY
- narrow strip of land, as for allowing an inland state access to the sea CORRIDOR
- part of a foreign state lying entirely within a state's territory ENCLAVE
- part of a state that is isolated within a nearby foreign state's territory EXCLAVE
- relating to a governor, as of a U.S. state GUBERNATORIAL
- rule, authority, or influence of one state over another HEGEMONY

state, condition (combining form) -OSIS, -TUDE

state of affairs as it currently exists STATUS QUO

state of mind, spirit of optimism and confidence, as among soldiers MORALE

state of mind (combining form) -THYMIA

statement, complaint, or protest, as in diplomatic matters or to the public authorities DEMARCHE

SPORTS AND GAMES

TRACK-AND-FIELD EVENTS, AND RELATED SPORTS

decathlon
heptathlon
pentathlon
pole vault

WINTER SPORTS

biathlon
bobsledding/ bobsleighing
langlauf/ cross-country skiing
skibobbing
skijoring
slalom
sledding
sled-dog racing
tobogganing

INDOOR GAMES

backgammon
charades
consequences
crambo
forfeits
go
Halma
jacks/ knucklebones
Mah-Jongg
pachisi
Parcheesi
pickup sticks
pinball/ bagatelle
reversi
spillikins/ jackstraws

MARTIAL ARTS AND SPORTS

aikido
Greco-Roman wrestling
jujitsu
karate
kendo
kung fu
sumo
tae kwon do

MOTOR, MOTORCYCLE, AND CYCLE SPORTS

autocross
cyclocross
drag racing
go-carting
Grand Prix
GT/grand touring
motocross/ scrambling
stock-car racing

SHOOTING AND BOWLING SPORTS

archery/ toxophily
biathlon
boccie
bowling
clay-pigeon shooting/ skeet shooting/ trapshooting
horseshoes
lawn bowling
quoits

TEAM AND BALL GAMES

American football/ football
bandy
baseball
basketball
court tennis/ royal tennis
cricket
croquet
Eton wall game
field hockey
fives
Gaelic football
hurling/ hurley
ice hockey
jai alai
korfball
lacrosse
lawn tennis
pelota
pushball
racquetball
rounders
rugby/royal football
shinny/ shinty
soccer/ association football
stoolball
volleyball

- statement based on evidence that is not or cannot ever be exhaustive GENERALIZATION
- statement or remark having no apparent relevance to what came before it NON SEQUITUR
- statement that is apparently self-contradictory or absurd though not necessarily untrue PARADOX
- statement that is arbitrary and unsupported DICTUM, IPSE DIXIT
- referring to a statement whose truth-value depends on real-life facts rather than on the meanings of its terms SYNTHETIC
- referring to a statement whose truth-value depends on the meaning of its terms rather than on real-life facts ANALYTIC

static or balanced condition, as in body chemistry and functions, or within a society or personality HOMEOSTASIS

stationary, fixed, unmoving STATIC, STABILE, SEDENTARY
- moving from place to place, mobile, as opposed to stationary AMBULATORY, AMBULANT, MIGRATORY

stationary (combining form) -STATIC, -STAT

stationery - mark stationery or other goods with the name, initials, or other form of identification of the owner PERSONALIZE

statistician in an insurance company who calculates risks, premiums, and the like ACTUARY

statistics - statistical chart in the form of a circle with sectors of varying size PIE CHART
- statistical chart in the form of a set of upright rectangles BAR GRAPH, HISTOGRAM
- statistical chart or diagram presented in the form of a picture PICTOGRAPH
- statistical variation, difference between any one number and the average DEVIATION
- statistically random STOCHASTIC
- interdependence in statistics of two random variables, increasing or decreasing simultaneously CORRELATION
- set of statistical data showing how often the various values of a variable occur FREQUENCY DISTRIBUTION, OGIVE
- use of statistics in the study of history CLIOMETRICS

statue See also chart at **sculpture**
- statue of a discus thrower, as in ancient Greece and Rome DISCOBOLUS
- statue of huge size COLOSSUS
- base block or slab, as of a column, statue, or trophy PLINTH
- destroyer of religious statues and sacred objects ICONOCLAST
- inscription on a statue, monument, or building EPIGRAPH
- referring to a statue or portrait in which the subject is depicted on horseback EQUESTRIAN
- referring to ancient statues of a conventional or stiff style ICONIC

statuette or small ornamental figure FIGURINE

status, reputation, or renown, as through success or wealth PRESTIGE, KUDOS, CACHET
- status or right, as of appearing in court, speaking at a meeting, and the like LOCUS STANDI
- status or role of a plant or animal within its ecological community NICHE
- important or high in status, position, or the like EXALTED
- order of power or status in a group PECKING ORDER, HIERARCHY

stay about, hang around aimlessly, or dawdle idly LOITER, LINGER
- stay in or at a place temporarily TARRY, SOJOURN
- stay unmoved or unchanged, especially in the face of outside pressures ABIDE, ENDURE, PERSIST, PERSEVERE
- staying only temporarily, passing through, as a farmworker might TRANSIENT, ITINERANT, MIGRANT, MIGRATORY

staying power, endurance STAMINA

steady, hardworking, and reliable YEOMANLY, STALWART
- steady, unchanging, and unpleasant UNRELIEVED
- steady, unhesitating, exhibiting no sign of doubt UNFALTERING, UNWAVERING
- steady, uniform, consistent INVARIABLE, UNDEVIATING

steak See also **beef, meat**
- raw minced steak with chopped onion, herbs, and raw egg STEAK TARTARE

steal See also **rob, robbery**
- steal, remove illegally, or use for one's own purposes without permission MISAPPROPRIATE, APPROPRIATE, CONVERT
- steal another person's ideas, writings, tunes, or the like and pass them off as one's own PLAGIARIZE
- steal back, or steal something to which one considers one has a right LIBERATE
- steal cattle or other livestock RUSTLE
- steal money or goods entrusted to one EMBEZZLE, PECULATE, DEFALCATE
- steal or use illegally, especially by publishing a work protected by another's copyright PIRATE
- steal something small or cheap, often in a sneaky way, swipe, nick FILCH, PILFER, PURLOIN
- steal the show from, draw attention away from UPSTAGE
- compulsive urge to steal things KLEPTOMANIA
- flee and hide, often after stealing goods ABSCOND
- ransack with intent to steal, loot RIFLE

stealthy, done or carried out in a secretive or underhand manner SURREPTITIOUS, CLANDESTINE, FURTIVE
- stealthily or secretly harmful, treacherous INSIDIOUS

steam-bath treatment or recreation of Finnish origin, typically followed by a cold plunge SAUNA

steam engine See illustration, page 521
- steam engine or locomotive that carries its water supply in tanks around the boiler TANK LOCOMOTIVE
- steam engine or locomotive with two large rear wheels, formerly used for hauling heavy loads TRACTION ENGINE
- steam engine or turbine of an ancient, simple design AEOLIPILE

steel of high quality, typically made by melting and fusing iron and charcoal CRUCIBLE STEEL
- steelmaking furnace in which fuel and ore are separated and heat reflected off the roof onto the ore REVERBERATORY FURNACE, OPEN-HEARTH FURNACE
- steelmaking process in which air is blown through molten iron BESSEMER PROCESS
- chemical elements used in conjunction with iron to make various kinds of steel COBALT, CHROMIUM, MANGANESE, VANADIUM, NIOBIUM, TITANIUM, MOLYBDENUM, TUNGSTEN
- coat steel with zinc to rustproof it GALVANIZE
- harden or toughen steel or other metal, as by alternate heating and cooling TEMPER
- harden the surface of iron or steel by heat and carbon treatment CASE HARDEN

steep - rather steep, sloping, inclined DECLIVITOUS
- very steep ABRUPT, PRECIPITOUS
- vertical or very steep PERPENDICULAR, SHEER

stem bearing a flower, fruit, or entire flower cluster PEDUNCLE
- stem bearing flowers, or the arrangement of flowers on it INFLORESCENCE
- stem creeping from the base of a plant, such as the strawberry, and

producing new roots and buds STOLON, RUNNER
- stem growing on or under the ground, as in the iris or grasses RHIZOME, ROOTSTOCK
- stem growing under the soil, like a bulb but with papery scale leaves, such as that of the gladiolus CORM
- stem growing under the soil, swollen and bearing buds, such as that of the potato or dahlia TUBER
- stem of a twining plant or creeper, or the plant itself BINE
- stem or arrangement of flowers attached singly to a stalk, with the youngest at the top RACEME
- stem or main axis, as of a flower cluster, compound leaf, or feather RACHIS
- stem or stalk, as of a mushroom or a fern or seaweed frond STIPE
- stem supporting a flower in a flower cluster PEDICEL
- grow into a long, thin stalk or stem, as a plant might SPINDLE
- joint or branching point on a stem NODE
- spongy core running through stems and branches PITH, MEDULLA
- stalk attaching a leaf to a stem PETIOLE

stencil having many curves, used by draftspersons and dressmakers FRENCH CURVE
- stencillike pattern, mold, plate, or the like, as in woodwork, for making or reproducing something accurately TEMPLATE

step See also **stairs**
- step, stage, or degree in a gradual progression GRADATION
- step in a straight staircase FLIER
- step in a winding staircase WINDER
- step taken by placing one foot ahead of and touching the other PIGEON STEP
- stepped formation, as of soldiers or ships, in offset parallel rows ECHELON
- stepping on the toes only while walking, as horses do DIGITIGRADE
- stepping on the whole foot while walking, as humans do PLANTIGRADE
- backward, unprogressive, as a step or decision might be RETROGRADE

step in, as to mediate or prevent INTERVENE

stepmother - adjective for a stepmother NOVERCAL

stereo HI-FI, RECORD PLAYER, PHONOGRAPH, GRAMOPHONE
- stereo recording or transmitting sound by means of two separate channels BINAURAL, STEREOPHONIC
- cabinet of a stereo system, television set, or the like, standing on the floor CONSOLE
- using four separate sound channels, as some stereo systems are QUADRAPHONIC
- using only one sound channel, rather than two as in stereo MONOPHONIC, MONAURAL, MONO

sterilize a female mammal by removing the ovaries SPAY
- sterilization of a male mammal CASTRATION
- sterilization of a man by cutting the sperm-carrying ducts VASECTOMY
- sterilization of a woman by tying off the fallopian tubes TUBAL LIGATION
- sterilizing vessel, using steam under pressure, much like a pressure cooker AUTOCLAVE

stethoscope - blowing or whispering sound heard through a stethoscope, typically caused by the flowing of the blood SOUFFLE
- crackling sound of diseased or fluid-filled lungs, as heard through a stethoscope RALE
- listening to body sounds, as through a stethoscope, for purposes of diagnosis AUSCULTATION

steward of a medieval royal household or manor SENESCHAL, CHAMBERLAIN, REEVE
- steward or chief butler MAÎTRE D'HÔTEL, MAJORDOMO

stick See also **join**
- stick, forked twig, or the like that allegedly quivers or dips when

Stairs

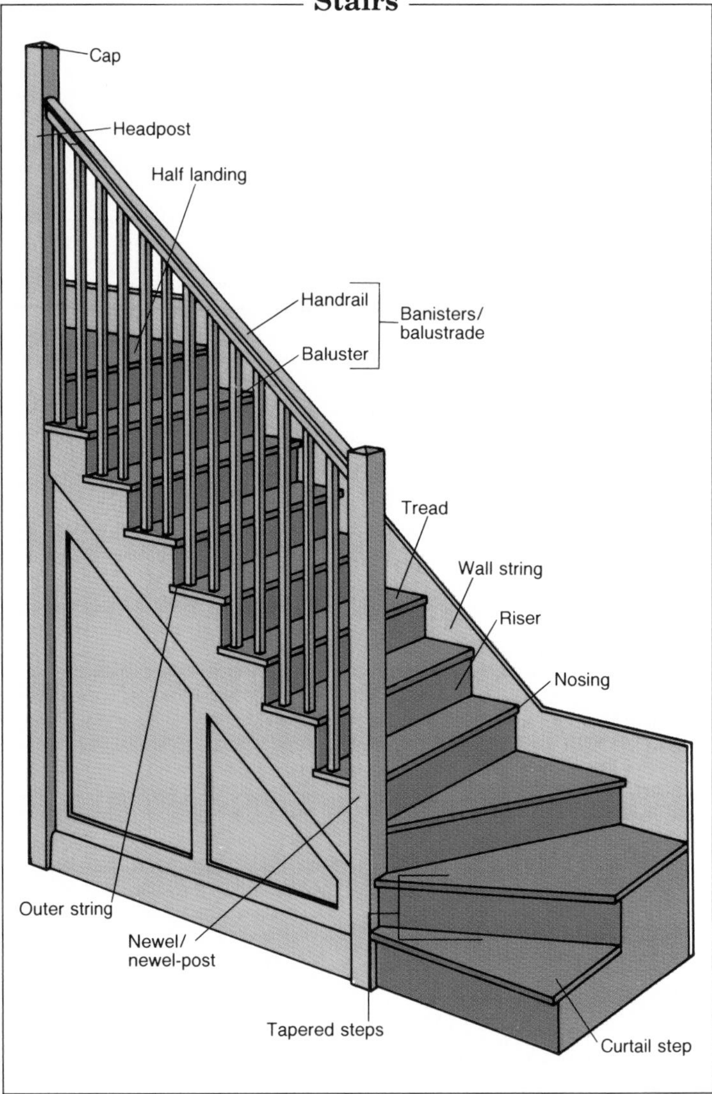

held above ground containing water or minerals DIVINING ROD, DOWSING ROD
- stick, ruler, or the like for beating children, especially on the hand FERULE
- stick fast, cling ADHERE, CLEAVE
- stick of perfumed substance, burned as incense JOSS STICK
- stick on which notches are cut, formerly used for keeping accounts or records TALLY
- stick or baton formerly used by a king or military commander to signal orders WARDER
- stick or pole, with a spring at the base, on which one can bounce along POGO STICK
- stick or rod from which lengths are cut for fastening adjoining wood or stone parts, or the fastener itself DOWEL
- stick or short cane carried by army officers SWAGGER STICK
- stick or short staff used as a police weapon, symbol of official authority, or the like BATON
- stick out, jut, project PROTRUDE
- stick together COHERE
- stick used for beating, or a beating with a stick, especially on the soles of the feet BASTINADO
- stick with a pointed or electrified tip for prodding animals or prisoners CATTLE PROD, GOAD
- sticking, holding, or clinging firmly TENACIOUS
- sticks, branches, or twigs tied in a bundle FAGOT
- building material of poles interlaced with reeds, sticks, or the like WATTLE
- bundle of sticks with an ax, carried as a symbol of the magistrates' authority in ancient Rome FASCES
- fence of pointed sticks forming a defensive barrier PALISADE, STOCKADE
- long, iron-tipped stick, used by hikers in the mountains ALPENSTOCK
- long stick with a curved blade used for rough pruning and harvesting fruit BILLHOOK
- small stick or wand used as a pointer, as by teachers FESCUE
- small thin stick for stirring or removing bubbles from a drink SWIZZLE STICK
- spiked walking stick whose handle opens into a flat seat SHOOTING STICK
- upright pointed stick forming part of a fence or the like PALE, PALING, PICKET

sticky ADHESIVE
- sticky, gummy, gluey GLUTINOUS, VISCOUS, VISCID
- sticky gum obtained from some plants RESIN, MUCILAGE

stiff, frosty, unfriendly, scornful or haughty ALOOF, DISDAINFUL, STANDOFFISH
- stiff, inelegant, and forced, as a strained way of speaking is STILTED
- stiff, starchy, conservative, prudish STRAITLACED
- stiff, strict, severe, as a law might be EXACTING, STRINGENT
- stiff, unbending, unwilling or unable to change UNADAPTABLE, INFLEXIBLE, INELASTIC, UNWAVERING, UNYIELDING, MONOLITHIC
- stiff and inflexible person, strict disciplinarian MARTINET, RAMROD
- stiff and very strict in matters of discipline PRUSSIAN, TEUTONIC
- stiffly and hypocritically self-righteous, holier-than-thou PHARISAICAL
- stiffly and pompously authoritative DOCTRINAIRE, OPINIONATED, PONTIFICAL
- stiffly austere and self-denying, especially in the cause of religious devotion ASCETIC, PURITANICAL
- stiffly committed to one's opinions or beliefs, unwilling to change or adapt one's views DOGMATIC, UNSHAKABLE, MONOLITHIC
- stiffly correct and strict observer of the rules, a religion, or the like PRECISIAN, FORMALIST, STICKLER, PURIST
- stiffly or excessively correct and hard to please, picky, choosy, fussy FASTIDIOUS, FINICKY, HYPERCRITICAL, PEDANTIC, PERSNICKETY
- thin strip of wood, whalebone, or the like for stiffening a corset BUSK

stiffness, cramp, or rigid muscular contraction, as in a fever RIGOR
- stiffness in artistic technique or criticism, overconcentration on form rather than meaning FORMALISM, STYLIZATION
- inflammation of the joints that results in pain, stiffness, and often deformity ARTHRITIS

still See also **calm, quiet**
- still, motionless, as a sailing ship is when there is no wind or current BECALMED
- still, not flowing, as pond water is STAGNANT
- still, stationary, unmoving or incapable of moving IMMOBILE
- still, unchanging, making no progress STATIC
- still, unmoving, very sluggish or passive INERT
- still in existence, surviving, not lost or extinct or destroyed EXTANT
- temporarily still or inactive DORMANT, LATENT

stimulate, agitate, or stir up discontent, riot, or the like FOMENT
- stimulate, arouse, inspire, startle, or spur into action GALVANIZE
- stimulate, inflame, or excite interest, love, or the like KINDLE
- stimulate, put life or energy into ANIMATE, INVIGORATE, VIVIFY
- stimulate, set in motion or action, prompt ACTIVATE, ACTUATE
- stimulate, urge on, spur, prod into action or movement GOAD, EGG ON
- stimulate, whip up, provoke, or take the initiative in something, especially wrongdoing or riot INCITE, INSTIGATE
- stimulate or increase appetite, desire, or interest WHET
- stimulate or inspire, provide an incentive MOTIVATE
- stimulating, lively, or cheering INVIGORATING, EXHILARATING

sting - having a sting, as a bee is ACULEATE

stinging or itching sensation, typically accompanied by weals on the skin URTICATION, HIVES, UREDO

stingy, miserly, grasping, cheap SKIN-FLINTY, CLOSE-FISTED, PENURIOUS, PARSIMONIOUS, PENNY-PINCHING
- stingy, miserly, and grasping person CHEAPSKATE, PENNY-PINCHER, PINCHPENNY, SKINFLINT, TIGHTWAD, CURMUDGEON
- stingy or unduly thrifty, unwilling to spend sufficient money, time, or effort SKIMPY

stinking, foul-smelling FETID, RANK, MALODOROUS, REEKING, NOISOME

stir up, disturb ROIL
- stir up trouble, rebellion, or the like FOMENT, INSTIGATE, PROVOKE, INCITE

stitch See also **sewing, embroidery**
- stitching of cloth with a decorative honeycomb pattern of tucks SMOCKING
- stitching or sewing together of the edges of a wound SUTURE

stock or range of jokes, pieces of music, roles, or the like to a performer REPERTOIRE
- stock or total quantity of goods on hand INVENTORY
- add new stocks or supplies, as in refilling a refrigerator REPLENISH

stock exchange See also **shares** and chart at **economics**
- stock exchange, especially that of Paris BOURSE
- stock-exchange average in London FT INDEX
- stock-exchange average in New York DOW JONES INDEX
- continuous strip of paper such as

that on which stock-exchange reports used to be printed TICKER TAPE
- referring to stocks and shares not quoted on the stock exchange UNLISTED
- short-term speculation on the stock exchange ARBITRAGE

stocky, heavily built PYKNIC, ENDOMORPHIC

stolen goods or property SWAG, LOOT, BOOTY, PLUNDER, SPOILS
- person who knowingly buys or stores stolen goods RECEIVER
- person who receives and sells stolen goods FENCE

stomach area MIDRIFF
- stomach lining of calves, or an extract of it used in making cheese RENNET
- stomach of an animal, or crop of a bird CRAW
- stomach or intestinal pains, especially in infants, from a buildup of gas COLIC, GRIPES
- stomach rumbling BORBORYGMUS
- stomach section in birds, often containing grit, for breaking down food GIZZARD
- stomach upset, indigestion DYSPEPSIA
- adjective for the stomach GASTRIC
- displacement of a part of the stomach through the diaphragm HIATUS HERNIA
- first stomach of a cow or other cud-chewing mammal, in which food is partly digested before returning to the mouth RUMEN
- fourth stomach of a cow or other cud-chewing mammal, where true digestion takes place ABOMASUM
- lower opening of the stomach for food to pass into the duodenum PYLORUS
- membrane lining the abdominal cavity and covering most of the stomach and other organs PERITONEUM
- part of the body containing the stomach and intestines ABDOMEN
- "pit of the stomach" SOLAR PLEXUS
- second stomach of a cow or other cud-chewing mammal RETICULUM
- third stomach of a cow or other cud-chewing mammal MANYPLIES, OMASUM, PSALTERIUM
- tube through which food passes from the pharynx to the stomach ESOPHAGUS, GULLET
- whitish chemical substance swallowed by a patient to make the stomach and intestines visible for X-ray photographs BARIUM MEAL

stomach (combining form) GASTR-, GASTRO-

stone See also **rock, gemstone,** and chart at **precious stones**
- stone band or molding along a wall, as an architectural ornament CORDON, STRINGCOURSE
- stone breakwater or jetty, protecting a harbor MOLE
- stone coffin or marble tomb, typically having a sculpture or inscriptions SARCOPHAGUS
- stone figure of grotesque appearance as on a cathedral roof, often serving as a rainwater spout from a gutter GARGOYLE
- stone fragment or chip SPALL
- stone or brick used in the top, usually sloping, section of a wall or roof COPING STONE, CAPSTONE
- stone or light volcanic rock used for scrubbing and polishing PUMICE
- stone or rock formation that protrudes sharply above the soil level, as on a plain OUTCROP
- stone or slab of stone used for paving FLAGSTONE
- stone or substance believed by alchemists to have the power of turning base metals into gold PHILOSOPHERS' STONE, ELIXIR
- stone pillar, four-sided and tapering up to a pyramidal top, of a kind used as a monument in ancient Egypt OBELISK
- stone slab, as laid flat over a grave LEDGER
- stone slab on top of a pillar, for supporting an arch or lintel SUMMER
- stone slab or pillar, with an engraved surface, as used in ancient times as a monument, gravestone, or the like STELE, STELA
- stone tablet that provided the key to ancient Egyptian hieroglyphics ROSETTA STONE
- stone tool used during the later Stone Age NEOLITH
- stonelike mass of mineral salts in the body, such as a gallstone or kidney stone CALCULUS
- adjective for stone LITHIC
- area or pit from which stone is extracted QUARRY
- cavity in a stone or rock lined with crystals GEODE
- engraved in stone LAPIDARIAN, LAPIDARY
- large standing stone, usually part of a prehistoric monument MEGALITH, MONOLITH, MENHIR
- metal clamp or cramping iron for fastening blocks of stone together AGRAFE
- metal pin for fastening blocks of stone together GUDGEON
- mound of stones serving as a memorial or landmark CAIRN
- person who shapes building stone, or is skilled at building with it MASON, STONEMASON
- prehistoric monument or chamber formed by stone pillars with a crossbeam DOLMEN, TRILITHON
- ring of stone pillars forming part of a prehistoric monument HENGE, CROMLECH
- shape or dress stone roughly with a broad chisel BOAST
- turn into stone LAPIDIFY, PETRIFY
- unbreakable stone, according to legend ADAMANT

stone (combining form) -LITE, -LITH-, LITHO-, LAPID-, PETR-, PETRI-, PETRO-

Stone Age - middle Stone Age MESOLITHIC
- new Stone Age NEOLITHIC
- old Stone Age PALEOLITHIC

Stonehenge - prehistoric pillarlike stone, as at Stonehenge, probably erected for religious purposes MEGALITH, MONOLITH, MENHIR

stonemason's chisel DROVE

stonework in a building MASONRY
- stonework prepared for moldings, sills, or the like DRESSINGS
- lacy ornamental pattern or stonework, as at the top of a Gothic window TRACERY

stool to which wrongdoers or suspects were formerly tied, as for ducking or public display CUCKING STOOL
- folding stool or desk for kneeling at during prayer, as by the English sovereign at the coronation FALDSTOOL

stoop, agree in a haughty or patronizing way to do or give something DEIGN, CONDESCEND, VOUCHSAFE

stop See also **end, prevent, hinder, obstruct**
- stop, cease, quit doing, discontinue DESIST, PRETERMIT
- stop, seize, or interrupt something, such as a message, in its course INTERCEPT
- stop, stoppage, immobility STASIS
- stop and confront someone unexpectedly ACCOST, WAYLAY
- stop doing or participating in, refrain or abstain FORBEAR
- stop or check the movement, development, or spread of ARREST
- stop or suspend a meeting, court proceedings, or the like temporarily ADJOURN, RECESS
- stop short, refuse, as a horse might at a jump JIB, BALK, SHY
- stopping, ceasing, termination CESSATION, SURCEASE
- stopping and starting at intervals, periodic INTERMITTENT
- come to a stop, or bring a ship to a stop HEAVE TO
- complete stop in progress or activity STANDSTILL
- old shipboard command to stop

AVAST
- suspended, or stopped temporarily, as a project might be IN ABEYANCE
stop (combining form) PARA-
stop-press space in a newspaper, for last-minute reports FUDGE
stoppage (combining form) -STASIS
stopping place for rest or refueling during a long journey STAGING POST
stopwatch or other instrument for measuring time very accurately CHRONOGRAPH
store, as in a granary GARNER
- store, typically small and fashionable, selling clothes, gifts, or the like BOUTIQUE
- store in a remote area, as in pioneering times, in which goods were often bartered TRADING POST
- store-lined roofed passageway, as through a building ARCADE
- store-lined street for pedestrians only MALL
- store of hidden arms, stolen goods, or the like, or its hiding place CACHE
- store or supply accumulated for future use STOCKPILE
- store restricted to military or other government personnel and their families PX, POST EXCHANGE
- store restricted to military personnel, diplomats, or the like COMMISSARY
- store selling goods at prices lower than the manufacturers' recommended prices DISCOUNT HOUSE
- store specializing in ham, sausage, and other cold cooked meats CHARCUTERIE
- storage place, warehouse DEPOSITORY, DEPOT, ENTREPÔT
- storeroom for cuttings and files in a newspaper office MORGUE
- code of lines and numbers, as on a library book or store item, typically read by a laser optical scanner UPC, UNIVERSAL PRODUCT CODE, BAR CODE
- funnel-shaped dispenser for bulk materials, as at a storage place for fuel or grain HOPPER
- large retail store selling a wide range of goods EMPORIUM
- secret store of money, drugs, or the like STASH
stork - large African stork MARABOU
- large Asian stork ADJUTANT BIRD
storm - interval of calm during a storm LULL
- lessen in intensity, decline or die down, as a storm or a feeling might SUBSIDE, ABATE, TAPER OFF
- still area at the center of a cyclonic storm EYE
stormy, as the weather, sea, or a

Steam Engine

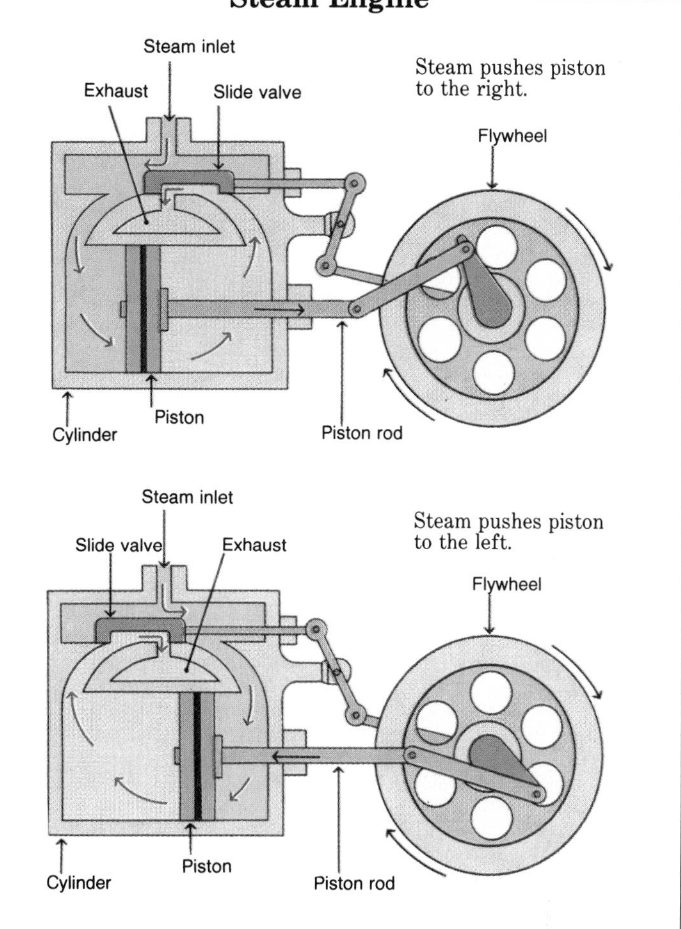

meeting or person might be BOISTEROUS, TURBULENT, TEMPESTUOUS, TUMULTUOUS
- stormy and wild, unpleasant, as weather might be INCLEMENT
story, especially a tale of adventure CONTE
- story, speech, sales talk, or the like that is glib or long-winded SPIEL
- story from one's past, usually related with nostalgia REMINISCENCE
- story of a person's life or experiences, as written by another person BIOGRAPHY
- story of a person's life or experiences, as written by himself or herself AUTOBIOGRAPHY, MEMOIRS
- story or drawn-out jokey anecdote whose supposed humor lies in the irrelevance or anticlimax of the punch line SHAGGY-DOG STORY
- story or picture in which the characters or scenes symbolize abstractions or ideas and convey a deeper meaning ALLEGORY
- story or rumor that is false or a deliberate hoax CANARD
- story with a moral, usually a beast fable APOLOGUE
- storytelling, or the story told NARRATION
- collection of poems, stories, or the like ANTHOLOGY
- doubtful, of very questionable authenticity, as an extraordinary story or anecdote might be APOCRYPHAL, SPURIOUS
- entertain or give pleasure to, as by telling stories REGALE
- events of a story as opposed to its dialogue, descriptions, and the like PLOT
- improve or enliven a report or story by adding colorful, often false, details EMBELLISH, EMBROIDER
- incoherent, disconnected, or disordered, as a report or story might be DISJOINTED
- make up or invent an excuse, story, or the like CONCOCT
- medieval verse story with comic,

satirical, or ribald themes FABLIAU
- short story relating some interesting or humorous incident ANECDOTE
- simple story which, usually indirectly, points to a moral or religious lesson PARABLE
- skilled teller of witty stories or anecdotes RACONTEUR

stove of a large iron make, usually burning coal or wood, with one or more ovens RANGE
- portable stove or heater, as for drying out a building under construction SALAMANDER

straight LINEAR
- straight, arrowlike SAGITTAL
- relating to straight lines RECTILINEAR

straight (combining form) ORTHO-

strain - straining or purifying by use of a filter FILTRATION
- reduce food to a pulpy consistency by mashing it or pressing it through a strainer PUREE

strained, long-winded, or tedious, as a speech might be LABORED
- strained, striving for effect, or forced AGONISTIC, VOULU
- strained, tense, or nervy OVERWROUGHT, AGITATED

strand twisted with others to make wool, rope, or the like PLY

strange, abnormal, irregular, inconsistent with or deviating from the norm ANOMALOUS
- strange, beyond normal nature, supernatural PRETERNATURAL, UNCANNY
- strange, inexplicable, conspicuously odd or very unconventional FANTASTIC, FREAKISH, BIZARRE, OUTRÉ, OUTLANDISH
- strange, odd, peculiar, especially in an interesting or amusing way ECCENTRIC
- strange, quirky, IDIOSYNCRATIC
- strange, unfamiliar, foreign to one's experience or nature ALIEN
- strange, unique, or remarkable and rare SINGULAR, SUI GENERIS
- strange and fascinating through being unfamiliar or foreign EXOTIC

strange (combining form) XENO-

strangers - person who is hostile to or scared of strangers and unfamiliar ideas XENOPHOBE

strangle, as with wire, typically in order to commit robbery or as a means of execution GARROTE
- strangle or choke THROTTLE
- strangle or stifle secretly, so as to leave the body unmarked BURKE

strap around an animal's body as to hold a saddle in place GIRTH, SURCINGLE
- straps for tying together the legs of a horse or cow HOBBLE
- leather strap split into strips at the end, used for beating children or prisoners TAWS
- leather straps, usually seven or nine, fastened to a wooden handle, used for beating children or prisoners CAT-O'-NINE-TAILS
- system of elastic straps used for tying down loads, as on a car roof SPIDER, OCTOPUS, SHOCK CORD

straw bedding for cattle LITTER
- straw mat used as a floor covering in a Japanese home TATAMI

stray and homeless child or animal WAIF
- stray, fall behind STRAGGLE, LAG
- stray from the main subject of one's speech or writing DIGRESS
- straying from the proper moral course, erring, wayward ERRANT

streak - streaked, grooved, or ridged STRIATE, STRIATED, STRIGOSE
- streaked or marked with several different colors VARIEGATED, PIED, BRINDLED

stream See also **river**
- stream flowing out of a lake, dam, or the like EFFLUENT
- stream of air or water forced backward by a propeller SLIPSTREAM, RACE
- stream of water or air directed at or into a part of the body for cleansing or healing DOUCHE
- stream or flow of people or things coming in, such as tourists arriving INFLUX
- stream or small river RIVULET, BROOK
- clear stream, or a sudden river flood from heavy rains or melting snow FRESHET
- narrow gorge or ravine, usually with a stream flowing through it FLUME
- small stream or a narrow tidal inlet CREEK

stream, flow (combining form) RHEO-

streamlined to reduce air resistance, as the design of a car might be AERODYNAMIC

street See also **road**
- street entertainer or musician performing for money from idlers or passersby BUSKER
- street urchin GUTTERSNIPE
- mechanical instrument played in the street, such as a barrel organ HURDY-GURDY

strength See also **strong**
- strength, power, or vitality THEW, SINEW
- strength of a metal or similar solid material to withstand a pulling force or longitudinal stress TENSILE STRENGTH
- strength of character, determination BACKBONE, SPUNK
- strength of mind, courage, and hardiness, especially in battle or against adversity FORTITUDE, VALOR, PROWESS
- strength to endure or resist, staying power, vigor STAMINA
- brute strength, muscular power BRAWN
- rest and regain one's strength after illness CONVALESCE, RECUPERATE

strengthen See also **support**
- strengthen, back up, or confirm an argument, proof, or the like CORROBORATE, SUBSTANTIATE, VERIFY, UNDERPIN
- strengthen, revive, enliven, impart new vitality to INVIGORATE, REVITALIZE
- strengthen, stabilize, secure CONSOLIDATE
- strengthen against danger, attack, or impact, prop up BOLSTER, BRACE, BUTTRESS
- strengthen or harden steel by heating and cooling TEMPER
- strengthen or increase the effectiveness of a drug, hormone, or the like by administering another POTENTIATE
- strengthen or reinforce a defensive position, wine, a decision, or the like FORTIFY
- strengthen the will or determination ANNEAL
- strengthening, returning, flowing strongly again, reemerging RESURGENT
- strengthening of a learned response, as by means of rewards REINFORCEMENT

stress, emphasize, or intensify, draw attention to in an emphatic way ACCENTUATE, UNDERSCORE, HIGHLIGHT
- stress for rhythm or meter in verse ICTUS
- stress or emphasize a point by constantly repeating it, dwell on, hammer home BELABOR
- referring to the syllable carrying the principal stress or accent in a sentence or word group TONIC, NUCLEAR

stretch, widen, expand DILATE, DISTEND
- stretch and exercise, as before beginning a race LIMBER UP
- stretch of a river REACH
- stretch of land, water, or sky EXPANSE
- stretch out or into PROTRUDE, OBTRUDE
- stretch over, bridge SPAN
- stretchable, capable of being drawn out without breaking, as some metals are TENSILE, EXTENSILE,

DUCTILE, TRACTILE
- stretched out on the ground, with arms and legs spread out SPREAD-EAGLE
- continuous stretching of a compressed or injured body part as a medical treatment TRACTION

stretcher for the wounded or sick LITTER

strict See also **stiff**
- strict, austere, moralistic, and self-denying, especially from religious considerations ASCETIC, PURITANICAL
- strict, demanding, severe, as a law, rule, or the like might be EXACTING, STRINGENT, IRONCLAD
- strict, relentless, not yielding to entreaty, not making allowances INEXORABLE, UNCOMPROMISING
- strict, rigid, severe, demanding RIGOROUS
- strict, severe, stern, and serious in life-style and morality AUSTERE
- strict, unyielding, rigorous, unshakable, stubborn ADAMANT, INFLEXIBLE, UNBENDING, OBDURATE, UNSWERVING
- strict and harsh, extremely severe, or cruel, as a law might be DRACONIAN
- strict and literal-minded believer in the Bible or other unalterable religious doctrine FUNDAMENTALIST
- strict and stiff in discipline, allowing little individualism PRUSSIAN, TEUTONIC
- strict and stiffly correct observer of the rules, a religion, or the like PRECISIAN, FORMALIST
- strict disciplinarian or authority MARTINET, RAMROD
- strict ruler, or a person favoring strict authority and obedience AUTHORITARIAN
- person who is strict in matters of correctness, as in use of words PURIST, STICKLER

strife - referring to destructive conflict or strife within a group INTERNECINE

strike See also **beat**
- striker or group of protesters positioned outside a place of work, as to discourage other workers or customers from entering PICKET
- anticipating and thwarting an opponent's moves, as a military strike might be PREEMPTIVE
- settlement of a strike or dispute by negotiating through a third party CONCILIATION, MEDIATION
- settlement of a strike or dispute by submitting to the judgment of a third party ARBITRATION, ADJUDICATION

strikebreaker SCAB

striking outstanding, conspicuous, as arguments might be SALIENT
- striking of a surface, as by sound on the ear or by a stick on a drum PERCUSSION

string, cord, or ribbon running inside a hem, as to tighten a sleeve or close a purse DRAWSTRING
- string worn around the neck, as for carrying a whistle LANYARD
- pad in a piano or other keyboard instrument that deadens a string's vibrations DAMPER
- plucking device for the strings of a harpsichord or related instrument QUILL
- referring to rope, string, or cable FUNICULAR
- small thin disc or plate, as of plastic, used for plucking the strings of a guitar, lute, or related instrument PLECTRUM, PICK
- strand making up string, rope, or thread PLY

string instruments See chart, page 527, and also **guitar, violin**
- string instrument, keyboard instrument, or any other instrument producing sound by means of vibrating strings CHORDOPHONE

strip, as of paper, that is twisted and formed into a ring to create a one-sided continuous surface MÖBIUS STRIP
- strip of leather THONG
- strip or deprive of something, such as clothes or rights DIVEST
- strip or path, such as that left behind by a scythe SWATH
- strip or slat of wood or metal, used especially in sheets as a backing for plaster, slates, tiles, or the like LATH

stripe or line of color LIST
- striped, grooved, or ridged STRIATE, STRIATED, STRIGOSE

stripteaser ECDYSIAST
- minimal genital covering worn by a stripteaser G-STRING
- small round patches covering a stripteaser's nipples PASTIES

stroke, fit, or brainstorm ICTUS
- stroke, often followed by paralysis, resulting from the bursting or blocking of a blood vessel in the brain CEREBRAL HEMORRHAGE, APOPLEXY

strong See also **strength**
- strong, clumsy, and unwieldy HULKING
- strong, sturdy, steadfast, as a supporter might be STALWART, STAUNCH
- strong, tough, long-lasting DURABLE
- strong against adversity or attack, quick to recover RESILIENT, RESISTANT
- strong and effective, as a medicine or alcoholic drink might be POTENT
- strong and healthy, surviving easily HARDY, ROBUST, RUGGED, VIGOROUS
- strong and large, awesome, impressive FORMIDABLE, REDOUBTABLE, HERCULEAN
- strong and undeniable, as a legal case or an argument might be AIRTIGHT, CAST-IRON, IRREFUTABLE
- strong in a masculine way, manly, or sexually potent VIRILE
- strong or clearly noticeable, as an accent might be PRONOUNCED
- strong or forceful, emphatic, vigorous, as a denial or objection might be STRENUOUS, VEHEMENT
- strongest or most widespread, having the greatest importance, authority, or force PREDOMINANT
- physically strong, stocky, muscular, thickset BURLY, BRAWNY
- so strong as to be unbeatable INVINCIBLE

strong point, one's special talent FORTE, MÉTIER

structure, framework, or pattern FABRIC
- structure, system, organization, or the like that is elaborate and complex EDIFICE
- structure or form, as of a plant or animal organism MORPHOLOGY
- structured, systematic, classified, as a body of knowledge might be ARCHITECTONIC

struggle See also **fight**
- struggle, agonizing effort THROES
- struggle for superiority, especially hand-to-hand GRAPPLE
- referring to contests or struggles AGONISTIC
- referring to infighting or destructive struggles within a group INTERNECINE

stubborn, pig-headed, opposing things just for the sake of it CONTRARY, PERVERSE, CUSSED, MULISH
- stubborn, hardened, habitual, or deep-rooted, as a criminal or vice might be INVETERATE
- stubborn, inflexible, unshakable, holding fast to opinions or refusing to make allowances INTRANSIGENT, UNCOMPROMISING, UNSWERVING, DIEHARD
- stubborn, obstinate, unyielding, wanting one's own way HEADSTRONG, WILLFUL, STIFF-NECKED
- stubborn and disobedient, as a spoiled child might be FROWARD, ADVERSE
- stubborn or relentless, refusing to go away, as pain or rain might

be UNREMITTING, INEXORABLE
- stubbornly disobedient or rebellious, insubordinate, unmanageable CONTUMACIOUS, REFRACTORY, INTRACTABLE, RECALCITRANT, UNRULY
- stubbornly persistent in the face of adversity, persevering, refusing to give up DOGGED, PERTINACIOUS, TENACIOUS
- stubbornly prejudiced, refusing to accept new social attitudes, ultraconservative UNREGENERATE, UNRECONSTRUCTED
- stubbornly refusing to forgive, modify, or back down IMPLACABLE
- stubbornly refusing to mend one's ways, hardened against good or moral influence INDURATE, OBDURATE, IMPENITENT, UNREPENTANT
- fast and immovable, as a stubborn stain is INERADICABLE, INGRAINED, PERSISTENT

stuck-up See also **proud**
- stuck-up, snobbish, high and mighty, haughty DISDAINFUL
- stuck-up and acting in a superior manner SUPERCILIOUS, PATRONIZING, CONDESCENDING

student about to receive a degree GRADUAND
- student in the first year of study at a university or college FRESHMAN, FRESHER
- student in the last year of study at a university or college SENIOR
- student in the next-to-the-last year of study at a university or college JUNIOR
- student in the second year of study at a university or college SOPHOMORE
- students' social organization FRATERNITY, SORORITY
- attend a course or class without receiving academic credit AUDIT
- graduate or former student of a school, college, or university ALUMNUS, ALUMNA
- supervise and keep watch over students at an examination MONITOR
- suspend a student from college or university RUSTICATE

studio or workshop of an artist or craftsman ATELIER

study See also **analysis, examine**
- study, deep reflection, laborious meditation LUCUBRATION, EXCOGITATION
- study, office, or other private room where one can remain undisturbed SANCTUM
- study course offered by a university or college to part-time students EXTENSION COURSE
- study group or meeting SEMINAR
- study intensely at the last minute for an exam CRAM, GRIND
- study leave for a term or year granted to a teacher after a number of years' work SABBATICAL
- study of or formal lecture or treatise on a subject DISQUISITION
- study or examine in detail CON, ANATOMIZE, DISSECT, SCRUTINIZE, PERUSE, TRAVERSE
- occurring outside the normal course of studies or timetable, as in a school or college EXTRACURRICULAR, EXTRAMURAL
- outline of a course of study or exam requirements CURRICULUM, SYLLABUS
- referring to two or more academic subjects or fields of study INTERDISCIPLINARY
- subject of study, branch of knowledge DISCIPLINE
- systematic account or written study of a particular subject MONOGRAPH, TREATISE, DISSERTATION

study (combining form) -GRAPHY, -ISTICS, -LOGY, -OLOGY, -ICS

stuffed, as mushrooms or a roast chicken might be FARCI

stuffing, fabric, and springs used in making a soft covering for furniture UPHOLSTERY
- stuffing and preparing the skins of dead animals for exhibiting TAXIDERMY
- stuffing of finely chopped and seasoned meat or fish FORCEMEAT
- stuffing of wool or cotton waste for furniture or mattresses FLOCK
- stuffing or padding material used in former times BOMBAST
- silky plant fiber used for stuffing cushions, for soundproofing, and the like KAPOK

stuffy, hot, and humid MUGGY

stunned, confused STUPEFIED

stupid See also **silly, fool**
- stupid, foolish, lacking understanding and human sensitivity INSENSATE
- stupid, muddled, confused ADDLEPATED
- stupid, slow-witted, or insensitive OBTUSE, PURBLIND
- stupidly and boringly routine STULTIFYING
- stupidly and boringly routine work CONVEYOR BELT, GRINDSTONE, TREADMILL
- stupidly insensitive, gross, unthinking, as a needlessly clumsy remark would be CRASS
- extremely stupid or foolish, senseless, as an impulsive blunder might be IMBECILIC, MORONIC, CRETINOUS

style, enthusiasm, vigor, vivacity BRIO, DASH, FLAIR, PANACHE, ÉLAN, VERVE
- style of a graceful, moving, or effective kind in speech or writing ELOQUENCE
- style of a light, bantering kind in speech or writing PERSIFLAGE, BADINAGE, RAILLERY
- style of language appropriate to a particular social setting or use REGISTER
- style of modern design, using industrial materials HIGH-TECH
- style of speech or writing, way of putting things in words PHRASEOLOGY, DICTION
- style of speech or writing that is pompous, high-flown, and showy FUSTIAN, GRANDILOQUENCE, BOMBAST, EUPHUISM, GONGORISM
- agreeable or appropriate in style FELICITOUS
- characterized more by style than by content, as showy language is RHETORICAL
- clear and easy to understand, as a prose style might be LIMPID, LUCID
- commonly used, popular, as the informal everyday local style of speech is COLLOQUIAL, DEMOTIC, VERNACULAR
- concise, often to the point of obscurity, as a literary style might be ELLIPTICAL
- concise and elegant, as a prose style might be LAPIDARY
- conversational or informal in style, characteristic of casual everyday speech COLLOQUIAL
- deliberately emotional or stirring in style, as a high-flown speech of protest would be ORATORICAL, DECLAMATORY
- effortless ease of style, flowing gracefulness, as in speech or movement FLUENCY
- excessively ornate or high-flown, as a literary style might be FLORID, AUREATE, TUMID, BAROQUE, ROCOCO, EUPHUISTIC, MANDARIN
- grand, lofty, or exalted, as a literary style or social circle might be RAREFIED
- impressive, grand, or highfalutin in style or speech ROTUND, SONOROUS, OROTUND
- inappropriate or ill-chosen, as a remark, style, or expression might be INFELICITOUS
- language of an elegant rhetorical style PERIODS
- language or speech of a distinctive style, exclusive to a profession or other group JARGON, ARGOT, CANT
- long-winded, indirect, or roundabout in style, as a speech might be PERIPHRASTIC, CIRCUMLOCUTORY,

PROLIX
- old-fashioned or outdated in style or idiom, no longer in common use OBSOLETE, OBSOLESCENT, ARCHAIC
- overrefined, excessively rich or precious, as a literary style might be DECADENT, FIN-DE-SIÈCLE
- pompously ornate or windy in style, but lacking any real content TURGID, FLATULENT
- simple and long-lasting in style, rising above changing fashions CLASSIC
- tending to use or characterized by very long words, as a writer's style might be SESQUIPEDALIAN, INKHORN
- writing of a more striking or elaborate style than the surrounding text PURPLE PATCH, PURPLE PASSAGE

subatomic particle forming part of an atom's nucleus, and having a positive electric charge PROTON
- subatomic particle forming part of an atom's nucleus, and without any electric charge NEUTRON
- subatomic particle having half-integral spin FERMION
- subatomic particle having integral spin BOSON
- subatomic particle of various kinds participating in strong interactions HADRON, BARYON, PROTON, MESON, PION, NEUTRON, KAON
- subatomic particle of various kinds participating in weak actions LEPTON, ELECTRON, MUON, TAU, NEUTRINO
- subatomic particle properties that are described by quantum numbers STRANGENESS; TOP, TRUTH; BOTTOM, BEAUTY; COLOR; SPIN; CHARM
- subatomic particle revolving around an atom's nucleus, and having a negative electric charge ELECTRON
- hypothetical subatomic particle thought to be the fundamental unit of known elementary particles QUARK

subconscious, as secret fears or painful memories might be REPRESSED

subdue or discipline one's body by self-denial or punishment MORTIFY

subject case in grammar NOMINATIVE
- subject of study, branch of knowledge DISCIPLINE
- subject that is remote or only vaguely understood HINTERLAND
- begin to discuss a subject BROACH
- relating to two or more academic subjects or fields of study INTERDISCIPLINARY

subject of (combining form) -LOGY, -OLOGY, -GRAPHY, -ICS, -ISTICS, -NOMY

submarine See illustration, page 529
- submarine observation vessel for staffed scientific research in deep-sea waters BATHYSCAPHE, BATHYSPHERE
- submarine's rudder on a horizontal axis HYDROPLANE
- device or system used for detecting enemy submarines ECHOLOCATION, SONAR
- optical instrument, as on a submarine, containing mirrors or prisms for viewing objects that are not in the direct line of sight PERISCOPE
- raised observation post or bridge on a submarine, usually housing the entrance CONNING TOWER, SAIL
- wake made by a submarine's periscope above the water FEATHER

submerge, cover completely in a liquid IMMERSE

submissive attitude, or respect DEFERENCE, HOMAGE, OBEISANCE, OBSEQUIOUSNESS, FAWNING

submit overrespectfully to another's wishes or decisions KOWTOW
- submit to or respect the wishes or opinion of someone else DEFER
- submitting, as to misfortune or to unfair treatment ACQUIESCENT, RESIGNED

subordinate See **secondary, servant**

subordinate (combining form) PARA-

subordination of a clause in grammar by means of a conjunction HYPOTAXIS
- linking of clauses in grammar by means of punctuation rather than by conjunctions or subordination PARATAXIS

subsidy, financial grant, such as an endowment SUBVENTION
- subsidy publisher, publisher producing but not marketing a book VANITY PRESS

substitute See also **agent**
- substitute, imitation ERSATZ
- substitute or agent, deputy, stand-in VICAR, PROXY, SURROGATE
- substitute or exchange COMMUTE
- substituted fraudulently SUPPOSITITIOUS, SPURIOUS
- relating to, serving as, performed or suffered by, or experienced through a substitute VICARIOUS

subtitle - translation shown above the stage or screen, rather than as a subtitle at its foot SURTITLE

subtle shade of meaning NUANCE
- subtle to a fault, overprecise, pedantic or dogmatic SCHOLASTIC, SOPHISTICAL
- subtly harmful, treacherous, or seductive INSIDIOUS
- making needless or oversubtle distinctions, nitpicking QUIBBLING, HAIRSPLITTING

subtlety, delicacy, precision, as in negotiations NICETY

subtraction - number or quantity from which another number is subtracted MINUEND
- number or quantity that is to be subtracted SUBTRAHEND

suburb from which many people commute to their place of work BEDROOM COMMUNITY
- suburb or quarter of a city, especially a French city FAUBOURG
- suburbs or outskirts of a town OUTSKIRTS, ENVIRONS, PRECINCTS

succeed, bear fruit, work out well, as a plan might FRUCTIFY
- succeed, meet the required standards PASS MUSTER
- succeed in doing, manage, as by scheming CONTRIVE
- succeed in life, thrive, do well, make out FLOURISH, PROSPER
- succeed in the face of opposition, win through PREVAIL
- succeed or replace somebody in a position or office SUPERSEDE
- succeed or thrive, typically by exploiting others BATTEN
- succeed to a throne, title, or the like, inherit ACCEDE TO

success of a book, movie, or the like with the reviewers, but not with the public at large SUCCÈS D'ESTIME
- success of a book, play, or the like, mostly because of its shock value SUCCÈS DE SCANDALE
- success of a spectacular or extraordinary kind SUCCÈS FOU
- success or achievement of a brilliant kind ÉCLAT
- success or realization of plans or wishes FRUITION
- definite, indisputable, widely acknowledged, as a victory or success might be RESOUNDING
- desire or striving for success and recognition, ambition ASPIRATION

successful, bearing results, as an idea or project might be FRUITFUL
- successful, thriving, doing well FLOURISHING
- successful or extremely brilliant person of very young age WHIZ KID, WUNDERKIND, CHILD PRODIGY
- successful or powerful, as a remedy might be EFFICACIOUS, POTENT

successive, ordered, following in a series SEQUENTIAL, CONSECUTIVE

sucker, as of a leech or octopus ACETABULUM

suction - relating to breathing or suction ASPIRATORY

sudden See also **surprise**
- sudden, brilliant, and fast, as a rise to fame might be METEORIC
- sudden, rapid, and uncontrolled,

without due care or planning HEADLONG, PRECIPITATE
- sudden, spontaneous, without planning, as a snap decision would be SPUR-OF-THE-MOMENT
- sudden and artificial development or device introduced to resolve a tricky situation or plot DEUS EX MACHINA
- sudden and powerful, as a disease might be FOUDROYANT
- sudden and entirely unexpected UNFORESEEN, UNANNOUNCED
- sudden and unexpected piece of good fortune, especially the sudden acquiring of money WINDFALL
- sudden and violent change or destruction CATACLYSM
- sudden and violent disruption, radical change UPHEAVAL
- sudden change of opinion or policy, U-turn VOLTE-FACE, ABOUT-FACE
- sudden decision or change of mood WHIM, CAPRICE, HUMOR
- sudden emphatic utterance, exclamation EJACULATION
- sudden insight or recognition, such as a mystical experience of the essence of an event EPIPHANY, REVELATION, ANACALYPSIS
- sudden jump in a sequence, as in a set of logical arguments SALTUS
- sudden or surprising event or development COUP DE FOUDRE
- sudden pain PANG
- sudden reversal in fortunes or the course of events, especially in a tragic play PERIPETEIA, PERIPETY
- suddenly lift or shift someone, as to stardom CATAPULT
- suddenly or quickly PRESTO
- acting suddenly, on whim rather than by planning IMPULSIVE, IMPETUOUS

sue - person or group that is sued by another or against whom a court action is brought DEFENDANT
- person or group that sues another or brings a civil action in court PLAINTIFF

suffering, agony TRAVAIL, ANGUISH
- suffering, as from a disease or disaster STRICKEN
- suffering, hardship, distress, or misfortune ADVERSITY, AFFLICTION
- suffering, tyrannized, or persecuted DOWNTRODDEN, OPPRESSED, MALTREATED
- suffering, under great strain or anguish ON THE RACK
- suffering and death for one's faith or cause MARTYRDOM
- suffering or great distress, especially from persecution TRIBULATION
- suffering or spiritual torment or ordeal CALVARY, PURGATORY, PRIVATE HELL
- sufferings of Jesus before and during the Crucifixion PASSION
- cause or means of severe or widespread suffering SCOURGE
- exist in a state of depression, weakness, or suffering LANGUISH
- occasion or place of great suffering GETHSEMANE
- unflinching steadfastness in the face of suffering STOICISM, FORTITUDE

suffering (combining form) -OTIC

suffocate STIFLE, SMOTHER, ASPHYXIATE

suffocation ASPHYXIATION, ASPHYXIA

sugar, starch, or a related compound CARBOHYDRATE
- sugar-coated and shiny, as cherries sometimes are GLACÉ
- sugar-coated, as preserved fruit might be CRYSTALLIZED
- sugar deficiency in the blood HYPOGLYCEMIA
- sugar excess in the blood, as in diabetes HYPERGLYCEMIA
- sugar of a brown, sticky, raw type MUSCOVADO
- sugar, starch, or another substance added to a drug to make it more suitable for administering EXCIPIENT
- sugar-processing plant REFINERY
- sugar substitute, artificial sweetener SACCHARIN, CYCLAMATE
- sugar syrup MOLASSES, TREACLE
- sugary, sweet, often excessively so SACCHARINE, MAWKISH
- brown crystallized sugar DEMERARA
- cane sugar, common edible sugar SUCROSE, SACCHAROSE
- coat food with flour, sugar, or the like, as by sprinkling DREDGE
- common sugar forming the basic energy source in plants and animals GLUCOSE
- corn or grape sugar DEXTROSE
- disease characterized by excess sugar in the blood and urine DIABETES MELLITUS
- fruit sugar, used in medicinal drips and as a preservative FRUCTOSE, LEVULOSE
- hormone secreted by the pancreas and regulating the blood-sugar level INSULIN
- milk sugar, used in baby foods and confectionery LACTOSE
- wood sugar, used in dyeing and tanning and in foods for diabetics XYLOSE

sugar (combining form) GLYC-, GLYCO-, -SACCHAR-, SACCHARO-, -OSE

suggest, hint, imply, let something be known indirectly INSINUATE, INTIMATE
- suggest, propose, or put forward a theory for consideration PROPOUND, PREDICATE, ADVANCE
- suggest, recommend, or support ADVOCATE, COMMEND
- suggest, refer to indirectly, hint at ALLUDE TO
- suggest strongly, prove, or indicate EVIDENCE

suggestion or association that is evoked by a word or thing, rather than its literal meaning CONNOTATION, OVERTONE
- suggestion or hint, something implied but not said directly IMPLICATION
- suggestion or hint of a veiled and typically offensive kind INNUENDO, ASPERSION, INSINUATION, IMPUTATION
- advance or seek support for a scheme, project, or suggestion FLOAT
- underlying suggestion or implied tendency or meaning UNDERTONE, UNDERCURRENT, IMPLICATION

suggestive, atmospheric, or memory-arousing, as an idea or story might be EVOCATIVE
- suggestive of sexual impropriety RISQUÉ, TITILLATING, INDELICATE
- suggestive or naughty pun, double meaning DOUBLE ENTENDRE

suicide attempt by a person who does not really want to die, usually as a cry for attention PARASUICIDE
- suicide by a Hindu widow who would cremate herself on her late husband's funeral pyre SUTTEE
- suicide or person who commits suicide FELO-DE-SE
- suicidal or self-destructive person, especially one who is part of a larger group LEMMING
- suicidally risky venture RUSSIAN ROULETTE
- Japanese ritual suicide by disembowelment HARA-KIRI, SEPPUKU
- Japanese suicide pilot during World War II, "divine wind" KAMIKAZE

suitable, appropriate, corresponding to what is right or needed FITTING, BEFITTING, BEHOOVING, MEET, FIT
- suitable, appropriate, relevant, as a comment might be APPOSITE, APROPOS, APT
- suitable, proper, conforming to good manners or taste BECOMING, DECOROUS, SEEMLY
- suitable for marriage, and typically very attractive, as a young woman might be NUBILE
- suitable or corresponding in character or type CONGRUENT, CONGRUOUS
- suitable or qualified for office, marriage, or the like ELIGIBLE
- suitable, harsh, deserved, or adequate, as a punishment might be CONDIGN
- be suitable, appropriate, or rele-

STRING INSTRUMENTS

aeolian harp/ wind harp	small boxlike instrument that sounds when blown by the wind	**oud**	lutelike instrument of northern Africa and western Asia
balalaika	plucked guitarlike, triangular Russian folk instrument with two to four strings	**pandura**	long-necked Persian lute
bouzouki	mandolinlike Greek folk instrument	**psaltery**	ancient and medieval instrument like a dulcimer, but plucked instead of struck
cimbalom	large Hungarian dulcimer	**rebab**	medieval Arabic bowed instrument with one to three strings, ancestor of the rebec
cithara/kithara	ancient Greek lyre, with a box-shaped frame	**rebec/rebeck/ ribibe**	medieval ancestor of the violin, with a body shaped like a half-pear
cittern/cithern	lutelike 16th-century instrument	**samisen**	three-stringed, banjolike Japanese instrument
clarsach/ clairschach	ancient Irish and Scottish harp	**sarod**	Indian instrument with two sets of strings, one plucked and the other acting as a drone
crwth/cruth/ crouth/crowd	ancient Celtic lyre-shaped instrument, played with a bow	**sitar**	long-necked Indian instrument made of gourds and wood
dulcimer	instrument with strings stretched over a soundboard and struck with hammers	**theorbo/ archlute**	two-necked 17th-century lute with extra bass strings
gittern	medieval four-stringed guitar	**ukulele**	small, four-stringed guitar of Portuguese origin, popular in Hawaii
hurdy-gurdy	medieval mechanical lute-shaped instrument in which a wheel, turned by a handle, acted as the bow	**viol**	any of a family of early violinlike instruments, with a fretted fingerboard, and usually six strings
kit/pochette	miniature violin, formerly used by dancing masters	**viola da gamba/ bass viol**	large viol, played between the legs like a cello
koto	box-shaped, 13-stringed, zitherlike Japanese instrument	**viola d'amore**	tenor viol, usually with seven gut strings plus several sympathetically vibrating wire strings
lute	medieval plucked instrument, usually with a body shaped like a half-pear, a bent neck, and a fretted fingerboard	**zither/zittern**	plucked, many-stringed Central European folk instrument, placed on the knees when played
lyre	harplike ancient Greek and Middle Eastern instrument		
mandolin	plucked instrument, related to the lute, with four pairs of strings		

vant PERTAIN, APPERTAIN, BEAR UPON
- occurring at a suitable or helpful time OPPORTUNE, PROPITIOUS

suitcase See also **case, bag**
- large suitcase with two hinged compartments PORTMANTEAU
- small bag or suitcase used as hand luggage VALISE

suitor - male suitor, lover, or sweetheart SWAIN

sulfur - old term for sulfur BRIMSTONE

sulfur (combining form) THION-

sulfuric acid VITRIOL

sulky expression POUT, MOUE

sultan's palace SERAGLIO
- wives, concubines, and female servants in a sultan's household HAREM

sum of many parts, whole, sum total AGGREGATE
- tiny, token, insignificant, as a sum of money might be NOMINAL

summary, list of main points, brief statement or outline of a subject ABSTRACT, APERÇU, EPITOME, SYNOPSIS
- summary, shortened or condensed version, as of a book DIGEST, ABRIDGMENT, COMPENDIUM, CONDENSATION
- summary at the beginning of a speech, book, or the like, listing the main points CONSPECTUS, SYNOPSIS, OUTLINE
- summary at the end of a speech, book, or the like, repeating the main points RECAPITULATION, RÉSUMÉ, SUMMATION, WRAP-UP
- summary of the contents of an academic course SYLLABUS
- summary or skeleton account of the plot of a dramatic or literary work SCENARIO
- summary that is very short but captures the main points ENCAPSULATION, OVERVIEW, PARAPHRASE, PRÉCIS
- summarized account of one's education, work experience, and the like, as for a prospective employer CURRICULUM VITAE, C.V., VITA, RÉSUMÉ
- summarized biography, a brief account of someone's life and

character PROFILE, POTTED BIO
- summarized record of the proceedings of a law court DOCKET
- summarized statement, as of the terms of an agreement, used in drafting a formal document AIDE-MÉMOIRE
- diagrammatic summary or outline SCHEMA
- formal summary of a proposed commercial, literary, or other venture PROSPECTUS

summer days from mid-July to September DOG DAYS
- summerhouse or garden pavilion, usually having a fine view GAZEBO, BELVEDERE
- sleep or remain in a dormant state throughout the summer, as some animals do ESTIVATE
- period of summery weather when summer is over INDIAN SUMMER

summon an assembly, call a meeting, or the like CONVOKE, CONVENE
- summon up a spirit by means of spells or incantations CONJURE, INVOKE
- summoning of a prisoner or accused before a court of law ARRAIGNMENT

summons to appear in court CITATION, SUBPOENA
- urgent, demanding, as a summons might be PEREMPTORY, IMPERIOUS

sun personified SOL
- adjective for the sun SOLAR
- brief flaming eruption of radiation from the sun FLARE
- bright surface layer of gases on the sun or other star PHOTOSPHERE
- flower or plant that turns toward the sun HELIOTROPE, TURNSOLE
- highest point of the sun ZENITH
- huge column of burning gas rising from the surface of the sun, as is visible during a total eclipse PROMINENCE, PROTUBERANCE
- layer of hydrogen and other gases, thousands of miles thick, around the sun or a star CHROMOSPHERE
- layer of ionized gases outside the sun's chromosphere, visible as a halo during an eclipse CORONA
- point farthest from the sun in the orbit of a planet or comet around the sun APHELION
- point nearest to the sun in the orbit of a planet or comet around the sun PERIHELION
- ring of light around the sun or moon, as when viewed through mist AUREOLE

sun (combining form) HELI-, HELIO-, SOL-

sunburn - skin condition induced by sunburn MELANOSIS

Sundays - any of the letters A to G applied to the Sundays in a given year to determine the church calendar DOMINICAL LETTER

sundial arm or similar object that casts a shadow to indicate the time GNOMON, STYLE

sunflower or related plant HELIANTHUS

sunglasses - darkening or changing color when exposed to light, as some sunglasses are PHOTOCHROMIC
- glare-reducing plastic, as used in some sunglasses POLAROID

sun-room, as for therapy SOLARIUM

sunshade shield fitted at the top of a car's windshield VISOR

sunspot MACULA
- darkest central area of a sunspot UMBRA
- lighter outer area of a sunspot PENUMBRA

sunstroke INSOLATION

superficial, routine, indifferent, as a quick inspection might be PERFUNCTORY, CURSORY
- superficial effort or merely symbolic gesture toward a goal or legal requirement TOKENISM
- superficially impressive or deceptively attractive outward appearance VENEER, GLOSS
- superficially or vulgarly attractive MERETRICIOUS
- person whose interest in the arts, antiques, or the like is an amateurish or superficial one DABBLER, DILETTANTE

superfluous See **excessive**

superhighway in a French-speaking country AUTOROUTE
- superhighway in a German-speaking country AUTOBAHN
- superhighway in Italy AUTOSTRADA

superhuman, "overman," "superman," the ideal superior human of the future, in Nietzsche's terminology ÜBERMENSCH

superior See **excellent, perfect**
- superior, outstanding, excelling others PREEMINENT, TRANSCENDENT
- superior in status, rank, or value SUPERORDINATE
- superior position or condition giving one an advantage over an opponent VANTAGE POINT

superiority, as of power, number, or weight PREPONDERANCE
- superiority, power, clear advantage ASCENDANCY, DOMINANCE

supernatural See also **spirit**
- supernatural force in an object or person, in South Pacific religions MANA
- supernatural or magical arts and alleged happenings THE OCCULT
- supernatural or psychic, beyond normal experience or scientific laws PARANORMAL
- supernatural power believed to reside on a magical object CHARM, FETISH, JUJU
- alleged perception by means of a sixth sense, supernatural powers, intuition, or the like EXTRASENSORY PERCEPTION, ESP, CLAIRVOYANCE, CRYPTESTHESIA
- allegedly having supernatural powers, or being in touch with the supernatural PSYCHIC, VISIONARY, CLAIRVOYANT, FEY
- appearance or manifestation of a god or supernatural force EPIPHANY, THEOPHANY, REVELATION, VISITATION
- relating to irrational, mystical, or supernatural experience TRANSCENDENTAL
- study of alleged telepathy and other supernatural phenomena PARAPSYCHOLOGY

superstition - object invested with superstition and used, carried, or worn for its magical powers CHARM, FETISH, JUJU, AMULET, RELIC
- plant, animal, or object invested with superstition in some societies, involved in various rituals and functioning as a symbol of a particular tribe, clan, or family TOTEM

supervisor of slaves or workers OVERSEER

supple, agile, loose-limbed, and nimble LITHE, LIMBER, LISSOM

supply See also **give**
- supply or provide FURNISH, PURVEY
- supply or source, as of raw materials LODE
- supply or store accumulated for future use STOCKPILE
- supply ship, provisioning vessel VICTUALLER, SUTLER
- supply that seems to be endless CORNUCOPIA
- add new stocks or supplies, as in refilling a refrigerator REPLENISH

support See also **strengthen**
- support, approve, or encourage COUNTENANCE, ENDORSE, SANCTION
- support, as for scaffolding or a table top, consisting of a horizontal bar on two pairs of splayed legs TRESTLE
- support, especially financial assistance SUBVENTION, SUBSIDY
- support, preach, or promote a new cause enthusiastically PROSELYTIZE
- support, propose, or recommend ADVOCATE, COMMEND, PROPOUND
- support, protection, sponsorship PATRONAGE, AEGIS, AUSPICES
- support, prove, back up, or confirm by convincing evidence

Submarine

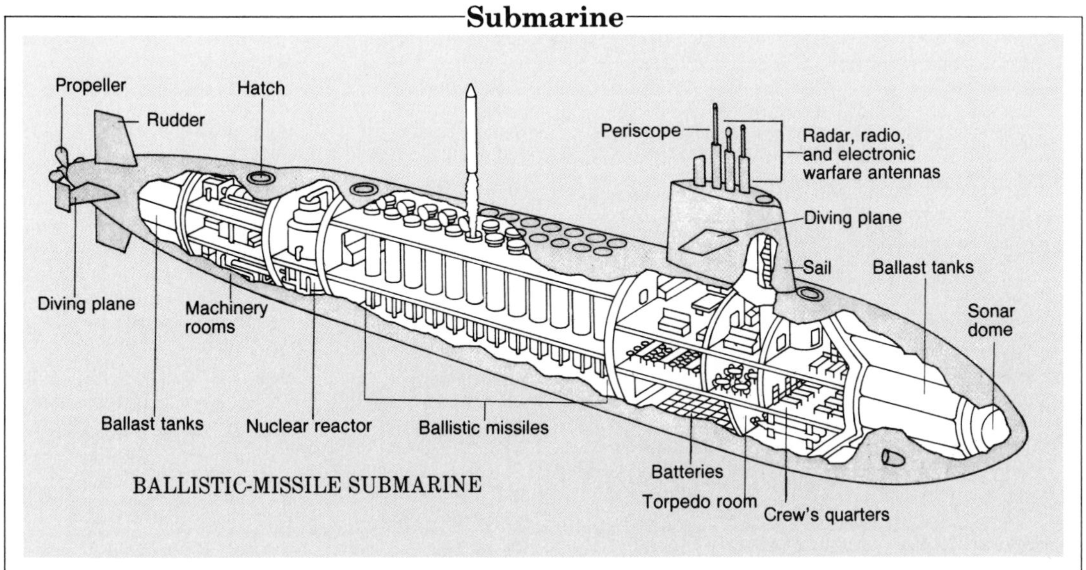

BALLISTIC-MISSILE SUBMARINE

VERIFY, SUBSTANTIATE, CORROBORATE, VOUCH FOR
- support, unity, and fellow feeling in a group, especially in the face of opposition SOLIDARITY
- support against danger, attack, or impact BOLSTER, BUTTRESS, BRACE, REINFORCE
- support at or for the back of something BACKSTAY
- support from below, hold up, keep from falling or sinking SUSTAIN, UNDERGIRD, UNDERPIN
- support or adopt a cause, faith, or ideal ESPOUSE, CHAMPION, ADVANCE
- support or base, as for a statue or column PEDESTAL, PLINTH
- support or principal sponsor of something or someone MAINSTAY
- support or stand having one leg, as for a camera MONOPOD
- support or stand having three legs, as for a camera TRIPOD
- support with money, finance SUBSIDIZE, PATRONIZE, SPONSOR
- supporting, as evidence might be CORROBORATIVE, COLLATERAL
- supporting beam in a building, placed horizontally, as between floors STRINGER, SUMMER
- supporting beam or bracket, as for a balcony CANTILEVER
- supporting framework of beams, struts, or the like for a bridge or roof TRUSS
- supporting or helping AUXILIARY, ANCILLARY
- supporting or stabilizing structure attached by spars, as to a boat, helicopter, vehicle, or building OUTRIGGER
- supporting structure or pillar, as for an arch or bridge PIER
- athletic supporter JOCKSTRAP
- heavy beam driven vertically into the ground as a foundation or support for a building PILE
- hinge or support on which a lever turns PIVOT, FULCRUM
- legally enforced financial support provided by a person to his or her ex-spouse ALIMONY, MAINTENANCE
- obtain or seek support, as for an election campaign RECRUIT, CANVASS, SOLICIT
- person who relies on someone else for financial support DEPENDENT
- stone or brick structure built for support against a wall, or anything that supports or sustains BUTTRESS
- surgical support, belt worn to keep a hernia from protruding TRUSS
- upright pole used as a support STANCHION

supporter, as of a political party, who is reliable and hardworking STALWART
- supporter, follower, or champion, as of a cause or theory EXPONENT, ADHERENT, PROPONENT
- supporter, person who argues in defense or justification of a cause or another person ADVOCATE, APOLOGIST
- supporter of the aims and ideals of a political or other group, without being a member of it FELLOW TRAVELER, CAMP FOLLOWER
- supporter or helper in some dubious or criminal activity ACCOMPLICE, ACCESSORY, CONFEDERATE
- supporter or promoter, especially one that finances a project, athlete, cultural activity, or the like SPONSOR, PATRON, ANGEL
- supporter or trusted follower, often willing to do the dirty work HENCHMAN, MYRMIDON
- supporters of a person or organization whose wishes have to be taken into account CONSTITUENCY
- early supporter of a new religion or cause, disciple APOSTLE
- enthusiastic supporter, fan, or follower, as of a particular sport DEVOTEE, AFICIONADO
- enthusiastic supporter of a political party or a cause PARTISAN, TRUE BELIEVER
- enthusiastic supporter of a religion, leader, or doctrine VOTARY

supporting (combining form) PRO-

supposed, assumed, merely conjectural or theoretical HYPOTHETICAL, SUPPOSITITIOUS
- supposed, unproved and often doubtful ALLEGED
- reputed or commonly considered, as a child's supposed father might be PUTATIVE

suppository - medicated vaginal suppository PESSARY

suppress comments, argument, or the like MUZZLE, GAG, STIFLE
- suppress something forcibly, such as a riot QUELL, QUASH

sure See **certain, confident**

surface appearance, gloss, or luster, especially one acquired by age or association PATINA, BURNISH
- surface curve of a liquid in a tube or container MENISCUS
- surface features, feel, or appear-

SURGICAL OPERATIONS

amniocentesis	piercing, through the abdominal wall, of the membrane surrounding a fetus, in order to withdraw a sample of fluid for testing for such defects as Down's syndrome and spina bifida, and to learn the gender of the baby
apicectomy	removal of part of the root of a tooth
appendectomy/ appendicectomy	removal of the appendix
arterioplasty	reconstruction of an artery
autograft/ autoplasty	replacement or repair of damaged tissue with sound tissue taken from the same person
cesarean section	delivering of a baby through an incision in the abdominal wall
cholecystectomy	removal of the gallbladder
cholelithotomy	removal of gallstones
colostomy	creation of an artifical anus in the abdominal wall when the natural passage is blocked permanently or cancerous
cordotomy	severing of nerve fibers in the neck to relieve chronic pain
craniotomy	removal of part of the skull
cryosurgery	freezing of small areas to destroy damaged or unwanted tissue, such as cataracts
cystectomy	removal of the bladder
D & C/dilatation and curettage	expansion of the neck of the womb and scraping away of its lining
debridement	removal of dead tissue and foreign matter from a wound
episiotomy	incision into the tissues between vagina and anus to ease delivery of a baby
fenestration	creation of a new opening in the labyrinth of the inner ear, to relieve deafness
gastrectomy	removal of all or part of the stomach
goniopuncture	draining of fluid from the eye, as a treatment for glaucoma
hepatectomy	removal of all or part of the liver
homograft/ allograft/ homoplasty	replacement or repair of damaged tissue or organs with tissue or organs taken from another person
hysterectomy	removal of the womb
ileostomy	formation in the abdominal wall of an opening for the ileum, to drain the intestine
iridectomy	removal of part of the iris of the eye, usually to create an artificial pupil
labioplasty	repair or reconstruction of damaged or deformed lips
laparotomy	incision into the abdominal cavity, usually as part of an exploratory operation
laryngectomy	removal of the larynx
lobotomy/ leukotomy	cutting of nerve fibers in the brain to relieve emotional disorders
lithonephrotomy/ nephrolithotomy	removal of a kidney stone
mastectomy	removal of a breast
necrotomy	removal of dead tissue, such as a dead piece of bone
nephrectomy	removal of a kidney
neurotomy	severing of a nerve
oophorectomy/ ovariectomy	removal of an ovary
orchidectomy orchiectomy/ testectomy	removal of a testicle
ostectomy	removal of a piece of bone
otoplasty	repair or reconstruction of the ears
phlebotomy/ venesection	opening or piercing of a vein
pneumonectomy	removal of all or part of a lung
rhinoplasty	reconstruction of the nose
rhizotomy	cutting of nerve roots where they leave the spinal cord, to relieve chronic pain
salpingectomy	removal or severing of a fallopian tube, usually for sterilization
thoracotomy	opening of the chest cavity
tracheostomy/ tracheotomy	cutting into and opening of the windpipe, as to assist breathing
vasectomy	cutting of a sperm-carrying duct, usually for sterilization

ance, as of a fabric or painting TEXTURE
- surface forming the boundary between liquids INTERFACE
- surface layer or finishing, as of fine wood VENEER
- surface of the body or a body part PERIPHERY
- grainy or crinkled surface, as on leather or paper PEBBLE
- having a dull, unglossy finish, as a painted surface might MAT, MATT
- on or near the surface, as a wound might be SUPERFICIAL
- process by which a thin film of substance accumulates on the surface of a solid ADSORPTION
- smooth surface on a bone or tooth FACET

surgical See chart, and also **medical**
- surgical cut INCISION
- surgical cutting or separating of tissue SECTION
- surgical removal of an organ or other body part EXCISION, ABLATION, AMPUTATION, EXTIRPATION
- surgical replacement of a limb, tooth, eye, or the like, or the artificial device used PROSTHESIS
- surgical rod, long and flexible, as for removing obstructions from the throat PROBANG
- surgical scraping or scooping instrument, as for removing dead tissue from the uterus CURETTE
- surgical stitching together of the edges of a wound SUTURE
- surgical thread, as used to close a blood vessel LIGATURE
- surgery for bone and joint disorders ORTHOPEDIC SURGERY
- surgery, such as a facelift, designed to improve one's physical appearance COSMETIC SURGERY
- surgery in which unwanted tissue is destroyed by sudden freezing CRYOSURGERY
- surgical transplant of animal tissue to humans ZOOPLASTY

surgical cut (combining form) -TOM-, -TOME, -TOMY, -OTOMY

surgical opening (combining form) -STOMY

surgical removal (combining form) -ECTOMY

surname, family name COGNOMEN

surplus See **excessive**

surprise See also **sudden**
- surprise, astonish, amaze ASTOUND, STAGGER
- surprise, bewilder, throw into confusion CONFOUND, BAFFLE, PERPLEX
- surprise, take aback, disturb the composure or calm of DISCONCERT, PERTURB, RUFFLE
- surprise, thrill, and startle, make people sit up and take notice ELECTRIFY, RIVET
- surprise attack on an enemy COUP DE MAIN
- surprise find, or bright new idea TROUVAILLE
- surprised and disbelieving, taken aback INCREDULOUS
- surprised and horrified, shocked, appalled AGHAST
- surprised and worried RATTLED, UNNERVED, FLUSTERED
- surprising and artificial development or device introduced to resolve a tricky situation or plot DEUS EX MACHINA
- by surprise, as when caught committing an offense RED-HANDED, IN FLAGRANTE DELICTO
- left speechless with surprise DUMBFOUNDED, NONPLUSSED
- show a feeling, especially surprise, clearly EVINCE
- sudden and shocking surprise, piece of unexpected bad news BOMBSHELL, BOLT FROM THE BLUE, THUNDERCLAP, COUP DE FOUDRE
- take by surprise, ambush WAYLAY
- taken by surprise, confronted unexpectedly CAUGHT UNAWARES, CAUGHT NAPPING
- utterly surprised, stunned FLABBERGASTED, STUPEFIED, THUNDERSTRUCK
- wide-eyed or open-mouthed with surprise AGAPE, BOUCHE BÉE

surrender See also **give up**
- surrender, accept or assent meekly ACQUIESCE, KOWTOW
- surrender, or admit CONCEDE
- surrender or give in, yield on agreed terms CAPITULATE
- surrender or giving up of something, as of land, territory, or rights CESSION
- surrender or hand over formally rights, territory, or the like CEDE
- surrender or voluntary relinquishing of a claim, privilege, or right WAIVER
- surrender to a superior force, temptation, or the like SUCCUMB
- surrender to another's authority, yield, bend the knee SUBMIT
- complete, absolute, unlimited, as the surrender of a warring nation might be UNCONDITIONAL

surround, encircle, hem in CINCTURE, COMPASS, ENVIRON
- surround completely, enfold, or swallow up ENGULF, ENVELOP
- surround or enclose protectively EMBOSOM, EMBOWER
- surround or include within its scope, take in COMPRISE, EMBRACE, ENCOMPASS
- surround with troops, besiege, lay siege to BELEAGUER
- surrounded, as an island is by water GIRDED

surrounding See also **boundary**
- surrounding, in the immediate vicinity, as the air is AMBIENT
- surrounding area, neighborhood ENVIRONS, VICINITY, PRECINCTS, PURLIEUS
- surrounding area, scope, sphere of operation or influence AMBIT, COMPASS, MILIEU, ORBIT
- surrounding band, as around the base of a tooth CINGULUM
- adjust or grow accustomed to new surroundings ACCLIMATIZE

surrounding (combining form) AMPH-, AMPHI-, PERI-, CIRCUM-

survey or inspect a stretch of land, an enemy's positions, or the like RECONNOITER, RECCE
- survey or view that is wide-ranging PANORAMA

surveyor's instrument, essentially a small moving telescope, for measuring horizontal and vertical angles THEODOLITE
- surveyor's instrument, essentially a telescope and spirit level, for measuring relative heights LEVEL
- surveyor's mark on a known object, used as a reference point for other measurements BENCH MARK
- surveyor's theodolite adapted to measure distances rapidly or directly TACHEOMETER, TACHYMETER
- electronic device used by surveyors for measuring fairly large distances by timing radio waves transmitted between the two points TELLUROMETER
- horizontal angle of a bearing in surveying, measured clockwise from a standard direction, especially north AZIMUTH
- moving marker on a surveyor's leveling rod VANE, TARGET
- striped pole used as a marker in surveying RANGE POLE

survive a crisis, danger, or the like WEATHER
- survive or continue in existence SUBSIST
- survival of the fittest NATURAL SELECTION

surviving, left over, remaining, continuing RESIDUAL, VESTIGIAL
- surviving, still in existence, not lost or extinct EXTANT
- surviving species from an earlier age RELICT
- capable of living or surviving independently VIABLE
- object surviving from a bygone civilization RELIC

suspend or refrain from enforcing a rule, penalty, or the like WAIVE
- suspend or transfer proceedings

ADJOURN

suspense - episode of a series, as on television, that ends in suspense CLIFFHANGER
- nervous, anxious, tense, in suspense ON TENTERHOOKS

suspension of an operation or activity for a time ABEYANCE
- suspension or delay, as of payments MORATORIUM
- suspension spring, as on a truck's back axle, consisting of a set of layered metal strips LEAF SPRING
- suspension that is based on fluid-filled cylinders rather than springs HYDRAULIC SUSPENSION
- suspension of very fine particles in a fluid medium, as in mist or paint COLLOID
- suspension of small globules of one liquid within another, as in homogenized milk EMULSION
- pharmacological term for a paste or suspension of solid particles in a liquid MAGMA
- scattering of particles, as in a colloid or suspension DISPERSION

suspicion - calm or dispel someone's suspicions LULL, ALLAY
- clear of blame or suspicion VINDICATE
- lay to rest the suspicion or hostility of, win round DISARM

suspicious, doubtful EQUIVOCAL
- suspicious, doubting, unwilling to trust or believe SKEPTICAL
- suspicious, wary, distrustful LEERY, CHARY
- suspicious or scared to an unreasonable degree PARANOID
- suspiciously or disapprovingly, the way one might look at a person or suggestion ASKANCE
- referring to behavior that is suspicious, stealthy, or secretive FURTIVE
- steal about, move in a suspicious way SKULK, SLINK, SIDLE, PROWL, LURK

swagger, bluster, or brag ROISTER
- swagger, boasting BRAGGADOCIO
- swagger, walk in a pompously affected way STRUT
- swaggering swordsman or adventurer SWASHBUCKLER

swallow or drink eagerly, gulp SWIG, SWILL
- swallow or take in food as if by swallowing INGEST
- swallowing or act of drinking, or the amount taken in DRAFT
- act of swallowing DEGLUTITION
- adjective for a swallow or related bird HIRUNDINE
- difficulty in swallowing, or refusal or inability to swallow APHAGIA
- inflammation of the tonsils or throat that makes swallowing difficult QUINSY

Swords

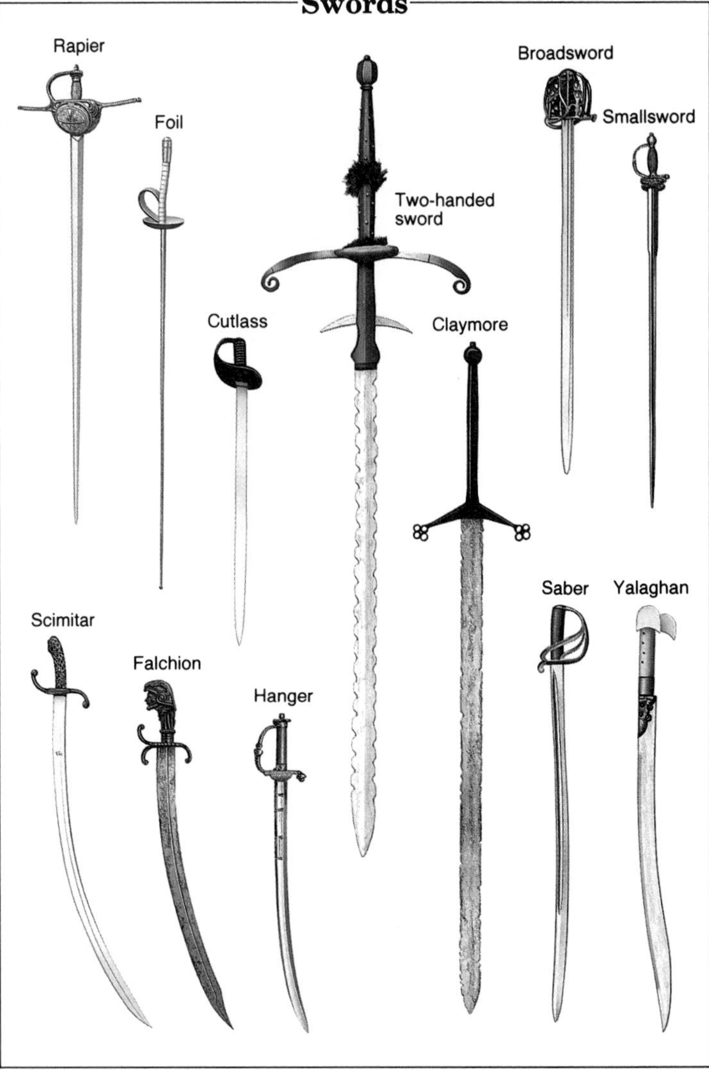

swamp, bog, or marsh SLOUGH, MIRE, QUAGMIRE
- swamp atmosphere MIASMA
- swamp gas METHANE
- swampy grassland area, especially Florida EVERGLADES
- swampy hollow, often filled with decaying plant matter, especiallly in the far north of Canada MUSKEG
- swampy stretch of land WASH, FEN, MORASS, SWALE
- swampy stretch of land or shallow lake in South Africa VLEI
- swampy tributary or sluggish backwater, especially in Louisiana BAYOU
- adjective for a swamp or marsh PALUDAL, PALUDINAL, PALUDIOUS, PALUDINE
- earliest, first, or original, as an ancient swamp might be PRIMEVAL
- light hovering over swampy ground, probably produced by flaming methane gas WILL-O'-THE-WISP, IGNIS FATUUS, JACK-O'-LANTERN, FRIAR'S LANTERN
- smelly and invisible vapor or gas, as rising from a swamp or rubbish heap EFFLUVIUM
- tree or shrub with aerial roots, flourishing in tropical coastal swamps MANGROVE

swan - female swan PEN
- male swan COB
- young swan CYGNET

swarm, as vermin might in a garden or on an animal INFEST
- swarm or teem, as if with ants FORMICATE
- swarming, abounding, full TEEMING, THRONGING

sway, swing from side to side FLUCTUATE, OSCILLATE, VACILLATE
- swaying, rippling, or other wavelike movement UNDULATION

swearword or profanity used as an exclamation EXPLETIVE
- swearword or term of abuse EPITHET
- swearword or vulgar language PROFANITY

sweat, especially when abundant or excessive DIAPHORESIS, HIDROSIS
- sweat gland ECCRINE GLAND
- sweat-inducing or -increasing SUDORIFIC, DIAPHORETIC
- spray, liquid, or other substance used to mask smells such as those of sweat or cooking DEODORANT

sweater See **clothes**

Swedish-style buffet meal SMORGASBORD

sweet, creamy paste used in candies and icings FONDANT
- sweet delicacy or crushed sesame seeds with honey HALVAH
- sweet delicacy or icing of ground almonds and sugar MARZIPAN
- sweet liquid in flowers, gathered by bees for making honey NECTAR
- sweet or rich to an excessive degree CLOYING, SACCHARINE
- sweet-voiced MELLIFLUOUS
- pastille that is sucked to sweeten the breath CACHOU
- rich, round sweet ball made of chocolate, egg, butter, and sometimes liqueur TRUFFLE

sweet corn INDIAN CORN, MAIZE

sweet pepper, red pepper PIMIENTO

sweetener - sugar substitute, artificial sweetener SACCHARIN, CYCLAMATE

sweetheart See **lover**

swell See also **increase**
- swell, bulge BILGE
- swell or expand by pressure from inside DISTEND, DILATE
- swell out, as sails might BILLOW
- swelling, becoming swollen or bloated TUMESCENT
- swelling, knob, knotty projection, or small growth NODE, NODULE, TUBERCLE
- swelling and inflammation of a lymph gland, especially in the armpit or groin BUBO
- swelling caused by a buildup of fluid in the tissues EDEMA
- swelling of the head, caused by a buildup of cerebrospinal fluid HYDROCEPHALUS
- swelling on a horse's back, typically causing stiffness SPAVIN
- swelling or bulging out TUMID, TURGID
- swelling or outgrowth of an organ or other body part APOPHYSIS
- swelling outward, bulging, as eyes might be PROTUBERANT
- subsidence of a swelling or swollen organ DETUMESCENCE

swerve or deviate from a path SHEER, VEER

swimming or floating NATANT
- art or action of swimming NATATION
- dancelike swimming to music, often for pairs of swimmers SYNCHRONIZED SWIMMING
- relating to or adapted for swimming NATATORIAL
- woman's topless swimming costume MONOKINI

swindle, fraudulent act or business scheme SCAM
- swindle in the form of taking for oneself money or property entrusted to one EMBEZZLEMENT, DEFALCATION, PECULATION

swing from branch to branch, as some apes and monkeys do BRACHIATE
- swing from side to side, sway FLUCTUATE, OSCILLATE, VACILLATE
- swinging, hanging loosely PENDULOUS

Swiss HELVETIAN
- Swiss breakfast food of cereals, nuts, raisins, and the like MUESLI
- Swiss state or a similar small regional unit CANTON
- sing in a voice wavering between normal and falsetto, as among Swiss, Austrian, or Bavarian folksingers YODEL

switch - switching, usually unintended, of the initial sounds of two or more words, as when one accidentally pronounces *a crushing blow* as *a blushing crow* SPOONERISM
- switching device in an electric circuit RELAY
- activate a mechanism by releasing a catch, trigger, or switch TRIP
- electrical coil producing a magnetic field, as used for activating switches SOLENOID

swollen, as a body part might be TUMESCENT, TUMID
- swollen, as through overeating or filling with water BLOATED, DISTENDED
- swollen area in an ulcer or around a wound that is healing PROUD FLESH, GRANULATION TISSUE
- swollen or bulging TURGID
- swollen or puffy condition, or the process leading to it TUMEFACTION

swoop down, as a bird of prey does on its victim STOOP

sword See illustration, and also **fencing**
- sword handle, hilt HAFT
- sword-shaped, long and narrow and pointed, as a leaf might be ENSIFORM, GLADIATE, XIPHOID
- sword thrust or lunge FOIN
- belt or sash crossing the chest from the shoulder, used for carrying a sword or bugle BALDRIC
- broad sword with only one cutting edge BACKSWORD
- carry a sword diagonally across the body PORT
- combatant with a sword in an arena in ancient Rome GLADIATOR
- former term for a sword of various kinds BRAND, BILBO, GLAIVE
- knob on a sword hilt POMMEL
- Malay sword or dagger with a wavy double-edged blade KRIS
- pierce or stab lightly, as with a sword PINK
- stick used instead of a sword in fencing SINGLESTICK
- stronger section of a sword blade, near the hilt FORTE
- weaker section of a sword blade, from the middle to the tip FOIBLE

sword (combining form) XIPH-, XIPHI-

sworn statement made in writing before a notary public or similar officer AFFIDAVIT
- sworn statement of a witness absent from court DEPOSITION

syllable - alphabetlike system of writing in which each symbol represents a whole syllable, as in Sinhalese SYLLABARY
- contraction of two syllables into one by fusing two adjacent vowel sounds SYNERESIS, SYNECPHONESIS, SYNIZESIS
- omission of an unstressed vowel or syllable, as in verse ELISION
- second-last syllable in a word PENULT
- stressed, carrying the principal accent in a word, as a syllable might be TONIC, NUCLEAR

syllogism See **logic**

symbol See also **punctuation, letter, mathematics, Greek**
- symbol, emblem, or trademark of a company LOGO, LOGOTYPE
- symbol, number, or letter, often of miniature size, written just above the level of another as in xy^2 SUPERSCRIPT
- symbol, number, or letter, often of miniature size, written just below the level of another as in H_2O SUBSCRIPT
- symbol, sign, or letter representing an entire word or phrase such as # for *number* LOGOGRAM, LOGOGRAPH
- symbol, picture, or object representing an abstract idea EMBLEM
- symbol or character in a writing

system, such as Chinese, that represents a thing or idea rather than the sound IDEOGRAM
- symbol or design, as on a flag or embroidery DEVICE
- symbol or image ICON
- symbol or kinship emblem, often a plant or animal, of a tribe, clan, or family TOTEM
- symbol or motif, as in literature, that keeps recurring ARCHETYPE
- symbol or pictorial character used in ancient Egyptian writing HIEROGLYPH
- symbol or sign, or its intended meaning or reference DENOTATION
- symbol that is nonverbal, as on a road sign GLYPH
- symbols, figures, or the like used systematically, as in music or mathematics, to represent elements or quantities NOTATION
- symbols and metaphors, as in poetry IMAGERY
- alphabet in which each symbol represents a whole syllable, as in Sinhalese SYLLABARY
- feminist or lesbian symbol of strength or solidarity, in the form of a double-headed ax LABYRIS
- printing symbol, †, as for indicating footnotes DAGGER, OBELISK
- printing symbol, ‡, as for indicating footnotes DOUBLE DAGGER, DIESIS
- printing symbol, *, as for indicating footnotes ASTERISK
- printing symbol, &, representing the word *and* AMPERSAND
- printing symbol, ☞, used to alert the reader to the passage following FIST, HAND, INDEX
- printing symbol of three stars, ⁂ or ⁂, used to alert the reader to the passage following ASTERISM
- printing symbol, §, used to indicate a footnote or mark off a section SECTION MARK
- proofreading symbol, resembling an inverted *V* or *Y*, indicating the position for an insert in a text CARET
- publisher's symbol or emblem on a book COLOPHON
- puzzle in the form of pictures or symbols representing syllables or words, such as *PRE4SS*, meaning *foreign press*, or *13579 VS. U*, meaning *the odds are against you* REBUS
- referring to meaning, as of words, gestures, or symbols SEMANTIC
- science or study of signs and symbols SEMIOTICS

symbolic, emblematic FIGURATIVE
- symbolic clothes, decorations, or characteristics, as of power or an official post TRAPPINGS, REGALIA
- symbolic story or picture in which the characters or scenes symbolize ideas and illustrate a deeper meaning ALLEGORY
- merely symbolic and superficial effort or gesture toward compliance with a law or social requirement TOKENISM

symbolize, be a typical example of EMBODY, TYPIFY
- symbolize or represent an idea as something concrete or human PERSONIFY, HYPOSTATIZE, REIFY

symmetry in a plant, animal, or organ, such that the two halves are mirror images of each other, though only when cut along one plane BILATERAL SYMMETRY
- symmetry in a plant, animal, or organ, such that the two halves are mirror images of each other when cut along any of two or more planes RADIAL SYMMETRY

sympathetic See also **kind**
- sympathetic, thinking along similar lines, sharing attitudes ATTUNED, ON THE SAME WAVELENGTH
- sympathetic relationship of mutual trust and emotional understanding RAPPORT

sympathize with, pity, feel sorry for COMMISERATE, CONDOLE
- sympathizer or comforter who causes only distress JOB'S COMFORTER

sympathy, pity, mercy COMPASSION
- sympathy and understanding so deep that one seems to share the other person's feelings EMPATHY, FELLOW FEELING
- sympathy for someone in distress or mourning COMMISERATION, CONDOLENCE
- arousing pity or sympathy PATHETIC

symptoms or signs of a nonpresent disease in a hysterical patient MIMESIS
- symptoms or signs jointly indicating or characterizing a disease, abnormality, or the like SYNDROME
- outward symptoms, symptoms that can be observed SIGNS, OBJECTIVE SYMPTOMS
- referring to the early stage of an infection or disease, before the symptoms or signs appear SUBCLINICAL
- study of disease symptoms or signs SYMPTOMATOLOGY, SEMIOTICS, SEMEIOTICS

synagogue sexton BEADLE, SHAMMES

synod delegate who represents the clergy in the Church of England PROCTOR
- presiding officer of a synod MODERATOR

synonym - word-finder book, classifying synonyms systematically or listing them alphabetically THESAURUS

syphilis LUES, SAINT JOB'S DISEASE, SAINT SEMENT'S DISEASE, MORBUS GALLICUS, POX, GREAT POX, FRANGHI, VÉROLE, MALUM VENEREUM, THE GREAT IMITATOR, TREPONEMIASIS
- adjective for syphilis LUETIC, SYPHILITIC
- hard, red, knotty growth or sore that is an early indication of syphilis CHANCRE

syringe or needle for injections beneath the skin HYPODERMIC
- syringe or similar instrument for directing a stream of air or water at or into a part of the body for cleansing or healing DOUCHE

syrup from sugar MOLASSES, TREACLE
- syrupy drink to which medicine can be added JULEP
- syrupy medicine for coughs and sore throats LINCTUS
- medicinal paste formed by mixing the drug with honey or syrup ELECTUARY

system, structure, organization, or the like that is elaborate and complex EDIFICE
- system of channels transporting watery body fluid between the tissues and the blood system or organs LYMPHATIC SYSTEM
- system of exercise, therapy, diet, or the like REGIMEN
- system or framework of scientific theories and concepts at any time, within which a scientist works PARADIGM
- systematic, structured, classified, as a body of knowledge might be ARCHITECTONIC
- medieval social system in Europe, in which vassals exchanged homage and service for land and protection from a lord FEUDALISM, FEUDAL SYSTEM
- political and economic system in Europe after the feudal system, based on increased trade MERCANTILISM, MERCANTILE SYSTEM
- running down of the energy in the universe or any other closed system ENTROPY

system (combining form) -NOMY

T

table See also **furniture**
- table consisting of a board or boards on top of hurdlelike supports TRESTLE TABLE
- table in church for the Communion bread and wine CREDENCE TABLE
- table leg, stair post, or the like, typically turned and decorated SPINDLE
- table of numbers for calculating discounts, interest, and the like READY RECKONER
- table of the chemical elements arranged according to their atomic properties and structures PERIODIC TABLE
- table with hinged leaves supported by movable pairs of legs GATELEG TABLE
- arranged in both rows and columns TABULAR
- hinged flap that can be raised and supported to increase the size of the table DROP LEAF
- panel that can be inserted in a table to increase the surface LEAF
- set of objects, such as small tables, designed for stacking one inside the other NEST

table wine VIN DE TABLE, TAFELWEIN

tablet of a medicated preparation for chewing or sucking LOZENGE, PASTILLE, TROCHE

tact, knowledge of appropriate behavior, especially in various social situations SAVOIR FAIRE

tactful, sensitive to the situation POLITIC, DIPLOMATIC, JUDICIOUS
- tactful in a quiet, wise, practical way PRUDENT, DISCREET

tactic or trick, as in a game, to secure an advantage STRATAGEM, PLOY, GAMBIT

tadpole POLLIWOG

tail, short and often erect, of a rabbit, hare, or deer SCUT
- tail assembly of an airplane EMPENNAGE
- tail of a fox BRUSH, BUSH
- tail with a distinctive shape or marking, as on a deer and certain dogs FLAG
- adapted for grasping, as a monkey's tail is PREHENSILE
- bony part or the solid part of an animal's tail DOCK
- bushy tip of the tail of a cow or other animal SWITCH
- having a tail CAUDATE
- relating to the tail, posterior, or hind parts of the body CAUDAL

tail (combining form) CAUD-, -UR-, URO-, -UROUS

tailor's adjustable pattern, for cutting different sizes DELINEATOR
- made-to-order, as clothes made by a tailor might be, or dealing in such items BESPOKE
- relating to a tailor SARTORIAL

tails, back of a coin or medal VERSO, REVERSE

take apart DISASSEMBLE, DISMANTLE, DISMEMBER, DISMOUNT
- take away from, cause to seem inferior DEROGATE, DETRACT, BELITTLE
- take away someone's property, by an official decree CONFISCATE, SEQUESTRATE, SEIZE
- take back, often publicly, a belief, accusation, or claim RECANT, RETRACT, DISAVOW, REVOKE
- take for oneself, typically without the owner's permission APPROPRIATE, ARROGATE
- take off one's hat or clothes DOFF
- take turns, alternate, proceed in a given order or sequence ROTATE

take advantage of, use selfishly and unjustly EXPLOIT
- person who takes advantage, often unfairly, of an opportunity OPPORTUNIST

take-off of a person, especially a celebrity IMPERSONATION, MIMICRY

talent, natural gift, speciality, strong point MÉTIER, FORTE
- talent, skill, knack, or fluency derived from practice or familiarity FACILITY, FLAIR
- talent or ability resulting from a special interest or leaning BENT, PENCHANT
- talented or skilled in a wide variety of ways VERSATILE
- inborn talent, quality, or gift ENDOWMENT, APTITUDE, ATTRIBUTE
- person with exceptional powers or talents PRODIGY

talk See **conversation, speak, speech, say, state**

talkative, extravagant in speech, compliments, and endearments GUSHY, EFFUSIVE, PROFUSE
- talkative, glib-tongued, willing to speak at length EXPANSIVE, LOQUACIOUS, VOLUBLE
- talkative, long-winded, and disorganized in speech or in writing DIFFUSE, MAUNDERING, PROLIX, RAMBLING
- talkative, open, responsive COMMUNICATIVE, FORTHCOMING
- talkative, wordy, windy, speaking more than is necessary VERBOSE, GARRULOUS
- talkative, scatterbrained, silly person FLIBBERTIGIBBET
- talkative person, liable to blurt out secrets BLABBERMOUTH
- person who is talkative, boastful, and vain, windbag POPINJAY

tall See also **high**
- tall and thin, and usually clumsy or ungainly LANKY, GANGLING
- tall and well-built, sturdy STRAPPING

tame, train, or breed animals to live with and be of use to humans DOMESTICATE

tan hides, as with alum or salt, especially to produce pale leather TAW

tangle, coil SKEIN
- tangle or catch in a net ENMESH
- tangled mass, as of matted hair SHAG

tank for water, as in the roof or attached to a toilet CISTERN
- tank in which solid waste is decomposed by bacteria SEPTIC TANK
- tank or other vehicle that moves on a Caterpillar, a continuous circular belt TRACKLAYING VEHICLE
- opening in a wall, tank, or the like, through which a gun is fired PORT
- revolving armored dome on a tank or warship in which guns are mounted TURRET

tap, as in a barrel FAUCET, SPIGOT
- tap, valve in a pipe regulating the flow of liquid or gas STOPCOCK
- tapping the chest or back and attempting a diagnosis from the sound produced PERCUSSION

tape or strong woven strip of cotton or nylon, as used for safety belts WEBBING
- tape used to protect areas during painting MASKING TAPE

tape recorder in which the tape passes between separate, open reels REEL-TO-REEL TAPE RECORDER

- tape-recorder system that reduces tape hiss DOLBY
- tape recording using separate electronic signals rather than a continuous fluctuating signal DIGITAL RECORDING
- distortion or rapid variation of pitch, as produced by a faulty tape recorder FLUTTER
- distortion or slow variation of pitch, as produced by a faulty tape recorder WOW
- pulley or rotating shaft of a tape recorder regulating the movement of the magnetic tape CAPSTAN

tapestry of a rich pictorial design GOBELIN
- hanging for a wall, especially a tapestry ARRAS

tapeworm or other parasitic worm HELMINTH

tapioca - starch from the root of a tropical plant, as used for making tapioca CASSAVA, MANIOC

tar-based liquid applied to wood as a preservative CREOSOTE
- black tarlike hydrocarbon used in roadmaking and roofing BITUMEN, ASPHALT

target for insults or criticism SCAPEGOAT, WHIPPING BOY
- target in archery, or its center CLOUT
- target in throwing games and contests COCKSHY
- target or post to be tilted at, as by horsemen QUINTAIN
- bull's-eye on a target, the white center circle BLANK
- outermost ring but one on a target MAGPIE

tarot See illustration
- fortune-telling with tarot or playing cards CARTOMANCY
- section of a tarot pack, the major or minor division ARCANA
- suits found in many tarot packs, corresponding to spades, hearts, diamonds, and clubs SWORDS, CUPS, PENTACLES, WANDS

tartan PLAID

task, assignment, or project UNDERTAKING
- difficult, laborious, or very straining, as a task might be HERCULEAN, ONEROUS

taste, act of tasting GUSTATION
- taste, flavor SAPOR, SAVOR
- taste carefully or appreciatively SAVOR, DEGUST
- tasty, flavorsome, or agreeable to eat PALATABLE
- common or crude, having vulgar tastes PLEBEIAN
- having good taste or judgment DISCERNING, DISCRIMINATING
- person considered a judge, as in matters of taste ARBITER, ARBITER ELEGANTIAE, PETRONIUS
- relating to the sense of taste GUSTATORY
- salty or spicy to the taste, rather than sweet SAVORY
- sharp or harsh, as a smell or taste might be ACRID, PUNGENT

Tarot

Tarots have been used both for fortune-telling and in a variety of card games since at least 1377, when they were known in Germany. Their history, however, goes back to ancient Egypt.

A complete tarot deck consists of 78 cards, of which 22 are the esoteric "Major Arcana." The other 56, the "Minor Arcana," can be used like the ordinary deck of playing cards, the four suits being swords (corresponding to spades), wands (clubs), cups (hearts), and pentacles (diamonds).

Tarot cards include some of the oldest symbols born in the human mind, such as the Sun, the Moon, the Lovers, the Devil, the Fool, the Hanged Man, the Emperor, Judgment, Death, and the Tree of Life. As the cards are laid out for divination, each card influences the meaning of its neighbor, and the tarot reader uses much intuition.

The illustration shows "minchiate" cards, an Italian form of tarot from the 18th century.

- sharp smell or taste TANG
- spicy and sharp, as a taste might be TART, PIQUANT
- wide-ranging, all-embracing, liberal and broad-minded, as one's tastes might be CATHOLIC, UNIVERSAL

tax, levy, or duty IMPOST
- tax-collecting department in Great Britain INLAND REVENUE
- tax-collecting department in the United States INTERNAL REVENUE SERVICE, IRS
- tax deduction from income WITHHOLDING TAX
- tax estimate ASSESSMENT
- tax levied in Anglo-Saxon England for opposing or placating the Viking invaders DANEGELD
- tax levied in former times for the building or repair of city walls MURAGE
- tax of a fixed amount for each member of a household CAPITATION, POLL TAX
- tax levied by a feudal lord on his vassals TALLAGE
- tax official in India in former times ZAMINDAR
- tax on money or property received as a gift or inheritance, death duty, formerly estate duty CAPITAL-TRANSFER TAX
- tax on tobacco, spirits, and certain other goods EXCISE
- tax paid by a feudal vassal in lieu of military service SCUTAGE
- tax paid by landowners to the king in medieval England GELD
- tax schedule or system of duties, especially on imports TARIFF
- avoidance of tax by cunning or illegal means EVASION
- free or excuse from a tax, duty, or the like EXEMPT
- impose or collect a tax, fine, membership fee, or the like LEVY
- in proportion to the value of the goods, as a tax or duty might be AD VALOREM
- referring to a country's treasury, finances, or tax matters FISCAL
- referring to a tax system in which the taxation rate decreases as the amount to be taxed increases REGRESSIVE
- referring to a tax system in which the taxation rate increases as the amount to be taxed increases PROGRESSIVE
- refund of part of a sum paid, as of one's taxes REBATE

taxonomy See **classification**

tea, coffee, or other drink, food, or drug that temporarily increases activity or efficiency STIMULANT
- tealike beverage from South America MATÉ, YERBA MATÉ, PARAGUAY TEA
- tealike beverage made from wild flowers, leaves, or the like HERB TEA, TISANE
- tealike drink made from the root of a medicinal Asian plant GINSENG
- teatime dance popular in the 1920's and 1930's THÉ DANSANT
- black China tea of various types BOHEA, CONGGOU, OOLONG, PEKOE, SOUCHONG
- fine variety of black tea from India DARJEELING
- orange whose rind yields a fragrant oil used in making perfume and in flavoring tea BERGAMOT
- Russian tea urn SAMOVAR
- staining substance, used in tanning, dyeing, and inks, found in bark, tea, and the like TANNIN
- steep tea or herbs in preparing a drink or extract INFUSE

teach forcefully, as by repetition INSTILL, INCULCATE
- teach or instruct, especially in an uplifting way EDIFY, ENLIGHTEN
- teach someone to accept something uncritically, as by biased education INDOCTRINATE, BRAINWASH

teacher, coach, or the like employed by two or more schools, and traveling from one to the other PERIPATETIC
- teacher, especially a private teacher TUTOR
- teacher or educator, especially a rather dogmatic one PEDAGOGUE
- teacher or instructor PRECEPTOR
- teacher or wise adviser MENTOR
- spiritual teacher or leader, as among Hindus or Sikhs GURU

teaching designed to instruct, often in an excessively dull or moralizing way DIDACTICS
- teaching or instruction TUITION
- teaching or learning by lessons heard during sleep HYPNOPEDIA
- teaching specially designed for slow learners REMEDIAL TEACHING

team's lucky object, animal, or person MASCOT

tear See also **break**
- tear down or demolish a building or city, destroy down to the ground RAZE
- tear or catch clothing on a nail, wooden stump, or the like SNAG
- tear the flesh, as with a knife or whip LACERATE
- tearing away or sudden amputation of a limb or other body part, either surgically or in an accident AVULSION
- apart or into pieces, as one might tear something ASUNDER

tearful, tending to weep, weepy LACHRYMOSE
- tearful or sentimental, as when drunk MAUDLIN

tears - adjective for tears LACHRYMAL
- small vase formerly used to hold mourners' tears LACHRYMATORY

tease a public speaker with interruptions HECKLE
- tease good-naturedly, kid, pull someone's leg BANTER, JOSH, RIB, RAG
- tease in a mocking or scoffing way TAUNT, GIBE, TWIT
- tease in a way that ridicules exaggerated claims, bring down a peg or two DEBUNK, DEFLATE
- tease or torment by withholding something desirable TANTALIZE

teasing, frivolous style, speech, or the like PERSIFLAGE
- teasing, playful conversation BANTER, BADINAGE, RAILLERY

technical or specialized vocabulary TERMINOLOGY, NOMENCLATURE, JARGON

technique, technology (combining form) -URGY

technology - person opposed to new technology LUDDITE

teens - beginning of sexual maturing, as in one's early teens PUBERTY
- phase of physical and psychological maturing, typically during one's teens ADOLESCENCE

teeth See also **tooth**
- teeth having sharp edges for tearing flesh, as in meat-eating animals CARNASSIAL TEETH
- teeth or notches in a series, as on a saw or leaf SERRATION
- arrangement, number, type, or growth of teeth in a mammal DENTITION
- dental structure with a false tooth or teeth permanently fixed to natural teeth BRIDGE, BRIDGEWORK
- dentist specializing in correcting the positioning of teeth ORTHODONTIST
- film or crust containing bacteria and other matter formed on the teeth PLAQUE
- fit of the teeth when the jaws are closed, bite OCCLUSION
- gap between the teeth DIASTEMA
- grind the teeth, as in anger GNASH
- growing continuously throughout life, as rodents' teeth are PERSISTENT
- having two successive sets of teeth, as humans and most other mammals are DIPHYODONT
- inflammation of the socket of the teeth PYORRHEA ALVEOLARIS, PERIODONTITIS
- mercury alloy, as used by dentists as a filling for teeth AMALGAM
- not having two successive sets of teeth, not diphyodont MONOPHYODONT

- plate or set of false teeth DENTURE
- referring to the tissues surrounding the teeth PERIODONTAL
- thin strong thread used to clean between the teeth DENTAL FLOSS
- yellowish, limy deposit building up on the teeth TARTAR, CALCULUS

teeth (combining form) DENT-, DENTI-, -ODON, -ODONT

teetotal, nondrinking, on the wagon TEMPERATE, ABSTINENT
- teetotaler ABSTAINER

telegraphic system for transmitting copies of documents by photoelectric scanning and reproduction FACSIMILE, FAX

telepathy See also **fortune-telling**
- alleged ability to foretell the future, as through telepathy FORESIGHT, PRECOGNITION, PRESCIENCE
- alleged perception by means of a sixth sense, telepathy, intuition, or the like EXTRASENSORY PERCEPTION, ESP, CRYPTESTHESIA, TELESTHESIA
- person with alleged telepathic powers, especially one able to predict future events CLAIRVOYANT
- study of telepathy and other psychic phenomena PARAPSYCHOLOGY

telephone coupled with a television set, allowing the people to see as well as talk to each other over a distance VIDEOPHONE
- telephone line connecting two distant exchanges LONG-DISTANCE LINE, TRUNK LINE
- telephone link between computers MODEM
- telephone link between heads of state for emergencies HOT LINE
- device in or part of a radio, television, telephone, or the like that takes in and converts incoming signals RECEIVER
- thin disc, as in a telephone ear-

TENNIS TERMS

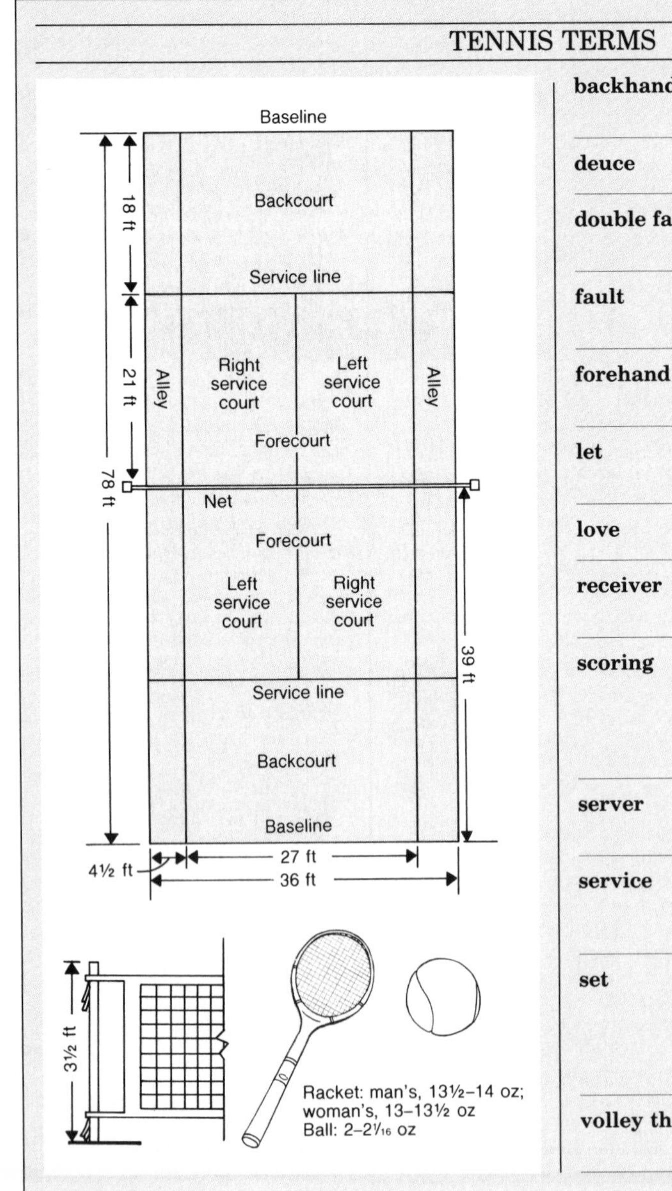

backhand shot	stroke in which the back of the hand is turned to the opponent
deuce	opponents being tied at 40
double fault	server faulting twice in a row and losing point
fault	failure of server to get the ball into the service court
forehand shot	stroke in which the palm of the hand is turned to the opponent
let	ball touching the net and yet falling into the opponent's court
love	zero score
receiver	player to whom the ball is served
scoring	first point, 15; second point, 30; third point, 40; fourth point, "game" and win (unless the score is deuce). Player must win by two points.
server	player serving the ball (has two chances on each point)
service	putting the ball in play by tossing it up and hitting it over the net into the service court
set	a tennis "round" (five sets for men, three sets for women). Winner of a set is the first to take six games. Must win by two games.
volley the ball	hit the ball on the fly after it crosses the net

piece or mouthpiece, whose vibrations are made to produce electric signals or vice versa DIAPHRAGM, TYMPANUM

telescope for viewing objects on land or on water rather than in space TERRESTRIAL TELESCOPE
- telescopelike toy producing varied symmetrical colored patterns when one looks in and rotates it KALEIDOSCOPE
- building housing telescopes for observing the stars OBSERVATORY
- eyepiece of a telescope, microscope, or the like OCULAR
- having fine threads for use in measuring, as the eyepiece of a telescope might be FILAR
- lens or set of lenses nearest to the object being viewed, in a telescope or microscope OBJECTIVE
- sliding tube within another, as in a telescope DRAWTUBE
- small telescope SPYGLASS
- small telescope attached to a larger one and used for locating the object to be observed FINDER
- surveyor's instrument, essentially a small telescope, for measuring angles THEODOLITE

television award, the equivalent of an Oscar EMMY
- television or radio announcements or linking items designed to avoid breaks between programs CONTINUITY
- television or radio network GRID
- television or radio program that has been prerecorded TRANSCRIPTION
- television program or movie intended as an accurate history or analysis but using actors and dramatic reconstructions DOCUDRAMA
- television program or movie presented as a nonfictional analysis or history DOCUMENTARY
- television system, as for security in shops, using cable or telephone links rather than broadcasting CLOSED-CIRCUIT TELEVISION
- television tube, oscilloscope tube, or similar electron-generating and -focusing vacuum tube CATHODE-RAY TUBE
- broadcast live a concert, speech, or the like, as on television RELAY
- cabinet of a television set, stereo system, or the like, standing on the floor CONSOLE
- cuing device producing a magnified script for someone speaking before television cameras TELEPROMPTER
- current information in printed form receivable on a specially adapted television set TELETEXT, VIEWDATA
- difference in brightness, as of a television picture CONTRAST
- estimates of the audience figures of a radio or television program RATINGS
- pattern of horizontal lines traced by a scanning electron beam, as on a television screen RASTER
- public appearance or presentation, as on television EXPOSURE
- ratio of a television picture's width to its height ASPECT RATIO
- referring to television in which members of the general public rather than professionals make the programs ACCESS, PUBLIC-ACCESS
- sharpness or clarity of outline, as of a photograph or television image DEFINITION
- tiny units that together make up a television image PIXELS

tell, inform, make familiar ACQUAINT
- tell, report, or repeat, especially a story or an account of a past event NARRATE, RECITE, RECOUNT, REHEARSE, RELATE
- tell a secret, reveal DISCLOSE, DIVULGE
- tell things apart, see or show the differences DIFFERENTIATE, DISTINGUISH, DISCRIMINATE
- entertain, especially by telling stories REGALE

teller of witty anecdotes or stories RACONTEUR

telling the future See also **fortune-telling, foretell**
- telling the future, prophetic MANTIC

telling the future (combining form) -MANCY

temper, irritability ASPERITY
- temper metal or glass ANNEAL
- temper or resentment, huff, as from a blow to one's pride PIQUE
- bad temper, ill humor SPLEEN, IRASCIBILITY, BILE
- easily provoked, as someone's temper might be HAIR-TRIGGER
- fit of temper TANTRUM
- quick-tempered, easily angered IRASCIBLE, INFLAMMABLE, VOLATILE

temperament, personality, or mood DISPOSITION
- changeable, as someone's temperament might be MERCURIAL
- gloomy, cold, and sluggish in temperament SATURNINE

temperature-controlled container, as for premature babies INCUBATOR
- temperature scales of various kinds CELSIUS, CENTIGRADE, REAUMUR, FAHRENHEIT, KELVIN, RANKINE
- abnormally high body temperature, as produced by fever HYPERPYREXIA, HYPERTHERMIA
- abnormally low body temperature HYPOTHERMIA, COLD STROKE, FROZEN SLEEP
- cooling power of the air based on both wind speed and air temperature WINDCHILL FACTOR
- surrounding, in the immediate vicinity, as the air or temperature might be AMBIENT
- switching or controlling device for regulating temperature, as in a refrigerator THERMOSTAT

temple See also **column**
- temple, as in Rome, for all the gods PANTHEON
- temple or shrine in Chinese communities JOSS HOUSE
- temple or shrine, typically a tapering tower with many stories PAGODA
- temple tower, in the shape of a steep pyramid, as in ancient Babylon ZIGGURAT
- entrance or porch of a temple PROPYLAEUM
- innermost chamber in the Temple in ancient Israel, which housed the Ark of the Covenant HOLY OF HOLIES, SANCTUM SANCTORUM, ORACLE

tempo - instrument indicating musical tempo by sounding out the beat METRONOME

temporarily, for the time being PRO TEMPORE, PRO TEM

temporary See also **short-lived**
- temporary, improvised, often as an emergency measure EXTEMPORANEOUS, EXPEDIENT, MAKESHIFT
- temporary or conditional, subject to change when permanent arrangements can be made STOPGAP, PROVISIONAL, INTERIM
- temporary stay or residence in a place SOJOURN
- temporary stop, pause RESPITE
- temporary suspending of operation or activity ABEYANCE

tempt, lure, attract ENTICE, INVEIGLE
- temptations, wheedling, or flattering BLANDISHMENTS
- tempting, fascinating ALLURING

ten-legged crustacean such as a lobster, or ten-tentacled mollusk such as a squid DECAPOD
- ten times, tenfold DECUPLE, DENARY
- ten-year period DECADE, DECENNARY, DECENNIUM
- based on the number ten, as a fraction, number system, or currency might be DECIMAL, DENARY

ten (combining form) DEC-, DECA-, DEK-

Ten Commandments DECALOGUE
- chest that contained the stone tablets with the Ten Commandments ARK OF THE COVENANT

tend, care for MINISTER TO
- tend or drift toward, as if irresist-

ibly attracted GRAVITATE

tendency, preference, leaning, liking APPETENCY, PREDISPOSITION, PROCLIVITY, PROPENSITY
- tendency of a physical body to remain at rest or in unchanged motion unless acted on by external forces INERTIA
- tendency or calling, as to a religious life VOCATION
- hypothetical tendency of the energy in the universe or a closed system to run down ENTROPY
- individual and habitual tendency or leaning, trend or bias of character BENT, DISPOSITION, INCLINATION
- liable to or showing a tendency for SUSCEPTIBLE TO
- strong tendency or inclination, definite and continued liking or favoring AFFINITY, PARTIALITY, PENCHANT, PREDILECTION

tendency toward (combining form) -PHIL-, -PHILIA

tendon above and behind the knee HAMSTRING

tennis See illustration and chart, page 538, and see chart at **sports**

tenon - slot into which a tenon is fitted when joining two pieces of wood, stone, or metal MORTISE

tenor with a strong voice, especially one suited to Wagnerian opera HELDENTENOR

tense, anxious, nervous, in suspense ON TENTERHOOKS
- tense, nervy, or strained OVERWROUGHT, AGITATED
- past perfect tense of a verb, as in *had climbed* PLUPERFECT

tension - remove the tension or danger from a situation DEFUSE

tent See also illustration at **tepee**
- tent of a large ornate kind, as used by medieval knights at tournaments or at war PAVILION
- tent of a very large and airy design, for balls, wedding parties, and the like MARQUEE
- tent or booth as used by the Israelites during the Exodus TABERNACLE
- tent or house used by Native Americans TEPEE, WIGWAM
- flap forming an entrance or extended roof for a tent FLY
- hooped rod supporting a canopy, as of a tent or covered wagon BAIL
- horizontal pole forming the ridge of a tent RIDGEPOLE
- put up a tent PITCH
- rope used to secure a tent GUY
- take down a tent STRIKE
- wooden block or strip with holes for securing and adjusting ropes, as of a tent or on a ship EUPHROE, ROPE KEY, TENT SLIDE

tentacled (combining form) ACTINO-

tenth of one's yearly income or production donated to the church or other cause TITHE

tenth (combining form) DECI-

tequila - tropical plant from which tequila is produced AGAVE

term at a university, forming half an academic year SEMESTER
- term at a university, forming one third of an academic year TRIMESTER
- term of endearment HYPOCORISM
- term that is less general than another and is embraced by it, as *dog* is by *animal* HYPONYM
- term that is more general than another and embraces it, as *animal* does *dog* SUPERORDINATE
- terms used in a particular science, art, profession, or the like NOMENCLATURE, TERMINOLOGY, JARGON
- learned in a showy sort of way, as deliberately "literary" terms are INKHORN

terrace or tree-lined garden walk in ancient Rome XYST, XYSTUS

terrify See also **scared, fear**
- terrify, paralyze with fear GORGONIZE, PETRIFY
- terrifying, thrilling book, movie, or the like CHILLER

territory administered by a country authorized by the League of Nations MANDATE
- territory needed for expansion, such as that formerly claimed by Germany LEBENSRAUM
- divide a territory into small warring states BALKANIZE
- foreign policy based on revenge or regaining of territory REVANCHISM
- incorporate territory into another country ANNEX
- policy of gaining territory that is historically or ethnically related to one's nation but under foreign control IRREDENTISM

terror (combining form) -PHOBE, -PHOBIA, -PHOBIC

terrorists - deliberate damaging or destruction of property, as by terrorists SABOTAGE
- military action taken against rebels or terrorist groups COUNTERINSURGENCY, PACIFICATION

test See also **examine**
- test, measure, or standard used for judgment or comparison YARDSTICK, CRITERION, TOUCHSTONE
- test for a part in a play, concert, or the like, by giving a sample performance AUDITION
- test for cancer of the cervix in women PAP TEST, SMEAR TEST
- test identifying a person's skills and potential, often used as an aid in career guidance APTITUDE TEST
- test in which a choice of possible answers is provided MULTIPLE-CHOICE TEST
- test something to assess its value

Theater

or quality ASSAY, APPRAISE
- test that will decide the effectiveness of something LITMUS TEST
- person or group whose reactions serve as a test for new ideas or opinions SOUNDING BOARD
- personality test based on the subject's interpretations of various abstract inkblot designs RORSCHACH TEST, INKBLOT TEST
- rigorous or decisive test ACID TEST

test-tube baby - referring to fertilization induced in an artificial laboratory environment, as when pro-

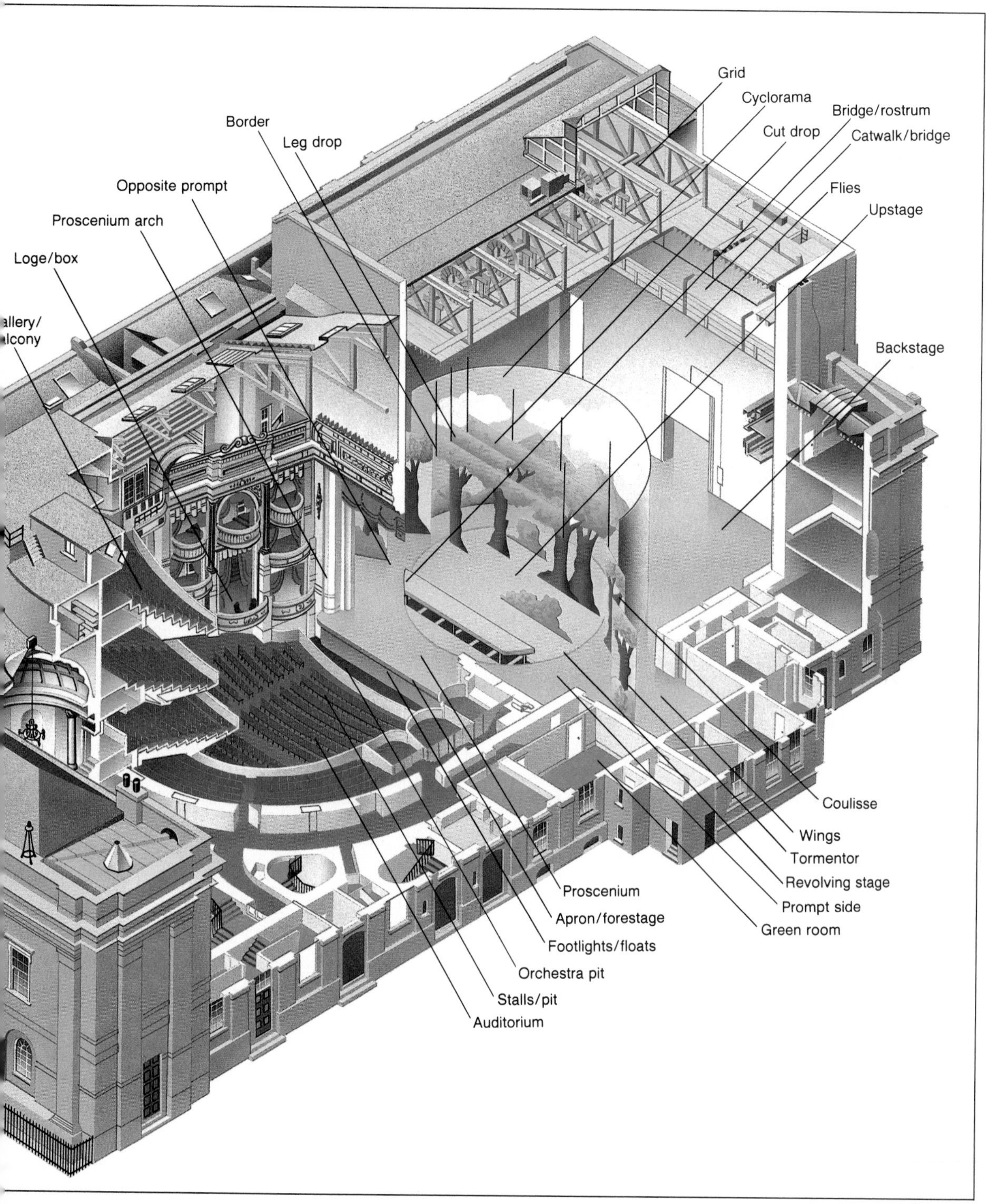

ducing a test-tube baby IN VITRO
testicle (combining form) ORCH-, ORCHID-, -ORCH, TEST-
testicles or ovaries GONADS
- area around and including the testicles GROIN
- condition in which the testicles have not descended into the scrotum CRYPTORCHIDISM, CRYPTORCHIDY
- external pouch of the male genital organs, containing the testicles SCROTUM
- long, coiled tube forming part of the sperm-bearing system attached to the testicles EPIDIDYMIS
- sperm-bearing duct connected by a tube to either of the testicles VAS DEFERENS
- surgical cutting of the sperm-bearing ducts near the testicles, used for sterilizing a man VASECTOMY
testify falsely in court PERJURE ONESELF
- person who makes an affidavit or testifies in writing under oath DEPONENT
testimony given under oath DEPOSITION
tetanus - grinlike expression, as from muscular contraction in tetanus RISUS SARDONICUS
- lockjaw, as in tetanus TRISMUS
text edited or revised critically to include the most plausible variant readings RECENSION, REDACTION
- text of a writer's works, together with collected notes and comments by scholars VARIORUM
- text of the songs and dialogue of an opera or operetta LIBRETTO
- text or passage from a classic or standard work that is considered authoritative LOCUS CLASSICUS
- text used by linguists for analyzing features of language beyond single sentences DISCOURSE
- change or corrupt a text by inserting material INTERPOLATE
- commonly accepted text or version of a work VULGATE
- compare texts in order to see where they differ COLLATE
- containing errors or changes, as the text of a copied manuscript might be CORRUPT, GARBLED
- correct and improve a text by critical editing EMEND
- critical analysis or explanation of a text, especially of the Bible EXEGESIS
- cut or delete a passage from a text EXCISE
- devise a version of a text, art object, or the like, on the basis of surviving fragments and other evidence RECONSTRUCT
- distort a text by expurgating it BOWDLERIZE
- edit or revise a text for publication REDACT
- extract from a text GOBBET
- fuse or blend two versions of a text to produce a full or reliable version CONFLATE
- insert or patch together a text in a strained and inharmonious way SPATCHCOCK
- note of critical commentary or explanation on a literary text ANNOTATION, GLOSS
- original text of a literary or musical work UR-TEXT, ARCHETYPE
- presenting texts or data in columns side by side for comparison SYNOPTIC
- scholarly comments, footnotes, variant readings, and so on in an edition of a text APPARATUS CRITICUS, CRITICAL APPARATUS
- variant reading in a particular edition of a text LECTION
textile See **fabric, cloth**
texture, firmness, as of a pudding CONSISTENCY
th - runic letter ð, representing the sounds /th/ and /<u>th</u>/, as used in Old and Middle English EDH, ETH
- runic letter þ, representing the sounds /th/ and /<u>th</u>/, as used in Old and Middle English THORN
thanks - "thank God" DEO GRATIAS
- in debt to, owing thanks to, grateful OBLIGED, INDEBTED, BEHOLDEN
that is, term introducing examples, "namely" VIDELICET, VIZ, I.E., ID EST
thatching - stalks of long grass, beans, peas, and other plants used for thatching HAULM
the or equivalent word in other languages, identifying specifically the noun or noun phrase that follows it DEFINITE ARTICLE
the end, word indicating the end of a book or manuscript, "finished" EXPLICIT, EXPLICITUS
- the end, word indicating the end of a play or the like, conclusion FINIS
the same, term used in references and footnotes to indicate a passage already referred to ID, IDEM
theater See illustration and chart, pages 540 and 543, and also chart at **drama**
- theater as a profession, the stage FOOTLIGHTS
- theater as an art DRAMATURGY
- theater award on Broadway, the equivalent of an Oscar TONY
- theater company performing a variety of plays during a season REPERTORY COMPANY
- theater that is unofficial, unorthodox, or away from the main theater areas FRINGE THEATER
- theatrical touring company or group TROUPE
- serious drama, as opposed to comedies, musicals, and the like LEGITIMATE THEATER
theatrical or overemotional behavior HISTRIONICS
theft of another person's writings, ideas, or the like, passing them off as one's own PLAGIARISM
- theft of another's property LARCENY
- theft of cattle or sheep, typically by driving them away RUSTLING
- theft of something small or cheap, minor thievery FILCHING, PILFERAGE, PURLOINING
- theft or illegal use, especially by publishing a work protected by another's copyright PIRACY
- theft or misuse of property or funds that have been entrusted to one MISAPPROPRIATION, EMBEZZLEMENT, PECULATION, DEFALCATION, CONVERSION
- flee and hide, as after committing a theft ABSCOND
theme in music SUBJECT
- theme, motif, or commonplace image in literature TOPOS
- theme, repeated idea, recurring verse, or the like REFRAIN, CHORUS, BURDEN
- theme or recurrent idea or symbol in a book, symphony, or the like MOTIF, LEITMOTIV, MOTTO
theology as a subject of academic study DIVINITY
- theological study of first things, such as creation ETIOLOGY
- theological study of last things, such as heaven ESCHATOLOGY
- theological training school for the clergy SEMINARY
theorem - problem or supplementary rule arising from a theorem, as in geometry RIDER
theoretical, in name only, not actual NOMINAL
- theoretical or imaginary rather than actual NOTIONAL
- theoretical rather than realistic or provable SPECULATIVE, CONJECTURAL
theory See also **philosophy**
- theory, as the basis of scientific experiments HYPOTHESIS
- theory, religious principle, body of beliefs, or the like DOGMA, DOCTRINE, CREED
- theory differing from the orthodox view HERESY, HETERODOXY
- theory or proposition put forward for argument THESIS, WORKING HYPOTHESIS
- theory that the universe came

gradually rather than suddenly into being, and that matter is created all the time STEADY-STATE THEORY, CONTINUOUS-CREATION THEORY
- theory that the universe originated by an explosion of a small dense mass and is merely expanding BIG-BANG THEORY, SUPERDENSE THEORY
- accepted, generally believed, as a theory might be RECEIVED
- assent to or believe in a theory, doctrine, or the like SUBSCRIBE, ADHERE
- blindly committed to a theory, dogmatic DOCTRINAIRE
- formulation or explanation of a theory EXPLICATION

theory (combining form) -LOGY, -OLOGY, -ISM

therapy See chart, page 544
- therapy, form of medical treatment MODALITY
- therapy for treating psychiatric patients, involving an electric shock to the brain ELECTROCONVULSIVE TREATMENT, ECT, ELECTROSHOCK THERAPY, EST
- therapy or therapeutic benefit through companionship of a cat, dog, turtle, bird, or other pet ZOOTHERAPY, ANIMAL THERAPY
- therapy through engaging in crafts or creative hobbies OCCUPATIONAL THERAPY
- untraditional or unorthodox, as a life-style or therapy might be ALTERNATIVE

therefore, consequently ERGO, THUS

thermometer for measuring very low temperatures CRYOMETER
- thermometer that records temperatures THERMOGRAPH
- electrical thermometer for measuring very high temperatures PYROMETER
- instrument consisting of two thermometers, one with a dampened bulb, whose differing readings produce a measure of the humidity in the air PSYCHROMETER, WET-AND-DRY-BULB THERMOMETER, WET-AND-DRY-BULB HYGROMETER
- mercury thermometer registering very small changes in temperature BECKMANN THERMOMETER

thesis or treatise, as for a higher academic degree DISSERTATION

thick and sticky, as some liquids are VISCID, VISCOUS
- thick-skinned mammal, such as the elephant or hippopotamus PACHYDERM

thicken, clot, or solidify, as blood might CONGEAL
- thicken, curdle, or jell into a semisolid mass COAGULATE
- thicken or condense, as by boiling or evaporation INSPISSATE
- thicken or curdle, as milk does CLABBER
- thickened at one end, club-shaped CLAVATE, CLAVIFORM
- thickener or starch used in cooking ARROWROOT
- thickening agent, such as cream or egg yolks, for soups, sauces, or the like LIAISON

thickness or width, as of a circle, piping, or wire DIAMETER

thief or rascal GANEF
- thieves' vocabulary or similar half-secret language CANT, ARGOT

thigh - thighbone FEMUR
- thighs and pelvic region LOINS
- junction of the inner thighs and trunk GROIN
- relating to the thigh CRURAL
- side of the body or thigh FLANK

thin, lean SPARE, MEAGER
- thin, lean, slender, but tough SINEWY, STRINGY, WIRY, WITHY
- thin, light, and partially see-through, as a fabric might be DIAPHANOUS, SHEER, TRANSLUCENT, GOSSAMER, CHIFFON

THEATER TERMS

amphitheater	outdoor auditorium, particularly in ancient Rome
apron	section of a conventional stage extending beyond the curtains into the auditorium
auditorium	seating area for the audience, as distinct from the stage
box set	flat pieces of scenery representing three walls, and usually the ceiling, of a room
coulisse	flat piece of scenery in the wings
decor	stage setting or scenery
drop scene	painted cloth behind which scenery is changed and in front of which short scenes are acted
fourth wall	apparent wall of a room represented by the proscenium arch, so that the audience appears to eavesdrop on the play's action
green room	backstage restroom for actors, especially in former times
grip	stagehand, helping to shift scenery
loge	box, or upper section of seats
odeum	theater or concert building in ancient Greece or Rome
orchestra	circular area in front of the stage, used by the chorus, in an ancient Greek theater
platform stage	Elizabethan stage, which projected into the central area, with the audience on three sides
proscenium	front part of a stage, or the arch framing it; performing area in front of the stage in an ancient Greek theater
rake	upward slope of the stage away from the audience
skene	two-story structure in an ancient Greek theater, providing changing and storage rooms
tableau curtains	curtains that draw up and outward from center stage
theater-in-the-round/ arena theater	theater in which the stage is almost entirely surrounded by the audience

- thin, pale, sickly person WRAITH
- thin, sharp fragment, splinter, as of glass or stone SLIVER
- thin, slender, slim and graceful, trim GRACILE, LITHE, SVELTE, SYLPH-LIKE, WILLOWY
- thin and bony, especially in an awkward way, lean, skinny, weedy ANGULAR, SCRAGGY, SCRAWNY, ECTOMORPHIC
- thin and exhausted-looking, pinched, peaky HAGGARD, GAUNT
- thin and fine, as hair might be WISPY
- thin and gaunt LANK
- thin and long-limbed ASTHENIC, RANGY
- thin and shriveled, withered SERE, SEAR, WIZENED
- thin and tall, and usually clumsy or ungainly LANKY, GANGLING, SPINDLY
- thin and untidy, as handwriting might be SPIDERY
- thin in consistency or density, diluted, weakened, as a gas or liquid might be RAREFIED, TENUOUS, ATTENUATED
- thin or weaken a cordial, concentrate, or other liquid, as by adding water DILUTE
- thin out, make or become less dense or compact RAREFY
- thin thread, fiber, wire, or the like FILAMENT
- thinner or narrow toward one end TAPERING
- abnormally thin, as through starvation, undernourished SKELETAL, EMACIATED, MACERATED, CADAVEROUS
- abnormally thin and weak, especially from nervous self-starvation ANOREXIC

thing as it appears to the mind or senses, according to Kantian philosophy, regardless of its underlying nature PHENOMENON
- thing in itself, according to Kantian philosophy, rather than as it appears to the mind or senses NOUMENON
- thing that exists in its own right, independently of other things ENTITY
- "things done," deeds, achievements RES GESTAE
- treat an idea or abstraction as a real or concrete thing REIFY

think See also **thought**
- think, consider, judge, reckon, have an opinion DEEM, OPINE
- think, hold thoughts, illusions, or the like ENTERTAIN
- think, suppose, take for granted or accept PRESUME, ASSUME
- think, work out, conclude DEDUCE, FIGURE
- think about or study something laboriously LUCUBRATE, BURN THE MIDNIGHT OIL
- think and make rough calculations about something, form a theory CONJECTURE, ESTIMATE, SPECULATE,

THERAPIES

acupuncture	insertion of fine needles into the skin to relieve pain or treat disease
aromatherapy	use of sweet-smelling oils to influence mood and treat disease
aversion therapy	eradication of harmful habits by associating them with something unpleasant
biofeedback	use of measuring instruments to monitor body responses and thereby help a patient control them
chemotherapy	use of chemicals to treat cancer, mental illness, and some other conditions
chiropractic	spinal manipulation to relieve various ailments
herbalism	use of herbal extracts to treat various ailments
homeopathy	use of minute amounts of drugs or natural remedies that in larger quantities would reproduce the effects of the disease being treated
hydrotherapy	use of water, usually in remedial swimming pools, to relieve pain in the muscles and joints, and treat disease
hypnotherapy	use of hypnosis to treat physical and mental disorders
irradiation/ radiation therapy	use of radiation to control disease, especially cancer
moxibustion	burning of mugwort, or moxa, leaves at particular points on the skin, often in association with acupuncture
naturopathy	use of natural remedies and healthy living habits to restore or improve well-being
osteopathy	manipulation of bones and joints to treat backache and muscle problems
phototherapy	use of light, including infrared and ultraviolet rays, to treat disease, especially tumors
physiotherapy	use of exercise, heat, or massage to treat injury or disability
primal therapy	treatment for neurotic behavior in which a patient is encouraged to "relive" painful experiences of early childhood, or allegedly even of birth
reflexology/zone therapy	use of massage, especially foot massage, to treat ailments elsewhere in the body
rolfing	use of deep massage to relieve muscular and emotional tension
shiatsu/acupressure	use of finger pressure at specific points on the body, and of massage, to relieve pain or treat disease

THEORIZE
- think deeply and at length, turn over in the mind MULL OVER, MUSE, RUMINATE, BROOD ON
- think hard, ponder deeply CEREBRATE
- think logically, reason RATIOCINATE
- think of or imagine something, especially some future possibility ENVISAGE
- think or consider carefully, reflect COGITATE, DELIBERATE, PERPEND
- think or consider deeply, ponder CONTEMPLATE, MEDITATE
- think or know by special insight, sense INTUIT
- think or ponder moodily BROOD
- think or reflect to oneself, search one's mind INTROSPECT
- think or work out in great detail EXCOGITATE
- think through, form an opinion APPRAISE, TAKE STOCK
- think up or invent something, especially in a devious way CONTRIVE, CONCOCT, FABRICATE
- think up or invent something, such as a plan CONCEIVE, DEVISE, FORMULATE, FASHION
- thinker, scholar, or philosopher, especially an oversubtle or devious one SOPHIST, CASUIST

thinking, thought CEREBRATION
- thinking of an imaginative and free-ranging rather than a strictly logical kind, often producing unexpected solutions to problems LATERAL THINKING, SERENDIPITOUS THINKING

third course of action, factor, or the like when there are supposed to be only two TERTIUM QUID
- third last, last but two ANTEPENULTIMATE
- third-ranking or third-level TERTIARY
- occuring every third year or lasting for three years TRIENNIAL
- one third of a three-month or three-part period TRIMESTER

third (combining form) TER-

thirst - satisfy one's thirst QUENCH, SLAKE
- unsatisfiable, as thirst or lust might be INSATIABLE

thirsty PARCHED

this, *those*, or similar word pointing out the person or thing referred to DEMONSTRATIVE, DEICTIC

this side (combining form) CIS-

thistle - thistlelike shrub with spikes of flowers ACANTHUS
- tuft of feathery bristles on a thistle or the like, helping to disperse the seeds PAPPUS

thorn, prickle, or spine, as on a rose ACULEUS
- thorny bush or shrub BRIAR, BRAMBLE

thorn (combining form) ACANTH-, ACANTHO-

thorough, covering all aspects COMPREHENSIVE, EXHAUSTIVE, ALL-ENCOMPASSING
- thorough, painstaking, diligent, or hard-working CONSCIENTIOUS, INDUSTRIOUS, SEDULOUS, ASSIDUOUS
- thorough, very careful or precise, paying close attention to detail METICULOUS, PUNCTILIOUS, SCRUPULOUS
- thorough, wide-ranging, sweeping EXTENSIVE

thoroughbred PEDIGREE
- thoroughbred horses, especially racehorses BLOODSTOCK

thoroughgoing, out-and-out ARRANT, EXTREME

thoroughly (combining form) CATA-

thought See also **think, thinking**
- thought, idea, mental image CONCEPTION
- thought, thinking, contemplation CEREBRATION, COGITATION
- thought, thinking, the mental faculty by which things become known or recognized COGNITION
- thought or intention that is deliberately held back and remains unrevealed ARRIÈRE-PENSÉE
- thought or study, deep reflection, laborious meditation LUCUBRATION
- alleged thought transference TELEPATHY
- arrange one's thoughts in order MARSHAL
- period or state of deep thought BROWN STUDY, REVERIE
- put one's thoughts into words, express FORMULATE
- referring to thought that is very disorganized INCOHERENT

thoughtful, absorbed, fully occupied mentally ENGROSSED, IMMERSED, INTENT
- thoughtful, attentive, and concerned, considerate SOLICITOUS
- thoughtful, reflective, meditative RUMINANT, PENSIVE, CONTEMPLATIVE, COGITATIVE
- thoughtful and careful in behavior, avoiding trouble CIRCUMSPECT, DISCREET, PRUDENT
- thoughtful and sensitive, carefully considered JUDICIOUS, POLITIC
- thoughtful and withdrawn, self-examining INTROSPECTIVE
- deeply thoughtful, lost in thought, distracted ABSTRACTED, PREOCCUPIED

thousand-year period MILLENNIUM
- thousand years, or group of 1,000 elements CHILIAD
- adjective for a thousand MILLENARIAN, MILLENARY

thousand (combining form) KILO-

thousand million, billion (combining form) GIGA-

thousand-millionth, billionth (combining form) NANO-

thousandth MILLESIMAL

thousandth (combining form) MILLI-

thread, thin wire, fiber, or the like FILAMENT
- thread, wire, or cord used in surgery, as for closing a blood vessel LIGATURE
- thread of gold or silver wire used in embroidery PURL
- thread that has separated from a fabric RAVEL
- threadlike or relating to thread FILAR
- threads running across the width in weaving or a fabric WOOF, WEFT
- threads running lengthwise in weaving or a fabric WARP
- ball of twine or thread CLEW
- cone-shaped roll of thread wound on a spindle COP
- loose coil of thread, wool, or the like SKEIN, HANK
- small lump in a thread or fabric, sometimes made deliberately for a knobbly appearance SLUB
- loosely twisted thread, as used in embroidery FLOSS
- spinning or twisting of silk, cotton, or the like into threads FILATURE
- tool for cutting an internal screw thread TAP
- tool parts with an internal thread used for cutting threads on screws, pipes, and the like DIE

thread (combining form) NEMAT-, NEMATO-

threat, risk, or danger MENACE, PERIL, JEOPARDY, HAZARD
- threat in the form of a perceived warning of future calamity OMEN, PORTENT, PRESAGE
- threat of disaster, causing constant anxiety SWORD OF DAMOCLES
- threat of punishment or revenge, denunciation COMMINATION
- threat or warning CAVEAT
- threats by means of a display of military power SABER RATTLING
- final terms offered in negotiating, carrying a threat of breakdown if rejected ULTIMATUM
- force or compulsion, as by means of threats DURESS, COERCION, CONSTRAINT

threaten, attack verbally, or denounce with great force BLUSTER, FULMINATE, INVEIGH
- threaten, endanger, put at risk JEOPARDIZE, HAZARD, IMPERIL
- threaten, look menacing, as the sky or weather might LOWER

- threaten or bribe someone into committing a wrongful act, especially perjury SUBORN
- threaten so as to silence or dissuade INTIMIDATE, DETER

threatening MENACING, MINATORY, MINACIOUS
- threatening, overhanging, unpleasant and likely to occur soon IMMINENT, IMPENDING
- threatening and prophetic, warning of some future calamity FOREBODING, OMINOUS, PORTENTOUS
- threatening or gloomy, as the expression on someone's face might be BALEFUL
- threatening or sulky frown SCOWL

three bent or curved branches constituting a pattern radiating from a center TRISKELION
- three in cards or dice TREY
- three in one TRIUNE
- three-leafed or having three leaflets, as clover is TRIFOLIATE
- three-legged stand or support TRIPOD, TRIVET
- three-legged stand, typically used for serving tea TEAPOY
- three-monthly or three-month TRIMESTRIAL
- three-part painting or carving, typically on three panels TRIPTYCH
- three people living together in a sexual relationship MÉNAGE À TROIS
- three-pronged fork or spear, as used by gladiators or carried by Neptune TRIDENT
- three-tiered Greek or Roman ship rowed with three banks of oars TRIREME
- three times, threefold TRIPLE, TREBLE, TRIPLICATE
- Three Wise Men MAGI
- division or separation into three parts TRICHOTOMY
- group of three TRIAD, TRIO, TRINITY, TROIKA
- group of three men TRIUMVIRATE
- leaf made up of three leaflets, or a design, symbol, or architectural ornament resembling this TREFOIL
- occurring once every three years or lasting for three years TRIENNIAL

three (combining form) TER-, TRI-

three-dimensional appearance, or a technique for representing it, in a drawing or painting PERSPECTIVE
- three-dimensional laser-produced photo or pattern HOLOGRAM
- three-dimensional picture or process based on images viewed through glasses with one red lens and one lens of a different color, such as green ANAGLYPH
- three-dimensional scene or tableau, as in museums, with models of figures exhibited against a background DIORAMA
- design, painting, or style of painting using shades of gray and aiming at a three-dimensional effect GRISAILLE
- optical instrument with twin lenses, producing a three-dimensional effect when used to view two similar photographs STEREOSCOPE
- pair of similar pictures that give a three-dimensional effect when viewed through special lenses STEREOGRAPH
- realistic painting that deceives the eye by its striking three-dimensional effect TROMPE L'OEIL

three-dimensional (combining form) STERE-, STEREO-

threshold at which a stimulus begins to evoke a response LIMEN
- below the threshold of perception or consciousness SUBLIMINAL

thrifty See also **miserly**
- thrifty, economical, unwasteful, prudent in spending CANNY, FRUGAL, PROVIDENT, SPARING
- thrifty or economical to the point of meanness PARSIMONIOUS
- thrifty or penny-pinching SCRIMPING, SKIMPING
- thrifty use and spending of resources HUSBANDRY, CONSERVATION
- aimed at thrift, regulating or limiting expenses, as a rule might be SUMPTUARY

thrill or shiver of fear or excitement FRISSON

thriving on (combining form) -PHILE, -PHILIC

throat See illustration at **mouth**
- throat and chest area THORAX
- throat or esophagus GULLET, GORGE
- throaty, relating to or pronounced in the throat GUTTURAL
- adjective for the throat or neck JUGULAR, GULAR
- band of color on the throat of a bird or other animal GORGET
- clear the throat loudly HAWK
- fold of skin hanging from the throat, as of some birds and lizards WATTLE
- loose fold of skin at the throat, as in cattle or many old people DEWLAP
- surgical cut or opening through the throat to help breathing TRACHEOSTOMY, TRACHEOTOMY
- surgical rod used for removing obstructions from the throat PROBANG

throne - attain the throne or other high office ACCEDE
- give up or relinquish the throne formally ABDICATE
- remove from office, power, the throne, or the like DEPOSE
- right of a person or family line to inherit a title, property, throne, or the like SUCCESSION
- seize by force and hold illegally the power, rights, throne, or the like of another USURP

through (combining form) DIA-, PER-

throughout, "here and there," used in references and footnotes to indicate the frequent occurrence of an item in a text PASSIM

throw away, get rid of, reject DISPOSE OF, DISCARD
- throw forward, launch or lob IMPEL, PROJECT, PROPEL
- throw from a great height, hurl down PRECIPITATE
- throw hard, fling, shower PELT
- throw or thrust into a position suddenly or unceremoniously PITCHFORK
- throw out, drive out, force out EJECT, EXPEL
- throw out of a window DEFENESTRATE
- throw overboard, or discard something burdensome JETTISON
- throw stones at, or stone to death LAPIDATE
- throwback, characteristic or individual affected by reversion to a more primitive state ATAVISM
- throwing the voice VENTRILOQUISM
- curved flight path through the air taken by something thrown, shot, or the like TRAJECTORY

thrush - flock or family of thrushes MUTATION
- poetic or regional term for a thrush THROSTLE

thumb or corresponding digit in an animal POLLEX
- thumb that can be placed against the fingertips, as in humans OPPOSABLE THUMB
- fleshy underpart of the top joint of a finger or the thumb PAD
- pad of muscle on the hand below the thumb HEEL, THENAR

thus, "so," term used in a printed text to indicate the deliberate reproduction of a mistaken or surprising wording or fact being quoted SIC

Tibetan Buddhist monastery LAMASERY

tick, mite, or related small creature ACARID
- tick off item by item TALLY
- infestation of the skin or hair with mites or ticks ACARIASIS

ticket or label, as might be tied on a package DOCKET
- person using a free ticket, as for a theater or train DEADHEAD
- person who resells tickets at an inflated price SCALPER

tidal flood BORE, EAGRE

- wave like a tidal wave, but caused by an underwater earthquake or volcanic eruption TSUNAMI

tide of maximum rise, occurring at the new or full moon of each month SPRING TIDE
- tide of minimum rise, occurring during the first and third quarter of the moon NEAP TIDE
- falling or receding tide EBB TIDE
- rising or incoming tide FLOOD TIDE
- seashore, specifically the area between high- and low-tide marks of the spring tide LITTORAL

tidy, careful, and systematic in work or behavior METHODICAL, ORDERLY, PAINSTAKING
- tidy or dress oneself very neatly PRIMP, PRINK, SPRUCE UP
- neat and tidy in dress or appearance TRIM, DAPPER, SPRUCE, WELL-GROOMED
- neat and tidy, orderly SHIPSHAPE

tie See also **join**
- tie, bond, connection LIGATURE, VINCULUM
- draw, tie, or deadlock, especially in a sports event STANDOFF
- scarflike neckband, arranged to resemble a very wide tie CRAVAT
- wide triangular tie knot, made with an extra turn WINDSOR KNOT

tie up, as by binding the arms, wings, or legs TRUSS
- sexual deviation in which one partner is tied up BONDAGE

tight - tightly closed, as a fist or teeth might be CLENCHED
- tightly fixed in place CRAMMED IN, IMMOVABLE, WEDGED IN
- tightly pressed down, as trodden earth might be COMPACTED
- tightly pressed together, very crowded, as ranks of troops might be SERRIED
- feeling of tightness or pressure, as in the chest CONSTRICTION
- pulled or stretched tight, as a rope might be TAUT

tightrope or slack-rope walker FUNAMBULIST
- tightrope walker or other performer of balancing feats EQUILIBRIST

tile, especially of wood, laid in overlapping rows on a roof SHINGLE
- curving roof tile overlapping or interlocking with the adjoining tiles PANTILE
- decorate, inlay, or pave with a mosaic of tiny tiles TESSELLATE
- thin mortar, as used between tiles GROUT

tilt, slope, slant INCLINATION, DEVIATION, CANT
- tilt or sway, as a ship might when sailing into the wind LIST, CANT, HEEL, CAREEN

tilting, or a post or target tilted at by horsemen QUINTAIN

timber beam between walls supporting a ceiling or roof JOIST
- timber beam placed horizontally in a building, as for supporting a floor STRINGER, SUMMER
- timber stake or heavy post SPILE
- horizontal timber beam over a window or doorway LINTEL

time See chart, page 548
- time between two periods or events INTERVAL, INTERIM
- time error, dating mistake, placing a person, thing, or event in the incorrect historical period ANACHRONISM
- time of greatest strength or success HEYDAY, PRIME
- time or distance between two limits SPAN
- time period, or continuation through time DURATION
- timekeeping instrument used when practicing music METRONOME
- times gone by, the old days LANG SYNE
- timing or pace, especially in music TEMPO
- adjective for time TEMPORAL
- arrange in slightly different but overlapping positions or time periods STAGGER
- dominant outlook and spirit of the times ZEITGEIST
- happening or existing at the same time SIMULTANEOUS, COINCIDENT, CONTEMPORANEOUS, CONTEMPORARY, COEXISTING
- immediately before or after in time CONTIGUOUS
- instrument for measuring tiny intervals of time CHRONOGRAPH
- location error, placing a person, thing, or event in the incorrect location, analogous to anachronism as an error in time ANACHORISM
- ordered according to time of occurrence CHRONOLOGICAL
- pass by, as time does ELAPSE
- period or point of time, especially when critical JUNCTURE
- referring to time going back to the distant past IMMEMORIAL, UR-
- science of measuring time, or the study of timepieces HOROLOGY
- scientific measurement or calculation of time CHRONOMETRY
- system allowing staggered working hours to employees FLEXITIME, FLEXTIME
- very long time, specifically a billion years AEON

time (combining form) CHRON-, CHRONO-, TEMP-, TEMPOR-

time limit - law setting a time limit for prosecuting a crime or bringing a legal action STATUTE OF LIMITATIONS

times (combining form) -FOLD

tin works, or tin-mining center or region STANNARY
- referring to or containing tin STANNIC, STANNOUS

tinder in the form of decayed wood or similar dry material TOUCHWOOD, PUNK

tiny See **small**

tiny (combining form) MICRO-, NANO-, -ULE

tip, gift of money in return for a service POURBOIRE, GRATUITY
- tip, small bribe, or charity, given in Eastern countries BAKSHEESH
- tip, small gift, or bonus PERQUISITE, BUCKSHEE
- tip or small bribe or conciliatory gift DOUCEUR
- tip or small bribe or gift in West Africa DASH
- metal ring or cap on the tip of a walking stick or umbrella to protect it against wear FERRULE

tip (combining form) ACRO-

tiptoe, walking with only the toes touching the ground, as dogs and horses are DIGITIGRADE
- spin on tiptoe or on the ball of a foot, as in ballet PIROUETTE

tire or doughnut shape TORUS
- tire with fabric cords running diagonally to stiffen the sidewalls CROSS-PLY TIRE
- tire with cords spread at right angles from the circumference to provide for flexible sidewalls RADIAL TIRE, RADIAL-PLY TIRE
- filled with or run by compressed air, as most tires are PNEUMATIC
- release air or gas from something, such as a tire DEFLATE
- system of cords in a tire WARP

tired FATIGUED, WEARY
- tired, run-down, drained, abnormally weak or feeble DEBILITATED, ENERVATED
- tired and lazy LANGUID, LETHARGIC, LISTLESS
- tired and sleepy, drooping, drowsy SOMNOLENT, SOPORIFIC
- tired and stale, dulled, having lost interest JADED, BLASÉ
- tired and worried in appearance CAREWORN, HAGGARD
- tired-eyed, as from lack of sleep BLEARY-EYED
- tired out, exhausted, shattered, done in DEADBEAT, FORSPENT, FORWORN, PROSTRATE
- tired through being drained of strength or energy DEPLETED, FLAGGING
- tired through overwork, or exces-

sive effort OVEREXTENDED, OVERTASKED, OVERTAXED
- feeling of being tired of life, desperate boredom ENNUI, TAEDIUM VITAE, WELTSCHMERZ
- slang terms for tired or exhausted TUCKERED OUT, BUSHED, FRAZZLED, WHACKED OUT
- spiritually tired and feeble, drained of moral force or vitality DECADENT, EFFETE

tiredness, lack of energy LANGUOR, LASSITUDE, LETHARGY, LISTLESSNESS, SLUGGISHNESS
- tiredness, lack of interest, mental dullness APATHY, HEBETUDE
- tending to cause tiredness or induce sleep SOMNOLENT, SOPORIFIC

tireless, untiring INDEFATIGABLE

tiring, demanding TAXING, GRUELING, EXACTING
- tiring or boring work DRUDGERY

tissue, in fibrous sheets, beneath the skin and encasing muscles FASCIA
- tissue of a single layer of tightly packed cells, covering body organs and surfaces EPITHELIUM
- tissue from which nails and teeth develop MATRIX
- tissue in a plant containing channels for conducting fluids VASCULAR TISSUE
- tissue of natural or synthetic material through which fluids can pass slowly MEMBRANE
- tissue structure, or the scientific study of it HISTOLOGY
- body tissue in which fat is stored ADIPOSE TISSUE
- wasting away of tissue, as through disease ATROPHY
- watery liquid from the body tissues LYMPH

tissue (combining form) HIST-, HISTO-

tit-for-tat injury, raid, punishment, or the like RETALIATION, REPRISAL, REQUITAL, TALION

title, formal name, or description STYLE, DESIGNATION, APPELLATION
- title given to a dead person placed at the first level on the way to sainthood in the Roman Catholic Church VENERABLE
- title of a category RUBRIC
- title of a work, stating its argument or theme LEMMA
- title of respect used for a man in Turkey and the Middle East EFFENDI
- title of respect in addressing an employer in East Africa BWANA
- title of respect for someone of superior status HONORIFIC
- title or inscription, as on a coin or coat of arms LEGEND
- "defender of the faith," one of the titles of the British sovereign FIDEI DEFENSOR
- referring to a title TITULAR
- use of a title or epithet, such as *Her Majesty*, in place of a proper name ANTONOMASIA

TNT - explosive power equivalent to one million tons of TNT MEGATON

to - uninflected verb form that in English often follows *to*, or the combination of *to* with that verb form, as in *to dream* INFINITIVE
- "to" when not used as a preposition INFINITIVE PARTICLE

to (combining form) AD-, EPI-

to wit, "namely," "that is to say," used to introduce a synonym, explanation, or missing word SCILICET, SC
- "to wit," "namely," used to introduce examples, lists, or explanations VIDELICET, VIZ, I.E., ID EST

toad of southern Africa, used in pregnancy testing XENOPUS, PLATHANDER, PLATANNA
- toad or frog, or adjective for a toad or frog ANURAN, SALIENTIAN, BATRACHIAN
- European toad whose fertilized

Time Chart

GEOLOGICAL TIME SCALE			
ERA	PERIOD	EPOCH	MAJOR EVENTS
CENOZOIC	QUATERNARY	**Holocene** From 10,000 years ago	Ice sheets melt, sea level rises. Towns and cities are built.
CENOZOIC	QUATERNARY	**Pleistocene** 1.8 million years ago	Ice Age. Mastodons die out. Modern humans emerge.
CENOZOIC	TERTIARY	**Pliocene** 5 million years ago	Large carnivores are the dominant land animals.
CENOZOIC	TERTIARY	**Miocene** 26 million years ago	Renewed uplift of Rockies. Apelike hominids appear.
CENOZOIC	TERTIARY	**Oligocene** 37 million years ago	Alps and Himalayas begin to rise. Mastodons and apes appear.
CENOZOIC	TERTIARY	**Eocene** 53 million years ago	Grasses develop and spread. Earliest horses appear.
CENOZOIC	TERTIARY	**Paleocene** 65 million years ago	Rocky Mountains take shape. Mammals diversify rapidly.
MESOZOIC	**Cretaceous period** 143 million years ago		Dinosaurs die out. Flowering plants develop.
MESOZOIC	**Jurassic period** 212 million years ago		Dinosaurs abundant. Birds appear. Conifers, cycads abound.
MESOZOIC	**Triassic period** 246 million years ago		Reptiles expand dramatically. First mammals appear.
UPPER PALEOZOIC	**Permian period** 289 million years ago		Insects appear. Amphibians increase. Trilobites die out.
UPPER PALEOZOIC	**Carboniferous period** 367 million years ago		Appalachians rise. Coal-forming forests flourish. Reptiles appear.
UPPER PALEOZOIC	**Devonian period** 416 million years ago		Sharks and other large fish are widespread. Vegetation increases.
LOWER PALEOZOIC	**Silurian period** 446 million years ago		Plants begin to invade dry land. Shelled cephalopods abound.
LOWER PALEOZOIC	**Ordovician period** 508 million years ago		Primitive fish and corals appear. Marine invertebrates diversify.
LOWER PALEOZOIC	**Cambrian period** 575 million years ago		Seas cover most of North America. Trilobites are common.
PROTEROZOIC / ARCHEOZOIC	**Precambrian period** 4 billion to 6 billion years ago		Earth's crust forms. Primitive plants and animals appear.

eggs are carried on the hind legs of the male MIDWIFE TOAD
- European "running toad" with a yellow-striped back, that swells up when alarmed NATTERJACK, BUFO CALAMITA

toadstool See **fungus, mushroom**

toady See **flatter**

toast See chart
- toast, drinking to someone's health PLEDGE
- toast, or salute formerly given on drinking someone's health WASSAIL
- toast on which a savory mixture is served CROÛTE
- toast that is very thin and crisp MELBA TOAST
- toasted or fried square of bread, served in soups or salads CROUTON
- wedge of toast or fried bread, typically served as a garnish SIPPET

tobacco case in which the humidity can be kept constant HUMIDOR
- tobacco leaf around a cigar WRAPPER
- tobacco of a strong coarse type, cut into shreds SHAG
- tobacco plug left in a pipe after smoking DOTTLE
- coarse, broken dried tobacco leaves CANASTER
- light Kentucky tobacco BURLEY
- pack down or stamp down tightly tobacco, concrete, or the like by means of light blows TAMP
- poisonous addictive chemical compound in tobacco NICOTINE
- strong, dark tobacco, of various kinds CAPORAL, PERIQUE, LATAKIA
- sweetened tobacco molded into oblong cakes CAVENDISH
- twisted roll of tobacco PIGTAIL
- wad of tobacco for chewing QUID

toboggan-like racing sled LUGE

toe, finger, or corresponding part in other animals DIGIT
- toe bones PHALANGES
- big toe HALLUX
- fleshy underpart of the top joint of a finger or toe PAD
- hoofed mammal, such as a deer or cow, having two or four toes on each foot ARTIODACTYL
- painful condition in the joints, especially those of the big toe, caused by an excess of uric acid GOUT
- painful swelling of the lower joint of the big toe BUNION
- spin on tiptoe or on the ball of a foot, as in ballet PIROUETTE

toe (combining form) DACTYL-, DACTYLO-

toenails - care of the feet and toenails PEDICURE

together, joined to form a whole INTEGRATED

TOASTS

Cheers! around the world

Albania	**Gëzuar!**
Austria	**Prost! Prosit!**
Belgium	**À votre santé! Gezondheid!**
Bulgaria	**Nazdrave!**
China	**Gun-bei!**
Denmark	**Skål!**
Finland	**Kippis! Skål! Hölkyn kölkyn!**
France	**À votre santé!**
Germany	**Prost! Prosit! Zum Wohl!**
Greece	**Stin yia ssas!**
Hong Kong	**Yum-sing!**
Ireland	**Slàinte!**
Israel	**L'chaim!**
Italy	**Salute! Ciao!**
Japan	**Kam pai!**
Mexico	**Salud!**
Netherlands	**Proost! Santjes!**
Norway	**Skål!**
Poland	**Na zdrowie!**
Portugal	**Saúde!**
Romania	**Noroc!**
Scotland	**Slàinte mhath!**
South Africa	**Geluk! Gesondheid!**
Spain	**Salud!**
Sweden	**Skål!**
Switzerland	**Prost! Zum Wohl! Santé! Salute!**
Thailand	**Chokdee!**
Turkey	**Şerefe!**
U.S.S.R.	**Na zdorovye!**
Wales	**Iechyd da!**
Yugoslavia	**Zieili!**

- together with, associated with, accompanying CONCOMITANT, COROLLARY

together (combining form) CO-, COM-, SYN-, SYM-

together with (combining form) -CUM-

toilet See **lavatory**

toilet water EAU DE COLOGNE

toiletries - small case for needles, toiletries, or the like ETUI

token, tiny, insignificant, as a sum of money might be NOMINAL

tolerant, broad-minded, as in matters of moral conduct PERMISSIVE
- tolerant, long-suffering, putting up patiently with provocation FORBEARING
- tolerant, mild, and forgiving of others' faults or crimes LENIENT
- tolerant, undogmatic, and liberal, especially in matters of church doctrine and ritual, Broad Church LATITUDINARIAN
- tolerant, unvengeful, willing to forgive and forget MAGNANIMOUS
- tolerant and obliging, yielding to others' wishes COMPLAISANT
- tolerant of other people's whims, desires, or faults INDULGENT

tolerate, allow, or approve COUNTENANCE, SANCTION
- tolerate, endure, put up with BROOK, STOMACH, WITHSTAND
- tolerate, forgive, or overlook an offense CONDONE

toleration or permission implied by the absence of an explicit prohibition SUFFERANCE

tolling of a bell, as at a funeral KNELL

tomb, burial vault SEPULCHER
- tomb, or impressive building housing a tomb MAUSOLEUM
- tomb in ancient Egypt, of oblong shape with sloping sides and a flat roof MASTABA
- tomb of stone, typically decorated with a sculpture or inscriptions SARCOPHAGUS
- tomb or coffin cover of dark material, often velvet PALL
- inscription on a gravestone, tombstone, or monument commemorating the person buried there EPITAPH

tomboy, young woman or girl attractive in a boyish way GAMINE

tomorrow, or shortly MAÑANA

tone color, sound quality produced by overtones rather than volume and pitch TIMBRE
- distinction or variation of a very fine or subtle kind, as of tone, color, or meaning NUANCE

tongs or long tweezers used by a surgeon FORCEPS

- tongs used to deliver babies FORCEPS
- hinged metal bars resembling tongs, used for lifting heavy objects such as building materials CRAMPONS

tongue See also **mouth**
- tongue-shaped, as some leaves are LINGULATE
- adjective for the tongue GLOSSAL, LINGUAL
- any of the tiny pimplelike bumps on the tongue PAPILLA
- fold or flap of skin, such as that under the tongue FRENUM
- implement having a wide-tipped or flexible blade, as for pressing down the tongue when examining the throat TONGUE DEPRESSOR, SPATULA
- sore or cyst under the tongue, caused by a blocked salivary gland or duct RANULA
- trilling of a flute or other wind instrument by a rapid vibration of the tongue FLUTTER-TONGUING
- U-shaped bone at the base of the tongue HYOID BONE

tongue (combining form) -GLOSS-, GLOSSO-

tonic RESTORATIVE
- tonic with a bitter taste, used to flavor drinks ANGOSTURA BITTERS

tool See chart
- tool, instrument IMPLEMENT, UTENSIL
- handle or binding of shock-absorbing material on a hammer or other tool WITHE
- shaft of a tool, such as the mounting of a dentist's drill MANDREL
- sharp part of a tool, such as the blade of a knife or plane BIT
- tongue or prong at the foot of the blade of a knife, tool, or the like for embedding into the handle SHANK, TANG

tooth See illustration, page 551, and also **teeth, mouth**
- tooth or notch, as on a saw or the edge of a leaf SERRATION
- tooth-shaped DENTIFORM
- tooth socket in the jawbone ALVEOLUS
- tooth that is broken, protruding, or out of line SNAGGLETOOTH
- toothlike projection, as on a gear wheel DENT, DENTATION, DENTICLE
- appear by breaking through the gum, as an emerging tooth does ERUPT
- beltlike band or surrounding structure, such as the ridge around the base of a tooth CINGULUM
- broad, flat back tooth, for grinding MOLAR
- long, pointed tooth, as of a snake or bat FANG
- pointed tooth beside a front tooth, for biting and tearing CANINE, EYETOOTH, LANIARY
- pull out something, such as a tooth, by force EXTRACT
- referring to a tooth jammed against another tooth, and unable to emerge normally IMPACTED
- sharp front tooth, for biting off INCISOR
- side tooth, for grinding, having two crests BICUSPID, PREMOLAR

tooth (combining form) DENT-, DENTI-, -ODON-

tooth decay DENTAL CARIES
- controversial addition of fluorine compounds to the public water supply as a measure to reduce tooth decay FLUORIDATION

toothed bar that meshes with a gear wheel RACK
- toothed metal wheel or disc, as used for perforating sheets of stamps or pressing dots onto an engraving plate ROULETTE
- toothed projection on a wheel or cylinder, as to engage a bicycle chain or the perforations on a film SPROCKET
- toothed wheel COG, COGWHEEL
- toothed wheel or bar engaged by a hinged catch to allow movement in one direction only RATCHET

toothpaste or tooth powder DENTIFRICE

top See also **best, good**
- top-to-toe CAP-A-PIE
- top up, refill REPLENISH
- topmost point, peak, or best or final development or achievement PINNACLE, ZENITH, APEX, APOGEE, MERIDIAN, SUMMIT, VERTEX, CREST, CROWN
- extreme, utmost, or top point, point of highest achievement ACME, NE PLUS ULTRA
- place something on top of something else, such as one film sequence over another SUPERIMPOSE
- reach or be at the top of SURMOUNT
- spinning top, shaped like an hourglass, that is thrown and caught on a cord held between the hands DIABOLO
- spinning top spun with the

TOOLS

AGRICULTURAL AND GARDENING TOOLS

billhook
cant hook
dibble/dibber
draw hoe
flail
grub hoe
mattock
maul
pitchfork
scuffle hoe
sickle

BLACKSMITH'S TOOLS

anvil
drift
flatter
fuller
hardie
mandrel
set hammer
swage

DRILLING TOOLS

auger
bit
broach
countersink
gimlet
reamer
rose reamer
twist drill
wimble

CUTTING TOOLS

bolster chisel
cleaver
cold chisel
drove/boaster
firmer chisel
gouge
paring chisel
router
scorper

HAMMERS AND MALLETS

ball peen hammer
bushhammer
claw hammer
cross peen hammer
joiner's mallet
sledgehammer
soft-faced hammer
soft-faced mallet
tack hammer

MARKING AND MEASURING TOOLS

calipers
center punch
miter box
miter square
mortise gage
plumb rule
scriber
T square

SAWS

backsaw
band saw
bucksaw
chain saw
circular saw
compass saw
coping saw
dovetail saw
flooring saw
fretsaw
hacksaw
jigsaw
log saw
pad saw
panel saw
pit saw
ripsaw
scroll saw

SHAPING TOOLS

adz
block plane
file
jack plane
rasp
smoothing plane
spokeshave

WRENCHES AND SPANNERS

allen wrench
box wrench
pipe wrench
socket wrench
spanner
stillson wrench
torque wrench

THATCHER'S TOOLS

eaves hook
eaves knife
long-straw rake
reed knife
shearing hook
yoke

WHEELWRIGHT'S TOOLS

auger
bruzz
felly pattern
traveler

fingers, sometimes having four sides with letters or numbers for use in games TEETOTUM
- four-sided spinning top with Hebrew letters DREIDEL

top (combining form) ACRO-

torch formerly used to light the way in dark streets LINK
- torch of former times, in the form of a pole-mounted cup burning oil or pitch CRESSET
- flaming torch FLAMBEAU

torment See also **tease**
- torment or tease by parading but withholding something desirable TANTALIZE
- torment or treat cruelly HARROW

tortoise's shell CARAPACE
- adjective for a tortoise or turtle CHELONIAN, TESTUDINAL
- bony plate covering the chest of a tortoise or turtle BREASTPLATE, PLASTRON

torture in which the victim is beaten on the soles of the feet BASTINADO
- torture in which the victim is hoisted on a rope and then dropped with a jerk STRAPPADO
- instrument of torture consisting of a coffinlike case lined with iron spikes, into which the victim was locked IRON MAIDEN
- instrument of torture for squeezing the fingers and thumbs PILLIWINKS
- instruments of torture of various kinds RACK, WHEEL, BOOT, THUMBSCREW

tot, small quantity of whisky or other drink DRAM, NIP, SLUG, TOUCH

total, or the addition process by which it is reached SUMMATION
- total, whole amount, sum of many parts AGGREGATE

total (combining form) HOL-, HOLO-, PAN-, PANO-, PANT-, PANTO-

totally, altogether, entirely IN TOTO

touch, join, be positioned next to, as pieces of land might ABUT
- touch, without intersecting, as two curves in geometry might OSCULATE
- touch or enter where one should not IMPINGE
- touch or handle a body part as an aid to diagnosis or as a therapy MANIPULATE, PALPATE
- touch or stroke lovingly or affectionately CARESS, FONDLE
- alleged ability to know facts about people or events by touching objects associated with them PSYCHOMETRY
- perceptible to the touch, capable of being felt PALPABLE, TANGIBLE
- relating to the sense of touch TACTILE, TACTUAL
- touch with the lips, kiss OSCULATE

touching, bordering, neighboring, alongside CONTIGUOUS, ADJACENT, ABUTTING, JUXTAPOSED
- touching or affecting POIGNANT
- touching without intersecting, as a line in geometry might TANGENT

touchy, easily offended UMBRAGEOUS

tough, austerely self-disciplined, having great fortitude SPARTAN
- tough, bold, and stout-hearted, as a warrior might be DOUGHTY
- tough, buoyant, able to recover quickly from misfortune or illness RESILIENT
- tough, spirited, and frisky, as a terrier might be FEISTY
- tough, unyielding, and inflexible, or firm of purpose or opinion ADAMANT, ADAMANTINE
- tough and firm against pressure or attack RESISTANT
- tough and hard to chew, as meat might be FIBROUS
- tough and long-lasting DURABLE, ENDURING
- tough and uncompromising, unsentimentally practical HARD-BITTEN, HARD-NOSED
- tough-minded and able to withstand grief, disappointment, or pain STOICAL
- tough-minded and impassive, showing little emotion STOLID, IMPASSIVE

tour guide on sightseeing expeditions CICERONE
- tour guide or interpreter in the Middle East formerly DRAGOMAN
- tour in which an electioneering politician briefly visits a series of small towns WHISTLE-STOP TOUR
- touring car, such as some sports cars GRAN TURISMO, GT
- touring group of entertainers TROUPE

tournament arena, as for chivalric combat LISTS
- tournament in medieval times, in which knights took part in horse races and riding displays CARROUSEL
- tournament of duels between knights, with lances on horseback JOUSTS, TILTING MATCH

tow - ring on a vehicle, into which a towing hook is inserted LUNETTE
- upright pivot pin, as on a rudder or towing vehicle PINTLE

toward (combining form) AD-, EPI-, -PROS-, -PETAL

Tooth

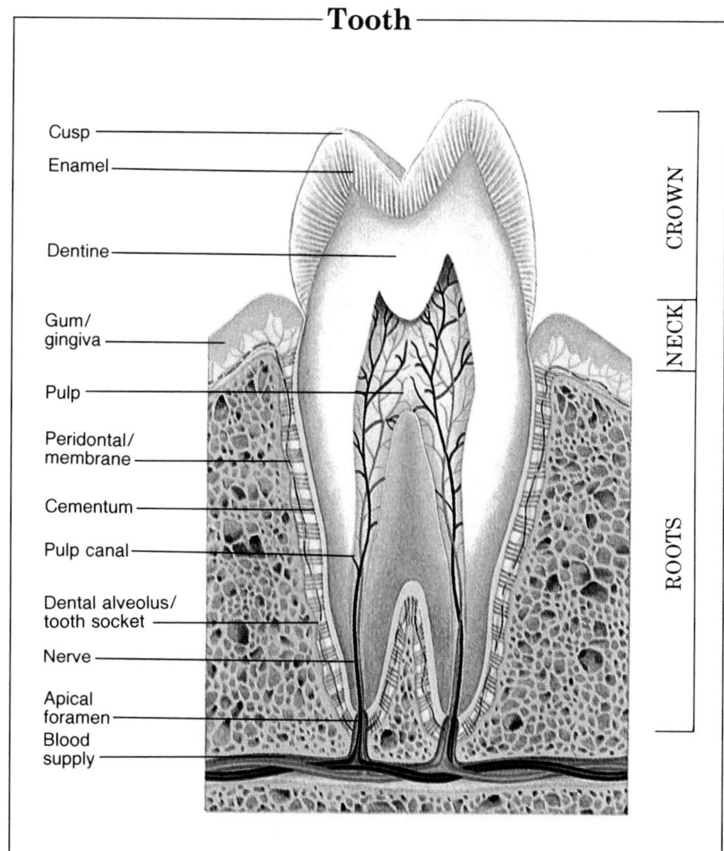

toweling or similar absorbent fabric with uncut loops on both sides TERRY, TERRY CLOTH

tower, mobile or makeshift, used in attacking castle walls TURRET, BELFRY
- tower formerly guarding the coast in various European countries MARTELLO TOWER
- tower or parapet in a medieval fortification BRATTICE
- freestanding bell tower CAMPANILE
- pyramid-shaped temple tower in ancient Babylon ZIGGURAT
- round, fortified tower built in ancient times in Scotland BROCH
- small tower TURRET
- small turret jutting from a wall or tower BARTIZAN
- tall cylindrical tower for storing grain or fodder SILO, ELEVATOR
- tall slender tower of a mosque, from which the muezzin summons the faithful to prayer MINARET

town See also **city**
- town, city, or self-governing community MUNICIPALITY
- town, outside a larger city, from which many people commute to work BEDROOM COMMUNITY, DORMITORY TOWN
- town crier's call for attention OYEZ
- town dweller OPPIDAN, BURGESS, URBANITE, CITIZEN
- town hall in Germany RATHAUS
- town or borough in Scotland BURGH
- adjective for a town MUNICIPAL, URBAN
- senior member of a town council ALDERMAN

toy consisting of a card or disc that is spun or twirled to produce a merged image of the partial words or pictures on either side THAUMATROPE
- toy consisting of an hourglass-shaped spinning top that is thrown and caught on a cord held between the hands DIABOLO
- toy spinning top spun with the fingers TEETOTUM
- toy with a rounded weighted base that always rights itself after being rocked or pushed down ROLY-POLY, TUMBLER
- toylike ornament with moving parts, usually of shiny metal, as found on office desktops EXECUTIVE TOY
- spinning toy of various kinds WHIRLIGIG

trace, small amount SEMBLANCE, MODICUM, SCINTILLA, IOTA, JOT, TITTLE
- traces left by something that has disappeared VESTIGES

track of visible foam or waves in water, as left by a ship WAKE
- track or trail, especially of a wild animal SPOOR, SLOT

trade, occupation, career VOCATION
- trade association or guild in the City of London LIVERY COMPANY
- trade restrictions imposed to protect a country's industries against competition from abroad PROTECTIONISM
- trade restrictions or similar measures imposed on a nation to put pressure on it to change its policies SANCTIONS
- trade through direct exchange of goods and services, without using money BARTER
- adjective for trade or commerce MERCANTILE
- practice or engage in one's trade PLY
- prohibition, as of foreign merchant ships, or arms trading, or of all trade EMBARGO

trademark, emblem, or symbol of a company LOGO, LOGOTYPE
- protected by a trademark, as a medicine might be PROPRIETARY, PATENT

trader, peddler, or supplier in former times CHAPMAN, CHANDLER

trading center where goods are held for reexport or transshipment ENTREPÔT
- trading center, marketplace, exchange RIALTO

traffic detour DIVERSION
- traffic holdup caused by an obstruction or narrow stretch of road, or the point of this holdup BOTTLENECK
- traffic jam CONGESTION, GRIDLOCK
- post on a traffic island, on the pavement to prevent parking, or the like, in Great Britain BOLLARD

tragedy See also chart at **drama**
- avenging justice, as in Greek tragedy NEMESIS
- excessive pride leading to downfalls, as in Greek tragedy HUBRIS
- "fatal flaw" in the character of a hero, which leads to his or her downfall, as in Greek tragedy HAMARTIA
- moment of recognition or insight by the hero, as at the climax of a Greek tragedy ANAGNORISIS
- purgation of the emotions through pity and fear, as when watching a drama CATHARSIS
- sudden change of fortune, usually from prosperity to ruin, as at the climax of a Greek tragedy PERIPETEIA

trail or tracks, especially of a wild animal SPOOR, SLOT

trailer - link bolt or hook, as at the back of a car, to which a trailer, camper, or the like is attached PINTLE

train, airplane, or the like carrying no passengers or cargo DEADHEAD
- train car of a comfortable and spacious design PULLMAN
- train car's enclosed entrance area VESTIBULE
- train cars, wagons, and locomotives ROLLING STOCK
- train compartment at the end of a continental European railway car, with seats on one side only COUPÉ
- train running on a single rail, often on an elevated track MONORAIL TRAIN
- bumper or grid in front of a train to clear the track COWCATCHER, FENDER
- car behind a steam locomotive, carrying fuel and water TENDER
- cord or chain in a railroad car that a passenger can pull in an emergency to stop the train COMMUNICATION CORD
- device for linking any two cars or trucks of a train COUPLING, DRAWBAR
- frame on the roof of an electric train engine or trolleybus, collecting current from an overhead wire PANTOGRAPH
- guard's van on trains, with eating and sleeping facilities for the crew CABOOSE
- low, open railroad freight car GONDOLA
- overhead cable for an electric train or trolleybus CATENARY
- railroad freight car that unloads through its floor HOPPER
- safety switch or lever, as on a train, that causes mechanical shutdown if released by the operator DEADMAN BRAKE
- shock-absorbing or cushionlike device, such as the steel pads between train cars BUFFER
- sleeping car, especially on a European continental train WAGON-LIT

trainee, contracted worker receiving instruction in a trade APPRENTICE
- trainee officer in the police or armed forces CADET
- contracted as a trainee, apprenticed ARTICLED

training, upbringing NURTURE
- training device consisting of a model, machine, or system reproducing actual conditions, such as a model flight deck for training pilots SIMULATOR
- training in a particular trade or skill that is to be the basis of a career VOCATIONAL TRAINING

traitor, deserter, faithless or disloyal person RECREANT, TURNCOAT
- traitor, especially one serving as the puppet leader of an occupying foreign power QUISLING
- traitor, person who abandons his or her religion, allegiances, or loyalties RENEGADE, APOSTATE
- traitor, person who betrays a partner DOUBLE-CROSSER
- traitor cooperating with enemy forces occupying his or her country COLLABORATIONIST, COLLABORATOR
- traitor or rebel who works secretly to undermine the government SUBVERSIVE
- traitor or refugee who abandons his or her country for that of an enemy DEFECTOR
- traitor or secret agent who deliberately incites people to illegal acts to entrap them AGENT PROVOCATEUR
- traitor or spy who infiltrates an organization to betray its secrets MOLE, PLANT, SLEEPER
- traitorous, treacherous, faithless PERFIDIOUS
- informer, police spy, traitor in the criminal world who betrays associates to the police STOOL PIGEON, STOOLIE
- person considered a traitor or collaborator through his or her undue acceptance of or cooperation with oppressors UNCLE TOM

tramp, down-and-out, bum DERELICT
- tramp, rogue, thief, or adventurer PICARO, PICAROON
- tramp or drifter, especially one that moves about as a stowaway on trains BUM, HOBO
- tramp or itinerant laborer in Australia SWAGMAN
- tramp who begs for money on the streets PANHANDLER
- former Scottish term for a tramp or beggar GANGREL
- wandering tramp or beggar, drifter VAGRANT, VAGABOND

tranquilizer, medical drug with a soothing or calming effect SEDATIVE, ATARACTIC
- tranquilizer or sleeping pill of a common synthetic make NITRAZEPAM, DIAZEPAM
- tranquilizing or pain-killing substance secreted by the brain ENDORPHIN

transfer a design by loosely shading or coloring its reverse side, and then tracing it onto a surface or paper underneath CALK, CALQUE
- transfer an estate, sovereignty, or the like, as by a will DEMISE
- transfer of a teacher, military officer, or the like for temporary duty elsewhere SECONDMENT
- transfer of property, interests, or rights in law ASSIGNMENT
- transfer of the ownership of property by means of a legal document CONVEYANCE

transform See **change, turn**

transformation, as of a caterpillar into a butterfly METAMORPHOSIS
- transformation or change of a spectacular kind TRANSFIGURATION, TRANSMOGRIFICATION

translate, as formerly from a Latin text, usually aloud, as a classroom exercise CONSTRUE
- translate in another language or form RENDER

translation, explanatory note, or commentary, as in the margin of a manuscript or text GLOSS
- translation shown above the stage or screen SURTITLE
- insert a new soundtrack into a movie, especially a translation of the dialogue DUB
- literal-translation aid, as used to cheat in a test PONY
- word for word, as a translation might be LITERAL, VERBATIM

translucent, as some fine fabrics are DIAPHANOUS, SHEER, GOSSAMER

transmigration of the soul METEMPSYCHOSIS

transmit something, such as a radio wave, through a given medium PROPAGATE

transparent, very clear or pure CRYSTALLINE, PELLUCID, LIMPID
- transparent or translucent, as some fine fabrics are DIAPHANOUS, SHEER, GOSSAMER
- transparent paper like wrapping material CELLOPHANE
- allowing the passage of light, as frosted glass does, but only in a diffused form, unlike transparent glass TRANSLUCENT
- preventing the passage of light, not transparent OPAQUE

transplant of animal tissue to humans ZOOPLASTY
- fail to accept a tissue graft or transplanted organ REJECT
- person who provides an organ for transplant DONOR
- person who receives a transplanted organ DONEE, RECIPIENT
- referring to medical drugs used to prevent rejection of a transplanted organ IMMUNOSUPPRESSIVE

transport or movement of goods or people from place to place TRANSIT, CONVEYANCE
- transportation or carrying, as of heavy supplies, or the cost of it PORTAGE
- transporting of goods as a business, or the charge for it HAULAGE
- organizing of any complicated project, especially one involving transport LOGISTICS

transposing of letters within a word, as in the development of *bird* from Old English *brid* METATHESIS

transvestism and female behavior of a man EONISM

trap See also **trick**
- trap, capture by trickery ENSNARE
- trap, enclosure, or the like, into which birds or game can be lured DECOY
- trap, entice, or tempt or lead astray by flattery or promises INVEIGLE
- trap, trick, dodge, devious scheme to gain the upper hand STRATAGEM, SUBTERFUGE, PLOY
- trap birds by means of a sticky substance spread on branches or twigs LIME
- trap for catching animals GIN
- trap for large animals, in which a heavy weight crushes the quarry DEADFALL
- trap for small animals or birds, typically a noose attached to a bent twig or branch SPRINGE, SNARE
- intended as a trap, treacherous, as a sneaky argument might be INSIDIOUS
- things in which one is trapped, caught, or confined TOILS

trappings or symbols, especially of royalty REGALIA

travel across or through TRAVERSE
- travel in stages or relays POST
- travel or wander far and wide, usually on foot PEREGRINATE
- travel slowly and laboriously, specifically by ox wagon TREK
- travels, typically long and far, and often by foot PEREGRINATIONS, PILGRIMAGE
- person who regularly travels a considerable distance between home and work COMMUTER
- planned route for one's travels ITINERARY
- yearning for travel or urge to travel, especially in foreign countries WANDERLUST

traveler, usually on foot WAYFARER
- traveler who journeys far and wide and frequently JET-SETTER, GLOBETROTTER
- travelers in a group or convoy across a desert CARAVAN

traveling from place to place, as some laborers, preachers, or judges are ITINERANT, MIGRANT
- traveling in disguise or under a false name INCOGNITO
- traveling musician in the Middle

Ages MINSTREL, TROUBADOUR, TROUVÈRE, JONGLEUR
- traveling scholar or student in the Middle Ages GOLIARD
- employed in a number of places, especially schools, and traveling between them PERIPATETIC
- relating to traveling VIATIC

traveling (combining form) -DROM-, VIAT-

tray, with a handle underneath, for carrying cement or plaster HAWK
- tray for bricks or mortar, carried over the shoulder on a pole HOD
- tray or platter, often made of silver, for serving food, presenting visiting cards, or the like SALVER, WAITER
- circular, revolving tray, used to hold food on a dining table DUMB WAITER, LAZY SUSAN
- small tray, sometimes on wheels, for a wine bottle, decanter, or the like COASTER

Trees

treacherous See also **traitor**
- treacherous, disloyal, faithless TREASONOUS, PERFIDIOUS
- treacherously and subtly harmful INSIDIOUS

treachery, disloyalty, breach of trust PERFIDY

treason See also **traitor**
- treason or other offense committed against a sovereign power LESE MAJESTY, LÈSE MAJESTÉ
- accuse of treason IMPEACH

treasure ship ARGOSY
- place where treasure is put for safekeeping REPOSITORY

treasury, government department that is in charge of funds or revenue in Great Britain EXCHEQUER
- referring to a country's treasury, finances, or tax matters FISCAL

treatment See **therapy, medical,** surgical

treaty See also **agreement**
- treaty or peace agreement CONCORD, ACCORD
- treaty restricting the increased production or deployment of nuclear weapons NONPROLIFERATION TREATY
- acceptance of an agreement or treaty ACCESSION
- affecting or undertaken by two parties, as a treaty might be BILATERAL, BIPARTITE
- amendment to, draft for, or supplement to a treaty or other document PROTOCOL
- announce formally the rejection of a treaty DENOUNCE
- give formal approval to a treaty and thereby confirm it RATIFY
- person, party, government, or the like that has signed and is bound to a treaty SIGNATORY

tree See illustration, page 554, and also **wood** and illustrations at **deciduous trees** and **evergreen**
- tree-lined terrace or garden walk in ancient Rome XYST
- tree of a cone-bearing, usually evergreen type, such as a pine or fir CONIFER
- tree or shrub of dwarf size, produced by rigorous pruning, or the traditional Japanese art of producing such plants BONSAI
- tree-shaped, resembling a tree DENDROID, DENDRIFORM, ARBORESCENT
- tree spirit, or divinity of the woods and trees, in mythology DRYAD, HAMADRYAD
- tree such as a conifer or yew, that produces naked seeds not enclosed in an ovary GYMNOSPERM
- tree trunk BOLE
- tree whose branches are cut back to the trunk to encourage new foliage POLLARD
- trees, hedge, or fence breaking the force of the wind WINDBREAK
- trees or forests of a particular region SILVA
- trees or shrubs in a thicket BOSK, BOSCAGE
- avenue or row of trees placed at regular intervals COLONNADE
- covered or shaded by trees or shrubs BOSKY
- cut a ring of bark from a tree trunk or branch to kill it or slow its growth RINGBARK, GIRDLE
- grove or small thicket of trees COPSE, COPPICE, SPINNEY
- having spread-out branches arranged in pairs, as some trees are BRACHIATE
- high, overhead cover, as of the foliage on treetops CANOPY
- knotty and twisted, as the trunk or branches of a tree might be GNARLED
- large roundish outgrowth of wood in a tree's trunk, branches, or roots BURL
- leafy upper part of a tree CROWN
- notch made in a tree being felled, or the cut end of a felled tree KERF
- place where trees and shrubs are cultivated for exhibition or study ARBORETUM
- plant of the common group including most trees and shrubs, characterized by two embryonic seed leaves DICOTYLEDON, DICOT
- referring to trees ARBOREAL
- retaining their leaves through winter, as most coniferous trees are EVERGREEN
- shedding all their leaves at a particular time each year, as some trees are DECIDUOUS
- study or cultivation of trees ARBORICULTURE, SILVICULTURE
- trimming of trees or hedges into ornamental shapes TOPIARY

tree (combining form) DENDR-, DENDRI-, DENDRO-, ARBOR-, SILV-

trellis or frame against which a shrub or fruit tree is trained to lie flat ESPALIER
- trellis or other framework carrying climbing plants and forming a covered walk PERGOLA

trench, channel, or groove, as for drainpipes or electric wires CHASE
- defensive bank, as behind a trench, giving protection from the rear PARADOS
- platform behind a parapet or in a trench, on which soldiers stand when firing BANQUETTE

trespass, intrude slowly on the property or rights of someone else ENCROACH, INFRINGE

trial See also **court**
- trial by combat in former times WAGER OF BATTLE
- trial in the Middle Ages, in which God's judgment was allegedly secured through exposing the accused to fire, immersion in water, or the like ORDEAL
- trial or acquittal in former times in which a number of people swore to the innocence of the accused COMPURGATION
- trial or inquest in England in former times ASSIZE
- trial period, as for membership of a profession or religious order PROBATION
- held in secret or behind closed doors, as a trial or hearing might be IN CAMERA
- negotiations between the defense and prosecution before a criminal trial, aimed at exchanging a guilty plea in court for a reduced charge PLEA BARGAINING
- preliminary trial or inquest HEARING
- privilege of clergymen in the Middle Ages to undergo trial in a church court rather than a secular court BENEFIT OF CLERGY
- referring to a judicial system where the judge in a criminal trial also acts as prosecutor INQUISITORIAL
- referring to a judicial system where the judge in a criminal trial rules on the case argued by a prosecutor ACCUSATORIAL

trial and error - referring to problem-solving techniques based on trial and error HEURISTIC

triangle See also **geometry**
- triangle with all three sides having different lengths SCALENE TRIANGLE
- triangle with three sides of equal length EQUILATERAL TRIANGLE
- triangle with two equal sides ISOSCELES TRIANGLE
- point of intersection of the three altitudes of a triangle ORTHOCENTER
- rule relating the lengths of the sides of a right-angled triangle PYTHAGOREAN THEOREM
- side of a right-angled triangle opposite the right angle HYPOTENUSE

triangular arrangement of numbers with each number being the sum of the two numbers just above it PASCAL'S TRIANGLE
- triangular in shape DELTOID
- triangular insert of material for enlarging or reinforcing a garment, bag, or the like GUSSET
- triangular section of wall or gable above the facade of a Grecian-

style building PEDIMENT
- triangular sheet of wood, metal, or plastic, used to construct certain angles and lines quickly in geometry or technical drawing SET SQUARE

tribal family group's symbol or kinship emblem, often a plant or animal TOTEM
- tribal grouping of related or intermarried clans PHRATRY, PHRATRIA

tribe(combining form) ETHN-, ETHNO-

tribute, expression of gratitude or appreciation TESTIMONIAL

trick See also **cheat, trap, fraud**
- trick, cheat, or defraud COZEN
- trick, crafty scheme, or the like, as to conceal or escape something SUBTERFUGE, EVASION, SHIFT
- trick, swindle, deception FLIMFLAM
- trick or ruse, especially where one appears to decline an advantage FINESSE, GAMBIT
- trick or ruse in various sports, in which one pretends to make a particular move in order to deceive an opponent FEINT
- trick or swindle in which the victim is defrauded after his or her trust has been won CONFIDENCE TRICK
- trick or tactic, as in a game, to secure an advantage by deceit STRATAGEM, PLOY, ARTIFICE, MANEUVER
- tricking or luring of someone as by the police, into crime, danger, or the like ENTRAPMENT
- tricks, either deceitful or playful WILES
- tricks, either mischievous or fraudulent SHENANIGANS
- easily deceived, tricked, or duped CREDULOUS, GULLIBLE
- magician's manual skill and speed in performing tricks SLEIGHT OF HAND, PRESTIDIGITATION, LEGERDEMAIN
- playful or clever trick or idea, prank DODGE, STUNT, WRINKLE
- victim of a trick, person fooled or used FALL GUY, PAWN, MARK, DUPE

trickery, cunning, ingenuity GUILE
- trickery, underhand or devious action SKULDUGGERY, CHICANERY
- trickery and plotting, deviousness, secret and hostile schemes MACHINATIONS
- secure or achieve by trickery or craftiness FINAGLE

trickster or con man MOUNTEBANK, CHARLATAN

tricky, crafty, cunning FOXY, SLY, WILY
- tricky, untrustworthy DEVIOUS, SHIFTY
- ruthlessly tricky, sly, or opportunistic, especially in politics MACHIAVELLIAN

trifling or hairsplitting distinction QUIBBLE, QUIDDITY
- trifling or utterly unimportant thing BAGATELLE

trillionth (combining form) PICO-

trimming See also **edge**
- trimming for hats, of twisted ribbon or cord TORSADE
- trimming of a flat, narrow braid forming zigzags RICKRACK
- trimming of lace or embroidery PURL
- trimming or edging, as for upholstery, consisting of a narrow tube of folded cloth, usually enveloping a cord PIPING
- trimming or fancy edging consisting of lace, braid, beadwork, or the like PASSEMENTERIE
- band of braid, lace, or embroidery forming a decorative border or trimming GALLOON
- gold or silver wire or cord used as a trimming, as on military uniforms BULLION FRINGE
- narrow and sometimes stiffened trimming used on clothes, curtains, and furniture GIMP, GUIPURE
- pleated or gathered lace or fabric used as a frilly trimming RUCHE, RUFFLE, FLOUNCE, FURBELOW
- richly embroidered border or trimming, as on clerical vestments ORPHREY

trinity - any of the three persons of the Holy Trinity HYPOSTASIS
- God's word, regarded as the second person of the Trinity LOGOS
- identical in essence or substance, as the three persons of the Trinity are sometimes interpreted as being CONSUBSTANTIAL
- relating to a trinity with an underlying unity TRIUNE

trinket, small, cheap, and flashy article or ornament BAUBLE, FURBELOW
- trinket, small inexpensive ornament or toy KNICKKNACK, NOVELTY, FOLDEROL
- trinket or small curio BIBELOT
- trinkets, showy or flashy objects or oddments BRIC-A-BRAC, FRIPPERY, GAUDERY, GEWGAWS, DOODAS

trip or stumble FALTER
- trip or pleasure outing, especially by public officials using public funds JUNKET
- coach or large bus hired for a trip CHARABANC, CHAR-À-BANC
- roam aimlessly or go on frivolous trips GAD ABOUT, GALLIVANT
- short trip, outing, usually to a designated destination EXCURSION
- short trip, outing, spree JAUNT

trite See **cliché**

triumphant, joyous, elated JUBILANT, EXULTANT

trombone - U-shaped section of tubing in a trombone that is moved outward and back to produce different notes SLIDE, GLIDE

troop formation of infantry in ancient Greece bearing overlapping shields PHALANX
- troop formation of stepped or offset parallel rows ECHELON
- troop formation or position subject to gunfire along its entire length ENFILADE

troops See also **soldier, services, military**
- troops or supplies sent to support those that are already in use REINFORCEMENTS
- troops protecting the front of a military unit VANGUARD
- troops stationed as a guard in case of surprise attack PICKET
- troops stationed at a military post or outpost GARRISON
- arrangement or order'y display, as of troops ARRAY
- assemble and prepare troops, as for an emergency MOBILIZE, MARSHAL, MUSTER
- assign accommodation to military officers or troops BILLET, QUARTER, CANTON
- dismiss or discharge troops from military service DEMOBILIZE, DEMOB, DISBAND
- march or emerge into a more open space, as a column of troops might DEBOUCH
- reassemble troops for a renewed attack RALLY
- remove troops or military control from an area DEMILITARIZE
- small selected unit of troops or ships sent on an assignment DETACHMENT
- station troops or weapons in an area, or make them ready for action DEPLOY
- withdraw troops from active conflict DISENGAGE

trophy - base block or slab, as of a column, statue, vase, or trophy PLINTH

troubadour or poet-musician of northern France in medieval times TROUVÈRE

trouble spot or explosive situation or person TINDERBOX, POWDER KEG
- make trouble, cause an uproar or disturbance RAISE CAIN

troublemaker, person who causes or heralds trouble STORMY PETREL

troublesome, burdensome ONEROUS, TOILSOME
- troublesome, unruly, given to fighting FRACTIOUS, BELLIGERENT

trousers See also **clothes**

- trousers with very narrow legs DRAINPIPES
- angle or fork formed by branches, steps, trouser legs, or the like CROTCH
- spreading or gradual widening, as of a trouser leg FLARE

truce between warring factions or armies ARMISTICE

truck in two sections, a tractor and a trailer, linked by a pivoting bar for greater maneuverability TRACTOR-TRAILER
- truck used in moving furniture VAN
- swing out of control into a V-shape, as a tractor-trailer might JACKKNIFE
- truck driver TEAMSTER
- weight of an unloaded truck or other commercial freight vehicle TARE

true, genuine, real, reliable AUTHENTIC, VERIDICAL, VERACIOUS, PUKKA, KOSHER
- true beyond question, indisputably certain VERITABLE, APODICTIC
- true by virtue of correspondence to facts in the real world rather than by the meaning of its words, as a proposition in logic might be SYNTHETIC, A POSTERIORI
- true by virtue of the meaning of its words rather than by correspondence to facts in the real world, as a proposition in logic might be ANALYTIC, A PRIORI
- true or indisputably accurate statement, belief, principle, or the like VERITY
- true to life, lifelike, as a very realistic novel or painting would be NATURALISTIC
- confirm as existent, true, correct, or genuine ATTEST, CORROBORATE, SUBSTANTIATE, VALIDATE, VERIFY

trump - play a trump in card games RUFF

trumpet fanfare TUCKET
- trumpet of an early kind with a high pitch CLARION
- trumpet's high register CLARINO
- blast or flourish on a horn or trumpet TANTARA, TANTIVY
- flourish, short ceremonial tune, or the like played on trumpets or other brass instruments FANFARE
- mute for a musical instrument, as on a trumpet SORDINO

trumpeter or proclaimer at royal announcements HERALD

trunk of a tree BOLE
- trunk of the body, or a sculpture of it TORSO
- elephant's trunk, or similar long flexible snout PROBOSCIS

trust - held in trust, or relating to a trust or trustee FIDUCIARY
- steal or misuse funds held in trust EMBEZZLE, DEFALCATE, PECULATE

trustee, person entrusted with something for safekeeping DEPOSITORY

truth, accurate correspondence to the facts VERACITY, FIDELITY
- truth that is universally acknowledged or self-evident AXIOM
- process of reaching the truth, as in Hegel or Socrates, by examining and exploiting contradictions DIALECTIC
- quality of appearing to be the truth VERISIMILITUDE
- straightforward, without any softening or decoration, as the plain truth is UNVARNISHED

truthful or genuine VERIDICAL, VERACIOUS

try, put to the test, evaluate or assess ASSAY
- try hard, make a conscious and earnest attempt ENDEAVOR
- try or strive for superiority against, take on CONTEND WITH, VIE WITH
- try or try out, especially in a careful or tentative way ESSAY
- trying something out, taking a chance ON SPEC
- first try, initial venture or attempt FORAY

tube, open at both ends, into which liquid is sucked to be measured or transferred PIPETTE
- tube, pipe, or canal for the passage of fluids, as in a building, a plant, or the human body DUCT
- tube inserted into a body cavity or channel for draining or introducing fluid CATHETER, CANNULA
- tube through which an ovum

Turtles

False map turtle

Green sea turtle

passes from the ovary FALLOPIAN TUBE, OVIDUCT
- tube with a narrow throat, used for measuring fluid flow rates, or to provide suction, as in a carburetor VENTURI
- tube with a very narrow bore CAPILLARY
- tube with internal mirrors producing an endless variety of symmetrical colored patterns when one looks through it and rotates it KALEIDOSCOPE
- diameter of the inside of a tube, of the bore of a gun, or of a bullet or shell CALIBER
- sliding tube within another, as in a telescope DRAWTUBE

tuberculosis of the lungs CONSUMPTION, PHTHISIS, TB

tuck - tapered tuck made in dressmaking DART

tummy rumbling BORBORYGMUS

tumor of the skin that is dark in color and malignant MELANOMA
- grow or spread abnormally, with fleshy outgrowths, as warts and some tumors do VEGETATE
- hard, slow-growing cancer tumor, as in the breast SCIRRHUS
- malignant cancer tumor of various kinds SARCOMA, CARCINOMA
- malignant tumor of the face that eats away at the bone and muscle behind the lips and nose RODENT ULCER
- referring to a tumor that does not seriously threaten a person's health BENIGN
- referring to a tumor that is spreading out of control and is resistant to treatment MALIGNANT
- small growth or tumor projecting from a mucous membrane, as in the nose POLYP
- soft tumor or swelling on the lower leg of a horse WINDGALL
- wart, corn, or similar benign growth or tumor PAPILLOMA

tumor (combining form) ONCO-, -CELE, -OMA

tuna or tunny, commonly eaten as canned tunafish ALBACORE

tune, musical passage STRAIN, ARIA, MEASURE, AIR
- tune accompanying and identifying a particular program or performer SIGNATURE TUNE
- tune added as counterpoint above a basic theme DESCANT
- tune added as counterpoint below a basic musical theme, usually played on a keyboard instrument, with the chords being indicated but the notes being left to the performer CONTINUO, THOROUGHBASS, FIGURED BASS
- tune or rhyme of a simple, catchy kind, as used in advertisements JINGLE
- tune or verse repeated regularly REFRAIN, CHORUS, BURDEN
- tunes played in succession as a single piece of music MEDLEY
- tuning fork or pitch pipe DIAPASON
- musical medley based on popular tunes QUODLIBET

tungsten WOLFRAM, W

tunic of chain mail HAUBERK, HABERGEON
- tunic worn by a medieval knight over his armor SURCOAT

tunnel - digging of a trench or tunnel toward or under an enemy position, fort, or the like SAP
- form a tunnel by digging EXCAVATE

turban, sash, skirt, or loincloth of cotton worn by men in India and some other countries LUNGI

turbine blade VANE

turf - legal right to dig peat or turf TURBARY

Turkish elite soldier or bodyguard in former times JANISSARY
- Turkish empire and dynasty from 1299 to 1922 OTTOMAN
- Turkish irregular cavalryman of a notoriously brutal band in the 19th century BASHI-BAZOUK
- Turkish language as written in Arabic script until 1930 OSMANLI
- Turkish or Balkan brandy or plum spirits, flavored with aniseed RAKI
- Turkish or Muslim emblem of power CRESCENT
- Turkish soldier, especially in the 19th century NIZAM
- Turkish viceroy in Egypt in former times KHEDIVE
- respectful term of address in Turkey, corresponding to *Mr.* or *Sir* BEY, EFFENDI

turn See also **change, twist**
- turn, curve, bend, or fold, as of a body part FLEXURE
- turn, whirl around, spin GYRATE, ROTATE, REVOLVE
- turn aside a fencing thrust, hostile question, or the like PARRY, WARD OFF
- turn aside, differ, or depart from the norm or standard, as of a policy or route DEVIATE
- turn aside from the main route, go by a roundabout way DETOUR
- turn aside or stray from the main subject DIGRESS
- turn aside or swerve away DEFLECT, DIVERT
- turn away one's eyes, gaze, or the like AVERT
- turn into a new form, or the next phase, as from a caterpillar to a butterfly METAMORPHOSE
- turn into a new form, especially one that is fantastic or bizarre TRANSMOGRIFY
- turn into a new sequence or order, rearrange PERMUTE
- turn into something radically new or better, change the appearance of TRANSFIGURE
- turn or change into a new form, convert TRANSFORM, TRANSMUTE, MUTATE
- turn or direct inward upon itself INTROVERT
- turn or fold a body part inside out or outward EVERT
- turn or fold a body part inward INTUSSUSCEPT, INVAGINATE
- turn or rotate while fastened or linked to another part or surface PIVOT, SWIVEL
- turn or swirl, as currents might in a stream EDDY
- turn out, come to pass TRANSPIRE
- turn to bone OSSIFY
- turn to salt SALIFY, SALINIZE
- turn to stone PETRIFY
- turn upside down or inside out INVERT
- in turn, by turns ALTERNATING
- relieve or stand in for somebody at work, by taking a turn SPELL

turn (combining form) -TROP-, TROPO-, -TROPIC, -TROPE

turnabout, U-turn, reversal of attitude or policy VOLTE-FACE

turning, act of twisting, or stress produced by it TORSION
- turning, twisting, winding CONTORTED, TORTUOUS, ANFRACTUOUS
- turning, whirling, revolving VERTIGINOUS
- turning force or the technical measurement of it TORQUE
- turning or applying for help to a person or thing, such as the courts RECOURSE

turning point, beyond which there is no going back RUBICON
- turning point, crucial time or event WATERSHED
- turning point or critical point in time JUNCTURE

turnip - shaped like a turnip, as some roots are NAPIFORM

turtle See illustration, page 557
- turtle's shell MAIL, CARAPACE
- adjective for a turtle or tortoise CHELONIAN, TESTUDINAL
- bony plate on the chest of a turtle BREASTPLATE, PLASTRON
- Mississippi mud turtle GRAPTEMYS
- painted turtle CHRYSEMYS
- turtle living in freshwater or brackish water TERRAPIN

tutorship or guardianship, or sub-

jection to it TUTELAGE
TV See **television**
twelfth night EPIPHANY
twelve - relating to the number 12 or to a twelfth DUODECIMAL, DUODENARY
twelve (combining form) DODECA-
twelve-tone - referring or relating to the twelve-tone system of music SERIAL, DODECAPHONIC
twenty - occurring once every 20 years, or lasting or existing for 20 years VICENNIAL
- referring to or based on the number 20 VICENARY, VIGESIMAL
twice a year BIANNUAL, BIENNIAL
twice (combining form) BI-, DUO-, DI-, SEMI-

Typefaces

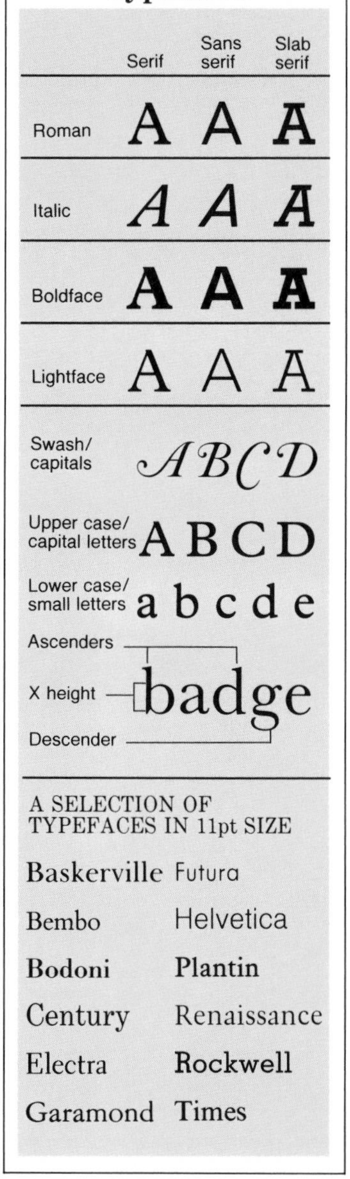

	Serif	Sans serif	Slab serif
Roman	A	A	A
Italic	*A*	*A*	*A*
Boldface	**A**	**A**	**A**
Lightface	A	A	A

Swash/ capitals *ABCD*

Upper case/ capital letters ABCD

Lower case/ small letters abcde

Ascenders

X height badge

Descender

A SELECTION OF TYPEFACES IN 11pt SIZE

Baskerville	Futura
Bembo	Helvetica
Bodoni	Plantin
Century	Renaissance
Electra	Rockwell
Garamond	Times

twig, flexible rod, whip, or the like SWITCH
- twig from a willow, as used in basketmaking OSIER
- twig or rope made of twigs, used for tying things together WITHE, WITHY
- twig or shoot cut for planting or grafting SLIP, SCION
twilight, dusk GLOAMING
- "twilight of the gods," destruction of the ancient gods in their battle with the forces of evil GÖTTERDÄMMERUNG, RAGNAROK
- referring to or resembling twilight, dim CREPUSCULAR
twin-hulled boat CATAMARAN
- individual born singly, not as a twin or in a litter SINGLETON
twin (combining form) ZYG-, ZYGO-
twining shootlike part serving to attach a climbing plant to its support TENDRIL
twinkling, as a cat's eye or similar gemstone is CHATOYANT
- twinkling or luminosity of a diamond or other precious stone FIRE
twins - referring to identical twins, derived from a single ovum MONOZYGOTIC
- referring to non-identical twins, derived from quite separate ova DIZYGOTIC
twist See also **turn**
- twist, interweave, or intertwine ribbons, hair, or the like BRAID, PLAIT
- twist, turn, or veer off course or to the side SLEW, SHEER
- twist, unpredictable action, as of fate QUIRK
- twist and turn as a river might MEANDER
- twist around, about, or together ENTWINE
- twist as if in pain or struggle WRITHE
- twist or curl, especially in a fingerprint WHORL
- twist or curl, such as a flourish under a signature CURLICUE
- twist or spiral shape HELIX, VOLUTE
- twist or spin on one's toe or ball of the foot PIROUETTE
- twist or weave branches or twigs PLEACH
- twist strands, as of wool or rope, together PLY
twisted and knotty, as the trunk of a tree might be GNARLED
- twisted facial expression, as of pain or disgust GRIMACE
- twisted or bent out of shape, as a person's features might be CONTORTED, DISTORTED
- twisted or corrupted, as a sick sense of humor is PERVERTED
- twisted to one side, amiss AWRY, ASKEW
- very twisted, involved, and confused CONVOLUTED
twisting, act of turning, or stress produced by it TORSION
- twisting force or the technical measurement of it TORQUE
- twisting, spiraling water current, whirlpool MAELSTROM, VORTEX
- twisting or winding, as a mountain road might be TORTUOUS, ANFRACTUOUS
twitch or spasm, especially in the face TIC
two aces or ones at dice AMBSACE
- two-chambered, as many legislative systems are BICAMERAL
- two dots placed above a vowel, as in *gemütlich* DIAERESIS, UMLAUT
- two-footed animal BIPED
- two-headed BICEPHALOUS
- two in card games or dice DEUCE
- two-sided BILATERAL
- two-year period BIENNIUM
- cut or divide into two equal parts BISECT
- divided into or having two parts BIPARTITE
- division or classification into two parts, such as conflicting opinions DICHOTOMY
- lasting or living for two years, or occurring once every two years BIENNIAL
- of two minds AMBIVALENT
two (combining form) AMBI-, BI-, DI-, DUO-, ZYG-, ZYGO-
two parts (combining form) DICH-, DICHO-
twofold, double, having two separate parts BINARY, DIPLOID, DUAL
tying or binding together LIGATURE
type See illustration
- type data or text, as onto a word processor KEYBOARD
- type or category of art, movies, or the like GENRE
- complete set of printer's type of any one style FONT, FOUNT
- flat top of the shaft of a piece of printer's type, forming the base for the raised letter or character SHOULDER
- having both edges of a column of type set flush with the margins JUSTIFIED
- part of a letter or character on a piece of printer's type that extends beyond or overhangs the main shaft KERN
- printer's unit of type size, equal to one seventy-second of an inch POINT
- printer's unit of type size, equal to one sixth of an inch PICA

- raised part of a piece of printer's type, bearing the letter or character to be printed BEVEL

typeface See illustration, page 559, and also **script**

typesetter COMPOSITOR, KEYBOARDER

typesetting COMPOSITION

- typesetting machine in which each letter is cast individually from hot metal MONOTYPE
- typesetting machine that casts a full line of type on a single metal slug LINOTYPE
- typesetting using projected light images PHOTOCOMPOSITION

typewriter device allowing paralyzed patients to type by blowing through a tube POSSUM

- typewriter type size with 10 characters to the inch PICA
- typewriter type size with 12 characters to the inch ELITE
- typewriter used in courts to record speech by means of phonograms, in a form of shorthand STENOTYPE
- device on a typewriter for setting automatic stops or column margins TABULATOR, TAB
- hinged bar on a typewriter for holding the paper down against the cylinder BAIL
- key on a typewriter that adjusts the mechanism to allow typing of capital letters SHIFT KEY
- roller on a typewriter CYLINDER, PLATEN
- small wheellike device supporting the printing characters on an electronic typewriter or word-processor printer DAISY WHEEL

typical, characteristic, providing good evidence of a state or event SYMPTOMATIC

- typical, conformist, or orthodox STEREOTYPICAL
- typical, original, or perfect example or model, on which all others are or seem to be based ARCHETYPE, PROTOTYPE
- typical, regular, and predictable STATUTORY
- typical, standard, everyday, in no way special STOCK, COMMONPLACE, UNIFORM, RUN-OF-THE-MILL, AVERAGE
- typical, standard, serving as an illustration EXEMPLARY, REPRESENTATIVE, TEXTBOOK, PARADIGMATIC
- typical or purest example or representative of its kind, essence EMBODIMENT, QUINTESSENCE, PERSONIFICATION, INCARNATION
- typical or representative example of a class or quality BYWORD, EPITOME, PARADIGM, TYPE
- typical pattern, standard of acceptability, or the like NORM
- typical person or thing, conforming to the standard image or attitude STEREOTYPE

tyrant or dictator AUTOCRAT, MONOCRAT, DESPOT, AUTARCH, OVERLORD

U

U-shaped lake formed from a river meander OXBOW, OXBOW LAKE, OXBOW CUTOFF, MORTLAKE
U-turn, about-turn, reversal of attitude or policy VOLTE-FACE
udder, breast, or teat DUG
ugly, deformed or monstrous GROTESQUE, MISBEGOTTEN, MISSHAPEN
- ugly, displeasing to one's artistic sensibilities UNESTHETIC
- ugly, grotesquely deformed person QUASIMODO
- ugly, plain, and shabby, as a girl might be DOWDY, FRUMPISH
- ugly, short, fat, and comic-looking man PUNCHINELLO
- ugly, unattractive ILL-FAVORED, UNSIGHTLY
- ugly feature on something BLOT, BLEMISH, STIGMA
- ugly or plain but attractive woman or girl JOLIE LAIDE
- ugly through injury, deformed, or badly damaged DISFIGURED, MUTILATED
- building, piece of furniture, or the like, noticeable because of its ugliness EYESORE, ABOMINATION
- coarsely ugly, red-faced, and bloated BLOWSY
- frighteningly ugly GRISLY, GRUESOME
- grotesquely ugly person GARGOYLE
- plain rather than actually ugly HOMELY
- unattractive rather than actually ugly UNPREPOSSESSING
- very ugly, hideous, offensive to look at REPULSIVE, REPELLENT

ulcer, as in the lining of the stomach, caused or irritated by digestive juices PEPTIC ULCER
- ulcer in the first part of the intestine DUODENAL ULCER
- ulcer in the lining of the stomach GASTRIC ULCER
- form an ulcer FESTER

ultimate point, furthest possible stage or degree NE PLUS ULTRA
umbrella - light and portable sunshade or umbrella PARASOL
- metal ring or cap on the tip of a walking stick or umbrella to protect it against wear FERRULE
- roll up a flag, umbrella, or the like FURL

unable or unwilling to move INERT
- unable to act effectively, unfit for a particular task UNEQUAL
- powerless, prevented from taking action, unable to act as desired IMPOTENT

unacceptable or unwelcome person PERSONA NON GRATA
unadaptability, inflexibility PERSEVERATION
unaffected, uninfluenced IMPERVIOUS, OBLIVIOUS
unambiguous, clear, plain, not open to doubt UNEQUIVOCAL
unanimous - without any dissenting votes, with no one contradicting, virtually unanimously NEM CON, NEMINE CONTRADICENTE
unarmed combat or self-defense techniques, such as kung fu and karate MARTIAL ARTS
unavoidable, certain to happen, inescapable INEVITABLE, INELUCTABLE
unaware, ignorant UNWITTING
unbalanced, not perfectly regular in pattern ASYMMETRIC
unbearable, intolerable, unendurable INSUFFERABLE, INSUPPORTABLE
unbeliever See **infidel**
unbiased, fair, unprejudiced IMPARTIAL
- unbiased, uninfluenced by any emotion or personal prejudice OBJECTIVE, DISPASSIONATE, DISINTERESTED

unbreakable, as a sacred rule should be INVIOLABLE, IRREFRANGIBLE, IRREFRAGABLE
- unbreakable, as a union or agreement might be INDISSOLUBLE

unbroken or continuous belief, course of action, or the like, usually in the face of discouragement PERSEVERANCE, STEADFASTNESS
uncalled-for, unjustified, without obvious cause GRATUITOUS
uncaring or unfeeling INDURATE, OBDURATE
uncertain, hesitant, or shy, as a smile might be TENTATIVE
- uncertain, hesitant, stumbling, as someone's speech might be FALTERING
- uncertain, of two minds, unable to make firm decisions INDECISIVE, IRRESOLUTE
- uncertain, of two minds, undecided UNRESOLVED, VACILLATING, WAVERING
- uncertain, questionable, still unresolved, as a point under debate would be MOOT
- uncertain, questionable, widely disputed CONTROVERSIAL
- uncertain, uncommitted, lukewarm, sitting on the fence LAODICEAN
- uncertain, undecided, skeptical, or doubtful DUBIOUS
- uncertain in attitude, holding simultaneously opposing views about one thing AMBIVALENT
- of uncertain length, size, or number, open-ended INDEFINITE, INDETERMINATE
- of uncertain meaning, open to various interpretations, as a puzzling answer might be AMBIGUOUS, EQUIVOCAL
- of uncertain size or number, usually because very large or numerous INCALCULABLE
- of uncertain outcome, failing to settle an issue decisively, as a battle might be INCONCLUSIVE

uncertainty - state of uncertainty or perplexity DILEMMA, QUANDARY
unchanging See also **stubborn, regular**
- unchanging, addicted by long use, as a drinker or liar might be CHRONIC, COMPULSIVE, DEPENDENT, HABITUAL, CONFIRMED, INVETERATE
- unchanging, always the same, constant INVARIABLE
- unchanging, immobile, stable, not fluctuating or decomposing readily STABILE
- unchanging, inflexible, thoroughgoing, especially in political views DYED-IN-THE-WOOL, UNCOMPROMISING
- unchanging, motionless, or producing no movement or change STATIC, STATIONARY
- unchanging, reliable, persevering, and firm of purpose STEADFAST, STAUNCH, UNFALTERING, UNDEVIATING, RESOLUTE
- unchanging, unaging, fixed forever IMMUTABLE
- unchanging, unbroken and unpleasant, as boredom might be UNRELIEVED
- unchanging, unrepentantly or obstinately prejudiced in social atti-

tudes UNREGENERATE, UNRECONSTRUCTED, UNREFORMED
uncle - relating to or resembling an uncle AVUNCULAR
unclear, imprecise, vague ELUSIVE, INTANGIBLE
uncoded, in ordinary language, not put in code EN CLAIR
uncombed or untidy, as hair might be UNKEMPT, DISHEVELED, UNGROOMED, TOUSLED
uncomfortable, forced, or inhibited manner or situation CONSTRAINT
uncommunicative, reserved, silent TACITURN
unconcerned about problems, carefree NONCHALANT, INSOUCIANT, DEBONAIR
unconnected, separate, individual, distinct DISCRETE
unconquerable INDOMITABLE
unconscious, as secret fears or painful memories might be REPRESSED
- unconscious, as through injury or disease COMATOSE
- unconscious, having no feeling INSENSATE, INSENSIBLE
- unconscious, mechanical, or spontaneous as sneezes, knee jerks, or similar responses are REFLEX, INVOLUNTARY
- unconscious or unaware OBLIVIOUS, UNMINDFUL
unconsciousness or stupor induced by drugs NARCOSIS
- unconsciousness together with a rigid bodily posture, as sometimes occurs in schizophrenia CATALEPSY, CATATONIA
- state or period of deep unconsciousness, as through injury COMA
uncontrollable See **disobedient, stubborn**
uncontrolled in one's sexual activity or body functions INCONTINENT
unconventional, rakish RAFFISH, DISREPUTABLE, OUTRÉ
- unconventional or provocative person ENFANT TERRIBLE
- unconventional or unorthodox, as a life-style or therapy might be ALTERNATIVE
- unconventional person with artistic interests BOHEMIAN
uncooperative See also **disobedient, stubborn**
- uncooperative, opposing others' wishes or suggestions unreasonably PERVERSE, CONTRARY
uncorrectable, unimprovable INCORRIGIBLE, IRREDEEMABLE
uncover, reveal, bring to light UNEARTH, EXHUME, DISINTER, EXPOSE
uncultivated, plowed but left unseeded, as a field might be, to regain fertility for a season FALLOW
undecided See also **uncertain**
- undecided, still before a judge or court, and therefore not to be discussed in public SUB JUDICE
- undecided, still not settled or finished PENDING
under, below, especially beneath the earth's surface NETHER
under (combining form) HYPO-, INFRA-, SUB-
undercarriage - capable of being drawn in or pulled back, as an airplane's undercarriage might be RETRACTABLE
undercoat - paint a surface with a sealer or undercoat PRIME
- apply an undercoat on canvas before painting on it SIZE
underdeveloped, immature, at a very early stage of development RUDIMENTARY, INCHOATE, EMBRYONIC, NASCENT
underground SUBTERRANEAN
- underground chamber, such as a church vault CRYPT, UNDERCROFT
- underground defensive shelter with a bank of gun emplacements aboveground BUNKER
- underground galleries and tunnels with niches or ledges for graves, especially those in Rome and Paris CATACOMBS
- underground railway system, as in New York SUBWAY
- underground railway system, as in Paris MÉTRO
undergrowth, or an area covered by it BRUSHWOOD, BRUSH, MAQUIS
- overgrown area, thick with shrubs and undergrowth THICKET, BRAKE
underhand, done or carried out in a secretive or stealthy manner SURREPTITIOUS, CLANDESTINE, SUBVERSIVE, FURTIVE
- underhand or devious action, trickery SKULDUGGERY
underlying layer, support, or principle SUBSTRATUM
- underlying motive kept concealed so as to deceive ULTERIOR MOTIVE
undermine a castle wall or other fortification, as by tunneling beneath it SAP
- enter secretly in order to destroy or undermine INFILTRATE
- secret undermining or the attempted destruction of a government or political system SUBVERSION
underside of an arch, staircase, or other overhang SOFFIT
understand, comprehend, take in APPREHEND, COMPASS, ENCOMPASS
- understand, form a mental picture of, be able to grasp CONCEIVE, PERCEIVE, DISCERN
- absorb mentally, take in, come to understand DIGEST
- penetrate to the meaning of, come to understand FATHOM
understandable INTELLIGIBLE, COMPREHENSIBLE
- understandable, easy to follow, straightforward ACCESSIBLE
- easily understandable, very clear LUCID, LUMINOUS
understanding, acute, INSIGHTFUL, DISCERNING, PERSPICACIOUS, PERCEPTIVE, SAGACIOUS
- understanding, opinions, or principles LIGHTS
- understanding of another that is so deep that one seems to enter into or share his or her feelings EMPATHY
- understanding or awareness PERCEPTION, COGNIZANCE, DISCERNMENT, SAVVY
- understanding or informal agreement between countries or powers ENTENTE CORDIALE
- understanding relationship of mutual trust and emotional sympathy RAPPORT
understood, implied, unspoken, as an informal agreement might be TACIT, IMPLICIT
undertaker FUNERAL DIRECTOR, MORTICIAN, EMBALMER, GRIEF THERAPIST
- undertaker's room where bodies are kept before burial CHAPEL
undertaking or project that may be risky or dangerous VENTURE, ENTERPRISE
undertone - softly, in an undertone, under one's breath SOTTO VOCE
underwater - breathing apparatus, using compressed air cylinders AQUALUNG, SCUBA
- underwater chamber from which construction or repair work is done CAISSON
- underwater research vessel for deep-sea exploration, in the form of a submarine with a large round observation cabin on the underside BATHYSCAPHE
- underwater vessel, open at the bottom, supplied with pressurized air DIVING BELL
- person living and working in an underwater building AQUANAUT
underwear and nightwear for women LINGERIE
underworld in classical mythology HADES, DIS
- referring to the underworld and its spirits and gods CHTHONIC, INFERNAL
undeveloped, immature, at a very early stage of development RUDIMENTARY, EMBRYONIC, NASCENT, INCHOATE
undignified, unsuitable, or unbe-

coming INFRA DIG, INFRA DIGNITATEM
undisciplined, rebellious, extremely disobedient DISAFFECTED, UNRULY, MUTINOUS, INTRACTABLE, REFRACTORY, RECALCITRANT
undo (combining form) DE-, DIS-
undoubtedly INDUBITABLY, UNQUESTIONABLY, ASSUREDLY, INCONTESTABLY, INDISPUTABLY, IRREFUTABLY
undress DISROBE, DOFF
- undressed or partially dressed DISHABILLE, DÉSHABILLÉ
unease or depression MALAISE, ANGST, APPREHENSION
uneasy, forced, or inhibited manner or situation CONSTRAINT
uneatable INEDIBLE
uneducated or illiterate UNLETTERED
unemotional See also **calm**
- unemotional, detached, and unbiased DISPASSIONATE, OBJECTIVE, IMPARTIAL, DISINTERESTED
- unemotional, expressionless, unexcitable PHLEGMATIC, IMPASSIVE, INSCRUTABLE, UNDEMONSTRATIVE, APATHETIC
- unemotional, unaffected by either pleasure or pain STOICAL, STOLID, IMPERVIOUS
unenthusiastic, half-hearted TEPID, LUKEWARM, LAODICEAN
- unenthusiastic, lazy, indifferent LACKADAISICAL, LANGUID
unequal (combining form) ANISO-
unerasable, permanent INDELIBLE, INERADICABLE, INGRAINED
unexcitable See **calm**
unexciting See **dull**
unexpected See also **surprise**
- unexpected, chance, accidental ADVENTITIOUS, FORTUITOUS, ALEATORY
- unexpected, inappropriate, out of place INCONGRUOUS, DISCORDANT, DISPARATE
- unexpected discovery or bright new idea TROUVAILLE
- unexpectedly, unplanned UNAWARES
- appear, occur, or interrupt unexpectedly INTERVENE
- occur as something unexpected or unnecessary SUPERVENE
- sudden and unexpected UNFORESEEN, UNANNOUNCED
- tendency to make lucky discoveries unexpectedly or by accident SERENDIPITY
unexplored country or subject matter TERRA INCOGNITA
unfair, unjustified, as a conclusion might be UNWARRANTED
- unfair and prejudiced attitudes or actions, as on the basis of race, sex, or age DISCRIMINATION
- unfair in a thoughtless or arrogant way HIGH-HANDED
- unfair or offensive, as a discriminatory comparison would be INVIDIOUS
- unfairly distributed or allocated, out of proportion, as a share might be DISPROPORTIONATE
- unfairly favoring one side over another PARTIAL, BIASED
- unfairness, as resulting from a biased or inconsistent law INEQUITY
unfaithful husband PHILANDERER, PHILOGYNIST
- unfaithful or wayward, as a husband or wife might be ERRANT
- unfaithfulness, especially adultery INFIDELITY
- husband of an unfaithful woman CUCKOLD
- husband of an unfaithful woman, who knows about and accepts her infidelity WITTOL
unfavorable or disapproving, as a particular sense or use of a word might be PEJORATIVE, DISPARAGING, DEPRECIATORY
- unfavorable to something or someone ADVERSE, INIMICAL
unfavorable (combining form) -DYS-
unfeeling or uncaring INDURATE
unfinished, still not settled or confirmed PENDING
unfold, unroll, spread out UNFURL
unforced, unprompted, as laughter might be SPONTANEOUS
unforgettable or enduring, as an impression might be INDELIBLE, INERADICABLE, INGRAINED
unfortunate See also **unlucky**
- unfortunate, inappropriate, or unsuitable INFELICITOUS
unfriendly, distant, or standoffish ALOOF, UNAPPROACHABLE
- unfriendly, threatening, or discouraging access or progress FORBIDDING
- unfriendly or hostile to something or someone ANTAGONISTIC, INIMICAL
- unfriendly or separated through having been antagonized ALIENATED, ESTRANGED
- unfriendly to outsiders, forming closed groups CLANNISH, EXCLUSIVE, CLIQUISH, XENOPHOBIC
ungrammatical or incorrect use of a word, phrase, or construction BARBARISM, SOLECISM, CATACHRESIS
ungrateful person INGRATE
unhappy See also **sad**
- unhappy, depressed, pessimistic IN THE DOLDRUMS
- unhappy, discontented, driven to a feeling of disloyalty DISAFFECTED, ALIENATED, ANTAGONIZED, ESTRANGED
- unhappy, discontented, or moody as a result of being thwarted DISGRUNTLED
- unhappy, ill-chosen, inappropriate, as a flippant remark might be INEPT, INFELICITOUS, UNFORTUNATE
- unhappy or distressed at some development, uneasy, disturbed DISQUIETED, DISMAYED
- be unhappy, fret REPINE, RUE, BEMOAN, LAMENT
unharmed, completely uninjured UNSCATHED
unhealthy condition MALADY, MORBIDITY, MALAISE
uniform and inflexible, as a large bureaucracy might be MONOLITHIC
- uniform of a group of servants, guild members, or the like LIVERY
- uniform or similar in kind or structure HOMOGENEOUS
- braid, fringed strap, or the like worn on the shoulder, as on a military uniform EPAULETTE, AIGUILLETTE
- civilian clothing, as distinct from one's uniform MUFTI, CIVVIES
- looped braid or cord used as a fastening, as formerly on a military uniform FROG
- not uniform or similar in kind or structure, mixed HETEROGENEOUS
unify See also **join**
- unifying, or promoting or relating to unity, specifically among the world's various religions ECUMENICAL
- unified pattern or structure that is more than the sum of its parts GESTALT, INTEGRAL WHOLE
unimportant See also **secondary**
- unimportant, inapplicable, or unrelated IRRELEVANT, IMMATERIAL
- unimportant, lightweight, having little effect INCONSEQUENTIAL, INSIGNIFICANT
- unimportant, minor, beside the point, not central to the issue at hand MARGINAL, INCIDENTAL, PERIPHERAL, PARENTHETICAL, ANCILLARY
- unimportant, not crucial or needed DISPENSABLE, EXPENDABLE
- unimportant, small-time, of secondary status MINOR-LEAGUE, SUBORDINATE
- unimportant, trifling, and petty, or foolish and silly TRIVIAL, FOOTLING, PIDDLING, PIFFLING, PALTRY
- unimportant, unworthy of serious attention, as an argument might be FRIVOLOUS, TRIVIAL
- unimportant, very small, not worth considering, as a sum of money might be MINIMAL, NEGLIGIBLE, PALTRY, PETTY, PICAYUNE
- unimportant and playful small talk, chitchat BADINAGE, BANTER, PERSIFLAGE
- unimportant and triflingly small, or invalid or inoperative, as a law might be NUGATORY
- unimportant but impertinent per-

son WHIPPERSNAPPER
- unimportant or worthless thing, trifle BAGATELLE
- unimportant person or thing NONENTITY, CIPHER, SMALL BEER
- unimportant person or thing taken up to make good a lack MAKEWEIGHT, PASSENGER
- event that turns out to be unimportant or disappointing after expectations have been raised NONEVENT, DAMP SQUIB

unimpressive, disappointing, failing to come up to expectations UNDERWHELMING

uninhabited, deserted DESOLATE

uninjured, completely unharmed UNSCATHED

unintended, unconscious, reflex INVOLUNTARY

unintentionally accidentally, without meaning to INADVERTENTLY, UNWITTINGLY

uninvolved, unprejudiced, uninfluenced by emotion or personal preference DISINTERESTED, DISPASSIONATE, OBJECTIVE, IMPARTIAL, EVENHANDED, DETACHED

union See also **labor union, join**
- union, especially of independent political parties forming a joint government COALITION
- union, league, or association of states, companies, or the like united for a common purpose CONFEDERATION, ALLIANCE, BLOC, CONFEDERACY
- union, league, or association of states, or a country formed by it, with a fairly strong central government FEDERATION
- union, often temporary, especially of political parties with common policies ALIGNMENT
- union between countries, specifically that between Nazi Germany and Austria in 1938 ANSCHLUSS
- union of business companies to finance and carry out projects jointly CONSORTIUM, SYNDICATE
- union of traders, companies, or the like to monopolize and regulate business to their common advantage CARTEL, TRUST
- union of traders, especially antique dealers, to hold auction prices down and share the profits among themselves RING
- union of two companies imposed by the stronger one TAKEOVER
- complete union or fusion, as of companies or political parties, to form a new, single entity AMALGAMATION, MERGER
- secret union of subversives or conspirators CABAL

union (combining form) -GAM-, PAN-, SYN-, SYM-, ZYG-, ZYGO-, JUG-

unique, beyond comparison or without rival INCOMPARABLE, UNRIVALED, UNPARALLELED
- unique, excelling all others PREEMINENT, TRANSCENDENT
- unique, impossible to equal or imitate successfully MATCHLESS, INIMITABLE, PEERLESS, NONPAREIL
- unique, individual, being the only one of its kind SUI GENERIS
- unique, unheard-of, never having happened before UNPRECEDENTED
- unique person or thing RARA AVIS
- uniquely able or beautiful person PARAGON, PHOENIX

unique (combining form) IDIO-

unit See also chart at **weights and measures**
- unit or grade in a classification system, such as a coin of a specified value DENOMINATION

unite See **join**

United Nations See chart, page 566
- administrative department of a large public or international organization such as the United Nations SECRETARIAT

United States government personified UNCLE SAM
- U.S. citizen YANKEE
- U.S. motto, "one (made out) of many" E PLURIBUS UNUM
- U.S. President or presidency THE WHITE HOUSE, THE OVAL OFFICE
- U.S. Southern states as a region or grouping DIXIE
- alliance of U.S. Northern states during the Civil War THE UNION
- alliance of U.S. Southern states during the Civil War THE CONFEDERACY
- easing of tensions between nations, especially between the United States and the U.S.S.R. DÉTENTE
- referring to the central government of the United States or Canada FEDERAL

unity of and mutual support within a group, especially in the face of opposition SOLIDARITY

universal, general, all-embracing CATHOLIC, ECUMENICAL
- universal, general, very widespread, as a disease might be EPIDEMIC, PANDEMIC
- universal remedy, cure-all, as sought by alchemists PANACEA, ELIXIR, CATHOLICON, AZOTH
- universal solvent believed by alchemists to be possible and discoverable ALKAHEST

universe See also chart at **astronomy**
- universe or society regarded as a single complex whole MACROCOSM
- universe or world regarded as an orderly system COSMOS
- belief that life and the universe have a purpose and guiding principle TELEOLOGY
- hypothetical elemental matter, probably neutrons, according to the big-bang theory of the spontaneous creation of the universe YLEM
- hypopthetical running down of the energy in the universe or any other closed system ENTROPY
- person, group, or system regarded as a small representation of the whole universe MICROCOSM
- referring to the whole universe, especially as distinct from the earth COSMIC
- study or theory of the origin and development of the universe COSMOGONY, COSMOLOGY
- theory that the universe came gradually rather than suddenly into being and is in a process of continuous generation of matter STEADY-STATE THEORY, CONTINUOUS-CREATION THEORY
- theory that the universe originated by an explosion of a small, dense mass, and is still expanding BIG-BANG THEORY, SUPERDENSE THEORY

universe (combining form) -COSM-, COSMO-

university See also **college**
- university, school, or college that one used to attend ALMA MATER
- university ceremony for conferring degrees COMMENCEMENT
- university class given by a teacher to an individual student or a very small number of students TUTORIAL, SUPERVISION
- university degree of the basic level, such as BA or BS BACCALAUREATE
- university degree ranking below a doctorate in some European countries LICENTIATE
- university department or its teaching staff FACULTY
- university education and the world of scholarship ACADEME, ACADEMIA
- university fraternity for academically gifted students and graduates PHI BETA KAPPA
- university governor or trustee REGENT
- university lecturer of senior rank just below professor, in Great Britain READER
- university lecturer or fellow of a British college DON
- university official in charge of discipline and the supervision of exams PROCTOR, MONITOR
- university official in charge of finances BURSAR
- university official in charge of

student records REGISTRAR
- university or college admission or enrollment MATRICULATION
- university or college course of study offered to part-time students EXTENSION COURSE
- university or college education TERTIARY EDUCATION
- university or college grounds CAMPUS
- university professor holding a professorship created by a royal grant, in Great Britain REGIUS PROFESSOR
- university's graduates collectively, or an assembly or conference of them CONVOCATION
- university's representative in business matters SYNDIC
- university term typically forming half an academic year SEMESTER
- BA honors exam or course at Cambridge University TRIPOS
- challenge a fellow student, at Oxford or Cambridge University, to drink a large amount of beer without stopping SCONCE
- complete and be awarded a degree at a university GRADUATE
- formal academic dress, especially at Oxford University SUBFUSC
- governing body of some universities SENATE
- graduate or former student of a school, college, or university ALUMNUS, ALUMNA
- higher division, with four subjects, of the liberal arts studied at a medieval university QUADRIVIUM
- highest-ranking academic officer of a university PROVOST
- lower division, with three subjects, of the liberal arts studied at a medieval university TRIVIUM
- men's club at a university FRATERNITY
- period of paid leave, especially for university teachers, for research or travel SABBATICAL
- permanent or secure employment status, as enjoyed by some university teachers TENURE
- referring to eight old and famous American universities, including Harvard, Princeton, and Yale IVY LEAGUE
- referring to nonresident students or to studies or activities outside the normal courses of a university or college EXTRAMURAL
- sheltered intellectual retreat from everyday life, as a university is sometimes considered to be IVORY TOWER
- student in the first year at a university FRESHMAN, FRESHER
- student in the second year at a university, college, or high school SOPHOMORE
- suspend or expel a student temporarily from a university RUSTICATE
- women's or girls' club, as at a university SORORITY

unjust in a shameful way INIQUITOUS
- unjust or unfair, not even-handed INEQUITABLE
- unjustly treated by a court or official ruling AGGRIEVED

unjustified, uncalled-for, needless, as an insult might be GRATUITOUS

unknowing, unaware UNWITTING

unknown, not famous or prominent OBSCURE, INCONSPICUOUS
- unknown and unhonored, as obscure heroes are UNSUNG
- unknown or unnamed, as an author or contributor might be ANONYMOUS, INNOMINATE
- unknown territory, unexplored country or subject matter TERRA INCOGNITA

unlawful, illegal, against the law ILLEGITIMATE, ILLICIT

unleavened bread, eaten by Jews during the Passover MATZO

unless - taking effect, as a divorce decree might, on a specificed date unless the court is shown cause why it should not NISI

unlucky, unfortunate HAPLESS, STAR-CROSSED
- unlucky, unpromising, threatening disaster, as a sign might be FOREBODING, UNPROPITIOUS, PORTENTOUS, INAUSPICIOUS, OMINOUS
- unlucky person, thing, or force, bringing misfortune JINX

unmanly, womanlike EFFEMINATE

unmarried person, especially one who has taken a religious vow of chastity CELIBATE
- live together as an unmarried couple COHABIT, POSSLQ
- man or woman that someone lives with and who has some of the rights of a spouse even though not legally married COMMON-LAW HUSBAND, COMMON-LAW WIFE

unmoving See **still**

unnamed, nameless or unknown, as an author or contributor might be ANONYMOUS, INNOMINATE

unnatural See **artificial**

unnecessary, excessive, beyond the required or regular number SUPERNUMERARY, SUPERFLUOUS, REDUNDANT
- unnecessary, inessential, capable of being left out DISPENSABLE, EXPENDABLE
- unnecessary, inessential, or irrelevant, as remarks might be EXTRANEOUS
- unnecessary, undeserved, or unjustified, as some criticism might be UNCALLED-FOR, UNWARRANTED, GRATUITOUS
- unnecessarily conscientious or observant, beyond the call of duty SUPEREROGATORY
- make unnecessary, as by anticipating OBVIATE, FORESTALL, PREEMPT

unnoticed - spreading or progressing almost unnoticed, as a disease might INSIDIOUS

unoriginal, conventional, and usually oversimplified image or opinion of someone or something STEREOTYPE
- unoriginal, copied from or based on an earlier example DERIVATIVE, IMITATIVE
- unoriginal, dull, or obvious remark INANITY, PLATITUDE, COMMONPLACE, CLICHÉ, BROMIDE
- unoriginal, dull, stale, antiquated, overused HACKNEYED, TRITE, SHOPWORN, MUSTY, THREADBARE, FLOGGED TO DEATH
- unoriginal, everyday, obvious, boring PREDICTABLE, TIMEWORN

unorthodox HETERODOX
- unorthodox opinion in religion, politics, or the like HERESY, HETERODOXY
- unorthodox or independent-minded thinker or group member MAVERICK

unpaid, as a job or position might be HONORARY
- unpaid rent, subscription, or other debt ARREARS
- unpaid work willingly undertaken VOLUNTARY WORK

unplanned, by chance, accidental FORTUITOUS, ADVENTITIOUS, ALEATORY
- unplanned, not asked for or suggested, as a compliment might be SPONTANEOUS, UNPROMPTED, UNSOLICITED
- unplanned, thrown together as a temporary expedient or substitute AD HOC, MAKESHIFT
- unplanned, unexpectedly, by surprise UNAWARES
- unplanned, without forethought, or unintentional, as manslaughter is UNPREMEDITATED
- unplanned or unprepared, as a speech might be IMPROMPTU, IMPROVISED, UNREHEARSED, EXTEMPORE, EXTEMPORANEOUS

unpleasant See also **disgusting, horrible, rude, spiteful**
- unpleasant, disagreeable, causing dislike or antipathy ABHORRENT, REBARBATIVE, REPUGNANT, OFF-PUTTING
- unpleasant, not to one's taste INSUFFERABLE, UNPALATABLE
- unpleasant and annoying, irksome, disturbing VEXATIOUS

UNITED NATIONS ORGANIZATIONS

PRINCIPAL UN ORGANS

New York:	The Hague:
General Assembly	The International Court of Justice
Security Council	
Economic and Social Council	
Trusteeship Council	
Secretariat	

OTHER UN ORGANS (PARTIAL LISTING)

	New York:
UNDP	UN Development Program
UNFPA	UN Population Fund
UNICEF	UN Children's Fund
UNITAR	UN Institute for Training and Research
	Santo Domingo:
INSTRAW	International Research and Training Institute for the Advancement of Women
	Geneva:
UNCTAD	UN Conference on Trade and Development
UNDRO	Office of the UN Disaster-Relief Coordinator
UNHCR	Office of the UN High Commissioner for Refugees
	Rome:
WFC	World Food Council
WFP	Joint UN/FAO World Food Program
	Vienna:
UNRWA	UN Relief and Works Agency for Palestine Refugees in the Near East
	Nairobi:
UNCHS	UN Center for Human Settlements (Habitat)
UNEP	UN Environment Program
	Tokyo:
UNU	UN University

SPECIALIZED AND/OR AUTONOMOUS UN AGENCIES

	Washington, DC:
IFC	International Finance Corporation
IMF	International Monetary Fund
IDA	International Development Association (together with IBRD: The World Bank)
IBRD	International Bank for Reconstruction and Development (together with IDA: The World Bank)
	Montreal:
ICAO	International Civil-Aviation Organization
	Geneva:
GATT	General Agreement on Tariffs and Trade
ILO	International Labor Organization
ITU	International Telecommunication Union
WHO	World Health Organization
WIPO	World Intellectual-Property Organization
WMO	World Meteorological Organization
	Berne:
UPU	Universal Postal Union
	London:
IMO	International Maritime Organization
	Paris:
UNESCO	UN Educational, Scientific, and Cultural Organization
	Rome:
FAO	Food and Agriculture Organization of the UN
IFAD	International Fund for Agricultural Development

UNITED NATIONS ORGANIZATIONS *Continued*

	Vienna:
IAEA	**International Atomic-Energy Agency**
UNIDO	**UN Industrial-Development Organization**
REGIONAL COMMISSIONS	
	Santiago:
ECLAC	**Economic Commission for Latin America and the Caribbean**
	Geneva:
ECE	**Economic Commission for Europe**
	Addis Ababa:
ECA	**Economic Commission for Africa**
	Baghdad:
ESCWA	**Economic and Social Commission for Western Asia**
	Bangkok:
ESCAP	**Economic and Social Commission for Asia and the Pacific**
UN OBSERVER MISSIONS AND PEACE-KEEPING OPERATIONS	
UNTSO	**UN Truce Supervision Organization**
UNDOF	**UN Disengagement Observer Force**
UNTAG	**UN Transition Assistance Group**
UNAVEM	**UN Angola Verification Mission**
UNFICYP	**UN Peace-Keeping Force in Cyprus**
UNIFIL	**UN Interim Force in Lebanon**
UNIIMOG	**UN Iran-Iraq Military Observer Group**
UNIMOGIP	**UN Military Observer Group in India and Pakistan**

- unpleasant and unhealthy UNWHOLESOME

- unpleasant or unfavorable, as a particular sense or use of a word might be PEJORATIVE, DISPARAGING, DEPRECIATORY

unpleasant (combining form) CACO-

unpractical, impracticable, or idealistic VISIONARY, UTOPIAN, QUIXOTIC

unpredictable, changing constantly QUICKSILVER, MERCURIAL

- unpredictable, or changeable in affections, wants, or aims FICKLE

- unpredictable, unstable, liable to changes VOLATILE

unprejudiced, open-minded, open to suggestion, prepared to change RECEPTIVE, AMENABLE

- unprejudiced, uninfluenced by emotion or personal preference OBJECTIVE, IMPARTIAL, DISINTERESTED, DETACHED, DISPASSIONATE

unprepared See **unplanned**

unprincipled, unscrupulous, not guided or restrained by conscience UNCONSCIONABLE

- unprincipled person changing his or her policies or opinions to serve personal interests TRIMMER, TIMESERVER, OPPORTUNIST, VICAR OF BRAY

unpromising, unlucky, threatening disaster, as a sign might be OMINOUS, INAUSPICIOUS, UNPROPITIOUS, PORTENTOUS

unprotected, open to danger or attack VULNERABLE, SUSCEPTIBLE

unqualified or unworthy to be chosen INELIGIBLE

unreadable ILLEGIBLE, INDECIPHERABLE

unreal, imagined, fanciful, or given to fantasizing CHIMERICAL

- unreal or imaginary object, illusion PHANTASM, FIGMENT OF THE IMAGINATION

unrealistic, excessively idealistic or romantic QUIXOTIC

- unrealistic, idealistic, impracticable VISIONARY, UTOPIAN

unreasonable, excessive UNCONSCIONABLE

- unreasonable, quite illogical IRRATIONAL

unreciprocated, as a person's love or passion for another might be UNREQUITED

unreformable, untamable, uncorrectable INCORRIGIBLE

unreformed, unreconciled to social changes UNRECONSTRUCTED, UNREGENERATE

unrehearsed See **unplanned**

unreliable, changeable in mood or opinion, hard to pin down MERCURIAL, VOLATILE, QUICKSILVER

- unreliable, dangerous, as thin ice might be TREACHEROUS

- unreliable, incapable of being defended, as a belief might be UNTENABLE

- unreliable, incapable of being defended, as an argument might be TENUOUS

- unreliable, not following any particular rule or pattern ARBITRARY, RANDOM, HAPHAZARD

- unreliable, occurring irregularly ERRATIC, FITFUL

- unreliable, rash, spontaneous, tending to be governed by emotion rather than reason IMPETUOUS, IMPULSIVE

- unreliable, unpredictable, inconstant, undependable SKITTISH, CAPRICIOUS, FICKLE, FLIGHTY, WHIMSICAL

- unreliable and untrustworthy, as a business agent might be DISREPUTABLE, FLY-BY-NIGHT

unrequested, without being ordered or asked for, as goods delivered by mail might be UNSOLICITED

unresponsive, as a disease might be to treatment, or a nerve to stimulation REFRACTORY

unrest See **rebellion**

unrestrained, excessive, beyond all reasonable limits INORDINATE, IMMODERATE

- unrestrained, immoral WANTON

- unrestrained or unchecked, as vegetation might be RAMPANT

unrewarded, without compensation or benefit in return GRATUITOUS, GRATIS, COMPLIMENTARY

unroll or open out something, such

as a flag UNFURL
unsatisfiable, as one's appetite might be INSATIABLE
unselective in a way that suggests lack of ability to choose or interest in choosing INDISCRIMINATE
unselfish, concerned for others' welfare ALTRUISTIC
unsettled, aimless, drifting person VAGABOND, VAGRANT, DRIFTER
unshiny finish or surface, as of a nonglossy paint or a photograph MAT, MATTE, TEXTURED
unskilled laborer, as on a building site, in Great Britain NAVVY
- unskilled work, such as domestic cleaning, that some consider undignified MENIAL WORK, STOOP WORK
unsophisticated, modest and unpretentious HOMESPUN
- unsophisticated, straightforward, honest, simple, innocent NAIVE, UNWORLDLY, GUILELESS, ARTLESS, INGENUOUS
- unsophisticated, unenlightened, ignorant BENIGHTED
- unsophisticated, unrefined, or unused to urban life RUSTIC
- unsophisticated, unrefined, unpolished, oafish BOORISH, PHILISTINE, UNCOUTH
- unsophisticated and rough people, the masses, the herd HOI POLLOI, PLEBS, RIFFRAFF, THE GREAT UNWASHED
- unsophisticated and unrefined person, boor PHILISTINE, YAHOO
- unsophisticated country person or out-of-towner BUMPKIN, HICK, RUSTIC, YOKEL, HAYSEED
- unsophisticated opinion, taste, or group of people LOWEST COMMON DENOMINATOR
- unsophisticated, homespun, or uninformed, typical of village-store conversation in the CRACKER-BARREL
unspeakable, indescribable UNUTTERABLE, INEFFABLE
unspoken, implied, understood, as an informal agreement might be TACIT, IMPLICIT
unstable See also **unreliable**
- unstable, changing, inconstant TURBULENT, VERTIGINOUS
- unstable, risky, or insecure PRECARIOUS
- unstable chemically or temperamentally LABILE, VOLATILE
- unstable person, typically aggressive, moody, and lacking in conscience PSYCHOPATH, SOCIOPATH
unstated though understood, inferred TACIT, IMPLICIT, IMPLIED
unsteady See also **unstable, unreliable**
- unsteady, constantly changing, as prices might be FLUCTUATING
- unsteady, tottery, wobbly, unbalanced, liable to fall PRECARIOUS, TEETERING
- unsteady, unreliable, unpredictable, undependable, inconstant CAPRICIOUS, ERRATIC, FICKLE, FLIGHTY, SKITTISH
- unsteady, winding from side to side or up and down SINUOUS, UNDULATING, IN FLUX
unsuccessful, failed, would-be MANQUÉ
- unsuccessful through lacking complete development ABORTIVE
unsuitable, inappropriate, or inopportune INFELICITOUS
unsure See **uncertain**
unsympathetic, impolite OFFHAND, IMPERSONAL, DISTANT
- unsympathetic treatment, curt consideration and dismissal SHORT SHRIFT
unsystematic, lacking a systematic order or arrangement RANDOM, HAPHAZARD, ARBITRARY, ALEATORY
untangle, disentangle UNSNARL
unthrifty or wasteful IMPROVIDENT, PRODIGAL, SPENDTHRIFT
untidy, and typically wet or limp BEDRAGGLED
- untidy, run down, or worn out, as through debauchery RADDLED
- untidy, scruffy SCRAGGLY, UNKEMPT
- untidy, shabby, lazy and careless in appearance or work SLOVENLY
- untidy, shabby, or old-fashioned, as a woman or her clothes might be DOWDY, FROWSY
- untidy, sloppy, careless SLIPSHOD, HAPHAZARD
- untidy handwriting SCRAWL
- untidy in appearance, as hair might be UNKEMPT, DISHEVELED, TOUSLED, UNGROOMED
- untidy or sluttish SLATTERNLY, BLOWSY
- untidily or irregularly spread out STRAGGLY
until, awaiting PENDING
untiring, tireless INDEFATIGABLE
untouchable, imperceptible to the touch IMPALPABLE, INTANGIBLE
- member of the lowest classes in Hindu society, an untouchable, technically outside the caste system, or the proudly assumed name of a follower of Gandhi HARIJAN
untransferrable, as rights or property might be INALIENABLE
untrue or untruthful MENDACIOUS
untrustworthy See **unreliable**
unusual See also **unique, strange, odd**
- unusual, out of the ordinary UNWONTED, UNORTHODOX
- unusual and hence valued person or thing RARITY, RARA AVIS
- unusually skillful or gifted EXCEPTIONAL
unutterable, unspeakable, indescribable INEFFABLE
unwanted, in the way SUPERFLUOUS, DE TROP, REDUNDANT
unwelcome or unacceptable person PERSONA NON GRATA
- unwelcome or uninvited INTRUSIVE
unwilling RELUCTANT
- unwilling, enforced, or compelled INVOLUNTARY
- unwilling, reluctant, opposed LOATH, AVERSE, DISINCLINED
- unwilling, reluctant, or forced, as admiration or a compliment might be GRUDGING
- unwilling to act, hesitant, shy BACKWARD
- unwilling to say much, somewhat secretive or withdrawn TACITURN, RETICENT, UNFORTHCOMING
unworthy of being chosen, or unqualified to be chosen INELIGIBLE
unyielding, unbudging, deaf to all pleas REMORSELESS, INEXORABLE, ADAMANT
up (combining form) ANA-
up-to-date, informed, knowledgeable about current affairs AU COURANT, AU FAIT, À LA MODE, HIP, WITH IT
upbringing, training NURTURE
upgrade an area socially, as when middle class residents move in GENTRIFY
upheaval, sudden and very violent change or disruption CATACLYSM
uphold, justify, or excuse by means of arguments or proof VINDICATE
upon (combining form) EPI-
upper surface of a body segment, as of an insect or lobster TERGUM
upper-class, as an accent might be PUKKA, U
- upper-class language, as *scent* rather than *perfume* is said to be U
- upper class or upper middle class collectively GENTRY, CARRIAGE TRADE
- person who has acquired upper-class wealth and pretensions but is not fully accepted socially UPSTART, PARVENU, NOUVEAU RICHE, ARRIVISTE, JOHNNY-COME-LATELY
upright VERTICAL, PERPENDICULAR, PLUMB
- upright pole or post, as for supporting a roof STANCHION
- upright post or strut of a ladder, door frame, window sash, or the like STILE
- upright, rib, or strip of a window, screen, or rock face MULLION
uprising See **rebellion**
uproot, pull up by, or as if by, the roots DERACINATE
- uprooted, rootless, separated

from one's homeland, social origins, familiar culture, or natural environment DERACINATED, DÉRACINÉ, LUMPEN

upset, agitated, worried DISQUIETED, PERTURBED
- upset, flustered, at a loss DISCONCERTED, DISCOMPOSED
- upset, sudden and violent disruption, radical change UPHEAVAL
- upsetting, extremely distressing HARROWING

upside down or inside out INVERTED

upstart, person of lowly background who is newly invested with wealth, power, or advanced social status PARVENU, ARRIVISTE, JOHNNY-COME-LATELY, NOUVEAU RICHE

upstream - migrating upstream from the sea to breed, as salmon are ANADROMOUS

upward slope ACCLIVITY

uranium ore PITCHBLENDE

urchin, waif, boy roaming the streets GAMIN, STREET ARAB, GUTTERSNIPE
- female urchin GAMINE

urge See also **tendency**
- urge, appeal for, apply for SOLICIT, SUPPLICATE
- urge, prod, get someone to do something by pressure or persuasion IMPEL, INDUCE
- urge, propose, or recommend a policy, view, or course of action ADVOCATE, CHAMPION, COMMEND, PROMOTE
- urge or arouse unrest or rebelliousness, stir up trouble FOMENT, INSTIGATE, INCITE
- urge or encourage, reassure, inspire, or egg on HEARTEN, EMBOLDEN, MOTIVATE
- urge or try to influence legislators to adopt a policy LOBBY
- urge strongly or appeal to earnestly EXHORT, ENTREAT, IMPORTUNE, BESEECH, ADJURE
- urge to hurry, nag, harass, goad CHIVY
- urging, encouraging HORTATORY
- channel or transform a sexual urge or other instinctual energy into a socially or culturally more acceptable activity SUBLIMATE
- irresistible and often irrational urge to perform a certain action COMPULSION
- pressure, promise of reward, goal, or the like that urges one to act STIMULUS, INCENTIVE

urgent, demanding, as a summons might be PEREMPTORY, IMPERIOUS
- urgent, essential, important IMPERATIVE, IMPELLING
- urgent, requiring immediate attention EXIGENT, PRESSING, COMPELLING
- urgently insistent in requests or demands, pestering IMPORTUNATE, CLAMANT, CLAMOROUS

urinal in public, especially as formerly found in the streets of Paris and other European cities PISSOIR, VESPASIENNE

urine of horses or camels STALE
- causing increased urine or urination DIURETIC
- lacking control of one's urinary or other body functions INCONTINENT
- pass urine, urinate MICTURATE
- thin, flexible tube inserted into a body channel, as for draining urine or introducing medication CATHETER
- tube or canal that conveys urine from the bladder out of the body URETHRA
- tube or duct that conveys urine from a kidney to the bladder URETER

urn of Russian origin, used for making tea SAMOVAR
- urn-shaped, shaped like a pitcher or urn, as some plants are URCEOLATE

use, make specific or practical use of UTILIZE, EMPLOY
- use an opportunity, take advantage of, turn to advantage EXPLOIT, UTILIZE, CAPITALIZE ON, PARLAY
- use in an irresponsible way, misuse, abuse PROSTITUTE, PERVERT
- use of and benefits from someone else's property, or the legal right to them USUFRUCT
- use up, consume EXPEND, EXHAUST
- use up, reduce greatly in quantity DEPLETE
- use up wastefully SQUANDER
- available for one's use AT ONE'S DISPOSAL
- disuse, state of being out of use or practice DESUETUDE
- make use of or turn to when forced to do so by difficulties HAVE RECOURSE TO, RESORT TO
- obtain and make use of AVAIL ONESELF OF
- practical or specific use for something APPLICATION

used to, accustomed to, familiar with ORIENTED, ATTUNED TO
- used to, accustomed to, hardened to INURED, HABITUATED, ACCLIMATIZED
- used to, accustomed to, in the habit of doing something WONT TO
- get used to, adapt or adjust to ACCOMMODATE ONESELF TO

useful, advantageous, or favorable in enabling something to happen CONDUCIVE
- useful and practical rather than just decorative UTILITARIAN, FUNCTIONAL
- useful only in furtherance of some other purpose SUBSERVIENT, INSTRUMENTAL
- useful or applicable in a wide variety of ways VERSATILE
- useful or usable, appropriate, giving sufficient service SERVICEABLE

usefulness or useful thing UTILITY

useless, of no benefit or advantage, in vain TO NO AVAIL, UNAVAILING, BOOTLESS
- useless, producing no worthwhile result, as unsuccessful efforts are FUTILE, FRUITLESS, VAIN, UNPROFITABLE
- useless, purposeless, serving no real purpose, as merely decorative language is OTIOSE
- useless, unsuccessful, or inadequate, failing to produce the desired effect INEFFECTUAL
- useless and expensive gift, project, or possession, requiring more trouble than it is worth WHITE ELEPHANT
- useless because of old age or illness SUPERANNUATED
- useless or unused because out of date OUTMODED, OBSOLETE, OBSOLESCENT
- deprive of force, make useless or ineffective ENFEEBLE, NULLIFY

U.S.S.R. See also **Russian**
- candor in airing and trying to remedy weaknesses in the Soviet system, "openness" GLASNOST
- easing of tensions between nations, especially between the United States and the U.S.S.R. DÉTENTE
- restructuring of government and society in the U.S.S.R. PERESTROIKA

usual, current, common or widespread PREVAILING, PREVALENT
- usual, expected, matter-of-course, or habitual CUSTOMARY, WONTED, PREDICTABLE
- usual, in line with customs or standards CONVENTIONAL, PRESCRIBED, CONSUETUDINARY
- usual, standard, stock, as the everyday diet of a region is STAPLE

uterus - abnormal positioning of a body organ, especially the uterus VERSION
- either of the pair of narrow tubes along which the eggs pass from the ovaries to the uterus FALLOPIAN TUBE, OVIDUCT, SALPINX
- emptying of the uterus, especially for an abortion, by means of suction through a tube VACUUM ASPIRATION
- legal term for the uterus of a mother VENTER
- mass of tissue linking the fetus to the uterus lining PLACENTA

- mucous membrane lining the uterus, shed during menstruation or childbirth DECIDUA
- placenta, umbilical cord, and uterus membranes expelled after the birth of a baby AFTERBIRTH, SECUNDINES
- slipping out of position of a body part or organ, such as the uterus PROLAPSE
- surgical operation involving opening the cervix and scraping the uterus DILATATION AND CURETTAGE, D & C
- surgical removal of the uterus HYSTERECTOMY
- surgical scraping or scooping instrument, as for removing dead tissue from the uterus CURETTE
- testing for the presence or position of a fetus by prodding the uterus BALLOTTEMENT
- withdrawal by syringe of fluid from a pregnant woman's uterus, to monitor the health of the fetus and determine its gender AMNIOCENTESIS

uterus (combining form) HYSTER-, HYSTERO-, METR-, METRO-, VENT-

utopia - fictional place or imaginary world where things are worse than in real life, the reverse of a utopia DYSTOPIA, CACOTOPIA

utter, complete, absolute RANK
- utter, out-and-out, notorious, as a knave is said to be ARRANT

utterance - short and mysterious, pithy, as an utterance might be GNOMIC

V

V-shaped pattern, as on a heraldic shield or a noncommissioned officer's stripes of rank CHEVRON

vacation See also chart at **holiday**
- vacation arranged and sold as a single unit, with transport, accommodation, and other elements priced jointly PACKAGE, PACKAGE TOUR, PACKAGED VACATION
- shared ownership of a vacation home, with an alternating use pattern TIME SHARING
- vacation organizer accompanying a tour TOUR GUIDE, COURIER
- vacation resort modeled on a ranch, featuring riding and camping DUDE RANCH

vaccination - slit or scratch the skin slightly, as for vaccination SCARIFY

vaccine dose following the main dose to increase or sustain its effectiveness BOOSTER
- vaccine for polio, formerly injected, based on a weakened or killed virus SALK VACCINE
- vaccine for polio, taken orally, based on a weakened but live virus SABIN VACCINE
- give a vaccine to, as by injection INOCULATE

vacuum formed at the top of an upright, sealed, inverted mercury-filled tube, as in a barometer TORRICELLIAN VACUUM
- referring to an incomplete vacuum PARTIAL

vacuum tube (combining form) -TRON

vagina - vaginal insert, as for contraception or as a medicated suppository PESSARY
- entrance to or chamber leading to a bodily cavity or canal, such as the vagina VESTIBULE
- external female genitals VULVA
- fold of skin lying behind the entrance to the vagina FOURCHETTE
- folds of tissue surrounding the opening of the vagina LABIA
- instrument inserted into the vagina or other body passage for examination or treatment SPECULUM
- membrane sometimes partially blocking the entrance to the vagina, as usually before loss of virginity HYMEN
- raised mass of fatty tissue over the pubic bones, which lie in front of the vagina MONS, MONS VENERIS, MONS PUBIS
- sensitive external genital organ in a woman, situated in front of the vagina CLITORIS
- surgical cut into the tissues around the vagina during childbirth to make the delivery easier EPISIOTOMY

vague, imprecise or indistinct ELUSIVE, INTANGIBLE
- vague, indecisive, hesistant SHILLY-SHALLYING, VACILLATING
- vague, uncertain, unclear, still not finally decided INDETERMINATE, INCONCLUSIVE
- vague, undecided, having conflicting feelings AMBIVALENT
- vague notion, hint that is unconfirmed or still not fully formed INKLING, INTIMATION
- vague or evasive, as an answer might be EQUIVOCAL, AMBIGUOUS

valid or reasonable, as a grievance might be LEGITIMATE
- approve something formally, such as a treaty, thereby making it valid and operative RATIFY

valley, between parallel faults in the earth's crust RIFT VALLEY
- valley, wide and open DALE, VALE
- valley or hollow, sunken area of land DEPRESSION
- ditch or small valley cut by rain- or floodwater GULLY
- high-lying steep-walled basinlike valley, often containing the head of a glacier or a small lake CIRQUE, CORRIE, CWM
- narrow, flat-bottomed, and steep-sided valley in Scotland or Ireland GLEN
- mouth of a valley as it opens out onto a plain EMBOUCHURE
- ravine, deep mountain pass, or steep-sided valley GORGE, CANYON, COULÉE, DEFILE, GULCH

Veal Cuts

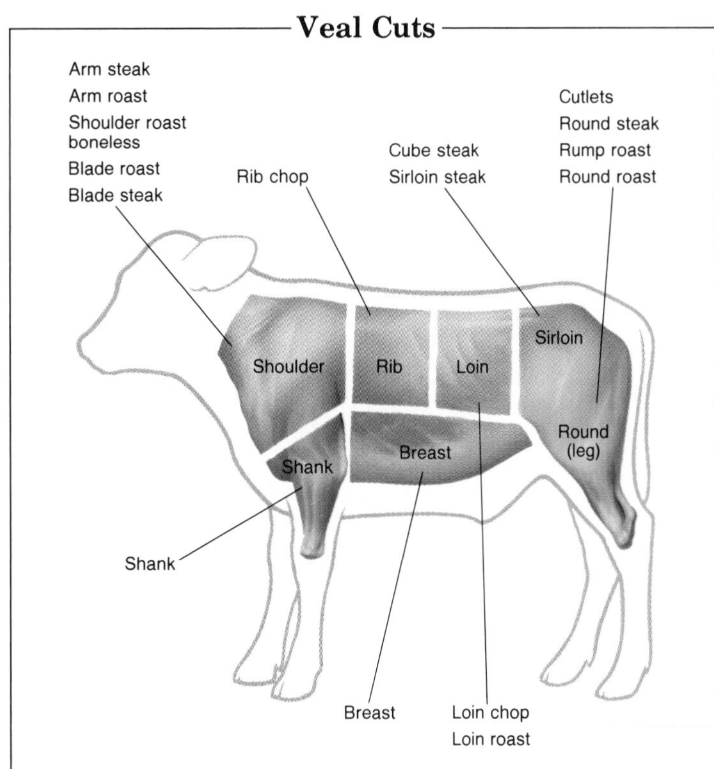

VEGETABLES

FLOWERS, LEAVES, STALKS, AND SHOOTS

broccoli/calabrese
cardoon
chard/leaf beet/ spinach beet
Chinese cabbage/ peh-tsai/pakchoi
collard/colewort
corn salad/ lamb's-lettuce
endive/scarole/ escarole
finocchio/florence fennel/sweet fennel
glasswort
globe artichoke
kale/borecole
kohlrabi/turnip cabbage
mung bean
romaine/cos lettuce
salad burnet/burnet bloodwort
sea kale/sea cole
sorrel

FRUITS

breadfruit
breadnut
chayote
eggplant/aubergine/ brinjal
squash
zucchini

PODS AND PULSES

adzuki bean
black-eyed pea/ blackeye bean/ cowpea
capsicum/pimiento/ sweet pepper
carob/St. John's bread/locust bean/ algarroba
chickpea/chestnut bean/dwarf pea/ chich/garbanzo
dhal/dal/pigeon pea
fava bean/broad bean
flageolet
gram
gumbo/okra/lady's fingers
haricot
lima bean
sugar pea

ROOTS AND TUBERS

cassava/manioc
celeriac
Chinese water chestnut
earthnut/pignut
Jerusalem artichoke
ramson
rutabaga/swede/ Swedish turnip/ Russian turnip
salsify/oyster plant/ vegetable oyster
scallion/shallot
scorzonera/black salsify
succory
sweet potato
taro/dalo/cocoyam/ eddo/dasheen
yam

- vast, steep-sided valley CHASM, ABYSS, GULF
- wide, flat-bottomed, and steep-sided valley or the grassland lying in it, especially in Scotland STRATH

valuable possession kept within a family by inheritance HEIRLOOM
- valuable possession, talent, or the like ASSET
- extremely valuable, impossible to replace IRREPLACEABLE
- highly valued and energetically competed for, as an award might be COVETED
- highly valued by its owner, often for sentimental reasons, as a treasured childhood possession or memory would be CHERISHED
- highly valued or respected, well-regarded ESTEEMED

value indicated on a check, stock certificate, or the like, as distinct from the real market value, NOMINAL VALUE, PAR VALUE, FACE VALUE
- value of a property or business once all debts are taken into account EQUITY
- value of an insurance policy that is voluntarily discontinued before it matures SURRENDER VALUE
- value or high regard placed on something PREMIUM
- in proportion to the value of the goods, as a tax or duty might be AD VALOREM
- loss in value, as of a car, as through age or wear DEPRECIATION
- rejection of all moral and social values NIHILISM, ANARCHISM
- rise in value of property ACCESSION, APPRECIATION
- traditional customs and values of a social group MORES

value system and beliefs of a society, as expressed in its arts MYTHOS
- value system or distinctive character of a particular people, artistic movement, or the like ETHOS

valve in a pipe for regulating the flow of liquid or gas STOPCOCK
- valve regulating the flow of vapor in an engine THROTTLE
- electronic valve helping to generate high-power microwaves, as in radar systems MAGNETRON
- heart valve regulating the flow of blood from the left atrium to the left ventricle MITRAL VALVE, BICUSPID VALVE
- mushroom-shaped valve, as in the exhaust or inlet system in an internal-combustion engine LIFT VALVE, POPPET VALVE
- simple valve, using either a ball or a hinged flap, allowing fluid flow in only one direction CLACK VALVE

vampire or witch LAMIA
vanish See **disappear**
vanishing See **short-lived**
vapor, smoke, or gas that is blown or breathed out EXHALATION
- vaporizing readily VOLATILE
- change into or produce vapor EVAPORATE
- smelly and invisible vapor or gas, as rising from a swamp or rubbish heap EFFLUVIUM
- turn directly from solid to vapor, or vice versa, without becoming liquid SUBLIMATE

vapor (combining form) ATMO-
vapor trail CONTRAIL
vaporizer ATOMIZER
variable or adaptable, as working hours might be FLEXIBLE
variation from a standard without going beyond a certain limit, leeway TOLERANCE, PLAY, LATITUDE
- variation or distinction of a very fine or subtle kind, such as a shade of meaning NUANCE
- variation or possible combination of elements PERMUTATION
- mutation of or abrupt variation within a species SALTATION

varied, assorted, various DIVERSE, MISCELLANEOUS, SUNDRY
- varied, having many different aspects or parts MULTIFARIOUS, DIVERSIFIED, MULTIFORM, VARIEGATED
- varied, several, many MULTIPLE, MANIFOLD, MYRIAD

variety of talents, uses, or the like VERSATILITY
variety, variant (combining form) -TROP-, TROPO-, -TROPIC
varnish for wooden floors or furniture SHELLAC, POLYURETHANE
- varnish or glossy black lacquer JAPAN, JAPAN BLACK

vase, especially one used for storing the ashes of the dead after cremation URN
- support for stems in a flower arrangement, such as a spiked board or pierced sponge in a vase FROG

vat in which clay or a similar substance is mixed with water when making pottery BLUNGER
Vatican See **pope**
vault, underground chamber, especially when under a church or cathedral UNDERCROFT, CRYPT
- vaulted or arched structure, cave, room, or the like FORNIX
- curved line at the intersection of two vaults GROIN

veal See illustration, page 571
- thin slice of meat, especially veal

VEGETABLE AND GRAIN DISHES

baba ganoush	Middle Eastern dish of puréed eggplants, garlic, tahini, lemon juice, and herbs
bhajia/bhagi	Indian dish of deep-fried, spiced, chopped vegetables
bubble and squeak	English dish of fried leftover mashed potato and vegetables
Caesar salad	Mexican salad of lettuce, garlic, cheese, croutons, and sometimes anchovies, in an egg, lemon juice, and oil dressing
champ	Irish dish of mashed potato and scallions, served with lumps of butter
colcannon	Irish dish of mashed potato and green vegetables, usually cabbage
couscous	North African dish of cracked wheat, steamed and served with spiced vegetables, fish, or meat, or with nuts or fruit
crudités	French hors d'oeuvre, consisting of fingers of raw vegetables served with a dip; crudely grated raw vegetables with a dressing
dhal/dal	Indian dish of puréed spiced pigeon peas or other pulses, onions, and ghee
dolma/ dolmades	Greek or Middle Eastern dish of stuffed vine leaves
duchesse potatoes	small baked cakes of mashed potatoes bound with egg
falafel/felafel	Middle Eastern dish of deep-fried balls of mashed chickpeas, onion, parsley, and coriander
fasolia	Greek bean salad in a garlic dressing
gado-gado	Indonesian vegetable salad with peanut sauce
gnocchi	Italian dumplings of pasta, seminola, or potato
guacamole	Mexican dip or salad of mashed avocado, lemon juice, garlic, and olive oil
hummus/ hummous	Middle Eastern dish of puréed chickpeas, often with olive oil, lemon, garlic, and tahini
imam bayildi	Turkish dish of eggplants, onions, tomatoes, and garlic
latke	potato pancake of traditional Jewish style
macédoine	mixture of diced vegetables
paella	Spanish dish of rice cooked in oil and stock with seafood, chicken, and vegetables
pakora	Indian fritters of chickpea flour
pease pudding	British dish of a thick purée of cooked dried peas
peperonata	Italian dish of peppers, tomatoes, onions, garlic, and olive oil
pilaf/pilau/ pilav/pulao	Middle Eastern dish of savory rice and vegetables
pissaladière	French yeast tart of tomato, onion, anchovies, olives, and garlic
polenta	Italian porridge of corn, farina, or semolina
raita	Indian dish of chopped cucumber, onion, or the like in yogurt
ratatouille	French stew of eggplant, onions, peppers, and tomatoes
risotto	Italian dish of rice cooked in oil and stock with onions and Parmesan cheese, often served with fish, poultry, or meat
rösti/roesti	Swiss dish of grated, fried potatoes
salade niçoise	French hors d'oeuvre of lettuce, tomatoes, olives, boiled eggs, and anchovies in a garlic dressing
sauerkraut	German dish of shredded, salted cabbage fermented in its own juice
stovies	Scottish dish of stewed potatoes
succotash	dish of lima beans and corn kernels
tabbouleh/ tabbouli	Middle Eastern salad of cracked wheat and vegetables in an oil and lemon-juice dressing
tahini/tahina	Middle Eastern sesame-seed paste
tsatsiki	Greek dish of cucumber, garlic, and yogurt
Waldorf salad	salad of apple, celery, and chopped walnuts in mayonnaise

SCALLOP, ESCALLOP, ESCALOPE, SCHNITZEL

vegetable See charts
- vegetables that are typically diced and cooked as a side dish JARDINIERE
- finely sliced or shredded, as vegetables may be JULIENNE

vegetarian, feeding on plants only, as many animals are HERBIVOROUS
- vegetarian who avoids all animal

products, including milk VEGAN
- vegetarian who eats only fruit FRUITARIAN
- vegetarian who lives on foods of plant origin but also on egg, milk, and cheese LACTO-OVO-VEGETARIAN

vegetation growing healthily VERDURE, HERBAGE
- vegetation of a region FLORA

vehicle See chart, and also chart at **horse-drawn vehicles**
- vehicle, means of transport CONVEYANCE
- vehicle that is old and broken down JALOPY, RATTLETRAP, BONE SHAKER
- vehicles traveling together in a group CONVOY

vehicle (combining form) -MOBILE

vein, especially in the legs, that has become abnormally knotted and swollen VARICOSE VEIN, VARIX
- vein, ridge, or rib, as on a leaf or insect's wing COSTA
- vein conducting blood directly from one organ to another, especially that between the digestive organs and the liver PORTAL VEIN
- vein in the neck JUGULAR VEIN
- vein just beneath the collarbone SUBCLAVIAN VEIN
- either of two large veins returning blood to the upper right chamber of the heart VENA CAVA
- in or into a vein, as an injection or drip might be INTRAVENOUS
- opening a vein for drawing or letting blood PHLEBOTOMY, VENESECTION
- patterning or system of veins, as on a leaf or insect's wing VENATION
- puncturing of a vein, as when injecting medicine VENIPUNCTURE
- referring to or containing veins VENOUS
- space surrounded by lines or veins, as on a leaf or insect's wing AREOLA
- tiny blood vessels forming a network in body tissue CAPILLARY
- tiny vein, as in the blood system or on a leaf VENULE
- vertical, cylindrical vein of ore PIPE

vein (combining form) PHLEB-, PHLEBO-, VEN-, VENI-, VENO-

velvet - velvety or fuzzy surface of raised fibers on a fabric NAP
- surface of soft loops or threads, as on velvet or a carpet PILE

vending machine DISPENSER
- vending machine, or room or restaurant dispensing food through vending machines AUTOMAT

vengeance See also **revenge**
- inflict or obtain vengeance EXACT, WREAK
- means of vengeance, criticism, or punishment SCOURGE

Venice - chief magistrate in Venice and Genoa in former times DOGE
- narrow boat, propelled by a single oar at the stern, on the canals of Venice GONDOLA
- nobleman of Venice in former times MAGNIFICO
- song of gondoliers in Venice, having a rhythm of rowing BARCAROLE
- steam- or motor-powered public-conveyance boat along the canals of Venice VAPORETTO

venom-injecting devices See illustration

Venus - relating to the Roman goddess Venus, the Greek goddess Aphrodite VENEREAN, VENEREAL, VENUSIAN, PAPHIAN

veranda or balcony along the outside of the upper level of a building LOGGIA
- veranda or entrance stairway at a house door STOOP
- veranda or paved outdoor area adjoining a house PATIO

verb, as in Latin or Greek, that is active in grammatical form but passive in meaning, as the English verb *to die* would be DEPONENT
- verb, especially the verb *be*, expressing or relating to existence SUBSTANTIVE VERB
- verb derived from a noun, such as *to jackknife* DENOMINATIVE
- verb form or construction used to indicate a fact or neutral attitude, as in *He was there* INDICATIVE MOOD
- verb form or construction used to indicate a hypothesis or imaginary situation, as in *if he were there* SUBJUNCTIVE MOOD
- verb form that does not show person, number, or tense, and which in its basic form in English is introduced with the particle *to* INFINITIVE
- verb such as *be, feel,* or *seem* that identifies the complement with the subject COPULA
- verb such as *be* or *sing* that does not follow the usual pattern of inflections IRREGULAR VERB
- verb such as *have, is,* or *can* that is used together with a main verb to indicate its tense, mood, voice, or aspect AUXILIARY VERB
- verb such as *must, will,* or *can* that usually occurs with another verb to express possibility, probability, or the like MODAL AUXILIARY, MODAL VERB
- verb such as *rise* that does not need or does not take a direct object INTRANSITIVE VERB
- verb such as *risk* that takes or needs a direct object TRANSITIVE VERB
- verb whose past tense or participle is formed from a root that is different from that of the present tense, as in *go* and *went* SUPPLETIVE VERB
- verbal idiom consisting of a verb and adverb, as in *turn it on* PHRASAL VERB
- verbal idiom consisting of a verb and preposition, as in *turn on him* PREPOSITIONAL VERB
- changes in the form of verbs, nouns, adjectives, and the like, as by adding suffixes, as with *take, takes, taking* INFLECTION
- form of a verb, ending in *-ing* in English, used like a noun, as in *Cooking is fun* GERUND
- form of a verb, usually ending in *-ing* or *-ed* in English, as used in forming tenses or as an adjective PARTICIPLE
- past perfect tense of a verb, as in *had climbed* PLUPERFECT
- referring to verb forms using auxiliary words rather than in-

VEHICLES

MOTOR VEHICLES

amphibian
berlin
Black Maria
cabriolet
camion
convertible
coupé/coupe
crawler
Dodgem car
dragster
DUKW/duck
fastback
float
jitney
juggernaut
limousine
moon buggy
moped
paddy wagon
pantechnicon
rig
roadster
scrambler
sedan
streetcar
utility
victoria

SNOW AND ICE VEHICLES

bobsled
drag
kibitka
luge
pung
skiddoo
skibob
skimobile
snowmobile, Sno-Cat
toboggan
troika
weasel

RAILROAD VEHICLES

caboose
bogie truck
dandy cart
fly coach
freightliner
pony engine
Pullman
tender
wagon-lit

HUMAN-POWERED VEHICLES

litter
palanquin
pedicab
penny-farthing
quadricycle
rickshaw/jinricksha
sedan chair/jampan
tandem
trishaw
unicycle/monocycle
velocipede

Venom-Injecting Devices

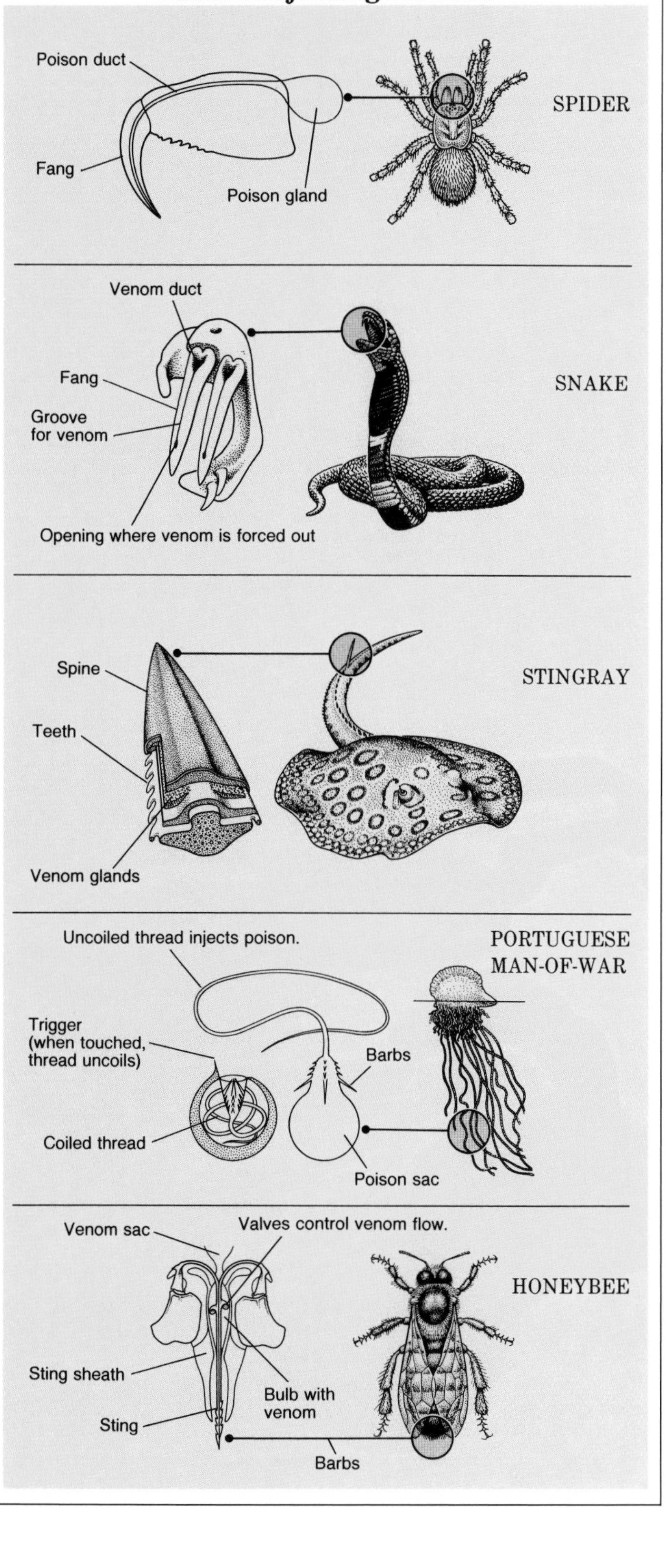

SPIDER
Poison duct
Fang
Poison gland

SNAKE
Venom duct
Fang
Groove for venom
Opening where venom is forced out

STINGRAY
Spine
Teeth
Venom glands

PORTUGUESE MAN-OF-WAR
Uncoiled thread injects poison.
Trigger (when touched, thread uncoils)
Barbs
Coiled thread
Poison sac

HONEYBEE
Venom sac
Valves control venom flow.
Sting sheath
Bulb with venom
Sting
Barbs

flections, as in *She did walk* rather than *She walked* PERIPHRASTIC
- vowel changes especially in strong verbs, as in *sing, sang, sung* ABLAUT, GRADATION

verdict of a jury, or similar formal pronouncement DELIVERANCE
- verdict of not guilty ACQUITTAL
- added clause, amendment, or qualification to a verdict, parliamentary bill, or the like RIDER
- deliver a verdict RENDER

verse See also **poem, poetry**
- verse of a poem STROPHE, STANZA, STAVE
- verse, line of poetry STICH
- verse mixing words from two or more languages MACARONIC VERSE
- verse or saying inscribed, as in a locket POSY
- verse repeated at regular intervals REFRAIN, CHORUS, BURDEN
- analysis of the metrical or rhythm patterns of verse SCANSION
- light verse, rhyming *aabba* and typically including a proper name LIMERICK
- pause in a line of verse, especially at a natural sense division CAESURA
- rhythmical stress in verse ICTUS
- study of verse forms and meters PROSODY
- trivial or predictably rhythmical verse DOGGEREL, CRAMBO

version - commonly accepted text or version of a work VULGATE

version, variant (combining form) -TROP-, TROPO-, -TROPIC

vertebra See also **bones**
- bony spur at the side of a vertebra TRANSVERSE PROCESS
- insertion of a syringe needle between the lower vertebrae to inject drugs or withdraw spinal fluid LUMBAR PUNCTURE
- second vertebra from the top AXIS
- top vertebra, supporting the skull ATLAS

vertebrate animal, including humans, or animal having a backbonelike supporting structure CHORDATE

vertical See **upright**

very, extremely, to a great degree EXCEEDINGLY, EXCEPTIONALLY

very (combining form) PER-

vessel See also **ship, boat, sail, glass, drinking, kitchen,** and chart at **laboratory**
- vessel or channel in the body DUCT, VAS
- relating to or containing vessels for conveying blood, sap, or other biological fluids VASCULAR

vessel (combining form) ANGIO-

vestry, room in a church in which

the sacred objects and vestments are stored SACRISTY, SACRARIUM

veteran performer TROUPER

vibrate and produce a corresponding sound when stimulated RESONATE
- vibrate or swing from one extreme to the other OSCILLATE
- vibrating element in a loudspeaker, buzzer, or the like ARMATURE

vibration, shaking and quivering movement TREMOR
- vibration in a string or other body caused by vibrations of the same frequency in a nearby body SYMPATHETIC VIBRATION
- point or region, as on a violin string, of minimum vibration NODE

vice See **immoral**

viceroy - wife of a viceroy, or woman viceroy VICEREINE, VICE-QUEEN

vicious See **cruel, spiteful, immoral**

victim of someone's exploitation STOOGE, PAWN, PUPPET, TOOL
- victim of someone's joke, plot, swindle, or the like, dupe or sucker BUTT, GULL, MARK, PATSY, PIGEON
- person or group victimized for the faults or distresses of others SCAPEGOAT, WHIPPING BOY, FALL GUY

victimize, discriminate against and oppress or ill-treat PERSECUTE

victory achieved very easily against a weak opponent, or as a formality through the withdrawal or absence of the opponent WALKOVER
- victory in which the victor too suffers great losses PYRRHIC VICTORY, CADMEAN VICTORY
- victory parade or ceremony in ancient Rome TRIUMPH, OVATION
- victory spoils, including captured weapons TROPHY
- victory symbol in ancient times LAURELS, BAYS
- definite, indisputable, widely acknowledged, as a victory or success might be RESOUNDING

video games, of various kinds NINTENDO, ATARI, SEGA, GENESIS, U-FORCE

view, illustration, or diagram of a machine or structure showing its parts separately EXPLODED VIEW
- view, typically covering a wide area PROSPECT, VISTA, PERSPECTIVE
- view or impression that is broad or general OVERVIEW, PANORAMA
- view revealing everything PANOPTIC VIEW
- accepted, generally believed, as a theory or view might be RECEIVED
- balcony, window, or tower offering a wide view MIRADOR
- dark chamber in which the image of an outside view is projected onto a surface by a lens CAMERA OBSCURA
- giving a general view of a whole subject SYNOPTIC
- overlooking, having a view from above COMMANDING, DOMINANT
- place or point that allows a particularly good overall view COIGN OF VANTAGE, VANTAGE POINT, RINGSIDE SEAT, CATBIRD SEAT
- summerhouse or gallery having a fine view BELVEDERE, BELVIDERE

Violin

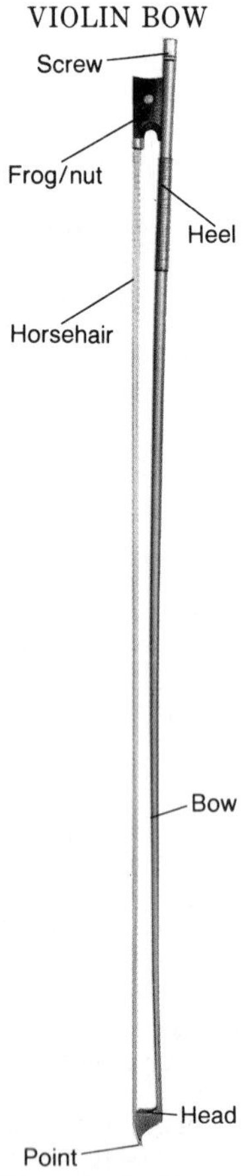

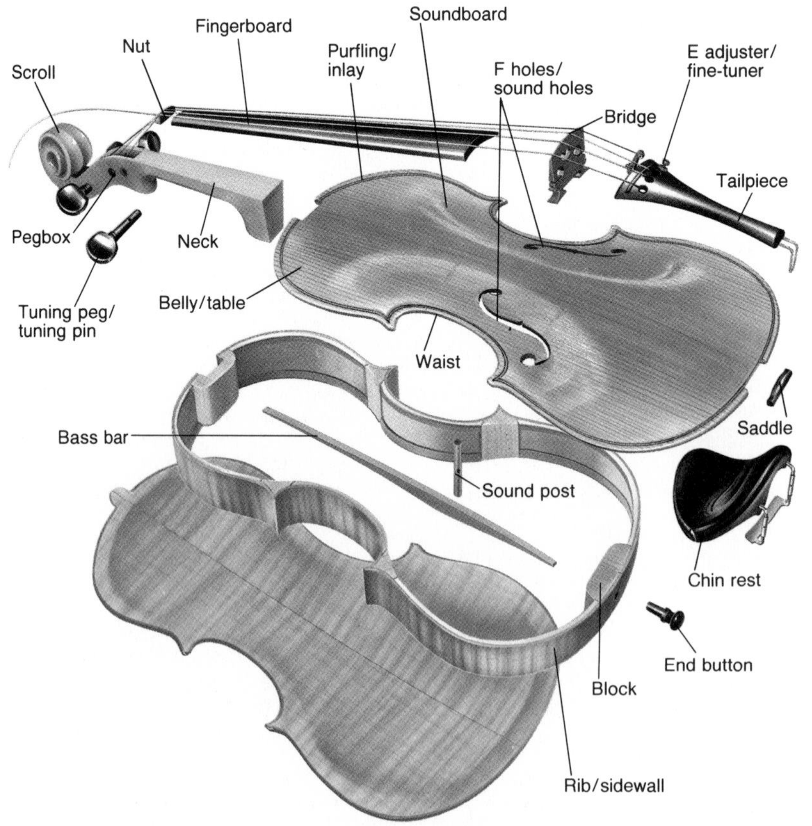

view (combining form) -SCAPE
viewing instrument with twin lenses, producing a three-dimensional effect when used to view two nearly identical photographs STEREOSCOPE
viewing (combining form) -SCOPY
vigor combined with style FLAIR, ÉLAN, BRIO, PANACHE
Viking NORSEMAN
- Viking boat LONGSHIP
- tax levied in Anglo-Saxon England for opposing or placating the Viking invaders DANEGELD
villa or country house in Russia DACHA
village or compound in Malaysia KAMPONG
- small or remote village HAMLET
- traditional fenced African village in southern Africa KRAAL
villain, criminal, or wrongdoer MISCREANT
- villain, petty criminal, person who behaves in an antisocial way DELINQUENT
- villain, quack, person using bogus claims to cheat others CHARLATAN, MOUNTEBANK
- villain, rascal, scoundrel, good-for-nothing, especially one with some lovable qualities SCAMP, RASCAL, RAPSCALLION, SCALAWAG, SCALLYWAG, SCAPEGRACE, NE'ER-DO-WELL, SCAPIN
- villain, rogue, knave, treacherous or morally unprincipled man BLACKGUARD, RECREANT, REPROBATE
- villain, wretch, especially a base, mean, sneaking coward CAITIFF, DASTARD
- former term for a villain or knave VARLET
vine - arch or frame of crisscrossing sticks, on which vines or creepers are trained to grow TRELLIS
- common woody vine of tropical rain forests LIANA
- covered walk or arbor with a latticework roof covered with roses, vines, or the like PERGOLA
- growing along the ground, as a vine or creeper might be PROSTRATE
- twining shootlike part, as on a grapevine, serving to attach a plant to its support TENDRIL
vinegar made from ale, malt vinegar ALEGAR
- referring to vinegar ACETIC
- small bottle for oil or vinegar, as used at table CRUET
- turn into vinegar ACETIFY
vineyard, estate DOMAINE
violence, killing, or bloody fighting, as in movies or on television GORE
- critical point beyond which a tense situation will erupt into war or violence FLASHPOINT
- referring to violence or conflict between neighboring or rival communities SECTARIAN
- uncalled-for, unjustified, without need or cause, as violence in a movie might be GRATUITOUS
violent, frenzied, or destructive in behavior RAMPAGING, ON THE RAMPAGE, BERSERK, AMOK
- violent, sensational, or gruesome, often in a deliberately artificial way GRAND GUIGNOL
- violent and sudden change, upheaval, or destruction CATACLYSM
- violent destruction, vandalism, confusion or injury of a wanton or widespread kind MAYHEM
- violent or cruel act OUTRAGE
- violent social disturbance UPHEAVAL, CONVULSION
violin See illustration, and also chart at **string instruments**
- violin or related instrument made in the 17th or 18th century by various outstanding craftsmen in Cremona, Italy GUARNERIUS, STRADIVARIUS, AMATI
- violin-shaped, as some leaves are PANDURATE
- violin-teaching method for young children, based on imitation and repetition SUZUKI METHOD
- bouncing the bow lightly off the strings of a violin or related instrument SPICCATO, JETÉ
- folksy term for a violin FIDDLE
- harsh sound sometimes produced by a violin or related instrument, resulting from faulty vibration WOLF
- played by plucking rather than bowing the strings, as a passage for the violin might be PIZZICATO
- small violin of a kind once used by dancing masters KIT, POCHETTE
VIP or famous person, often famous chiefly for being famous CELEBRITY, PERSONAGE
- VIP or high-ranking person BIGWIG, DIGNITARY, GRANDEE
virgin birth, reproduction without fertilization PARTHENOGENESIS
- virgin or nymph in paradise, according to the Koran HOURI
- virgin priestess in ancient Rome, tending the sacred fire in the temple of the goddess Vesta VESTAL VIRGIN
- virgin who is nevertheless sexually active, or even promiscuous DEMI-VIERGE
Virgin Mary - taking up of the Virgin Mary into heaven, or the feast day commemorating it, August 14, in the Roman Catholic Church THE ASSUMPTION
virginal (combining form) PARTHEN-, PARTHENO-
virginity CHASTITY
- deprive of virginity DEFLOWER
virtue, goodness, moral uprightness RECTITUDE
- virtues, traditionally the basic moral qualities, of justice, prudence, fortitude, and temperance CARDINAL VIRTUES
- piously and narrow-mindedly convinced of one's own virtues SELF-RIGHTEOUS, SANCTIMONIOUS, HOLIER-THAN-THOU
virus in its complete inert form before its invades and infects a cell VIRION, VIRAL PARTICLE
- virus of a group that multiplies in the stomach or intestines, causing gastrointestinal diseases, and also diseases such as polio and meningitis ENTEROVIRUS
- virus of a harmless kind in the respiratory and digestive systems REOVIRUS
- virus of various groups causing respiratory infections that produce symptoms like those of the common cold ADENOVIRUS, RHINOVIRUS
- insect-borne virus, causing diseases such as yellow fever ARBOVIRUS
- weaken a virus, as for use in a vaccine ATTENUATE
vise or clamp used to hold a tool or workpiece, as in a drill or lathe CHUCK
visible, easily noticed, obvious CONSPICUOUS
- visible, or detectable by any of the senses PERCEPTIBLE
- visible to the naked eye, without the need of a microscope MACROSCOPIC
vision See also **eyesight**
- vision, prophecy, or revelation of a great disaster APOCALYPSE
- perception on the outer edge of the field of vision PERIPHERAL VISION
visit a place regularly FREQUENT, HAUNT
visitor, guest, or the like who expects or accepts too much hospitality or generosity FREELOADER, SPONGER, SCROUNGER, CADGER
- frequent visitor, as to a club HABITUÉ, FREQUENTER
visual or visible OCULAR
visual defect (combining form) -OPIA
vital See **essential**
vitamin A, as found in eggs and fish liver oils, essential for normal vision RETINOL
- vitamin B_t, enabling the heart muscle to burn fatty acids CARNITINE

- vitamin B_x, used in compounds that prevent sunburn PARA-AMINOBENZOIC ACID, PABA
- vitamin B_1, as found in meat, essential for breaking down and absorbing carbohydrates THIAMINE
- vitamin B_5, as found in many animal and plant food sources, used to fight pelagra and other diseases, and to remedy schizophrenia NIACIN, NICOTINIC ACID
- vitamin B_6, fighting various body deficiencies, and having three active forms PYRIDOXAL, PYRIDOXAMINE, PYRODOXINE
- vitamin B_{12}, as found in liver, essential for red blood cell formation COBALAMIN, CYANOCOBALAMIN
- vitamin B_{15}, slightly controversial substance fighting ailments such as arthritis, asthma, and skin disorders PANGAMIC ACID
- vitamin B_{17}, found in almond seeds, known as a controversial cancer medication LAETRIL, AMYGDALIN
- vitamin C, as found in fruit and vegetables, essential in avoiding scurvy ASCORBIC ACID
- vitamin D, as found in milk, fish, and eggs, essential for normal bone growth CALCIFEROL, SUNSHINE VITAMIN
- vitamin E, a group of viscous oils, as found in wheat germs and similar sources, important for reproductive and other body functions, occurring in four forms ALPHA-, BETA-, GAMMA-, DELTA TOCOPHEROL
- vitamin F, including linoleic acid, important for normal body functioning ESSENTIAL FATTY ACID
- vitamin G, or vitamin B_2, as found in milk and egg yolks, essential for breaking down carbohydrates RIBOFLAVIN
- vitamin H, a B-complex vitamin produced by all living organisms BIOTIN
- vitamin K, a group of fat-soluble vitamins that enhance blood clotting KOAGULATION FACTOR
- vitamin M, or vitamin B_c, as found in leaf vegetables, essential for the normal production of red blood cells FOLIC ACID
- vitamin P, imprecise name for a group of substances nourishing the walls of blood vessels, as found in plant food sources BIOFLAVONOIDS
- vitamin T, found in certain yeasts, promoting regeneration of injured body tissues TORUTILIN
- vitamin U, as found in cabbage juice, assumed to provide relief for ulcers METENOIC ACID
- amounts of vitamin contents INTERNATIONAL UNITS, IU, MICROGRAMS
- amounts of vitamin potency RECOMMENDED DAILY ALLOWANCE, RDA, MINIMUM DAILY REQUIREMENT, MDR

viva - "may it flourish," motto similar to "viva," used with the name of a place or institution FLOREAT

vocabulary exclusive to a profession or other group JARGON, CANT, ARGOT
- vocabulary of a particular language, person, profession, subject, or the like LEXICON, LEXIS
- vocabulary of technical or very specialized terms TERMINOLOGY, NOMENCLATURE
- vocabulary or small specialized dictionary often accompanying or supplementing a difficult or technical text GLOSSARY
- relating to the words or vocabulary of a language LEXICAL

voice See also **pronunciation, sound**
- voice, put into words VOCALIZE
- voice-amplifying device consisting of a wide tapering tube, as used at protest demonstrations MEGAPHONE
- voice-production, especially by an entertainer, giving the impression

Volcano

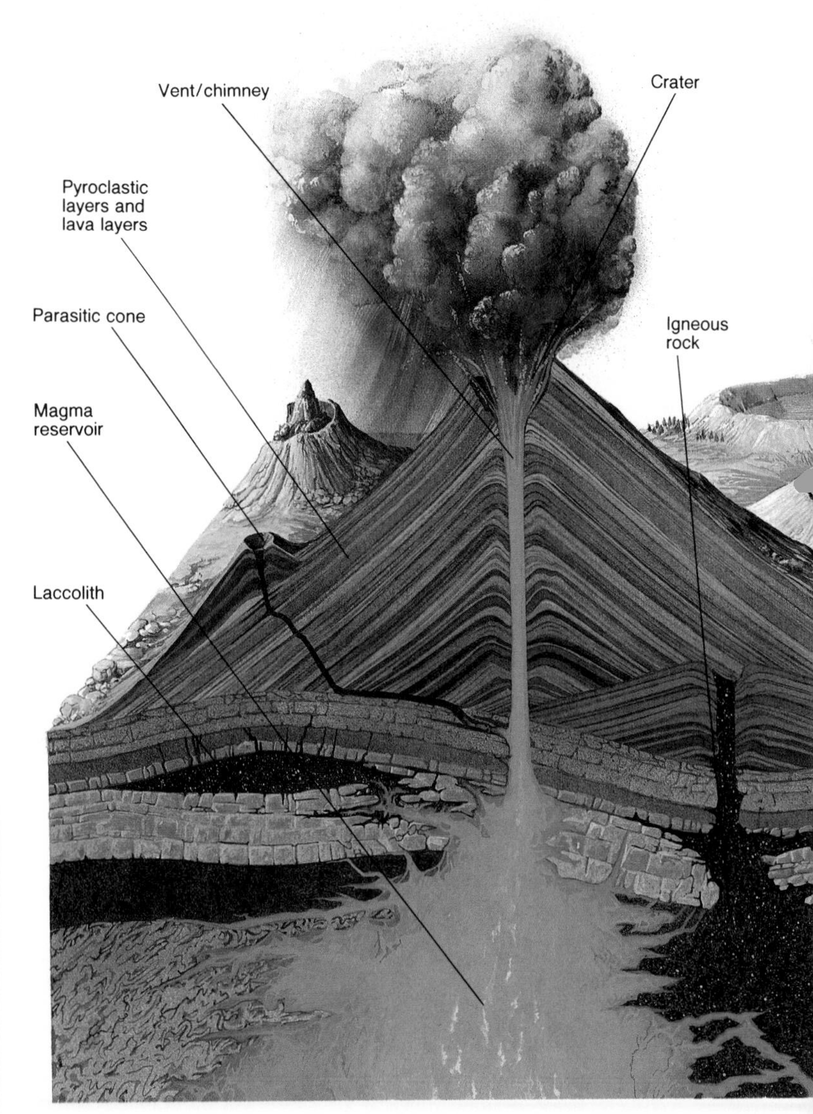

that the sound originates elsewhere, as from a dummy VENTRILOQUISM
- voice training through singing the *do-re-mi* syllables TONIC SOL-FA, SOLFEGGIO, SOLMIZATION
- adjust the pitch or tone of one's voice MODULATE, INFLECT
- having many voices, often with different melodic parts, as a piece of music might be POLYPHONIC
- referring to a voice that is deep, full-throated, or loud BOOMING, SONOROUS, OROTUND, RESONANT
- referring to a voice that is high-pitched and shrill REEDY
- referring to a voice that is hoarse, deep, and often emotional HUSKY
- referring to a voice that is nasal or choky ADENOIDAL
- referring to a voice that is rich and full-toned MELLOW, FRUITY
- referring to a voice that is unpleasantly loud STRIDENT, STENTORIAN
- referring to a voice that is very smooth and sweet MELLIFLUOUS
- referring to the voice generally VOCAL
- light rhythmical, springy flow or swing, as in a person's voice or walk LILT

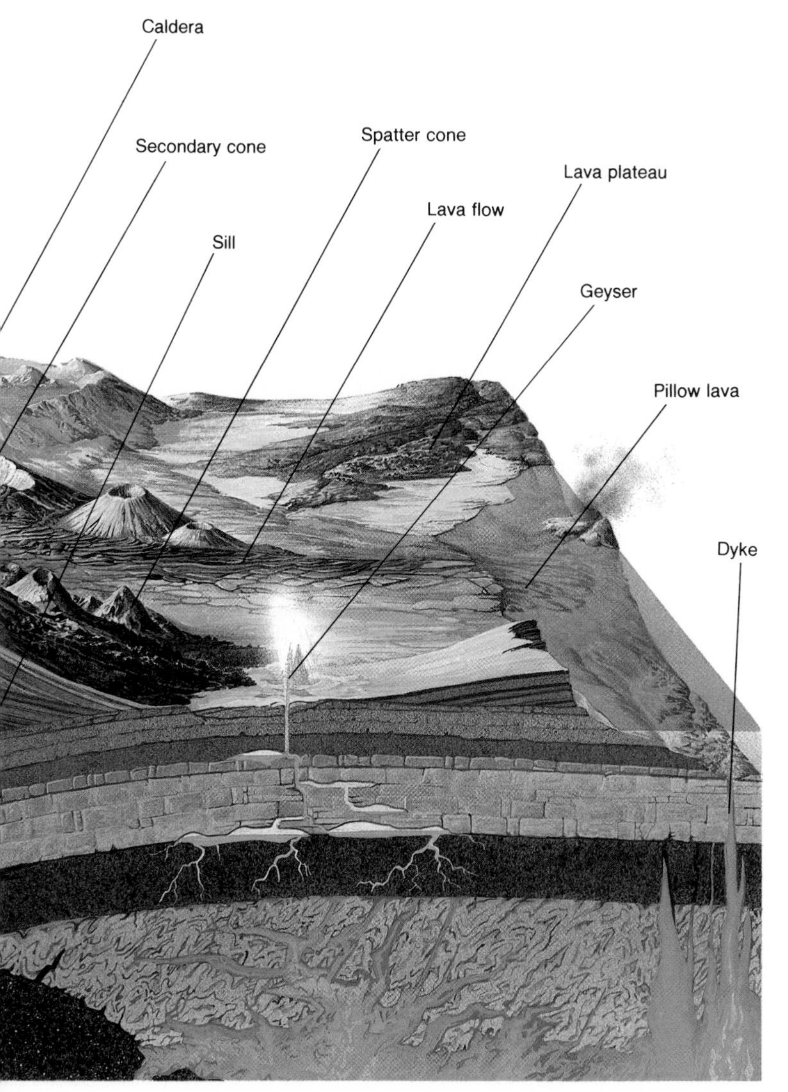

- loss of one's voice through injury, disease, or emotional disorder APHONIA
- range of the voice REGISTER, DIAPASON
- rise and fall of the pitch of the voice INTONATION, MODULATION, CADENCE, INFLECTION
- trembling or caused by trembling, as the voice of a frightened person might be TREMULOUS

voice (combining form) -PHON-, PHONO-, -PHONE, -PHONY

volcanic See also **volcano**
- volcanic and other rocks such as granite, produced from cooled magma IGNEOUS ROCKS
- volcanic glass that is black and shiny OBSIDIAN, PITCHSTONE
- volcanic lava fragments SCORIA, SLAG, CINDERS
- volcanic rock, light and porous, used for scrubbing and polishing PUMICE
- volcanic rock that can be ground for making cement TRASS
- destructive flowing cloud of burning gas emitted in certain volcanic eruptions NUÉE ARDENTE
- jet of steam, gases, and smoke issuing from the ground in volcanic regions SOFFIONE, FUMAROLE
- oval cavity, originally a bubble, in volcanic rock, filled with quartz or similar mineral AMYGDULE
- vent in the ground in an otherwise extinct volcanic region, emitting carbon dioxide MOFETTE

volcano See illustration
- expel fumes violently, as a rumbling volcano might ERUCT
- expel lava forcefully and abundantly, as a volcano might ERUPT
- inactive but not extinct, as a volcano might be DORMANT
- matter thrown out of an erupting volcano EJECTA
- referring to a volcano or volcanic eruption VULCANIAN, VULCANIC
- small cone or exposed rock-filled vent of an extinct volcano PUY
- still active, not extinct, still in danger of erupting, as a volcano might be EXTANT
- vent in or near a volcano, emitting sulfurous gases and often water vapor SOLFATARA

voluntary, unforced, unprompted, as laughter might be SPONTANEOUS

vomit, often without bringing up anything HEAVE, RETCH
- vomit or bring up partly digested food REGURGITATE
- vomit or spew out DISGORGE
- causing vomiting, as a medicine might be EMETIC
- illness, combining bulemia and

anorexia nervosa, in which compulsive eating is followed by self-induced vomiting BULMOREXIA
- illness consisting of compulsive overeating, often followed by self-induced vomiting BULIMIA, BULIMIA NERVOSA
- sick feeling, urge to vomit NAUSEA

von, *de*, or similar preposition accompanying a title or surname, indicating noble rank NOBILIARY PARTICLE

vote See also **election**
- vote against or veto someone, especially from membership of a club BLACKBALL, OSTRACIZE
- vote by the electorate on a proposal or issue of public importance REFERENDUM
- vote by the electorate to accept or refuse a proposal, program, or government PLEBISCITE
- vote cast for someone not listed on a ballot, by writing his or her name down WRITE-IN VOTE, WRITE-IN
- vote for the candidate most likely to defeat a candidate one dislikes, rather than for the candidate one positively favors PROTEST VOTE, TACTICAL VOTE
- vote of approval at a meeting, expressed by cheering rather than by a formal ballot ACCLAMATION
- vote of the chairperson or the presiding officer that decides the outcome when the votes in an assembly are tied CASTING VOTE
- vote or right to vote SUFFRAGE, FRANCHISE
- appeal for or request something earnestly, such as votes or funds SOLICIT
- campaign for votes from people or a region in an election campaign CANVASS
- decision or statement discussed and voted on at a meeting RESOLUTION, MOTION
- electoral system in which parties are represented according to the proportion of votes that they win PROPORTIONAL REPRESENTATION
- give voting rights or full citizenship rights to ENFRANCHISE
- majority in an election in which the winner fails to secure more than half of the total votes or seats RELATIVE MAJORITY, PLURALITY
- majority in an election in which the winner secures more than half of the total votes or seats ABSOLUTE MAJORITY
- person casting a vote on behalf of another PROXY
- person who checks or counts votes at an election, in Great Britain SCRUTINEER
- person who counts the votes in an election, assembly, legislature, or the like TELLER
- refrain from voting ABSTAIN
- without any dissenting votes, with no one contradicting, virtually unanimously NEM CON, NEMINE CONTRADICENTE

voting district PRECINCT
- voting rights, the vote SUFFRAGE, FRANCHISE
- voting system in which each voter is allowed as many votes as there are candidates, to be distributed as he or she wishes CUMULATIVE VOTING
- voting system in which the voter indicates his or her choices in order of preference PREFERENTIAL VOTING
- study of voting patterns and electoral systems PSEPHOLOGY

voucher, certificate, or other formal document DOCKET
- exchange coupons, vouchers, or the like for goods REDEEM

vow of faith and promise of support by members of a church COVENANT
- referring to a vow or wish, as a prayer or religious offering might be VOTIVE

vowel sound that changes in quality during the syllable, such as the /ī/ sound in *fine* DIPHTHONG
- change in the vowel sound of a verb, as in *sing, sang, sung* GRADATION, ABLAUT
- omitting or slurring of an unstressed vowel or syllable, as to make a line of verse scan ELISION
- pair of vowels run together as /œ/ or /æ/ in Latin LIGATURE, DIGRAPH, DIPHTHONG
- repetition or similarity of the vowels in a series of words, as for poetic effect ASSONANCE
- two dots placed above a vowel, as in *gemütlich* DIAERESIS, UMLAUT
- unstressed midcentral vowel sound, as in the last syllable *Anna* or *teacher*, or the symbol /ə/ that represents it SCHWA

voyage, long journey or wanderings PEREGRINATIONS

vulgar See also **rude, showy**
- vulgar, unrefined, coarse, oafish BOORISH, UNCOUTH, PHILISTINE
- vulgar and showy, flashy or cheap-looking TAWDRY, TINSELLY, GAUDY, GARISH, RAFFISH, BRASH
- vulgar and unrefined person, lout PHILISTINE, YAHOO
- vulgar language or swearword PROFANITY
- vulgar opinion, taste, or group of people LOWEST COMMON DENOMINATOR
- vulgar or crude, having common or coarse tastes PLEBEIAN
- vulgar or rough people, the masses, the herd HOI POLLOI, RIFFRAFF, PLEBS, THE GREAT UNWASHED
- vulgar tongue, the ordinary spoken language rather than the refined or written form of a language VERNACULAR
- vulgarly or superficially attractive MERETRICIOUS, SPECIOUS
- vulgarly sentimental BATHETIC, MAUDLIN, MAWKISH

vulture, hyena, insect, or the like that feeds on dead animals, rotting meat, or other decaying organic matter SCAVENGER

wafer See **Communion**
wage earners - referring to industrial wage earners in manual-labor jobs BLUE-COLLAR
wages, fees, or other form of profit from one's job or office EMOLUMENT
wagon See also chart at **horse-drawn vehicles**
- wagon builder WAINWRIGHT
- canvas-covered wagon, used by American pioneers PRAIRIE SCHOONER, CONESTOGA WAGON
- defensive camp formed by a circle of covered wagons CORRAL, LAAGER
- hooped rod supporting the canopy of a covered wagon BAIL
- old-fashioned or regional term for a farm wagon WAIN
- open wagon used to transport condemned prisoners to the place of execution, as during the French Revolution TUMBRIL
- pivoted bar linking a wagon, plow, or the like to the side straps or traces of the horse's harness SWINGLETREE, WHIFFLETREE, WHIPPLETREE
wail, lament for the dead KEEN
- wail as if lamenting ULULATE
- wail weakly, whimper, whine MEWL, PULE
waist or bodice of a dress CORSAGE
- waistline, particularly when large GIRTH
waistcoat for a woman GILET
- waistcoat pocket, originally designed for a pocket watch FOB
wait, linger TARRY, LOITER, LAG
waiter in France (or in French) GARÇON
waiting state, intermediate or transitional condition LIMBO
waiting room, entrance hall, or reception area FOYER, VESTIBULE, LOBBY
wakefulness VIGILANCE
waking signal, usually by bugle, in the armed forces REVEILLE
walk See also **move**
- walk about casually, usually for pleasure, stroll, stretch one's legs AMBLE, PERAMBULATE
- walk aimlessly from place to place RAMBLE, ROAM, ROVE
- walk along without apparent worry or care SWAN, DALLY
- walk at a leisurely pace, typically in a public place PROMENADE
- walk casually or furtively SIDLE, SLINK
- walk casually or wearily TRAIPSE
- walk determinedly, brushing all aside WADE
- walk heavily, march long distances, plod FOOTSLOG, TRUDGE
- walk in an affected or prim way, with very short steps MINCE
- walk in an idle or leisurely way, stroll SAUNTER, MOSEY, SASHAY
- walk in a proud or pompously affected way STRUT, SWAGGER
- walk or move haltingly or unsteadily STAGGER, TOTTER, HOBBLE
- walk or run awkwardly LOLLOP, WADDLE, GALUMPH
- walk slowly, lag behind DAWDLE, LOITER
- walk swiftly with long steps STRIDE, PACE, STEP OUT, MOVE OUT
- walk taken for the good of one's health CONSTITUTIONAL
- walk unsteadily or clumsily, shuffle SHAMBLE
- walk with conspicuous movements to express impatience, anger, or the like FLOUNCE
- walk with short, unsteady steps, as very young children do TODDLE
walking about, able to walk AMBULATORY, AMBULANT
- walking area, typically covered, such as an aisle or cloister AMBULATORY
- walking or moving from place to place, as in the course of one's business ITINERANT, PERIPATETIC
- walking with both heel and toes touching the ground, as humans are PLANTIGRADE
- walking with only the toes touching the ground, as cats are DIGITIGRADE
- flat stretch of ground for walking along, especially along a seashore ESPLANADE, PROMENADE
- instrument gauging the distance covered while walking, according to the number and length of steps taken PEDOMETER
- style of walking or carrying oneself, bearing GAIT, CARRIAGE, DEPORTMENT
walking (combining form) -GRADE
walking stick made from the stem of the rattan palm MALACCA CANE
- walking stick whose handle opens into a flat seat SHOOTING STICK
- walking stick with a spike at the tip PIKESTAFF
- metal ring or cap on the tip of a walking stick FERRULE
wall See also **brickwork, fortification, castle**
- wall consisting of two layers with a small space between them for insulation CAVITY WALL
- wall hanging made from a heavy woven textile TAPESTRY, ARRAS
- wall-like partition dividing up a ship, aircraft, or spacecraft BULKHEAD
- wall of a body cavity or organ PARIES
- wall or roof covering of overlapping boards WEATHERBOARDING, CLAPBOARDING
- wall painting MURAL
- wall painting made on dry plaster SECCO
- wall painting made on fresh damp plaster FRESCO
- boarding running along the foot of an interior wall BASEBOARD, SKIRTING BOARD
- bricks jutting out from a wall, typically meant as ornaments CORBELING
- circular wall, especially one supporting a dome TAMBOUR
- coating of cement, plaster, or the like covering a wall or other surface RENDERING
- coating of cement, sand, and lime forming a hard finish on outside walls STUCCO
- construction or prop pressing against a wall to strengthen it BUTTRESS, PIER
- decorative slab, memorial tablet, or the like, as mounted on a wall or monument PLAQUE
- decoratively patterned plasterwork on walls PARGETING
- exterior angle of a wall QUOIN, COIGN
- facing of rectangular tiles fixed on an external wall in imitation of stone blocks STONE CLADDING
- fortified wall surrounding a castle, town, or the like, or the area protected by it ENCEINTE

- gluey glaze, filler, or coating, as for paper or walls, made of wax, clay, resin, or the like SIZE
- hole or niche in a wall for supporting a beam COLUMBARIUM
- hollow plug, as of plastic, typically inserted into a hole in the wall as a mooring for a nail or screw RAWL, RAWL PLUG
- imprison, shut up within walls IMMURE
- inward-curving surface between a ceiling and wall, or a concave molding COVE, COVING
- lower section of a wall, distinguished by different decoration such as paneling DADO, WAINSCOT
- molding running along the top of a building or wall CORNICE
- opening in a wall, wider inside than out, for a door or window EMBRASURE
- ornamental ridge running along the top of a roof or wall CRESTING
- outside the walls or boundaries, as of a castle, city, or university EXTRAMURAL
- plaster of a coarse, gravelly kind applied to outside walls ROUGHCAST, SPATTER DASH
- plaster used as a finishing or sealing coating on walls GROUT
- projecting from the surrounding wall or surface PROTUBERANT, PROUD
- protective row of spikes or broken glass fitted to the top of a wall CHEVAUX-DE-FRISE, CHEVAL-DE-FRISE
- referring to a wall MURAL
- rough finish for outside walls, produced by small pebbles embedded in the plaster PEBBLE DASH, ROCK DASH
- roughened with a metal brush, as a wall might be KEYED
- scaling, by ladders, of a castle wall, rampart, or the like, as during a military attack ESCALADE
- section or space set back from the main surface of a wall, as for a statue or bookcase ALCOVE, RECESS, NICHE
- strip of ornamental plasterwork, stone, wood, or the like on a building or wall MOLDING
- tall frame used to scale fortress walls during a siege in ancient times TURRET, BELFRY
- top layer of bricks, tiles, or the like, usually sloping, of a wall COPING
- triangular section at the top of a wall, supporting a roof GABLE

wander about aimlessly MAUNDER, MEANDER, RAMBLE, ROAM
- wander about, especially in an enjoyable and sociable way GAD ABOUT, GALLIVANT
- wander from the main subject of one's speech or writing DIGRESS, DEVIATE

wandering See also **traveling**
- wandering, erratic PLANETARY
- wandering about, drifting, homeless VAGABOND, VAGRANT
- wandering from the main topic or course, as in a speech DIGRESSION, EXCURSION, EXCURSUS
- wandering in search of adventure, as medieval knights were ERRANT
- wandering medieval musician MINSTREL, TROUBADOUR, JONGLEUR
- wandering or traveling from place to place, as in search of work ITINERANT, MIGRANT
- wandering scholar or student in the Middle Ages GOLIARD

wanderer, specifically a member of a pastoral people moving about in search of food or grazing land NOMAD

waning, as the moon might be DECRESCENT

war See also **military**
- war memorial or other monument honoring a dead person or dead people buried elsewhere CENOTAPH
- war or phase of a war in which little fighting is done or little change in the military balance occurs SITZKRIEG, PHONY WAR, STANDOFF
- war waged by the giants against the gods in Greek mythology GIGANTOMACHY, GIGANTOMACHIA
- aggressive, hostile, warlike BELLIGERENT, BELLICOSE, HAWKISH, MILITANT
- arms or other goods that a neutral nation cannot legally supply to a warring nation CONTRABAND OF WAR
- display of military power or threatening of war by one country in its dealings with another SABER RATTLING, GUNBOAT DIPLOMACY
- murderous, marked by mutual slaughter, as a bloody war is INTERNECINE
- payments demanded as compensation from the losing side in a war REPARATIONS
- person forced from his or her home or homeland, especially by a war, refugee DISPLACED PERSON, DP
- person moved from a war zone to a safe area EVACUEE
- politician or adviser favoring aggression or war HAWK
- politician or adviser favoring conciliation or avoidance of war DOVE
- prepare for war, as troops might MOBILIZE
- provocative act or event that prompts or justifies a war CASUS BELLI
- referring to nonnuclear warfare or weapons CONVENTIONAL
- referring to the period after a war, especially the American Civil War POSTBELLUM
- referring to the period before a war, especially the American Civil War ANTEBELLUM
- referring to war MARTIAL
- right of a nation at war to use or destroy the property of a neutral nation on condition that full compensation is paid ANGARY
- simple living conditions, as imposed in wartime AUSTERITY
- slaughter or massacre, especially in war CARNAGE
- victor's harsh decree or settlement imposed on a defeated enemy after a war DIKTAT
- wearing down or slow exhaustion of enemy forces during a war ATTRITION

war (combining form) -MACHY, -MACHIA

ward - relation between ward and guardian TUTELAGE

wardrobe or large, heavy cabinet ARMOIRE
- wardrobe or small room for hanging clothes GARDEROBE
- wardrobe specially prepared by a bride TROUSSEAU

warehouse for storing goods before payment of duty or before export or transshipment BONDED WAREHOUSE
- warehouse or similar place for storage DEPOSITORY, DEPOT, ENTREPÔT, REPOSITORY, REPERTORY

warm - wine warming to room temperature after it is opened CHAMBRÉ
- warm-blooded, as mammals are HOMOIOTHERMIC, HOMEOTHERMIC
- warm up by stretching and exercising, as before a race LIMBER UP
- warmed up before serving, as leftover food might be RÉCHAUFFÉ
- warming dish CHAFING DISH
- warming rack or stand, next to a fireplace FOOTMAN
- warmish, lukewarm TEPID
- warmth-producing CALEFACIENT
- not warm-blooded, cold-blooded, as reptiles are POIKILOTHERMIC

warn, give a useful hint TIP OFF
- warn or advise against a particular action, caution ADMONISH
- warn or indicate that something is about to happen PRESAGE, HARBINGER, HERALD

warning, guide, or sign BEACON
- warning against touching or interfering, "do not touch me" NOLI ME TANGERE
- warning of an event before it occurs PREMONITION
- warning or caution CAVEAT, CAVE

- warning or elaborate complaint JEREMIAD, DENUNCIATION
- warning signal or alarm, typically on a bell TOCSIN
- gentle warning or scolding ADMONITION
- Latin maxim warning the buyer to beware CAVEAT EMPTOR
- remedial, improving, as advice or a warning might be SALUTARY
- sign or warning of a coming event AUGURY, AUSPICE, PORTENT, OMEN, PRODIGY, PRESAGE

warrior - full equipment of weapons and armor belonging to a warrior PANOPLY

warship See also **ship**
- armored cylinder protecting the turret of a warship BARBETTE
- fleet or grouping of warships ARMADA, SQUADRON, FLOTILLA
- revolving armored dome or drum on a tank or warship, in which guns are mounted TURRET

wart, corn, or other small benign growth PAPILLOMA
- wart on the sole of the foot PLANTAR WART
- wart or any similar horny growth on the skin KERATOSIS
- wart or wartlike growth VERRUCA
- wartlike growth or projection, as on a legume's root, the skin, or a bone TUBERCLE
- destruction of warts or other unwanted tissue by means of electric sparks FULGURATION, ELECTRODESICCATION
- grow or spread abnormally, with fleshy outgrowths, as warts and some tumors do VEGETATE

wash by flushing out or flooding with water SWILL OUT, SLUICE, DOUSE
- wash or purify ceremonially LUSTRATE
- wash out a wound, the eye, or the like with water or a medicinal solution IRRIGATE
- washing of the body, as in religious ceremonies ABLUTION
- washing out of an organ, such as the stomach LAVAGE
- washing substance as used for industrial and household cleaning DETERGENT
- low basinlike bathroom fixture on which one sits to wash one's private parts BIDET
- purify, separate, or remove a substance, such as ore, by washing and straining it ELUTRIATE
- remove soluble parts from a substance such as soil by washing it out with water LEACH, LIXIVIATE, ELUVIATE

washbowl - bedside table, movable stand, or the like containing a washbowl COMMODE

wasp's nest, or colony of wasps or hornets VESPIARY
- referring to a wasp VESPINE

waste, spend or use extravagantly SQUANDER
- waste, spend or use up in an inefficient or wasteful way DISSIPATE
- waste liquid, as from a factory or sewage works EFFLUENT
- waste material from a furnace after smelting or refining SLAG, SINTER, CINDER, SCORIA
- waste matter discharged from the body EXCREMENT, EXCRETA, FECES, EGESTA, ORDURE, DEJECTA
- waste time DAWDLE, DALLY, TARRY, LOLLYGAG
- waste time, money, or the like FRITTER AWAY, FRIVOL AWAY
- wasting away of the body or part of the body PHTHISIS, ATROPHY, EMACIATION, MACERATION
- wasting disease, especially tuberculosis of the lungs CONSUMPTION
- wasting of the body or of an organ as a result of lengthy disease TABES
- wasting time, or causing a delay DILATORY, PROCRASTINATING
- extraction of useful substances from waste material RECOVERY, RECYCLING

wasteful, excessive, unrestrained WANTON, IMMODERATE
- wasteful or unthrifty IMPROVIDENT, SPENDTHRIFT
- irresponsibly and recklessly wasteful or extravagant PRODIGAL, PROFLIGATE

wasteland DEVASTATION, DESOLATION

watch See also **clock**
- watch or clock of a very precise kind, especially one used at sea CHRONOMETER
- watch or clock that can be primed to strike the hour or quarter hour REPEATER
- watch or guard kept during the hours of sleep VIGIL
- watch that is wound by a small attached knob projecting outside the casing STEM-WINDER
- watch with a hinged metal lid protecting the face HUNTER
- watch with a sweep-second hand CHRONOGRAPH
- adjust watches to register the identical time SYNCHRONIZE
- art of making watches or clocks, or the study of them HOROLOGY
- display of symbols, as on a quartz watch, produced by liquid crystals LCD
- fine coiled spring helping to regulate the movement of a watch HAIRSPRING
- glass or plastic cover of a watch face LUNETTE, CRYSTAL
- referring to a watch, clock, or meter that indicates readings by changing numbers rather than by moving hands on a dial DIGITAL
- referring to a watch, clock, or meter with traditional hands and dial to indicate readings ANALOG
- second hand of a watch SWEEP-SECOND HAND
- small, notched winding knob on an old-fashioned watch CROWN
- waistcoat pocket, originally designed for a pocket watch FOB

watchful, alert, on the lookout for danger VIGILANT, ON THE QUI VIVE, ARGUS-EYED

watchtower of a fortress BARBICAN

water-borne barrier, as of logs or empty drums BOOM
- water cask or drinking fountain on a ship SCUTTLEBUTT
- water channel or canal that is made by humans AQUEDUCT
- water channel or ditch in South Africa SLOOT
- water channel or small dam, or the gate or valve holding back or regulating the water SLUICE
- water channel such as a ravine or gully GULLET
- water collecting in a ship's hull BILGE WATER
- water-cooled smoking pipe, used in the East HOOKAH, NARGHILE, HUBBLE-BUBBLE, KALIAN
- water drops formed on surfaces from cooling air CONDENSATION
- water-dwelling, as some plants are HYDROPHILOUS, HYDROPHYTIC, AQUATIC
- water nymph in classical mythology NAIAD
- water or air stream directed at or into a part of the body for cleansing or healing DOUCHE
- water pipe on a pavement, with nozzles for hoses HYDRANT
- water pipe or channel CONDUIT, CULVERT
- water-raising apparatus, as used in ancient times, typically a spiral device within a tube ARCHIMEDES' SCREW
- water-raising apparatus, as used in Egypt, consisting of a pivoted pole with a bucket and a counterweight on the end SHADOOF
- water spirit in Germanic folklore, usually hostile to humans NIX
- water spirit in Scottish folklore, in the form of a horse that would drown its riders KELPIE
- water spirit or nymph UNDINE
- water tank, as on the roof or un-

derground for storing rainwater CISTERN
- addition of fluorine compounds to the public water supply as a measure to reduce tooth decay FLUORIDATION
- alleged water divining by means of a rod or wand RHABDOMANCY, DOWSING
- artificial water channel, as for providing power or transporting logs FLUME
- backward flow of air or water, as from a propeller or a wave on the beach BACKWASH
- channel for excess water, as around the side of a dam SPILLWAY
- channel or bay through which water flows inland INLET, ESTUARY
- cover with water, flood INUNDATE
- cultivation of plants without soil, using nutrients dissolved in water HYDROPONICS, AQUICULTURE
- curved surface of water or other liquid held in a tube or container MENISCUS
- deprived of water or moisture, dry DEHYDRATED, DESICCATED
- dip lightly into the water, as a bird might DAP
- fit for drinking, as uncontaminated water is POTABLE
- fizzy mineral water that is either natural or artificially aerated SELTZER WATER, CLUB SODA
- floating mass of tiny animal or plant organisms on a large body of water PLANKTON
- flowing with a violently agitated movement, as river water might be TURBULENT
- legal trial in the Middle Ages, in which God's judgment was allegedly secured through exposing the accused to fire, immersion in water, or the like ORDEAL
- level at which the ground is saturated by water WATER TABLE
- living, growing, or occurring in or on water AQUATIC
- living both on land and in water, or relating to both land and water AMPHIBIOUS
- measure the depth of water, as with a weighted line SOUND, FATHOM, PLUMB
- muddied through sediment or foreign particles, as river water might be TURBID
- operated by or involving water pressure HYDRAULIC
- plunge beneath the water, soak completely IMMERSE, SUBMERGE
- process discarded glass, water, and so on for reuse RECYCLE
- remove salt, as from sea water DESALINATE
- rippling movement in water EDDY, PURL
- rising, lowering, or distortion of the surface of water or other liquid, as when held in a tube, because of surface tension CAPILLARITY, CAPILLARY ACTION
- shallow stretch of water SHOAL
- sheet of water flowing over a weir or dam wall NAPPE
- slightly salty, as water might be BRACKISH, BRINY
- stick, forked twig, or the like that allegedly quivers or dips when held above ground containing water or minerals DIVINING ROD, DOWSING ROD
- stretch of land intermittently covered by water WASH, FLOOD PLAIN
- strong swift current of water, or its channel RACE
- supply water to a region, farmland, or the like IRRIGATE
- thin or weaken a cordial, concentrate, or other liquid, as by adding water DILUTE, ADULTERATE
- track of visible foam or waves in water, as left by a ship WAKE
- uninterrupted stretch of water along a river or canal REACH
- unmoving, not flowing, as pond water is STAGNANT
- upright outdoor water pipe with a tap STANDPIPE
- very clear, as pure water is LIMPID, PELLUCID

water (combining form) -AQU-, AQUA-, HYDR-, HYDRO-

OLD WEAPONS

arbalest	large crossbow used to fire arrows, stones, and other missiles
assegai	light spear of southern Africa
ballista/onager	ancient catapultlike device used to hurl missiles
belfry	movable siege tower used to attack enemy walls
caltrops	spiked balls placed in the path of troops
flail	swinging bar attached to a long handle, used in close combat
gladius	short double-edged sword of ancient Rome
Greek fire	flaming chemical substance, used as a kind of firebomb, mainly by the Byzantine navy
halberd/ gisarme	pikestaff topped by an axlike blade and a spike
javelin/lance	long, pointed spear
mace	club with a spiked metal head
parazonium	ancient Greek dagger
partisan	pikestaff topped by a long double-edged blade
pilum	long, heavy spear of ancient Rome
quarterstaff	long wooden staff, tipped with iron
spatha	blunt-pointed sword of ancient Rome; long sword used by Britons and Saxons
spontoon	pikestaff topped by a pointed metal head and crossbar
trebuchet/ mangonel	medieval catapultlike device used to hurl missiles
trident	three-pronged weapon used by Roman gladiators
twibil	double-edged battle-ax
waddy	tapered stick used by Australian Aborigines as a club or missile
wommera	notched stick used by Australian Aborigines to launch a spear

water buffalo CARABAO
water clock CLEPSYDRA
water ice SORBET
water lily or related plant LOTUS, NYMPHAEA, NUPHAR
water on the brain HYDROCEPHALUS, HYDROCEPHALY
water ski consisting of a single board AQUAPLANE
water vapor - containing as much water vapor as possible, as a humid atmosphere might be SATURATED
- containing large amounts of water vapor, as moist air is HUMID, MUGGY, CLOSE
- lose or give off water vapor through pores, as from the surface of a leaf TRANSPIRE
water wheel See illustration at **windmill**
- water wheel rimmed with buckets that dip into a stream or pool, used in irrigation systems NORIA
- referring to a water wheel driven by water flowing beneath UNDERSHOT
- referring to a water wheel driven by water flowing over its top OVERSHOT
- watercourse directing water into a mill, turbine, or water wheel HEADRACE
watercolor painting or wash AQUARELLE
- watercolor pigment mixed with gum to make it opaque, or a painting or the method using such pigments GOUACHE
waterfall CHUTE
- waterfall, or series of small waterfalls CASCADE, CATARACT
watering place, resort area with mineral springs SPA
waterproof IMPERMEABLE
- waterproof rubber shoes worn over standard shoes GALOSHES
- waterproof sheet of canvas used as a covering TARPAULIN
- pitch or tarry mixture, as used in waterproofing BITUMEN, ASPHALT
watershed - area bounded by watersheds, in which all water drains into one river system CATCHMENT AREA, DRAINAGE BASIN
watertight chamber from which underwater construction or repair work is done CAISSON
- watertight enclosure or compartment, as for construction on a riverbed COFFER
- make a boat watertight by sealing or packing the seams, as with tar CAULK, PAY
waterway linking two larger bodies of water STRAIT, SOUND
- clean or deepen a harbor or waterway by means of a scooping machine DREDGE
watery, containing, relating to, or dissolved in water AQUEOUS
- watery chemical solution used as a disinfectant and bleaching agent JAVELLE WATER
- watery liquid from the body tissues LYMPH
wave - wavelike, wavy UNDULANT
- wave moving upstream in a river estuary, as caused by tidal currents BORE, EAGRE
- wave or reveal a weapon or similar object openly or defiantly BRANDISH, FLOURISH
- wave or swell of the sea, smoke, sound, or the like BILLOW
- wave the arms about to convey meaning GESTICULATE
- backward pull of waves toward the sea when receding after breaking on the shore UNDERTOW
- broken wave of the sea, as on a shore COMBER, BREAKER, ROLLER
- huge wave resulting from an earthquake or volcanic eruption on the seabed TSUNAMI
- loud, deep, and resonant, as the sound of waves crashing on the shore is PLANGENT
- referring to waves, such as light waves, of the same frequency or related phases COHERENT
- rise and fall as waves do in the open sea SURGE, HEAVE, SWELL
- transmit a wave through a medium, in physics PROPAGATE
wavelength - invisible radiation having wavelengths between those of visible light and microwaves INFRARED
- invisible radiation having wavelengths between those of visible

WEATHER AND CLIMATE TERMS

anticyclone	area of high atmospheric pressure, with winds spiraling outward
backing	referring to a change of wind direction anticlockwise, as from south to southeast to east, at a particular place
Beaufort scale	scale of wind force, ranging from 0 for calm to 12 for hurricane
black ice/ glazed frost	thin coating of transparent ice
col	area of intermediate pressure separating two anticyclones or two depressions
convection	transfer of heat by massive movement within the atmosphere, typically upward
cyclone	tropical storm with violently rotating winds around a low-pressure center
depression/low	area of low atmospheric pressure in temperate latitudes, with winds spiraling inward
dust devil/ sand column	rapidly moving column of dust whipped up by a swirling of wind around an intense low-pressure area
front/ discontinuity	boundary between air masses of different temperature and humidity
greenhouse effect	heating of the earth's surface by retention of infrared radiation, caused by increasing carbon dioxide in the atmosphere
haar	cold sea mist or fog on the British northeast coast
hoarfrost	powdery, white coating of small ice crystals
hurricane	intense, tropical disturbance—force 12 on the Beaufort scale—in the West Indies and Gulf of Mexico
inversion/ inversion layer	increase of temperature with height, or the layer of the atmosphere where this occurs

continued

light and X-rays ULTRAVIOLET

wavy, having winding lines, movements, decorations, or the like VERMICULATE, UNDULATE

wax modeling CEROPLASTICS

- wax or polish something, such as a car SIMONIZE
- wax polish or similar polishing agent LUSTER
- bronze-casting technique in which a mold is formed around a wax model, which is then melted and drained off LOST-WAX PROCESS, CIRE PERDUE
- pointed writing instrument, as used on wax tablets in ancient times STYLUS

wax (combining form) CERO-

waxing, as the moon might be INCRESCENT

waxy or waxlike CERACEOUS

- waxy substance formed from oils in a whale's head, as used for cosmetics and candles SPERMACETI
- waxy substance secreted by the ear, earwax CERUMEN
- waxy substance secreted by whales, used as a fixative in making perfume AMBERGRIS

way in which someone or something works or something is used MODUS OPERANDI

- way of working or living together MODUS VIVENDI
- go one's way WEND

weak, bland, lacking all real force, as a character or comment might be ANODYNE, ANEMIC, INSIPID

- weak, feeble, frail, doddering like an old woman ANILE
- weak, limp, lacking energy and vitality LETHARGIC, LANGUID
- weak, powerless, lacking force or competence, as a king might be IMPOTENT, INEFFECTUAL
- weak, unaccented, as a syllable might be ATONIC
- weak and small PUNY
- weak and unconvincing, as an excuse or argument might be TENUOUS, FLIMSY, UNTENABLE
- weak area or vulnerable aspect SOFT UNDERBELLY, ACHILLES' HEEL
- weak or ineffectual, drained of energy and vitality, as through self-indulgence EFFETE, DEGENERATE, DECADENT
- weak through age, illness, overuse, or the like DECREPIT, INFIRM
- weak-willed, indecisive, lacking purpose or perseverance IRRESOLUTE
- weak-willed, lacking courage or strength of character SPINELESS, LILY-LIVERED
- weak-willed, passive, slack, wishy-washy SUPINE, FECKLESS
- weakly built, liable to collapse, as a building might be RICKETY
- weakly defended, open to attack PREGNABLE, VULNERABLE
- weakly sentimental and affected, as someone's manner or poetry might be NAMBY-PAMBY, MAWKISH, MAUDLIN
- chronically weak and sickly VALETUDINARIAN

weak person, especially one lacking courage or determination, MILKSOP, WIMP, SISSY, NINNY

- weak person, ineffectual or powerless man EUNUCH, MEDIOCRITY
- weak person, once strong or honorable but now spineless or feeble BROKEN REED
- weak person, overprotected and pampered MOLLYCODDLE
- weak person, team, or the like, easily defeated PUSHOVER
- weak person, timid and retiring man MILQUETOAST

weaken, deprive of initiative, energy, and other qualities traditionally regarded as masculine EMASCULATE

- weaken, go limp, as a flower might WILT
- weaken, grow feeble or disheartened FLAG, SAG, LANGUISH
- weaken, make useless STULTIFY
- weaken, tire out or wear down by sapping energy or vigor ENERVATE, ENFEEBLE, DEBILITATE, DEVITALIZE
- weaken in a stealthy way, as in preparing to overthrow a regime UNDERMINE, SUBVERT
- weaken or make thin, as disease or dilution might ATTENUATE
- weaken or thin a cordial, concentrate, or other liquid, as by adding water DILUTE, ADULTERATE

WEATHER AND CLIMATE TERMS *Continued*

isobar	line on a weather map linking places that have the same atmospheric pressure
isohyet	line on a weather map linking places that have the same rainfall
isotherm	line on a weather map linking places that have the same temperature
jet stream	narrow, fast-moving, generally westerly airstream at high altitude
monsoon	major pressure and wind system that reverses direction with the seasons, as in southern and southeastern Asia
occluded front/ occlusion	front formed in a depression when the cold front overtakes the warm front
ridge	elongated area of high pressure between two depressions
rime/frost feathers	frost in the form of granular ice crystals on the windward side of objects
thermal	vertically rising current of warm air, used by glider pilots
tornado	intense cyclone with winds whirling at more than 200 miles per hour
trough	elongated area of low atmospheric pressure between two areas of higher pressure
typhoon	intense cyclone in the China sea, with winds whirling at more than 100 miles per hour
veering	referring to a change of wind direction clockwise, as from south to southwest to west, at a particular place
waterspout	rapidly moving column of cloud and water whipped up by a small, intense, short-lived low-pressure area over the sea
wedge	area of high pressure between two depressions, narrower than a ridge

WEIGHTS AND MEASURES

UNIT	WHAT IT MEASURES
ENERGY AND MOTION	
bar/barye/pascal	pressure
dyne/newton/poundal	force
erg/joule/kilowatt-hour	work or energy
knot/mach	speed
watt	power
HEAT, LIGHT, AND SOUND	
angstrom	wavelength of light
calorie/therm	heat
candela	luminous intensity
decibel/phon	loudness
fresnel/hertz	frequency
kelvin	temperature
lumen	luminous flux, the rate of flow of luminous energy
ELECTRICITY AND MAGNETISM	
ampere	electric current
coulomb	electric charge
farad	electric capacitance, the capacity to store an electric charge
gauss/tesla	magnetic flux density, the direction and magnitude of magnetic force
henry	electric inductance, the property of enabling an electromagnetic force to be generated
maxwell/weber	magnetic flux, the strength of a magnetic field through an area
oersted	magnetic field strength
ohm	electric resistance
siemens	electric conductance
volt	electric potential and electromotive force
ATOMIC PHYSICS	
becquerel/curie	radioactivity
dalton/AMU/atomic mass unit	mass of an isotope
rad/gray	energy absorbed from radiation
rem/REM	radiation dose
roentgen	X-rays or gamma rays

UNIT	VALUE
METRIC UNITS	
grade	one-hundredth of a right angle
gram	about 0.002 pound avoirdupois
hectare	100 ares, or 2.47 acres
micrometer/micron	10_6 meters, about 1/25,000 inch
stere	volume equivalent of 1 cubic meter
ton or metric ton	10 quintals, or 0.98421 long tons

continued

- weaken or wither, waste away, as a body part might ATROPHY
- weaken the reputation or position of, as by scandal COMPROMISE
- weakened and pale, as through fever or starvation ETIOLATED
- weakened or seriously injured or disabled INCAPACITATED
- weakened to the point of exhaustion, drained of strength or resources DEPLETED

weakness, chronic loss or lack of strength, as through disease DEBILITY, ASTHENIA, CACHEXIA, TABES
- weakness, flaw, small but fatally vulnerable spot ACHILLES' HEEL
- weakness, minor personal failing, small fault of character FOIBLE
- weakness and failing powers because of illness or old age INFIRMITY

weakness (combining form) -ASTHEN-

wealth, riches, or money, especially if acquired in a dubious way PELF, LUCRE
- wealth regarded as a corrupting influence MAMMON
- mine or other source of great wealth GOLCONDA, EL DORADO
- source of great wealth or good luck BONANZA

wealthy See **rich**

weapons See chart, page 584, and also **bomb, missile, knife, gun, club, sword**
- weapons or arms, especially heavy guns ORDNANCE
- weapons and ammunition MUNITIONS
- weapons manufacturer or repairer ARMORER
- weapons or defense policy designed to discourage enemy attack DETERRENT
- weapons supply greater than required for victory OVERKILL
- referring to a weapon or bomb that produces a violent fire INCENDIARY
- referring to nonnuclear warfare or weapons CONVENTIONAL
- remove weapons from a person or group DISARM
- search a person, as for concealed weapons, using quick hand move-

WEIGHTS AND MEASURES *Continued*

UNIT	VALUE
IMPERIAL UNITS: LINEAR MEASURE	
1 cable	about 608 feet
1 chain	4 rods, or 22 yards
1 fathom	6 feet
1 furlong	10 chains, or 220 yards
1 hand	4 inches
1 league	3 nautical miles
1 rod/1 pole/1 perch	5½ yards
IMPERIAL UNITS: LIQUID MEASURE	
1 barrel	31½-35 gallons
1 firkin	9 gallons
1 fluid drachm	60 minims, or ⅛ fluid ounce
1 gill/noggin	5 fluid ounces, or ¼ pint
1 hogshead	2 barrels
1 minim	1/480 fluid ounce
IMPERIAL UNITS: DRY MEASURE	
1 bushel	4 pecks
1 peck	8 quarts
IMPERIAL UNITS: JEWELERS' WEIGHTS	
1 carat	1/24 (4.1667%) gold
1 grain	1/480 ounce troy
1 ounce troy	1/12 pound troy, or 1.097 ounces avoirdupois
IMPERIAL UNITS: AVOIRDUPOIS WEIGHTS	
1 dram	27 11/32 grains, or 1/16 ounce
1 drachm	3 scruples
1 scruple	20 grains
ARCHAIC AND FOREIGN UNITS	
barleycorn	⅓ inch (length of a barley grain)
catty/kati	about 1⅓ pounds (China)
crore	10 million (India)
cubit	18 to 21 inches
ell	45 inches (cloth)
hide	100 to 120 acres
kilderkin	about 18 gallons
lakh	100,000 (India)
maund	about 82 pounds (India)
morgen	2.116 acres (South Africa)
mutchkin	0.9 pint (Scotland)
picul	133.33 pounds (China)
pipe	105 gallons (wine)
pood	36.11 pounds (Russia)
rood	¼ acre (and other values)
shekel	about ½ ounce (ancient Hebrew)
span	9 inches; tip of thumb to tip of little finger of an extended hand
tael	usually 1⅓ ounces (Asia)
tierce/terce	42 wine gallons; about 33 gallons
verst	0.6629 miles, just over kilometer (Russia)
virgate	about 30 acres; about 1/4 acre

ments FRISK
- station troops or weapons in an area, or make them ready for action DEPLOY
- store of hidden weapons, stolen goods, or the like, or its hiding place CACHE
- storehouse or factory for weapons ARMORY, ARSENAL
- wave a weapon or similar object about in a threatening, boastful, or showy way BRANDISH, FLOURISH

wear away, wear down, as through the action of wind or water ERODE, CORRADE
- wearing away by chemical action, as of rusting metals CORROSION
- gradual wearing down, as of rock or enemy forces ATTRITION

weasel, ferret, badger, otter, or related mammal MUSTELINE
- tree-dwelling mammal resembling the weasel PINE MARTEN

weather See chart, pages 585–586, and also **wind**
- balloon-borne instrument used to collect and transmit weather information RADIOSONDE
- dangerous lack of protection from the weather EXPOSURE
- look menacing and dark, as the sky or weather might LOWER
- mild, as the weather or one's temper might be CLEMENT, TEMPERATE, EQUABLE
- period of settled weather around

the winter solstice HALCYON DAYS
- science of weather conditions and forecasting METEOROLOGY
- stormy and wild, as weather might be INCLEMENT
- unfavorable, as winds or weather might be ADVERSE, CONTRARY

weathercock VANE, WEATHER VANE

weaving - boat-shaped device holding the bobbin in weaving, and used for passing the weft threads through the warp threads SHUTTLE
- device on a loom that keeps the cloth stretched during weaving TEMPLE
- heavy decorative weaving used as a wall hanging TAPESTRY, ARRAS
- loom, invented in the early 19th century, for mechanical pattern weaving JACQUARD LOOM
- parallel cords or wires in a loom, separating the warp threads for the shuttle HEDDLES
- reel around which yarn is wound in weaving SPINDLE, BOBBIN, QUILL
- threads running crosswise in weaving or in a woven fabric WOOF, WEFT, FILLING, PICKS
- threads running lengthwise in weaving or in a woven fabric WARP

webbed, as a duck's feet are PALMATE

wedding See also **marriage**
- wedding ceremony NUPTIALS
- noisy mock serenade, as with pots and pans, made to a newly married couple at their wedding CHARIVARI, SHIVAREE

wedge, as for locking printing type, raising a cannon, or the like QUOIN, COIGN
- wedge or wooden block stopping a barrel, wheel, or boat from rolling or sliding CHOCK, SCOTCH
- wedge-shaped SPHENIC, CUNEAL, CUNEATE
- ancient writing system in the Middle East, using wedge-shaped characters CUNEIFORM

weed with fleshy leaves, sometimes eaten as a salad PURSLANE
- weeding spade SPUD, HOE
- clinging bristly seed pod of various weeds, such as burdock BUR
- weedkiller HERBICIDE
- growing vigorously and widely, as weeds might RANK
- growing wild, especially on cultivated land, as wild flowers or weeds might be AGRESTAL

weekday that is not a feast day, on some Christian church calendars FERIA

weekly HEBDOMADAL

weeping continually, tearful LACHRYMOSE

weigh down, burden, or hinder ENCUMBER

weight hanging on a cord, as used in fishing, depth sounding, or determining a vertical line PLUMB
- weight lifted for exercise, typically consisting of a small bar with a fixed metal ball at each end DUMBBELL
- weight lifted for exercise or in competitions, consisting of a metal bar with heavy removable metal discs at both ends BARBELL
- weight of a person, especially of a heavy person AVOIRDUPOIS
- weight of an unladen vehicle, or of the container or wrapping material of goods TARE

weight (combining form) BARO-

weightlifting - lifts of various kinds in weightlifting, to raise the weight above the head PRESS, SNATCH, JERK
- lift in weightlifting in which the weight is raised to shoulder height, and held there CLEAN

weights and measures See chart, pages 587–588

weird See also **odd**
- weird, nightmarish or surreal KAFKAESQUE

weld or unite two metal parts by means of melted alloy SOLDER
- welder or other metalworker in heavy industry BOILERMAKER
- gas mixture used for the high-temperature flame in welding OXYACETYLENE
- mask for shielding the eyes, as worn by welders VISOR

welfare work or humanitarian feelings, charity PHILANTHROPY

well drilled through impermeable rocks to reach water that is under pressure ARTESIAN WELL
- pivoted pole with a bucket on the end for drawing water from a well SWEEP, SWIPE

well (combining form) EU-

Welsh, Welshman, Welshwoman CAMBRIAN
- Welsh language CYMRIC
- Welsh name for Wales CYMRU
- Welsh people CYMRY
- Welsh terms of endearment, as in addressing a child DEL, BACH
- British group of Celtic languages, including Welsh and Cornish BRYTHONIC LANGUAGES
- ice-gouged, steep-walled hollow on a Welsh mountain CWM
- medieval anthology of Welsh legends MABINOGION

werewolf LOUP-GAROU, LYCANTHROPE

West Indies - various kinds of religions in the West Indies, combining African and Christian rituals VOODOO, OBEAH
- heavily rhythmical form of popular music originating in the West Indies REGGAE
- light rhythmical form of popular music originating in the West Indies SKA
- religious and political movement among black West Indians, involving veneration of the late Haile Selassie, former Ethiopian emperor RASTAFARIANISM
- slave on the run in the West Indies in former times, or a descendant of such a slave MAROON
- song from the West Indies, with a syncopated rhythm, and lyrics typically improvised on a humorous or topical theme CALYPSO

Western countries or regions THE OCCIDENT

wet, fill, soak completely SATURATE
- wet, soggy, marshy PLASHY, PALUDIAN, PALUDOUS, PALUDINE, PALUDAL, PALUDINAL
- wet and sticky, as the air might be HUMID, MUGGY
- wet and untidy, as one's hair or clothes might be BEDRAGGLED
- wet or wash with a flow of water SLUICE, SWILL
- wet thoroughly, drench DOUSE
- wet through, sopping SODDEN
- wetting, helping to retain moisture, as glycerin is HUMECTANT
- unpleasantly cold and wet, chilly and damp DANK, CLAMMY

wet (combining form) HYGRO-

whale See illustration, page 590
- whale, porpoise, or similar aquatic mammal CETACEAN
- whale's fat forming in a layer beneath its skin BLUBBER
- whale's air hole on the top of its head BLOWHOLE, SPIRACLE
- whalelike mammal with small paddlelike forelimbs MANATEE, DUGONG, SEA COW
- arctic whale with teeth and, in the male, a long spiral tusk NARWHAL
- black-and-white toothed whale, killer whale ORC, GRAMPUS
- dive down quickly and deep, as a whale or large fish might SOUND
- either of the flaps of the tail of a whale or related animal FLUKE
- herd or school of whales GAM, POD
- large toothed whale, hunted for its valuable oil, the sperm whale CACHALOT
- shrimplike sea creatures forming the principal food of some whales KRILL
- small pale whale of northern seas, the white whale BELUGA
- spearlike instrument used to kill whales HARPOON
- strip a whale, seal, or the like of

its skin or blubber FLENCH, FLENSE
- surface or leap from the water, as a whale might BREACH
- toothless, plankton-eating whale of various kinds, the whalebone whale MYSTICETE, BALEEN WHALE
- waxy cholesterol substance secreted by whales, used as a fixative in making perfume AMBERGRIS
- waxy substance formed from oils in a whale's head, used for cosmetics and candles SPERMACETI
- whalebone whale with a furrowed throat and chest, and a dorsal fin COMMON RORQUAL, FINBACK, RAZORBACK

whalebone, flexible hornlike material from the upper jaw of certain whales, as formerly used for making corset stays BALEEN
- carved or engraved articles of ivory, whalebone, or the like SCRIMSHAW

wheat - cereal food produced by boiling and then drying coarsely ground wheat BULGUR, CRACKED WHEAT
- dish of hulled wheat, boiled in milk, sweetened, and spiced FRUMENTY
- hard wheat granules left over after the grinding of flour, used in milk puddings SEMOLINA
- hard wheat whose flour is used in making pasta DURUM WHEAT
- North African dish of crushed steamed wheat granules served with various meats or vegetables COUSCOUS
- protein mixture in wheat flour, used in glues GLUTEN
- resembling or made of grain, especially wheat FRUMENTACEOUS
- species of wheat with reddish grains, widely cultivated in ancient times SPELT

wheel - wheellike cage that spins when a pet mouse or hamster runs along inside it for exercise SQUIRREL CAGE
- wheel or cylinder with a toothed rim, as to engage a bicycle chain or film perforations SPROCKET
- wheel or disc whose axis is off-center and which converts rotary to reciprocating motion ECCENTRIC
- wheel or roller within a tractor tread, as on a tank BOGIE
- wheel rotated by the tread of a prisoner, pet mouse, or the like TREADMILL
- wheel-shaped, or resembling a wheel TROCHAL
- wheel used by a potter LATHE
- wheel with a grooved rim, as on a pulley SHEAVE
- wheel's spindle, as in a watch or clock ARBOR
- wheels slanting toward each other at the bottom DISHED WHEELS
- abrasive wheel for sharpening knives CARBORUNDUM WHEEL
- "big wheel," giant amusement-park wheel FERRIS WHEEL
- center of a wheel, through which the axle passes HUB, NAVE
- curved metal plate on the rim of a wooden wheel STRAKE
- heavy or noisy rolling movement of a wheel TRUNDLE
- inward-turned alignment of front wheels to improve steering TOE-IN
- one-wheeled vehicle, as pedaled by acrobats UNICYCLE, MONOCYCLE
- outward tilt of a vehicle's front wheels CAMBER
- pivot of metal at the end of a wooden shaft or axle, as for a wheel to turn on GUDGEON
- projecting rim or edge, as on a wheel or beam, for strengthening, attaching, or the like FLANGE
- small flywheel on a spinning wheel WHORL, WHARL
- small stabilizing wheel attached on each side of the rear wheel of a child's bicycle TRAINING WHEEL, FAIRY WHEEL, OUTRIDER
- small swiveling wheel on each leg of an item of furniture, for easy moving CASTOR
- small toothed wheel on the spur on a cowboy's boot ROWEL
- spinning flywheel maintaining a stable angle or direction in a frame

Whales

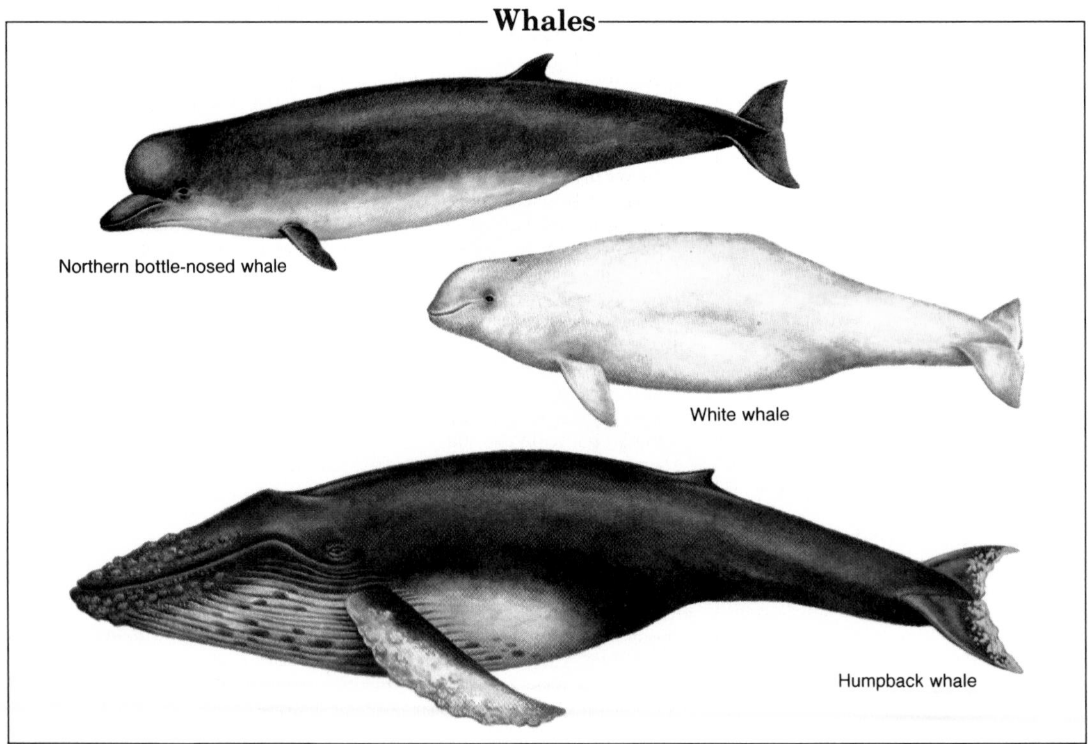

of pivoted supports GYROSCOPE
- wedge or block placed under a wheel, log, or the like, to immobilize it on a slope SCOTCH, CHOCK
wheezing or whistling sound from the chest, caused by partial blocking of the air channels RHONCHUS
whether you like it or not, willy-nilly NOLENS VOLENS
whey, watery part of milk SERUM
whimsical or peculiar action or notion CAPRICE, VAGARY, QUIRK
whip, flexible rod, twig, or the like SWITCH
- whip, flog, or scourge, as for religious discipline or sexual gratification FLAGELLATE
- whip mark on the flesh WEAL, WALE
- whip of stiff leather, especially of rhinoceros or hippopotamus hide, in South Africa SJAMBOK
- whip to the point of stripping the skin from FLAY
- whip used for punishment SCOURGE
- whip used formerly in Russia for flogging KNOUT
- whip with a leather loop at the tip, used by horseriders CROP
- whiplike leather strap split into strips at the end, used for beating children or prisoners TAWS
- handle of a whip, fishing rod, or the like STOCK, BUTT
whirling, revolving VERTIGINOUS
- Muslim ascetic, sometimes engaging in ecstatic, whirling dancing DERVISH
whirlpool, whirlwind, or similar fast-rotating flow VORTEX
- whirlpool or dangerous swirl in the sea MAELSTROM
- whirlpoollike shape or line SPIRAL, HELIX, VOLUTE, WHORL
- current or swirl moving against the main current, often creating a miniature whirlpool EDDY, GULF
whirlwind TOURBILLION, TORNADO, TWISTER
- whirlwind in an arid area drawing up a column of dust DUST DEVIL
- whirlwind or hurricane in the China sea TYPHOON
- whirlwind or hurricane in tropical areas CYCLONE
- whirlwind that forms over the sea and draws up a column of water WATERSPOUT
whiskers or sensitive hairs, as at either side of a cat's mouth VIBRISSAE
- whiskers spreading in a roughly triangular shape down the side of the face MUTTONCHOPS, MUTTONCHOP WHISKERS
- feeler or "whisker" on a fish such as the catfish BARBEL
whiskey distilled illicitly, especially in Southern states MOONSHINE, MOUNTAIN DEW, WHITE LIGHTNIN'
- whiskey, brandy, or other strong spirits AQUA VITAE, EAU DE VIE
- whiskey factory DISTILLERY
- whiskey that is distilled illicitly in Ireland POTEEN
- blend or dilute whiskey or other alcoholic spirits RECTIFY
- Irish or Scottish term for whisky USQUEBAUGH
- leftover impure spirits from the distillation of alcoholic drinks, especially whiskey FEINTS, FAINTS
- tot or small quantity of whiskey or other drink DRAM
whispering or rustling, as of the wind, or surf SOUGH, SUSURRATION
whistling noise produced when loudspeaker noise reenters a microphone FEEDBACK
- cord worn around the neck, as for carrying a whistle LANYARD
white See also **color**
- white, cold, and smooth or hard, like marble MARMOREAL
- white of an egg ALBUMEN
- white or gray, as through old age HOARY
- white person in New Zealand, as distinct from a Maori PAKEHA
- person or animal having abnormally white skin and hair through lack of normal pigmentation ALBINO
- protein occurring in the white of an egg ALBUMIN
- referring to the so-called white race CAUCASIAN
white (combining form) LEUC-, LEUCO-, LEUKO-, ALB-, CAND-
white ant TERMITE
White Friar CARMELITE
white whale BELUGA
whiten, as by cutting off light or soaking in acid BLANCH
- whitened through lack of sunlight, as grass or other green plants might become ETIOLATED
whole, entire INTEGRAL
- whole, sum total, sum of many parts AGGREGATE
- whole, unbroken, still in one piece, having all its parts INTACT
- whole, undivided UNITARY
- whole, unified pattern or structure that is more than the sum of its parts GESTALT
- whole number or zero INTEGER
- wholeness, fullness, completeness PLENITUDE, PLENUM
- wholeness, unity, undivided or unbroken condition INTEGRITY
- breaking down a whole into its component parts in order to examine it ANALYSIS
- combining of parts or elements to form a whole SYNTHESIS
- form into a whole, make solid or united CONSOLIDATE
- set of well-matching parts, such as garments, effecting a unified whole ENSEMBLE
- something that completes a whole COMPLEMENT
- universe or society regarded as a single, complex whole MACROCOSM
whole (combining form) HOL-, HOLO-
whooping cough PERTUSSIS
wick - charred end of a candlewick SNUFF
wicked See also **evil, immoral**
- wicked, vile, hateful ABOMINABLE, ODIOUS, HEINOUS
wickerwork - cane from a tropical Asian palm, as used for wickerwork furniture RATTAN
wide, open stretch of land, sea, or sky EXPANSE
- wide-ranging, all-embracing, liberal and broad-minded, as one's interests might be CATHOLIC
- wide-ranging, general, comprehensive, giving or having a broad view SYNOPTIC
- wide-tipped and flexible blade, as for spreading paint SPATULA
- widely applicable, talented, or the like VERSATILE
- person with wide-ranging knowledge or interests, as distinct from a specialist GENERALIST, POLYMATH, UNIVERSALIST, COMPREHENSIVIST
widen, expand DILATE, DISTEND
widespread, as a disease might be EPIDEMIC, PANDEMIC
- widespread, common, or deeply rooted within a particular region or group ENDEMIC
- widespread, occurring in quite separate regions, as some species are ALLOPATRIC
- widespread, scattered widely DIFFUSE, DISPERSED, BROADCAST
- widespread, very common or frequent PREDOMINANT, RIFE
- widespread, wide-ranging, embracing many aspects or a wide area EXTENSIVE, COMPREHENSIVE
- widespread or current PREVAILING, PREVALENT, REGNANT
widow having a title or property derived from her late husband DOWAGER
- widow's clothing while in mourning WEEDS
- widow's share, during her lifetime, of her late husband's property or the interest on it DOWER
- formal or old-fashioned term for a widow RELICT
- former Hindu custom in which a widow cremated herself on her late husband's funeral pyre SUTTEE

- practice, in keeping with Old Testament law, of marrying one's brother's widow LEVIRATE

width, height, or length DIMENSION
- width or thickness, as of piping or wire DIAMETER

wife or husband SPOUSE
- wife or husband, especially of a monarch CONSORT
- wife or husband, regarded as a helper HELPMATE, HELPMEET
- wife's scolding of her husband in private, or similar private reproach CURTAIN LECTURE
- wife swapping or husband swapping SWINGING
- adjective for a wife UXORIAL
- common-law wife or husband POSSLQ
- crime or state of having two wives or husbands at any one time BIGAMY
- custom or state of having only one wife at a time MONOGAMY, MONOGYNY
- custom or state of having two or more wives or female mates at a time POLYGAMY, POLYGYNY
- dominated by a nagging or willful wife HENPECKED
- group of wives and concubines in a Muslim household HAREM
- killing of one's wife UXORICIDE
- legal right to the help, company, and affection of one's husband or wife CONSORTIUM
- man who has married and killed several wives BLUEBEARD
- man whose wife commits adultery with his knowledge and his condoning it WITTOL
- man whose wife has committed adultery CUCKOLD
- referring to an excessive devotion to one's wife UXORIOUS
- secondary wife in some societies CONCUBINE

wig, especially a long curly wig PERIWIG, PERUKE
- wig or hairpiece covering a bald spot TOUPEE
- wig that is long at the back FULL-BOTTOMED WIG
- decorative wig or hairpiece, especially for a woman POSTICHE

wild, intemperate, or overindulgent behavior EXCESSES
- wild, savage, especially when formerly domesticated FERAL
- wild, untamed, living in the wild UNDOMESTICATED
- wild, violently out of control, ranting and raving, as in a fit of madness HYSTERICAL, BERSERK, RUNNING AMOK, RAMPAGEOUS, FRENZIED, FRENETIC, FRANTIC
- wild, without any order, pattern, or control ANARCHIC, CHAOTIC
- wild headlong rush, as of startled

Windows

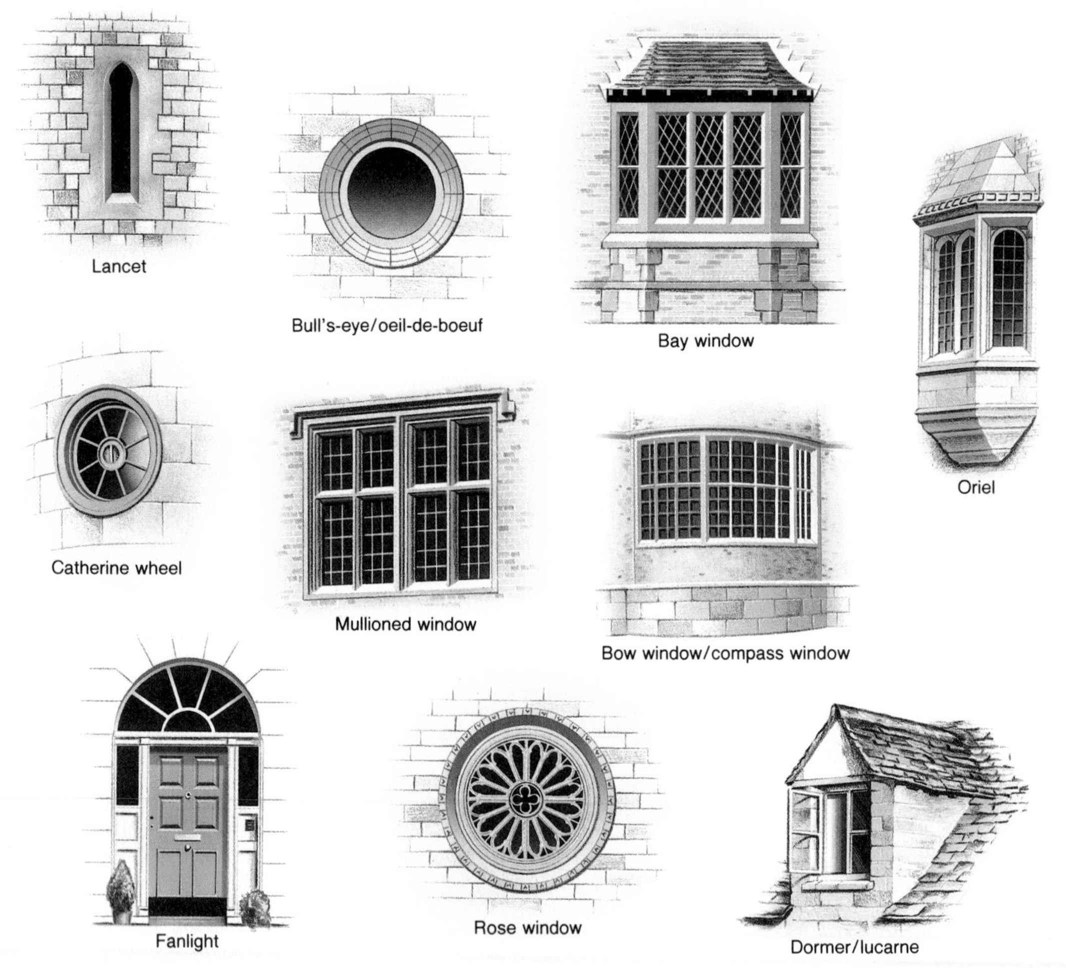

Lancet

Bull's-eye/oeil-de-boeuf

Bay window

Oriel

Catherine wheel

Mullioned window

Bow window/compass window

Fanlight

Rose window

Dormer/lucarne

cattle or horses or of a panic-stricken crowd STAMPEDE
- wild or mischievous adventure, caper, prank ESCAPADE
- referring to wild and ecstatic revels or orgies, in the style of an ancient Greek cult CORYBANTIC, CYPRIAN, DIONYSIAC
- uncontrolled, irresponsibly uninhibited, as wild behavior is EXTRAVAGANT, UNBRIDLED, MADCAP

wild ass ONAGER
wild boar or male elephant with impressive tusks TUSKER
wild duck MALLARD
wild flowers - growing wild, especially on cultivated land, as wild flowers or weeds might be AGRESTAL, AGRESTIAL
wildlife reserve SANCTUARY
will - addition to a will CODICIL
- deprive an heir of his or her inheritance, as by cutting the heir out of one's will DISINHERIT
- estate to be left in a will by a husband to his widow JOINTURE
- leave money or property to someone in a will BEQUEATH
- leaving a valid will when dying TESTATE
- leaving no valid will when dying INTESTATE
- legal proof of the validity of a will PROBATE
- liable to alteration or cancellation, as a will might be AMBULATORY, ALTERABLE
- lowest level of will or desire, typically without any action taken to fulfill it VELLEITY, INCLINATION
- money or property left in a will LEGACY
- pass on property, especially land or buildings, by a will DEVISE
- person appointed by a testator to carry out the requirements of his or her will EXECUTOR, EXECUTRIX
- person exerting or trying to exert a sinister influence over another's will SVENGALI
- person who makes a will LEGATOR, TESTATOR
- person who receives charity, a favor, money from a will, or the like BENEFICIARY
- transfer an estate, sovereignty, or the like, as by a will DEMISE

will-o'-the-wisp, flickering light sometimes seen over marshy ground IGNIS FATUUS, JACK-O'-LANTERN, FRIAR'S LANTERN
willful, based on or acting on personal whim or prejudice CAPRICIOUS, ARBITRARY
- willful, stubbornly self-willed, unwilling to cooperate or back down PERVERSE, CONTRARY

willing, act of choosing VOLITION
- willing, eager to please, cooperative OBLIGING, COMPLIANT, COMPLAISANT
- willing, without constraint and without payment VOLUNTARY
- willingly or freely given, generous UNSTINTED, UNGRUDGING
- willing or inclined, prepared to do a particular job DISPOSED
- willingness or promptness

WINDS

austral wind	south wind
berg wind	warm, dry wind blowing down from the South African plateau to the coast
bise	cold, dry, northerly wind in Switzerland, France, and Italy
bora	cold, squally, dry wind blowing from the mountains of central Europe to the northern Adriatic area in winter
boreal wind	north wind
chinook/snow eater	warm, dry wind blowing down the eastern side of the Rocky Mountains in Canada and the United States
chinook/wet chinook	warm, wet wind blowing from the Pacific onto the coasts of Oregon and Washington
doctor	any local wind that offsets unpleasant weather
favonian wind	west wind
föhn/foehn	warm, dry wind blowing down the northern sides of the Alps
harmattan	dry, dusty, northeasterly wind blowing from the Sahara to the West African coasts
helm wind	strong easterly wind on the northern Pennines, England
khamsin/ chamsin	hot, southerly wind blowing from the Sahara to the eastern Mediterranean from March to May
levanter	easterly wind in the westernmost Mediterranean
libeccio	strong southwesterly wind in Italy
mistral	violent, cold, dry, generally northerly wind blowing down the Rhône valley in France
pampero	violent, cold, southwesterly wind on the pampas of South America
Santa Ana	hot, dry, northeasterly wind blowing down from the mountains in southern California
simoom/ samiel	swirling, burning, sand-laden wind of Asian and African deserts
sirocco	southerly wind blowing in spring from the Sahara, being hot, dry, and dusty in North Africa, but humid in southern Europe
trade wind	tropical wind that blows from the northeast in the northern hemisphere, and from the southeast in the southern hemisphere
tramontana	cold, dry, north wind blowing down from the mountains in Italy and Spain
willy-willy	desert whirlwind in Australia; intense tropical storm in northwestern Australia
zonda	warm, humid, northerly wind in South America

WIND INSTRUMENTS

alpenhorn/ alphorn	long wooden tube producing a single powerful note
aulos	ancient Greek oboelike instrument
bassoon	low-pitched woodwind instrument, with a double wooden tube, and a double-reed mouthpiece
bombardon	large low-pitched tubalike instrument used in brass and military bands
clarion	shrill, medieval trumpet
contrabassoon/ double bassoon	woodwind pitched one octave lower than an ordinary bassoon
cornet	valved instrument, similar to a trumpet, used chiefly in brass bands
didgeridoo	Aboriginal Australian instrument, consisting of a long bamboo pipe that produces a droning noise
English horn/ cor anglais	double-reed woodwind instrument, similar to an oboe but lower-pitched
euphonium	tenor tuba, used especially in brass and military bands
fife	high-pitched flute in former times; flute in a modern "fife and drum" band
flageolet	six-holed woodwind instrument, similar to a flute, but blown at the end rather than the side
flügelhorn/ fluegelhorn	valved instrument, similar to a cornet, used chiefly in brass bands
French horn	circular, coiled brass instrument with a wide bell
harmonica/ mouth organ	small, box-shaped instrument played by sucking and blowing through metal reeds
hautbois/ hautboy/ hoboy	early form of oboe
helicon/ sousaphone	large spiral brass instrument that coils around the player's body
hunting horn/ cor de chasse/ waldhorn	simple early form of the French horn
kazoo	children's instrument with a membrane that turns the player's hum into a buzzing sound
krummhorn/ cromorne	deep-pitched medieval instrument, with a double reed
musette	small French bagpipe
oboe	woodwind with a double reed and a cone-shaped tube, pitched between a flute and clarinet
ocarina/sweet potato	small, simple egg-shaped clay or metal instrument with finger holes
panpipes/ syrinx	set of short vertical pipes or reeds, played by blowing over their tops
piccolo	small, high-pitched flute
post horn	simple brass instrument with no valves, having a limited range of notes
sackbut	trombonelike instrument used in the middle ages
sarrusophone	bassoonlike brass instrument, with a double reed
serpent	deep-toned, S- or double-S-shaped wind instrument, used mainly in the 18th century
shawm/shalm	early double-reed woodwind, forerunner of the oboe
trombone	brass instrument, bent back twice on itself, with a U-shaped slide
tuba	large valved brass instrument, with a bass pitch

ALACRITY

willow shoots or similar flexible twigs used to make baskets WICKER
- willow twig, or rope made of such twigs, used for tying things together WITHE, WITHY
- willow with long twigs used in basket making OSIER

willy-nilly, whether you like it or not NOLENS VOLENS

win, triumph or overcome through greater power or ability PREVAIL
- win achieved very easily against a weak opponent, or as a formality through the withdrawal or absence of the opponent WALKOVER

wind See chart, page 593, and also **weather**
- wind-blown, dispersed as by wind, fanned WINNOWED
- wind caused by the earth's rotation GEOSTROPHIC WIND
- wind or airstream moving very fast at high altitudes JET STREAM
- wind or windstorm that is snowy and very violent BLIZZARD
- belt of calm or light winds at sea along the equator DOLDRUMS
- blowing or gusting fast and noisily, as the wind might BLUSTERY
- buildup of gas in the digestive tract, causing belching and breaking of wind FLATULENCE
- carry lightly, as the wind carries the smell of flowers WAFT
- diagram showing wind directions

and frequency WIND ROSE
- facing or moving in the direction toward which the wind is blowing LEEWARD, DOWNWIND
- gentle wind or breeze, especially the west wind ZEPHYR
- gust of wind, or wind-driven shower or snow flurry SCUD
- instrument for measuring wind speed ANEMOMETER
- plant, such as the dandelion, whose fruits or seeds are spread by the wind ANEMOCHORE
- referring to a downward wind or air current, especially one flowing down a slope KATABATIC
- referring to a rising wind or air current, especially one rising along a slope ANABATIC
- relating to the wind AEOLIAN, EOLIAN
- scale of wind velocities BEAUFORT SCALE
- sighing sound, as the wind might make SUSURRATION, SOUGH
- sudden, violent burst of wind, typically with rain or snow SQUALL
- tapering cloth tube fixed to a pole to indicate wind direction, as at airfields WIND SOCK, WIND CONE, WIND SLEEVE, AIR SOCK, DROGUE
- unfavorable, blowing in an inconvenient direction, as winds might be ADVERSE, CONTRARY
- upright pivoting plate, typically of metal and shaped like a cock or arrow, used to indicate wind direction VANE, WEATHERCOCK

wind (combining form) ANEM-, ANEMO-, VENT-, VENTO-

wind instruments See chart
- band of metal fastening the reed to the mouthpiece of a wind instrument such as a clarinet or saxophone LIGATURE
- device to reduce or muffle sound, especially of a wind instrument MUTE, SORDINO
- flared end of a wind instrument such as a clarinet or trumpet BELL
- lip, wooden plug, or other obstruction serving in place of a reed to initiate the vibration in certain organ pipes and wind instruments FIPPLE
- mouthpiece of a wind instrument, especially a brass one, or the position and use of the lips in playing it EMBOUCHURE

winding, twisting and turning CONTORTED, TORTUOUS, ANFRACTUOUS
- winding knob of a watch CROWN
- winding or curving gracefully, as the movements of a snake might be SINUOUS
- winding or twisting path, as of a river MEANDER

windmill See illustration
- windmill-operated pump GIN
- arm of a windmill, carrying a sail WHIP
- blade of a windmill, catching the wind SAIL, SWEEP, VANE

window See illustration, page 592
- window above a door, as to admit light from one room to another FANLIGHT, TRANSOM WINDOW, VASISTAS
- window blinds that can be raised and lowered, and whose horizontal slats can be angled VENETIAN BLIND
- window consisting of two sliding frames set in grooves in a fixed frame SASH WINDOW

Windmills and Water Mills

SMOCK MILL

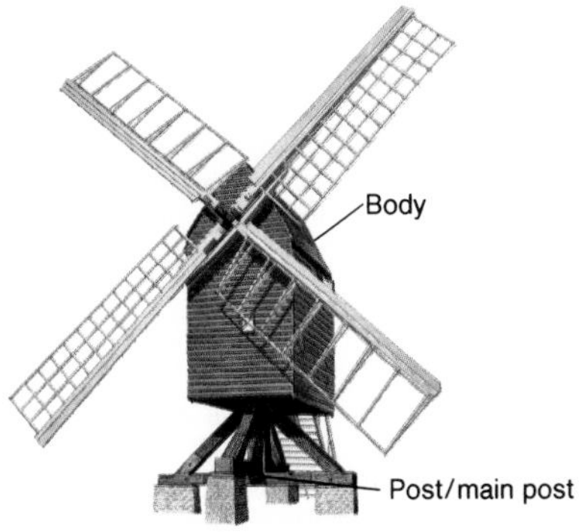

POST-MILL

TOWER MILL

WATER MILL: UNDERSHOT WHEEL

WATER MILL: OVERSHOT WHEEL

- window frame with hinges along one side CASEMENT
- window glass of former times, circular in shape, with a lump in the center from the worker's rod CROWN GLASS
- window with horizontal adjustable glass slats JALOUSIE, LOUVER WINDOW
- windows formed by small pieces of glass fastened by lead strips LEAD LIGHTS
- circular or semicircular window, panel, or the like ROUNDEL
- crescent-shaped recess or additional window above a main window LUNETTE
- crisscrossed strips of wood or metal, as in a screen or window LATTICE
- decorative frame or molding around a door, window, or recess ARCHITRAVE
- horizontal dividing bar or strip in a window TRANSOM
- lacy ornamental pattern or stonework, as at the top of a Gothic window TRACERY
- leaflike shape in the tracery of Gothic windows FOIL
- legal right to unobstructed light through a window that has been used for at least 20 years ANCIENT LIGHTS
- length of board or fabric at the top of a window, used to hide curtain fixtures PELMET
- person who installs window glass GLAZIER
- rubber or leather blade, fixed to a handle, for wiping liquid, as in cleaning windows SQUEEGEE
- short decorative skirt of drapery hung along the top of a window, shelf, or the like VALANCE
- small, usually triangular, window in the front door of a car VENT WINDOW
- small window FENESTELLA
- small window, usually circular, in the side of a ship PORTHOLE
- thin lead strip securing the panes in stained-glass windows CAME
- throwing a thing or person out of the window DEFENESTRATION
- triangular molding or recess, usually decorated, above a door or window PEDIMENT, FRONTISPIECE, GABLE
- upper horizontal beam or support, as of a window LINTEL
- upright dividing bar or strip in a window MULLION
- upright post or strut of a ladder, door frame, window sash, or the like STILE
- upright side of a door post or window frame JAMB
- wall or panel with windows, designed for light or ventilation, typically inset in a roof CLERESTORY
- wooden bar or strip securing the panes in a window or door GLAZING BAR, MUNTIN, MUNTING, MULLION

windpipe TRACHEA
- tubes that carry air from the windpipe to the lungs BRONCHI, BRONCHIAL TUBES

wine See chart
- wine of high quality, identified by year and region VINTAGE
- wine cask or beer barrel of large capacity TUN
- wine cellar or pantry BUTTERY
- wine cup used at Mass CHALICE
- wine expert ENOLOGIST, OENOLOGIST
- wine glass with a stem GOBLET
- wine-loving BACCHANT
- wine making or grape growing VINICULTURE, VITICULTURE
- wine merchant VINTNER
- wine or water bottle at table CARAFE, DECANTER
- wine store, sometimes selling groceries too, in Spanish-speaking countries BODEGA
- wine that is sugared, spiced, and then heated MULLED WINE
- wine that is still fermenting MUST, STUM
- wine vessel of silver, with handles, that is drunk from in turn, as by guests at a banquet LOVING CUP
- wine waiter SOMMELIER
- wine's fragrance BOUQUET
- winery or wine cellars of a French vineyard CAVE
- basic local wine VIN ORDINAIRE, TAFELWEIN
- clarifying of wine, beer, or the like, as by adding isinglass FINING
- clear wine, beer, or cider of its dregs RACK
- crust forming in bottles of old wine, especially port, or a wine containing this crust BEESWING
- dilute or add impurities to a substance, such as wine ADULTERATE
- expert in wine, art, or the like, or a person of refined tastes CONNOISSEUR
- fee or price charged at a restaurant for serving wine brought in by the customer CORKAGE
- fine wine, certified quality wine APPELLATION CONTRÔLÉE, QUALITÄTSWEIN
- finest wine of its type in France PREMIER CRU
- grape skins, pips, and stems left over after the juice has been extracted for wine making RAPE, POMACE, PUMACE
- mature and rich, not acidic, as a good wine is MELLOW
- person who drinks excessive amounts of wine WINE BIBBER
- pour a liquid from one container to another, as when separating wine from its sediment DECANT
- reddish substance in grape juice deposited as a crust in wine vats TARTAR, ARGOL, ARGAL
- referring to dry wine SEC
- referring to extremely dry wine, especially champagne BRUT
- referring to sweet wine DOUX
- referring to wine, wine drinking, or excessive wine drinking VINOUS
- referring to wine brought to room temperature after it is opened CHAMBRÉ
- sediment or residue in wine, coffee, or other liquid LEES, DREGS

wine (combining form) VIN-, VINI-, VINO-

wing See also **bird**

WINES

FRANCE	**Muscat/ Muscatel**	HUNGARY	**Soave**
Alsace	**Sancerre**	**Tokay**	**Valpolicella**
Beaujolais	**Sauterne**	ITALY	PORTUGAL
Bergerac	GERMANY	**Asti spumante**	**Aveleda**
Bordeaux/ claret	**Liebfraumilch**	**Barbera**	**Dão**
Burgundy/ Bourgogne	**Mosel**	**Bardolino**	**Douro**
Chablis	**Nierstein**	**Barolo**	**Madeira**
Champagne	**Rhine wine/ hock**	**Chianti**	**Mateus Rosé**
Côtes-du-Rhône	**Riesling**	**Dolcetto**	**Oporto**
Entre-deux-Mers	**Sekt**	**Frascati**	**vinho verde**
Graves	**Sylvaner**	**Lacrima Christi**	SPAIN
Mâcon	GREECE	**Lambrusco**	**Málaga**
Médoc	**retsina**	**Marsala**	**Navarra**
		Orvieto	**Rioja**
			Valdepeñas

- wing, feather, fin, or similar projecting body part PINNA
- wing, tail plane, flap, or other surface of an aircraft affecting lift or stability in flight AIRFOIL
- wing of a bird, specifically the rear section holding the flight feathers PINION
- winged or feathered PENNATE
- winglike, winged, or wing-shaped ALAR
- winglike membrane between the fore and hind limb of a bat or flying squirrel PATAGIUM
- feathered part of a bird's wing in the position corresponding to the thumb ALULA, BASTARD WING
- having wings or winglike projections ALATE, ALAR
- underside of a wing, corresponding to the human armpit AXILLA

wing (combining form) -PTER-, -PTERO-

wink or blink NICTITATE
- wink or blink repeatedly or involuntarily PALPEBRATE
- suggesting a plot or secret, as a knowing wink or nudge might be CONSPIRATORIAL

winter - adjective for winter HIBERNAL, HIEMAL
- pass the winter in a very inactive, semisleeping state, as some animals do HIBERNATE

wipe out, rub out, erase EFFACE

wiper - rubber or leather blade resembling a windshield wiper, fixed to a handle and used for wiping liquid, as in cleaning windows SQUEEGEE

wire, thin thread, fiber, or the like FILAMENT
- wire coil producing a magnetic field when carrying an electric current, as used for activating switches SOLENOID
- wire used for electric contact, as in a crystal radio set CAT WHISKER
- ornamental work consisting of fine, twisted wire, especially of gold or silver wire FILIGREE
- produce wire, metal or plastic sheeting, or the like by pressing through a nozzle or die EXTRUDE
- unit of measure of the diameter of wire ($1/_{1,000}$ inch) MIL

wisdom - widely accepted wisdom or belief, often of a hackneyed, standard, and unquestioned kind RECEIVED WISDOM, CONVENTIONAL WISDOM

wisdom (combining form) -SOPHY, SAP-, PRUD

wise, having wisdom SAPIENT
- wise, showing or having good judgment, well-advised DISCERNING, SAGACIOUS, JUDICIOUS
- wise adviser or prophet, apparently infallible authority ORACLE
- wise and respected leader or adviser SOLON, NESTOR
- wise or learned person, expert PUNDIT, LUMINARY
- wise teacher, judge, philosopher, or the like SAGE, GURU

wish or hope that is fanciful and unrealistic PIPE DREAM, CASTLE IN THE AIR, CASTLE IN SPAIN
- wish or tendency, without any action taken to fulfill it VELLEITY
- help to attain someone's wishes, often unworthy wishes GRATIFY, PANDER TO
- obey a rule or order, carry out someone's wish or demand, or the like COMPLY
- respect or submit to the wishes or opinion of someone else DEFER

wishbone or similar forked bone or body part FURCULA

wit, spirit, liveliness ESPRIT
- wit of a wry, delicate, but pointed kind ATTIC SALT, ATTIC WIT
- biting or cutting, as wit can be CAUSTIC, TRENCHANT, PUNGENT, MORDANT
- sparkling or brilliant, as a person's wit might be LAMBENT, CORUSCATING, SCINTILLATING
- sparkling or brilliant, reminiscent of fireworks, as a person's wit might be PYROTECHNIC

witch SORCERESS, SIBYL
- witch, wizard, sorcerer, or male witch WARLOCK
- witch or female vampire LAMIA
- witch's attendant spirit, often assuming animal form FAMILIAR
- witches' gathering, or a group of 13 witches COVEN

witch-hunt against suspected communist sympathizers in the United States in the 1950's MCCARTHYISM
- witch-hunter who questions suspects INQUISITOR

witchcraft, black magic, devil worship, or the like DIABOLISM
- witchcraft, use of supernatural power, as with the help of evil spirits SORCERY, WITCHERY, SORTILEGE, ENCHANTMENT
- witchcraft and other allegedly supernatural arts THE OCCULT

with (combining form) -CUM-, CO-, COM-, SYN-, SYM-, SYMP-

withdraw, often publicly, a former belief or claim RECANT, RETRACT, DISAVOW
- withdraw as a member, break away from an alliance, or the like SECEDE, DISSOCIATE, DISAFFILIATE
- withdraw from or go back on a promise or deal RENEGE
- withdraw from or leave a fortress, infected area, or the like EVACUATE
- withdraw or annul officially a law, regulation, or the like RESCIND, REVOKE, REPEAL
- withdraw or cancel an order or command COUNTERMAND

withdrawn into seclusion, isolated CLOISTERED, SEQUESTERED
- withdrawn person, living alone, as for religious reasons HERMIT, RECLUSE

withered, dry, shriveled, as a dead leaf would be SERE

within or internal, existing inside as a force or essence IMPLICIT, IMMANENT, INHERENT, INTRINSIC

within (combining form) END-, ENDO-, ENTO-, INTRA-, INTRO-

without meaning to, without realizing INADVERTENTLY
- without reference to, without consideration of, regardless of IRRESPECTIVE OF

without (combining form) A-, AN-

witness in court considered unfairly biased HOSTILE WITNESS
- witness who gives testimony in writing under oath, for submission to the court DEPONENT
- witness's evidence or declaration given in court TESTIMONY
- witness's sworn statement, used when he or she is absent from court DEPOSITION
- be evidence or proof of, be a witness for ATTEST, TESTIFY
- deliberate giving of false evidence by a witness under oath PERJURY

witty, brilliant, or vivacious SCINTILLATING
- witty, high-spirited literary work JEU D'ESPRIT
- witty or fanciful thought or expression CONCEIT
- witty or humorous in a dry, ironical way WRY
- witty reply in a conversation BACKCHAT, RETORT, REPARTEE
- witty saying, clever remark MOT, BON MOT, WITTICISM

wizard, witch doctor MEDICINE MAN, SHAMAN
- wizard in ancient times MAGUS
- wizard or magician SORCERER
- wizard or male witch WARLOCK
- wizard's attendant spirit, often assuming animal form FAMILIAR

wobble or spin in flight, as a missile or aircraft might YAW

wolf - wolfman, person who thinks he is a wolf LYCANTHROPE
- adjective for a wolf LUPINE
- group or pack of wolves ROUT

woman leader of a tribe or large family MATRIARCH
- woman living with and supported

by a man without being married to him CONCUBINE, MISTRESS
- woman or girl who behaves like, or is, a prostitute COCOTTE, TART, FILLE DE JOIE, HARLOT, HOOKER, HUSSY, FLOOZY, TROLLOP, BAWD, CHIPPY, STRUMPET, LADY OF THE NIGHT
- woman or girl who indulges in flighty or flirtatious behavior SOUBRETTE, COQUETTE
- woman or girl who is attractive though not pretty JOLIE LAIDE
- woman or girl whose charm or attractiveness make her a favorite BELLE
- woman or sweetheart who is idealized, as Don Quixote's sweetheart was DULCINEA
- woman or wife in Polynesian or Maori cultures WAHINE
- woman oracle, prophetess SIBYL
- woman fighting for voting rights for women SUFFRAGETTE
- woman who behaves in a conceited or dominating way, as a temperamental leading actress or singer might PRIMA DONNA
- woman who intimidates people through her ugliness or her behavior GORGON, DRAGON
- woman who is aggressive, spiteful, quarrelsome, and scolding HARRIDAN, HARPY, SHREW, HELLCAT, TERMAGANT, VIRAGO, VIXEN
- woman whose husband is frequently absent or separated or divorced from her GRASS WIDOW
- woman whose husband is so severely alcoholic that he has ceased to be a companion GLASS WIDOW
- woman whose sexual charms or scheming can lead her admirers into danger FEMME FATALE, MATA HARI, JEZEBEL, SIREN, VAMP
- woman with an insatiable sexual appetite, which is typically associated with frigidity NYMPHOMANIAC
- woman with scholarly or literary interests BLUESTOCKING
- womanly, characteristic of or appropriate to a woman FEMININE
- woman's dressing room, bedroom, or private sitting room BOUDOIR, BOWER
- women-only party HEN PARTY
- women with contrived sex appeal, or photographs of them, as in advertising CHEESECAKE
- women's clothes worn by a man, or vice versa DRAG
- women's hats MILLINERY
- women's liberation movement FEMINISM
- women's or girls' club, as at a university SORORITY
- women's work or preoccupations DISTAFF
- womanlike, unmanly EFFEMINATE
- abnormal development of male traits in a woman VIRILISM
- bust, waist, and hip measurements of a woman VITAL STATISTICS
- cantankerous old woman GRIMALKIN
- column in an ancient Greek building, in the form of a sculpture of a loosely robed woman CARYATID
- dirty, untidy, or sluttish woman SLATTERN, DRAB
- dull and old-fashioned, as a woman's clothing or appearance might be DOWDY, FRUMPISH
- elderly and dignified or wealthy woman, often a widow DOWAGER
- elderly woman, especially a grandmother GRANDAM, GRANDAME
- elderly woman, typically unattractive BELDAM, BELDAME, HAG, CRONE
- external sexual organs of a woman PUDENDA, MULIEBRIA
- girl or very young woman who, though sexually immature, is attractive to men NYMPHET, LOLITA
- graceful and slender woman or girl SYLPH
- group of women, usually wives, concubines, or female family of a Muslim man HAREM
- hatred of women MISOGYNY
- kept or sexually promiscuous woman living on the fringes of respectable society, as in the 19th century DEMIMONDAINE, DEMIREP
- money or property handed over by a woman to her husband on their marriage DOWRY
- old-fashioned term for a young woman WENCH
- outstandingly attractive woman STUNNER, LOOKER
- plump or full-bosomed, as some women are BUXOM
- respectable older woman, who accompanies or supervises a young or unmarried woman in public CHAPERON, DUENNA
- scolding, nagging woman or wife XANTHIPPE
- seclusion of women from view, especially in India PURDAH
- sensually built, with a very shapely figure, as a woman might be VOLUPTUOUS, LUSCIOUS, ZAFTIG
- small and slim in build, trim, dainty as a woman or girl might be PETITE
- suitable and ready for marriage, as an attractive young woman is said to be NUBILE
- terrifying woman, evil female demon LAMIA
- unrestrained by social conventions, as a liberated woman is EMANCIPATED
- warriorlike woman VALKYRIE, AMAZON, BATTLE-AX
- young French working woman GRISETTE
- young woman in the 1920's who enjoyed defying the conventions of society FLAPPER
- young woman in a harem ODALISQUE
- young woman or girl who acts in a high-spirited and cheeky or tomboyish way HOYDEN
- young woman or girl who is naive or innocent INGENUE
- young woman or maiden DAMSEL, DEMOISELLE

woman (combining form) -GYN-, GYNO-, GYNECO-

womanhood or femininity MULIEBRITY

womanizer, seducer LOTHARIO, DON JUAN, LADYKILLER, RAKE, PHILOGYNIST, PHILANDERER

womb See **uterus**
- mass of tissue linking the fetus to the womb lining PLACENTA
- surgical removal of the womb HYSTERECTOMY

womb (combining form) HYSTER-, HYSTERO-, METR-, METRO-

wonder See also **think**
- year of wonders ANNUS MIRABILIS

wonderful, extraordinary PHENOMENAL, STUPENDOUS, PRODIGIOUS
- wonderful to relate MIRABILE DICTU

wood See illustration
- wood-eating XYLOPHAGOUS
- wood engraving, wood-block printing XYLOGRAPHY
- wood-fiber mixture from which paper is made PULP
- wood floating on or washed up by the sea, a river, or a lake DRIFTWOOD
- wood from newly felled trees TIMBER, LUMBER
- wood used for smoking food and making walking sticks HICKORY
- boarding made of thin sheets of wood glued together PLYWOOD
- coat wood with varnish SHELLAC, FRENCH-POLISH, JAPAN
- cut small shavings from wood WHITTLE
- dry wood, used for starting fires TINDER, PUNK, TOUCHWOOD, KINDLING
- hard brown wood from a south Asian tree TEAK
- inlaid work, as in wood MARQUETRY, MARQUETERIE
- mosaic of inlaid wood INTARSIA
- referring to wood LIGNEOUS, XYLOID
- shiny surface layer or finish, as of fine wood VENEER
- sliding front of a rolltop desk, or similar covering consisting of strips of wood pasted on a stretch of canvas TAMBOUR

Wood

SOFTWOODS

Eastern red cedar

Douglas fir

Western hemlock

Redwood

Ponderosa pine

Sugar pine

White pine

Sitka spruce

"Softwood" is the wood of coniferous (or evergreen) trees.

"Hardwood" is the wood of angiospermous (or deciduous) trees.

HARDWOODS

White ash

Quaking aspen

American basswood

American beech

Yellow birch

Black cherry

Rock elm

Sweet gum

Shagbark hickory

Sugar maple

Red oak

White oak

American plane

Tulip tree

Black walnut

Black willow

- strip of wood cut lengthwise from a tree trunk FLITCH
- strip of wood trimmed from a plank LIST
- tar-based liquid applied to wood as a preservative CREOSOTE
- utensils made of wood TREENS
- very dark wood, as used in making black piano keys EBONY
- very lightweight wood, from a tropical American tree, as used for making model boats BALSA

wood (combining form) LIGN-, LIGNI-, LIGNO-, XYL-, XYLO-

wood alcohol CARBINOL, METHANOL, METHYL ALCOHOL

wood grouse CAPERCAILLIE

wooded, having many trees ARBOREOUS

wooden defensive barrier of upright posts or stakes STOCKADE
- wooden frame for confining an offender and exposing him or her to public abuse PILLORY, STOCKS
- wooden or woodlike XYLOID, LIGNEOUS
- wooden paneling fixed to the walls of a room WAINSCOTING
- wooden strip or plank forming part of a barrel, ship's hull, or the like STAVE
- wooden strip used in flooring, for supporting roof tiles, securing sails, or the like BATTEN
- wooden strips in a mosaic pattern, as used on floors PARQUET
- wooden table leg, handrail support, or the like, typically turned and decorated SPINDLE
- wooden tray or plate for carving or serving food TRENCHER

woods, small stretch of trees COPPICE, THICKET, COPSE
- woods, woodland, or undergrowth sheltering game COVERT
- woods or woodland area BOSCAGE, BOSK
- wood nymph, spirit or deity of the woods and trees, in Greek mythology DRYAD, HAMADRYAD
- open area in the woods or other overgrown land CLEARING
- relating to woods or forests SYLVAN

woodwinds See **wind instruments**

woody tissue of plants XYLEM

wool-bearing, or covered in woolly hair LANIFEROUS
- wool or cotton wadding used as stuffing BATTING, FLOCK
- wool recycled from unfelted cloth SHODDY
- woollike or fluffy in appearance or texture FLOCCULENT
- fat from sheep's wool, used in cosmetics and ointments LANOLIN
- long woolly nap, as on coarse cloth or a carpet SHAG
- lump in wool or cloth BURL
- loose coil of thread, wool, or other yarn SKEIN, HANK
- open and clean raw cotton or wool fibers by means of a spiked drum WILLOW
- shear, trim, or cut the hair, wool, or horns of POLL
- silky wool from a llamalike South American mammal ALPACA
- soft downy wool from a Himalayan goat CASHMERE
- strand twisted with others to make wool, rope, or the like PLY
- unravel and straighten wool or similar fiber by combing it TEASE

woolly, covered with woolly hairs, as leaves might be LANATE

word See also **verb, noun**
- word, expression, idea, or action that is overused CLICHÉ
- word in which sound echoes meaning ONOMATOPOEIA
- word, name, or phrase forming a main heading and fully explained in a dictionary or encyclopedia HEADWORD, MAIN ENTRY, DEFINIENDUM, LEMMA
- word, name, or phrase spelled out by the first letters of the lines of a poem or message ACROSTIC
- word, phrase, or construction used incorrectly or ungrammatically BARBARISM, SOLECISM
- word, phrase, or form indicating respect HONORIFIC
- word, such as a noun or verb, having reference to the real world rather than just to relationships within a sentence CONTENT WORD, NOTIONAL WORD
- word, such as a pronoun, conjunction, or article, indicating a grammatical, logical, or textual relationship FUNCTION WORD
- word, such as *and*, indicating equal alternatives CONJUNCTIVE
- word, such as *but*, expressing contrast or opposition DISJUNCTIVE
- word, such as *sociology*, with elements from two or more languages HYBRID
- word, such as *this* or *those*, pointing out the person or thing referred to DEMONSTRATIVE, DEICTIC
- word as regarded as a series of sounds or letters rather than as a unit of meaning VOCABLE
- word at the top of a page of a dictionary, telephone directory, or the like, indicating the alphabetical range of that page GUIDE WORD, RUNNING HEAD, CATCHWORD
- word borrowed from another language, such as *cul-de-sac* LOAN WORD
- word coined specially for a single occasion and not intended for use anywhere else NONCE WORD
- word element, such as *un-* or *micro-*, added at the beginning of a word or stem PREFIX, (INITIAL) COMBINING FORM
- word element, such as *-ing* or *-graphy*, added at the end of a word or stem SUFFIX, (FINAL) COMBINING FORM
- word element, such as *un-*, *micro-*, *-ing*, or *graphy-*, added to a word or stem either at the beginning or at the end AFFIX
- word formation, or a word so formed, from a supposed derivative, such as *laze* from *lazy* BACK-FORMATION
- word formed by fusing parts of two or more other words, such as *chortle* from *chuckle* and *snort* BLEND, PORTMANTEAU WORD
- word formed from a more basic word, as through the addition of a prefix or suffix such as *indecisive* from *decide* DERIVATIVE
- word formed from the initial letters of other words and pronounced (unlike an acronym) letter by letter, such as *USA* LETTERWORD
- word formed from the initial letters or syllables of other words and pronounced (unlike a letterword) as a word, such as *NATO* ACRONYM
- word having the opposite meaning from another, such as *refuse* in relation to *accept* ANTONYM
- word having the same or nearly the same meaning as another, such as *refuse* in relation to *decline* SYNONYM
- word having the same pronunciation and the same spelling as another, but with different meaning and origin, such as *flag* (piece of cloth) and *flag* (to hang loose), or *lie* (untruth) and *lie* (to recline), word that is both a homograph and homophone HOMONYM
- word having the same pronunciation as another and the same or a different spelling, but with different meaning and origin, such as *flag* (piece of cloth) and *flag* (the hang loose), or *some* and *sum* HOMOPHONE
- word having the same spelling as another and the same or a different pronunciation, but with different meaning and origin, such as *flag* (piece of cloth) and *flag* (to hang loose), or *tear* (in the eyes) and *tear* (to pull apart) HOMOGRAPH
- word in a foreign language, close-

ly resembling a word in one's own language but differing from it in meaning, such as the French *actuel,* which means "present-day, current" FALSE FRIEND, FAUX AMI
- word in fashionable use that suggests one is knowledgeable in a particular field BUZZWORD
- word list, specialized dictionary LEXICON, GLOSSARY, VOCABULARY
- word now obsolete except in certain idioms or phrases, such as *fro* in *to and fro* FOSSIL
- word occurring only once in a text, ancient language, or the like HAPAX LEGOMENON, HAPAX
- word of a kind serving as a noun or pronoun, such as *hat, me,* or *the rich* SUBSTANTIVE
- word of a kind that can stand alone, typically expressing emotion, such as *alas!* INTERJECTION
- word of a kind that is usually positioned before a noun or noun phrase, and indicates relationships in position, time, or the like, such as *to, of,* and *despite* PREPOSITION
- word of a kind that joins words, clauses, or phrases, such as *and, or,* and *while* CONJUNCTION
- word of a kind that limits or specifies a noun and is placed before descriptive adjectives, such as *the, your,* or *many* DETERMINER
- word or expression no longer in everyday use, such as *yonder* ARCHAISM
- word or expression that fits the context appropriately MOT JUSTE
- word or formula repeated in meditation MANTRA
- word or phrase as an expression of style LOCUTION
- word or phrase borrowed from another language by a literal or close translation of each element, such as G.B. Shaw's coinage of *superman* from Nietzsche's term *Übermensch* CALQUE, LOAN TRANSLATION
- word or phrase intended to characterize a person or thing, often part of a name or title, as in *Richard the Lionheart* EPITHET
- word misused through confusion with a similar-sounding word, such as *pineapple* for *pinnacle, kosher nostril* for *cosa nostra,* or *forte* (the two-syllable Italian music term meaning "loud") and *forte* (the one-syllable French word meaning "strength, strong point") MALAPROPISM
- word or phrase that is neutral or acceptable, substituted for one that is blunt or offensive, such as *passed away* for *died* EUPHEMISM
- word or phrase that is unpleasant or offensive, substituted for a neutral or favorable one, the reverse of a euphemism DYSPHEMISM, CACOPHEMISM
- word or phrase that seems to have a second, typically saucy meaning DOUBLE ENTENDRE
- word or phrase used for identification or recognition, as among members of a group WATCHWORD, SHIBBOLETH
- word or phrase whose letters are rearranged from or into another word or phrase, as with *stop* and *spot,* or *the United States of America* and *attaineth its cause: freedom* ANAGRAM, TRANSPOSITION
- word or proposition that is less general than another and is embraced by it, as *poodle* is by *dog* HYPONYM
- word or proposition that is more general than another and embraces it, as *furniture* does *chair* SUPERORDINATE
- word or word element, such as *'em,* lacking an independent accent and typically linked with a preceding word ENCLITIC
- word or word element, such as *piglet* or *-let,* indicating small size, unimportance, youth, affection, or the like DIMINUTIVE
- word or word element, such as *superstar* or *super-,* indicating increase in size or intensity AUGMENTATIVE
- word or word element with a fixed meaning and not divisible into smaller elements MORPHEME
- word or words reading the same backward as forward, such as *madam,* or *Doc, note, I dissent. A fast never prevents a fatness. I diet on cod* PALINDROME
- word printed or typed separately at the foot of a page to indicate the first word of the following page CATCHWORD
- word related in origin to another word, through sharing a root, as *sing* is to *song* PARONYM, COGNATE
- word structure of a given language, including inflections and derivatives MORPHOLOGY
- words and phrases exclusive to a profession or other group JARGON, ARGOT, CANT
- words suggesting yet evading a promise or commitment WEASEL WORDS
- words used by or available to a person, group, or entire language VOCABULARY, LEXICON, LEXIS
- adjective for a word or words VERBAL, LEXICAL
- adopt a foreign word or phrase fully into the language NATURALIZE, ASSIMILATE
- alteration of a borrowed word or expression to make it fit familiar patterns of the language, as when *asparagus* is called *sparrowgrass,* or when *girasole,* Italian for "sunflower," becomes *Jerusalem* in *Jersusalem artichoke* FOLK ETYMOLOGY, POPULAR ETYMOLOGY, HOBSON-JOBSON
- altered form of a word, differing from the original or correct form CORRUPTION, ALTERATION, MODIFICATION
- change in the form of a word, especially a noun or pronoun, showing its function in a sentence, as with *he* and *him* CASE
- change in the form of a word to indicate tense, gender, and the like as in *cry, crying, cries* INFLECTION, ACCIDENCE
- change in the sense or tone of a word to a less favorable one, as with *hussy,* which once meant "wife, housewife" DETERIORATION, PEJORATION
- change in the sense or tone of a word to a more favorable one, as with *nice,* which once meant "stupid" AMELIORATION, MELIORATION, ELEVATION
- change of a word's sound or spelling by the transposing of sounds or letters within the word, as in the development of *bird* from Old English *brid* METATHESIS
- choice of words, mode of expression, as of a particular person or group PHRASEOLOGY, PARLANCE, DICTION
- code or puzzle in which a word or phrase is represented by pictures, symbols, or numerals, as in representing the phrase *I hate Ellen Pound* by a picture of an eye followed by *H8 LN #* REBUS
- combination or arrangement, especially of words typically occurring together, as of *victimless* with *crime* COLLOCATION
- core part of a word to which affixes such as *un-* or *-ing* can be added STEM
- describe fully the grammar of a word in its context PARSE
- earliest known form or root of a word or word element ETYMON
- express one's ideas in words FORMULATE, VERBALIZE
- game in which one player or team produces a word or line rhyming with a cue from the other CRAMBO
- game in which one player or team represents in mime, typically syllable by syllable, a word or phrase

for the others to guess CHARADE
- incorrect use of words, choice of the wrong word for the context CATACHRESIS
- index of all the words in a text, such as the works of Shakespeare, listing every occurrence of each word CONCORDANCE
- invent or make up a new word COIN
- loss or accidental omission of words or letters in a piece of writing LIPOGRAPHY
- loss or cutting off of a letter, syllable, or sound at the beginning of a word, as with *squire* from *esquire* APHAERESIS, APHESIS, FRONT-CLIPPING
- loss or cutting off of a letter, syllable, or sound from the end of a word, as with *prof* from *professor* APOCOPE, BACK-CLIPPING
- loss or cutting off of a letter, syllable, or sound from the middle of a word, as with *fo'c'sle* from *forecastle* SYNCOPATION, SYNCOPE
- loss or cutting off of a syllable or sound from the middle of a word, as when pronouncing *deteriorate* as though it were spelled *deteriate* HAPLOLOGY
- meaning of a word in normal use ACCEPTATION
- meaning or explicit reference of a word DENOTATION
- newly invented word or expression NEOLOGISM, COINAGE
- object of meaning, the idea or thing referred to by a word, phrase, or sign REFERENT
- omission of a word or words from a sentence, as for compression or dramatic effect ELLIPSIS
- origin and development of a word, or the study of such origins ETYMOLOGY, DERIVATION
- pair of words, or one of the pair, deriving via different routes from a single source, as with *royal* and *regal* DOUBLET
- pair of words differing in only one small respect, helping to identify a language's distinctive sounds or features, such as *back* and *pack*, or *photography* and *phytography* (the description of plants) MINIMAL PAIR
- pass or toss something back and forth, such as words in an argument BANDY
- piece of writing that deliberately excludes any word containing a particular letter of the alphabet LIPOGRAM
- piece of writing that is deliberately composed entirely of words containing only one particular vowel UNIVOCALIC
- pronounce words unclearly, as by running them together SLUR
- provide evidence for or prove the use of a word, especially its first recorded use ATTEST
- referring to meaning, as of words, gestures, or symbols SEMANTIC
- referring to the words or vocabulary of a language LEXICAL
- referring to very long words POLYSYLLABIC, SESQUIPEDALIAN, INKHORN
- referring to words or expressions that are no longer generally recognized and are very rarely, or never, used ARCHAIC
- referring to words or expressions that are still generally recognized but are rarely used OBSOLETE
- referring to words or expressions that are still generally recognized but are used less and less often OBSOLESCENT
- shorten a word or words by combining or leaving out some of the sounds or letters, as in *can't* CONTRACT
- spelling or pronunciation differing slightly from another form of the same word VARIANT
- splitting up of a word by an expression put between its parts, as in *what place soever* for *whatsoever place*, or in British slang inserts like *abso-flaming-lutely* TMESIS
- study or science of the meaning of words, or of meaning in general SEMANTICS
- study or science of the way words are built or change in use MORPHOLOGY
- study or science of the way words link into sentences SYNTAX
- surrounding speech or writing of a specified word or passage refining its meaning CONTEXT
- switching, usually unintended, of the initial sounds of two or more words, as when *a crushing blow* comes out as *a blushing crow* SPOONERISM
- symbol representing an entire word or phrase, such as % for *per cent* LOGOGRAM
- write or engrave words, as in a gift book or by incision into a hard surface INSCRIBE

word (combining form) -LOG-, -LOGUE, LOGO-, LEX-, LEXIC-, VERB-, VOC-, -ONYM

word blindness, reading difficulties ALEXIA, DYSLEXIA

word-for-word, as a translation might be LITERAL
- word-for-word, using the very same words VERBATIM, AD VERBUM

word processor See **computer**

wordiness, longwindedness VERBIAGE, VERBOSITY, PROLIXITY
- wordiness, roundabout or evasive speech or writing CIRCUMLOCUTION, PERIPHRASIS

wordy in a boring way, long-winded PROLIX, VERBOSE
- wordy or talkative LOQUACIOUS, VOLUBLE, GARRULOUS

work, occupation, career VOCATION
- work, such as domestic cleaning, that is routine and unskilled or considered undignified MENIAL WORK
- work, typically numbered in sequence, of a composer OPUS
- work at which one is skilled and happy MÉTIER, FORTE, VOCATION
- work done without pressure and without any payment VOLUNTARY WORK
- work or operate in harmony or at the same time SYNCHRONIZE
- work regarded as a pointless waste of time BOONDOGGLE
- work that is boring and often tiring and unpleasant DRUDGERY
- work that is very easy but yields a high income GRAVY TRAIN
- work that requires very little or no effort but yields income SINECURE
- work together, as on a scholarly or artistic project COLLABORATE
- work together harmoniously COORDINATE
- working hard and dutifully DILIGENT, ASSIDUOUS, CONSCIENTIOUS, SEDULOUS
- working in conjunction, cooperating IN TANDEM
- working properly, in working order OPERATIONAL, FUNCTIONAL, OPERATIVE
- assign work, duties, or powers to one's agent, subordinate, or the like DELEGATE, DEPUTE
- belief in the virtues of hard work WORK ETHIC
- fixed amount or spell of work or duty STINT, SHIFT
- hard or dirty domestic work in a military camp or barracks, often imposed as punishment FATIGUE
- "law" or mock-scientific principle to the effect that work expands to fill the time available for its completion PARKINSON'S LAW
- person who is addicted to work WORKAHOLIC
- person who regularly travels a considerable distance between home and work COMMUTER
- relieve or stand in for somebody at work, by taking a turn SPELL
- share of work given to or re-

quired by a participant QUOTA
- study or application of biology and engineering in work and the workplace BIOTECHNOLOGY, ERGONOMICS, ENGINEERING PSYCHOLOGY, HUMAN ENGINEERING
- task allotted to a person or group ASSIGNMENT, COMMISSION

work (combining form) ERG-, ERGO-, OPER-

work of art, usually fairly small OBJET D'ART
- work of art or literature OEUVRE

work out, deduce, or guess at from known information EXTRAPOLATE
- work out an answer, as by calculating DETERMINE
- work out or prove by reasoning, DEDUCE, INFER, DERIVE

workable, possible, practicable, realistic VIABLE

worker See also **servant**
- worker, especially a skilled industrial worker OPERATIVE
- worker fighting against modernization or technical advance LUDDITE
- worker in the U.S.S.R. regarded as especially zealous or productive STAKHANOVITE
- worker qualified at his or her craft but still employed by someone else JOURNEYMAN, JOURNEYWOMAN
- worker receiving instruction in a trade, trainee APPRENTICE, ROOKIE
- worker who defies a strike by continuing to work or replaces a worker on strike SCAB
- worker who performs tasks, often unpleasant tasks, purely for the money HIRELING
- worker's supervisor OVERSEER, FOREMAN
- assign new tasks to workers REDEPLOY
- metalworker, such as a welder, in heavy industries such as shipbuilding BOILERMAKER
- peasant or unskilled worker, especially in Latin America PEON
- reduction in the number of workers, through retirement or resignation rather than through dismissal ATTRITION
- referring to industrial wage earners or workers in manual labor jobs BLUE-COLLAR
- referring to office workers and other nonmanual workers WHITE-COLLAR
- wandering or traveling from place to place, as a farm worker or casual laborer might be ITINERANT, MIGRANT

working class or lower class, especially the class of industrial wage earners PROLETARIAT

working hours - adaptable or variable, as working hours might be FLEXIBLE
- system allowing staggered working hours to employees FLEXITIME, FLEXTIME

works - collection or full list of works, especially by a particular writer CORPUS, OEUVRE, CANON

workshop, factory, or the like where pay and working conditions are very poor SWEATSHOP
- workshop or studio of an artist or craftsman ATELIER

world See also **earth**
- world of fashion, high society BEAU MONDE, HAUT MONDE
- world of the dead, the underworld NETHERWORLD
- fictional place or imaginary world where things are better than in real life UTOPIA
- fictional place or imaginary world where things are worse than in real life DYSTOPIA, CACOTOPIA
- person, group, or system regarded as a small representation of the whole world MICROCOSM
- regarding the world as the center of the universe, as in early astronomy GEOCENTRIC

world (combining form) -COSM-, COSMO-

world languages See **international**

world view, philosophical standpoint WELTANSCHAUUNG

worldly, earthly, of this life SUBLUNARY
- worldly, ordinary TERRESTRIAL, MUNDANE
- worldly rather than spiritual or religious SECULAR, TEMPORAL

worldwide, universal ECUMENICAL

worm See illustration
- worm-eaten or worm-infested VERMICULATE
- worm in the intestines, tapeworm HELMINTH
- worm of a type having segmented bodies, including the earthworms and leeches ANNELID
- worm of a type having long, unsegmented bodies, often parasitic, including the hookworm NEMATODE, ROUNDWORM
- worm remedy, expelling or destroying intestinal worms VERMIFUGE, ANTHELMINTIC, VERMICIDE
- wormlike, relating to worms, or caused by worms VERMICULAR
- wormlike creature having one pair of legs on each body segment CENTIPEDE
- wormlike creature having two pairs of legs on each body segment

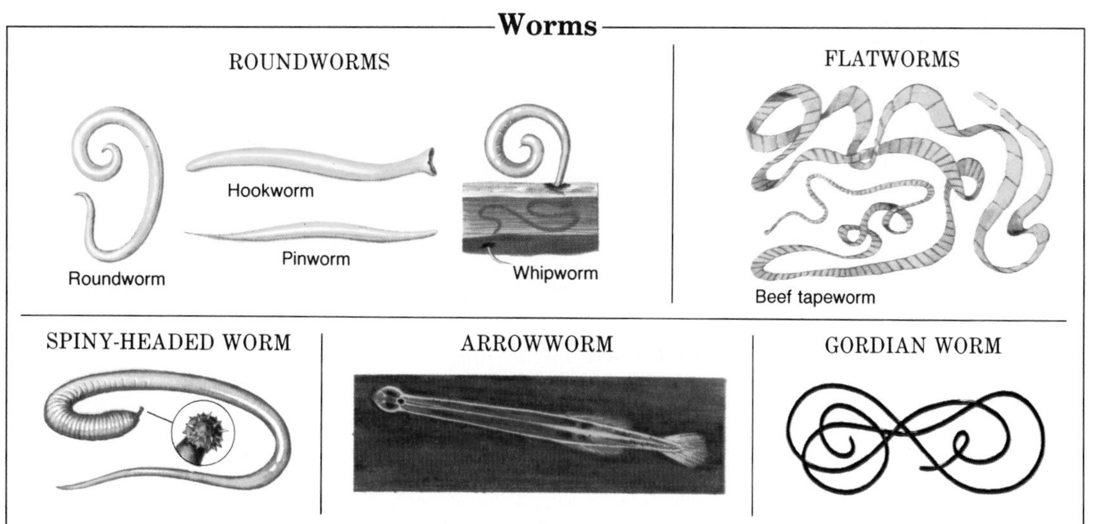

MILLIPEDE
- wormlike young hatched from the egg of an insect LARVA
- parasitic flatworm of various kinds, including the flukes, having suckers and a tough skin TREMATODE
- resembling or relating to an earthworm LUMBRICOID
- shaped like a worm VERMIFORM
- silky protective capsule spun by larvae such as those of silkworms, to house the pupa COCOON

worm (combining form) VERMI-, HELMINTH-

worn out, drained of one's natural force and vitality, as through inbreeding or indulgence EFFETE
- worn out, exhausted, strained HAGGARD
- worn out, run down, or untidy, as through debauchery RADDLED
- worn out, severely weakened, exhausted or enfeebled DEBILITATED, DEPLETED, ENERVATED, ETIOLATED
- worn out or broken down through age or overuse DECREPIT, DILAPIDATED
- worn out or degraded, as through oversophistication or debauchery DECADENT, DEGENERATE

worried, distressed, very nervous FRAUGHT, PERTURBED, AGITATED, DISQUIETED, EXERCISED, DISCOMFITED
- worried, fretful, very tense, in suspense ON TENTERHOOKS
- worried, nervous, or concerned SOLICITOUS
- worried or troubled repeatedly, plagued by problems BESET, BEDEVILED, BELEAGUERED
- very worried or emotionally upset UNNERVED, UNSTRUNG, DISCOMPOSED, DISTRAIT, DISQUIETED, DISTRAUGHT, OVERWROUGHT

worry, annoy repeatedly, pester, badger HARASS, HECTOR
- worry or burden, such as a debt MILLSTONE
- worry or uneasiness, anxious state DISQUIETUDE, CARK, APPREHENSIVENESS, VEXATION, DISCOMFITURE
- worry or vague unease, feeling of unspecific but powerful anxiety ANGST
- worrying or dangerous experience, of short duration MAUVAIS QUART D'HEURE
- free one's mind of a worry, grief, anxiety, guilt, or other burden DISBURDEN
- object or thought causing persistent but often needless worry BUGBEAR, BUGABOO
- sudden worry or dismay that throws everything into confusion CONSTERNATION

worsen, complicate, or intensify something, such as an injury or difficulty AGGRAVATE, EXACERBATE, COMPOUND
- worsen, decline in value, quality, health, or the like DETERIORATE, DEGENERATE
- worsen, return to an earlier and inferior stage or condition, take a step backward REGRESS, RETROGRESS, RELAPSE
- worsen, weaken or cheapen, reduce in quality, corrupt or devalue DEBASE, DEGRADE, DEMEAN
- gradual worsening in the sense of a word with time, as with *hussy*, which once meant "wife, housewife" DETERIORATION, PEJORATION

worship of the dead NECROLATRY
- offering of worship, thanksgiving, or the like OBLATION
- relating to worship DEVOTIONAL

worship (combining form) -LATRY

worthless, insignificant, trifling PALTRY, NUGATORY
- worthless but showy TRUMPERY
- worthless or unimportant thing BAGATELLE, TRIFLE

worthy, qualified, appropriate, as for a job or post ELIGIBLE

would-be, unsuccessful MANQUÉ

wound, injury LESION, TRAUMA
- wound or hurt someone's feelings, as by insults or severe criticism SCARIFY, LACERATE
- wound or injure very severely, causing serious disfigurement or disability MAIM, MUTILATE
- wound or injury, as caused by an accident or surgery TRAUMA
- burn flesh or tissue with a corrosive chemical or a very hot or very cold instrument, as in treating wounds CAUTERIZE
- discharge pus, as a wound might SUPPURATE, MATURATE, FESTER
- formation of small beads of new tissue on the surface of a wound during healing GRANULATION
- joining of broken bones, the edges of a wound, or the like COAPTATION
- on or near the surface, as a wound might be SUPERFICIAL
- sewing or stitching together of the edges of a wound SUTURE
- swollen area around a healing wound PROUD FLESH, GRANULATION TISSUE

woven See **weaving, fabrics**

wrap a newborn baby tightly with clothes or strips of cloth SWADDLE
- wrap closely, envelop, as in furs SWATHE
- wrap up in a scarf or blanket, as for warmth or disguise MUFFLE

wrath - become liable or subject to something such as debts or someone's wrath INCUR

wreath or crown of flowers worn on the head GARLAND, CHAPLET, CORONAL
- wreath or crown of leaves and branches, presented as an award or token of honor in ancient times BAYS, LAURELS

wreckage from a shipwrecked ship WRACK
- wreckage or cargo remaining afloat after a ship has sunk FLOTSAM, JETSAM

wrestle or come to grips GRAPPLE

wrestling - held in a headlock in wrestling IN CHANCERY
- wrestling hold with leverage against the opponent's neck and surrounding parts NELSON
- Japanese style of wrestling, in which one tries to force one's opponent out of the ring or to the ground SUMO
- referring to a wrestling contest in which the usual weight divisions are disregarded CATCHWEIGHT
- style of wrestling in which holds are restricted to the upper body GRECO-ROMAN WRESTLING
- throws of various kinds in wrestling FLYING MARE, CROSS-BUTTOCK
- wrestling with the hands only INDIAN WRESTLING, ARM WRESTLING

wrinkle, crease, fold up RUCK, RUMPLE, PURSE, PUCKER
- wrinkled and shriveled, as an elderly person's face might be WIZENED

wrist bone CARPAL, CARPUS

write, set down in writing, as one might a poem INDITE
- write hastily and untidily SCRAWL, SCRIBBLE
- write or engrave words, as in a gift book or by incision into a hard surface INSCRIBE
- write or play a musical composition in a different key TRANSPOSE
- write or spell in the letters of another alphabet TRANSLITERATE
- write or talk at length and in detail on a subject ELABORATE, EXPATIATE, ENLARGE, DILATE
- write or type out a copy of a recording, shorthand notes, or the like TRANSCRIBE
- able to read and write LITERATE
- itch or urge to write CACOËTHES SCRIBENDI
- unable to read or write ILLITERATE

write off an asset gradually, or prepare for its replacement by paying into a sinking fund AMORTIZE

writer See also **author**
- writer, artist, or the like living in an unconventional way BOHEMIAN
- writer, journalist, artist, or the

like who is self-employed and tends to undertake only short-term projects FREE LANCE, FREE-LANCER
- writer of fables or fantasies FABULIST
- writer or artist who favors a real-life representation of everyday subject matter REALIST, NATURALIST
- writer or journalist SCRIBE
- writer who writes a memoir or book on behalf of somebody else GHOST WRITER
- writer's complete works or output OEUVRE, CORPUS, CANON
- writers, artists, or other grouping whose aims or methods seem experimental, very daring, and ahead of their times AVANT-GARDE
- assumed name of a writer PSEUDONYM, PEN NAME, NOM DE PLUME
- line under the title of a magazine or newspaper article giving the writer's name BYLINE
- list of works by or about a particular writer BIBLIOGRAPHY
- referring to or written by an unnamed writer ANONYMOUS
- share of the proceeds paid by a publisher to a writer from sales of his or her work ROYALTY
- world of hack writers and mediocre journalists GRUB STREET

writing See also **handwriting, style, alphabet, speech, highfalutin,** and illustration at **script**
- writing desk, typically with a hinged top closing over small drawers ESCRITOIRE, SECRETAIRE, SECRETARY
- writing disability caused by brain disease AGRAPHIA, DYSGRAPHIA, APHASIA
- writing instrument, as used on wax tablets in ancient times STYLUS
- writing or copying room in a monastery SCRIPTORIUM
- writing or speaking effortlessly in a graceful, flowing way FLUENT
- writing or speech of an elegant, high-flown style PERIODS
- writing or speech that is pompous, high-flown, and showy FUSTIAN, BOMBAST, EUPHUISM, GRANDILOQUENCE
- writing or speech that is roundabout or evasive CIRCUMLOCUTION, PROLIXITY, PERIPHRASIS
- writing system, as in Chinese, in which each word is represented by a single character or symbol LEXIGRAPHY
- writing system, especially one based on an alphabet ORTHOGRAPHY
- writing that is more striking or elaborate than the surrounding text, often in an overblown way PURPLE PATCH, PURPLE PASSAGE
- ancient system of writing in which lines go alternately from left to right and from right to left ("like oxen in plowing"), or, correspondingly, the time-saving alternate-line reversal of high-speed computer printers BOUSTROPHEDON
- bureaucratic speech or writing that is wordy and often empty GOBBLEDYGOOK, OFFICIALESE, BUREAUCRATESE, WASHINGTONESE
- long and typically dull speech or piece of writing DIATRIBE, SCREED
- outpouring of emotion in speech or writing EFFUSION
- person employed in writing, either by taking dictation or by making neat copies of handwritten documents AMANUENSIS
- picture representing a word or idea, as in a writing system such as hieroglyphics PICTOGRAM
- piece of writing that deliberately excludes throughout a particular letter of the alphabet LIPOGRAM
- piece of writing that deliberately permits the use of only one of the vowels throughout UNIVOCALIC
- scientific study of writing systems GRAMMATOLOGY
- study of handwriting, as for psychological analysis or detection of forgery GRAPHOLOGY
- symbol or character in a writing system, such as Chinese, that represents a thing or idea rather than the sound IDEOGRAM

writing (combining form) -GRAM, -GRAPH, SCRIPT-

writings of a deep, scholarly, often dry kind LUCUBRATIONS
- writings of doubtful authorship or reliability APOCRYPHA
- writings or drawings, often witty or obscene, scribbled typically on walls in public places GRAFFITI
- writings produced by a writer in his or her earlier years before reaching a mature style JUVENILIA
- complete collection of writings by a particular writer CORPUS, OEUVRE, CANON
- passing off as one's own the writings, tunes, ideas, or the like of another PLAGIARISM

written study or systematic examination of a particular subject TREATISE, DISSERTATION, THESIS

wrong See also **mistake, false, incorrect**
- wrong, erring, straying from the moral course, wayward ERRANT
- wrong or unjust in a shameful way INIQUITOUS
- distress or anger arising from a sense of being injured or wronged GRIEVANCE
- prove a statement or argument wrong REFUTE, REBUT, CONFUTE
- provoke something, often something wrong, or provoke someone into doing it INSTIGATE

wrong (combining form) CACO-, MAL-, MIS-, DIS-, DYS-, PARA-

wrongdoer, criminal, or villain MISCREANT, REPROBATE, KNAVE, MALEFACTOR, TRANSGRESSOR, DELINQUENT

wrongdoing, especially by a public official MALFEASANCE, MALVERSATION

wrongful act in civil law, other than breach of contract TORT

wrongly CATA-, MAL-

X, Y, Z

X-ray ROENTGEN RAY
- X-ray or gamma-ray examination, or the technique involved RADIOGRAPHY
- X-ray technique in which brain tissue or other soft tissue is scanned and a computer provides a three-dimensional image COMPUTERIZED AXIAL TOMOGRAPHY, CAT SCAN
- X-ray technique that shows up only the section of tissue wanted TOMOGRAPHY
- technique that produces images from the responses of a magnetic field, avoiding the radiation hazards of X-rays NUCLEAR MAGNETIC RESONANCE, NMR
- medical treatment, particularly of cancer, by means of X-rays or similar radiation, or radioactive chemicals RADIOTHERAPY
- reveal or make visible an internal body part by means of surgery, X-rays, or NMR VISUALIZE
- whitish preparation containing barium sulfate, swallowed before an X-ray examination of the alimentary canal BARIUM MEAL

X-ray (combining form) -GRAM

X-shaped, crossing, intersecting DECUSSATE

xylophone of Latin American style MARIMBA

yacht See also **sail, boat**
- yacht's keel that can be raised when not in use CENTERBOARD, DROP KEEL, SLIDING KEEL, CHEESECUTTER
- chairman of a yacht club COMMODORE
- dinghy or small service boat towed or carried by a yacht or ship TENDER
- docking basin or mooring area for yachts MARINA

yard in which railroad cars, engines, and so on are collected and then joined up to form new trains SHUNTING YARD

yarn or fabric made from recycled wool SHODDY
- ball of twine, yarn, or thread CLEW
- bundle or measure of yarn HANK
- knot or lump in yarn or cloth BURL
- loose coil of thread; wool, or other yarn SKEIN
- small lump in yarn or a fabric, sometimes made deliberately to produce a knobbly appearance SLUB
- smooth yarn used in making braids and fringes GENAPPE
- tightly twisted woollen yarn made from long fibers WORSTED

yawning or drowsiness OSCITATION
- yawning or drowsy OSCITANT

year in which farm land is left to lie fallow, observed every seventh year by the ancient Jews and in modern Israel SABBATICAL YEAR
- year of origin, especially of a wine VINTAGE
- year of remarkable events ANNUS MIRABILIS
- year of rest, restitution, or celebration JUBILEE
- years important to one's development, especially in childhood FORMATIVE YEARS
- adjective for a year ANNUAL

yearly, annually PER ANNUM
- yearly payment of an allowance, dividends, or the like ANNUITY

yearn or long for something intensely PINE, HANKER
- yearning or sentimental longing for something in the past, especially one's childhood home NOSTALGIA

yeast or similar substance added to dough to aid fermentation LEAVEN

yellow See also **color**
- yellow-flowering crop producing a valuable oil seed and used for fodder RAPE, COLZA
- pale sickly yellowish in color or complexion SALLOW

yellow (combining form) XANTHO-, FLAV-

yellowing of the skin and eyes, or an illness producing it JAUNDICE, ICTERUS

yes - answering yes, expressing assent or agreement AFFIRMATIVE

yes-man, servile follower LACKEY, FLUNKY, MINION, TOADY, SYCOPHANT, LICKSPITTLE

yield See also **give up**
- yield control or possession of, release or abandon RELINQUISH
- yield or hand over formally rights, territory, or the like CEDE
- yield or give up a claim or right voluntarily, as to a trial by jury WAIVE
- yield or surrender, end one's resistance CAPITULATE
- yield out of pity, withhold a planned punishment or victory blow RELENT
- yield overrespectfully to another person's wishes or decisions KOWTOW, TRUCKLE, FAWN
- yield to a superior force, temptation, or the like SUCCUMB
- yield to a whim or craving INDULGE, GRATIFY

ZODIACAL SIGNS

SIGNS	DATES	SIGNS	DATES
Capricorn: the Goat	Dec. 23–Jan. 19	**Cancer: the Crab**	June 23–July 23
Aquarius: the Water Carrier	Jan. 20–Feb. 19	**Leo: the Lion**	July 24–Aug. 23
Pisces: the Fishes	Feb. 20–Mar. 21	**Virgo: the Virgin**	Aug. 24–Sept. 23
Aries: the Ram	Mar. 22–Apr. 20	**Libra: the Scales/ the Balance**	Sept. 24–Oct. 23
Taurus: the Bull	Apr. 21–May 21	**Scorpio: the Scorpion**	Oct. 24–Nov. 22
Gemini: the Twins	May 22–June 22	**Sagittarius: the Archer**	Nov. 23–Dec. 22

- yield to or comply with another's decision or opinion DEFER TO
- yield to someone's authority, bend the knee SUBMIT
- yield to someone's urging, consent or agree to a request ACCEDE, CONCEDE, ACQUIESCE

yielding or giving up of something, as of territory or rights CESSION
- yielding or voluntary relinquishing of a claim, right, or privilege WAIVER
- yielding overeagerly, submissive SERVILE, OBSEQUIOUS, FAWNING

yoga of a form emphasizing exercises HATHA-YOGA
- sitting position, with crossed legs and hands resting on knees, as used in yoga and meditation LOTUS POSITION

yoke (combining form) ZYG-, ZYGO-, CONJUG-

yolk of an egg VITELLUS

young See also **animal**
- young and immature JUVENILE, ADOLESCENT, PUERILE
- young and immature or inexperienced CALLOW
- young and inexperienced person, organization, or the like FLEDGLING, STRIPLING
- young child or animal that is still unweaned SUCKLING
- young person who is extremely clever or successful for his or her age WHIZ KID, WUNDERKIND, CHILD PRODIGY
- make young again, restore to youthful appearance or energy REJUVENATE

young (combining form) -LING, JUV-

young man kept as a lover by an older woman GIGOLO, TOYBOY
- young man who is very good-looking APOLLO, ADONIS

young woman, girl, maiden DAMSEL
- young woman or girl who is slim and attractive in a boyish way GAMINE
- young woman undergoing a formal presentation to society, as at a ball DEBUTANTE

youth, adolescent boy STRIPLING
- give renewed youth or vitality to REJUVENATE
- time of one's youth or immaturity, especially the time of one's minority, during which one is legally under age NONAGE

youthful, young, fresh, springlike VERNAL

z - /z/, /s/, or related hissing sound SIBILANT

zebra - zebralike mammal, now nearly extinct, of southern Africa QUAGGA

Zen riddle or brainteaser designed to free the mind from the constraints of logic KOAN

zenith - point in the heavens directly beneath the observer, diametrically opposite the zenith NADIR

zero, nothing NAUGHT, AUGHT, NIL, NICHTS, NIX, ZILCH, GOOSE EGG
- zero, the symbol 0 CIPHER

zest, enthusiasm, dash, vigor FLAIR, ÉLAN, PANACHE, FLAMBOYANCE, PIZZAZZ, VERVE, BRIO, OOMPH
- zest, hearty enjoyment of life JOIE DE VIVRE
- zest, vitality or enjoyment, liveliness ANIMATION, VIVACITY, VIVACIOUSNESS, GUSTO

zigzag braid, flat and narrow, as used to trim clothing RICKRACK
- zigzag course, especially in sailing when trying to progress into the wind TACK
- zigzag path, as taken by a sailing ship TRAVERSE
- cut a zigzag or scalloped edge on PINK

zinc - coat or rustproof steel or iron with zinc GALVANIZE

zip code ZONE-IMPROVEMENT PLAN
- zip code in Great Britain POST CODE

zodiac See chart, and also chart at **astrology**
- plot of the relative positions of planets and signs of the zodiac at a given time HOROSCOPE

zone on the earth's surface lying between the tropics TORRID ZONE
- zones on the earth's surface lying between the polar regions and the tropics TEMPERATE ZONES
- zones on the earth's surface lying within the polar regions FRIGID ZONES
- sensitive to sexual stimulation, as certain zones of the body are EROGENOUS

zoo JARDIN ZOOLOGIQUE, TIERGARTEN
- small zoo or display enclosure of wild animals MENAGERIE

zygote, fertilized ovum OOSPERM, OOKINETE, TRAVELING VERMICULE

ACKNOWLEDGMENTS

Many of the illustrations in this book are taken from or adapted from the following books published by Reader's Digest or Drive Publications:

ABC's of the Human Body; America's Fascinating Indian Heritage; Back to Basics; Book of British Birds; Book of the British Countryside; Car Maintenance Course; Complete Guide to Needlework; The Cookery Year; Eat Better, Live Better; Family Health Guide and Medical Encyclopedia; Family Medical Adviser; Fascinating World of Animals; Guide des Chiens; Guide to Places of the World; Household Hints & Handy Tips; Household Manual; The Reader's Digest Illustrated Book of Dogs; Reader's Digest Illustrated Encyclopedic Dictionary; Into the Unknown; Inventions That Changed the World; Joy of Nature; Library of Modern Knowledge; Nature Lover's Library; Reader's Digest New D-I-Y Manual; North American Wildlife; The Past All Around Us; Traditional Crafts in Britain.

Abbey Buildings: Brian Delf. **Aircraft:** Precision Illustration. **Arch:** Malcolm McGregor. **Armor:** Malcolm McGregor. **Astrological Signs:** The Granger Collection, New York. **Atmosphere:** Malcolm McGregor. **Atom:** From *The World Book Encyclopedia;* © 1990 World Book, Inc.; by permission. **Backgammon:** Courtesy of Selchow & Righter Co. **Baseball:** Reproduced from *Book of 1000 Family Games.* **Baskets:** Drawings (left) from *The World Book Encyclopedia;* © 1990 World Book, Inc.; by permission. Photos (top to bottom right) Lee Boltin; Jerry D. Jacka, Heard Museum; Lee Boltin; Carmelo Guadagno, Museum of the American Indian, Heye Foundation. **Basketball Court:** Reproduced from *Book of 1000 Family Games.* **Bats:** Reprinted with permission of Macmillan Publishing Company from *Macmillan Illustrated Animal Encyclopedia,* edited by Dr. Philip Whitfield; copyright © 1984 by Macmillan Publishing Company. **Beef Cuts:** Harriet Pertchik. **Books of the Bible:** Taken from *The Lion Encyclopedia of the Bible,* edited by Pat Alexander; copyright © 1986 by Lion Publishing; used by permission. **Bicycle:** Precision Illustration. **Bird:** (top) D.W. Ovenden; (bottom) Norman Arlott. **Bones:** Charles Raymond. **Bookbinding:** (top) Hayward & Martin; (bottom) Precision Illustration. **Brain:** Pavel Kostal. **Bread:** John Cook/Whitecross Studios. **Brickwork Bonds:** Edward Williams. **Bridges:** Precision Illustration/Aerofilms. **Butterflies:** From the book, *Webster's New World Dictionary* © 1984; used by permission of the publisher, New World Dictionaries/Simon & Schuster, Inc. New York, N.Y. 10020. **Camels:** Michael Woods. **Car:** Spectron Artists. **Castle:** Brian Delf. **Cats:** From *The World Book Encyclopedia;* © 1990 World Book, Inc.; by permission. **Chameleon:** Reprintedwith permission of Macmillan Publishing Company from *Macmillan Illustrated Animal Encyclopedia,* edited by Dr. Philip Whitfield; copyright © 1984 by Macmillan Publishing Company. **Cheese:** Mitchell Beazley Publishers, London. **Church:** Brian Delf. **Clerical Clothing:** Malcolm McGregor. **Clouds:** Professor Scorer. **Columns:** Malcolm McGregor. **Cricket:** Hayward & Martin. **Crocodile:** Reprinted with permission of Macmillan Publishing Company from *Macmillan Illustrated Animal Encyclopedia,* edited by Dr. Philip Whitfield; copyright © 1984 by Macmillan Publishing Company. **Crosses:** Pavel Kostal. **Deciduous Trees:** Ian Garrard. **Digestive System:** Jane Hurd Studio. **Dinosaurs:** Charles Pickard. **Dogs:** (top to bottom left) (1) Jean Coladon; (2,3,4) Francoise Bonvoust; (5,6) Guy Michel; (top to bottom right) (1) Gregoire Sobieski; (2,3,4) Joel Blanc; (5) Line Mailhe; (6) Guy Michel; (following page top to bottom left) (1) Jean Coladon; (2) Guy Michel; (3) Jean-Marie Le Faou; (4) Guy Michel; (top to bottom right) (1) Joel Blanc; (2) Michel Janvier; (mongrels) Guy Michel. **Ear:** Pavel Kostal. **Earth:** Gary Hincks. **Egg:** Pavel Kostal. **Embroidery Stitches:** Reproduced from *Complete Guide to Needlework.* **Evergreens:** Rebecca Merrilees. **Eye:** Pavel Kostal. **Feather:** Sidney Woods. **Fish:** Mick Loates. **Flags:** Pavel Kostal. **Flowers:** Pavel Kostal. **Football Field:** Reproduced from *Book of 1000 Family Games.* **Footprints:** Enid Kotschnig. **Fractures:** Malcolm McGregor. **Frogs:** John D. Dawson. **Garden Predators:** Lee Ames & Zak Ltd. **Gemstones:**(diamond) De Beers; (remainder) Institute of Geological Sciences, British Museum (Natural History)/Illustrated by Pavel Kostal. **Geometric Shapes:** Precision Illustration. **Glacier:** Gary Hincks. **Grasses:** Ian Gerrard. **Gun:** Precision Illustration. **Hand:** Ray Skibinski. **Harness:** Malcolm McGregor. **Hats:** Malcolm McGregor. **Heart:** Malcolm McGregor. **Heraldry:** Reader's Digest Studio. **Herbs:** (top to bottom far right) Kathleen Smith; (Borage) Pat Cox; (Chives) Donald Myall; (Horseradish & Angelica) Colin Emberson; (remainder) Shirley Ellis. **Hockey Field:** Reproduced from *Book of 1000 Family Games.* **Horse:** David Nockels. **Hunting Skills:** David Cook. **Igloo:** Vic Kalin. **Insect:** Pavel Kostal. **Internal-Combusion Engine:** Julian Baker/Maltings Partnership. **Jet Engine:** John Crump. **Kangaroo:** Reprinted with permission of Macmillan Publishing Company from *Macmillan Illustrated Animal Encyclopedia,* edited by Dr. Philip Whitfield; copyright © 1984 by Macmillan Publishing Company. **Kites:** Enid Kotschnig. **Knots:** Pavel Kostal. **Lamb Cuts:** Harriet Pertchik. **Language:** Copyright © 1981 by Houghton Mifflin Company; reprinted by permission from *The American Heritage Dictionary of the English Language.* **Leaf Shapes:** Malcolm McGregor. **Lightning:** Enid Kotschnig. **Map Projections:** Reader's Digest Studio. **Metamorphosis:** Richard Bonson and Eric Robson. **Moon:** (center) Patricia Ryan; (remainder) Lick Observatory Photographs. **Mouth, Nose, and Throat:** Pavel Kostal. **Mushroom:** Pavel Kostal. **Nerve Cell:** Richard Bonson. **Nervous System:** Richard Bonson. **Newt:** Reprinted with permission of Macmillan Publishing Company from *The Macmillan Illustrated Animal Encyclopedia,* edited by Dr. Philip Whitfield; copyright © 1984 by Macmillan Publishing Company. **Oceans:** Globes from *The World Book Encyclopedia;* © 1988 by Rand McNally, R.L. 90-S-88. **Oil:** Launcelot Jones. **Orchestra:** Mitchell Beazley Publishers, London. **Organ:** Brian Delf. **Papal Vestments:** Marcos Oksenhendler/*New York Daily News.* **Pasta:** John Cook/Whitecross Studios. **Pests:** Ed Lipinski. **Piano:** Pavel Kostal; (piano action) Piano Warehouse, London. **Pinniped:** Reprinted with permission of Macmillan Publishing Company from *Macmillan Illustrated Animal Encyclopedia,* edited by Dr. Philip Whitfield; copyright © 1984 by Macmillan Publishing Company. **Planets:** Gary Hinks. **Pork Cuts:** Harriet Pertchik. **Primates:** Reprinted with permission of Macmillan Publishing Company from *Macmillan Illustrated Animal Encyclopedia,* edited by Dr. Philip Whitfield; copyright © 1984 by Macmillan Publishing Company. **Radio Waves:** Hayward & Martin. **Rainbow:** John Deeks. **Rebus:** Reproduced from *Reader's Digest Illustrated Encyclopedic Dictionary.* **Rhinoceros:** Reprinted with permission of Macmillan Publishing Company from *Macmillan Illustrated Animal Encyclopedia,* edited by Dr. Philip Whitfield; copyright © 1984 by Macmillan Publishing Company. **River:** George Buctel. **Rodents:** Reprinted with permission of Macmillan Publishing Companny from *Macmillan Illustrated Animal Encyclopedia,* edited by Dr. Philip Whitfield; copyright © 1984 by Macmillan Publishing Company. **Roof Shapes:** Hayward & Martin. **Roots:** John Murphy. **Saddle:** Precision Illustration. **Sailing:** Precision Illustration, Norman Lacey. **Seeds:** Ann Savage. **Semaphore:** Reproduced from *Reader's Digest Illustrated Encyclopedic Dictionary.* **Shellfish:** Norman Weaver and Charles Pickard. **Shells:** From the book, *Webster's New World Dictionary* © 1984; used by permission of the publisher, New World Dictionaries/Simon & Schuster, Inc. New York, N.Y. 10020. **Ships:** From the book, *Webster's New World Dictionary* © 1984; used by permission of the publisher, New World Dictionaries/Simon & Schuster, Inc. New York, N.Y. 10020. **Shoe:** Precision Illustration. **Skin:** Judy Skorpil. **Snakes:** John D. Dawson. **Spiders:** John D. Dawson. **Stairs:** Hayward & Martin. **Steam Engine:** From *The World Book Encyclopedia;* © 1990 World Book, Inc.; by permission. **Submarine:** From *The World Book Encyclopedia;* © 1990 World Book, Inc.; by permission. **Swords:** Precision Illustration. **Tarot:** Robert Harding Picture Library. **Tennis:** Reproduced from *Book of 1000 Family Games.* **Theater:** Precision Illustration. **Tooth:** Malcolm McGregor. **Trees:** Tree illustrations by S.R. Badmin; leaf and fruit illustrations by Vanna Haggerty. **Turtles:** Reprinted with permission of Macmillan Publishing Company from *Macmillan Illustrated Animal Encyclopedia,* edited by Dr. Philip Whitfield; copyright © 1984 by Macmillan Publishing Company. **Veal Cuts:** Harriet Pertchik. **Venom-Injecting Devices:** Eric Robson. **Violin:** Launcelot Jones. **Volcano:** Gary Hincks. **Whales:** Reprinted with permission of Macmillan Publishing Company from *Macmillan Illustrated Animal Encyclopedia,* edited by Dr. Philip Whitfield; copyright © 1984 by Macmillan Publishing Company. **Windmills and Watermills:** (windmills) Brian Delf; (watermills) Roy Castle. **Windows:** Precision Illustration. **Woods:** From the book, *Webster's New World Dictionary* © 1984; used by permission of the publisher, New World Dictionaries/Simon & Schuster, Inc. New York, N.Y. 10020. **Worms:** From the book, *Webster's New World Dictionary* © 1984; used by permission of the publisher, New World Dictionaries/Simon & Schuster, Inc. New York, N.Y. 10020.